GLOBAL EDUCATION MONITORING REPORT

Inclusion and education:

ALL MEANS ALL

The Education 2030 Incheon Declaration and Framework for Action specifies that the mandate of the *Global Education Monitoring Report* is to be "the mechanism for monitoring and reporting on SDG 4 and on education in the other SDGs" with the responsibility to "report on the implementation of national and international strategies to help hold all relevant partners to account for their commitments as part of the overall SDG follow-up and review". It is prepared by an independent team hosted by UNESCO.

The designations employed and the presentation of the material in this publication do not imply the expression of any opinion whatsoever on the part of UNESCO concerning the legal status of any country, territory, city or area, or of its authorities, or concerning the delimitation of its frontiers or boundaries.

The *Global Education Monitoring Report* team is responsible for the choice and the presentation of the facts contained in this book and for the opinions expressed therein, which are not necessarily those of UNESCO and do not commit the Organization. Overall responsibility for the views and opinions expressed in the Report is taken by its Director.

This publication can be referenced as: UNESCO. 2020. *Global Education Monitoring Report 2020: Inclusion and education: All means all.* Paris, UNESCO.

This report and all related materials are available for download here: http://bit.ly/2020gemreport

Foreword

It has never been more crucial to make education a universal right, and a reality for all. Our rapidly-changing world faces constant major challenges – from technological disruption to climate change, conflict, the forced movement of people, intolerance and hate – which further widen inequalities and exert an impact for decades to come. The COVID-19 pandemic has further exposed and deepened these inequalities and the fragility of our societies. More than ever, we have a collective responsibility to support the most vulnerable and disadvantaged, helping to reduce long-lasting societal breaches that threaten our shared humanity.

In the face of these challenges, the messages of the 2020 GEM Report on inclusion in education are even more poignant. It warns that education opportunities continue to be unequally distributed. Barriers to quality education are still too high for too many learners. Even before Covid-19, one in five children, adolescents and youth were entirely excluded from education. Stigma, stereotypes and discrimination mean millions more are further alienated inside classrooms.

The current crisis will further perpetuate these different forms of exclusion. With more than 90 per cent of the global student population affected by Covid-19 related school closures, the world is in the throes of the most unprecedented disruption in the history of education. Social and digital divides have put the most disadvantaged at risk of learning losses and dropping out. Lessons from the past – such as with Ebola – have shown that health crises can leave many behind, in particular the poorest girls, many of whom may never return to school.

This Report's core recommendation for all education actors to widen their understanding of inclusive education to include all learners, no matter their identity, background or ability comes at an opportune time as the world seeks to rebuild back more inclusive education systems.

This Report identifies different forms of exclusion, how they are caused and what we can do about them. As such, it is a call to action we should heed as we seek to pave the way for more resilient and equal societies in the future. A call to collect better data, without which we cannot understand or measure the true scope of the problem. A call to make public policies far more inclusive, based on examples of effective policies currently in force, and by working together to address intersecting disadvantages, just as we saw Ministries and government departments are capable of when addressing Covid-19.

Only by learning from this Report can we understand the path we must take in the future. UNESCO stands ready to help States and the education community so that, together, we can develop the education the world so desperately needs and to ensure that learning never stops.

To rise to the challenges of our time, a move towards more inclusive education is non-negotiable – failure to act is not an option.

Audrey Azoulay
Director-General of UNESCO

Foreword

Education makes an essential contribution to building inclusive and democratic societies, where differences of opinion can be freely expressed and where the wide range of voices can be heard, in pursuit of social cohesion and in a celebration of diversity.

This year's *Global Education Monitoring Report* reminds us that education systems are only as inclusive as their creators make them. Disadvantage can be created by these systems and their contexts. It exists where people's needs are not taken into account.

Inclusion in education is about ensuring that every learner feels valued and respected, and can enjoy a clear sense of belonging. Yet many hurdles stand in the way of that ideal. Discrimination, stereotypes and alienation do exclude many. These mechanisms of exclusion are essentially the same, regardless of gender, location, wealth, disability, ethnicity, language, migration, displacement, sexual orientation, incarceration, religion, and other beliefs and attitudes.

The Report reminds us of continuing and disturbing education disparities, including in ensuring access to all, which should be the foundation of inclusion. But an 'all means all' approach to inclusion also means dropping any stigmatizing labels assigned to children. Adopting learning approaches on account of such labels limits their potential, ignoring the benefits that varied learning approaches can bring to all children.

Thus, how education systems are designed is critical. Countries can choose what counts in deciding whether their education system is on the right track or not. They can choose to address an inclusion agenda in a piecemeal approach, or they can tackle the entire set of challenges head on.

There are dilemmas and tensions involved in reaching the ideal of full inclusion. Moving from where we are now to having systems which cater for every learner's needs, including those with severe disabilities, is difficult. This Report does not deny that the full ideal of inclusion may have its downsides too. Well-intended efforts to include can slide into pressure to conform, wear down group identities, and drive out languages. Recognising and helping an excluded group in the name of inclusion could serve to marginalize them at the same time. There are also practical challenges in deciding on the speed of change, whether for richer countries looking to move away from systems which were originally based on segregation, or for poorer countries looking to create an inclusive system from scratch.

In full recognition of these challenges, though, the Report asks whether it really is necessary to seek justifications for inclusive education to be pursued. It notes that debating the benefits of inclusive education can be seen as tantamount to debating the benefits of the abolition of slavery, or indeed of apartheid. Inclusion in education is a process, and not only a desired end point. On that journey, many changes can be made easily – in gestures made by teachers, in the ethos school leaders create for their learning environments, in the way families make decisions when school choices are presented to them, and in what we, as a society, decide we want for our future.

Inclusion is not just a choice for policymakers. Imposed from above it will never work. So, the question you, as readers, are asked in the report is whether *you* are ready to challenge the current mindset and ready to decide that education is for everyone and must strive to be inclusive of all.

The Right Honourable Helen Clark
Chair of the GEM Report Advisory Board

Helen Clark

Acknowledgements

This report would not have been possible without the valuable contributions of numerous people and institutions. The *Global Education Monitoring Report* (GEM Report) team would like to acknowledge their support and thank them for their time and effort.

Invaluable input was provided by the GEM Report Advisory Board's members and its chairperson, Helen Clark. Special thanks also go to our engaged and committed funders, without whose financial support the GEM Report would not be possible.

We would like to acknowledge the role of UNESCO and its leadership. We are very grateful to many individuals, divisions and units at UNESCO headquarters, notably in the Education Sector and the Bureau for the Management of Support Services, for facilitating our daily work. The UNESCO Institute for Statistics (UIS) played a key role by supporting access to its data through the UIS Data API. We would like to thank its director, Silvia Montoya, and her dedicated staff for their close collaboration, notably as part of our partnership with the UIS on the World Inequality Database on Education and in the framework of the Technical Cooperation Group on the Indicators for SDG 4 – Education 2030. Additional thanks go to colleagues at the International Institute for Educational Planning, the UNESCO Institute for Lifelong Learning, the UNESCO-UNEVOC International Centre for Technical and Vocational Education and Training and the UNESCO field office network.

The GEM Report team would like to thank the researchers who produced background papers informing the GEM Report's analyses: Ehaab Dyaa Abdou, Anjlee Agarwal, Joyceline Alla-Mensah, Parul Bakhshi, Jan Berkvens, Alisha Braun, Liliane Garcez, Martin Gustafsson, Seamus Hegarty, Marion Hersh, Paula Frederica Hunt, Soohyun Kim, Maxwell Opoku, Pauliina Patana, Helen Pinnock, Richard Rose, Jamil Salmi, Aemiro Mergia Tadesse and Laura Rodriguez-Takeuchi.

We are grateful to several institutions and their research staff who also produced background papers: Education Sub Saharan Africa (Ranjit Majumdar, Tracy Hart), Georg Eckert Institute (Eckhardt Fuchs, Marcus Otto, Simiao Yu), Idara-e-Taleem-o-Aagahi (Muhammad Afzan Munir, Hamza Sarfaraz, Baela Raza Jamil, Monazza Aslam), Oxfam India (Anjela Taneja, Randeep Kaur, Sanjeev Rai, Shamaila Khalil, Sanghamitra Mishra), Pratham Education Foundation (Samyukta Lakshman, Rukmini Banerji, Arjun Agarwal), Sightsavers – Royal Commonwealth Society for the Blind (Guy Le Fanu, Gareth Roberts, Lianna Jones, Clare McGill, Elena Schmidt), UNESCO Institute for Information Technologies in Education (Tao Zhan, Natalia Amelina) in partnership with Peoples' Friendship University of Russia, UNICEF Innocenti Centre (Dominic Richardson) and University of Oulu (Elina Lehtomäki).

We are grateful for the expertise and guidance of the GEM Report's Advocacy Working Group on inclusion and education: Nafisa Baboo (Light for the World), Julia McGeown and Sian Tesni (International Disability and Development Consortium), Sirtaj Kaur (Global Partnership for Education), Catherine Howgego and Matt Clancy (United Kingdom Department for International Development), Rosmarie Jah and Wongani Grace Taulo (UNICEF), Emilie Sidaner (World Food Programme), Rebecca Telford (United Nations High Commissioner for Refugees), Rubén Ávila (International Lesbian, Gay, Bisexual, Transgender, Queer and Intersex Youth and Student Organisation), Robie Halip (Indigenous Peoples Major Group), Priscille Geiser (International Disability Alliance) and Deboleena Rakshit (Promundo).

Additional thanks go to numerous institutions that hosted consultations on the GEM Report's 2020 concept note, as well as the many individuals and organizations that provided input during the consultation process. Particular thanks go to the Foundation to Promote Open Society, the Inclusive Education Special Interest Group of the Comparative and International Education Society, the German Commission for UNESCO and the UK Forum for International Education and Training.

We are grateful to Florence Migeon (UNESCO) and the organizing team of the Cali International Forum on Inclusion and Equity in Education and to Natasha Graham (UNICEF) and Jennifer Pye (IIEP) for the invitation to the Technical Round Tables on inclusion of children with disabilities in education sector planning. Maria Martinho and Mario Spiezio (UNDESA) kindly shared data on accessibility in schools. Paula Reid (Zero Project) shared background information on innovative practices in inclusive education.

We have benefitted greatly from our partnership with the following organizations in the context of the two forthcoming regional reports on inclusion and education: on the Latin America and Caribbean edition with the UNESCO Regional Bureau for Education in Latin America and the Caribbean (Claudia Uribe, Carlos Vargas Tamez, Ximena Rubio Vargas) and the SUMMA Education Research and Innovation Laboratory for Latin America and the Caribbean (Javier Gonzalez, Ismael Tabilo); and on the Central and Eastern Europe, Caucasus and Central Asia edition with the European Agency for Special Needs and Inclusive Education (Cor J. W. Meijer, Amanda Watkins) and the Network of Education Policy Centres (Lana Jurko, Dženana Husremović).

A group of independent experts reviewed the draft of the GEM Report's thematic part and provided valuable feedback. For their input we thank Nafisa Baboo, Verity Donnelly, Daniel Mont, Diane Richler, Nidhi Singal and Roger Slee. Lani Florian kindly reviewed the chapter on teachers.

Special thanks go to the GEM Report's first cohort of fellows, supported by the Foundation to Promote Open Society: Madhuri Agarwal, Gabriel Bădescu, Donald Baum and Enrique Valencia Lopez.

The report was edited by Jessica Hutchings, whom we thank for her tireless work. Our thanks also go to Justine Doody for editing our communication materials.

We also wish to acknowledge those who worked tirelessly to support the production of the report, including Rebecca Brite, Blossom, Erin Crum and FHI 360 (Shannon Dyson, Kay Garcia, Krista Gill and Aziza Mukhamedkhanova).

Many colleagues within and outside UNESCO were involved in the translation, design and production and printing of the 2020 GEM Report and its related materials and we would like to extend to them our deep appreciation for their support.

Specific thanks go to Burness Communications Inc., Anne Derenne, Dean Swift, Housatonic Design Network and Rooftop for their support to the outreach of the GEM Report; to Association Valentin Hauy for producing Braille and easy-to-read versions of the summary; and to Humanity and Inclusion, Foundation to Promote Open Society, Save the Children, UNHCR and UNICEF for extensive use of their photos.

Finally, we would like to thank the short-term consultants and interns who provided much input to the GEM Report team: Gabriela Mathieu, Ulrich Janse van Vuuren, Walter Gomez Velarde and Jiaheng Zhou. Thanks also to the students of the Université Paris 1 Panthéon-Sorbonne, Sorbonne School of Economics, who contributed to the development of country profiles: Alexandra Methot, Diallo Kindi Mohamed, Kyeonghun Joo and Yang Yang.

The *Global Education Monitoring Report* team

Director: Manos Antoninis

Daniel April, Bilal Barakat, Madeleine Barry, Nicole Bella, Erin Chemery, Anna Cristina D'Addio, Matthias Eck, Francesca Endrizzi, Glen Hertelendy, Milagros Lechleiter, Priyadarshani Joshi, Katarzyna Kubacka, Kate Linkins, Kassiani Lythrangomitis, Alasdair McWilliam, Anissa Mechtar, Claudine Mukizwa, Yuki Murakami, Carlos Alfonso Obregón Melgar, Judith Randrianatoavina, Kate Redman, Maria Rojnov, Anna Ewa Ruszkiewicz, Will Smith, Laura Stipanovic, Morgan Strecker, Rosa Vidarte and Lema Zekrya.

The *Global Education Monitoring Report* is an independent annual publication. The GEM Report is funded by a group of governments, multilateral agencies and private foundations and facilitated and supported by UNESCO.

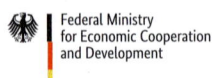    

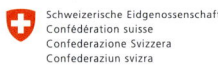 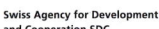   

For more information, please contact:
Global Education Monitoring Report team
UNESCO, 7, place de Fontenoy
75352 Paris 07 SP, France
Email: gemreport@unesco.org
Tel.: +33 1 45 68 07 41
www.unesco.org/gemreport
https://gemreportunesco.wordpress.com

Any errors or omissions found subsequent to printing will be corrected in the online version at www.unesco.org/gemreport

Global Education Monitoring Report series

2020   *Inclusion and education: All means all*

2019   *Migration, displacement and education:*
        Building bridges, not walls

2017/8 *Accountability in education: Meeting our commitments*

2016   *Education for people and planet:*
        Creating sustainable futures for all

EFA Global Monitoring Report series

2015   *Education for All 2000–2015: Achievements and challenges*

2013/4 *Teaching and learning: Achieving quality for all*

2012   *Youth and skills: Putting education to work*

2011   *The hidden crisis: Armed conflict and education*

2010   *Reaching the marginalized*

2009   *Overcoming inequality: Why governance matters*

2008   *Education for All by 2015: Will we make it?*

2007   *Strong foundations: Early childhood care and education*

2006   *Literacy for life*

2005   *Education for All: The quality imperative*

2003/4 *Gender and Education for All: The leap to equality*

2002   *Education for All: Is the world on track?*

Contents

List of figures, tables and text boxes

FIGURES

TABLES

TEXT BOXES

HIGHLIGHTS

Identity, background and ability dictate education opportunities.

In all but high-income countries in Europe and Northern America, only 18 of the poorest youth complete secondary school for every 100 of the richest youth. In at least 20 countries, mostly in sub-Saharan Africa, hardly any poor rural young women complete secondary school.

Discrimination, stereotyping and stigmatization mechanisms are similar for all learners at risk of exclusion.

While 68% of countries have a definition of inclusive education, only 57% of those definitions cover multiple marginalized groups.

Despite progress, many countries still do not collect, report or use data on those left behind.

Since 2015, 41% of countries, representing 13% of the global population, have not had a publicly available household survey to provide disaggregated data on key education indicators; the region with the lowest coverage is Northern Africa and Western Asia. Recent data from 14 countries using the Child Functioning Module suggest that children with disabilities constitute 15% of the out-of-school population. They face complex barriers. Those with a sensory, physical or intellectual disability are 2.5 times more likely to have never been in school than their peers without disabilities.

Millions are missing out on the opportunity to learn.

In middle income countries, despite a 25-percentage point increase in the past 15 years, only three quarters are still in school by age 15. Of those, only half are learning the basics, a rate that has been stagnant over the period. And many assessments overestimate how well students are doing: three quarters of students who did no better in multiple choice questions than random guessing were considered proficient in reading in a regional assessment of 15 countries in Latin America.

A key barrier to inclusion in education is the lack of belief that it is possible and desirable.

One in three teachers in 43 mostly upper-middle- and high-income countries in 2018 reported that they did not adjust their teaching to students' cultural diversity.

While some countries are transitioning towards inclusion, segregation is still prevalent.

In the case of students with disabilities, laws in 25% of countries (but over 40% in Asia and in Latin America and the Caribbean) make provisions for education in separate settings, 10% for integration and 17% for inclusion, the remainder opting for combinations of segregation and mainstreaming. In OECD countries, more than two-thirds of all immigrant students attend schools where at least half the students are immigrants.

Financing needs to target those most in need.

Across 32 OECD countries, socio-economically disadvantaged schools and classrooms are more likely to have less qualified teachers. Conditional cash transfers in Latin America since the 1990s have increased education attainment by between 0.5 and 1.5 years. One in four countries has some form of affirmative action programme to help the marginalized get access to tertiary education. About 40% of low- and lower-middle-income countries have not taken any measures to support learners at risk of exclusion during the Covid-19 crisis.

Teachers, teaching materials and learning environments often ignore the benefits of embracing diversity.

Some 25% of teachers in 48 education systems report a high need for professional development on teaching students with special needs. Just 41 countries worldwide recognize sign language as an official language. In Europe, 23 out of 49 countries do not address sexual orientation and gender identity explicitly in their curricula.

This photo symbolises the potential strength, power and confidence of the many girls in Solomon Islands if we are given the chance to complete our secondary education.

CREDIT: Plan International

1

Introduction

How far away is inclusion in education?

KEY MESSAGES

Education resources and opportunities are distributed unequally

- An estimated 258 million children, adolescents and youth, or 17% of the global total, are not in school. The number out of school in sub-Saharan Africa is growing.

- In low- and middle-income countries, adolescents from the richest 20% households are three times as likely as those from the poorest to complete lower secondary school; of those who complete, students from the richest households are twice as likely as those from the poorest households to reach minimum proficiency in reading and mathematics.

- In 10 low- and middle-income countries, children with disabilities were 19% less likely to achieve minimum proficiency in reading than those without disabilities.

International declarations have made commitments to non-discrimination since 1960 and to inclusion since 1990; inclusion permeates the 2030 Agenda, with its call to leave no one behind

- Several Sustainable Development Goals and targets refer directly to equity, inclusion, diversity, equal opportunity or non-discrimination, including SDG 4 on education.

- The 2006 UN Convention on the Rights of Persons with Disabilities (CRPD) guaranteed the right to inclusive education but stopped short of precisely defining inclusion in education. The struggle of people with disabilities has shaped perspectives on inclusion in education.

- In 2016, General Comment No. 4 to CRPD Article 24 described inclusive education as involving 'a process … to provide all students … with an equitable and participatory learning experience and environment that best corresponds to their requirements and preferences'.

Layers of discrimination deny students the right to be educated with their peers or to receive education of the same quality

All over the world, discrimination is based on gender, remoteness, wealth, disability, ethnicity, language, migration, displacement, incarceration, sexual orientation, gender identity and expression, religion and other beliefs and attitudes; the Covid-19 pandemic has added new layers of exclusion.

- In sub-Saharan Africa, teachers may fear teaching children with albinism.

- Stateless children and youth in Gulf States cannot enrol in public education institutions.

- Rohingya who are internally displaced or refugees have had no access to formal public schools.

- Roma children in Europe are segregated and more likely to be placed in special schools.

- In Latin America, learning materials omit or misrepresent the history of Afro-descendants.

Inclusion is not just an economic but also a moral imperative, yet belief in the inclusion principle should not obscure the difficult questions

- Inclusion may inadvertently intensify pressure to conform. Group identities, practices, languages and beliefs may be jeopardized, undercutting a sense of belonging.

The international community's commitment in 2015 to 'ensure inclusive and equitable quality education and promote lifelong learning opportunities for all' as the fourth Sustainable Development Goal (SDG 4) is one of the clearest examples of the overall pledge to leave no one behind, contained in the United Nations (UN) 2030 Agenda for Sustainable Development. The 2030 Agenda brought together aspirations of poverty reduction and environmental sustainability, underpinned by a drive for social justice that builds on the human rights instruments of the past 70 years.

Transforming our World, the foundation document of the 2030 Agenda, refers extensively to equity, inclusion, diversity, equal opportunity and non-discrimination. It calls for empowering vulnerable people and meeting their needs. Several SDGs refer to inclusion and equality (**Table 1.1**). Others simply state that a goal should be reached 'for all', either explicitly, in the case of social goals, or implicitly, in the case of environmental goals.

TABLE 1.1:
Equity and inclusion in *Transforming our World: The 2030 Agenda for Sustainable Development*

Main text: Equity and inclusion	Sustainable Development Goals
A world with **equitable** and universal access to quality education at all levels, to health care and social protection … (§7)	Ensure **inclusive and equitable** quality education and promote lifelong learning opportunities for all (SDG 4)
… a world of universal respect for human rights and human dignity, the rule of law, justice, **equality and non-discrimination**; of respect for race, ethnicity and cultural **diversity**; and of **equal opportunity** permitting the full realization of human potential … (§8)	Achieve **gender equality** and empower all women and girls (SDG 5) Promote sustained, **inclusive** and sustainable economic growth, full and productive employment and decent work for all (SDG 8)
A world in which every woman and girl enjoys full **gender equality** and all legal, social and economic barriers to their empowerment have been removed. A just, **equitable**, tolerant, open and socially **inclusive** world in which the needs of the most **vulnerable** are met. (§8)	Build resilient infrastructure, promote **inclusive** and sustainable industrialization and foster innovation (SDG 9) Reduce **inequality** within and among countries (SDG 10) Make cities and human settlements **inclusive**, safe, resilient and sustainable (SDG 11) Promote peaceful and **inclusive** societies for sustainable development, provide access to justice for all and build effective, accountable and **inclusive** institutions at all levels (SDG 16)
Main text: Leaving no one behind	**SDG 4 targets**
… we pledge that **no one will be left behind** (Preamble)	… ensure that all girls and boys complete free, **equitable** and quality primary and secondary education … (4.1)
… we will endeavour to **reach the furthest behind first** (§4)	… ensure **equal** access for all women and men to affordable and quality technical, vocational and tertiary education … (4.3)
No one must be left behind (§24; health)	… eliminate gender **disparities** in education and ensure **equal** access to all levels of education and vocational training for the **vulnerable**, including persons with disabilities, indigenous peoples and children in **vulnerable** situations (4.5)
Quality, accessible, timely and reliable disaggregated data will be needed to help with the measurement of progress and to ensure that **no one is left behind** (§48; data)	… ensure that all learners acquire the knowledge and skills needed to promote … gender **equality** … appreciation of cultural **diversity** … (4.7)
A robust, voluntary, effective, participatory, transparent and integrated follow-up and review framework to ensure that **no one is left behind** (§72; follow-up and review framework)	… provide safe, non-violent, **inclusive** and effective learning environments for all (4.a)
… people-centred, gender-sensitive, respect human rights and have a particular focus on the poorest, most **vulnerable** and **those furthest behind** (§72; follow-up and review processes)	

Source: United Nations (2015).

EDUCATION FOR ALL IS THE FOUNDATION OF INCLUSION IN EDUCATION

Equity and inclusion have become the heart of the 2030 Agenda as unequal distribution of resources and opportunities persists. Characteristics commonly associated with inequality of distribution include gender, remoteness, wealth, disability, ethnicity, language, migration, displacement, incarceration, sexual orientation, gender identity and expression, religion, and other beliefs and attitudes.

Some mechanisms contributing to inequality are universal while others are specific to social and economic contexts, as the Covid-19 pandemic has laid bare. Advantage and disadvantage are transmitted over generations as parents impart resources, such as income, skills and networks, to their children. Organizations and institutions may favour some groups over others and propagate social norms and stereotypes that exclude more vulnerable groups from opportunities. Individuals form groups that extend advantage to members and block it to others. Public institutions may be designed to correct imbalances or may be beholden to vested and powerful interests (UNDP, 2019).

Despite progress in reducing extreme poverty, especially in Asia, it affects 1 in 10 people. Children are more at risk, especially in sub-Saharan Africa, where extreme poverty affects 49% of children, accounting for 52% of extremely poor children globally (**Figure 1.1a**). Inequality is growing in some parts of the world. Even where it is falling, it often remains unacceptably high among and within countries. The income share of the poorest 50% of the population in Asia and Northern America has decreased since 2000. Elsewhere it has stagnated well below the share in Europe, the most equal region (**Figure 1.1b**).

Key human development outcomes are also unequally distributed. In 30 low- and middle-income countries, children under age 5 from the poorest 20% of households were more than twice as likely to be stunted (41%) as those from the richest 20%, severely compromising their opportunity to benefit from education (**Figure 1.2**).

Education is an opportunity with the potential to transform lives. Yet an estimated 258 million children, adolescents and youth, or 17% of the global total, are not in school. The number out of school in sub-Saharan Africa has passed that of Central and Southern Asia and is growing. The share of sub-Saharan Africa in the global total increased from 24% in 2000 to 38% in

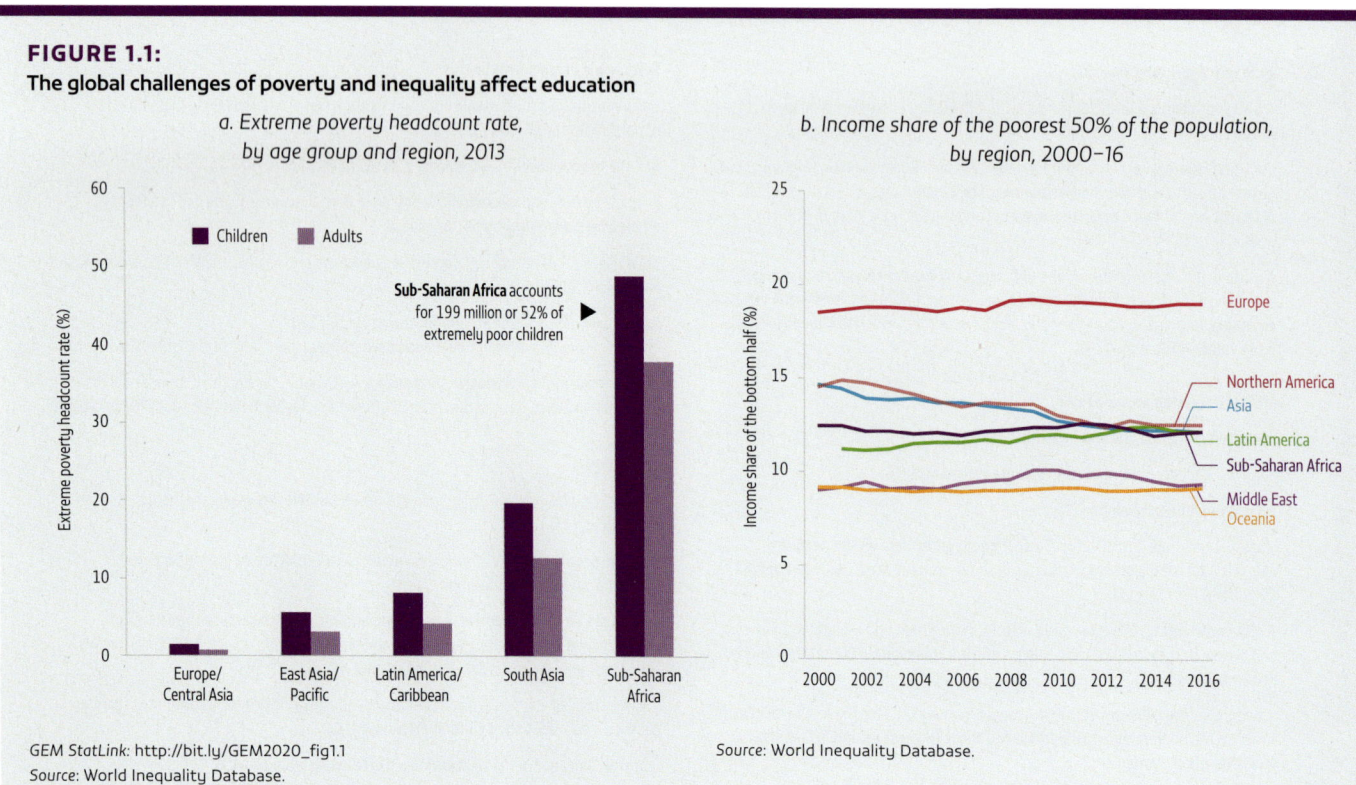

FIGURE 1.1:

The global challenges of poverty and inequality affect education

a. Extreme poverty headcount rate, by age group and region, 2013

b. Income share of the poorest 50% of the population, by region, 2000–16

GEM StatLink: http://bit.ly/GEM2020_fig1.1
Source: World Inequality Database.

Source: World Inequality Database.

2018 (**Figure 1.3**). Those most likely to be excluded are disadvantaged due primarily to poverty but also language, location, gender and ethnicity (**Figure 1.4**).

Globally, the success of efforts to reach the furthest behind first is mixed. Primary and secondary school completion has improved on average and for all major groups as defined by sex, location and wealth. The improvement has been marginally faster for children living in rural areas relative to the average. The same is true for primary school completion among the poorest. Arguably, in neither case are they catching up: At the current rate, closing the gap will take decades. In the case of secondary school completion, the poorest are falling further behind (**Figure 1.5**).

Factors associated with potential disadvantage also affect academic achievement. Results from the 2018 Programme for International Student Assessment (PISA) showed that gender and, to a greater degree, socio-economic status, as defined by factors such as parental education and education resources at home, are associated with wide variation in reading and mathematics proficiency among 15-year-olds. Using the wealth parity index

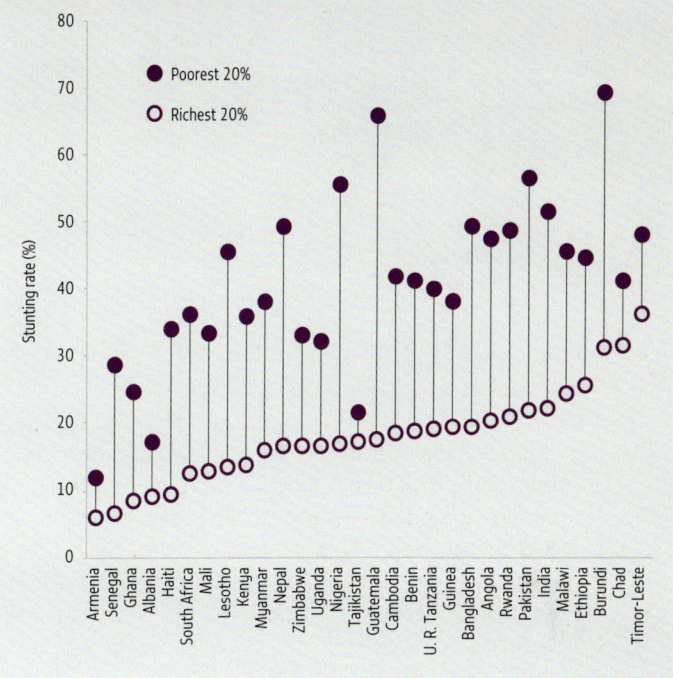

FIGURE 1.2:

The poorest children are more than twice as likely to be malnourished as the richest

Stunting rate, poorest and richest 20% of households, selected low- and middle-income countries, 2014–18

GEM StatLink: http://bit.ly/GEM2020_fig1_2
Source: DHS STATcompiler.

FIGURE 1.3:

A quarter of a billion children, adolescents and youth are not in school

a. Out-of-school rate of primary and secondary school-age children, adolescents and youth, by region, 1990–2018

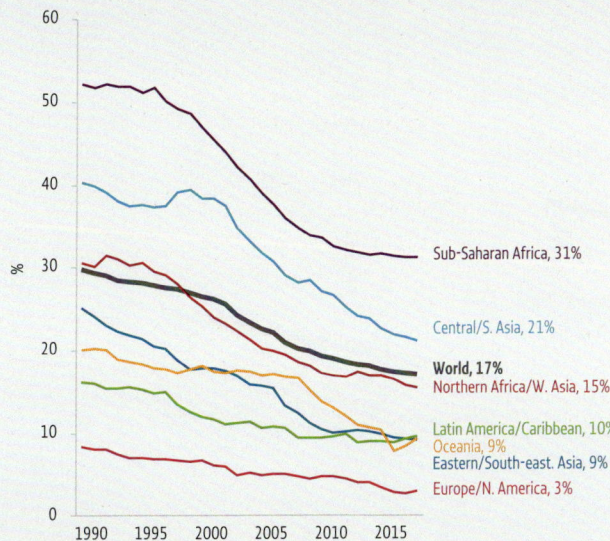

b. Out-of-school primary and secondary school-age children, adolescents and youth, world and selected regions, 1990–2018

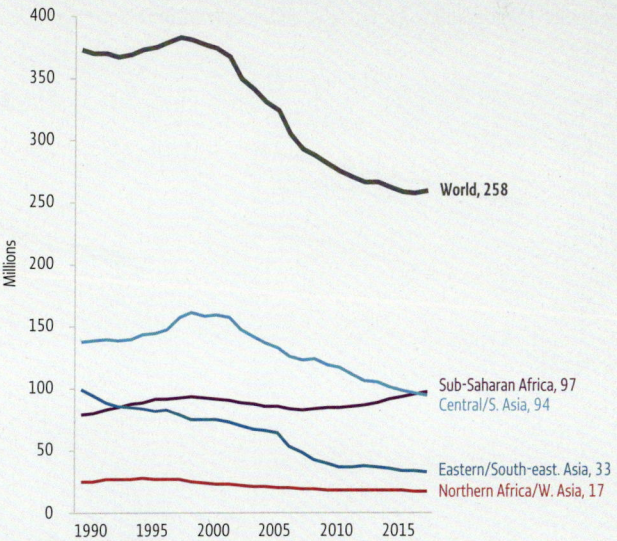

GEM StatLink: http://bit.ly/GEM2020_fig1_3
Source: UIS database.

FIGURE 1.4:

There are large wealth, linguistic, regional and ethnic differentials in school attendance

Out-of-school rate, by population group, selected countries, 2016

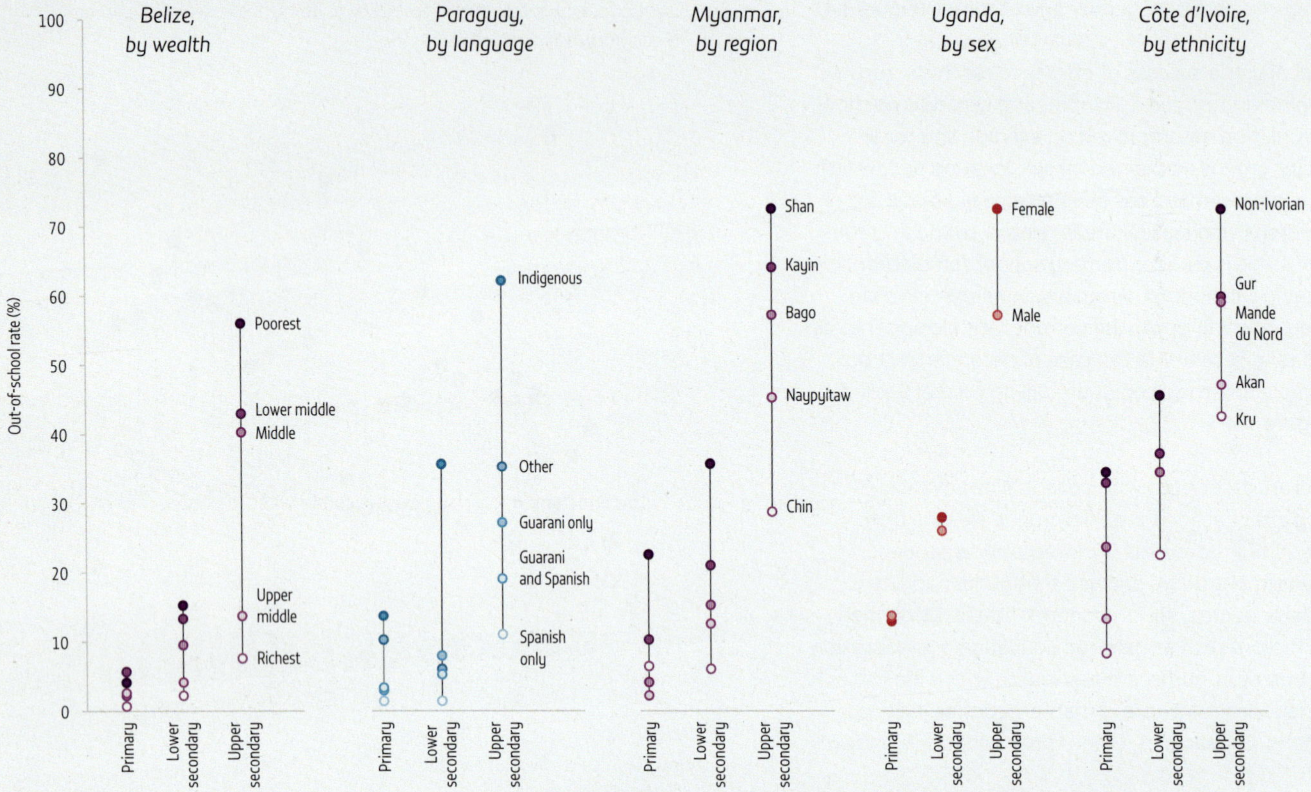

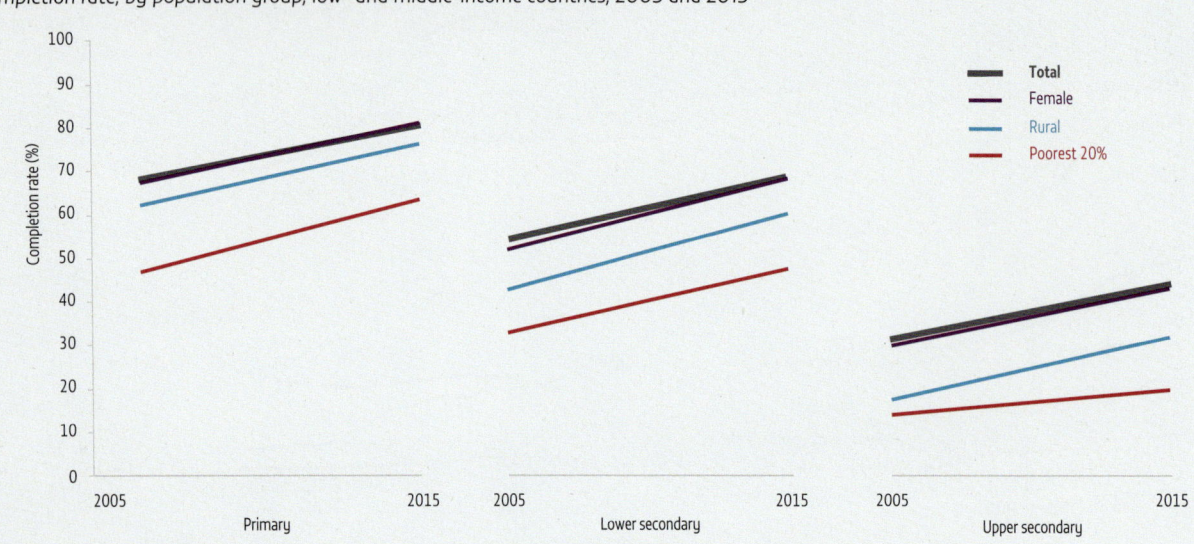

GEM StatLink: http://bit.ly/GEM2020_fig1_4
Source: World Inequality Database on Education.

FIGURE 1.5:

The promise of reaching the furthest behind first is not being kept

Completion rate, by population group, low- and middle-income countries, 2005 and 2015

GEM StatLink: http://bit.ly/GEM2020_fig1_5
Source: GEM Report team estimates based on household survey data.

as a measure (the ratio of the scores of the most disadvantaged students relative to the least), those in the bottom socio-economic quarter did worse than those in the top quarter in all countries (**Figure 1.6**).

The gap is underestimated, since students from lower socio-economic strata are more likely to leave school before age 15 and not take the test. In all regions except Europe and Northern America, adolescents from the richest households were three times as likely to complete lower secondary school as those from the poorest households. Among those who completed lower secondary school, students from the richest households

are twice as likely to have basic skills as those from the poorest households. Only 18 of the poorest youth complete secondary school for every 100 of the richest youth (**Figure 1.7**).

Grade 4 students in middle and high-income countries who were taught in a language other than their mother tongue typically scored 34% below native speakers in reading tests. Moreover, exclusions mean inequality is underestimated in achievement comparisons. Countries participating in PISA may exclude inaccessible or special schools. Students may be excluded, notably those with

FIGURE 1.6:

Socio-economic status is a major predictor of learning achievement

Adjusted parity index in achievement of minimum proficiency in reading and mathematics, by gender and wealth, countries participating in the 2018 Programme for International Student Assessment

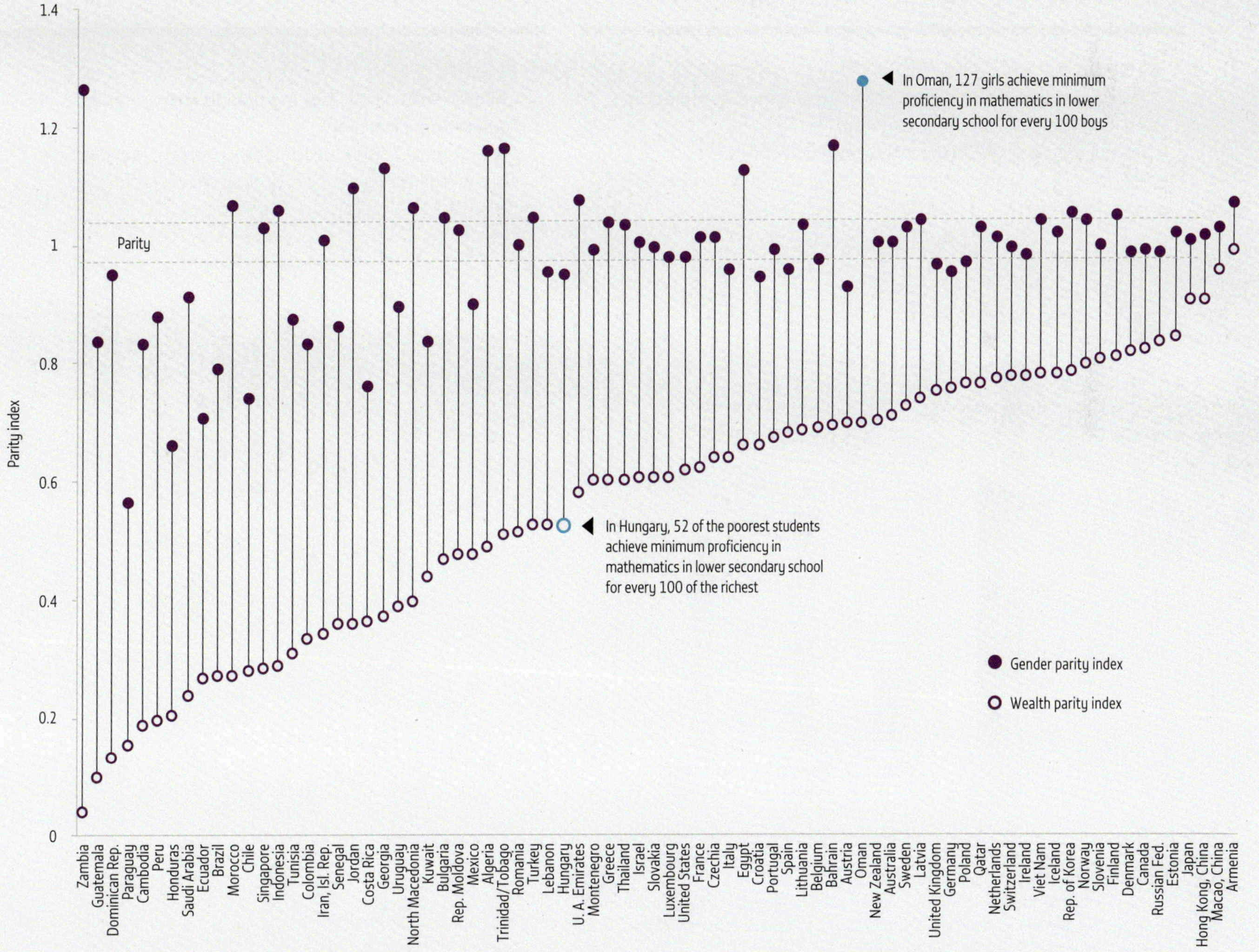

In Oman, 127 girls achieve minimum proficiency in mathematics in lower secondary school for every 100 boys

In Hungary, 52 of the poorest students achieve minimum proficiency in mathematics in lower secondary school for every 100 of the richest

● Gender parity index
○ Wealth parity index

GEM StatLink: http://bit.ly/GEM2020_fig1_6
Source: UIS database.

limited proficiency in the language of assessment and students with selected disabilities (OECD, 2019).

Children with disabilities are particularly at risk of exclusion from education. Until recently, there was no consensus on defining and measuring disability, and its links with school attendance and learning achievement were obscure. The Washington Group Short Set of Questions on Disability (see **Chapter 3**) has been gaining momentum, although even the UN Disability Statistics Database contains few results that use the questions (United Nations, 2019). They were adopted in the sixth round of the UNICEF Multiple Indicator Cluster Surveys and other surveys that collect a combination of information on disability, school attendance and foundational proficiency skills in reading and mathematics. In 10 low- and middle-income countries, children with disabilities were 8 percentage points, or 19%, less likely to achieve minimum proficiency in reading than those

without disabilities (**Figure 1.8**). Yet in all 10 countries, especially the poorest, the majority of children, regardless of disability status, were at high risk of exclusion, as they did not achieve minimum proficiency in reading.

INCLUSION IN EDUCATION IS NOT JUST A RESULT; IT IS A PROCESS

Low rates of entry, progression and learning are just the final, visible outcomes of socio-economic processes that marginalize, disappoint and alienate scores of children, youth and adults. A 'toxic mix of poverty and discrimination' results in them being 'excluded because of who they are' (Save the Children, 2017, p. 1). Powerful social and economic mechanisms related to the distribution and use of opportunities, especially early in life, have major, lasting effects on inclusion in education. Education system mechanisms that play out daily in

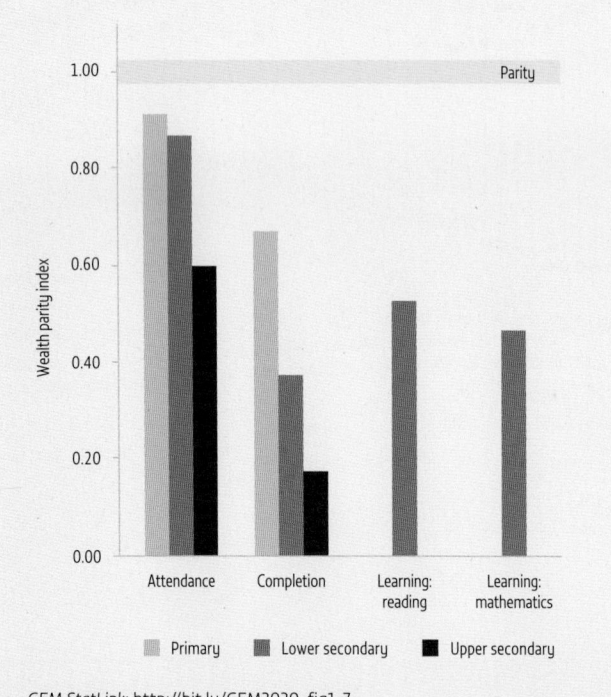

FIGURE 1.7:
There are large wealth disparities in attendance, completion and learning
Wealth parity index in attendance, completion and minimum proficiency in reading and mathematics, by education level, selected countries, 2013–17

GEM StatLink: http://bit.ly/GEM2020_fig1_7
Note: Sample excludes high-income countries in Europe and Northern America.
Source: GEM Report team analysis using household surveys (attendance and completion) and UIS database (learning).

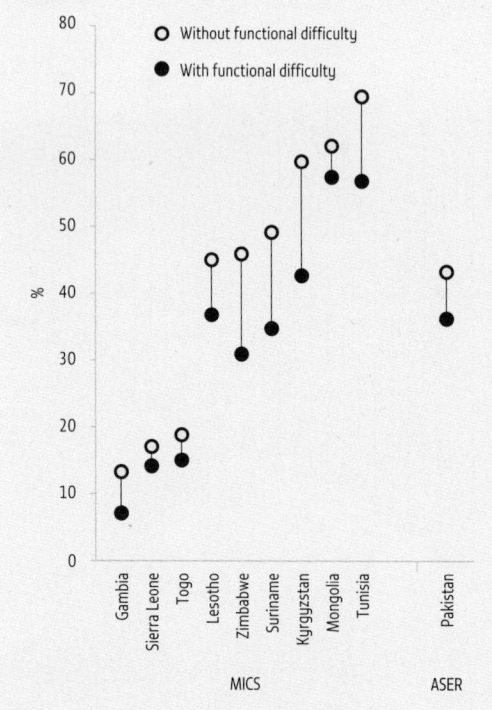

FIGURE 1.8:
Children with disabilities lag behind their peers in foundational learning
Percentage of 7- to 14-year-olds who achieve foundational skills in reading, by disability status, selected countries, 2017–19

GEM StatLink: http://bit.ly/GEM2020_fig1_8
Source: GEM Report team analysis of MICS and ASER Pakistan data.

classrooms, schoolyards, parent–teacher meetings, community gatherings, local government coordination structures and ministerial councils also have an impact. The purpose of this report is to detail processes that fail many students but also to highlight bold steps to address the challenges of diversity.

An 'inclusive and equitable' education is at the core of the SDG 4 ambition. Defining equitable education requires distinguishing between equality and equity, two terms occasionally misunderstood. In a cartoon that has appeared in various versions, a panel labelled equality shows children of varying heights standing on same-sized boxes trying to write on a blackboard, the shortest ones struggling. In the equity panel, they stand on differently sized boxes, all able to write comfortably. However, the representation is misleading (**Figure 1.9**). There is equality in both panels: of inputs in the first, of outcomes in the second. Equality is a state of affairs (what): a result that can be observed in inputs, outputs or outcomes, e.g. achieving gender equality. Equity is a process (how): actions aimed at ensuring equality.

Inclusion is more difficult to define. As used in this report, it mirrors equity. It is a process: actions and practices that embrace diversity and build a sense of belonging, rooted

in the belief that every person has value and potential and should be respected. Yet inclusion is also a state of affairs, a result, whose multifaceted nature makes it difficult to pin down.

While SDG 4 envisions inclusive education as encompassing all children, youth and adults, such education has historically been associated with, and often conceptualized as, education for children with disabilities. The struggle of people with disabilities has therefore shaped the understanding of inclusion.

THE STRUGGLE OF PEOPLE WITH DISABILITIES SHAPES PERSPECTIVES ON INCLUSION IN EDUCATION

Education was recognized as a human right in 1948. In 1960, the UNESCO Convention against Discrimination in Education specified what governments must do to prevent 'nullifying or impairing equality of treatment in education' (Article 1). It focused on ensuring that all learners enjoyed equal access to, and quality of, education with respect to human dignity but did not include disability among characteristics that could lead to 'distinction, exclusion, limitation or preference' in education. In 1994, the Statement at the World

FIGURE 1.9:
A popular representation of equality and equity is misleading

ADENE

Conference on Special Needs Education in Salamanca, Spain, made a strong and clear case for inclusive education: '[Those] with special educational needs must have access to regular schools', albeit with the proviso 'unless there are compelling reasons for doing otherwise' (UNESCO and Spain Ministry of Education and Science, 1994, Art. 2 and 3).

The 2006 UN Convention on the Rights of Persons with Disabilities (CRPD) guaranteed the right to inclusive education. Article 24, aiming to realize the right to education of people with disabilities 'without discrimination and on the basis of equal opportunity', committed countries to 'ensure an inclusive education system at all levels and lifelong learning'. The article's first paragraph captured its spirit: Inclusive education would ensure the development of the 'sense of dignity and self-worth' of people with disabilities and of 'their personality, talents and creativity, as well as their mental and physical abilities to their fullest potential' to enable them to 'participate effectively in a free society'. The second paragraph contained the key means of fulfilling the right, including access to education 'on an equal basis with others in the communities in which they live' and 'support required, within the general education system' (United Nations, 2006).

Although absent in earlier drafts, the commitment to inclusion in school placement not only broke with the historical tendency to exclude children with disabilities from education altogether or to segregate them in special schools, but also distinguished inclusion from integration. Ensuring access to mainstream schools but placing children with disabilities in separate classes for much of the time, not providing them with needed support or expecting them to adapt to available services is at odds with the goal of inclusion, which involves changes in school support and ethos (de Beco, 2018). This approach reflected radical changes in perception of disability over the last 50 years that led to the social model of disability, which the CRPD takes as its foundation (**Box 1.1**).

The CRPD stopped short of a precise definition of inclusion in education. The term therefore remains contentious, lacking a tight conceptual focus, which may have contributed to ambivalence and confused practices (Slee, 2020). While the CRPD endorsed actions that could lead to enrolment in mainstream schools, it did not suggest that special schools violated

BOX 1.1:

The evolving interpretation of disability has shaped education provision

Evolving perceptions of people with disabilities shaped three approaches to their education (Al Ju'beh, 2015). The charity model viewed people with disabilities as victims or objects of pity. They were considered uneducable and excluded from education, although some religious institutions provided education alongside care. The medical model considered disability a condition to be treated, making health professionals primarily responsible for education. Starting in the 1970s, the social model contrasted the biological condition (impairment) with the social condition (disability). In this approach, disability is not an individual attribute. It emerges because individuals face barriers they cannot overcome in certain environments. It is the system and context that do not take the diversity and multiplicity of needs into account (Norwich, 2014). The social model is linked to the rights-based approach to inclusion and the idea that education needs to be available, accessible, acceptable and adaptable (Tomaševski, 2001).

In 2001, the World Health Organization issued the International Classification of Functioning, Disability and Health, which synthesized the medical and social models of disability. Although it listed 1,500 disability codes, it stated that disability resulted not only from physical conditions and biological endowment but also from personal or environmental contexts (WHO, 2001).

This new perspective led to the abandonment of the term handicap. Disability results from interaction between people with impairments and their contexts (Rimmerman, 2013). Functioning and capability approaches are central to the social model's focus on what a person has difficulty doing. Society and culture determine rules, define normality and treat difference as deviance.

The concept of obstacles suggests that many people are at risk of education exclusion. Social and cultural mechanisms drive exclusion on the basis of ethnicity or poverty, for instance. In education, the concept of barriers to participation and learning is replacing that of special needs and difficulties.

the convention (de Beco, 2018). Some argue that, in favouring an anti-discrimination over a needs-based perspective, Article 24 privileged 'mainstream educational environments as its presumed substantive standard rather than the provision of quality instruction in an appropriate setting (including specialized settings) tailored to the particular educational needs of each individual student' (Anastasiou et al., 2018, pp. 9–10). Reports to countries by the Committee on the Rights of Persons with Disabilities confirm a clear position that embraces a 'transition from special and segregated education towards the inclusive model' (Cisternas Reyes, 2019, p. 413).

Ultimately, the CRPD gave governments a free hand in shaping inclusive education, which may be seen as implicit recognition of the dilemmas and tensions involved in overcoming obstacles to full inclusion (Forlin et al., 2013). While exclusionary practices by many governments in contravention of their CRPD commitments should be exposed, limits to how flexible mainstream schools and education systems can be should be acknowledged.

In addressing inclusion in education as a question of where students with disabilities should be taught, there is potential tension between the desirable goals of maximizing interaction with others (all children under the same roof) and fulfilling learning potential (wherever students learn best) (Norwich, 2014). Other considerations include the speed with which systems can move towards the ideal and what happens during transition (Stubbs, 2008), and the trade-off between early needs identification and the risk of labelling and stigmatization (Haug, 2017).

Education serves multiple objectives. Efforts to pursue them simultaneously can be complementary or conflicting. Policymakers and educators confront delicate, context-specific questions related to inclusion. They need to be aware of opposition by those with an interest in preserving segregated delivery rather than addressing inclusion. Perpetuating the misconception of people with disabilities as fundamentally different can make segregation a self-fulfilling prophecy.

However, rapid change may be unsustainable, potentially harming those it is supposed to serve. Including children with disabilities in mainstream schools that are not prepared, supported or accountable for achieving inclusion can intensify experiences of exclusion and provoke backlash against making schools and systems

more inclusive. Appropriation of the language of inclusion by those who advocate for exceptions can aggravate backlash: '[Instead] of providing a framework for the consideration of disability as a relationship between individual impairments or differences and combinations of curriculum, pedagogy, assessment and school and classroom organisation and culture, the term "special educational needs" became an overarching category of defective pathology' (Slee, 2020, p. 22).

These ambiguities led the Committee on the Rights of Persons with Disabilities to issue General Comment No. 4 on Article 24 in 2016, following a two-year process involving submissions from countries, non-government organizations (NGOs), organizations for people with disabilities, academics and disability advocates. It defined inclusion as

> a process of systemic reform embodying changes and modifications in content, teaching methods, approaches, structures and strategies in education to overcome barriers with a vision serving to provide all students of the relevant age range with an equitable and participatory learning experience and environment that best corresponds to their requirements and preferences. Placing students with disabilities within mainstream classes without accompanying structural changes to, for example, organisation, curriculum and teaching and learning strategies, does not constitute inclusion. Furthermore, integration does not automatically guarantee the transition from segregation to inclusion. (Committee on the Rights of Persons with Disabilities, 2016, p. 4)

The committee described the right to inclusive education as encompassing

> a transformation in culture, policy and practice in all formal and informal educational environments to accommodate the differing requirements and identities of individual students, together with a commitment to remove the barriers that impede that possibility. It involves strengthening the capacity of the education system to reach out to all learners. It focuses on the full and effective participation, accessibility, attendance and achievement of all students, especially those who, for different reasons, are excluded or at risk of being marginalized. Inclusion involves access to and progress in high-quality formal and informal education without discrimination. It seeks to enable communities, systems and

structures to combat discrimination, including harmful stereotypes, recognize diversity, promote participation and overcome barriers to learning and participation for all by focusing on well-being and success of students with disabilities. It requires an in-depth transformation of education systems in legislation, policy, and the mechanisms for financing, administration, design, delivery and monitoring of education. (Committee on the Rights of Persons with Disabilities, 2016, p. 3)

INCLUSION IN EDUCATION CONCERNS ALL LEARNERS

Two key takeaways from General Comment No. 4 are central to this report. First, as the description of the requirements makes clear, inclusive education involves a process that contributes to the goal of social inclusion. The attainability of this goal should not affect the resolve of those responsible for implementing this process or those holding them accountable for fulfilling their commitment. Inclusive education should embody the principles of dialogue, participation and openness, bringing all stakeholders together to resolve emerging tensions and dilemmas. Decisions should be based on human dignity, without compromising, discounting or diverting from the long-term ideal of inclusion.

At the same time, the efforts of policymakers and educators should not override the needs and preferences of those affected. Beyond upholding the fundamental human rights and principles that provide moral and political direction for education decisions, fulfilling the inclusive ideal is not trivial. Delivering sufficient differentiated and individualized support requires perseverance, resilience and a long-term perspective. In Ethiopia, the academic achievement and academic self-concept of deaf and hard-of-hearing primary school students who transitioned into mainstream schools decreased, compared with peers who remained in special schools (Mulat et al., 2018). In Fiji, the needs of students with intellectual disabilities were more appropriately met in special education settings because mainstream schools were not adequately resourced (Tones et al., 2017). Moving students from special to mainstream schools is not automatically a solution unless the requisite human and financial resources exist to provide inclusive education effectively.

Moving away from education systems whose design suits some children and obliges others to adapt cannot happen by decree. Prevailing attitudes and mindsets must be challenged. 'The correct approach is not to seek justification for the limits to the goal of inclusive education, but rather to establish the legitimacy of making efforts towards that goal despite such limits. We must investigate whether it is possible to incorporate the element of actual achievability into the ideal of inclusive education' (de Beco, 2018, p. 408).

The second takeaway of General Comment No. 4 is that inclusive education is much broader in scope. It entails a 'process of addressing and responding to the diversity of needs of all children, youth and adults' (UNESCO, 2009, p. 8), to eliminate barriers to the right to education and change the culture, policy and practice of mainstream schools to accommodate and effectively include all learners. While 68% of countries have a definition of inclusive education, only 57% of those definitions cover multiple marginalized groups.

It is not only learners with disabilities who are excluded through discriminatory mechanisms. For instance, the disproportional referral of minorities to special education indicates how cultural biases are embedded in identification of special needs. All over the world, layers of discrimination on the basis of gender, remoteness, wealth, disability, ethnicity, language, migration, displacement, incarceration, sexual orientation, gender identity and expression, religion and other beliefs and attitudes deny students the right to be educated with their peers or to receive education of the same quality (**Figure 1.10**) (**Boxes 1.2–1.6**). The Covid-19 pandemic has added new layers of exclusion related to accessibility of distance learning opportunities, which also affect new categories of the population.

Belief in the principle of inclusion should not obscure the difficult questions and potential drawbacks raised by including groups of learners at risk of exclusion. In some contexts, inclusion may inadvertently intensify pressure to conform. Group identities, practices, languages and beliefs may be devalued, jeopardized or eradicated, undercutting a sense of belonging. The right of a group to preserve its culture and the right to self-determination and self-representation are increasingly recognized. Inclusion may be resisted out of prejudice but also out of recognition that identity may be maintained and empowerment achieved only if a minority is a majority in a given area. Rather than achieve positive social engagement, in some circumstances inclusion policies may exacerbate social exclusion. Exposure to the majority may reinforce dominant prejudices, intensifying minority disadvantage. Targeting assistance can also lead to stigmatization, labelling or unwelcome forms of inclusion (Silver, 2015).

FIGURE 1.10:
All means all

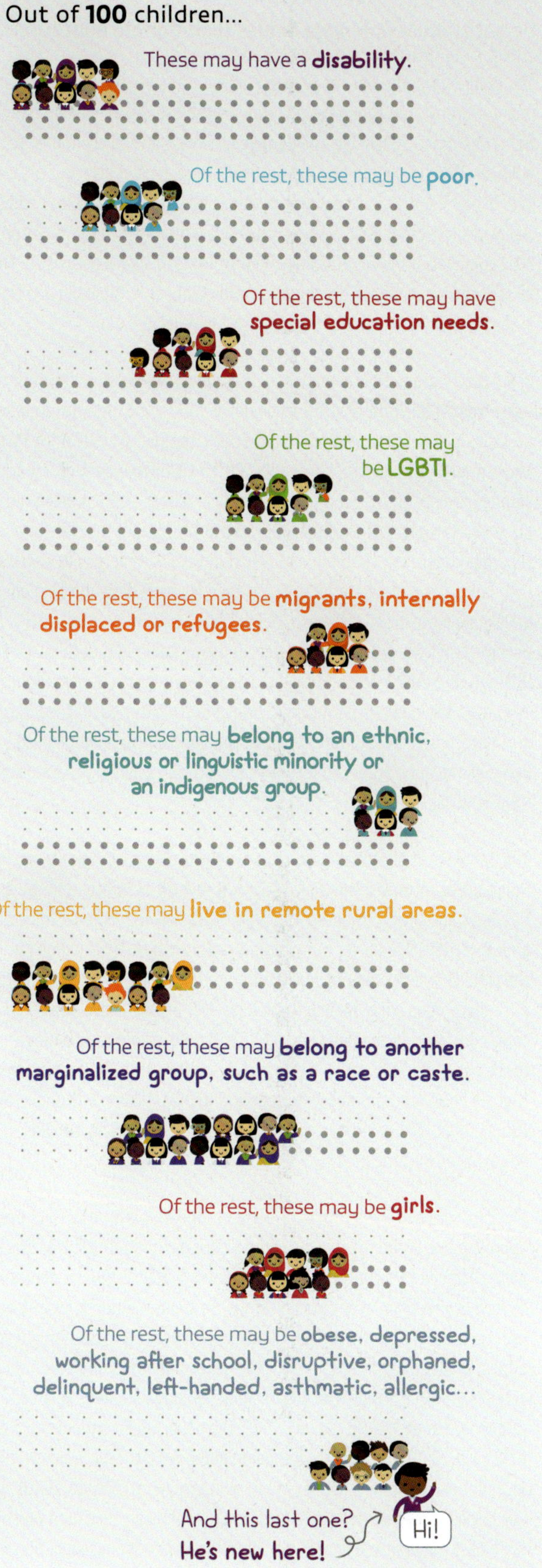

Out of **100** children...

These may have a **disability**.

Of the rest, these may be **poor**.

Of the rest, these may have **special education needs**.

Of the rest, these may be **LGBTI**.

Of the rest, these may be **migrants, internally displaced or refugees**.

Of the rest, these may **belong to an ethnic, religious or linguistic minority or an indigenous group**.

Of the rest, these may **live in remote rural areas**.

Of the rest, these may **belong to another marginalized group, such as a race or caste**.

Of the rest, these may be **girls**.

Of the rest, these may be **obese, depressed, working after school, disruptive, orphaned, delinquent, left-handed, asthmatic, allergic**...

And this last one? He's new here!

Hi!

BOX 1.2:

The education and even the lives of children with albinism in sub-Saharan Africa are at risk

People with albinism are at high risk of exclusion in sub-Saharan Africa, specifically in education. In some countries, a belief that their body parts bring luck, wealth and success has led to mutilations and killings: There have been over 700 attacks and other violations in 28 countries since 2006 (Action on Albinism, 2019). The appearance and vision impairment of people with albinism mark them as different, resulting in violence, stigmatization, discrimination and social exclusion (Burke et al., 2014). The UN Human Rights Council urged countries to address 'the root causes of attacks and discrimination against persons with albinism, notably by proactively combating superstition and stigma vis-à-vis albinism, including through education and awareness-raising campaigns' (Human Rights Council, 2013, p. 17).

Although people with albinism can be considered legally blind, they can read if they have access to large-print text. However, in sub-Saharan Africa, children with low vision, including those with albinism, are primarily educated in special schools for the blind (Lynch et al., 2014). In Malawi, those with albinism are mainly educated by itinerant teachers for the blind (Lynch and Lund, 2011). In Zimbabwe and parts of Zambia, children with albinism attend mainstream schools, where inclusion can be challenging. Teachers may fear teaching these children (Miles, 2011), and lack of education and correct information in the community increases the probability of teachers drawing on local myth in their approaches (Baker et al., 2010).

In the United Republic of Tanzania, about 1 in 2,650 people has albinism. Only half of children with albinism complete primary school (Baker, 2018). Those in school often have difficulty reading and need vision devices to participate. Lack of this support negatively affects their learning, often resulting in their transfer to special schools. As part of its 2012–17 inclusive education strategy, the government incorporated a guide for teachers of students with albinism in the teacher education curriculum. To address the threat of attack, however, the government placed hundreds of these children in 'protectorate centres', separated from their peers. The centres were overcrowded and understaffed, and had inadequate education infrastructure (Standing Voice, 2017).

In June 2015, the Human Rights Council appointed the first independent expert on human rights, including the right to education, for people with albinism. The 2017–21 Regional Action Plan on Albinism in Africa, presented to the council in 2017, focused on education equality and non-discrimination in access and learning (United Nations General Assembly, 2017a). In May 2017, the African Commission on Human and Peoples' Rights endorsed the plan and urged states to adopt and implement it. In May 2018, the Pan-African Parliament passed a resolution endorsing it (Action on Albinism, 2019). The plan made provision for reasonable accommodation by 2021. This led the United Republic of Tanzania's Prime Minister's Office to instruct the Ministry of Industry and Trade to produce assistive devices and to reduce their cost when not produced domestically. Yet the risk of education exclusion remains high (Pedneault and Labaki, 2019). The independent expert's mission report on the United Republic of Tanzania made several recommendations related to full implementation of the inclusive policy and the allocation of necessary resources (United Nations General Assembly, 2017b)

BOX 1.3:

Stateless people in some Arab countries lack access to public education

An estimated 10 million people worldwide are stateless, lacking a recognized nationality. The *bidoon* (without) in Bahrain, Kuwait, Saudi Arabia and the United Arab Emirates have difficulty gaining access to education due to uncertainty surrounding their nationality (Institute on Statelessness and Inclusion, 2017). In Kuwait, the *bidoon* are without nationality (Beaugrand, 2017). They fall into three categories: those born to people who did not apply for nationality or did not have the necessary documentation when Kuwait became independent in 1961; those who were employed by the Kuwait army and police forces and settled in Kuwait with their families in the 1960s; and those born to a Kuwaiti mother and a stateless or foreign father (Human Rights Watch, 2011). The government disputes the estimate of 100,000 *bidoon* (Human Rights Watch, 2019c), considering 34,000 eligible for citizenship and the rest migrants or their descendants (*Middle East Eye*, 2016).

While the *bidoon* received social and economic benefits similar to citizens in the 1960s and 1970s, including free education, instability after the 1980s led to the removal of benefits. Kuwait's nationality law became stricter, e.g. revoking Kuwaiti women's right to pass citizenship on to their children if the father was not Kuwaiti in 1980. The *bidoon* do not receive the civil identification cards necessary to enrol in most schools and training institutions. Instead, they receive security cards, which protect them from deportation and allow registration in the private schools to which they are limited.

In 1986, the government created a parallel private school system and transferred 50,000 *bidoon* students from public schools (Beaugrand, 2010). The private schools are believed to be under-resourced and to have lower standards. Parents pay annual fees of US$860 to US$1,550 plus textbook and uniform costs (Human Rights Watch, 2011), although the government set up a fund to subsidize 70% of the fees (Elgayar, 2014). Many but not all *bidoon* children receive funds, including children who lack valid security cards or do not pass annual examinations (Human Rights Watch, 2011).

Bidoon students are ineligible for scholarships to study abroad and were banned from Kuwait universities in 1987. They have access to the Kuwait branch of the Arab Open University, which welcomes stateless people; one-quarter of its graduates were *bidoon* in 2007 (Beaugrand, 2010). The government presented plans to grant citizenship to some *bidoon* while expecting others to obtain foreign passports, which would allow them to remain in Kuwait legally, for instance through an agreement with Comoros to grant passports in exchange for infrastructure investment (Zacharias, 2018). The Ministry of Education recently rejected a parliamentary proposal to register *bidoon* children in public schools (Amnesty International, 2019).

Kuwait is the most visible example of a larger regional issue. Qatari women married to foreigners could not pass nationality on to their children, leading to expulsions and family separations. In 2018, these children were allowed to gain permanent residency, giving them access to public education. However, 100 residency permits are given per year, and the children are still deprived of Qatar citizenship. They may apply for it only after 25 years of permanent residency (MENA Rights Group, 2018).

BOX 1.4:

Persecution of Rohingya denies their right to education

The Rohingya, a Muslim minority in Rakhine state, Myanmar, are one of the most discriminated against ethnic groups. The 1982 Citizenship Act denied them Myanmar citizenship and deprived them of several economic, social and political rights (Parashar and Alam, 2019). Campaigns of persecution, including in 1978 and 1991/92, led hundreds of thousands to flee, mainly to neighbouring Bangladesh (Human Rights Watch, 2009). Exacerbation of the situation since 2012 culminated with the displacement of 742,000 after August 2017. Nearly all settled in and around the refugee settlements of Kutupalong and Nayapara in the Cox's Bazar district of Bangladesh (UNHCR, 2020).

In Rakhine state, school attendance rates were the lowest in the country, apart from Shan state: at the primary level, 76%, compared with a national average of 83%; at the secondary level, 49%, compared with 60% (Myanmar Ministry of Health and Sports and ICF, 2017). An independent review contained witness reports of neglect and humiliating practices, such as being taunted by teachers for lack of citizenship, seated at the back of the class or placed in separate classrooms. Rohingya students did not have access to instruction in their language and were effectively banned from entering the only university in Rakhine state in 2012 (Human Rights Council, 2018). Rohingya could not become teachers without citizenship, and non-Rohingya teachers avoided Rohingya schools, leading to high teacher absenteeism (Human Rights Watch, 2019a). Following inter-communal conflict in 2012, camps for the internally displaced, where about one-quarter of the Rohingya population lived, had minimal or no access to formal public schools (Plan International and REACH, 2015).

The Bangladesh government refuses to register the vast majority of the Rohingya as refugees. However, in 2016, it revised its Strategy for Myanmar Refugees and Undocumented Myanmar Nationals to recognize education among potential areas for humanitarian intervention. This change facilitated the establishment of about 3,000 temporary learning centres during the 2017–18 refugee crisis. Mainly funded by UNICEF, they have been providing early education to children aged 4 to 6 and non-formal basic education to those aged 6 to 14 (Human Rights Watch, 2019a). A recent mapping found that 126 NGO programmes were serving 166,000 children and adolescents (Dupuy et al., 2019) – just over half of the 311,000 5- to 17-year-olds enumerated in camps.

The curriculum in the temporary learning centres is informal. The government approved two components up to grade 2 but did not indicate whether it would accredit this education (Human Rights Watch, 2019a). It denies access to formal education in or outside camps. Students cannot sit examinations or receive completion certification, which prevents them from pursuing education beyond grade 8. In 2019, the government ordered seven secondary schools in Teknaf subdistrict not to allow Rohingya students to attend (Human Rights Watch, 2019b). In January 2020, the government announced that, as of April 2020, 10,000 Rohingya children in grades 6 to 9 in camps would enrol in a pilot programme using the Myanmar curriculum (Ahmed, 2020). While the decision goes some way to offer the Rohingya an education prospect, it violates the principle of inclusion of refugees in national education systems.

Roma children in Europe are frequently segregated in education

The Roma are the largest ethnic minority in Europe, numbering between 10 million and 12 million. They live in poverty and suffer prejudice, intolerance and discrimination (FRA, 2014). Their education attainment is low. Across nine countries in 2016, their early childhood education participation rate was 53%. About 6% of 16- to 24-year-olds had never attended school, with country shares as high as 42% in Greece. The secondary school completion rate of 18- to 24-year-olds was 34% among men and 29% among women (FRA, 2016).

Roma children suffer various forms of segregation in education. The shares of those attending classes where all or most learners were Roma ranged from 14% in Portugal to about 60% in Bulgaria, Hungary and Slovakia. In Bulgaria, 27% of Roma children attended schools where all their classmates were Roma, according to the Second Survey on Minorities in Europe (FRA, 2016). In Hungary, segregation has increased, with the proportion of basic schools with a Roma population of at least 50% rising from 10% in 2008 to 15% in 2017 (European Commission, 2019a). Roma children were also segregated on separate floors or in separate classes (Albert et al., 2015).

Roma children are disproportionally diagnosed with intellectual disabilities and placed in special schools, as in Hungary (Van den Bogaert, 2018) and Slovakia (Amnesty International and European Roma Rights Centre, 2017). The Council of Europe issued a position paper on fighting school segregation through inclusive education, which drew attention to new forms of discrimination, such as Roma-only private schools (Council of Europe, 2017). In 2013, European Council recommendations on effective integration measures obliged member states to end 'inappropriate placement' of Roma students in special schools (European Council, 2013, Para. 1.3). Nevertheless, in 2016, 16% of Roma children aged 6 to15 in the Czech Republic and 18% in Slovakia attended special schools (FRA, 2016).

In line with its 2000 Racial Equality Directive, which prohibited discrimination in education on racial and ethnic grounds, the European Union (EU) started infringement procedures against the Czech Republic (2015), Slovakia (2015) and Hungary (2016), telling them to end discrimination against Roma children in education and ensure equal access to quality education (European Commission, 2016). A letter of formal notice was sent to Slovakia in 2015, but the European Commission concluded in October 2019 that measures taken had been insufficient to redress the situation and warned the country that if it did not take action by the end of 2019, the matter could be referred to the European Court of Justice (European Commission, 2019b). A European Court of Human Rights ruling in Horváth and Kiss v. Hungary in 2013 obliged the country to 'undo a history of racial segregation' (European Court of Human Rights, 2013, p. 34), but local actors have been trying to undermine the decision (Zemandl, 2018).

A joint EU and Council of Europe project, Inclusive Schools: Making a Difference for Roma Children, aims to increase understanding of the benefits of inclusive education among teachers and the public, set up support mechanisms and resources for pilot inclusive schools, provide support to teachers to practice inclusive teaching and support removal of barriers for vulnerable groups (Council of Europe, 2019).

Afro-descendants in Latin America have endured a legacy of limited education opportunities

Latin America and the Caribbean has the world's largest concentration of Afro-descendant populations, with estimates ranging from 120 million to 170 million (Rodríguez and Mallo, 2014). Brazil is home to the majority (112 million), equivalent to 55% of its population (IBGE, 2017). The smaller populations in other countries are often concentrated. For instance, 8 in 10 people in Choco department, Colombia, are Afro-descendant (World Bank, 2018). Across Latin America, legislation protecting their rights has contributed to increases in the numbers of people identifying as Afro-descendant (World Bank, 2018). Among 12 countries with a population census in the 2010 round, 11 incorporated a question for people of African descent (ECLAC, 2017a).

These populations, whose ancestors were victims of the slave trade, continue to experience structural inequality. In Brazil, the poverty headcount rate is 26% for Afro-descendants and 12% for others; in Colombia, the respective rates are 41% and 27%. In Ecuador, 16% of the urban population but 30% of the Afro-descendant population live in slums; in Nicaragua, the respective rates are 59% and 93% (World Bank, 2018). Education can play a key role in reducing such inequality. The Organization of Ibero-American States included education equity for Afro-descendant populations in its Goals 2021 agenda (OEI, 2010).

Despite progress in many countries, inequality persists in education attendance, attainment and achievement. In 7 of the 11 countries with relevant data, attendance rates for Afro-descendants aged 12 to 17 were lower than for their non-Afro-descendant peers (ECLAC, 2017b). The probability of Afro-descendants completing secondary education was 14% lower than non-Afro-descendants in Peru and 24% lower in Uruguay in 2015 (World Bank, 2018).

Historically, learning materials have given rise to stereotypes, discrimination and racism. In some countries, the history of Africa and Afro-descendants, if not omitted or misrepresented, appeared only in relation to food, music and dance (Chagas, 2017; Mena García, 2009). UN experts recommended to Ecuador that 'textbooks and other educational materials reflect historical facts accurately as they relate to past tragedies and atrocities, in particular slavery, the trade in enslaved Africans and colonialism, so as to avoid stereotypes and the distortion or falsification of these historic facts, which may lead to racism, racial discrimination, xenophobia and related intolerance' (OHCHR, 2019). Guatemala was a pioneer in making Garifuna an official language in 2003 (Muñoz, 2003), but bilingual instruction opportunities are limited (ECLAC, 2018).

Countries have introduced affirmative action laws and policies to redress discrimination. In Colombia, a project to train early childhood educators in strengthening pedagogy based on ancestral African knowledge aimed to support children in asserting their identity (Torres Fuentes, 2014). A 2012 law introduced a 10% quota for Afro-Colombian students entering public universities and technical schools by 2024 (Paschel, 2016). Ecuador's Plan for the Elimination of Racial Discrimination and Ethnic Exclusion set a 10% quota for admission to secondary and higher education of Afro-Ecuadorians, indigenous peoples and the Montubios, a mestizo population (Ecuador Ministry of Heritage Coordination, 2009). A 2016 agreement recognized eight guardian schools of Afro-Ecuadorian knowledge (Antón, 2020). Besides legislation, 14 countries have policies to promote racial equality or better targeting of policy (ECLAC, 2017a)

WHY DOES INCLUSIVE EDUCATION MATTER?

Careful planning and provision of inclusive education can deliver improvement in academic achievement, social and emotional development, self-esteem and peer acceptance. Including diverse students in mainstream classrooms and schools can prevent stigma, stereotyping, discrimination and alienation. Ensuring that classrooms and schools are well resourced and well supported implies costs: to adapt curricula, train teachers, develop adequate and relevant teaching and learning materials and make education accessible. There are potential efficiency savings from eliminating parallel structures and using resources more effectively in a single, inclusive mainstream system. As few systems come close to the ideal, reliable estimates of the full cost are scarce. An economic cost–benefit analysis is therefore difficult, not least because the benefits are hard to quantify and extend over generations.

An economic justification for inclusive education, while valuable for planning, is not sufficient. It has been argued that debating the benefits of inclusive education is equivalent to debating the benefits of abolishing slavery (Bilken, 1985) or apartheid (Lipsky and Gartner, 1997). Inclusion is a moral imperative and a condition for achieving all the SDGs, particularly sustainable, equitable and inclusive societies. It is an expression of justice, not of charity, whatever the differences, biological or otherwise, and however they may be described. Thinking about the education of students with disabilities or special needs should be tantamount to thinking about what all students may need. All students require teaching methods and support mechanisms that help them succeed and belong.

Inclusive education promotes inclusive societies, where people can live together and diversity is celebrated. It is a prerequisite for education in and for democracies based on fairness, justice and equity (Slee, 2020). It provides a systematic framework for identifying and dismantling barriers for vulnerable populations according to the principle 'every learner matters and matters equally' (UNESCO, 2017, p. 12). It counteracts education system tendencies that allow exceptions and exclusions. The 2017/18 *Global Education Monitoring Report* described the trend of undue emphasis on evaluating schools along a single dimension, such as reading and mathematics scores, that determined resource allocation. Such practices force schools in some countries to be selective or to label students likely to perform below average.

GUIDE TO THE REPORT

The 2020 *Global Education Monitoring Report* recognizes the contexts and challenges facing countries in providing inclusive education; the groups at risk of being excluded from education and the barriers individual learners face, especially when various characteristics intersect; and the fact that exclusion can be physical, social (in interpersonal and group relations), psychological and systemic, as requirements may exclude, for instance, the poor (e.g. fees) or migrants and refugees (e.g. documentation). It addresses these challenges through seven elements, considering how they contribute to local and system-level inclusion of learners vulnerable to exclusion. Recommendations at the end of this chapter summarize the next steps needed to achieve the 2030 Agenda targets.

The thematic part of the report is organized into eight chapters. Chapter 2 analyses the role of legal tools in supporting development of inclusive education. Laws express the national interpretation of international conventions, which have formulated the commitment to inclusion, but also adaptation of these concepts to reflect the complexities and barriers specific to their contexts. It addresses vague or contradictory laws and policies that can hinder inclusion and universal access to the different levels of education. A short section looks at the inclusion challenges for laws and policies through the lens of Covid-19.

Chapter 3 assesses challenges in collecting data on and for inclusion in education. It reviews experiences of defining vulnerable groups, including learners with disabilities, and challenges of identification and labelling. It then considers qualitative aspects, such as segregation, administrative data and qualitative measures of inclusion.

Chapter 4 addresses two related aspects. First, education ministries are at the heart of the inclusion effort but need to work with ministries and agencies in other sectors, subnational education authorities and NGOs. Success in inclusive education rests on good governance of these complex partnerships. Second, financing is crucial in ensuring education for all and targeting the schools and students most in need. In addition to general equity-oriented funding mechanisms, a twin-track approach calls for financing the education of groups, such as learners with disabilities.

Chapter 5 discusses the politically equally complicated issue of how curricula and learning materials are adapted to the principles of inclusive education. It looks at the stakeholders involved in curriculum and textbook development and how groups at risk of exclusion are neglected, under-represented or misrepresented, including in images. Curricula can also exclude through irrelevant content and inflexible delivery. Last, the chapter examines assessment and accommodations.

Chapter 6 looks at how teachers can support transition from special needs to mainstream education, what their needs are and how governments help them prepare. It also explores education support personnel, the degree to which they are available and their relation to teachers, towards ensuring inclusive practice. Finally, it covers the extent to which staff make-up reflects student diversity.

Chapter 7 examines three school-level factors. First, a whole-school approach based on an inclusive ethos is a prerequisite for inclusion and requires head teachers to be prepared for the challenging task. Second, physical accessibility, from road conditions to building design to water and sanitation, can be a major barrier, requiring a universal design approach. Third, technology can provide significant support to students with disabilities, but cost constraints and teacher preparedness remain obstacles.

Chapter 8 examines communities' crucial role in achieving inclusive education. Students can hold or be subject to discriminatory attitudes, which affect school climate and safety, well-being and learning. Parents of vulnerable children, like other parents, may support more inclusive education but also be apprehensive. Grassroots and civil society organizations have promoted inclusion through education service provision, advocacy and scrutiny of government actions.

The report asks the following questions:

- What are the key policy solutions for each element of inclusive education to ensure achievement of SDG 4?
- How can common obstacles to implementation of these solutions be anticipated and overcome?
- What arrangements are needed to coordinate among government sectors and tiers and with other stakeholders to overcome overlapping dimensions of exclusion?

- How do education systems monitor exclusion, in terms of both individual education success and systemic factors, and how can current practices be improved?
- What financing channels are used around the world? How are they monitored, and how do they affect local practice?

To the extent possible, it examines these questions in view of changes over time. However, inclusion is a complex area that is only beginning to be documented on a global scale. A contribution of this report is having collected information on all countries, from Afghanistan to Zimbabwe, and developed profiles of how they are addressing the challenge of inclusion in education. The report features analysis of these profiles, notably in Chapter 2 on laws and policies. The profiles are available on a new *Global Education Monitoring Report* website, Profiles for Enhancing Education Reviews (PEER), and can be used by countries to share experiences and learn from each other, especially at the regional level, where contexts are similar. They can serve as a baseline to review qualitative progress by 2030.

The monitoring part of the report, Chapters 9 to 21, serves two purposes. First, it reviews the latest evidence on the SDG 4 monitoring indicators to assess quantitative progress towards the international education targets. Second, it identifies monitoring challenges and advances for each target. An introduction (Chapter 9) presents a brief set of developments in the SDG 4 monitoring framework over the past year and selected issues with data availability in three key areas: household surveys, learning assessments and teacher data – the latter two with reference to sub-Saharan Africa. Chapters 10 to 19 address the seven targets and three means of implementation. Chapter 20 reviews the role of education in three other SDGs: gender (SDG 5), climate change (SDG 13) and partnerships (SDG 17). Chapter 21 looks at domestic public and external aid and household finance.

RECOMMENDATIONS

ALL MEANS ALL: LEARNER DIVERSITY IS A STRENGTH TO BE CELEBRATED

The world has committed to inclusive education not by chance but because it is the foundation of an education system of good quality that enables every child, youth and adult to learn and fulfil their potential. Gender, age, location, poverty, disability, ethnicity, indigeneity, language, religion, migration or displacement status, sexual orientation, gender identity and expression, incarceration, beliefs and attitudes should not be the basis for discrimination against anyone in education participation and experience. The prerequisite is to see learner diversity not as a problem but as an opportunity. Inclusion cannot be achieved if it is seen as an inconvenience or if people harbour the belief that learners' levels of ability are fixed. Education systems need to be responsive to all learners' needs.

As the world enters the final decade of action to achieve SDG 4 and fulfil the commitment to 'inclusive and equitable quality education' and 'lifelong learning opportunities for all', the following 10 recommendations take into account the deep roots of barriers and the wide scope of issues related to inclusion, which threaten the world's chance to achieve the 2030 targets by the deadline.

1 **Widen the understanding of inclusive education: It should include all learners, regardless of identity, background or ability.**
Although the right to inclusive education encompasses all learners, many governments are yet to base their laws, policies and practices on this principle. While 68% of countries have a definition of inclusive education in their laws, policies and practices, only 57% of definitions cover multiple marginalized groups. In 26% of countries, the definition of inclusive education covers only people with disabilities or special needs.

Education systems that celebrate diversity, and rest on a belief that every person adds value, has potential and should be treated with dignity, enable all to learn not only the basics but also the broader range of skills needed to build sustainable societies. This is not about setting up an inclusive education department. Rather, it is about not discriminating against anyone, not rejecting anyone, making all reasonable accommodations to cater for diverse needs, and working towards gender equality. Interventions should be coherent from early childhood to adulthood to facilitate lifelong learning, and thus an inclusive perspective should be adopted in education sector plan preparation.

2 **Target financing to those left behind: There is no inclusion while millions lack access to education.**
A quarter of a billion children and youth remain out of school, and many learners leave school early. Two African countries ban pregnant girls from school, 117 countries allow child marriage, and 20 countries have not ratified the Minimum Age Convention to prevent child labour. About one in four countries has affirmative action programmes for access to tertiary education.

Once legal instruments are in place to address these barriers, governments need a twin-track approach that allocates general funding to foster an inclusive learning environment for all learners, as well as targeted funding to follow the furthest behind as early as possible. Non-education financing policies are critical. Since the 1990s, social protection programmes in Latin America have increased education attainment by 0.5 to 1.5 years. Upon access to school, early interventions can considerably reduce the potential impact of disability on progression and learning.

3 **Share expertise and resources: This is the only way to sustain a transition to inclusion.**
Laws in 25% of countries (but over 40% in Asia and in Latin America and the Caribbean) provide for education of students with disabilities in separate settings, 10% in integrated settings and 17% in inclusive settings, the remainder opting for combinations of segregation and mainstreaming. In many ways, achieving inclusion is a management challenge. Human and material resources to address diversity are scarce. Historically they have been concentrated in a few places as a legacy of segregated provision and are unequally distributed. In several countries, resource centres or itinerant specialist teachers are used to transition to inclusion. Mechanisms and incentives are needed to move them flexibly to ensure that specialist expertise supports mainstream schools and non-formal education settings.

4 **Engage in meaningful consultation with communities and parents: Inclusion cannot be enforced from above.**

Parents may hold discriminatory beliefs about gender, disability, ethnicity, race or religion. Some 15% of parents in Germany and 59% in Hong Kong, China, feared that children with disabilities disrupted others' learning. Fixed beliefs may mean families with choice avoid disadvantaged local schools or mainstream schools if they feel these do not cater for their children's needs. In Australia's Queensland state, 37% of students in special schools had moved from mainstream schools. Governments should open space for communities to voice their preferences as equals in the design of policies on inclusion in education.

In OECD countries, the share of students who felt they belonged in school fell from 82% in 2003 to 73% in 2015. Schools should increase interaction within and outside of school walls on the design and implementation of school practices through parent associations or student pairing systems. Everybody's view should count.

5 **Ensure cooperation across government departments, sectors and tiers: Inclusion in education is but a subset of social inclusion.**

Ministries sharing administrative responsibility for inclusive education must collaborate on identifying needs, exchanging information and designing programmes. A mapping of inclusive education implementation in 18 European countries showed substantial division of labour. Cross-sector collaboration can provide one-stop shops, the ideal in service delivery to individuals and households with multiple and complex needs.

Not all programmes that target disadvantaged groups can be delivered at the same location; however, they should be linked to maximize synergies. In Colombia, social programmes are tied to multidimensional poverty index scores for each family, which they can consult to see what support they are eligible for. Some 89% of countries have school health and nutrition programmes.

Decentralization can exacerbate inequality when it does not fully take into account local governments' uneven capacity for resource mobilization. In the United Kingdom, while the number of children and youth with an education, health and care plan rose

by 33% between 2015 and 2019, funding to local councils increased by only 7%. Central governments need to ensure human and financial support for local governments to carry out clearly defined inclusive education mandates.

6 **Make space for non-government actors to challenge and fill gaps: They must also make sure they work towards the same inclusion goal.**

Government must provide leadership and maintain dialogue with NGOs to ensure that education service provision leads to inclusion, meets standards and is aligned with national policy, and does not replicate services or compete for limited funds.

Government should also create conditions enabling NGOs to monitor fulfilment of government commitments and stand up for those excluded from education. A 2001 NGO campaign in Armenia resulted in a new legal and budget framework to roll out inclusive education nationally by 2025.

7 **Apply universal design: Ensure inclusive systems fulfil every learner's potential.**

All children should learn from the same flexible, relevant and accessible curriculum, one that recognizes diversity and responds to various learners' needs. Yet many countries still teach students with disabilities a special curriculum, offer refugees only the curriculum of their home country to encourage repatriation, and tend to push lower achievers into slower education tracks. Curriculum challenges arise in several contexts, from internally displaced populations in Bosnia and Herzegovina to gender issues in Peru, linguistic minorities in Thailand, Burundian and Congolese refugees in the United Republic of Tanzania and indigenous peoples in Canada. In Europe, 23 of 49 countries did not address sexual orientation and gender identity expression explicitly.

Spoken and signed languages and images in textbooks should make everyone visible while removing stereotypes. In India's Odisha state, multilingual education covered about 1,500 primary schools and 21 tribal languages of instruction. The share of females in secondary school English language textbook text and images was 44% in Indonesia, 37% in Bangladesh and 24% in Punjab province, Pakistan.

Assessment should be formative and allow students to demonstrate learning in a variety of ways.

In seven sub-Saharan African countries, no teacher had minimum knowledge in student assessment to improve learning. School infrastructure should not exclude anyone, yet some 335 million girls still attend primary and secondary schools that lack facilities essential for menstrual hygiene. The huge potential of technology should be exploited.

8 Prepare, empower and motivate the education workforce: All teachers should be prepared to teach all students.

Teachers need training on inclusion. Some 25% of teachers in 48 middle- and high-income countries reported a high need for professional development on teaching students with special needs. Across 10 francophone sub-Saharan African countries, just 8% of grade 2 and 6 teachers had received in-service training on inclusive education. Inclusive approaches should not be treated as a specialist topic but as a core element of teacher education, whether initial education or professional development. Such programmes need to focus on tackling entrenched views of some students as deficient and unable to learn. Head teachers should be prepared to implement and communicate an inclusive school ethos.

A diverse education workforce also supports inclusion by offering unique insights and serving as role models to all students. In India, the share of teachers from scheduled castes, which constitute 16% of the country's population, increased from 9% in 2005 to 13% in 2013.

9 Collect data on and for inclusion with attention and respect: Avoid labelling that stigmatizes.

Since 2015, 41% of countries, representing 13% of the global population, have not had a publicly available household survey to provide disaggregated data on key education indicators. Education ministries must collaborate with other ministries and statistical agencies to collect population-level data coherently so as to understand the scale of disadvantage for the marginalized.

On disability, the use of the Washington Group Short Set of Questions and the Child Functioning Module should be prioritized. Administrative systems should aim to collect data for planning and budgeting in provision of inclusive education services, but also data on the experience of inclusion. However, the desire for detailed or robust data should not take priority over ensuring that no learner is harmed. Portugal recently legislated a non-categorical approach to determining special needs.

10 Learn from peers: A shift to inclusion is not easy.

Inclusion represents a move away from discrimination and prejudice, and towards a future that can be adapted to various contexts and realities. Neither the pace nor the specific direction of this transition can be dictated, but much can be learned from sharing experiences through teacher networks, national forums, and regional and global platforms. We must work together to build a world that sees diversity as something to celebrate, not a problem to rectify. The *Global Education Monitoring Report* country profiles are intended to contribute to this peer learning process.

The 2020 GEM Report recommendations have been endorsed by two governments and eight organizations that champion inclusion.

We look forward to the GEM Report every year; the data and analysis are invaluable in aligning DFID policy and programmes with the latest global evidence. We are pleased this year's GEM Report focuses on inclusive education where so much progress remains to be made.

Baroness Sugg, UK Special Envoy for Girls' Education, Department for International Development UK

The GLAD Network welcomes the GEM Report and its comprehensive approach to inclusive education. The report recognizes that inclusive education requires a profound cultural shift at the early childhood, primary, secondary and post-secondary levels with one system of education for all learners that ensures support to include learners with disabilities.

Vladimir Cuk, IDA, Penny Innes, DFID UK, and Jon Lomøy, Norad, Global Action on Disability Network

---

Education is every child's right, not just a privilege for a few. The 2020 GEM Report is a welcome step towards celebrating diversity among learners. It establishes inclusion at the heart of education to enable children to reach their full potential.

Alice P. Albright, CEO, Global Partnership for Education

Inclusive education is the only way to achieve SDG 4 for all children − including all children with disabilities − whoever they are and wherever they are. The 2020 GEM Report gives an impetus and a direction to effectively transform education systems in ways that include all learners and prepare for more inclusive societies able to fully embrace diversity.

Ana Lucia Arellano, President, International Disability Alliance

---

We wholeheartedly welcome the 2020 GEM Report on inclusion in education, which highlights that that we should celebrate diversity in all learners, rather than see it as a problem as is too often the case.

Dom Haslam, Chair, International Disability and Development Consortium

---

The 2020 GEM Report calls on governments to effectively create inclusive education systems for all learners, including children who are, or are perceived to be, lesbian, gay, bisexual, transgender or intersex. IGLYO welcomes its broad approach and its commitment to work across sectors to advocate for everyone's right to quality education.

Euan Platt, Executive Director, IGLYO

If we want to realize a future without violence or discrimination, and to achieve gender equality in our lifetimes, creating policies and structures for inclusive education is one of the most impactful ways to invest in change; the 2020 GEM Report provides a roadmap on how to get there.

Gary Barker, President and CEO, Promundo

The theme of this year's report, inclusion in education, is particularly important for those children who have been uprooted from their homes and communities. Their inclusion in national education systems in countries of asylum allows them the chance to learn, grow, and contribute to the societies in which they live, and better prepares them for the time when they can return home in safety and in dignity.

Filippo Grandi, United Nations High Commissioner for Refugees

---

The evidence in this report points to an unmistakable learning crisis − millions of children and young people are struggling to develop the skills they need. This crisis disproportionately affects children and young people in emergencies, girls, and children with disabilities. We must not leave these children behind.

Henrietta H. Fore, Executive Director, UNICEF

Helping all children reach their full potential means investing in the health, nutrition and well-being of every learner, not just in their learning. This integrated approach creates a tremendous opportunity to achieve SDG 4 − and all the other SDGs. The 2020 GEM Report urges us to think about schoolchildren's many different needs holistically and join forces across sectors to meet them.

David Beasley, Executive Director, World Food Programme

PEER

Profiles Enhancing Reviews in Education

A new online tool to support the monitoring of national education laws and policies

education-profiles.org

CONTEXT AND OBJECTIVES

The *Global Education Monitoring Report* has a twin mandate from the Education 2030 Framework for Action: to monitor progress on education in the Sustainable Development Goals and to report on implementation of national and international education strategies to help hold partners accountable for their commitments. To better fulfil its mandate, the GEM Report has developed PEER, an online resource providing systematic, comprehensive information on national laws and policies. The first set of country profiles reviews inclusion and education, the theme of the 2020 GEM Report.

The profiles are intended to motivate national policy dialogue and regional peer learning on SDG 4 issues. They respond to countries' interest in exchanging comparable, up-to-date education system information to enrich their perspectives on solutions to challenges. The profiles can also facilitate monitoring of policy trends.

PEER covers all countries except those of the European Union and selected neighbouring countries, whose education laws and policies are available in the European Commission's Eurydice network descriptions of national education systems.

METHODOLOGY: INCLUSION AND EDUCATION

The first country profiles elaborate on the 2020 GEM Report theme of inclusion and education. The profiles were primarily prepared through literature review, complemented, for selected countries, by commissioned research to add subnational examples. The Global Campaign for Education contributed information on inclusion in selected countries.

The profiles, each about 2,000 words long, are available in English, French or Spanish.

Countries were invited, through their delegation at UNESCO, to review, update and validate the information. Validation is indicated. Countries are encouraged to provide comments and additions to help ensure a comprehensive, up-to-date, accurate and concise overview of laws and policies on inclusion and education.

CONTENT: INCLUSION AND EDUCATION

Information was compiled in seven areas:

1 Definitions

2 School organization

3 Laws, plans, policies and programmes

4 Governance

5 Learning environments

6 Teachers and support personnel

7 Monitoring and reporting.

Building on an analysis of this qualitative information, selected indicators were coded to identify and summarize patterns in country approaches to inclusion and education. These indicators are used in the report, notably in **Chapter 2** on laws and policies.

Country overview pages provide links to further education system information resources on selected themes.

NEXT STEPS

Future profiles will cover additional themes. Ongoing work on education financing laws and policies targeting disadvantaged groups, for instance, will provide qualitative evidence on a thematic indicator of SDG target 4.5 on equity. These profiles will review education financing mechanisms, as well as social policies and programmes providing resources to schools, students and households.

Work has begun on a systematic mapping of national approaches to the regulation of non-state education providers, the theme of the 2021 GEM Report.

The GEM Report is seeking national, regional and international partners to help develop PEER and ensure that it is relevant for their needs.

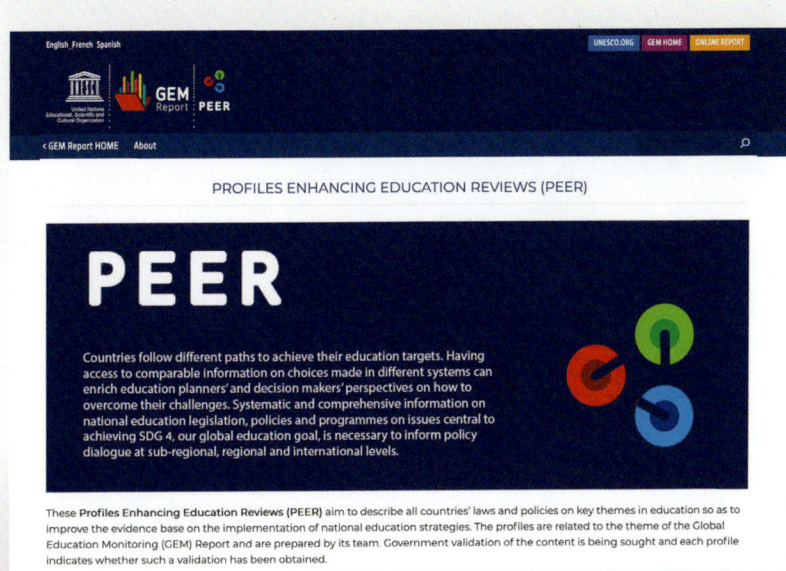

The winning entry in the GEM Report's 2020 Photo competition was Robert Lumu's photograph of a 9-year-old boy, sitting and reading with his peers at his school in Central Uganda, where albinism is still considered a curse.

CREDIT: Robert Lumu/UNESCO

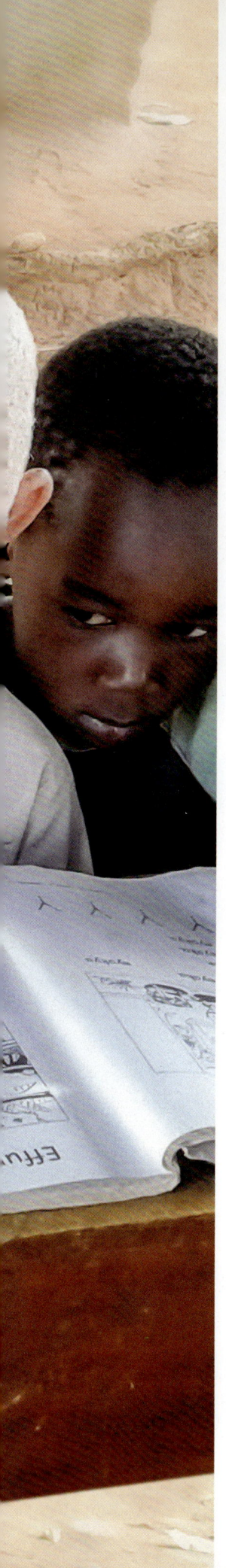

2

Laws and policies

What foundations are needed?

KEY MESSAGES

The inclusion aspirations of international conventions are often not reflected in national laws

- Worldwide, general or inclusive education laws under education ministry responsibility focus on people with disabilities in 79% of countries, linguistic minorities in 60%, gender equality in 50% and ethnic and indigenous groups in 49%.

- Laws under health, gender and social welfare ministry responsibility regulate and promote inclusion in education for people with disabilities in 74% of countries, gender equality in 46%, ethnic minorities and indigenous groups in 28% and linguistic minorities in 25%.

Countries are introducing inclusive laws and policies for children with disabilities

- Worldwide, laws emphasize segregation in 25% of countries, partial segregation in 48%, integration in 10% and inclusion in 17%.

- Policies tend to be more ambitious, emphasizing segregation in 5% of countries, partial segregation in 45%, integration in 12% and inclusion in 38%.

- Policy planning is often weak, however, resulting in inconsistencies and poor implementation.

Inclusive early childhood care and education improves chances throughout children's lives

- However, access is lower for the children who need it most. Ireland provides free services for refugee children under age 5 to support their integration.

- Quality, especially in terms of interactions, integration, and child-centredness based on play, determines inclusion. A review of programmes in 121 countries found that two-thirds involved parents.

Automatic promotion supports disadvantaged children if enhanced with remedial support

- In Brazil, automatically promoted students enjoyed modest but persistent benefits in the transition from the lower to upper primary education cycle.

- In India, children who repeated a primary grade were less likely to complete primary school, yet a dozen states abandoned the no-repetition policy in 2017.

Equity and inclusion strategies are needed in technical, vocational and tertiary education

- Just 11% of 71 countries had formulated a comprehensive tertiary education equity strategy.

- About one in four countries have some form of affirmative action for university admission.

Responses to the Covid-19 crisis have not paid enough attention to inclusion of all learners

- About 40% of low- and lower-middle-income countries have not supported learners at risk of exclusion, such as the poor, linguistic minorities and learners with disabilities.

- Only 12% of households in the least developed countries have internet access at home. Even low-technology approaches cannot ensure learning continuity. Among the poorest 20% of households, 7% owned a radio in Ethiopia and 8% in the Democratic Republic of the Congo.

- In France, up to 8% of students had lost contact with teachers after three weeks of lockdown.

The main obstacle to inclusion in education is the absence of explicit educational legislation on the learner's right to be treated with dignity in all school contexts.

Francisco Gomes de Matos, co-founder of ABA Global Education and Board president, Brazil

Laws and policies set the framework for achieving inclusion in education. At the international level, binding legal instruments and non-binding declarations, led especially by the United Nations (UN) but also by regional organizations, have expressed the international community's aspirations. They have strongly influenced the national legislative and policy actions on which progress towards inclusion hinges. However, despite good intentions enshrined in laws and policies on inclusive education, governments often do not take the follow-up actions necessary to ensure implementation. Barriers remain high for access, progression and learning, and disproportionately affect more disadvantaged populations. Inside education systems, these populations face discrimination, rejection and reluctance to accommodate their needs. Exclusion is most manifest in the segregation of learners with different needs into separate classrooms and schools.

This chapter consists of two parts. The first discusses the evolution of international instruments and declarations, and variation in national legislation and policy frameworks. The analysis builds largely on a systematic mapping based on the Profiles Enhancing Reviews in Education (PEER) website, which describe how every country in the world approaches inclusion in education. The second part addresses policy issues at education levels throughout the life cycle. It covers early childhood education, early identification of needs, the choice between repetition and automatic promotion in basic education, remedial and second-chance programmes, the distinct challenges in technical, vocational and tertiary education, and the digital divide. This last also offers an entry point for a discussion of the multiple challenges to inclusion posed by Covid-19.

INTERNATIONAL INSTRUMENTS AND DECLARATIONS HAVE SHAPED INCLUSIVE EDUCATION

While the right to education was first expressed in the 1948 UN Universal Declaration of Human Rights, it was the 1960 UNESCO Convention against Discrimination in Education that specifically obliged countries to address explicit and implicit barriers in education. It defined discrimination as 'any distinction, exclusion, limitation or preference which, being based on race, colour, sex, language, religion, political or other opinion, national or social origin, economic condition or birth', results in individuals being treated unequally in education (Article 1). The convention referred to the effects of discrimination as depriving people of access, relegating them to education quality 'of an inferior standard', 'establishing or maintaining separate educational systems or institutions' and 'inflicting … conditions which are in-compatible with the dignity of man' (Article 1). It accepted that, under certain conditions, single-sex schools and schools catering to religious or linguistic communities did not constitute discrimination (UNESCO, 1960). Of the 105 countries that are party to the convention, around half have ratified it.

The 1989 UN Convention on the Rights of the Child is the human rights treaty with the greatest number of signatories (196, including all UN Member States except the United States). Two articles were dedicated to the right to education, and a separate article made reference to education for children with disabilities, recognizing the 'special needs of a disabled child' and calling on 'assistance … provided free of charge' and 'designed to ensure that the disabled child has effective access to and receives education … in a manner conducive to the child's achieving the fullest possible social integration and individual development' (Article 23) (United Nations, 1989).

The 1990 World Declaration on Education for All, adopted in Jomtien, Thailand, called on countries to commit actively 'to removing educational disparities'.

> Underserved groups: the poor; street and working children; rural and remote populations; nomads and migrant workers; indigenous peoples; ethnic, racial, and linguistic minorities; refugees; those displaced by war; and people under occupation, should not suffer any discrimination in access to learning opportunities (Article 3, §4).

People with disabilities were not included in the list but were mentioned where the declaration called for steps to 'provide equal access to education to every category of disabled persons as an integral part of the education system' (Article 3, §5). The declaration thus distinguished between disabled persons and the underserved (UNESCO, 1990).

The Statement and Framework for Action of the 1994 World Conference on Special Needs Education in Salamanca, Spain, further established the principle that 'schools should accommodate all children regardless of their physical, intellectual, social, emotional, linguistic or other conditions' and therefore that 'children and youth with special educational needs should be included in the educational arrangements made for the majority of children' (Framework, p. 6), i.e. 'the school that would be attended if the child did not have a disability' (Framework, p. 17). The statement urged states to 'adopt as a matter of law or policy inclusive education' (Statement, p. ix) and recognized the need for schools to 'include everybody, celebrate differences, support learning, and respond to individual needs' (Preface, p. iii). It helped shift the focus from the learner to the system, recognizing that schools would need to be restructured (UNESCO and Spain Ministry of Education and Science, 1994). The 2000 World Education Forum in Dakar, Senegal, acknowledged that inclusive education emerged 'in response to a growing consensus that all children have the right to a common education in their locality regardless of their background, attainment or disability' (UNESCO, 2000, p. 18).

In 2006, the right to inclusive education was established in the UN Convention on the Rights of Persons with Disabilities (CRPD), which has been ratified by 181 countries, the latest being Saint Kitts and Nevis in October 2019. Nine other countries are signatories (Bhutan, Cameroon, Lebanon, Solomon Islands, Saint Lucia, Tajikistan, Tonga, United States and Uzbekistan) and eight are not (Botswana, Equatorial Guinea, Eritrea, the Holy See, Liechtenstein, Niue, South Sudan and Timor-Leste) (OHCHR, 2020). Article 24 specified that 'States Parties shall ensure an inclusive education system at all levels' aimed at the 'full development of human potential and sense of dignity and self-worth, and the strengthening of respect for human rights, fundamental freedoms and human diversity' and the development by people with disabilities 'of their personality, talents and creativity, as well as their mental and physical abilities, to their fullest potential' (United Nations, 2006).

Articles 33 and 34 specified that a country that ratified the convention must submit a report within two years and every four years thereafter. Countries' reports and shadow reports by civil society organizations should explain progress made towards securing the rights set out in the convention (UNDESA, 2019). The Committee on the Rights of Persons with Disabilities, composed of

18 independent experts, reviews the reports and makes recommendations to countries. Signature of an optional protocol enables the committee to examine individual complaints related to violations of the convention (OHCHR, 2019).

Global actions are complemented by regional-level initiatives and processes to promote the education rights of people with disabilities. Article 16 of the legally binding 2018 Protocol to the African Charter on Human and Peoples' Rights on the Rights of Persons with Disabilities in Africa established that people with disabilities have a right to education on an equal basis with others and called on parties to provide inclusive quality education for people with disabilities, along with reasonable accommodation, individualized support, training for education professionals and support for sign languages (African Union, 2018). However, unlike the CRPD, Article 16, despite its broad scope, allowed for continued segregation when it called for making 'appropriate schooling choices' available to people with disabilities 'who may prefer to learn in particular environments' (Biegon, 2019). For the protocol to enter into force, at least 15 of the 55 African Union countries need to ratify it. As of December 2019, six had signed but none had ratified (African Commission on Human and Peoples' Rights, 2019).

CRPD Article 24 was hotly debated, for instance on questions related to 'best interest' of the child, scope and coverage and where education should take place (UNDESA, 2004a, 2004b, 2004c, 2004d). During negotiations among states in final drafting, the text shifted from the right of children with disabilities to education (maintained until the sixth session) to their right to inclusive education. However, the issue of placement, or where education should take place, was not settled, and the final text does not include an obligation to educate children with disabilities in mainstream schools (Kanter, 2019).

Such tensions led the Committee on the Rights of Persons with Disabilities, in September 2016, to formulate General Comment No. 4 on Article 24 (Committee on the Rights of Persons with Disabilities, 2016). It acknowledged the persistent discrimination against people with disabilities, which denies many the right to education; a lack of awareness about barriers that impede fulfilment of the right and a lack of knowledge about inclusive education, its potential and implications; and the need for clarification and definition of inclusive education

and strategies for implementation (Hunt, 2020). General Comment No. 4 interpreted CRPD signatories' provisions and obligations regarding the right to inclusive education. It clarified the meaning and intention of the right to inclusive education and defined inclusive education more thoroughly than either the Salamanca Declaration or the CRPD. It is 'the de facto global development policy on inclusive education', outlining the critical policy considerations and implementation guidelines (Hunt, 2020).

Yet tensions also exist concerning the content of General Comment No. 4. For instance, interpretation of segregation divides those focused on inclusion in learning and those focused on placement. A submission by four international deaf people's organizations was clear:

> Although the term 'special schools' could have the appearance of being segregated, 'specialised schools' does not necessarily mean education that 'excludes' or segregates. The best quality education is provided in a learning environment where the individual child can be fully included such by providing for a full sign language environment, whether this is in a specialised deaf/sign language school or in a fully accessible mainstream school ... States Parties should provide the option of different schooling types to facilitate choice' (World Federation of the Deaf et al., 2015, p. 6).

Australia and Germany did not consider segregation negative with respect to parental choice. Spain suggested that, to reach full inclusion, some students, e.g. those with autism spectrum disorder, needed to be in separate classrooms first to establish the routines needed for integration. Others, including Argentina, Bahrain and Plan International, took a more positive stance towards inclusion (OHCHR, 2016).

Previously, the committee did not explicitly discourage education taking place outside the mainstream system and sometimes considered special education acceptable. Its concluding observations on Spain in 2011 recommended that parents should be consulted on decisions to place a child with disability in a special school (Committee on the Rights of Persons with Disabilities, 2011). More recently, a stricter position considers exclusionary or segregated education a form of discrimination that violates the CRPD and its provisions for equal opportunity (Degener and Uldry, 2018). In its concluding observation on Spain in April

"

The broader vision of inclusion in education of all learners is still largely lacking in legislation worldwide

"

2019, the committee reiterated that 'measures should be taken to view inclusive education as a right, and grant all students with disabilities, regardless of their personal characteristics, the right to access inclusive learning opportunities in the mainstream education system, with access to support services as required' (Committee on the Rights of Persons with Disabilities, 2019, p. 10).

The struggle for inclusive education for people with disabilities has been led by the community at the forefront of promoting their rights, on the basis of three key elements (**Box 2.1**). A number of conventions on other potentially disadvantaged groups also promote the right to inclusive education (**Box 2.2**). Together, these calls for proactive provision of inclusive education shaped the vision of the 2015 Incheon Declaration:

> Inclusion and equity in and through education is the cornerstone of a transformative education agenda, and we therefore commit to addressing all forms of exclusion and marginalization, disparities and inequalities in access, participation and learning outcomes. No education target should be considered met unless met by all. We therefore commit to making the necessary changes in education policies and focusing our efforts on the most disadvantaged, especially those with disabilities, to ensure that no one is left behind (Article 7) (UNESCO, 2015a).

This approach, which recognized that mechanisms of exclusion were common, regardless of background, ability or identity, underpinned the use of the term 'inclusive' in the formulation of SDG 4.

LAWS ON INCLUSION TEND TO FOCUS ON STUDENTS WITH DISABILITIES

Within this evolving global framework, countries have stepped in to translate international commitments into national legislation. Laws vary in the extent to which they refer to the right to education for all or are targeted to specific groups at risk of exclusion in education, often those with disabilities.

The broader vision of inclusion in education of all learners is still largely lacking in legislation worldwide. Of 194 countries, Chile, Italy, Luxembourg, Paraguay and Portugal have inclusive education laws covering all learners (**Box 2.3**). Italy was the first to close special schools in order to mainstream students with disabilities, in 1977. Other laws, directives and guidelines have since extended the law's reach, including a 2012 Directive, which organized inclusion of all students with learning difficulties, including those related to socio-economic, linguistic and cultural disadvantage (Italy Ministry of Education, Universities and Research, 2012).

By contrast, 11 countries have inclusive education laws that exclusively cover people with disabilities. Colombia's 2017 decree determined that students with disabilities should be educated in the same institutions as the rest of the population. The decree also institutionalized 'individual plans of reasonable supports and adjustments' to make learning relevant for students with disabilities, respecting their learning styles and rhythms (GEM Report Education Profiles[1]).

Globally, 16 countries mention inclusive education in their general education laws. Peru adopted an inclusive education law in 2018 which incorporated article 19A on inclusive education in the general education law. It states that education is inclusive in all stages, forms, modalities, levels and cycles, and encourages education institutions to adopt measures to ensure conditions of accessibility, availability, acceptability and adaptability in provision of education services and to develop personalized education plans for students with special education needs (GEM Report Education Profiles).

GEM Report analysis shows that laws for which education ministries are responsible, whether general or focused on inclusion, typically target individual groups, primarily people with disabilities. Among countries examined, 79% have laws referring to education for people with disabilities, 60% for linguistic minorities,

---

1   A new GEM Report tool for systematic monitoring of national education laws and policies, accessible at www.education-profiles.org.

BOX 2.1:

Three key elements guarantee the right to inclusive education for people with disabilities

Three elements are essential to guarantee the education rights of people with disabilities: non-discrimination, zero reject and reasonable accommodation (Hunt, 2020).

The right to education without discrimination in any aspect of education encompasses all internationally prohibited grounds for discrimination. It receives the highest protection when it is set out in national constitutions. For instance, the 2005 Constitution of the Democratic Republic of the Congo states that '[n]o Congolese person may, in matters of education ... , be subjected to any discriminatory measure, whether by statute or by an act of the executive, on grounds of religion, family origin, social condition, residence, views or political convictions, or membership of a certain race, ethnicity, tribe, cultural or linguistic minority' (Article 13).

The concept of zero reject is closely associated with non-discrimination, and the two are often referenced together. Zero reject explicitly recognizes the right of anyone to (public) education, regardless of circumstance. It addresses direct exclusion, e.g. when a person is deemed non-educable, but also non-direct exclusion, e.g. when a person is required to pass a test without accommodation or support as a condition for school entry (Committee on the Rights of Persons with Disabilities, 2016). The US Individuals with Disabilities Education Act adopted the zero-reject principle to ensure that all children receive free and appropriate public education no matter how severe their disability (US Department of Education, 2019). The principle prohibits exclusion from education not only of people with disabilities but also of ethnic minorities and indigenous people.

An inclusive education system also considers the need for reasonable accommodation and individualized support beyond accessibility. Reasonable accommodation enables learners to gain access to education on an equal basis, and those involved must be included in discussions about their requirements. For instance, transport provision for children with disabilities is essential to the right to inclusive education. Whereas accessibility measures ensure access for various people and are designed to benefit various groups, reasonable accommodation ensures non-discrimination for individual people with disabilities. Failure to provide reasonable accommodation constitutes discrimination on disability grounds (Hunt, 2020).

BOX 2.2:

Global efforts to promote inclusive education are aligned with efforts to defend the rights of various groups

While the rights of people with disabilities have been at the heart of the inclusion in education agenda, parallel work in support of other vulnerable groups has also supported this push. For instance, in response to the 1979 UN Convention on the Elimination of All Forms of Discrimination against Women, the 1991 General Recommendation 18 of the Committee on the Elimination of Discrimination against Women called for measures to ensure that girls and women with disabilities have equal access to education, acknowledging the intersection of vulnerabilities.

The right of refugees to education in host countries was guaranteed in the 1951 UN Convention Relating to the Status of Refugees, later expanded with a 1967 protocol to remove time and geographical restrictions. The 146 parties to the convention and 147 parties to the protocol committed to refugees receiving 'the same treatment as is accorded to nationals with respect to elementary education' and 'treatment as favourable as possible, and, in any event, not less favourable than that accorded to aliens generally in the same circumstances with respect to education other than elementary education' (Article 22). The 1990 International Convention on the Protection of the Rights of All Migrant Workers and Members of Their Families recognized the right to education of immigrant children irrespective of their official migrant status (Article 30), although only one in four countries have ratified the convention (OHCHR, 2020).

The 1989 ILO Indigenous and Tribal Peoples Convention affirmed the relevance of curriculum, the importance of being taught in the mother tongue and the need for 'history textbooks and other educational materials [to] provide a fair, accurate and informative portrayal of the societies and cultures of these peoples' (Article 31). The 23 countries that have ratified the convention (Central African Republic, Denmark, Dominica, Fiji, Luxembourg, Nepal, Norway, the Netherlands, Spain and 14 Latin American countries) have accepted the duty to respect, fulfil and protect indigenous peoples' rights. The 2007 UN Declaration on the Rights of Indigenous Peoples acknowledged their right 'to establish and control their educational systems and institutions providing education in their own languages, in a manner appropriate to their cultural methods of teaching and learning' (Article 14).

BOX 2.3:

Portugal has comprehensive inclusive education legislation

In July 2018, following 18 months of preparation, Portugal passed Decree-Law 54/6 on inclusive education. Article 1 specifies that inclusion is 'a process that aims to respond to the diversity of the needs and potential of each and every one of the pupils'. Article 5 calls on schools to create 'a school culture where everyone will find opportunities to learn and the conditions for full realization of this right, responding to the needs of each pupil, valuing diversity and promoting equity and non-discrimination in accessing the curriculum and the progression in the educational system' (Portugal Presidency of the Council of Ministers, 2018).

Previously, inclusive education provision was enshrined in Decree-Law 3/2008, which provided for specialized support in mainstream schools and for special schools (Portugal Presidency of the Council of Ministers, 2008). While the framework for students with communication, learning, mobility, autonomy, interpersonal relationship and social participation difficulties who required highly differentiated and specialized support and resources had developed continuously, other groups at risk of exclusion, due to social, cultural or economic disadvantage, were being left behind.

The new law expands coverage and support for children and youth with a range of needs. The introduction to the law refers to inclusive education as a process intended to respond to the diversity of students. It recognizes the curriculum and the student as core elements of the inclusion process and requires adjustment to teaching and learning processes. The law rests on the principles of equity, universal design for learning, school and professional autonomy, and curriculum diversification through accommodation and adaptation. The preamble, which states that it should no longer be necessary to categorize students in order to intervene, seeks to ensure that all students reach the same standard at the end of compulsory schooling, 'even if it is through differentiated learning paths that allow each student to progress in the curriculum in a way that ensures their educational success'.

The law requires schools to have a multidisciplinary team, composed of a teacher, a special education teacher, a psychologist and three members of the pedagogical council. It also introduces learning support centres intended to support inclusion, create learning resources and assessment tools for curriculum components and organize the post-education transition. In creating these centres, Portugal applies the expertise and resources of its formerly separate special education system to support inclusion of all students in mainstream classrooms.

50% promoting gender equality and 49% for ethnic and indigenous groups.

Litigation is increasingly used to fight discrimination and inequality in education. The European Court of Human Rights adopted a vulnerability approach to redress structural inequality on the grounds of sex, sexual orientation, disability, race and ethnicity. D.H. and Others vs. Czech Republic was brought in 2000 by 18 Czech Roma students assigned to special primary schools with simplified curriculum. The court ruled the students had been denied their right to education because enrolment criteria did not take into account characteristics specific to Roma, resulting in racial discrimination and segregation (European Court for Human Rights, 2007). Later rulings included Oršuš and Others vs. Croatia, which

> " Globally, 16 countries mention inclusive education in their general education laws "

called for the state to provide linguistic support enabling Roma children to enter mainstream classes, and Horváth and Kiss vs. Hungary, which found that Roma children were misdiagnosed because of 'socio-economic disadvantage and cultural differences' (Broderick, 2019).

Similar judgements have been made with reference to the revised 1996 European Social Charter, notably to Article 15, which calls on education and training for learners with disabilities to occur 'in the framework of general schemes wherever possible', and Article 17 on the right to education (Quinlivan, 2019). In some countries, legislation excludes learners with severe disabilities from mainstream education. In the Flanders region of Belgium, under the 2014 law on measures for students with special education needs, known as the M-decree, only children able to follow common core curriculum have access to mainstream education; this effectively excludes most of those with intellectual disabilities. In 2017, the European Committee of Social Rights found Belgium in breach of the charter, arguing that the eligibility requirements were not justified, that the country made insufficient provision for reasonable accommodation, and that the education system was discriminatory on grounds of intellectual disability (European Committee of Social Rights, 2017). In 2002, Autism Europe initiated a collective complaint of insufficient education provision for people with autism in France. The complaint was declared admissible, and the committee concluded that France had violated the charter (Council of Europe, 2018a).

Courts have also protected rights pertaining to sexual orientation and gender identity and expression. In 2002, the Supreme Court of Canada established that lesbian and gay students and same-sex parents had the right to be protected from discrimination and to see their lives reflected in curricula. In its concluding statement, the judgement said: 'The distaste of some parents for books that do not conform with their personal beliefs cannot shape the policy of a pluralist education system that has proclaimed its commitment to accepting and celebrating diversity' (Canada Supreme Court, 2002). In India, following a 2014 Supreme Court ruling recognizing the status of transgender, eunuch and intersex people (hijras), the University Grants Commission called on universities to include the category on all application forms (*Economic Times*, 2015; India Supreme Court, 2014).

In addition, courts have ruled on bullying, often triggered by a disability or learning difficulty. High court decisions in Colombia (Colombia Constitutional Court, 2016) and Mexico (Mexico Supreme Court, 2015) ruled that bullying negatively affected victims' dignity, integrity and education, and indicated that the education sector should protect students from violence based on personal characteristics.

Conversely, the absence of laws protecting the right to education for some groups at risk of exclusion can be an important obstacle, as in the case of Venezuelan migrants and asylum seekers in Trinidad and Tobago (**Box 2.4**).

In many countries, health, gender and social welfare ministries have legal instruments to regulate and promote inclusion of some groups in education. Among countries examined, 74% had laws referring to disability, 46% to gender equality, 28% to ethnic and indigenous groups and 25% to linguistic minorities.

A 2018 law in Pakistan prohibits discrimination against transgender people in education and establishes their right to education and a 3% quota for transgender

---

BOX 2.4:

Venezuelans in Trinidad and Tobago face challenges in getting access to education

As of May 2020, governments in Latin America and the Caribbean reported 5.1 million Venezuelan migrants, refugees and asylum-seekers, including about 80,000 in the non-Spanish-speaking Caribbean countries of Aruba, Curaçao, Guyana, and Trinidad and Tobago (R4V, 2020). The latter number may be a fraction of what other countries in the region receive, but huge in relative terms; for instance, the 17,000 migrants and refugees in Aruba represent 15% of the population. The true figures are likely to be higher, as many government sources only account for Venezuelans with regular status. For instance, the Regional Inter-Agency Coordination Platform reports 24,000 Venezuelans are in Trinidad and Tobago, but other estimates suggest there are over 40,000 (Teff, 2019).

A National Policy to Address Refugee and Asylum Matters in the Republic of Trinidad and Tobago was approved in 2014, but there is no legislation (Teff, 2019). Children of registered asylum seekers cannot attend school. The government spent two weeks registering Venezuelans in April 2019, granting six-month renewable work permit exemptions at five registration centres, but with no guarantee to education (Trinidad and Tobago Office of the Prime Minister, 2019).

Non-government organizations (NGOs) work to ensure that Venezuelan children have access to education. For instance, Living Water Community (LWC) accommodated 600 Venezuelan children in six child-friendly spaces as of December 2019, with a plan to set up four more spaces for 400 additional children. The Ministry of Education granted access to the primary education curriculum and appointed a teacher to work with LWC to secure certification.

The Equal Place Education Programme (UNHCR, 2019) helps Venezuelan children get access to accredited education. Developed by the office of the United Nations High Commissioner for Refugees, UNICEF, LWC and the Trinidad and Tobago Venezuela Solidarity Network, it delivers tailor-made learning at no cost on two globally recognized platforms: NotesMaster, in English, and Dawere, in Spanish. This allows children to have the last two years of the Colombian and Venezuelan Bachillerato validated. The programme is certified by the Caribbean Examination Council.

---

children in mainstream public and private education institutions. It also stipulated that service providers should ensure equal opportunity in both academic and extracurricular activities, such as sports (Munir et al.,

2020). In the Republic of Korea, a law on education in island and remote areas prescribes customized measures related to school infrastructure and teaching and learning materials (GEM Report Education Profiles). In the Russian Federation, a 1999 federal law protects indigenous minorities, including in education. A 2006 law in the Yamalo-Nenets Autonomous Okrug on indigenous minorities includes provisions for education support and promotion of native languages (IITE, 2020).

LAWS ON INCLUSION OF STUDENTS WITH DISABILITIES VARY IN AMBITION

Countries are increasingly introducing legislation to facilitate inclusion of children with disabilities in mainstream schools. Adopting an inclusive education approach for students with disabilities necessitates amendments and adjustments to existing laws to ensure coherence. However, laws promoting inclusion in education may coexist with laws promoting special education in separate settings, preventing a shared understanding of inclusive education and obstructing implementation.

The GEM Report estimates that 25% of countries have provisions for education in segregated settings, especially in Central and Southern Asia, Eastern and South-eastern Asia, and Latin America and the Caribbean. Some 48% combine mainstreaming with separate settings, usually for those with severe disabilities; 10% privilege integration; and 17% have legislative provisions to

educate people with disabilities in inclusive settings, with the highest prevalence observed in Europe and Northern America and in Oceania (**Figure 2.1**). These findings are consistent with other reviews showing that, despite an increasing trend towards inclusion, countries rely on various combinations of special education and inclusion to educate children and youth with disabilities (Anastasiou and Keller, 2014, 2017).

In the Islamic Republic of Iran, which revised its special education law in 2004, the 2016 Charter on Citizenry Rights affirmed that 'no one should be deprived of the opportunity to acquire knowledge or job skills due to their disabilities' and included regulations to support those registered in mainstream schools with resource teachers. However, there is no legal guarantee of the right to inclusive education. A 2015 regulation specified that students who could not 'study in regular educational environments' would be placed in segregated special education centres (Human Rights Watch, 2019b). All children are screened at age 6 for ability to be enrolled in first grade. Those who fail are referred for professional evaluation. In 2014, 1.2 million children were assessed at 862 fixed centres and at 17 mobile bases for nomadic populations. About 13% were referred, and over 90% of those were placed in special schools (Samadi and McConkey, 2018).

In Iraq, a 2011 ministerial decree authorized the Ministry of Education to create special classes and schools to educate students who are 'slow learners or have visual or

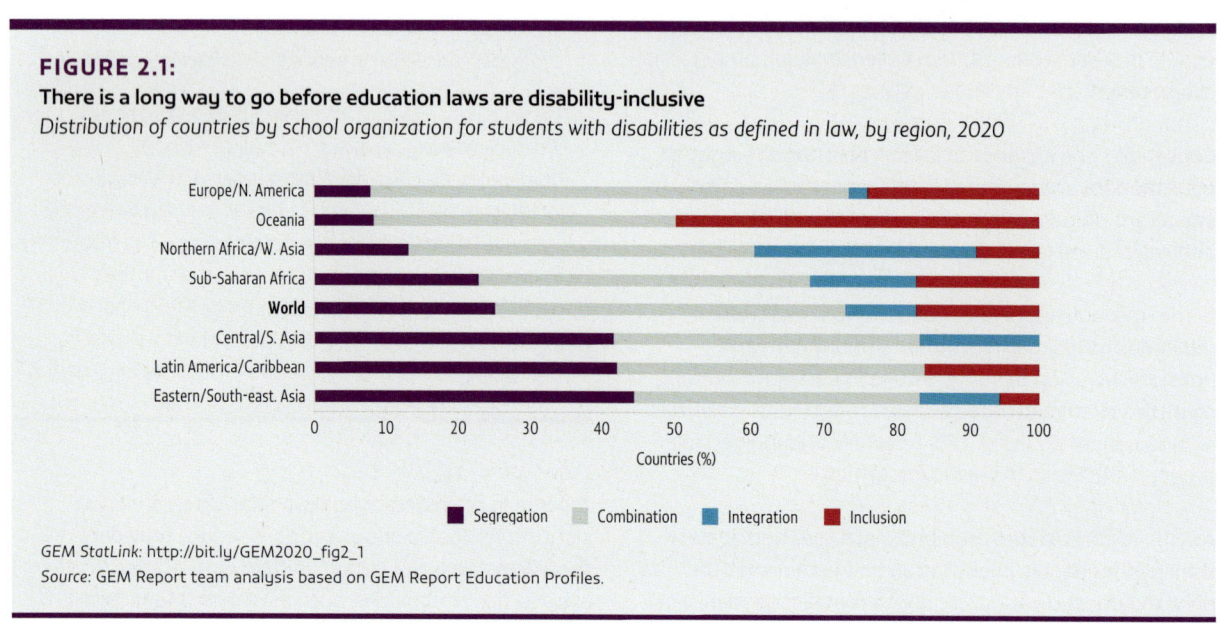

FIGURE 2.1:

There is a long way to go before education laws are disability-inclusive

Distribution of countries by school organization for students with disabilities as defined in law, by region, 2020

GEM StatLink: http://bit.ly/GEM2020_fig2_1
Source: GEM Report team analysis based on GEM Report Education Profiles.

hearing weakness' (Article 14). The decree did not mention offering integration opportunities for those students or specify other forms of physical or mental disability. Children with disabilities attend separate classes. As of 2019, there were 1,325 schools with special classes for children with disabilities, of which 107 were in rural areas (GEM Report Education Profiles).

In Lebanon, the 2000 law on the rights of people with disabilities granted education rights while allowing segregation to continue. In practice, school admission is at the discretion of head teachers, who may turn down children with disabilities, leaving them no alternative to specialized institutions run by private organizations funded by the Ministry of Social Affairs, which the Ministry of Education and Higher Education may not recognize as schools (Human Rights Watch, 2018a). In Myanmar, Article 41b of the 2014 education law specified that people with disabilities were to receive education through special education programmes and services based on a curriculum designed to cater for the needs of visually impaired, hard of hearing, mentally disabled and other learners (GEM Report Education Profiles).

Most countries combine mainstreaming with separate setting arrangements, usually for learners with severe disabilities. But lack of definition of severe disabilities can lead to arbitrary decisions. In Djibouti, Article 15 of the 2000 education law established that children with physical or mental disabilities preventing them from following structured education were exempt from compulsory education (Djibouti Government, 2000). In Mauritania, Article 9 of the 1975 education law specified that students could be 'permanently excluded, by decision of the regional director of basic education … after advice from the teachers council, [due to] a mental or physical state incompatible with school work on the basis of the medical certificate' or behaviour compromising the proper functioning of the school (Mauritania Government, 1975). In Oman, a 2017 ministerial decree stated that students with disabilities, especially visual impairment and other physical disabilities, could be accepted only in fully equipped schools (Abdou, 2020).

India's 2016 Rights of Persons with Disabilities Act translated the CRPD principles into the national context and established a right to inclusive education. However, it introduced ambiguity and the possibility of segregation, stating that 'every child with a benchmark disability has access to free education in an appropriate environment … in a neighbourhood school, or in a special school of his choice'. Further, children with multiple disabilities and severe disability have the right to opt for home-based education as per the 2012 Right to Education (Amendment) Act. For instance, the Kerala state education law referred to special schools and the possibility of homeschooling children with severe and multiple disabilities (UNESCO, 2019b).

South Africa's 1996 schools law stated that the right to education of children with special needs was to be fulfilled in mainstream public schools through support services and measures 'where reasonably practicable'. In the Russian Federation, Moscow permits education provision in separate or correctional classes when students with disabilities cannot receive education in inclusive settings. Article 5.1 of a 2010 law committed to provision of conditions for inclusive education in public education institutions for people with disabilities (GEM Report Education Profiles).

Some laws focus on integration. Amendments to Armenia's education law in 2014 made a commitment to introduce a universal inclusive education system by 2025. A 2016 action plan provided for reorganization of special education institutions into pedagogical and psychological assistance centres supporting general education by 2022 (GEM Report Education Profiles).

Among the countries whose laws emphasize inclusion, Colombia, a 2017 decree, acknowledged inclusive education for people with disabilities as a permanent process. Responding to a 2011 Constitutional Court judgement, which emphasized the government's duty to move from segregated or integrated to inclusive education where all children study and learn together, the decree valued diversity in a common learning environment, without discrimination or exclusion, and guaranteed rights-based support and reasonable adjustments to remove barriers through practices, policies and culture (Colombia Ministry of National Education, 2017). Ghana's 2008 education law defined inclusive education as a 'value system' that 'holds that all persons … are entitled to equal access to learning' and that 'transcends the idea of physical location, but incorporates the basic values that promote participation, friendship and interaction' (Article 5.4).

In 40% of countries, disability law also regulates inclusion in education. In Burkina Faso, a 2010 law on protection and promotion of the rights of people with disabilities noted that inclusive education was guaranteed at all education levels and that '[a]ny institution of initial and in-service training of teachers/literacy educators ... shall take into account inclusive education in its training programmes' (Article 12). Senegal's 2010 law on people with disabilities guaranteed children and adolescents with disabilities free education in mainstream schools as close as possible to their homes (GEM Report Education Profiles).

EDUCATION POLICIES VARY IN EMPHASIS ON INCLUSION

Countries are at various stages in developing inclusive education policies to implement legislative provisions and put enabling environments in place. A GEM Report review showed variation in placement types, instruction arrangements, staffing, teacher preparation, infrastructure, administrative structures and funding.

The review found that 17% of countries had a comprehensive inclusive education policy addressing all learners. In Bhutan, the 2017 Standard for Inclusive Education defines inclusive education as 'the process of valuing, accepting and supporting diversity in schools and ensuring that every child has equal opportunity to learn'. Ghana's 2015 policy defines it as an approach that accommodates all children in schools 'regardless of their physical, intellectual, social, emotional, linguistic or other conditions'. Nigeria's 2017 policy endorses the UNESCO definition, calling it the 'process of addressing all barriers and providing access to quality education to meet the diverse needs of all learners in the same learning environment' (GEM Report Education Profiles).

References to inclusion exist in 75% of countries' education sector plans or strategies. Attention to people with disabilities in education remains the norm: 67% of countries have such policies or plans, for which education ministries are fully or partly responsible.

Indonesia provides education according to a model whereby children with special needs may attend mainstream schools, special education units or special schools. The country has strengthened the inclusiveness of its education system, decreasing the number of students in special schools and expanding access of those with disabilities to mainstream schools from pre-primary

through tertiary education: 1,600 schools, or 11% of the total, provided inclusive education at the various levels in 2018. Following evaluation of the implementation of the previous Master Plan, the 2019–24 Master Plan for Inclusive Education Development endorses a broad concept of inclusive education. It will be implemented in three phases, with roll-out expected to begin in 2021 (GEM Report Education Profiles).

Malawi's 2017–21 National Strategy on Inclusive Education covers all children likely to be excluded from and within the education system, and its 2015–19 National Education Plan endorses an inclusive approach, referring to children and youth who have been marginalized or excluded, such as girls, children with disabilities, people living in remote villages and those from poor households. A pillar of Morocco's 2015–30 strategic vision guarantees the right of access to education and training for people with disabilities (GEM Report Education Profiles).

Nepal's government is drawing up an action plan to create disability-friendly education infrastructure and facilities, improve teacher training and develop a flexible curriculum by 2030. However, the government has yet to articulate, in law or policy, inclusive education standards in line with international standards and how to ensure them (Human Rights Watch, 2018c). Spain's Basque Country has a comprehensive diversity-based plan for inclusive schools declaring that excellence is achieved when all students reach maximum development of their personal abilities (Basque Country Department of Education, 2019).

Some 5% of countries still have policy provisions to deliver education in separate settings, while 45% combine mainstreaming with other provisions for children with extreme disabilities (**Figure 2.2**). In Pakistan's Punjab province, under the 2012 inclusive education policy framework, students with mild and moderate disabilities are admitted to mainstream primary and lower secondary schools whose teachers are trained by master trainers of the Department of Special Education. The Seychelles' inclusive education policy states that mainstreaming learners with disabilities should be an integral part of national plans for achieving education for all. Learners should be placed in special schools 'only in exceptional cases' and, in such cases, 'their education need not be entirely segregated' (GEM Report Education Profiles).

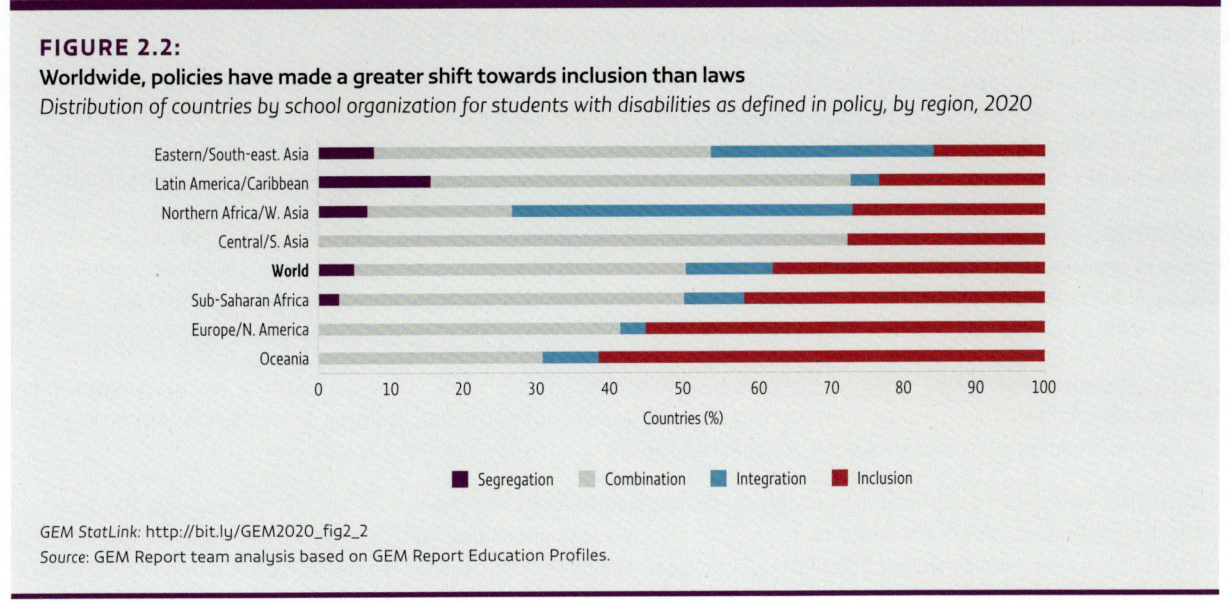

FIGURE 2.2:
Worldwide, policies have made a greater shift towards inclusion than laws
Distribution of countries by school organization for students with disabilities as defined in policy, by region, 2020

GEM StatLink: http://bit.ly/GEM2020_fig2_2
Source: GEM Report team analysis based on GEM Report Education Profiles.

In comparison with laws, which are slower to change, policies are much more geared towards providing education in inclusive settings for students with disabilities. Some 38% of countries have adopted such policies, GEM Report analysis finds. Inclusion of special needs students in mainstream classrooms is, to varying degrees, part of every Canadian province's education policy. The province of New Brunswick's inclusive education policy was a pioneer in establishing that segregated programmes and classes 'must not occur' (New Brunswick Government, 2013).

In India, inclusive practices are found in relation to early intervention for children with disabilities. Tamil Nadu state set up a State Resource Centre for Inclusive Education. Andhra Pradesh and Maharashtra states arranged transport for children and their parents, as they closed small schools. Bihar state ensured representation of parents of learners with disabilities on school management committees (Oxfam India, 2020). Overall, though, delivering education in inclusive settings is relatively less preferred in Central and Southern Asia and in Northern Africa and Western Asia.

The move towards inclusion follows different paths at different speeds due to contextual factors. In Fiji, a special education school was established in the mid-1960s for children affected by poliomyelitis, which was followed by other special schools. As these were located in main urban

areas and on the two main islands, access for children in rural areas and on outer islands was limited. An inclusive education policy supporting access for children with disabilities to neighbourhood mainstream schools was first endorsed in 2010 and reviewed in 2016. The Special and Inclusive Education Policy Implementation Plan 2017–2020 supports a staged approach promoting both special and inclusive education options. Special schools are part of the plan, enabling students with particular disabilities to learn key skills, such as sign language or Braille, that complement mainstream education (Fiji Ministry of Education, Heritage and Arts, 2016).

Many countries deploy special resources equitably to provide adequate support in mainstream education and in the transition to inclusion. In Sichuan province, China, the Shuangliu District Special Education School's 1+5+N model aims to integrate learners with special education needs through a three-level resource system. The main, first-level resource centre for the district, founded by the local government, provides professional help to other resource room centres (1); secondary resource rooms

> ❝ 42% of countries in sub-Saharan Africa are considered to be pursuing inclusive policies ❞

BOX 2.5:

Sub-Saharan African countries deploy a range of tools to include students with disabilities

Sub-Saharan African countries have taken steps towards policies that support full inclusion of students with disabilities in mainstream schools. In all, 42% of countries in the region are considered to be pursuing inclusive policies, although a coherent approach towards inclusion remains a challenge. Countries are exploring possibilities by using special schools, resource centres, itinerant teachers and satellite classes. However, there is also a marked absence of standardized monitoring tools and of rigorous evaluations of the implementation of policies and programmes at national level (Jolley et al., 2018).

Angola's 2017 National Policy of Special Education has a target of including 30,000 children with special education needs in mainstream schools by 2022. The policy will be implemented in 6,000 primary schools (GEM Report Education Profiles). It aims to transform special schools into support centres providing guidance for inclusion of children with disabilities in mainstream schools, along with capacity building and training for teachers (Section VI) (Lobo d'Avila et al., 2019).

In Ethiopia, inclusive schools are mainstream schools where learners with and without disabilities learn in the same classrooms. Teaching assistants, such as sign language interpreters, may be available. Schools are grouped into 7,532 clusters to facilitate resource sharing. Among these, 213 schools, or 2.9%, have established inclusive education resource centres (Tadesse Mergia, 2020).

Ghana's 2015 inclusive education policy framework envisages transforming special schools into resource centres to assist mainstream education while maintaining special units, schools and other institutions for students with severe and profound disabilities. Special schools were expected to cooperate with mainstream schools accommodating children with special education needs, work closely with assessment centres for periodic screening and diagnosis and ensure that their staff were trained in the centres. The policy went beyond physical accessibility and incorporated basic values promoting participation, friendship and interaction (Ghana Ministry of Education, 2015).

Kenyan students with disabilities attend special schools, integrated schools and special units within mainstream schools targeted at those with hearing and visual impairments, intellectual disabilities and physical disabilities. The 2018 sector policy for learners and trainees with disabilities extends education provision in mainstream schools. It recognizes special schools' pivotal role in the transition towards inclusive education and relies on education services provided by existing arrangements, as well as home-based education, especially for those with severe disabilities and in vulnerable circumstances. Currently, 1,882 primary and secondary mainstream schools provide education for students with special needs (GEM Report Education Profiles).

Malawi has taken a twin-track approach. Children and youth with severe disabilities are educated in special schools or special needs centres, while those with mild disabilities are mainstreamed. The Education Sector Implementation Plan II aims to strengthen inclusive education in all schools to avoid segregation. Special schools at each education level are being transformed into resource centres, as specified in the 2007 National Policy on Special Needs Education (GEM Report Education Profiles).

In Nigeria, missionaries began segregation in the 1970s and governments later followed suit. The 2004 education policy formalized public special schools. While inclusion was affirmed for various learner groups, separate interventions led to segregated education provision. The 2017 National Policy on Inclusive Education tries to harmonize modalities to provide a unified system. It plans to realize inclusive education by rehabilitating and upgrading special schools to serve as resource centres catering for the needs of people with disabilities and training teachers on inclusion (GEM Report Education Profiles). Most state government-run special schools target one or two impairments. Enugu state supports three schools as special education centres integrating children with and without disabilities. Lagos state set up a few inclusive primary schools, providing trained teachers and materials for children with disabilities in same or separate classes. Poorer states have only one or two special schools, which provide both boarding and day services (Pinnock, 2020).

South Africa has introduced inclusive schools to develop 'cultures, policies and practices that celebrate diversity, respect difference and value innovation and problem-solving'. Known as 'full-service' schools, in the sense that they cater for the full range of learning needs, they are also expected to support neighbouring ordinary schools (South Africa Department of Basic Education, 2010). A National Education Excellence Award for the Most Improved Full-Service School was introduced in 2014 (South Africa Department of Basic Education, 2016a). A school that received the award counted school-based support teams; institutionalized screening, identification, assessment and support; curriculum differentiation; direct learner support; and collaboration with the community as factors of success (Martin, 2015). Goal 26 of the 2015/16–2019/20 Five Year Strategic Plan seeks to increase the number of schools that effectively implement the inclusive education policy and have access to centres offering specialist services (South Africa Department of Basic Education, 2016b). The most recent annual report does not provide an update on this goal but mentions the appointment of Transversal Itinerant Outreach Team Members in provinces (South Africa Department of Basic Education, 2019).

Itinerant teachers also work in some regions of the United Republic of Tanzania, providing teacher and student support, with a focus on adaptation and material preparation for visually impaired learners (Mnyanyi, 2014). They are trained, managed and overseen by Tanzania Society for the Blind and employed by the government through district education offices. They are provided with a motorbike and associated recurrent costs. Itinerant teachers also perform vision screening, refer children to medical facilities and organize community sensitization and counselling (Light for the World and Imprint Consultants, 2016).

established in five mainstream schools (5) receive help from the district special education centre and help all other resource centres in regular schools (N) (European Agency for Special Needs and Inclusive Education and UNESCO, 2019).

Some countries have established satellite classes, i.e. special classes in mainstream schools, including Australia (for students with autism spectrum disorder) and China. In Zhejiang province, China, satellite classes, defined as a placement for students with disabilities 'between special schools and supplementary reading classes', follow the principles of resource pooling, proximity and two-way coordination. They are directed at students with intellectual disabilities, cerebral palsy and autism spectrum disorder. Per-capita funding of satellite students is at least 10 times that of mainstream students at the same level in the same area (China Ministry of Education, 2015). The Cook Islands has set up satellite classes in isolated villages on small islands to offer early childhood and early primary level programmes, while older students attend larger schools in more central locations (GEM Report Education Profiles). Sub-Saharan African countries are at various stages of developing policies to include students with disabilities (**Box 2.5**).

INCLUSIVE EDUCATION POLICIES TARGET SEVERAL POPULATION GROUPS

Education policies strong on inclusiveness often target other vulnerable groups. The GEM Report found that education or other ministries had responsibility for education policies targeted at gender equality in 71% of countries, linguistic minorities in 46% of counties, and ethnic and indigenous groups in 37% of countries.

In Bangladesh, the 2010 National Education Policy recognized children's right to receive education in their mother tongue. The 2012 Pre-Primary Education Expansion Plan and 2016–20 Seventh Five Year Plan highlighted the importance of respecting all children's traditions, culture and heritage, including in the curriculum (GEM Report Education Profiles).

In the Plurinational State of Bolivia, under the Institutional Strategic Plan for the Ministry of Education and Sectoral Plan for Integral Development of Education for Living Well 2016–2020, historically excluded groups, including indigenous populations, people with disabilities,

rural and remote populations, street children and pregnant teenagers who drop out, are targeted through a range of programmes. The government established the Plurinational Competency Certification System to certify skills and experiences gained in trades or occupations outside formal education. An average of 25,000 people a year, often from previously neglected indigenous groups and rural areas, receive post-literacy certification (UNESCO, 2019a).

Ireland's 2019 Action Plan for Education aims to help individuals achieve their full potential through learning and contribute to national development. Various instruments across education levels and groups uphold this mission. The 2005 Delivering Equality of Opportunity in Schools Plan, the main policy instrument to support schools with higher concentrations of disadvantaged students, was relaunched in 2017 with more than 100 actions to tackle disadvantage. As of 2019, almost 900 schools were taking part in the programme. Travellers and Roma constitute a vulnerable group. The Department of Justice and Equality coordinates the cross-government National Traveller and Roma Inclusion Strategy. With support from the Department of Education and Skills, Department of Children and Youth Affairs, and Child and Family Agency, the strategy adopts an inclusive approach to education to improve attendance, participation and engagement and reduce early school leaving (UNESCO, 2019a).

Kenya's 2015 Policy Framework for Nomadic Education paid special attention to inclusion and vulnerability within nomadic communities, especially for girls and children with special needs. To facilitate access to and participation in education, the policy called for establishing more mobile schools, introducing open and distance learning and introducing innovative and flexible community-based education interventions (GEM Report Education Profiles).

The Philippines Department of Education issued a gender-responsive basic education policy in 2017 that called for an end to discrimination based on gender, sexual orientation and gender identity. The policy outlined measures for education administrators and school leaders, including enriching curricula and teacher education programmes with content on bullying, discrimination, gender, sexuality and human rights (Thoreson, 2017). It is one of numerous examples of

BOX 2.6:

Schools are beginning to respect diversity in sexual orientation and gender identity and expression

Globally, 42% of lesbian, gay, bisexual and transgender and intersex youth reported having been 'ridiculed, teased, insulted or threatened at school' (Richard and MAG Jeunes LGBT, 2018, p. 11) because of their sexual orientation and gender identity status, primarily by their peers. About 37% reported feeling rarely or never safe at school, with the highest prevalence in the Arab States and sub-Saharan Africa.

Legislation can reinforce discriminatory behaviour or make it impossible to address issues related to gender identity and sexual orientation in education. About 68 countries criminalize consensual same-sex sexual acts. Barbados rejected all recommendations in its 2013 UN Universal Periodic Review that urged decriminalization of same-sex sexual acts. About 31 countries have laws and regulations restricting the right to freedom of expression in relation to sexual orientation issues on individuals, educators or the media. While morality codes have been almost ubiquitous in the Arab States, new legal tools criminalize expressions of affirmation or support for homosexuality. For instance, a 2017 resolution of the Ministry of Education and Sciences in Paraguay prohibits the dissemination and use of education materials referring to 'gender theory and/or ideology' (Mendos, 2019). In May 2019, the Kenyan High Court upheld a colonial-era law that criminalized same-sex intercourse (Kyama and Pérez-Peña, 2019).

Countries are beginning to pay attention to gender identity. In 2015, Malta passed the Gender Identity, Gender Expression and Sex Characteristics Act (see **Box 14.1**). Later that year, the Ministry for Education and Employment published the Trans, Gender Variant and Intersex Students in Schools Policy. In 2016, the Council of Europe Parliamentary Assembly called on member countries to promote respect and inclusion and disseminate objective information (Council of Europe, 2016). As of 2018, 21 of its 47 members had national or regional action plans explicitly prohibiting and addressing school bullying based on sexual orientation and gender identity and expression (UNESCO, 2018b).

Although countries are moving towards recognition of the rights of people with diverse gender identities, incoherent laws and policies persist. In Lithuania, while the 2017 Law on Equal Treatment obliged secondary and post-secondary education institutions to guarantee equal opportunity for all students regardless of sexual orientation, an article of the 2011 Law on the Protection of Minors against the Detrimental Effect of Public Information prohibits dissemination of information on concepts of marriage and family values that differ from those in the Constitution and Civil Code (LGL, 2018).

There are fewer examples of such recognition outside Europe and Northern America. Chile's Ministry of Education issued school guidelines to support inclusion of transgender students without discrimination and violence (Right to Education Initiative, 2017). In India's Delhi National Capital Territory, cooperation between the transgender rights NGO Society for People's Awareness, Care and Empowerment and the Directorate of Education resulted in 27 schools being certified as trans-friendly. The schools have taken measures inclusive of transgender and gender non-conforming children, including making at least one toilet gender-neutral and raising awareness to prevent bullying (*New Delhi Times*, 2019). In South Africa, some 20 Cape Town schools have made similar provisions, including gender-neutral uniforms and allowing students to use new names (BBC News, 2019).

---

the increasing attention education systems are paying to the right of everyone to safe and inclusive learning environments (**Box 2.6**).

LACK OF LAW AND POLICY IMPLEMENTATION HINDERS INCLUSION

Even if laws are enacted and policies announced, follow-up actions to achieve inclusion depend on national context, as shaped by historical, political, cultural and socio-economic factors; political will to include some disadvantaged groups; resistance to new forms of education provision; attitudes; and coordination capacity. Policy planning is often weak, resulting in inconsistencies across the system and poor execution. For instance,

a global review of teacher education programmes for inclusion identified challenges in change management (Rieser, 2013).

Ensuring that laws are translated into policies that are adapted to take learners' needs into account is only the first step. Most countries lag in ensuring effective fulfilment of these often ambitious commitments. In a review of 85 country reports on CRPD implementation regarding inclusive education programmes and services, submitted to the Committee on the Rights of Persons with Disabilities, a striking disconnect between laws, policies and practice was a common theme. Jordan acknowledged that most schools were not well prepared to practice inclusion, as insufficient measures had been taken for transport, access and safe use of the physical environment and for curricula harmonization, especially in basic education. South Africa reported new segregated schools and a lack of provisions for children with severe intellectual disabilities (Leonard Cheshire Disability, 2017).

Throughout sub-Saharan Africa, while teachers follow individualized teaching strategies, role modelling, peer support and group strategies to promote inclusion of students with intellectual and developmental disabilities, lack of human and material resources for inclusive education is a concern (Okyere et al., 2019a). An analysis of the experiences of children with intellectual and developmental disabilities in inclusive schools in Accra, Ghana, argues that, despite steady progress and a strong legislation and policy framework, students with disabilities must perform the same tasks within the same time frame as their peers without disabilities, occupy desks placed far from teachers and are often physically punished by teachers for behavioural challenges; moreover, teaching is not differentiated (Okyere et al., 2019b).

Malawi increasingly encourages learners with special needs to enrol in mainstream schools, yet lack of facilities forces many to transfer to special schools, e.g. learners with visual impairment moved to schools for the blind (GEM Report Education Profiles). In evaluating its efforts to implement the national inclusive education policy, the Namibian government noted a shortage of resource schools in rural areas, lack of accessible infrastructure, inadequate awareness and unfavourable attitudes towards disability (Namibia Ministry of Education, Arts and Culture, 2018a).

India has made considerable efforts to expand the rural school network since the 2009 Right to Education Act, which required primary schools to be located no more than 1 km from a child's home. However, expansion was achieved by increasing the number of small schools with inadequate infrastructure, resulting in an ongoing process of rationalizing education resource distribution. While primary education is ensured in most rural villages, school distribution rationalization in remote rural areas has affected school distance for secondary and higher education, particularly for girls and learners with disabilities (Oxfam India, 2020).

In Nepal, according to the 2017 Disability Rights Act and the Inclusive Education Policy for Persons with Disabilities, children should be able to attend schools in their communities without discrimination,

but other provisions allow for educating children with disabilities separately. Government efforts focusing on infrastructure and facilities, teacher education and flexible curricula by 2030 need to be aligned with international standards (Human Rights Watch, 2018c; Nepal Law Commission, 2017).

In Turkey, despite a comprehensive legislative framework supporting inclusion in education, implementation challenges include negative attitudes, deficient physical infrastructure and teachers' lack of knowledge and skills (Hande Sart et al., 2016). Viet Nam's 2010 disability law was not effective in preventing education segregation, according to the concluding observations of the Committee on Economic, Social and Cultural Rights in late 2014 (Fiala-Butora, 2019). The government has since issued regulations on training, data collection, materials, equipment and assessment to support the education of people with disabilities. Article 15 of the 2019 education law identifies inclusive education as the preferred mode of education, committing to adopt policies to support implementation (Hai et al., 2020). However, the challenge remains high: 53% of people believed that children with disabilities should study in a special school either in principle or depending on their disability level (Viet Nam General Statistics Office, 2018).

INCLUSIVE POLICIES NEED TO BE PURSUED AT ALL EDUCATION LEVELS AND AGES

While inclusion policies in education generally target population groups, they also take into account differing needs regarding access to and progress through education levels. The following section addresses this lifelong perspective and the distinct challenges of the different stages.

INCLUSIVE EARLY CHILDHOOD CARE AND EDUCATION CAN HELP LEVEL THE FIELD

Poor nutrition, safety, health and learning in the early years can result in developmental delays and disabilities. Inclusive early childhood care and education (ECCE) gives children better chances throughout life. Preschool can have a positive influence on learning outcomes (Elango et al., 2015). Yet ECCE access tends to be lower for the children most in need, even in countries that provide universal legal entitlement (Melhuish et al.,

> **Poor nutrition, safety, health and learning in the early years can result in developmental delays and disabilities**

2015). In 34 European countries, ECCE participation is significantly lower among children who have immigrant or less educated mothers, live in rural areas or come from poor families (Ünver et al., 2016). In Albania, poverty, lack of registration, discrimination and lack of parental awareness of the benefits limit preschool enrolment of Roma children (Council of Europe, 2018b), despite measures to facilitate access (European Commission/EACEA/Eurydice, 2019). In Montenegro, a campaign to raise parental awareness in disadvantaged northern municipalities used innovative approaches, such as art performances in city centres, increasing enrolment by 20% between 2014 and 2015 (UNICEF, 2019).

In India, the Integrated Child Development Services of the Ministry of Women and Child Development, launched in 1975, offers six services to pregnant and lactating women and to children from birth to age 6, including non-formal preschool education for 3- to 6-year-olds. About 1.36 million rural childcare centres (anganwadi) were operational in 2018 (India Ministry of Women and Child Development, 2018). In parallel, private provision has been growing (Wadhwa et al., 2019): already in 2011, 28% of villages in Assam, 42% in Telangana and 93% in Rajasthan had at least one private preschool (Kaul et al., 2017). However, the quality of education is not age-appropriate: the education service does not receive sufficient attention at the anganwadi centres, while private preschools do not offer age-appropriate pedagogy (Bhattacharjea and Ramanujan, 2019).

Groups at risk of exclusion from ECCE include refugees, ethnic and linguistic minorities, and children with disabilities. Countries tend to rely on NGOs for services reaching these groups, although there are promising attempts to embed provision in government systems. In Armenia, with support from Save the Children, Syrian refugee children attend four-hour classes in two general education preschools in Yerevan (Armenia Government, 2016). Ireland's Community Childcare Subvention Resettlement programme provides free services for refugee children under age 5 to support their integration (Ireland Government, 2019). In Uganda, within the Comprehensive Refugee Response Framework, the government has introduced policies to increase

numbers of certified caregivers and centres providing good-quality integrated early childhood development services (Uganda Ministry of Education and Sports, 2018; UNHCR, 2018a, 2018b).

Cambodia's 2015–18 Multilingual Education National Action Plan enabled ethnic minority learners to take preschool and the first three years of primary school in five languages other than Khmer. The programme is implemented in 5 provinces, reaching 92 state and community preschools, and has since been expanded to one more language (Ball and Smith, 2019). The government has committed to increase the number of multilingual teachers by 25% by 2023 (Cambodia Ministry of Education, Youth and Sport, 2019).

Access to ECCE for children with disabilities is a particular challenge in rural areas. In rural Namibia, early childhood development programmes often take place outside formal structures (Ngololo Kamara et al., 2018). By contrast, in Cuba, children with disabilities are included in mainstream early childhood development programmes. Support is provided to all children, even in rural areas, thanks in part to Educa tu hijo (Educate your child), which serves more than 5,000 children with disabilities (Cuba Government, 2019).

Quality contributes to inclusive early childhood care and education

Even if ECCE services are accessible, their quality largely determines whether they contribute to inclusion. Three broad dimensions of quality related to inclusion are worth mentioning: modalities based on interactions, efficiency based on integration, and child-centred curriculum based on play.

Increasingly, inclusive early childhood development services aim to be accessible and equitable for all, even when their aim is to support children with developmental delays and disabilities. For those children, early childhood interventions are becoming increasing individualized and delivered at home, moving away from services delivered by experts in clinical settings. A review of 426 inclusive early childhood development and early childhood intervention programmes in 121 countries found that two-thirds involved parents in service delivery. Governments still need to overcome a range of barriers: absence of administrative data documenting developmental delays, inadequacy of community outreach efforts to identify children at risk, lack of caregiver power to demand services and inadequate service quality supervision. Programmes are successful when staff are trained and interventions enjoy political support and an enabling policy environment (Vargas-Barón et al., 2019).

A review of 32 inclusive early childhood education programmes in Europe identified active participation as the overarching objective to ensure children learn and develop a sense of belonging. Positive interaction with adults and peers, involvement in play and other daily activities, a child-centred approach, personalized learning assessment, and accommodation, adaptation and support are essential components (European Agency for Special Needs and Inclusive Education, 2016). In France, where all children are entitled to free pre-primary school (recently extended to age 2), classes for children with autism spectrum disorders have opened in preschools, and other children are taught to understand their classmates' needs in order to communicate. In Latvia, Chinese immigrant parents spend time with children and teachers during the first month of preschool before children are left with teachers for increasing lengths of time. In Sweden, all children have the right to ECCE from age 1 and to free services for 15 hours per week from age 3. Children under age 1 with special education needs may start free ECCE for 15 hours per week. Support is offered to the entire preschool class, adjusting the number of staff or children as appropriate (European Agency for Special Needs and Inclusive Education, 2016; European Commission/EACEA/ Eurydice, 2019).

Lack of understanding of the holistic nature of early childhood services hinders inclusion, as does absence of coordination among health, nutrition and education providers (see **Chapter 4**). Considerable progress in service integration has been made in Latin America. In a 2016 presidential decree, Brazil initiated Criança Feliz (Happy Childhood) to promote comprehensive child

development in the early years through home visits and inter-sector collaboration. By January 2018, 25 of 27 federal units had joined the programme (Girade, 2018). Colombia's De Cero a Siempre (From Zero to Forever), initiated in 2011 and passed into legislation in 2016, is based on an integrated package of services that each child should receive from birth to age 6. It integrates services horizontally among government departments and vertically between the national and subnational government levels (Santos Calderón, 2018).

Shifting from teaching strategies that risk not engaging children to those better aligned with their interests is also key to building inclusive learning. Learning through play can help develop skills and capabilities, improve interactions with peers and foster cooperation to solve problems. While the concept is mainstreamed in high-income countries, most attempts to introduce play in low- and middle-income countries' curricula remain peripheral and tend to benefit from support of multilateral organizations and foundations (**Box 2.7**). In Kenya, an innovative attempt at inclusion through sport from early childhood on has received government support (**Box 2.8**).

EARLY IDENTIFICATION IS CRUCIAL TO RESPOND APPROPRIATELY TO DIVERSE LEARNER NEEDS

Early identification is vital in meeting individual learning needs and preventing delay (Braun, 2020). Some signs of dyslexia, such as inability to develop oral language, phonological awareness or motor skills, tend to appear early (**Box 2.9**). Definitions of special education needs, which vary by country, are at the heart of identification procedures grounded in law or administrative rules. Lack of identification may prevent provision of adequate support: An Irish court decided that a school unaware that a student had a disability could not be required to make reasonable accommodation (Whyte, 2019).

In 21 eastern and southern African countries, it is usually parents who inform schools or school staff who notice the disability. Formal identification and screening systems are rare (Education Development Trust and UNICEF, 2016).

> 66
>
> In Europe, active participation is the overarching objective to ensure children learn and develop a sense of belonging
>
> 99

BOX 2.7:

Low- and middle-income countries are exploring learning through play as a route to inclusion

Few learning through play approaches have become part of formal curricula in low- and middle-income countries. Serbia adopted the Years of Ascent preschool curriculum framework in 2018. It is child centred and uses a pedagogy based on play that engages children, families and schools. Designed for ages 6 months to 6.5 years, it emphasizes curriculum coherence and continuity of learning (UNICEF, 2019).

In Viet Nam, in line with the 2005 education law's call for preschools to 'help children develop holistically by organising play activities', the 2009 early childhood education curriculum emphasized holistic development. With the support of VVOB, a Belgian non-profit organization, the Ministry of Education and Training developed a two-module training programme for preschool teachers, which supports them in monitoring children's well-being and involvement and in identifying children at risk of not learning. Teachers found lower well-being and involvement during teacher-led academic learning than during play activities (VVOB, 2018).

Interventions are small-scale in most countries and run by NGOs. Kidogo in Kenya targets children under age 6 living in slums. Emphasizing learning through play, problem solving and social-emotional skills, using the national curriculum, it facilitates holistic care in child-friendly environments with trained and certified caregivers, nutritious meals and parental engagement (Jordan et al., 2015). In Nicaragua, the Fabretto foundation early education programme provides education services for children aged 2 to 6 in more than 80 public schools in underserved rural communities. It trains teachers, focusing on play-based learning strategies inspired by holistic education approaches adapted to meet student needs (Center for Education Innovations, 2018b).

South Africa adopted a National Strategy on Screening, Identification, Assessment and Support in 2014 to provide standardized procedures (South Africa Department of Basic Education, 2014). The policy, aligned with the Integrated School Health Policy, targets out-of-school children as well as learners in mainstream and special schools who encounter learning barriers. Assessment and support are not based on predefined categories of disability but on level and nature of learning needs. At admission, teachers screen all children, record results in learner profiles and become case managers.

In Belize, teachers advise head teachers to place students they consider as having 'exceptional learning needs' on a referral list for itinerant resource officer assessment (Belize National Resource Centre for Inclusive Education, 2019). As officers visit each school infrequently, many children wait months to be assessed. Officers help teachers develop individualized education plans adapted to learning needs and support school placement of children not in school (UNICEF, 2013). In Saint Vincent and the Grenadines, under the 2005 Education Act, the education minister refers children whom the chief education officer identifies as having learning difficulties to medical, education and social services for treatment or assistance (St Vincent and the Grenadines Government, 2005).

BOX 2.8:

In Kenya, learning through sport is a route to inclusion of children with intellectual disabilities

Unified Champion Schools is a programme of Special Olympics, a sports organization dedicated to children and adults with intellectual disabilities. The programme, which operates in 14 countries, aims to promote inclusion in schools through sports activities that break down barriers and change attitudes, from early childhood through adolescence. It has four components: play-based, early childhood motor skills development for 2- to 7-year-olds; teams of youth with and without intellectual disabilities training together and competing in sport and play; clubs and student organizations working on advocacy efforts to increase inclusion throughout school life; and awareness activities, engaging the whole school community in understanding, supporting and practicing inclusion (Special Olympics, 2019).

In Kenya, in partnership with the Ministry of Education and UNICEF, Unified Champion Schools has helped assess and refer children identified with intellectual disabilities, following up with workshops on inclusive education with families, teachers and school leaders. The project has enrolled nearly 600 students with intellectual disabilities and has helped develop positive attitudes towards these students in participating schools. Special Olympics contributed to the development of the national inclusive education policy, including drafting an easy to read version. Unified Champion Schools, in partnership with Catholic Relief Services, continues Special Olympics Kenya's work on early childhood development for children with intellectual disabilities through the Young Athletes programme. Identifying children in need of services early helps support families, providing a hopeful vision for their children's future and disproving widely held myths about ability to learn (Special Olympics Kenya, 2018).

BOX 2.9:

Early identification of dyslexia fosters inclusion, but countries struggle to develop processes

Dyslexia exists among speakers of all languages (Shaywitz et al., 2008; Ziegler and Goswami, 2005). When it is undiagnosed, the risk of illiteracy and social exclusion is higher. Although lack of teacher training and knowledge are challenges, when teachers are trained, 90% of children with dyslexia can be educated in mainstream classrooms. Approaches for these students can benefit all those learning to read (Dyslexia International, 2014).

A longitudinal study in Finland that followed a sample of children from birth to adolescence suggested that first indications of risk of dyslexia can be observed nearly at birth. Brain event-related potentials measured at three to five days from birth are significantly correlated with reading ability at grade 2 (Lyytinen et al., 2015). Detecting risk early can support inclusion.

> A study in Finland suggested that first indications of risk of dyslexia can be observed nearly at birth

In low- and middle-income countries, such as Indonesia, the concept of dyslexia and instruments supporting early identification are relatively underdeveloped (Rofiah, 2015). Standard Indonesian, the primary language of instruction, has a transparent orthography and nearly a one-to-one letter-to-sound correspondence. Dyslexia is expected to manifest through lower reading speed. A research project to develop identification tests and assess reading development found that 17% of grade 1 and 14% of grade 2 students were at risk of dyslexia (Jap et al., 2017). The Dyslexia Association of Indonesia has developed an online early identification system (Dewi et al., 2017).

A study in Qom, Islamic Republic of Iran, estimated that 5% of students aged 6 to 14 were dyslexic (Pouretemad et al., 2011). However, screening tests remain at the level of research studies in university medical departments and are not yet part of formal procedures (Delavarian et al., 2017; Faramarzi et al., 2019). To some extent, this reflects the broader challenge of scientific knowledge being disconnected from education practice, partly as a result of 'pervasive disagreements about the definition of [learning disabilities], diagnostic criteria, assessment practices, treatment procedures, and educational policies', as noted in the United States (Fletcher et al., 2018, p. 2).

Samarpan in India's Madhya Pradesh state is a community-based early intervention to identify, screen, treat and rehabilitate children under age 5 with developmental delays or physical disability. Its early intervention clinics use a holistic approach involving officials concerned with public health, family welfare, women and child development, social justice and empowerment and revenues (NITI Aayog and UNDP, 2015). In other countries, health authorities maintain a strong role. In the Lao People's Democratic Republic, the Centre for Medical Rehabilitation, under the Ministry of Health, is responsible for examining and diagnosing children up to age 18 and directing those identified with disabilities to extended support (Lao PDR Government, 2016).

Some question whether early identification is desirable because the stigma of labels often aggravates exclusion in the name of inclusion. It has also led to segregated education, with referred individuals separated to receive 'appropriate support' (Ainscow, 1991; Algraigray and Boyle, 2017). In promotion of inclusion and equity, special education needs identification and assessment may engender difference and marginalization. Identification may also lead to lower teacher expectations (Tomlinson, 1982), peer rejection (Keogh and MacMillan, 1996), exclusion from participation in standardized testing, and disproportionality: over-representation of poor and minority students in special education (Cruz and Rodl, 2018; Gordon, 2017).

Disproportionality has been thoroughly studied in the United States, where black students are identified with disabilities at higher rates than their peers. Recent studies corroborate the findings, under certain conditions (Braun, 2020). In Florida, black and Hispanic students are under-represented in physical disabilities and over-represented in intellectual disabilities. They tend to be overidentified with disabilities in schools with few minorities. Every 10 percentage point increase in the share of minority students was associated with a 0.9 point decline in the disability gap with white students (Elder et al., 2019). Over-representation of groups in special education is often due to bias in procedures, testing material or people. For instance, students with immigrant backgrounds are often misdiagnosed as having special education needs, partly because literacy tests are not offered in their home language (Adair, 2015; Sanatullova-Allison and Robison-Young, 2016).

AUTOMATIC GRADE PROMOTION WITH REMEDIAL SUPPORT HELPS DISADVANTAGED STUDENTS

Grade repetition, practiced worldwide, is an inclusion challenge. In 2016, the lower secondary school repetition rate was 10.2% in Luxembourg and 8.5% in Spain. In the United States, 18 states require students to repeat grade 3 if they do not achieve reading proficiency (Modan, 2019). Repetition is more common in poorer countries and slightly more common in lower secondary than in primary education, although countries vary: In 2017, respective repetition rates for primary and secondary education were 10% and 21% in Morocco, 9% and 12% in South Africa, 9% and 5% in Guatemala and 13% and 5% in Rwanda (**Figure 2.3**). The inclusion challenge is that disadvantaged students have a higher probability of repeating. In Rwanda, the probability of repeating a grade more than once was 15 percentage points higher for children with difficulties speaking and being understood

and 9 points higher for those with behavioural issues (Rwanda Ministry of Education and UNICEF, 2017).

Policymakers must choose between enforcing repetition or allowing promotion. A common concern is that repetition may increase early school leaving, but demonstrating this requires careful research design. Traditional perceptions of the benefits of repetition may be stronger determinants of policy than evidence (Goos et al., 2013).

A meta-analysis of studies done over two decades in the United States showed no effect of grade repetition on achievement; the analysts recommended attention to both general repetition policy and its details, especially support to those repeating (Allen et al., 2009). The negative effect on social-emotional outcomes, such as low self-esteem (Martin, 2011) and disruptive behaviour (Jimerson and Ferguson, 2007) should be examined.

International experiences of automatic promotion policies vary. In Brazil, primary education was split into two four-year cycles in 1997, and the continued progression policy prescribed automatic promotion for all but grades 4 and 8. However, the policy was not applied uniformly across the country, and the extent to which it was implemented related to school characteristics. A study that controlled for selectivity in implementation found that automatically promoted cohorts showed modest but persistent benefits in the transition from the lower to upper primary education cycle (Leighton et al., 2019).

In Cameroon, a ministerial order established automatic promotion in primary education in 2006 in response to repetition rates reaching 30% in the 1990s. Repetition rates have halved since 2005 but remain around 12%. The order envisaged promoted low achievers receiving remedial education. A survey of grade 6 students in the two English-speaking regions found that the regions applied automatic promotion but not the other prescriptions. Most teachers opposed automatic promotion (Endeley, 2016). In Ethiopia, an analysis of automatic promotion for grades 1 to 3 found that it had a negative effect on student motivation, attitudes towards school, attendance and behaviour, as well as on teacher classroom management (Ahmed and Mihiretie, 2015). Similar concerns have been expressed in India despite the positive impact of automatic promotion (**Box 2.10**).

Namibia adopted semi-automatic promotion in 1996. Up to grade 10, students who did not achieve minimum

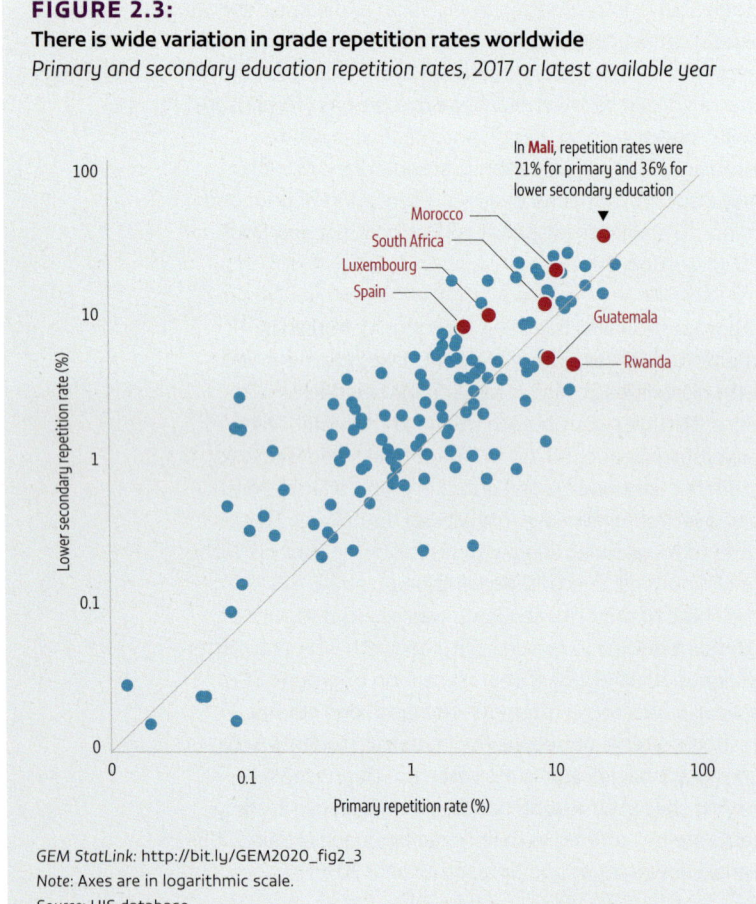

FIGURE 2.3:
There is wide variation in grade repetition rates worldwide
Primary and secondary education repetition rates, 2017 or latest available year

GEM StatLink: http://bit.ly/GEM2020_fig2_3
Note: Axes are in logarithmic scale.
Source: UIS database.

requirements a second time were promoted; as of grade 10, failing students were not allowed to repeat (UNICEF, 2015). An evaluation found that repetition did not decline, weak learners received no support and promotion requirements were not consistently applied (Sichombe et al., 2011); primary school repetition was still 16% in 2017. In 2018, the education ministry developed a secondary education repetition policy to ensure that no learner would be more than three years older than the age for grade, and that lagging students would receive individualized support and counselling in close collaboration with parents. School promotion committees would discuss borderline cases. The ministry also made provisions for fair assessment of learners with hearing and visual impairments (Namibia Ministry of Education, Arts and Culture, 2018b).

Remedial programmes can be effective but need to be sustained

Automatic promotion's effectiveness depends on whether struggling students receive support. Remedial learning interventions target children at risk of falling behind and leaving school early. They take multiple forms but tend to be delivered in core subjects to small groups after school. Chile's National Student Assistance and Scholarship Board, under the Ministry of Education, targets students from disadvantaged families at risk of dropout with two programmes: school repetition support, which offers social-emotional support through a multidisciplinary team that includes social workers and psychologists, and Habilidades para la vida (Skills for life), which targets schools with high levels of socio-economic vulnerability (Santiago et al., 2017).

Evaluations of remedial programmes tend to come from high-income countries. A programme in Japan for grade 3 and 4 students with low academic performance was found to have a small positive effect on Japanese language test scores but not on mathematics scores. The evaluation found positive effects on study practices and hours of study (Bessho et al., 2019).

In the United States, remedial programmes benefit poorer students. Parents also benefit as childcare needs are eased when programmes take place during after school. However, good-quality instruction and regular attendance are key for lasting positive effects (McCombs et al., 2017). Grade 6 Florida students whose previous year's state test scores had fallen below a threshold were randomly assigned to take two mathematics classes

---

■ **BOX 2.10:**

Some Indian states are abandoning automatic promotion despite its benefits

Section 16 of India's 2009 Right of Children to Free and Compulsory Education (RTE) Act stipulates that no child 'admitted in a school shall be held back in any class or expelled from school till the completion of elementary education' (grades 1 to 8). Many raised concerns over negative effects on learning quality, as automatic promotion is often misunderstood as absence of evaluation.

In 2017, these concerns led to a proposal to rescind the no-repetition policy through the Right to Education (2nd Amendment) Bill, which reintroduced the possibility of repetition if a student failed grade 5 (end of primary) or grade 8 (end of lower secondary) examinations. A dozen states and union territories (UTs), including Assam, Bihar and Uttar Pradesh, abandoned the policy, citing apparent negative effects on quality of learning and performance in higher grades (Maadhyam, 2017).

> **"** Analysis for this report suggests that children who repeated a primary grade were less likely to complete primary school and more likely to leave school early **"**

Analysis for this report suggests that children who repeated a primary grade were less likely to complete primary school and more likely to leave school early. Using two external factors (the extent to which states and UTs differed in applying no-repetition policy before the adoption of the RTE Act, and the age of the child), the analysis shows that the no-repetition policy lowered dropout rates, with a larger decrease among primary school-aged children in states and UTs that implemented the policy after adoption of the RTE Act (Agarwal, 2020). This is important, as the probability of repeating remains higher for children who belong to scheduled castes.

---

instead of one. Learning improved after a year, but when they returned to one class, gains shrank by up to 50% the following year and up to 80% the year after (Taylor, 2016). In another programme, grade 9 students in Chicago doubled the time spent on algebra, with an emphasis on problem-solving skills. An evaluation showed a positive impact on test scores, graduation rates and rates of transition to higher education. The effects were stronger among students with low reading skills, as mathematical concepts were presented verbally (Cortes et al., 2015).

A few examples come from middle-income countries, notably evaluations of those that have used the Teaching at the Right Level programme, which originated in India (see **Chapter 6**). The World University Service of Canada's Equity in Education in Refugee Camps in Kenya provides remedial education to grade 7 and 8 girls in Dadaab and Kakuma refugee camps who are at high risk of early school leaving. An assessment found that attendance was large but irregular, and the effect on learning outcomes positive only for food-secure households. There were no statistically significant effects on primary completion examination scores or school attendance (de Hoop et al., 2019).

In Lima, Peru, an evaluation of a remedial inquiry-based science education programme for grade 3 students at disadvantaged schools who scored in the bottom half of their class found that scores improved, although gains were small and concentrated among boys (Saavedra et al., 2019). In Serbia, the Roma Teaching Assistant Programme assigned one Roma assistant each to eligible primary schools. They were free to allocate their time as needed during classes and after school; for instance, they could collect information about children not enrolling or leaving school early, gather documents, visit families and cooperate with the community. An evaluation found that the programme helped increase grade 1 Roma student attendance (Battaglia and Lebediniski, 2015, 2017).

A review of low- and middle-income countries found that most had remedial education strategies in their sector plans (Schwartz, 2012). Implementation was hindered by lack of appropriate learning materials, overcrowded classrooms and inadequate teacher training and time. Gambia's 2016–30 Education Sector Plan includes an After School Support Programme (Gambia Ministries of Basic and Secondary Education and Higher Education, Research, Science and Technology, 2016). The 2016–20 education sector plan in the Lao People's Democratic Republic includes remedial instruction for children with poor learning outcomes (Lao PDR Ministry of Education and Sports, 2015).

SECOND-CHANCE PROGRAMMES MATTER BUT ARE COSTLY

Poverty and social norms are pushing many families to send their children to work before they reach the minimum legal working age or to marry and have children early. Governments are denying many of these children a second chance in education by not enforcing rules,

not setting rules or, in a few cases, even setting rules that violate children's rights (**Box 2.11**). Second-chance education programmes target adolescents and youth who have never been to school or left early without qualification. These programmes are effective when targeted to some marginalized groups, but the cost and the need for well-trained, highly motivated educators are concerns (OECD, 2016).

Argentina introduced Plan FinEs (Plan for Primary and Secondary Education Completion) in 2008 to offer people age 18 or over an opportunity to complete primary or secondary school (Argentina Ministry of Education, 2019). States and civil society collaborate on implementation and delivery takes place outside schools, e.g. in clubs and churches, which individuals were more likely to frequent in daily life. The programme appears only to have prompted some to switch from mainstream adult education. Education quality has been questioned, not least because teachers are under pressure to ensure that students obtain certification (Beech, 2019).

Bangladesh's Reaching Out-of-School Children II aims to give a second chance to out-of-school 8- to 14-year-olds in 148 rural, disadvantaged subdistricts and selected slums. Combining formal and non-formal education, including pre-vocational skills training, and delivered in learning centres (Ananda schools), it provides opportunities to complete primary and transition into secondary education. The schools are owned and managed by communities and supported by the government and NGOs. The schedule is flexible, and each cohort has the same teacher up to graduation. Books, uniforms and stationery are free, and children receive a stipend. Almost 750,000 children are enrolled in 22,000 learning centres at a total cost of US$137.5 million, equivalent to about US$90 per student-year. The average completion rate is 92% (World Bank, 2019a, 2019b).

In Nepal, Marginalized No More is one of 41 projects in the second phase of the Girls' Education Challenge, funded by the UK Department for International Development after a redesign prompted by recommendations in a performance review of the first phase (ICAI, 2016). The project involves a nine-month accelerated learning programme for girls from the marginalized Musahar community, which has untouchable status. Community educators teach basic reading, writing and numeracy. It aims to reach 10,500 girls (Girls' Education Challenge, 2018a; Street Child, 2020). A project run by Sang Sangai, an NGO, involves a nine-month course for girls from

BOX 2.11:

A second education chance is often denied to children who start work, marry or have children early

It is estimated that 114 million 5- to 14-year-olds were working in 2016. This was equivalent to 9.6% of the global age group, down one percentage point from 2012. Of those, 36 million, or 32%, were out of school, and the education chances of many of those attending school also suffer (ILO, 2017). Almost all countries have ratified the 1999 ILO Convention on the Worst Forms of Child Labour, but 20 countries, including Bangladesh and Myanmar, have not ratified the 1973 ILO Minimum Age Convention. Many countries permit child labour before the end of compulsory education. For instance, in Peru and Paraguay, the minimum employment age is 14 but the end of compulsory schooling is age 17 and 18, respectively. An increase in the duration of compulsory education reduced boys' child labour rates in China and Turkey (Alper Dinçer and Erten, 2015; Tang et al., 2020).

Recent estimates of the shares of 20- to 24-year-old women married before age 18 are 21% worldwide and 41% in western and central Africa (UNICEF, 2018). Equivalent estimates for men are lower by about 40% in South Asia and 60% in sub-Saharan Africa (UNICEF, 2020). Article 16 of the Convention on the Elimination of All Forms of Discrimination Against Women prohibits forced and child marriage, but 20 countries, including many with a high prevalence of child marriage, such as Bangladesh and Niger, have expressed reservations on the article (UNESCO, 2018). Bangladesh's legal provision against child marriage punishes parents or guardians but does not declare such marriages void (Blomgren, 2013). At least 117 countries set the minimum age of marriage below 18 (Pew Research Foundation, 2016). Sudan has the lowest minimum ages: 10 for boys and puberty for girls for Muslim marriages, 13 for girls and 15 for boys for non-Muslim marriages (El Nagar et al., 2018).

The estimated adolescent birth rate globally is 44 births per 1,000 girls aged 15 to 19 in 2015-20, down from 53 in 2000-05. However, the rate is 115 in western and central Africa and as high as 229 in the Central African Republic. These girls' chance to complete their education is compromised, and many governments actively thwart their efforts to return to school. Human Rights Watch, an international NGO, reported that, among 48 sub-Saharan African countries, Equatorial Guinea, Sierra Leone and the United Republic of Tanzania totally banned the presence of pregnant girls and young mothers in public schools (Human Rights Watch, 2019). Activists brought a case against Sierra Leone at the Court of Justice of the Economic Community of West African States, which ruled the ban discriminatory in December 2019 and ordered its immediate lifting. In March 2020, the government complied, announcing two new policies focusing on 'radical inclusion' and 'comprehensive safety' of all children in the education system (Peyton, 2020). Still, 20 countries in sub-Saharan Africa have no laws, policies or strategies supporting girls' right to go back to school after pregnancy (Human Rights Watch, 2018).

A few countries recently took steps in the right direction. In 2018, Burundi overturned a ministerial decree that would have banned pregnant girls, and the boys who got them pregnant, from school, while Mozambique revoked a decree that forced pregnant girls to take classes at night. In 2019, Zimbabwe amended its education law to protect pregnant girls from exclusion (Human Rights Watch, 2019).

disadvantaged groups with no or minimal prior schooling and a three-month bridging course to help those who left school catch up before re-enrolling. About 80% of those who took part transitioned to school (RDC Nepal, 2019).

Tunisia's Ministries of Education, Vocational Training and Employment, and Social Affairs have partnered with two national NGOs and France Education International to develop a second-chance education model for 12- to 18-year-olds who left school early. The aim is to integrate it with the national M3D project, which seeks to prevent early school leaving among 5- to 16-year-olds (France Education International, 2019).

NGOs have developed innovative solutions that combine education and sport to support reintegration of street children, involving, for instance, capoeira in Haiti and

boxing in Mombasa, Kenya (Ferguson, 2017). In Ethiopia, the Retrak NGO offers street children safe and secure accommodation, three meals a day, basic health care, life skills training, psychosocial support, intensive counselling and catch-up classes, depending on their numeracy and literacy level, to facilitate reintegration into formal education (Yohannes et al., 2017).

TECHNICAL AND VOCATIONAL EDUCATION AND TRAINING CAN CONTRIBUTE TO INCLUSION

Technical and vocational education and training (TVET) is often considered inclusive by definition because, at least in some countries, it tends to serve populations commonly excluded from mainstream education. However, it faces the same challenges as other education levels (Alla-Mensah, 2020).

Some countries focus skills policy on inclusion of people with disabilities; examples include the 2011 National Skills Development Policy in Bangladesh (ILO, 2017a) and the 2012 National Plan for Vocational Integration of People with Disabilities in Costa Rica (ILO, 2017c). The International Labour Organization and the Ethiopian Centre for Disability and Development supported the federal TVET agency in preparing national guidelines for inclusion of people with disabilities, enabling admission in all skills training centres in all regions (ILO, 2017c). In India, Article 19 of the 2016 Rights of Persons with Disabilities Act provides for concessional loans to support vocational training in all mainstream formal and non-formal training programmes (India Parliament, 2016). Bangladesh, Brazil and South Africa have used TVET institution admission quotas for people with disabilities (ILO, 2017c).

Other countries embrace a wider definition of inclusion in TVET. In the Lao People's Democratic Republic, the Strategic Plan for the Development of Technical and Vocational Education and Training from 2006 to 2020 emphasized women, the poor, people with disabilities and ethnic minorities (Lao PDR Ministry of Education, 2007). Malawi's TVET law and policy also take a broad perspective on inclusion (**Box 2.12**).

In Myanmar, the National Education Strategic Plan 2016–21 emphasized creating equal learning opportunities for TVET in rural and urban areas, bridging TVET levels, providing scholarship programmes for the disadvantaged and offering more pathways from TVET to higher education (Myanmar Ministry of Education, 2016).

Girls' Education Challenge includes projects that facilitate transition to work or self-employment. In northern Afghanistan, Empowering Marginalized Girls, run in partnership with the government, targets inclusion of rural girls in training, including a six-month vocational course on income-generating skills, such as jewellery making, rug weaving, baking and car mechanics. Girls receive a US$400 starter kit upon graduation and can receive additional entrepreneurial training (Center for Education Innovations, 2018a).

In Bangladesh, a randomized control trial of an intervention that provided 144 hours of training over 18 months to 12- to 18-year-old girls found that those who received education tutoring support and gender-related life skills training were 31% less likely to marry before age 18; the figure was 23% for those who received livelihood training in entrepreneurship, mobile

---

BOX 2.12:

Poverty, disability and gender equality concerns threaten inclusion in technical and vocational education and training in Malawi

Malawi's 1999 law and 2013 policy on technical, entrepreneurial and vocational education and training govern its TVET system. They, and the strategic plan of the national authority implementing training programmes, identify disadvantaged individuals as priorities. A recent study of the TVET system, which included interviews in 15 public, private and community technical colleges, as well as community skills development centres, identified obstacles to inclusion (Malawi Ministry of Labour, Youth, Sports and Manpower Development, 2018a).

Tuition subsidies, bursaries, scholarships and attachment allowances for students during work experience were available, but targeting was ineffective. Students still paid some fees, which especially penalized the poorest. Women received less than one-third of bursaries. Only 9% of the TVET levy, a key source of funding, was spent on direct support to students in 2016/17 (Malawi Ministry of Labour, Youth, Sports and Manpower Development, 2018a).

Facilities lacked accessibility features, such as ramps, wide doorways and good pathways between buildings, and colleges and hostels lacked disability-friendly toilets. Mobility support was insufficient, and bursaries did not take into account additional costs, such as for wheelchairs. Learning equipment instructions were not available in Braille, and learning materials were not available in large print. Discriminatory employer attitudes and behaviours also need to be overcome.

Gender stereotypes were pervasive in study programmes, attitudes and behaviours, and gender-based violence by instructors, administrators and peers was common. About 29% of female college students had experienced disrespectful or demeaning language from other students. A companion analysis in three colleges showed that one in four female students had been asked to have or had had sex with an instructor (Malawi Ministry of Labour, Youth, Sports and Manpower Development, 2018b). Female student security was also an issue. Just one college had a lockable gate. In several hostels, female students' rooms could not be locked. Codes of conduct have been published for instructors, administrators and trainees, accompanied by a trainee orientation programme, as part of the EU-funded Skills and Technical Education Programme (Heath, 2019).

phone servicing, photography and basic first aid (Amin et al., 2018).

Many programmes in Latin America are built on partnerships and ties that combine TVET with other public services fostering inclusion. In Brazil, a component of the National Programme for Access to Technical Education and Employment targeted 1.7 million beneficiaries of the Brasil sem Miséria (Brazil without Poverty) plan, 53% of whom were Afro-descendants (Abramo et al., 2019). Part of a process to move from poverty alleviation to poverty exit strategies, it relies on ensuring education and training quality for its success (Fenwick, 2015). Programmes such as Mi Primer Empleo Digno (My First Decent Job) in the Plurinational State of Bolivia and Con Chamba Vivís Mejor (Life's Better with a Job) in Honduras provide subsidies to cover transport and meal costs. Childcare services are also provided under the Support for Argentine Students Programme, the ProJovem National Youth Inclusion Programme in Brazil and the +Capaz and Women Heads of Household programmes in Chile (Abramo et al., 2019).

Partnerships with non-state actors are also important. Since 2016, the Inclusive Employment Model has operated in selected Colombian cities, focusing on Afro-descendant and indigenous communities, people with disabilities, adolescent mothers, and internally displaced and other people suffering the consequences of conflict. The aim is to enhance their skills and employability through better inter-agency coordination and collaboration between mayors and firms, relying on national business association support and changes in recruitment processes (Fundación Corona et al., 2020).

INCLUSION IN TERTIARY EDUCATION SHOULD TARGET ACCESS AND COMPLETION

Ensuring inclusive and equitable access to higher education is essential for social justice and economic efficiency, an objective reflected in SDG target 4.3, albeit limited to gender equality. Expansion of tertiary education has been unprecedented, but accompanied by persistent vertical and horizontal inequity. The vertical dimension looks at who enters and who graduates. Even when they gain access, students from under-represented groups tend to have lower completion rates. The horizontal dimension concerns the kind of institutions attended and the labour market

opportunities that various qualifications and degrees offer graduates.[2]

Many countries are implementing policies and programmes to support equitable access to higher education for students from under-represented groups, definitions of which vary widely by country (Salmi and Sursock, 2018). A survey of 71 countries found that 11% had a comprehensive equity strategy, while another 11% had a policy for one group. Students with disability were the most frequently targeted (Salmi, 2018). The Global University Disability and Inclusion Network was founded in 2019 to expand the share of students with disabilities enrolled in post-secondary education (AHEAD, 2019).

A meta-analysis of 75 impact studies focusing on the effects of equity-oriented interventions in 11 middle- and high-income countries shows that most looked at access rather than completion, with few looking at several interventions implemented together, focusing instead on piecemeal interventions (Herbaut and Geven, 2019). The most effective policies are those that combine financial aid with measures to overcome non-financial barriers (OECD, 2008; Salmi and Bassett, 2014). Well-targeted and efficiently managed financial aid, such as grants, scholarships and student loans, can play a significant role. In addition, many countries and tertiary education institutions have outreach and bridging programmes with secondary schools, affirmative action and reformed admission procedures, and retention programmes to improve completion rates (**Figure 2.4**).

Not all financial measures promote equitable access
The most common tuition fee policy is no or low fees for students enrolled in public institutions. Such subsidies lower costs but have a regressive effect when they are unconditional, as they benefit more students from richer households, especially if access is restricted (Guerra Botello et al., 2019).

Many countries grant in-kind financial support through highly subsidized food, housing and transport. As these measures also tend not to be targeted, they dilute, if not outright subvert, their effectiveness in reaching equity objectives. For instance, most Francophone countries in Africa offer subsidized canteens and dormitories,

---

2   This section is based on Salmi (2020).

FIGURE 2.4:
Countries apply various measures to enhance equitable access to tertiary education

Share of countries applying a range of equity and inclusion measures in higher education, 2018

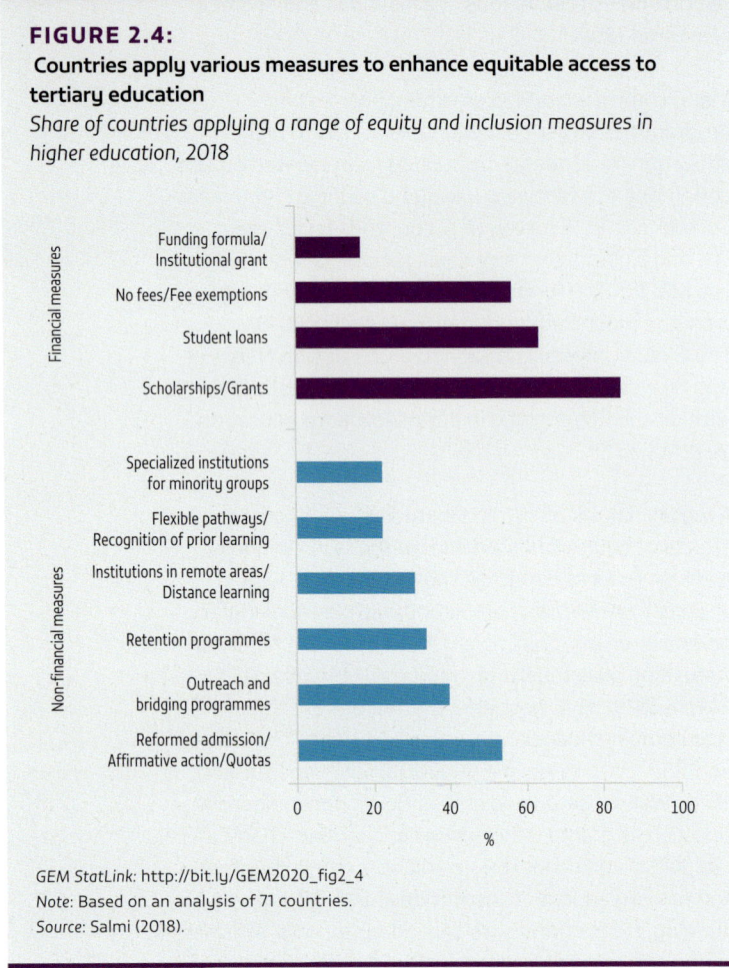

GEM StatLink: http://bit.ly/GEM2020_fig2_4
Note: Based on an analysis of 71 countries.
Source: Salmi (2018).

but only Senegal and Tunisia restrict these subsidies to poor students.

Some countries use selective fee exemptions. Canada's New Brunswick and Ontario provinces, Chile, Italy, Japan and South Africa target free tuition to the poorest (Usher and Burroughs, 2018). However, many poor students in Chile are enrolled in recently established private universities, which are neither government-subsidized nor tuition-exempt. Countries may regulate fee levels in public universities or, as in Azerbaijan, private universities. Regulation can also be indirect. Côte d'Ivoire established a reference price used to calculate scholarship amounts for poor students in private institutions (Salmi, 2020).

Brazil's ProUni University for All programme, launched in 2006, is a variation on a voucher programme to support equitable access. The government uses tax incentives to buy places in private universities for academically qualified poor students not admitted to top public universities because of limited places and low entrance examination scores (Salmi, 2017).

Fee exemptions are not just prompted by equity concerns; Egypt and countries in Eastern Europe, Central Asia and Anglophone sub-Saharan Africa waive fees for secondary school graduates with the best academic results, which may entrench inequality.

Some countries use regulations, funding formulas or competitive grants to encourage tertiary education institutions to admit students from groups at risk of exclusion. In Indonesia and Viet Nam, public universities must provide financial aid to at least 20% and 10% of their respective student populations. In Mexico, private universities must provide grants or scholarships to at least 5% of their students. In England (United Kingdom), each higher education provider commits, through an Access and Participation Plan, to spend a fixed proportion of tuition fee income on scholarships and bursaries.

Funding formulas are used to allocate resources to institutions that promote a national equity agenda. In Ireland, block grants to tertiary education institutions are largely based on enrolment and cost of disciplines but provide a 30% premium for each student from government-defined priority groups.

In Australia, as part of the Higher Education Participation and Partnerships Program, the Higher Education Disability Support Program covers costs for sign language interpreters, note taking and examination assistance. A performance-based allocation had not been effective in attracting students with disabilities, probably due to its small size (KPMG, 2015). A recent reform merged the core and performance-based elements and will allocate funds based on a combination of individual claims and a formula (Australia Department of Education, Skills and Employment, 2020). Australia stands out in successfully addressing the needs of deaf students. By contrast, resource constraints in South Africa mean National Student Financial Aid Scheme guidelines do not allow for human support, and some students in India pay out of pocket for sign language interpreters (Chiwandire and Vincent, 2019). India does offer a small incentive under the Higher Education for Persons with Special Needs programme for universities to establish resource units and invest in accessibility features and special equipment (India University Grants Commission, 2012).

More than 70 countries offer student loans, which vary by repayment terms, capital source, expenses covered, eligibility rules and applicability to private and distance institutions. There are three main loan models. First, mortgage-style loans are the most common but also at the highest risk of financial unsustainability due to high administrative costs, interest rate subsidies and defaults. The repayment burden can be high for the poorest graduates (Chapman et al., 2014). Colombia presents an example of an effective loan programme (**Box 2.13**).

Second, guaranteed and shared-risk mortgage-style loans involve governments working with private banks to increase the leverage ratio. Large programmes of this nature have a mixed record. Chile introduced a shared-risk programme in 2006 to expand loan opportunities in the rapidly growing private sector but eliminated it six years later because of unaffordable debt levels for many graduates.

Finally, universal income-contingent loans, such as those in Australia and New Zealand, tend to have higher repayment rates and are more equitable, since graduates pay a fixed proportion of income and are exempt from repayment if they are unemployed or their income is below a given threshold. Administration is simpler and cheaper because loan recovery is handled through existing mechanisms, such as income tax administration and social security.

Non-financial measures are needed to increase equitable access

Besides financial barriers to tertiary education, marginalized groups face inadequate academic preparation, poor access to information, low education expectations and self-confidence, lack of cultural capital, inflexible admission processes and inaccessible learning environments (Salmi, 2020).

Outreach and bridging programmes provide early counselling on academic career prospects. An online survey of all 18- and 19-year-old undergraduate applicants in the 2015 admissions cycle in the United Kingdom showed that those who knew by age 10 that they would apply to university were 2.6 times more likely to enrol in a university that admits applicants with higher qualifications than those who did not know until age 16 or later (UCAS, 2016).

Affirmative action measures, which admit members of a disadvantaged group who would otherwise be excluded, include quotas or other preferential treatments, such as bonuses on admission scores (**Box 2.14**). Supporters say these measures are essential because discrimination and stereotypes continue to hinder education opportunities. Critics argue that the reasons for lack of opportunities cannot be addressed through affirmative action.

To reach underserved populations, some countries have set up virtual universities with an explicit equity focus, such as Colombia's 241 regional higher education centres and India's Swayam Project. Tunisia's Virtual University supports the academic work of at-risk students enrolled in brick-and-mortar universities, especially in remote regions (Salmi, 2018).

THE DIGITAL DIVIDE HINDERS INCLUSION IN EDUCATION

At the end of 2018, 3.9 billion people, or 51.2% of the global population, were internet users (ITU, 2018d). Online resources open opportunities for further education and skills acquisition. The 2015 Qingdao Declaration recognized that expansion of digital technology and

---

BOX 2.13:

Colombia has developed a world-class student loan programme

In 1950, Colombia set up the world's first student loan institution, Instituto Colombiano de Crédito Educativo y Estudios Técnicos en el Exterior (ICETEX) (Colombian Institute for Education Loans and Overseas Technical Studies). It provides subsidized loans to students from the poorest families and from ethnic and racial minorities, as well as students with disabilities. For the poorest students, the loans are interest-free. Since the mid-2000s, ICETEX has mobilized additional resources from government and multilateral donors, extending coverage to about 20% of the total student population, the highest coverage rate in Latin America and one of the highest among low- and middle-income countries.

ICETEX has also improved its collection record and management practices. It reduced operating costs from 12% in 2002 to 3% in 2010. It entered into partnerships with universities to provide financial, academic and psychological support to beneficiaries. It supplements loans with scholarships for the poorest students to cover living expenses. ICETEX wants to raise further funds to finance more poor students and eliminate dropout for financial reasons. It is migrating from mortgage-style to income-contingent loans, with technical assistance from Australia, which should help reduce the burden on graduates from the poorest households (Salmi, 2020).

BOX 2.14:

Mandatory reservation quotas or reformed admission criteria are used frequently in tertiary education

About one in four countries have some form of affirmative action for tertiary education admission (Jenkins and Moses, 2014), reflecting specific circumstances but also tensions. Austria's 2017 National Strategy on the Social Dimension of Higher Education set targets for probability of admission of under-represented groups relative to dominant groups for 2020 and 2025 and aims to increase 'non-traditional' admissions from 4,000 to 5,300. The number of degree programmes with less than 30% men or women are to be halved. Institutions are to increase the share of second-generation immigrants from 22% to 30% (Austria Ministry of Science Research and Economy, 2017).

In Brazil, in the early 2000s, state and federal universities began applying quotas reserving seats for disadvantaged groups. Some universities that introduced racial quotas also established committees to confirm candidates' racial identity. These were strongly debated because they contradicted the legal right to self-identification (Daflon et al., 2013). In 2012, a law extended a 50% quota of all places at federal institutions for public secondary school students, especially those of African or indigenous origin or from families with income up to one and a half times the minimum salary per capita. The quota increased access to tertiary education for black students but only where universities adopted a race-conscious policy (Vieira and Arends-Kuenning, 2019). Students who benefited from the quota came from families with incomes up to 50% lower than those who did not (Norões and McCowan, 2016). Beneficiaries had the same level of performance as other students (Wainer and Melguizo, 2017).

India has required since the 1950s that 15% of students admitted to public universities should belong to a scheduled caste and 7.5% to a scheduled tribe, reflecting population shares. Studies have shown that quotas secure places for targeted disadvantaged groups but at the potential cost of displacing other disadvantaged groups, such as women (Bertrand et al., 2010). Scheduled caste students are more likely than others to fall behind once enrolled (Frisancho Robles and Krishna, 2016). Dalits face caste-based humiliation, being addressed in offensive ways, and face further obstacles in having their complaints resolved (Bhattacharya et al., 2017; Thorat et al., 2007). Scheduled caste activists strongly opposed a 2019 law extending quotas by reserving 10% of places for poor members of upper castes, which will apply to all public and private tertiary education institutions (Jyoti, 2019; Niazi, 2019).

Since 1998, a programme in Malaysia has given better university admission and course enrolment chances to ethnic Malays and natives of Sabah and Sarawak, or bumiputra. In 2019, the government announced that the pre-university matriculation programme ethnic quota (90% of seats reserved for bumiputra) would remain in place. In response to protests, the total number of students admitted to the pre-university programme was increased from 25,000 to 40,000 (Yi, 2019). New Zealand universities have admission programmes for students of Māori and Pasifika descent (University of Auckland, 2019; Victoria University of Wellington, 2019).

In 2019, the Government of Pakistan introduced a policy that established admission quotas for students with disabilities. Tertiary education institutions were asked to exempt candidates with disabilities from admissions tests, relax age limits, provide fee concessions and offer appropriate examination modalities (Pakistan Higher Education Commission, 2019).

In Romania, university admission is based on standardized test scores but, depending on past demand, a few places in public universities, mostly in the social sciences, are reserved for Roma students. Candidates need to provide a certificate issued by a Roma organization attesting their ethnic affiliation. Those admitted are guaranteed tuition grants and paid accommodation on campus. Needs-based state scholarships are available, as are some external funding opportunities (Pantea, 2014).

In Sri Lanka, 40% of all available places in tertiary education institutions are reserved for those with the best scores. Remaining places are distributed as follows: 55% of students in many fields must have studied in the same district as the institution in the last three years; 40% of seats are reserved for those who studied in one of the other 25 districts; and 5% are reserved for students from one of Sri Lanka's 16 economically disadvantaged districts (Sri Lanka University Grants Commission, 2018).

connectivity, which can change the world of teaching and learning, was not benefitting everyone (UNESCO, 2015b). One in four people in Latin America and nearly one in three in Africa mention affordability as a top constraint on internet use. Women are 17% less likely than men to use the internet in the Arab States and Asia and the Pacific and 25% less likely in Africa. Large gender gaps also appear in more complex tasks, such as programming and use of large data sets. The digital divide widens when gender intersects with other characteristics, such as age, education, location and income (ITU and UNESCO, 2019). Rural people are also over-represented among non-users, even in high-income countries, such as Australia (Hodge et al., 2017).

Bridging the digital divide requires reducing or eliminating affordability and access obstacles. To that end, countries are supporting deployment of free Wi-Fi. The Dominican Republic is installing 5,000 free public Wi-Fi hotspots. Madagascar initiated an effort to connect schools and hospitals with free broadband, particularly in remote areas. Thailand is rolling out connectivity to 4,000 villages at a cost of US$ 325 million (ITU and UNESCO, 2019).

Digital literacy skills are crucial, yet they are unequally distributed. In the United States, the share of digitally literate adults was 59% among those who had not completed secondary school, 83% among those who had completed secondary school and 95% among those with tertiary education (Mamedova and Pawlowski, 2018). In countries that participated in the Programme for the International Assessment of Adult Competencies, 10% of adults reported having no computer experience, and a further 14% either failed or opted out of the core skills test (Martin, 2018). In Mexico, 78% of adults over age 55 were not internet users (Martínez-Alcalá et al., 2018).

Provincial authorities in Argentina, such as La Plata and Rio Negro, have undertaken initiatives focusing on senior citizens' digital literacy skills. The Algarrobo Abuelo campaign in San Luis connected senior citizens to the internet, preloaded tablets with applications and services to help them with daily tasks and offered individualized instruction. Retired volunteers helped peers develop skills (ITU, 2018a, 2018b, 2018c). The Access to Information programme in Bangladesh has over 5,000 digital centres in rural areas, connecting almost 6 million visitors each month. The centres have trained more than 3,000 women in business, digital and hardware repair skills needed to open information technology repair centres, which are lacking in rural areas (ITU, 2018b).

In Sri Lanka, visitors at 300 centres in public libraries and houses of worship have access to a programme that provides training in digital skills to people in rural areas who lack connectivity (E-Nenasala, 2019). In the United Kingdom, the Good Things Foundation has helped over 2 million people develop digital skills through 5,000 community partners offering internet access at discounted rates and a free Learn My Way curriculum of basic computer skills (ITU, 2018b). Viet Nam's farmer's union, in partnership with Google, is training 30,000 farmers in basic digital skills (Viet Nam Government and World Bank, 2019).

CONCLUSION

Many countries are establishing more inclusive education systems. Sound legislative frameworks, often inspired by international commitments, are a sign of progress, but they often take time to establish. Policies tend to be more advanced. However, neither laws nor policies are sufficient, as the implementation record remains weak. Subsequent chapters on data; collaboration with sectors and actors outside education; development of curricula, materials and learning environments; and adoption of inclusive approaches by teachers, school leaders and communities detail the efforts that need to accompany laws and policies to make inclusive education a reality.

Achieving inclusion requires a whole-system approach. It is a process that unfolds over time and spans education levels, from ECCE to TVET skills development, tertiary education and opportunities for lifelong learning. Education systems, step by step, are embracing inclusion in education irrespective of students' ability, background and identity. Responding to diversity of needs in education is necessary to accomplish broad social inclusion objectives.

COVID-19:

A NEW LAYER TO THE CHALLENGE OF EDUCATION INCLUSION

In the course of a few weeks, the Covid-19 pandemic overwhelmed many national health systems. Uncertainty over its deadliness led governments around the world to impose lockdowns and curtail economic activity, threatening billions of livelihoods. One key measure to limit the risk of contagion was school and university closures. At the peak of the closure period in April 2020, 91% of the global student population was affected in 194 countries. Only a handful of countries, including Belarus, Nicaragua and Tajikistan, kept all schools open throughout, although a few high-income countries, including Australia, the Russian Federation and Sweden, kept some schools open. Covid-19 thus precipitated an education crisis, fuelled by the deep and multiple inequalities discussed in this report. While these inequalities have long existed, many were obscured in classrooms. Lockdowns and school closures suddenly brought them into sharp relief.

During this period, millions of people had to make tough decisions: Individuals had to decide whether to respect or evade quarantine restrictions, medical staff needed to choose among patients' competing needs and authorities had to decide how to allocate economic support. The management of education also posed moral dilemmas. The disruption of learning confronted policymakers with the 'do no harm' principle – the requirement that no plan or programme should be put in place if there is a risk of it actively harming anyone at all. Unfortunately, just as education policymakers look to the future to make an opportunity out of a crisis, it has become apparent that many of the solutions tried pose a risk of leaving many children and young people further behind.

EFFORTS TO MAINTAIN LEARNING CONTINUITY MAY EXACERBATE EXCLUSION

The consequences of the health and financial crisis for inclusion in education were both immediate and gradual. Education systems responded with distance learning solutions, all of which offered less or more imperfect substitutes for classroom instruction. In addition, closures interrupted support mechanisms from which many disadvantaged learners benefit. Forcing these learners to spend more time at home may not have been conducive to learning. Economic difficulties resulting from lockdowns are expected to have medium- to long-term impact. Governments will need to respond to the loss of revenue in the ensuing recession and to competing, urgent demands from various sectors. Households,

especially those near or below the poverty line, will also need to make hard decisions about resource allocation, which may lead to withdrawing children from school.

No current learning continuity solution ensures learning for all

The world was caught by surprise when the global pandemic struck, even though, in retrospect, it is arguable that it should have been anticipated. It had been estimated that the probability of an influenza pandemic causing at least 6 million deaths globally in any given year was 1%, or a 25% probability in a generation (Madhav et al., 2018). The 2014–15 Ebola virus epidemic in western Africa was all too recent to have been erased from planners' memories. Yet the challenge was too large for any education system to respond effectively. School closures placed unprecedented challenges on governments, teachers, students and parents aiming to ensure learning continuity.

The poorest countries have relied relatively more on radio. For instance, 64% of low-income countries used this approach for primary education, compared to 42% of upper-middle-income countries. The use of radio had weakened over the years, although there had been exceptions, such as Sierra Leone, which broadcast education radio programmes five days a week in 30-minute sessions during the Ebola crisis (Powers and Azzi-Huck, 2016). In mid-March, Kenya began running primary and secondary school lessons on public radio (Kenya Institute for Curriculum Development, 2020). In Madagascar, a non-government association of about 30 local radio stations offered education programmes (Verneau, 2020).

By contrast, 74% of lower-middle income countries used television programmes in primary education, compared with 36% of low-income countries. Country income is also a crucial factor in differences in adoption of online learning platforms. In primary and secondary education, they were used by about 55% of low-income, 73% of lower-middle-income and 93% of upper-middle-income countries (**Figure 2.5**).

High-income countries capitalized on recent investments in education technology to mobilize online learning platforms, whether synchronous (real-time) or not. In France, the Centre national d'enseignement à distance (National Distance Education Centre)

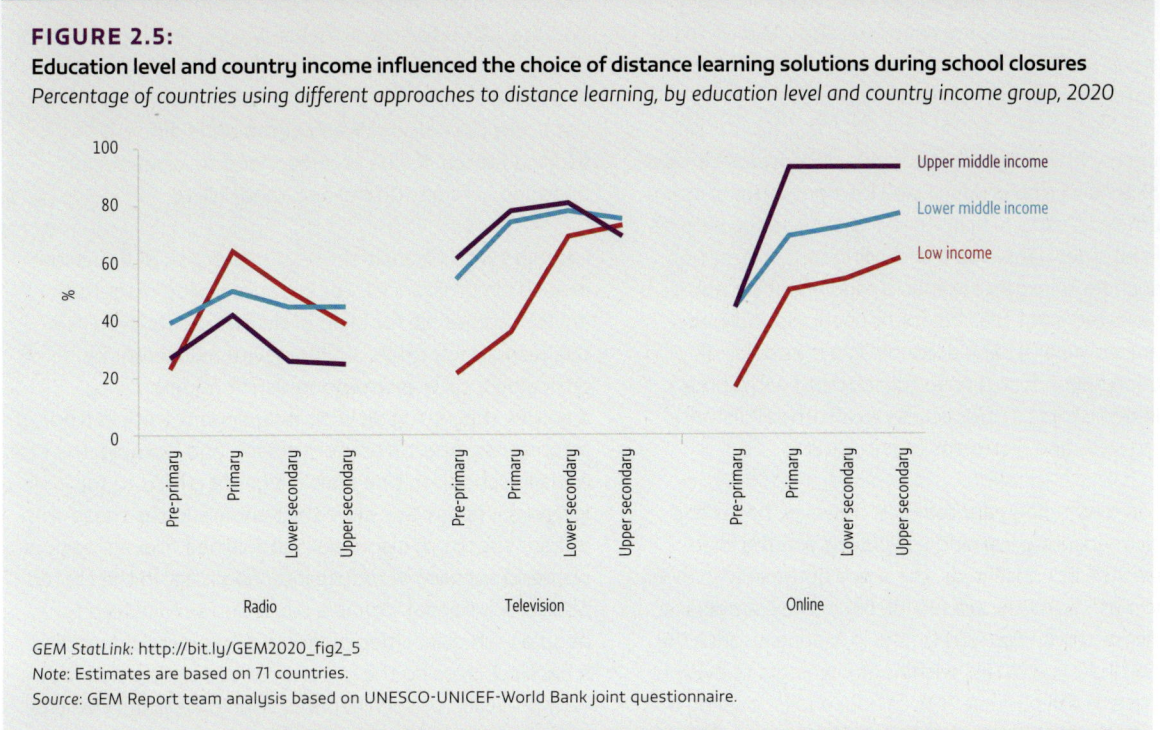

FIGURE 2.5:

Education level and country income influenced the choice of distance learning solutions during school closures

Percentage of countries using different approaches to distance learning, by education level and country income group, 2020

GEM StatLink: http://bit.ly/GEM2020_fig2_5

Note: Estimates are based on 71 countries.

Source: GEM Report team analysis based on UNESCO-UNICEF-World Bank joint questionnaire.

expanded the number of users allowed on its 'My class at home' e-learning platform from 6 million (Autin, 2020) to 15 million (France Inter, 2020). But even as governments increasingly rely on technology, the digital divide lays bare the limitations of this approach. Not all students and teachers have access to adequate internet connection, equipment, skills and working conditions to take advantage of available platforms.

In OECD countries, 1 in 20 students, and almost 1 in 10 of those attending disadvantaged schools, lack an internet connection at home. The latter share rises to 1 in 4 in Chile, 1 in 2 in Turkey and almost 3 in 4 in Mexico (OECD, 2020). Not all internet connections are strong enough to download data or take part in video calls. In Italy, while 95% of households are connected, 1 in 4 have a connection below 30 Mbps, lower than required to download and stream education content (AgCom, 2020).

Technology was previously an essential part of the education experience only for some students and teachers, mostly at the upper secondary level. In 11 countries, including Germany, the Republic of Korea and Uruguay, at most 1 in 4 grade 8 students reported using information and communication technology weekly, in or outside school, to work online with other students, and at most 1 in 3 used it to write and edit documents (Fraillon et al., 2019).

Most teachers and school administrators had to switch overnight to new tools to deliver lessons, distribute content, correct homework and communicate with students and their parents. Working from home is nearly impossible for those who look after children or other family members. In 2018, head teachers reported only 5 in 10 teachers had the technical and pedagogical skills to integrate digital devices in instruction in the Netherlands and just 3 in 10 in Japan (OECD, 2020). A survey in the United States found that only 43% of teachers felt prepared to facilitate remote learning and just 1 in 5 said school leaders provided guidance (ClassTag, 2020). Few high-income countries could afford to train teachers at short notice. In the United Arab Emirates, the Ministry of Education trained 42,000 teachers using courses such as 'Be an online tutor in 24 hours' and 'Design an online course in 24 hours' (Mojib, 2020). In any case, teachers using online platforms have had to learn much more during the crisis than just a few technical skills.

Low- and middle-income countries are at a far more disadvantaged starting point for an effective transition to online learning platforms. In Burkina Faso, Burundi and Chad, at least 85% of the population did not even have access to electricity in 2018 (World Bank, 2020). The share of households with internet access at home was 47% in developing countries and 12% in the least developed countries in 2019, compared with 87% in developed countries. Internet bandwidth per internet user was 91 kbit/s in developing countries and 21 kbit/s in the least developed countries, compared with 189 kbit/s in developed countries (ITU, 2019).

In Morocco, while 71% of households had internet access in 2019, 93% was by phone. Fixed internet infrastructure is insufficient, especially in rural areas. As about 90% of mobile internet data is paid according to consumption, it is much more expensive than a regular subscription, but the latter is not feasible for households without regular income or a bank account. The ministries of education and industry have collaborated with three mobile operators to offer access to all official distance learning sites and platforms (Kadiri, 2020).

Even low-technology approaches, however, have little chance of ensuring learning continuity. Among the poorest 20% of households, the share of those who owned a radio was 7% in Ethiopia (2016), 8% in the Democratic Republic of the Congo (2014), 14% in Madagascar (2016) and 30% in Kenya (2014), with none owning a television. The share of the poorest 20% of households owning a television was 5% in Nepal (2016), 10% in Yemen (2013), 13% in Guatemala (2014/5), 14% in Pakistan (2017/8) and 22% in Cambodia (2014) (DHS Program, 2020).

Recognizing that not even low technology solutions will work, a few countries have tried to deliver education materials to students' homes. In Peru, the Ministry of Education instructed local government authorities to coordinate delivery of textbooks to schools, homes or other points (Peru Ministry of Education, 2020). But even when distance learning options are available and accessible, several conditions negatively affect disadvantaged students' opportunity to learn. They have to rely more on the support of parents and guardians with little or no education. They need a good home environment but about 30% of 15-year-old students lack access, for instance, to a quiet place to study in Malaysia, the Philippines and Thailand (OECD, 2020). Poorer children suffer more from the consequences of lockdown. A phone survey of 14- to 18-year-olds in Ecuador showed that those from the poorest quartile were more likely than their richer peers to spend more time on work or household chores than on education (Asanov et al., 2020).

Insufficient attention has been paid to inclusion of all learners

Schools can perform many functions outside of education. Ideally, they provide a safe haven, a social arena, and vital goods and services, from sanitary towels in India (India Ministry of Health and Family Welfare, 2016) to school meals, which are critical for poor households. Japan continued delivering school meals in some districts, and provision continued in Argentina, Catalonia (Spain), and Washington and California (United States). China provided food to students in boarding schools (Chang and Yano, 2020).

Learners with disabilities are at higher risk of exclusion in such circumstances. For instance, many resources are not accessible for blind or deaf students even if the technology exists. Children with mild learning difficulties, such as attention deficit hyperactivity disorder, may struggle with independent work in front of a computer. Apart from technology and learning, the loss of daily school routine adds a layer of difficulty for learners who are sensitive to change, such as those with autism spectrum disorders. Schools had to scale back or suspend support to reduce infection risks. In the United States, a proposal to waive education service fees for people with disabilities mandated by federal law caused a backlash, forcing the government to issue guidance on how provision of such services should be continued (US Department of Education, 2020). Teachers struggled to provide the reassurance that only personal contact can offer (Tugend, 2020).

By increasing social isolation, the pandemic also increased the risk of marginalized students disengaging further from education and leaving school early. In France, after just three weeks of lockdown, up to 8% of students had lost contact with their teachers. In the US city of Los Angeles, about one-third of students were out of reach, 15,000 secondary school students did not connect or do any homework, and for more than 40,000 students, or one-third of the total secondary school population, contact with teachers was on a less than daily basis (Blume and Kohli, 2020).

The experience of the 2014–15 Ebola epidemic in three west African countries is also a reminder of potential effects of Covid-19 on girls' and young women's education. More time at home exposes them to domestic chores, sexual violence or teenage pregnancy risks. The evidence on the last is mixed. Some studies in Sierra Leone indicate localized increases (Elston et al., 2016) but at national level the rate of girls aged 15 to 19 who had a live birth fell from 26.4% in 2010 (Statistics Sierra Leone and UNICEF-Sierra Leone, 2011) to 19.3% in 2017 (Statistics Sierra Leone, 2018). It is essential nevertheless for communities to support continuity in girls' learning and maintain contact to prevent dropout. In five sub-Saharan African countries, CAMFED, an international

NGO, has deployed community workers to respond to challenges created by the pandemic (CAMFED, 2020).

Overall, about 40% of low- and lower-middle-income countries have not supported learners at risk of exclusion during the Covid-19 pandemic, such as those living in remote areas, the poor, linguistic minorities and learners with disabilities (**Figure 2.6**). But there are also good examples of response. In Sri Lanka, a toll-free study-support telephone service was introduced to help grade 11 students in science, mathematics and English for three languages of instruction: Sinhala, Tamil and English. Action has also been taken to launch a toll-free tuition service, accessible via normal telephone, with the help of a private telecommunication service provider.

Assessing the effect of school closures on Covid-19 infection rates has been filled with uncertainty, as conclusive evidence is yet to emerge (Brauner et al., 2020; Esposito and Principi, 2020), making the issue at times quite divisive. Some teachers who belong to vulnerable groups are concerned that their health is at risk. Only a minority of countries can enforce strict social distancing rules in schools. But schools reopened: as of the end of May 2020, national school closures were in effect in 150 countries, affecting 68% of the global student population.

Depending on the academic year structure, school closures affected school calendars, teacher training and licensing schedules, and examinations. The Central Board of Secondary Education in India cancelled grade 10 and 12 examinations, the national open school examination and the joint entrance examination (Firstpost, 2020). Indonesia cancelled its national examination, declared it would not be required for graduation or university entry, and issued guidance on the use of school examination scores for graduation at other levels (Indonesia Ministry of Education and Culture, 2020). The United Kingdom cancelled its General Certificate of Secondary Education examination and will award qualifications based on moderated teacher judgements (Thomson, 2020). One concern is that such judgements may be affected by stereotypes about particular types of students.

Overall, the setback on learning is expected to be considerable, although its magnitude is difficult to pin down. Research in the United States that examined the 'summer slide', the loss of learning during the long school break between grades, found that students lost nearly 20% of the school year's gains in reading and 27% in mathematics skills between grades 2 and 3, and 36% of their gains in reading and 50% in mathematics between grades 7 and 8 (Kuhfeld, 2018; Kuhfeld and Tarasawa,

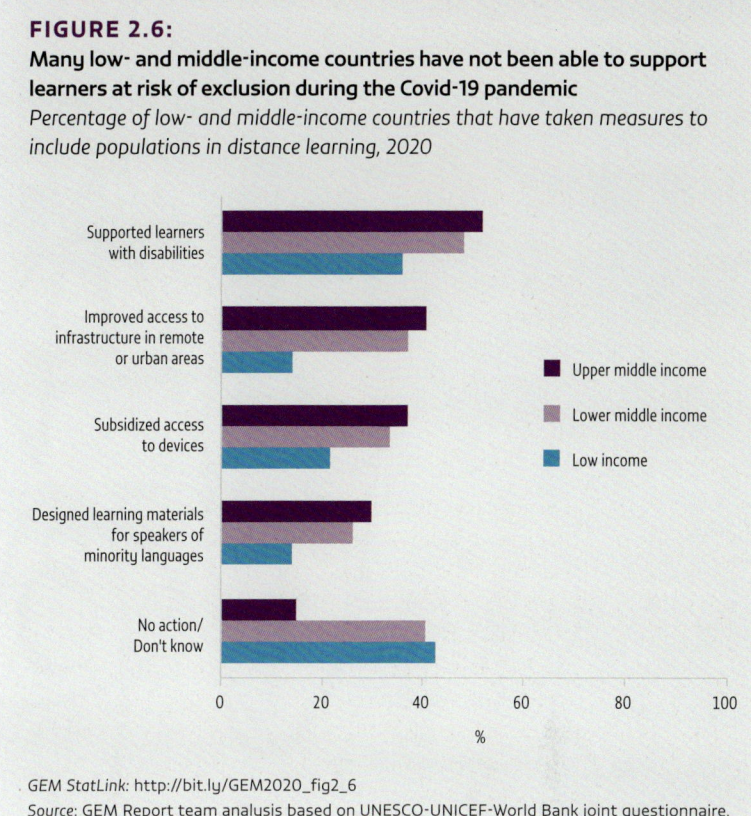

FIGURE 2.6:

Many low- and middle-income countries have not been able to support learners at risk of exclusion during the Covid-19 pandemic

Percentage of low- and middle-income countries that have taken measures to include populations in distance learning, 2020

GEM StatLink: http://bit.ly/GEM2020_fig2_6
Source: GEM Report team analysis based on UNESCO-UNICEF-World Bank joint questionnaire.

2020). The concern is that the gaps are greater for disadvantaged students who have fewer resources at home (Cooper et al., 1996), which would increase socio-economic gaps. Among low- and middle-income countries, 17% are planning to recruit more teachers, 22% to increase class time and 68% to introduce remedial classes when schools reopen. How such classes are planned and targeted will be critical to whether disadvantaged students can catch up.

The Covid-19 crisis has shown that the issue is not just about technical solutions to tackle the digital divide. Although distance learning has captured many headlines, only a minority of countries have the basic infrastructure to focus on the pedagogical challenges of online approaches to teaching and learning. Most children and youth have suffered a short-term direct, but hopefully temporary, loss of learning. Concern remains about more lasting effects, likely to be brought about indirectly by the recession, which will throw millions of people back into poverty. Governments need to take a close look at the inclusion challenges highlighted in this report to rebuild education systems that are better and accessible to all learners.

In Colombia, Maria Angel, 8 years old, from Venezuela, works on math problems in one of Save the Children's recently established Temporary Learning Centers (TLCs) in Maicao's informal settlements.

CREDIT: Jenn Gardella / Save the Children

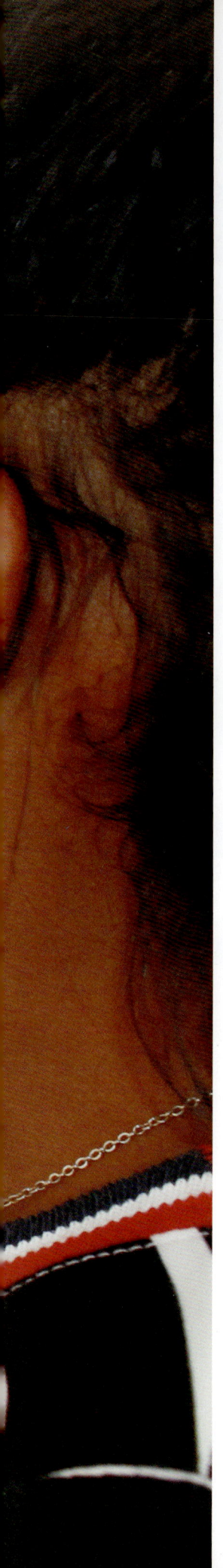

3

Data

Who is excluded?

KEY MESSAGES

What data are collected and how they are used determine whether inclusion is served

■ Identifying groups makes the disadvantaged ones visible but can reduce children to labels, which can be self-fulfilling. After all, everybody potentially faces barriers to inclusion.

■ Not all children facing inclusion barriers belong to an identifiable or recognized group, while others belong to several. Portugal has a non-categorical approach to determine special needs.

Censuses and surveys help monitor outcomes at population level but their use is not straightforward

■ Surveys put a spotlight on intersecting characteristics. In at least 20 countries, hardly any poor, rural young woman completed secondary education.

■ Formulating questions on nationality, ethnicity, religion, sexual orientation and gender identity can touch on sensitive personal identities, be intrusive and trigger persecution fears. Kenya added new ethnic group categories and intersex as a gender option in its 2019 census.

Statistical measurement of disability is beginning to catch up with the social model

■ Data from 14 low- and middle-income countries in 2017–19 using the Child Functioning Module questions showed a disability prevalence among children of 12%, ranging from 6% to 24%.

■ Those with a sensory, physical or intellectual disability were 4 percentage points more likely to be out of school than their primary school age peers, while the figure for lower secondary age was 7 points and, for upper secondary, 11 points.

■ Using national definitions, the share of students in Europe deemed to have special education needs ranges from 1% in Sweden to 20% in Scotland. These variations reflect institutional rather than population differences. Comparing disability prevalence is difficult: Learning disability is the largest category of special needs in Germany but unknown in Japan.

Some countries do not capture even basic data, while others monitor students' experiences

■ A review of 11 sub-Saharan African education ministries found Cameroon and Nigeria had no enrolment data on children with visual impairments.

■ One in four 15-year-old students reported feeling like outsiders at school; the share exceeded 30% in Brunei Darussalam, the Dominican Republic and the United States.

■ New Zealand monitors whether students feel cared for, safe and secure, along with their ability to establish and maintain positive relationships, respect others' needs and show empathy.

School-level data point to persistent exclusion and segregation

■ In OECD countries, more than two-thirds of immigrant students attended schools where at least half the students were immigrants.

■ Socio-economic segregation is persistent: Half the students in Chile and Mexico would have to be reassigned schools to achieve a uniform socio-economic mixture, and there has been no change in two decades.

The main obstacle to inclusion in education is the lack of reliable data on learners with special needs, hence making it difficult to plan for them.

Catherine Asego, Project Coordinator at African Population and Health Research Center, Kenya

Data are critical to support inclusion in education. The 2006 United Nations (UN) Convention on the Rights of Persons with Disabilities, for instance, explicitly called for collection of statistical and research data. The purpose is twofold. First, data can highlight gaps in education opportunities and outcomes among learner groups. They can identify those at risk of being left behind and the barriers to inclusion. Second, with data on who is being left behind and why, governments can develop evidence-based policies and monitor their implementation (e.g. via resources, equipment, infrastructure, teachers and teaching assistants, anti-bullying strategies, parental involvement) and the results.

In defining results, inclusion-specific outcomes cannot easily be distinguished from general education outcomes (Armstrong et al., 2010). The European Agency for Special Needs and Inclusive Education suggested that, in addition to data on attendance and learning, feelings of belonging, mutual respect and social esteem should be monitored (Watkins et al., 2014). Qualitative data on such experiences can capture fine-grained information that paints a drastically different picture than quantitative categorical data. For instance, in an 'inclusive classroom' in Canada, students with learning difficulties were made to solve problems on a different blackboard than others, with their backs to the rest of the class (Jordan and McGhie-Richmond, 2014).

Unlike population- or system-level indicators, such measures should describe learners' individual experiences rather than those of groups or categories. The more inclusive the school, the less useful categorical data become, as fewer children require identification for support. One approach to a set of indicators involves systematically examining levels of authority, from schools to education ministries, and a range of results, not just outputs and outcomes but also processes (**Table 3.1**).

TABLE 3.1:
Potential indicators of inclusion in education, by level of authority and result

Level	RESULT		
	Inputs	Processes	Outputs and outcomes
System	Policy	Climate	
	Teacher education	School practice	
District	Professional	Collaboration	Participation
	development	Shared	Achievement
	Resources and finances	responsibility	Post-school outcomes
School	Leadership	Support to individuals	
	Curriculum	Role of special schools	

Source: Loreman et al. (2014).

> "
> Measuring inclusion is tied
> to how countries define it
> "

Information on processes is difficult to collect and even more difficult to compare among schools or groups, let alone among countries. Frameworks for voluntary self-evaluation by schools or for programme evaluations are not necessarily suitable for official country-level monitoring of inclusion. Measuring inclusion is tied to how countries define it. While some aspects are part of most definitions, such as whether all students feel welcome in school, no single list of indicators is suitable everywhere. Criteria need to be locally determined and account for context, as vulnerabilities vary by place (Ainscow, 2005).

This chapter reviews the promise and potential obstacles of various approaches to collecting and analysing data to identify exclusion and to prompt action. It then looks at how countries collect data to monitor the effects of actions to make education systems more inclusive.

DATA ON INCLUSION: THE GROUPS COUNTRIES MONITOR VARY

Countries face a dilemma in deciding what data to collect on inclusion. On the one hand, the concept should not be fragmented by group because inclusion cannot be achieved one group at a time. 'In the process of pointing to the exclusion of specific groups, attention is focused on the "markers of difference" and thus difference is in fact created by comparison to an implicit norm' (Armstrong et al., 2010, p. 37). Education systems and environments become inclusive by breaking down barriers for the benefit of all children. Such barriers may be higher for some groups than for others: '[I]ssues raised by the presence of students with disabilities have cleared the path for nondisabled students who share similar experiences' (De Vroey et al., 2016, p. 110). In any case, many types of vulnerability are not outwardly apparent (Moyse and Porter, 2015; Porter et al., 2013), making it impossible to distinguish neatly between students with and without disabilities or special needs.

> "Data collection should not be fragmented because
> inclusion cannot be achieved one group at a time"

On the other hand, categorizing students is important to shine a light on specific groups and help make them visible to policymakers (Florian et al., 2006; Simon and Piché, 2012). Certain groups of children may be excluded not only by omitting them from textbooks, placing them at the back of the class or never calling on them, but also by lack of explicit recognition in data collection. Lack of data both results from and contributes to their invisibility.

Resolving this dilemma requires different kinds of data at different levels. Outcomes can be monitored at the population level; service delivery can be monitored at the student level through administrative systems that identify needs. Understanding the purposes and types of inclusion-related data can therefore ease dilemmas of identification: Identifying groups for statistical or policy purposes need not create a false dichotomy between 'normal' and 'special' groups that distorts efforts at inclusion. For instance, collection and use of administrative data can occur without assigning corresponding labels in the classroom. In some high-income countries, voluntary equal-opportunity questionnaires collect information on gender, sexual orientation, ethnicity and other characteristics. Results are used only to monitor diversity in universities or workplaces.

CENSUSES AND SURVEYS PROVIDE INSIGHTS INTO INCLUSION IN EDUCATION

Population censuses and household surveys provide valuable information on the education status of those at risk of being marginalized, but like any tool they have advantages and disadvantages.

Censuses aim to cover all residents and, done properly, do not intentionally exclude any group from the count. They have advantages over surveys, which miss some populations because of their small sample sizes or by design (e.g. prisons and orphanages tend not to be sampled) (United Nations, 2005). However, even they are known to undercount marginalized populations, such as nomads, seasonal and migrant workers, domestic servants, the homeless, and those living in areas affected by conflict or insecurity, most of whom are among the poorest (Carr-Hill, 2013). More generally, censuses are costly and therefore infrequent and contain few questions.

Surveys, especially those from cross-national and hence more standardized programmes, have put a spotlight on the education progression of population groups defined by single characteristics or their intersections. For instance, in low-income countries, 69 young women completed secondary school for every 100 young men, 23 rural residents for every 100 urban residents and 5 among the poorest 20% for every 100 of the richest. In at least 20 countries with data, mostly in sub-Saharan Africa, hardly any poor, rural young woman completed upper secondary school (**Figure 3.1**).

Multiple characteristics intersect to push people deeper into education disadvantage. There are gender gaps among those already disadvantaged by poverty, for instance. Analysis of World Inequality Database on Education data shows that in Eastern and South-eastern Asia, lower secondary completion among the poor is, on average, 7 percentage points lower than the national average, dropping to 11 points lower among those who in addition experience gender disadvantage and, among those, 12 points lower if they are also in a disadvantaged location.

Censuses and surveys are the bases for key national and global statistics that are the foundation of policies to address disadvantage. Globally, an estimated 385 million children live in households in extreme poverty (UNICEF and World Bank, 2016). Malnutrition affects one in three children under age 5, with 200 million suffering from stunting or wasting, compromising their development potential (UNICEF, 2019). There are 140 million classified as orphans, of whom 15 million have lost both parents (UNICEF, 2017).

Many countries identify specific groups as vulnerable in constitutions, social inclusion legislation, education legislation or documents directly related to inclusive education. The group most identified is people with disabilities, but women and girls, rural or remote populations and the poor are also commonly recognized. Few countries link recognition of specific groups with a mandate to collect data on their inclusion in education, however.

Disaggregation of enrolment statistics into male and female has long been standard. While most censuses ignore non-binary gender identities, this is beginning to change. Canada's 2011 census allowed respondents to

FIGURE 3.1:

In at least 20 countries, hardly any poor, rural young woman completed upper secondary school

Upper secondary school completion rate, by sex, location and wealth, selected countries, 2013–18

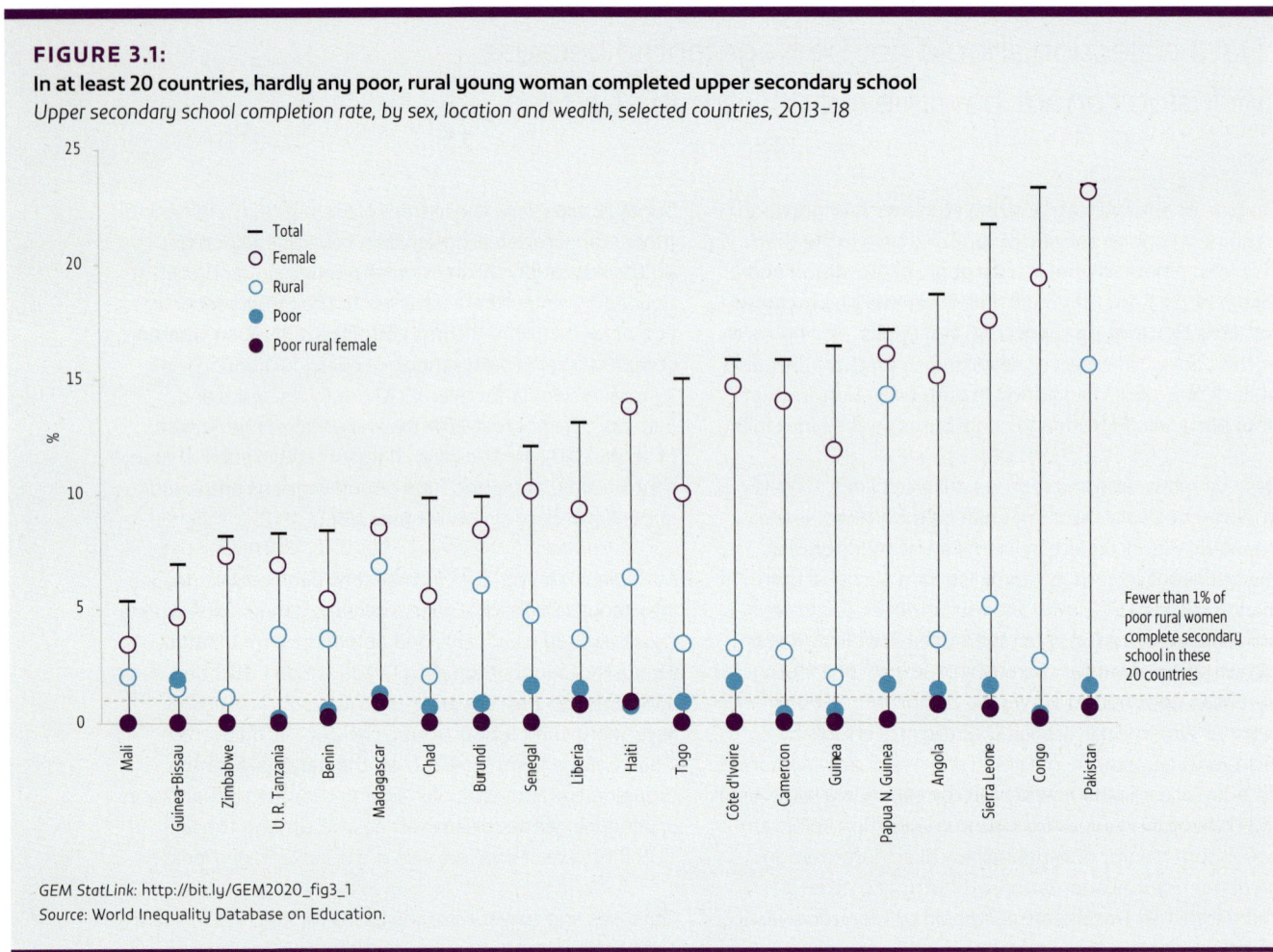

GEM StatLink: http://bit.ly/GEM2020_fig3_1
Source: World Inequality Database on Education.

leave the binary response blank and enter a comment. It is now testing a 'third gender' option in its tools (Grant, 2018). India, Nepal and Pakistan, which have a historically established gender minority identity, had already taken this step, although the term 'third gender' was poorly accepted among the target group (Park, 2016). Kenya added 'intersex' as a specific third gender option in its 2019 census (Bearak and Ombour, 2019).

The Kenyan census also added new ethnic group categories, some of which were previously subsumed under larger categories. Who is recognized in a census or survey may reflect political power and representation. Data that highlight inequality among groups are not always welcome for political reasons; groups in power may question their reliability and worry that drawing attention to such gaps will fuel resentment among the disadvantaged. A global analysis of 138 censuses in the

> " Data that highlight inequality among groups are not always welcome for political reasons "

2000 round showed that more than one-third had no ethnic classification (Morning, 2008). Political changes can have a major impact on how groups are captured. The number of Latin American countries that incorporated at least one ethnicity question in their census increased from 6 in 1980 to 13 in 2000. Today, all countries in the region except the Dominican Republic have census questions about ethnicity (Valencia Lopez, 2020).

Some censuses have captured the low education attainment and literacy rates of disadvantaged ethnic minorities and indigenous groups, such as the Ainu

> Censuses and surveys are the bases for key national and global statistics that are the foundation of policies to address disadvantage

indigenous group of Hokkaido prefecture in Japan and the Lolo in Viet Nam (UNDESA, 2017). Surveys have also served an important function in highlighting the relative education progress of various ethnic groups. Successive waves of household surveys, for instance in Ethiopia and Nigeria, show that attainment levels of groups lagging behind tend to follow the national trend, with mixed signs of catching up (**Figure 3.2**).

Questions on nationality, ethnicity or religion touch on sensitive points of personal identity and can be intrusive unless answering is strictly voluntary. They may also trigger fear of persecution. Whether to include a citizenship question on the 2020 US census, for instance, was highly political and ultimately rejected by the Supreme Court (Wines, 2019). A similar citizenship question on the American Community Survey had a 6% non-response rate in 2016, the only non-response rate that has been increasing. Non-response is as high as 12% among foreign-born Hispanics who fill in the survey without being interviewed (O'Hare, 2018). Latino children are among

the most undercounted populations in the country, despite being major beneficiaries of large education programmes whose budgets are allocated at least partly based on census estimates. For instance, they make up 37% of learners in the US$8 billion Head Start programme (The Leadership Conference Education Fund, 2018).

Various factors hamper identification of immigrants for policy purposes. First, it matters whether countries define immigrants as foreign nationals or as those born abroad. Identifying second-generation immigrants is still more complicated (UNESCO, 2018). Even with clear definitions, censuses in high-income countries often undercount immigrants. For instance, the 2001 UK census undercounted the overall population by an estimated 6%. Some groups, such as young men from ethnic minorities in London, were particularly undercounted, with implications for local authorities' education planning (United Kingdom House of Commons, 2010; United Kingdom Office of National Statistics, 2015).

FIGURE 3.2:
Surveys allow education attainment to be disaggregated by ethnicity
Primary school completion rate, by ethnicity, Ethiopia and Nigeria, 2000–18

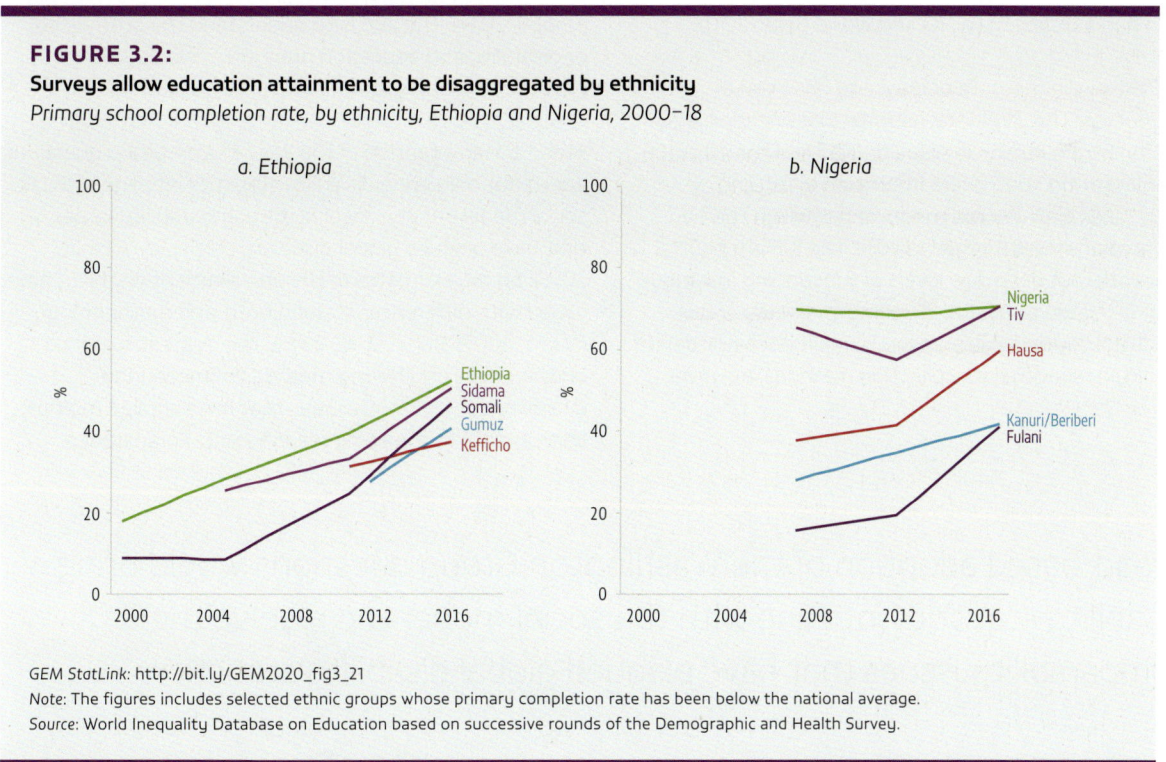

GEM StatLink: http://bit.ly/GEM2020_fig3_21
Note: The figures includes selected ethnic groups whose primary completion rate has been below the national average.
Source: World Inequality Database on Education based on successive rounds of the Demographic and Health Survey.

Statistical offices use techniques to adjust overall census results, but these cannot replace fine-grained mapping of the marginalized enabling targeted policies to improve equity and inclusion in education. One approach for hard-to-reach populations is snowball sampling, where respondents provide leads to further participants. It was used to rapidly assess migrant and refugee education levels in Europe, where further studies confirmed the results' robustness. For instance, two waves of migrant and refugee surveys along the Balkan corridor found that 76% of those aged 25 to 64 in 2015 and 2016 had secondary or tertiary education, exactly the same estimate reached by a formal longitudinal survey in Germany, the principal destination country (Aksoy and Poutvaara, 2019).

MEASUREMENT OF DISABILITY HAS EVOLVED ALONG WITH ITS DEFINITION

While formulating appropriate questions on ethnicity or gender identity in censuses and surveys is often a question of politics, the main issues in the case of questions on disability have been attitudes and knowledge. For instance, if disability is seen as bringing shame to the family, certain questions trigger fear of stigmatization and elicit unpredictable responses. A commonly referenced estimate from around 2004 was that 15% to 20% of adults but only 5% of children up to age 14 had a disability (WHO and World Bank, 2011).

Agreeing a valid measure of disability has been a long process. The 2001 International Classification of Functioning, Disability and Health (ICF) and the 2007 ICF for Children and Youth were important in moving from a medical to a social model of disability. The two classifications were merged in 2012. The ICF is a neutral framework that describes levels of functioning in various domains related to health, including 'major life areas' such as education (Hollenweger, 2014). It does not define disability or specify data collection methods, however.

The UN Statistical Commission set up the Washington Group on Disability Statistics in 2001. Its Short Set of Questions, aligned with the ICF and suitable for inclusion in censuses or surveys, was agreed in 2006 (Groce and Mont, 2017). The six questions cover critical functional domains and activities: seeing, hearing, mobility, cognition, self-care and communication. For instance, the cognition question is, 'Do you have difficulty remembering or concentrating?' Response options for all questions are 'No – no difficulty', 'Yes – some difficulty', 'Yes – a lot of difficulty' and 'Cannot do at all' (WHO and World Bank, 2011).

One limitation was that the questions were developed for adults and did not adequately capture developmental disabilities in children. After extensive consultation and testing, a Module on Child Functioning was developed in collaboration with UNICEF (Loeb et al., 2018; Massey, 2018). Its first large-scale application is in the sixth wave of UNICEF's Multiple Indicator Cluster Surveys (MICS). Crucially, the module queries difficulties with learning and recognizes the importance of freedom from anxiety and depression. An earlier analysis in five European countries suggested that between 10% and 20% of children had mental health problems (Braddick and Jané-Llopis, 2008).

An additional module developed by UNICEF covers a broader range of inclusion and participation dimensions, such as attitudes, accessibility, transport and affordability (Cappa, 2014). The aim is to understand the prevalence of disability and education outcomes, the education environment and specific barriers to education.

Broad-based adoption of the Washington Group questions would not only bring disability statistics into line with the social model but also resolve the comparability issues that have plagued global disability statistics (Altman, 2016). So far, estimates of the prevalence of disability have varied with differences in definitions and methodology (Mont, 2007; Singal et al., 2015). The clearest evidence on the effect of differing methods of measuring disability comes from studies that have applied multiple instruments to the same respondents. For instance,

> ❝ Broad-based adoption of the Washington Group questions would bring disability statistics into line with the social model and resolve the comparability issues that have plagued global disability statistics ❞

Incorporation of inclusion indicators into EMIS is an emerging best practice

studies have shown that approaches focused on impairments yield different results than those focused on activities (Fotso et al., 2019). A study in Cameroon and India found that self-reporting missed around half of those with disabilities. Clinical measures missed between 14% and 22%. Even activity limitations did not fully capture barriers to participation in daily activities (MacTaggart et al., 2014).

For adults, the Model Disability Surveys, which the World Health Organization developed in collaboration with the World Bank in 2012, contain questions on barriers to education. Respondents who never entered education or who had left are asked whether accessibility was the main reason; those currently in education are asked what would make it easier for them to get an education. A version suitable for integration into existing household surveys was developed in 2016 (WHO, 2019). In Chile and Costa Rica, where this survey has been used, around one in five adults was found to have a disability. In Chile, 12% had a mild to moderate disability and 8% a severe disability (Chile Ministry of Social Development, 2016). An analysis of data from Chile found that those with mental disorders identified essentially the same environmental disabling or enabling factors as those experiencing difficulties due to non-communicable diseases (Kamenov et al., 2018). In Costa Rica, about 55% of respondents with disabilities reported that education centres were not accessible and lacked ramps, visual and audio alerts, grab bars and other adaptations. Less than 5% reported receiving any type of education support or accommodation (Costa Rica National Institute of Statistics and Census, 2019).

New measures offer new perspectives on education of children with disabilities

While the Washington Group questions have gained currency (Groce and Mont, 2017), many information sources are not aligned with them. The most recent estimates on disability prevalence and its effects on education thus rely on sources that are not fully comparable. A UNESCO Institute for Statistics (UIS) analysis showed that 15- to 29-year-olds with disabilities in 37 countries were less likely than their peers to have attended school; in Egypt, Indonesia and Viet Nam, they were half as likely (UIS, 2018).

Two collections of disability-disaggregated education statistics for a large number of countries were made available as part of the Global Disability Summit and the first UN flagship report on disability and development (Leonard Cheshire and Department for International Development, 2018; United Nations, 2018). Both have a preference for, but are not limited to, Washington Group definitions.

Without consistent definitions, surveys show wildly varying estimates of child disability prevalence, from below 1% to over 50% (Cappa, 2014). Even the same questions can lead to a wide range of estimates if they are interpreted differently in different contexts. For instance, in the second wave of MICS in the mid-2000s, estimates of disability among 2- to 9-year-olds ranged from 3% in Uzbekistan to 49% in the Central African Republic (UNESCO, 2014).

In 14 countries with estimates based on the MICS Module on Child Functioning in 2017–19, prevalence estimates of functional difficulty among 5- to 17-year-olds vary by domain and, within each domain, by country. In the sensory domain, the average prevalence was 0.4% for hearing difficulties and 0.6% for seeing difficulties. In the mobility domain, walking difficulties affected 3% of children in Sierra Leone. Cognitive and psycho-emotional difficulties were far more common, especially in conflict and post-conflict settings. In Sierra Leone, 9% of children and adolescents were depressed. In Iraq, 16% suffered from anxiety (**Figure 3.3a**). The share of those with a functional difficulty in at least one domain was 12% on average, varying from 6% in Mongolia to 24% in Tunisia (**Figure 3.3b**).

Children, adolescents and youth with disabilities accounted for 12% of the in-school population, but 15% of the out-of-school population. In general, the lower the out-of-school rate, the more likely it is that children with disabilities will be among those out of school, suggesting that those with disabilities are among the hardest to reach (**Figure 3.4**). Relative to their peers of primary, lower secondary and upper secondary school age, those with a disability were more likely to be out of school by 1, 4 and 6 percentage points, respectively, and those with a sensory, physical or intellectual disability by 4, 7 and 11 percentage points (**Figure 3.5**). But the latter were 2.5 times more likely to have never been in school as their peers without disabilities.

FIGURE 3.3:

Cognitive and psycho-emotional difficulties are the most common disabilities among children and adolescents

Prevalence of functional difficulties among 5- to 17-year-olds, selected countries, 2017–19

GEM StatLink: http://bit.ly/GEM2020_fig3_3
Source: MICS Survey Findings Reports.

FIGURE 3.4:

Children with disabilities constitute 15% of out-of-school children

Percentage of children, adolescents and youth with functional difficulties in the in-school and out-of-school population, by education level, selected countries, 2017–19

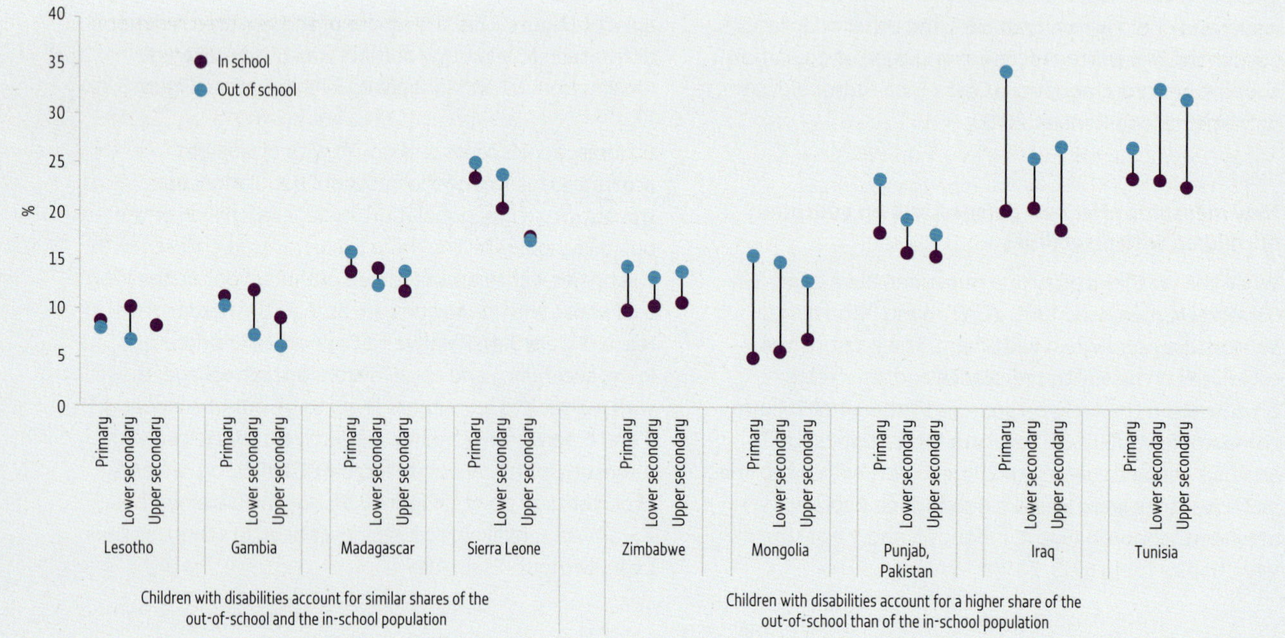

GEM StatLink: http://bit.ly/GEM2020_fig3_4
Source: GEM Report team analysis based on MICS data.

> Life at the intersections of disability with race, class, gender, sexual orientation and gender identity expression is more than the sum of each vulnerability

THE INTERSECTIONS OF DISABILITY WITH OTHER CHARACTERISTICS NEED TO BE TAKEN INTO ACCOUNT

Characteristics that expose individuals to risk do not affect everybody the same way. For instance, life at the intersections of disability with race, class, gender, sexual orientation and gender identity expression is more than the sum of each vulnerability (Connor, 2014). From a statistical point of view, sample size is a challenge for analysis of intersecting disadvantage. Standard household surveys suffer from rapidly shrinking samples and larger estimation errors as the focus shifts to individuals with multiple specific characteristics. Consequently, analyses of intersections involving the relatively rare characteristic of disability are largely limited to census data, which offer much greater sample sizes but do not yet apply a consistent definition of disability. But it is important not to underestimate the risk that, for instance, poor people with disabilities may be twice excluded: from society generally but also within the disability movement.

With respect to the intersection between disability and gender, an analysis across cohorts based on census data from 19 countries suggested that males with disabilities have seen the slowest growth in primary and secondary completion and adult literacy (Male and Wodon, 2017; Wodon et al., 2018). As for the intersection between disability and income, moderate and severe disabilities reduce school attendance at all levels (Fotso et al., 2018), although the poor with disabilities are often more vulnerable to exclusion. Often disability is the result of illnesses and accidents that push already poor people deeper into poverty (Singal, 2014).

Intersecting vulnerabilities may mean some go unaddressed. Language difficulties and behavioural, social and emotional difficulties often coincide (Hartas, 2011).

FIGURE 3.5:

The disability disadvantage is largest at the upper secondary education level

Percentage of out-of-school children, adolescents and youth with and without functional difficulties, by education level, selected countries, 2017–19

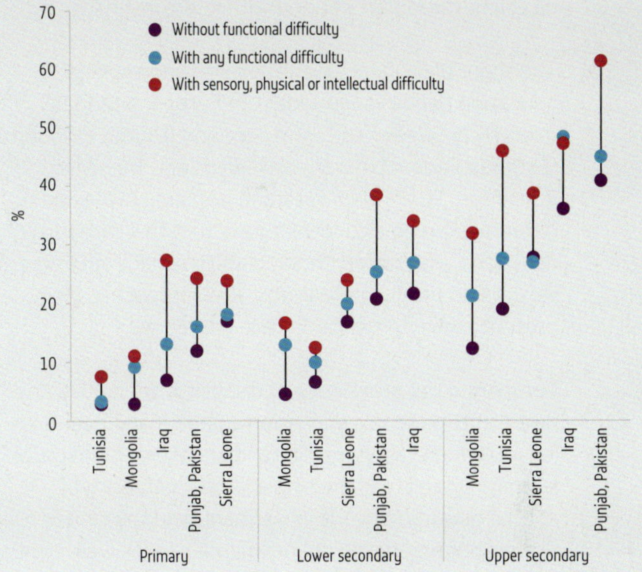

GEM StatLink: http://bit.ly/GEM2020_fig3_5
Source: GEM Report team analysis based on MICS data.

Yet bilingual students with disabilities, for instance, are likely to be in classrooms that address their academic or linguistic needs but not both (Cioè-Peña, 2017). Half of children with disabilities in the United Kingdom also experience learning difficulties (Porter et al., 2008; Porter et al., 2013). In studies of children and adolescents with epilepsy, one-quarter met criteria for depression (Ettinger et al., 1998) and half for learning difficulties (Fastenau et al., 2008). Children identified as gifted and talented often experience emotional difficulties coping with their exceptionality and social distance from peers. Giftedness may not be recognized in children with autistic spectrum disorders. A significant minority of gifted students may also have poor reading skills (Al-Hroub, 2010; Munro, 2002). Such children are less likely to receive appropriately challenging learning opportunities.

DIAGNOSTIC CRITERIA TO IDENTIFY SPECIAL EDUCATION NEEDS CAN BE ARBITRARY AND CONTENTIOUS

Not all children with disabilities have special education needs, nor do all children with special education needs have a disability (Keil et al., 2006; Porter et al., 2011). Special needs identification is a distinct issue from disability measurement and with less consensus.

The share of students identified as having special education needs varies widely. In Europe, it ranges from 1% in Sweden to 21% in Scotland (United Kingdom) (European Agency for Special Needs and Inclusive Education, 2018). Such variation is mainly explained by differences in how countries construct this category of education. Institution, funding and training requirements vary, as do policy implications. The approaches also present measurement and data challenges.

Comparing the prevalence of disability, difficulties and disadvantage across education systems and over time is problematic, even for clinical diagnoses. For instance, learning disability is the single largest category of special education needs in Germany and the United States, but practically unknown in Japan (Powell, 2014). In the United States, the cut-off intelligence quotient score for intellectual disability was reduced from 85 to 70 in 1965 (Harry, 2014).

Like intellectual disability, autism spectrum disorder is recognized as a condition at the extreme end of a continuum. Neither medical nor education considerations give unambiguous guidance on the point at which a behaviour becomes a disorder. The determination partly depends on context. Whatever the underlying biochemistry of attention deficit hyperactivity disorder, in some settings the boundary of orderly behaviour determines the diagnosis. Pre-primary and even early childhood education settings have become more academic. Ever younger children, whose age-appropriate behaviour is free play, spend more time in school and their teachers have higher expectations. In the United States, between 1998 and 2010, the proportion of children attending full-day kindergarten increased from 56% to 80%, while the proportion of teachers who expected children to read in kindergarten rose from 31% to 80% (Bassok et al., 2016). Moreover, measurement difficulties limit the availability of global data. For instance, the existence of autism is established in low- and lower-middle-income countries (Abubakar et al., 2016; Ametepee and Chitiyo, 2009), but prevalence estimates are scarce (Elsabbagh et al., 2012).

> "
> There is wide variation in education ability and behaviour within categories of disability
> "

With the exception of learning difficulties, diagnostic criteria for disabilities are not inherently related to education. Accordingly, they have no particular implications for curriculum and teaching (Norwich, 2014). There is wide variation in education ability and behaviour within categories of disability (Florian, 2014). Many conditions, including epilepsy and other chronic health conditions, are diagnosed outside education and for non-education purposes. Such information may be relevant even for schools that adopt a non-categorical approach.

There is a clear case for school-based screening to enable some straightforward interventions. Short-sightedness is not generally considered a disabling impairment because it is easy and cheap to treat with glasses. In a randomized experiment in a poor rural area of China, dropout halved among myopic lower secondary school students when they were provided with free corrective glasses (Nie et al., 2020). Yet school-based screening is not yet common. An analysis of 10 countries participating in the Programme d'analyse des systèmes éducatifs de la CONFEMEN, a cross-national learning achievement survey in francophone African countries, showed that, in 4 countries, less than 3% of grade 2 teachers reported that eye tests took place (Wodon et al., 2018). Other research found that a majority of students with refractive errors, such as myopia, were not wearing glasses in Malawi (Kaphle et al., 2015) and South Africa (Naidoo, 2007).

Labels affect those labelled and are self-confirming

Data collection must be careful to do no harm. Identification of children with specific conditions must strike a balance. On the one hand, identification can inform teachers of the needs of students, including those with 'invisible impairments'. Schools rely on this information to target accommodations accordingly. On the other hand, there is a risk of peers, teachers and administrators reducing children to a label and behaving towards them according to stereotypes (Virkkunen et al., 2012). Low expectations triggered by a label, such as learning difficulties, can become a self-fulfilling prophecy.

Special needs labels make the labelled students vulnerable. Teachers may take a deterministic view that these students' ability and potential are fixed and cannot be changed by additional effort (Hart and Drummond, 2014). Labels can also shape expectations for a group. For instance, before children with Down's syndrome began benefiting from inclusive education, their learning environments were constrained and their developmental outcomes often limited. These limits were misinterpreted as inherent to what such children could achieve (Buckley, 2000).

Stigma attached to special needs categories varies, affecting the data collected. A label's status can change over time, confusing debates about whether labelling as such is harmful. It is frequently noted that children do not require labelling to exclude another child (Frederickson, 2010; Kauffman and Badar, 2014).

Socio-economic characteristics can drive special needs categorization status. Interaction of variation in underlying factors with variation in identification has been researched extensively in the United States.

> Low expectations triggered by a label, such as learning difficulties, can become a self-fulfilling prophecy

For instance, better-off families were more likely to be able to afford and actively seek a diagnosis to ensure that their dyslexic children benefit from services and accommodations (Hanford, 2017). Autism may be on the cusp of a similar development, with mainly richer families demanding access to services that come with the diagnosis, particularly early intervention (Marks and Kurth, 2013). The pattern was observed across all racial and ethnic groups, with the largest gap among Asians: 10.7 per 1,000 among the richest 8-year-olds compared with 3.9 among the poorest (Durkin et al., 2010). By contrast, in Europe, most studies indicate children on the autism spectrum were more likely to be diagnosed in households with low socio-economic status (Delobel-Ayoub et al., 2015). Moreover, US children at a given ability level were disproportionately more likely to be designated as having an intellectual disability if they

ADENE

> " Portugal recently legislated a non-categorical approach to determining special needs "

belonged to racial and ethnic minorities. In some states, minorities could officially be up to five times likelier to be in special education categories without triggering discrimination concerns (Harry, 2014; Marks and Kurth, 2013).

Whether labels are formally or informally assigned and whether they are made public or kept private are important considerations for assessing the implications of labelling (Riddick, 2000). Screening and providing evidence-based general advice to schools on inclusive teaching may work better than identifying affected students (Tymms and Merrell, 2006). Voluntary self-identification is frequently the only data source in higher and adult education. Individuals respond at least in part according to whether they identify with a category. Many vulnerable students resist feeling different; others express a sense of relief at a disability determination and may form and express a strong group identity (Southwell, 2006).

Support can be monitored without diagnosing students

The potentially detrimental effects of diagnoses, labels and categories can be minimized so they inform rather than determine practice (Norwich, 2014). Doing so affects the kind of data reported. Portugal recently legislated a non-categorical approach to determining special needs (GEM Report Education Profiles[1]). Such moves, in a break from categories defined in terms of medical conditions, focus instead on level of support given. The medical approach promotes a 'wait to fail' attitude: Diagnosis outside the learning setting is accompanied by an expectation that the student will fail without intervention.

In the United States, under the Response to Intervention approach, the criterion for attesting a learning disability is whether a learner progresses in response to mainstream classroom instruction and, subsequently, to intense support of a fixed duration (Norwich, 2014). The idea is

---

1 A new GEM Report tool for systematic monitoring of national education laws and policies, accessible at www.education-profiles.org.

'to rule out the possibility that poor achievement may simply be the result of poor instruction' (Harry, 2014, p. 84). A similar graduated response based on learning outcomes rather than diagnoses has been proposed in eastern and southern Africa (Sarton and Smith, 2018).

A non-categorical approach has implications for data. Instead of aggregate statistics on the number of students with specific conditions, data refer to the number of students who received support. The use of special education needs categories for instructional purposes can be separated from the use of a reduced set of categories for resource allocation (Norwich, 2014).

DATA FOR INCLUSION: THE POLICIES AND RESULTS COUNTRIES MONITOR VARY

Data on the education attainment and achievement of various groups help describe their situation and prompt policy responses from education ministries. Implementation of these responses also needs to be monitored, within a clear result framework, to achieve progress on making systems more inclusive. This section analyses three key monitoring areas: progress towards inclusion and desegregation in schools, collection of qualitative data on inclusive teaching practices, and inclusive approaches to data collection.

MONITORING STUDENT SEGREGATION OCCURS AT SEVERAL LEVELS

A key tenet of inclusion is ensuring that the diversity of the school-aged population is represented in every classroom. In practice, this goal is undermined by the existence of special schools and by residential and other geographical disparities.

Information on the share of students with disabilities in special schools is incomplete

A key system-level question is the extent to which children are in the same classrooms regardless of background. While enrolment in separate schools is the most easily identified, statistics on intermediate arrangements, such as mainstream classes with special support or special and mainstream schools on shared premises, are rarely available. This scarcity reflects the variety of possible and potentially concurrent arrangements and the lack of standardized nomenclature

> **Inclusion is undermined by the existence of special schools and by residential and other geographical disparities**

and clear-cut boundaries (Hornby, 2015). Existing data are mainly time series for individual countries, some of which have shown significant progress towards an inclusive approach. For instance, in Brazil, segregation was the norm 20 years ago, but after a policy change the share of students with disabilities in mainstream schools rose, from 23% in 2003 to 81% in 2015 (Hehir et al., 2016).

Good data are also available for some regions. In Europe, large variation is observed. Scotland (United Kingdom) and Sweden have a similar share of students in special schools (just under 1%). However, those students in Scotland are a small minority of the more than 20% identified with special education needs. By contrast, few Swedish students are identified with special needs and they are concentrated in special schools (**Figure 3.6**).

FIGURE 3.6:

The share of students with special education needs in special schools varies greatly across Europe

Share of primary and secondary school students designated with special education needs among all students and in special schools, selected European education systems, 2014/15

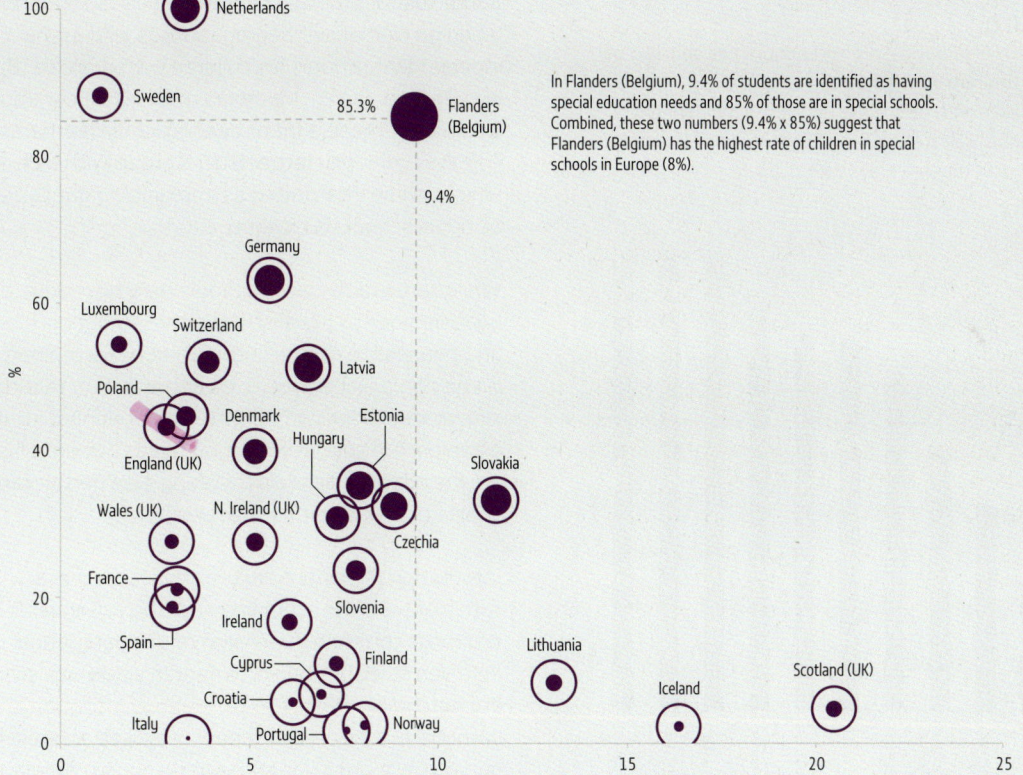

In Flanders (Belgium), 9.4% of students are identified as having special education needs and 85% of those are in special schools. Combined, these two numbers (9.4% x 85%) suggest that Flanders (Belgium) has the highest rate of children in special schools in Europe (8%).

GEM StatLink: http://bit.ly/GEM2020_fig3_6

Note: The share of the circle filled represents the share of students in special schools in relation to the highest value, recorded in the Flanders region of Belgium (8%).

Source: European Agency Statistics for Inclusive Education (2018).

The UN Economic and Social Commission for Asia and the Pacific also reported a wide range in the percentage of primary school-aged children with disabilities attending special schools, from 0% in Timor-Leste and Thailand to 97% in Kyrgyzstan, with an average of almost 20% (United Nations, 2018).

Systematic statistics of this kind are not available at the global level, only at the country level and for some regions. The shares of children with disabilities enrolled in mainstream and special schools in most low- and lower-middle-income countries with data, as recorded in education sector plans, show that most children with disabilities tend to be enrolled in mainstream schools, although there are exceptions, such as the Central African Republic (28%) (**Figure 3.7**). However, these data may reflect only a fraction of all children with disabilities.

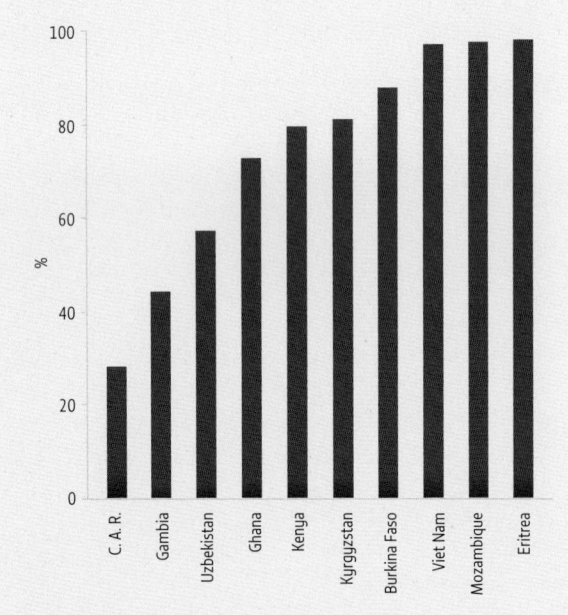

FIGURE 3.7:
Children with disabilities in poorer countries tend to be enrolled in mainstream schools
Share of children with disabilities enrolled in mainstream primary schools, selected low- and lower-middle-income countries, education sector plans since 2008

GEM StatLink: StatLink: http://bit.ly/GEM2020_fig3_7
Source: GEM Report team calculations based on Global Partnership for Education (2018), tables 2.2 and 2.3.

> Gender is the most common dimension of disaggregation. Yet even statistics on enrolment in single-sex schools are patchy

Self-segregation blurs the boundaries of inclusion

Special education may nominally be a parental choice. It may also reflect a preference for self-exclusion (Shakespeare, 2006). This applies as well to schools that cater to specific groups, such as single-sex, minority language and religious community schools. Their contribution to inclusion is ambiguous: Indigenous schools, for instance, can provide 'an inclusive environment where marginalised voices are heard and where their traditions, cultures and experiences are privileged' but 'can also re-inscribe marginality and deficit understandings of the "other" through their focus on a fixed and reductionist group identity' (Keddie, 2014, p. 57).

Some special schools see themselves as supporting a benign kind of self-segregation, as with some independent schools for children with dyslexia (Burden and Burdett, 2005). Members of the Deaf community, a subset of those hard of hearing, consider themselves a linguistic minority rather than a group with a disability, which can be interpreted as implying a right to separate bilingual schools (Goswami, 2004).

While some faith-based schools may be motivated by resistance to pluralistic societies, others exhibit an openness to others and, with non-discriminatory admission policies, would reject the notion that they are segregated. Provision for gifted and talented students is often part of special education needs but not all schools for the gifted or schools fostering elite performance in sports or arts count as special schools.

Internationally comparable statistics on these types of separate schooling are scarce. Gender is the most common dimension of disaggregation. Yet even statistics on enrolment in single-sex schools are patchy (see **Focus 14.1**). Religious affiliation is sometimes captured in school censuses or household surveys, although variations in response categories and lack of clear boundaries between faith-based and non-government organization schools make cross-country comparisons difficult. Every two years, for instance, the United States surveys private schools, which account for about 10% of total enrolment in primary and secondary education. The survey provides a breakdown between religious and non-religious schools and, among the former, distinguishes between schools that are Catholic or conservative Christian, belong to associations with another specific religious orientation, and are unaffiliated (National Center for Education Statistics, 2016). In sub-Saharan Africa, household surveys in 16 countries indicated that faith-based schools accounted for 11% to 14% of enrolment, an estimate that corresponded reasonably well, on average, with the administrative data collected in some countries (Wodon, 2014). How Islamic schools are captured in statistics depends on the status of the schools in various countries (**Box 3.1**).

Even when voluntary, high levels of segregation are a warning sign. Preferences adapt to available alternatives. As argued above with respect to private schooling, parents are not obliged to wait for systems to change (Swift, 2003). Flight from mainstream schools by those facing barriers could be understood as a response to lack of inclusiveness (Shaw, 2017).

Residential segregation drives the concentration of disadvantaged students in certain schools

Spatial segregation among schools may persist even when each is inclusive of its students. Poor or migrant families are often clustered in certain localities and schools (Nieuwenhuis and Hooimeijer, 2016). Such schools are not identified as schools for immigrants in education statistics; there is therefore no direct equivalent to special school enrolment statistics.

In the United States, the 1968 desegregation policy led to a rapid decline in the share of black students attending intensely segregated schools (where at least 90% of the student population belonged to a minority group). However, the share increased in all regions between 1991 and 2011, especially in the South, where more than half of black students live: There the share increased from 26% to 34%, although the South remains the least segregated region. The highest share was observed in the north-east (51%) (Orfield and Frankenberg, 2014).

BOX 3.1:

Islamic schools span inclusion and self-segregation in parts of the world

In several countries where Islam is the religion of the majority or of a sizeable minority, religious schools have helped expand access to education. The extent to which these schools are part of the formal system – and therefore captured in statistics – depends on historical context.

In Southern and South-eastern Asia, there has been intense debate about tradition vs modernization in education (Park and Niyozov, 2008). While unrecognized religious schools remain, recognized madrasas that teach the official curriculum have been introduced since the 1980s and have been credited with expanding access to students from poorer households, for instance in Bangladesh and Indonesia (Asadullah and Chaudhury, 2016; Asadullah and Maliki, 2018). In Bangladesh, madrasas accounted for 1.2 million or 6% of primary school students (grades 1 to 5) in 2016 and 2.1 million or 17% of secondary school students (grades 6 to10) in 2018, according to the school census. The number of unregistered schools remains limited (Bangladesh Bureau of Education Information and Statistics, 2018; Bangladesh Directorate of Primary Education, 2017). In Indonesia, the percentage of students in madrasas was 10% in primary, 23% in lower secondary and 20% in upper secondary education in 2012. There are 7 million enrolled in registered, publicly supported madrasas across all levels and 8 million enrolled in unregistered madrasas, often with boarding facilities, monitored by the Ministry of Religious Affairs (Asadullah and Maliki, 2018).

While the share of students in religious schools in these two countries has remained fairly constant, Turkey has expanded, adapted and diversified the public religious schools known as *imam hatip* (Aşlamacı and Kaymakcan, 2017; Çakmaklı et al., 2017). A turning point came in 2013, when *imam hatip* expanded from the upper secondary to lower secondary level. Between 2012 and 2017, the share of students in these schools increased from 0% to 12% in lower secondary and from 5.6% to 11% in upper secondary education (Butler, 2018).

In sub-Saharan Africa, Islamic schools are the preferred choice of poorer families but have remained at the margins of the education system, comparatively speaking. While a few countries, such as Côte d'Ivoire and Mauritania, have formal Islamic schools, no more than 3% of primary school children enrol in them, the exception being Gambia at 11%. Most of the schools are non-formal, and many children attend both a formal secular school and a non-formal Islamic school (d'Aiglepierre and Bauer, 2018). Senegal has a large variety of non-formal Islamic schools, known as *daara*, including neighbourhood schools, most of whose students also attend public schools, and boarding schools. A few have been formalized, including a handful in the public education system (Dia et al., 2016). Such variety makes it hard to monitor the percentage of children attending the various types. A citizen-led assessment of households estimated that 16% of 9- to 16-year-olds attended a *daara* but could not further distinguish the types (Fall and Cisse, 2017).

In countries of the Organisation for Economic Co-operation and Development that participated in the Programme for International Student Assessment (PISA), socio-economic segregation was a persistent challenge. More than two-thirds of immigrant students attended schools where at least half the students were immigrants (OECD, 2015). Another analysis using PISA data showed that half the students in Chile and Mexico but less than one-third in Scandinavian countries would have to be reassigned schools to achieve a uniform socio-economic mixture. Such segregation barely changed between 2000 and 2015 (**Figure 3.8**). High socio-economic segregation among schools is also found in China (Yuxiao and Chao, 2017). Data from Latin America suggest that

> " In the Czech Republic and Slovakia, most Roma children were educated in majority Roma schools "

segregation by ethnic origin is more widespread than segregation by socio-economic status (Murillo and Martínez-Garrido, 2017).

The purpose of the analysis matters. Official statistics on desegregation in South Africa have focused on school-level analysis of the extent to which all population groups have gained access to formerly white schools. An analysis of grade 12 examination data for this report shows that 98% of white students are from schools that include non-white students. Among schools attended by white students, half have 65% or more non-white students, and half have 28% or more black students (Gustafsson, 2019).

The contentious debate about whether schools in the United States are desegregating or resegregating hinges on the difference between the extent to which groups are evenly distributed and the extent to which they are exposed to each other (Chang, 2018; Reardon and Owen, 2014). In Providence, Rhode Island, the share of schools with 90% or more minority students increased from 36% in 2000 to 74% in 2015. Yet segregation decreased in terms of even distribution of groups across schools (Barshay, 2018).

Policies to counter residential and school segregation must take their complex interaction into account. In San Francisco, California, families from historically disadvantaged neighbourhoods get a bonus in the school lottery that increases their chance of getting their first choice. Inadvertently, this benefits middle-class families who are gentrifying these neighbourhoods; they receive the bonus on top of their existing advantage and make more ambitious and strategic choices in the lottery than their neighbours who are the intended beneficiaries (Goldstein, 2019).

Roma children are much less likely than non-Roma to attend school; those who do attend are often educated separately. In the Czech Republic and Slovakia, most Roma children were educated in majority Roma schools. Special needs identification serves to segregate Roma children in special schools or in segregated classes within mixed schools, with separate entrances and cafeterias.

FIGURE 3.8:
Socio-economic segregation among schools is a persistent challenge
Dissimilarity index of distribution of socio-economic top and bottom 50% of students across schools, selected countries, 2000–15

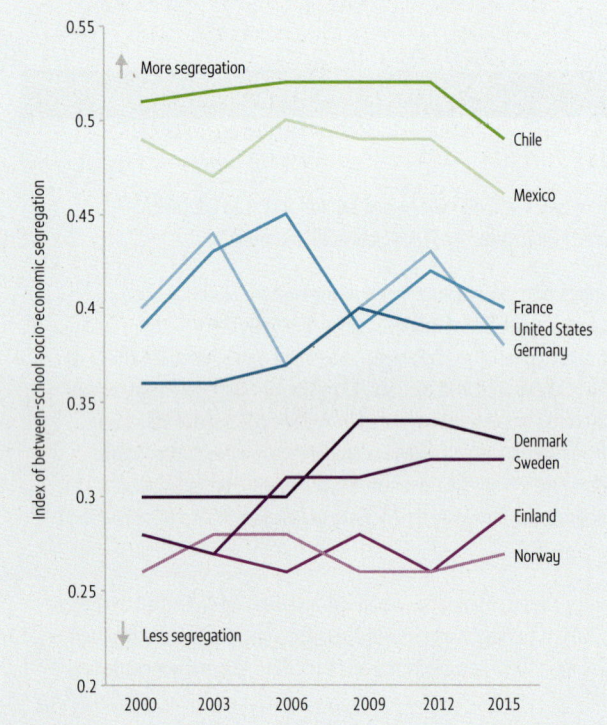

GEM StatLink: http://bit.ly/GEM2020_fig3_8
Notes: The dissimilarity index reflects the differing distribution of two groups (e.g. students of high and low socio-economic status) among specific units (e.g. schools). It is equal to half the sum of absolute differences in proportions between the two groups across schools. It ranges from zero (where the proportion of both groups in every school is equal to the proportions found in the population, i.e. there is no segregation) to one (where there is complete segregation of students, i.e. all schools have only one group of students represented).
Source: Based on Gutiérrez et al. (2020).

"

Feelings of relating and belonging affect learning

"

At least 5% of Roma in Croatia, Hungary, the Republic of Moldova and Romania, and at least 10% in Slovakia and Bulgaria, attended segregated classes in mainstream schools (Brüggemann, 2012)

Some countries with concentrations of indigenous, ethnic, linguistic and other cultural minority communities identify them using geographical areas as proxies instead of trying to determine individual students' identities. Bangladesh has used such an approach to target ethnic minorities, populations on flood-prone river islands and in coastal or *haor* (wetland) areas, those vulnerable to the *monga* (lean season of rice production), families working on tea plantations and, most recently, Rohingya refugees. Each group lives in fairly clearly demarcated parts of the country (Begum et al., 2019). In Nepal, the government introduced an equity index in 2014, with the support of UNICEF and other development partners, to assess education disparity within and across districts for needs-based school-level planning (UNICEF, 2018).

MONITORING OF INCLUSION IN SCHOOLS SHOULD BE AMBITIOUS

Monitoring inclusive teaching in classrooms is challenging. Comprehensive reviews confirm a lack of evidence on any special pedagogy for teaching children with special needs (Davis et al., 2004; Nind and Wearmouth, 2004; Rix and Sheehy, 2014). Evidence on specific inclusive pedagogies is also lacking for special schools (Hedegaard-Soerensen et al., 2018). Teachers who can effectively teach students with special needs are the most effective teachers overall (Jordan and McGhie-Richmond, 2014).

Information on the education outcomes of children belonging to various groups gives at best a limited view of their experiences of exclusion and inclusion. Students can be physically in a class but not belong to the class socially (Ferguson, 2008). Learners can be subject to humiliating treatment whether they belong to a specific group or not.

Few data on student experiences exist, and outsiders have only limited and irregular opportunities to observe classrooms (Kuper et al., 2018; Price, 2018). A study of dropout in Norway found that '[t]eachers' displays of ignorance, sarcastic remarks and absent leadership are the main topics in the adolescents' statements':

> Finally, feeling a little nervous ... I raised my hand and was ready to give my answer. The teacher

smiled at me and said in front of everyone, 'Tom, our troublesome little boy, has finally decided to participate and show us his worldly wisdom.' Everyone laughed. At that moment I decided that I would never talk in front of that teacher or that class again. Not ever (Lund, 2014, p. 100).

Feelings of relating and belonging affect learning (Alton-Lee, 2003; Porter et al., 2013). An environment that allows students to be persistently mocked cannot be genuinely inclusive, even if ridicule is directed not at a disability or group membership but at physical appearance, motor skills, an uncommon name or new-student status (Dare et al., 2017; Oravec, 2012).

Cross-national learning achievement surveys tend to ask questions on sense of belonging. In the 2018 PISA, around 1 in 10 students in Belarus, Norway and Spain, but over 1 in 3 in Brunei Darussalam, the Dominican Republic and the United States, reported feeling like outsiders at school (**Figure 3.9**). From this and other questions, such as whether they feel lonely at school, an index of sense of belonging has been calculated. Schools in every participating country fall far short of making students from all socio-economic backgrounds equally feel like they belong (**Figure 3.10**).

The Index for Inclusion is the most prominent holistic framework of school-level indicators across the domains of inclusive cultures, policies and practices (Booth and Ainscow, 2002). While its applicability in developing countries has been questioned, both because of lack of resources and the risks a tick-box approach entails, the index can be adapted to local contexts through school self-evaluations and value frameworks (Carrington and Duke, 2014). It has been translated into 40 languages and adapted and used in many countries. In Brazil, it has helped schools identify inclusion barriers and informed teacher and civil servant professional development since 2006 (Index for Inclusion Network, 2019).

The index does not generate a one-dimensional value for simple aggregation and comparison of schools, however. To inform policy and monitor implementation and outcomes, detailed data must be captured in an education management information system (EMIS). Yet almost half of low- and middle-income countries have no EMIS that is inclusive, for instance of children with disabilities (United Nations, 2018).

FIGURE 3.9:
Many students feel like outsiders at school

Percentage of students who agree or strongly agree that they feel like outsiders or left out at school, selected countries, 2018

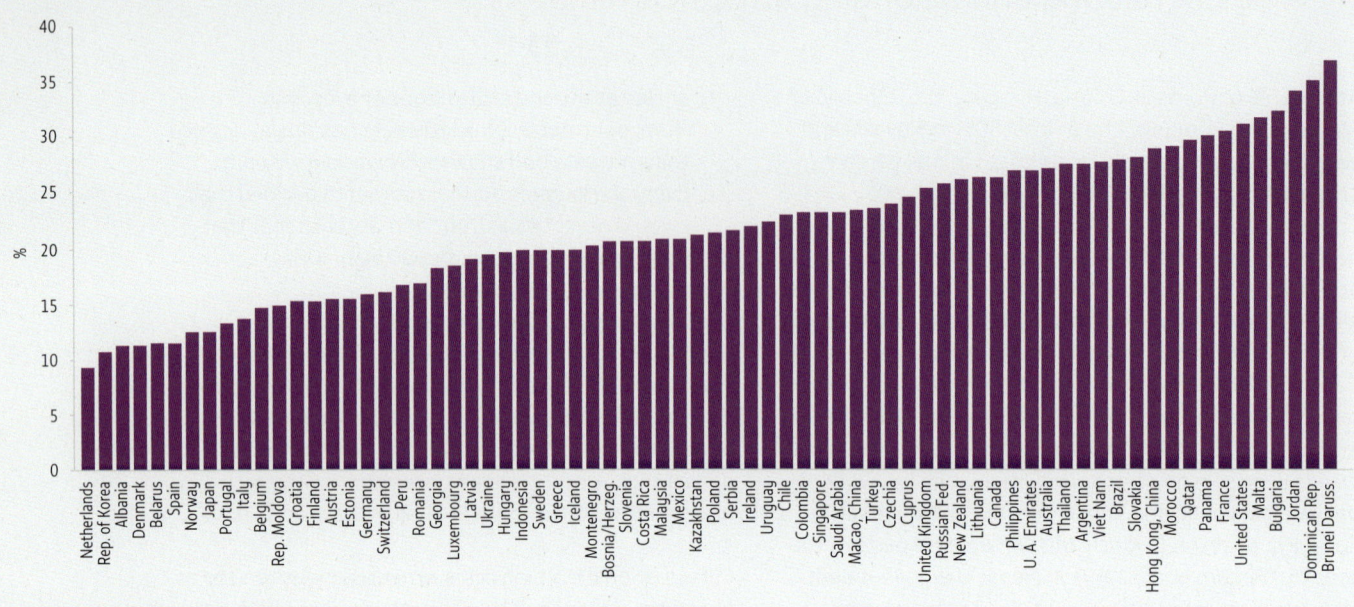

GEM StatLink: http://bit.ly/GEM2020_fig3_9
Source: OECD (2019).

FIGURE 3.10:
Disadvantaged students feel they do not belong at school

Index of sense of belonging, by socio-economic status, selected countries, 2018

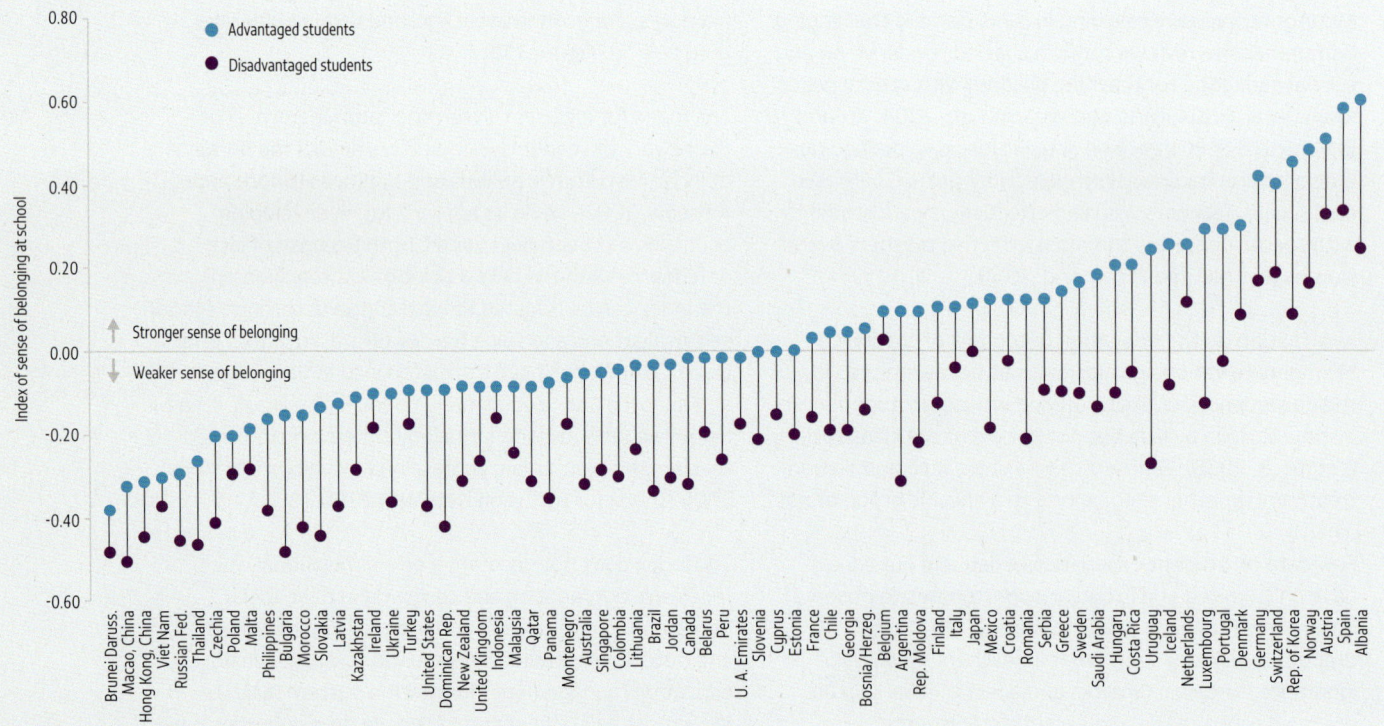

GEM StatLink: http://bit.ly/GEM2020_fig3_10

Notes: The index of sense of belonging is based on responses to the following questions: 'I feel like an outsider (or left out of things) at school', 'I make friends easily at school', 'I feel like I belong at school', 'I feel awkward and out of place in my school', 'Other students seem to like me' and 'I feel lonely at school'. The value of zero is the average for OECD countries.
Source: OECD (2019).

> " In 14 countries, the share of children with a functional difficulty in at least one domain was 12% "

The scope and quality of the data, where available, often remain limited. In a survey of education ministries in 11 sub-Saharan African countries on children with visual impairments, conducted for this report, Cameroon and Nigeria could not provide enrolment data, while Ghana, Kenya and Zambia could provide data for children in special and integrated schools but not mainstream ones. Moreover, some ministries stressed the potential lack of data reliability (Sightsavers, 2020).

Incorporation of inclusion indicators into EMIS is an emerging best practice. UNICEF recently produced a guide on adding disability-related questions to school censuses, including a recommended minimum set related to inclusion. Feasible and universally applicable questions include incidence of in-service teacher training on teaching children with disabilities and whether schools' main entrances are wide enough for wheelchairs. Gearing school-level data collection towards inclusion can be incremental. India simply added a column to forms collecting information on various facilities on whether they were accessible to students with disabilities (UNICEF, 2016).

The UIS reviewed approaches to collecting administrative data on disability in 71 low- and middle-income countries to determine the extent to which they aligned with the social model of disability, along with what measures could contribute to both national policy and Sustainable Development Goal (SDG) 4 monitoring. Administrative data from Rwanda demonstrated the value of combining detailed information on education and disability: Enrolment of children with multiple disabilities was found to have dropped from 348 in grade 1 to 87 in grade 6 in 2018. However, few systems collect sufficiently detailed data on disability or education programmes and outcomes (**Figure 3.11**): Costa Rica, Fiji, Indonesia, the Marshall Islands and Puerto Rico (United States) include information on psychosocial or behavioural difficulties, while 14 systems identify four common domains: vision, hearing, physical and intellectual impairments (UIS, 2019).

The review recommends replacing general questions on school accessibility with specific questions related to availability of accommodations, such as Braille materials and modified furniture. Existing questions, e.g. on availability of internet for pedagogical purposes, can be extended with an additional question on availability of screen readers for students with visual impairment.

Leveraging of EMIS for inclusion can and should go much further. New Zealand systematically monitors soft indicators at the national level, including on whether students feel cared for, safe and secure, and on their ability to establish and maintain positive relationships, respect others' needs and show empathy (New Zealand Education Review Office, 2016). Fiji's EMIS may be one of the most comprehensive examples with respect to disability (**Box 3.2**).

In Colombia, inclusion indices go beyond primary and secondary schooling, having also been prepared for early childhood and higher education. The National Accreditation Council established the higher education assessment to guide institutional self-assessment of inclusion. Across Latin America, there has been an initiative for a harmonized regional education information system on students with disabilities (UNESCO, 2011).

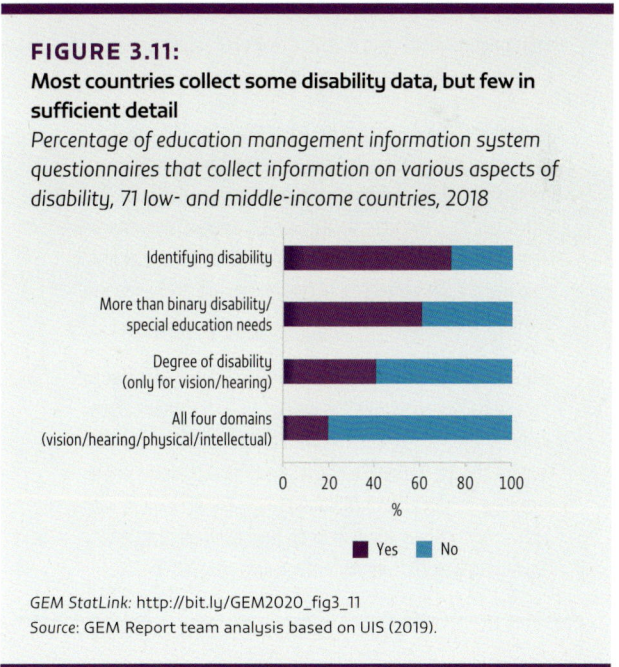

FIGURE 3.11:
Most countries collect some disability data, but few in sufficient detail
Percentage of education management information system questionnaires that collect information on various aspects of disability, 71 low- and middle-income countries, 2018

GEM StatLink: http://bit.ly/GEM2020_fig3_11
Source: GEM Report team analysis based on UIS (2019).

BOX 3.2:

The education management information system in Fiji focuses on inclusion

Across Pacific Island states, there have been efforts to improve indicators for disability-inclusive education (Sharma, 2016). The evolution of Fiji's EMIS is an instructive example of good practice. The online, individual-level system replaced the previous school-level system in 2013; technical and financial support came from the Australia-funded Access to Quality Education Program.

While disability disaggregation was possible from the beginning, the system was initially limited: Teachers gave simple responses to whether disabilities on a list were present and there were no instructions or training on how to respond (Sprunt, 2014). The system was expanded in 2013 to include a more sophisticated disability disaggregation toolkit based on the MICS Module on Child Functioning. Standard questions improve the chance of data being comparable with findings from sample surveys using the same questions (Fiji Ministry of Education, Heritage and Arts, 2016, 2017).

Among other components, teachers receive a guidebook and are trained to assess the difficulties students experience, compared with children of the same age. They are encouraged to complete a student learning profile for any child who consistently performs poorly. The form is meant to be completed with parents, taking clinical assessments into account when appropriate. Parents and teachers review the assessments and agree on any need for targeted support.

Student-level information in the system is complemented with school information, including an accessibility audit. Involvement by disabled persons' organizations and students with disabilities and their families is encouraged. The system records information on the services needed and those available. Crucially, the estimated cost of closing any gaps between the two is also recorded.

Schools provide information on out-of-school children with disabilities known to them, as well as on engagement, such as home visits. There are links with the national teacher data system and the national literacy and numeracy assessment database. Schools are encouraged to assess all children without undue concern over the effects on their average test results (Fiji Ministry of Education, Heritage and Arts, 2017).

> " Collecting data on inclusion can itself be part of making schools and systems more inclusive "

During the first phase, 8 countries used a reduced questionnaire with 14 of 42 originally proposed qualitative and quantitative indicators on the normative and policy framework along with statistical information. One finding was that relatively low shares of mainstream primary schools received students with disabilities, ranging from 40% in Brazil to 2.5% in Paraguay (UNESCO, 2013).

DATA COLLECTION SHOULD PROMOTE INCLUSION

Monitoring, evaluation, accountability and learning should not only serve the function of collecting data on inclusion but also be inclusive in methodology and actively foster inclusion (Save the Children, 2016). Collecting data on inclusion can itself be part of making schools and systems more inclusive. The choice of indicators directs attention to issues that may have been ignored. School self-assessments are part of finding solutions to overcoming barriers to inclusion. The Fiji EMIS data collection process, for instance, improves teacher awareness and encourages more nuanced thinking about inclusion.

The Monitoring Framework for Inclusive Education in Serbia, initiated by UNICEF and the government's Social Inclusion and Poverty Reduction Unit, is a well-elaborated framework suitable for national adoption. It includes indicators for inter-sectoral monitoring and identifies minimal and optimal indicator sets, including for identifying disparity among school authorities, municipalities and schools in terms of inclusion success. It has clear reporting cycles and assigned roles for information collection. It also envisages consolidation of information from school and municipal reports, the national statistical office, the national EMIS, other organizations' research, and special surveys (Serbia Social Inclusion and Poverty Reduction Unit and UNICEF, 2014). The framework has been integrated within the overall school quality assurance policy and quality standards for schools (Nedeljkovic, 2019).

> Comprehensive data collection that helps monitor equity and inclusion without creating stigma at the individual level is possible

The Inclusive Futures in Rwanda programme similarly went beyond data collection and monitoring. By establishing monitoring teams, the project was able to monitor and evaluate its own data collection process, as well as evaluate the impact of the standards, tools, roles and norms it proposed, which are now included in the ministry guide to inclusive education (Murenzi and McGeown, 2015; Rwanda Education Board, 2016).

Inclusive data collection asks questions of all concerned, from head teachers and teachers to government officials, local partners, parents and students. Community-based surveys can respond to this challenge. A community-based EMIS in Tajikistan that collected information on out-of-school children and attendance of enrolled children both motivated community solutions and informed district policies (Save the Children, 2016). Perhaps the best-known inclusion-oriented data collection initiative is that of the People's Action for Learning Network, whose citizen-led learning assessments collected and widely shared data on education attainment and achievement in schools and households to raise awareness and a sense of ownership in the community, notably in India and Pakistan (Rose and Sabates, 2017).

For non-academic outcomes especially, it is important to consult with children and young people directly and elicit their views, not only to monitor outcomes but also to foster inclusive practices (Messiou, 2008). Article 12 of the UN Convention on the Rights of the Child explicitly requires student consultation. This is possible even if the child has communication difficulties or limited formal language skills (Fayette and Bond, 2017). Ensuring that children can express dissent, including non-verbally, and that all children's voices are heard is a crucial consideration (Porter, 2014).

CONCLUSION

Data on inclusion deliver a clear message: Many millions continue to be excluded from education access and success. Among them, disproportionately, are women; people living in poverty; ethnic, religious and linguistic minorities; people with disabilities; and, especially, those experiencing intersecting sources of discrimination and disadvantage. To reach the excluded requires understanding who they are and the barriers they face.

Many countries still struggle to collect meaningful data for inclusion of educationally disadvantaged populations. Comprehensive data collection that helps monitor equity and inclusion without creating stigma at the individual level is possible. Inclusion of data on qualitative experiences at the school level in the national EMIS is a promising approach. Comprehensive data on inclusion must cover inputs, processes and outcomes at all levels of the system.

Monitoring education inequality at the system level requires identifying specific groups. Whether involving ethnicity or poverty, such categorization will always be imperfect. With respect to disability, data collection needs to use standardized best-practice instruments based on the Washington Group's set of questions and the Module on Child Functioning that adapts them to children.

By contrast, inclusion at the individual learner level is best served by avoiding categorization and labels as much as possible. Assumptions about what learners can or cannot do, based on assigned categories, should be replaced with understanding of every individual's abilities and their experience of exclusion and inclusion.

Schoolchildren eat midday meals
at Mondalpara High School,
Mondalpara Gaighata, West Bengal.

CREDIT: UNICEF/Altaf

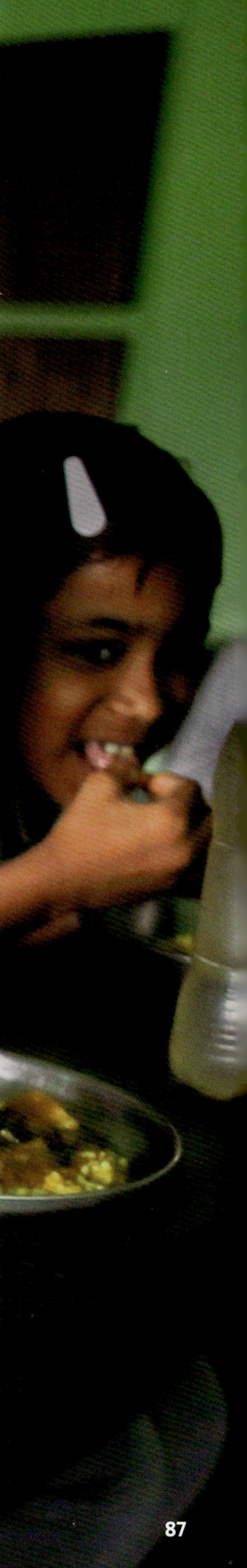

Governance and finance

How should countries manage and finance inclusion?

KEY MESSAGES

Inclusive education requires horizontal collaboration to share information, set standards and sequence support services, but implementation is often thwarted

- Kenya established Educational Assessment and Resource Centres with multidisciplinary professional teams, but one-third of county-level centres had only one officer.

- Services need to be complementary. In Colombia, social programmes are tied to a poverty index score for each family, which they can consult to see the services they are eligible for.

- Standards need to be coherent. In Jordan, the ministries of education and social development set separate standards for licensing and accrediting special education centres.

- Governments need capacity to regulate NGOs. China aims to put in place an effective system to purchase services from them and pass relevant legislation by the end of 2020.

Inclusive education requires vertical collaboration among government levels for local authorities to fulfil their mandates

- In the Republic of Moldova, an inclusive education reform stumbled because savings from reducing the number of children in residential institutions were not transferred to the local government institutions and schools absorbing the students.

- In the United Kingdom, the number of children with special needs increased by 33% between 2015 and 2019, while the funding local councils received rose by only 7%.

Equity and inclusion will not be achieved without adequate funding reaching schools and students according to need

- Governments finance local authorities or schools. In Indonesia, poorer districts with lower capacity to raise revenue struggle and inter-municipal inequality in attainment has grown.

- Education programmes may target students and families through exemptions (e.g. from fees), cash transfers (e.g. scholarships) or in-kind transfers (e.g. school meals). A 2018 law in Finland aims to reduce fees to minimize the effects of socio-economic background.

- Social protection financing policies and programmes also target students and families, affecting equity and inclusion in education. Since the 1990s, conditional cash transfer programmes in Latin America have increased education attainment by 0.5 to 1.5 years.

- About 310 million schoolchildren in low- and middle-income countries receive a daily meal at school. A government-led school feeding programme in Ghana targeting priority districts increased test scores, especially among girls, poor children and those from northern regions.

Providing education for students with disabilities involves extra and often mounting costs

- Evidence from Europe and Northern America suggests it costs about 2 to 2.5 times more to educate students with disabilities.

- Many high-income countries are trying to remove incentives to increase the number of students with special needs, shifting funding to block grants to local authorities.

The main barrier to inclusion in education is the lack of public policy and financial support.

Anne Kole, public health policy advisor at EURORDIS and parent, France

Education governance encompasses a dense network of institutions, rules and norms that determine policy formulation, implementation and monitoring. As the 2009 *EFA Global Monitoring Report* proposed, a review of governance arrangements in education should capture not only formal administrative and management systems but also informal processes that distribute power in these systems and determine decision making at all levels. Other chapters of this report cover aspects of education governance that have an impact on inclusion, such as standard-setting processes through laws and policies (see **Chapter 2**), monitoring and evaluation mechanisms (see **Chapter 3**) and communities' role in holding government to account (see **Chapter 8**).

This chapter focuses on mobilization of the organizational and financial actors required to make education systems inclusive. Weak collaboration, cooperation and coordination of stakeholders within the system (from early childhood to adult education), across sectors (e.g. reaching out to health and social protection), across government levels (from central to local) and between government and non-state institutions (e.g. civil society or the private sector) can impede implementation of ambitious laws and policies (**Figure 4.1**).

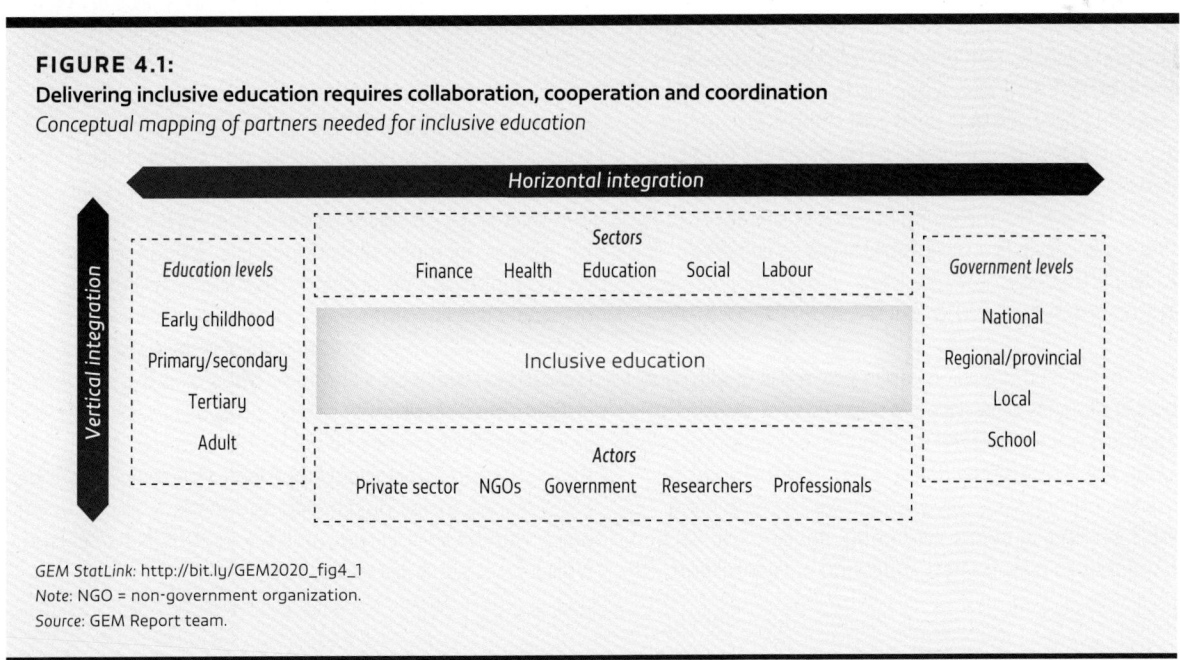

FIGURE 4.1:
Delivering inclusive education requires collaboration, cooperation and coordination
Conceptual mapping of partners needed for inclusive education

GEM StatLink: http://bit.ly/GEM2020_fig4_1
Note: NGO = non-government organization.
Source: GEM Report team.

The chapter addresses collaboration, cooperation and coordination from two viewpoints. First, considering the need to break down silos in policy formulation and implementation, which is the hallmark of the United Nations (UN) 2030 Agenda for Sustainable Development, it looks at how education ministries establish strong partnerships between education levels, between government levels, with other sectors and with non-government stakeholders. Second, it looks at the financing of services for equity and inclusion, including mechanisms to allocate education resource to regions, schools and students. It also looks at social protection programmes that target vulnerable groups and can affect education, concluding with a review of financing mechanisms for disability-inclusive education.

DELIVERING INCLUSIVE EDUCATION REQUIRES MULTIPLE ACTORS TO WORK TOGETHER

Ensuring equal education opportunities for those at risk of exclusion is not the sole responsibility of education policy designers. It requires mobilizing multiple actors and aligning the administrative systems supporting various facets of vulnerable populations' lives. Responsibilities for delivering inclusive education need to be shared horizontally among government departments or government and non-government actors, as well as vertically across education or government levels, taking their respective advantages into account.

Integrating services has two main benefits. First, it allows for greater consideration of a child's full set of needs, including health, well-being, participation, social justice and equality. Services that form part of holistic care are more accessible and more likely to be taken up. Greater awareness of services and how they are linked also increases uptake. By improving needs identification and promoting accessibility, integrated services can also positively affect outcomes for those with complex needs (CfBT Education Trust, 2010; Corter, 2019; OECD, 2015).

Second, integrated provision can improve the quality and cost-effectiveness of services, leading to cost savings. Integration can be achieved through case management whereby one service provider acts as a referral point for access to another. It can also be achieved by providing multiple services at single sites or by reducing transaction costs related to travel, safety, nutrition or mental and

> Weak collaboration, cooperation and coordination of stakeholders can impede implementation of ambitious laws and policies

emotional health. Co-locating services can reduce duplication. Cooperative arrangements, in which various service professionals communicate and work together on behalf of individual users, can also improve service quality (OECD, 2015; Statham, 2011).

Interministerial responsibility-sharing arrangements are common

Government agencies generally share administrative responsibilities for delivery of inclusive education. A mapping of inclusive education implementation in 18 European countries, mostly regarding students with disabilities, showed substantial division of labour. Education ministries tend to be responsible for providing additional teachers, running mainstream and special schools and providing learning materials. In most countries, health ministries bear responsibility for screening, assessment and rehabilitation services, while social protection ministries tend to provide financial aid and advice (**Figure 4.2**). Regional and local authorities lead on physical accessibility or extracurricular support. Transport and public works ministries are also involved in promoting infrastructure accessibility (European Agency for Special Needs and Inclusive Education, 2016).

Structures bringing together government entities to coordinate service delivery are a common first step towards integration. In New Zealand, the Ministerial Committee on Disability Issues is the government focal point on implementation of the UN Convention on the Rights of Persons with Disabilities and the national disability strategy. It also outlined priorities for cross-government action in the Disability Action Plan 2014–2018, which aimed to transform the support system, ensure personal safety, promote access and increase employment and economic opportunities. Regular reports documented progress on these priorities. For instance, developing policy options for children under age 8 with disabilities was on track in 2018 (New Zealand Office for Disability Issues, 2015, 2018).

FIGURE 4.2:

To ensure inclusion, education ministries share responsibility with other ministries and local government

Division of administrative responsibilities for inclusive education in 18 European countries, 2014–15

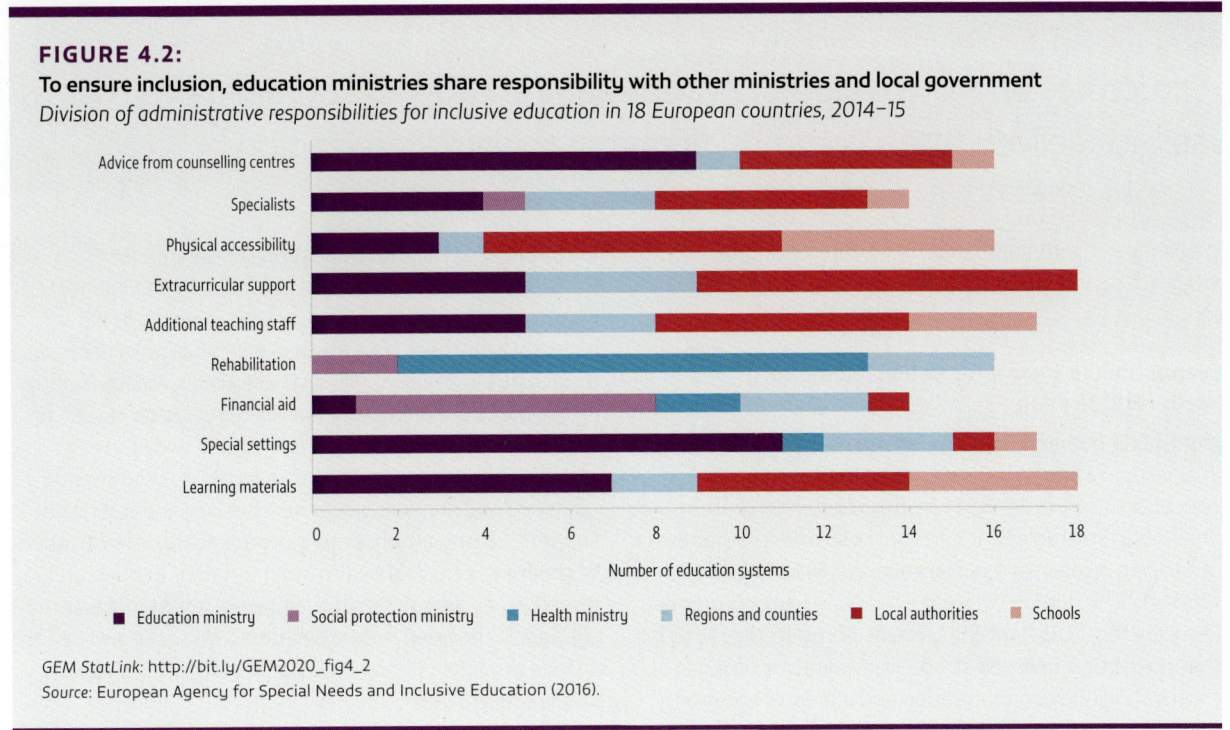

Number of education systems

- ■ Education ministry
- ■ Social protection ministry
- ■ Health ministry
- ■ Regions and counties
- ■ Local authorities
- ■ Schools

GEM StatLink: http://bit.ly/GEM2020_fig4_2
Source: European Agency for Special Needs and Inclusive Education (2016).

However, sharing responsibility does not always imply collaboration, cooperation and coordination. Deep-rooted norms, traditions and bureaucratic cultures hinder smooth transition from traditional siloed service delivery to innovative collaboration and cooperation between education and other sectors. Variable access to and quality of social services create additional, overlapping obstacles to effective integration. Inadequate training, ineffective communication with educators, lack of shared vision or overarching policy framework, and variation in standards across regions also inhibit efficient service provision (Lawrence and Thorne, 2016; Lord et al., 2008).

Serbia's government established local coordination mechanisms among the education, health and social sectors to identify needs and provide support to all children (Serbia Prime Minister's Office, 2019). However, coordinating state financing structures was challenging, and local coordinating body recommendations were not binding for service providers (NOOIS, 2018). Kyrgyzstan, the Lao People's Democratic Republic, Tajikistan and Uzbekistan cited lack of coordination as

a challenge hindering planning and implementation of inclusive education programmes for children with disabilities (Global Partnership for Education, 2018a). In Sierra Leone, the 2011 National Disability Act established a national commission for people with disabilities, composed of representatives of several ministries and NGOs, with responsibility for issuing disability certificates to recognize rights and provide access to services (Sierra Leone Government, 2011). However, implementation has been very slow as a result of lack of staff and financing (Tigere and Moyo, 2019).

HORIZONTAL COLLABORATION IS A PRECONDITION FOR INCLUSIVE EDUCATION

As education outcomes are strongly correlated with health, poverty and social exclusion, integrated service delivery that encourages collaboration across social services can efficiently address disadvantaged students' challenges. Economic, social, cultural or physical vulnerability is not best addressed when sectors work in isolation. Horizontal integration connects services but also professions, policy groups and non-government actors across sectors to make education services more inclusive and holistic (Munday, 2007; OECD, 2015). This section discusses types of collaboration, highlighting the context-specific opportunities and

> " Variable access to and quality of social services create additional, overlapping obstacles to effective integration "

> ❝ Structures bringing together government entities to coordinate service delivery are a common first step towards integration ❞

challenges governments face when attempting to integrate services.[1]

Sectors should share information related to needs identification

Identifying populations to be served is a crucial first step in developing integrated services to improve inclusive education. Early childhood identification, intervention and prevention strategies are far more cost-effective, in terms of tackling disability, disadvantage, vulnerability and social exclusion, than corrective measures later (European Commission, 2016; UNESCO, 2006). Some studies suggest that prevention-oriented strategies facilitate inter-agency cooperation and communication and a greater focus on the family than do correction-oriented strategies (CfBT Education Trust, 2010).

In Nordic countries, identification of risk and needs for specialized support starts before birth. In Finland, maternity and child health clinics reach virtually all expecting mothers, as a medical examination is necessary to receive a maternity grant. These clinics, located within municipal health centres, monitor the physical health of mothers and young children and offer a wide range of other services, including health education, child-rearing guidance and support, social services and mental health support. Strong emphasis is placed on early identification of children's physical health and mental or behavioural disorders, as well as family well-being. Additional tailored support is provided in coordination with social and health service providers (Finland National Institute for Health and Welfare, 2019).

Croatia harmonized procedures for assessing the needs of learners with autism spectrum disorders and established committees that included representatives of all education and support stakeholders (European Agency for Special

---

1 This section is based on Patana (2020).

ADENE

> Identifying populations to be served is a crucial first step in developing integrated services to improve inclusive education

Needs and Inclusive Education, 2016). In the Republic of Korea, Dream Start centres identify vulnerable families based on administrative data records and subsequent letters and home visits (Republic of Korea Ministry of Health and Welfare, 2019).

Kenya established Educational Assessment and Resource Centres to increase the number of children assessed and expand education access and transition from primary to secondary and vocational schools for children with disabilities. Multidisciplinary teams of professionals were to involve the community in early identification, assessment, intervention and placement of children with special needs in integrated programmes. However, a national survey in 2016/17 found that one-third of county-level centres had only one officer, just 15% had speech therapists, and staff had not been trained to use the revised assessment tool. The 2018 Sector Policy for Learners and Trainees with Disabilities aims to address these weaknesses (Kenya Ministry of Education, 2018). Ultimately, lack of implementation means relatively few learners with disabilities are enrolled in mainstream schools and segregated education persists (Kiru, 2019).

In South Africa, the National Strategy on Screening, Identification, Assessment and Support was one of six elements in the 2001 Education White Paper, a broader commitment to improve inclusive education, integrate learners with special needs into the education system and better respond to the needs of children at risk of marginalization and learners in special education. The strategy, a result of collaboration among agencies, schools and stakeholders, paved the way for additional services through district- and institution-based support teams and special school centres. Education professionals, parents, schools and districts complete a Support Needs Assessment to identify barriers to learning and develop a support strategy to overcome them. Guidelines help parents and service providers navigate the process (South Africa Department of Basic Education, 2014). However, studies point to slow implementation and differences in practices and beliefs (Donohue and Bornman, 2014).

The Framework for the Assessment of Children in Need and their Families, initially developed in England and Wales (United Kingdom), was adapted in more than 15 countries, including Canada, New Zealand and the Russian Federation (Léveillé and Chamberland, 2010). The Common Assessment Framework, used as part of the Every Child Matters strategy in England (United Kingdom), took a standardized approach to assessing children and their families, identifying their needs and providing support in a coordinated manner. It sought to provide additional coordinated services to those below the threshold of intensive support (e.g. child protection) to encourage a client-centred approach (Holmes et al., 2012; OECD, 2015).

Some multidisciplinary social programmes that disburse cash benefits conditional on children's use of a range of education and health services determine access to benefits on the basis of household income and means tests. In Colombia, Más Familias en Acción (More Families in Action) is a cash transfer programme conditional on school attendance and health service use. It serves 2.7 million poor families targeted through two complementary mechanisms. First, three registries are used to certify vulnerability: beneficiaries of the extreme poverty programme Red Unidos (United Network), victims of displacement and those enumerated in the Indigenous Census. Second, the National Planning Department's multidimensional Beneficiary Identification System for Social Programmes index uses proxy characteristics to estimate living standards. The programme's management information system uses information technology to improve operational efficiency and reduce families' participation costs (Medellín and Sánchez Prada, 2015).

Countries lacking technical means to identify children and families most in need have simpler ways of targeting. For instance, Cambodia's Second Education Sector Support Project used geographical targeting based on district gross enrolment ratios to expand disadvantaged children's access to early childhood care and education (ECCE). A synergistic approach involving 14 ministries increased interventions' impact (World Bank, 2018).

Standard setting is essential for sectors to communicate

When developing and implementing integrated service delivery, clear definition of standards and objectives is key to ensuring their effectiveness and quality. Well-defined, measurable standards outline actors' responsibilities, the desired outcomes of integration and the dimensions

> **"** Some studies note that lack of clearly defined standards and framework is a major impediment to integrating education and health services **"**

in which policies will be evaluated. Some studies note that lack of clearly defined standards and framework is a major impediment to integrating education and health services (Lawrence and Thorne, 2016).

Chile established an Agency for Quality Education to pool information across government sectors for monitoring and evaluating education outcomes (OECD, 2017a). The country had already reformed its ECCE curriculum, for instance creating an inter-institutional commission that brought together stakeholders and professionals from various sectors involved (Kaga et al., 2010) (**Box 4.1**).

Standards and guidelines are also necessary for development of collaborative practices, capacity and joint working. Rwanda's Inclusive Futures project

BOX 4.1:

Chile's Crece Contigo early childhood programme set clear standards

Chile Crece Contigo (Chile Grows with You) is a comprehensive early childhood programme covering prenatal to age 4. Through strong political will and consensus-based policy development, it provides coordinated services across all relevant sectors. Municipalities coordinate education, health and social teams. A coordinating body at the Ministry of Social Development and a 2009 law that institutionalized the programme and provided a permanent budget line facilitated national expansion. Resources were allocated to the health and education ministries through transfer agreements and to municipalities through direct transfer agreements. The agreements specified technical standards for institutions, providing a quality control mechanism.

The programme is part of the social protection system, which includes psychosocial support for extremely poor families. Successful expansion was also a result of incremental improvements to existing systems, which promoted collaboration among the health, social protection and education sectors and built on municipal social protection programmes. Local health and education teams' skills and competences have increased. Progress is inter-sectoral and participatory, indicating continuous feedback to the local level (Milman et al., 2018).

developed inspection standards to assess classroom inclusivity so as to increase enrolment of children with disabilities and improve their learning outcomes. For instance, inspectors determined whether learning materials were accessible to all students with special education needs. The Rwanda Education Board helped define, harmonize and monitor the standards using their inspectors, which helped develop capacity and promote sustainability (Murenzi and McGeown, 2015).

Since 1995, the Early Head Start and Head Start programmes in the United States, which provide comprehensive early education, health and social services to disadvantaged children and youth, have included performance standards mandating service providers to work towards improving coordination and communication among them and to record their efforts. The programmes have been effective in promoting cooperation and establishing partnerships among local providers, ensuring access to a variety of services to help families be self-sufficient, including families of children with disabilities (Vogel and Xue, 2018).

Problems arise where standards are not harmonized. In Jordan, the 1993 disability law transferred responsibility for the education of most students with special needs to the Ministry of Education from the Ministry of Social Development, which retained responsibility for diagnosis, care, training and rehabilitation of those with mild to severe learning difficulties (Abu-Hamour and Al-Hmouz, 2014). The Higher Council for Affairs of Persons with Disabilities was established to coordinate actors at the national level. However, lack of coordination persisted. The Ministry of Education had a special education directorate, while the Ministry of Social Development and the Higher Council set their respective separate standards for licensing and accrediting special education centres (Jordan Government, 2016). The 2017 disability law aimed to resolve these issues, and the 10-year strategy to implement the law's inclusive education commitments envisaged developing inclusive school standards and curriculum development standards (Jordan Ministry of Education, 2020; Tabazah, 2017).

Integration allows services to be sequenced

Case management and co-location are key in efforts to integrate services for vulnerable children and youth, although the sequencing of services depends on education and child and family welfare structures (OECD, 2015; Sloper, 2004). Where access to child and maternity clinics, ECCE and other specialized services is free and universal, basic education and health services often act as an entry point for referral to additional, more specialized, multidisciplinary services.

Most children can be reached through schools, which can play a central role in support, for instance through school-based health. A policy review of global nutrition in 160 countries showed that 89% had some type of school health and nutrition programme (WHO, 2018). South Africa's Integrated School Health Policy, initiated in 2012, provides a package of basic health services at all schools. They include preventive measures for physical and emotional health, and treatment for visual impairment, mental health and HIV/AIDS (South Africa Department of Basic Education, 2015). In the United States, school-based health centres offer co-located, multidisciplinary support to primary and secondary school students through case management. They have reduced gaps in access to health services among disadvantaged groups, such as students with disabilities and racial minorities, for preventive care, treatment of chronic illness and health risk behaviour reduction (Arenson et al., 2019). In Nordic countries, health, mental health and social support are available to all learners in compulsory education (Nordic Welfare Centre, 2019).

'One-stop shops' are the ideal in service delivery to individuals and households with multiple and complex needs. Some are universal, such as Sweden's family centres, which provide preventive, low-threshold support services to all. These multidisciplinary, co-located services seek to identify mental, physical and social challenges early and provide integrated services to address them. Case managers help ensure that families in need get access to specialized services (Kekkonen et al., 2012). Norway's 0-to-24 Cooperation seeks to bring together four ministries to support all children and young people, recognizing that inclusive service provision is not a child-specific need (UNESCO, 2019a). Smoother coordination between education and health authorities is at the heart of a recent white paper on early intervention and inclusive communities, which focuses on grade 1 to 4 students at risk of falling behind in reading, writing and mathematics (Norway Government, 2019).

> " 'One-stop shops' are the ideal in service delivery to individuals and households with multiple and complex needs "

Other initiatives target families at risk of exclusion or disadvantage. The United Kingdom's Sure Start provides education, health and social services, focusing on socially deprived areas. It offers co-located, nearby and home-based services to children under age 5 and their families, aiming to prevent intergenerational transmission of disadvantage and improve children's cognitive and language development, education and other outcomes (Bate and Foster, 2017). Countries including Australia (Children's Contact Services) and Hungary (Sure Start) have similar targeted initiatives (Patana, 2020).

Arrangements of this type also show great potential for reaching disadvantaged and disengaged youth. Brazil's Public Employment Service established Estação Juventude (Youth Station) to address difficulties related to the large number of unintegrated programmes targeting youth (OECD, 2014). It combines information on education and employment opportunities with personalized, multidisciplinary services that address young people's specific needs and facilitate their autonomy and social inclusion. The services are set up in partnership with state and municipal governments; the infrastructure depends on local needs and the social partners taking part (Brazil National Secretariat of Youth, 2017). Related initiatives have been established in countries including Finland (Ohjaamo), France (Missions Locales), New Zealand (Youth Service) and the United Kingdom (Connexions) (Patana, 2020).

In Colombia, several social programmes are linked. The links are facilitated partly by unified databases: Vulnerable families can consult their multidimensional poverty index score and check which programmes they are eligible for. Links are promoted by design. Beneficiaries of Más Familias en Acción, the health and education conditional cash transfer programme, have priority to join Jóvenes en Acción (Youth in Action), another conditional transfer programme providing academic training and life skills relevant to the labour market for poor and vulnerable youth. Many families benefiting from Más Familias en Acción are also registered in Red Unidos, the extreme poverty programme. Administrators guide families on access to public services appropriate to their situations. A handbook lists available programmes, including those related to education and training (Medellín and Sánchez Prada, 2015).

Horizontal collaboration between government and non-government actors is needed

In many countries, non-government actors play a major role in provision of inclusive education (see **Chapter 8**). Governments contract out specific services to NGOs, although regulation of the organizations varies substantially. In Malta, for instance, the government finances NGOs supporting children and adults with dyslexia and other learning difficulties (Bezzina, 2018). However, service agreements would benefit from a stronger focus on quality assurance standards (European Agency for Special Needs and Inclusive Education, 2015).

In India, through the Assistance to Disabled Persons Scheme, established in 1981, NGOs serve as implementing agencies, buying and fitting aids and appliances for children with disabilities. There are registry requirements, income eligibility requirements and periodic revision of eligible aids or appliances for those with visual, hearing, locomotor, mental and multiple disabilities. The government website includes details of institutions that have received grants and information on suspended or blacklisted NGOs, e.g. those that during monitoring visits could not prove distribution of funds (India Ministry of Social Justice and Empowerment, 2017, 2019).

Some countries are moving to formalize relationships with NGOs to make them more robust and transparent. In Indonesia, most national and international NGOs relied on donor funding (Davis, 2013). A 2018 presidential regulation made it easier for them to bid on government contracts to provide services for hard-to-reach populations, including those in remote areas, ethnic and religious minorities and people with disabilities (Jackson, 2018). In countries where donors have greater influence and provide significant financing for inclusive education, the government's role in managing or regulating NGOs may be more tenuous, as NGOs can be more wary of formalized, hierarchical arrangements and contracts (Rose, 2011).

Governments need to develop capacity to regulate NGOs. The Chinese government's 2013 State Council Office's Guidance on Purchasing Services from Society supported local authorities in purchasing public services, including education. The government aims to have an effective purchasing system in place and pass relevant legislation at the local level by 2020. However, an analysis of integrated family service centres in Guangzhou contracted to NGOs suggested that local-level officials needed more training to develop contracts and evaluation arrangements and manage relationships with the NGOs (Kwan Chan and Lei, 2017).

VERTICAL COLLABORATION IS CRITICAL FOR INCLUSIVE EDUCATION

Vertical integration of governance and financing promotes cooperation and coordination among government or education levels to harmonize standards, share data, ensure full funding of commitments and improve monitoring and evaluation of student outcomes.

Local governments need support to provide inclusive education

A common criticism of centralized governance systems is that, through one-size-fits-all policies and limited autonomy at lower levels, they are less likely to promote local ownership. In principle, decentralization aligns needs with preferences and improves accountability. However, underfunding of mandates granted to local actors and failure to develop local capacity may worsen inequality.

For instance, China is constitutionally a unitary state, and provinces have limited autonomy in raising revenue. Yet it is the world's most decentralized country in terms of subnational share of total expenditure (85%), which has resulted in unfunded mandates. Only 5% of education, which is a joint mandate, is centrally funded. While provinces step in to equalize allocations at the county level, a recent reform aims to increase central government's role in reducing regional disparity and improve public service delivery (Wingender, 2018).

To strike the right balance between centralized and decentralized systems, governments ideally maintain a

> " Underfunding of mandates granted to local actors and failure to develop local capacity may worsen inequality "

> **Several countries have recently undergone decentralization, with local institutions assuming increased responsibility for inclusive education**

level of control, for instance developing and monitoring delivery standards and managing funding transfers, while striving to strengthen local institutional capacity (European Agency for Special Needs and Inclusive Education, 2017a). Overlaps or gaps in responsibilities can prevent local governments and schools from delivering inclusive education that meets standards. In Iceland, overlapping roles and responsibilities between the Ministry of Education and municipalities led to disagreement over funding and hampered formal collaboration among bodies and agencies. Local and school stakeholders argued that, while language around inclusive education had changed, practices had not. Only the municipality of the capital, Reykjavík, developed a formal inclusive education policy. Regional variation in implementation led to demand for guidance on minimum standards (European Agency for Special Needs and Inclusive Education, 2017b).

An analysis of inclusive education in Europe found that many implementation weaknesses were linked to governance mechanisms that did not ensure sufficient resources or allow for inter-institutional cooperation and coordinated provision. Local authorities lacked capacity to use resources efficiently, and schools lacked staff to assist learners (European Agency for Special Needs and Inclusive Education, 2016).

Several countries have recently undergone decentralization, with local institutions assuming increased responsibility for inclusive education. Colombia's Ministry of National Education provides guidelines for inclusive education and works with national institutes for the blind and the deaf to create inclusive programmes. Regional education departments implement the policy. They carry out identification and enrolment campaigns for children with disabilities, in coordination with other government entities, then develop progressive implementation plans (Colombia Ministry of National Education, 2017).

As part of its commitment to fulfil the right to inclusive education enshrined in the 1997 General Education Act, the Dominican Republic has established regional resource centres since 2004. These promote whole-school

improvement processes to enable development of inclusive education through support, counselling, educator and administrator training, and guidance to families (Dominican Republic Ministry of Education, 2008; UNESCO, 2018).

In Nepal, authority for education delivery was decentralized through the 1999 Local Self-Governance Act and strengthened with a new federal political structure (Nepal Ministry of Education, 2016). A midterm evaluation of the current school sector programme and an initial inclusive education workshop found that, while some central government posts were being shifted, provincial and local government capacity to support decentralized education service delivery was weak (Asian Development Bank, 2019; Hunt and Poudyal, 2019).

The Republic of Moldova Ministry of Education cooperates with the Institute of Education Sciences and the Republican Centre of Psycho-pedagogical Assistance to develop and manage inclusive education policy implementation. At the district level, the Education Directorate, inclusive education officers and the psycho-pedagogical assistance service implement the policy, identify needs and support professional development. At the local level, multidisciplinary intra-school commissions, individualized education plan teams, resource centres for inclusive education and assistance personnel have direct contact with parents and families to ensure child protection (Republic of Moldova Ministry of Education, Culture and Research, 2017).

Many European countries frame cooperation with formal agreements. In Italy, national- and regional-level framework agreements regulate, integrate and coordinate the policies of entities involved in education, social and health interventions. In the Netherlands, there are agreements with school alliances and communities responsible for youth care, health and social services. In Portugal, municipalities and the Ministry of Education sign contracts governing implementation of national policies: Primary and secondary schools can enter into formal agreements with the ministry that increase their autonomy in curricular and pedagogical organization,

> Decentralization can exacerbate inequality when it does not take fully into account local governments' uneven capacity for mobilizing resources

human resource management, social support and financial management (European Agency for Special Needs and Inclusive Education, 2016).

Local government inclusive education mandates need to be fully funded

Ensuring that resources match local- and school-level service delivery commitments requires central governments to monitor the situation and support entities that struggle to raise the necessary resources. Decentralization can exacerbate inequality when it does not take fully into account local governments' uneven capacity for mobilizing resources, a concern that applies across social spending commitments.

In the Republic of Moldova, a reform sought to support inclusive education, moving children out of residential institutions, most of which were Ministry of Education boarding schools. An evaluation showed that the reform stumbled because savings from reducing the number of children in residential institutions were not transferred to the local government institutions and schools absorbing the students (Evans, 2013).

In the United Kingdom, central government funding for students with special education needs is provided to local councils' education budgets. While the number of children and youth with an education, health and care plan rose by 33% between 2015 and 2019, from 240,000 to 320,000, funding to local councils increased by 7% (Weale, 2019).

In the US state of Wisconsin, the cost of special education eligible for state aid increased by 18% between 2008 and 2018, but state aid remained flat and fell as a share of total special education spending, from 29% to 25%. Federal aid also remained flat. Cash-strapped districts have therefore diverted resources from mainstream education, as they must cover the cost of, for instance, speech language pathology, physical therapy, classroom aids, modified curriculum, counselling, transport and school nursing (Wisconsin Taxpayer, 2019).

Transition between education levels requires coherence and coordination

Transition between education levels requires coordination to ensure that delivery continues smoothly. An analysis of early childhood to primary education transition policies in 30 high-income countries found growing attention to this issue in strategy and policy documents. Early childhood

> About three in four countries noted that they provided specialist support, such as psychologists or care workers, for children with special needs during transition

education responsibilities are increasingly integrated within education ministries to facilitate collaboration, including for inclusive education. Austria developed a national strategy on transition, recognizing that its decentralized context meant several early childhood centres were not coordinating well with primary schools. Japan uses a five-level scale to evaluate collaboration quality among municipal stakeholders, assigning the top score when reviews have been undertaken to improve transition. Schools use self-evaluation and develop plans for collaboration and exchange at the beginning of each school year (OECD, 2017b).

Regarding the added challenges children from disadvantaged backgrounds face, policies to fill transition gaps include language support and financial support for early childhood education participation. About three in four countries noted that they provided specialist support, such as psychologists or care workers, for children with special needs during transition. The Netherlands Ministry of Education developed agreements with the 37 largest municipalities to track, and provide extra funding for, their efforts on targeted programmes for disadvantaged children, including collaborating with parents during transition (OECD, 2017b).

The transition between secondary and post-secondary education and integration into society is often much harder (Moriña, 2017). An evaluation of inclusive education provision in Iceland showed that municipal goals were ambitious at the preschool and compulsory education levels but less so at the upper secondary level (European Agency for Special Needs and Inclusive Education, 2017b). An analysis of how young people with disabilities experienced transitioning to tertiary education in Austria, the Czech Republic, Ireland and Spain found a lack of financial support and service delivery measures (Biewer et al., 2015).

THERE ARE SEVERAL ROUTES TO FINANCING EQUITY AND INCLUSION IN EDUCATION

Achieving equity and inclusion requires adequate funding reaching schools and students according to need. Countries pursue policies of varying form and intensity to mitigate the education impact of vulnerabilities such as poverty, ethnicity, disability and remoteness. In general, three funding levers are important in analysing financing for equity and inclusion in education.

First, governments pursue an overall policy of financing local authorities or schools. Such policies range from those aimed at ensuring that every authority or school receives the same level of resources per student (equality) to those meant to take characteristics of areas or schools (or their student populations) into account (equity). Policies may vary by type of school or by type of financial, human resource or material input, with approaches for distribution of maintenance grants, for instance, differing from those for teacher appointments or equipment purchases. More rarely, allocations may be determined by outcomes or have a performance element. General policies focusing on equality may be complemented by specific programmes compensating for disadvantage.

Second, education financing policies and programmes may target students and their families rather than authorities and schools. These may be in the form of cash (e.g. scholarships) or exemptions from payment (e.g. of fees), or in kind (e.g. school meals).

Third are financing policies and programmes, also targeting students and families, that are not education-specific but may affect equity and inclusion in education. These tend to be social protection programmes, such as conditional cash transfers or child grants with an education component that aim to address poverty, for instance with a gender dimension. Targeting mechanisms tend to be well articulated and regularly evaluated.

For each funding lever, the key aspects to consider when examining the potential impact on equity are whether specific policies or programmes to reallocate resources to disadvantaged areas or populations exist (and, if so, using what targeting criteria); the absolute volume or relative depth of spending (e.g. average transfer size); and the coverage in terms of percentage of schools, students or families reached.

> General policies focusing on equality may be complemented by specific programmes compensating for disadvantage

SOME COUNTRIES CONSIDER EQUITY IN THEIR FUNDING TO REGIONS OR SCHOOLS

Several countries devolve funds to the local level and may include a fiscal redistribution element to reduce disparity.

Poorer countries generally lack capacity for fund redistribution. As a first step, however, some have allocated funds transparently to districts or schools through capitation grants. Since 2003, Rwanda has provided schools with a simple capitation grant allocated to teaching and learning materials (50%), school maintenance (35%) and teacher training (15%), combined with a teacher salary top-up. The grant has provided basic funds to all schools and helped improve textbook availability, but its effect on teacher training is unknown, especially after that part of the grant was recentralized in 2012 (Milligan et al., 2017; Williams, 2017). No adjustment is made for schools needing more

funding (Rwanda Ministry of Finance and Economic Planning, 2017). Parental contributions to schools in richer areas exacerbate inequality (Paxton and Mutesi, 2012). Better targeting of the grant to poorer schools is needed to achieve universal secondary education (Department for International Development, 2016), a policy concern in many sub-Saharan African countries (**Box 4.2**).

Mauritania has been considering introducing education priority zones to coordinate activities addressing school disadvantage in selected geographical areas. The 2014–17 education sector action plan allocated 1.3% of resources to development of such zones, covering 150 schools, with an emphasis on promoting revenue-raising activities such as horticulture and school-managed shops where students could procure lower-cost materials (Mauritania Government, 2015).

BOX 4.2:

Sub-Saharan African countries struggle to finance recent commitments to provide free secondary education

In recent years, many sub-Saharan African countries have committed to delivering free secondary education, pursuing a range of funding strategies with mixed outcomes. There is a notable lack of attention to the equity implications of education expansion, when most countries are yet to achieve universal primary completion.

Uganda was the first to introduce a universal secondary education policy in 2007. For the first 10 years, it was financed through a public–private partnership. Up to one-third of students had access to over 800 publicly funded, privately managed schools in 2016. Some analyses have focused on the cost-effectiveness of this delivery mode (O'Donoghue et al., 2018), while others have highlighted its unaffordability (Malouf Bous and Farr, 2019). In 2018, the government decided to phase out such schools and instead support government school construction (Ahimbisibwe, 2018). However, the education share in the budget declined from 20% in 2004 to 12% in 2017, according to the UNESCO Institute for Statistics, and is projected to continue declining to 10.3% in 2019/20, casting doubt on the sustainability of the commitment (Mutegeki, 2019).

Kenya did away with secondary school tuition fees in 2008. The fees had accounted for about 40% of the total cost to households, which still paid for infrastructure, boarding and school uniforms. In 2016/17, the cost of the policy amounted to US$320 million, close to 2% of the budget or almost double the cost of the earlier free primary education policy. An evaluation found that the policy increased females' education attainment by about 0.75 years, decreased their probability of marriage before 18 by around 25% and increased their likelihood of skilled work by 28% (Brudevold-Newman, 2017).

The United Republic of Tanzania abolished lower secondary education fees in 2015. There had been significant increases to the education budget, which doubled between 2011/12 and 2015/16 (UNICEF, 2017). A simulation exercise estimated that the policy might increase lower secondary enrolment by over 50% by 2025, costing at least US$840 million per year by 2024 and representing an increase in the budget share of lower secondary education, from 19% in 2018 to 35% in 2024, to fund the additional 75,000 teachers and 30,000 classrooms. The analysis recommended cost-saving measures, especially on construction, to keep the expansion fiscally sustainable (Asim et al., 2019).

In Ghana, basic education has been free since 1992. A free upper secondary school policy was introduced in 2017 to meet increasing demand. While education has been well funded, education as a share of total recurrent public expenditure (excluding debt service) was expected to decrease, from a peak of 32.3% in 2015 to 21.3% in 2019 and 19.9% in 2020 (Global Partnership for Education, 2018b), which may be at odds with the free secondary school policy.

However, as of 2019 there had been no implementation progress (Aïdara, 2019).

Many countries that attempt to redistribute funds struggle to make an impact on inequality. Education financing in Argentina, a federal country, is in three parts. First, there are automatic transfers from the federal government to provincial governments. Rules for some of them are set in the 2006 education financing law, which takes rural and out-of-school populations into account (Argentina Government, 2006). However, these transfers do not sufficiently account for provincial differences (Rivas and Dborkin, 2018). Second, the ministries of education and public administration make non-automatic transfers to provinces and municipalities in implementing their nationwide programmes. Their effect on inequality is hard to estimate. Third, provinces co-finance education from their revenue, which provides the bulk of total education spending (Bertoni et al., 2018). As this revenue varies a lot, it is a major source of inequality. There are calls for a more centralized model to address interprovincial inequality, as well as for a review of non-automatic transfers to increase their effect on inequality (Claus and Sanchez, 2019). A recent comparison with other Latin American countries gives an idea of the lost redistribution potential (González, 2019).

In Indonesia, different mechanisms are used for the two main types of education expenditure. First, teacher salaries and allowances are paid through the General Allocation Grant. This unconditional grant transfers resources to local governments to cover salary costs. It also attempts to compensate for the difference between local needs and revenue, but inequality has been increasing (Akita et al., 2019; UNDP, 2019). Second, a capitation grant covers schools' operational and, since 2009, quality-related costs. Some districts complement this with a school grant. However, districts vary significantly in revenue-raising capacity, and the poorest struggle (OECD and ADB, 2015). Some studies focusing on inputs found that decentralization resulted in lower budgets and teachers with fewer qualifications in poorer schools. Teachers also spent less time in classrooms in rural areas (Leer, 2016). Another study, focusing on outcomes, found that decentralization increased inter-municipal inequality in attainment (Muttaqin et al., 2016).

Provinces in Sri Lanka also receive funds through two main channels. First, they receive block grants for salaries and recurrent non-salary expenditure. Almost all schools receive education quality input funds according to a formula that takes student population, school size and grade coverage into account. Second, provinces receive grants for capital expenditure, notably the Province Specific Development Grant, whose allocation is determined by four factors to equalize intra-provincial disparity: per capita income (40%), infrastructure (30%), health (15%) and education (15%), the latter in the form of an index based on enrolment and pass rates for five examinations (Sri Lanka Finance Commission, 2014). However, considerable disparity exists among districts in both resource allocation and examination results; in the latter case, within-district disparity was even higher than inter-district disparity. In addition to late, partial or non-receipt of funds, smaller schools with fewer resources have limited ability to raise funds, exacerbating disparity (Ranasinghe et al., 2016).

In assessing the inclusivity of budget practices, the value of targeting groups instead of targeting factors more broadly associated with underlying disadvantage is debatable. For instance, while students with immigrant backgrounds are a common policy concern in many high-income countries, migrant status is rarely explicitly included as a factor in financing schools. Belgium, England (United Kingdom), Israel and the Netherlands have either reduced or removed the focus on migrant status in favour of related factors, such as socio-economic status and parental education level (UNESCO, 2019b).

School feeding programmes can promote equity and inclusion

About 310 million schoolchildren in low- and middle-income countries receive a daily meal at school, with Brazil, China and India having some of the largest programmes (WFP, 2019a). Such programmes are a key part of poverty reduction strategies, using schools as venues to address malnutrition. They can also promote equity and inclusion by increasing poor students' attendance and learning outcomes, as improved nutrition and health can affect attention and cognitive functions (Bundy et al., 2018).

> **Many countries that attempt to redistribute funds struggle to make an impact on inequality**

> " A systematic analysis of 15 school feeding programmes found that overall they increased attendance "

Successful programmes provide meals of high nutritional quality and target children who might not otherwise get a meal at home. One concern has been inadequate emphasis on raising family awareness about nutrition and snack quality (Kristjansson et al., 2016). A systematic analysis of 15 school feeding programmes found that, despite wide variability, overall they increased attendance, particularly in contexts of food insecurity and low attendance rates. Evidence on learning outcomes has been less consistent (Snilstveit et al., 2015).

A randomized control trial evaluated a large-scale, government-led school feeding programme in Ghana, introduced after poverty and food insecurity rankings were developed to target priority districts. It found that the programme increased test scores, especially among girls, poor children and those from northern regions. The effect was the result of increased school participation and reduced time doing household chores. The study also countered earlier findings and criticisms that the programme did not target areas most in need (Aurino et al., 2018).

Many governments struggle to develop equitable and inclusive school feeding programmes. The civil war in Yemen left 53% of the population severely food insecure; about 2 million children under age 5 required treatment for acute malnutrition (Humanitarian Information Unit, 2018). The country relaunched school feeding in 2018 with the support of the World Food Programme, distributing high-energy biscuits and date bars to all primary schools across 13 governorates, reaching almost 400,000 students. More than half the snacks were locally produced and procured to shorten commodity lead times and support the local economy. A review of the context as part of World Bank's Systems Approach for Better Education Results identified an urgent need for a national school feeding policy that would lead to budget commitments, effective and efficient logistics and procurement focused on local sourcing and community participation, and a monitoring and evaluation system. An inter-sectoral steering committee was set up in 2019 to coordinate actions towards a national school feeding programme (WFP, 2019b).

The social aspect of school meals should not be ignored. Meaningful inclusion through sharing of school meals can be difficult to achieve in some contexts, as with the discrimination observed in the implementation of India's midday meal programme (**Box 4.3**).

EDUCATION PROGRAMMES TARGETING STUDENTS COMPENSATE FOR DISADVANTAGE

Education policies may target not only regions and schools but also individual learners and their families to ease financial and other constraints.

Several countries offer fee exemptions to increase access to education for girls, the poor and other vulnerable

---

BOX 4.3:

Caste discrimination mars the midday meal programme in India

India's midday meal programme was launched in 1995 to combat poverty and malnutrition and to promote primary school access and other education objectives. It went nationwide in 2001, after the Supreme Court ruled the midday meal a legal entitlement for all primary school children. The world's largest national school feeding programme, it serves more than 100 million children. Several studies have documented resulting increases in enrolment, attendance, retention and learning (Drèze and Khera, 2017). Effectiveness depends on the nutritional components and whether schools actually receive the intended grains or funds (Accountability Initiative, 2013).

One programme objective, using school meals for socialization to combat discrimination, has had challenges. A parliamentary committee condemned the practice of untouchability in the midday meal programme, observed in 144 districts (India Committee on the Welfare of Scheduled Castes and Scheduled Tribes, 2013). Several reports, qualitative studies and media articles have documented caste-based discrimination in midday meals. Lower-caste children (Dalit) were made to sit separately from their upper-caste peers (National Campaign on Dalit Human Rights, 2017), and scheduled-caste children received less food (Sabharwal et al., 2014). In addition, schools and parents have resisted employing cooks from scheduled castes. A study based on 709 households in the seven poorest states in eastern and central India found that the percentage of scheduled-caste cooks and helpers was very low due to the practice of untouchability, despite a 2004 Supreme Court directive to give preference to them (Reddy, 2018; Sabharwal et al., 2014; Samal and Dehury, 2017).

> **Several countries offer fee exemptions to increase access to education for girls, the poor and other vulnerable groups**

groups. In Benin, girls are exempt from secondary and tertiary tuition fees (Benin Ministry of Pre-Primary and Primary Education, 2018). Finland launched a EUR 5 million pilot in 2018 giving discretionary transfers to municipalities that provide free ECCE to 5-year-olds. A 2018 law aims to reduce fees to minimize the effects of socio-economic background on learning outcomes (Eurydice, 2018). The programme is being evaluated to assess whether it increases participation rates and how municipalities organize their costs (Finnish Education Evaluation Centre, 2019). Viet Nam granted preschool tuition fee exemptions to poor and remote households in 2018 (Viet Nam Ministry of Planning and Investment, 2018).

Scholarships are another common measure. Their equity and inclusion effects strongly depend on the targeting mechanism. Several programmes have increased inclusion of girls. A large-scale female secondary school stipend programme introduced in Bangladesh in 1994 increased attainment by 14% to 25%, delayed marriage, reduced number of offspring and improved decision-making autonomy (Hahn et al., 2018). Primary school poverty- and merit-targeted scholarships targeting grade 4 students in rural Cambodia led to higher attainment (Barrera-Osorio et al., 2018). An evaluation of secondary school scholarships in Ghana found that beneficiaries attained more years of secondary school, had higher reading and mathematics test scores, adopted more preventive health behaviour and earned more, largely because women's tertiary enrolment rates doubled (Duflo et al., 2017).

In Indonesia, Bantuan Siswa Miskin, a cash transfer for poor students, expanded its coverage and improved its targeting in 2013 (World Bank, 2017a). Although households were not obliged to change spending patterns, poor families' education expenditure increased (Anindita and Sahadewo, 2020).

The equity and inclusion impact of financing policies to promote access to tertiary education is contested. An analysis of 71 countries found that 32% had defined participation targets for any specific group. By contrast, 60 countries had scholarships, bursaries or grant

programmes; 45 had student loan programmes; and 40 had tuition fee reduction policies (Salmi, 2018). The Plurinational State of Bolivia offered solidarity scholarships to students from poor, indigenous and Afro-descendant backgrounds to attend private university (Bolivia Ministry of Education, 2018). In Georgia, while most scholarships were merit-based, between 6% and 10% were needs-based with a merit component, to support students from schools in conflict-affected or remote areas or serving linguistic minorities (World Bank, 2014). Ireland gave tertiary education institutions access to a Fund for Students with Disabilities to help provide services and support (Salmi, 2018).

Disparity in distribution of resources needs to be addressed

Governments need to ensure equity not only in education financing flows but also in distribution of inputs. Teachers, for instance, are often unequally distributed. Across 32 Organisation for Economic Co-operation and Development countries, socio-economically disadvantaged schools and classrooms are more likely to have less qualified teachers (Qin and Bowen, 2019). Teachers in poorer areas of Mexico were less qualified and had less education than teachers in richer areas (Luschei and Chudgar, 2016). In Zambia, on average, rural schools have four vacancies while urban schools are overstaffed by four teachers (Figueiredo Walter, 2018).

In low- and middle-income countries, resources and services to support learners with disabilities tend to be scarce and mechanisms to ensure their equal distribution underdeveloped. CBM, an international NGO, works with local NGOs to help governments fill gaps. In Cambodia, early intervention centres for children with hearing impairment offer appropriately fitted quality hearing aids and ear moulds with expert aftercare support. Speech and language therapists develop receptive skills lip-reading and expressive skills. In North East India, special schools were transformed into resource centres, which, in addition to hosting specialists, have become hubs that share knowledge, develop teacher capacity, carry out early interventions, distribute assistive devices,

> "
> Equitable distribution of textbooks
> and learning materials is necessary for
> inclusive access to learning opportunities
> "

early learning kits and audio books, and produce inclusive teaching and learning materials. In Papua New Guinea, the Network of Callan Services includes 19 resource centres, which offer screening and prepare children with disabilities for placement in mainstream education. An inclusive education institute trains resource centre staff and mainstream teachers (CBM, 2018).

Equitable distribution of textbooks and learning materials is necessary for inclusive access to learning opportunities. In Timor-Leste, textbook distribution is unequal across regions due to weak transport links (Smart and Jagannathan, 2018). In India, several schools in eight New Delhi districts experienced months of textbook delivery delays (Prakash, 2017). Less than 10% of existing published materials were accessible for visually impaired people (World Blind Union, 2016). Bangladesh's curriculum and textbook board reached 963 of an estimated 40,000 visually impaired children under 15 with Braille textbooks in 2016 (Sarker, 2019).

Some studies caution that textbook distribution policies, while necessary for inclusive learning, are not sufficient. Free textbook distribution in two Kenyan districts had no impact on dropout except among grade 8 students, whose transition to secondary education rate improved, and no impact on learning except among the top fifth of students. A potential explanation was that the textbooks were too difficult to be of much use to weaker students (Glewwe et al., 2009) (see **Chapter 5**). A randomized control trial evaluation of a free primary school textbook programme in Sierra Leone showed that attendance did not increase, as teachers restricted access to textbooks out of uncertainty they would continue receiving them in the future (Sabarwal et al., 2014).

SOCIAL PROGRAMMES TARGETING STUDENTS CAN COMPENSATE FOR EDUCATION DISADVANTAGE

Social protection programmes are a key example of how cross-sector collaboration can contribute to inclusion in education. In particular, cash transfers conditional on school attendance and use of health services, which

were rolled out in Latin America in the 1990s, have been extensively evaluated and found to have consistently positive effects on enrolment, dropout and completion (Snilstveit et al., 2015). Evidence of their long-term effects shows they have increased education attainment by between 0.5 and 1.5 grades (Molina Millán et al., 2019).

Public expenditure on these programmes varies by country, from 0.01% of gross domestic product (GDP) in Belize to 0.61% in Argentina. Population coverage also varies, from 1.2% in El Salvador to 51% in the Plurinational State of Bolivia. While all programmes target by poverty, some also target by location or disability (**Table 4.2**).

A review of 35 studies found that making transfers conditional on school attendance had a greater effect on attendance than targeting unconditional transfers to poor people, but the difference was not statistically significant. Positive effects were greater when conditionality was monitored (Baird et al., 2014). In Ecuador, Bono de Desarollo Humano (Human Development Grant) targeted households that had children under age 16 and were classified as vulnerable according to the Social Registry's socio-economic index. Ultimately, the programme's conditionality on school attendance was not enforced; however, an evaluation of effects over 10 years found a significant increase in secondary school completion: up to two percentage points (Araujo et al., 2017).

Conditional and unconditional programmes targeting the poor and having an effect on inclusion exist in many other parts of the world. Some have a long history, while others were inspired by lessons and developments in Latin America. In Indonesia, Program Keluarga Harapan (Family Hope Programme) began providing quarterly cash transfers to very poor households in 2008. Initially equivalent to 15% to 20% of income, their real value fell to 7% within six years. Eligible households have certain demographic characteristics, such as children under age 15 or children aged 16 to 18 who have not completed nine years of education. Conditions for payments include an 85% school attendance rate. A six-year follow-up evaluation showed enrolment rates among 13- to 15-year-olds rose by up to nine percentage points, equivalent to halving the share of those out of school. Increases of between four and seven percentage points were observed in the secondary school completion rate among 18- to 21-year-olds, with the effect concentrated among young men (Cahyadi et al., 2018). The government aimed to scaled up the programme from 3.5 million to

> Conditional cash transfers in Latin America since the 1990s have increased education attainment by between 0.5 and 1.5 grades

TABLE 4.2:
Conditional cash transfer programme coverage in Latin American countries

Country: Programme	Targeting criteria	Percentage of GDP (year)	Average transfer, US$ per month	Beneficiaries: **Share of population** Number
El Salvador: Programa Comunidades Solidarias	Location, poverty	**0.18%** (2016)	15–20	**1.2%** 0.38m households
Costa Rica: Avancemos	Location, poverty, academic performance	**0.18%** (2017)	53–70	**3.7%** 0.18m students
Chile: Subsistema de Seguridades y Oportunidades	Poverty	**0.03%** (N/A)	9	**4.4%**
Guatemala: Mi Bono Seguro	Location, poverty, pregnant/breastfeeding	**0.05%** (2017)	65–168	**5.9%** 0.98m people/0.15m households
Ecuador: Bono de Desarrollo Humano	Location, poverty	**0.24%** (2017)	50–150	**6.3%** 1.9m people/0.41m households
Panama: Red de Oportunidades	Location, poverty	**0.06%** (2017)	25	**8.2%** 0.33m people/0.05m households
Argentina: Asignación Universal por Hijo	Poverty, disability	**0.61%** (2016)	75–98	**9.0%** 3.9m people/2.2m households
Uruguay: Asignaciones Familiares – Plan de Equidad	Poverty, disability	**0.34%** (2015)	44–305	**11.0%** 0.38m people/0.14m households
Paraguay: Tekoporâ	Poverty, disability	**0.16%** (2016)	4–104	**11.6%** 0.78m people/0.14m households
Belize: Building Opportunities for Our Social Transformation	Poverty	**0.01%** (2012)	22–247	**16.9%** 0.48m people/0.88m households
Honduras: Bono Vida Mejor	Location, poverty	**0.25%** (2017)	12–14	**17.5%** 1.6m people/0.27m households
Dominican Republic: Progresando con Solidaridad	Poverty	**0.37%** (2017)	8–92	**33.3%** 3.5m people/0.97m households
Bolivia, P. S.: Bono Juancito Pinto	Poverty, disability, public schools	**0.18%** (2017)	29	**51%** 2.2m students/1.16m households

Source: United Nations Economic Commission for Latin America and the Caribbean.

10 million households by the end of 2018, equivalent to 14% of the population (World Bank, 2017c).

Turkey has run a conditional cash transfer programme since 2003. An initial evaluation found large positive effects on the secondary school enrolment rate among 14- to 17-year-olds, especially in rural areas, where the probability of being enrolled increased by 17% and, for boys, as much as 23% (Ahmed et al., 2007). The government later scaled up the programme and extended it in May 2017 to reach Syrian and other refugee children. It is implemented through a partnership of the Ministry of Family, Work and Social Services, Ministry of National Education, Turkish Red Crescent, European Commission and UNICEF. By June 2019, more than 500,000 students regularly attending school were receiving a transfer of between US$6 and US$10 per month; 83% of the families also benefited from Emergency Social Safety Net grants of US$20 per family member per month (Turkey Government and European Commission, 2019).

PROVIDING EDUCATION FOR STUDENTS WITH DISABILITIES INVOLVES ADDITIONAL COSTS

Beyond general financing to promote equity and inclusion, financing disability-inclusive education requires additional focus by governments. The challenge for policymakers is that spending throughout the education system, even if it mainstreams students from vulnerable groups, may fail learners with disabilities, especially since fulfilling their need for specific support is costlier. A twin-track approach to financing is needed both to address exclusion from general programmes and to introduce specific targeted programmes (IDDC and Light for the World, 2016).

Three main issues confront policymakers. First, they need to interpret national legislation by defining standards for services to be delivered and costs they will cover. Second, they need to be able to meet increased costs when special needs identification rates rise, and design ways to prioritize, finance and deliver targeted services for a wide range of needs. Third, they need to define results in a way that maintains pressure on local authorities and schools to avoid further earmarking services for children with diagnosed special needs and further segregating settings at the expense of other groups or general financing needs (Center for Inclusive Policy, 2019).

Costing education delivery for people with disabilities is related to the overall challenge of costing their living expenses. People with disabilities and their families need to pay for additional health services and the higher cost of routine activities that require assistive devices, adaptations, additional services and caregivers. These sizeable costs vary by severity of disability and household composition: Those living alone or in small households rely more on private caregivers and transport (Mitra et al., 2017). In the United Kingdom, the extra cost for people with disabilities is about US$750 per month, on average, or almost half their income (John et al., 2019).

Households with people with disabilities also earn less because of limited employment opportunities, including as a result of lower education attainment, and because other household members have to be caregivers. In Cambodia, the probability of a household being poor almost doubled, from 18% to 34%, if it had a member with a disability (Palmer et al., 2016). In Nepal, some 40% of people with visual, hearing and physical impairments cited financial challenges as a major barrier to pursuing their education (Lamichhane, 2015). As a result, disability is associated with higher poverty.

Well-resourced systems pursue a variety of disability-inclusive education funding mechanisms

Even in richer countries, good information on school financing is usually lacking, especially on how resources are allocated to special and inclusive settings or, in the latter case, how spending is distributed between general and specific uses. A project mapping how 16 European countries finance inclusive education found that 5 had information available (European Agency for Special Needs and Inclusive Education, 2016). Thus, few countries can analyse cost-effectiveness or estimate the financial impact of policy changes. The problem is more acute in poorer countries.

Patchy historical information from Europe and Northern America suggested that students with disabilities cost about 2 to 2.5 times more to educate than other students (Chambers et al., 2004; OECD, 2000). Costs varied widely by impairment and type of expenditure. In the US city of New York, the cost of educating students with special needs was 3 times higher, hiring paraprofessionals was 12 times higher and transport was 20 times higher (**Figure 4.3**). Educating students with special needs accounted for 31% of total education expenditure in 2017 (New York City Department of Education, 2018).

Even within one country, such as Australia or the United States, it is difficult to compare expenditure on special education across school districts (Cornman et al., 2019; Sharma et al., 2015). It is much more difficult to compare costs among countries, as they vary in various respects. They may vary in terms of the extent

> A twin-track approach to financing is needed both to address exclusion from general programmes and to introduce specific targeted programmes

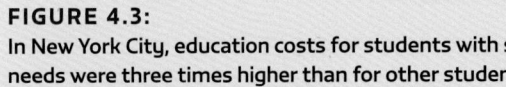

FIGURE 4.3:

In New York City, education costs for students with special needs were three times higher than for other students

Ratio of expenditure per student, by student type, New York City, 2017

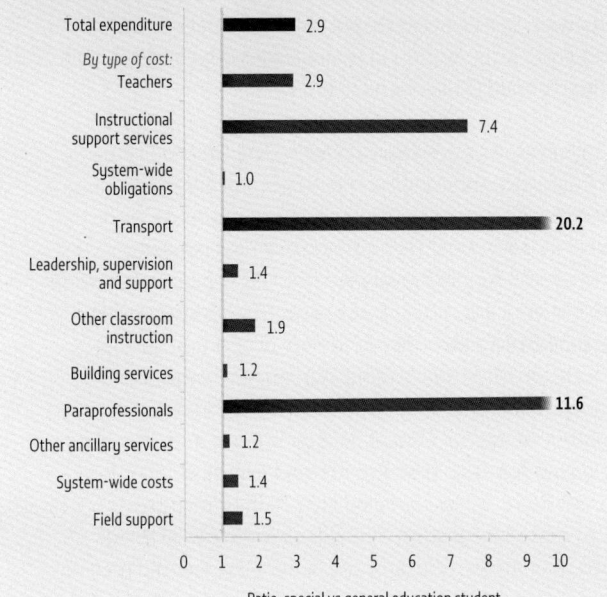

GEM StatLink: http://bit.ly/GEM2020_fig4_3

Note: Expenditure types are presented by descending order of magnitude.

Source: New York City Department of Education (2018).

> " The cost of delivering education for learners with disabilities has been rising in high-income countries, in some cases because more students are being identified as needing support "

increases for teachers (47%) and transport (41%). While the school transport programme serves both children living far from school (91%) and those with a diagnosed disability (9%), the latter account for almost half its budget because the number of children requiring escorts and individual services has risen (Ireland Department of Public Expenditure and Reform, 2017).

There are competing explanations for the growing number of children identified as having special education needs in some countries. It may be prompted by local authorities and schools applying standards loosely to ease teachers' work or by parents exerting pressure as they seek opportunities to support their children. Others contend that local authorities and schools apply standards strictly, but the prevalence of some disabilities is increasing. For instance, researchers cannot definitively attribute the increasing reported prevalence of autism spectrum disorders to changes in the clinical definition (encompassing more people), better diagnosis efforts (identifying more people) or simply more people with the disorders (CDC, 2019).

In the United States, the Individuals with Disabilities Education Act says the federal government must provide each state with 40% of the per-student expenditure multiplied by the number of special education students (Griffith, 2015). In fact, it provides only 18% (National Council on Disability, 2018), and the states make up the shortfall. Some analyses have attributed part of the growth in expenditure to districts responding to funding mechanisms that encourage increasing the number of students with disabilities (Cullen, 2003).

Additional support for students with disabilities is provided at the state level by various funding mechanisms and combinations thereof. In total, 27 states apply either a single weight to the general funding formula for mainstream schools or multiple weights (e.g. by type of impairment or instructional arrangement required). Eight states distribute resources, such as support personnel or specialists, instead of money, based on the number of students requiring special education services.

to which provision is through mainstream or costlier special schools. Cost structures may vary, depending on how services are procured. There is also wide variation in the percentage of students identified with special needs, a number that changes at different rates through changes in legislation and policy but also for different impairments and across different population groups.

The cost of delivering education for learners with disabilities has been rising in high-income countries, in some cases because more students are being identified as needing support. In Croatia, increased expenditure on transport and co-financing for nutrition and special teaching aids, along with a rising number of learners with special education needs, are the main cost drivers (European Agency for Special Needs and Inclusive Education, 2016). In Ireland, public expenditure for disability and special education support increased by 38% between 2011 and 2017, in line with the increase in students qualifying for such support, although those diagnosed with an autism spectrum disorder increased by 84%. There were above-average cost

> "
> Governments need to foster synergies and encourage networks to share resources, facilities and capacity development opportunities
> "

Five states reimburse districts for all or part of their spending. One in four states provides additional funding for very-high-cost students (Dachelet, 2019). For instance, Florida combines multiple weights and additional funding for high-cost students. It ranks students in five support levels and awards districts 3.7 and 5.6 times more for each student at support levels 4 and 5, respectively (Florida Department of Education, 2019).

Countries have tinkered with their funding mechanisms with mixed results. Schools in the Netherlands used to receive funding based on the number of students identified as having special needs. As this encouraged schools to declare more such students, the relevant budget was shifted in the mid-1990s to regional institutions, which allocated some funds to mainstream schools with the expectation that collaboration with special schools would grow. However, the reform was applied inconsistently across regions, and the number of students in special education kept rising. As a result, the funding model changed back in 2003. The 2014 inclusive education policy shifted back again, calling for regional partnerships to improve resource sharing and school collaboration. However, this shift has also encountered difficulties, as regions with higher school participation rates had lower budgets (Gubbels et al., 2018).

Several European countries have changed their inclusive education funding mechanisms in response to growing numbers of students diagnosed with special needs and to potential perverse incentives in funding mechanisms. Finland reformed its funding system in 2009, when the share of full-time students in special education reached 8.5% (a 3 percentage point increase in 10 years) but also out of concern over delivery differences among municipalities. It shifted from a weighted (by number of students in special education) to an unweighted capitation grant, except for students with severe disabilities in extended compulsory education. The aim was to strengthen support in mainstream education, offered at three levels: general and occasional, for all students; intensified and systematic, for those needing regular support based on a pedagogical assessment and a learning plan; and special, based on a pedagogical statement and an individualized education plan. A parallel project, Kelpo, helped develop municipal and school capacity to implement the reform. Although

the reform broadly met its aims, incentives for segregated provision still exist, while part-time special education and early intervention in mainstream education remain underfunded (Pulkkinen, 2019).

Similar reforms are taking place in the United States. In California, the funding mechanism avoided creating incentives to increase the number of students with special needs, but the number rose nevertheless, and overall funding levels did not keep pace. A statewide special education task force recommended a funding increase and a stronger focus on integrating special education into mainstream primary and secondary education. It also proposed abolishing the parallel system of special education governance and distributing released funds to districts instead (Hill et al., 2016). In Vermont, rising costs led to a 2018 reform to accelerate integration of children with special needs into mainstream classrooms, where they would receive targeted instructional time. The changes are being rolled out without increased funding; the funding mechanism is moving away from reimbursements to block grants, increasing flexibility in how money is spent. The reform discourages using paraeducators in favour of highly skilled professionals to support all learners (Morando Rhim, 2018).

A review of financing practices across Europe concludes that there is no ideal way to fund inclusive education, since countries vary, 'depending on their history, their understanding of inclusive education, and levels of decentralisation'. However, it argues that governments need to foster synergies and encourage networks to share resources, facilities and capacity development opportunities, for instance through block grants under service agreements with local authorities or school clusters. Such autonomy and flexibility would need to be accompanied by quality assurance mechanisms to monitor whether local authorities and schools achieve inclusion-specific results (Ebersold et al., 2019, p. 245).

Poorer systems are also building disability-inclusive education funding mechanisms

Poorer countries are exploring, but often struggling with, how to finance the shift from special to inclusive education. Ghana set aside funds for inclusive education policy implementation, with various cost-sharing agreements among sectors. For instance, the Ministry of Transport was to set aside 5% of the road sector fund for inclusive education, especially for children with disabilities (Ghana Ministry of Education, 2013). Progress has been limited, but the education and health ministries have coordinated to promote annual health screenings and referrals for early detection and support (IIEP, 2018).

In Nepal, the budget discussion for the 2016–23 school sector development plan addressed the shift from special schools to a more inclusive approach. Reform strategies included modules in pre-service teacher education and capacity building of national- and district-level staff. However, the expenditure framework noted that inclusive education was one of several 'other item' costs, which amounted to 3.4% of the total school sector cost categories. A separate budget line on 'inclusive education' was only explicitly noted for the secondary school development programme, amounting to just 0.02% of secondary school activities (Nepal Ministry of Education, 2016).

In some countries, there are efforts to cost inclusive education. Malawi developed a costing model for inclusive education in its strategy document, which estimated the cost at US$29 million over five years. However, this estimate does not take into account the need to recruit additional teachers to support inclusion (ActionAid et al., 2020). Namibia's sector policy on inclusive education costed its outcomes, which, in addition to the main resource allocation policy, included establishment of regional inclusive education units, transformation of some schools into inclusive schools and transformation of special classes and schools to resources. These initiatives amounted to almost half the policy implementation costs (Namibia Ministry of Education, 2013) (**Figure 4.4**).

Some countries have increased their budgets to improve education access for students with disabilities but maintain a target-group-based approach. Armenian Ministry of Finance transfers to regional education departments were based on just over US$200 per student per year, but the allocation was four to five times higher for students with special education needs (Center for Educational Research and Consulting, 2013). Mauritius's 2018/19 budget set aside funds to establish a Special Education Needs Authority. In addition, the annual per capita grant for teaching aids, utilities, furniture and equipment for special needs students was quadrupled. A taxi fare grant was being expanded from tertiary to primary and secondary school students (Mauritius Government Information Service, 2019). The United Republic of Tanzania doubled the size of its primary school capitation grant (US$4.3 per student) for enrolled students with disability (ActionAid et al., 2020).

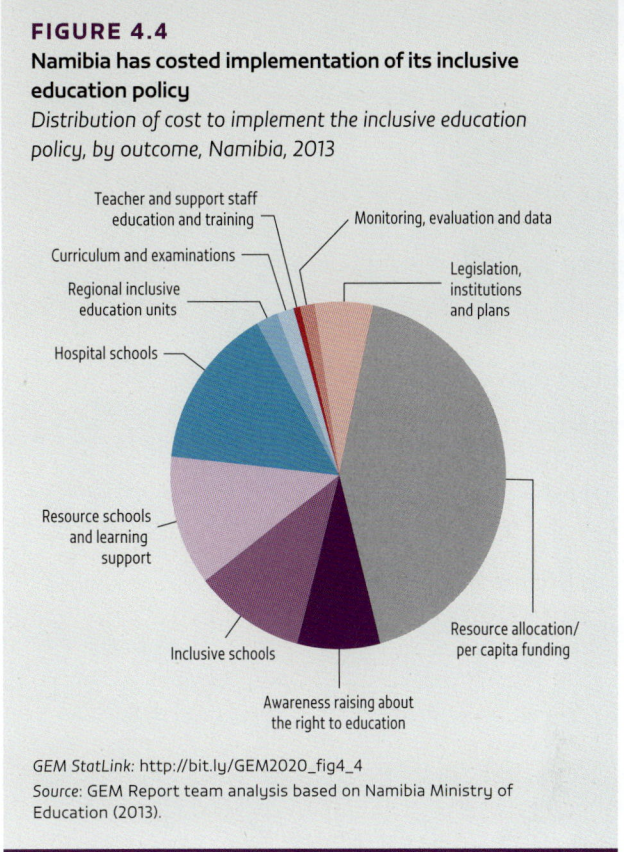

FIGURE 4.4

Namibia has costed implementation of its inclusive education policy

Distribution of cost to implement the inclusive education policy, by outcome, Namibia, 2013

GEM StatLink: http://bit.ly/GEM2020_fig4_4
Source: GEM Report team analysis based on Namibia Ministry of Education (2013).

CONCLUSION

Education ministries need to collaborate with other ministries, local governments and non-government partners, and to link education levels, to promote inclusion. Disjointed services and communication protocols, inadequate coordination efforts, insufficient capacity and financing lead to poor implementation and weak accountability. The potential of integrated service delivery initiatives, for instance in early needs identification or transition between education levels, is yet to be realized in many countries.

Countries also need to transform funding mechanisms to promote inclusion. The way they finance regions, schools and students should have a much stronger emphasis on equity, with better use of data and a larger share of resources reallocated to compensate for disadvantage. Even as marginalized groups are mainstreamed, a twin-track approach targeting them is needed, since the cost of serving their support needs is much higher, especially for students with disabilities. Education planners need to recognize synergies with social cash transfer programmes, which often have a strong impact on education attendance and attainment.

A special needs classroom in the Primary wing of
Adarsha Saula Yubak Higher Secondary School,
Bhainsipati, Lalitpur, Nepal.

CREDIT: GPE/NayanTara Gurung Kakshapati

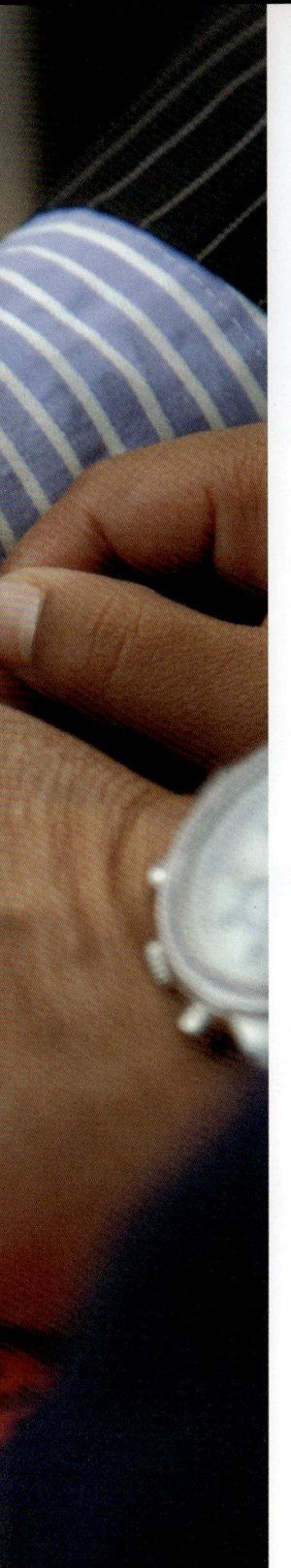

5

Curricula, textbooks and assessments

How can students learn if the system reminds them of their exclusion?

5

KEY MESSAGES

Curricula should adapt to learners' diverse needs and aspire to an inclusive society

■ The refugee education policy in the United Republic of Tanzania promotes repatriation of Burundian and Congolese refugees, limiting their inclusion chances in Tanzanian society.

■ A national language policy calls for the use of first language in Thailand, but the use of Malay as a language of instruction is limited to pilot projects. Odisha in India uses 21 tribal languages in instruction. Just 41 countries worldwide, 21 of them in the European Union, recognize sign language as an official language.

■ Among 49 European countries, 19 had inclusive national curricula that made it compulsory to address sexual orientation, gender identity and gender expression, 7 made it optional and 23 did not address the issue explicitly.

■ Australia recognizes four levels of adjustment (extensive, substantial, supplementary, and support with quality differentiated teaching practice) for four categories of disability (cognitive, physical, sensory and social-emotional): 19% of students received adjustments.

■ Multigrade teaching is applied either by design or by necessity in rural contexts from Guatemala to Switzerland.

■ Curricula can alienate if they are irrelevant to local contexts. In Namibia, mobile schools delivering the national curriculum did not make good use of pastoralist communities' environment.

Textbooks can exclude by perpetuating stereotypes through omission and misrepresentation

■ The share of females in secondary school English language textbook text and images was 44% in Indonesia, 37% in Bangladesh and 24% in Punjab province of Pakistan.

■ Textbooks may mitigate or exacerbate the degree to which minority groups are received, or perceive themselves, as 'other'. A trilingual education policy in Kazakhstan made it possible to increase provision of new Tajik, Uighur and Uzbek primary school textbooks.

■ In Bahrain, civil education teachers opposed applying the curriculum's Western conception of citizenship and diversity because they believed it might increase tensions.

■ The rights of people with disabilities were mentioned in 9% of secondary school social science textbooks around 2010, up from 2% in the 1970s.

Good-quality assessment is fundamental to inclusive education but testing that does not accommodate different needs can exclude learners

■ Formative and summative assessments need to be more closely related. In seven sub-Saharan African countries, no teacher had minimum knowledge in student assessment.

■ A review of studies of test accommodations in the United States showed that extended time tended to improve test scores for students with disabilities, whereas oral delivery did not.

Inclusion in education is what I aspire to; however, the reality of the situation is that the design of our environment and curriculum offers challenges and barriers to achieving it.

Sarah Rhodes, senior lecturer in Learning and Teaching at University of Wolverhampton, UK

Inclusion is not just about ensuring everyone is in school or eliminating physical segregation. An inclusive learning experience requires inclusive curriculum, textbooks and assessment practices. The curriculum has been described as 'the central means through which the principle of inclusion is put into action within an education system' (IBE, 2008, p. 22). It reflects what is meant to be taught (content) and learned (goals). It needs to be coherent with how it is to be taught (pedagogical methods) and learned (tasks), as well as with the materials to support learning (e.g. textbooks, computers) and the methods to assess learning (e.g. examinations, projects).

Curricula exclude when they do not cater to learners' diverse needs and do not respect human and citizenship rights. Textbooks can perpetuate stereotypes by associating certain characteristics with particular population groups. Inappropriate images and descriptions can make students with non-dominant backgrounds feel misrepresented, misunderstood, frustrated and alienated. While good-quality assessment is a fundamental part of an inclusive education system, testing regimes that do not accommodate various needs can exclude learners. Finally, the links among curricula, textbooks and assessments are often ignored, with one being changed while others are not.

This chapter addresses these three interlinked aspects of learning, showing how a number of factors need to be aligned for inclusive curricular, textbook and assessment reforms to be successful. Capacities need to be developed so that stakeholders work collaboratively and think strategically. Partnerships need to be in place so that all parties own the process and work towards the same goals. Successful attempts to make curricula, textbooks and assessments inclusive entail participatory processes during design, development and implementation to ensure that all students' needs are reflected.

INCLUSIVE CURRICULA TAKE THE NEEDS OF ALL LEARNERS INTO ACCOUNT

The International Bureau of Education defines an inclusive curriculum as one that 'takes into consideration and caters for the diverse needs, previous experiences, interests and personal characteristics of all learners. It attempts to ensure that all students are part of the shared learning experiences of the classroom and that equal opportunities are provided regardless of learner differences' (IBE, 2019).

> **There are political tensions regarding the kind of society people aspire to achieve through education**

This definition draws attention to three concepts pursued in this section. First, there are political tensions regarding the kind of society people aspire to achieve through education, for inclusion is an exercise in democracy. Second, there are practical challenges in ensuring flexibility in order to serve diverse contexts and needs without segregating learners. Third, there are technical challenges in ensuring that the curriculum serves equity by being relevant and in creating bridges that do not cut off some learners.

The curriculum is not just 'a set of plans made for guiding learning' but also the 'actualization of those plans' (Glatthorn et al., 2018, p. 3). It entails distinct phases, from design to development, implementation and evaluation, each of which affects how inclusive curricula are (**Table 5.1**). Throughout, a conscious effort is made to ensure that students master particular content, referring to the intended curriculum. In practice, what students receive and learn is also affected by social and cultural norms, which contribute to what is sometimes called the hidden curriculum.

During the curriculum's design phase, education systems need to decide on the breadth and depth of the inclusion paradigm they will follow. In the development phase, the commitment to inclusion is tested in the ways in which diversity is tackled and other viewpoints to broaden student understanding are taken into account. It is at this stage that certain content is eliminated and new content is added. Original ideas encounter resistance if there is too little or too much attention to certain minorities. Parents may find it hard to reconcile some topics with their personal, cultural or religious beliefs. Teachers may realize the new curriculum requires them to teach new skills or take more inclusive pedagogical approaches. Even if these hurdles are overcome, an inclusive curriculum's effectiveness is really put to the test during the implementation phase, when the intended curriculum is interpreted and enacted in schools. Without proper understanding and mastery of the expected pedagogies, the reform could easily lose steam (Berkvens, 2020).

TABLE 5.1:
Phases of curriculum development

Phase Characterization	Participants	Questions	Enabling or constraining factors
Pre-design and design Written curriculum (as embodied in approved texts)	▪ Ministry of Education ▪ Teacher organizations	Who is pushing for inclusion and on the basis of what paradigms?	There is usually a genuine interest in inclusive education.
Development Supported curriculum (as shaped by resources allocated to deliver it)	▪ Curriculum department ▪ Publishing houses ▪ Teacher organizations ▪ Students, parents and organizations through consultations	Who is included in the process and at what stages? Who makes the final decisions, and what are they based on?	A focus on the general curriculum and the basic knowledge, skills and attitudes to be mastered by all may result in a heavy and overloaded curriculum. Not enough time may be allocated to subjects, or textbooks may not be available or appropriate.
Implementation Taught curriculum (as observed in class)	▪ Teacher education institutions and universities ▪ School leaders and teachers ▪ School boards	Are teachers and school principals prepared? How?	Opportunities for teacher education and professional development and other support may be insufficient. If teachers are forced to follow the curriculum with fidelity but have limited autonomy, the inclusiveness objective may be diluted.
Evaluation Assessed curriculum (as tested)	▪ School inspectorate ▪ Curriculum department ▪ Examination department	Is school inspection prepared to assess the new curriculum? What is assessed at the end of education? Who is involved in measuring the success of the inclusive curriculum?	The role of formative evaluation may be neglected, and national examinations may neglect the importance of non-academic areas of learning for inclusiveness.

Source: GEM Report team analysis based on Berkvens (2020) and Glatthorn et al. (2018).

INCLUSIVE CURRICULA NEED TO RESPECT HUMAN RIGHTS

An inclusive education should reflect the aspiration of a society committed to social inclusion (Tedesco et al., 2013). Some countries develop a broad inclusive curriculum that encompasses all population groups. They recognize the value of acknowledging and respecting diversity. The Kenyan Institute for Curriculum Development developed a curriculum framework in 2016 based on inclusion, among other principles. It aims to enable learners to appreciate diversity in terms of race, ethnicity, gender, language, culture and religion, and respect learners' various needs and abilities, 'valuing these within an inclusive learning environment' (Njeng'ere Kabita and Ji, 2017, p. 9).

However, in many countries, implementation is a stumbling block. Inclusive curriculum implementation needs to tackle head-on the inclusion of groups whose existence may have been ignored, hidden, parallel or pushed to the margins of societies and education systems. Governments are likely to encounter backlash related to teachers not being prepared, parents not accepting or people not understanding, even when proposed reforms are meant to fulfil commitments made in national laws and international conventions.

In Norway, where the core curriculum puts great emphasis on culture as a source of enrichment in education, the physical education curriculum states that schools with students with immigrant backgrounds should teach games from their home countries (Norway Ministry of Education and Research, 2015). By contrast, the refugee education policy in the United Republic of Tanzania supports the principle of repatriation. In Kigoma region, 150,000 school-age refugee children receive education in three refugee camps, where the Burundian and Congolese national curricula are used for the respective nationals (U. R. Tanzania Ministry of Education, Science and Technology, 2018). This segregation limits their chances of inclusion in further education in Tanzanian schools.

In Thailand, historical grievances of the Muslim population in the four southern provinces close to the Malaysian border are rooted in perceptions of state discrimination on the basis of ethnicity and religion (Lo Bianco, 2019; UNICEF, 2014). The conflict has an education component, and local militants have attacked schools. Thai has been the single language of instruction, with the use of the Patani dialect of Malay prohibited in schools. In 2004, the separatist insurgency led to the resumption of a preschool bilingual programme that had been discontinued in 1983 (Arphattananon, 2011). The first national language policy in 2010 called for use of first language (Warotamasikkhadit and Person, 2011), but political instability has hindered its implementation. In 2015, two teacher education institutions, one of which was in southern Thailand, started to train teachers in multilingual education (Kosonen, 2017). The use of Malay as a language of instruction is limited to pilot projects. A joint project by UNICEF and Mahidol University for students up to grade 6 introduced new teaching materials meeting Ministry of Education standards; it was found to double the use of Thai words among grade 3 students (Mahidol University and UNICEF, 2018; Premsrirat, 2019).

In Bosnia and Herzegovina, displacement during and after the 1990s war in the former Yugoslavia homogenized several areas of the country by ethnicity. As part of efforts to encourage the return of refugees and internally displaced people in a fraught post-war environment, the Two Schools Under One Roof policy was established to bring into a single building children of different ethnicities who had previously studied separately. This temporary solution was considered only a first step towards full integration but 56 schools still segregate children on the basis of ethnicity, offering distinct curricula on the same school premises (OSCE, 2018; Surk, 2018).

In many parts of Europe, Roma and traveller children are at high risk of exclusion in education through curriculum deficiencies. They are disproportionately likely to be taught a reduced curriculum because they are often sent to remedial classes and special schools (Council of Europe, 2017). Moreover, the core curriculum does not reflect their history. The Council of Europe's Committee of Experts on Roma and Traveller Issues is working towards a recommendation on the inclusion of their history in curricula and teaching materials (Council of Europe, 2019).

In a national survey in the United States, 72% of respondents said significant changes to the curriculum on Native American history and culture were needed.

> " Inclusive curriculum implementation needs to tackle head-on the inclusion of groups whose existence may have been ignored "

> "
> Roma and traveller children are likely to be taught a reduced curriculum because they are often sent to remedial classes and special schools
> "

According to teachers, 'history of Native American peoples' and 'pre-Columbian American history and culture' have worse coverage and accuracy than any other subjects (First Nations Development Institute, 2018). Another survey, conducted in 28 states, 26 of which had federally recognized tribal nations, indicated that only 12 required Native American material to be taught in some or all public school grades (National Congress of American Indians, 2019).

The issue of religion and education is complex for most societies. In France, a secular public education system means that religion is only taught in the curriculum as part of history and does not include discussions over belief and spirituality or over religious diversity in today's society. A commitment to religious neutrality, which can be traced back to a specific historical context, stifles attempts to review the role of religion in public education, even though this may be a factor that weakens social cohesion (Localmultidem, 2007). In other contexts, religious minorities are presented as alien and curricula portray the history of the majority religious community as superior. Such domination even extends to physical discrimination (Amor, 2001). For instance, hate speech has been repeatedly used in education institutions against the Ahmadi community in Pakistan (FIDH and HRCP, 2015).

Countries around the world struggle to address sexual orientation, gender identity and gender expression in curricula (**Box 5.1**). They tend to omit affirmative inclusion of such identities and realities. An inclusive education index covering 49 European countries found that 19 had inclusive national curricula that made it compulsory to address sexual orientation, 7 made it optional and 23 did not address the issue explicitly (Ávila, 2018).

Inclusive curricula are an exercise in democracy

A common denominator in making a curriculum inclusive is preventing the preferences of the majority population from violating the needs of minority populations at risk of exclusion. Inclusive education is aligned with democratic values, notably protection of the rights of all and active participation (Education International, 2019).

A prime example is citizenship education, discussed below in the section on textbooks. Inclusiveness and democratic values can also be served through curricula that shift away from knowledge and towards competences. Communication, collaboration, critical thinking and problem solving have been slowly making inroads into curricula and instructional approaches. While some countries promote such competences to make their workforces internationally competitive, others see them as integral to strengthening inclusion. In Mexico, as part of the curriculum for compulsory education rolled out in August 2018, inclusion is to be strengthened through enhanced participation, active pedagogies, curriculum flexibility, and citizenship and peace education (UNESCO, 2019). The Ministry of Preschool Education in Uzbekistan approved a revised curriculum in September 2018 that moves to a competence-based model through early learning development standards. It is being piloted in selected preschools (Uzbekistan Ministry of Education, 2019).

Good intentions can be derailed, however. In Peru, the basic education curriculum's long-term vision is students who value diversity through intercultural dialogue in a democratic context (Peru Ministry of Education, 2016). As part of a commitment to develop competences for democratic participation and living together, the curriculum recognized diversity in sexual orientation. After this was legally challenged by pressure groups, the government had to develop a communication strategy to defend the curriculum content (Peru Ministry of Education, 2017).

Teachers in Ghana considered their involvement in curriculum development essential, but 46% felt their participation in design was low or very low and 90% felt their contributions had not been taken into account (Abudu and Mensah, 2016). Often, curriculum development efforts are initiated through cooperation with international organizations. While the latter tend to have a relatively good understanding of contemporary international trends and examples, they may not be sufficiently steeped in local context, which can drive a wedge between curriculum intentions and realities (Berkvens, 2020).

BOX 5.1:

Progress in recognizing sexual orientation, gender identity and gender expression in curricula is mixed

Many curricula either ignore homosexuality, bisexuality and non-binary gender identities or treat them as deviant or abnormal. Coupled with stereotypes and discrimination in everyday school life, this can have negative effects on the well-being of lesbian, gay, bisexual, transgender and intersex (LGBTI) students. In the United States, the 2017 GLSEN School Climate survey found that two-thirds of students had not been exposed to representation of LBGTI people and history in school. It also found that students in schools with inclusive curricula were less likely to feel unsafe at school because of their sexual orientation (42% vs 63%) or to be often or frequently exposed to biased language (52% vs 75%) (Kosciw et al., 2018).

A survey of 6,000 teachers in Japan showed that between 63% and 73% felt the curriculum should cover sexual orientation, gender identity and gender expression (Doi, 2016). The current curriculum does not properly reflect diversity in sexual orientation. The 2016 curriculum revision missed an opportunity to address this issue (Doi and Knight, 2017). A 2011 review of curricula in 10 eastern and southern African countries found that none addressed sexual diversity appropriately (UNESCO and UNFPA, 2012). Namibia's life skills curriculum in grades 8 and 12 at least refers to the issue of diversity in sexual orientation (UNESCO, 2016b).

Around the world, countries realize the need to embed sexual orientation, gender identity and gender expression in curricula. High-income countries are taking the lead. Following recommendations by the LGBTI Inclusive Education Working Group, Scotland (United Kingdom) announced it would be 'the first' to embed LGBTI-inclusive education in the curriculum across all state schools by 2021 (Scotland Government, 2018). The state of Berlin in Germany focused on concepts such as difference, tolerance and acceptance to introduce sexual diversity in the primary curriculum. In Canada's Ontario province, grade 8 students learn to connect sexual orientation and gender identity with the concept of respect (UNESCO, 2016b).

California was the first US state to introduce a regulatory framework for inclusion of LGBTI people's contributions in history and social science curricula. In 2019, Colorado, Illinois, New Jersey and Oregon followed (Illinois Safe Schools Alliance, 2019). By contrast, seven states have discriminatory curriculum laws. South Carolina's school board guidelines on sexuality education say that 'the program of instruction ... may not include a discussion of alternate sexual lifestyles from heterosexual relationships' (South Carolina Code of Laws, 2013). The Texas Health and Safety Code states that sexuality education content should emphasize 'that homosexuality is not a lifestyle acceptable to the general public and that homosexual conduct is a criminal offense' under state law (Texas Health and Safety Code, 2018). Discriminatory language can also be found in the state's education regulations and curriculum guidelines (Rosky, 2017). In Utah, civil society mobilization led to the repeal of a statutory prohibition against 'advocacy of homosexuality' as a step towards stopping discrimination based on sexual orientation and gender identity in public schools (Wood, 2017).

Some low- and middle-income countries have inclusive curricula with respect to sexual orientation and gender identity. Mongolia includes sexual behaviour and diversity in its sexual and reproductive health curriculum in grades 6 to 9. In Nepal, the health and physical education curriculum in grades 6 to 9 discusses health and well-being of sexually and gender diverse learners, with a particular focus on the hijras, a transgender and intersex group recognized in Southern Asia as a third gender (UNESCO, 2015). Thailand's new course and textbooks on physical and health education in grades 1 to 12, introduced in May 2019, cover sexual diversity (Thai PBS News, 2019).

This is why a fully participatory process in curricular reform is so important. Between 2012 and 2016, Finland undertook a comprehensive curricular reform to improve basic education's quality and equity. Four values underlie the new curricula: uniqueness of each student and right to a good education; humanity, equality, democracy and general knowledge and ability; cultural diversity as richness; and necessity of a sustainable way of living. The new curricula lay the learning and teaching foundations but are adapted at the local level to take local needs into consideration. The curricula were developed through a participatory process in which teachers played an instrumental role (Halinen, 2018; Pietarinen et al., 2016).

INCLUSIVE CURRICULA SHOULD BE FLEXIBLE

Inclusive curricula do not lower standards or reduce knowledge, which would compromise students' future opportunities; rather, they are flexible and involve interactive or group work to facilitate learning and enhance achievement (Flecha, 2015). Flexibility can refer to processes or outcomes (e.g. number of words to be mastered) (O'Mara et al., 2012). Accommodations are curricular adaptations that maintain the curriculum standards and expected outcomes but focus on processes, for instance through basic interventions, such as enlarged print (Mitchell, 2014), or more complex ones, such as collaborative teaching (Tremblay, 2013), to enable student participation and access to information.

> ## " Inclusive curricula do not lower standards or reduce knowledge "

Modifications also follow the curriculum standards but allow for different individual student outcomes. For instance, while all students may be assigned the same task, one student may be assigned fewer and more targeted questions. Lack of time is a common challenge in implementing curriculum differentiation (Ware et al., 2011). Some students who need more intense or differentiated support can receive individualized education plans, although care should be taken to ensure that these are part of an inclusive curriculum (**Box 5.2**).

A flexible curriculum is one key to including children with disabilities while minimizing the stigma of following a different programme (Hunt, 2020). Some countries have made curriculum accessibility a priority for inclusion. Australia recognizes four levels of adjustment (extensive, substantial, supplementary, and support with quality differentiated teaching practice) for four categories of disability (cognitive, physical, sensory and social-emotional). In total, 19% of students received adjustments (Australia Education Council, 2017). New Zealand's teaching guides stress that accessibility

and flexibility are key characteristics of an inclusive curriculum (New Zealand Ministry of Education, 2017).

In Portugal, a 2017 legislative order increased school autonomy in curriculum management and flexibility. In the pilot phase of an autonomy and curriculum flexibility project in 2017/18, 302 schools could adapt the curriculum to various learning needs and teachers could tailor delivery to make lessons more inclusive. The 2018 law for inclusion formally offered all schools more autonomy to manage curricula (European Commission, 2019; Hunt, 2020; Portugal Presidency of the Council of Ministers, 2018). In the Russian Federation, students with disabilities are entitled to adapted education programmes, supported by special textbooks and training equipment for collective and individual use (GEM Report Education Profiles[1]). The inclusive education policy framework in Dubai, United Arab Emirates,

---

1 A new GEM Report tool for systematic monitoring of national education laws and policies, accessible at www.education-profiles.org.

BOX 5.2:

Individualized education plans may or may not be part of an inclusive curriculum for students with disabilities

In many countries, students with disabilities receive support services according to individualized education plans with clear objectives and the intermediate steps needed to reach them. Teachers and support personnel develop these plans together with parents and students (McCausland, 2005). In Hong Kong, China, all mainstream schools are requested to include students with special needs using a three-tier intervention model. The first tier integrates students with mild or temporary difficulties into mainstream classrooms. The second involves small group learning and pull-out programmes for those with persistent learning difficulties. The third covers support for learners with severe learning difficulties and is based on an individualized education plan, regularly reviewed with parents (GEM Report Education Profiles). In the Maldives, the 2013 inclusive education policy stipulated that schools should establish individualized education plans for gifted and talented children, children with various learning disabilities and children who need additional learning support, to be reviewed twice per year (GEM Report Education Profiles). In Saudi Arabia, individualized education plans are defined in the Regulations of Special Education Institutes and Programmes (Alkahtani and Kheirallah, 2016).

Such plans often originate in a medical interpretation of impairments and tend to focus on what needs to be fixed. In that sense, there is a risk of individualized education plans slowing down support for inclusive education. They have been criticized as leading to exclusion from classroom peer interactions and feedback opportunities (Carrington and MacArthur, 2012; Florian, 2013). Challenges include lack of communication between schools and families, lack of training and clear information on the roles of teachers and other actors (Carrington and MacArthur, 2012), and negative attitudes and insufficient teacher training impeding student progression. Individualized education plans should be seen not as a gateway to services for children with disabilities but as an accountability mechanism for students who need more structured support (Hunt, 2020).

uses curriculum adjustments and flexible curriculum pathways (Dubai KHDA, 2017). In the United States, the Education for All Handicapped Children Act was seen as guaranteeing the right to special education, but a 1997 amendment reinterpreted the right as specially designed instruction to ensure access to the general curriculum (United States Code, 2011; United States Office of the Federal Registers, 2019).

Curriculum adaptation need not be limited to rich contexts. In Namibia, in response to the 2013 inclusive education policy, the government reviewed the national curriculum for basic education and issued a supplement on inclusive education, encouraging adaptation of subject content with suitable methodologies and materials in response to learner diversity (GEM Report Education Profiles). In a poor rural district in South Africa, teachers highlighted several ways they adapted the curriculum to students with special needs, including through teaching strategies, individual work, group work and extra work (Adewumi et al., 2017).

Nor does adaptation necessarily refer exclusively to students with disabilities. Flexible time frames for particular subjects are one example. Multigrade classrooms expose students to diverse content, allowing some to revisit earlier grade material and reinforce their

> **New Zealand's teaching guides stress that accessibility and flexibility are key characteristics of an inclusive curriculum**

understanding of concepts (Little, 2006). Adaptation has been applied either by design or by necessity in rural contexts from Guatemala (McEwan, 2008) to Switzerland (Smit and Humpert, 2012). In Myanmar, the 2016–21 education sector plan envisions development of a local curriculum, consisting of five classes per week in primary school and four in secondary school and including ethnic languages, culture and arts. Schools can adapt and improve the curriculum. The Ministry of Education spells out standards for special education programme content targeted to diverse learners (GEM Report Education Profiles). In Sri Lanka, schools have similar freedom to adapt the curriculum to the local environment (GEM Report Education Profiles).

In practice, curriculum adaptation faces many obstacles, such as insufficient teacher preparation. Teachers and education support personnel in Australia's Victoria state reported that they lacked training on implementing differentiated teaching and adjustments

(Victoria State Government, 2016). Ethiopia issued guidelines for curriculum differentiation in 2012 and a master plan in 2016, but delays in implementation have been reported (Ethiopia Ministry of Education, 2012, 2016; Mergia, 2020).

Lack of resources is another frequent constraint. In Malawi, students with disabilities cannot benefit from information and communications technology, computer studies or science in the general curriculum because of lack of resources for adjustments (Munde-Mana, 2019). A review of education sector plans in 51 low- and lower-middle-income countries showed that 1 in 5 planned to adapt or modify curricula to suit children with disabilities' needs, and fewer still had clear plans for how to proceed, Kenya being one exception (Global Partnership for Education, 2018). Insufficient attention can be another barrier. In Turkey, mathematics and computing are among subjects not adapted to the needs of students with impairments, especially to hearing and sight (OHCHR, 2019b).

While curriculum flexibility helps in responding better to learners' needs, it presents technical complexities concerning the organization of learning and teaching. Ultimately, some curricula may have been poorly designed in the first place and too costly to amend. Just as inaccessible school buildings generated demand for universal design (see **Chapter 7**), a movement for Universal Design for Learning has been conceived as 'a set of principles for curriculum development that give all individuals equal opportunities to learn' (AHEAD, 2017). A holistic perspective to learning goes beyond learners' strengths and weaknesses to consider conditions and approaches that make each learner most likely to learn (**Box 5.3**).

> ❝
> Curriculum adaptation faces many obstacles, such as insufficient teacher preparation
> ❞

BOX 5.3:

Universal Design for Learning goes beyond inclusive environments to ensure inclusive teaching

Inclusive education rests on the idea that barriers to learning emerge not from learners but from their interaction with education system components, including curriculum. The Universal Design for Learning concept encapsulates approaches to maximize accessibility and minimize barriers to learning. Developed in the mid-1990s at the Center for Applied Special Technology in the US state of Massachusetts, it exploits the flexibility of digital technology to design learning environments that accommodate diverse learner needs. Initially focused on learners with disabilities, its scope rapidly expanded to encompass education developments that could improve all learners' access to curricula (Meyer et al., 2016).

Universal Design for Learning, grounded in neuroscience and education research, seeks to provide flexible approaches to curriculum design that can be adjusted for individual needs. As 'brain functions and characteristics fall along a continuum of systematic variability', it views student differences not as a problem but as 'an actively positive force in learning for the group as a whole' (Meyer et al., 2016, p. 9). These differences can be built into the curriculum, which would be flexible and adapted to diverse needs through teaching and learning methods, including technology.

This vision supports a shift to a learner-centred education system and away from labels. It calls for multiple means of representation (the 'what' of learning: present information and content in various ways), action and expression (the 'how' of learning: differentiate the ways students can express what they know) and engagement (the 'why' of learning: stimulate interest and motivation for learning) to ensure the needs of all students are met (New Zealand Ministry of Education, 2015).

In 2008, the term Universal Design for Learning was included in the US Higher Education Opportunity Act. In 2010, it was mentioned in the US Department of Education's National Education Technology Plan as a framework to benefit all learners, especially the underserved (US Department of Education, 2010). Other countries, such as New Zealand, are seeking to embed Universal Design for Learning principles in teacher class planning (New Zealand Ministry of Education, 2015). The Ghanaian inclusive education policy has also endorsed the approach (GEM Report Education Profiles).

INCLUSIVE CURRICULA PROMOTE EQUITY THROUGH RELEVANCE AND CLEAR PATHWAYS

Inclusive curricula should be close to students' contexts, focus on relevant skills and be coherent so as to create better linkage between education levels.

Curricula alienate learners in many poorer countries

The appendix to the first General Comment to Article 29(1) of the Convention on the Rights of the Child emphasizes that 'the curriculum must be of direct relevance to the child's social, cultural, environmental and economic context' (United Nations, 2001, p. 4). Yet in many low- and lower-middle-income countries, curricula tend to be insensitive to local and learner contexts. This lack is manifested in overambitious curricula delivered at a pace disadvantaged students cannot keep up with, skills that do not meet the needs of marginalized populations and languages of instruction different from those learners speak. These and other consequences run counter to a scenario in which 'children should be able to relate what they learn to their context, to find a deep understanding of their immediate world along with the tools for its care and transformation, and discover their own culture in their native language' (Schmelkes, 2018, p. 14).

The pace of curriculum delivery is often too fast for vulnerable students

Evidence from citizen-led assessments in Southern Asia and sub-Saharan Africa highlights the large gap between curriculum objectives and learning outcomes. Students are often expected to progress at an unrealistic pace, too fast to follow the curriculum, leading to lower cumulative learning. Remedial education and curriculum simplification are needed, but countries have lacked the resources for the former (Pritchett and Beatty, 2012) while, with respect to the latter, observers note that systems, especially in sub-Saharan Africa, bear the elitist stamp of colonial legacy, catering to more privileged students and certain types of knowledge (Nyamnjoh, 2012).

In recent years, many sub-Saharan African countries have undertaken ambitious curricular reforms. Eswatini adopted a competence-based curriculum framework in 2018 to help children develop 'according to [their] talents and capabilities as opposed to the current system of making children … compete according to pre-determined

targets' (European External Action Service, 2018). A recent review of 25 countries in the region showed that 13 had attempted similar ambitious reforms. However, although no rigorous evaluations have been done, the overwhelming evidence is that the reforms have not been successful, whether because of design flaws or implementation bottlenecks, such as lack of professional development (Fleisch et al., 2019).

A survey of primary mathematics curriculum enacted in Uganda highlighted inequality in implementation. Three higher-order topics aiming for computational proficiency and conceptual understanding of mathematical ideas (number sense, operations and measurement) received disproportionately more attention, on average, relative to what the curriculum standards prescribed, than the lower-order topics of reciting, memorizing and recalling mathematical facts, especially in grades 1 to 3. Moreover, measurement was least emphasized in rural areas and most emphasized in urban areas. Urban teachers also prioritized the ability to communicate and demonstrate understanding of mathematical ideas, while rural teachers focused on reciting, memorizing and recalling. Since measurement got more emphasis in primary school leaving examinations, rural children were at a disadvantage (Atuhurra and Alinda, 2018). As another dimension of inequality, private school teachers and students complemented English instruction with better quality and better suited support material available on the open market (Ssentanda et al., 2019).

Curricula are not sufficiently relevant for some marginalized groups

Curriculum relevance receives insufficient attention despite evidence it plays a large role in inclusion and learning. Pastoralists are one group not served by national curricula. In Kenya, the curriculum developed to serve the 2008 nomadic education policy incorporated traditional knowledge, was adjusted to the nomadic

> " Students are often expected to progress at an unrealistic pace, too fast to follow the curriculum "

calendar and included the use of radio and mobile phones for outreach. Yet the content changes did not go far enough, and there were doubts about implementation (e.g. a lack of mother tongue reading materials) and parental approval (Ng'asike, 2019). In Namibia, mobile schools introduced to serve pastoralist communities, such as the Himba and Zemba, delivered the national curriculum, which was considered contrary to their beliefs and did not help them make better use of their environment (Haïlombe, 2011). After curriculum relevance emerged as a priority for the African Union at the first international conference on curriculum for sustainable learning in 2018, a cluster on curriculum development for all levels of education was created as part of the Continental Education Strategy for Africa implementation (African Union, 2016, 2018).

India's tribal people are seldom depicted in curricula and textbooks. When they are, the material often provokes a sense of inferiority among tribal students, as it promotes the dominant class's caste, gender and religious values (Darak, 2018). Maharashtra developed a state curriculum adapting the 2005 national curriculum, but although it allows assessments to be administered orally to tribal children who do not understand Marathi, the state language, there are few other curriculum and pedagogical aids to bridge mainstream curriculum and tribal ways of life (Centre for Budget and Policy Studies, 2017).

Bolivia's Plurinational Base Curriculum is based on four pillars: decolonisation, intra- and inter-culturalism, productive education and communitarian education. Created to address indigenous, rural and Afro-descendant people's demands (Cortina, 2014), it has national (60%), regional (30%) and local (10% to 20%) components. Indigenous peoples' education councils elaborate regional education curricula that correspond to indigenous cultures (Altinyelken, 2015).

> " In Bolivia, indigenous peoples' education councils elaborate regional education curricula that correspond to indigenous cultures "

Home languages need to be promoted

Learning in the mother tongue is vital, especially in primary school, to avoid knowledge gaps and increase the speed of learning and understanding what is taught (UNESCO, 2016a). This is particularly important in sub-Saharan Africa, where implementation has lagged, despite home language introduction in many countries' curricula. In Uganda, which has 41 languages in addition to the two national languages, the 2007 curriculum mandated use of local languages in grades 1 to 3 before a switch to English in grade 4 (UNICEF, 2016). Teachers needed more support in early grades to manage mother tongue instruction, and transition to English was a challenge for children whose teachers lacked skills to teach English as a subject (Ssentanda, 2014). Language of instruction policy, although important, is not sufficient to make curricula more inclusive. South Africa has committed to 11 official languages in the constitution and in education. Yet learning outcomes have been consistently low. While this is partly related to gaps in language of instruction policy implementation, implementation needs to be combined with core pedagogical interventions (Fleisch, 2018).

In Armenia, the model general education curriculum for national minorities allocates 41 hours per week to teaching their language and literature in all 12 grades. The criteria and programme for Kurdish and Assyrian languages have been approved (UNECE, 2014). In Georgia, the national curriculum mandates teaching in a native language (Armenian, Azeri or Russian) as well as a state language in minority schools (UNESCO, 2018).

In India's Odisha state, multilingual education has been in effect since the mid-2000s. Its coverage has expanded to about 1,500 primary schools and 21 languages of instruction (UNICEF, 2019), for which online dictionaries have been published (Global Voices, 2019). After evaluation of the initial phase, which showed positive effects on learning outcomes, the state government announced a policy for tribal children in 2014, the first of its kind in the country (Odisha Government, 2014). In preparation for and support of the policy, it developed curriculum and culture-specific learning materials in tribal languages, as well as teacher training manuals. The community was actively involved in the curriculum design. Priority was given to recruiting teachers fluent in the respective languages. A state resource group, including teachers, linguists, international

"
Own language is a right and an essential part of any group's ethnic identity
"

agencies, anthropologists and tribal language experts, was formed (Mohanty, 2017, 2019).

A review of language policies in six South-eastern Asian countries noted that only Myanmar recognized three languages – mother tongue, Burmese and English – in its language policy, introduced in 2016 (Bradley, 2019). Cambodia developed a multilingual education curriculum using Khmer and five indigenous languages. An evaluation positively appraised the 2014–18 Multilingual Education National Action Plan but called for providing the curriculum and materials for pre-primary and primary schools in more languages and strengthening teacher capacity (Ball and Smith, 2019).

Own language is a right and an essential part of any group's ethnic identity (Expert Mechanism on the Rights of Indigenous Peoples, 2010); it has been among the fundamental claims of indigenous organizations (ECLAC, 2014). South and central America has some 560 indigenous languages in 21 countries and territories. In six countries, some indigenous languages are official; in three, they are recognized as regional languages; in a further seven countries and territories, some are used as languages of instruction (World Bank, 2015). In Chile, indigenous languages were incorporated into schools with over 50% indigenous enrolment in 2010. In 2013, this was extended as a voluntary initiative in schools with at least 20% indigenous enrolment (Webb and Radcliffe, 2013). The curriculum framework for indigenous languages has been implemented in Aymara, Mapuzugun, Quechua and Rapa Nui. Study plans and programmes have also been developed (Chile Ministry of Education, 2019).

The United Nations (UN) Standard Rules on the Equalization of Opportunities for Persons with Disabilities stress the need for governments to consider the use of sign language in educating deaf children (United Nations General Assembly, 1994). About 34 million children worldwide have disabling hearing loss (WHO, 2018). Nearly 95% of deaf children are born to hearing parents, for whom sign language knowledge is crucial. Local sign languages introduce deaf children to basic expression and communication skills and need to be recognized as their mother tongue. Just 41 countries worldwide recognize sign language as an official language. Of these, 21 are in the European Union, in line with a 1988 European Parliament resolution (World Federation of the Deaf, 2017).

The UN Convention on the Rights of Persons with Disabilities explicitly requires states to provide for sign language in many aspects of life, including education. Sign language is thus a means of fostering access to curricula. In the context of deaf children, access to mainstream schools with reasonable accommodations requires sign language interpretation of the national language. However, International Sign notwithstanding, there are hundreds of national sign languages, with their morphologies, phonologies and syntax (Hohenberger, 2007). For instance, Dutch Sign Language has seven dialects (Mercator, 2017).

Deaf people's organizations strive for bilingual education with sign language as the language of instruction and the national language as the written language. A number of countries recognize sign language for instruction, including Ethiopia in its 2016 education law. In the United States, 45 of the 50 states do (National Association of the Deaf, 2018). However, recognition does not imply implementation. Faroese Sign Language was recognized as official in June 2017. The government intends to provide for teaching of and in sign language, and a sign language dictionary has been prepared, but the measure has not yet been implemented (OHCHR, 2019a).

Zimbabwe Sign Language has no direct links with spoken languages and has no descriptive grammar. The government recognized it as an official language in the 2013 Constitution, but its role in instruction is unclear. Most deaf children lack an appropriate environment to learn it at home and arrive at boarding schools without

"
Just 41 countries worldwide recognize sign language as an official language. Of these, 21 are in the European Union
"

a spoken or signed language. They learn it among themselves, with each school developing a separate system (Kadenge and Muzengi, 2018). Teachers in mainstream rural primary schools lack dictionaries, and large class sizes affect their ability to pay attention to deaf learners' needs (Musengi and Chireshe, 2012). Some teachers believe the sign language is a deficient communication system that deaf students can learn informally and independently (Musengi, 2019). Some fear it interferes with learning the spoken language and are uncomfortable with the role of teaching assistants (Musengi et al., 2012). Zimbabwe recently began to assess teacher performance and publicly examine deaf children, which it is hoped will have a positive influence on negative attitudes (Kadenge and Muzengi, 2018).

The Kenyan Constitution promotes development and use of Kenyan Sign Language, Braille and other communication formats and technology accessible to people with disabilities. Since most deaf children in low-resource settings start primary school with little or no language, the role of local sign languages as mother tongues is essential in introducing them to basic expression and communication skills and opening the pathway for progression in formal education (Deaf Child Worldwide, 2018; VSO and Deaf Child WorldWide, 2018). Teaching reading in a way that is not primarily sound-based but centres on sign language helps deaf children understand the meaning of and remember written words (Wauters et al., 2001). Such teaching requires specific teaching skills and reading materials (Royal Dutch Kentalis, 2019). eKitabu's Studio KSL project integrates Kenyan Sign Language videos into digital children's storybooks featuring locally relevant stories and characters, packaged in the open standard EPUB format for wide access. The storybooks contain sign language glossaries and questions for teachers and children to use together (All Children Reading, 2018).

Incoherent curricula may deepen education exclusion

Use of different or non-standard curricula for some groups hinders inclusion (Garner et al., 2012). In England and Wales (United Kingdom), results from the Deployment and Impact of Support Staff project suggested that students with special education needs were often involved in one-to-one interaction with a teaching assistant and removed from class. In 87% of cases when they were not in class, they were known to be doing a different task than their peers (Blatchford et al., 2009).

In many countries, students with disabilities are explicitly taught a special education curriculum. In Kenya, the basic education curriculum framework includes a special needs education framework. Students who can follow the regular curriculum can receive it with adaptations, while for those who may not be able to (e.g. those with 'mental handicap, deaf blindness, autism, cerebral palsy, multiple handicaps, and profound disabilities'), four levels of education have been designed: foundation, intermediate, pre-vocational and vocational. Yet the modality is stage-based, not age-based (Kenya Institute of Curriculum Development, 2017). In Malaysia, special education curriculum, also known as alternative curriculum, was developed in line with the 2013 Special Education Regulations. Tailored curricula were also designed for specific groups, such as blind learners. No curricula for students with learning disabilities, such as autism, have yet been introduced (GEM Report Education Profiles).

Choice options, whether for schools or students, may hurt disadvantaged learners. In Austria, school autonomy over curriculum provides a means of boosting schools' attractiveness but creates a hierarchy among schools, as they can choose students from a surplus of applications. Most often, the most vulnerable and marginalized students end up in the 'leftover' classes or schools (Altrichter, 2019). In the United Kingdom, students with lower achievement levels were encouraged to take certain vocational qualifications, which helped them – and their schools – obtain higher scores but did not necessarily help them learn what they needed most; hence a 2016 reform removed these qualifications from the school performance tables (Spielman, 2017).

Building pathways instead of dead ends between education levels is a key challenge for inclusion. In Brazil, the primary education structure supports both vertical articulation

> " In many countries, students with disabilities are explicitly taught a special education curriculum "

> " A textbook development approach that employs inclusive language, represents diverse identities and integrates human rights serves the purpose of inclusion "

(learning continuity and progression through the primary cycle) and horizontal (among areas of knowledge) (Opertti et al., 2018). In Finland, the 2014 National Core Curriculum for Basic Education aims to promote education continuity and ensure that learners can progress through the levels and cycles (Finnish National Board of Education, 2014).

TEXTBOOKS CAN EXCLUDE THROUGH OMISSION AND MISREPRESENTATION

Textbooks, as an essential part of enacted curricula, are crucial for promoting inclusion (Fuchs and Bock, 2018). A textbook development approach that employs inclusive language, represents diverse identities and integrates human rights serves the purpose of inclusion (UNESCO, 2017). Civic education, social studies, history, geography, religion and ethics textbooks, in particular, should encompass human and citizen rights. This also implies that inclusion and exclusion in different social and historical contexts should be represented to foster awareness of challenges.

Even when textbooks deal with diversity and multiculturalism, they may avoid critical discussion of complex and controversial topics. Diversity may appear as a special topic rather than a normal feature of social coexistence. Ethnic or religious groups may be marginalized, and certain minority stereotypes perpetuated (Niehaus, 2018).

Textbooks and the legitimate knowledge they convey emerge from complex power dynamics (Apple and Christian-Smith, 1991). They can perpetuate biases and stereotypes through visual or written content but also by omission. This section highlights representations and misrepresentations in textbooks through examples drawn primarily from an analysis of textbooks from 28 countries conducted for this report (Fuchs et al., 2020).

HOW MINORITIES ARE REPRESENTED IN TEXTBOOKS IS KEY TO THEIR INCLUSION

Representation of ethnic, linguistic, religious and indigenous minorities in textbooks depends largely on historical and national context. Factors influencing countries' treatment of minorities include the presence of indigenous populations; the demographic, political or economic dominance of one or more ethnic groups; the history of segregation or conflict; the conceptualization of nationhood; the role of immigration; and various combinations of these factors. Textbooks may acknowledge minority groups in ways that mitigate or exacerbate the degree to which they are received, or perceive themselves, as 'other' (Fuchs et al., 2020).

In New Zealand, a lower secondary school social studies textbook introduces the term 'superdiversity' and depicts migration as a continuous phenomenon, from the first Polynesian settlers to the most recent migrants from Eastern and South-eastern Asia. It addresses historical ethnic and religious discrimination, with victims ranging from resident Germans during the two world wars to Polynesian immigrants whose homes were raided by the police in the 1970s and 1980s to vandalism of Jewish graves in 2004, which led to the establishment of Te Ngira, a diversity action programme. The textbook focuses extensively on the indigenous Māori culture, ensuring that nearly all chapters feature examples relating to their history, customs and skills. There is notable use of Māori terms to describe specific cultural concepts, which goes beyond isolated content elements, pointing to indigenous practices in society (Fuchs et al., 2020).

Countries with a history of ethnic, tribal and religious conflict tend to cultivate a self-image as a plurinational state. They emphasize the common aspects of the constituent cultures and how diversity enriches the nation. Mostly they focus on the welfare of the state and how individual citizens can fulfil civic duty. Some try to reflect on how power relations affect representation of individual groups.

> "
> Textbooks may acknowledge minority groups in ways that mitigate or exacerbate the degree to which they are received, or perceive themselves, as 'other'
> "

China recognizes 56 ethnic groups (Mullaney, 2010). Analyses of secondary school history textbook content, language and organization have documented how representation of non-Han people changed in the late 1970s from non-Chinese to Chinese, following the principle of interethnic equality. History textbooks have since covered minority histories and contributions to China, even downplaying the role of Han figures that could be relatively controversial for other ethnic groups (Baranovitch, 2010). However, the process has not always been uniform (Yan and Vickers, 2019). Other analyses argue that moral education textbooks both under-represent minorities and are more likely to use stereotypes in their imagery (Chu, 2018). With respect to language of instruction, the 1984 Regional Ethnic Autonomy Law stated that schools should use textbooks in their own languages and also use these languages for teaching, whenever possible (China Government, 2001). In Xinjiang province, Uighur was replaced as language of instruction in primary and secondary education in 1999 and a bilingual education policy adopted, which was extended to preschools in 2005. While there are two teachers in many bilingual preschool classrooms, one of them Uighur-speaking, most were instructed and trained to teach in Chinese only (Chen et al., 2018).

In Indonesia, the grade 10 civic education textbook presents official identity-forming principles: Bhinneka Tunggal Ika (unity in diversity or, literally, out of many, one) and Pancasila (five principles: belief in god, just and civilized humanity, national unity, representative democracy and social justice). The textbook describes religious, ethnic, sub-ethnic and linguistic diversity with respect, and speaks in favour of openness, tolerance, inclusion and respect for human rights. At the same time, it does not shy away from sociocultural and inter-religious conflicts or human rights violations, providing detailed information on abuses of power and violent riots in recent national history. The textbook emphasizes domestic inclusiveness and does not refer to the various ethnic and tribal groups as minorities (Fuchs et al., 2020).

Following the break-up of the Soviet Union, Central Asian countries developed state language schools and tried to strengthen state language teaching. However, the collapse of textbook supply chains had a damaging influence on education quality. For instance, in Kazakhstan, less than 40% of sanctioned textbooks were available in Kyrgyz and Russian and even less in Uzbek and Tajik. In Kazakhstan and Kyrgyzstan, primary and secondary schools choose target languages for subjects based on teacher capacity, context and resources. The most successful pilot schools became resource centres for new schools, providing multilingual content and teaching materials. The High Commissioner on National Minorities of the Organization for Security and Co-operation in Europe supported the creation of an Uzbek language textbook development and publishing centre in Osh, Kyrgyzstan. The recent adoption of a trilingual education policy in Kazakhstan made it possible to increase provision of new Tajik, Uighur and Uzbek primary school textbooks and learning materials (Stoianova and Angermann, 2018).

In Bangladesh, within the framework of the 2010 National Education Policy, which recognized the right of all children to receive mother tongue education, the Mother Tongue-based Multilingual Education programme has been introduced in five indigenous languages in pre-primary education (GEM Report Education Profiles). Non-government organizations (NGOs) often step in to provide mother tongue pre-primary education for indigenous children, as in the BRAC Education for Ethnic Children project (Ali, 2016). In these preschools, teachers communicate in ethnic languages and Bengali using teaching materials based on local culture (Sharif, 2014). Among minorities, Santals often suffer from exclusion and early school dropout (Sarker and Davey, 2009; Siddique and Vlassopoulos, 2020). Moreover, Santals have no textbooks because of lack of agreement on whether to use Bangla, Roman or Ol Chiki, a Santal script developed in the 1920s (Sharif, 2014). In 2017, a parliamentary standing committee asked the government to resolve the issue

(*New Age*, 2017). India has recognized Santali as an official language (Choksi, 2017), and Ol Chiki script has been included in university curricula (Anderson, 2015).

In Nepal, the Curriculum Development Centre developed primary school textbooks and supplementary reading materials in 22 languages (GEM Report Education Profiles). In the Philippines, textbooks have been prepared and translated in 14 languages to support the curriculum for indigenous people. Indigenization of learning materials is encouraged in the Occidental Mindoro and Oriental Mindoro areas (GEM Report Education Profiles).

The Bahraini grade 9 civic education textbook, introduced after a reform in 2005, covers citizenship extensively, with emphasis on national unity and how individual citizens can contribute to it. It characterizes Bahraini society by its Arab and Islamic identity while also emphasizing the country's multi-ethnicity, its geographical position, the importance of intercultural exchange and the regional tensions that lead to different interpretations of citizenship (Fuchs et al., 2020). However, applying a Western conception of citizenship based on liberal values, which was at least partly influenced by collaboration with international advisers during curriculum preparation, has not been problem-free. Teachers found it difficult when students raised controversial issues. Discussion was not being used as a structured activity, and teachers took an avoidance approach, as most opposed explicitly acknowledging diversity in Bahraini society because they believed it might increase tensions (Selaibeekh, 2017).

In Egypt, history textbooks have made great strides in shedding negative depictions of various religions. For instance, they cast Christian values of justice, equality and tolerance in a positive light and have removed references to relatively controversial historical figures that might have been offensive to some minorities. Nevertheless, there is a sense that the overall historical narrative favours the Arab Muslim identity over other perspectives and voices, which could undermine the aim of inclusiveness. For instance, the history of the Coptic minority, although consistently included, took up

> " Nepal developed primary school textbooks and supplementary reading materials in 22 languages "

disproportionately less space and did not acknowledge its contributions (Abdou, 2016, 2017).

In Cameroon's grade 9–10 civic education textbook, diversity is particularly emphasized in relation to human rights, although national unity is given preference over diversity in the context of citizenship. The upper secondary civic education textbook in Nigeria emphasizes multi-ethnic national identity even more strongly, as the concept of government majority is linked to both effective representation of various ethnic interests and duties of care towards them (Fuchs et al., 2020). In South Africa, representation of races varies across subjects. For instance, white people are represented in 18% of visuals in history and social science and 28% in mathematics and life skills. Some stereotypes are also apparent with respect to representation in sports, with white people in more privileged positions (South Africa Department of Basic Education, 2019).

Three grade 9 and 10 civic education textbooks from Latin America show a generally inclusive approach. The Argentinian textbook critically examines racism and xenophobia. The foreword to the Mexican textbook defines inclusion as one of 10 basic principles (e.g. peaceful conflict resolution, respect). The Peruvian textbook reflects on the country as a multi-ethnic nation-state, explicitly including specific ethnic minorities and indigenous groups within a human rights and citizenship framework under the heading 'We are a diverse nation'. However, it repeatedly focuses on the indigenous population as an ethnic minority, with textual and visual depiction predominantly of people in traditional costume, posing a risk of stereotyping (Fuchs et al., 2020).

An analysis of textbooks from the Canadian provinces of British Columbia and of Labrador and Newfoundland points to examples that ask students to think as settlers. Such a narrative may be considered insensitive, undermining indigenous peoples' historical grievances based on prior presence (Schaefli et al., 2019). However, representation of indigenous people has been improving. The Quebec government spent CAD 1.6 million in 2018 to replace the word Amerindian and modify other indigenous content in recently finalized history textbooks (Banerjee, 2018). By contrast, in the United States, 87% of national and state history standards related to indigenous peoples focus on pre-1900 history, limiting discussion and representation of indigenous peoples. Of existing state standards, 17 had no post-1900 indigenous standards (Shear et al., 2015).

WOMEN ARE UNDER-REPRESENTED IN TEXTBOOKS

In many countries, girls and women are under-represented in textbooks or, when included, depicted in traditional roles. In Afghanistan, women were almost absent from grade 1 textbooks published in the 1990s. Since 2001, they have been more present but in passive and domestic roles as mothers, caregivers, daughters and sisters. They are mostly represented as dependent, with teaching being the only career open to them (Sarvarzade and Wotipka, 2017). A review of 95 primary and secondary compulsory education textbooks in the Islamic Republic of Iran showed that women accounted for 37% of images. About half the images showing women were related to family and education, while work environments appeared in less than 7%. There were no images of women in about 60% of textbooks for Farsi and foreign language, 63% for science and 74% for social science (Paivandi, 2008). In India, the Maharashtra State Bureau of Textbook Production and Curriculum Research revised many textbook images in 2019. For instance, grade 2 textbooks show men and women sharing household chores, along with a female doctor and a male chef. Students are asked to note these images and talk about them (News18, 2019).

The share of females in secondary school English language textbook text and images was 44% in Malaysia and Indonesia, 37% in Bangladesh and 24% in Punjab province, Pakistan. Women were represented in less prestigious occupations and as introverted and passive (Islam and Asadullah, 2018). A Malaysian primary school textbook suggested girls risked being shamed and ostracized unless they protected their modesty. The Ministry of Education acknowledged weaknesses in quality control and sent a sticker to cover the graphic in question (Lin, 2019).

Respondents to a public consultation on gender discrimination in textbooks in the Republic of Korea pointed out that doctors and scientists were shown as mainly male, dancers, housewives and nurses as mainly female. Early childhood education textbooks depicted rabbits and foxes as female and lions and tigers as male (Republic of Korea Ministry of Gender Equality and Family, 2018). In the United States, a study of introductory economics textbooks found that 18% of characters mentioned were female, mostly portrayed in relation to food, fashion or entertainment (Stevenson and Zlotnick, 2018). A report on how women's history was reflected in pre-primary, primary and secondary social studies found that 53% of mentions of women in state standards referred to domestic and family roles and 2% to entry into the workforce (Maurer et al., 2018).

> " In Chile, the grade 6 science textbook had 2 female vs 29 male characters "

> **"**
> The rights of people with disabilities were mentioned in 9%
> of secondary school social science textbooks around 2010,
> up from 2% in the 1970s
> **"**

Chilean grade 4 history textbooks had 2 female characters for every 10 male, and their historical contributions were represented with stereotyped views linked to domestic chores. The grade 6 science textbook had 2 female vs 29 male characters (Covacevich and Quintela-Dávila, 2014). Women's under-representation was also observed in Italy, despite its participation in a European Union project in which textbook publishers agreed to a code to improve gender equality (Scierri, 2017). In Spain, the share of female characters was 10% in primary school and 13% in secondary school textbooks. One-fifth of more than 12,000 images were of women (López Navajas and López García-Molins, 2009).

An analysis of preschool textbooks in Morocco found that 71% of images depicting women showed them doing voluntary work and 10% doing paid work (Cobano-Delgado and Llorent-Bedmar, 2019). In Turkey, primary school textbooks presented unequal social roles and a patriarchal understanding of family unquestioningly, and secondary school textbook language exhibited sexism, although these problems were somewhat reduced after the 2004 curricular reform (Çayir, 2014). In Uganda, secondary school physics textbooks generally did not mention the gender of objects and subjects. However, use of gendered nouns (e.g. boy) and pronouns (e.g. his) gave the text gender connotations, while illustrations referred to men (Namatende-Sakwa, 2018).

REPRESENTATION OF DISABILITY IN TEXTBOOKS REQUIRES MORE ATTENTION

The main challenges with representation of disability in textbooks are neglect and misrepresentation. A global analysis showed that the rights of people with disabilities were mentioned in 9% of secondary school social science textbooks around 2010, up from 2% in the 1970s (UNESCO, 2016c).

There was only one mention related to disability in the text of seven secondary school English language textbooks in the Islamic Republic of Iran (Hodkinson et al., 2016). In South Africa, a government review found that people with physical disabilities accounted for 2% of visuals and 1% of text mentions, and that intellectual disabilities were not represented. An exception was the Life Orientation textbook, which considered disability more extensively and covered various types, such as physical impairment, sensory impediment and learning disorder. A volunteer activity section depicted young people with disabilities helping less fortunate children (Fuchs et al., 2020; South Africa Department of Basic Education, 2019).

In Spain, 0.6% of primary school physical education textbooks published between 2006 and 2013 involved people with disabilities, chiefly people with physical disabilities using a wheelchair (Moya-Mata et al., 2017). The Turkish grade 11 social studies textbook covered disability under 'negative deviance', which also included criminals and those with mental deficiencies or psychological disorders (Çayir, 2014). A study of 96 primary school textbooks in the United Kingdom showed that 0.3% of characters in illustrations and 0.8% in photographs were people with disabilities (Hodkinson et al., 2016). Such limited exposure can generate negative attitudes.

> **"**
> Disability is often misrepresented
> in children's reading books.
> Characters with disabilities
> tend to be positioned as inferior
> **"**

Disability is often misrepresented in children's reading books. Connotations of something outside the norm convey an exclusionary message. Characters with disabilities tend to be positioned as inferior (Curwood, 2013; Wopperer, 2011), often as victims, dependent or objects of pity (Beckett et al., 2010). Even award-winning books, often recommended reading in schools, may have been written years ago, with an outdated understanding of disability (Leininger et al., 2010).

A review of 28 textbooks for this report suggests that changes are under way. Some two-thirds mention the situation of people with physical or mental disabilities, generally through legislative amendments. They use keywords, such as anti-discrimination law and accessibility. In some cases, disability is extended to include the chronically ill and the elderly. Although people with disabilities are still rarely depicted in non-disability-related contexts, a Canadian textbook shows people with disabilities as autonomous individuals, activists and public figures, such as a sports personality greeting young people. A Romanian textbook section on non-violence in schools shows a sprinter with one arm and a man in a wheelchair playing a guitar (Fuchs et al., 2020).

Lack of textbooks in alternative formats hinders curriculum accessibility, especially for visually impaired people. The 2013 Marrakesh Treaty tried to address the fact that only 1% to 7% of the world's published books were accessible due to copyright barriers, among other challenges (WIPO, 2016). In Greece, many textbooks are either not translated into Braille or inaccurately translated (National Confederation of Disabled People, 2019). In Malawi, curriculum revision is often not matched by revision of learning materials in Braille (Malawi Government, 2016).

RELIABLE, RELEVANT AND FORMATIVE ASSESSMENT PROMOTES INCLUSION

Information from learning assessments is critical to guide teaching for all students.[2] Yet assessment tends to be associated with standardized tests administered in a controlled way at the end of an education cycle to large numbers of students, often to the disadvantage of the more vulnerable. When used for accountability purposes, such high-stakes assessments can lead to the adoption of negative practices, such as selective admission, strict discipline policies, student reassignment and greater focus and time given to those most likely to succeed. According to head teacher reports across countries taking part in the 2015 Organization for Economic Co-operation and Development Programme for International Student Assessment, 38% of tested students were in schools where academic performance was an important determinant of admission. In Bulgaria, Croatia, Hong Kong (China), Hungary, Japan, Singapore, Thailand and Viet Nam, more than 8 in 10 schools used performance as a criterion. By contrast, Finland, Greece, Norway, Spain and Sweden rarely based admission on student performance (OECD, 2016).

While exclusionary practices are common, assessment and inclusion need not be seen as contrary. However, to support inclusive education, assessment systems need to abide by principles that promote learning for all students. A review of assessment systems in 29 European countries provides useful entry points into these principles. First, all students' learning progress and achievement should be identified and valued, and all students should have the opportunity to demonstrate their progress and achievement. Second, assessment procedures should be complementary, coherent with the goal of supporting learning and teaching,

---

2   This section draws on Hegarty (2020).

> 66
>
> High-stakes assessments can lead to negative practices, such as selective admission, strict discipline policies, student reassignment and greater focus and time given to those most likely to succeed
>
> 99

> "
> **Standardized tests can provide important diagnostic information, but it is how the information is used that makes the difference**
> "

and coordinated, avoiding segregation through labelling. Third, students should be entitled to reliable and valid assessment procedures that accommodate and, where possible, are modified to meet their needs (European Agency for Development in Special Needs Education, 2007, 2008).

A RENEWED FOCUS ON FORMATIVE ASSESSMENT IS NEEDED

To serve its purpose, assessment should be valid and not driven by external factors. Language skills assessment administered in a student's second language may be biased, as it will be insufficiently accurate in measuring actual linguistic proficiency. If test content or administration favours some test takers over others, or if their learning experiences are substantially different in relation to what is being tested, it can be difficult if not impossible to interpret test scores or to make equitable decisions on that basis.

Assessment should focus on students' tasks: how they tackle them, which ones prove difficult and how some aspects can be adapted to enable success. A shift in emphasis from high-stakes summative assessments at the end of the education cycle to low-stakes formative assessments over the education trajectory (i.e. from the outcome to the process of assessment) underpins efforts to make assessment fit for the purpose of inclusive education (Laveault and Allal, 2016; Opertti and Ji, 2017). An appropriate connection needs to be made between summative and formative assessment. Standardized tests can provide important diagnostic information, but it is how the information is used that makes the difference.

Teachers need a degree of autonomy to identify the assessment practices that best serve a broader set of learning goals. In New Zealand, a national survey of assessment practices in primary and secondary schools attended by students with high or very high needs enumerated 24 approaches, some of which were highly valued and frequently used by teachers, such as observations, work samples, anecdotal records and portfolios (Bourke and Mentis, 2010).

In the United Republic of Tanzania, the Toa Nafasi (Provide a Chance) Project uses assessment to target interventions in 10 public primary schools. It assesses grade 1 children in literacy, numeracy and cognitive skills and collects information on social behaviour, adaptive activities and motor skills through observation and interviews. Administered to all children by trained teachers on a one-to-one basis, it takes up to 20 minutes per child. It is used to identify which children need specific classroom small-group interventions and individual tutoring in literacy and mathematics and group games to promote executive functioning and social skills. Five such sessions per week, each lasting 30 to 45 minutes, are devoted to literacy, mathematics, games and art. An evaluation found that about one in four children screened in three successive year cohorts was selected to receive the interventions. Significant progress was recorded at 6- and 12-month intervals for each cohort (Stone-Macdonald and Fettig, 2019).

However, in poor and rich countries alike, such assessment approaches are scattered and unsystematic. A review of assessment approaches in Germany noted numerous examples of individualized teaching and assessment in heterogeneous learning groups, but they were unevenly dispersed across locations and types of schools (Prengel, 2016). A review of approaches to inclusive education in Uganda identified isolated examples of learning assessment for children with disabilities, such as the approach used in three schools by Sense International, an NGO for deaf-blind children (Enable-Ed and Uganda Society for Disabled Children, 2017). There is scope to collect information systematically to evaluate approaches' effectiveness and suitability for daily use so that they can be adopted in mainstream education (Lebeer et al., 2011).

> "
> **It is up to governments to ensure that inclusive education and assessment policies are consistent**
> "

> "
> In many poorer countries, a core underlying problem is that there is insufficient attention to monitoring of learning outcomes
> "

ASSESSMENT SHOULD BE COHERENT WITH INCLUSIVE EDUCATION

Often, assessments are held responsible for exclusion when it is the entire legislative and policy framework that is exclusionary. Where opportunities to continue education are rationed and determined by an examination, more vulnerable students' education may be ended prematurely or diverted towards less desirable pathways. Placement in special schools, for instance, is often based on psychological or achievement tests, complemented by teacher and other professional reports, another form of assessment. Yet the outcomes vary by country, depending on whether special schools are the exception or the rule. Often assessment becomes just a tool to implement exclusionary laws and policies (Hegarty, 2020).

It is up to governments to ensure that inclusive education and assessment policies are consistent. Teachers in South Africa's Eastern Cape province pointed to inconsistency between the 2001 Education White Paper 6 and the 2014 Screening, Identification, Assessment and Support (SIAS) strategy on the one hand, which promote curriculum differentiation, and Curriculum and Assessment Policy Statements that contradict them (Geldenhuys and Wevers, 2013). SIAS is also under-resourced. The SIAS strategy entails all children being screened in grade 1 and the results recorded in a learner profile, a legal document that follows students when they move schools. In consultation with parents, teachers are to complete a support needs assessment as a basis for an individualized support plan. If teacher support is insufficient, a school-based support team draws up a plan, which in turn is referred to district-level support if the objectives are not met (Adewumi et al., 2017). District officials have been trained, but the strategy has not sufficiently informed pre-service and in-service teacher education, which affects uptake of the otherwise clear procedures (Kelly and McKenzie, 2018; McKenzie et al., 2018).

In many poorer countries, a core underlying problem is that there is insufficient attention to monitoring of learning outcomes. Preoccupation with high-stakes examinations, often mistakenly considered equivalent to assessment for learning, usually takes over.

A study based on Service Delivery Indicator surveys in seven sub-Saharan African countries showed that roughly 1 in 10 teachers had minimum knowledge in general pedagogy and none had minimum knowledge in student assessment. While teachers use some practices, such as structuring, planning, asking questions and giving feedback, to promote learning in classrooms, less than 1 in 10 applied all practices (Bold et al., 2017).

ASSESSMENT SHOULD PROVIDE ACCOMMODATIONS

As in the case of curriculum, accommodations are ways to adapt tests to remove barriers that distract from the measurement of learning outcomes. They include changes to test content, format or administration that remove irrelevant obstacles for certain test takers without compromising test validity or giving unfair advantage to individual test takers. They aim to ensure that all students are assessed and, in the case of high-stakes tests, ranked fairly. To the extent that they are successful, accommodations provide an important mainstream experience for students who otherwise risk being excluded or ranked below their true ability.

The Gordon Commission on the future of assessment in education in the United States examined issues related to students with disabilities or at risk of being assessed unfairly (ETS, 2013). Braille or large-print versions of tests, written replacements for oral components, extra time in timed tests, use of voice recording or an assistant to record responses, and access to bilingual glossaries or other second-language support are among the tools being tried (Thurlow, 2013; World Bank et al., 2019). For students with language disabilities, assessments that rely on language communication need to use different communication modes, such as non-linguistic or visual modes, which could be more effective in providing feedback.

Various reviews have assessed the effectiveness of test accommodations in the United States. The use of audio presentation in mathematics enhanced scores for primary but not secondary school students (Laitusis et al., 2012). A review of five types of accommodations for grade 3 to 8 students with attention deficit hyperactivity disorder showed no association with improved standardized test scores in reading and mathematics (Pritchard et al., 2016). A major review of 53 studies published in 2013–14, from preschool to post-secondary education, offered a mixed picture. Extended time tended to improve test scores for students with disabilities, whereas oral delivery did not. Two studies examining calculator use showed positive if nuanced support for enhanced performance by students with disabilities (Rogers et al., 2016).

Methodological limitations make it hard to reach straightforward conclusions. Small sample size, weak study design and insufficient control over how accommodations are applied, including simultaneous implementation of various accommodations, get in the way of interpreting results. Some accommodations are used for very different kinds of impairments even if grouped under a common label, such as learning disabilities (Thurlow, 2013). A positive effect of accommodations not to be underestimated involves perception. Students feel that accommodations help them perform better, and teachers believe they are beneficial to student performance and self-esteem (Rogers et al., 2016).

Importantly, the validity of assessing the effectiveness of standardized test accommodations has been questioned on theoretical grounds, as they appear to fit students to a model, for instance in the case of students with dyslexia (Reid, 2016). The emphasis should instead be on students with impairments and how the assessment can support them in demonstrating learning. Australia's Queensland state has developed an approach to high-stakes assessment for grade 12 students that avoids accommodations. The process starts with identifying and transparently setting down learning expectations to be assessed based on the state curriculum and individualized education programmes, where necessary. The assessment modality takes student impairments into account without minimizing the requirement or opportunity to demonstrate learning. Ultimately, a moderation process based on peer review of work samples ensures comparability of learning goals and consistency of judgement standards (Cumming and Maxwell, 2013). Reports from the assessment regulator showed evidence of high levels of comparability in schools' application of the standards (Queensland Government, 2017).

CONCLUSION

Curricula, textbooks and assessments are key building blocks of inclusive education systems. Curriculum choices are of fundamental importance to promote the values of an inclusive and democratic society. Curricula need to reassure all groups at risk of exclusion that they are at the core of the education project, whether in terms of content or implementation. Curricula need to be flexible and adapted to diverse needs. They should not lead to dead ends in education but offer pathways for continuous education opportunities.

Textbooks, as a component of curriculum, can omit or misrepresent group characteristics, perpetuating stereotypes and undermining any pretence to inclusion. Through textbooks, minorities and vulnerable groups can see themselves included as equal contributors to national development, rather than relegated to a marginalized position in society, and can see their differences treasured and respected, rather than caricatured.

Assessments are often organized unduly narrowly. Critics see governments sending conflicting signals through assessments about their commitment to inclusion. If appropriately designed and focused on learning, they are essential for steering teachers and students towards targeted interventions. General Comment 4 to Article 24 on the right to inclusive education of the UN Convention of the Rights of Persons with Disabilities is clear: 'Standardised assessments must be replaced by flexible and multiple forms of assessments and recognition of individual progress towards broad goals that provide alternative routes for learning' (UN Committee on the Rights of Persons with Disabilities, 2016, p. 9).

Lesieli Latu teaches students with disabilities at Ngele'ia Primary School in Nuku'alofa, Tonga. The class is part of an inclusive education pilot programme.

CREDIT: Connor Ashleigh/DFAT

6

Teachers

What is teaching for inclusion?

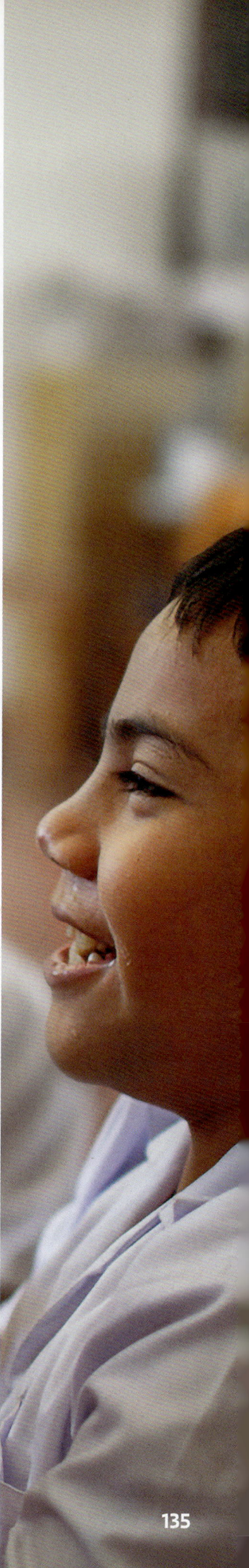

KEY MESSAGES

Inclusive teaching requires teachers to recognize the experiences and abilities of every student and to be open to diversity

- Inclusive approaches to teaching connect classroom and life experiences in problem-solving activities and require teachers to make a range of options available to all, not some, students.

Teachers tend to have positive attitudes towards inclusion but also doubts about its feasibility

- Teachers may have entrenched views about students' potential to learn. In Lebanon, teachers did not believe all students with disabilities could be successfully included.

- Teachers may not be immune to social biases and stereotypes. In the United States, 31% believed inequality was mainly due to African Americans lacking motivation.

- Such biases are detrimental to student learning. In Italy, girls assigned to teachers with implicit gender bias underperformed in mathematics and chose less demanding schools.

Teachers need to be prepared to teach students with varied backgrounds and abilities

- Some 25% of teachers in middle- and high-income countries reported a high need for professional development on teaching students with special needs.

- Across 10 francophone sub-Saharan African countries, just 8% of grade 2 and 6 teachers had received in-service training in inclusive education.

- Training on inclusion tends to focus on teaching skills for specialists. But in New Brunswick province of Canada, a quarter of all teachers were trained to help students with autism spectrum disorders.

- Mainstream and special school teachers tend to be trained separately and the latter are more likely to be negative about inclusion as the best way to educate all students. In Belarus and Norway, transition to inclusive education has been challenging for specialized teachers.

- Education officials who monitor implementation of inclusive teaching also need training. In Zanzibar (United Republic of Tanzania), nearly 70% of school inspectors, examiners and curriculum developers had attended one- to three-day training courses on inclusion.

It is not sufficient for teachers to have knowledge; they also need good working conditions

- In Cambodia, teachers questioned the feasibility of applying child-centred pedagogy in a context of overcrowded classrooms, scarce teaching resources and overambitious curricula.

- Support personnel accompany a transition towards inclusion, but a survey of unions suggested they were always available in no more than 22% of countries.

Teaching-force composition often does not reflect the diversity of classroom composition

- In India, the share of teachers from scheduled castes, which constitute 16% of the country's population, increased from 9% to 13% between 2005 and 2013.

If teachers understand what inclusion means and leave their comfort zone, taking advantage of opportunities to develop skills for children to help them recognise and respect diversity, they can be agents of change.

Maria Teresa Moreno Zavaleta, teacher, Peru

An important element of inclusive education involves ensuring that all teachers are prepared to teach all students. Inclusion cannot be realized unless teachers are agents of change, with values, knowledge and attitudes that permit every student to succeed. Throughout the world, variations in how teachers are prepared reflect standards and qualifications that differ across national contexts. But a common theme is that education systems are moving away from identifying problems with learners and towards 'identifying barriers to learning and participation and providing anticipatory responses, planning for all learners up front' (European Agency for Special Needs and Inclusive Education, 2015, pp. 14–15).

This chapter shows how this shift challenges teachers to be active agents for inclusion and to reflect on how approaches to teaching can be inclusive of all learners. Inclusive teaching requires teachers to recognize the experiences and abilities of every student and to be open to diversity. They need to be aware that all students learn by connecting classroom with life experiences, and thus embed new ideas and skills in problem-solving activities. While many teacher education and professional learning opportunities are designed accordingly, entrenched views of some students as deficient, unable to learn or incapable mean that teachers sometimes struggle to see that each student's learning capacity is open-ended.

Consequently, teachers' attitudes often mix commitment to the principle of inclusion with doubts about their preparedness and how ready the education system is to support them. Ensuring that teachers rise to the challenge requires training. It also requires support, appropriate working conditions and autonomy in the classroom to focus on every learner's success. The chapter also describes the challenge of making the teaching workforce more representative of social diversity.

> "
> Inclusive teaching requires teachers to recognize the experiences and abilities of every student and to be open to diversity
> "

INCLUSIVE TEACHING ADAPTS TO STUDENT STRENGTHS AND NEEDS

A teacher education for inclusion project identified four core values and associated competence areas (European Agency for Special Needs and Inclusive Education, 2012). Instilling these values – supporting all learners, working with others, valuing learner diversity and engaging in professional development – should lead to teachers who have high expectations for all learners (**Table 6.1**). The framework's implications for teacher attitudes, methods and professionalism should be addressed head-on and not as afterthoughts in teacher education.

Inclusive approaches to teaching are based on recognition that many students are not actively participating in the learning process. Such approaches reject methods that label and segregate students on the basis of characteristics, strengths or weaknesses. An example that has received a lot of attention is the Teaching at the Right Level (TaRL) programme in India, which was developed in response to students being left behind. It shifted attention from age and grade as organizing principles to students' actual learning levels. The programme has been applied in multiple contexts and can be used during and outside school hours, including during the summer holidays (**Box 6.1**).

Inclusive approaches to teaching also require teachers to take responsibility for all students by making a range of options available to everybody in the classroom rather than offering a set of differentiated options only to some (Florian and Spratt, 2013). For instance, adapted, learner-centred approaches that establish measurable academic goals, address strengths and challenges related to learning, and mitigate social and behavioural challenges may be particularly suitable for students with disabilities (Hayes et al., 2018). To meet the standard of inclusion, these approaches should be applied in ways that do not exclude some students from opportunities available to others.

POSITIVE TEACHER ATTITUDES TOWARDS INCLUSION ARE COMBINED WITH SCEPTICISM

Evaluating teacher attitudes towards inclusion is not straightforward. A review of teacher attitude studies in six countries, including Australia, Canada and India, found that few assessed the various cognitive, affective and behavioural components of attitudes (Ewing et al., 2017).

Still, many studies found that teachers had positive attitudes towards inclusion but also had reservations,

TABLE 6.1:
Core values and competence areas of inclusive teaching

Core values	Competence areas
Support all learners	■ Promote academic, practical, social and emotional learning for all ■ Engage effective teaching approaches in heterogenous classes based on understanding of a variety of learning processes and how to support them
Work with others	■ Work with parents and families to engage them effectively in learning ■ Work with other education professionals, including collaboration with other teachers
Value learner diversity	■ Understand inclusive education (e.g. it is based on belief in equality, human rights and democracy for all) ■ Respect, value and view learner diversity as an asset
Engage in professional development	■ Be reflective practitioners (i.e. systematically evaluate one's own performance) ■ View initial teacher education as the foundation for ongoing professional learning

Source: Based on European Agency for Special Needs and Inclusive Education (2012).

BOX 6.1:

Inclusive pedagogies are a reaction to more traditional, passive modes of teaching and learning

The non-government organization (NGO) Pratham developed TaRL in urban India in 2002 in response to the realization that schools were failing to equip students with basic reading, writing and mathematics skills. The approach has since been expanded to rural areas and outside India (Pratham, 2020).

As a pedagogical approach, TaRL was designed with a remedial mindset, aiming to enable children left behind to catch up. It departs from more traditional approaches by emphasizing clearly articulated learning goals instead of covering an entire textbook. It focuses on active teaching through simple daily activities that involve children working in groups. The instructional process starts with a basic assessment of children's learning levels and forming groups for instruction by level rather than grade. Other assessments track progress and make corrections to the course. As children progress, they move quickly into more advanced groups. Teaching–learning activities are based on the belief that children learn best through a combination of activities carried out in big groups, small groups and individually, some shared by all groups and others tailored to group level.

Evaluations have shown learning gains compared with traditional teaching. The Read India programme, which uses the TaRL approach, focuses on basic Hindi and mathematics skills acquired during intensive learning camps. An evaluation in two districts in Uttar Pradesh randomly assigned schools to four groups. The first received a 10-day camp plus another 10-day camp during the summer. The second received a 20-day camp plus another 10-day camp during the summer. The third received TaRL material without academic support. No activities took place in the fourth group. Children in the first two groups gained between 0.7 and 1 levels, on average, in language and mathematics compared with almost no progress in the third group. By the end of the learning camps, 49% of participants could read paragraphs and stories, compared with 24% in the control group. By 2017, the model was in use in over 4,000 schools across India, reaching over 200,000 children (Banerjee et al., 2017).

As of 2019, variations of the TaRL approach are being applied in 12 countries in Africa and 3 in Asia. For instance, the Catch Up programme, piloted in 80 schools in Zambia, increased the share of students able to complete a two-digit subtraction from 32% to 50% and the share of those able to read a simple paragraph or story from 34% to 52%. The programme was to be scaled up to 1,800 schools in 2019 (Teaching at the Right Level, 2019b). In Ghana, the STARS programme, run in partnership with the Ministry of Education and other public authorities, focuses on equipping teachers of grades 4 to 6 to understand the reasons behind low achievement and to offer appropriate responses (Teaching at the Right Level, 2019a).

TaRL shares features with other inclusion-oriented teaching approaches. Escuela Nueva, which began in Colombia in 1975, has expanded to 14 other countries, including the Philippines and Viet Nam (Le, 2018). It promotes active and participatory learning, with teachers serving as facilitators. It fosters skills development in multigrade instruction and encourages collaborative teacher relationships and parental and community engagement (Colbert and Arboleda, 2016). Save the Children's Literacy Boost programme has been implemented in more than 30 countries (Save the Children, 2019). It aims to improve children's reading skills by training teachers to keep students engaged. In Ethiopia, girls participating in the programme were 43% more likely to stay in school than their peers in schools without it (Dowd et al., 2013).

either because they were not empowered to overcome certain barriers or because they believed the education system and learning environment were not supportive. A survey found that teachers in Finland questioned the feasibility of inclusion and its merit for all students without fundamental shifts in the system and investment levels. Some respondents saw inclusion policies as a cover for cost-cutting (Honkasilta et al., 2019). In Japan, teachers expressed generally positive attitudes towards inclusion but had concerns about implementation, partly due to lack of belief in their ability to carry out activities that would achieve inclusion (Yada and Savolainen, 2017).

These country-specific studies were somewhat corroborated in the comparative Organisation for Economic Co-operation and Development (OECD) Teaching and Learning International Study (TALIS), which examined the attitudes and competences of lower secondary school teachers in 48 education systems

> " Many studies found that teachers had positive attitudes towards inclusion but also had reservations "

in 2018, mostly in upper-middle- and high-income countries. Finland and Japan were among the countries where teachers adapted their teaching the least to students' cultural diversity. One reason may be both countries' relative ethnic homogeneity and recent exposure to immigration. By contrast, almost all teachers in Colombia, Portugal and the United Arab Emirates adapted their teaching in diverse classrooms (**Figure 6.1**).

In Cambodia, teachers' perceptions of the possibility of inclusion of students with disabilities depended on the type of disability to be accommodated. At least half the respondents considered inclusion of students with learning, physical, visual and hearing impairments 'very possible' or 'possible'. However, less than 20% felt the same in the case of students who were blind or deaf, had intellectual disabilities or had severe and multiple disabilities (Kartika and Kuroda, 2019). In Lebanon, a survey of teachers who were part of the National Inclusion Project, which aimed to remedy exclusion of students with disabilities in mainstream schools, found positive attitudes towards inclusion but a general belief that not all students with a disability could be successfully included (Khochen and Radford, 2012). Positive experiences affect

> "
> Positive experiences affect
> teachers' attitudes positively
> "

teachers' attitudes positively. In Bangladesh, success at teaching children with disabilities and perceived school support for inclusive teaching practices were associated with more positive attitudes towards inclusive education (Ahmmed et al., 2012).

Ultimately, teachers may not be immune to social biases and stereotypes. A study comparing the general and teacher populations in the United States between 1985 and 2014 found that educators had less negative racial attitudes. However, these differences could be explained by educational attainment. A small minority of teachers still had racial attitudes detrimental to student learning and development. For instance, in 2014, 4% of pre-primary, primary and secondary school teachers believed inequality was mainly due to African Americans having less innate ability to learn, and 31% believed it was mainly due to African Americans lacking motivation or willpower to pull themselves out of poverty (Quinn, 2017). In Mexico,

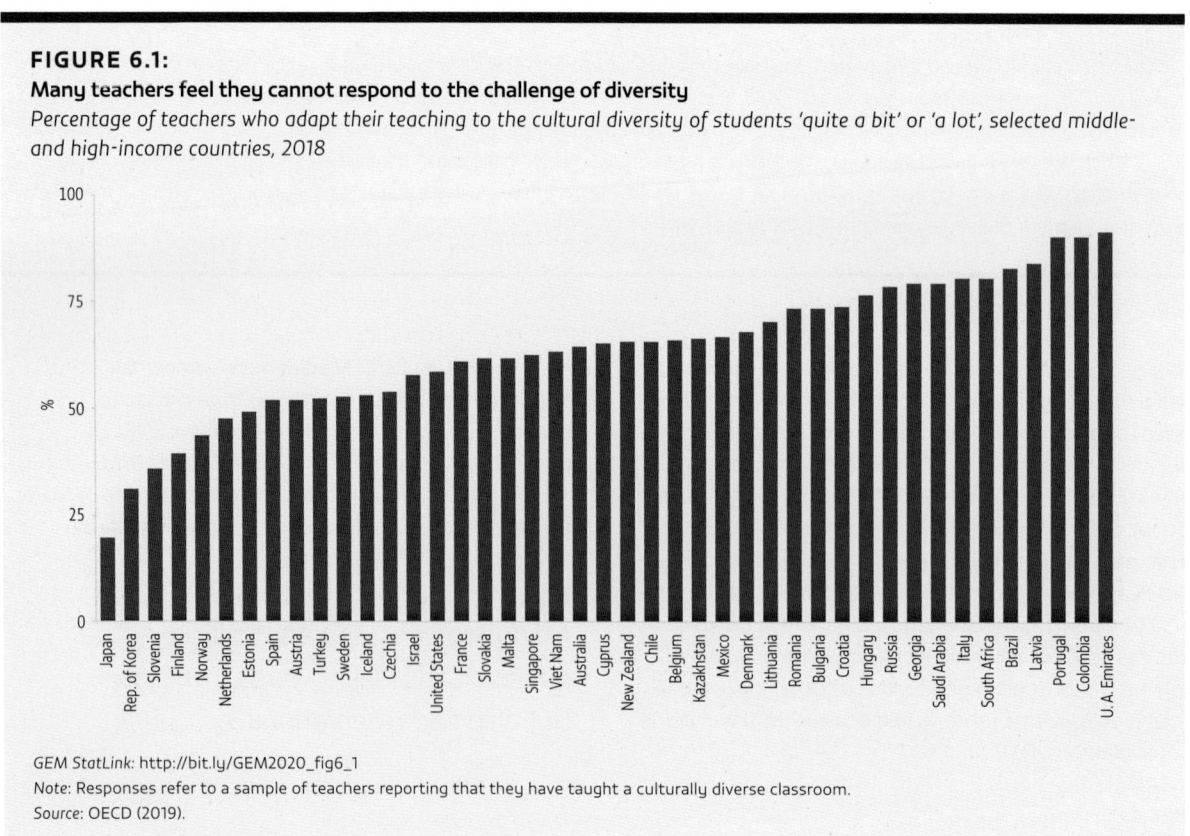

FIGURE 6.1:
Many teachers feel they cannot respond to the challenge of diversity
Percentage of teachers who adapt their teaching to the cultural diversity of students 'quite a bit' or 'a lot', selected middle- and high-income countries, 2018

GEM StatLink: http://bit.ly/GEM2020_fig6_1
Note: Responses refer to a sample of teachers reporting that they have taught a culturally diverse classroom.
Source: OECD (2019).

ADENE

prejudice influenced teacher attitudes towards inclusion of Mayan children (Osorio Vázquez, 2017). Roma parents in Europe cited discriminatory teacher behaviour, such as bullying and ostracization, as a key safety consideration for their children (Albert et al., 2015; O'Nions, 2010).

Attitudes affect student achievement, even when they are not explicit. In Italy, girls assigned to teachers with implicit gender bias underperformed in mathematics and chose less demanding schools, following teachers' recommendations (Carlana, 2019).

TEACHERS NEED COMPREHENSIVE TRAINING ON INCLUSION

Lack of preparedness for inclusive teaching may result from gaps in teachers' knowledge about pedagogies and other aspects of inclusion. Teacher education can address issues ranging from instructional techniques and classroom management to multi-professional teams and learning assessment methods. To be of good quality, teacher education must be relevant to teachers' needs, cover multiple aspects of inclusive teaching for all learners and include follow-up support to help teachers integrate new skills into classroom practices (European Agency for Special Needs and Inclusive Education, 2010, 2015).

> " Teachers' attitudes affect student achievement, even when they are not explicit "

In fact, the idea that specialized knowledge is needed can marginalize issues of diversity in teacher education (Cochran-Smith and Dudley-Marling, 2012). Overcoming the legacy of preparing different types of teachers for different types of students is a dominant concern, alongside questions about the level of preparedness and reflection among teacher educators (Florian and Pantić, 2017; Symeonidou, 2017).

Overall, teachers around the world lack access to comprehensive training on inclusion. Analysis of information collected for the GEM Report Education Profiles[1] determined that out of 168 countries analysed, 61% provided elements of training on inclusion. However, this analysis does not contain sufficient information on coverage and quality. An alternative approach is to ask teachers directly about their experience of training.

1   A new GEM Report tool for systematic monitoring of national education laws and policies, accessible at www.education-profiles.org

> " Analysis of information collected for the GEM Report Education Profiles determined that out of 168 countries analysed, 61% provided elements of training on inclusion "

Even in countries where most teachers are trained and qualified, many of them report a lack of training on inclusion or teaching of vulnerable groups. For instance, among OECD countries participating in TALIS, only 35% of teachers reported that teaching in multicultural and multilingual settings was included in their formal teacher education or training, while 62% reported receiving training to teach in mixed-ability settings (OECD, 2019).

The situation is much more challenging in countries with fewer resources, where many teachers are not trained according to national standards (Education International, 2018). Across 10 sub-Saharan African countries that participated in the Programme d'analyse des systèmes éducatifs de la CONFEMEN learning achievement survey, just 8% of grade 2 and 6 teachers had received in-service training in inclusive education – the lowest among the topics included in the relevant question (Wodon et al., 2018). Teachers in Bangladesh reported a lack of both pre- and in-service opportunities for professional development on meeting the needs of students with disabilities (Rahaman, 2017). In Morocco, teachers lacked training on adaptive methods for ensuring learning among children with disabilities or special needs (UNICEF, 2015a).

FEW COUNTRIES PROVIDE PRE-SERVICE TEACHER EDUCATION ON INCLUSION FROM A BROAD PERSPECTIVE

Inclusion-oriented pre-service teacher education programmes tend to focus on content knowledge about how to address challenges various types of learners might encounter. The risk of this approach is that modules on special education end up emphasizing differences between learners and reinforcing the very divisions that create barriers to inclusion (Florian, 2019). Research on teacher education for inclusive education suggests that inclusive approaches should be a core element of general teacher preparation rather than a specialist topic (Rouse and Florian, 2012).

A review for this Report on teacher education for inclusion in Argentina, Ethiopia, Ghana, the Lao People's Democratic Republic and Zanzibar (United Republic of Tanzania) found policies on training for inclusion in all the countries at the primary education level and a clear trend to extend teacher development for inclusion to early childhood care and education, secondary education and higher and adult education. However, most efforts focused on students with disabilities, though there

ADENE

> **Inclusive approaches should be a core element of general teacher preparation rather than a specialist topic**

were some efforts towards a whole-school approach and system transformation to build inclusive school communities and cultures (Lehtomäki et al., 2020).

A few countries provide examples of how inclusion training can be embedded in a wider system of initial teacher education. To graduate from the Upper Austria College of Education, student teachers must have inclusive pedagogical competences and knowledge to teach students with various needs. Inclusive content is embedded in each subject (European Agency for Special Needs and Inclusive Education, 2015). In South Africa, guidelines on inclusive teaching and on responses to learner diversity emphasize the principle of inclusion and the practice of adapting curriculum to diverse needs (South Africa Department of Basic Education, 2010, 2011).

Ghana's Inclusive Education Policy recognized learner diversity in terms of disability, socio-economic background and ethnicity. One objective was to ensure that all teachers were equipped to deal with diverse students through the promotion of Universal Design

for Learning and learner-friendly methods, including in teacher education (Ghana Ministry of Education, 2015). In the Lao People's Democratic Republic, the 2016–20 Education and Sports Sector Development Plan aims to build on previous efforts to include all students in education, though progress has been slow (Lao PDR Ministry of Education and Sports, 2015) (**Box 6.2**).

Inclusion-focused teacher education can have a positive impact on attitudes about inclusion. A study comparing Canadian and German pre-service vocational teacher education found Canadian teachers more likely to have positive attitudes regarding inclusion and their capacity to create inclusive classrooms, partly because of the more prominent role inclusion played in training (Miesera and Gebhardt, 2018). In the Seychelles, teachers who had inclusive education training reported higher endorsement of the inclusion of children with disabilities in mainstream classrooms and more positive beliefs about the practice (Main et al., 2016).

BOX 6.2:

Laos has adopted a broad inclusion framework for educating teachers, but implementation is slow

The government of the Lao People's Democratic Republic first made a commitment to leave no learner behind in the early 2000s. The 2003–15 National Plan of Action on Education for All called for ongoing support and training for teachers on how to interact with parents of children with special needs, and for head teachers and managerial staff to support teachers in making schools more inclusive. It also called for an inclusive teacher education curriculum by 2008 (Lao PDR Ministry of Education, 2005).

While teachers introduced elements of student-centred teaching, they were not adequately empowered to create content or adapt material to reflect students' daily lives and cultural backgrounds. Generally, teachers lacked confidence to break with old routines and stereotypes about girls, ethnic minorities and students with disabilities (Chounlamany, 2014). Moreover, while 20% of head teachers and 38% of teachers surveyed believed the development of teacher capacity was a priority for achieving inclusion, all of them identified teaching materials as the highest priority resource still required (Catholic Relief Services, 2016).

Under the 2016–20 Education and Sports Sector Development Plan, a system of continuous professional development for inclusive education is meant to be developed to provide teachers with pedagogical skills to address the diverse learning needs of girls, ethnic minorities and children with disabilities, as well as students in multigrade classrooms (Lao PDR Ministry of Education and Sports, 2015). By 2018, a pre-service training programme for curriculum writers and a training module aimed at enabling teachers 'to understand disability and gender issues' were still being developed. Another effort at the Inclusive Education Centre at the Ministry of Education and Sports focused on strengthening trainer capacity (BEQUAL, 2018).

> "
> Linguistic and ethnic diversity together with gender are common focuses of teacher education programmes
> "

INCLUSION-ORIENTED PRE-SERVICE PROGRAMMES TEND TO FOCUS ON INDIVIDUAL GROUPS

Most pre-service programmes focus on preparing teachers to address the needs of specific groups, notably students with disabilities. In Ukraine, bachelor's and master's curricula include topics on meeting the needs of people with disabilities, often directed at specialists. For instance, there are courses for psychologists in special schools, psychological and pedagogical support for children with mental disabilities, practical speech therapy methods, and approaches facilitating social development in children with visual impairment (Ukrainian Step by Step Foundation, 2015). In Viet Nam, a 2007 decision established the need for teachers and education managers to be trained in inclusive education. Training institutions in Kon Tum and Ninh Thuan provinces developed pre-service modules on inclusive education of children with disabilities (UNICEF, 2015b). At the national level, education faculties at Hanoi Pedagogy University, Ho Chi Minh City Pedagogy University, Ho Chi Minh City National Pedagogy College and the National Pedagogy College provide formal training in special education. An optional sign-language module is available at the undergraduate level and in short-term, non-formal training courses (OHCHR, 2019).

Students belonging to linguistic and ethnic minorities, such as indigenous groups, are another common focus of teacher education programmes, especially in Latin America. In Colombia, the National Bilingual Programme helps professionalize bilingual teachers and their education (Mora et al., 2019). In Costa Rica, a 2019 decree stipulates that indigenous educator training and participation in curricula formulation and implementation should be promoted and facilitated (GEM Report Education Profiles). In Peru, the National Bilingual Intercultural Education Plan recognizes initial and in-service teacher education as the most critical aspect of implementation (Peru Ministry of Education, 2016). In 2016, Peru had 38,000 bilingual teachers (with varying levels of training), but at least 17,000 new trained teachers are required to meet demand (GEM Report Education Profiles). The capacity to develop such teachers remains limited. The National Intercultural University of the Amazon, for instance, does not have trained indigenous or intercultural teaching staff (Espinosa, 2017).

Gender is another focus of pre-service education programmes. Cuba's Sexuality Education Programme seeks to strengthen teacher education on sexuality and preventing HIV and other sexually transmitted infections, with a gender and sexual rights approach, throughout the basic curriculum, electives and post-graduate studies (Cuba Ministry of Education, 2011). Despite these many examples, more attention needs to be given to determining effective ways to prepare teachers for work in inclusive settings.

IN-SERVICE INCLUSION-RELATED PROGRAMMES RESPOND TO HIGH TEACHER DEMAND

There is often high demand among teachers for professional development on inclusion. Some 25% of teachers in the 2018 TALIS reported a high need for professional development on teaching students with special needs, and in Brazil, Colombia and Mexico the share was over 50%. About 15% reported a high need for personalized learning training, rising to over 40% in Japan and Viet Nam (**Figure 6.2**). In the Netherlands, one in five teachers with at least two decades of experience reported considerable difficulty dealing with students with post-traumatic stress disorder, and 89% said they had encountered at least one such student (Alisic et al., 2012).

A few countries offer training on disability as part of a larger support system. In Singapore, all teachers in mainstream schools receive training aimed at developing a basic understanding and awareness of disability. In addition, some teachers in every school undergo more extensive training aimed at developing deeper knowledge and skills to support students with disabilities. Specially trained Allied Educators in primary schools work closely with teachers to identify and provide additional learning and behavioural support to students with mild disabilities (OHCHR, 2016). In Canada's New Brunswick province, a comprehensive inclusive education policy introduced training opportunities for teachers to support students with autism spectrum disorders (**Box 6.3**).

More commonly, in-service teacher education for inclusion tends to focus on specific skills to address the needs of students with disabilities and other target groups. Teachers need knowledge to identify special needs and refer students to complementary services.

Fiji's 2016 Policy on Special and Inclusive Education recognized the need to train teachers in screening and referring disabilities (Fiji Ministry of Education, Heritage and Arts, 2016). In Gujarat state, India, health and education services cooperated to create a training programme for early identification of students with dyslexia and other special needs. The programme started in 2019, training 80 educators to pick up early signs of disorders and connect affected students to relevant services (Shastri, 2019). In South Africa, the Department of Basic Education aimed to ensure each school had at least one teacher trained to screen and support students, although this target was not met (The Right to Education for Children with Disabilities Alliance, 2016).

Concerning ethnic minorities, one aim of Cambodia's 2015 Teacher Policy Action Plan was to promote continuous professional development through incentives and credits on inclusive education and multilingualism, especially for remote and underperforming schools (Cambodia Ministry of Education, Youth and Sport, 2015). A component of the 2014–18 Multilingual Education National Action Plan focused on a pilot programme of teacher and education official training. An evaluation of the plan called for a recruitment strategy to deploy and retain indigenous teachers with good command of an indigenous language (Ball and Smith, 2019). The 2019–23 Multilingual Education National Action Plan aims to include a multilingual education programme at a regional teacher training centre (GEM Report Education

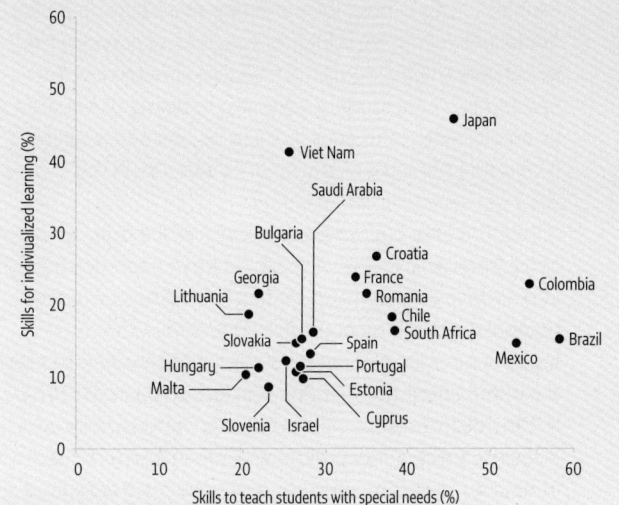

FIGURE 6.2:
Teachers need more opportunities for professional development on inclusion
Percentage of teachers reporting a high need for training in two inclusion-related areas, selected middle- and high-income countries, 2018

GEM StatLink: http://bit.ly/GEM2020_fig6_2
Note: Education systems selected are those in which teachers reported a higher-than-average need for professional development on teaching students with special needs, i.e. students in whom a special learning need has been formally identified because of mental, physical or emotional disadvantage.
Source: OECD (2019).

BOX 6.3:

New Brunswick offers teachers training to support students with autism spectrum disorders

The Canadian province of New Brunswick has been a pioneer in promoting inclusive education for three decades. The roots go back to a home-grown movement in which teachers played a prominent role (Porter and Towell, 2017). The province's efforts received international recognition after it approved a legally binding policy on inclusive education in 2013 (Zero Project, 2016). An earlier evaluation had found challenges; for instance, the many support personnel deployed were focusing more on working directly with students with special needs than on supporting mainstream classroom teachers. To address this, professional development in some areas, including autism spectrum disorders, needed to be strengthened (Porter and AuCoin, 2012).

In response, the Department of Education and Early Childhood Development created the Autism Learning Partnership in 2012. A training course, consisting of online introductory and advanced learning programmes and continued education opportunities, it is supported by a team of behaviour analysts, psychologists, researchers and educators (New Brunswick Government, 2019). In 2015, the prevalence of autism spectrum disorders was 1.3% among 6- to 17-year-olds in the anglophone sector, which makes up 68% of the population (Canada Public Health Agency, 2018).

About 25% of all education personnel, including education assistants and behaviour interventionists, completed the course. Advanced training was offered in 49% of schools and was completed by one in three resource teachers. As part of continuing education opportunities, 30 teachers were supported to certify as behaviour analysts. Trained staff work with all children in the preschool autism programme. Preliminary research found that introductory learning programme participants had increased confidence in their ability to understand how autism characteristics affect learning, provide support to students with autism spectrum disorders and recognize adaptation and response strategies to help students (New Brunswick Government, 2019).

> " In most countries, teacher education related to inclusion and safety of LGBTI students is a neglected and contentious area "

Profiles). In Colombia, inclusive higher education policy guidelines recognize educators as central actors who, to achieve the policy vision, must be able to develop pedagogy, value student diversity in terms of equity and interculturality, and generate discussion and analysis (Colombia Ministry of National Education, 2013).

In high-income countries, two approaches that are highly consistent with inclusive teaching have been developed in response to increasing immigration. The culturally responsive teaching approach to teacher education focuses on skills and dispositions teachers need to teach diverse student populations (Villegas and Lucas, 2007). In the second approach, content and language integrated learning, teacher development courses support teachers in helping students who may not speak the language of instruction, enabling diverse learner groups to use languages as both a communication and learning tool (Coyle et al., 2010).

Gender is a relatively common inclusion-related topic in in-service training. Chile's 2015–18 Education for Gender Equality Plan introduced ongoing teacher education at the national level on gender, discrimination, inclusive schooling, sexuality and sexual diversity in the classroom (Chile Ministry of Education, 2017). In Nepal, the National Centre for Educational Development incorporated a gender awareness module in its teacher professional development programme (OHCHR, 2017).

In Uganda, the 2015–19 National Strategy for Girls' Education aimed to introduce gender training as part of teacher education, with a focus on science teachers and on ensuring response to girls' needs and interests (Uganda Ministry of Education and Sports, 2015). However, the budget for in-service training for primary teachers' colleges had been scrapped since 2013, undermining implementation (Uganda Ministry of Finance, Planning and Economic Development, 2018). The National Teacher Policy launched in 2019 has renewed the government's focus and has included development and a pilot of guidelines to equip teachers with basic knowledge about gender concepts and skills for gender-responsive pedagogy in science, technology, engineering and mathematics. (UNESCO, 2019).

In most countries, teacher education related to inclusion and safety of lesbian, gay, bisexual, transgender and intersex (LGBTI) students is a neglected and contentious area. Less than half of teachers surveyed in Albania said they felt well informed on LGBTI rights, and two-thirds reported that they did not react when LGBTI adolescents were bullied (Pink Ambasada, 2018). Backlash in the media halted a series of workshops in Tirana schools aimed at eliminating discrimination based on sexual orientation in a pilot project of the Ministry of Education, Sport and Youth (ILGA Europe, 2019). Scotland's LGBTI Inclusive Education Working Group, established by the government, recommended pre-service and in-service training to raise awareness among teachers and ensure that they maintained 'their awareness of current LGBTI issues for learners, sustaining their confidence to teach' (Scottish Government, 2018).

Some countries invest in teacher education to ensure that gifted children stay motivated and feel included in the classroom. In Panama, the National Directorate for Special Education began assessing exceptional abilities in 2011 and developed a related programme in 2016. Training and mentoring for teachers, school professionals and administrative workers have raised awareness and developed skills (GEM Report Education Profiles).

Non-government organizations often lead professional development opportunities

In many countries, especially low- and middle-income countries, NGOs fill resource and capacity gaps in government provision of in-service teacher education on inclusion (see **Chapter 8**). In Chad's Lac region, the international NGO Humanity and Inclusion has conducted campaigns sensitizing teachers and other education personnel to the need to educate all students. The programme includes training on differentiated pedagogical models and psychology-informed pedagogy. Between 2017 and 2021, the training aims to support 47 teachers, 4 education inspectors and 3 pedagogical counsellors (Humanity and Inclusion, 2018).

Non-state stakeholders are active not only in lieu of but also in support of government teacher education policies for inclusion. For instance, Burkina Faso's 2012–21 education sector plan provided for measures to improve inclusion of children with disabilities, though few interventions had been carried out and no comprehensive strategy introduced by 2018 (Global Partnership for Education, 2018). Humanity and Inclusion has created an inclusive education module at national teacher education schools and provided further training to a cohort of teachers who visit schools to give one-to-one support (Humanity and Inclusion, 2017). In the Lao People's Democratic Republic, Catholic Relief Services trained teachers in the Xaybouathong district on general inclusive education theory and on teaching methods for children with disabilities (Catholic Relief Services, 2016).

In-service training is particularly crucial in contexts where there is practically no pre-service training. In South Sudan, an NGO-run course on school-related gender-based violence aimed to provide teachers with knowledge and skills to understand their role in prevention, response and non-violent teaching and discipline practices. It also prepared them to be mentors in school clubs to help girls and boys break free from gender stereotypes and build skills to protect themselves from violence and abuse (CREW, 2017).

SPECIAL AND MAINSTREAM EDUCATION TEACHERS ARE OFTEN TRAINED SEPARATELY

It is often taken for granted that special schools employ trained professionals. However, even the most basic expectations may not be realized in the poorest countries. In Niger, for instance, only 10 of the 162 teachers working in special needs and inclusive schools were trained to work with children with disabilities (FNPH, 2018).

Where teacher training exists for special education, it tends to be delivered in different institutions or programmes from mainstream education. This can perpetuate segregation and hinder progress towards making education systems inclusive. In Kazakhstan, special education teachers are trained in higher education institutions with support from the National

Applied Research Centre of Correctional Pedagogy or in corresponding regional professional development institutions (OECD, 2009; OECD and World Bank, 2015). Singapore requires teachers in special schools to have certified training, and the government provides scholarships for special education teachers to pursue master's degrees and professional development grants (OHCHR, 2016).

Separate training systems can increase scepticism among participating teachers. In Canada, teachers who received professional development in special education or were trained as special education teachers were much more likely than mainstream teachers to express negative views about inclusion as the best way to educate all students. Professional development systems that concentrate on special needs education may be too narrowly focused and ignore the wider context of inclusion (Woodcock and Hardy, 2017). In addition, the transition to more inclusive systems can be challenging for specialized teachers. In Belarus and Norway, there was uncertainty about the role of training systems that had served special needs educators as the countries moved towards inclusive systems, and special education professionals were concerned about being replaced by generalists (Hannås and Bahdanovich Hanssen, 2016).

Some initiatives bring mainstream and special education training closer together. An outreach project of the School for the Deaf in Hossana, Ethiopia, provides in-service training for mainstream and special education teachers, along with awareness-raising programmes for families, community members and education officials. It focuses on the teaching and learning of deaf and hearing-impaired students in mainstream settings throughout the country to improve the quality of education in inclusive classrooms and create access to education for children in the target group who are out of school (Lehtomäki et al., 2020).

Callan Services for Persons with Disabilities is a partnership of stakeholders advocating for inclusion in Papua New Guinea. Among other activities, it established the Callan Inclusive Education Institute to upgrade

> " In many countries NGOs fill resource and capacity gaps in government provision of in-service teacher education on inclusion "

> **Professional development systems that concentrate on special needs education may be too narrowly focused and ignore the wider context of inclusion**

staff knowledge and skills at Inclusive Education Resource Centres, which raise awareness, screen for disabilities, provide rehabilitation and preparation for mainstream education, and place children with disabilities in mainstream classrooms with long-term support. The institute also provides training for mainstream teachers and resource centre staff on how to work with and train mainstream teachers (CBM, 2018a, 2018b).

FOLLOW-UP IS NEEDED FOR TRAINING TO BE EFFECTIVE

Research that evaluates teacher education for inclusion points to positive changes in attitudes but not necessarily in classroom behaviour.

Some approaches prepare teachers alongside their educators. In Kenya, Leonard Cheshire Disability trained 130 teachers and 30 teacher educators in five districts. The five-day programme focused on inclusion of girls with disabilities. It provided practical guidance on teaching methods, followed by refresher training with a manual and wider activities for continued support. Results showed increased self-efficacy in both groups and more positive beliefs about inclusive education among teachers. However, neither group intended to adopt inclusion practices as a result of the training, possibly due to a lack of practical ways to follow up on the training (Carew et al., 2019).

Some initiatives explicitly focus on teacher educators. In Ethiopia, the Federal Technical and Vocational Education Institute and its satellite campuses have been engaged in an institutional capacity-building project focused on developing curricula on inclusive education and related modules for pre- and in-service training for technical and vocational education teachers (Lehtomäki et al., 2020).

Training is also needed for education officials who monitor implementation of inclusive teaching. In Zanzibar (United Republic of Tanzania), in-service training on inclusive education was extended to a range of officials at all education levels. In January 2015, the Ministry of Education and Vocational Training appointed and trained one staff member from each of the 15 departments to serve as an inclusive education focal point. By May 2019, nearly 70% of school inspectors, as well as examiners and curriculum developers, had attended one- to three-day training courses. Local and national inclusive education advisers and assistants took part in more intensive training involving seven study modules; a workshop on screening, identification, assessment and support for students; and six-week introductions to sign language and Braille (Lehtomäki et al., 2020).

Such cascade models are commonly used as a less costly training approach, with workshops and training sessions focusing on a few teachers selected for their capabilities or key positions in teacher networks. They then serve as master teachers, training their peers (IBE, 2017). However, cascade models have been criticized because they can dilute content, omit context, lead to misinterpretation and undervalue the knowledge of local teachers, who are often not involved in preparation (Bett, 2016).

TEACHERS NEED SUPPORT TO ENSURE INCLUSIVE TEACHING

To adapt teaching to students' needs and backgrounds, it is not sufficient for teachers to have knowledge and skills. They also need support and appropriate working conditions (Hehir et al., 2016). High pupil/teacher ratios, lack of education support, weak professional teacher networks and lack of autonomy over content can prevent teachers from making classrooms inclusive.

In Cambodia, despite teachers' strong support for child-centred pedagogy, classroom practices relied on more traditional, passive methods. Teachers questioned the feasibility of applying child-centred pedagogy in a context of overcrowded classrooms, scarce teaching resources and overambitious curricula (Song, 2015). In India's Tamil Nadu state, teachers who did engage in child-centred, activity-based learning methods reported difficulty in adhering to the principles of tailored, one-to-one or small group teaching methods in large and under-resourced classrooms (Singal et al., 2018). In South Africa, while teachers favoured inclusion, they perceived the education system to be too under-resourced to enable implementation and saw policy idealism as disconnected from the challenging reality of schools, undermining inclusive teaching and learning (Engelbrecht et al., 2016).

Inclusion can also suffer as a result of pressure on teachers to comply with accountability mechanisms, which can lead to tension between external policy and professional autonomy (Ben-Peretz and Flores, 2018). This is especially true if policy calls for a standardized approach, which may conflict with meeting the diverse needs of students (European Agency for Special Needs and Inclusive Education, 2012). Teaching to the standardized content requirements of a learning assessment can make it more difficult for teachers to adapt their work, for instance to reflect students' cultural backgrounds.

NETWORKS ARE CRUCIAL TO SUPPORT INCLUSIVE PRACTICES

Cooperation among teachers in different schools can support them in addressing the challenges of diversity, especially in systems transitioning from segregation to inclusion. Ideally, cooperation should be based on complementary skills. This is a challenging task, since teachers from mainstream and special schools are not encouraged to interact, their careers diverging as early as the pre-service level. Sometimes such collaboration is absent even among teachers at the same school. In Sri Lanka, a study found that few teachers in schools with special needs units reported collaborating with or receiving support from the other stream, partly due to the units' segregation (Furuta and Alwis, 2017).

In Kenya, a small-scale intervention focused on establishing inclusion committees consisting of students, teachers and head teachers in mainstream and special schools, as well as people in the community. Members met regularly to discuss the best ways to make schools more inclusive and developed modes of co-teaching and collaborating. The project empowered teachers to champion inclusion and sensitized communities to the need to include students with disabilities in education (Elder and Kuja, 2019).

As part of a move from segregation to inclusion, Namibia's Ministry of Education encouraged the transformation of special schools into resource centres and advised them to collaborate with mainstream teacher education institutions to develop skills. Collaboration included co-teaching (Namibia Ministry of Education, 2013).

Singapore's Ministry of Education established 16 Satellite Partnerships between mainstream and special schools to encourage integration. Between 2015 and 2017, the Buddy'IN programme, aimed at integrating graduating students from mainstream and special schools to improve acceptance of people with disabilities, covered 200 students (OHCHR, 2016).

In Ho Chi Minh City, Viet Nam, as part of a programme run by a local NGO in partnership with CBM, an international NGO, blind students can choose between attending the mainstream school or remaining in segregated classes in a resource centre with boarding facilities. Students who moved to the mainstream school reported missing the resource centre's extracurricular activities and vocational training. In response, the centre and school worked together, with the centre offering more support to the school, including in-service teacher education (CBM, 2018b).

EDUCATION SUPPORT PERSONNEL CAN PROMOTE OR PREVENT INCLUSION

Education support personnel, from teaching assistants and school nurses to psychologists and drivers, cover a wide range of professional, technical and administrative functions (Education International, 2017). In some settings, a rise in the supply of support personnel, especially teaching assistants but also occupational therapists, behavioural therapists and autism support personnel, has accompanied the opening of mainstream education to students with special needs. Globally, however, the provision is largely lacking. Respondents to a survey of teacher unions reported that support personnel were largely absent or not available at all in at least 15% of countries, somewhat available in about 29% to 44% and always available in about 5% to 22%, depending on the type of support personnel (Education International, 2018).

> **It is not sufficient for teachers to have knowledge and skills. They also need support and appropriate working conditions**

> ❝
> In some settings, a rise in the supply of support personnel has accompanied the opening of mainstream education to students with special needs
> ❞

Classroom learning or teaching assistants can be particularly helpful in providing more attention to students with special needs (Blatchford et al., 2009; Masdeu Navarro, 2015). As part of an inclusive education programme in Zimbabwe, classroom assistants were introduced in selected primary schools to assist children with disabilities. Teachers were appreciative but split over whether assistants should primarily play a carer or an expert advisory role (Deluca et al., 2017).

Support personnel cannot replace teachers. Nor can they compensate for overcrowded classrooms or lack of special education teachers. As part of Ireland's transition to inclusion, since 2017, mainstream schools have had more autonomy and flexibility to engage special education teachers and support personnel. Primary school guidelines on supporting students with special needs in mainstream schools state that special education support should be solely for 'pupils with identified special education needs, including those pupils for whom English is an Additional Language', and cannot be used to reduce the pupil/teacher ratio. Special education teachers cannot have sole responsibility for delivery of curriculum to any class (Ireland Department of Education and Skills, 2017, p. 5). The Cook Islands inclusive education policy emphasized the importance of teaching assistants but placed ultimate responsibility for learning in the hands of teachers (**Box 6.4**).

At the tertiary level, support personnel enable the students at risk of exclusion to complete their studies. The Young Mums programme in Melbourne, Australia, run by an education support personnel team in collaboration with Swinburne University, provides a safe space for mothers aged 15 to 20 with challenging family histories to complete their education or vocational qualifications. The programme aims to fill education and welfare system gaps in child care provision, helping teenage mothers concentrate on learning (Swinburne University, 2018).

SUPPORT PERSONNEL NEED TRAINING AND DEFINED ROLES AND RESPONSIBILITIES

Some question the benefits of teaching assistants in inclusion. Parents may fear assistants create dependency and undermine teacher accountability. Limited training or unclear responsibilities may restrict support personnel's effectiveness. Although increased professional development has enabled support personnel to gain formal qualifications in recent years, the majority enter schools without specific training (Rose, 2020).

The role of support personnel is to supplement, not supplant, teachers' or special educators' work, yet they are often put in positions that demand much more. As support personnel are increasingly central in fostering inclusion, increased professional expectations, accompanied by often low levels of professional development, can lead to lower-quality learning and be counterproductive where inclusion is sought.

BOX 6.4:

Education support personnel have been deployed in the Cook Islands

The Cook Islands Inclusive Education Policy, introduced in 2002 and reviewed in 2011, focused on taking a more inclusive approach by transferring students with physical and learning special needs from special units to mainstream schools (Cook Islands Ministry of Education, 2014).

To achieve this, the policy recognized the role of support personnel, particularly teaching assistants. They receive specialist training, and many gain a New Zealand-issued Certificate in Teacher Aiding. Their role is to provide 'one on one support to an individual child or support a small group within a class, depending on the level of need' (Cook Islands Ministry of Education, 2014, p. 21). They work at all levels from early childhood to secondary education. In 2017, 64 teaching assistants were employed (Cook Islands Ministry of Education, 2017a).

The assistants are meant to work with teachers to assure the best quality learning environment for students with certified special needs. Ultimate responsibility and duty of care for all children remains with teachers; a supervisory teacher must be present at all times (Cook Islands Ministry of Education, 2017b). Teachers write weekly plans based on the learning outcomes of the inclusive education programme and give assistants direction and opportunity for feedback (Cook Islands Ministry of Education, 2010).

Inadvertent detrimental effects associated with excessive or inappropriate use of teaching assistants include interference with peer interaction, decreased access to competent instruction, and stigmatization (Chopra and Giangreco, 2019; Rose, 2020).

If not properly prepared and organized, special support and collaboration to promote transition to inclusive education can do more harm than good. In Australia, the access of students with disabilities to qualified teachers was somewhat impeded by overdependence on unqualified support personnel. In some instances, students received more instruction from teaching assistants than from qualified teachers. The situation is exacerbated when teachers consider teaching assistants responsible for individual students, enabling the teachers to abdicate professional responsibility for these students (Butt, 2018).

South Africa established District-Based Support Teams as part of the process of moving students with disabilities to mainstream schools. Their key functions were to promote classroom and organizational support and provide specialized learner, administrative and teacher support and curricular and institutional development. However, the teams focused on students and were unable to equally support teachers (Makhalemele and Payne-van Staden, 2018).

Training support personnel is necessary, but not sufficient, to ensure an inclusive learning environment and effective cooperation with teachers. A review of studies from 11 high-income countries, including Canada, Italy and Norway, found that teaching assistants often had unclear responsibilities and limited collaboration with and supervision by teachers. It also noted that their efficacy in raising learning outcomes and inclusion was mixed. For instance, teaching assistants often taught students with disabilities in small, separate groups, effectively excluding them from the wider classroom (Sharma and Salend, 2016).

In England (United Kingdom), teaching assistants often took responsibility for instruction but were rarely adequately trained and prepared. Their role should be reconsidered in terms of providing support to maintain learner engagement, fostering independence when children are in difficulty and encouraging students to use their own learning strategies. Ideally, teachers and assistants need to be trained together (Radford et al., 2015).

> "
> The role of support personnel is to supplement, not supplant, teachers' or special educators' work, yet they are often put in positions that demand much more
> "

Teachers may be unaware of their obligation to direct teaching assistants' work and collaborate with them. Rectifying this may necessitate school management support or professional development opportunities. Relevant competences include conducting planning meetings, developing supplemental plans for teaching assistants and monitoring their day-to-day professional activities (Chopra and Giangreco, 2019).

MANY EDUCATION SYSTEMS STRUGGLE TO ACHIEVE DIVERSITY IN THE TEACHING PROFESSION

Teaching staff diversity can signal the value of inclusion to students and society in general. A review of the benefits of hiring people with disabilities pointed to benefits for both employers (e.g. lower turnover and higher levels of retention, innovation and productivity) and employees (e.g. improved quality of life, enhanced self-confidence and larger social networks) (Lindsay et al., 2018). Teachers with minority backgrounds can serve as role models. In India's Jharkhand state, increasing representation of various ethnic groups among teachers was associated with increased student enrolment of different groups (Borker, 2017). In the United States, teacher diversity has had a positive effect on student performance and student perception of teachers, particularly among students with minority backgrounds (Cherng and Halpin, 2016; Egalite et al., 2015).

By contrast, homogenous teaching staff may struggle to find common ground with diverse student and parent populations. Yet in most countries the staff composition is not representative of the population. In England (United Kingdom), a study found that, as most teachers came from middle-class backgrounds, they were not always able to listen to and take into account comments from working-class parents (Gazeley, 2012).

Some countries make explicit efforts to increase teacher representativeness, for instance hiring teachers with disabilities (**Box 6.5**). Some interventions are aimed specifically at teaching children with disabilities.

BOX 6.5:

Teachers with disabilities make a unique contribution to education systems

There is little comparative evidence on teachers with disabilities worldwide. A study of further and higher education teachers with dyslexia in England (United Kingdom) and Finland found that it equipped them with a deep understanding of their role as educators and the importance of empathy towards students. They could advise colleagues on being more aware of students' difficulties with dyslexia, contributing to greater inclusion (Burns and Bell, 2010). Similarly, a study in the United Kingdom during school placement of six student teachers with dyslexia found that they brought strengths to their work, including a better understanding of students' difficulties (Griffiths, 2012).

In Nepal, educated individuals with visual impairments are actively recruited as teachers in mainstream schools: Out of the approximately 1,000 people in Nepal with visual impairments and a university degree, around 400 worked as teachers in mainstream schools. A survey found that both students and principals perceived these teachers positively, despite some challenges in classroom management, support (e.g. materials in Braille), help with marking examinations or training in use of computers. Students reported that the teachers' strengths were positive attitudes, good communication skills and more attention paid to social and moral lessons (Lamichhane, 2016). However, teachers with disabilities often face serious obstacles. About 81% of teachers with disabilities in the United Kingdom reported having been discriminated against because of their disability during their teaching career (NASUWT, 2015).

The government of Bangladesh, with donor support, recruited 650 primary school teachers with disabilities, about 70% of them women (OHCHR, 2018).

Lack of diversity extends to ethnic and cultural under-representation. Data from Europe showed that teachers with migrant backgrounds were under-represented relative to the student body. Teachers with minority backgrounds in the United States, such as African-American or Hispanic teachers, are increasingly under-represented relative to the student population (**Figure 6.3**). Under-representation is fuelled by barriers at each step, from entering initial teacher education to remaining in the profession (Donlevy et al., 2017). In India, there has been progress in terms of historically disadvantaged groups: Between 2005 and 2013, the share of teachers from scheduled castes, which constitute

> " A review of the benefits of hiring people with disabilities pointed to benefits for both employers and employees "

16% of the country's population, increased from 9% to 13% (Census India, 2011; NUEPA, 2016).

LACK OF DIVERSITY IN THE TEACHING PROFESSION STEMS FROM STRUCTURAL INEQUALITY

Lack of teacher diversity can be partly explained by structural factors, reflecting disparity and exclusion within education, for instance. Low representation of a group among students in higher education or specific fields translates into low representation among graduating teachers, which in turn contributes to low representation in the teaching profession.

For instance, students with disabilities pursue tertiary education at lower rates, and still fewer graduate, thus being unable to become teachers. In 11 sub-Saharan African countries, primary and secondary completion rates of students with disabilities were significantly lower than for students without (Wodon et al., 2018). Similarly, the scarcity of female science and mathematics teachers is a consequence of low female representation in these fields in higher education (UNESCO, 2016).

Some policies provide incentives. In the Australian state of Queensland, teachers willing to work in rural and remote areas may be entitled to rent subsidies and financial benefits, depending on location and degree of remoteness (Queensland Department of Education, 2019). In the Central African Republic, teachers in conflict-affected areas are recruited from local populations (GEM Report Education Profiles).

Diversity can also be hindered by corrupt hiring practices. In Afghanistan, many teaching positions are reportedly gained through bribery or nepotism. Financial and other obstacles to entry may effectively block candidates from diverse socio-economic backgrounds and can also exacerbate gender disparity. For every 100 male teachers, there are 66 female teachers and the ratio drops as low as 10 in some provinces, including Uruzgan and Zabul. This creates an obstacle to girls' education in regions where traditional values prohibit girls being taught by men.

The Ministry of Education has taken measures to reduce corruption in teacher recruitment (Bakhshi, 2020).

Moreover, lack of diversity can result from intentional hiring and firing decisions. For instance, historical analysis of teacher employment patterns following school integration in the southern United States showed that integration was associated with reduced employment of African-American teachers. The reduction was not a necessary result of the policy but a conscious choice of school administrators, boards of education and federal-level policymakers. A school district transitioning from fully segregated to fully integrated reduced its employment of African-American teachers by 32% (Thompson, 2019).

CONCLUSION

Teachers are a foundation of an inclusive education system. As education systems accommodate more diverse student populations, classrooms are changing. Teachers around the world are increasingly likely to encounter students with varied backgrounds and experiences, strengths and weaknesses.

While many countries have made progress in preparing teachers to support all students, collaborate with others, value diversity and engage professionally, others struggle to change attitudes, equip teachers with the skills needed to support all students, and provide supportive working environments. Teachers may not receive sufficient or appropriate pre-service education or in-service professional development. Lack of training can compromise their ability to promote the learning potential of all students.

Questions remain about what constitutes high-quality training and how it should be delivered in different parts of the world. As this chapter has shown, a range of efforts are under way, but they are inconsistent. Teacher attitudes reveal continuing reservations about the feasibility of providing inclusive education to all.

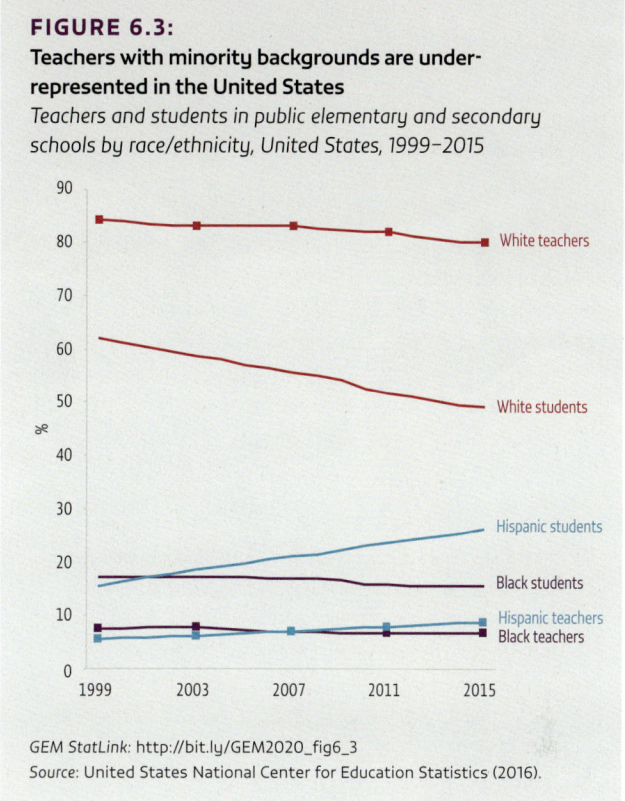

FIGURE 6.3:
Teachers with minority backgrounds are under-represented in the United States
Teachers and students in public elementary and secondary schools by race/ethnicity, United States, 1999–2015

GEM StatLink: http://bit.ly/GEM2020_fig6_3
Source: United States National Center for Education Statistics (2016).

Such misgivings are often based on discriminatory beliefs, which may stem from personal convictions or reflect wider social norms. Scepticism can also reflect system inefficiency, as when teachers are given insufficient autonomy or guidance to build effective collaboration with peers and support personnel.

Teacher diversity often lags behind population diversity, sometimes as a result of structural problems preventing members of marginalized groups from acquiring qualifications, teaching in schools once qualified and remaining in the profession. Systems should recognize that these teachers can bolster inclusion by offering unique insights and serving as role models to all students.

A Gay-Straight Alliance school bus during the Seattle Pride in 2008, United States.

CREDIT: jglsongs

7

Schools

Is school inclusiveness only about infrastructure?

KEY MESSAGES

School ethos, the explicit and implicit values and beliefs, as well as the interpersonal relationships, that define a school's atmosphere, has been linked to student well-being

- The share of students in OECD countries who felt they belonged in school fell from 82% in 2003 to 73% in 2015.

- The strength of school ethos can be gleaned from how clearly school values are expressed, how strong measures are to tackle bullying and how close student–teacher relationships are, but also how flexibly the school handles student health conditions and how warmly it welcomes new students.

The overall promotion of an inclusive culture relies on visionary school leaders

- Nearly one-fifth of head teachers in middle- and high-income countries, and as many as half in Croatia, had no instructional leadership training. Yet teachers of students with special needs in mainstream schools reported lower professional development needs if they experienced better instructional leadership.

- About 15% of head teachers in middle- and high-income countries, and as many as 60% in Viet Nam, reported a high need for professional development in promoting equity and diversity.

- School leaders can learn by sharing expertise. In Hong Kong, China, schools with strong whole-school approaches serve as resource centres for other schools.

School culture often falls short of inclusive ideals

- School bullying and violence cause exclusion. One-third of 11- to 15-year-olds have been bullied in school.

Safe and accessible schools are crucial for inclusion

- Comparable evidence on schools that have adapted infrastructure and materials for students with disabilities remains elusive because national standards vary, monitoring capacity is weak and data are not verified independently. Even so, no schools in Burundi, Niger or Samoa met national standards. In Slovakia, only 15% of primary schools did.

- A study of 7,000 children in 11 countries in Africa, Asia and Latin America showed that more than one-quarter of girls reported never or seldom feeling safe on the way to school.

- Incorporating accessibility and universal design features into school infrastructure is cost-effective. Doing so from the outset increases total cost by 1%. Adapting after completion can increase it by 5% or more, depending on the modifications.

Assistive technology can make the difference between participation and marginalization

- Assistive devices are inputs (e.g. adapted keyboards), outputs (e.g. screen readers), alternative and augmentative communication (replacing speech) and assistive listening systems (improving sound clarity). Such technology improves graduation rates, self-esteem and optimism.

*Schools should work by considering where children are from and that they
do not start education with the same preparations or home situations.*

Els Heijnen-Maathuis, senior education advisor

Countries have taken steps to make education systems more inclusive through laws and policies to mainstream students with a wide range of needs into regular education. Many of these students have had the opportunity to be educated with their peers. However, as this report has shown, being mainstreamed does not necessarily create a sense of belonging.

Inclusion in education cannot happen without inclusive schools, which the Salamanca Declaration defined as 'institutions which include everybody, celebrate differences, support learning and respond to individual needs' (UNESCO, 1994, p. iii). Schools committed to inclusion are dedicated to the belief that each student can and will learn and succeed, and that diversity is of value to all students (Falvey and Givner, 2005). In an inclusive school, all students are welcomed, feel they belong, realize their potential and contribute to daily school life. Inclusive schools ensure that all students, regardless of gender, ethnicity, sexual orientation, socio-economic background or education need, are engaged and achieving by being present, participating and learning (New Zealand Government, 2014).

Effective and supportive school leadership is instrumental (though not sufficient) in building such environments. An inclusive school culture can increase students' motivation so that they take greater responsibility for their behaviour and learning and have a greater sense of belonging. This chapter documents good practices in an inclusive school ethos, and potential barriers. It looks at what schools can do to build inclusive cultures and management processes. It then examines how schools can be more accessible in terms of physical infrastructure and use of technology.

INCLUSION AND A SENSE OF BELONGING DEPEND ON SCHOOL ETHOS

School ethos, a term sometimes used interchangeably with school culture or climate, refers to the explicit and implicit values and beliefs, as well as interpersonal relationships, defining a school's atmosphere and guiding behaviour (Donnelly, 2000). The concept was popularized 40 years ago, when its impact on school outcomes, beyond other measurable factors, was identified (Rutter et al., 1979). School values and norms have since come to be considered an important factor in schools' academic performance (Bennett, 2017). In the United States, the Maryland Safe and Supportive School Climate Survey included questions related to sense of belonging and equality of treatment. Responses from about 25,000 secondary school students were used to develop a measure of school climate associated with a learning-conducive environment, which helps predict student achievement outcomes (Bradshaw et al., 2014).

> " **Schools committed to inclusion are dedicated to the belief that each student can and will learn and succeed** "

Some governments highlight the importance of ethos in their education policies. For instance, Curriculum for Excellence in Scotland (United Kingdom) took a positive ethos as the 'starting point for learning' (Scottish Government, 2008, p. 20).

A positive school ethos has been linked to social and emotional development, feelings of well-being and improved behaviour (Goldberg et al., 2019). Actively promoting a sense of belonging in school is associated with reduced aggression and connections with risky groups, such as gangs (Roffey, 2013). In Australia, a randomized control trial of a school ethos change initiative, using strategies to make staff and students feel more connected and valued through communication, professional development and community outreach, reduced student risk behaviour and substance abuse (Bond et al., 2004). A replication of the experiment in Canada had similar effects (Hawe et al., 2015).

School ethos can be evaluated in terms of the nature of school values and norms, the degree to which these are consistently held among staff and the extent to which students accept them and share the school's education perspective. While it is a difficult concept to capture, there have been attempts to operationalize it. A study of secondary schools in Stockholm, Sweden, assessed school ethos using teacher ratings of clarity of the expression of school values, strength of measures to tackle bullying and violence, and closeness of student–teacher relationships, along with staff turnover (Granvik Saminathen et al., 2018).

As a first step in embracing inclusive values, schools can develop a mission statement to articulate their collective intent to value and accommodate student diversity and promote respect for all school community members. Such statements can be publicized. An action plan can outline school goals, and strategies can be formulated to guide efforts. However, such measures do not constitute an inclusive ethos in and of themselves. Crucially, inclusive norms must guide school community members' practices. 'Achieving an inclusive school ... is more than just developing a value statement that addresses inclusion. ...

ADENE

An inclusive school is based on the philosophy that the whole school shares in the responsibility for inclusion' (NBACL, 2011, p. 6). A study of secondary schools in England (United Kingdom) showed that both the most and the least successful schools had value statements, but the latter had not integrated them into practice (Glover and Coleman, 2005). In a context of marketization, there is a risk of schools having an incentive to develop superficial identities and mission statements in an effort to attract parents (Faas et al., 2018).

A comparison of inclusive schools in Portugal, the United Kingdom and the United States (Kugelmass, 2006) noted that their inclusive culture was manifest in their uncompromising commitment to and belief in inclusion, perception of diversity among students and staff as a resource, and commitment to inclusive ideals communicated across the school and to the community. Another key element was a collaborative interaction style among staff and students (**Box 7.1**).

This is not to suggest that there are off-the-shelf, best-practice approaches to developing an inclusive ethos. Such approaches do not emerge mechanically through organizational restructuring or adoption of particular practices. Schools develop different ways to put their inclusive philosophy to work. Indeed, the inclusion logic can extend in very different directions (**Box 7.2**).

A WHOLE-SCHOOL FRAMEWORK IS NEEDED TO BUILD A SENSE OF BELONGING

Cross-national assessments, such as PISA, have been used to measure students' sense of belonging in school. In OECD countries, while a majority of students reported that they did not feel awkward, lonely or like outsiders, and that they made friends at school, the share of students who felt they belonged in school fell from 82% in 2003 to 73% in 2015. This is partly because of increasing shares of students with immigrant backgrounds, but levels of native students' sense of belonging have also declined (OECD, 2017, 2019a).

A whole-school framework can help build sustainable inclusive change (McMaster, 2013). A synthesis of research on school belonging identified six strategies, involving students, parents, the community and staff, to help students feel more connected to school. The strategies are based on trusting and caring relationships that promote open communication among these groups. Families also need to be encouraged

> " In OECD countries, the share of students who felt they belonged in school fell from 82% in 2003 to 73% in 2015 "

to participate actively at home and in school life. Programmes need to develop student skills for active engagement. Classroom management and teaching methods should foster positive learning environments. Teachers need to receive the right professional development and support. Ultimately, decision-making processes should also facilitate student, family and community engagement, academic achievement and staff empowerment (Centers for Disease Control and Prevention, 2009).

A meta-analysis of 51 studies confirmed that parental involvement in school life through effective communication and information sessions was strongly

---

BOX 7.1:

Collaborative relationships are one of the foundations of inclusive schools

Approaches based on an inclusive school ethos foster collaboration among school leaders, teachers, staff, students and parents. They lead all school stakeholders to be involved and allow students to develop a sense of belonging. Analysis for this report of results from the 2015 Programme for International Student Assessment (PISA) of the Organisation for Economic Co-operation and Development (OECD) showed that students who had positive interactions with other students or did not feel threatened by other students had greater collaborative problem-solving skills, even after accounting for socio-economic background.

Low socio-economic status was associated with low collaborative problem-solving skills in most countries: Differences in status explained about 15% of the skills variance, and in about one-third of countries it accounted for as much as 20% to 30% (OECD, 2017). Yet, PISA data suggested that more disadvantaged students valued teamwork more than their peers. The data also showed a gap in collaborative problem-solving skills between immigrant and non-immigrant students. After accounting for gender and socio-economic status, immigrant students scored 26 points below non-immigrant students, on average, across OECD countries (Bădescu, 2020).

BOX 7.2:

An inclusive school ethos can extend to a wide range of student categories

The need for inclusion goes beyond well-identified categories of special education needs. Many conditions do not fall under the concept of disability or may not be directly related to academic achievement. Yet neglecting them can affect students' sense of belonging or achievement in other domains, such as arts and sport (Rix and Sheehy, 2014).

Many chronic illnesses may not lead to a disability classification yet can have significant effects on children's education. In the United States, it was estimated that one in four children suffered some chronic condition (Van Cleave et al., 2010). Asthma is the most common serious chronic health condition among children. Its prevalence, which exceeds 10% globally, has been increasing in low- and middle-income countries, including countries as varied as Kenya, Lebanon, Paraguay and Thailand. It may be as high as 30% in some countries, including Australia and New Zealand (WAO, 2011). Asthma is explicitly included as a subcategory of special education need in a range of countries but far from all (United Arab Emirates Ministry of Education, 2009; Department for Education, 2015). For affected students, a school's inclusiveness partly depends on how it handles associated treatment. Affected students may regularly miss school for medical appointments (Fleming et al., 2019). Inclusion in this case entails flexibility, which potentially benefits a wider student population: Finding ways to minimize the social and learning impact of absence due to illness can also benefit students who are absent for other reasons or who re-enter after dropout (Gleason et al., 2016; Wheeler et al., 2006).

Being left-handed is not generally recognized by law as a vulnerability. But left-handed students have to adapt to tools, instruments, classroom furniture and schools designed for the right-handed majority. Historically, secondary schools in the United States were oriented to let sunlight in from the left so the writing hand would not cast a shadow over what was being written (Kamenetz, 2018). Discrimination has taken the form of forced conversion to right-hand writing (Meng, 2007). Inclusive schools should provide left-handed tools, such as scissors and furniture. In the Philippines, a new law mandates provision of neutral desks to 10% of the student population at all levels, including technical, vocational and higher education, within a year. Once rules and regulations are formulated, administrative penalties may be imposed for non-compliance (Philippines Senate, 2019).

Being a newcomer to a school can be stressful, especially if it implies other challenges, such as being forced to change schools due to behaviour. In the United States, most primary and secondary school students experience at least one non-promotional school change during their education career (Rumberger, 2015). While evidence is mixed, on balance, changing schools typically has a negative effect on learning outcomes (Centre for Education Statistics and Evaluation, 2016; Schwartz et al., 2017). A longitudinal analysis in the United Kingdom showed that children who had experienced peer problems were more likely to move schools and that school mobility was a risk indicator for anxiety and depression (Winsper et al., 2016). Where lack of inclusion makes new students feel like outsiders, the stress response may lead to a vicious circle of challenging behaviour and further involuntary school changes (Park, 2014).

associated with students' sense of belonging (Allen et al., 2018). Schools need to reach out to parents and the wider community to promote their ethos and vision of inclusion. Parents and other community members need to take part in school activities or school management committees. However, PISA results indicated that only 12% of parents in OECD countries volunteered in extracurricular activities and 17% participated in school government (OECD, 2019b).

An inclusive and supportive school ethos can help students dealing with psychological trauma. Displaced students tend to be particularly at risk. In the state of Victoria, Australia, refugee well-being committees help students adapt to a new environment and connect them to psychological support units (Foundation House,

2016). Poverty can also make students vulnerable to stress, trauma and their negative mental health effects, which can lead to behavioural difficulties (Blitz et al., 2016). Schools with responsive and supportive environments adopt multi-tiered strategies to address the effects of trauma on students. Psychological support staff in schools, to help address symptoms without stigmatization or referral to segregated education services, greatly aid student well-being (Phifer and Hull, 2016).

Empowering students to participate as active, responsible citizens within the school community is also crucial. Opportunities to be involved in decision making, practise communication skills and cooperate through student

> *Parents and other community members need to take part in school activities or school management committees*

councils and advisory bodies are important, especially in schools with high diversity (Johnson, 2003).

SCHOOL LEADERS PLAY A KEY ROLE IN PROMOTING INCLUSION

Head teachers are responsible for applying laws and regulations on inclusion and promoting equitable access to learning. Where anti-discrimination laws or inclusive frameworks are lacking or ambiguous, head teachers need to take extra steps, for instance to ensure a fair admission policy. Ultimately, the overall promotion of an inclusive culture and shared values relies particularly on visionary school leaders, especially where teachers are sceptical or unprepared for inclusive practices. Head teachers can develop a shared vision of inclusion, guide inclusive pedagogy, communicate the value of inclusive approaches and plan professional development activities (Ainscow, 2011; Schuelka, 2018). School leaders need to give staff time and space to develop a critical understanding of their own beliefs, assumptions, prejudices and behaviours, which can sustain division rather than promote inclusion. This is essential, as staff need to identify barriers to inclusion and recognize their responsibility for finding solutions.

School leaders have a responsibility to ensure that all children, especially the most disadvantaged, receive adequate learning support. Head teachers who create and communicate a culture of high expectations without compromising inclusiveness have been a key factor in improving schools in poor areas (European Agency for Special Needs and Inclusive Education, 2018b; Muijs et al., 2010). Leaders and staff at London schools that substantially improved outcomes for disadvantaged students shared common motivations and had strong convictions that they could have a positive impact on these students (Baars et al., 2018).

Head teachers can demonstrate inclusive teaching practices. Those with experience teaching disadvantaged or special needs students can coach less experienced teachers. A cross-country study of teachers who taught special needs students in mainstream schools found that those who experienced better instructional leadership reported lower professional development needs (Cooc, 2018). School leaders can also build competence in inclusion by learning from schools with exemplary practices or sharing expertise and resources with other schools (Ainscow et al., 2016; Armstrong and Ainscow, 2018). Some governments facilitate school support networks and provide incentives for schools to collaborate. In Hong Kong, China, the government launched a programme in which schools with strong whole-school approaches to inclusive education serve as resource centres for other schools (Poon-McBrayer and Wong, 2013). Some European countries have set up specialized consultancies to assist schools in supporting special needs students. In Sweden, schools receive help from local resource centres, supported by the Swedish National Agency for Special Needs Education and Schools (European Agency for Special Needs and Inclusive Education, 2017c). Special schools are perhaps uniquely placed to share expertise with their mainstream counterparts but face challenges of their own (**Box 7.3**).

As the range of school leader tasks has become increasingly complex, covering vision, strategic thinking, learning focus, resource management, communication, problem solving and pedagogical leadership, it is increasingly evident that a team approach is needed (European Agency for Special Needs and Inclusive Education, 2018b). Schools with inclusive cultures are more likely to be characterized by a leadership style that encourages participation in these functions, along with democratic decision making.

System factors can undermine school leaders' efforts to promote inclusion

By one estimate, school leadership accounts for over one-quarter of the difference in student learning across schools that is attributable to school-level variables (Leithwood et al., 2008). But system-specific factors can thwart school leaders' efforts to create an inclusive learning environment. For instance, schools that are

BOX 7.3:

Special school principals face particular challenges

The challenges special school leaders face are both similar to and distinct from those of their mainstream peers, especially in planning and resource management. For instance, they may face more challenges with staff recruitment, retention and training. In the United States, a shortage of special education teachers has been exacerbated by high attrition rates and increased numbers of students with special needs. Head teachers report difficulty hiring special needs support staff, such as physiotherapists and speech and language therapists (Scott and McNeish, 2013). They must also organize professional development to keep staff up to date on mainstream developments, norms and curricula. And they must ensure that teachers balance teaching and care responsibilities, which can involve a greater role for head teachers in mentoring and in demonstrating practice (Bubb, 2009).

Special schools maintain relationships with health and social services. Health professionals and others may provide advice on student care and teaching plans; schools may mediate between parents and these services. Partnership with parents is more significant and continuous than is the case for many mainstream students. In addition, as systems increasingly mainstream students with special needs, there is an increasing role for special schools in building the capacity of mainstream schools (Ainscow et al., 2003).

In recent years, several European countries have been converting special schools into resource centres. This strengthens links between special and mainstream education and supports the shift towards inclusive education without making existing institutions redundant. Lithuania has two national resource centres (for the visually impaired and hearing impaired) and a project to reorganize four special schools into resource centres is under way (European Agency for Special Needs and Inclusive Education, 2017a). Slovenia's move towards mainstreaming includes conversion of special schools into resource centres at which mobile specialist teachers are based (European Agency for Development in Special Needs Education, 2013; European Agency for Special Needs and Inclusive Education, 2017b). Portugal has gone furthest along this route. Since 2009, it has converted most special schools into resource centres and provides support through specialized professionals (European Agency for Special Needs and Inclusive Education, 2019).

This trend is global. Malawi has transformed 140 special primary schools and 37 special secondary schools into resource centres. In Namibia, some special schools have become resource schools to provide consultancy and support to mainstream schools. The United Republic of Tanzania has outlined plans for similar reforms. Viet Nam has established inclusive education development support centres in 20 provinces and cities (GEM Report Education Profiles[1]).

---

1 A new GEM Report tool for systematic monitoring of national education laws and policies, accessible at www.education-profiles.org.

evaluated on test-based student performance standards may have incentives to screen out marginalized students.

Autonomy and room to make decisions about a school's direction and organization are fundamental in ensuring equity. Discretion does not mean head teachers cannot be held accountable, but leadership accountability mechanisms should be aligned with other policies to support inclusion, which is often lacking in practice. A review of European policy documents related to school leadership found a lack of explicit focus on inclusive school leadership (European Agency for Special Needs and Inclusive Education, 2018b).

Yet too much decision-making autonomy can undermine inclusion, as can incentives if parents push for less inclusion. South Africa has anti-discrimination legislation and racial desegregation in schools, but head teachers have autonomy to determine catchment boundaries. In Johannesburg, this is a factor in increased exclusion of

> " Schools that are evaluated on test-based student performance standards may have incentives to screen out marginalized students "

poor suburban children from better-performing schools (Bell and McKay, 2011). Head teachers are instrumental in supporting dialogue with the community and building trust with parents. They need to be especially committed to identifying marginalized families and persist in including them in the school community (Campbell, 2011).

Understanding how to allocate school resources to implement inclusive education is critical. Head teachers may need to organize professional development or decide how to schedule support staff, such as teaching assistants, language specialists and school psychologists (Hehir et al., 2017). Lack of resources can be a barrier. School leaders may need to lobby school boards or local government for material, financial and human resources (Cobb, 2014).

School leaders need specialized training to promote inclusion

To build inclusive schools, head teachers need knowledge and understanding of inclusion (Garner and Forbes, 2013; Jahnukainen, 2014). Leadership support and professional development for inclusion should focus less on administration and more on learning and achievement, and cover areas such as evidence-informed decision making and use of data (European Agency for Special Needs and Inclusive Education, 2018b).

Head teachers may not receive formal leadership or administrative training. In countries that participated in the 2018 OECD Teaching and Learning International Survey (TALIS), nearly one-fifth of head teachers had no instructional leadership training. The share was one-third in Australia and Lithuania and half in Croatia (OECD, 2019c). Across the 47 participating education systems, 15% of head teachers reported a high need for professional development in promoting equity and diversity, with the share reaching more than 60% in Viet Nam (**Figure 7.1**). Less than one-quarter of the 31 countries taking part in the World Bank Systems Approach for Better Education Results assessment on teachers required principals to participate in an induction or mentoring programme (Wilichowski and Molina, 2018).

Training in special education is obligatory for trainee head teachers in only eight US states (Lynch, 2012). Leadership courses often focus on law and compliance requirements rather than on leading strong instructional programmes for students with diverse

> **Understanding how to allocate school resources to implement inclusive education is critical**

needs (Osterman and Hafner, 2009). Lack of training and professional development often extends over the career (Burdette, 2010). An Estonian pilot project on organizational measures supporting inclusion of special needs learners in mainstream schools offers continuing training programmes for teachers and school leaders, and inclusive education implementation is a cross-cutting priority (European Agency for Special Needs and Inclusive Education, 2018a). Ireland established a Centre for School Leadership in 2015 (Fitzpatrick Associates, 2018).

SCHOOL CULTURE OFTEN FALLS SHORT OF INCLUSIVE IDEALS

The 2018 TALIS offered insights into school policies to promote diversity and equity in diverse environments. Across 47 education systems, head teachers of 64% of schools reported having organized multicultural events, such as cultural diversity days, and 70% of schools supported activities encouraging expression of students' ethnic or cultural minority identity. These figures are likely overestimates, however, as teachers reported rates around 10 percentage points lower on these questions (**Figure 7.2**). Somewhat unexpectedly, the head teacher share was four percentage points lower and that of teachers nine points lower for schools with a more diverse ethnic and cultural student background. For all participating systems, about one in five schools does not follow explicit policies against gender and socio-economic discrimination, and the share is as much as half in some countries, including Belgium and Italy (OECD, 2019c).

Bullying and school violence lead to exclusion

Typically, one-third of 11- to 15-year-olds have experienced bullying in school, although the range is wide, from less than 10% in Armenia to more than 50% in Lithuania, Nepal and the Philippines (UNESCO, 2019). In countries that participated in the 2015 Trends in International Mathematics and Science Survey, 45% of grade 4 students reported having been bullied at least once a month, and the share ran as high as 78% in South Africa (Mullis et al., 2016).

FIGURE 7.1:

Many head teachers need professional development related to inclusion

Percentage of lower secondary school head teachers who reported a high need for professional development in promoting equity and diversity, selected countries and territories, 2018

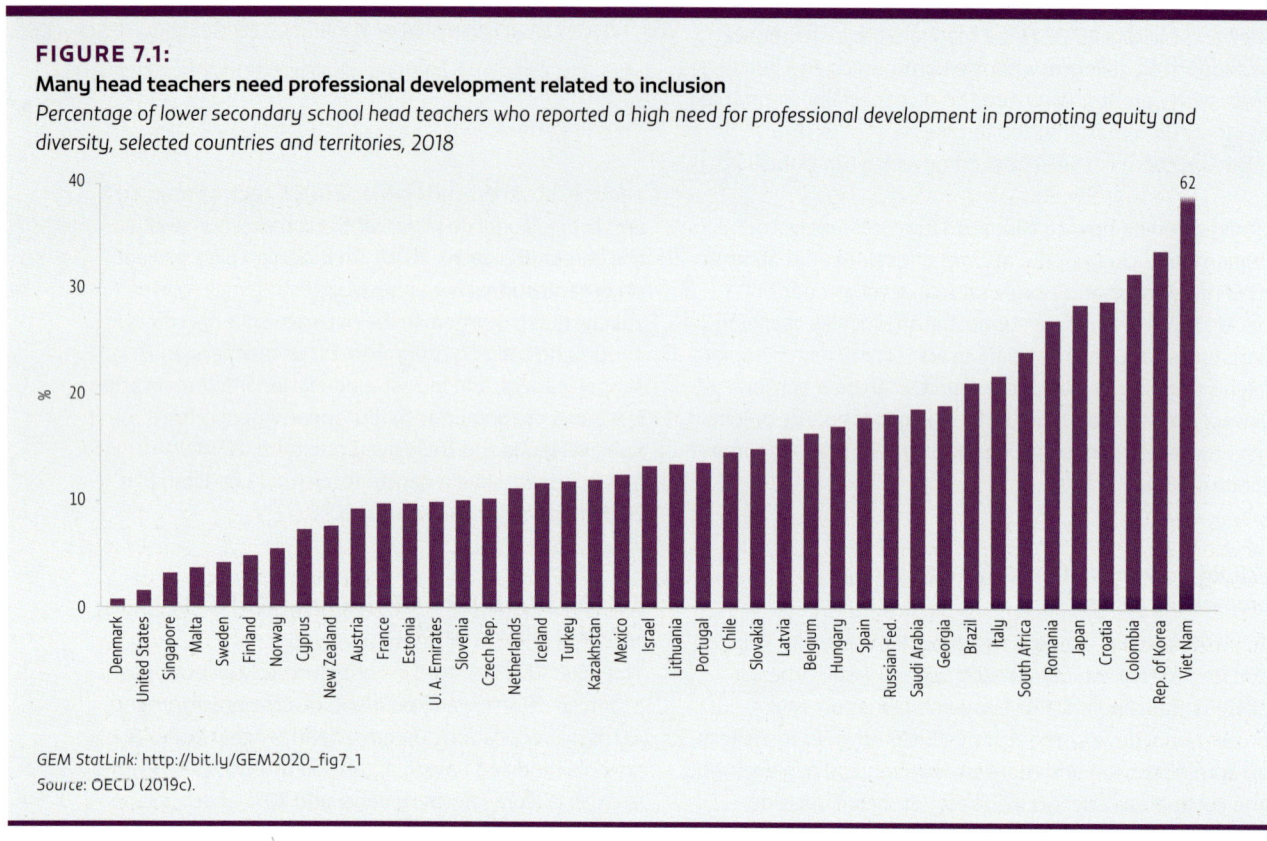

GEM StatLink: http://bit.ly/GEM2020_fig7_1
Source: OECD (2019c).

FIGURE 7.2:

Many schools are not implementing inclusive policies and practices

Selected diversity- and equity-related school practices, by type of respondent, in education systems that participated in the 2018 TALIS

GEM StatLink: http://bit.ly/GEM2020_fig7_2
Source: OECD (2019c).

Generally, the students most likely to be victimized are those perceived as differing from social norms or ideals. They include sexual, ethnic and religious minorities, and low-income and special needs students. Lesbian, gay, bisexual, transgender and intersex students (LGBTI) are often at significant risk, reporting higher rates of bullying than other groups (Schuster et al., 2015). In New Zealand, LGBTI students were three times as likely to be bullied as their peers (UNESCO, 2017).

Findings on the experiences of students with disabilities paint a bleak picture. A study in Australia found that 56% had experienced bullying in the previous 12 months, more than the twice the rate observed in the general school-aged population (Gotlib, 2018). In Uganda, 84% of children with disabilities had experienced violence at the hands of peers or staff in the past week, compared with 53% of those without disabilities (Devries et al., 2018). In the United Kingdom, in addition to being bullied more than non-autistic students, students with autism spectrum disorder reported less social support from classmates and friends (Humphrey and Symes, 2010).

> "
> The 2018 TALIS shows that about one in five schools does not follow explicit policies against gender and socio-economic discrimination
> "

In the United States, students with intellectual disabilities, emotional disturbance disorders and orthopedic impairment appear to be at greater risk than their peers without disabilities (Blake et al., 2012).

The development of a school-wide inclusive ethos, in which students both feel valued and value each other, can be expected to reduce negative behaviour such as bullying. Measures of teacher-reported inclusive school ethos (Modin et al., 2017) and of student-reported sense of belonging, for instance, in the Progress in International Reading Literacy Study (UNESCO, 2018), have been strongly associated with lower bullying rates.

Schools have a responsibility to combat bullying with targeted interventions. A study of schools in England (United Kingdom) found that, while those characterized by equality of opportunity, social cohesion and good leadership showed less bullying, the strongest predictors were school policies and practices directly targeting or dealing with bullying (Muijs, 2017). A meta-analysis of 53 programmes confirmed the effectiveness of school-based anti-bullying initiatives (Ttofi and Farrington, 2011).

Schools should put in place classroom management practices, guidance services and policies that identify staff responsibilities and actions to prevent violence and bullying and to intervene when necessary. Teacher codes of conduct need to refer explicitly to violence and abuse and ensure that penalties are clearly stipulated and consistent with legal frameworks for child rights and protection. Lack of firm intervention by head teachers, teachers and staff can increase the prevalence of violence among students. Students and staff should be confident that sanctions will follow transgressions (UNESCO, 2017). In Italy, successful school-based interventions to combat bullying have involved improved playground supervision, disciplinary methods, classroom rules and classroom management (UNESCO, 2019).

However, punitive approaches should not displace provision of student support and cultivation of a respectful atmosphere. Punitive zero-tolerance approaches can unfairly marginalize some students and encourage more covert forms of bullying (Borgwald and

Theixos, 2012). In the United States, a pilot on working with troubled and violent children in schools involved assigning counsellors to work closely on behavioural change. Results showed a promising 80% reduction in suspensions, disciplinary referrals and peer aggression incidents (UNESCO, 2017).

Successful large-scale anti-bullying programmes, such as Kiva in Finland and Zero in Norway, have included teacher education. In France, new teachers are expected to complete training on violence management (Roland et al., 2010; Salmivalli et al., 2011; UNESCO, 2017). In the United Kingdom, schools with less bullying kept records of bullying incidents, organized professional development, talked to parents of bullies and victims, had policies on teacher roles during breaks and developed behaviour codes collaboratively (Muijs, 2017). Peru launched a national monitoring initiative, the Specialized System against School Violence. Victims and witnesses in schools registered in the system can report cases of violence in the school setting. The system specifies follow-up actions to be completed by a designated staff member (UNESCO, 2019).

Interventions to prevent school violence and bullying can be more effective when students are involved in planning and implementation. Save the Children's Violence Free Schools project in Afghanistan emphasizes involvement of children to prevent abuse, bullying and gender-based violence. A key element is the establishment of a child protection committee, a parent–teacher–student association and a student council in each school (UNESCO, 2017). In China, India and New Zealand, several schools and universities have established student-led, school-based clubs where LGBTI students can meet and interact safely. Open to all learners, they aim to challenge discrimination and homophobic bullying (UNESCO, 2016).

Schools should also combat violence and bullying by teachers. In Uganda, the Good Schools Toolkit, developed by the non-government organization (NGO) Raising Voices, aims to develop a collective vision for schools, create a nurturing learning environment, use more progressive learning methodology and strengthen school governance. Two lead teachers and two student representatives in each school coordinate activities, which include outreach to parents and the community. A randomized control trial found that the initiative reduced incidents of physical violence by school staff by 42% (Knight et al., 2018).

SAFE AND ACCESSIBLE SCHOOLS MATTER FOR INCLUSION

Safe and accessible schools are crucial for all children, especially those with disabilities.[2] The condition of school access routes, buildings and other facilities often violates key dimensions of the right to education, such as accessibility, acceptability and adaptability (**Table 7.1**). Among the infrastructure features that can affect access and inclusion are conditions on the way to school, often neglected as a factor leading to exclusion (**Box 7.4**).

2   This section draws on Agarwal (2019).

In some of the world's poorest countries, lack of classroom furniture forces children to sit on the floor, making for unacceptable learning conditions. The pupil/desk ratio in the United Republic of Tanzania in 2016 was 5:1 vs the recommended 3:1. Moreover, averages tend to hide wide discrepancies at the expense of disadvantaged areas: The ratio was 7:1 in the Geita, Rukwa and Simiyu regions (U. R. Tanzania Ministry of Education, 2016). In Uganda, among the Karamoja subregion's four districts with data, the ratio ranged from 5:1 to 124:1 (Brown et al., 2017).

In most countries, school facilities' overall quality may be inadequate. A recent review of empirical studies around the world concluded that a number of classroom features affected learning, and many are essential to inclusion. They include good-quality electric lighting or abundant daylight without glare, shelter from the sun's heat, windows big enough for ventilation, lack of nearby

TABLE 7.1:
Selected infrastructure conditions related to accessibility, acceptability and adaptability

Going to school	Water, sanitation and hygiene
■ Well-maintained routes free of obstacles and busy traffic ■ Sidewalks or designated pathways along the route	■ Accessible toilets integrated with regular toilets ■ Toilets with doors and roofs for safety and privacy ■ Hand- and foot-activated water and handwashing facilities ■ Signs identifying water, sanitation and hygiene facilities
Entering the school	**Play**
■ Wide entrance for children with wheelchairs ■ Firm, even, level and well-maintained ground surface	■ Space with a sitting area and overhead protection connected to a wheelchair-accessible route ■ Firm surface
Moving through the school	**Emergency evacuation**
■ Wide hallways for children with wheelchairs ■ Handrails on stairs and ramps ■ Well-lit hallways, walkways and stairs	■ School evacuation plan for children with disabilities ■ Classrooms not overcrowded ■ Visual and audio alarms
Entering and using classrooms	**Communication**
■ Naturally lit classrooms with shading and ventilation ■ Movable desks and tables if needed ■ Signs identifying rooms and amenities ■ Low window sills allowing children to see out if seated	■ Quiet classroom environment: minimal background noise from fans and mechanical equipment ■ Good lighting illuminating face of teacher/sign-language interpreter

Source: Topping (2014).

BOX 7.4:

Many journeys to school are filled with obstacles and risks

Millions of children, whether in remote rural or densely built urban areas, face significant barriers to reach school every day, affecting their attendance. Lack of safety and threats of violence also affect access, particularly for girls. In a study of 7,000 children in 11 countries across Africa, Asia and Latin America, more than one-quarter of girls interviewed reported never or seldom feeling safe on the way to or from school (Plan International, 2014). In Benin City, Nigeria, a survey of secondary school students found that dangerous driving was the most significant challenge children faced en route to school, with 15% having been injured in a road traffic accident during the previous six months (Ipingbemi and Aiworo, 2013).

Some measures, such as free or subsidized transport and upgrading of pedestrian routes or walkways, may require relatively large investments. Others, such as volunteer-run services, may have more minor cost implications. The benefits, however, can be substantial. For instance, a survey of head teachers in several sub-Saharan African countries estimated that more adequate transport would increase enrolment of disabled students by one-quarter (Access Exchange International, 2017).

For those in relatively close proximity to schools, 'walking school bus' programmes group children to walk safely to and from school or a school bus stop, escorted by adults. The route picks up children at designated meeting points or homes along the way (Access Exchange International, 2017). In San Francisco, United States, a team of parents and neighbourhood community organizations launched the Tenderloin Safe Passage programme in 2008; it now covers 15 blocks in the eponymous city neighbourhood. Trained volunteers posted at high-risk corners provide an adult presence for more than 200 children daily (Hoodline, 2018). Children at greater distance from schools face different challenges. In Brazil, more than 35,000 school buses were purchased and more than 170,000 bicycles procured under two nationwide programmes between 2008 and 2013 to support transport for rural students (Brazil Government, 2014).

Lack of paved routes or transport can leave children with disabilities homebound. One-tenth of students with disabilities in Botswana and one-quarter in Mozambique reported having stopped attending due to difficulty getting to school (UNDESA, 2019a). Motorized vehicles may be the most effective transport to school, and governments have an important role, as costs are significant. The local government in Curitiba, Brazil, finances a fleet of 60 buses, fully accessible with wheelchair lifts, taking 2,500 students with special needs to school each day. Costa Rica gives subsidies to caregivers of disabled children for the transport services they provide (Access Exchange International, 2017).

external noise, large simple areas for older students and more varied areas for younger students, easy access to outside spaces, wide corridors and visual variety in room layout (Barrett et al., 2019). While elements such as air conditioning and high-quality furnishings imply large costs, others, such as engaging classroom and school layouts, may require little more than imagination.

Unfortunately, schools are often designed and built without fully considering the needs of students, staff and community members. Sanitation facilities are an example. In many countries, including Mali, Mauritania and Senegal, most primary schools lack separate toilets for girls (**Figure 7.3**). This is recognized as an important factor in attendance of girls who have begun menstruating, especially in sub-Saharan Africa, where a high percentage of students are over-age.

THE FULL NEEDS OF STUDENTS WITH DISABILITIES ARE RARELY CONSIDERED IN SCHOOL DESIGN

Children with disabilities face significant barriers in and around schools. The importance of facilities suitable for students with disabilities in ensuring inclusion is recognized in global indicator 4.a.1 of the Sustainable Development Goals, which refers to the proportion of schools with access to 'adapted infrastructure and materials for students with disabilities'. Burundi, Niger

> " Schools are often designed and built without fully considering the needs of students, staff and community members "

FIGURE 7.3:

In many poorer countries, single-sex toilets are the exception, not the norm

Percentage of primary schools with single-sex toilets, selected countries, 2016–18

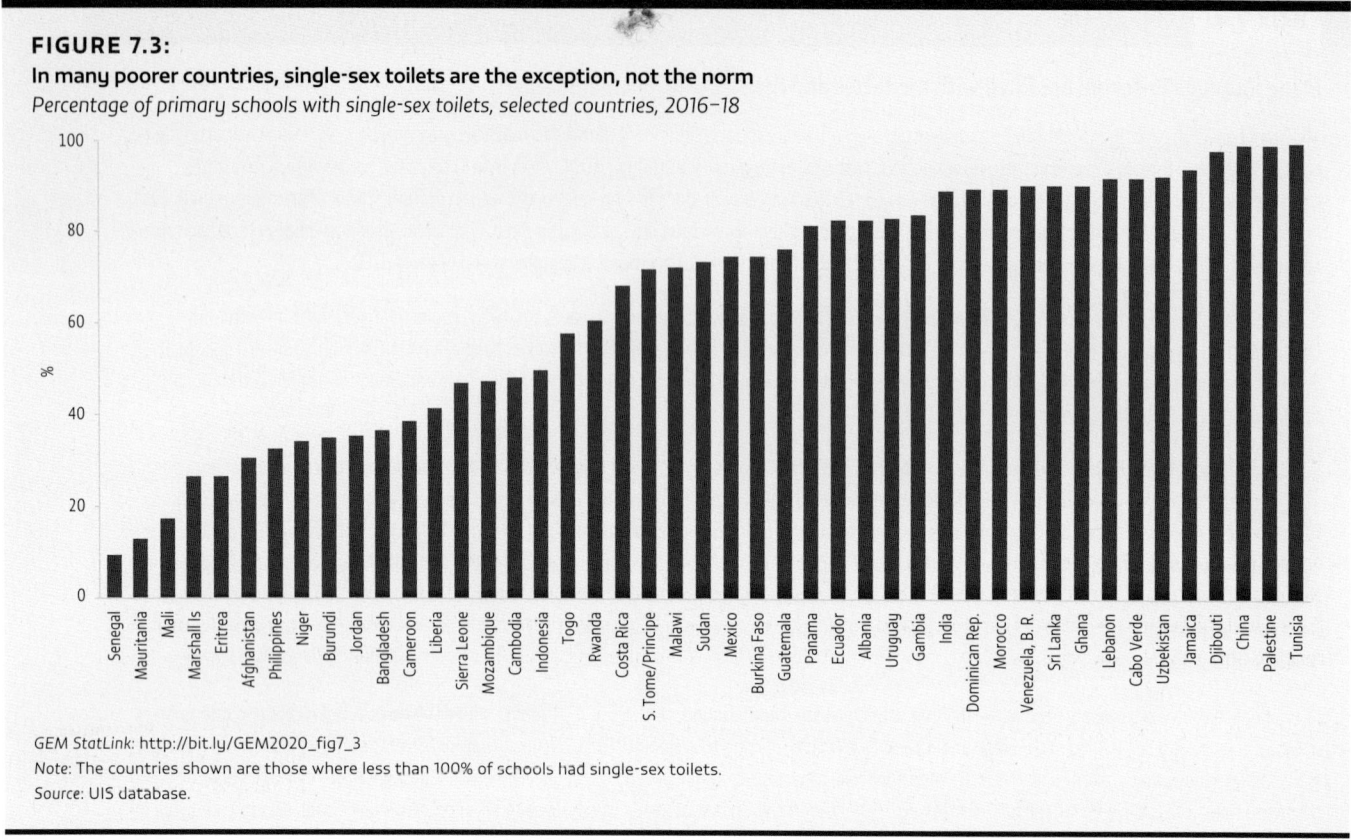

GEM StatLink: http://bit.ly/GEM2020_fig7_3

Note: The countries shown are those where less than 100% of schools had single-sex toilets.

Source: UIS database.

and Samoa reported that no primary or lower secondary school in their territory met these criteria. Few schools met basic standards even in richer countries, such as Slovakia, where the shares were only 14% for primary and 21% for lower secondary schools (**Figure 7.4**).

Further breaking down averages within countries shows that standards are not equally enforced between urban and rural areas, levels of education, or public and private schools. Public schools are more likely to comply in India and Jamaica, while private schools are more likely to comply in Malaysia and Peru.

Informative, cross-country comparable evidence remains elusive, for three reasons. First, although many countries have national standards, they vary. In Victoria state, Australia, the School Building Authority standards include norms for car and bus parking spaces (Victoria Department of Education and Training, 2019). In Malaysia, local authorities require public buildings to meet the Malaysian Standard Codes of Practice on Access for Disabled Persons, enabling people with disabilities to use them as members of the general public, as visitors or for employment (Kamarudin et al., 2012).

“

The importance of facilities suitable for students with disabilities in ensuring inclusion is recognized in global indicator 4.a.1 of the Sustainable Development Goals

”

A recent report argued that adapted infrastructure should be defined globally as 'any built environment related to education facilities that has been built or modified to enable accessibility by all users, including those with different types of disability' and refer to 'pathways, entry, evacuation and/or use of a building and its services and facilities (including at a minimum, educational, recreational, and water, sanitation and hygiene facilities). Examples of adaptations include ramps, hand rails, widened doorways, modified toilets, clear signage, and tactile markers' (UIS, 2018, p. 15). Despite progress, this standard has not yet taken effect.

Second, as this definition suggests, schools may meet some but not all elements of a given set of standards. Third, even if standards were agreed, monitoring capacity tends to be weak, as data are reported by schools and not independently verified by external inspectors who could comment on facilities' quality and not just their availability. Governments rarely organize such monitoring. In 2015, Burkina Faso carried out a study

> **Detailed monitoring of school design is commonly the result of research or citizen action**

of 6,685 schools with 14,762 buildings and found that half had ramps (UNDESA, 2019b). India's Department of Empowerment of Persons with Disabilities conducts accessibility audits of public buildings in 48 cities, obliging governments to retrofit buildings to meet accessibility standards (Agarwal, 2019). In Malaysia, in both new and retrofitted public buildings, including schools, an access audit examines adherence to codes (WHO, 2011).

More commonly, detailed monitoring is the result of research or citizen action. In Ghana, a review of 20 senior secondary schools that were ranked in the top fifth for academic performance and physical infrastructure evaluated accessibility on the basis of international

FIGURE 7.4:
Countries struggle to ensure that schools have adequate provisions for students with disabilities
Percentage of schools with adapted infrastructure and materials for students with disabilities, by education level, selected countries, 2016–18

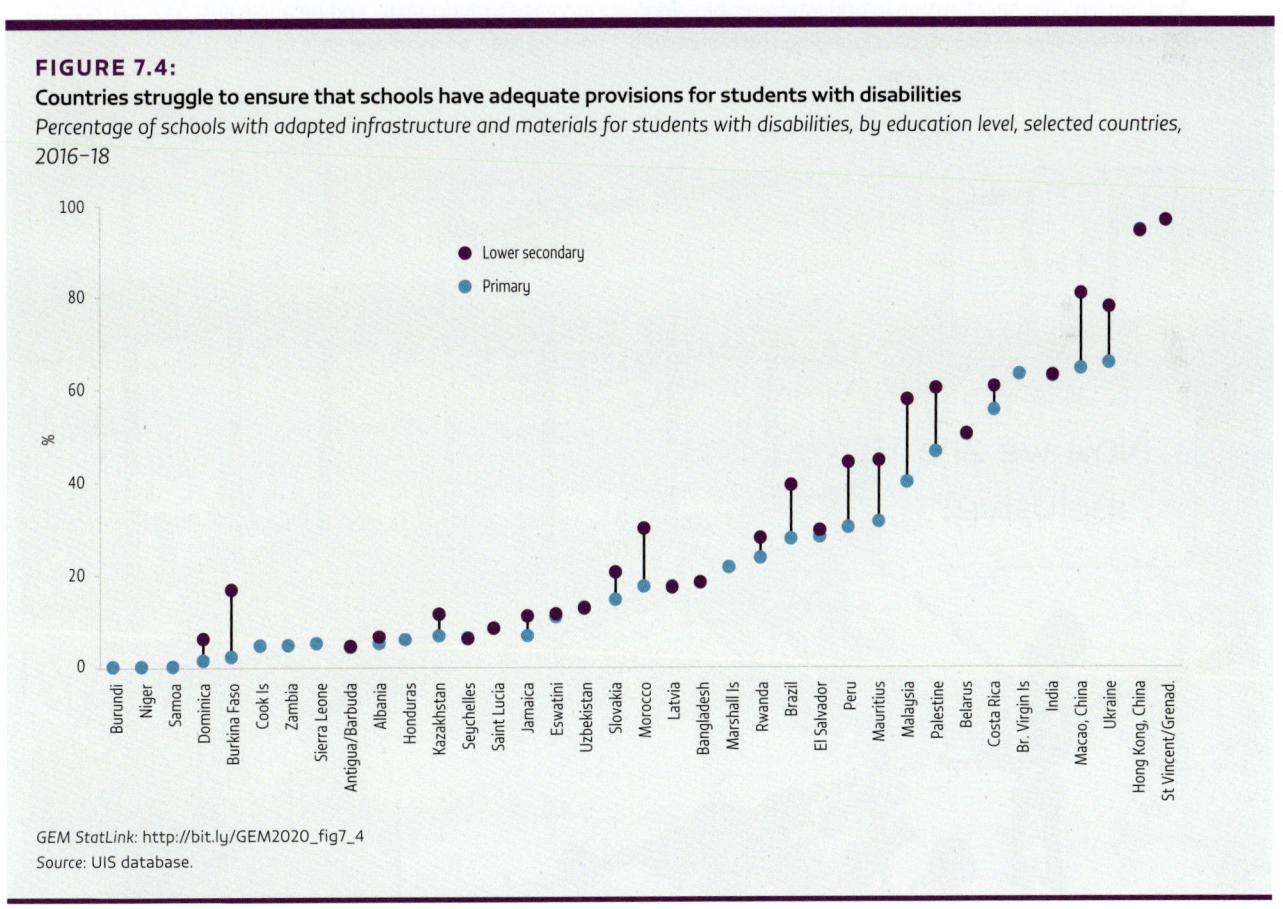

GEM StatLink: http://bit.ly/GEM2020_fig7_4
Source: UIS database.

> " Universal design aims to increase functionality and be applicable to everyone's needs, regardless of age, size or ability "

building standards and national legislation. Most schools fell significantly short. For instance, there were no restrictions in just 3% of cases of vertical circulation (between floors) and 10% of cases of horizontal circulation, and 83% of buildings had severe restrictions in sanitation facilities (Danso et al., 2012).

Crowdsourced data, mostly from high-income countries, suggest that 47% of education facilities are accessible to people using wheelchairs (UNDESA, 2019a). In France, a disability helpline was developed to accommodate concerns reported by families of students with disabilities and to offer solutions in cooperation with local education authorities and school inspectorates (UNDESA, 2019a). In India, an audit by the Comptroller and Auditor General found significant discrepancies in the limited number of accessibility measures captured in education monitoring information systems. An app developed by the Ministry of Social Justice and Empowerment allows citizens to upload images of inaccessible schools, enabling the ministry to take follow-up action (Agarwal, 2019).

UNIVERSAL DESIGN IS AN EFFICIENT WAY TO MAKE SCHOOL BUILDINGS INCLUSIVE

Where accessible infrastructure is provided, it is often the result of specialized optional measures to support a few children, but not necessarily all. Rather than promoting the addition of accessibility features, the United Nations (UN) Convention on the Rights of Persons with Disabilities adopted the concept of universal design: 'the design of products, environments, programmes, and services to be usable by all people to the greatest extent possible, without the need for adaptation or specialised design' (United Nations, 2006, p. 4). Universal design aims to increase functionality and be applicable to everyone's needs, regardless of age, size or ability.

Whether for school buildings, public walkways or physical appliances, universal design can be used to evaluate existing designs, guide the design process and educate designers and users about the characteristics of more usable products and environments. Seven principles of universal design were developed by a group of architects, product and environmental designers, and engineers: equitable use for people with diverse abilities; flexibility in use to accommodate a range of individual preferences and abilities; simple and intuitive use, regardless of user experience, knowledge, language skills or level of concentration; perceptible information that is effectively communicated, regardless of surrounding conditions or sensory abilities; tolerance for error to minimize the consequences of accidents caused by unintended actions; low physical effort; and appropriate size and space for approach, reach, manipulation and use, regardless of user's body size, posture or mobility (Centre for Excellence in Universal Design, 2019).

Incorporating accessibility and universal design features into school infrastructure is cost-effective. In Ethiopia, including access features in a school toilet amounted to less than 3% of the cost (Jones, 2011). Incorporating full-access facilities from the outset is estimated to increase the total cost by 1%, while adaptation after completion can increase it by 5% or more, depending on the modifications (United Nations, 2019).

India has taken steps in recent years to promote accessibility via policy and legislation. The 2016 Rights of Persons with Disabilities Act mandates provision of accessible transport systems and universal design in public buildings and education facilities. The draft National Education Policy states that universal design should be applied to schools' building design, sports facilities and general environments so all children benefit. In each state, a committee of cognitive scientists, early childhood education experts, artists and architects is to be formed to design school spaces 'that are truly inviting and inspiring places to spend time and learn'. Funding is promised for existing schools to adapt their facilities (Agarwal, 2019).

Aid programmes have helped disseminate universal design principles. All schools built under Indonesia's Basic Education Programme, with support from Australia, had to install accessible toilets, handrails and ramps. The government later adopted similar measures for all new schools. Australia released a universal design guide to promote adherence to accessibility principles in all construction projects it supported (AusAID, 2013). A school self-assessment tool, based on national standards and the Centre for Studies on Inclusive Education index, was also developed (Agarwal, 2019). The Kiribati Education Improvement Programme, which has been rehabilitating primary schools since 2013, is also designed to comply with national infrastructure standards and Australian Aid's universal design principles. Features include accessible paths between buildings, ramps, wider doors, grab rails and wheelchair-accessible toilet facilities (Coffey, 2016).

TECHNOLOGY CAN MAKE THE DIFFERENCE BETWEEN PARTICIPATION AND MARGINALIZATION

Technology has considerable but largely unused potential to support inclusive education. In relation to the universal design for learning (see **Chapter 5**), it supports the focus on inclusive means of representing information, expressing knowledge and engaging in learning (Rose et al., 2002). Assistive devices help overcome barriers preventing vulnerable students from fully benefiting from curriculum. To realize its potential, technology needs to be used with appropriate pedagogy. It also needs to be personalized to accommodate students' differing and sometimes conflicting needs (Foley and Ferri, 2012). Yet differentiated learning supported by technology is rarely used, largely due to lack of relevant teacher education. In low- and middle-income countries, lack of infrastructure can exacerbate the challenges of using technology.[3]

---

3 This section draws on Hersh (2020).

> " Differentiated learning supported by technology is rarely used, largely due to lack of relevant teacher education "

> Stigma can be reduced by technological designs that are small, attractive and similar to general-purpose ones and that challenge stereotypes

Information and communication technology (ICT) can support creative and cooperative learning environments and promote inclusion of students with disabilities. Computers with specialized software can be used to record, edit and share ideas, help in completing assignments on time and improve motivation. Yet ICT's implications for the needs of students and staff with disabilities are often not considered in advance.

The use of ICT in education frequently involves computer-aided learning using tablets that can serve students with disabilities. For instance, in Western Australia state, teachers in an education support centre who were trained to use popular apps to support literacy and mathematics considered tablets suitable for students with autism spectrum disorder, attention deficit disorder and those requiring multisensory input, as they were customizable, portable and comprehensive (Johnson, 2013). Use of multimedia, concept mapping or organizing software, and dictation with speech recognition can improve the writing skills of children and adults with learning difficulties (Batorowicz et al., 2012). Symbol production software has been found to improve the reading comprehension of adults with mild learning disabilities (Jones et al., 2007).

ASSISTIVE TECHNOLOGY CAN GREATLY SUPPORT STUDENTS WITH DISABILITIES

Some general-purpose technology, such as alternative and augmentative communication apps, can meet learner needs and have the advantage of being more readily available, cheaper, more familiar and less stigmatized than specialized technology (McNaughton and Light, 2013). People with minimal technical knowledge can fairly easily develop personalized content for language intervention, for instance for learners with autism spectrum disorders (Shane et al., 2012). Where this is not possible, assistive technology is increasingly available (Ahmad, 2015) and can make the difference between marginalization and participation, not only in school but also in community life and lifelong learning (**Box 7.5**). The UN Convention

on the Rights of Persons with Disabilities states that '"universal design" shall not exclude assistive devices for particular groups of persons with disabilities where this is needed' (United Nations, 2006, p. 4).

Assistive technology in schools has been found to increase rates of graduation, post-secondary education, paid employment and earning above minimum wage (Bouck et al., 2011). It can also improve academic orientation, enjoyment, self-esteem, optimism and subjective well-being, as a study in Ireland has shown (Wynne et al., 2017). Student and staff attitudes are important: A study of university students with disabilities in the United Kingdom found that some used such technology only at home due to concerns over stigma (Seale et al., 2010). Stigma can be reduced by designs that are small, attractive and similar to general-purpose devices and that challenge stereotypes (Bichard et al., 2007). Reliability and availability of technical support, involvement of potential users and their families in decision making, and ease of use, particularly the time required to programme a device, also affect use (Baxter et al., 2012).

In high-income countries, enabling learners to use their own devices with assistive technology already installed is another way to encourage uptake (Hersh and Mouroutsou, 2015). Yet while many students are frequent, highly proficient technology users familiar with a wide range of learning strategies, others may be unable to commit the time and effort required to use such technology successfully (Seale et al., 2010). As there are trade-offs between assistive technology and other forms of support, both options need to be offered and seen as complementary.

Availability of assistive technology varies greatly by country, education level and disability type (**Box 7.6**). In Estonia, schools provide a text-to-speech converter, screen reader, e-learning platforms and online dictionaries and handbooks free of charge (Hersh and Mouroutsou, 2019). In Italy, schools are required to provide computers

BOX 7.5:

There is a large variety of assistive technology for education

There are no agreed definitions related to technology for inclusive education (Robyler and Doering, 2013). While education technology supports the teaching and learning of all learners, assistive technology refers to 'technologies, equipment, devices, apparatus, services, systems, processes and environmental modifications used by disabled and/or older people to overcome the social, infrastructural and other barriers to [learning] independence, full participation in society and carrying out [learning] activities safely and easily' (Hersh and Johnson, 2008, p. 196).

Assistive devices may refer to input technology, such as big key, on-screen, Braille/chording or other keyboards; options for controlling computer input by eye, head or foot; joysticks, including sip and puff mouth-controlled joysticks; ways to emulate mouse operations, such as multiple switch scanning; single-switch entry devices to scan and choose letters, numbers, symbols and graphics using any body part under consistent control; speech input/dictation software; and text input improvement software that reduces the amount of typing, for instance through natural pointing gestures or word prediction.

Assistive devices can also refer to output technology, especially for learners with visual impairments. Examples include screen readers and magnifiers, refreshable displays enabling text to be read using Braille cells, and Braille note-takers. Three-dimensional printers produce tactile diagrams raised above the paper surface; Braille embossers print Braille documents; closed-circuit television (CCTV) produces magnified images with various text and background colours for partially sighted people; digital accessible information systems produce talking books; and scanners with optical character recognition convert scanned images of text to editable text files that can be read with screen readers or Braille displays. Teachers with minimal Braille knowledge can use free Braille Easy software to produce Braille mathematics representations from computer text. Software such as LaTex, BlindMath, LAMBDA and LeanMath use access overlay and hot-key techniques to improve accessibility (Ashraf et al., 2017).

Alternative and augmentative communication systems replace speech. There are stand-alone versions and apps for mobile and other devices. Picture exchange communication systems feature 'object' and 'action' pictures used to ask for objects. Proloquo2go is a flexible app using symbols, with a large core vocabulary, options to add symbols and photos, and an output choice of 100 natural-sounding voices, including children's voices, in various languages (Hersh, 2019).

Assistive listening systems improve sound clarity and reduce background noise. In audio induction loops, cable placed around a room or building transmits signals to users' hearing aids. With frequency modulated microphone and receiver systems, speech into a microphone is received through small earpieces. Infrared listening systems amplify audio devices. Another example for the hearing impaired is software that recognizes sign language and converts it to text. Software that converts text to sign language is still limited (Hersh, 2019).

---

equipped with assistive technology to students with disabilities, although there is no standard set-up. In the Republic of Korea, modified keyboards, mouse emulators, screen magnifiers and screen readers are available in special education schools but only for specific students in mainstream schools. Additional technology can be supplied on request to mainstream and special schools (Hersh and Mouroutsou, 2019).

In low- and middle-income countries, availability of assistive technology is limited. In Nigeria, there is limited use of assistive hardware (e.g. large key keyboards, mouse alternatives) and software (e.g. screen readers, magnifiers, print-to-Braille converters, Braille-to-speech synthesizers, speech-to-text converters, memory/organization devices, voice-over on devices); the main users in education are the hearing impaired and people with learning disabilities. Irregular electricity supply hampered the use of available devices (Ajuwon and Chitiyo, 2015).

> " In low- and middle-income countries, availability of assistive technology is limited "

Countries are improving inclusion of various groups through assistive technology

Visual impairment

Portugal established a network of 41 reference schools to educate blind and partially sighted students in regular classes in mainstream schools. The schools provided screen readers, refreshable Braille displays, Braille embossers, scanners, electronic calculators, electronic pocket magnifiers and CCTV. Computers with assistive and other software, as well as the learning content management system Moodle, were also used. Specialist and regular teachers worked together, without a technology adviser. Specialist teachers had more knowledge of the tools used (Ramos and de Andrade, 2016).

In Georgia, blind and partially sighted children mainly use a slate and stylus to write, and there is limited availability of Braille displays, CCTV and magnifiers. In Romania, digital recorders and Braille materials are available only in special schools. Romania also developed Robobraille, free software that produces accessible document formats (Hersh, 2019). In Serbia, screen readers are used less frequently in rural than in urban schools (Ault et al., 2013).

In Brazil, teachers at a school for visually impaired students developed tactile graphics for use in mathematics and science classes. While the school has equipment and technicians to do this on a large scale, low-cost materials are used to facilitate reproduction by teachers (Bernardo and Rust, 2018). In Grenada, five visually impaired students were supported in transferring from special to mainstream schools in 2004, using computers with screen readers, magnifiers, special keyboards and various Braille tools. Two trained professionals and a trained instructor visited the schools and assisted students, who then took the Caribbean Secondary Education Certificate. It was the first time blind students passed an examination at this level. Two of the students became teachers, one at his old school (UNESCO, 2011).

Hearing impairment

ICT-based approaches for learners with hearing disabilities include lecture recordings, subtitles (closed captions) and digital materials. Lecture recordings allow repeat review at students' own pace. A survey of deaf people in Poland and the United Kingdom found that they preferred subtitles for recorded materials and a combination of subtitles and sign language for lectures (Hersh, 2013). Subtitles are also useful to non-native speakers.

Text highlighting and captions for digital materials have proved useful. Microphone and receiver systems linked to students' hearing aids have been used in universities in Scotland (United Kingdom) and Tunisia. In the former case, a hearing-impaired student, supported by a lecturer always speaking facing the class and giving pointers to lab technicians, obtained top marks in an engineering class (Hersh, 2019).

At Bauman Moscow State Technical University, the Principal Educational, Research and Methodological Center for the deaf and hearing impaired offers bachelor's and master's degree programmes in computer science and engineering. It uses ICT, including a smart board with associated software, internet resources, scanners and printers, to support alternative communication in the classroom and improve access to information. After an evaluation of their needs, students receive a personalized resource package, including individual and group hardware, as well as communication and rehabilitation services, such as special software, assistive listening devices and sign language translation (Bauman University, 2019).

Autism spectrum disorder and other learning disabilities

Timers, computer software, online learning environments and personal digital assistants have been effective for learners with autism spectrum disorders, but provision of a single mobile device with multiple apps would probably have advantages in mainstream education (Southall, 2013). The voice output communication aid Proxtalker, which stores vocabulary on sound tags and retrieves it with radio frequency identification technology, has been used on an individual basis and could be beneficial on a larger scale (ACE Centre, 2019).

A smartphone app used in special schools in Brazil supports autistic students and those with cognitive impairments in using picture exchange communication systems (Manrique et al., 2016). In a special education college in north-eastern England (United Kingdom), autistic students and those with dementia or low literacy use touchscreen technology with about 50 symbols to support vocational learning in horticulture, travel and daily living skills. The approach can be used with any instructions that can be presented in sequence (Hersh, 2014).

In Toronto, Canada, a five-month trial in special needs classes in two schools found that a mobile app inputting vocabulary and linking words with pictures increased confidence, ease of learning, social interaction, a sense of community and peer-assisted learning, despite difficulty understanding voices, manipulation problems due to the small size, and charging and storage difficulties (Campigotto et al., 2013).

Touchscreen mobile devices for communication and self-prompting have been effective for people with developmental disabilities, although studies have mostly been small scale, involved one product (Proloquo2go) and assessed limited skills. While learners mastered them to varying degrees, they did not show spontaneous communication, indicating a need for more research on teaching spontaneous communication (Stephenson and Limbrick, 2015).

FINANCING AND TEACHER EDUCATION ARE CHALLENGES IN USE OF ASSISTIVE TECHNOLOGY

Huge disparities in access to even the most basic infrastructure, including electricity and the internet, mean that much of the potential of education and assistive technology for inclusion remains untapped and far out of reach for many in the world's poorest countries. Beyond that, barriers to the introduction of assistive technology relate to funding and teacher education.

There are various approaches to financing individual and institutional access to assistive technology. The federal and state governments in Australia provide direct payments to schools and universities to support students with disabilities. In the Republic of Korea, support centres provide assistive technology. Direct payments are made to students in Slovakia. University students can obtain funding for ICT and assistive technology in Estonia (PRIMUS Programme), Poland (Student II Programme of the National Rehabilitation Fund) and the United Kingdom (Disabled Students' Allowance) (Hersh and Mouroutsou, 2015).

Successful introduction and use of ICT and assistive technology in inclusive education requires their integration with appropriate pedagogical approaches used by well-trained teachers. Many teachers, however, lack relevant training. Developing expertise requires assistive technology professional development plans, time for teachers to share assistive technology strategies in meetings, and time to attend assistive technology training and professional development (Messinger-Willman and Marino, 2010). And teacher attitudes and beliefs can have a significant impact on successful ICT use. In Bangladesh, teachers with positive attitudes, even those with less ICT knowledge than others, found it easier to integrate ICT into their teaching (Khan et al., 2012).

Pre- and in-service education is needed to develop teacher knowledge. In Kazakhstan, a 36-hour training course for primary school teachers focuses on using ICT in teaching children with disabilities. It involves both theoretical knowledge about inclusive education and practical skills in using ICT in an inclusive environment. Four modules cover ICT use in inclusive education, teacher readiness, assistive technology, and software for creating interactive exercises. Project materials include websites, videos, online education media and links to networks of education communities (Oralbekova et al., 2016). Such institutionalized training is the exception worldwide, though. More often, the emphasis is on project-based and one-off courses.

CONCLUSION

An inclusive school ethos is key to making all students feel they belong and can realize their potential. Effective and supportive school leadership, while not enough in itself, is highly conducive to an inclusive school climate. For school leaders to effectively promote an inclusive school environment, they need autonomy to make the right decisions. They also require specialized training. Head teachers, like teachers more generally, must combat bullying and school violence, which constitute one of the most important drivers of exclusion.

Adequate physical infrastructure and effective use of technology can further foster an inclusive school environment. Safe and accessible schools are important for each child, and even more so for children with disabilities. Therefore, school design must follow universal principles that address the needs of all students and staff. While general-purpose education technology can support inclusive learning, assistive technology can play a crucial complementary role.

Anis, 13 years old, at a Save the Children-supported
Temporary Learning Space in a village in southern Idlib governorate
in northwestern Syria. Before he was displaced, he was injured
during an airstrike and became paralyzed. He is now in fourth grade.

CREDIT: Save The Children

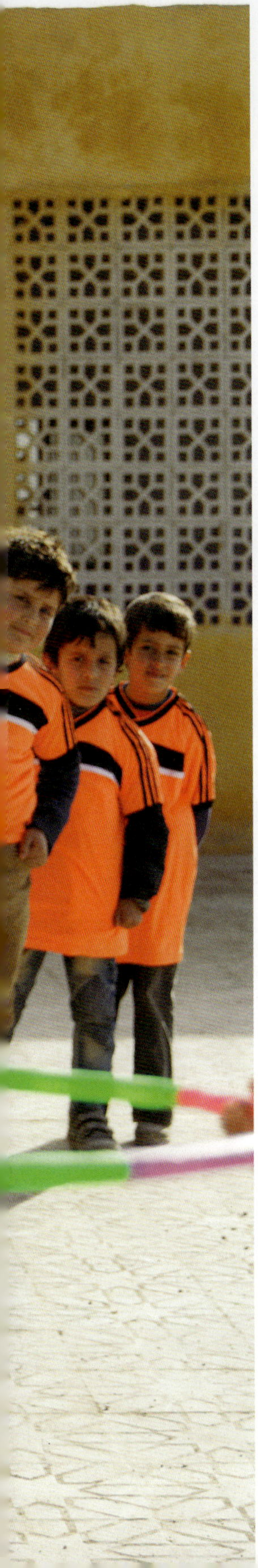

CHAPTER

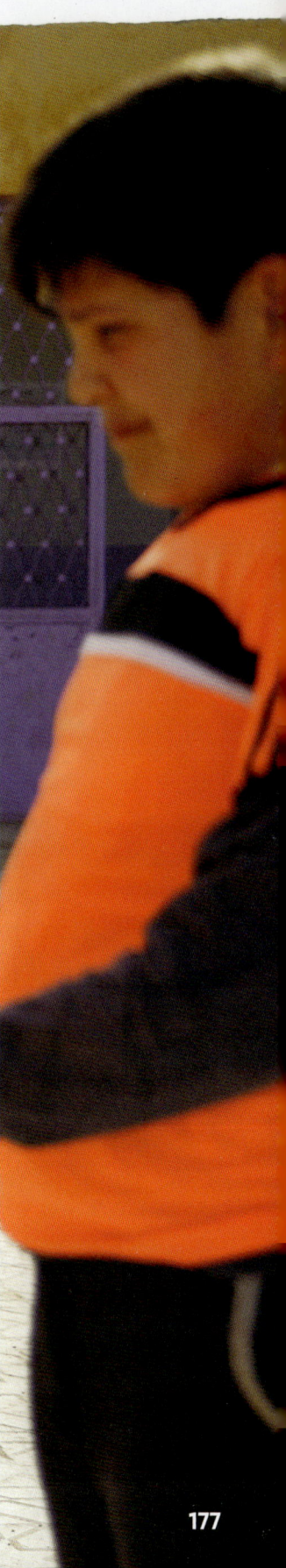

8

Students, parents and communities

What role do parents and the community play?

KEY MESSAGES

Students' attitudes towards inclusion vary according to their experiences and background, but some groups are at risk of being discriminated against and alienated from school

- Students hold largely neutral beliefs and feelings towards peers with disabilities, but a minority of negatively predisposed students can make students with disabilities feel isolated.

- Peer attitudes can improve through contact with a diverse student body from an early age. In Barbados, those with a friend at school with a disability had more positive attitudes.

- Examples abound of students discriminating against peers from minority groups, whether it is the Roma in Cyprus, indigenous groups in Ecuador, immigrants in the Republic of Korea, Syrian refugees in Turkey, Muslims in the United States or the Muhamasheen, a marginalized social group associated with garbage collection, in Yemen.

- In São Paulo, Brazil, grade 8 mathematics teachers were more likely to give white students a passing grade than their equally proficient and well-behaved black classmates.

Parents can drive, but also resist, inclusive education

- Among parents, 15% in Germany and 59% in Hong Kong, China, feared that children with disabilities disturbed other students' learning. In Australia's Queensland state, 37% of students in special schools had moved from mainstream schools.

- School choice exacerbates parental tendency to self-segregate, for instance in Chile (by income), in Denmark (between migrants and natives), in Lebanon (along sectarian lines) and in Malaysia (by ethnicity).

- Home schooling is a test for inclusion. Countries in Europe are banning the practice in law.

- Parents can organise networks to press for inclusive education. In the Russian Federation, they sued the government for access to schools for children with cerebral palsy.

- Parents with disabilities or from marginalised backgrounds are more likely to be poor, less educated and face barriers coming to school or working with teachers. In Viet Nam, children of parents with disabilities had 16% lower attendance rates.

Organizations for people with disabilities, disabled people's organizations, grassroots associations and international NGOs active in development and education play key roles

- Civil society is an advocate and watchdog for the right to inclusive education. It monitors progress on government commitments and defends against right violations. In Armenia, an NGO campaign resulted in a decision to roll out inclusive education nationally by 2025.

- Civil society organizations provide education services on government contract or their own initiative. They support groups governments do not reach (e.g. street children) or offer alternatives. Afghanistan supports community-based education. Yet NGO services should align with policy and not replicate services or compete for limited funds.

Societal norms often are the biggest barrier to inclusion.

Simona, preschool teacher, Italy

Breakthroughs towards inclusion have sometimes been the result of efforts by inspirational and committed pedagogical and education leaders who played key roles in breaking down discrimination barriers and empowering vulnerable groups. In other cases, they have been the result of groups campaigning to challenge injustices suffered by others or because their own needs had been systematically neglected and they organized to hold those responsible to account.

A move towards inclusion cannot be sustained solely through interventions by experts or mobilization by advocates, however. Societies need to embrace inclusion as a goal. Everyone needs to contribute – in the schoolyard, at school management committee meetings, during local and national elections. Inclusive societies require social and political transformation whereby everyone respects others' rights and believes in fulfilling everyone's potential. Such transformation requires active participation, not passive reception of instructions and guidelines.

Efforts to build inclusive education systems can easily be undermined by certain behaviour towards vulnerable groups, which may be unconscious and without reflection. Children can ostracize disadvantaged peers through jokes or intentional aggression. Parents can block efforts to form inclusive classrooms, whether because they belong to a privileged group and do not want their children's progress negatively affected or because they believe their children's or community's special needs are better served through separate provision. Grassroots organizations established to protect vulnerable children's rights can become an obstacle to making overall systems inclusive, regardless of whether attempts to preserve a status quo come from conviction or self-interest. This chapter discusses how students', parents' and communities' attitudes and behaviours can shift the balance towards or against inclusion in education.

VULNERABLE STUDENTS WISH TO BE INCLUDED BUT RISK BEING ISOLATED

An inclusive school offers conditions that promote all students' well-being. It promotes participation, cultivates a sense of belonging and rejects discrimination. Establishing friendships is a critical aspect of an education experience and may even be the main motivation for attending school. Conversely, difficulty making friends is a key obstacle to thriving at school. Having at least one good friend may serve an important protective function (Avramidis et al., 2018; Bollmer et al., 2005).

> Inclusive societies require social and political transformation whereby everyone respects others' rights and believes in fulfilling everyone's potential

Segregation in mainstream classrooms clearly decreases children's chances of seeing their friends and participating in activities during and after school (Finnvold, 2018). Yet inclusive settings can also expose vulnerable students to abusive behaviour and other challenges.

STUDENTS WITH DISABILITIES HAVE MIXED ATTITUDES TOWARDS INCLUSION

Taking vulnerable students' views and experiences into account is fundamental in designing truly inclusive education systems. Yet documenting and addressing their interests is not straightforward. Eliciting views of children at risk of exclusion in a way that treats them equally, respects their rights and empowers them to reveal their concerns without feeling singled out and targeted requires careful research design. Among studies that tried to assess their beliefs on inclusive education and their daily experiences in various education settings, several found that vulnerable students preferred inclusive settings. The sheer variability of cases and contexts, however, makes it difficult to draw general conclusions. Type of vulnerability, type of school currently attended, prior experience at a different type of school, level of specialized support and how discreetly it is provided are among the factors that can shape student preferences.

In the United Kingdom, 65% of children with mild to moderate learning difficulties in both mainstream and special schools gave positive reports about their current education experience. Among those in special schools, 74% had previous experience in mainstream schools. Of those, twice as many expressed negative as expressed positive views. One-third of students in special schools said they would have preferred mainstream school (Norwich and Kelly, 2004). Diaries and drawings by students on the autism spectrum have been used as complementary tools in research to capture how these children experience social isolation as they struggle with social interaction and communication with peers. The order and predictability that many children with related conditions prefer can easily be disrupted by the disorder of schools, especially at the secondary education level, adding to anxiety (Humphrey and Lewis, 2008).

Even when they are in mainstream schools, vulnerable students may appreciate the opportunity to receive learning support in separate settings, for reasons ranging from more attention and higher quality to less noise.

> " In the United Kingdom, one-third of students in special schools said they would have preferred mainstream schools "

Primary school students with special education needs in Botswana reported that they appreciated being in inclusive classrooms but that parts of the curriculum remained inaccessible (Mukhopadhyay et al., 2019). A study of academically talented students found that they preferred homogenous groups to improve learning outcomes but were less certain about the impact of such arrangements on social outcomes, including the opportunity to be recognized for their academic abilities in a mixed group (Adams-Byers et al., 2004).

Students with dyslexia can suffer low self-esteem and a feeling of helplessness when they attribute their struggle with reading to a lack of ability that is beyond their control. An early diagnosis is necessary to separate the learning difficulty from the understanding of their ability and to build self-esteem (Glazzard, 2010). It is also important for learners to remain motivated (Elbeheri et al., 2017). A study of dyslexic students in South Africa suggested that they preferred special schools where they felt normal to mainstream schools, which deepened their sense of difference from other students (Leseyane et al., 2018).

PEER ATTITUDES TOWARDS STUDENTS WITH DISABILITIES CAN IMPROVE THROUGH CONTACT AND KNOWLEDGE

While vulnerable students have a preference for being fully included in education, their attitude is conditioned by a host of factors, not least of which are peers' attitudes. Eliciting information on these attitudes is not straightforward. The reliability of information is affected by studies' quality and the extent to which they are free of bias. Respondents to attitude surveys have been shown to provide answers they think interviewers and society at large want to hear (Lüke and Grosche, 2018). Still, students appear to hold largely neutral beliefs, feelings and intentions towards peers with disabilities, although a minority of negatively predisposed students can make students with disabilities feel isolated (de Boer et al., 2012). Attitudes tend to vary by type of disability: Students with behavioural problems and intellectual disabilities are the most vulnerable. In Canada, primary school students in inclusive schools were more prejudiced against children with intellectual disabilities than against those with physical disabilities (Nowicki, 2006).

Positive peer attitudes are important for the success of inclusive education. Overall, there is limited evidence on the effectiveness of interventions aimed at influencing attitudes towards students with disabilities (Scior, 2011). Existing interventions stress early contact with vulnerable groups and awareness raising to increase the level of knowledge about particular vulnerabilities.

A review of 35 studies showed that 22 claimed contact with people with disabilities had a positive effect on attitudes (MacMillan et al., 2014). In Barbados, where less than half of students reported having a friend with a disability, those with either a personal friend or a friend at school with a disability had more positive attitudes (Blackman, 2016). In Saudi Arabia, contact with children with intellectual disabilities in an inclusive school resulted in positive student attitudes (Alnahdi, 2019).

Interaction should be fostered early on to increase acceptance of diversity. In inclusive early childhood care and education settings, students with disabilities gain in peer acceptance, friendships and cognitive development (Odom et al., 2011). Awareness can be most influenced at preschool age, when children exposed to people with disabilities can develop a basic understanding of disabilities and share the emotional state of people with disabilities (Hong et al., 2014). A study of grade 8 students in Austria's Styria state showed that intensive contact with students with special needs through common school projects was more effective for improving attitudes towards peers with disabilities than mere coexistence in an inclusive classroom (Schwab, 2017, 2018).

Pairing students to support peers with disabilities, both in school and in the community, is a key intervention to increase acceptance and empathy, although inclusion

in mainstream schools does not guarantee inclusion outside school. A randomized controlled experiment examined the effectiveness of peer instead of adult paraprofessional support on academic and social outcomes of students with severe disabilities in inclusive classrooms. Compared with students receiving support only from adults, peer support increased interaction and led to academic engagement and social participation, including friendships that lasted after the intervention (Carter et al., 2016). Studies that collected information on both quality and quantity of contact concluded quality rather than quantity reduced prejudice. In fact, controlling for quality of contact, more contact increased prejudice against students with intellectual and developmental disabilities (Keith et al., 2015).

Improved knowledge can help shape student attitudes towards peers with disabilities. Interventions to improve understanding of peers with autism spectrum disorders through detailed explanations and suggestions on how to interact with them can play a role (Campbell and Barger, 2014). An online autism awareness-raising programme involving university students in Lebanon and the United States helped increase knowledge and reduce stigma (Obeid et al., 2015). An analysis of 20 studies on school-based interventions to improve student attitudes towards children with disabilities from kindergarten through secondary school in the Republic of Korea showed positive effects, especially when interventions were contact-based and used role play (Chae et al., 2019).

STUDENTS FROM MINORITY AND VULNERABLE GROUPS ARE AT RISK OF BEING STEREOTYPED AND DISCRIMINATED AGAINST

Majority populations tend to stereotype minority and vulnerable groups because of a predisposal to categorize, simplify and develop group identities. Stereotypes affect the type of information majority groups collect about minority groups and can lead to expectations that perpetuate stereotypes, contributing to negative attitudes and discriminatory actions. In education,

> " Pairing students to support peers with disabilities, both in school and in the community, is a key intervention to increase acceptance and empathy "

> **In education, stereotypes and negative peer attitudes lead to less acceptance and to isolation and bullying**

stereotypes and negative peer attitudes lead to less acceptance and to isolation and bullying.

Stereotypes affect a sense of belonging

Students may internalize stereotypes, which compounds negative effects on their sense of belonging and education achievement. In Turkey, Syrian refugees complained that negative stereotypes led to feelings of depression, stigmatization and alienation from school (Çelik and İçduygu, 2018).

Students at risk of being stereotyped may fear confirming a negative stereotype. This feeling has a negative impact on test performance (Lyons et al., 2018). A study in the United States showed that presenting a reading test as a diagnostic of abilities adversely affected the performance of African-American children, who were aware of racial stereotypes (Wasserberg, 2014).

Stereotypes can lower expectations and self-esteem. A study in Switzerland is one of many confirming that girls internalize the stereotype that they are less suited than boys for science, technology, engineering and mathematics, which discourages them from pursuing degrees in these fields (Makarova et al., 2019). A survey of US schools showed that 87% of lesbian, gay, bisexual, transgender, queer and questioning students experienced peer harassment or assault in 2017. They had lower self-esteem, did less well on examinations and were twice as likely as other students to report that they did not want to pursue post-secondary education (Kosciw et al., 2018).

Negative attitudes towards minorities lead to student bullying

Students around the world harbour negative attitudes towards minorities. Children with immigrant backgrounds in the Republic of Korea are three to five times as likely as native students to be victims of school violence but less likely to bully others (Bae et al., 2019; Lee et al., 2019). In northern Sri Lanka, a legacy of the caste system persists, with children of families associated with

sanitation-related occupations bullied in school (Lall, 2016). Adolescents from ethnic minorities in Viet Nam have reported being singled out for bullying and physical assault (Pells et al., 2016). In Yemen, children of the Muhamasheen, a historically marginalized social group associated with garbage collection, face persistent discrimination, abuse by teachers and bullying by peers (Equal Rights Trust, 2017).

Roma students in Cyprus suffer bullying, negative language and social isolation (Symeou et al., 2009). In Serbia and Slovenia, the poorer the Roma students, the more negative their experiences with respect to fear of rejection by peers and teachers (Macura-Milovanović et al., 2013). Afro-descendant and indigenous students in Ecuador have been ignored or excluded from collective projects (Martinez Novo and de la Torre, 2010). In the US state of California, 53% of Muslim students reported being made fun of, verbally insulted or abused at school because of their identity, more than double the average national rate (CAIR, 2017). Albino students in the United Republic of Tanzania were bullied by peers who did not understand the condition (Ngalomba, 2016). A recent spate of aggressive acts against this population led to the opening of special schools and shelters or the withdrawal of albino children from school (Pedneault and Labaki, 2019).

Stereotypes tend to persist, especially if reinforced through the social status of particular groups. However, increased contact with minority groups in schools can help break these stereotypes. For instance, students with Albanian immigrant backgrounds were initially less accepted by native students in Greece. However, a three-year longitudinal study in lower secondary schools showed that they were increasingly accepted as their involvement with local culture increased (Asendorpf and Motti, 2017). A study involving 6,000 grade 6 students in the United States showed that the more school diversity increased, the more likely students were to make friends from different ethnic groups, and these friendships led to more positive interethnic attitudes (Graham, 2018).

Minority and vulnerable students experience teacher prejudice and discrimination

Teachers can be instrumental in fighting but also in perpetuating discrimination in education, affecting the self-esteem and academic achievement of minority and vulnerable groups. In São Paulo, Brazil, grade 8 mathematics teachers were more likely to give white students a passing grade than their equally proficient and well-behaved black classmates. This bias corresponded to a 4% difference in the probability of retention and a 5% reduction in the probability of black students being at the top of their class (Botelho et al., 2015). Studies on teachers' assessment of pre-primary students in the United States showed that they judged boys' proficiency to be above girls' when both performed and behaved similarly (Cimpian et al., 2014; Cimpian et al., 2016).

Teachers in China had less favourable perceptions of rural migrant students – and their parents – than of their urban peers. Conversely, the latter reported that their teachers, across subjects, asked them to participate in class and praised them more than their migrant peers. Children left behind in rural areas by parents migrating to urban areas felt their teachers were less likely to call on or praise them (Cherng and Han, 2018). In Spain, secondary school teachers' low expectations affected immigrant students' academic achievement and probability of dropout (Prats et al., 2017).

In parts of the world, certain groups, such as boys, ethnic minorities and children with disabilities, are more likely to be subject to corporal punishment in school (Gershoff, 2017). Children aged 8 from disadvantaged families in Peru were more likely to receive such punishment than children from more privileged families. School violence, including by teachers, is the main reason children dislike school, with shares ranging from one-quarter in India to over half in Viet Nam (Ogando Portela and Pells, 2015).

Vulnerable students are at risk of mistreatment in both basic and higher education. A study on university students with disabilities in the Czech Republic revealed that they faced institutional, attitudinal and disability-specific barriers, including inflexibility, less welcoming approaches by administrators and the absence of guiding protocols. Problems included difficulty following lectures and making contact with others, lecturers' unwillingness to make slides and handouts accessible and other students' reluctance to share their notes (Strnadová et al., 2015). The heavy legacy of oppression and systemic discrimination against indigenous populations in Australia and Canada is being addressed through various policy initiatives (**Box 8.1**).

PARENTS CAN DRIVE INCLUSIVE EDUCATION BUT ALSO RESIST IT

Attitudes towards inclusion in education reflect attitudes towards social inclusion in general. Parents who hold discriminatory beliefs about gender, disability, ethnicity, race or religion may be unlikely to support inclusive classrooms and schools. Parents of vulnerable children may favour special education and resist inclusion in mainstream schools if they believe the children will not receive sufficient attention. Parents living on the margins of society may be powerless to prevent discrimination.

SOME PARENTS HOLD DISCRIMINATORY BELIEFS

Discriminatory norms can be diffused in populations through lack of information or through inaccurate information. In parts of the world, some parents mistakenly believe disability is infectious or a form of divine punishment (Mariga et al., 2014). In the Central African Republic, children – mostly boys – with physical or mental disabilities are considered witches and chased from home and community, depriving them of shelter, let alone access to education (Tesemma, 2011).

Moreover, parents may refuse the additional cost of admitting minority students, adopting a 'not in my backyard' attitude and being unwilling to take into account the social benefits of inclusion. They may worry their children will lose out by being taught with vulnerable students, especially in cultures that emphasize academic achievement. In Germany, 15% of parents feared that their children might adopt negative behaviour of other children, and 16% that children with disabilities might slow down their children's learning (Lohmann et al., 2019).

> " A study in the United States showed that the more school diversity increased, the more likely students were to make friends from different ethnic groups "

8

BOX 8.1:

Despite radical changes in policy and attitudes, indigenous students in Australia and Canada still face difficulty in being included

Indigenous populations in Australia and Canada have historically been subjected to discrimination and abuse, including in education. Both countries' governments have issued formal apologies for past mistreatment, and reconciliation processes are under way (Australia Government, 2008; Canada Government, 2008).

Racism has had a negative impact on the schooling experience of Aboriginal and Torres Strait Islanders in Australia. Long-term effects include negative beliefs about indigenous peoples' intelligence and academic performance (Moodie et al., 2019). The experience of racism has negatively affected Aboriginal children's well-being and increased the risk of emotional and behavioural difficulties (Macedo et al., 2019; Priest et al., 2012). While cultural integration and inclusion policies improved indigenous students' situation at nearly all education levels, discrimination in schools persists (Bodkin-Andrews and Carlson, 2016). In New South Wales and Victoria, 40% of students with indigenous backgrounds reported having been racially discriminated against by peers and 20% reported discrimination by teachers (Australian National University, 2019). The Longitudinal Literacy and Numeracy Surveys for Indigenous Students, which followed students through grades 3 to 6, also found that indigenous students' average achievement in English and mathematics was lower than their non-indigenous peers, although the gap was mitigated by a positive learning environment and teacher–student relations (Purdie et al., 2011).

In Canada, between the 1870s and the 1990s, 150,000 First Nation, Inuit and Métis students aged 4 to 16 attended, mostly forcibly, a network of boarding schools aimed at weakening family ties and promoting assimilation into dominant Canadian culture. Indigenous students were isolated, divided, neglected and abused in these poorly located, built and maintained residential schools (OECD, 2017). The system was described as physical, biological and cultural genocide (Truth and Reconciliation Commission of Canada, 2015a). While the schools had been closed by 1997, 20 years later, an independent body was still proposing 94 further actions, notably calling on the federal government to draft legislation giving indigenous parents and communities responsibility, control and accountability in their children's education (Truth and Reconciliation Commission of Canada, 2015b).

Various provincial governments have taken measures in recent years. In Alberta, the First Nations, Métis, and Inuit High School Completion Coach Project was introduced in 2016/17 to develop positive relationships in the school community (Edmonton Public Schools, 2018). In 2016, the Alberta Teachers' Association and other stakeholders signed a commitment with the province's education department to ensure that all students learned the histories and cultures of indigenous people, notably through Walking Together: Education for Reconciliation, a professional learning project. Its resources, including the Stepping Stones series, aim to increase knowledge in line with teaching quality standards (Alberta Teachers' Association, 2019). In south-western Ontario, the Fourth R: Uniting Our Nations programmes promote inclusive education and improve transition from primary to secondary school for indigenous students through mentoring, cultural leadership courses and camps, and student advisory committees (Crooks et al., 2015). Yukon has developed First Hunt, First Fish and Spring Camp, three programmes aimed at empowering First Nation students to build a sense of self-worth and pride in themselves, their cultural heritage and their language (Yukon Government, 2019).

In Hong Kong, China, 59% of parents felt that students with special needs disturbed other students' learning and 39% that they used too many school resources (Sin et al., 2012). It is not uncommon for parents to oppose admission of children with developmental disorders, such as autism, despite government efforts towards more inclusive education systems (Chia, 2017).

Parents around the world have opposed admitting poor and marginalized children, whether out of prejudice or lack of solidarity and unwillingness to share costs. Students with disabilities are not the only minority targeted: Parents in Greece voiced xenophobic concerns over establishing a refugee reception facility and threatened to occupy schools in protest (Simopoulos and Alexandridis, 2019).

As part of a research project aimed at consulting with parents on lesbian, gay, bisexual, transgender, queer and questioning content in curriculum, supported by the New South Wales state government in Australia, 34 in 39 primary and secondary schools declined to participate. Many cited the project as 'incompatible with the parent community' (Ullman and Ferfolja, 2016). In 2019, after the UK Parliament voted for primary-level sex and relationship education that would include

> " In Hong Kong, China, 59% of parents felt that students with special needs disturbed other students' learning "

> " Inclusive approaches should be a core element of general teacher preparation rather than a specialist topic "

lesbian, gay, bisexual and transgender topics, there were demonstrations in front of a primary school in Birmingham that had introduced lessons about same-sex relationships. About 400 parents signed a petition to stop the lessons and threatened to withdraw their children, with the result that the classes were suspended (Stewart, 2019; *The Economist*, 2019; Parveen, 2019).

The media are a powerful force, capable of perpetuating and dismantling stereotypes among parents. Coverage of vulnerable groups can be a bellwether, leading changes in attitudes. Media discourse can be negative for inclusive education, depicting children with disabilities as deviant and a threat to other students' education, or presenting special schools as the only option for addressing their needs (Runswick-Cole, 2008). Conversely, accurate and balanced representation of disability as part of everyday life can challenge misconceptions and make an important contribution towards inclusion (United Nations, 2019).

Parents can influence education policies through elections, and the media play a large role in the nature of the debate. In 2017, inclusive education proved a decisive issue in state elections of North Rhine-Westphalia, Germany, with the electorate divided between support for inclusive schools and support for choice and the value of special schools (Bernewasser, 2018). Several media outlets presented inclusive education negatively, emphasizing the cost and giving insufficient space to experts (Thoms, 2017). Plans to generalize inclusive education were rolled back in 2018 (North-Rhine Westphalia Ministry of Schools and Education, 2018). Only primary schools are inclusive, while conditions at secondary schools make it very difficult to accommodate students with learning disabilities (Stein, 2019).

As part of a school desegregation project run by Roma non-government organizations (NGOs) in Bulgaria, supported by the Open Society Institute and the Roma Education Fund, 20,000 Roma children were integrated into mainstream schools over a 12-year period. The NGOs engaged in discussions with local authorities, school directors and non-Roma parents, and the effort was accompanied by a sustained media campaign. Roma parents were encouraged to become members of school boards. The project resulted in considerably increased

student motivation and improved education participation and achievement (Nicoletti and Kunz, 2018; Ryder, 2015).

PARENTS OF VULNERABLE CHILDREN TEND TO SUPPORT INCLUSION BUT OFTEN HAVE RESERVATIONS

In much of the world, parents of children with disabilities have few, if any, school options. There may be no inclusive schools catering for children with disabilities in rural areas in low- and middle-income countries, reducing parents' choices to no schooling, placement in a local school with no resources, or education in an appropriate school far from home.

When realistic choices are available, parents of vulnerable children wish to send them to schools where they can achieve their academic potential but, more particularly, where their well-being and opportunities for social development are ensured. In India, parents of children with disabilities were initially concerned about teasing, sanitation, teacher attitudes and academic expectations, but they later recognized improvement in both the academic and social domains (Hooja, 2009). In Nigeria, parents with greater knowledge may support teaching children with disabilities in mainstream schools (Torgbenu et al., 2018). Among parents of children with disabilities in the United States, positive views of inclusion were more likely among those with higher levels of education (Leyser and Kirk, 2004).

Parents also need to be confident that mainstream schools will understand and respond to their children's needs. Even some well-informed parents prefer early identification and placement in special needs sections or special schools, fearing that mainstream schools are unprepared. A review of parental attitude studies showed that parents of children with disabilities were neutral about the concept of inclusive education but not in favour when it concerned inclusion of their child (de Boer et al., 2010).

In some cases of severe disability, difficulties increase with age, and under-resourced mainstream schools may not be able to offer enough support. A study in England (United Kingdom) focused on children with

> "
> A review showed that parents of children with disabilities were neutral about the concept of inclusive education but not in favour when it concerned inclusion of their child
> "

autism spectrum disorder that made them less likely to respond to demands. As the school schedule became more demanding, these children were more likely to be excluded, forcing parents to look for schools that better met their needs (Brede et al., 2017). A study in the Netherlands found that other parents were the most negative about inclusion of children with profound intellectual and multiple disabilities in primary school classrooms (de Boer and Munde, 2015). A key school choice decision is the transition between primary and secondary education (Byrne, 2013; Makin et al., 2017).

Parents take several factors into account in choosing from a range of inclusive and special schools. Especially in richer countries, where more options may be available, parents examine the availability of special education needs programmes, school and class size, distance from home, teacher interpersonal skills, frequency of parent–teacher communication and possibilities for parental involvement. They also look for a positive attitude towards children with disabilities, allowing school and family values to align and their children to maintain their support system (Mawene and Bal, 2018).

Choice also depends on parents' assessment of their children's ability to learn and, in the case of moderate to severe disabilities, their eventual ability to work. Popular beliefs about disability can distort parental perspectives about their child's potential (Chu and Lo, 2016). Parents who believe their child has a condition that sets them apart from society (medical model) favour special schools to focus on life skills, while parents who believe social, institutional and attitudinal barriers prevent inclusion (social model) prefer inclusive schools because they encourage social integration (Mawene and Bal, 2018). Parents with negative attitudes towards inclusive education tend to have little faith in the mainstream school system (Opoku, 2019).

In Australia's Queensland state, a survey of parents of children with disabilities attending public schools – whether special or mainstream – showed that half favoured special classes, possibly because 70% believed their child required more patient teachers, more substantial changes in classroom procedures and more special training for teachers than they thought were available in mainstream settings (Elkins et al., 2003). Data from the Australian Institute of Health and Welfare previously suggested that 29% of children with disabilities who started in a mainstream school either left school, went to segregated classes or, in one-third of cases, moved to a special school. In Queensland, 37% of students in special schools in 2015 had moved from mainstream schools. A survey of 80 parents who transferred their child to one of the 42 special schools found that insufficient provision for academic learning in the mainstream school, coupled with lack of an inclusive ethos, led to emotional strain (Mann et al., 2018). In addition, about 12% of children with disabilities in Australia were denied a place in a mainstream school (Children and Young People With Disability Australia, 2017).

At times, parents go so far as to bribe officials to recognize a special need to gain advantage in assessment or support. To increase the chances of university admission, some parents in the United States falsely claimed that their children had learning disabilities, allowing them to take entrance examinations alone, where bribed officials could provide answers (Pierpoint, 2019).

School choice has implications for inclusion and segregation

In countries where school choice is possible or even actively encouraged, a portfolio of options beyond the local school usually means families with adequate financial means are more likely to avoid disadvantaged schools and send their children to schools that cater to their academic or social aspirations. This choice can lead to enrolment patterns that increase segregation and reduce social cohesion.

In Europe, when the share of immigrants becomes disproportionally high in less affluent neighbourhoods, parents of native students may respond by moving to other schools (Brunello and De Paola, 2017). In Denmark, an increase by 7 percentage points over 15 years in the share of students in larger municipalities whose parents were born outside the EU or OECD was associated with a rise of 1 percentage point in the share of natives attending private school (Gerdes, 2013).

In Chile, school segregation by income is among the highest in the world. A study calculated the percentage of students at the bottom of the socio-economic distribution who should have been moved to achieve homogeneity across schools and reflect changes over time. It showed that the level of segregation and worsening trend resulted not only from high levels of income inequality and residential segregation but also from a school choice mechanism with exclusionary selection practices and from price discrimination (Valenzuela et al., 2014).

In the United States, a range of school choice policies contribute to growing segregation by income and race (Roda and Wells, 2013). An evaluation of a policy in Chicago that tried to increase information to poor families about school quality showed that, while such families left failing schools, they went to other low-performing schools (Rich and Jennings, 2015). When white parents choose schools, they use racial composition and factors for which race is a proxy, such as school safety, quality of facilities and academic performance (Billingham and Hunt, 2016). In 11 southern states where a major desegregation effort took place in the late 1960s in response to the civil rights movement, those gains have been eroding, owing partly to demographic trends related to immigration and partly to school choice policies. The share of black students attending a school with less than 10% white students rose, from 23% in 1980 to 36% in 2014 (Frankenberg et al., 2017).

"
Parents with negative attitudes towards inclusive education tend to have little faith in the mainstream school system
"

In other countries, even in the absence of government policy actively encouraging school choice, parental decisions lead to self-segregation. In Lebanon, the vast majority of parents favour private schools along sectarian lines. Segregation shows no sign of abating, not only because of social divisions but also because of the perceived lower quality of public schools and indirect public support to private schools (Baytiyeh, 2017; Shuayb, 2016). In Malaysia, the education system is expected to support national unity. However, alternative private streams, organized by ethnicity and differentiated by quality, have developed in parallel, contributing to ethnic stratification despite government measures to desegregate schools (Raman and Sua, 2010).

Migration poses challenges to inclusion. The Gulf Cooperation Council countries rely on migrant workforces to such an extent that, in some countries, immigrants constitute more than half the student population. Migration is managed through short-term contracts and high migrant turnover. As a result, ministries of education do not make substantive efforts to integrate immigrant children but encourage the development of private schools, where access and quality are linked to ability to pay. These schools offer an extensive range of curricula, mostly in line with the country of origin of the student body. For instance, 194 private schools in Dubai, United Arab Emirates, offer 17 different curricula. Students are taught in the language of their home country or in English and use textbooks from the country of origin (Kippels and Ridge, 2019).

In some immigrant host countries, there is a tendency for groups to establish independent schools along ethnic, linguistic or religious lines. In Canada, school choice in Muslim communities navigates between the desire for education in private Islamic schools, in line with home values, and public secular schools, in line with the realities of a multicultural society (Zine, 2007). In the Netherlands, Hindu schools respond to parents' need for a sense of belonging and their high teacher expectations. The schools are aligned with the national education system through multiple links, including curricula (e.g. intercultural and citizenship education) and monitoring. A key question is whether a voluntary and affirmative parental decision to educate children separately is a legitimate response for minorities and, if so, what conditions and criteria allow the avoidance of school ghettoization to the detriment of inclusion (Merry and Driessen, 2012). Homeschooling is an example of how parental preference for self-segregation can test the limits of inclusive education, despite the potential that distance and online mainstream education offer for inclusion (**Box 8.2**).

PARENTS CAN SUPPORT THE REALIZATION OF INCLUSIVE EDUCATION

Parents are best placed to know the needs of their children and well placed to assess the coherence of various interventions (Sayeed, 2009). They can support teachers with valuable information, a practice which can also make parents feel listened to and respected. Parents highly value mainstream school–home communication (Stevens and Wurf, 2020). Parents need to communicate and cooperate effectively with teachers and have access to information about the school's organization and requirements and their children's achievements and challenges. They can also help reinforce the school programme through activities at home. Some countries have policies to capitalize on parental knowledge. In Georgia, parents of children with disabilities must be involved in decision making regarding the best school model and in the formulation of individual education plans (Tchintcharauli and Javakhishvili, 2017).

For parents to play a greater role in promoting the interests of vulnerable children and fulfilling the vision of inclusive education, their participation in school activities and decision-making bodies is highly desirable. However, it is often challenging, either because parents are marginalized themselves or because of challenges related to time, distance, language and other factors (Page et al., 2007). A study showed that most immigrant parents in the province of Quebec, Canada, were not involved in school committees due to work or their perception that the school was unapproachable and remote from their lives (Beauregard et al., 2014).

In the United States, 47% of students living at or above the federal poverty level had a parent serving on a school committee in 2015/16, compared with 27% of those

> " In the Netherlands, Hindu schools respond to parents' need for a sense of belonging and their high teacher expectations "

BOX 8.2:

Homeschooling expands but also tests the limits of inclusion

Educating children at home is illegal in many countries, especially in Europe. In Germany, a family whose request for exemption from compulsory primary school for religious reasons was rejected by the school supervisory authority appealed to the European Court of Human Rights. The court sided with the national body on multiple grounds, notably in asserting that the obligation of the state extended beyond the acquisition of knowledge to

> the education of responsible citizens who participate in a democratic and pluralistic society. The acquisition of social competence in dealing with other persons who hold different views and in holding an opinion which differed from the views of the majority could only materialise through regular contact with society. ... Given the general interest of society in the integration of minorities and in avoiding the emergence of parallel societies, the interference with the applicants' fundamental rights was proportionate and reasonable. (Council of Europe, 2006, p. 26)

The European countries that still allow homeschooling do so under tight restrictions.

Some countries are increasingly making the option available under relatively simple conditions. The Philippines and Ukraine recently issued regulations easing homeschooling requirements (Donnelly, 2019). The highest prevalence of homeschooling occurs in the United States, where the Department of Education estimated that the number of homeschooled children increased from 850,000 in 1999 to 1.8 million in 2012, or 3.4% of the school-age population (US Department of Education, 2012). As to the main reasons for homeschooling, 34% of parents cited concerns over the school environment (safety, drugs, peer pressure), while 12% cited physical health, mental health or some other special need. About 51% cited a desire to provide religious instruction, although only 16% gave that as the main reason (McQuiggan et al., 2017).

Some systems provide the services of a teacher or teaching assistant to children who do not attend mainstream school, ranging from a few hours per day to a few hours per month. In Western Australia, parents of children with an autism spectrum disorder can homeschool them with support from the Schools of Isolated and Distance Education, originally established as part of the state's Department of Education to educate children in remote areas (Chamberlain, 2019; McDonald and Lopes, 2014). Public schools in Des Moines, United States, offer a dual enrolment programme for homeschooled children. Parents can choose between unassisted or assisted instruction. Those choosing unassisted instruction develop an education plan and select the curriculum and instruction methods. A licensed teacher conducts a year-end evaluation. Parents choosing assisted instruction are assigned a teacher who makes regular home visits to advise on the child's schooling, including the education plan and instruction methods. Homeschooled students can also take part in school music lessons, sports teams and any class of interest (Johnson, 2013).

---

living below it. Some 65% of parents who completed university or professional education served on a committee, while 25% of parents without a secondary school certificate did so. Parental participation was 34% for black students, compared with 49% for white students, and 25% for parents who did not speak English at home, compared with 46% of parents who did (McQuiggan et al., 2017). In some societies, women are not expected to play an active role in public life and are heavily under-represented on school-based management committees. In a representative survey of primary schools in four Nigerian states, the percentage of women on such committees ranged from 12% in Jigawa to 32% in Kwara (Antoninis, 2010).

As the next section will show, parents often organize in networks or associations outside schools to press for more inclusive education (Stubbs, 2008). They build links and foster partnerships with local and national education authorities, organize meetings to present new approaches and support teacher development. Parents can also change policy and practice through the courts. A group of parents in Petrozavodsk, the Russian Federation, sued the government and subsequently protested for access to mainstream schools for children with cerebral palsy (Meresman, 2014). Parents of children with disabilities in South Africa campaigned for removing school fees for children with disabilities (Human Rights Watch, 2019). After parents of children with dyslexia in the United States state of Ohio filed a class action against their district because schools were not identifying dyslexia or providing adequate help, schools began training staff to identify and evaluate students with learning disabilities (Hanford, 2018).

Parents also need support

Parents of vulnerable children often find themselves in a distressing situation. In many cultures, they react with shock and shame to the birth of a child with a disability; they are psychologically, emotionally and socially unprepared. They may feel despair, helplessness and hopelessness. They may experience pressure from their own families: In Lagos, Nigeria, couples have separated because of family pressures. Often, it is mothers who give up employment to look after children with disabilities (Brydges and Mkandawire, 2020). Parents with disabilities present particular concerns (**Box 8.3**).

Parents of children with disabilities, especially poorer parents, may be unaware of education opportunities and need information on inclusive education and their rights. They need support in finding out about early identification and intervention, medical and therapeutic services, and early childhood education and schooling. Early intervention and inclusive development are crucial. Early intervention for deaf or hard-of-hearing children enables access to sign language, reducing the risk of linguistic deprivation, which makes them vulnerable to abuse and can lead to cognitive delays, mental health challenges and post-traumatic stress disorder (Humphries et al., 2012).

Disadvantaged parents of students with disabilities are likely to feel less empowered regarding education. They may see teachers and other professionals as more knowledgeable, raising barriers to communication. In Bhutan, most parents of at least partially integrated children with special education needs had minimal or no communication with school, due at least in part to a culture of deference to teachers, especially among people from rural areas or with little education (Jigyel et al., 2018). Parents need support and counselling to monitor their children's progress and become more confident in dealing with schools (Hornby, 2010).

They also need support managing their children's sleep, behaviour, nursing, comfort and care. Early intervention programmes for children with disabilities that help families take care of their children at home can lead to a virtuous circle whereby parents grow more confident, use other support services and are more likely to enrol their children in mainstream schools. Mutual support programmes, involving information from others they trust who have had similar experiences, also help parents cope. Parent and family groups can provide solidarity, support, confidence and information (Mariga et al., 2014).

BOX 8.3:

Parents with disabilities can struggle to secure their children's education

Parents with disabilities are more likely to be poor and have lower education levels (Inclusion International, 2006). Their children may have increased responsibility at home, or parents may be unable to take them to school. The parents may experience more stress, reducing their capacity to monitor and support their children's education. In Viet Nam, children of parents with disabilities had 16% lower attendance rates and lower attainment levels. Outcomes were more negative for boys and when the mother was the disabled parent. Tuition fee exemptions and transport assistance improved attendance (Mont and Nguyen, 2013).

Parental disability may be unknown to the school. In the United States, there are at least 4 million parents with disabilities with children under age 18. As with any parent, access to information and communication is crucial to involvement in education. Lack of physical facilities and modes of communication can prevent parents with disabilities from coming to school or working with teachers. Schools may be unaware that these parents cannot attend meetings because the building is inaccessible or that they do not respond to letters due to visual impairment. Parents may be unwilling to acknowledge a disability because they fear their parenting capacities will be called into question (Through the Looking Glass, 2013).

In Australia, parents with disabilities are over-represented in child protection and legal proceedings, mainly due to prejudice and absence of adequate support services (Booth et al., 2005). In Israel, social workers have a legal obligation to support parents with intellectual disabilities in the exercise of their parental rights. They are asked to make efforts to ensure that children remain with their parents and are obliged to treat parents with intellectual disabilities like any others. Nevertheless, a majority of social workers had negative or ambivalent attitudes regarding the parental capacities of those with intellectual disabilities (Gur and Stein, 2020).

COMMUNITIES AND ORGANIZATIONS SUPPORT GOVERNMENTS AND HOLD THEM TO ACCOUNT FOR INCLUSIVE EDUCATION

Social mobilization to promote inclusive education often goes beyond spontaneous activities by concerned parents and vulnerable people. Organized civil society activity of various forms has played a fundamental role in demanding quality education. Such activity includes advocacy and watchdog functions to hold governments accountable for national and international commitments, along with provision of education services at various levels, especially in support of learners with disabilities (**Box 8.4**). Nevertheless, the role of civil society organizations (CSOs) as education providers has challenges, for instance in the extent to which they complement or substitute for government services and the extent to which they support special or inclusive education.[1]

ORGANIZATIONS ACT AS ADVOCATES AND WATCHDOGS FOR THE RIGHT TO INCLUSIVE EDUCATION

Grassroots NGOs and CSOs have long advocated for inclusive education at the local, regional and national levels whenever governments have not met the needs of vulnerable groups. Relying on their comparative advantages of innovation, specialization and responsiveness, they collect data and other evidence to monitor implementation of government commitments, campaign for fulfilment of rights and defend against violations of the right to inclusive education, especially for those with disabilities.

International NGOs commission research to underpin their advocacy. For instance, World Vision analysed how 28 education sector plans endorsed by the Fast Track Initiative addressed the challenges of disability and inclusion (World Vision, 2007). Light for the World and the Open Society Foundations funded research on the current state and future challenges of financing inclusive education (IDDC and Light for the World, 2016).

Several organizations have run successful advocacy campaigns to change public opinion and push for changes in policy, practice and service delivery to fulfil the right to education for all (Lang and Officer, 2009). In Armenia, Bridge of Hope ran an advocacy campaign starting in 2001 to switch to inclusive schools. Ultimately, it succeeded, with a new legal and budget framework to roll out inclusive education nationally by 2025 and transfer funding from special to inclusive mainstream schools and support centres (Tadevosyan and Ghukasyan, 2015). In Paraguay, Fundación Saraki elaborated guidelines for inclusive education to ensure implementation of the law on inclusion (Paraguay Ministry of Education and Sciences

---

BOX 8.4:

Various organizations have shaped education for people with disabilities

Four broad types of NGOs and CSOs have been instrumental in the development of education for children with disabilities. First, there are organizations for people with disabilities, often having a philanthropic or religious affiliation. While several have tended to respond through medical care, interventions and rehabilitation, many demonstrate an increased understanding of the social model. Second, disabled people's organizations (DPOs) are representative organizations or groups of people with disabilities, who constitute most of the staff, board members and volunteers. Their efforts, with a strong advocacy focus, are directed towards removing barriers that restrict life choices. Third are parent associations, described above. Fourth, some international NGOs active in development and education have played a major role in promoting inclusive education in the global agenda.

The United Nations (UN) Convention on the Rights of Persons with Disabilities (CRPD) acknowledged these organizations' role in helping those with disabilities gain access to services and realize their basic human rights over the course of their lives. However, in keeping with efforts to promote and implement inclusive education, the CRPD positions governments at the centre of service delivery, assigning organizations a greater role in raising public awareness. Nevertheless, NGOs and CSOs have been key providers of education services for children with disabilities. They have supported mainstream schools in including them by supplying teaching aids and appliances, developing infrastructure and supporting the workforce with training and support staff. Some have worked directly with children and their families to support inclusion.

---

1 This section draws extensively on Singal (2020).

et al., 2018). The Open Society Institute in Tajikistan set up a working group of DPOs, parents' organizations and education ministry staff to improve understanding of inclusive education and explore inclusive practices, which resulted in budget increases (Dastambuev, 2015). Yet advocacy activities and engagement may tread a fine line. In China, a three-year campaign by NGOs pushed forward a national policy on reasonable accommodation for university entrance examinations. In 2016, however, new legislation preventing NGOs from receiving any form of overseas funding had a disproportionately negative effect on the nascent disability rights movement, which relied heavily on such funding (Huang, 2019).

Many organizations provide information on rights, access to services and how to influence decisions that affect the education of children with disabilities. They support families in reporting rights violations and help disseminate knowledge online (Meresman, 2014). In the slums of Mumbai, India, the Spastics Society promoted inclusive education with support from UNICEF. Parents were initially cool to the idea. Those with disabled children felt they were better off in special schools, where they would not be teased; others thought their children would lag behind. Parent support groups and parent–teacher–therapist meetings were set up to address these fears, and parents with both concerns were enlisted to remove barriers and became resource persons (Alur, 2010). In Kazakhstan, NGOs inform parents about school options, legislation and the benefits of inclusive education (Rollan and Somerton, 2019).

DPOs have been crucial in a worldwide movement to demand full civil rights (Rieser, 2009). They have shifted the disability discourse from a charity-based to a rights-based perspective. They have also joined forces with NGOs in advocacy campaigns. For instance, the International Disability and Development Consortium launched a call to action on investing in disability-inclusive education to pressure governments and donors to deliver on the SDGs. The Global Partnership for Education endorsed the call (IDDC, 2018).

Article 33(2) of the CRPD requires DPOs to be either represented, even at the board level, or closely cooperating with independent monitoring mechanisms. Some DPOs are preparing and submitting parallel reports to the UN Committee on the Rights of Persons with Disabilities (de Beco, 2014). The Federation of Organisations of Disabled People in Angola, the Namibian Association of Differently Abled Women and the National Federation of People with Disabilities in Namibia have been active in such reporting (Singal, 2020).

Organizations defend vulnerable groups' right to education around the world

Many NGOs are engaged in supporting vulnerable groups' education when governments leave a void due to lack of will, capacity or resources. For instance, the Open Society Foundations established the Barvalipe schools in 2011 in Albania, the Republic of Moldova, Serbia, Spain and Turkey to empower the Roma population and provide them with advocacy skills to raise awareness of their communities' situation, including in education (OSCE and ODIHR, 2015). Retrak Ethiopia reintegrated hundreds of street children into school, many of whom passed the national examination allowing them entry into secondary school (Yohannes et al., 2017). In El Salvador and Guatemala, Toybox has supported 20,000 street children in school since the 1990s with local partners Viva El Salvador and Conacmi. One of their projects helps children obtain birth registration, which is required to enrol for and sit examinations (Theirworld, 2018). ChildHope, with local partner Centro de Estudios Sociales y Publicaciones, supported over 9,000 street-connected children in Lima to increase their safety at school and build their confidence, among other objectives (Dave, 2017).

Ultimately, however, non-engagement by the state can undermine some interventions' chances of long-term success. In Peru, the German technical assistance programme worked closely with indigenous organizations and NGOs to include teacher training in intercultural bilingual education within a larger project of decentralizing

"

Disabled people's organizations have shifted the disability discourse from a charity-based to a rights-based perspective

"

decision making in education. Yet the programme was abandoned, partly because the government decided to limit decentralization and reduce admissions to teacher education institutes (Cortina, 2014a, 2014b).

Despite their good intentions, care should be taken to ensure NGOs do not become an obstacle to inclusion, especially those involved in service provision. For instance, in the case of the Roma, some NGOs have been criticized for supporting this vulnerable population but at the same time depriving it of agency (van Baar, 2013). They may also have perpetuated a portrayal of this group based on its most marginalized members (Timmer, 2010). To obtain recognition and funding, there is incentive for some NGOs to present a given group as a problem, reinforcing difference and separation from the rest of the population (Timmer, 2017).

SEVERAL ORGANIZATIONS PROVIDE A RANGE OF INCLUSIVE AND SPECIALIZED EDUCATION SERVICES

Grassroots NGOs and CSOs provide education services, whether on government contract or their own initiative. These services may fill gaps or be alternatives to government services. They may cover the full needs of learners with disabilities, help form a bridge to formal education or be auxiliary. Many organizations pilot approaches that are then rolled out or even taken up by governments. In poorer countries, NGOs often deliver education to hard-to-reach children whom governments cannot or do not want to serve (Srivastava et al., 2015).

NGOs were the first to provide services in much of the world. For instance, the Association of Deaf Uruguayans established an institute of Uruguayan Sign Language and helped establish the Association for Parents and Friends of Deaf Uruguayans, which supports schools for the deaf to help children participate independently in social and economic life (Meresman, 2014). As a result of such efforts, many governments recognize NGOs as equal partners in achieving inclusive education objectives. The Master Plan for Special Needs Education/Inclusive Education in Ethiopia 2016–25 sees delivery of inclusive education as the shared responsibility of the government, NGOs, DPOs and communities (Federal Democratic Republic of Ethiopian Ministry of Education, 2016). The Ghana Inclusive Education Policy calls on NGOs to mobilize resources, advocate for increased funding, contribute to infrastructure development and engage in research, monitoring and evaluation (Ghana Ministry of Education, 2015).

> NGOs were the first to provide inclusive and special education services in much of the world

However, where NGOs provide education instead of governments, concerns can arise over governments' role (Srivastava et al., 2015). There is a risk of segregation when NGOs focus on setting up special schools for specific groups instead of adopting an inclusive approach. Governments need to provide the appropriate policy environment. In Rwanda, the Ministry of Education recognized the important roles community-based and faith-based organizations and NGOs play in education service provision in its 2018 special needs and inclusive education policy. It also noted, however, that service quality was uncoordinated and lacked standards (Rwanda Ministry of Education, 2018). One project operationalizing the policy is Expanding Access to Inclusive Basic Education, run by Humanity and Inclusion and funded by UNICEF. Aiming to develop a culture of inclusion, it has trained educators at 480 teacher education colleges and plans to train 3,160 pre-service teachers in 2020. In addition, it has trained 55 district education staff to support target schools (McGeown, 2019).

In India, some NGOs have paved the way for governments to take over their work in inclusive education. In Tamil Nadu, under the Sarva Shiksha Abhiyan primary education programme, NGO responsibility for inclusive education was eventually transferred to the government (Furuta and Thamburaj, 2014). The government adopted provision of an inclusive school environment for children with special needs and children from disadvantaged groups as a primary education objective for 2019–20. A State Resource Centre for Inclusive Education was set up in Chennai for children with special needs (Tamil Nadu School Education Department, 2019). Other NGOs, which may continue to operate in parallel, have shifted from special schools to a more inclusive model and are scaling up services. One organization, the Spastics Society of India, established special schools for children with cerebral palsy and physical disabilities in 1973 and, over the years, has turned them into inclusive schools. It runs centres in 16 states and many parts of Mumbai. It aims to provide a holistic model of development by combining education, treatment and socio-economic development. It helps teachers develop individualized education plans and provides specialized aids and assistance in the classroom to students with disabilities (Singal, 2020).

> " A key challenge is to counter negative attitudes, stereotypes
> and discrimination and prevent their further development,
> as they can hamper the education of vulnerable students "

NGOs face several challenges as providers of inclusive education. Organizations often do not collaborate but replicate services and compete for limited funds. International NGOs, with greater resources and experience, may be effective in influencing national policies but sometimes do not engage with local NGOs. Dependence on resources from international development partners can result in some national NGO strategies being driven by their funders, which may make organizations more accountable to their donors than to their members. The Cambodian Disabled People's Organization depended on resources from donors that used different concepts of disability and rights than its own (Nuth, 2018). In Papua New Guinea, an inclusive curriculum was introduced with funding from external donors, but local stakeholders felt it reflected Western education influences (Le Fanu, 2013). More collective efforts need to be directed towards developing national NGO capacity (Charema, 2007). There is very little systematic and rigorous evaluation of the effectiveness of NGO-run projects (Srivastava et al., 2015).

Organizations provide education to vulnerable groups around the world

Organizations provide education to various vulnerable groups. In Shanghai, China, migrant children were barred from taking secondary school entrance examinations. They had three options after graduating from lower secondary school: entering the job market, continuing education in their rural hometowns or attending vocational schools in the city. Changban, an NGO providing education to children of migrant workers, ensured that 60% of its students opted for vocational schools in Shanghai. After graduating, they started work in companies, opened stores or pursued higher education in their hometowns (Xiong and Li, 2017).

In a slum in the Gomti Nagar area of Lucknow, India, the Study Hall Educational Foundation runs a school for over 800 girls from poor families, from preschool through grade 12, with an emphasis on empowering them for equal participation in society. While the school equips girls with necessary skills, it provides a separate alternative to mainstream school (Sahni, 2019). During

armed conflict in the Bajaur and Kurram tribal agencies of Pakistan, NGOs made important contributions to education for children of the tribal population in 2007–12. They increased enrolment and decreased dropout rates through targeted interventions, such as school reconstruction. However, the sustainability of education delivery remains to be addressed (Khan et al., 2018). In Somalia, in 2012–13, the Candlelight NGO provided basic education for children from pastoral communities through mobile schools, audio radio teaching and a camel library (Candlelight, 2015).

In much of the world, community-based education (CBE) has been instrumental in expanding services in areas governments find hard to reach. In some cases, governments can eventually take over CBE structures, which rely on local people in resource-constrained environments, as in Afghanistan (**Box 8.5**).

CONCLUSION

Students, parents, organizations and communities are the pillars on which to build a favourable environment in support of inclusive education. A key challenge is to counter negative attitudes, stereotypes and discrimination and prevent their further development, as they can hamper the education of vulnerable students. Parents can be valuable allies but need sufficient information and positive interactions with schools. Parents of children with disabilities may be sceptical about sending them to mainstream schools without reassurances that the children will be fully supported and not alienated or marginalized.

While the state bears the duty of education, grassroots NGOs and CSOs often step in, especially in poorer countries, to provide education services for populations not reached by governments. Such organizations also lead the way in putting pressure on governments to fulfil their national and international obligations to guarantee the right to inclusive education for all. This role is recognized in formal monitoring mechanisms. Government leadership, dialogue among all parties and a coordinated approach, aligned with national education policies, are essential.

BOX 8.5:

Community-based education has been a success for inclusion in Afghanistan

Afghanistan is marked by several exclusion challenges: security issues that expose schools as targets for attacks; cultural beliefs that systematically exclude girls and children with disabilities; and poverty, which exacerbates geographical and climate challenges in remote mountainous areas. CBE has been a key mechanism in addressing these challenges. The system is primarily made up of community-based classes and accelerated learning programmes jointly established and implemented by provincial and district education departments, communities and NGOs (Afghanistan Ministry of Education, 2018).

A CBE policy was developed in 2018 through multi-stakeholder consultations to improve existing practices, define standards and articulate institutional stakeholders' roles and responsibilities. The policy document specifies criteria to be met when establishing community-based classes. For instance, a community can request a class if the nearest public school is more than 3 km away and there are 20 to 35 school-age students. The Ministry of Education is responsible for oversight of textbooks and learning materials, but an implementation partner can provide government textbooks and additional books if so agreed. The expectation is that institutionalizing CBE will help sustain education delivery in villages, improve working conditions of community-based teachers and increase coordination of CBE within the ministry (UNESCO, 2019).

The policy recognizes the need to ensure continuation of education beyond the primary level. Certification at the end of primary education is recognized by the ministry and allows graduates to attend a government hub school to ensure transition to secondary education. However, transition is likely to remain a challenge, especially for girls who never attended the nearest primary hub school.

Sustainability is another challenge. There is an understanding between the Citizens' Charter project and the ministry to link CBE policy to existing community development councils, opening up potential additional funding and management through community block grants. The goal is to bring financing from all sources on-budget through a Community-Based Education Transition Unit to improve the sustainability and national ownership of the ministry (UNESCO, 2019).

Community-based schools are mostly managed by school management committees or *shuras* (village councils). Some parents support teacher salaries and make in-kind contributions. However, there is very limited social accountability in terms of equity and inclusion. Exclusionary practices that permeate the community inevitably also affect the learning process (Bakhshi, 2019).

The schools, with an estimated 334,000 students in 2016, are credited with having expanded access to education (Afghanistan Ministry of Education, 2016). The role of international donors has been key. In 2017/18, a programme funded by the United States Agency for International Development was operating in 8,440 community-based classes and accelerated learning programmes, with 171,300 students, 53% of whom were girls (USAID, 2019b). Yet evaluations of effectiveness and relevance are rare. A randomized field experiment to evaluate the effectiveness of CBE, teacher recruitment and community mobilization in six provinces showed some improvement in attendance and learning outcomes, although increasing parental support for education remains a challenge, despite efforts to use culturally embedded messages for raising awareness of the role of education (Burde et al., 2017; Burde et al., 2015).

A group of girls in a circle at a peer-led village workshop designed to inform and empower girls, in Sylhet, Bangladesh.

CREDIT: Tom Merilion/ Save the Children

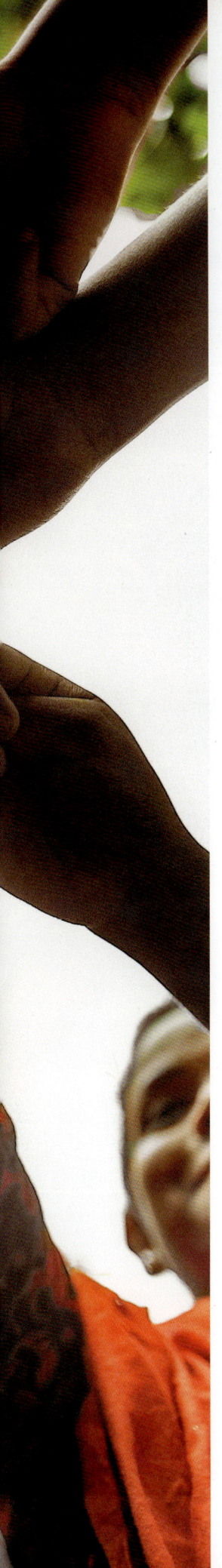

9

Monitoring education in the Sustainable Development Goals

9

KEY MESSAGES

Following its 2020 Comprehensive Review, the Inter-agency and Expert Group (IAEG) on SDG Indicators adopted the completion rate as a second global indicator for target 4.1, filling an important gap in the SDG 4 monitoring framework.

The IAEG also upgraded the last two SDG 4 global indicators whose methodology had been questioned: the proportion of 3- to 5-year-olds who are developmentally on track and the extent to which sustainable development and global citizenship are mainstreamed in education systems.

An agreement was reached to develop minimum regional benchmarks for seven SDG 4 indicators, an unfulfilled commitment from the Education 2030 Framework for Action.

Data gaps remain in key areas of the SDG 4 monitoring framework:

- In 2015–19, household survey data were publicly available for 59% of countries, corresponding to 87% of the population. The lowest coverage rates are in Northern Africa and Western Asia in population terms (46%) and Oceania in country terms (29%).

- Good-quality data on learning outcomes is lacking. In Africa, since 2014, only 14 of 54 countries have reported data on reading proficiency in early grades; 10 of those are francophone countries that took part in the PASEC assessment.

- There is a shortage of data on teachers. Only one of the six most populous countries in sub-Saharan Africa has reported the number of primary education teachers since 2015. Countries also struggle to distinguish between trained and qualified teachers. In 2019, the UNESCO General Conference approved a process to establish an international standard classification for teachers to improve comparability in the definition of trained teachers.

In assessing whether SDG monitoring contributes to equity and inclusion:

- Indicators need to be disaggregated by individual characteristics.

- Indicator development and data collection processes should be inclusive.

- Multiple sources, including non-traditional and unofficial data, such as satellite/drone imagery, sensor networks and commercial data, should be used.

- An inclusive paradigm should be used in interpreting indicators. For instance, learning gains should not be seen as an achievement if they result from excluding more children from tests.

Inclusive education is but a natural progression of human rights into the education system. It is the need of the hour.

Percy Cardozo, programme head and counsellor, India

As an introduction to the review of progress on education in the Sustainable Development Goals (SDGs), this chapter reviews the latest developments concerning the SDG 4 monitoring framework, then discusses selected data gaps preventing a fuller picture on equity, learning and teachers globally and with particular reference to sub-Saharan Africa.

THERE HAVE BEEN POSITIVE DEVELOPMENTS IN THE SDG 4 MONITORING FRAMEWORK

Throughout 2019, United Nations (UN) Member States and multilateral agencies worked to refine the SDG monitoring framework. The Inter-agency and Expert Group (IAEG) on SDG Indicators convened in Beirut in March and in Addis Ababa in October to review proposed methodologies for global indicators that had been insufficiently developed, among other tasks. The IAEG carried out the 2020 Comprehensive Review of the original list of 232 global indicators adopted by the UN General Assembly in 2017. The Technical Cooperation Group (TCG) – the IAEG's counterpart, convened by UNESCO and the UNESCO Institute for Statistics (UIS) to develop the SDG 4 monitoring framework, including global and other education-specific thematic indicators – convened in Yerevan in August. This section summarizes key developments related to SDG 4.

The IAEG approved a UIS proposal to adopt primary, lower secondary and upper secondary completion rates as a second global indicator for target 4.1. This decision addressed a gap in the global monitoring framework, as the target's other global indicator, the proportion of children achieving minimum proficiency in reading and mathematics, refers only to those in school. It was among just 6 of more than 200 new global indicator proposals approved in the 2020 review. The proposal leaves open the possibility that the completion rate will be estimated in the future with a statistical model to overcome typical problems associated with household survey data, such as timeliness, volatility and multiple sources. The GEM Report team has developed such a model (Barakat et al., 2019) and reported results and projections as part of the SDG 4 review for the High-level Political Forum (UNESCO, 2019b) (see **Chapter 10**). It has committed to discussing further development of the model within the framework of the TCG in 2020.

> " The IAEG approved a UIS proposal to adopt primary, lower secondary and upper secondary completion rates as a second global indicator for target 4.1 "

India has.

> " Setting global benchmarks is difficult because starting points vary across countries; however, most countries have yet to set national benchmarks, even though it is 2020 "

The IAEG upgraded two global indicators from tier III (no established methodology) to tier II (established methodology but countries do not regularly produce data): global indicator 4.2.1 on the development of 3- to 5-year-olds, following approval of a plan by its custodian agency, UNICEF, at the end of a long consultation and methodological development process (see **Chapter 11**); and global indicator 4.7.1 on education system efforts to mainstream sustainable development and global citizenship, after two failed proposals. While the latter indicator still presents significant challenges, the revised proposal introduces some discipline, notably by ensuring that countries provide references to support subjective responses. A slight reformulation of the indicator means it is now identical to global indicators 12.8.1 and 13.3.1 (see **Chapter 16**). There are now no tier III SDG 4 global indicators (except for the portion of indicator 4.2.1 referring to children under age 3). Tier III indicators would have been dropped at the end of the 2020 Comprehensive Review.

The 12 global indicators (**Table 9.1**) are complemented by 30 thematic indicators for a total of 42 indicators (see the introduction to the statistical tables in the annex) aimed at enriching the perspective on progress towards SDG 4. Starting with the 2019 data release, the UIS reports on one additional indicator: 4.2.3 on the percentage of children under age 5 experiencing positive and stimulating home learning environments. This brings the total the UIS reports on to 33 of the 42 global and thematic SDG 4 indicators.

One outstanding monitoring issue is the commitment made in the Education 2030 Framework for Action that called on countries to establish 'appropriate intermediate benchmarks (e.g. for 2020 and 2025)' towards achieving SDG 4, seeing these as 'indispensable for addressing the accountability deficit associated with longer-term targets' (UNESCO, 2016, Art. 28). Setting global benchmarks is difficult because starting points vary across countries; however, most countries have yet to set

national benchmarks, even though it is 2020. The most promising way forward is to set minimum benchmarks for countries in a region.

The Framework for Action requires benchmarks to be set through an inclusive process. The most important development in the last TCG meeting was an agreement in principle to develop minimum regional benchmarks for seven SDG 4 indicators (UIS, 2019a). The proposal would require mobilization of SDG 4 regional steering committees to review and set regional benchmarks in 2020. EU countries set benchmarks for seven education indicators to be achieved by 2020 through a similar process, which is being repeated for new benchmarks to be achieved by 2030 (European Commission, 2019; European Council, 2020).

MAJOR DATA AVAILABILITY CHALLENGES REMAIN FOR SEVERAL GLOBAL INDICATORS

Progress has been made in formulating, endorsing and refining an expanded SDG monitoring framework, but much more effort is needed to ensure that countries report on the global indicators across the SDGs. Custodian agencies need to communicate indicators' meaning, significance and methodologies to national authorities. National authorities need to collect data and build their capacity to analyse, report and use them. Funders need to coordinate their data collection and capacity-development programmes. This section discusses data gaps in three key SDG 4 areas, which can be addressed through improved coordination among these three groups of actors.

EQUITY: FOUR IN TEN COUNTRIES HAVE NO RECENT, PUBLICLY AVAILABLE SURVEY TO DISAGGREGATE EDUCATION DATA

The SDGs emphasize equity. The Intersecretariat Working Group on Household Surveys, which has a broad mandate to promote household survey methodological development and common standards, has pointed out that at least 80 of the 232 SDG global indicators depend on household surveys (UNSC, 2019).

Household and other surveys are the foundation for disaggregating global education indicators by individual characteristics. Examples include completion (4.1), early childhood education participation (4.2), adult education

[handwritten: holders of the data →]

TABLE 9.1:

SDG 4 and other education-related global indicators, by custodian agency and classification tier

[handwritten: Unesco Institude for Satistics.]

Indicator		Custodian agency	Tier
SDG 4			
4.1.1	Proportion of children and young people (a) in grades 2/3; (b) at the end of primary; and (c) at the end of lower secondary achieving at least a minimum proficiency level in (i) reading and (ii) mathematics, by sex	UIS	I
4.1.2	(New) Completion rate (primary education, lower secondary education, upper secondary education)	UIS	I
4.2.1	Proportion of children under 5 years of age who are developmentally on track in health, learning and psychosocial well-being, by sex	UNICEF	II/III
4.2.2	Participation rate in organized learning (one year before the official primary entry age), by sex	UIS	I
4.3.1	Participation rate of youth and adults in formal and non-formal education and training in the previous 12 months, by sex	UIS	II
4.4.1	Proportion of youth and adults with information and communications technology (ICT) skills, by type of skill	UIS and ITU	II
4.5.1	Parity indices (female/male, rural/urban, bottom/top wealth quintile and others such as disability status, indigenous peoples and conflict-affected, as data become available) for all education indicators on this list that can be disaggregated	UIS	I/II depending on indicator
4.6.1	Proportion of population in a given age group achieving at least a fixed level of proficiency in functional (a) literacy and (b) numeracy skills, by sex	UIS	II
4.7.1	Extent to which (i) global citizenship education and (ii) education for sustainable development are mainstreamed in (a) national education policies; (b) curricula; (c) teacher education; and (d) student assessment	UIS	II
4.a.1	Proportion of schools offering basic services, by type of service (new simplified formulation adopted by the IAEG; no changes to the metadata, which still refer to electricity; internet; computers; adapted infrastructure and materials for students with disabilities; water; single-sex toilets; and handwashing facilities)	UIS	II
4.b.1	Volume of official development assistance flows for scholarships by sector and type of study	OECD	I
4.c.1	Proportion of teachers with the minimum required qualifications, by education level (new simplified formulation adopted by the IAEG; no changes to the metadata)	UIS	II
Other SDGs			
1.a.2	Proportion of total government spending on essential services (education, health and social protection)	ILO, UIS and WHO	II
5.6.2	Number of countries with laws and regulations that guarantee full and equal access to women and men aged 15 years and older to sexual and reproductive health care, information and education	UNFPA	II
8.6.1	Proportion of youth (aged 15–24 years) not in education, employment or training	ILO	I
	12.8.1 = 4.7.1	UIS	II
	13.3.1 = 4.7.1	UIS	II

Notes: Tier classifications are defined as follows:

Tier 1: Indicator is conceptually clear, has an internationally established methodology and standards are available, and data are regularly produced by countries for at least 50% of countries and of the population in every region where the indicator is relevant.

Tier 2: Indicator is conceptually clear, has an internationally established methodology and standards are available, but data are not regularly produced by countries.

Tier 3: No internationally established methodology or standards are yet available for the indicator, but methodology/standards are being (or will be) developed or tested.

Source: UNSD (2020).

[handwritten: examine data → children missing from the data.]

participation (4.3), youth and adult information and communication technology skills (4.4) and adult literacy (4.6). Such surveys are also the basis for calculating global indicator 4.5.1, the parity index, by gender, location and wealth. Surveys should be frequent, their questions comparable and their data publicly available to allow open discussion.

Surveys are increasingly becoming publicly available. The main international household survey programmes, the Demographic and Health Surveys (DHS) and the Multiple Indicator Cluster Surveys (MICS), have made data available for more than 20 years. The Living Standards Measurement Study, which pioneered cross-national household surveys in the late 1980s, is part of a 2015 World Bank commitment to address data gaps: Only 63 out of 155 countries had at least two household surveys between 2002 and 2011 to estimate poverty; it aims to ensure one household survey of this kind is carried out every three years (Sánchez-Páramo and Fu, 2019; Serajuddin et al., 2015).

Some projects have invested in harmonizing data from various sources and making them available free for research purposes. The University of Minnesota's IPUMS project is the largest collection of publicly available and harmonized individual-level census data, covering 82 countries (IPUMS, 2019). The Luxembourg Income Study Database is the largest database of harmonized household income and expenditure microdata, drawing on about 50 mostly high-income countries (LIS, 2019).

International organizations have supported statistical capacity development programmes, including efforts to make national statistical agency data more accessible. The now-defunct International Household Survey Network helped countries make survey data publicly available in the 2000s through the National Data Archive (NADA), a survey cataloguing software, and the establishment of international reporting standards (IHSN, 2013). The World Bank's Microdata Library, which includes more than 3,000 surveys, uses NADA (World Bank, 2019). The Partnership in Statistics for Development in the 21st Century, which reports on measures of statistical capacity, shows that, while 66% of countries in Africa used NADA in 2018, the region lagged others in making a data portal available (64% of countries in 2018) and in national statistical office user outreach (44% in 2017) (PARIS21, 2019).

> "
> A review of household survey coverage for this report showed that data were available for 59% of countries, corresponding to 87% of the population
> "

A review of household survey coverage for this report showed that data were available for 59% of countries, corresponding to 87% of the population. Northern Africa and Western Asia has the lowest coverage in population terms (46%). Repeated rounds of the DHS in Egypt, Jordan and Yemen and of the MICS in Algeria, Iraq, Palestine, Sudan and Tunisia helped increase coverage, but there have been no data since 2014 in Egypt and Sudan. Public access to data from Morocco, Turkey and, especially, Gulf Cooperation Council countries has been restricted; for instance, Oman's data from the 2014 MICS are not public. Oceania has the lowest coverage in country terms (29%) (**Table 9.2**). After severe technical obstacles, the 2016–18 Papua New Guinea DHS is the first publicly available household survey data set from the region in years. It provides valuable insight into baseline education indicators to evaluate progress towards SDG 4 (**Box 9.1**).

The review of household survey country coverage for this report may overstate data availability. Some surveys are not nationally representative. More importantly, the quality of education questions included in background information in surveys designed to collect information on health or household living conditions may be unsatisfactory from an education point of view.

TABLE 9.2:
Coverage of publicly available household survey data, by region, 2015–19

Region	Countries (%)	Population (%)
World	**59**	**87**
Sub-Saharan Africa	71	89
Northern Africa and Western Asia	42	46
Central/S.Asia	71	94
Eastern and South-eastern Asia	61	88
Oceania	29	83
Latin America and the Caribbean	43	87
Europe and Northern America	83	96

Source: GEM Report team analysis.

Papua New Guinea successfully concluded a Demographic and Health Survey to establish a baseline for key SDG 4 indicators

Papua New Guinea, a country of immense cultural diversity, has rugged terrain that hampers data collection. The latest DHS took 27 months (October 2016 to December 2018) to collect data, in 4 phases, on 19,200 households. Challenges included 'inaccessibility because of the geography of the country and severe weather patterns, refusal by respondents to participate in the survey, need for security due to law and order situations, outstanding payments owed to service providers, absence of reliable communication services, and late disbursement of funds to support teams in the field' (Papua New Guinea National Statistical Office and ICF, 2019, p. 4). Fieldwork was not completed in 4% of the clusters in the sample.

DHS data from 1996 and 2006 were not publicly available (Pacific Community, 2013). The third round is the first to make data accessible on the DHS website, allowing baseline estimations for selected education development indicators. Results show that Papua New Guinea faces considerable challenges to achieve target 4.1, compared with other resource-rich countries. Average completion rates at all education levels are almost identical to those of Angola but well below those of neighbouring Timor-Leste. Moreover, inequality by wealth is high. About 40% from the poorest wealth quintile complete primary school, compared with 84% from the richest; 2% from the poorest but 40% from the richest complete upper secondary school. Nationally, 4 in 10 children do not complete primary, and barely 1 in 6 youth completes upper secondary, on average (**Figure 9.1**).

FIGURE 9.1:
Papua New Guinea faces a large challenge to achieve target 4.1
Completion rates, by wealth quintile, Papua New Guinea, 2016–18, compared with Angola, 2015–16, and Timor-Leste, 2016

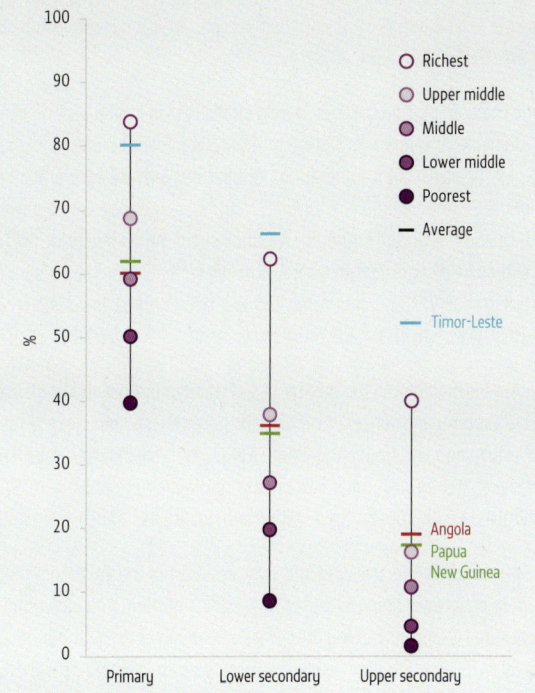

GEM StatLink: http://bit.ly/GEM2020_fig9_1
Source: GEM Report team analysis of DHS data.

> Surveys should be frequent, their questions comparable and their data publicly available to allow open discussion

Ensuring that data on key indicators are disaggregated is necessary to promote discussion on equity and inclusion. However, it is only a first step and far from sufficient. Ensuring that SDG 4 monitoring is itself inclusive involves several factors (**Box 9.2**).

LEARNING: ONLY 3 IN 10 AFRICAN COUNTRIES HAVE RECENTLY REPORTED ON LEARNING OUTCOMES

Learning assessments are the source of information on global indicator 4.1.1 but also a potential source of information on selected thematic indicators, including knowledge of environmental science (4.7.4) and bullying (4.a.2). Many countries report their cross-national assessment results, but national assessments are also used, for instance for data on reading skills in countries including China (lower secondary education) and India (primary education).

BOX 9.2:

An equity and inclusion focus in monitoring should not stop at disaggregation

Assessing whether SDG monitoring contributes to equity and inclusion entails several components. First and foremost, the process of developing the SDG monitoring framework has been inclusive, with systematic participation of countries, civil society and multilateral agencies (Fukuda Parr and McNeill, 2019; Fukuda Parr and Muchhala, 2020).

Second, SDG monitoring efforts have drawn attention to groups at risk of exclusion that were largely invisible in the Millennium Development Goals (MDGs). Disability, ethnicity and migratory status, for instance, have gained in prominence. Yet disaggregation of indicators by, say, indigenous status does not amount to true inclusion of indigenous perspectives and priorities (Yap and Watene, 2019). There is also a concern that the indicator framework is narrower in scope than the ambitious inclusive agenda it should serve (Bexell and Jönsson, 2018). To some extent, the narrower framework reflects a realistic assessment of the costs and benefits of investing in data collection. However, given different actors' conflicting approaches to development, some argue the narrower framework is the result of more powerful actors imposing their perspective (Burke and Rürup, 2019). Global indicators should not undermine the SDGs' transformational potential (Pérez Piñán and Vibert, 2019).

Third, it is important to include multiple partners in overcoming challenges in implementing the monitoring framework. Open initiatives have emerged, such as the Global Partnership for Sustainable Development Data, a multi-stakeholder network that goes beyond international agencies and national statistical offices to include citizen and civil society groups, foundations, enterprises/private actors, academia and others (GPSDD, 2019a). The Inclusive Data Charter, launched in 2018 by 10 partners, is another example. It includes multilateral agencies, non-government organizations, and governments, including those of Colombia, Ghana, the Philippines and the United Kingdom. The charter promotes five principles consistent with the spirit of the SDGs: All populations must be included in the data; all data should be disaggregated wherever possible; data should be drawn from all available sources; there must be accountability in and for data collection and statistics production; and data capacity must be improved, including through increased financing. Signing up to the charter requires a commitment to develop an action plan, which is made publicly available (GPSDD, 2019b).

Including all available data sources is manifest in the greater use of non-traditional and unofficial data sources for monitoring the SDGs, compared with the MDGs, including satellite/drone imagery and sensor networks, and commercial data. Several research institutions have called for greater use of 'citizen science' for SDG monitoring to increase coverage and frequency (Fritz et al., 2019). This involves risks. The Inclusive Data Charter maintains that broader data sourcing must not come at the cost of transparency, accountability or national capacity (Mahajan, 2019). The UN Statistical Commission emphasizes national statistical offices' continued responsibility, especially for standard setting and quality assurance, even in the context of a data revolution (Merry, 2019).

An inclusive paradigm should inform the understanding and interpretation of the indicators themselves. No indicator should be interpreted as having improved when, in practice, more people are being excluded from measurement. Any indicators defined on the in-school population must be contextualized with an indication of who is excluded. Gains in learning outcomes as a result of excluding more children from tests cannot be recognized as an achievement. An inclusive perspective motivates recognition that gender parity indices are a useful operational proxy for basic equality in access but also that much more comprehensive measurement is needed to understand gender inequality in education. The gender equality in education monitoring framework employed in the GEM Report's *Gender Report* edition is based on these premises (UNESCO, 2019a).

The UIS inventory of learning assessments contains valuable information on the grades at which national and cross-national learning assessments are conducted, as well as some of their technical properties. For Africa, which has the lowest percentage of children and adolescents reaching minimum learning proficiency, all but a handful of 54 countries conduct a learning assessment at the end of primary or lower secondary school. There are fewer national examinations in early grades, but even at that level, 42 countries have done assessments since 2010.

As these figures may overstate the availability of assessment data with the right properties for monitoring SDG 4, however, coverage of indicator 4.1.1 may be much lower. Of the 42 early grade assessments done

since 2010, 38 have been done since 2014 (**Figure 9.2a**). There are 24 of the 42 whose assessments (a) report the share of learners performing at the various proficiency levels instead of average scores, (b) provide sufficient information on proficiency levels to determine a minimum acceptable level and (c) employ state-of-the-art psychometric scoring (**Figure 9.2b**). Of those, only 21 are from 2014 or later (**Figure 9.2c**). The corresponding number is 17 countries for the end of primary and 9 for the end of lower secondary education, where data tend to come from national examinations. As a result of further limitations in some assessments, the availability of quality-assured, usable learning data for indicator 4.1.1 is even lower. The UIS database shows that 26% of African countries have reported data on reading proficiency in early grades since 2014, corresponding to 28% of the

> **The UIS database shows that 26% of African countries have reported data on reading proficiency in early grades since 2014, corresponding to 28% of the population**

population; 10 of those are francophone countries that took part in the Programme d'analyse des systèmes éducatifs de la CONFEMEN (PASEC) in 2014 (**Figure 9.2d**).

Considerable capacity and financial constraints need to be overcome to ensure African countries carry out nationally representative, sample-based national or cross-national assessments every three to five years that meet quality standards. Many governments have not been sufficiently supportive. For instance, the 2013 round of the Southern and Eastern Africa Consortium for Monitoring Educational Quality assessment faced serious delays in the release of country reports and doubts about the validity of results (Spaull, 2016).

Donors have also not risen to the challenge of filling the coordination and financing gap. For instance, there is insufficient information how regional assessments, such as the 2019 round of PASEC, which involved 15 francophone African countries, secure adequate and predictable financial support both for the secretariat and for country operations. Within the Global Coalition for Education Data framework, a multilateral agency initiative, the UIS has recently attempted to create a virtual registry of donor support to learning assessments. Such information is currently not shared. In the absence of publicly available information on how donors fund data collection and capacity development for global indicator 4.1.1, it is impossible to hold them to account for remaining gaps and to develop joint, coordinated plans for filling these gaps in every country.

QUALITY: DATA ON QUALIFIED AND TRAINED TEACHERS ARE SCARCE AND DIFFICULT TO COMPARE

Administrative data provide information on teacher-related indicators. About 58% of sub-Saharan African countries have reported data on primary and 25% on upper secondary education since 2016. Of the six most populous countries, only the United Republic of Tanzania has regularly reported the number of teachers in primary education. The Democratic Republic of the Congo and South Africa last reported in 2015, and there are no data in the UIS database for Ethiopia, Kenya (other than UIS estimates) and Nigeria.

FIGURE 9.2:
Sufficiently good learning assessments for SDG 4 reporting remain rare in Africa
Availability of reading or mathematics learning assessments in grades 2/3, by assessment characteristics, Africa

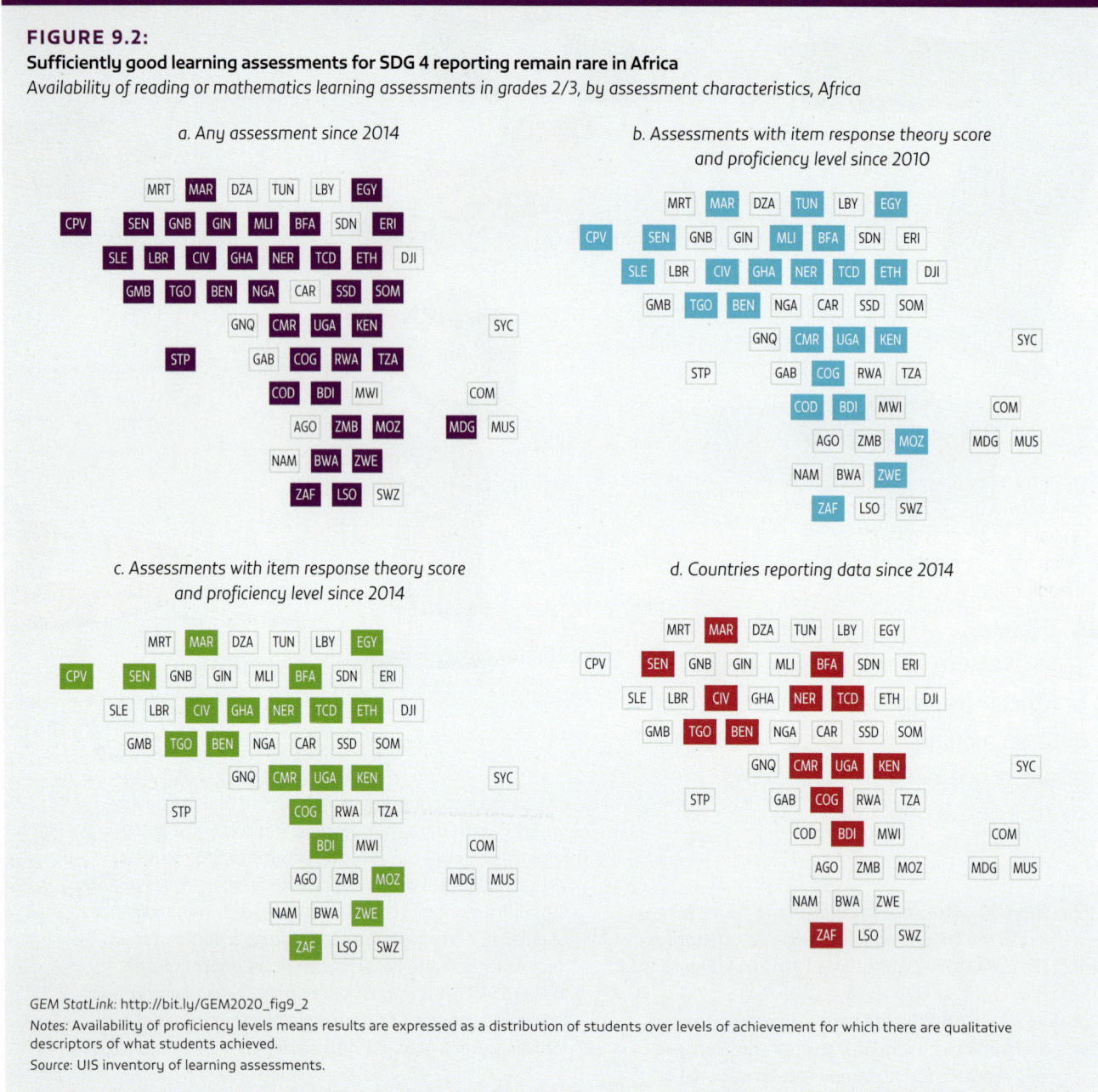

a. Any assessment since 2014

b. Assessments with item response theory score and proficiency level since 2010

c. Assessments with item response theory score and proficiency level since 2014

d. Countries reporting data since 2014

GEM StatLink: http://bit.ly/GEM2020_fig9_2

Notes: Availability of proficiency levels means results are expressed as a distribution of students over levels of achievement for which there are qualitative descriptors of what students achieved.
Source: UIS inventory of learning assessments.

Without information as basic as teacher numbers, it is not possible to report on global indicator 4.c.1, the percentage of trained teachers, and other thematic indicators related to trained and qualified teachers. Trained or qualified is an important distinction. Qualified refers to academic qualifications, such as an undergraduate degree, required to teach. This is separate from teacher training. A teacher can be qualified, trained, both or neither.

In practice, the distinction may not be straightforward, depending on country context, or may clash with established terminology whereby a qualified teacher is

one who has been trained. Target 4.c indicator definitions are not part of the UIS survey questionnaire but are included in an accompanying 40-page manual (UIS, 2018). Data collection tools in high-income countries often do not distinguish between the concepts. This may change, as such countries are being given the opportunity to complete the UIS questionnaire on teacher statistics, which makes the distinction, and can indicate whether they do not collect data because of statutory recruitment requirements, i.e. schools cannot legally hire teachers who lack requisite academic qualifications and a teacher training certificate. In other countries, even given a meaningful distinction, administrative data may include only one of the two categories. Less than one-quarter of countries report distinct values for qualified and trained teachers (**Figure 9.3**). Some countries report that all teachers are both trained and qualified, potentially indicating lack of distinction.

More generally, data interpretation and comparability between countries suffer from lack of clarity in the definition of trained teachers. A recent review of available data from the International Standard Classification of Education for 46 teacher education programmes in 39 countries has shown, for instance, that the usual entry level for primary school teachers was after completion of secondary education for an average programme duration of two years. However, these averages mask diversity in entry points and duration between countries. In addition, there are other important teacher preparation programme characteristics, including length and conditions of probationary or induction periods and additional certification or licensing processes (UIS, 2019b). UIS will attempt to tackle this challenge with a new international standard classification for teachers, a process approved by the UNESCO General Conference

in November 2019. The classification would code programmes by level (e.g. primary teachers), minimum level of education to participate and duration in years.

GUIDE TO THE MONITORING PART – IN PRINT AND ONLINE

As with each edition of the report, the next 12 chapters provide an update on progress in education in the SDGs. Chapters 10 to 19 review progress towards the seven targets (4.1 to 4.7) and three means of implementation (4.a to 4.c), Chapter 20 discusses issues related to education in three other SDGs and Chapter 21 reviews education financing. In addition, each chapter focuses on selected issues that shed light on various challenges to monitoring.

As of January 2020, the print version of the report is complemented by an online monitoring version, SCOPE (Scoping Progress in Education) available at Education-Progress.org, which provides a synthetic narrative on key issues regarding SDG 4.

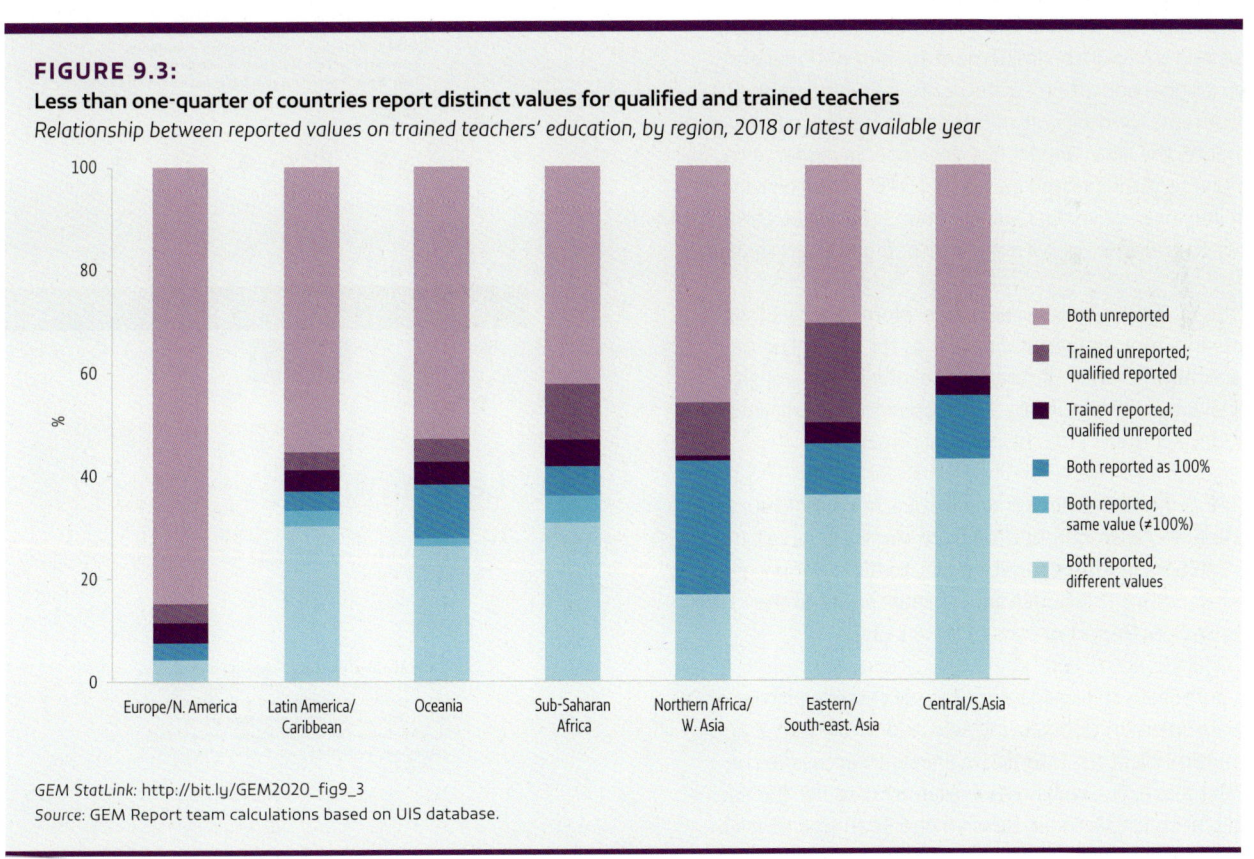

FIGURE 9.3:

Less than one-quarter of countries report distinct values for qualified and trained teachers

Relationship between reported values on trained teachers' education, by region, 2018 or latest available year

Legend:
- Both unreported
- Trained unreported; qualified reported
- Trained reported; qualified unreported
- Both reported as 100%
- Both reported, same value (≠100%)
- Both reported, different values

Regions: Europe/N. America, Latin America/Caribbean, Oceania, Sub-Saharan Africa, Northern Africa/W. Asia, Eastern/South-east. Asia, Central/S.Asia

GEM StatLink: http://bit.ly/GEM2020_fig9_3
Source: GEM Report team calculations based on UIS database.

SCOPE
Scoping Progress in Education

A new interactive online report to support the monitoring of progress towards Sustainable Development Goal 4

education-progress.org

CONTEXT AND OBJECTIVES

The *Global Education Monitoring Report* has a twin mandate from the Education 2030 Framework for Action: to monitor progress on education in the Sustainable Development Goals and to report on implementation of national and international education strategies to help hold partners accountable for their commitments. To better fulfil its mandate, the GEM Report has developed a resource to complement the printed edition: SCOPE, an online report enabling interactive data visualizations that allow comparison between countries or with regional and global averages.

On the SCOPE website, users can explore, create, download, share and print images and data files for use online or in presentations. Aimed at the general public, the website is of special interest to journalists and opinion makers, who can introduce content into the political discourse.

SCOPE brings together administrative, household survey and learning assessment data from various sources, notably the UNESCO Institute for Statistics, to highlight progress towards SDG 4. It includes and updates some of the most popular GEM Report graphs of recent years.

The purpose is to provide a concise, accessible picture of global education trends using selected SDG 4 global and thematic indicators. Interactive links give access to the UIS database. The website is available in Arabic, Chinese, English, French, German, Russian and Spanish and will be refreshed with data updates and stories from countries and regions.

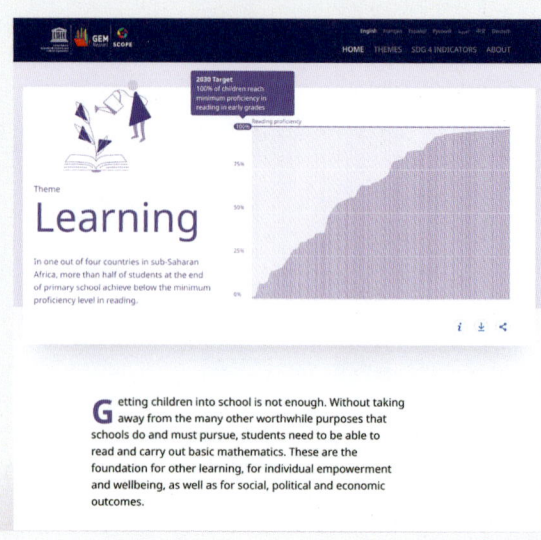

CONTENT

SCOPE content is organized into five themes, each with a core indicator showing level of progress.

Access covers progress in school attendance and over-age participation. It shows the impact of population growth on out-of-school numbers. In sub-Saharan Africa, for instance, the primary school-aged population more than doubled between 1990 and 2017. As a result, even though the rate of out-of-school children more than halved during this period, the number of children out of school barely changed. The website article on access also presents completion rate estimates based on the GEM Report's recent model. One interesting finding is how completion rates differ depending on whether they include those who complete an education level between three and five years later than the official graduation age or those who complete even later than that.

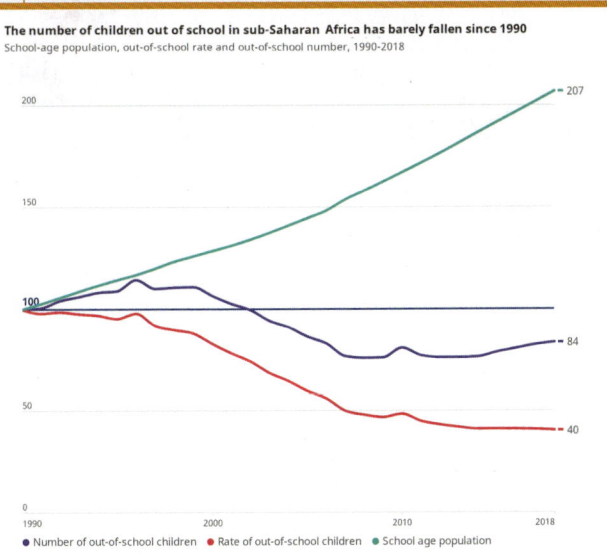

The number of children out of school in sub-Saharan Africa has barely fallen since 1990
School-age population, out-of-school rate and out-of-school number, 1990-2018

- ● Number of out-of-school children
- ● Rate of out-of-school children
- ● School age population

Equity complements the World Inequality Database on Education. It shows gender parity rates over time by income group and region. It demonstrates, for instance, the pace of change towards gender parity in lower secondary education in Central and Southern Asia. It also depicts the increasing prevalence of disparity at the expense of boys, particularly in tertiary education. Household survey data show that education gaps between females and males are not as wide as those between rural and urban areas and between the poor and the rich. Intersecting parity indices for poverty and gender highlight how gender gaps are greatest among the poorest.

Learning shows the low level of reading and mathematics skills in many poor countries. Many children cannot read a single word after three years of schooling. Data from citizen-led assessments in India and Pakistan highlight how learning results depend on whether assessments cover children not in school. Adult illiteracy remains widespread in many countries, especially among women. Visualizations of rates of change in literacy show whether they owe to literate youth reaching adulthood or adults receiving education.

Quality shows the impact the abolition of fees in sub-Saharan Africa between 1990 and 2000 had on increasing pupil/teacher ratios. It shows rates of trained teachers by country and region over time and the existence of appropriate learning environments, including adequate water and sanitation, electricity, internet, and freedom from violence and bullying.

Finance shows government, donor and household contributions to education spending. It depicts the amounts main donors allocate to poor countries, to basic education and as a share of national income over time. It itemizes how much the top 10 donors give to each education level in various countries, evidencing how little is allocated to basic education in the poorest countries.

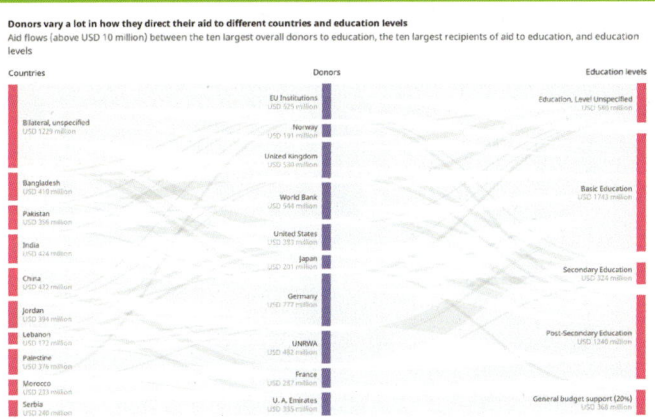

Donors vary a lot in how they direct their aid to different countries and education levels
Aid flows (above USD 10 million) between the ten largest overall donors to education, the ten largest recipients of aid to education, and education levels

Due to extensive heat, children from a public elementary school attend a class outdoors in Yucatán state, Mexico.

CREDIT: Juan Alfonso Rangel Terrazas/ UNESCO

KEY MESSAGES

Globally, 1 in 12 primary school-age children, 1 in 6 lower secondary school-age adolescents and 1 in 3 upper secondary school-age youth are out of school. In 2018, sub-Saharan Africa surpassed Central and Southern Asia as the region with the largest out-of-school population. Sub-Saharan Africa's share of the school-age population will have doubled to 25% between 1990 and 2030.

In low-income countries, as enrolment rates stagnated, completion rates continued to increase, but not enough to ensure universal completion by 2030.

Over-age participation is a challenge. In 20 low- and middle-income countries, at least 30% of 15-year-olds were still in primary school; in Malawi, the share was 75%.

High-income countries have many hidden out-of-school populations, a result of temporary and permanent exclusion, which disproportionately affects disadvantaged groups.

Learning outcomes in rich countries have not progressed. The share of 15-year-olds without basic reading skills even increased in OECD countries, from 19% in 2003 to 22% in 2018.

Less than 3% of 15-year-olds, including those out of school, were proficient readers in Cambodia, Senegal and Zambia.

Some assessments are too difficult for average learners in some countries. Up to 37% of students failed to score above the random guessing threshold on regional assessments in mathematics in Latin America and in southern and eastern Africa.

CHAPTER 10

TARGET 4.1

Primary and secondary education

By 2030, ensure that all girls and boys complete free, equitable and quality primary and secondary education leading to relevant and effective learning outcomes

GLOBAL INDICATOR

4.1.1 – *Proportion of children and young people (a) in Grade 2 or 3; (b) at the end of primary education; and (c) at the end of lower secondary education achieving at least a minimum proficiency level in (i) reading and (ii) mathematics, by sex*

4.1.2 – *Completion rate (primary education, lower secondary education, upper secondary education)*

THEMATIC INDICATORS

4.1.3 – *Gross intake ratio to the last grade (primary education, lower secondary education)*

4.1.4 – *Out-of-school rate (primary education, lower secondary education, upper secondary education)*

4.1.5 – *Percentage of children over-age for grade (primary education, lower secondary education)*

4.1.6 – *Administration of a nationally-representative learning assessment (a) in Grade 2 or 3; (b) at the end of primary education; and (c) at the end of lower secondary education*

4.1.7 – *Number of years of (a) free and (b) compulsory primary and secondary*

Target 4.1 focuses on the need for universal access to schooling of good quality that leads to relevant learning outcomes. This chapter tackles attendance, completion and learning outcomes, drawing attention to their interaction.

SCHOOL ATTENDANCE AND COMPLETION

Globally, 1 in 12 primary school-age children (59 million), 1 in 6 lower secondary school-age adolescents (61 million) and 1 in 3 upper secondary school-age youth (138 million) are out of school. Just over half of out-of-school children and adolescents are in sub-Saharan Africa. As of 2018, the region also hosts the largest out-of-school population, surpassing Central and Southern Asia for the first time (**Table 10.1**).

These figures reflect a refinement of the out-of-school rate indicator calculation, approved in 2018. About 4 million primary school-age children in pre-primary education are now considered to be in school, since children in pre-primary education almost universally make the transition to primary school even if they enter late (**Focus 10.1**).

In some countries, upper secondary education is not of uniform duration, with some programmes shorter than the age bracket used for calculation of out-of-school rates. For instance, in five European countries offering vocational tracks leading to secondary qualification within two rather than three years, such as Croatia and Denmark, at least 10% of upper secondary school-age

youth are recorded as out of school. Care must be taken when interpreting upper secondary out-of-school rates to account for country contexts that allow some youth to graduate from upper secondary programmes earlier than the indicator assumes. Conversely, significant numbers of school-age children in high-income countries may be effectively out of school but not recognized as such (**Focus 10.2**).

The completion rate, which the Inter-agency and Expert Group on SDG Indicators approved as a new global indicator for target 4.1 in November 2019 (see **Chapter 9**), has reached 85% for primary, 73% for lower secondary and 49% for upper secondary education (**Table 10.2**). While the attendance rate among primary school-age children and the primary completion rate are close, the rates diverge in secondary education.

The two indicators need not agree when adolescents and youth start school late and repeat classes, eventually leaving school early. The attendance rate captures rapid increases, such as those caused by fee abolition in several sub-Saharan African countries in recent years. The completion rate captures learners who make it to the final grade, including those completing later than the expected age (**Focus 10.1**). The gap between the two rates is larger in poorer countries, where both late entry and repetition are higher. Progress in enrolment

> As of 2018, sub-Saharan Africa hosts the largest out-of-school population

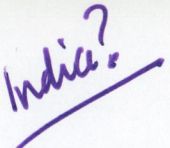

TABLE 10.1:
Selected indicators on school participation 2018

	Primary Out-of-school children		Lower secondary Out-of-school adolescents		Upper secondary Out-of-school youth	
	(000)	(%)	(000)	(%)	(000)	(%)
World	**59 141**	**8**	**61 478**	**16**	**137 796**	**35**
Sub-Saharan Africa	32 214	19	28 251	37	37 026	58
Northern Africa and Western Asia	5 032	9	3 998	14	8 084	30
Central and Southern Asia	12 588	7	16 829	15	64 745	45
Eastern and South-eastern Asia	5 697	3	9 016	10	17 870	21
Latin America and the Caribbean	2 267	4	2 544	7	7 159	23
Oceania	210	5	109	5	408	25
Europe and Northern America	1 133	2	731	2	2 503	7
Low income	20 797	19	21 243	39	26 176	61
Lower middle income	30 444	9	30 706	17	87 730	44
Upper middle income	6 570	3	8 444	7	20 615	20
High income	1 330	2	1 085	3	3 275	8

Source: UIS database.

TABLE 10.2:
Completion rate, by level, 2018

	Primary	Lower secondary	Upper secondary
World	**85**	**73**	**49**
Sub-Saharan Africa	65	40	28
Northern Africa and Western Asia	85	76	53
Central and Southern Asia	85	74	37
Eastern and South-eastern Asia	95	82	59
Latin America and the Caribbean	90	80	60
Oceania	...	83	48
Europe and Northern America	99	97	88
Low income	56	28	13
Lower middle income	84	71	42
Upper middle income	94	84	59
High income	99	97	88

Sources: UIS database and World Inequality Database on Education.

FIGURE 10.1:
Primary school enrolment rates have stalled in sub-Saharan Africa, but completion rates continue to rise slowly
Primary adjusted net enrolment and completion rates, 2000–18

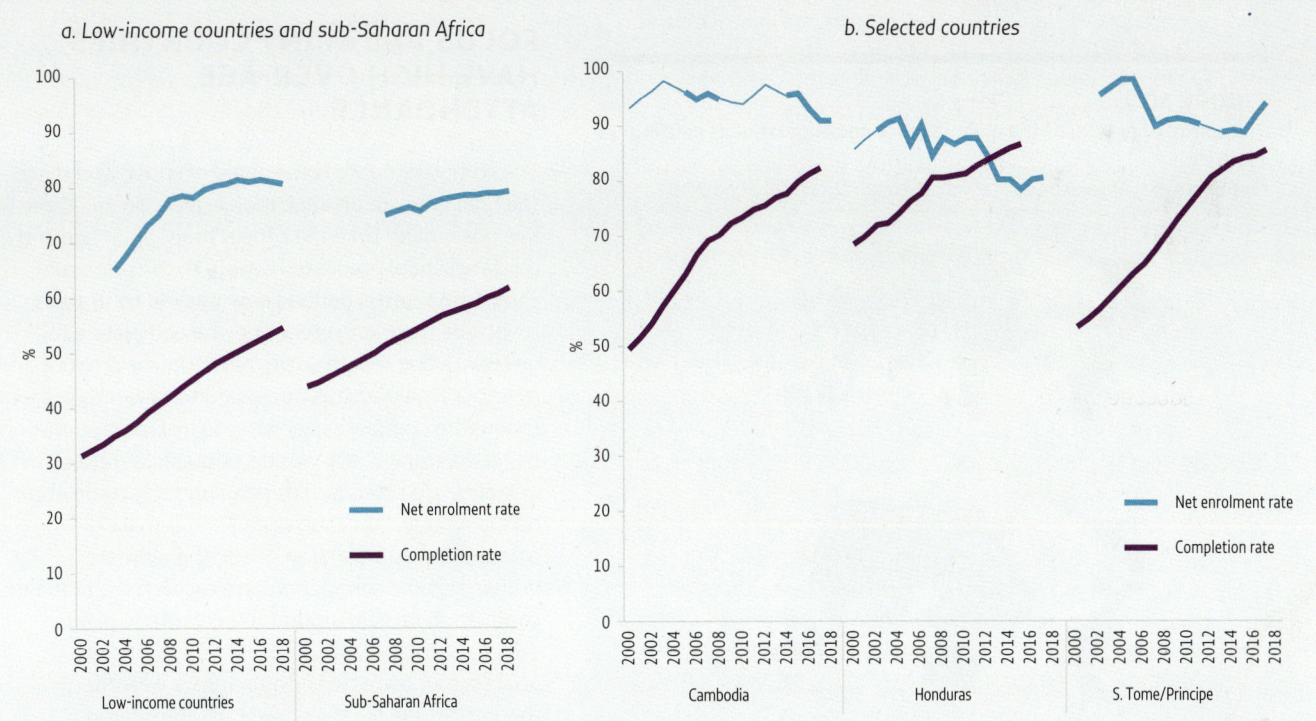

GEM StatLink: http://bit.ly/GEM2020_fig10_1
Note: Lines in country trends are thicker when representing actual data and thinner when based on interpolations.
Sources: UIS and GEM Report team analysis.

> gap between the net enrolment and completion rates in low-income
> ntries shrank from 35 percentage points in 2008 to 26 points in 2018 **"**

Sub-Saharan Africa will account for one-quarter of school-age children by 2030

About 700 million children have been born between 2015 and 2019, and the number has likely stopped growing (United Nations, 2019). Thus, the share of secondary school students will grow relative to primary school students. However, the effect is small relative to changes in enrolment rates. The shift is happening slowly. Between 2000 and 2015, the global share of upper secondary among all school enrolments increased from around 15% to just under 20%, mostly at the expense of the share of primary enrolments.

More importantly, the number of births has peaked in some countries and regions but continues to grow in others. As a result of these demographic differences, the geographical distribution of school-age children and enrolments is changing dramatically. In terms of shares of the school-age population, sub-Saharan Africa, Europe and Latin America were of comparable weight in 1990, but the weight of secondary schooling is shifting to sub-Saharan Africa. Its share of the school-age population, which was 12% in 1990, is expected to reach 25% by 2030 (**Figure 10.2**). A global conversation about secondary education in 2030 amounts to a conversation about sub-Saharan Africa.

FIGURE 10.2:
The centre of gravity of the global school-age population is shifting to Africa
Cartogram proportional to the school-age population, 1990 and 2030

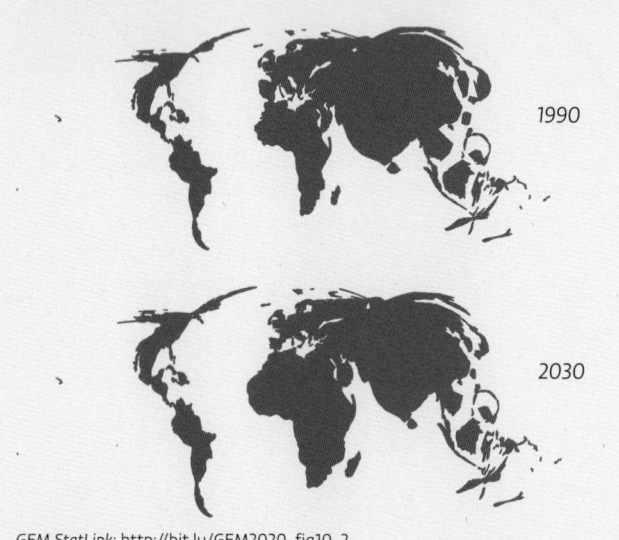

1990

2030

GEM StatLink: http://bit.ly/GEM2020_fig10_2
Note: Regions are scaled in proportion to size of school-age population.
Sources: UIS database and United Nations (2019).

rates has stalled since the mid-2000s in low-income and sub-Saharan African countries. Continuing rapid population growth is a potential cause (**Box 10.1**). The completion rate, however, continues to increase, although at a pace insufficient to reach universal primary completion in these countries by 2030 (UNESCO, 2019b). The gap between the net enrolment and completion rates in low-income countries shrank from 35 percentage points in 2008 to 26 points in 2018 (**Figure 10.1a**).

The closing gap is evident in country data. Cambodia has reported universal primary enrolment since the early 2000s, when barely one in two children completed. The gap has been closing rapidly, but at least one in six children still does not complete primary school on time (**Figure 10.1b**). However, half of those not completing on time ultimately do so, which means that the ultimate completion rate is 92%.

FOCUS 10.1: MANY COUNTRIES HAVE HIGH OVER-AGE ATTENDANCE

The completion rate is the share of those who reach the final grade of an education level at an age three to five years older than the official graduation age. If the primary school graduation age is 11, the primary completion rate is defined over ages 14 to 16 so as to include the many students who complete a few years late due to late entry, repetition or dropout and re-entry. However, it is necessary to take into account those who complete even later to interpret education trends in some of the world's poorest countries. In Malawi, the standard (timely) primary completion rate is 49%, but an estimated 73% ultimately complete. In sub-Saharan Africa, the ultimate primary school completion rate exceeds the standard completion rate by around 10 percentage points.

Students who are two or more years over the theoretical age for their grade are considered over-age. However, this definition does not capture the depth of over-age participation, i.e. the large number of years by which many learners are older than classmates who entered on time and

FIGURE 10.3:

Many adolescents are still in primary school in low- and middle-income countries

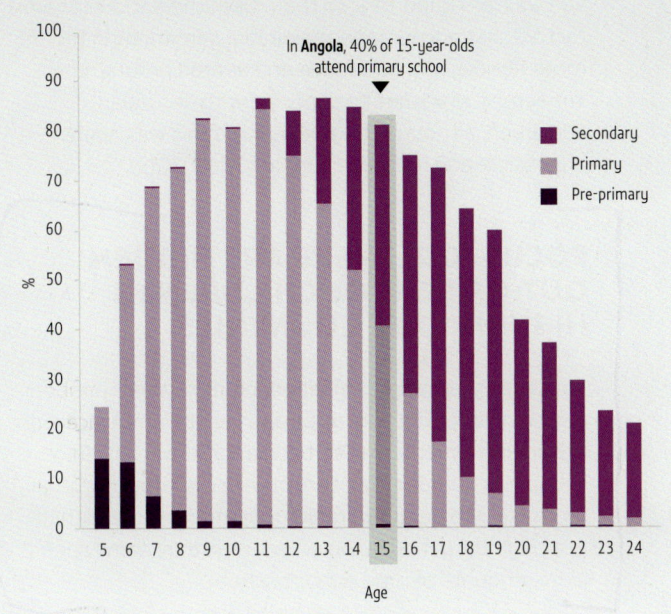

a. School attendance, by education level and age, Angola, 2015/16

In **Angola**, 40% of 15-year-olds attend primary school

Legend:
■ Secondary
■ Primary
■ Pre-primary

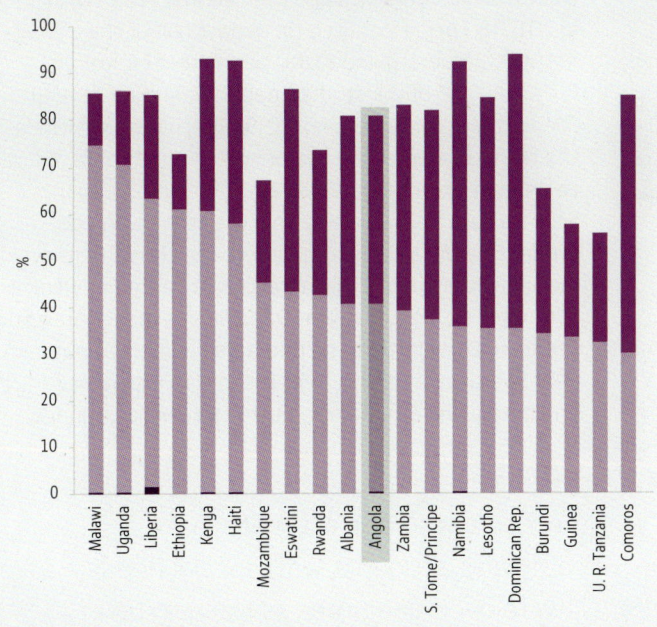

b. School attendance of 15-year-olds, by education level, selected countries, 2015/16

GEM StatLink: http://bit.ly/GEM2020_fig10_3
Source: GEM Report team analysis based on DHS and MICS data.

never repeated. In Angola, 19% of 24-year-olds were still in secondary school in 2015/16. This is a knock-on effect from lower levels: For instance, 4 in 10 15-year-olds attended primary school (**Figure 10.3a**). In 20 selected low- and middle-income countries, at least 30% of 15-year-olds were in primary school; in Malawi, the share was 75% (**Figure 10.3b**).

High levels of over-age participation represent a positive development in the short term if over-age students were previously more likely to drop out. Yet rising expectations for appropriate minimum schooling may create a backlog transitional generation of late entrants and re-entrants. The UNESCO Institute for Statistics (UIS) estimates that, globally, 1.6% of children are not expected ever to enter school. Because primary school entry was not universal in 2018, reaching universal secondary school completion by the class of 2030 requires late entry. Barring rapid turnaround in timely entry and dropout trends, over-age participation will increasingly be required.

An analysis of 16 countries with Multiple Indicator Cluster Survey (MICS) data since 2015 shows that, in most, a substantial majority of out-of-school children, adolescents and youth had missed at most two years of schooling and could re-enter without being severely over-age. This includes Nigeria, which has a large number of out-of-school children (**Figure 10.4**).

Having missed one or two years of school is a severe disadvantage. However, the high baseline levels of over-age enrolment among those currently in school means re-entrants would be no older than their peers. Accelerated education programmes condensing several years of schooling may be more appropriate for those more than two years behind. Ten aspirational principles for effective programmes in humanitarian settings could be adapted to general contexts (Myers et al., 2016).

FIGURE 10.4:
Most out-of-school children are not too old to re-enter
Gap between years of schooling completed and theoretical grade for age, selected countries, 2015–18

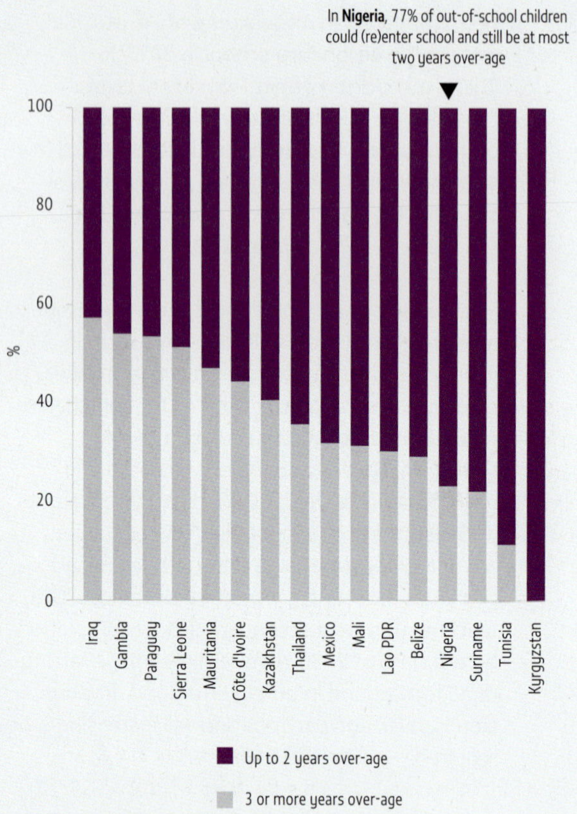

In **Nigeria**, 77% of out-of-school children could (re)enter school and still be at most two years over-age

Legend:
- Up to 2 years over-age
- 3 or more years over-age

GEM StatLink: http://bit.ly/GEM2020_fig10_4
Source: GEM Report team analysis of MICS data.

Aligning accelerated programmes with the national education system is key. While the programmes may issue final certification, credible pathways into the formal system are a concern. In the Speed School model in Burkina Faso, Mali, Niger (Kebede, 2018), Ethiopia and Uganda (Lowden, 2019), the curriculum of the first 3 years of primary education is condensed into 9 to 10 months. The model is designed as a temporary intervention. Classroom space and eligible children are identified through community outreach, and teaching is initially conducted in the local language. A crucial element is close collaboration with 'link schools' in the formal system that receive graduates.

Not all accelerated programme participants, especially older adolescents, wish to (re-)enter the formal system by the shortest route. A study of accelerated education programmes for 10- to 18-year-olds in refugee settings in Uganda showed that no participants wanted to transition into the formal primary school system. Being the right age was less important to them than the socio-economic factors that encouraged their initial enrolment in the more flexible, more inclusive accelerated programmes. Yet almost all wished to continue with secondary education, although they recognized this was almost impossible due to lack of supply (Oddy, 2019).

[handwritten: Demark's rate of school exclusion]

FOCUS 10.2: THERE ARE HIDDEN OUT-OF-SCHOOL CHILDREN IN HIGH-INCOME COUNTRIES

Education authorities in high-income countries are responsible for the education and well-being of students excluded from school (Thomson and Russell, 2009). Yet some categories of students are disproportionally more likely to be temporarily or permanently excluded. Although they may be on school registers, some spend large amounts of time outside school.

According to one estimate in England (United Kingdom), students with special needs were over nine times as likely to be permanently excluded (Daniels and Cole, 2010). In 2017/18, they accounted for almost half of the official 411,000 temporary and 8,000 permanent exclusions (5.1% and 0.1% of the student population, respectively) (Department for Education, 2019). This does not include the many students who are 'off-rolled', or encouraged to unenroll voluntarily to pre-empt formal expulsion. Schools have both leverage and incentive to off-roll: Students avoid a stain on their records, and schools avoid including them in disciplinary exclusion statistics. Recent estimates suggest that 1 in 10 students experiences an unexplained exit during secondary education. About 24,000 students, or 4 in 10 of those who experience an unexplained exit, do not return to a publicly funded

> **66**
> According to one estimate in England, students with special needs were over nine times as likely to be permanently excluded
> **99**

> In the United States, the out-of-school suspension rate of students with disabilities (10.6%) was twice as high as the national average (5.3%)

school by the spring term of grade 11 (Hutchinson and Crenna-Jennings, 2019).

While antisocial behaviour can significantly disrupt learning for all, removing students interferes with their education progression and can perpetuate a failure cycle, culminating in prison (Christle et al., 2007; Cuellar and Markowitz, 2015). In the United States, through zero-tolerance measures, such as mandatory suspension and law enforcement referral, schools in disadvantaged areas may initiate a so-called school-to-prison pipeline (Lewis and Vásquez Solótzano, 2006). A discretionary suspension or expulsion nearly triples the likelihood of a student being in contact with juvenile justice in the following year. Adults who as students went to schools with above-average suspension rates experienced 15% to 20% higher incarceration rates. High suspension rates also negatively affect education attainment (Bacher-Hicks et al., 2019). Yet learners excluded from school retain their right to education, even in prison (see **Focus 12.2**).

Children are funnelled into the juvenile and criminal justice systems for often minor infractions. Such disciplinary policies disproportionately affect black students, who represent 31% of school-related arrests, around twice their share of the student body, and are suspended and expelled three times as often as white students (US Department of Education Office for Civil Rights, 2014). In a Mississippi school district, children as young as 10 were routinely arrested and taken to jail in handcuffs whenever teachers requested. Some were held for days before being given access to a lawyer. At schools in the district, including special schools, students were suspended and expelled for more than 10 days at 7 times the state rate (Kauffman, 2012). Black girls were strongly affected, representing the fastest-growing group in the juvenile justice system (Morris, 2016). Unlike their white peers, they received out-of-school rather than in-school suspensions (National Women's Law Center, 2015). Nationwide, 9.6% of black girls in public primary and secondary schools received out-of-school suspensions in 2013/14, compared with 1.7% of white girls (US Department of Education, 2019).

The high rate of exclusion of special needs students underscores the need for more proactive behavioural supports to prevent further marginalization and exacerbation of education difficulties. In the United States, one study suggested that 19.5% of students with disabilities had been suspended at least once in the academic year (Sullivan et al., 2014). Nationwide, the out-of-school suspension rate of students with disabilities (10.6%) was twice as high as the national average (5.3%) (US Department of Education, 2019). Many of these children have learning disabilities or histories of poverty and neglect; they should benefit from additional education and counselling services, not face zero-tolerance policies. Even when students were extremely disruptive, teachers may have provoked or escalated the behaviour, and school rules may have been inappropriate (Razer et al., 2013). The New York Police Department recently signed a policy limiting police officers' responsibilities in the New York City public schools – the nation's largest district, serving 1.1 million students. The policy is part of a school climate effort that includes hiring 285 new school social workers. Out-of-school suspensions will be limited and support provided for educators to practice positive discipline techniques (Miller, 2019).

LEARNING

Data on global indicator 4.1.1 come from national and cross-national learning assessments. While China (lower secondary education) and India (primary education) base their reports on reading skills on national assessments, most countries so far base theirs on cross-national assessments.

Two major international learning assessments were conducted in 2018. The Pacific Islands Literacy and Numeracy Assessment (PILNA) underwent its third round since 2012, under the umbrella of the Pacific Community Educational Quality and Assessment Programme. PILNA collects information on grade 4 and 6 student learning outcomes (corresponding to 'end of primary', as captured by global indicator 4.1.1b). The 2018 round covered 15 countries, 900 schools, 41,000 students and 10 languages (UNESCO, 2019a). The regional aggregates, which are the only publicly available information, show 83% of grade 6 students scored above the minimum threshold in numeracy (compared with 68% in 2015) and 63% in literacy (compared with 46% in 2015) (Pacific Community, 2019).

FIGURE 10.5:
Even the richest countries are not moving towards the global target on reading proficiency

Distribution of reading proficiency levels, countries participating in the 2003 and 2018 Programme for International Student Assessment (PISA) and the 2017 PISA for Development (PISA-D)

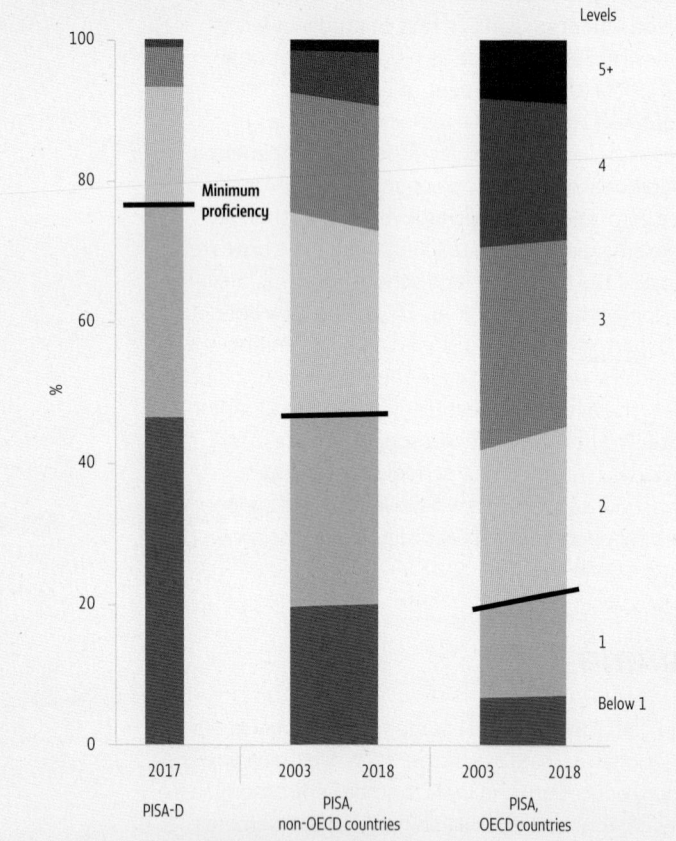

GEM StatLink: http://bit.ly/GEM2020_fig10_5

Notes: The figure shows unweighted averages of proficiency levels in 7 non-OECD countries that took part in the 2017 PISA-D and 8 non-OECD and 29 OECD countries that took part in the 2003 and 2018 PISA. Proficiency levels are mapped to the 2003 scale based on score point thresholds as follows: level 1 = 2018 level 1a; level 5+ = 2003 level 5 and 2018 levels 5 and 6. Students achieved minimum proficiency level if they reached at least level 2.

Source: GEM Report team analysis based on 2003 and 2018 PISA and 2017 PISA-D data.

> The most striking finding from the 2018 PISA is the lack of progress in the past 15 years

19% in 2003 to 22% in 2018, and remained essentially constant in non-OECD countries at 47% (OECD, 2019) (**Figure 10.5**).

INEQUALITY IN LEARNING OUTCOMES IS UNDERESTIMATED

The United Nations 2030 Agenda for Sustainable Development called for disaggregating results by population group. There are several indications that inequality in learning outcomes is underestimated, for two reasons. Assessments look only at those in the school system (Chmielewski, 2019) and information on achievement of the most disadvantaged is incomplete.

Learning assessments do not yield information on all children

Being school based, neither national nor cross-national learning assessment results capture all children's learning achievement. This issue began receiving attention as more upper-middle-income countries, where significant numbers leave school before age 15, began participating in PISA. Three-quarters of 15-year-olds in the six middle-income countries that took part in the 2003 and 2018 PISA rounds were in school, including in Brazil, Indonesia and Turkey, an increase of 25 percentage points. In Indonesia, the percentage of 15-year-olds in school and participating in PISA increased from 46% to 85%. The apparent stagnation in the percentage of those reaching minimum proficiency could therefore count as progress, since results take into account the performance of many relatively disadvantaged adolescents who would not previously have taken the test, even if the rate of progress is below that required to achieve SDG 4.

The Organisation for Economic Co-operation and Development (OECD) conducted the seventh round of the Programme for International Student Assessment (PISA) since 2000. It provides results for reading and mathematics among 15-year-olds (roughly corresponding to 'end of lower secondary', as captured by global indicator 4.1.1c) in education systems in 80 mostly high- and upper-middle-income countries. The most striking finding is the lack of progress in the past 15 years. The percentage of 15-year-olds not achieving minimum proficiency (level 2) increased in OECD countries from

Challenges in comparing results between countries with low and high attendance levels were more prominent with PISA for Development (PISA-D), conducted in nine mostly lower-middle-income countries in 2017. Attendance rates in the seven countries for which reports have been published were lower than in the six lower-middle-income countries that took part in the 2018 PISA. The share of 15-year-olds enrolled in grade 7 and above was 61% in Ecuador and less than 30% in Cambodia and Senegal (**Figure 10.6a**).

FIGURE 10.6:

Less than 3% of 15-year-olds in Cambodia, Senegal and Zambia have minimum proficiency in reading

Lower-middle-income countries participating in the 2018 PISA and in the 2017 PISA for Development

a. Distribution of 15-year-olds by grade

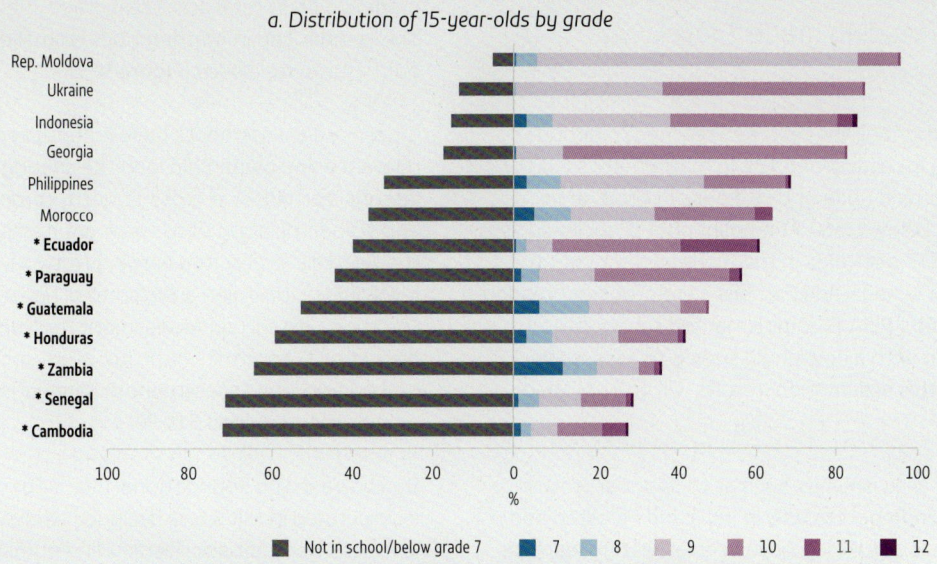

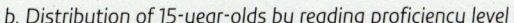

b. Distribution of 15-year-olds by reading proficiency level

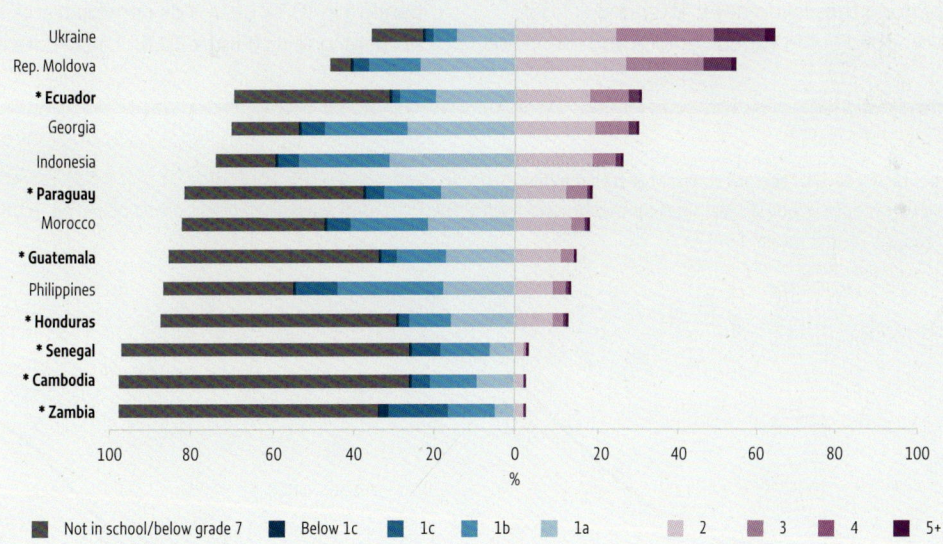

* Countries that took part in the 2017 PISA-D.

GEM StatLink: http://bit.ly/GEM2020_fig10_6

Notes: Not in school/below grade 7 includes a small percentage of eligible students who may have been excluded for other reasons (e.g. small school size). Panel b assumes that all those not in school or below grade 7 would have scored below minimum proficiency level.

Source: GEM Report team analysis based on 2003 and 2018 PISA and 2017 PISA-D data.

> " The most striking result in the 2018 ASER data from India is the slow pace of acquisition of the most basic skills, such as reading grade 2-level text "

Of those who took the test, 23% reached minimum proficiency in reading and 12% in mathematics (OECD, 2018). Assuming none of those out of school or in school but below grade 7 had minimum proficiency, less than 3% of 15-year-olds in the three poorest countries (Cambodia, Senegal and Zambia) were proficient readers (**Figure 10.6b**). PISA-D complemented school-based assessment with a household survey to assess the validity of this assumption; results will be published in 2020.

Citizen-led assessments, such as the Annual Status of Education Report (ASER) in India and Pakistan and Uwezo in eastern Africa, have been assessing learners both in and out of school for years and continue to do so regularly, providing valuable insights, albeit only at basic skills levels, which are probably below the minimum proficiency level. They allow comparison of learning outcomes among those who never attended school, those who dropped out in various grades and those still

in school. The most striking result in the 2018 ASER data from India is the slow pace of acquisition of the most basic skills, such as reading grade 2-level text. Among 15-year-olds who completed or were still in school at grade 5, 22% in rural areas had grade 2-level reading skills. The gender gap in mathematics is smaller in early grades but never quite closes (**Figure 10.7**).

Citizen-led assessments have emphasized contextual relevance and ownership, and the sharing of process lessons learned, over cross-country comparability and standardization of assessment items. In 2019, the People's Action for Learning Network of organizations involved in citizen-led assessments began piloting a common Citizen-Led Assessment for Numeracy in 1 rural district of 13 countries (Kipruto, 2019). It consisted of an oral one-on-one assessment of foundational numeracy among children aged 5 to 16.

By contrast, the Foundational Learning module, incorporated in MICS 6, is designed to ensure comparability in assessment of basic literacy and numeracy skills. The emerging results, estimated for those both in and out of school, show that low-income countries in sub-Saharan Africa struggle to make the kind of progress in early grades expected from observation of countries in Asia. In Togo, barely 1 in 10 14-year-olds demonstrates fundamental numeracy skills (**Figure 10.8**). These data are alarming,

FIGURE 10.7:

In rural India, it takes several years in school to master basic skills

Percentage of 15-year-olds with basic grade 2-level skills in reading and mathematics in rural India, by highest grade achieved, 2018

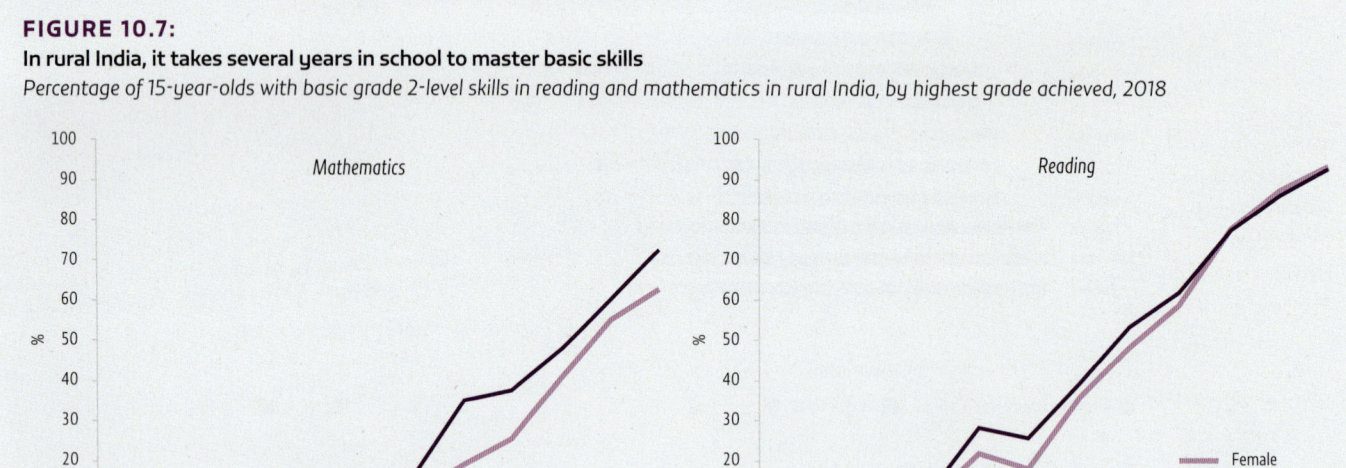

GEM StatLink: http://bit.ly/GEM2020_fig10_7

Notes: Basic skills in reading are defined as being able to read a grade 2-level story. Basic skills in mathmatics are defined as being able to carry out a division of a three-digit by a single-digit number. 0 = never attended school. Analysis excludes points with fewer than 100 observations.

Source: GEM Report team calculations based on 2018 ASER data.

> ❝
> The lower the score of students participating in the three PISA rounds between 2009 and 2015, the more likely they were not to report on the majority of questions related to background ❞

not least because the assessed skills, once linked to the proficiency measure, are likely to be below the minimum level, as in the case of citizen-led assessments.

More work is needed to understand socio-economic gaps in learning

The utility of learning assessments in dealing with inclusion depends on whether they provide information about the learning of those at risk of being left behind. The mobilization around SDG 4 has led to considerable progress in the quantity and quality of data collected on learning outcomes and their distribution among population groups. MICS 6 data offer novel insights into the association of learning proficiency with background characteristics, such as wealth, language, maternal education and disability, and their interaction.

The Foundation Learning module was administered in two languages in the 2018 Lesotho MICS and three languages in the 2019 Zimbabwe MICS. The use of English instead of local languages is associated with higher inequality in the distribution of learning outcomes and lower performance of learners from the poorest households. In Lesotho, among students from the poorest 20% of households, the share demonstrating fundamental reading skills was 8% when the assessment was in English but 27% for assessment in Sesotho. In Zimbabwe, the share of the poorest quintile demonstrating fundamental reading skills was 6% in English, 13.5% in Ndebele and 21% in Shona (**Figure 10.9**).

MICS data are an exception in this regard, however. Data on learning outcomes often do not fully capture disadvantaged children. Two dimensions have been underappreciated. First, statistical analyses of learning outcomes by student characteristics may inadvertently under-represent low performers, who are less likely to provide background information. For instance, the lower the score of students participating in the three PISA rounds between 2009 and 2015, the more likely they were not to report on the majority of questions related to background (**Figure 10.10**). Second, even when background information is complete, many assessments

are too difficult to allow low performers to demonstrate their learning, which hampers interpretation of data on minimum proficiency (**Focus 10.3**).

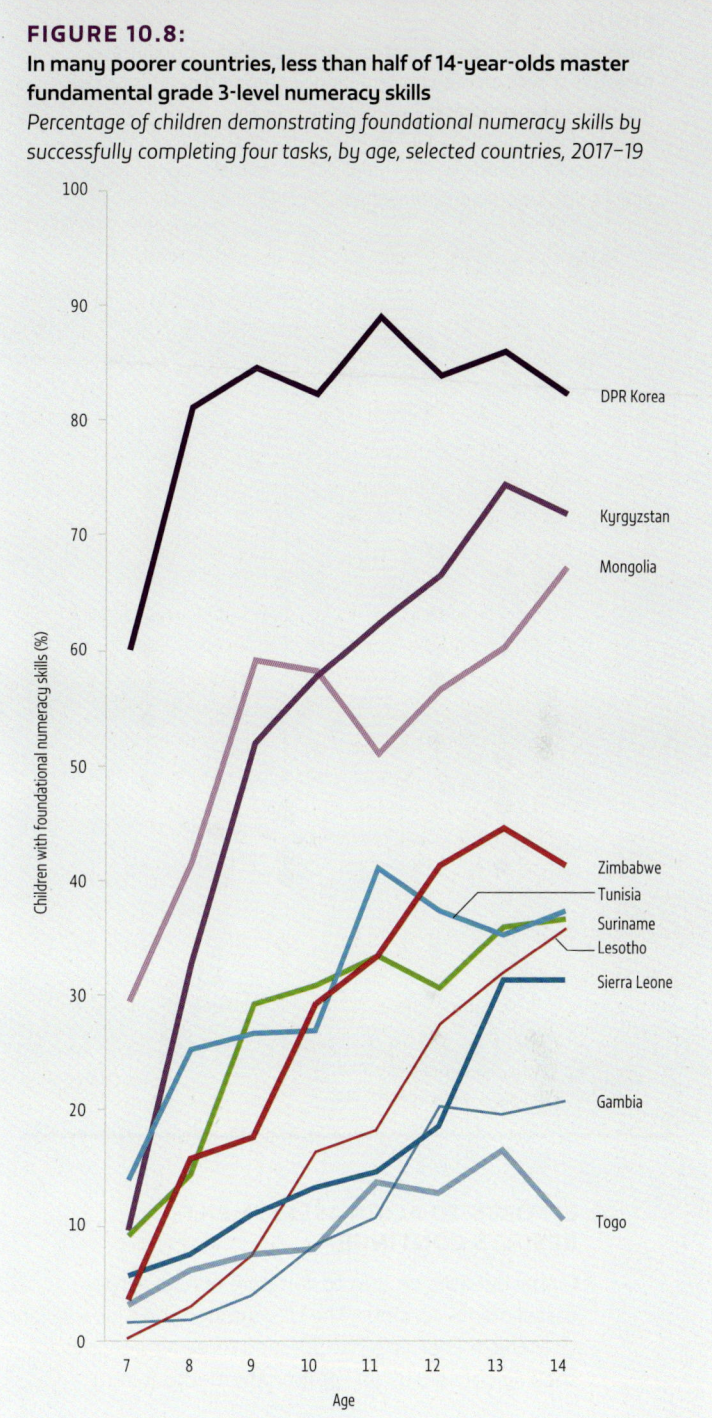

FIGURE 10.8:
In many poorer countries, less than half of 14-year-olds master fundamental grade 3-level numeracy skills
Percentage of children demonstrating foundational numeracy skills by successfully completing four tasks, by age, selected countries, 2017–19

GEM StatLink: http://bit.ly/GEM2020_fig10_8
Source: MICS Survey Findings Reports.

FIGURE 10.9:

English as a language of instruction has a disproportionate negative effect on reading proficiency among disadvantaged learners in Lesotho and Zimbabwe

Percentage of children aged 7 to 14 who demonstrate foundational reading skills by successfully completing three tasks, by language and wealth, Lesotho and Zimbabwe, 2018–19

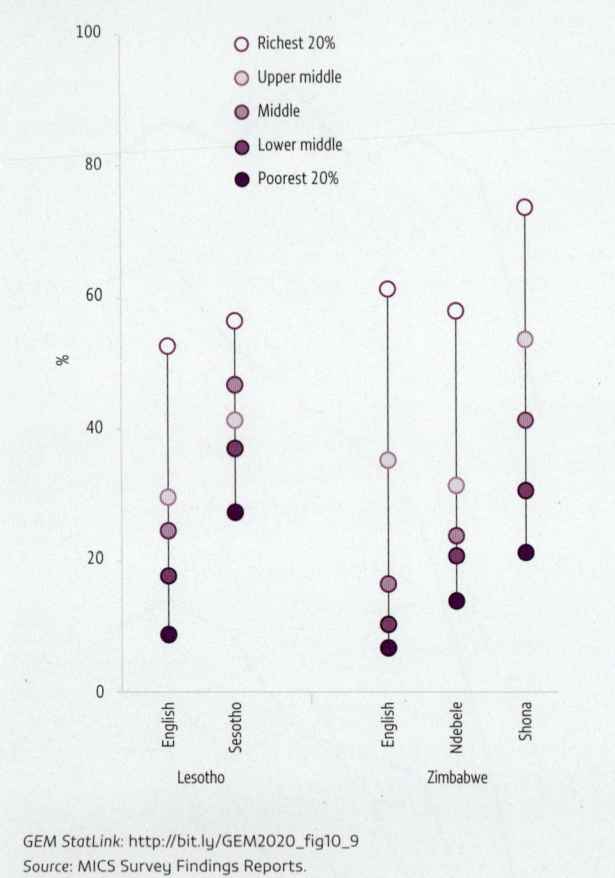

GEM StatLink: http://bit.ly/GEM2020_fig10_9
Source: MICS Survey Findings Reports.

FIGURE 10.10:

Poor readers are less likely to respond to background questions in learning assessments

Average Programme for International Student Assessment reading score, by share of missing responses in the individual background questionnaire, 2009, 2012 and 2015

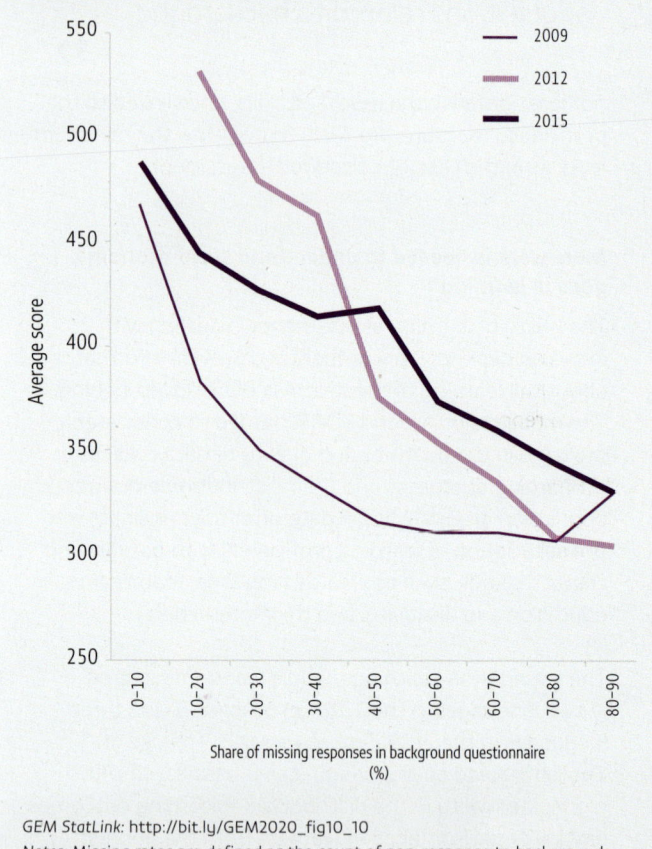

GEM StatLink: http://bit.ly/GEM2020_fig10_10
Notes: Missing rates are defined as the count of non-response to background questions with non-zero observations.
Source: Kim and Richardson (2020), based on PISA 2009, 2012 and 2015.

EFFORTS TO ALIGN ASSESSMENT RESULTS CONTINUE

Global debates on how to compare results across assessments continue. The UIS, through the Global Alliance to Monitor Learning, has pursued three approaches in seeking consensus on appropriate methodology.

The first and simplest uses statistical techniques to link proficiency scales to a common standard. The World Bank relies on this approach for its definition of the learning poverty indicator, which is a variation on global indicator 4.1.1b (World Bank, 2019).

There has been progress towards implementing the second approach linking entire tests. Students from three Latin American countries that took part in the Latin American Laboratory for Assessment of the

> " The UIS, through the Global Alliance to Monitor Learning, has pursued three approaches in seeking consensus on comparing assessment results "

> "
> Without the ability to distinguish levels and trends among the lowest performers, it is difficult to tell whether interventions aimed at them work
> "

Quality of Education (LLECE) study and those from three francophone African countries that took part in the Programme d'Analyse des Systèmes Educatifs de la CONFEMEN (PASEC) would sit not only for the new rounds of their respective surveys but also for a survey administered by the International Association for the Evaluation of Educational Achievement (IEA), such as the Progress in International Reading Literacy Study (PIRLS) (UIS, 2019).

The third, non-statistical approach may enable greater use of national assessments to inform SDG 4 reporting. National experts review items and reach consensus on how they align with agreed international benchmarks. Piloted in Bangladesh and India in 2019, the approach was endorsed at the sixth meeting of the Technical Cooperation Group in August 2019 and will be used in six countries (Montoya and Senapaty, 2019).

FOCUS 10.3: IT IS TIME TO EXAMINE LOW PERFORMANCE IN LEARNING ASSESSMENTS

Meeting the monitoring purpose of ensuring that no one is left behind in learning depends on the ability to differentiate degrees of low performance. If an assessment is too difficult, some learners will not be able to answer any question correctly. Scores then suffer from a 'floor effect', with too many students scoring zero. When, for instance, 40% of learners in a country score zero, it would be helpful to know whether there are variations at this very low performance level. Without the ability to distinguish levels and trends among the lowest performers, it is difficult to tell whether interventions aimed at them work.

The challenge is particularly obvious in international assessments calibrated to a common scale rather than geared towards the range of proficiency among a

FIGURE 10.11:

International assessments do not identify the very lowest and highest performers

Distribution of student scores compared with idealized underlying normal distribution, selected countries, 2015

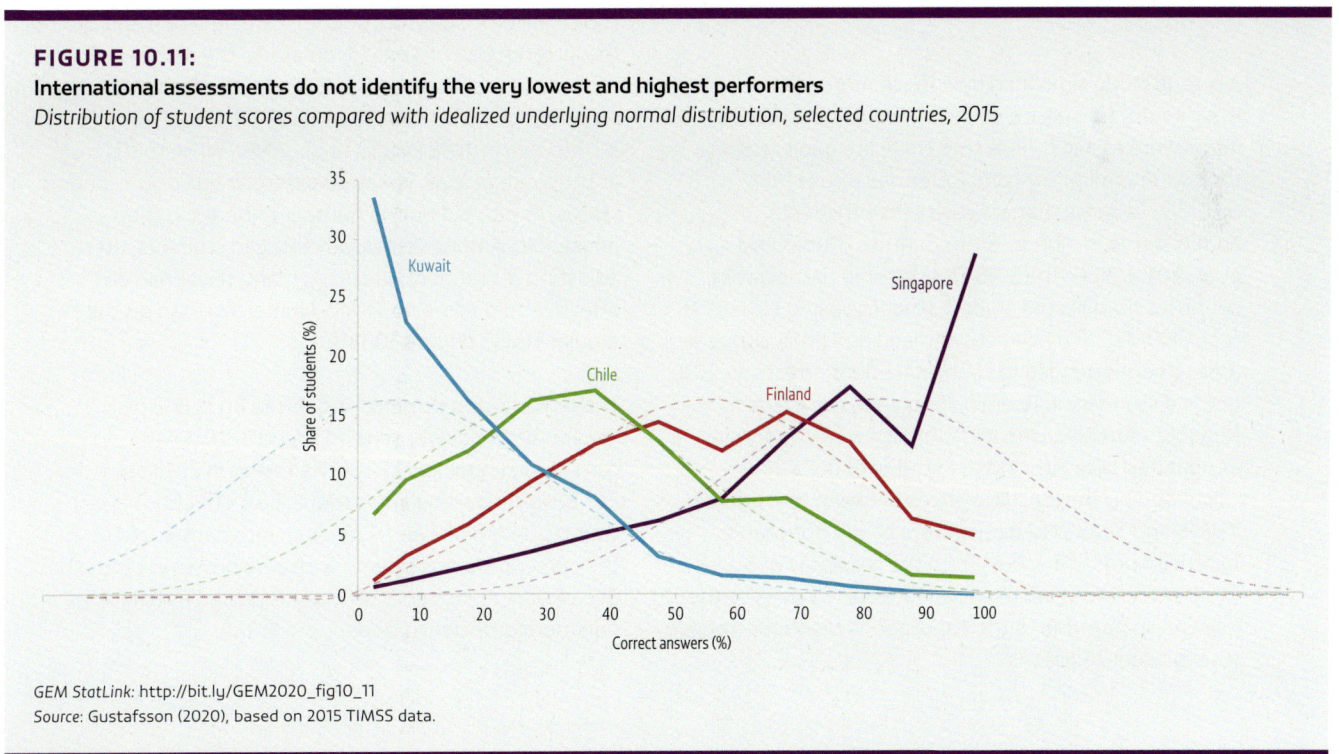

GEM StatLink: http://bit.ly/GEM2020_fig10_11
Source: Gustafsson (2020), based on 2015 TIMSS data.

country's learners. For instance, among countries that took part in the 2015 IEA Trends in International Mathematics and Science Study (TIMSS), many students in Kuwait ran up against the scale floor, while in Singapore, they were limited by the scale ceiling. This makes the gap between the countries appear smaller than it is (**Figure 10.11**).

Even national assessments built on assumptions around grade-level competences may be poorly targeted. In many developing countries, skills specified in the curriculum tend to be well above what students in that grade actually learn (Pritchett and Beatty, 2012) (see **Chapter 5**). A test focused only on specified competences is likely to be too difficult for many students.

Item response theory (IRT) is one way to ensure assessments better differentiate among students at the low end of achievement. IRT scores take into account the difficulty of each item. If two students answer the same number of questions correctly, but one student correctly answers more difficult questions, that student receives a higher IRT score. Capacity for IRT scoring is weak in many countries, but investing in such capacity has several benefits, including more informative results regarding low-performing schools and students. IRT scoring can also be used to refine each student's score, using individual background data to predict variation across students with a raw score of zero (Martin et al., 2016).

A recent study simulated how much more reliable PISA results for specific countries would be if test items were easier. It finds that there are good reasons for low- and middle-income countries to use PISA or TIMSS variants that are easier than the tests administered in high-income countries (Rutkowski et al., 2019). Since the 2015 TIMSS, some participating countries have tested grade 4 students using either the regular TIMSS or a new, less demanding TIMSS Numeracy assessment intended to counteract floor effects. In 2015, grade 4 students in Bahrain, Indonesia, the Islamic Republic of Iran, Kuwait and Morocco were randomly assigned to take either test. In terms of IRT scores calculated by the IEA, differences between the regular TIMSS and TIMSS Numeracy were barely noticeable. In other words, IRT scores from the regular TIMSS are fairly successful at differentiating students even at the low end, in part due to the imputations mentioned above (Gustafsson, 2020a).

> " A recent study finds that there are good reasons for low- and middle-income countries to use PISA or TIMSS variants that are easier than the tests administered in high-income countries "

Relying on tests set at too high a level of difficulty is nevertheless problematic because the comparison of IRT scores does not account for random guessing for multiple choice. Floor effects may come into play even before scores hit zero. With multiple choice questions, in particular, what is informative about a learner's knowledge is not the raw number of correct answers. It is how much better they did than would be expected with random guessing. This number can be estimated, including for a mix of multiple choice questions and items requiring learners to construct responses (Burton, 2001).

For example, 34% of students in Kuwait scored zero on 12 constructed response questions, while 3% scored zero on 15 multiple choice questions. When the results are adjusted for random guessing, it appears likely that the achievement of around 25% of students was actually too low for estimation on the multiple choice part (Gustafsson, 2020b). Largely as a result of the introduction of TIMSS Numeracy, the number of countries considered by the IEA to suffer from reliability problems due to floor effects declined, from five in 2011 to two in 2015 (Mullis et al., 2016). While this is true at the average level, variation emerged by socio-economic status, as defined by the number of books in the household. Among less disadvantaged students, after adjusting for random guessing, many fewer had an effective zero score on TIMSS Numeracy than on the regular TIMSS (**Figure 10.12**).

The regional assessments organized by LLECE in Latin America (whose third round in 2013 was commonly known as TERCE, its fourth in 2019 as ERCE) suffer particularly serious floor effects. In every country, in grade 3 and 6 reading and mathematics, the percentage of students with zero scores exceeds the percentage of students officially reported as below the minimum proficiency level.

FIGURE 10.12:
Standard versions of well-known cross-national assessments are too difficult for disadvantaged learners

Percentage of students with adjusted scores of zero, by type of assessment and household poverty, selected countries, 2015

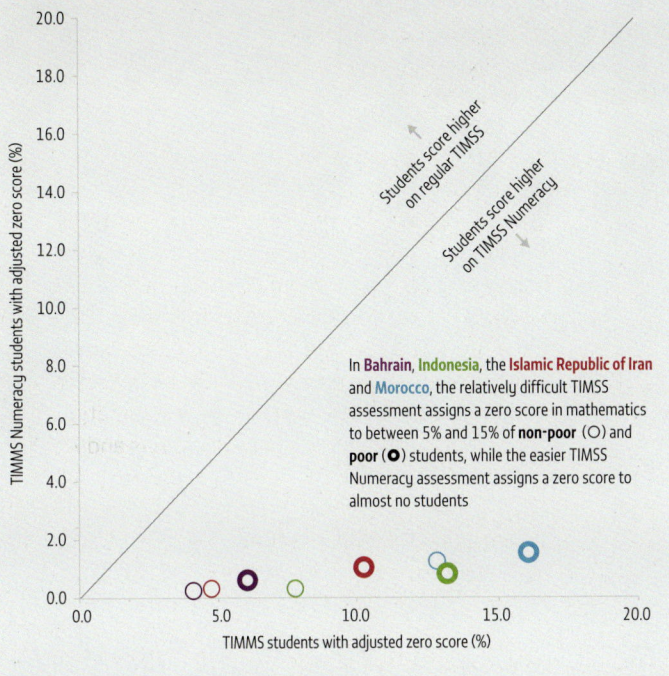

In **Bahrain**, **Indonesia**, the **Islamic Republic of Iran** and **Morocco**, the relatively difficult TIMSS assessment assigns a zero score in mathematics to between 5% and 15% of **non-poor** (O) and **poor** (◉) students, while the easier TIMSS Numeracy assessment assigns a zero score to almost no students

GEM StatLink: http://bit.ly/GEM2020_fig10_12
Note: Non-poor households have more than 10 books.
Source: GEM Report team based on 2015 TIMSS data analysis by Gustafsson (2020).

FIGURE 10.13:
In Latin America, significant numbers of learners are assumed to meet minimum proficiency when they displayed no real evidence of learning

Percentage of grade 3 students with zero correct responses in reading above the random guessing threshold, by assigned level of proficiency, selected Latin American countries, 2013

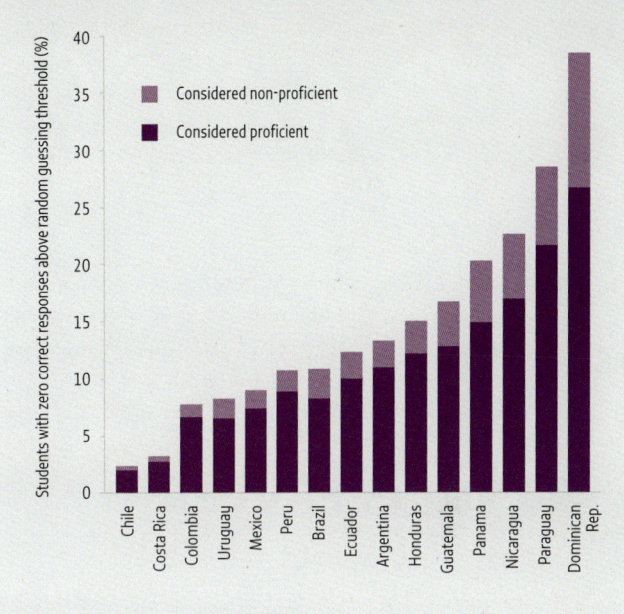

GEM StatLink: http://bit.ly/GEM2020_fig10_13
Source: GEM Report team based on 2013 LLECE data analysis by Gustafsson (2020).

For grade 3 mathematics in TERCE, learners who had raw scores indistinguishable from random guessing but who were nevertheless considered proficient can be identified (**Figure 10.13**). Likewise, three-quarters of students who did no better on multiple choice questions than random guessing were considered proficient in reading. These students may have higher IRT scores than those in the bottom group (considered below minimum proficiency level), but after controlling for random guessing, there is insufficient information on students from both groups to say much about what they can and cannot do. In other words, LLECE assessments do not include enough easy items to produce meaningful information about the most marginalized students (Gustafsson, 2020b).

Comparing the magnitude of floor effects against average performance across large-scale assessments yields both good and bad news. Some assessments

are clearly too difficult for average learners in some countries, especially in mathematics, with up to 37% of students failing to score above the random guessing threshold on regional assessments in Latin America and southern and eastern Africa (Gustafsson, 2020b).

The good news is that calibrating difficulty so average students can answer at least half the questions correctly generally seems to allow the vast majority of students to display measurable performance and limit the floor effect to, at most, 10%. However, the comparison also shows that the assessments that largely manage to reduce floor effects to acceptable levels have fewer multiple choice and more constructed response items. While the very large floor effects seen in some countries can be eliminated, completely eliminating them would involve substantially different approaches to testing that are costly and more complex to develop, score and compare across countries.

Save the Children will reach more than 15,000 girls and boys in need in urban Port-au-Prince, Haiti, working with teachers, parents and community leaders to improve the quality of education the children receive.

CREDIT: Susan Warner/Save the Children

KEY MESSAGES

Participation in pre-primary school the year before primary school entry age was 67% in 2018, with shares ranging from 9% in Djibouti to 100% in Cuba and Viet Nam. Globally, average participation has been rising by just over two percentage points every five years.

_____

Participation can be increased rapidly by attaching reception classes to primary schools (as in the Lao People's Democratic Republic) and expanding public provision (as in Algeria). Morocco plans to introduce pre-primary classes in all public schools to achieve universal preschool by 2028.

_____

Children from poor households often lack stimulating home environments. In Paraguay, 90% of children in the richest households and 40% of children in the poorest benefitted from stimulating adult engagement.

_____

The new UNICEF tool to assess early childhood development, with 20 questions in three domains (learning, psychosocial well-being and health), will lead to standards on whether children are 'developmentally on track' by ages 24, 36 and 48 months.

_____

Many young children start attending primary school early due to childcare constraints, which results in underperformance as much as for those who attend over-age. In Nigeria, just 12% of children start school on time having attended pre-primary education.

CHAPTER 11

TARGET 4.2

Early childhood

By 2030, ensure that all girls and boys have access to quality early childhood development, care and pre-primary education so that they are ready for primary education

---

GLOBAL INDICATOR

4.2.1 – *Proportion of children under 5 years of age who are developmentally on track in health, learning and psychosocial well-being, by sex*

4.2.2 – *Participation rate in organized learning (one year before the official primary entry age), by sex*

THEMATIC INDICATORS

4.2.3 – *Percentage of children under 5 years of age experiencing positive and stimulating home learning environments*

4.2.4 – *Gross early childhood education enrolment ratio in (a) pre-primary education and (b) early childhood educational development*

4.2.5 – *Number of years of (i) free and (ii) compulsory pre-primary education guaranteed in legal frameworks*

Ensuring all children are prepared and not behind when entering school is an important part of reducing inequality. Continuity between the pre-primary and primary levels is important but should not mean pre-primary education becoming increasingly academic. Early childhood and primary education should be different in purpose, organization and structure (UNICEF, 2019) (**Focus 11.1**).

PARTICIPATION

Interpreting data on early childhood education participation depends on the age group definition, institutional arrangements and early entry patterns. Participation generally increases with age, reaching its highest level the year before primary school entry age, the focus of global indicator 4.2.2. Participation was 67% in 2018 (**Table 11.1**), with shares ranging from 9% in Djibouti to 100% in Cuba and Viet Nam.

In Djibouti, the enrolment rate gap relative to regional averages for sub-Saharan Africa and for Northern Africa and Western Asia has grown since 2000 (**Figure 11.1**). Not only are enrolment levels very low, but 93% of enrolment is in private preschools, with only 24 public preschools in operation in 2016. Although the official age range is two years, public preschool education lasts one year for cost efficiency reasons. Attempts to pilot preschool classes in public primary schools

> 66
>
> In Djibouti, not only are enrolment levels very low, but 93% of enrolment is in private preschools
>
> 99

TABLE 11.1:
Early childhood education participation indicators, 2018

	Pre-primary gross enrolment ratio (%)	Participation one year before primary school entry age (%)
World	**52**	**67**
Sub-Saharan Africa	33	42
Northern Africa and Western Asia	32	50
Central/S.Asia	26	59
Eastern and South-eastern Asia	82	87
Latin America and the Caribbean	78	96
Oceania	76	80
Europe and Northern America	86	64
Low income	24	41
Lower middle income	37	61
Upper middle income	78	83
High income	83	91

Source: UIS database.

fell through because they were used instead for primary-level instruction (Djibouti Ministry of National Education and Professional Training, 2017). The new government strategy aims to ensure that all 5-year-olds, of which there were about 19,000 in 2019, attend one year of preschool by 2030 (Djibouti Ministry of National Education and Professional Training and UNICEF, 2019).

Average participation worldwide has been rising at a rate of just over two percentage points every five years. Some of the fastest progress in the 2010s was observed in Azerbaijan (from 30% at the decade's beginning to 69% at its end), Burundi (19% to 45%), Guinea (23% to 42%), the Lao People's Democratic Republic (38% to 67%) and the Philippines (41% to 83%) (**Figure 11.2**).

> ❝ Participation has declined, even from low starting points, in some countries, including Eritrea, Mali and Morocco ❞

Countries increase participation either by expanding early childhood and pre-primary education systems or by attaching reception classes to primary schools. After piloting a programme in 2002, the Laotian government introduced a grade 0 reception class in primary schools in 2006 and instituted pre-primary education expansion in the 2007 education law. In parallel, kindergartens not attached to primary schools catered for 3- to 5-year-olds. However, enrolment levels remain low for ethnic minorities, which account for 38% of the population (Inui, 2020). A World Bank-funded programme in selected northern districts will carry out an impact evaluation in 2020 of two alternative approaches to delivering education for 3- to 5-year-olds: informal community child development groups and multi-age teaching (which would expand preschools to children under 5) (World Bank, 2019).

Participation has declined, even from low starting points, in some countries, including Eritrea, Mali and Morocco (Figure 11.2). Morocco lacks a public pre-primary education system; the share of private institutions, mostly attached to mosques, in total enrolment was 87% in 2018, and enrolment levels have stagnated over the past two decades. By contrast, enrolment in Algeria increased sharply in the mid-2000s, largely through expansion of the public system (**Figure 11.3**). Following recommendations from its Higher Council of Education, Training and Scientific Research, Morocco undertook to generalize pre-primary education, aiming to increase enrolment in 2018/19 by 100,000 and the share of public institutions to 16%. A 2019–22 action plan includes an enrolment rate target of 67% by 2021/22 and pre-primary classes in all public schools as intermediate steps towards universal pre-primary education by 2027/28 (Morocco Higher Council of Education Training and Scientific Research, 2017; Zerrour, 2018).

Pre-primary education varies by country from one to four years. Participation among children across the age range was 52% in 2018, with shares by income group ranging from 24% in low-income to 83% in high-income countries (Table 11.1). Country rates range from 1% in Chad to 115% in Belgium and Ghana. Few countries report enrolment in early childhood education development

FIGURE 11.1:

Djibouti has the world's lowest early childhood education participation rate

Rate of participation in organized learning one year before primary school entry age, Djibouti, selected regions and world, 2000–18

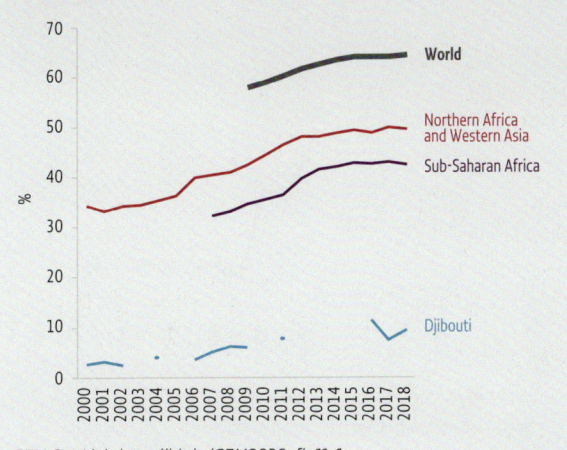

GEM StatLink: http://bit.ly/GEM2020_fig11_1
Source: UIS database.

FIGURE 11.2:

Participation among pre-primary school-aged children is increasing rapidly in some countries

Rate of participation in organized learning one year before primary school entry age, 10 countries with the largest positive and negative change between 2010 and 2018

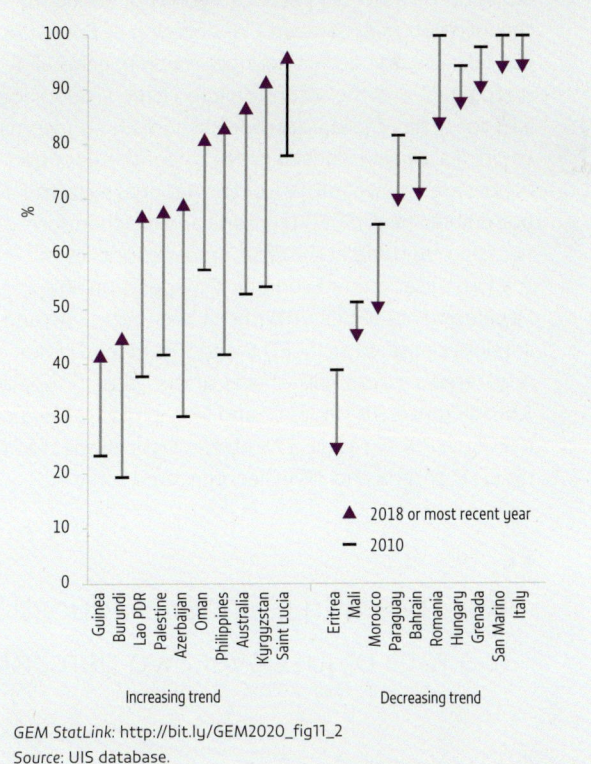

GEM StatLink: http://bit.ly/GEM2020_fig11_2
Source: UIS database.

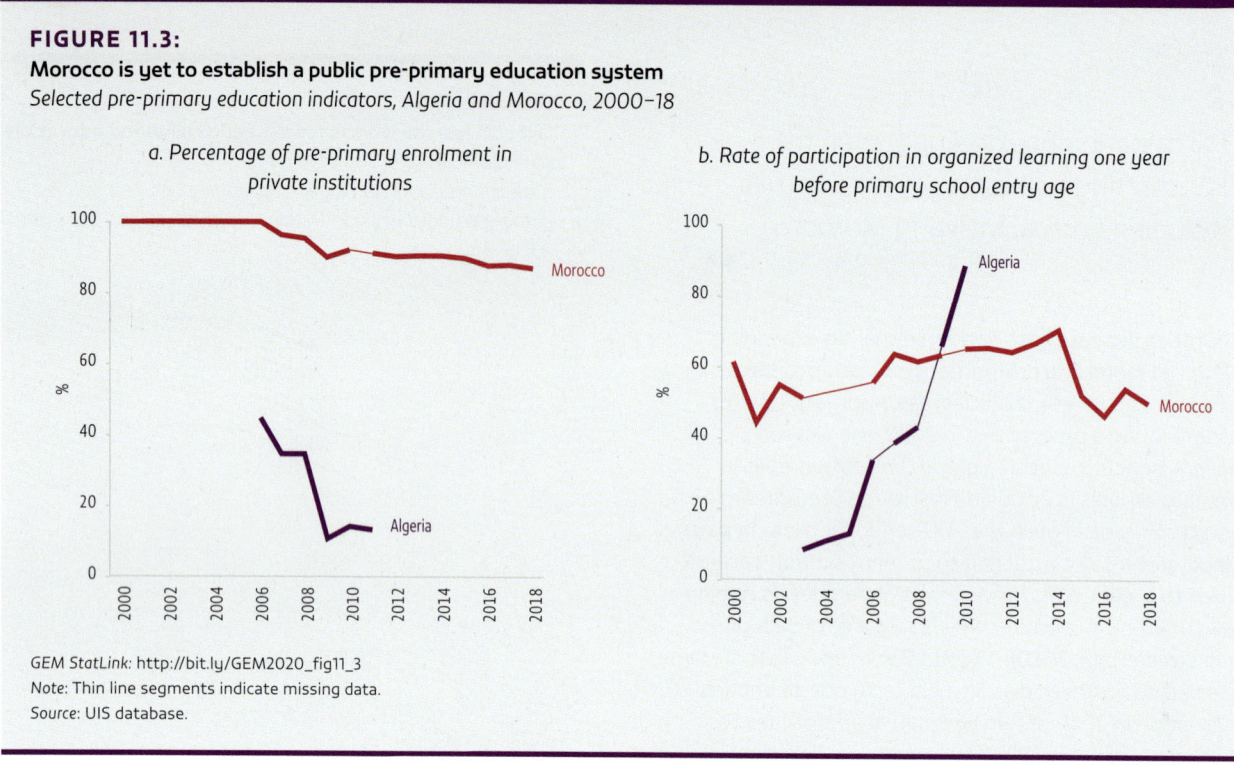

FIGURE 11.3:
Morocco is yet to establish a public pre-primary education system
Selected pre-primary education indicators, Algeria and Morocco, 2000–18

a. Percentage of pre-primary enrolment in private institutions

b. Rate of participation in organized learning one year before primary school entry age

GEM StatLink: http://bit.ly/GEM2020_fig11_3
Note: Thin line segments indicate missing data.
Source: UIS database.

programmes, which may begin at age 1. Among those that do, variation in enrolment within income groups is greater than for pre-primary education (**Figure 11.4**).

The distinction between early childhood education development programmes and pre-primary education is reflected in subcategories of level 0 in the International Standard Classification of Education (ISCED). The first covers younger children, generally up to age 2, and the second children from around age 3 to the start of primary school. In some high-income countries, certain kinds of provision for the younger cohort are an integral part of the national system but do not meet ISCED 0 criteria and are therefore not fully captured in the data. Across countries in the Organisation for Economic Co-operation and Development (OECD), 26% of children under 3 attend services classified as ISCED 0 and 10% attend other registered services, with shares of the latter including 32% in France, 27% in Japan and 59% in the Netherlands (OECD, 2019). By age 3, 77% attend institutions that meet ISCED 0 criteria and 3% other registered services.

EARLY CHILDHOOD DEVELOPMENT

Global indicator 4.2.1 is the percentage of children under age 5 developmentally on track in health, learning and psychosocial well-being. The indicator provisionally drew on the Early Childhood Development Index (ECDI) based on the Multiple Indicator Cluster Surveys (MICS). It measures the percentage of children on track in at least three of four domains. However, concerns over its validity led the Inter-agency and Expert Group on SDG Indicators (IAEG) to classify the indicator as tier III (no established methodology) and to ask UNICEF, as custodian agency, to develop a robust measure for children aged 24 to 59 months. In March 2019, the IAEG upgraded the indicator to tier II (established methodology, but countries do not regularly produce data). The United Nations Statistical Commission adopted the new methodology in March 2020.

Since 2015, UNICEF has systematically reviewed available tools; identified items that measure child development in the indicator's three domains; carried out cognitive

" Average early childhood education participation has been rising at a rate of just over two percentage points every five years "

FIGURE 11.4:
Few in poor countries benefit from pre-primary education

Gross enrolment ratios for early childhood education development and pre-primary education, 2018

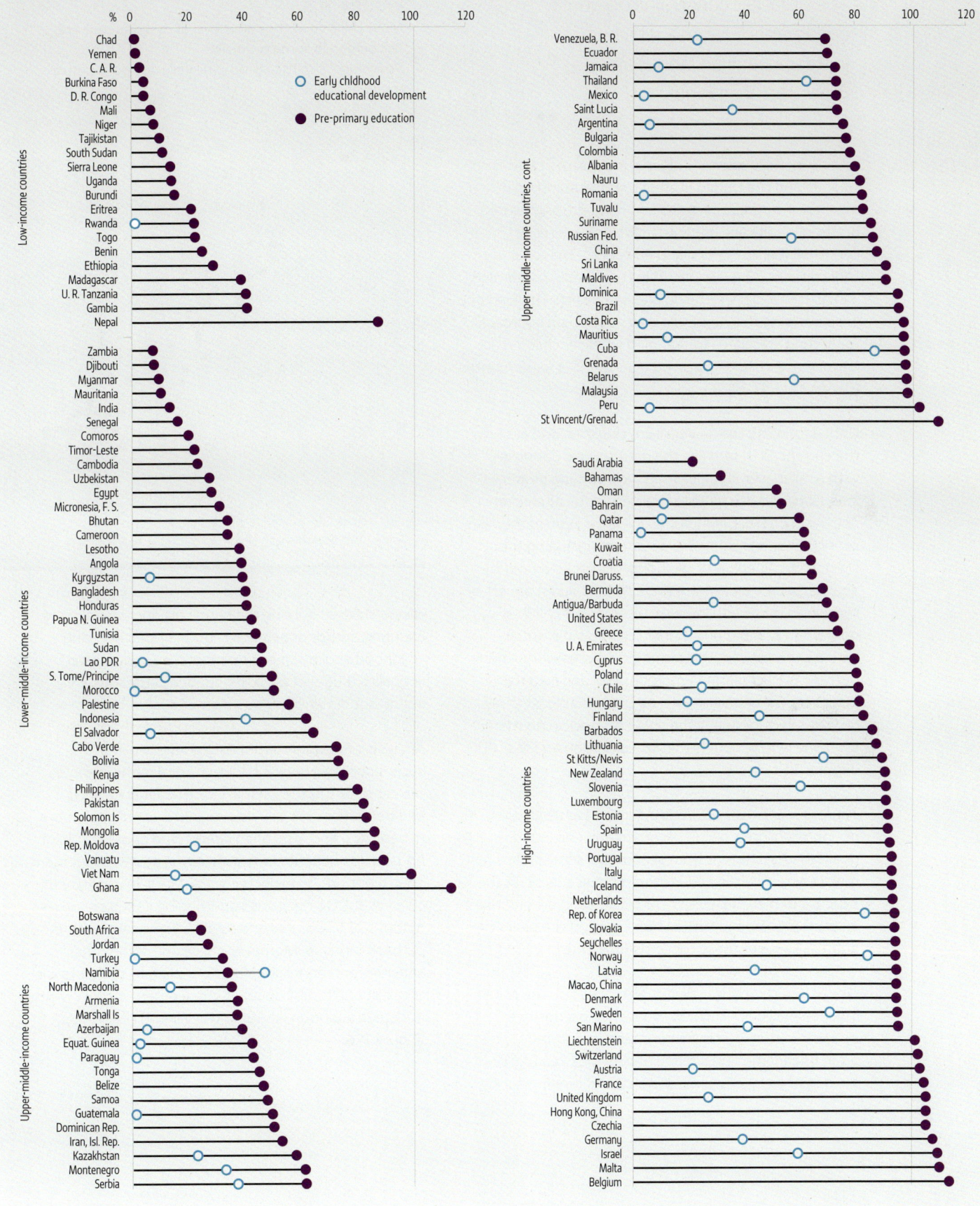

GEM StatLink: http://bit.ly/GEM2020_fig11_4

Source: UIS database.

> The greatest constraint on adult engagement is time, which is instead spent on labour and livelihood challenges

testing in six countries (Bulgaria, India, Jamaica, Mexico, Uganda and the United States) to understand how mothers interpret questions and respond; and piloted draft questions and administrative procedures in three countries (Belize, Mexico and Palestine). The resulting tool contains 20 questions: 11 in the domain of learning, 5 in psychosocial well-being and 4 in health. The last step in elaborating this new ECDI is to develop an approach for setting standards for defining whether children are 'developmentally on track' by ages 24, 36 and 48 months (Cappa et al., 2019).

Until data using the new tool are collected and analysed, the current ECDI remains the data source. Countries with similar overall values may have varying degrees of inequality and vary substantially in terms of children not being on track in multiple domains. Even in the countries with the poorest outcomes, including the Democratic Republic of the Congo, Guinea, Nigeria and Sierra Leone, no more than 2% of children are off track in all domains. However, the share of children on track in at most one domain can be substantial, with significant variation among countries with similar overall ECDI scores. In Cameroon, Mali and Nigeria, just over 60% of children are on track in at least three domains, but in Nigeria the share on track in no more than one is 10%, double that of Cameroon and Mali (5%) (**Figure 11.5**).

There is scepticism about standardized assessment of young children, partly because early childhood is qualitatively different from school age. Assessment may make early childhood education more academic at the expense of play. Australia deploys an early development instrument across all institutions every three years to address some of these concerns (**Box 11.1**).

One SDG 4 thematic indicator also draws on the MICS. The percentage of children experiencing a positive and stimulating home environment is captured by adult engagement in a range of activities: reading or looking at picture books; telling stories; singing songs;

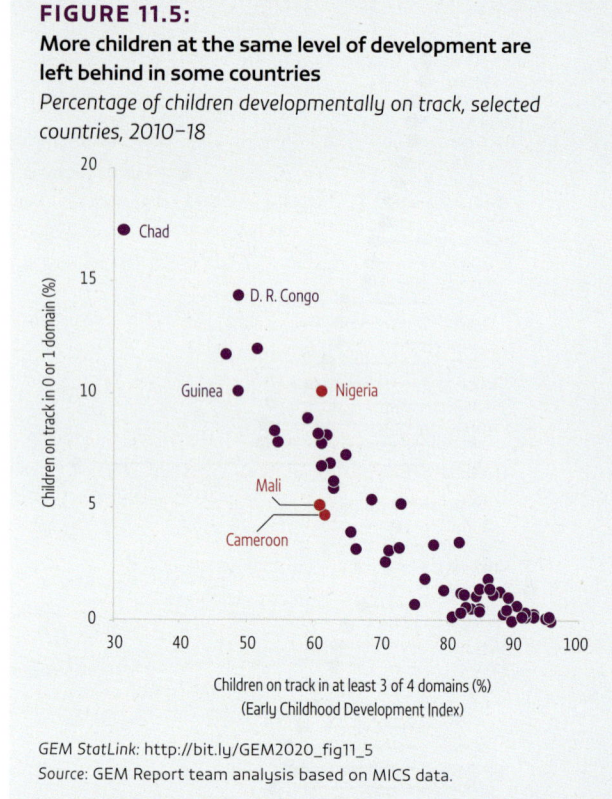

FIGURE 11.5:

More children at the same level of development are left behind in some countries

Percentage of children developmentally on track, selected countries, 2010–18

GEM StatLink: http://bit.ly/GEM2020_fig11_5
Source: GEM Report team analysis based on MICS data.

taking children outside the home; playing; and naming, counting and/or drawing. Although home and early childhood education environments are likely related in quality (Kuger et al., 2019), this indicator adds an important dimension.

Analysis of disaggregated data shows striking socio-economic gaps. Children from poor households are consistently the least likely to experience such adult engagement. In Paraguay, 90% of children in the richest 20% and 40% of children in the poorest 20% of households benefit from stimulating adult engagement. This might not be expected were it largely a matter of culture. But telling stories and singing songs are no less markers of traditional and rural than modern culture, perhaps more so. Moreover, these and some other activities are monetarily free. The pattern suggests the greatest constraint on adult engagement is time, which is instead spent on labour and livelihood challenges (**Figure 11.6**).

BOX 11.1:

Australia regularly assesses whether children are developmentally on track

The Australia Early Childhood Development Census (AECD) is a nationwide data collection tool that measures whether young children are developmentally on track when they start school (Boller and Harman-Smith, 2019). It was adapted from Canada's Offord Centre Early Development Instrument, which also informed the development of the new ECDI. The AECD has been implemented every three years since 2009. Coverage is universal. In 2015, data were collected for over 300,000 children, or 97% of the target group. Data for every child are collected by teachers but reported at community, state/territory and national levels. The 2018 round cost US$18 million, which included coordination, training and research support in and between data collection years.

The 2018 results show that the most disadvantaged children, e.g. those in remote areas, Aboriginal and Torres Strait Islanders and those with home languages other than English, are closing the developmental gap in three domains. Teachers work with a cultural consultant when completing the questionnaire to reflect the capabilities of children from historically marginalized communities.

A 2010 evaluation confirmed the AECD's promise as a tool to inform policy and programme design, improve early childhood development and help evaluate long-term strategies. It identified a need to contract complex aspects of delivery to specialists and strengthen community engagement and capacity. Key actions include intense groundwork to promote use of data in municipal and community decision making, ownership by local community and programme leaders, a uniform measure across communities, and key stakeholder and leader buy-in for scaling.

FIGURE 11.6:
Children from poor households do not receive as much stimulating adult engagement
Percentage of children experiencing a positive and stimulating home environment, selected countries, 2015–18

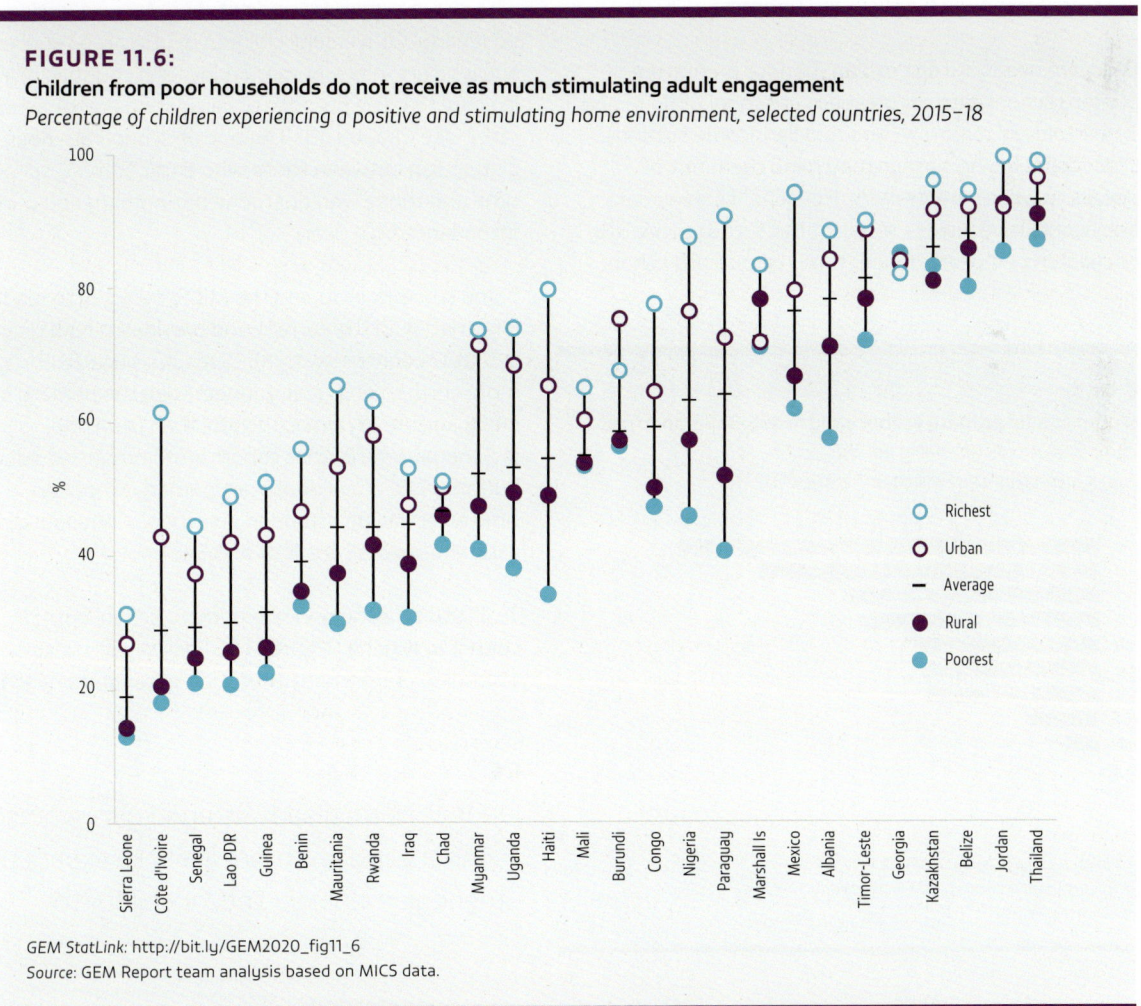

GEM StatLink: http://bit.ly/GEM2020_fig11_6
Source: GEM Report team analysis based on MICS data.

FOCUS 11.1: EARLY ENTRY IS MORE COMMON THAN BELIEVED

Target 4.2 aims to ensure that all children enjoy age-appropriate education opportunities before primary school, but assessment is hampered by the significant number who attend primary school early. Across 10 sub-Saharan African countries with age 7 entry, a significant number of 5-year-olds attend primary school (**Figure 11.7**).

Early school entry can be harmful. In Viet Nam, disadvantaged girls who start school early are more likely to experience teenage marriage and/or childbirth (Nguyen and Lewis, 2019). Under-age children are as likely to underperform as those over age, if not more so (Dyer et al., 2019). As with the problem of over-age enrolment (see **Chapter 10**), the standard of surveying attendance from age 5 may truncate the actual age distribution of enrolment. Surveys without this limitation show that primary school attendance may begin as much as three years early (Barakat and Bengtsson, 2017).

Childcare needs are one explanation for premature primary school entry or presence at school of 5-, 4- and 3-year-olds in some low- and middle-income settings. Older schoolgoing siblings may mind them out of necessity while parents work. Household survey data are inconclusive: Across 17 recent MICS, the probability of children one year younger than the primary school

entry age attending primary rather than pre-primary education is higher in some countries for children with a sibling in primary school, but lower in others. Selection effects operate in two directions. Children with no primary school-age siblings are more likely to come from smaller and likely wealthier families and to be the first born. Children with siblings in the relevant age range who are out of school are more likely to live in disadvantaged areas with no pre-primary provision.

Early school entry statistics reveal little about the transition between levels. As a matter of policy, whether primary school-age children without pre-primary education should attend preschool first is open to question.

Children one year younger than the primary school entry age count towards global indicator 4.2.2, regardless of whether they attend pre-primary or primary education. The indicator does not distinguish between children who attend both in sequence at the expected ages and those who skip pre-primary and enter primary education a year early. Conversely, children of primary school entry age who are in pre-primary education count as being in school for the purpose of calculating out-of-school rates (see Chapter 10). The out-of-school rate does not distinguish between those who enter primary school on time and those who postpone pre-primary and primary attendance by a year.

Some surveys, including the MICS, collect attendance information in the current and previous school year. In 9 of 17 countries with MICS results since 2015, more children one year younger than the primary school entry age are in primary school than preschool. In Senegal, 64% of that cohort are in organized education, but only 19% of children start primary school on time after having attended preschool. Corresponding estimates in Mali are 90% and 5%.

To illustrate, early and late primary school entry coexist in Nigeria (**Figure 11.8**). Basically all those attending pre-primary education enter primary school,

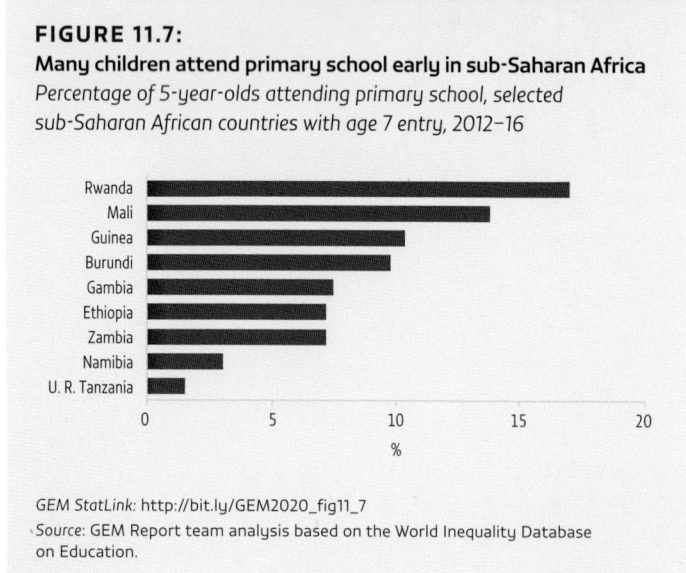

FIGURE 11.7:
Many children attend primary school early in sub-Saharan Africa
Percentage of 5-year-olds attending primary school, selected sub-Saharan African countries with age 7 entry, 2012–16

GEM StatLink: http://bit.ly/GEM2020_fig11_7
Source: GEM Report team analysis based on the World Inequality Database on Education.

> 66
>
> In Viet Nam, disadvantaged girls who start school early are more likely to experience teenage marriage and/or childbirth
>
> 99

FIGURE 11.8:

In Nigeria, 12% of children start school on time with pre-primary education

School experience among children one year before and at primary school entry age, Nigeria, 2016

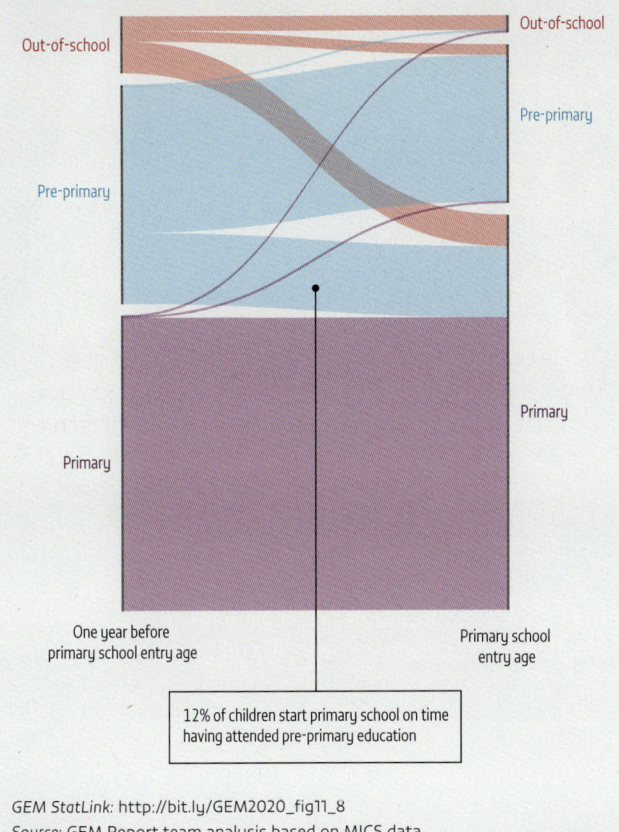

12% of children start primary school on time having attended pre-primary education

GEM StatLink: http://bit.ly/GEM2020_fig11_8
Source: GEM Report team analysis based on MICS data.

although not necessarily immediately: Two-thirds at primary school entry age remain in pre-primary education. A majority of primary school-aged children without pre-primary education enter primary school. Thus, although a large majority attend organized learning one year before primary school entry age, a small minority represent the ideal of on-time primary school entry with pre-primary education.

One approach to improving the situation of primary school-aged children who have not previously attended pre-primary education is accelerated school readiness: Ethiopia's programme offers 150 hours over the summer months prior to entry (UNICEF, 2019).

System-wide recommendations depend on analysis of differences in average outcomes between the two pathways. This requires information on learning outcomes at a higher grade, age upon entering primary school, and pre-primary education attendance. Case-by-case considerations determine which pathway is more appropriate. Some systems are moving away from age-based entry and progression in early grades towards pooled reception grades, which offer flexibility in entrance age and time at a stage before progressing. The approach is practiced in some German states and was recently proposed in Canada's New Brunswick province (Sweet, 2019).

Nur (yellow scarf), 16 years old, prepares her tools while attending a workshop on installing and repairing solar panels that are ubiquitous in Kutupalong-Balukhali mega-camp, Cox's Bazar, Bangladesh.

CREDIT: UNICEF/Brown

KEY MESSAGES

New data show adult education and training participation rates in the previous month to be 1% for low-, 2% for lower-middle-, 3% for upper-middle- and 16% for high-income countries; and, in the previous 12 months, 11% for upper-middle- and 48% for high-income countries.

In OECD countries, adults with high skills are three times as likely to participate in training as adults with low skills: 58% vs 20%.

In the EU, almost 60% of adults do not participate in adult learning because they see no need for it. Cost and inconvenient training schedules or locations are pressing institutional barriers. Lack of time and family responsibilities are common situational barriers, especially for women.

The 2015 Mandela rules guarantee the right of 10.7 million prisoners to education but there are hardly any data to monitor fulfilment. Access to education in US prisons would save governments US$366 million per year in incarceration costs.

Global participation in tertiary education reached 224 million in 2018, equivalent to a gross enrolment ratio of 38%.

In Northern Africa and Western Asia, tertiary education participation has expanded rapidly and gender parity has been reached, but country paths differ. In Tunisia, enrolment rates have stagnated, while gender disparity has grown at men's expense.

CHAPTER 12

TARGET 4.3

Technical, vocational, tertiary and adult education

By 2030, ensure equal access for all women and men to affordable and quality technical, vocational and tertiary education, including university

---

GLOBAL INDICATOR

4.3.1 – *Participation rate of youth and adults in formal and non-formal education and training in the previous 12 months, by sex*

THEMATIC INDICATORS

4.3.2 – *Gross enrolment ratio for tertiary education by sex*

4.3.3 – *Participation rate in technical-vocational programmes (15- to 24-year-olds) by sex*

TECHNICAL, VOCATIONAL AND ADULT EDUCATION

Under the Belém Framework for Action and in line with the 2015 Recommendation on Adult Learning and Education, the fourth *Global Report on Adult Learning and Education* (GRALE) combines policy reviews with quantitative data analyses and case studies. The report finds insufficient progress in adult education. Almost one-third of countries with data report participation rates below 5%; one-quarter report between 5% and 10%. Participation increased the slowest or not at all among marginalized groups, including adults with disabilities. In all, 152 of 198 countries responded to the GRALE survey. Of those, 103 reported participation rates based on actual figures rather than estimates. As GRALE is a quadrennial survey, other sources are used for routine annual reporting (UIL, 2019).

Global indicator 4.3.1 captures the rate of youth and adult participation in formal and non-formal education and training in the previous 12 months, by sex. For 2019, estimates based on the International Labour Organization's database of labour force surveys were included for the first time to monitor the indicator, increasing coverage from 45 to 106 countries, of which 70 have been added since 2015. As the *Global Education Monitoring Report 2017/8* noted, survey alignment with the indicator is imperfect. Challenges include lack of standardization in adult education and training questions and variation in age range (e.g. adult being defined as age 15+ or 18+). Variation in reference period is the most consequential issue. The indicator's 'previous 12 months' is inspired by the EU Adult Education Survey (AES), one of only two cross-national surveys dedicated to adult education, alongside the Organisation for Economic Co-operation and Development (OECD) Programme for the International Assessment of Adult Competencies (PIAAC). Many labour force surveys use a shorter reference period, usually one month.

For participation rates calculated for different reference periods to be comparable, the distribution of training duration, participation in multiple activities within the same 12-month period, and seasonal effects must be known. The reference period correlates with overall participation level, further complicating comparison: The 12-month measure is largely limited to high-income countries. Across 71 countries, the median adult education participation rate with the previous month as the reference period is 1% for low-, 2% for lower-middle-, 3% for upper-middle- and 16% for high-income countries. With the previous 12 months as the reference period, it is 11% for upper-middle- and 48% for high-income countries (**Figure 12.1**). It is important not to mix data for different reference periods.

Some countries show considerable gender gaps in adult education and training, regardless of reference period. Female participation rates exceed male rates in Baltic (e.g. by 14 percentage points in Estonia, 9 in Latvia) and Scandinavian countries (e.g. by 12 percentage points in Finland, 9 in Sweden) (Eurostat, 2019). A potential reason is gender segregation in education and employment. Too few males attend tertiary and vocational education and training in health, education and welfare: 9% in Estonia and 16% in Finland, well below the EU average of 23% (European Institute for Gender Equality, 2019). In addition, these countries have above-average labour market gender segregation by occupation and/or by sector (Burchell et al., 2014). Women are more likely to work, for instance, as nurse and healthcare assistants and/or in the public sector, where opportunities for training are higher.

> **"**
> Some countries show considerable gender gaps in adult education and training
> **"**

FIGURE 12.1:

Estimates of participation in adult education vary according to the reference period

Percentage of adults who participated in formal or non-formal adult education, by reference period, 2018 or most recent year

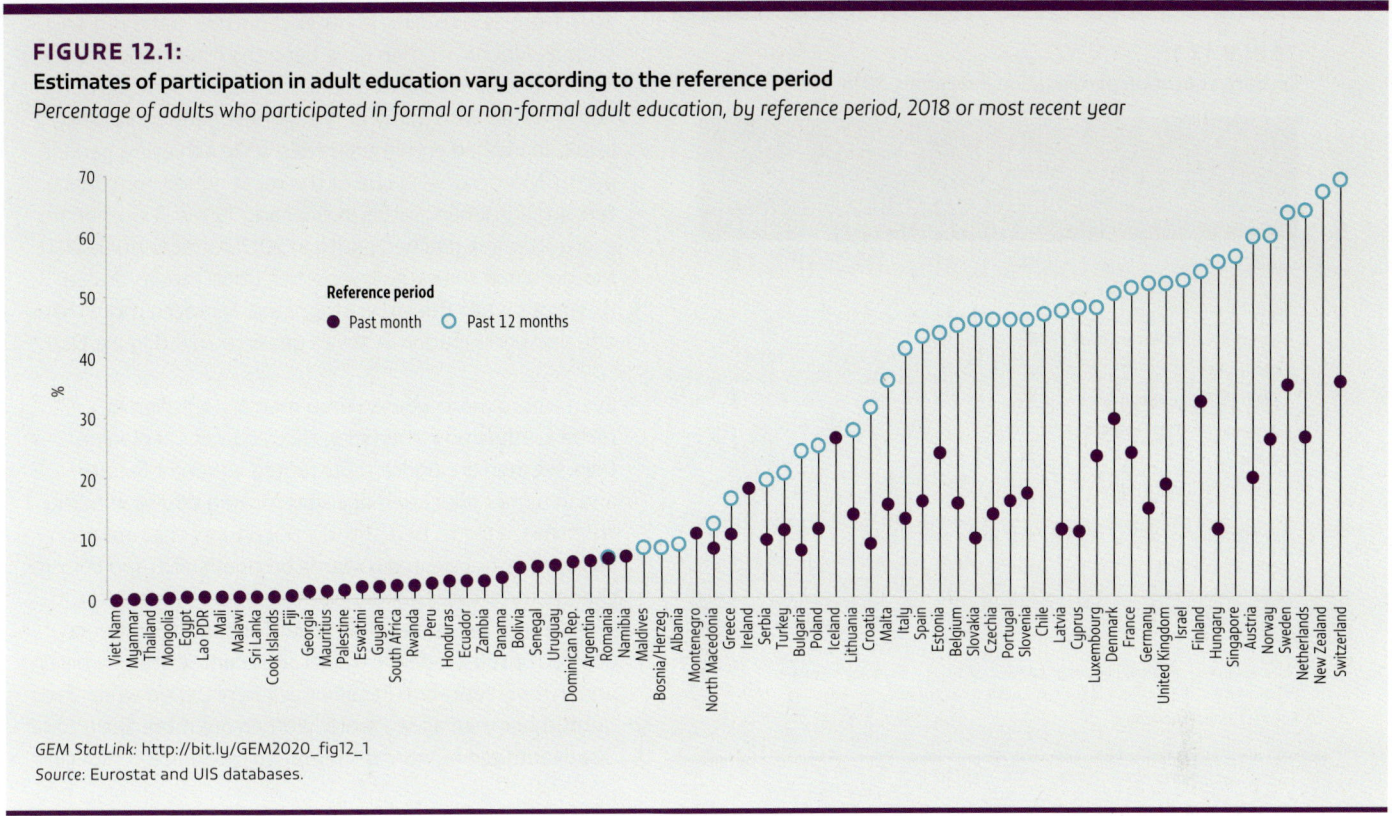

GEM StatLink: http://bit.ly/GEM2020_fig12_1

Source: Eurostat and UIS databases.

More work is required to achieve consistent disaggregation of indicator 4.3.1 by socio-economic status across surveys. In OECD countries, adults with high skills are three times as likely to participate in training as adults with low skills: 58% vs 20% (OECD, 2019a). Those in low-skill occupations are less likely to have to upgrade skills. Disadvantaged young people may be less likely to perceive themselves as learners outside school and to seek opportunities, which feeds a cycle of education disadvantage (Wikeley et al., 2009). A review of OECD countries' adult training systems' capacity showed that they struggled to reach under-represented groups, including the unemployed, migrants and adults with low education attainment, especially in the context of challenges such as ageing populations, globalization and digitalization. Inadequate finances constrain most systems. Other obstacles include low quality and relevance of training and inadequate skills assessment and governance mechanisms (OECD, 2019a).

Labour force surveys are a key source of data on adult learning opportunities, indicating the dominant role of work-related training. Some observers argue for renewed attention to the social construction of inequality and related barriers to adult participation in education (Rubenson, 2018). For instance, difference in time availability affects male vs female participation (**Focus 12.1**). Prisoners, a vulnerable group, may have more time than the general population, yet prison education is often a lost opportunity (**Focus 12.2**).

TERTIARY EDUCATION

Global participation in tertiary education reached 224 million in 2018, equivalent to a gross enrolment ratio of 38%. Shares ranged from 9% in low-income to 75% in high-income countries. Globally, 19% of tertiary students are enrolled in short-cycle programmes (International Standard Classification of Education [ISCED] 5), 68% in bachelor's degree programmes (ISCED 6), 11% in master's (ISCED 7) and 1% in doctorate (ISCED 8). Eastern and South-eastern Asia has the highest share enrolled in short-cycle programmes (33%); Europe and Northern America has the highest in master's (20%) (**Table 12.1**).

Northern Africa and Western Asia have had among the most rapid expansions of tertiary education participation since 2013. Yet country experiences vary. Tunisia had among the highest participation rates as recently as 2010 but has since stagnated at around 35%. Saudi Arabia enrolment rates more than doubled between 2009 and

TABLE 12.1:
Tertiary education participation indicators, 2018

	Gross enrolment ratio (%)	Share of students enrolled in tertiary education (%)			
		ISCED 5	ISCED 6	ISCED 7	ISCED 8
World	**38**	**19**	**68**	**11**	**1**
Sub-Saharan Africa	9	20	70	9	2
Northern Africa and Western Asia	46	19	71	9	1
Central/S.Asia	26	3	83	13	1
Eastern and South-eastern Asia	45	33	61	6	1
Latin America and the Caribbean	52	10	84	5	1
Oceania	73	26	57	14	3
Europe and Northern America	77	21	56	20	3
Low income	9	8	82	8	1
Lower middle income	25	6	83	11	1
Upper middle income	53	28	63	7	1
High income	75	21	58	18	3

Note: ISCED 5 = short-cycle programmes; ISCED 6 = bachelor's degree programmes; ISCED 7 = master's; ISCED 8 = doctorate.
Source: UIS database.

2017, from 32% to 70%. In other countries in the region, such as Algeria, women have been the main beneficiaries of rapid increases in tertiary education enrolment. By contrast, Saudi Arabia, with some of the highest gender disparity levels, increased enrolment levels while achieving gender parity. Morocco, with one of the most gender-unequal tertiary enrolment ratios in the early 1990s (3 women for every 10 men), reached parity in 2017. As recently as 2011, Morocco had the same low participation rate as Sudan (16%), but while the latter stagnated, Morocco more than doubled participation in seven years to 36% (**Figure 12.2**).

Even where more women than men are enrolled in tertiary education, they may face an unequal playing field. Women are under-represented as senior faculty and in higher education decision-making bodies in many countries, a signal of institutional cultures that are not inclusive or not geared towards broader social and cultural change for greater gender equality. Conventional faculty recruitment processes that reward linear, full-time, uninterrupted academic trajectories contribute to women's under-representation in senior academia, even when they outnumber men as students. Women are more likely to be disadvantaged by norms that fail to recognize competing

FIGURE 12.2:
Not all countries experience rapid expansion of tertiary education
Tertiary education indicators, selected Northern African and Western Asian countries and regional averages, 1990–2018

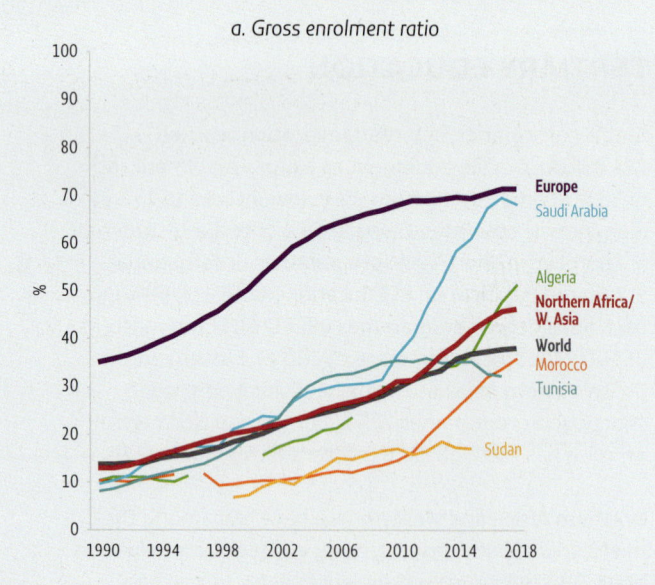

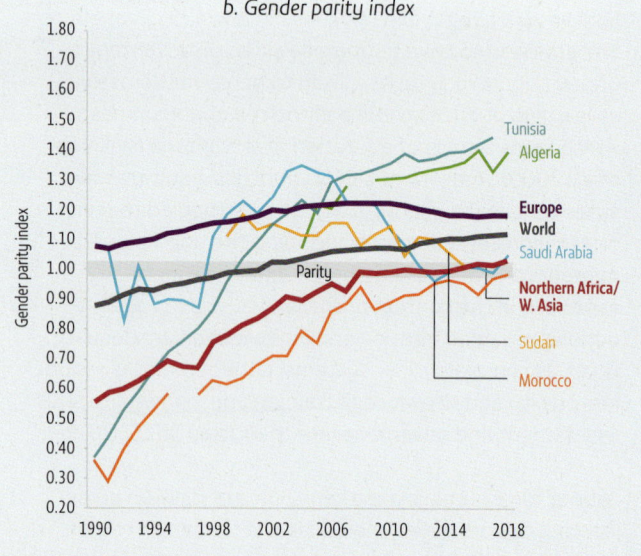

GEM StatLink: http://bit.ly/GEM2020_fig12_2
Source: UIS database.

> " Women are under-represented as senior faculty and in higher education decision-making bodies in many countries "

commitments, such as care responsibilities. In 2010, Australia's Group of Eight leading universities embraced the principle of merit relative to opportunity in faculty recruitment and assessment (Rafferty et al., 2010). The approach encourages a holistic, multidimensional evaluation of academic achievement beyond a narrow focus on number of publications, and takes into account career breaks, other commitments and individual circumstances. Official EU guidance endorses incentives and, if necessary, legal sanctions to encourage use of gender quotas and targets in universities (European Commission, 2018).

Inclusive assessment of merit should apply to students. Poor students in the United States score lower on standardized university admission tests (Perry, 2019). As a countermeasure, a company responsible for one such test introduced a numerical adversity score based on neighbourhood and school socio-economic factors (Escobar, 2019). However, just as academics' career breaks cannot be assessed by how many publications having a baby is 'worth' (Klocker and Drozdzewski, 2012), this measure was withdrawn in recognition that disadvantage cannot be fairly measured by a single number (Hartocollis, 2019).

Disadvantaged young people face multiple obstacles in gaining access to tertiary education, including information and networking barriers. Counsellors and advisers are particularly important for these learners, yet minorities, students with disabilities, those living in rural or poor areas and other disadvantaged students are often the least likely to receive adequate counselling on higher education opportunities (**Box 12.1**).

Even when provided with information and support, members of groups under-represented at universities are less likely to know how to game the system. Wealthy parents in the United States spend significant energy and resources on university admission, giving rise to illegal admission scandals, backdoor admission and surrogate test-takers

BOX 12.1:

Disadvantaged youth need more support to enter tertiary education but receive less

As part of a general support system, counsellors can play an important role in steering young people towards tertiary education. However, services are often not targeted where needed. In the United States, students who benefit from one-on-one counselling are more than three times as likely to attend college and almost seven times as likely to apply for financial aid. Yet too few students benefit: The median number of students per counsellor is 455, nearly twice the recommended 250:1 ratio (American School Counselor Association, 2019; Chrisco Brennan, 2019). Spatial distribution of access to counsellors is inequitable. College guidance is often inadequate or non-existent in rural secondary schools. However, virtual models are emerging to fill the gap. College Possible's Navigate programme combines counselling via phone, text and email. A pilot by College Advising Corps, a non-profit organization, relies on videoconferencing (Friess, 2019). In New York City, college students may act as near-peer counsellors (Gonser, 2019).

Access to counsellors is even more limited in France, particularly in more disadvantaged areas, with a ratio of 1,200:1 in some secondary schools (Mayer, 2019). A high workload limits advisers' time with students and ability to provide academic guidance. A 2018 survey by the national council that evaluates education policy showed that half of 18- to 25-year-olds were dissatisfied with the counselling received in secondary school and did not feel supported by the institution at this critical stage. By contrast, in Finland, counselling is part of learning starting in primary education. Lower secondary students receive two hours of compulsory counselling per week with specialist teachers, who coordinate company visits, occupational films and individual interviews with students and parents on areas of interest (Hoibian and Millot, 2018).

Recognizing and accepting diversity is an important challenge. Counsellors' perceptions, sociocultural biases and gender stereotypes can affect students' education and career choices (US Department of Education, 2018). This may explain some of women's under-representation in tertiary science, technology, engineering and mathematics. An online random survey of high school counsellors in the US state of Wisconsin found that, even though they believed female students outperformed males in mathematics and were more likely to succeed, they were less likely to recommend mathematics over English to female students (Welsch and Windeln, 2019). White counsellors may underestimate the quality of historically black colleges and universities and fail to make appropriate recommendations to black students (Miller, 2020).

In-service training and continuing education can help counsellors identify and correct discriminatory guidance. In school districts with large minority student populations, counsellors are trained in early identification and support for students with potential for tertiary education. Other interventions seek to support underprepared college-oriented students. College access programmes, for instance, may encourage disadvantaged grade 9 minority students to be more ambitious in their choice of classes in order to meet college admission requirements (US Department of Education, 2018).

(Robbins, 2019; Tough, 2019). Parents in a 2019 national college admission fraud paid bribes for forged test scores and sports qualifications for elite university entry. The fraud also involved cheating on standardized admission tests by faking eligibility for extra time reserved for those with learning disabilities or with physical or mental impairments (Durkin, 2019). Such abuse of inclusive education policies victimizes intended beneficiaries by undercutting support for legitimate accommodation (Golden and Burke, 2019; Juneja, 2019).

Student precarity is rising as the number of marginalized students in tertiary education grows. In late 2019, French students protested for more affordable housing, food and health services (RFI, 2019). In the United States, around half of undergraduates are reportedly food insecure, and up to one in five housing insecure (Broton and Goldrick-Rab, 2017). More than one-quarter of university students have dependent children (Institute for Women's Policy Research, 2014). Less than one-third of single mothers graduate within six years of enrolment (Institute for Women's Policy Research, 2018).

FOCUS 12.1: ADULTS FACE MULTIPLE BARRIERS IN PURSUING EDUCATION OPPORTUNITIES

Analysing barriers to adult education and learning requires a clear framework. The PIAAC survey refers to barriers as factors preventing adults from participating in formal or non-formal education. Only non-participants in education are asked these questions; those already participating are not asked what prevented them from further increasing their participation. By contrast, the AES distinguishes between those not interested in education or training and those willing to participate, and investigates barriers to participation among the latter.

How barriers are categorized matters. A long-standing categorization (Cross, 1981) describes factors preventing participation as situational (e.g. life circumstances, such as family responsibilities or lack of time), dispositional (e.g. determined by previous learning experiences and personal disposition towards learning) and institutional (e.g. structural conditions hampering access, such as cost, lack of support, rigid schedules or limited provision) (UIL, 2019).

> Student precarity is rising as the number of marginalized students in tertiary education grows

Dispositional barriers are generally less investigated in surveys and thus underestimated (Rubenson, 2011). Yet, when measured, they are the strongest factor hindering adult learning in most countries (**Figure 12.3**). On average, across EU countries, almost 60% of respondents do not participate in adult learning mainly because they see no need for it. Cost and inconvenient training schedules or locations are the most pressing institutional barriers. Lack of time and family responsibilities are the most common situational barriers, according to both PIAAC and AES data.

Analysis of complementary PIAAC evidence for this report supports or extends these findings. Respondents in Greece and Turkey are most affected by situational barriers. Lack of time was a recurring concern in Japan, the Republic of Korea and Singapore, where respondents reported being too busy at work. In terms of institutional barriers, training cost prevented between 25% and 30% of adults in Greece, Israel and Slovenia from participating; in Finland, around one in five cited inconvenient locations or schedules.

France stands out in terms of lack of employer or public service support, with only slight improvement between the 2011 and 2016 AES rounds. This is despite the Compte Personnel de Formation (Personal Training Account), a programme introduced in 2014 that allows employees to convert accumulated time credits into grants, as well as training leave, part-time work or early retirement. Financial incentives only partly address the barriers. They need to be combined with non-financial instruments, such as counselling services and information awareness campaigns (OECD, 2019b).

While men were slightly more likely to mention scheduling as a barrier, women in all countries except Denmark were far more likely to mention family responsibilities (**Figure 12.4**). The tendency is higher in southern Europe, with up to two-thirds of female respondents in some countries unable to participate for this reason.

FIGURE 12.3:
Negative previous learning experiences discourage many adults from participating in adult education
Distribution of main barriers to adult education participation among non-participants, selected European countries, 2016

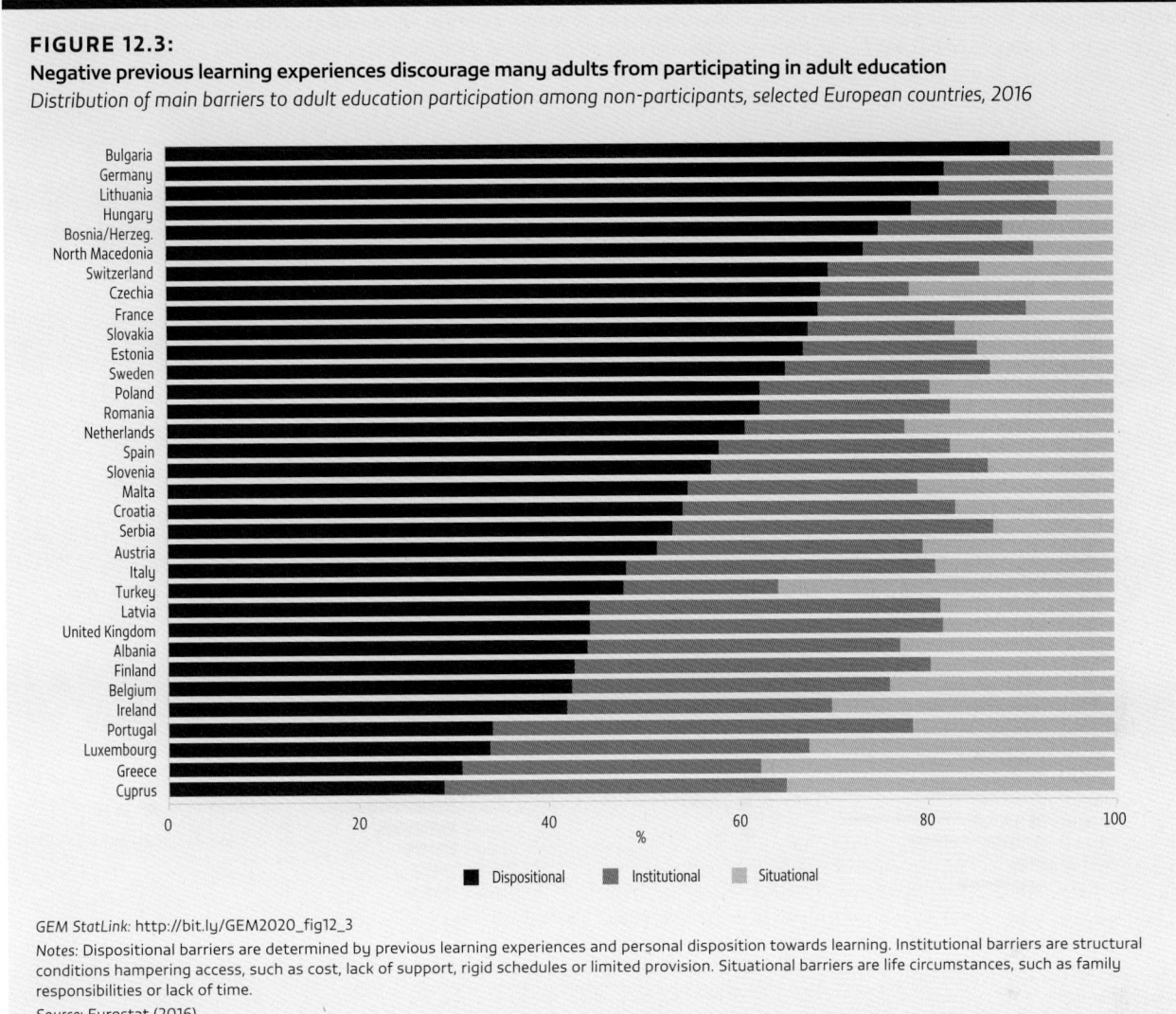

GEM StatLink: http://bit.ly/GEM2020_fig12_3

Notes: Dispositional barriers are determined by previous learning experiences and personal disposition towards learning. Institutional barriers are structural conditions hampering access, such as cost, lack of support, rigid schedules or limited provision. Situational barriers are life circumstances, such as family responsibilities or lack of time.
Source: Eurostat (2016).

A comparative study based on 14 time-use surveys and 5 household surveys in 19 countries found that men allocated slightly more time to learning, leisure and social activities. Albania, Ghana, Pakistan and the Republic of Moldova reported the highest gender imbalances: Ghanaian women spent almost two hours per day less than men on such activities (Rubiano-Matulevich and Viollaz, 2019). Women were more likely to see cost as an obstacle but less likely to have scheduling conflicts, probably reflecting their lower labour force participation and higher part-time employment rates.

FOCUS 12.2: PRISON EDUCATION IS A RIGHT AND AN INVESTMENT

An estimated 10.7 million people were in penal institutions in 2018. The 10 countries with the highest prison populations were the United States (2.1 million), China (1.7 million), Brazil (690,000), the Russian Federation (583,000), India (420,000), Thailand (364,000), Indonesia (249,000), Turkey (233,000), the Islamic Republic of Iran (230,000) and Mexico (204,000) (Walmsley, 2018). There are no global data on prisoner access to education or success of prison education programmes.

FIGURE 12.4:

Women in European countries were almost twice as likely as men not to participate in adult education for family-related reasons

Adults citing family responsibilities and course schedules as barriers to participation in adult education, by sex, selected European countries, 2016

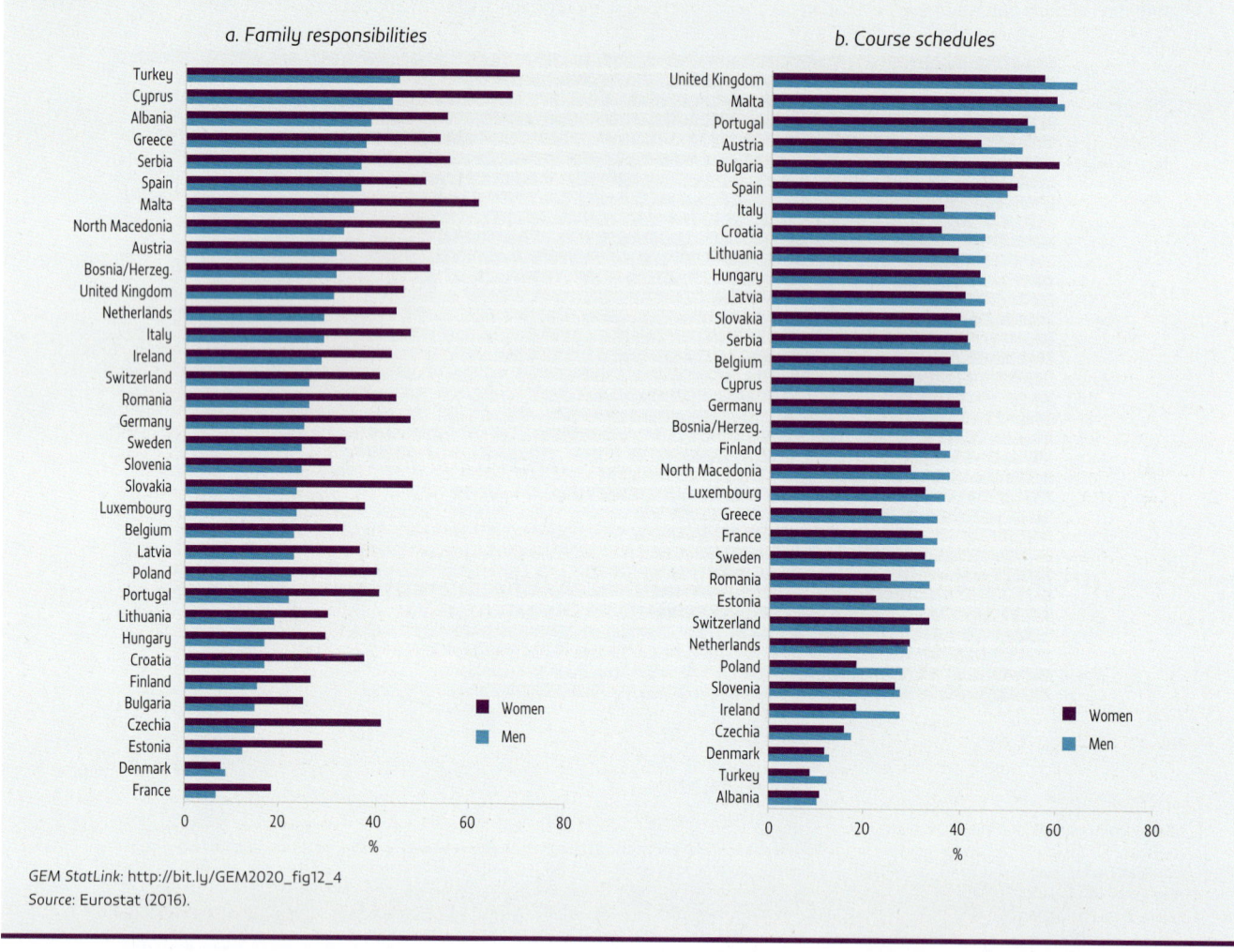

GEM StatLink: http://bit.ly/GEM2020_fig12_4
Source: Eurostat (2016).

Multiple arguments support prisoners' right to education (Vorhaus, 2014). The Standard Minimum Rules for the Treatment of Prisoners, adopted in 1955 and approved through United Nations Economic and Social Council resolutions in 1957 and 1977, were revised and relaunched in 2015 as the Mandela rules. These maintain the original reference to prisoners' right to education, vocational guidance and training, namely that 'the education of prisoners shall be integrated with the educational system of the country so that after their release they may continue their education without difficulty' and that 'the education of illiterates and young prisoners shall be compulsory' (UNODC, 2015). The rules have guided national legislation. For instance, India's National Prison Manual maintains that the '[e]ducation of illiterate adolescents and adult prisoners shall be compulsory'

and attempts to link prison education with mainstream education (India Ministry of Home Affairs, 2003).

Beyond being a right, prison education has important benefits for prisoners, prisons and societies. An opportunity to learn skills and gain work experience helps prisoners stay away from crime after release. It can support order, safety and security in prisons, making them more positive environments (UNODC, 2017). Studies show that higher education levels correlate with lower recidivism rates (Farley and Pike, 2018). A meta-analysis in the United States found that prison education reduced probability of recidivism by 13 percentage points. Increased chance of employment is a key factor, with vocational education having twice the effect of other education types (Davis et al., 2013).

> " A meta-analysis in the United States found that prison education reduced probability of recidivism by 13 percentage points "

A recent study estimates that access to prison education saves state governments an estimated US$366 million per year in incarceration costs (Oakford et al., 2019).

National prison systems struggle to cater for varied needs. Prisoners are disproportionately likely to come from challenging social backgrounds, have had limited or no education and struggle with literacy: 10% of prisoners in Guinea are reportedly literate (Prison Insider, 2019). Disadvantage in prison education is associated with age, sex and disability. A review in England (United Kingdom) found that providing programmes meeting the whole range of individual needs was a complex challenge (Coates, 2016).

Young prisoners are likelier to have access to education. A review of adolescent prisoners in eight Latin American and Caribbean cities found that 70% attended some kind of formal education programme (UNICEF and Universidad Diego Portales, 2017). By contrast, less than one-quarter of all prisoners in most European countries participated in education and training (Costelloe et al., 2012). Female prisoners in India are entitled to education, but provision is largely limited to basic literacy instruction, and tailored provision is necessary for self-study (India Ministry of Women and Child Development, 2018). In the United Kingdom, 32% of new prisoners were recorded or self-reported as having learning difficulties or disabilities in 2014/15 (Coates, 2016). According to the European Prison Rules, '[e]very prison shall seek to provide all prisoners with access to educational programmes which are as comprehensive as possible and which meet their individual needs while taking into account their aspirations' (Council of Europe, 2006). Yet programmes meeting the needs of prisoners with disabilities are often lacking (Council of Europe, 2018).

A recent UNESCO study advances the transformative potential of prison libraries. These provide access to reading material and information, including legal information and support for formal qualification, leading to improved literacy and a culture of reading and lifelong learning. Brazil enables sentence reduction based on reading; participants can submit up to 12 book reviews per year to earn 48 days of remission (Krolak, 2019). Prison libraries may be subject to arbitrary censorship, however. More than 15,000 titles are banned from prison libraries in the US state of Texas, including prizewinning fiction and political biographies (Schaub, 2016). Sign language learning materials are banned because they could enable prisoners to communicate without drawing guards' attention (Miller, 2016).

Funding is one of the biggest challenges prisoners face. In 1994, US prisoners were banned from receiving Pell grants, the main form of federal student aid, until a 2015 pilot initiative reinstated access (Nadworny, 2019).

Online and distance learning can facilitate access. An estimated 80% of prisoners in Kenya and Uganda have never met with a lawyer (Gertz, 2017). The African Prisons Project gives prisoners access to distance law courses at British universities (Sawahel, 2017). Incarcerated students in Nigeria receive a 50% tuition fee discount at the National Open University (Farley et al., 2016). For prisoners without regular or frequent internet access, this is an obstacle to distance learning. Australia's University of Southern Queensland introduced Making the Connection, which offers courses and programmes loaded on notebooks or servers rather than rely on hard copy or the internet (Sawahel, 2017).

Governments around the world have introduced prison education programmes. Singapore's Digitalisation of Inmate Rehabilitation and Corrections Tool gives inmates tablets not only to maintain contact with family but also to access books and e-learning sources and to study towards a diploma (Justice Trends, 2019). In Europe, Prison Education: Basic Skills and Blended E-Learning aims to improve prison education by making basic skills learning easily accessible (Torlone and Vryonides, 2016). In the United States, the Incarceration Nations Network partners with organizations, correctional facilities and universities to create Prison-to-College Pipelines. Based on this model, South Africa's Ubuntu Learning Community, established in partnership with Stellenbosch University and the Department of Correctional Services, provides access to public university-level education (Lindeque, 2018).

Many initiatives rely on non-government organizations and volunteers. In England (United Kingdom), the Shannon Trust has supported prisoners teaching prisoners to read in 124 prisons (Moss, 2017). Almost all prisons in the US state of California provide face-to-face tertiary education classes taught by educators from nearby universities, including for inmates serving life sentences (D'Orio, 2019).

In Cochabamba, Bolivia, an 11-year-old girl uses from the computer lab in a school supported by Save the Children.

CREDIT: SCUS/Save the Children

KEY MESSAGES

ICT skills are important for work but unequally distributed. The use of basic formulas in spreadsheets, one of nine skills monitored, is possessed by 7% of adults in lower-middle-income countries, 20% in 19 upper-middle-income countries and 40% in high-income countries.

Recent disaggregated data on spreadsheet skills from 10 poorer countries show large disparities by age; by gender (at women's expense in low- and lower-middle-income countries and at men's expense in upper-middle-income countries); and, especially, by wealth: for instance, 3% of women from the poorest quintile had this skill vs 35% from the richest in Suriname and 39% in Mongolia.

New ICT skills to be monitored in coming years will include the abilities to set up effective security measures to protect devices and accounts and to change privacy settings for personal data.

In Europe, ICT skills are acquired relatively less through workplace training: Only 10% of respondents took part in on-the-job ICT training in 2018. Rather, skills are developed through free online training and/or self-study, especially among the young.

Over 90% of entrepreneurs in Africa and the Arab States and over 80% in Asia and the Pacific are in the informal sector. They require entrepreneurship training tailored for microenterprises with limited growth prospects.

CHAPTER 13

TARGET 4.4

Skills for work

By 2030, substantially increase the number of youth and adults who have relevant skills, including technical and vocational skills, for employment, decent jobs and entrepreneurship

---

GLOBAL INDICATOR

4.4.1 – *Percentage of youth/adults with information and communications technology (ICT) skills, by type of skill*

THEMATIC INDICATORS

4.4.2 – *Percentage of youth/adults who have achieved at least a minimum level of proficiency in digital literacy skills*

4.4.3 – *Youth/adult educational attainment rates by age group and level of education*

Target 4.4 captures learning that prepares youth and adults to participate in the world of work. It refers to 'decent jobs and entrepreneurship' (**Focus 13.1**), but the variety of labour market contexts and required job skills covered makes monitoring global progress difficult.

In addition to youth and adult literacy and numeracy skills, captured in target 4.6, technology-related skills increasingly affect work life. Digital skills in particular are a desirable outcome of education and a factor enabling access to it, helping overcome spatial inequality in provision (Xie et al., 2017). Global indicator 4.4.1 is an indirect measure of computer-related skills in use of information and communication technology (ICT). Household survey respondents report whether they carried out any of nine activities in the previous three months, from copying or moving files or folders to connecting and installing new devices.

Although the number of countries reporting ICT skills data has increased since the indicator became part of the SDG monitoring framework, two problems affect monitoring. First, the number of low- and middle-income countries reporting is still insufficient for robust regional estimates. Existing data nevertheless demonstrate wide disparity in ICT skills distribution. The median share of adults who used a basic arithmetic formula in a spreadsheet is 7% in 10 lower-middle-income countries, 20% in 19 upper-middle-income countries and 40% in 41 high-income countries. Second, analysis of trends in ICT skills is limited by a change in methodology that means only figures since 2015 are comparable. Even since then, however, some large year-on-year changes can be observed that are difficult to explain. Averaging available data over 2015–17 to smooth fluctuations shows that skills such as handling spreadsheets and sending messages with attachments are highly correlated (**Figure 13.1**).

Individual-level data are not available in the International Telecommunication Union (ITU) and UNESCO Institute for Statistics (UIS) databases. The databases nevertheless make it possible to infer disparity in ICT skills distribution within countries by comparing the number of skills a proportion of adults have. Some middle-income countries rank much higher in number of skills possessed by at least 20% of adults, suggesting an elite minority (**Figure 13.2a**). Skills are more evenly distributed in countries such as Denmark and Norway, where at least half of adults have those six skills (**Figure 13.2b**).

The sixth round of the Multiple Indicator Cluster Surveys includes a module with questions on the nine ICT skills. The data, yet to be included in the ITU and UIS databases, cover adults aged 15 to 49 and allow disaggregation of skills by individual characteristics. Clear gender patterns emerge across 10 countries administering the questions: Women in the seven low- and lower-middle-income countries are less likely to have used, for instance, a basic arithmetic formula in a spreadsheet while parity exists in the three upper-middle-income countries. Young women in Mongolia, Suriname and Tunisia are even slightly more likely than men to have this skill. These three countries also have a distinctive age profile, showing the rapid pace of ICT adoption by the younger generation (**Figure 13.3**).

The surveys show wide socio-economic disparity in distribution of basic ICT skills. In seven poorer countries, the probability of women in the poorest 60% having the spreadsheet skill is below 1%. In the three richer countries, 3% of women from the poorest quintile had this skill vs 27% in the richest in Tunisia, 35% in Suriname and 39% in Mongolia (**Figure 13.4**).

In 2019, the ITU, as co-custodian agency of global indicator 4.4.1, reviewed and adjusted the nine ICT skills questions. It reformulated four skills descriptions to broaden their scope. For instance, sending emails with

> "
> The number of low- and middle-income countries reporting on ICT skills is still insufficient for robust regional estimates
> "

> ❝
> In seven low- and lower-middle-income countries, the probability of women in the poorest 60% being able to do basic arithmetic in a spreadsheet is below 1%
> ❞

attachments was expanded to sending any message with attachments. The ITU dropped the most widely practiced basic skill: copying or moving files or folders. It added two skills: setting up effective security measures to protect devices and accounts, and changing privacy settings to limit sharing of personal data or information. The changes are not expected to be reflected in reported data for a few years but will likely make interpreting some trends more difficult.

How people acquire skills is a key question. EU ICT surveys, which help monitor Digital Single Market Strategy implementation, offer insight into the relative importance of acquisition at school, work and home. Despite the relevance of ICT skills for work, training opportunities are not predominantly part of professional development. Analysis of Eurostat data for this Report shows that 10% of respondents had on-the-job training in 2018. One in five adults participated in at least one general activity to improve computer, software and application expertise. Skills acquisition mainly occurs via free online training and/or self-study, especially among the young: 25- to 29-year-olds are twice as likely to seek online training as 55- to 64-year-olds.

FIGURE 13.1:

The prevalence of information and communication technology skills is highly correlated

Percentage of adults possessing eight basic ICT skills, selected countries, 2015–17

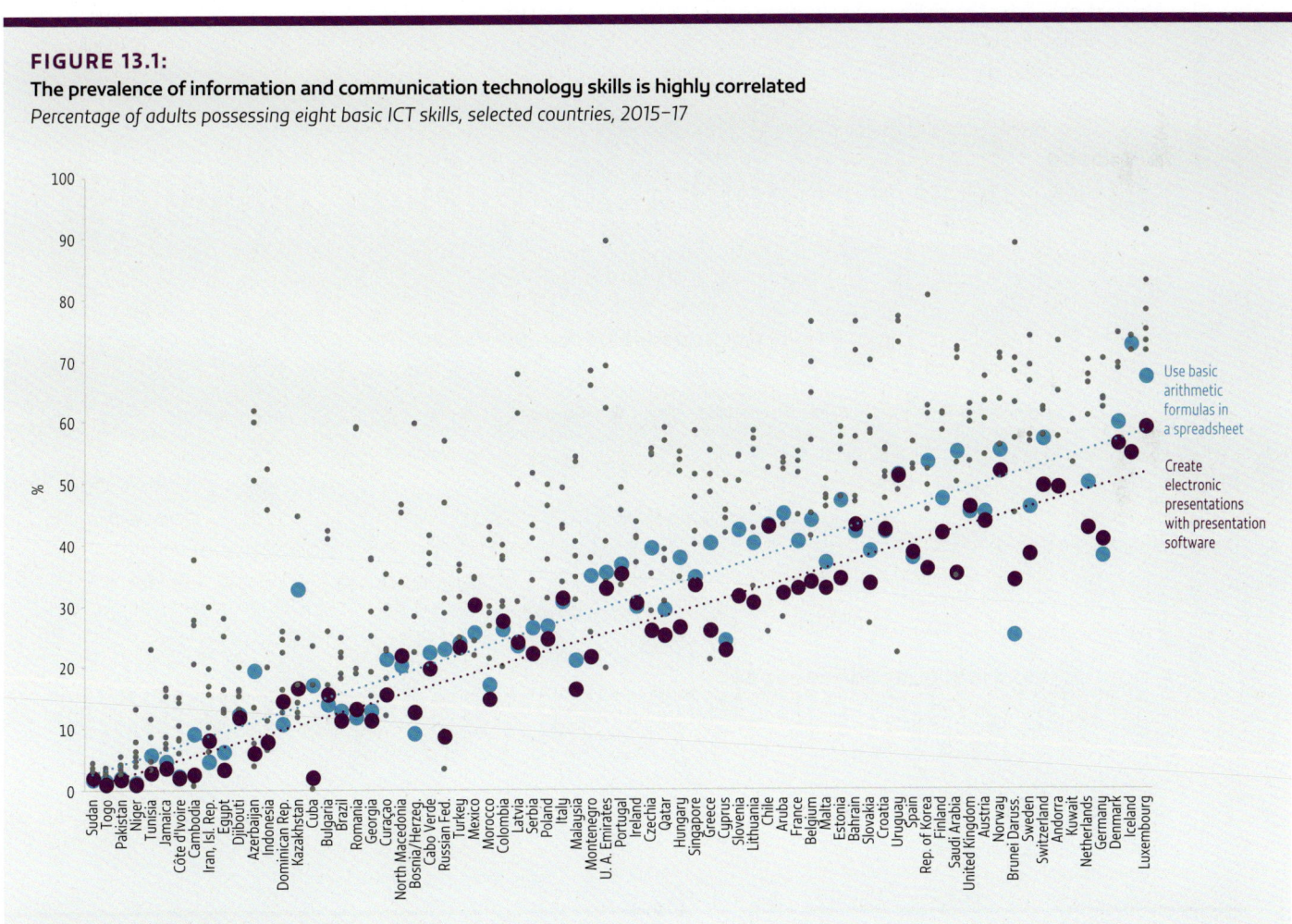

GEM StatLink: http://bit.ly/GEM2020_fig13_1

Notes: Countries are ordered according to median value of reported ICT skills. One of the nine skills in the indicator definition is not included (write a computer program using a specialized programming language). The two lines are linear trends for two of the eight skills.

Sources: ITU and UIS databases.

"
Despite the relevance of ICT skills for work, training opportunities are not predominantly part of professional development
"

FIGURE 13.2:
Most adults lack most information and communication technology skills in most countries
Number of basic ICT skills, selected countries, 2015–17

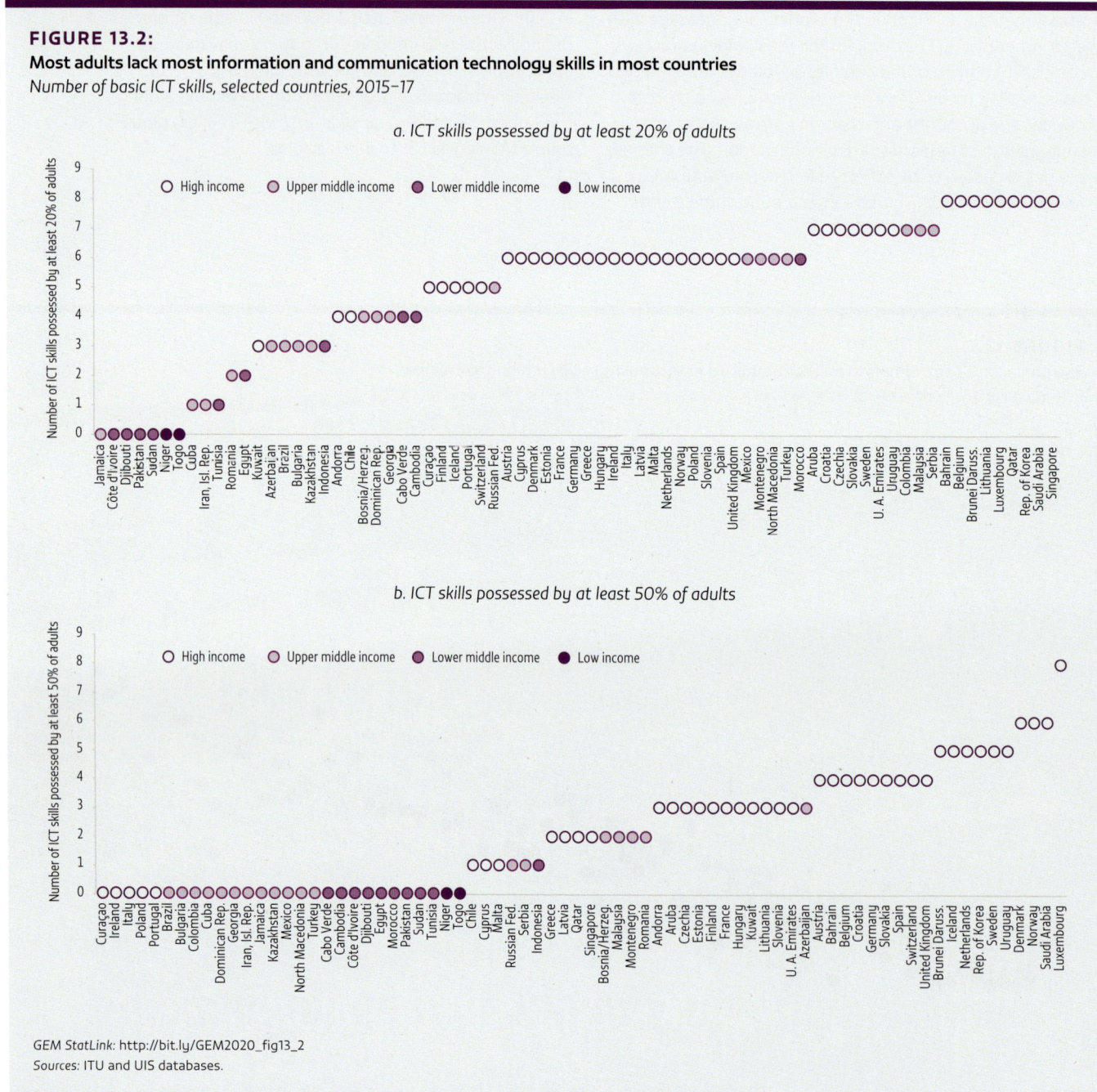

a. ICT skills possessed by at least 20% of adults

b. ICT skills possessed by at least 50% of adults

GEM StatLink: http://bit.ly/GEM2020_fig13_2
Sources: ITU and UIS databases.

FIGURE 13.3:

Women in low- and lower-middle-income countries are less likely to have basic information and communication technology skills

Percentage of 15- to 49-year-olds who used a basic arithmetic formula in a spreadsheet, selected countries, by age and sex, 2017–19

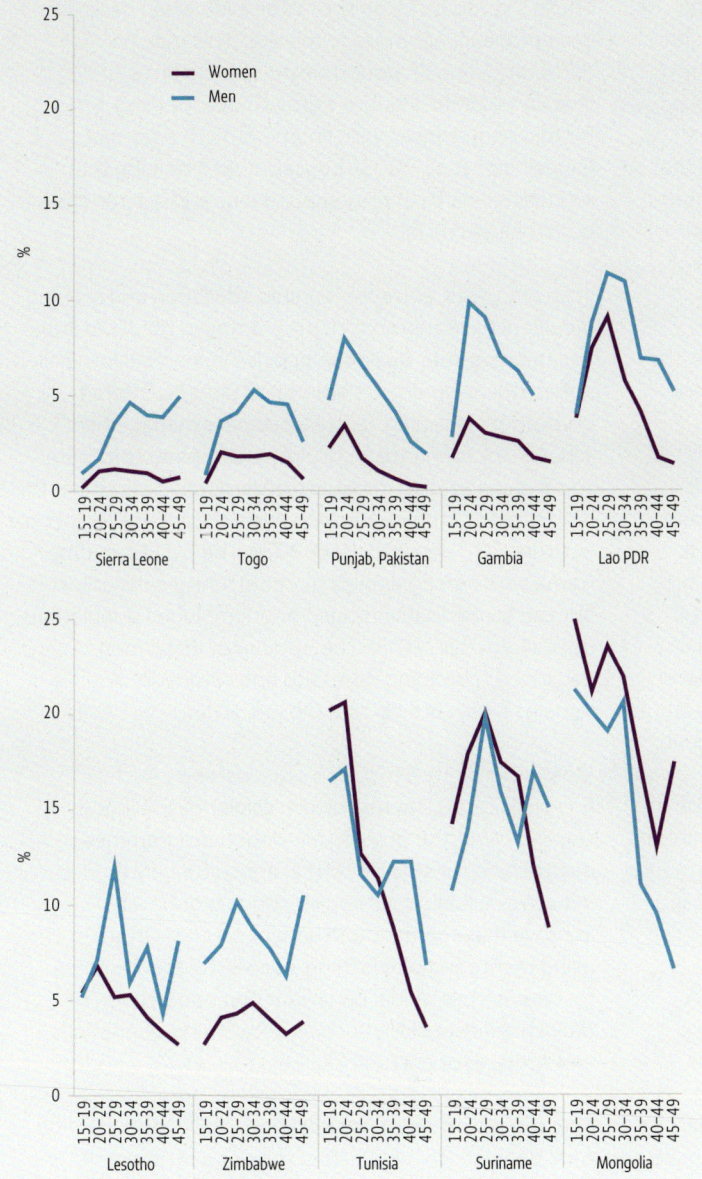

FIGURE 13.4:

There is wide socio-economic disparity in distribution of basic information and communication skills in upper-middle-income countries

Percentage of 15- to 49-year-old women who used a basic arithmetic formula in a spreadsheet, selected countries, by wealth, 2017–19

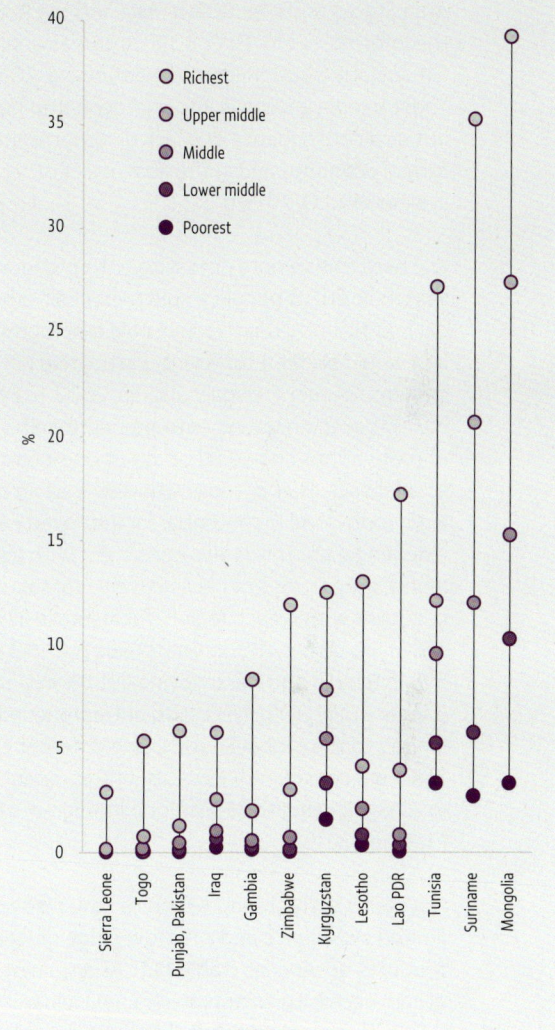

GEM StatLink: http://bit.ly/GEM2020_fig13_3
Source: MICS Survey Findings Reports.

GEM StatLink: http://bit.ly/GEM2020_fig13_4
Note: Mongolia, Suriname and Tunisia are upper-middle-income countries. The others are low- and lower-middle-income countries.
Source: MICS Survey Findings Reports.

FOCUS 13.1: NECESSITY ENTREPRENEURSHIP HAS SKILLS IMPLICATIONS

Entrepreneurship and associated skills encompass a spectrum of businesses, from high-tech start-ups to bakeries and tea stalls. For many of the 3.4 billion people living on less than US$5.50 per day (World Bank, 2018), entrepreneurship is not a choice. Unlike opportunity entrepreneurs, survival or necessity entrepreneurs do not build on innovative business ideas that create value and jobs. Over 90% of entrepreneurs in Africa and the Arab States and over 80% in Asia and the Pacific are in the informal sector (ILO, 2018). International Labour Organization (ILO) Recommendation No. 204 noted that 'most people enter the informal economy not by choice but as a consequence of a lack of opportunities in the formal economy and in the absence of other means of livelihood' (ILO, 2015, p. 2).

It is hard to estimate necessity entrepreneurship, as 'the vast majority of people would prefer self-employment over sufficiently unattractive paid employment and would prefer a sufficiently attractive job over self-employment' (Jayachandran, 2020, p. 24). A global review based on young entrepreneurs' self-assessment of motivations showed that about one-quarter saw it as a fallback. Half of those who saw it as an opportunity were motivated by potential for improved earnings or independence. This is also consistent with a pattern of higher proportions of necessity entrepreneurs in poorer countries within each region, for instance 32% in India but 11% in Singapore, 41% in Guatemala but 16% in Uruguay, 51% in Bosnia and Herzegovina but 5% in Denmark (Singer et al., 2015). Necessity entrepreneurship is not limited to the Global South. Using different criteria, about 31% were considered necessity entrepreneurs in Germany in 2013–17, rising to 38% among immigrants (Leifels and Metzger, 2019).

Necessity entrepreneurs tend to have less education, limited experience and a narrow range of ideas for products or services (**Table 13.1**). As a training target group, necessity entrepreneurs are 'vulnerable, unemployed or inactive individuals' who are potential entrepreneurs or 'informal or micro and small enterprise owners' (Valerio et al., 2014, p. 34). Needed skills depend on context. Necessity entrepreneurs tend to copy existing business activities and need both business and cognitive skills to avoid entering unprofitable activities (Webb and Fairbourne, 2016).

> "
> Education and training that include necessity entrepreneur needs and aspirations are crucial
> "

Many policies and programmes do not differentiate between necessity and opportunity entrepreneurs. Those that do focus on the latter, even when necessity entrepreneurs are more numerous. This may be deliberate; many favour training to build firms that can sustain economic growth over training for microenterprises with limited growth potential (Lingelbach et al., 2005). Education and training that include necessity entrepreneur needs and aspirations are nonetheless crucial.

In recent years, entrepreneurship education and training providers have customized programmes. The ILO's Start and Improve Your Business includes vulnerable low-skilled potential entrepreneurs among its targets. Offered in vocational training centres, business management schools, microfinance institutions, company corporate social responsibility initiatives or remotely, it is one of the largest programmes, reaching more than 10 million people between 2011 and 2015 (ILO, 2017). The EU EntreComp framework mostly applies to opportunity entrepreneurs but can serve disadvantaged or unemployed populations (McCallum et al., 2018). The number of institutions dedicated to training necessity entrepreneurs at scale remains small (Brewer and Gibson, 2016).

Most programmes focus on practical skills, such as financial literacy for microloan recipients, livelihood training as part of poverty alleviation programmes, and training for small, informal agriculture enterprises. Initiatives usually focus on starting up or how to improve management and administration. Often using mentoring or coaching, successful programmes foster entrepreneurial behaviour and opportunity or growth mindset skills, such as networking, aspiration, and spotting opportunities.

The non-government organization PRIDE in rural Bangladesh administers skills and attitudes training for income-generating activities to women. It provides marginalized women opportunities to meet entrepreneurs and develop peer and community networks to exchange information and advice. Building social capital through training influences aspirations, mindset and confidence, empowering entrepreneurs within their communities (Cummings et al., 2019).

TABLE 13.1:
Profiles and education needs of necessity and opportunity entrepreneurs

Characteristics	Necessity entrepreneurs	Opportunity entrepreneurs
Primary driver	'Push factors' of economic survival	'Pull factors' of personal satisfaction, wealth accumulation and employment creation
Skill level	Generally unskilled	Skilled
Education level	Low	At least secondary school education; may have attended university
Starting a business	Unfamiliar with bureaucratic formalities	Familiar with bureaucratic formalities
Location	Rural and urban areas	Primarily urban areas
Employment	Often self-employed	Employer
Financial resources	Extremely limited; at best, supported by microfinance or family loans	Often have some; unqualified for microfinance; may leverage resources with bank loans
Growth potential	Limited	High
Nature of business	Small retail or other unskilled services	Retail or wholesale skilled services, import/export, light manufacturing
Appropriate entrepreneurship education and training programmes	Entrepreneurship training in specialized institutions, vocational training centres, finance institutions or as part of development programmes (employment, financial literacy, microfinance, livelihood training, women's empowerment); greater focus on finance and business management than entrepreneurial mindset	Entrepreneurship education and training in specialized or tertiary education institutions; focus on more advanced finance and business development topics and entrepreneurial mindset (e.g. leadership, spotting opportunities, managing risks)
Examples	Start and Improve Your Business (ILO, global) FINCA International (global) Economic Empowerment of Adolescent Girls and Young Women (Liberia) Academy for Creating Enterprise (Philippines) Women's Organisation (United Kingdom) SFEDI Passport to Enterprise and Employment, qualification programme in prisons (United Kingdom)	Ministry of Employment, Technical Education and Vocational Training (Madagascar) National curriculum entrepreneurship module (Montenegro) Auchi Polytechnic School of Business (Nigeria) Institute of Entrepreneurship (South Africa) Lancaster University Enterprise Education Development (United Kingdom) Embedding Entrepreneurship Education Teaching Toolkit (selected European countries and Australia)
	Both types of entrepreneur	
	Brazilian Micro and Small Enterprise Support Service IMKAN GO and IMKAN GROW (with UNIDO Entrepreneurship Curriculum Programme/EU EntreComp) (Egypt)	

Source: GEM Report team analysis based on Mersha et al. (2010).

The Brazilian Micro and Small Enterprise Support Service, a non-profit known by its Portuguese acronym, SEBRAE, designed and delivers entrepreneurial training programmes focusing on practical skills and mindset, combined with support such as loans and an online interactive library with information on norms and legislation. In 2013, SEBRAE trained 4.9 million people online and over 10 million face to face. Content and type of class, lecture or workshop are customized to local needs and vary by region and stage of business development (Roberts and Myrrha, 2016).

In the Philippines, the Academy for Creating Enterprise offers necessity entrepreneurs an eight-week residential model and an on-site training programme. Training relies heavily on case studies and 'discovery learning'. The case study approach encourages discussion and multiple solutions to business problems, developing not only financial and technical but also problem-solving skills (Brewer and Gibson, 2016).

Gender dynamics matter in microenterprise business management, especially in contexts of household inequality. Ghanaian women hid income and savings, and limited business growth, to ensure husbands' continued responsibility as providers and to plan long-term household consumption. Entrepreneurship training requires additional focus on gender empowerment in such settings (Friedson-Ridenour and Pierotti, 2018).

Scalable training for entrepreneurial mindset skills remains rare. An alternative approach is to focus on opportunities that rely on business skills over innovative thinking, e.g. supporting micro-franchising and entrepreneurial education on running specific, proven business models in context. Micro-franchise entrepreneurs benefit from a clear blueprint and mentoring and technical training. However, the difficulty of building and managing supply chains limits scalability, especially for non-profit organizations seeking employment and poverty alleviation through micro-franchising (Webb and Fairbourne, 2016).

Shumi, 16 years old, who avoided
early marriage, sits on a bed reading a
book at home in Sylhet, Bangladesh.
Shumi benefited from a Save the Children
project funded by UK aid.

CREDIT: Tom Merilion/Save The Children

KEY MESSAGES

Global gender parity figures are easy to communicate but can miss those left furthest behind through intersecting disadvantages. Lower secondary completion rates are 28% in Côte d'Ivoire and Rwanda, but 2% among poor rural females in the former and 10% in the latter.

Measures of disparity by wealth typically compare the poorest and richest 20% of households. But poorer households tend to have more children. In India, the poorest households have 25% of all children, compared with 15% for the richest.

The MICS household survey uses best practice in disability measurement based on functional difficulties but differentiated between children aged 5 to 17 and adults age 18 and above. In Sierra Leone, disability prevalence falls from 16.6% among 17-year-olds to 0.3% among 18-year-olds, hampering the interpretation of education indicators that straddle these age groups.

Single-sex schools are an exception in most education systems but gender segregation in separate classes or schools is common in countries as diverse as Chile, Ireland, Israel and Singapore and is prevalent in many Muslim-majority countries.

While self-identification is the predominant approach, Latin American countries also use other criteria to measure indigenous identity in surveys. In Mexico, 30% identify as indigenous, while 9% are identified as such through official criteria and 6% on the basis of language.

CHAPTER 14

TARGET 4.5

Equity

By 2030, eliminate gender disparities in education and ensure equal access to all levels of education and vocational training for the vulnerable, including persons with disabilities, indigenous peoples and children in vulnerable situations

---

GLOBAL INDICATOR

4.5.1 – *Parity indices (female/male, rural/urban, bottom/top wealth quintile and others such as disability status, indigenous peoples and conflict-affected, as data become available) for all education indicators on this list that can be disaggregated*

THEMATIC INDICATORS

4.5.2 – *Percentage of students in primary education whose first or home language is the language of instruction*

4.5.3 – *Extent to which explicit formula-based policies reallocate education resources to disadvantaged populations*

4.5.4 – *Education expenditure per student by level of education and source of funding*

4.5.5 – *Percentage of total aid to education allocated to least developed countries*

Globally, there is gender parity in pre-primary through secondary education enrolment (**Table 14.1**). However, averages hide continuing country-level gender disparity. In one-quarter of low-income countries, for every 100 males, fewer than 87 females are enrolled in primary education and fewer than 60 in upper secondary, at which level only 25% of countries have achieved parity. While there is full information on gender enrolment gaps, there is little information on gender enrolment segregation in single-sex schools (**Focus 14.1**).

Global gender parity figures across education levels are easy to communicate but insufficient for identifying those left furthest behind. Intersecting disadvantage severely affects education opportunities of children and youth. In low-income countries, females from the poorest 20% of households are consistently less likely to progress: 12 poor women attend post-secondary education for every 100 poor men. The ratio is much more favourable, although still not equal, for the richest women. In lower-middle-income countries,

up to secondary education completion, the poorest females experience a similar if smaller gap. But their relative chances improve in post-secondary education, reflecting the fact that average disparity at that level is at the expense of men in all but low-income countries (**Figure 14.1**).

How far countries let the most disadvantaged fall behind is evident in country rankings for a given education indicator, such as completion, and its value for the most disadvantaged group by sex, location and wealth (usually the poorest rural females). The average lower secondary education completion rate is around 28% in Côte d'Ivoire and Rwanda, but while completion is close to zero among the most disadvantaged in the former, the latter, although still low in absolute terms, does better at 10%. Completion is marginally higher in Cameroon (43%) than Cambodia (41%), but it drops by 41 percentage points for the most disadvantaged in Cameroon, compared with a 25 point drop in Cambodia. Similarly, Nepal does better than the Philippines (**Figure 14.2**).

TABLE 14.1:
Adjusted gender parity index of gross enrolment ratio, by education level, 2018 or latest available year

	Pre-primary	Primary	Lower secondary	Upper secondary	Tertiary
World	**0.98**	**1.00**	**0.99**	**0.98**	**1.16**
Sub-Saharan Africa	0.99	0.96	0.90	0.84	0.74
Northern Africa and Western Asia	0.99	0.96	0.93	0.96	1.03
Central and Southern Asia	0.94	1.08	1.04	0.96	1.00
Eastern and South-eastern Asia	0.99	1.00	1.01	1.03	1.20
Latin America and the Caribbean	1.01	0.98	1.01	1.10	1.43
Oceania	0.98	0.97	0.90	0.90	1.69
Europe and Northern America	0.99	1.00	0.99	1.00	1.39
Low income	1.00	0.94	0.87	0.80	0.62
Lower middle income	0.96	1.03	1.02	0.96	1.05
Upper middle income	1.00	1.00	1.00	1.05	1.25
High income	1.00	1.00	0.97	1.00	1.33

Source: UIS database.

FIGURE 14.1:

Poverty exacerbates gender disparity in education

Median gender parity index, by education level, low- and lower-middle-income countries, 2013–18

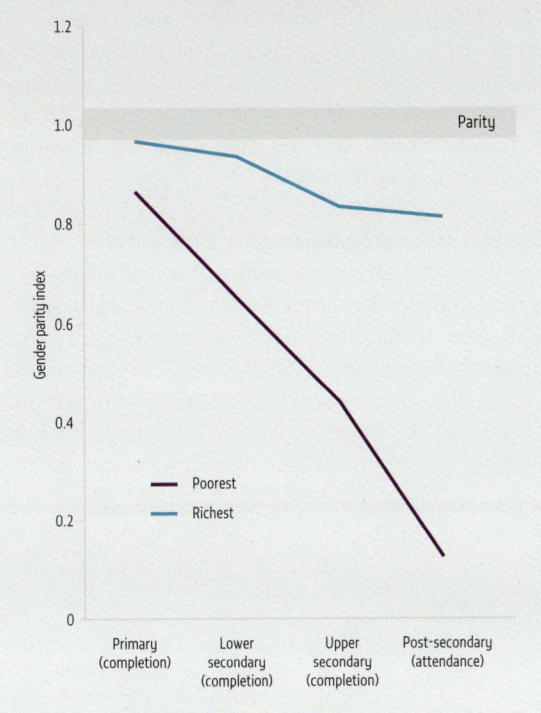

Low-income countries

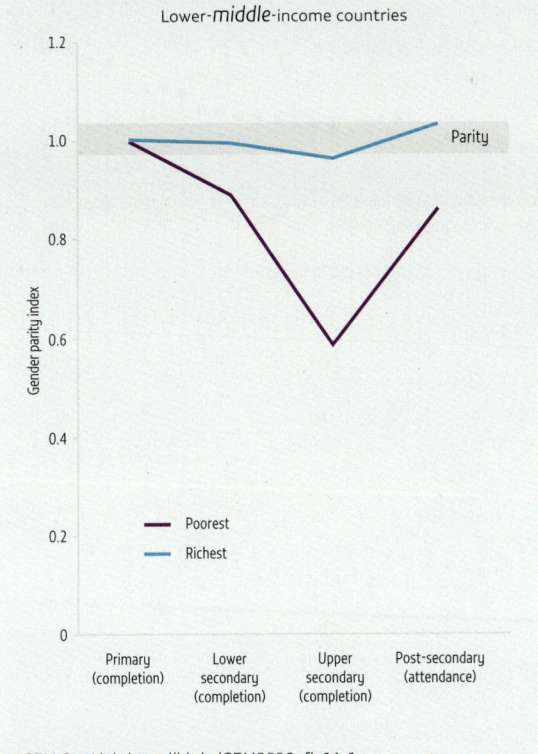

Lower-*middle*-income countries

GEM StatLink: http://bit.ly/GEM2020_fig14_1
Source: World Inequality Database on Education.

FIGURE 14.2:

Countries with similar education indicator averages may differ in those left furthest behind

Country ranking in lower secondary education completion rates for the national average and most disadvantaged group, selected countries, 2013–18

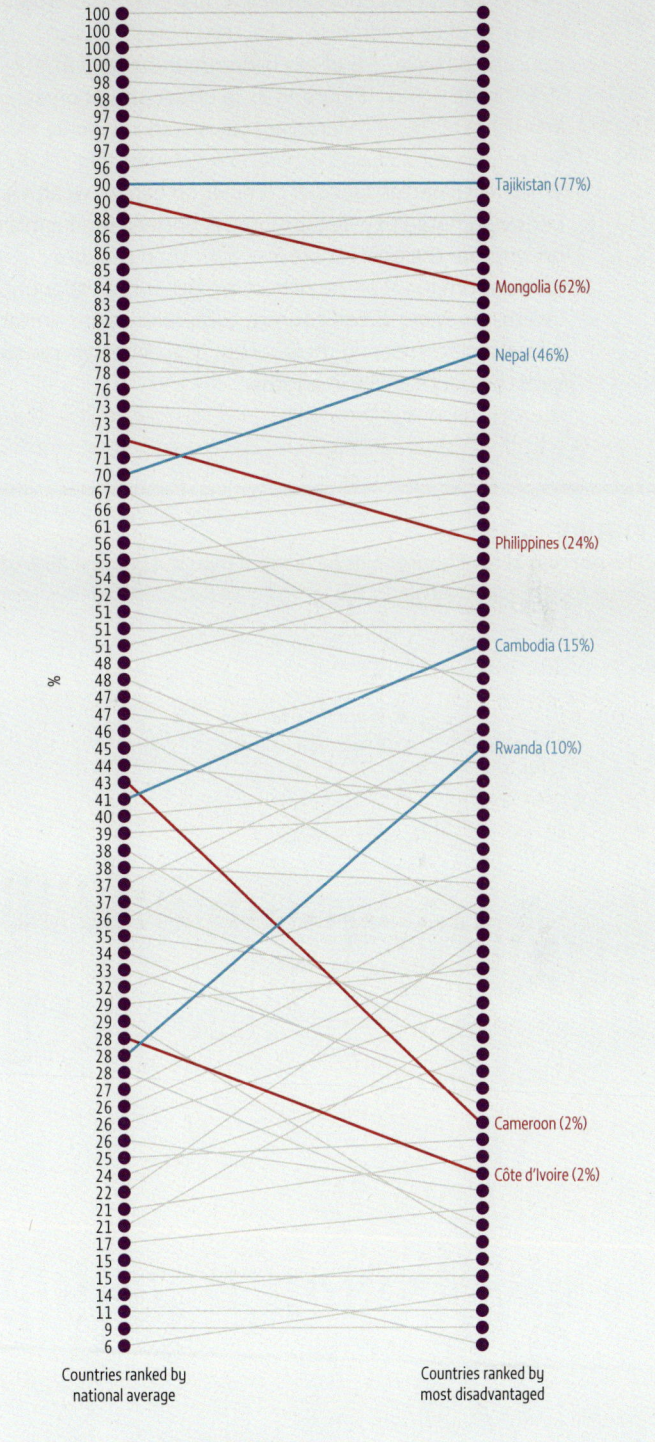

GEM StatLink: http://bit.ly/GEM2020_fig14_2
Note: The most disadvantaged group is defined in terms of sex, location and wealth.
Source: World Inequality Database on Education.

Disparity by wealth commonly compares the bottom and top 20% of households, not of children. Yet, in most societies, poorer families have more children, on average: The poorest 20% of households tend to have more than one-fifth of all children. In India, the poorest 20% of households have 25% of all children, compared with 15% for the richest (**Figure 14.3**). In effect, the poorest and richest 20% of children are compared in Liberia vs the poorest 25% and richest 15% in Myanmar. Whether the attendance or completion gap by wealth is underestimated or overestimated is unclear. It depends on whether the poorest are less poor than thought (underestimation) or the richest are richer than thought (overestimation). Cross-country comparisons are similarly distorted if comparing the poorest 20% of children in one with the poorest 25% in another.

The most marginalized groups with intersecting disadvantage suffer the worst education poverty, but data are scarce. Survey sample frames may not capture groups such as street children and nomads. Even when included, they may be difficult to identify, as with indigenous groups (**Focus 14.2**). Moreover, tools focused on such groups may not align with education indicator definitions, as in the case of the new questions capturing disability (**Box 14.1**).

To monitor inclusion in learning, national and cross-national learning assessments must be inclusive. In 2019, the Technical Cooperation Group on SDG 4 indicators decided reporting on thematic indicator 4.5.2 (percentage of primary education students whose first or home language is the language of instruction) could be based on information

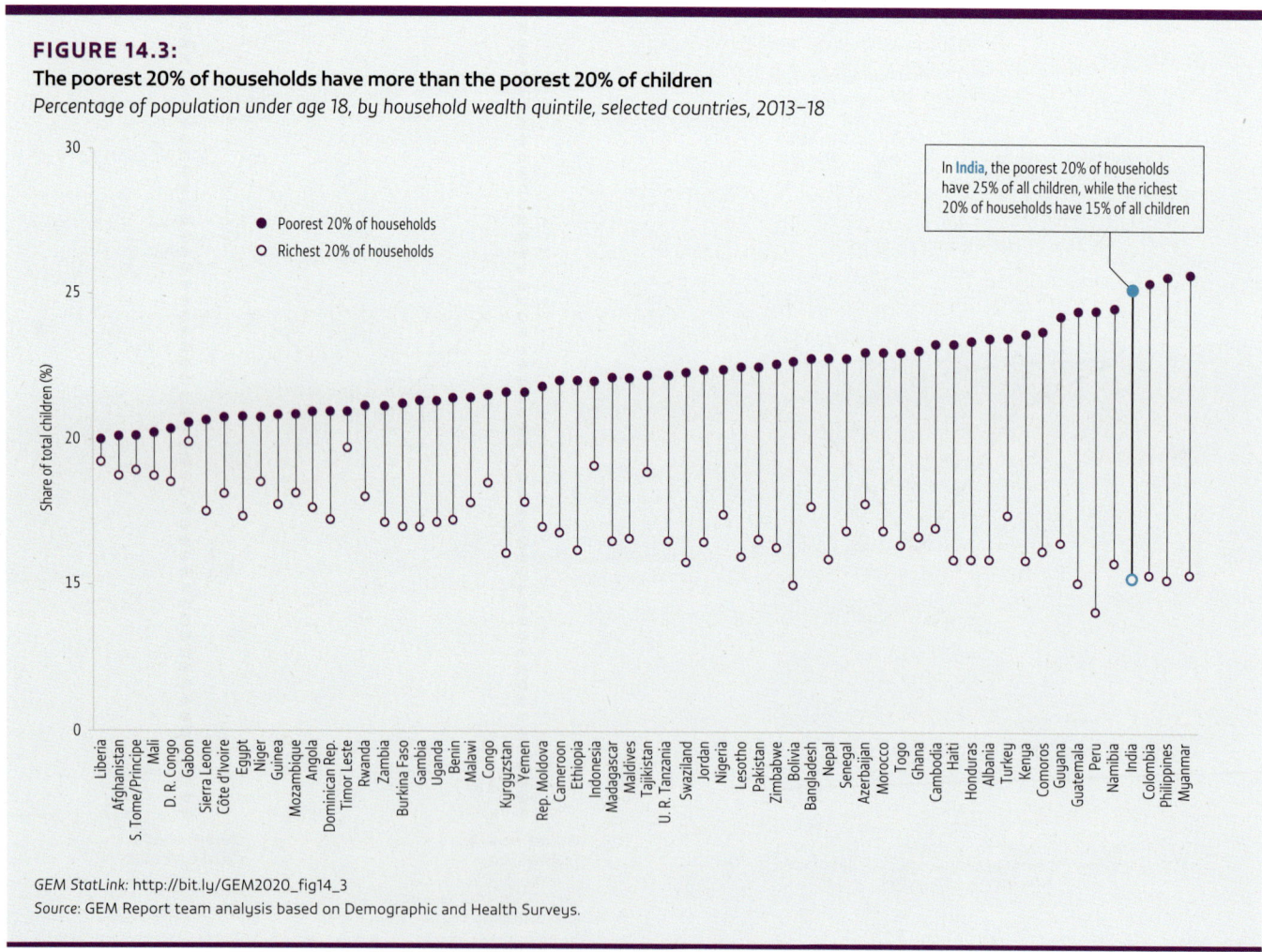

FIGURE 14.3:

The poorest 20% of households have more than the poorest 20% of children

Percentage of population under age 18, by household wealth quintile, selected countries, 2013–18

In **India**, the poorest 20% of households have 25% of all children, while the richest 20% of households have 15% of all children

- ● Poorest 20% of households
- ○ Richest 20% of households

GEM StatLink: http://bit.ly/GEM2020_fig14_3

Source: GEM Report team analysis based on Demographic and Health Surveys.

BOX 14.1:

Discontinuity in disability definitions can affect education indicators

The sixth round of the UNICEF Multiple Indicator Cluster Surveys (MICS) is the first to use the best practice in disability measurement, the Washington Group Short Set of Questions, which is based on functional difficulties (see **Chapter 3**). Part of its sophistication is consideration of age-appropriate functional domains. Yet the standard Short Set underestimates the prevalence of child disability by omitting functions relevant to their life stage. The MICS 6 Module on Child Functioning overcomes this by applying different disability measures for children under age 5 and those aged 5 to 17 than for adults age 18 and above.

However, age does not determine some functional domains. The appropriate meaning of disability does not change at age 18. Changes in relevant domains may occur slowly, as they relate to developmental stages for which age is a proxy. Others may change suddenly in response to situational changes, such as being in or out of school.

Threshold ages do not align with the definitions of several education indicators. Pre-primary education enrolment may refer to ages 3 to 5. When the age for the final grade of primary education is 13, the primary completion rate is defined for the age group 16 to 18. In many countries, upper secondary enrolment and attendance rates also refer to the age group 16 to 18. The youth literacy rate is defined over the age group 15 to 24. What these and other indicators have in common is that they straddle two age groups for whom disability has been assessed in different ways.

The different approaches' dramatic effect on estimates of disability prevalence hampers interpretation of education indicators disaggregated by disability. In Sierra Leone, disability prevalence falls from 16.6% among 17-year-olds to 0.3% among 18-year-olds (**Figure 14.4a**), while the lower secondary education completion rate is defined for ages 17 to 19 (**Figure 14.4b**). Average education outcomes for those with and without functional difficulties are impossible to interpret if having a functional difficulty is measured differently for individuals in an indicator age group.

There is no satisfactory solution, other than not disaggregating indicators affected by discontinuity in disability measurement. Disaggregating functional difficulties by domain shows anxiety to be the largest source of difference in prevalence rates between the Module on Child Functioning and the Washington Group Short Set for adults, albeit not the only one. However, trying to align the two by ignoring the effect of this domain would not result in valid measurement. A non-standard literacy rate for ages 18 to 24 could be calculated, or both the Module on Child Functioning and the Washington Group questions could be administered to ages 15 to 24.

FIGURE 14.4:

Interpreting education disability gaps is difficult when the measure and prevalence of disability change at age 18

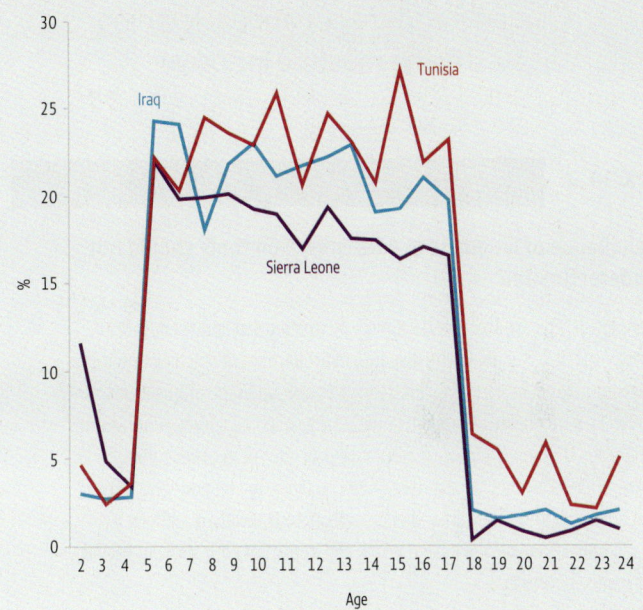

a. Prevalence of disability, by age, Iraq, Sierra Leone and Tunisia, 2017–18

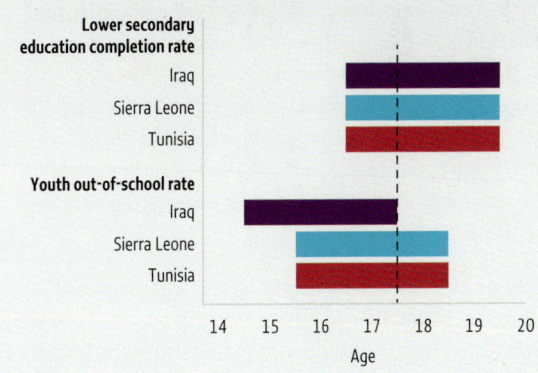

b. Age range of selected education indicators, Iraq, Sierra Leone and Tunisia

GEM StatLink: http://bit.ly/GEM2020_fig14_4
Note: The out-of-school rate age group refers to youth of upper-secondary-school age.
Source: GEM Report team.

on language used in assessments until information on language of instruction became available. Data on many other education indicators are collected using survey instruments whose accessibility is poorly documented or studied. In practice, surveys may not be available in languages respondents or enumerators fully understand, compromising data quality (**Box 14.2**).

> **"**
> To monitor inclusion in learning, national and cross-national learning assessments must be inclusive
> **"**

BOX 14.2:

The challenge of language in data collection tools should not be underestimated

Household surveys are an essential source of information about education systems, especially for analysing disparity in attainment and achievement by various characteristics. However, inattention to the language of questions can compromise data quality. Major cross-national household survey programmes have rigorous training and quality assurance procedures. In other survey contexts, such as humanitarian crises, minority language respondents often rely on unsupported local staff and enumerators to translate questions. This has implications for the design, reach and impact of education, especially in emergency contexts.

Research by Translators Without Borders, a non-government organization, shows that many enumerators cannot understand surveys due to language barriers or cannot understand responses. Understanding abbreviations is especially difficult. In north-eastern Nigeria, just 31% of respondents understood ORS (oral rehydration salts), and 43% understood IED (improvised explosive device). Only 1 in 24 enumerators could explain the meaning of extremism. For open-ended questions, enumerators must typically choose from a list of answers best matching the response. Enumerators reported not always understanding the English answer options and having difficulty identifying which best matched the response. In such cases, they may instead select answers they are confident they understand (TWB, 2019).

Even basic household data can be lost. The Rohingya word for young girl and adult woman is the same, potentially distorting the estimated number of children in households. For sensitive issues, translations may be stigmatizing, as is often the case with disability and mental health terms. Surveys should be based on a good mapping of languages spoken where enumeration will take place (TWB, 2020). They should be in plain language and put in local context, and terms that enumerators might find hard to translate and use should be discussed. Enumerators should translate responses back into the survey language to ensure they have captured their essence. Recording and translating a sample of responses is a good quality control. Using home language is key to developing data collection tools.

FOCUS 14.1: HOW MANY CHILDREN ATTEND SINGLE-SEX SCHOOLS?

Disaggregation of enrolment by sex is routine in international education statistics, but comparative cross-country data on single-sex vs co-education enrolment are scarce. Cross-national learning assessments, such as the Programme for International Student Assessment and the Trends in International Mathematics and Science Study (TIMSS), which collect information on student class and sex, offer valuable insights.

In about 60% of education systems in the mostly upper-middle and high-income countries that took part in the 2015 TIMSS, less than 5% of primary schools were single-sex. However, gender segregation in separate classes or schools is common in countries as diverse as Chile, Ireland, Israel and Singapore and is prevalent in many Muslim-majority countries. The prevalence of single-sex schools generally increases in secondary education, for instance from close to zero for primary to almost one in five for lower secondary education in England (United Kingdom) (**Figure 14.5**).

In most countries, the proportion of students in single-sex schools corresponds to the proportion of such schools. Exceptions relate to the size and type of schools that tend to be single-sex. In the Islamic Republic of Iran, single-sex primary schools (66%) enrol 84% of grade 4 students, partly because public single-sex schools are larger than private co-education schools. By contrast, single-sex primary schools in the Russian Federation (8%) account for 1% of grade 4 enrolment, as single-sex religious and/or private schools are smaller, on average.

Although sudden changes in school system structure are rare, comparisons over time for the countries that participated in the 2007 and 2015 TIMMS capture some shifts. Single-sex schooling decreased in Australia and the Republic of Korea. The latter shifted to co-education schools in the 1980s, and a recent policy decisively favours co-education (Dustmann et al., 2018). The situation is more complex in Western Asia. In Jordan, the share of single-sex lower secondary schools increased by 8 percentage points and the share of students attending them by 12 points. One reason may be the influx after 2011 of Syrian refugees, who attended public single-sex schools. The share of single-sex schools decreased in Bahrain and Kuwait. While public schools remain segregated in Gulf Cooperation Council countries, the changes are attributable to an increasing share of mixed private international schools.

FIGURE 14.5:

In many countries, the share of single-sex schools is large

Percentage of single-sex schools attended by grade 4 and 8 students, selected countries, 2015

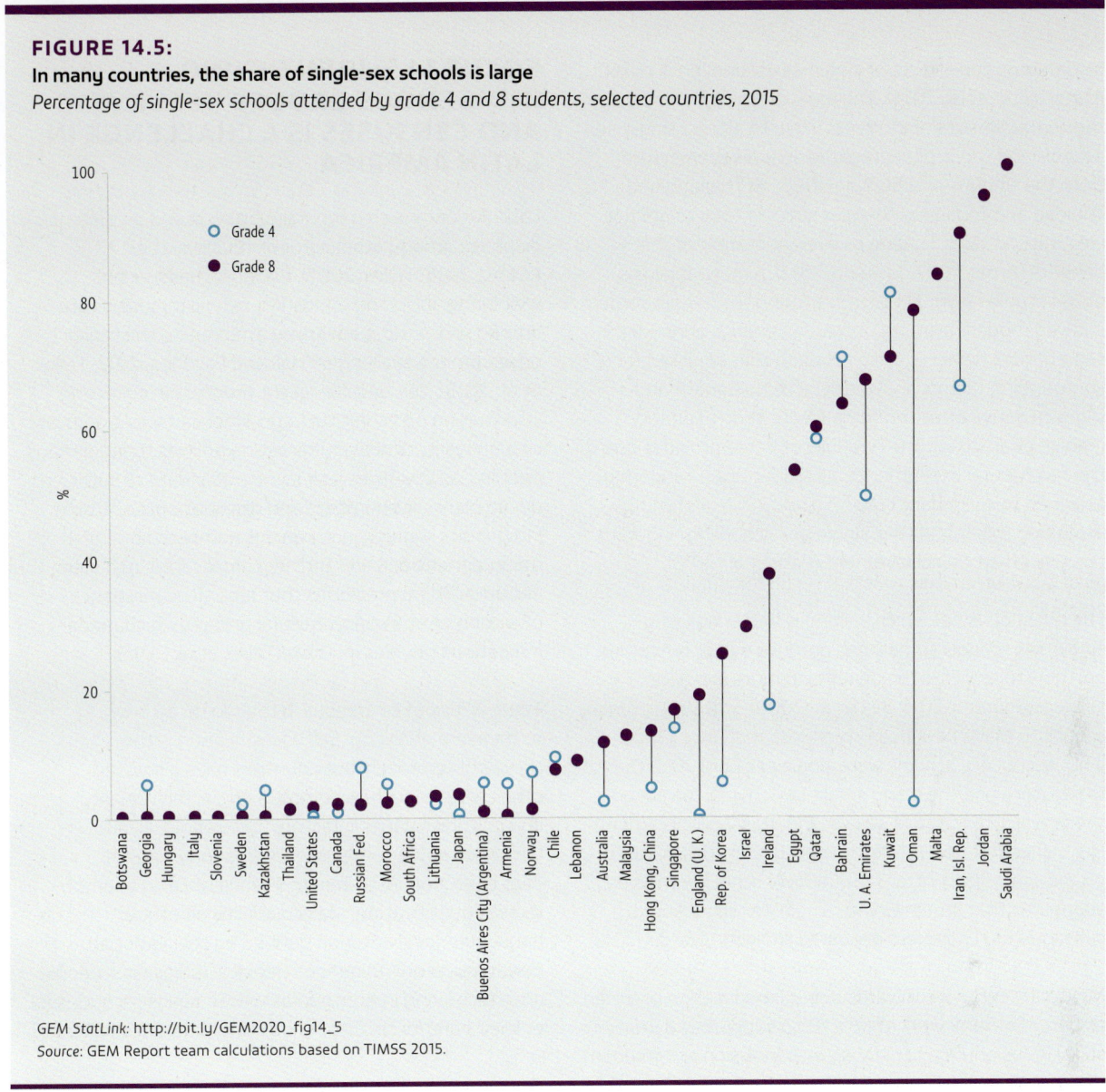

○ Grade 4
● Grade 8

GEM StatLink: http://bit.ly/GEM2020_fig14_5
Source: GEM Report team calculations based on TIMSS 2015.

The United Arab Emirates introduced co-education primary schooling in 2018 (Dajani and Rizvi, 2018).

From a gender inclusion perspective, single-sex schooling may be an acceptable temporary compromise when the de facto alternative in some culture- or country-specific contexts is females not attending (Marcus and Page, 2016; Sperling and Winthrop, 2015). Parents may prefer to send daughters to single-sex schools once they reach adolescence; lack of such provision in parts of Pakistan is one reason reported for low female enrolment (Aslam and Kingdon, 2008).

Some argue that gender social dynamics are educationally counterproductive (Bigler et al., 2014). Females may show greater affinity for and achievement in science, technology, engineering and mathematics when less exposed to negative gender stereotypes about ability and to males monopolizing equipment (Marcus and Page, 2016). Yet single-sex schooling is unlikely to affect choices, attainment or achievement unless it challenges dominant notions of masculinity and femininity (Smyth, 2010). The counterargument is that single-sex schooling can prevent females from developing social skills needed to navigate unsegregated workplaces and adult life (Fabes et al., 2013; Wong et al., 2018).

Evidence on the effects of single-sex schooling is mixed (Unterhalter et al., 2014). The main difficulty is isolating the characteristics of students likely to attend single-sex schools and those of segregated schools themselves from the single-sex-schooling effect. In Thailand and Trinidad and Tobago, single-sex schools tend to attract wealthier females, leading to overestimation of the benefits (Arms, 2007; Jackson, 2012). A meta-analysis of 184 studies from 21 countries found that, while some showed modest learning outcome benefits of gender segregation, higher-quality research that adjusted for confounding factors showed little to no benefit and a slight negative effect on female education aspirations (Pahlke et al., 2014). The Republic of Korea provides one of the few natural experiments, as students are randomly assigned to secondary schools (Link, 2012). A study exploiting this found that single-sex schooling had a small positive effect on achievement (Park et al., 2013).

The question is not which setting is better but why single-sex schools sometimes produce better outcomes and how to replicate the benefits in more inclusive settings (Riordan, 2015; Sax et al., 2009). State-run primary schools in Malta have been co-educational since 1980, while secondary schools were single sex until 2013. Due to this history and the many single-sex church-run schools, the prevalence of single-sex secondary schools is among the highest for non-Muslim-majority countries. A study on the centralized lottery for Catholic school admission suggested that students with single-sex schooling subsequently chose less gendered subjects (Giardili, 2019).

Malta's recent move towards public co-education occurred as part of a framework of policies to support and promote social inclusion. One benefit is easier inclusion and freedom of expression of lesbian, gay, bisexual, transgender and intersex students, who may be particularly excluded in single-sex schools premised on a homogeneous gender identity. With its 2015 Gender Identity, Gender Expression and Sex Characteristics Act, Malta adopted Europe's first comprehensive education policy focused on their needs; it included confidentiality and ended gender segregation in uniforms and some sports (Ávila, 2018).

> "
> Despite recent progress in collecting information on ethnicity, Latin America faces significant challenges in effectively targeting policies to indigenous peoples
> "

FOCUS 14.2: IDENTIFYING INDIGENOUS GROUPS IN SURVEYS AND CENSUSES IS A CHALLENGE IN LATIN AMERICA

Latin America is characterized by wide and persistent disparity among ethnic groups (Bustillo et al., 2018; ECLAC, 2016; Telles, 2007). By most measures of well-being, including education, ethnic minorities are among those most adversely affected by the region's development challenges (Hall and Patrinos, 2012; Telles et al., 2015). Yet, despite recent progress in collecting information on ethnicity, Latin America faces significant challenges in effectively targeting policies to indigenous peoples, as countries lack comparable data of sufficient quality on exact numbers and distribution. Capturing indigenous identity in surveys is hampered by its many dimensions and further complicated by historical nation-building processes that embraced *mestizaje*, or mixing of ethnic and cultural groups, which made indigenous peoples invisible (Telles et al., 2015).[1]

There is lack of consensus in the region on how to measure ethnicity. Self-identification is the prevalent approach, but countries have also used other criteria, such as common origin, territoriality and cultural-linguistic factors (Del Popolo, 2008). Countries apply these criteria in various ways in data collection instruments. For instance, in addition to self-identification, Mexico applies an official household-level criterion defined by the National Commission on Indigenous Peoples: Indigenous people are those living in households whose heads (or spouses) or their parents speak an indigenous language (CDI, 2017).

Demographic shifts have blurred ethnic boundaries and given rise to fluid indigenous identities and imperfect congruence between criteria (**Figure 14.6**). Indigenous population estimates vary considerably, depending on the criterion used (INEE, 2017; Telles and Torche, 2019). Six countries in the region have data on both self-identification and linguistic criteria: the Plurinational State of Bolivia, Ecuador, Guatemala, Mexico, Paraguay and Peru. Peru has the highest proportion of self-identified indigenous people (almost two in three). In Paraguay, 1.7% self-identify as indigenous, while about three in four speak an indigenous language – the highest proportion in the region. Ecuador has the lowest proportion of indigenous speakers among the six countries (4.8%).

1 This Focus is based on Valencia Lopez (2020).

Self-identification is the increasingly dominant criterion, consistent with the International Labour Organization's Indigenous and Tribal Peoples Convention. However, used alone, it can provide inconsistent estimates of education inequality. Education outcomes of speakers of indigenous languages are often worse than those of self-identified indigenous people who speak only Spanish (INEE, 2017; Planas et al., 2016). Across four national household surveys in 2018, school attendance among 15- to 17-year-olds in the Plurinational State of Bolivia, Guatemala, Mexico and Peru was 3 to 20 percentage points lower among speakers of an indigenous language than among all those identifying as indigenous (Valencia Lopez, 2020). Skin colour tends to be a better predictor of years of schooling than the census criterion, especially after controlling for social class (Flores and Telles, 2012). Recent research in Brazil, Mexico and Peru showed persistent inequality by skin colour, language and, in some countries, self-identification, after controlling for social class (Telles et al., 2015; Villarreal, 2014).

Indigenous groups defined by different criteria may have distinct education needs. Education policy responses in countries with low concordance of self-identification and indigenous language vary. Mexico enforces intercultural indigenous curricula in schools with high levels of self-identified indigenous groups, but whether these are administered in an indigenous language should depend on whether students speak it, not on whether they self-identify as indigenous (Valencia Lopez, 2020).

One reason for the discrepancy in education outcomes between indigenous groups identified according to identity or language may be insufficient household- or school-level language transmission and a resulting shift in identity. There is evidence that indigenous individuals do not identify their children as having their ethnicity, reflecting cross-generation fluidity (Villarreal, 2014). Individuals may also change how they perceive their ethnic identity.

Longitudinal data from Mexico's national household living conditions survey offer insights into the fluidity of ethnic identity. The ethnicity question is comparable over time, and responses are individual rather than by household head as proxy. Individuals who identified as indigenous in the first wave in 2002 exhibited high levels of fluidity: Half had changed ethnic identity at least once by 2009. Education level is associated with more constant self-declaration of ethnicity, consistent with the ethnic pride hypothesis. Speaking an indigenous language

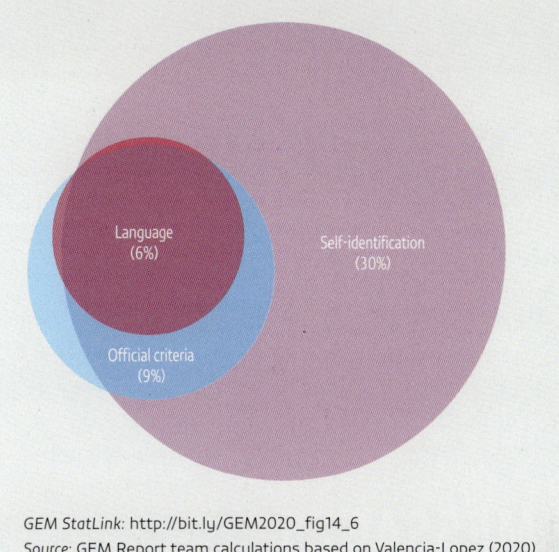

FIGURE 14.6:
Official identification criteria capture most speakers of indigenous languages in Mexico but only a fraction of those who self-identify as indigenous
Percentage of indigenous people according to three definitions and overlaps, Mexico, 2018

Language (6%)

Self-identification (30%)

Official criteria (9%)

GEM StatLink: http://bit.ly/GEM2020_fig14_6
Source: GEM Report team calculations based on Valencia-Lopez (2020).

> " Education outcomes of speakers of indigenous languages are often worse than those of self-identified indigenous people who speak only Spanish "

is also associated with a lower likelihood of individuals later declaring themselves non-indigenous. Living in a city reduces the likelihood of consistent indigenous identity.

Urban migration and loss of indigenous language proficiency over generations result in complex processes of negotiating identity. Anthropological research has documented how the presence of indigenous peoples in urban areas led to new forms of indigenous identity expression (Gomez Murillo, 2008). In Guatemala and Mexico, urban migration resulted in loss of indigenous languages, once the main marker of indigenous identity, as indigenous peoples gained access to local, predominantly Spanish-speaking labour markets (Telles and Torche, 2019; Yoshioka, 2010).

In Nazirpur, Bangladesh, a senior villager gives a class to a group of women. In this village, local teachers and NGOs educate members of the community who then go on to educate other women.

CREDIT: Arindam Dutta/UNESCO

KEY MESSAGES

The share of adults who achieved minimum literacy proficiency in 2017–18 was 74% in Kazakhstan, 49% in Mexico, 29% in Peru and 28% in Ecuador. In the United States, the share of adults achieving minimum numeracy proficiency decreased from 72.4% in 2012–14 to 70.8% in 2017.

Some 21% of Ghanaian and 29% of Kenyan working-age urban adults had minimum literacy proficiency, but 85% and 95%, respectively, could read a short sentence, regardless of comprehension.

In Eastern and South-eastern Asia, the share of women among illiterate youth decreased from 74% in 1990 to 48% in 2018, while their share among illiterate adults stagnated at 70%.

Even if universal primary completion is achieved by 2030, the proportion of adults who have not completed primary school may remain above 10% in sub-Saharan Africa until the 2050s.

About 70 to 80 languages each are spoken in the Central African Republic, Mali and South Sudan, where only one in three adults can read. In Chad, just 1% of adult women can read in the Lac and Wadi Fira regions.

A review of 17 literacy programmes for people with learning difficulties in the United States found that the most effective used strategies such as graphic organizers, accessible texts and application of skills in context.

CHAPTER 15

TARGET 4.6

Literacy and numeracy

By 2030, ensure that all youth and a substantial proportion of adults, both men and women, achieve literacy and numeracy

---

GLOBAL INDICATOR

4.6.1 – *Percentage of population in a given age group achieving at least a fixed level of proficiency in functional (a) literacy and (b) numeracy skills, by sex*

THEMATIC INDICATORS

4.6.2 – *Youth/adult literacy rate*

4.6.3 – *Participation rate of illiterate youth/adults in literacy programmes*

Proficiency in literacy and numeracy skills varies, a fact recognized in global indicator 4.6.1, which has made an important contribution to the global debate. Assessing these skills is technically complex and costly, pending adoption of more efficient and affordable tools. The Literacy Assessment and Monitoring Programme (LAMP) of the UNESCO Institute for Statistics (UIS) advanced methodology in the mid-2000s and piloted or fully estimated literacy and numeracy in 10 low- and middle-income countries in 2006–11 (UIS, 2017). It has since developed a short module, known as mini-LAMP, for potential use in multipurpose household surveys (UIS, 2018).

The Organisation for Economic Co-operation and Development's Programme for the International Assessment of Adult Competencies (PIAAC), which focuses primarily on high-income countries, is the main tool for assessing youth and adult literacy and numeracy. Six countries, four of which were upper-middle-income, took part in the third and final round (2017–18) of the first PIAAC cycle, which began in 2011. Minimum literacy proficiency (level 2) involves matching text and information and/or paraphrasing or making low-level inferences given competing information. Some 74% of youth and adults in Kazakhstan, 49% in Mexico, 29% in Peru and 28% in Ecuador are at level 2 or above in literacy (**Figure 15.1**). In the United States, the only country to be surveyed twice during the first PIAAC cycle, the percentage of adults below minimum proficiency in numeracy increased, from 27.6% in 2012–14 to 29.2% in 2017 (OECD, 2019).

A third cross-national survey measured literacy. The World Bank's Skills Toward Employment and Productivity (STEP) sampled urban areas in 17 middle-income countries and territories between 2012 and 2015 (World Bank, 2015). While not nationally representative, results were benchmarked, as STEP used the PIAAC scale. Some 21% of Ghanaian and 29% of Kenyan working-age urban adults had minimum proficiency in 2012, while 39% (Ghana) and 65% (Kenya) reached the lower threshold of locating a piece of information in a short text (level 1). These estimates were lower than the most rudimentary directly assessed measure of literacy: According to the 2014 Demographic and Health Surveys (DHS), 85% of Ghanaian and 95% of Kenyan urban adults aged 15 to 49 could read a very short sentence, regardless of comprehension (**Figure 15.2**).

In the absence of nationally representative assessments, the fallback option is to continue monitoring the adult literacy rate based on the outdated binary concept of literacy. The 2019 UIS youth and adult literacy data provide new estimates for 72 countries, including 21 whose last estimates dated from 2010 or earlier. Globally, 86% of adults aged 15 and above and 92% of youth aged 15 to 24 are literate. Women are less likely to be literate, but the gap is closing in the younger generation. Gender gaps remain particularly large in Central and Southern Asia (15 percentage points), sub-Saharan Africa (14 points)

> ❝
> Some 74% of youth and adults in Kazakhstan, 49% in Mexico, 29% in Peru and 28% in Ecuador are at level 2 or above in literacy
> ❞

FIGURE 15.1:
Almost 40% of adults in assessed upper-middle-income countries are below minimum literacy proficiency

Percentage of adults aged 16 to 65, by literacy proficiency level, countries participating in the Programme for the International Assessment of Adult Competencies, 2011–18

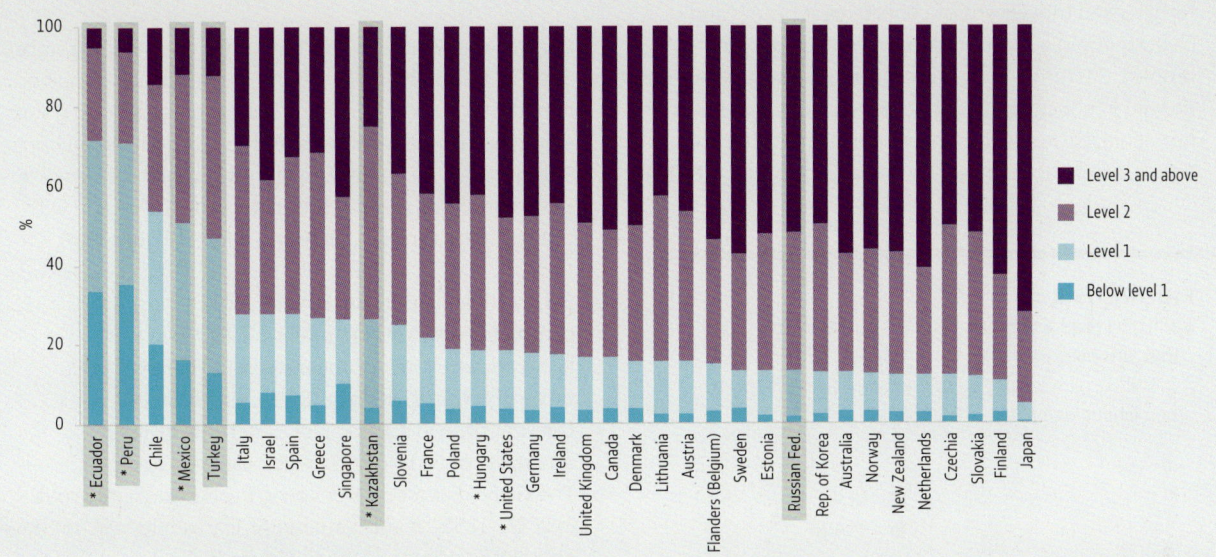

* Countries that took part in the third round of the first PIAAC cycle (2017–18).
GEM StatLink: http://bit.ly/GEM2020_fig15_1
Notes: Upper-middle-income countries are highlighted. Russian Federation figures represent all but the Moscow municipal area. United Kingdom figures refer to England and Northern Ireland. Level 1 tasks involve reading short texts on familiar topics using basic vocabulary knowledge and locating a piece of information identical to or synonymous with information in the question. Level 2 tasks involve matching text and information and/or paraphrasing or making low-level inferences given competing information.
Source: OECD (2019).

and Northern Africa and Western Asia (11 points) (**Table 15.1**).

The share of illiterate female youth has decreased in the three regions, and consequently the world, since around 2005, although the decrease in Eastern and South-eastern Asia since 1990 has been steeper (**Figure 15.3a**). The share of illiterate adult women, however, has remained constant for the past 20 years at around 63%. Eastern and South-eastern Asia may have the highest gender parity index (moving towards parity) and highest adult female literacy rate but also has

> " Globally, 86% of adults aged 15 and above and 92% of youth aged 15 to 24 are literate "

TABLE 15.1:
Youth and adult literacy rates, 2018

	Youth (15–24)			Adults 15+		
	Total	Female	Male	Total	Female	Male
World	**91.7**	**90.4**	**92.9**	**86.3**	**82.8**	**89.8**
Sub-Saharan Africa	76.7	73.7	79.8	65.8	58.9	72.9
Northern Africa and Western Asia	88.9	87.1	90.7	80.1	74.3	85.5
Central/S.Asia	89.9	88.0	91.6	73.9	66.0	81.5
Eastern and South-eastern Asia	98.9	98.9	98.9	95.8	94.1	97.4
Latin America and the Caribbean	98.5	98.7	98.4	93.9	93.5	94.3
Oceania	…	…	…	…	…	…
Europe and Northern America	…	…	…	…	…	…
Low income	75.6	72.3	78.8	63.2	55.6	71.1
Lower middle income	89.7	88.0	91.4	77.2	70.9	83.4
Upper middle income	98.3	98.3	98.4	95.2	93.7	96.6
High income	…	…	…	…	…	…

Source: UIS database.

the highest share of women among illiterate adults (**Figure 15.3b**). Among women over age 65 in the region, 75% are illiterate.

Demographic changes – notably in life expectancy, fertility and movement of cohorts over time – and investment in education determine regional literacy profiles. Eastern and South-eastern Asia began investing heavily in education over two generations ago but did not achieve the second-lowest number of illiterate adults, after Latin America and the Caribbean, until 2015.

FIGURE 15.2:
Ability to read a sentence is not equivalent to comprehension
Adult literacy indicators, by sex and proficiency level, urban Ghana and Kenya, 2012–14

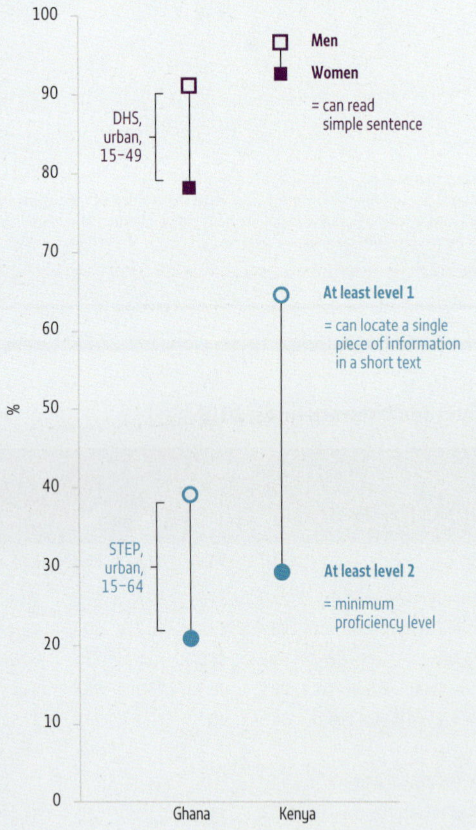

GEM StatLink: http://bit.ly/GEM2020_fig15_2
Notes: DHS = Demographic and Health Survey. STEP = Skills Toward Employment and Productivity.
Source: GEM Report team analysis using STEP data and DHS final reports.

> In 2050, 11.5% of sub-Saharan African adults will not have completed primary school

Central and Southern Asia has by far the most illiterates aged 25 to 64 (269 million), and the share has remained constant for about 25 years, but progress among youth since the late 1990s is expected to start having an impact. Sub-Saharan Africa has the highest number of illiterate youth and thus is expected to become the region with the highest number of illiterate adults (**Figure 15.4**).

Even achieving universal upper secondary school completion with literacy skills by 2030 will not bring about universal adult literacy. There will still be all of today's illiterate youth, estimated for the first time in 2018 at just under 100 million, and most of today's 773 million illiterate adults. The *Global Education Monitoring Report* estimates that, in 2050, 11.5% of sub-Saharan African adults will not have completed primary school (**Figure 15.5**).

Literacy statistics refer to official languages. The number of illiterates who speak minority or non-official languages and live where the language of instruction differs from that spoken at home is unknown. Almost two decades ago, UNESCO quoted an unverified Summer Institute of Linguistics estimate that over half of illiterates belonged to this category (UNESCO, 2003). Regardless of the estimate's accuracy, the share may be high and is unlikely to decline, since the share of sub-Saharan Africa in the total illiterate population continues to increase. The region has the largest population of children not taught in the language spoken at home (UNDP, 2004).

The five sub-Saharan African countries with the world's lowest adult literacy rates have high linguistic diversity. Chad, with an adult literacy rate of 22%, has 133 languages. The Central African Republic, Mali and South Sudan have 70 to 80 languages each (**Figure 15.6**). According to Ethnologue, at least two-thirds of these languages – as many as 9 in 10 in Mali – are either institutional ('developed to the point that [a language] is used and sustained by institutions beyond the home and community') or stable ('the norm in the home and community that all children learn and use', even if not sustained by formal institutions) (Eberhard et al., 2020).

FIGURE 15.3:

The share of illiterate women has been constant for 20 years

Share of illiterate females, by region, 1990–2018

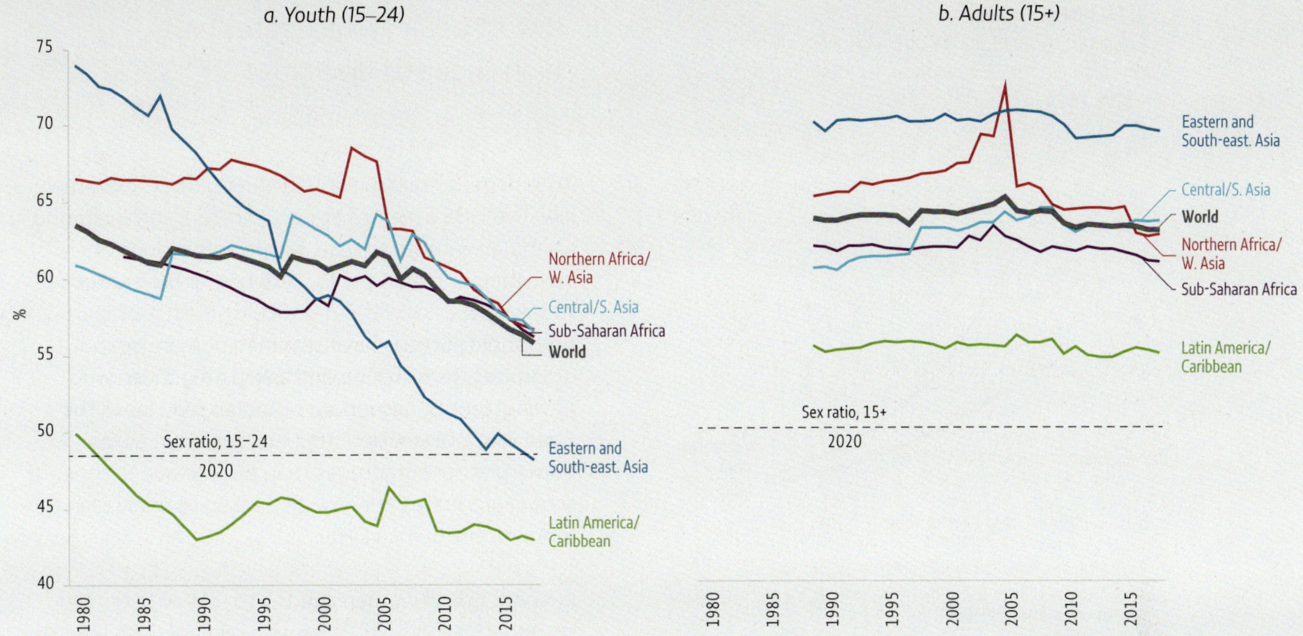

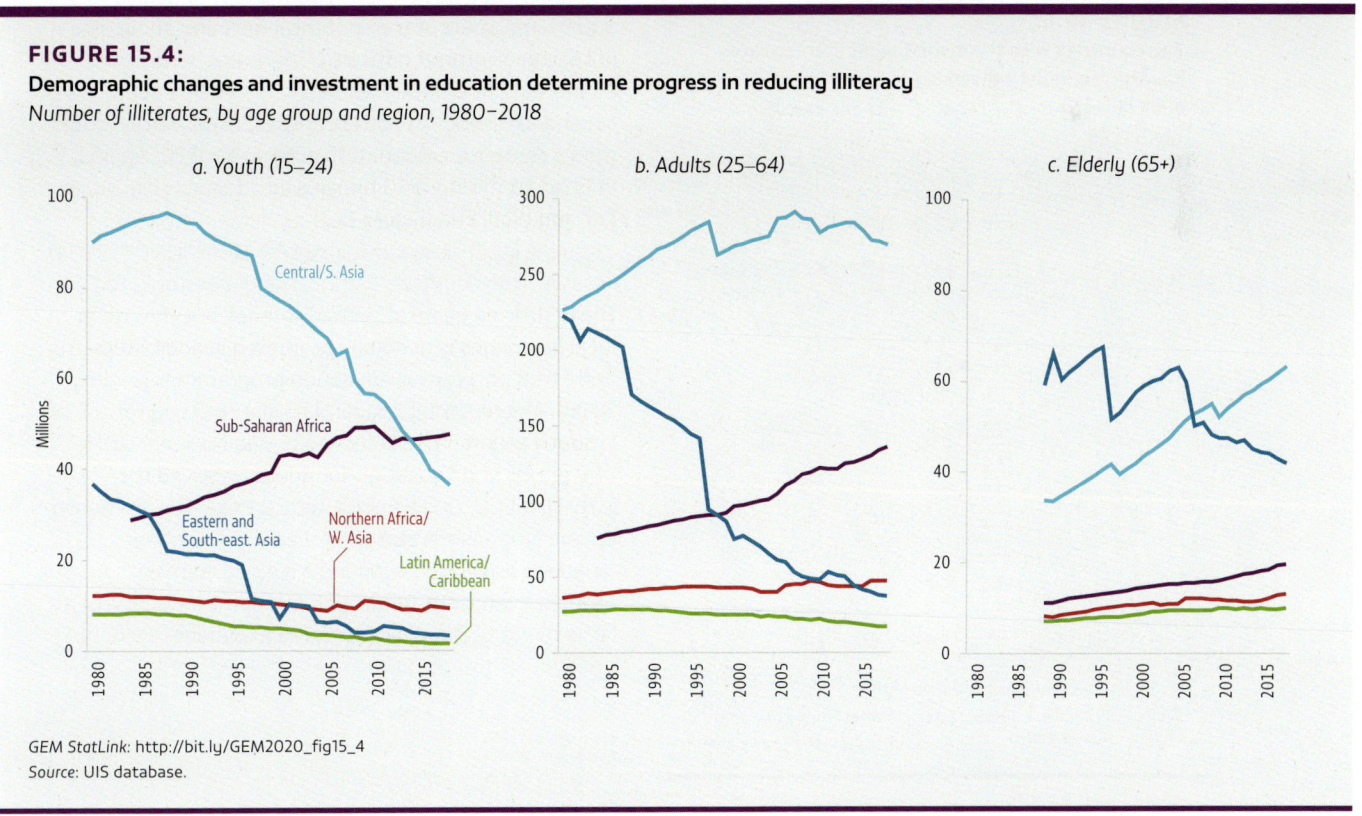

GEM StatLink: http://bit.ly/GEM2020_fig15_3
Source: UIS database.

FIGURE 15.4:

Demographic changes and investment in education determine progress in reducing illiteracy

Number of illiterates, by age group and region, 1980–2018

GEM StatLink: http://bit.ly/GEM2020_fig15_4
Source: UIS database.

FIGURE 15.5:

Even with universal secondary school completion by 2030, literacy programming will still be needed in 50 years

Projected share of adults aged 25+ who will not have completed primary education, sub-Saharan Africa and world, 2020–70

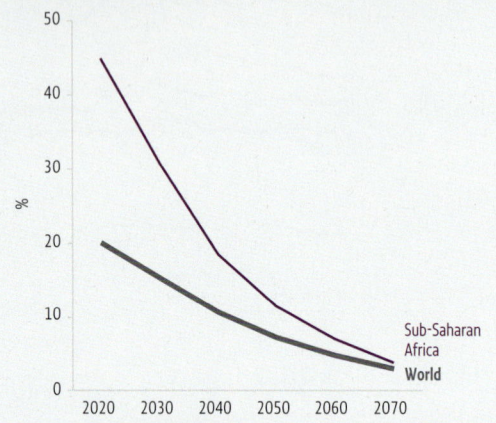

GEM StatLink: http://bit.ly/GEM2020_fig15_5

Note: Projections are based on universal primary and secondary school completion by 2030.

Source: GEM Report team calculations based on Wittgenstein Centre (2019).

FIGURE 15.6:

The countries with the lowest adult literacy rates have high linguistic diversity

Adult literacy rate, five countries with the lowest rate, 1990–2018

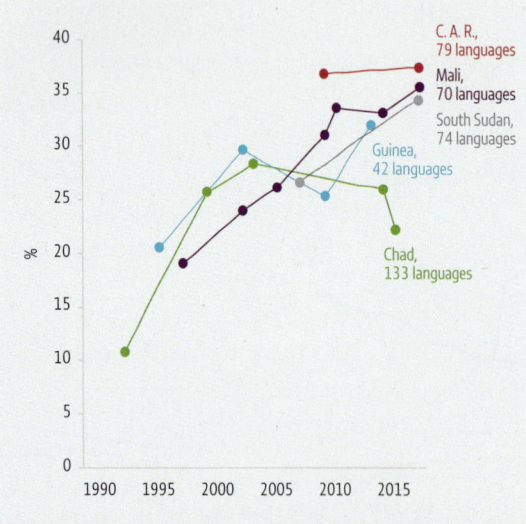

GEM StatLink: http://bit.ly/GEM2020_fig15_6

Sources: UIS database (literacy rates); Eberhard et al. (2020) (number of languages).

> **The five sub-Saharan African countries with the world's lowest adult literacy rates have high linguistic diversity**

Adult female literacy in Chad and Guinea is extremely low. The DHS assesses literacy directly, administering a simple sentence to read. Responses include an indication of reading skills, i.e. whether the sentence was read with or without difficulty. Such multipurpose household surveys have assumed primary school graduates were literate and asked only those who never attended secondary school to read (as in the Chad DHS). Given mounting evidence that some primary school graduates may be illiterate, secondary school graduates are now also asked to read (as in the more recent Guinea DHS).

In Chad, 15% of women aged 15 to 49 had attended secondary school. Of those who had not, 1.7% read the sentence without difficulty, and 5.5% read part of the sentence, meaning one in five read without difficulty. In Guinea, 4% had attended post-secondary education. Of those who had not, 11% read without difficulty, and 9% read part of the sentence, meaning about one in two read without difficulty. This is not surprising, as the sample included women who had attended secondary school. In both countries, 1 in 6 women could read a sentence without difficulty. In 12 of 20 regions in Chad, at most 1 in 10 females could read – 1 in 100 in Lac and Wadi Fira (**Figure 15.7**).

Most African countries use local languages only for the first three years of primary school, but the use of local languages is generally promoted in adult literacy and other non-formal education programmes (Alidou, 2006). Algeria's Multilingual National Strategy for Literacy programme, launched by the National Office of Literacy and Education for Adults, received the 2019 UNESCO King Sejong Literacy Prize. The 18-month course emphasizes starting to learn in the home language as key to becoming a lifelong learner. Students can learn Tamazight, the home language of a large minority. Rural and/or female students account

FIGURE 15.7:
At most, 1 in 10 women can read a sentence in most regions of Chad and Guinea
Female literacy rate, adults aged 15 to 49, by region, 2014 and 2018

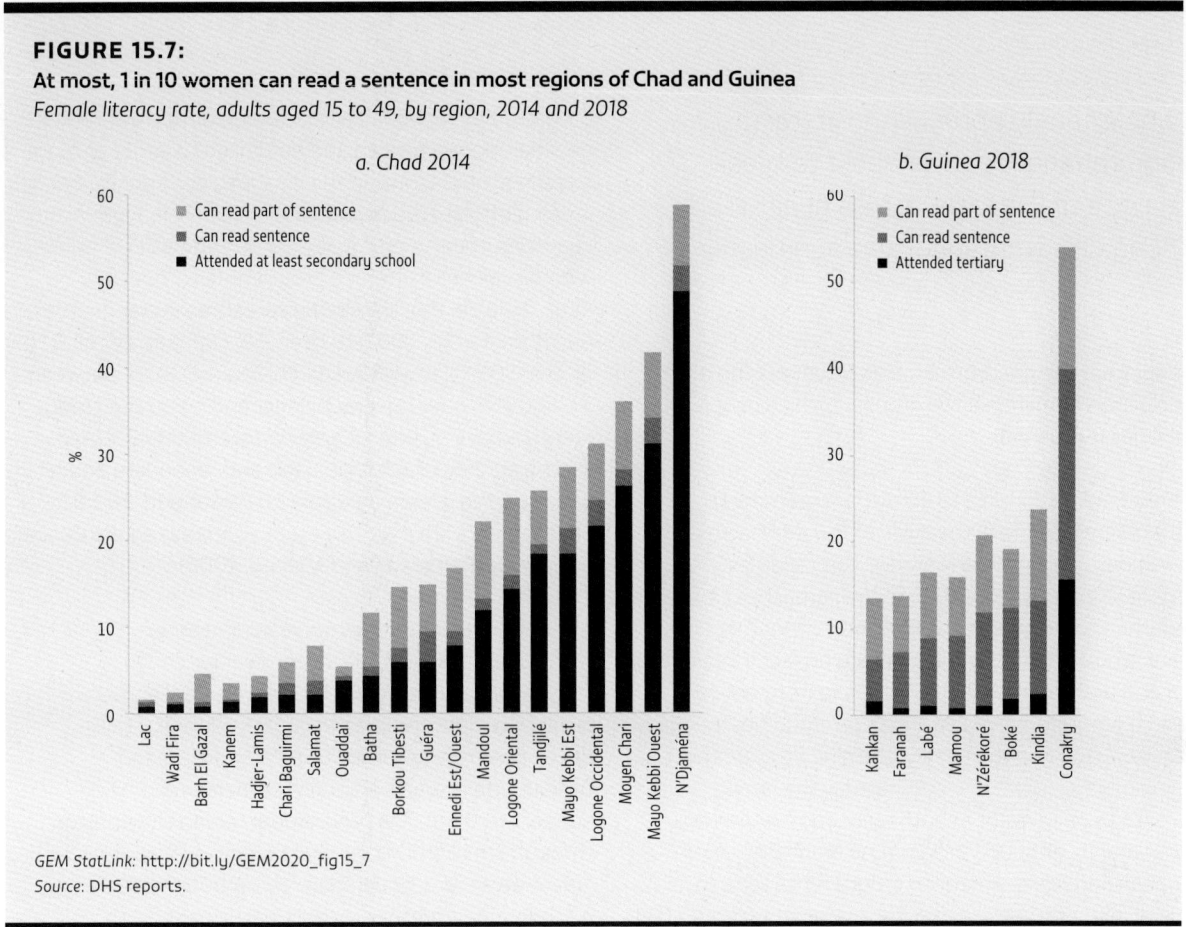

GEM StatLink: http://bit.ly/GEM2020_fig15_7
Source: DHS reports.

for about 90% of participants (UNESCO, 2019a). Senegal outsourced adult literacy programmes to civil society organizations, giving local providers a choice of six languages (Robinson, 2016).

South Africa's Kha Ri Gude adult literacy programme offers classes in all 11 official local languages, along with sign language and Braille. Yet teachers often

> 66
> South Africa's Kha Ri Gude adult literacy programme offers classes in all 11 official local languages, along with sign language and Braille
> 99

face multilingual and heterogeneous groups of learners without adequate training. Teachers may speak but not write the local language or may not have pedagogical strategies to support bilingual or multilingual classroom practices (Hanemann and McKay, 2019). In some countries, such as Ecuador, local languages are even written and read using competing alphabets, each with its own political connotations, which affects how people interact with literacy programmes (Limerick, 2017).

Too little is known about literacy programme participation globally. The UIS country questionnaire on literacy statistics will include a module to fill the gap with respect to SDG thematic indicator 4.6.3 (participation rate of illiterate youth/adults in literacy programmes). Yet individual participation statistics do not always provide a complete picture.

> "
> A whole-family approach to literacy
> programming may work best to break
> the cycle of low rates across generations
> among disadvantaged communities
> "

Among other things, information is often missing on participation of marginalized groups, such as people with disabilities (**Focus 15.1**).

A whole-family approach to literacy programming may work best to break the cycle of low rates across generations among disadvantaged communities (European Commission, 2012). Such approaches can strengthen community cohesion and development. Recent studies on the Family Literacy project in Hamburg, Germany (Rabkin et al., 2018), a participatory action research programme in pastoralist communities in Kenya (Ng'asike, 2019) and the Family Learning Programme in Mozambique (UNESCO, 2019b) show the family approach to be relevant in both high- and low-literacy environments, although programme emphasis varies. European and North American programmes tend to focus on parental literacy with the intent to improve child literacy. Sub-Saharan African programmes tend to target the community and focus on the value and transmission of local culture, language and traditional knowledge.

FOCUS 15.1: LITERACY PROGRAMMES SHOULD STRIVE TO REACH PEOPLE WITH LEARNING AND OTHER DISABILITIES

Learning difficulties and disabilities represent a barrier to acquiring the listening, speaking, reading and writing skills necessary to communicate in learning and participate in society. Adults with these challenges are more likely to be unemployed, poor or receiving government assistance (Patterson and Mellard, 2008).

In low- and middle-income countries, literacy programmes for adults with learning difficulties tend to be small, poorly funded and not linked to larger or more sustained efforts within the disability community or adult literacy efforts (Groce and Bakhshi, 2011). In high-income countries, there is no consensus on estimates of adults with disabilities in literacy programmes (Copeland et al., 2016). In the United States, estimates range from 6% (Kutner et al., 2007) to over 25% (Tamassia et al., 2007) or over 50% (National Research Council, 2012). Between 5% and 25% have dysgraphia (depending on the study), and 10% have dyslexia (Dyslexia International, 2014). In Kansas, 29% of adults in basic and secondary education self-reported a learning disability (Patterson, 2008). Such learners are over-represented among adults lacking basic skills (Patterson and Mellard, 2008).

A variety of programmes serve adult learners with disabilities. Australia's two-year Latch-On literacy programme gives adults with intellectual disabilities opportunities to continue literacy skills development. The curriculum is responsive and flexible, and researchers train teachers and provide support to them. The programme facilitates inclusion through small group courses, an individual approach where necessary, and access to computer technology. A student newsletter connects participants with young adults across the country (Latch-On, 2020). The International Dyslexia Association developed a toolkit to advocate for best literacy practices and recommend useful software and apps (International Dyslexia Association, 2019). The Dyslexia Association of Ireland runs a free information service, adult seminars on dyslexia and full-time training courses for unemployed adults with dyslexia. The course offers a Major Award in Employability Skills at level 3 and daily specialist literacy tuition (Dyslexia Association of Ireland, 2016). South Africa's Kha Ri Gude programme, which reaches 4.7 million of the country's 9.6 million illiterate adults, specifically targets citizens with disabilities. It has hired 60 sign language teachers and is developing Braille materials and other accommodations (South Africa Department of Basic Education, 2019).

"

Evidence on the effectiveness of strategies, accommodations, interventions and models to help adult learners with disabilities reach their full potential remains scarce

"

Evidence on the effectiveness of strategies, accommodations, interventions and models to help adult learners with disabilities reach their full potential remains scarce. In the United States, a report identified evidence-based reading and writing accommodations for adults with learning disabilities, such as software (e.g. word prediction, speech recognition, word processing) and extended time for assignments (National Research Council, 2012). Many adult reading programmes are based on the Orton Gillingham-Stillman Approach, a multisensory method combining visual, auditory and tactile–kinaesthetic instruction to enhance memory and learning (LDA, 2015). A review of 17 programmes found that the most effective adopted a variety of strategies, e.g. using graphic organizers and accessible texts and applying skills in context (Copeland et al., 2016).

A mother and her two children stand before a poster which the children contributed to making, as they arrive for class at New Winthorpes Primary School in St. John's, Antigua and Barbuda.

CREDIT: UNICEF/LeMoyne

KEY MESSAGES

In 2016/17, 83 countries responded to a consultation on whether the guiding principles of the 1974 Recommendation on peace and non-violence, human rights and fundamental freedoms, cultural diversity and tolerance, and human survival and well-being were reflected in their education policies, curricula, teacher training and student assessments.

- Only 12% of countries fully reflected the guiding principles.

- Several countries reported they assessed students even if curricula did not entirely include certain areas related to sustainable development and global citizenship or if teachers were not fully trained in them. In Burundi, Colombia and Myanmar, students were assessed even though neither condition was met.

- Prevention of gender-based violence was taught in 93% of countries but prevention of violent extremism in only 34%

- About 8 in 10 countries reported revising textbooks to deliver the principles, although change was constrained by the slow process of curricular reform and textbook development and roll-out.

The next consultation will introduce simplified questions, expand coverage to all target 4.7 dimensions and require governments to document their responses.

The leading role of school-age children in climate protests is significant, showing that today's schooling, as devised and provided by adults, will be irrelevant if tomorrow's planet is uninhabitable.

CHAPTER 16

TARGET 4.7

Sustainable development and global citizenship

By 2030, ensure that all learners acquire the knowledge and skills needed to promote sustainable development, including, among others, through education for sustainable development and sustainable lifestyles, human rights, gender equality, promotion of a culture of peace and non-violence, global citizenship and appreciation of cultural diversity and of culture's contribution to sustainable development

GLOBAL INDICATOR

4.7.1 – *Extent to which (i) global citizenship education and (ii) education for sustainable development are mainstreamed in: (a) national education policies, (b) curricula, (c) teacher education and (d) student assessment*

THEMATIC INDICATORS

4.7.2 – *Percentage of schools that provide life skills-based HIV and sexuality education*

4.7.3 – *Extent to which the framework on the World Programme on Human Rights Education is implemented nationally (as per the UNGA Resolution 59/113)*

4.7.4 – *Percentage of students by age group (or education level) showing adequate understanding of issues relating to global citizenship and sustainability*

4.7.5 – *Percentage of students in the final grade of lower secondary education showing proficiency knowledge of environmental science and geoscience*

Climate change, environmental degradation, technological development, conflict, and population growth and movements exert significant pressures on lives. Whether learners acquire knowledge of the challenges and constructive attitudes and behaviours to deal with them is crucial. Building on universal pre-primary, primary and secondary education, which ensure students can read, think and become lifelong learners, target 4.7 covers issues central to transformational SDG ambitions but difficult to act on.

UNESCO's 1974 Recommendation concerning Education for International Understanding, Cooperation and Peace and Education relating to Human Rights and Fundamental Freedoms offered guiding principles on peace and non-violence, human rights and fundamental freedoms, cultural diversity and tolerance, and human survival and well-being. Although it predates target 4.7 by 40 years, the 1974 Recommendation aligns with its call for countries to promote education for sustainable development and global citizenship.

In view of conceptual and practical challenges, the Inter-agency and Expert Group (IAEG) on SDG Indicators twice rejected a proposal to upgrade global indicator 4.7.1 based on the 1974 Recommendation's consultation and reporting process to tier II status (established methodology, but countries do not regularly produce data). A revised approach was endorsed in November 2019 (**Focus 16.1**).

Analysis of country responses to the 2016/17 consultation on the 1974 Recommendation revealed interesting patterns. Although coverage rose from 57 countries in the fifth consultation to 83 in the sixth (UNESCO, 2018), reporting was not globally representative: More than half the countries were in Europe, Latin America and the Caribbean.

Responses were analysed according to whether they reflected 1974 Recommendation principles fully, somewhat, a little or not at all in three domains – education policies and frameworks, curricula and in-service teacher training – and whether learning assessments included corresponding content. Half the countries displayed one of the four most common response patterns. Of 68 countries with information on the 4 domains, 9 (12%) fully reflected or included the guiding principles in all domains (**Figure 16.1**).

Many countries report students are assessed on relevant education content, even if curricula do not entirely include it. Few countries fully train teachers in the content their policies and curricula prescribe and on which students are assessed. In Burundi, Colombia and Myanmar, for instance, students are assessed even though teachers are not trained.

Such discrepancies may arise because domains are not necessarily equally applicable to all education levels. Almost all countries report including the principles in primary and secondary school curricula, mainly in civics (70% of countries), social studies (51%), geography (44%) and history (43%). Coverage is significantly lower in pre-primary, post-secondary, adult and non-formal education.

Almost all countries reporting on the question teach equality, inclusion, non-discrimination, and environmental sustainability and caring for the planet (**Figure 16.2**).

> **"**
>
> Target 4.7 covers issues central to transformational SDG ambitions but difficult to act on
>
> **"**

> The share of countries reporting fully adequate teaching and resource materials ranged from 18% for peace and non-violence to 26% for human rights and fundamental freedoms

While the principles do not mention gender equality, 93% of countries teach prevention of gender-based violence. Some 66% teach prevention of violent extremism and 71% education for global citizenship.

Other information was collected on the four domains. First, countries reported they implement the principles in various ways in their education programmes. At the policy level, 68 in 76 countries, or 89%, implemented the principles through a task force, working group or similar mechanism. In classrooms, the most reported approaches were learner-centred (88%), participatory and interactive (84%), and innovative and creative teaching (70%). Less than half the countries used research and experimentation.

Second, 8 in 10 countries reported revising textbooks to deliver the principles (**Focus 16.2**). The share reporting fully adequate teaching and resource materials ranged from 18% for peace and non-violence to 26% for human rights and fundamental freedoms. Third, more than 60% of European countries trained less than 60% of teachers to apply the principles. However, there is no further information on topics teachers were trained in. Fourth, in learning assessments, 81% of countries focused on knowledge, 72% on skills and competences, 62% on values and 42% on attitudes and behaviours, although several reported plans to reinforce the latter dimensions in assessments.

Analysis dating as far back as the early 20th century shows an 'ebb and flow of inclusionary educational orientations' (Jiménez and Lerch, 2019). Among countries reporting on 1974 Recommendation implementation in 2016/17, one-fifth said it had improved from five years earlier. None of the 12 participating sub-Saharan African countries reported progress. Almost half the countries cited insufficient financial, technical or human resources as the main

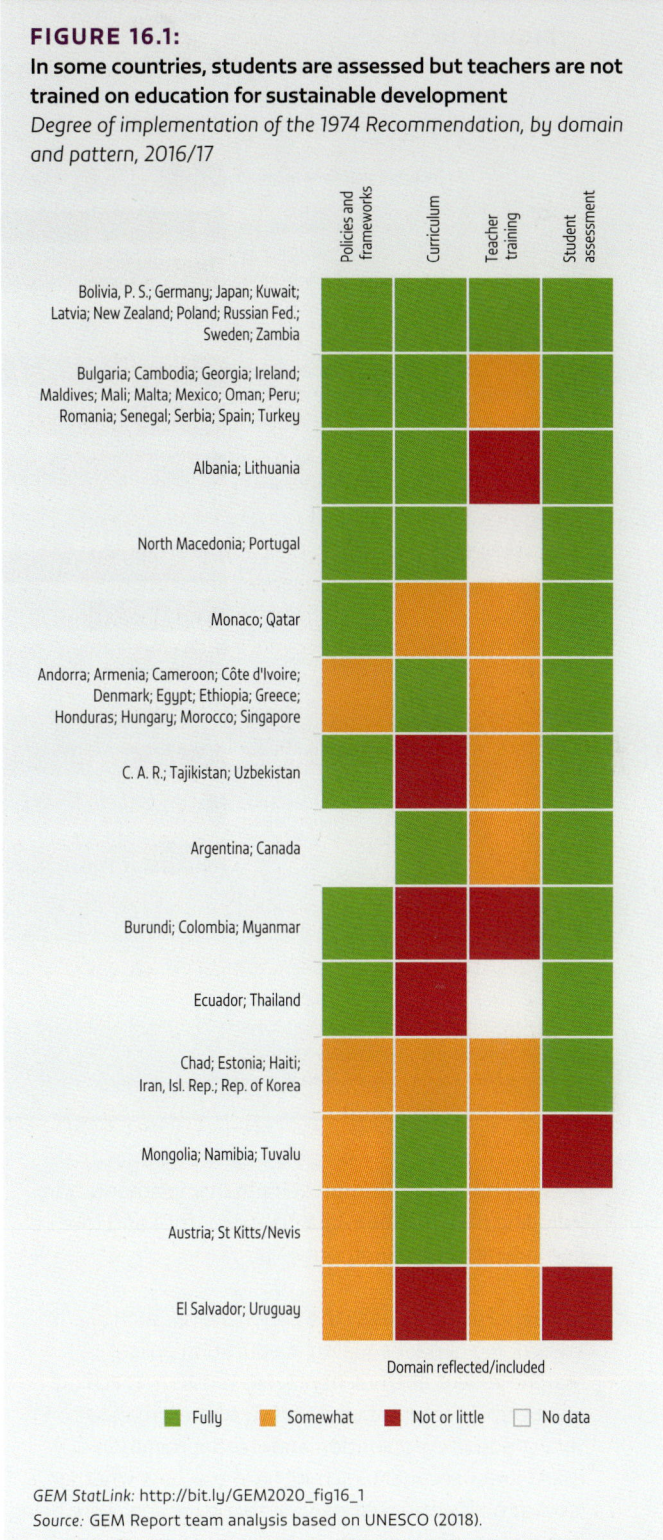

FIGURE 16.1:

In some countries, students are assessed but teachers are not trained on education for sustainable development

Degree of implementation of the 1974 Recommendation, by domain and pattern, 2016/17

GEM StatLink: http://bit.ly/GEM2020_fig16_1
Source: GEM Report team analysis based on UNESCO (2018).

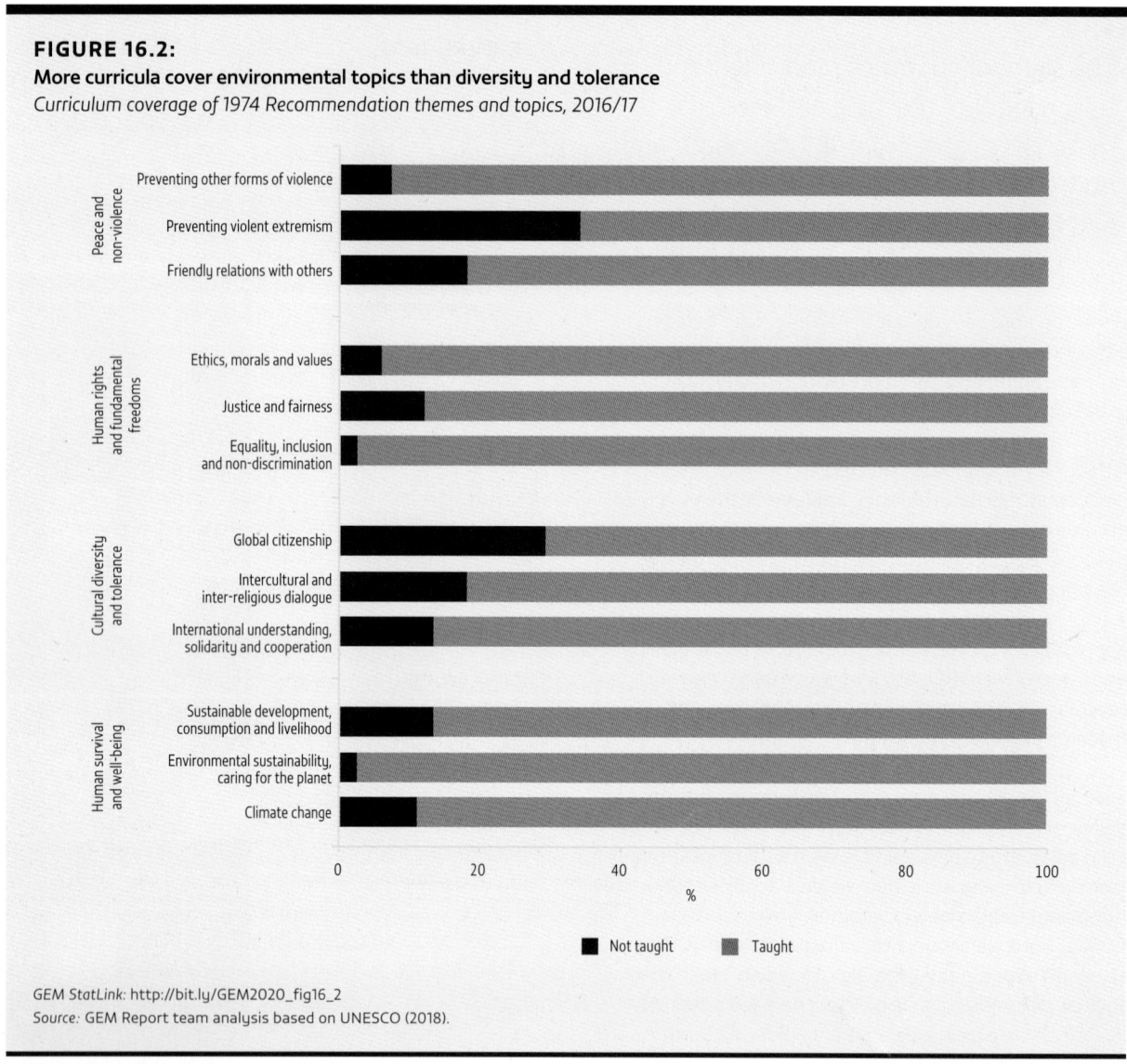

FIGURE 16.2:
More curricula cover environmental topics than diversity and tolerance
Curriculum coverage of 1974 Recommendation themes and topics, 2016/17

GEM StatLink: http://bit.ly/GEM2020_fig16_2
Source: GEM Report team analysis based on UNESCO (2018).

reason for no or little improvement in implementation, including two in three in sub-Saharan Africa and four in five in Central and Southern Asia.

Self-reported actions at the national level, such as embedding gender equality in education policy, may be absent at the school level. The 2018 Teaching and Learning International Survey of the Organisation for Economic Co-operation and Development (OECD) asked lower secondary school head teachers whether 'explicit policies against gender discrimination' were being implemented in their school. In the Flanders region of Belgium and in Italy, Malta, New Zealand and Singapore, around half affirmed they were (OECD, 2019).

> **Data are lacking not only on the target's global indicator but also on most of its thematic indicators**

Data are lacking not only on the target's global indicator but also on most of its thematic indicators. Young people's knowledge and feelings are difficult to measure, although their recent climate actions have sent a clear message (**Box 16.1**). Monitoring target 4.7 therefore necessitates alternative efforts and piecing together insights from multiple sources (Smart et al., 2019).

BOX 16.1:

Climate strikes by children erupted in 2019

Children's anger may be the most important and effective campaign for climate action. As many of the communities most affected by climate change are in low- and middle-income countries, it is unsurprising that climate justice activism by children emerged there. In Latin America, Belizean Madison Pearl Edwards and Ecuadorian Nina Gualinga have stood against threats to biodiversity from climate change and fossil fuel industries since ages 9 and 8 (WWF, 2018). Established in 2006, the African Youth Initiative on Climate Change links the issue with sustainable development, including poverty reduction, and allows youth activists across the continent to share ideas, strategies and lessons (African Youth Initiative on Climate Change, 2020).

Although the recent spotlight on Swedish climate activist Greta Thunberg arguably reflects media bias towards Western stories (Unigwe, 2019), there is a compelling logic to climate activism in the form of school strikes. One week in September 2019 saw the largest climate mobilization in history, with some 7.6 million taking to the streets (Global Climate Strike, 2019). While built on scientific consensus, schoolchildren's leading role on climate is significant. Younger generations will be more exposed than political decision makers to climate change's long-term impact. Behind the school strikes is the fact that today's schooling, devised and provided by adults, will be irrelevant if tomorrow's planet is uninhabitable.

Education has immediate benefits, but from a capability perspective, which values individual agency, it can also deliver on the promise of greater future capability. Older generations undermine this promise by claiming a bright future through education while destroying its very possibility. Teachers have supported school boycotts. An Education International resolution encouraged affiliates to 'stand in full solidarity with all students striking or protesting against climate change' and schools 'not to take action against students' (Education International, 2019). Schools for Climate Action argues that schools and educators have legal child protection mandates, and inaction on climate change amounts to child neglect (Preston, 2019).

Government failure to curb carbon emissions, long after the damaging impact on future generations has been established, is the basis of constitutional lawsuits by youth in Europe and in countries elsewhere, including Canada, Colombia, India, Pakistan, the Philippines, Uganda and the United States (Our Children's Trust, 2019).

> **Few countries have mechanisms to track progress in cognitive, social and emotional skills, reflecting implementation challenges**

A Pew Research Center survey on US adults' scientific knowledge included three items related to environmental science and geoscience. It asked whether (a) oil, natural gas and coal were fossil fuels; (b) the tilt of Earth's axis in relation to the sun determined the seasons; and (c) deforestation led to increased erosion. Knowledge depended on education attainment. Between 78% and 87% with postgraduate degrees answered correctly, compared with 48% to 55% of those with at most high school diplomas (Kennedy and Hefferon, 2019). However, levels of scientific knowledge among US adults in other areas, notably related to climate change, are not clearly correlated with education (see **Chapter 20**).

The OECD's Programme for International Student Assessment (PISA) has twice asked questions related to target 4.7. The 2006 PISA collected information on integration of environmental science issues into curricula and found that 98% of students in OECD countries were taught environment or sustainability topics (Buckler and Creech, 2014). The 2018 PISA was the first to collect information on intercultural knowledge and analytical and critical thinking in a module on 'global competence'. Students reported skills and attitudes such as empathy and responsibility (OECD, 2017). The OECD will present results in October 2020 in association with AFS Intercultural Programs, a non-profit active in international secondary school exchange, volunteerism and intercultural learning.

The skills dimension is no better covered, despite growing interest in other than strictly academic education outcomes (The Aspen Institute, 2019). Few countries have mechanisms to track progress in cognitive, social and emotional skills, reflecting implementation challenges (Vista et al., 2018). Such systems require high levels of trust. Privacy protection is arguably more important when it comes to data on student attitudes than it is with respect to their learning assessment scores.

Measurement challenges risk sidelining target 4.7 in the SDG 4 agenda – a double loss, as its issues can contribute to other targets' achievement. Learning has inseparable cognitive, social and emotional dimensions.

Fostering their development is positively correlated with attendance, completion rates and test scores (e.g. Durlak et al., 2011). A review of 27 studies from around the world found that 8 in 10 employers considered social and emotional skills the most important for success but also the rarest (Cunningham and Villasenor, 2016).

FOCUS 16.1: PROGRESS IN MONITORING AND REPORTING ON TARGET 4.7 HAS BEEN INCREMENTAL

Global indicator 4.7.1 asks to what extent countries mainstream education on sustainable development and global citizenship. Monitoring has reached a turning point. Examining the considerations that drove the discussions is instructive.

UNESCO developed a methodology to report on the indicator based on the quadrennial monitoring of implementation of the 1974 Recommendation during the sixth consultation in 2016/17. As discussed above, countries report on incorporation of 1974 Recommendation principles and topics in four domains. Limitations of the approach included the questionnaire being both too ambitious (e.g. several complex and/or unclear questions and lack of clear definitions for key terms) and not ambitious enough (e.g. lack of dimensions related to gender equality and human rights). Countries self-reported without being required to provide evidence.

A proposal to upgrade the indicator to tier II was rejected at the eighth IAEG meeting in November 2018, and further work was requested. Questions included whether data collection instruments should be based on self-reporting by governments, review of official documents by non-government respondents, or both; how often data should be collected; which levels and types of education should be covered; and whether climate change education should be included in data collection. Proposed adjustments included questionnaire clarification, expanded coverage to all target 4.7 dimensions and supporting documentation requirements.

Alternative sources to the 1974 Recommendation consultation were also tabled, generally accompanied by calls for simplification, fewer questions and tighter focus on primary and secondary education or indicator domains (UIS, 2019a). One proposal focused on a coding method developed by the UNESCO International Bureau of Education for the 2016 *Global Education Monitoring Report*, which included six categories: human rights; gender equality; peace, non-violence and human security; health and well-being; sustainable development; and interconnectedness and global citizenship. Curriculum and textbook keyword searches would determine coverage of a category (UIS, 2019c).

Another proposal built on background questionnaires of the International Association for the Evaluation of Educational Achievement's International Civic and Citizenship Education Study. Focused on curricula, it would have put forward working definitions of key concepts (UIS, 2019b). The Council of Europe's Charter on Education for Democratic Citizenship and Human Rights Education was also proposed, as it followed an established country consultation process similar to that of the 1974 Recommendation, albeit at a regional level and only for some target dimensions.

In August 2019, the sixth meeting of the Technical Cooperation Group sought to reclassify 4.7.1 as tier II, based on the 1974 Recommendation process, with an additional demand for self-reporting to be validated by supporting documents submitted by governments. In December 2019, the IAEG endorsed the approach and approved a revised formulation merging it with indicator 12.8.1 on sustainable consumption and production and 13.3.1 on climate action: 'Extent to which (i) global citizenship education and (ii) education for sustainable development are mainstreamed in (a) national education policies, (b) curricula, (c) teacher education, and (d) student assessment'. UNESCO and the UNESCO Institute for Statistics will refine the questionnaire and metadata, based on feedback from the IAEG and other experts, for inclusion in the seventh consultation.

> **"** Proposed adjustments to global indicator 4.7.1 included questionnaire clarification and supporting documentation requirements **"**

FOCUS 16.2: SLOW TEXTBOOK DEVELOPMENT THREATENS PROGRESS TOWARDS TARGET 4.7

Target 4.7 calls for incorporating new perspectives into education policies, curricula, teacher education and learning assessments. Some curricula, such as Chile's new youth and adult education curriculum, are being changed to include environmental sustainability and climate change and, gradually, human rights, gender equality, citizenship and a culture of peace (Hanemann, 2019). However, considering the urgency of the challenges, change is slow, and few curricula cover social and emotional skills (Vista et al., 2018).

Change is limited by the mechanics of curricular reform and textbook development and the practicalities of roll-out. Half of today's children may have left school by the time content following new policy affects practice. While curricular reform is conceived as linear or cyclical, contemporary views see it as an ongoing process of renewal. Even curriculum innovations that need not wait for curricular reform progress through multiple steps before becoming expected learning in classrooms.

There are no systematic international data on curriculum development to inform estimates of typical curricular reform duration from instigation to implementation. The process can be complex, requiring careful, time-consuming consultation and negotiation. Reform may take five years – more, if politically contentious – if all stages receive due attention (Pingel, 2010). Duration depends on the scope of changes, consultation, piloting and validation. Reforms pushed too fast are likely rushed and incomplete. Aligning curricula with target 4.7 may

> " Half of today's children may have left school by the time content following new policy affects practice "

mean introducing content in isolation rather than as a cross-cutting element. Romania introduced textbooks on the history of minorities within two years, but teachers had not been trained when they arrived in classrooms (OECD, 2001). Contemporary history textbooks did not appear in schools in eastern German states for up to 10 years after the fall of the Berlin Wall (Pingel, 2010), the same time it took South African textbooks to appropriately address apartheid (Engelbrecht, 2006). Some former history textbooks in India were in print for 25 years (Greaney, 2006).

Practically speaking, books need replacing. While textbook shelf life has limited impact on the pace of new content entering classrooms, replacing textbooks only when no longer usable may prolong delays. There are no systematic statistics, but the World Bank estimates that textbooks in sub-Saharan Africa last two to three years (Fredriksen and Brar, 2015). To address chronic shortages, reduce costs and increase the viability of a second-hand market, efforts have been made to increase durability, with a target life at the secondary education level of five to six years. Some schools achieve eight years or more. In education systems that cannot afford to replace textbooks prematurely, it may take up to five years past publication for all learners to have access to new content (World Bank, 2008).

In Malawi, Marlita Sylvester, 15 years old, says,
"I love school, but it poses major challenges for me.
It is difficult to get to and from school. The road from
home to school is two kilometres, and I depend on a
friend pushing the wheelchair".

CREDIT: Jonas Gratzer/Save the Children

KEY MESSAGES

About 45% of schools in low-income countries and 78% in lower-middle-income countries have basic water supply. Some 335 million girls attend schools that lack essential menstrual hygiene management facilities.

Schools need different adaptations for students' different functional difficulties. Validating the information is complex. Regardless, less than 5% of primary schools in Albania, Honduras and Zambia reported meeting national standards.

While 102 countries have endorsed the 2015 Safe Schools Declaration, enforcement is lacking. In Burkina Faso, Mali and Niger, school closures doubled between 2017 and 2019, disrupting education for more than 400,000 children.

Bullying and school violence targeted at lesbian, gay, bisexual and transgender students occurs everywhere. In the United States, they were three times more likely than heterosexual students not to go to school at least once in the previous 30 days because they felt unsafe.

In South-eastern Asia, children who experienced ambient temperatures well above average attained 1.5 fewer years of schooling than those who experienced average temperatures. In Barcelona, Spain, exposure to high pollution levels in school reduced cognitive development.

Children experience physical exhaustion, violence and harassment, and exposure to significant danger on their way to and from school. In Brazil, the longer the commute, the worse the impact on academic performance. In Delhi, India, young women preferred colleges of lower quality if accessible by a safer route.

CHAPTER 17

TARGET 4.a

Education facilities and learning environments

Build and upgrade education facilities that are child, disability and gender sensitive and provide safe, non-violent, inclusive and effective learning environments for all

GLOBAL INDICATOR

4.a.1 – *Proportion of schools offering basic services, by type of service*

THEMATIC INDICATORS

4.a.2 – *Percentage of students experiencing bullying in the last 12 months*

4.a.3 – *Number of attacks on students, personnel and institutions*

Safe, welcoming environments are a right but also benefit learning (Barrett et al., 2019; Theirworld, 2019). The physical environment affects some learners more than others, as with access to adequate sanitation for girls. Some 335 million girls attend primary and secondary schools lacking facilities essential for menstrual hygiene (UNICEF, 2019a). Ensuring access to such facilities fulfils a right to dignity, even if building a girls' toilet block is no more sufficient for making a school gender-responsive than building a ramp is for making a classroom truly disability-inclusive (Naylor, 2019).

On average, 45% of schools in low-income countries have basic water supply. In lower-middle-income countries, 78% have basic water supply, 81% have sanitation facilities and 69% have basic handwashing facilities. In its 2019 data, the UNESCO Institute for Statistics complemented its school water supply, sanitation and hygiene facility estimates with those of the World Health Organization (WHO) and UNICEF's Joint Monitoring Programme (JMP) for countries not reporting official statistics. In primary education, where the two sources are comparable, there is largely agreement. Where sources diverge, there is no consistent pattern. In some cases, the difference is marginal. In others, e.g. Costa Rica, wide variation reflects differing methodologies. JMP estimates are based on a statistical model averaging the time trend across available estimates (**Figure 17.1**).

High-income countries report all schools meet the basic standard for three dimensions of global indicator 4.a.1. However, facilities may not be in good condition. Moreover, physical learning environment quality encompasses more than the aspects captured by the indicator, including factors underestimated in learners' well-being and achievement (**Focus 17.1**). Similarly, having sanitation facilities does not mean they are wheelchair accessible. The JMP database provides information on accessibility for 18 countries. In El Salvador, Fiji, Tajikistan, the United Republic of Tanzania and Yemen, less than 1 in 10 schools with improved sanitation had accessible facilities (**Figure 17.2**).

One dimension of 4.a.1 captures 'adapted infrastructure and materials for learners with disabilities'. Measurement is hampered for two reasons: lack of clarity owing to multiple combinations of functional difficulty types and possible adaptations, not all of which might be met at once; and concerns over validation of the information (see **Chapter 3**). It is not possible to establish whether a school meets the infrastructure adaptation standard if it has Braille signposting but no ramps, or whether it meets the materials adaptation standard if it provides screen readers but no large-print books. Whether the indicator should measure the proportion of schools adapted for at least one disability or the proportion adapted for almost any disability was put to the Technical Cooperation Group meeting in August 2019. It decided against the latter. Regardless of exactly how countries are reporting, few schools seem to meet accessibility standards. No more than 1 in 20 primary schools in Albania, Honduras and Zambia has adaptations (**Figure 17.3**).

A safe learning environment means not being actively at risk. If learners cannot reach school safely, their learning environment is unsafe. Many children run a risk of natural hazards, armed violence, sexual harassment and dangerous traffic to get to school (**Focus 17.2**).

On average, 45% of schools in low-income countries have basic water supply

"

FIGURE 17.1:

Most primary schools in many poor countries lack basic water, sanitation and hygiene facilities

Percentage of schools with basic drinking water, sanitation facilities and handwashing facilities, by data source, selected countries, 2018

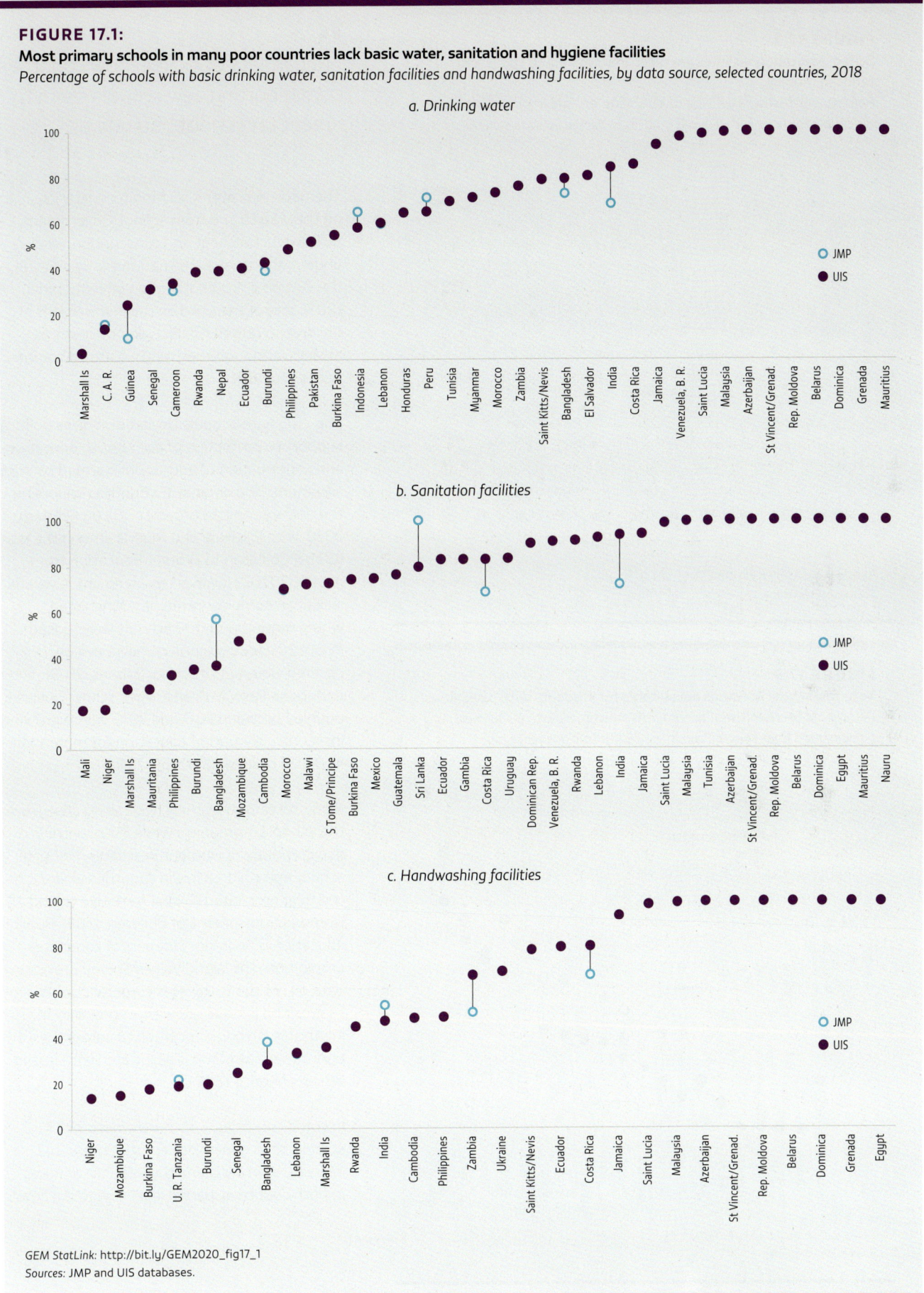

a. Drinking water

b. Sanitation facilities

c. Handwashing facilities

GEM StatLink: http://bit.ly/GEM2020_fig17_1

Sources: JMP and UIS databases.

FIGURE 17.2:
School sanitation facilities are often inaccessible to those with reduced mobility

Percentage of schools with improved sanitation, and improved sanitation accessible to those with reduced mobility, selected countries, 2016

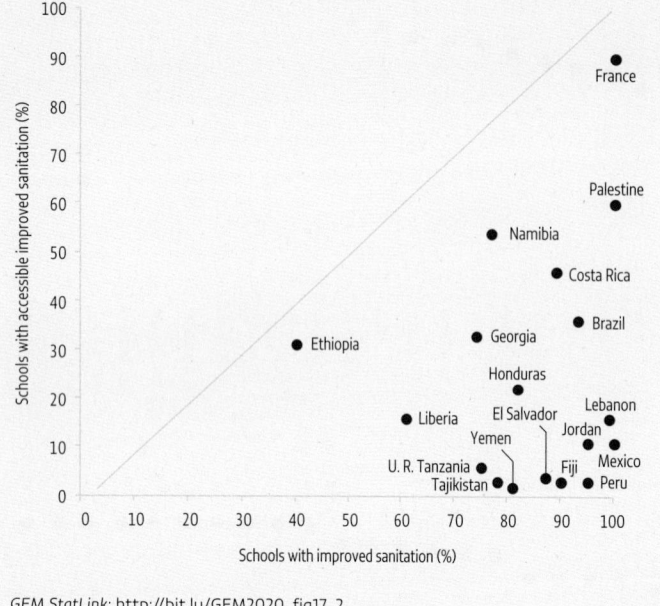

GEM StatLink: http://bit.ly/GEM2020_fig17_2
Source: JMP database.

FIGURE 17.3:
Very few school buildings are suitable for students with disabilities

Percentage of schools with adaptations for learners with disabilities, by education level, selected countries, 2018 or most recent year

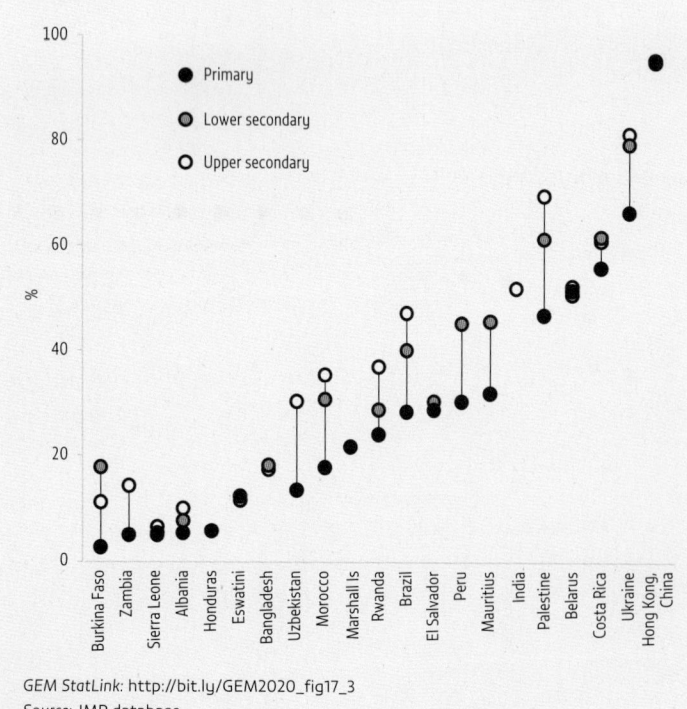

GEM StatLink: http://bit.ly/GEM2020_fig17_3
Source: JMP database.

> Regardless of exactly how countries are reporting, few schools seem to meet accessibility standards

Thematic indicator 4.a.3 monitors attacks on the way to and from school. Government military recruitment and conscription, legal under national and international laws such as the Optional Protocol to the Convention on the Rights of the Child on the Involvement of Children in Armed Conflict, do not count as attacks, although they may violate education rights (**Box 17.1**).

The 2015 Safe Schools Declaration gives political support to protection of the right to education and continuation of education in armed conflict situations. The original 37 countries endorsing the declaration had grown to 102 by February 2020, with Fiji, Haiti and Nigeria among the latest (Global Coalition to Protect Education from Attack, 2020). However, enforcement is severely lacking in some countries. In Afghanistan, where more than 1,000 schools were closed in late 2018 due to conflict, half a million children were out of school (Munns, 2019). In Burkina Faso, Mali and Niger, school closures doubled between 2017 and 2019 due to growing insecurity, disrupting education for more than 400,000 children (UNICEF, 2019b).

Many threats to learners' well-being arise from the school community. While 132 countries ban corporal punishment in schools, half of all school-age children live in countries where it is not fully prohibited (Global Initiative to End All Corporal Punishment of Children, 2019). Public education is an important part of complete prohibition. The World Values Survey provides data on attitudes towards corporal punishment that can be juxtaposed with its prevalence in schools. Strong opposition to corporal punishment at home is associated with less in schools (**Figure 17.4**).

In some countries, it is more widespread in schools than general lack of support would indicate, as in India and the Republic of Korea. In both countries, partial legal protection against

BOX 17.1:

Indefinite conscription is a major obstacle to education in Eritrea

Since 2003, in the context of the border war with Ethiopia, the Eritrean government has required all secondary school students to spend their final year at a specialized school in Sawa military camp. They are under military command even while studying, and must spend five months in military training (Bader, 2019). Afterwards, they join the army or train to work for the government as civilians. Despite a statutory limit of 18 months of national service, conscripts have often waited 5 or 10 years to be discharged. As recently as 2016, the government justified indefinite national service on the grounds that the country had not formally demobilized and remained on war alert. While length of conscription is decreasing, there have been no mass discharges of cohorts who have served several years (EASO, 2016). The government signed a peace agreement with Ethiopia in July 2018 but has made no formal changes to its compulsory conscription policy.

It is estimated that military service has pushed more than half a million of the country's nearly 5 million people into exile, most at aged 18 to 24. Some students leave school or opt for early marriage and motherhood to escape Sawa and conscription. Schools offer poor-quality education because teachers are often demotivated or absent, having had no choice of assignment or location (Bader, 2019).

Calls are mounting to allow students to complete secondary education at other public schools, enforce the national service limit, give teachers adequate training and choice about their professional futures, and make aid to education conditional on such changes (Bader, 2019). The award of the 2019 Nobel Peace Prize to Ethiopian Prime Minister Abiy Ahmed, not least for his initiative to resolve the conflict with Eritrea, has drawn attention that could lead to a chance to ensure a peace dividend for Eritrean youth.

FIGURE 17.4:
Corporal punishment in schools aligns with social attitudes
Percentage of adults who agree it is never justified for parents to beat their children and estimated prevalence of corporal punishment in schools, 2007–14

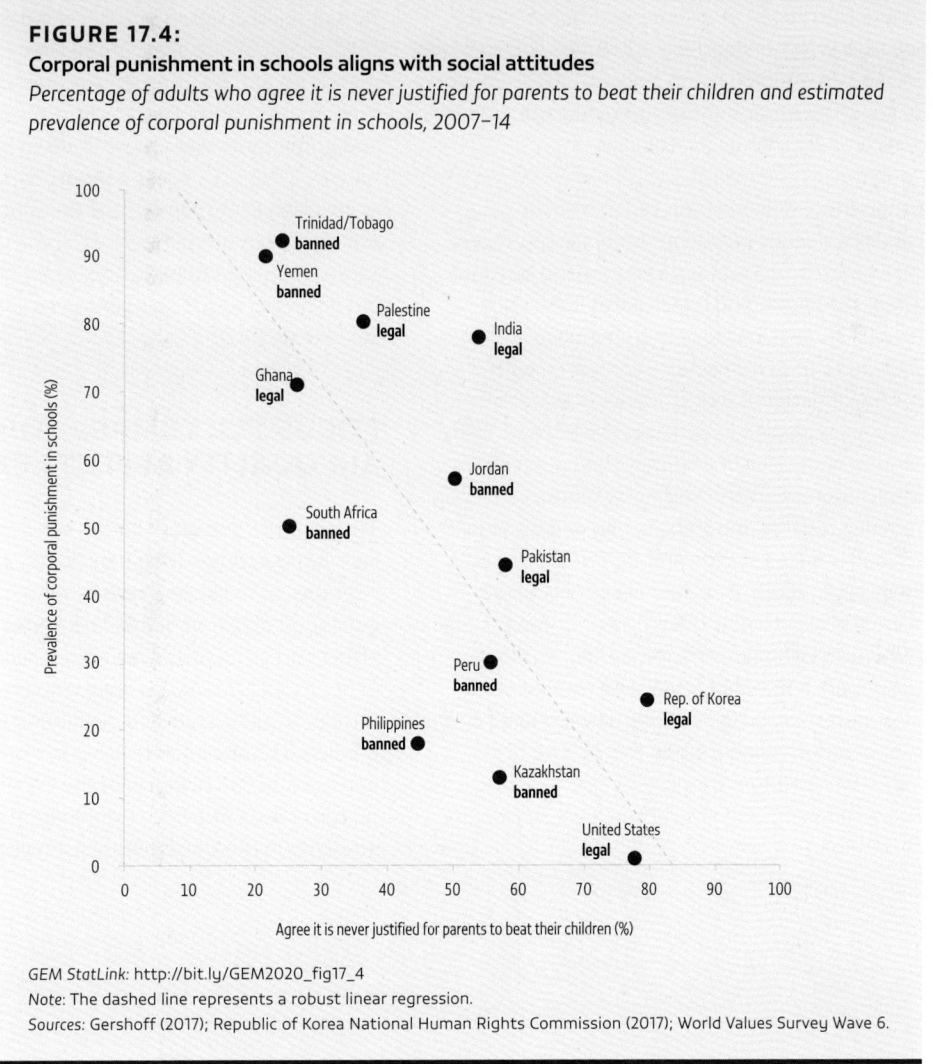

GEM StatLink: http://bit.ly/GEM2020_fig17_4
Note: The dashed line represents a robust linear regression.
Sources: Gershoff (2017); Republic of Korea National Human Rights Commission (2017); World Values Survey Wave 6.

> " Many children run a risk of natural hazards, armed violence, sexual harassment and dangerous traffic to get to school "

corporal punishment exists for some jurisdictions, types of school or age groups. Recent research suggests that parents in India distinguish between home and school, with 90% approving of corporal punishment in school. Parents may take a cue from teachers, a large majority punishing children beaten at school further. For underprivileged children, daily corporal punishment by teachers is practically universal (Agrasar, 2018).

In the Philippines and South Africa, where significant numbers of students are exposed to teacher violence despite bans, many people do not reject corporal punishment at home. Evidence from Viet Nam suggests that exposure to corporal punishment at home has a strong negative effect on learning outcomes and spillover effects on peers' learning (Le and Nguyen, 2019). Ensuring that bans are effective, and maximizing education quality, may require broader change in attitudes.

Bullying and school violence targeted at lesbian, gay, bisexual and transgender students occurs everywhere. In the United States, 12.5% of lesbian, gay and bisexual students reported not going to school at least once in the previous 30 days because they felt unsafe at or on their way to and from school, compared with less than 4.6% of heterosexual students (Kann et al., 2016). Research exploiting variation in the introduction of state anti-bullying laws found that they reduced victimization, depression and suicidal ideation, especially among female students and lesbian, gay and bisexual teenagers, and reduced suicide among females by up to 16% (Rees et al., 2020). Few countries collect such data, leaving the task to non-government organizations (NGOs). Where reporting mechanisms exist, students may under-report homophobic violence for fear of further stigmatization. A UNESCO technical brief provides guidance on strengthening routine monitoring of this issue in national and international surveys, including on terminology, sampling, and ethical and legal challenges (UNESCO, 2019b).

Avoiding cyberbullying is a key aspect of education for digital skills, even for young children. It is a central plank of the Power of Zero campaign led by No Bully, a US NGO aiming to strengthen the ability of children aged 5 to 8 to use the internet positively. It identifies four essential online skills: 'harness opportunities of the digital world for play, creativity, expression and connection; keep safe and respond effectively to risks and challenges of the online world; develop a commitment to zero bullying; and use their online power for good' (Power of Zero, 2018).

The proportion of cyberbullied children aged 11 to 16 in Belgium, Denmark, Ireland, Italy, Portugal, Romania and the United Kingdom rose from 7% in 2010 to 12% in 2014. Lack of more recent data is troublesome. Despite growing concern, with countries including Italy and Lebanon providing teacher training on online safety and prevention and reporting of cyberbullying, there are fewer data on cyberbullying than on other types of bullying (UNESCO, 2019a). The last round of Health Behaviour in School-aged Children in 2013/14 indicated that 10% of children in Canada and Europe were cyberbullied through messages and 8% through pictures. Girls were more likely to be cyberbullied through messages than boys, and immigrants were more likely to be cyberbullied than natives (UNESCO, 2018). School policies play a crucial role in ensuring that members of the school community do not hurt each other. However, some policies promoting safety may lead to exclusion, especially if sanctions are disproportionate and enforced with zero tolerance (see **Focus 10.2**).

FOCUS 17.1: TEMPERATURE AND AIR QUALITY AFFECT LEARNING

Temperature and air pollution can significantly affect learning outcomes (Barshay, 2020). A study on the relationship between extreme temperatures and education attainment in 29 countries found adverse effects on schooling, even among wealthier households. In South-eastern Asia, a child who experiences temperatures 2 standard deviations above average is predicted to attain 1.5 fewer years of schooling (Randell and Gray, 2019). Analysis of the impact of extreme heat on the college entrance examination results of 10 million students in the United States showed that those who experienced hotter days before an examination had lower achievement and that extreme heat was especially detrimental for poor and minority students. A 1.8°C increase in average school year temperatures lowered learning outcomes by 1%, as did 6 days above 32.2°C. Air conditioning almost entirely offset these effects (Goodman et al., 2018).

Experimental studies in China and Costa Rica confirmed the negative effects of extreme temperatures (Porras-Salazar et al., 2018; Wang et al., 2018). A meta-analysis of studies from temperate climates suggests that a decrease from 30°C to 20°C in classrooms would increase test performance by 20%, on average, the optimal temperature estimated to be below 22°C. The effects of extreme temperatures are considered more severe for children in classrooms than adults in offices, where the estimated optimum temperature threshold is higher (Wargocki et al., 2019). In the 2015 Trends in International Mathematics and Science Study, over 30% of head teachers in Bahrain, the Islamic Republic of Iran, Kuwait, Oman, Saudi Arabia, Turkey and the United Arab Emirates reported that insufficient cooling in schools substantially affected student learning (UNESCO, 2017).

Air pollution can reduce cognitive ability significantly and perhaps irreversibly, given suspected neurotoxicity (Costa et al., 2017). Analysis of chess player behaviour estimated that a standard deviation increase in dust raised both the probability of making an error and the magnitude of errors (Kunn et al., 2019). Even temporary exposure to dust reduced Israeli students' examination performance and post-secondary education attainment (Ebenstein et al., 2016). A cohort study of almost 3,000 children in Barcelona, Spain, found that, adjusting for socio-economic status, those exposed to high pollution levels in school had less cognitive development growth than peers in less polluted schools (Sunyer et al., 2015). In the United States, children attending schools downwind of a major highway, and as a result experiencing more air pollution, had lower test scores, more absences and more behavioural incidents than peers attending otherwise similar schools located

> " Poor ventilation and high CO_2 concentration in classrooms can substantially reduce student performance "

upwind of a highway. Effects were larger for busier roads and continued after children left downwind schools (Heissel et al., 2019). Schools in India, Mexico and Thailand close when air pollution exceeds certain levels (The Economist, 2019).

Cars and power plants are widely recognized external sources of air pollutants. Buildings can magnify or emit pollutants, for instance from building materials, devices and volatile chemicals in furnishings (Baron, 2019). Poor ventilation and high CO_2 concentration in classrooms can substantially reduce student performance (Bakó-Biró et al., 2012). Indoor air quality is often much poorer than is thought. In the United Kingdom, a study on London schools found higher levels of damaging air pollution inside classrooms than outside, putting children at risk of lifelong health problems (Mumovic et al., 2018).

Although evidence comes from the Global North, implications are worrying for the Global South, where pollution levels are higher, industrialization is increasing and global warming effects are likely stronger, presenting mounting challenges in providing suitable learning environments. A study examining the effect of a 2°C rise in global temperature by 2050 forecasts that 22% of cities will experience climate conditions not currently experienced by any major city (Bastin et al., 2019). The tropics face increasingly frequent extreme weather. At higher temperatures and humidity, sweat cannot cool the body (Matthews, 2019). Governments need to ensure that buildings not only provide suitable learning environments but are carbon neutral and limit other pollutants. Building design can play a role, but mechanical ventilation and air filtration, and their associated costs, need to be planned for.

FOCUS 17.2: SAFE SCHOOLS MUST BE SAFE TO REACH

In poorer countries, there is little political support and therefore limited budget for improving children's safety on the way to and from school. Children experience physical exhaustion, violence and harassment, and exposure to significant danger on their routes. Journeys may be long and arduous, especially in rural areas with poor infrastructure and public transport. This disproportionately affects poor children whose parents cannot afford public transport or commute long distances to work and cannot accompany children to school. Some children walk several hours. Evidence from Brazil showed that the longer the commute, the worse the impact on academic performance (Tigre et al., 2017). In Delhi, India, young women were willing to enrol in a college of lower quality if it was accessible by a safer route (Borker, 2018).

Violence against girls and neighbourhood violence are common. In Haiti, 27% of women who received money for sex before age 18 listed schools and school neighbourhoods as the most common location for solicitation (Rames et al., 2016). Rape on the school commute was a parental worry in many countries in Africa (Greene et al., 2011). Students in urban and peri-urban areas of South Africa cited violence as a major fear (International Forum for Rural Transport and Development, 2010). Evidence from Brazil showed that exposure to violence and homicide on the way to school, in areas surrounding schools or at home negatively affected repetition, dropout and achievement (Koppensteiner and Menezes, 2017). Walking instead of taking a bus through violent neighbourhoods in Baltimore, United States, increased absenteeism (Burdick-Will et al., 2019). Introduction of a bus service at Marquette University in the US state of Wisconsin reduced crime in the neighbourhood, especially along the route (Heywood and Weber, 2019).

> 66
>
> In Delhi, India, young women were willing to enrol in a college of lower quality if it was accessible by a safer route
>
> 99

Students face physical risks, such as ditches that especially younger children find difficult to cross. Flash floods in the wet season can be lethal for children unable to swim – a gendered risk, as girls are less likely to know how. Wildlife presents significant dangers (International Forum for Rural Transport and Development, 2010). Students in Kenya's Kakuma refugee camp collaborated with graduate students at the University of Geneva to geolocate incidences of snakebite with mobile phones. An app mapped snake sightings to help identify safe routes (Moser-Mercer, 2018).

Traffic accidents rank at or near the top of the most significant dangers. Children walking to school are disproportionately affected because many schools are located along major highways, and children have more limited impulse control, slower reaction time and poorer risk perception than adults (Silverman, 2016). Traffic is especially dangerous in poorer countries (Silverman and Billingsley, 2015) and neighbourhoods (Lin et al., 2019). Rapid, unplanned growth contributes to poor road conditions and inadequate urban traffic design, putting pedestrians and other vulnerable road users at risk, especially when combined with lack of stringent vehicle safety standards.

Despite having far fewer vehicles, poorer countries have a far higher risk of accidents and fatal accidents. There are 6.2 fatalities among 5- to 14-year-olds per 100,000 people in low-income countries, which average 8 vehicles per 1,000 people, compared with 1.7 in high-income countries, where the average is 528 (**Figure 17.5**). An International Road Assessment Programme survey of nearly 250,000 km of roads in 60 countries found that more than 80% with a traffic flow over 40 km/h and used by pedestrians had no pavements (Welle et al., 2016).

Traffic education is important. The Global Initiative for Child Health and Mobility, coordinated and funded by the FIA Foundation, aims to ensure safe and healthy school journeys for all children by 2030 (FIA Foundation, 2016). Within the SDG framework, it campaigns for speed limits, viable footpaths and cycle lanes (FIA Foundation, 2020). Finding a safe place to cross the road is more difficult for those with intellectual disability, as their ability to focus and ignore irrelevant stimuli is weaker. Road safety education should take into account their attention and cognitive style using virtual reality technology (Alevriadou, 2010).

> Traffic accidents rank at or near the top of the most significant dangers

Systemic solutions are needed. The Safe System approach to traffic planning is a promising evidence-based initiative, pioneered in Sweden as Vision Zero. It recognized that, while human fallibility is inevitable, serious injuries and fatalities are not. Road system design should ensure that human error has no serious outcomes (Welle et al., 2016). The Republic of Korea reduced child traffic injuries by 95%, from 1,766 in 1988 to 83 in 2012, using a comprehensive approach that combined safe school routes, road safety legislation and education, and measures such as free car seats for low-income households (Silverman, 2016).

Many successful initiatives and system designs are yet to be widely adopted. In Kenya, Global Road Safety Partnership and WHO worked with government to lower speed limits, reducing traffic injuries among students. Thailand's 7 Percent Project coalition tackles the issue of the more than a million children who ride to school on their parents' scooters, of whom only 7% wear helmets. Uruguay's Safely Back to School campaign resulted in legislation requiring all school transport vehicles to have three-point, height-adjustable seat belts, which has become a reference for other Latin American countries (Silverman and Billingsley, 2015).

FIGURE 17.5:

Children in poorer countries with fewer vehicles are more likely to die in traffic accidents

Road fatalities of children aged 5 to 14 per 100,000 people and road vehicles per 1,000 people, by country income group, 2014

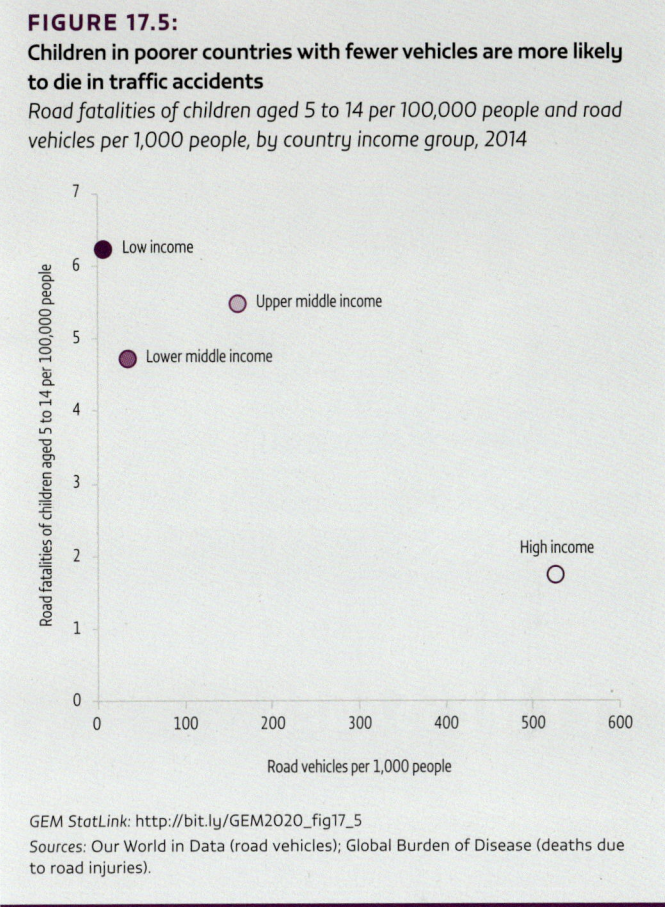

GEM StatLink: http://bit.ly/GEM2020_fig17_5

Sources: Our World in Data (road vehicles); Global Burden of Disease (deaths due to road injuries).

Engineering master's student from Syria on a scholarship at the German Jordanian University (GJU) near Madaba, Jordan.

CREDIT: UNHCR/Antoine Tardy

KEY MESSAGES

Aid for post-secondary education amounted to US$6.1 billion in 2018; of that, US$3.1 billion represented scholarships and imputed student costs.

Some lower-middle-income countries, including Eswatini and the Republic of Moldova, receive the highest level of scholarship aid per capita. Overall, small island developing states tend to receive some of the highest per capita scholarship flows, as highly specialized degrees are seldom available in those countries and necessitate study abroad.

The top 50 scholarship aid providers, amounting to 94% of the estimated total number of scholarships targeted to sub-Saharan African students, offered some 30,000 new scholarships in 2019 for 2020 entry. Scholarships reached the equivalent of 0.4% of the 8.1 million sub-Saharan African tertiary education students.

China increased total scholarships to African students for 2019–22 to 50,000, or 5,000 more scholarships per year. The German Academic Exchange Service increased scholarships to the region by 900 between 2014 and 2017.

Some 30% of scholarships to African students can be classified as inclusive, in the sense that they offered full funding and met at least one developmental objective; but most providers cannot provide detailed information on scholars' background.

University selection procedures and learning environments are often poorly aligned to the needs of vulnerable sub-Saharan African students.

CHAPTER 18

TARGET 4.B

Scholarships

By 2020, substantially expand globally the number of scholarships available to developing countries, in particular least developed countries, small island developing States and African countries, for enrolment in higher education, including vocational training and information and communications technology, technical, engineering and scientific programmes, in developed countries and other developing countries

GLOBAL INDICATOR

4.b.1 – *Volume of official development assistance flows for scholarships, by sector and type of study*

Target 4.b is one of few in the United Nations (UN) 2030 Agenda for Sustainable Development with a 2020 deadline. While it focuses on number of scholarships available, there is no comprehensive database of scholarships for reporting. Research conducted for this report aims to fill the gap, focusing on numbers and trends among sub-Saharan African students. Well-targeted scholarships can promote equity, but the target is open to criticism as other targets have a stronger equity emphasis. Scholarships available to sub-Saharan African students cover a fraction of upper secondary school graduates, for instance. The analysis in this chapter addresses questions of whether scholarships contribute to equity and which particular programmes do so (**Focus 18.1**).

Aid for post-secondary education amounted to US$6.1 billion in 2018, of which US$3.1 billion represented scholarships and imputed student costs, i.e. expenditure in publicly financed tertiary education institutions for students from developing countries. Total expenditure on scholarships and imputed student costs is US$3.5 billion if aid to other sectors is considered. Imputed costs are high in countries with largely free higher education, such as France and Germany (**Figure 18.1**). However, both counties have been revising their policies. France increased tuition fees for non-EU nationals in April 2019, e.g. from EUR 170 to EUR 2,770 per year for bachelor's programmes (Hansrod, 2019). The German state of Baden-Württemberg reintroduced tuition fees for international students in 2017/18 (Gardner, 2016). Countries that charge fees for public tertiary education tuition could be expected to have more resources available to provide more scholarship aid.

However, the United Kingdom, the largest scholarship provider charging tertiary education fees, allocates just 12% more scholarship aid than Germany and 28% less than France.

Aid to post-secondary education projects other than scholarships and imputed student costs may support academic mobility. In 2017, the European Union allocated US$52 million to support post-secondary projects. Its Intra-Africa Academic Mobility Scheme supports tertiary education cooperation with African countries to increase the number of highly trained professionals in the region (European Commission, 2019).

While larger student populations attract more scholarship aid, countries with similar student populations differ widely in average amount of scholarship aid per student. Some lower-middle-income countries, such as Eswatini and the Republic of Moldova, receive the highest level of scholarship aid per capita (**Figure 18.2a**). Overall, however, it is small island developing states that receive some of the highest per capita scholarship flows. Pacific islands receive far more scholarship aid per capita than Caribbean islands, with sub-Saharan African island states in the middle (**Figure 18.2b**). Highly specialized degrees are seldom available in those countries and necessitate study abroad.

> " Total expenditure on scholarships and imputed student costs is US$3.5 billion if aid to other sectors is considered "

FIGURE 18.1:

France and Germany account for most aid to post-secondary education through scholarships and imputed student costs

Aid to post-secondary education, 2015–17

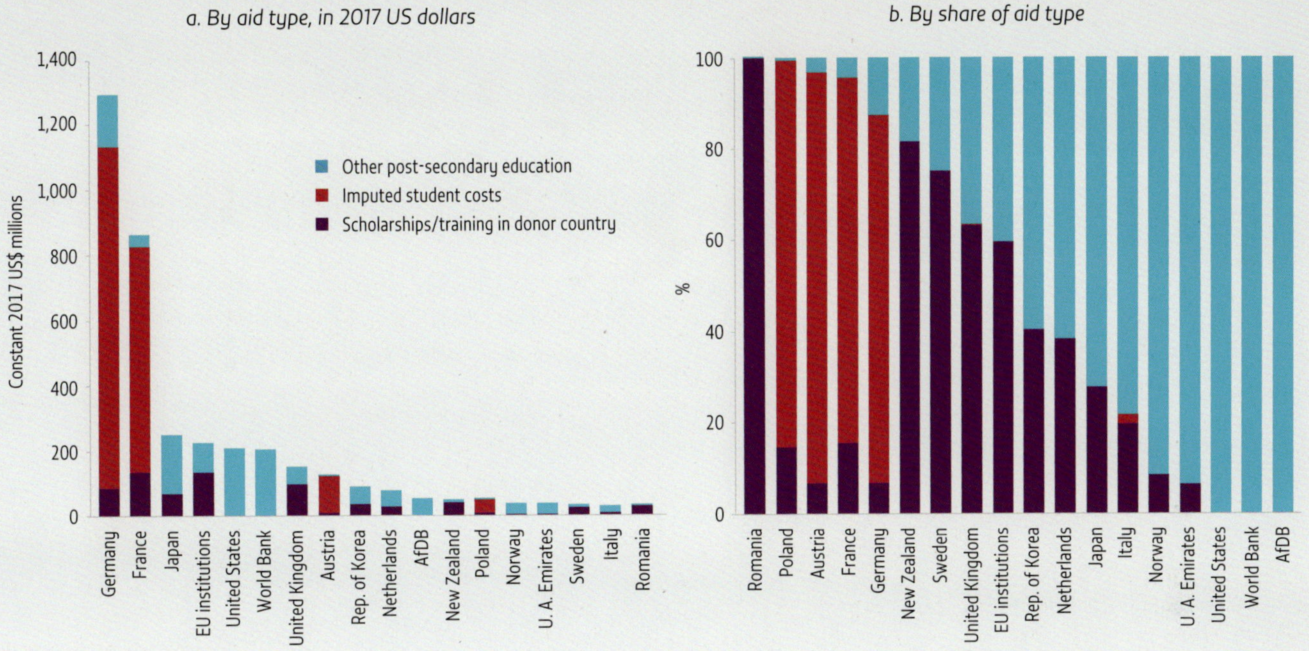

a. By aid type, in 2017 US dollars

Legend:
- Other post-secondary education
- Imputed student costs
- Scholarships/training in donor country

b. By share of aid type

GEM StatLink: http://bit.ly/GEM2020_fig18_1
Source: GEM Report team analysis based on the OECD-DAC CRS database (2019).

FOCUS 18.1: SCHOLARSHIPS FOR SUB-SAHARAN AFRICAN STUDENTS ARE INCREASING IN NUMBER BUT NEED TO BE INCLUSIVE

Target 4.b calls for monitoring the number of scholarships available to developing countries, but there is no data collection mechanism. Past editions of the *Global Education Monitoring Report* proposed ways to fill the gap, but there has been insufficient funding interest. In-depth analysis of scholarship opportunities for sub-Saharan African students, conducted for this report, is a further step.[1]

The top 50 scholarship aid providers offered some 30,000 new scholarships in 2019 for 2020 entry.

---

1   This Focus draws on research by Education Sub Saharan Africa (ESSA).

> " A small number of large providers accounted for most scholarships in sub-Saharan Africa "

They amounted to 94% of the estimated total number of scholarships targeted to sub-Saharan African students, according to a mapping of more than 200 providers. In other words, a small number of large providers accounted for most scholarships in the region. Undergraduate scholarships accounted for 56% (**Figure 18.3**). Scholarships reached the equivalent of 0.4% of the 8.1 million sub-Saharan African tertiary education students.

Government initiatives dominate scholarship provision for sub-Saharan African students. The Chinese government, through various agencies, was the single

FIGURE 18.2:

Countries with more students receive more scholarship aid, but small island developing states receive higher levels per capita

Volume of official development assistance for scholarships, by region and tertiary education enrolment, 2018

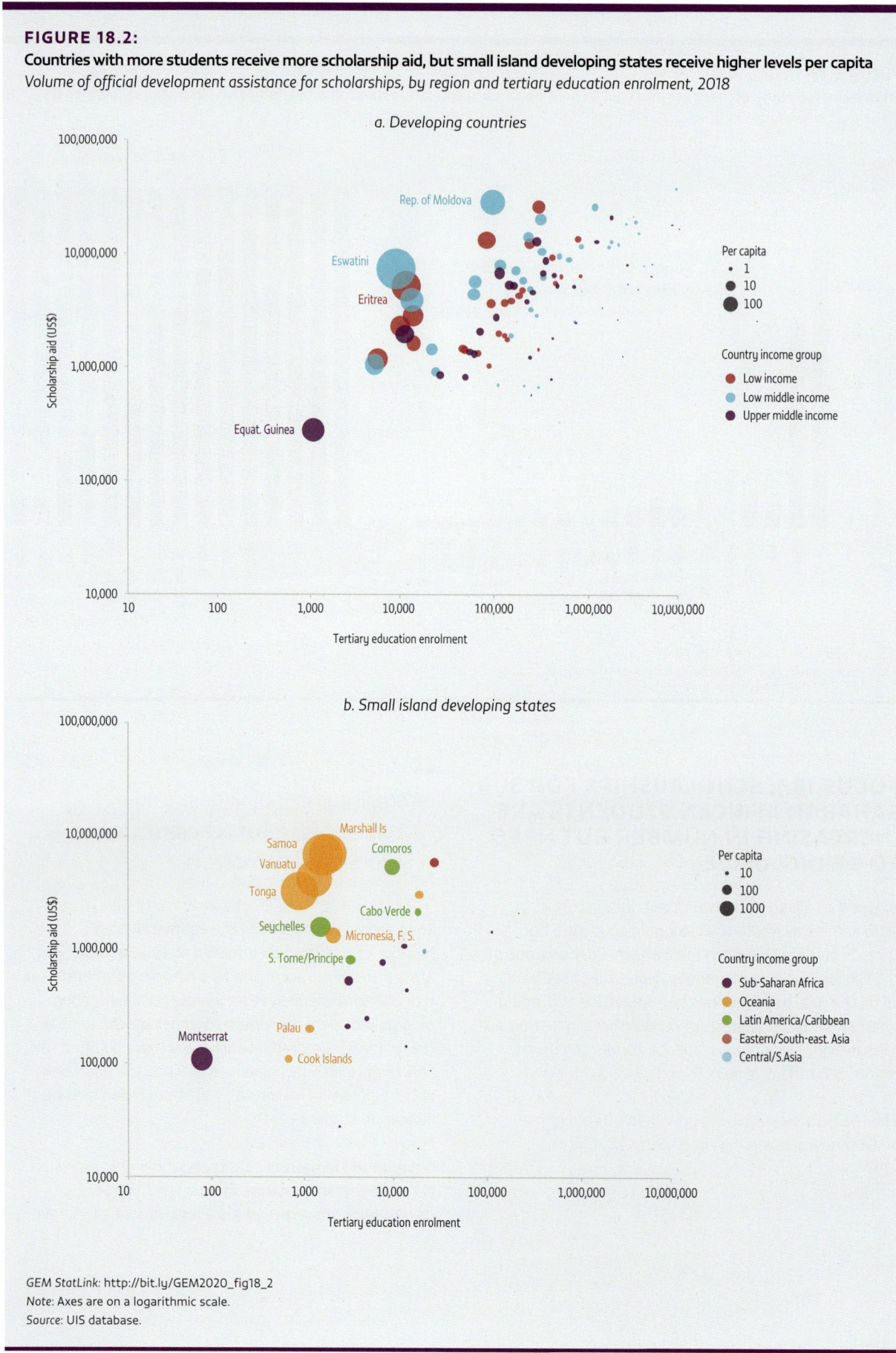

GEM StatLink: http://bit.ly/GEM2020_fig18_2
Note: Axes are on a logarithmic scale.
Source: UIS database.

> " At least 10 of the top 50 providers and 30 smaller programmes have launched initiatives or expanded programming in the last five years "

FIGURE 18.3:

A majority of tertiary education scholarships for sub-Saharan African students are for undergraduate study

Distribution of tertiary education scholarships for sub-Saharan African students offered by the largest 50 providers, by degree type, 2019

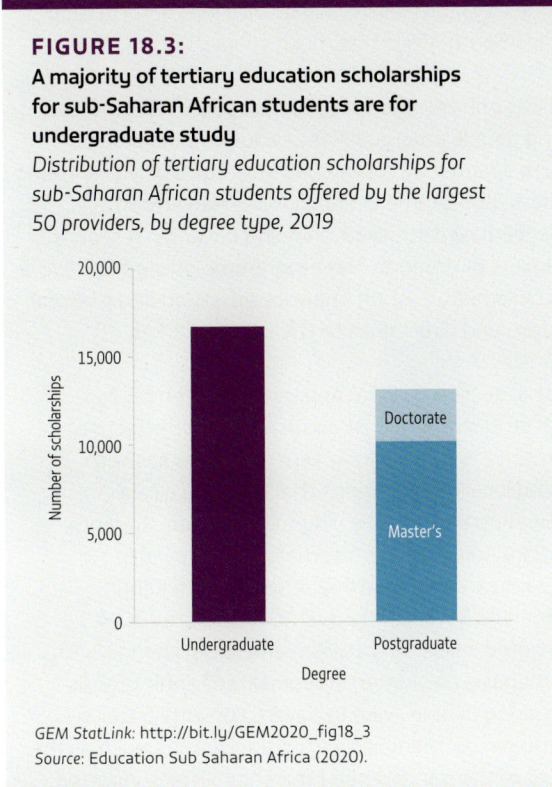

GEM StatLink: http://bit.ly/GEM2020_fig18_3
Source: Education Sub Saharan Africa (2020).

and 30 smaller programmes have launched initiatives or expanded programming in the last five years.

In 2018, China increased total scholarships (new and ongoing) for 2019–22 to 50,000, up from 30,000 in the previous three years. This represents an additional 5,000 scholarships per year, or 16% of the estimated 2019 total. DAAD, the German Academic Exchange Service, increased scholarships to the region by 900 between 2014 and 2017. In 2018, the UK government pledged a further 100 scholarships annually through its Chevening programme. The World Bank recently launched a programme with more than 500 postgraduate scholarships for western Africa. In 2015, India announced 50,000 scholarships over the next five years in a pledge to the African Development Bank. Smaller programmes continue to emerge, but philanthropic scholarship funding was heavily concentrated among a small number of large providers and reliant on their continued interest. The MasterCard Foundation was estimated to account for four times the volume of scholarship funds as the second-biggest philanthropic programme.

Scholarships must be well-targeted to affect sustainable development. They must create opportunities otherwise unavailable. Assessing inclusion is difficult. Donors and providers tend not to have verifiable metrics; they may not even have inclusion objectives. One approach to defining programmes as inclusive is to consider those that offer full funding (tuition and living expenses) and have one or more of the following objectives: (a) access and empower young people from marginalized groups, (b) prepare applicants for decent work, and (c) promote sub-Saharan African universities through programming involving long-term partnerships with institutions, including local education non-profit and non-government organizations (NGOs).

Some 30% of scholarships can thus be classified as inclusive, and 31 of the top 50 providers as offering inclusive scholarships. All 10 international organizations in the top 50 are classified as offering inclusive scholarships and account for 28% of the total number of such opportunities. The African Union, the EU Erasmus+

largest provider, with over 12,000 opportunities annually. The next-largest government providers were South Africa, the Russian Federation, the United Kingdom, Turkey, Egypt, India, Germany and Japan. International organizations, including the UN High Commissioner for Refugees, the African Union, the European Union and the World Bank, were also prominent in the top 25. Corporations, including public enterprises and corporate foundations, represented 5 of the top 50 providers. The MasterCard Foundation and ABSA Bank contributed 95% of all corporate scholarships.

Although aid for scholarships has been stagnant since 2010 (UNESCO, 2018), opportunities in sub-Saharan Africa have increased since 2015 and will likely increase over the next five years. At least 10 of the top 50 providers programme, DAAD, the KfW Development Bank and the World Bank have launched or accelerated inclusive programmes. One particular inclusion concern is related to the approximately 60% of recipients who study outside sub-Saharan Africa. They often face application processes, selection procedures and learning environments that are challenging for sub-Saharan African applicants, and existing programmes do not cater sufficiently to their needs.

Only 6% of the poorest 20% in sub-Saharan Africa complete upper secondary education, and almost none attend post-secondary. As part of the mapping for this report, the feasibility of collecting data on key performance indicators for inclusive scholarship programmes was trialled anonymously with 20 scholarship providers (10 in the top 50) that exemplified good practice in scholarship programming. One objective was to ascertain how many scholarships were awarded to members of disadvantaged groups. Most providers could not provide detailed background information, e.g. whether recipients had rural backgrounds or a disability. Almost all providers measured the share of female recipients. Two programmes targeted women exclusively; the share in other programmes ranged from 32% to 57%, with most at the upper end of the range.

Whether scholarships benefit recipients is another important indicator – in particular, whether recipients complete their studies, stay in or return to sub-Saharan Africa, and/or transition into decent work or further education. A few programmes involved agreements with graduates compelling them to return to home countries. Few were legally binding.

All providers tracked programme completion. In all but two cases, completion rates were 85%, including programmes operating at African universities. This contrasts favourably with low undergraduate and postgraduate completion rates across the region, including in South Africa. However, in the absence of student background information, high rates may reflect privileged backgrounds. Movement information was generally available one but not three or five years after graduation. Many providers aside from the 20 studied more closely, especially those offering scholarships for study outside Africa, had student return rates of 25% to 45%. Providers operating in South Africa generally had good information and above 90% success rates when

> **" General calls for applications often fail to reach students at risk of exclusion "**

it came to graduates finding quality jobs. Information outside South Africa was much sparser.

Five key principles to target and support marginalized young people emerged. First, inclusive scholarships require adequately researched strategies. The Dell Young Leaders programme in South Africa had strong evidence-based strategic planning based on research on drivers of dropout. The programme offered funding to supplement existing financial aid, study and pastoral support, and direct links to the labour market.

Second, general calls for applications often fail to reach students at risk of exclusion. A cost-effective alternative is to build long-term relationships with trusted local organizations that can play a role in nominating and interviewing marginalized students. The Ford Foundation's International Fellowship programme sponsored 562 scholars from Kenya, Nigeria and South Africa over 10 years, until 2014. It targeted leaders in activism and social change, with an emphasis on women, marginalized ethnic groups and young people living in poverty or with disability. Long-term partnerships with organizations, such as the Forum for African Women Educationalists, supported successful targeting.

Third, marginalized students need tailored programmes to support their university experience, including orientation, study and life skills training, mentoring and pastoral support, workplace preparation and psychosocial support. The Moshal Scholarship Program in South Africa introduced an early warning system to monitor students' academic progress. It offered monthly face-to-face support meetings and responded quickly to major life events.

Fourth, scholarship providers would benefit from tracking graduates' pathways to livelihood opportunities and refining planning and modelling to improve employment outcomes. Alumni tracking showed that disadvantaged graduates faced prejudice and obstacles in finding decent work, even when qualified. The Regional Universities Forum for Capacity Building in Agriculture, a pan-African organization offering students from rural communities postgraduate scholarships at local universities, closely aligned degrees with agricultural opportunities in students' communities, resulting in 75% of graduates finding decent work in the formal sector or as entrepreneurs.

Fifth, providers often operate in isolation, with no culture of cooperation and few platforms to facilitate coordination. This was reflected in a strong geographical bias, with most programmes either targeted to, or taken up by, students from a small number of the more developed anglophone countries. A notable example of cooperation, emphasizing the importance of providing scholarship opportunities to a wider group of francophone, lusophone and low-income countries, was the Ashinaga Africa Initiative, a Japanese non-profit organization. Working with national governments, local NGOs, international universities and staff on the ground, it has sponsored 184 undergraduates from 44 countries since 2014, the vast majority being first-generation scholars.

"I love my teacher Nana. She teaches me and plays with me. I am also strong because I do karate", said Mohammad, 16 years old, with his Makani facilitator. He is attending Life Skills in his local UNICEF-supported Makani Centre in Zarqa, Jordan.

CREDIT: UNICEF/Herwig

KEY MESSAGES

Global data on teacher training is patchy and often not of good quality. Apparent progress in the share of trained teachers, for example in Cameroon and Liberia, is contradicted by implausible large year-on-year changes or discrepancies between school census and teacher education provider data.

Primary pupil/teacher ratios in sub-Saharan Africa have declined since 2010, to levels last seen in the mid-1990s, but remain very high at 40:1 and reach over 50:1 in Malawi and the United Republic of Tanzania.

Preschool teachers are less likely to be trained, even in high-income countries such as Iceland, where only 64% of staff had been trained.

Data on teaching assistants is limited, even in high-income countries. In Chile, the Netherlands and the United Kingdom, pupil/teacher ratios fall by 15% to 20% when teaching assistants are included – and more in pre-primary education.

Many high-income countries specify statutory working time for teachers, which often bears little relation to actual working hours. But the latter are difficult to estimate. Teachers tend to report more hours when they add up time spent on specific tasks than when they report the total number of working hours in a week. The public tends to perceive teachers as working fewer hours than they do.

CHAPTER 19

TARGET 4.c

Teachers

By 2030, substantially increase the supply of qualified teachers, including through international cooperation for teacher training in developing countries, especially least developed countries and small island developing States

---

GLOBAL INDICATOR

4.c.1 – *Proportion of teachers with the minimum required qualifications, by education level*

THEMATIC INDICATORS

4.c.2 – *Pupil-trained teacher ratio by education level*

4.c.3 – *Percentage of teachers qualified according to national standards by level and type of institution*

4.c.4 – *Pupil-qualified teacher ratio by education level*

4.c.5 – *Average teacher salary relative to other professions requiring a comparable level of qualification*

4.c.6 – *Teacher attrition rate by education level*

4.c.7 – *Percentage of teachers who received in-service training in the last 12 months by type of training*

Progress towards SDG 4 is impossible without teachers trained to take on multiple challenges. Patchy global data show that many lack adequate training. In sub-Saharan Africa, 49% of pre-primary, 64% of primary, 58% of lower secondary and 43% of upper secondary school teachers received minimum training according to national standards. Female teachers are as likely to be trained as male colleagues (**Table 19.1**).

In the 2010s, many countries have data showing increases in the share of trained teachers, e.g. by 23 percentage points in Cameroon and Liberia (**Figure 19.1**). Due to data quality issues, however, there is doubt as to how much change such trends reflect. In Cameroon, the share rose by 21 percentage points between 2010 and 2012, had fallen by the same amount by 2015 and increased by 23 points by 2017. Such large year-on-year changes are not plausible. In Liberia, a review of school census data found information discrepancies between teacher education providers

> " In sub-Saharan Africa, 49% of pre-primary, 64% of primary, 58% of lower secondary and 43% of upper secondary school teachers received minimum training according to national standards "

and graduates of initial three-week to nine-month programmes awarding the minimum qualification (C Certificate) (Ginsburg et al., 2018).

While training (preparation to be a teacher) differs from qualification (having a specific level of formal schooling), many countries do not report on trained and qualified teachers separately (see **Chapter 9**). Data on pupil/trained teacher ratios (thematic indicator 4.c.2) and pupil/qualified teacher ratios (thematic

TABLE 19.1:
Percentage of trained teachers, by education level, 2018

	Pre-primary			Primary			Lower secondary			Upper secondary		
	Total	Female	Male	Total	Female	Male	Total	Female	Male	Total	Female	Male
World	..	..	..	85	87	81	84	85	82	..	..	..
Sub-Saharan Africa	49	47	56	64	63	65	58	59	58	43	47	41
Northern Africa and Western Asia	82	82	84	86	85	87	84	85	83	86	87	85
Central and Southern Asia	..	..	..	73	73	72	78	78	77	81	89	75
Eastern and South-eastern Asia	..	..	..	..	..	..	..	..	..	..	..	..
Latin America and the Caribbean	76	76	66	90	90	87	83	82	83	82	83	81
Oceania	..	..	..	..	..	..	..	..	..	..	..	..
Europe and Northern America	..	..	..	..	..	..	..	..	..	..	..	..
Low income	44	45	36	72	74	70	..	..	..	..	..	..
Lower middle income	..	..	..	76	79	73	78	80	76	79	84	74
Upper middle income	..	..	..	..	..	..	..	..	..	..	..	..
High income	..	..	..	..	..	..	..	..	..	..	..	..

Source: UIS database.

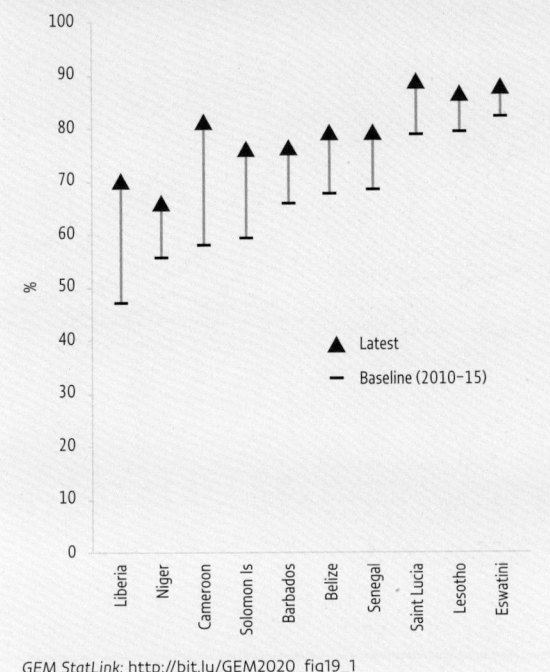

FIGURE 19.1:
Several countries have increased the share of trained primary school teachers
Percentage of trained primary school teachers, countries with the largest increases in the 2010s

▲ Latest
— Baseline (2010–15)

GEM StatLink: http://bit.ly/GEM2020_fig19_1
Source: UIS database.

> **Teacher satisfaction with salary ranged from 10% in Iceland to 39% in Turkey, but most staff reported overall job satisfaction, from 79% in Korea to 98% in Israel**

the ratio fell from 32:1 to 27:1 at the secondary education level (grades 9 and 10) and remained constant at 38:1 for higher secondary education (grades 11 and 12). Conversely, two other striking facts in the Indian national data are not captured in the internationally comparable data. Implementation of the Right to Education law led to a sharp decrease in the pupil/teacher ratio between 2011/12 and 2012/14, from 41:1 to 25:1 for primary education (grades 1 to 5) and 34:1 to 17:1 for upper primary (grades 6 to 8) (**Figure 19.3a**). Secondary and higher secondary education ratios in a handful of northern Indian states, including Bihar, Jharkhand and Uttar Pradesh, were over twice the national average (**Figure 19.3b**).

Education support personnel, including teaching assistants and specialists, such as sign language interpreters, are present in many classrooms, especially in inclusive settings. How they affect pupil/teacher ratios is not clear-cut (**Focus 19.1**). Ratios based on headcount may not account for teachers' varying working hours (**Focus 19.2**).

indicator 4.c.4) are therefore patchy. Overall pupil/teacher ratios are more readily available. They remain extremely high in several countries, especially in sub-Saharan Africa. Primary education ratios have declined since 2010, returning to levels reached in the mid-1990s. The Central African Republic, Malawi and the United Republic of Tanzania have struggled to achieve a ratio of 50:1, as has Rwanda, despite its recent progress from a high starting point. Secondary education ratios have declined in sub-Saharan Africa and Central and Southern Asia (**Figure 19.2**).

Southern Asia saw a sudden increase in the upper secondary education ratio in 2013. While the internationally comparable data suggest this increase was driven by India, the Indian national data do not reflect this trend. Between 2008/09 and 2014/15,

Pre-primary school teachers are less likely to be trained. The Starting Strong Teaching and Learning International Survey of the Organisation for Economic Co-operation and Development (OECD) collected data in nine countries on early childhood care and education (ECCE) staff characteristics, work practices, beliefs about child development and views on the profession and the sector. While the teachers typically had post-secondary education, not all were trained to work with children: The share with training in Iceland was 64%. Satisfaction with salary ranged from 10% in Iceland to 39% in Turkey, but most staff reported overall job satisfaction, from 79% in Korea to 98% in Israel (OECD, 2019b).

Target 4.c considers teachers a 'means of implementation'; however, their key individual and collective role as active agents of educational

FIGURE 19.2:

In sub-Saharan Africa, the primary education pupil/teacher ratio remains above 1990 levels

Pupil/teacher ratio, by education level and region, 1990–2018

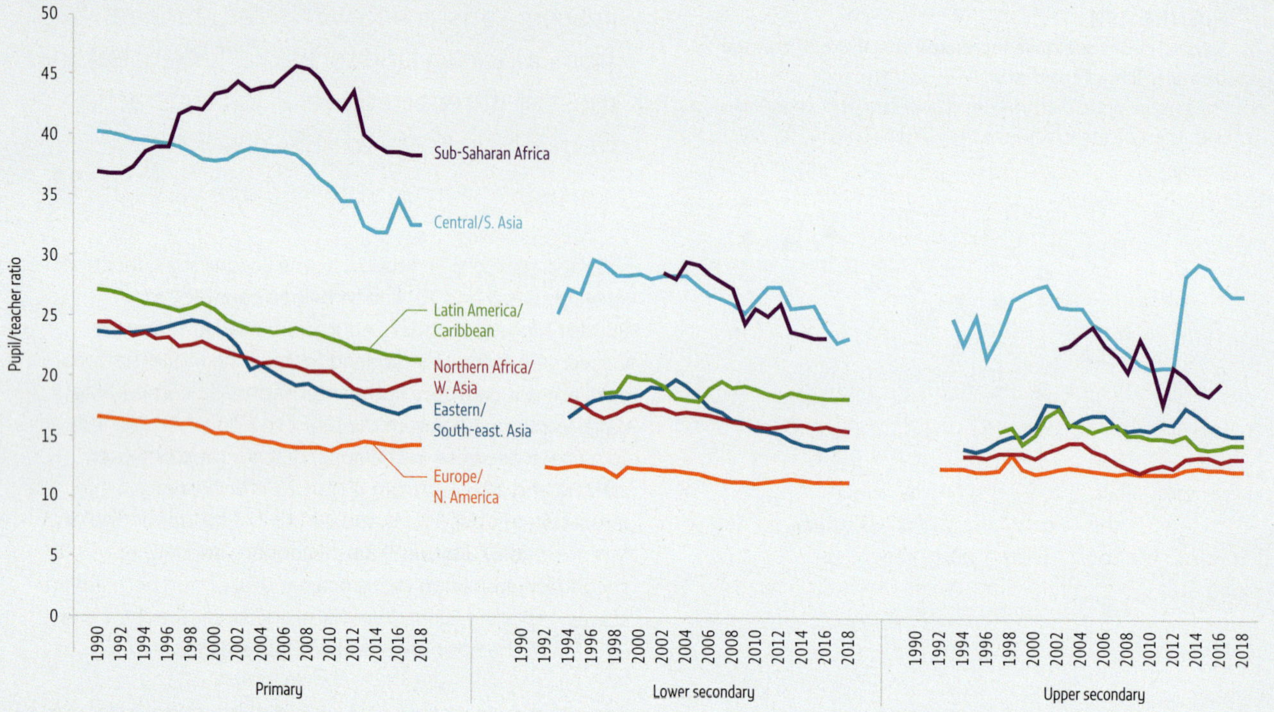

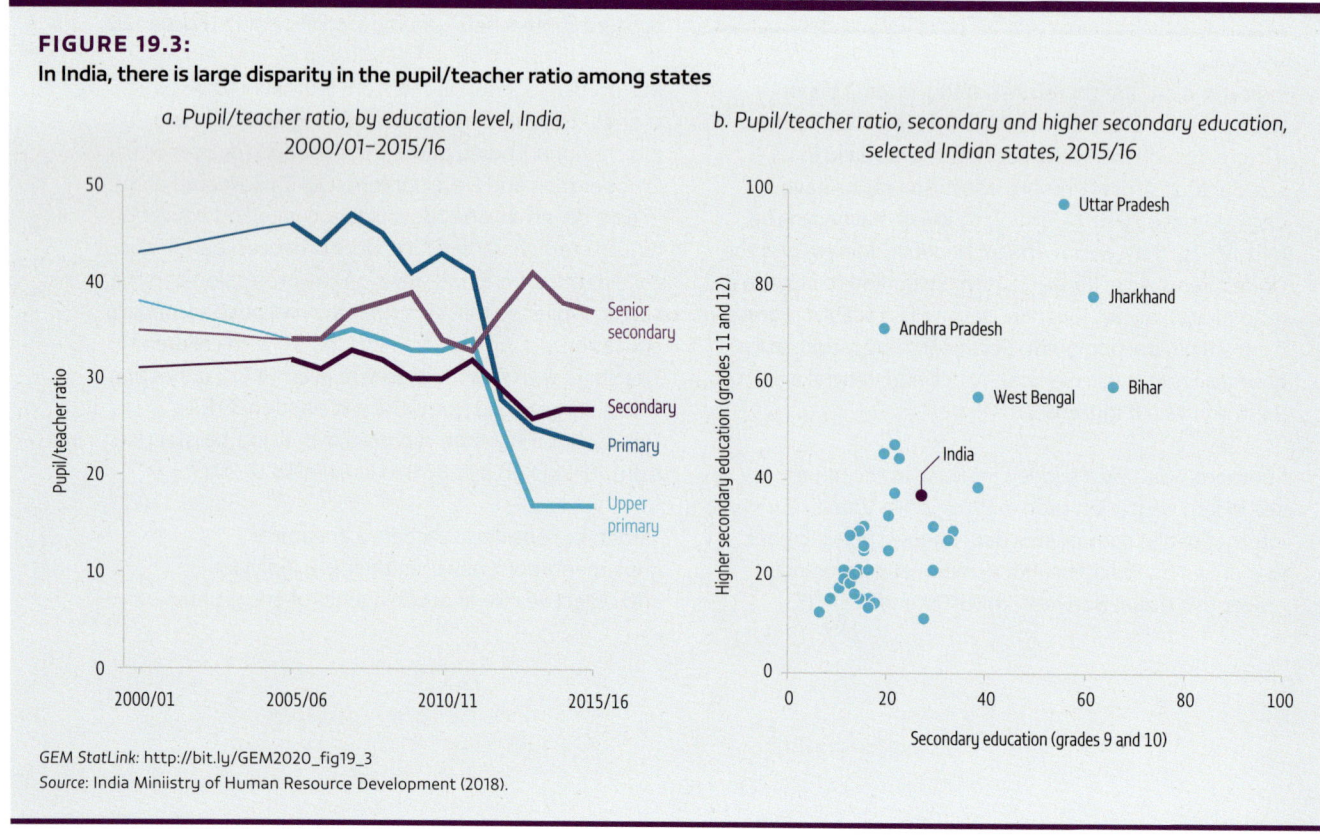

GEM StatLink: http://bit.ly/GEM2020_fig19_2
Source: UIS database.

FIGURE 19.3:

In India, there is large disparity in the pupil/teacher ratio among states

a. *Pupil/teacher ratio, by education level, India, 2000/01–2015/16*

b. *Pupil/teacher ratio, secondary and higher secondary education, selected Indian states, 2015/16*

GEM StatLink: http://bit.ly/GEM2020_fig19_3
Source: India Miniistry of Human Resource Development (2018).

development must be emphasized. The Transforming the Education Workforce report has called for (a) diagnostic tools to improve workforce design and management, (b) research and evaluation to explore what makes teachers effective and at what cost and (c) networks and coalitions for change at all levels. It has identified strong leadership, evidence-based policies, workforce empowerment, communication with key stakeholders and implementation monitoring as factors for success in workforce reforms (Education Commission, 2019).

Recognizing that systems-level information needs to be complemented by an understanding of classroom practice, the World Bank developed the Teach classroom observation tool. It aims to measure the time teachers spend on instruction and how that time is spent (**Table 19.2**). Two 15-minute observations are made. After each, observers assign scores against low, medium and high benchmarks (World Bank, 2019). Some critics question the tool's validity, partly because of findings that classroom observation scores depend on factors such as time of day, activity type, number of adults in the room and observer characteristics (H. Kim, 2019; Helyn Kim et al., 2018). It is sometimes assumed that teacher absenteeism is the main problem, but this is open to question: In Uganda, learner absenteeism is about 40% higher than teacher absenteeism (Uwezo, 2018). Others raise the concern that using Teach as an evaluation tool might be seen as undermining teacher professionalism, although its designers deny any such intent (Edwards, 2019).

> **"**
> In Uganda, learner absenteeism is about 40% higher than teacher absenteeism
> **"**

FOCUS 19.1: EDUCATION SUPPORT PERSONNEL VARY ACROSS COUNTRIES

Teaching assistants are an important part of inclusive education (see **Chapter 6**). Their presence can have implications for calculating and interpreting pupil/teacher ratios. Teaching assistants are meant not to fulfil teaching duties but to help teachers and take on some non-pedagogical responsibilities in inclusive settings (Rose, 2020). This Focus looks at how national and international data collection identifies teachers and teaching assistants and how including teaching assistants may affect pupil/teacher ratios.

Education support staff definitions and labels in data collection instruments vary across countries and education levels. Terms used include learning support assistants, non-teaching assistants, learning support staff, teaching assistants, teacher aides and classroom support staff. The umbrella terms 'learning support staff' and 'education support personnel' also refer to staff who provide classroom support to teachers (Masdeu Navarro, 2015; Rose, 2020).

TABLE 19.2:
Measures of teaching quality in three areas of the World Bank Teach framework

Classroom culture	Instruction	Socio-emotional skills
▪ Offering a supportive learning environment (treating all students respectfully, using positive language, etc.) ▪ Creating positive behavioural expectations (acknowledging positive behaviour, managing negative behaviour)	▪ Facilitating lessons (articulating lesson objectives, connecting learning materials across knowledge areas) ▪ Checking student understanding (using questions, prompts, etc.) ▪ Giving feedback to clarify misunderstanding and identify successes ▪ Encouraging critical thinking (asking open-ended questions, assigning tasks requiring active analysis of content)	▪ Instilling autonomy (providing opportunities to make choices and assume classroom roles) ▪ Promoting perseverance (acknowledging efforts rather than natural abilities) ▪ Fostering social and collaborative skills (encouraging peer interaction, perspective taking, etc.)

Source: World Bank (2019).

At the international level, the joint data collection manual of the UNESCO Institute for Statistics, OECD and Eurostat (UOE) defines 'educational personnel' as 'all those employed in educational institutions covering both instructional and non-instructional institutions' (UOE, 2019, p. 41), regardless of assignment to specific programmes or International Standard Classification of Education levels. It identifies four functional categories: instruction; professional (academic, health or social) support (e.g. counsellors, librarians, education media specialists, attendance officers); management and administration; and school maintenance and operations. Teacher aides in tertiary education include 'all students employed on a part-time basis for the primary purpose of assisting in classroom or laboratory instruction or in the conduct of research' (UOE, 2019, p. 44). These are usually graduate student teaching assistants, teaching fellows or research assistants (OECD, 2018).

At the national level, definitions are often blurry, even in differentiating between teaching and support personnel. Cambodia's broad definition makes monitoring the use of teachers' aides challenging: Teaching staff include those 'in charge of teaching every day, librarians, operational activity teachers, art teachers/home economics teachers, lab staff, computer trainers, primary school principals in school with 6 classes or less and vice-principals with 10 classes or less, general secondary school principals in school with 4 classes or less and vice-principals with 7 classes or less' (Cambodia Ministry of Education Youth and Sport, 2017, p. iii). South Africa collects data on educators, i.e. 'any person who teaches, educates or trains other persons or who provides professional education services' (South Africa Department of Basic Education, 2018, p. 34).

Support personnel are present for many reasons (logistics, discipline, support, etc.) and in settings that vary in terms of inclusiveness. Comparable international data on inclusion-related use of support personnel are not generally available. Countries in UOE data collection may vary in the extent to which inclusion is mainstreamed (OECD, 2018). A review of education management information systems in 40 countries in Africa, Asia, Latin America and the Caribbean showed that data on aides supporting teachers in inclusive settings were scant at best (UNICEF, 2016).

> " Comparable international data on inclusion-related use of support personnel are not generally available "

Across education levels, there is little variation among the few countries with UOE data, such as the Czech Republic, Lithuania and Sweden, on when pupil/teacher ratios include teaching assistants. The assistants' impact is more perceptible in Chile, the Netherlands and the United Kingdom, where ratios decrease by between two and four percentage points, or 15% to 20%, when teaching assistants are included. The effect is largest at the ECCE level in Chile and the United Kingdom; in the latter, the ratio decreased from 65:1 to 7:1, the lowest among countries with data (**Figure 19.4**).

FOCUS 19.2: THERE IS WIDE DISPARITY IN TEACHERS' WORKING HOURS

Instruction is the main teaching task, but others, including professional development, collaboration and outreach, take substantial time. Head teachers may be primarily involved in school management but also take on teaching responsibilities and other tasks. The Education 2030 Framework for Action recognizes teachers' right to decent working conditions (UNESCO, 2016). Work time is an important aspect of this, with potential implications for reward and support mechanisms, but it is not assessed uniformly across countries.

The OECD collects data on the statutory number of hours full-time teachers are expected to work according to national policy. Teaching time is converted into 60-minute periods, excluding breaks of 10 minutes or longer, except at the pre-primary and primary education levels, for which short breaks are included if teachers are responsible for classes during breaks. The OECD differentiates between teaching and non-teaching time. A full-time teacher teaching for 60% of the average teaching time is counted as one full-time teacher for headcount indicators and as 0.6 of a full-time equivalent (OECD, 2018).

FIGURE 19.4:
In some high-income countries, including teaching assistants reduces pupil/teacher ratios by between 15% and 20%
Pupil/teacher ratios with and without teaching assistants, by education level, selected countries, 2018

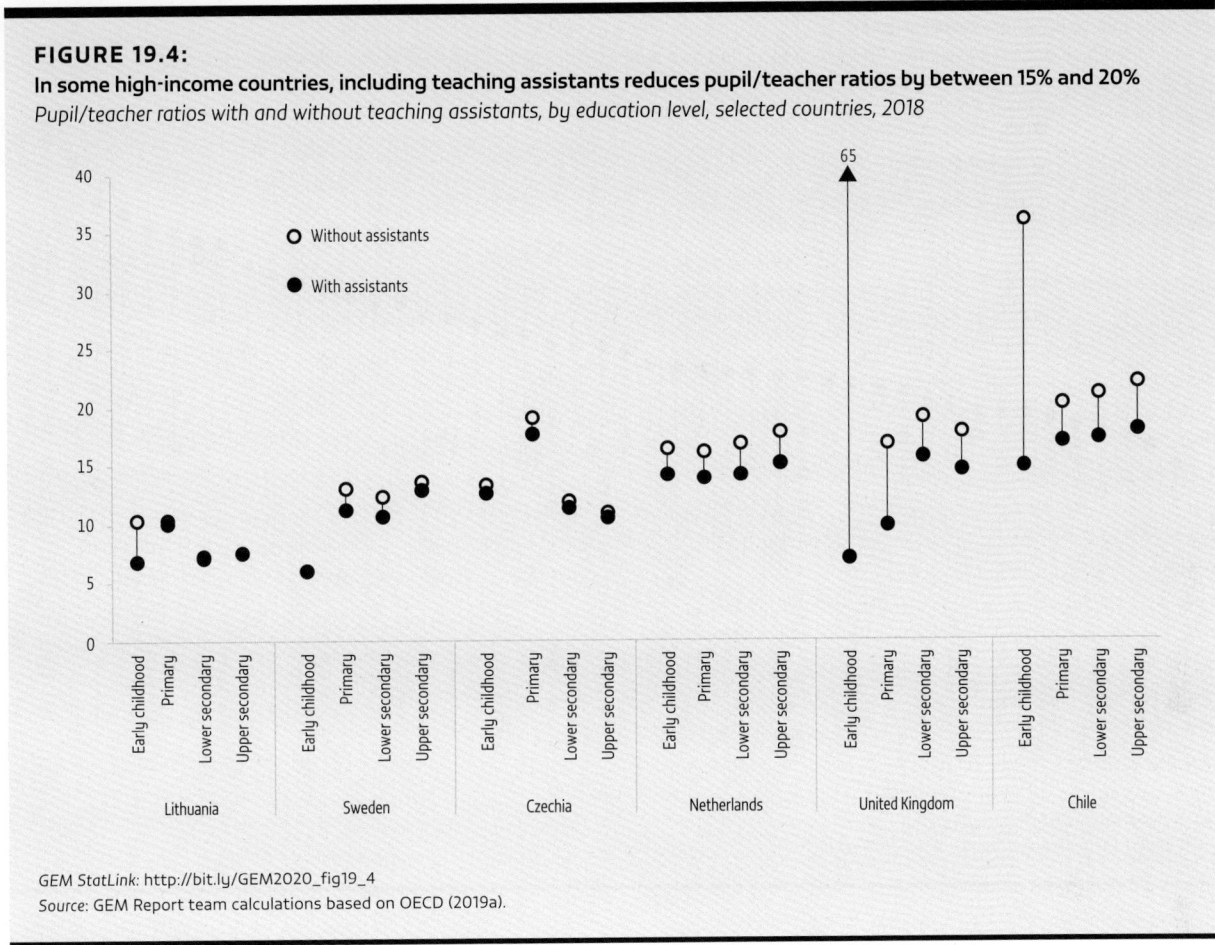

GEM StatLink: http://bit.ly/GEM2020_fig19_4
Source: GEM Report team calculations based on OECD (2019a).

Direct surveys are another means of collecting information. The 2018 OECD Teaching and Learning International Survey (TALIS) asked teachers and head teachers in 48 education systems in middle- and high-income countries to report their total work time. It included questions about time spent per week on non-instruction tasks, e.g. class preparation, parent visits and marking, including over the weekend and in other non-school-regulated time. Head teachers indicated time spent developing curriculum, teaching, observing classrooms, evaluating students, and mentoring and professionally developing teachers (OECD, 2019c).

> With few exceptions, when teachers estimated time spent on specific tasks during the previous week, the number of working hours was greater than estimates of total working hours

With few exceptions, when teachers estimated time spent on specific tasks during the previous week, the number of working hours was greater than estimates of total working hours (**Figure 19.5**). The discrepancy may reflect cognitive errors in estimating time, especially for past tasks (Schuhmacher & Burkert, 2013). Estimating actual work time is therefore not straightforward.

More than half of OECD countries specify statutory working time per year (OECD, 2019a), allowing comparison with TALIS self-reported weekly estimates.

FIGURE 19.5:
Teachers struggle to estimate hours worked
Teacher-estimated previous week's working hours as a total and as a sum of time spent on various tasks, selected countries, 2018

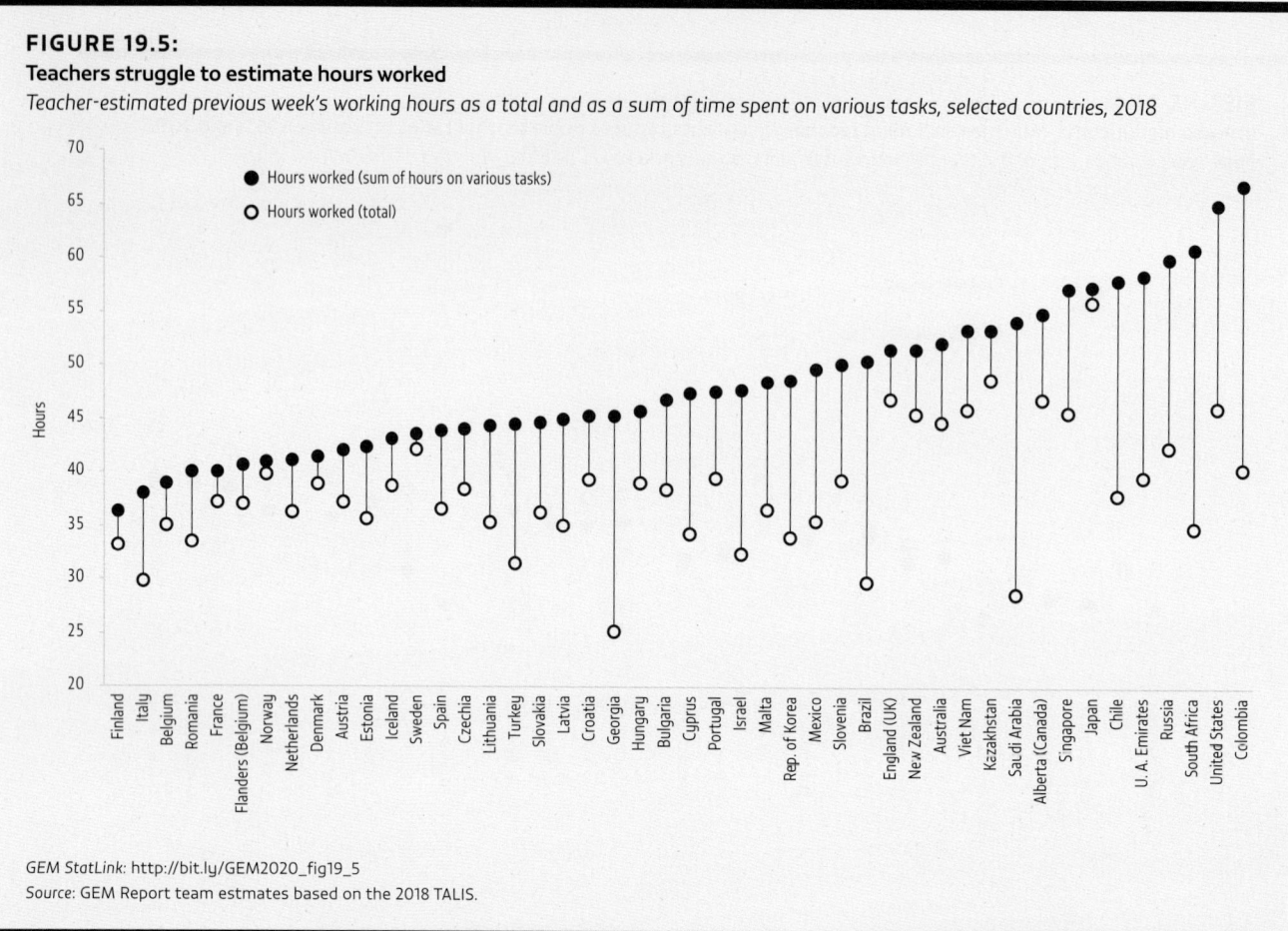

● Hours worked (sum of hours on various tasks)
○ Hours worked (total)

GEM StatLink: http://bit.ly/GEM2020_fig19_5
Source: GEM Report team estmates based on the 2018 TALIS.

Countries vary in amount of time allocated for teaching and learning, including number of teaching weeks per year: At the lower secondary education level, Estonia allocated 35 weeks and Germany 40 (OECD, 2019a). The Varkey Foundation's Global Teacher Status Index offers another potential comparison. It collects data on public perceptions of teachers' working hours (Dolton, Marcenaro, De Vries, & She, 2018). These tend to be lower than teacher-reported estimates (**Figure 19.6**). A trade union analysis of official UK data suggests that teachers work, on average, over 12 unpaid hours per week, more than workers in any other sector (Henshaw, 2019).

Statutory hours, as reported by the OECD *Education at a Glance* report, and self-reported estimates, as reported in TALIS, are at odds in many countries. In Israel, statutory teaching time is 25 hours per week, while teachers report

> " A trade union analysis of official UK data suggests that teachers work, on average, over 12 unpaid hours per week, more than workers in any other sector "

less than 22; in the Flanders region of Belgium, statutory teaching time is just under 16 hours per week, but teachers report more than 18. Discrepancies may reflect differences in teachers' daily work relative to system regulations but also different reference periods. Statutory teaching time reflects an average week; surveys, such as TALIS, often ask teachers to report on the previous week, which may not be representative.

FIGURE 19.6:

The public underestimates teachers' working hours

Teachers' working hours per week based on self-reporting, government reporting based on statutory expectations, and public perceptions, selected countries, 2018

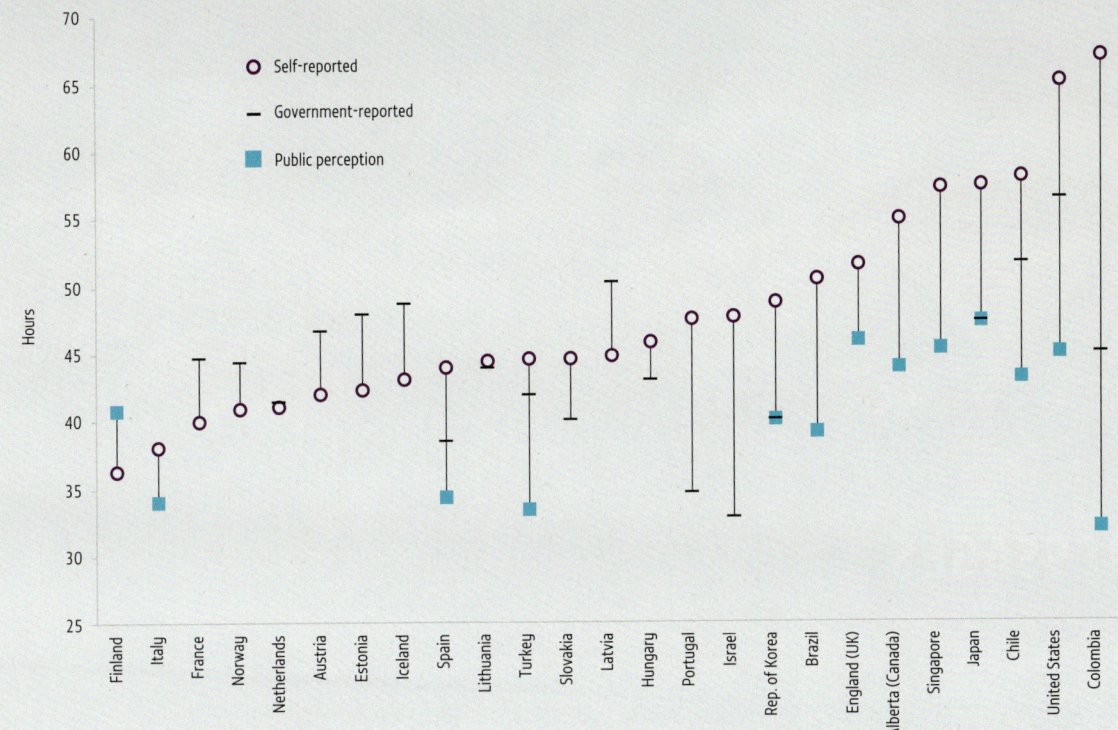

○ Self-reported

— Government-reported

■ Public perception

GEM StatLink: http://bit.ly/GEM2020_fig19_6

Notes: The government-reported statutory number of hours was based on estimated annual number of working hours divided by number of teaching weeks for lower secondary school teachers, except for the Netherlands, for which number of teaching weeks for primary school teachers was used.

Source: GEM Report team estmates based on OECD (2019a, 2019b) and Dolton et al. (2018).

Students wash their hands
at Khokkham Primary School,
Pak Ou District, Lao People's
Democratic Republic.

CREDIT: GPE/Kelley Lynch

KEY MESSAGES

Improved female education outcomes improve health outcomes. An additional year of education in Zimbabwe, following a reform to expand access to secondary education, is associated with a three percentage point increase in the probability of women working outside the home and a 21% decline in child mortality.

Education is an effective means of combatting climate change. Educating girls and women is ranked 6th out of 80 solutions to combat climate change from 2020 to 2050 by Project Drawdown. Closing the annual education financing gap of US$39 billion in low- and lower-middle-income countries could yield a reduction of 51.48 gigatons of emissions by 2050.

Nevertheless, there is no evidence that education is targeted in domestic and international investment to address and respond to climate change, which reached US$579 billion in 2017–18 but was allocated mostly to sustainable transport, renewable energy generation and energy efficiency.

As indigenous peoples and local communities manage at least 17% of the total carbon stored in the forestlands of 52 tropical and subtropical countries, it is vital to protect their knowledge. Yet climate change partnerships are characterized by a focus on technical knowledge rather than transformative perspectives of how people are linked with each other and natural systems.

CHAPTER

Education in the other SDGs – a focus on gender equality, climate change and partnerships

(Global indicators from goals other than SDG 4 that are education-related)

GLOBAL INDICATOR

1.a.2 – *Proportion of total government spending on essential services (education, health and social protection)*

5.6.2 – *Number of countries with laws and regulations that guarantee full and equal access to women and men aged 15 years and older to sexual and reproductive health care, information and education*

8.6.1 – *Proportion of youth (aged 15–24 years) not in education, employment or training*

4.7.1/12.8.1/13.3.1 – *Extent to which (i) global citizenship education and (ii) education for sustainable development are mainstreamed in (a) national education policies, (b) curricula, (c) teacher education, and (d) student assessment*

Education is key in achieving all SDGs. This chapter discusses aspects of education's relationship with gender equality (SDG 5) and climate change (SDG 13), focusing on linkages, monitoring and professional capacity development, including through partnerships (SDG 17).

EDUCATION'S RELATIONSHIP WITH GENDER EQUALITY IS STRONG BUT MEDIATED BY NORMS

Women's education has long been strongly associated with economic, health and social benefits. Education is linked to increased female labour force participation (Heath and Jayachandran, 2016). In Turkey, increasing compulsory schooling from five to eight years in 1997 increased enrolment among rural girls and the likelihood of women working outside the home and in jobs that provide social security benefits (Erten and Keskin, 2018). Women's labour force participation fell from 34% in 1990 to 23% in 2005 but rose to 34% in 2018. It remains among the lowest in the world (OECD, 2019).

Systematic reviews of causal links confirm that improved female education outcomes improve health outcomes, e.g. reducing child mortality (Mensch et al., 2019). An additional year of education in Zimbabwe, following a reform to expand access to secondary education in 1980, is associated with a three percentage point increase in probability of women working outside the home and a 21% decline in child mortality (Grépin and Bharadwaj, 2015).

Girls' education attainment and child marriage are strongly linked (Birchall, 2018; Male and Wodon, 2018).

In Uganda, pregnancy was a leading reason for early school-leaving, especially among girls from the lowest income quintile (Wodon et al., 2016). Delaying marriage and childbearing requires a combination of safe-space programmes, life skills training, better reproductive health knowledge, and livelihood opportunities or incentives for schooling (Chakravarty et al., 2016). Innovative education approaches are required to combat long-standing gender norms and discrimination. Interventions focused on community norms may change views of masculinity that condone violence (Jewkes et al., 2015).

Interventions to reduce schooling costs and increase supply improve education access. School construction, school water and sanitation as well as cash transfers have some of the strongest effects (Evans and Yuan, 2019). In India, a nationwide initiative to build single-sex toilets substantially increased enrolment and lowered dropout among adolescent girls, who benefited from privacy, safety and reduced vulnerability to illness. The higher share of female teachers in schools with single-sex toilets had an additional positive impact on these outcomes (Adukia, 2017). In the state of Bihar, girls were provided with bicycles to facilitate access to secondary school. The programme helped increase their enrolment by 32% and led to a 12% increase in the number who passed the secondary school certificate examination (Muralidharan and Prakash, 2017).

> " An additional year of education in Zimbabwe is associated with a 21% decline in child mortality "

> " It is important to look at education opportunities in the context of gender norms and values, institutions outside education, education laws and policies, education systems and development outcomes "

Gender discrimination can turn synergy between development goals into a trade-off. Good nutrition positively influences ability to learn. Where child marriage is common, however, recent evidence suggests better nutrition contributes to earlier dropout because it precipitates menstruation (Khanna, 2019).

The association between girls' education and development outcomes is not straightforward and may materialize only in specific circumstances.

The Global Gender Gap Index's education attainment, economic opportunity and political empowerment sub-indices for 148 countries highlight the issue. Countries with similar gender disparity in education attainment appear at the top (Lao People's Democratic Republic) and the bottom (Saudi Arabia) of the sub-index on female economic opportunity, which captures labour force participation and pay gaps. By contrast, Guinea has one of the lowest education attainment sub-index scores but one of the highest for economic opportunity (**Figure 20.1a**). There is a closer association of the education attainment sub-index with that on political empowerment, which captures, for instance, women in parliament and ministerial positions (**Figure 20.1b**). School attendance is insufficient to realize education's potential for women. It is important to look at education opportunities in the context of gender norms and values, institutions outside education, education laws and policies, education systems and development outcomes (UNESCO, 2019).

FIGURE 20.1:

Education attainment is necessary but not sufficient to empower women

Global Gender Gap Index, relationship of female education attainment with other sub-indices, 2018

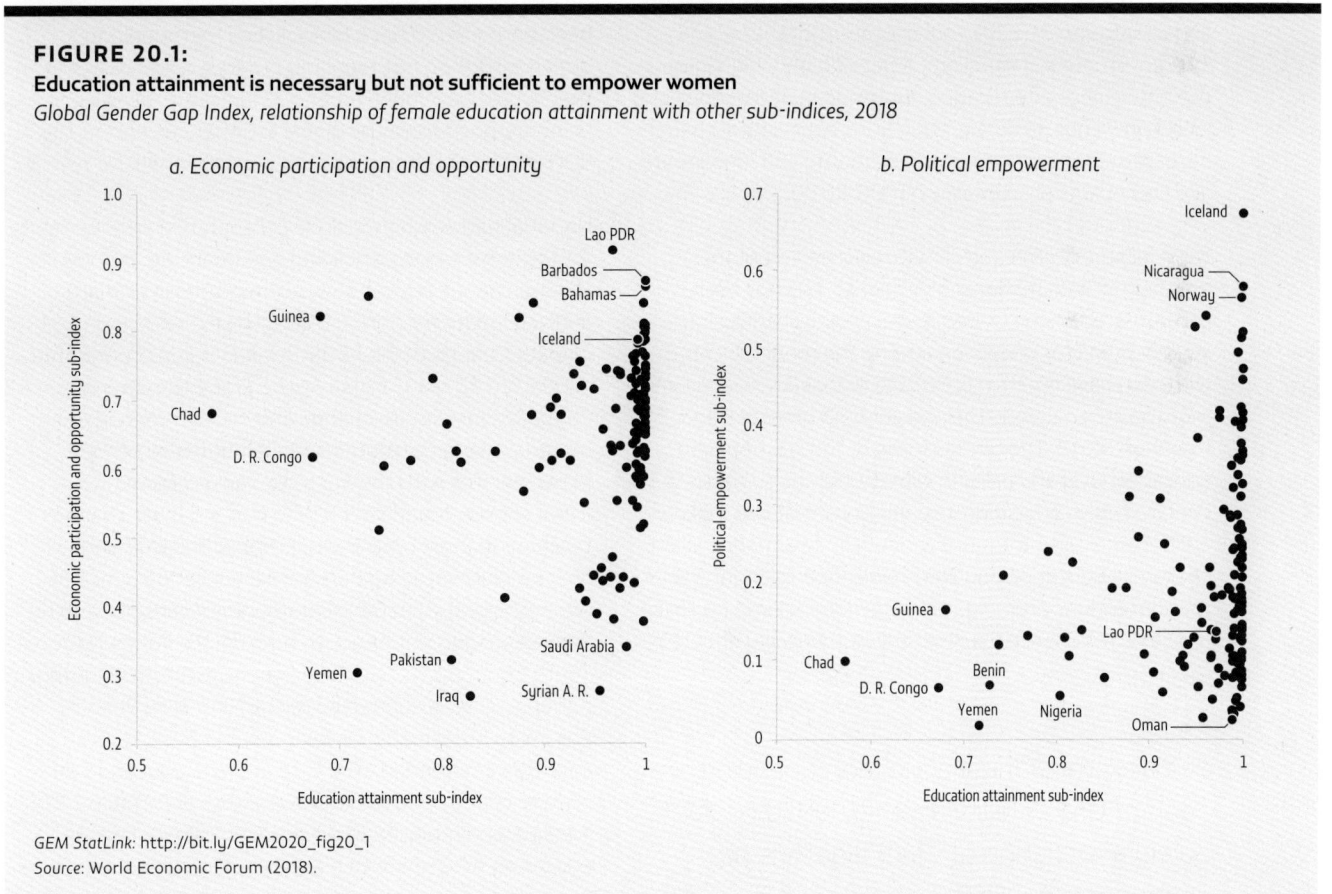

GEM StatLink: http://bit.ly/GEM2020_fig20_1

Source: World Economic Forum (2018).

EDUCATION'S RELATIONSHIP WITH CLIMATE CHANGE MITIGATION AND ADAPTATION MUST BE STRENGTHENED

Education is recognized as necessary to combat climate change. A main channel is education's effect on lowering fertility rates and population growth. Project Drawdown developed scenarios to estimate the potential 2020–50 climate impact of 80 solutions: It ranked educating girls sixth and family planning seventh. Closing the annual financing gap of US$39 billion over 2015–30 for reaching universal pre-primary, primary and secondary education of good quality in low- and lower-middle-income countries, estimated by the *Global Education Monitoring Report*, could yield a reduction of 51.48 gigatons of emissions by 2050, an 'incalculable' return on investment (Hawken, 2017).

The United Nations Framework Convention on Climate Change (UNFCCC) and the 2015 Paris Agreement underscore education's role in climate change mitigation and adaptation. The 2018 special report of the Intergovernmental Panel on Climate Change highlighted the importance of education, informed by indigenous and local knowledge, in accelerating both behavioural change necessary for a carbon-neutral economy and innovation and technological adaptation (IPCC, 2018).

Yet education's effect on climate science acceptance, another potential channel of influence, has not been corroborated. In the United States, political affiliation is a greater predictor of opinion among the more educated, who may have greater confidence in their knowledge and more ability to defend their position (Drummond and Fischhoff, 2017). The tenuousness of the link between education level and belief in climate change suggests a need to evolve education interventions that can make a difference. Misinformation about climate change is a challenge. Education and communication to counteract misconceptions promulgated in classrooms and on social media can be especially relevant (Lewandowsky et al., 2017).

> Closing the annual education financing gap of US$39 billion over 2015–30 could yield a reduction of 51.48 gigatons of emissions by 2050

International knowledge partnerships are advancing climate action. UNESCO developed the Green Citizens Platform. The UNFCCC maintains the UN CC:e-Learn initiative, which helps countries develop climate change learning. In response to the 2017 Doha Work Programme, 102 of 195 member states have a designated education focal point for action on climate empowerment to advance climate change mitigation education (Kwauk, 2020). Despite such recognition, there has been no substantive progress in monitoring climate change education. A study commissioned by the *Global Education Monitoring Report* showed that, while nearly three-quarters of national curriculum frameworks mentioned sustainable development, only one-third referenced climate change (IBE, 2016).

Two developments should increase focus and attention on monitoring. In March 2020, SDG global indicators 12.8.1 (on responsible consumption and production) and 13.3.1 (on climate change) were merged with global indicator 4.7.1 (on sustainable development and global citizenship). In November 2019, these indicators had been upgraded to tier II (established methodology, but countries do not regularly produce data); as tier III, they would have been among 32 indicators at risk of being dropped from the global list of 232 as part of the SDG monitoring framework 2020 comprehensive review.

National partnerships include collaborative arrangements for technical capacity building and financing. In Tonga, climate change education was integrated in primary and secondary education through the Coping with Climate Change in the Pacific Island Region programme, supported by the German Agency for International Cooperation. Climate change and disaster management materials were translated and distributed to schools. In partnership with the Australian government, a civil society organization prepared a climate change teaching manual for primary schools. These efforts are complemented by non-formal education aimed at strengthening vulnerable communities' capacity and by active engagement of youth through the Tonga National Youth Congress (Tonga Government, 2019). In voluntary national reviews submitted to the High-level Political Forum on Sustainable Development in 2019, several countries mentioned efforts to improve education on climate change and general awareness of it (**Table 20.1**). Weakness in monitoring progress on climate change education may relate to bias towards technical solutions to climate change effects or a disconnect between the education and climate action communities.

TABLE 20.1:
Selected voluntary national review responses on education and climate change

Algeria	A tripartite partnership (environment, energy and education) developed a course teaching basic concepts of causes and consequences of climate change and risk reduction measures, an eco-friendly guide for environmental clubs and a guide on education and pedagogy linked with climate change.
Ghana	Climate change has been integrated into curriculum to be taught in primary schools starting in 2019/20 and later in secondary schools. The Environmental Protection Agency will train teachers on new teaching and learning materials. Four public universities have introduced climate change courses to promote research and policy analysis.
Mauritius	The Climate Change Information Centre, established in 2013, developed a toolkit with 111 actions to help combat climate change. Some 600 youth leaders and 750 primary and secondary school teachers were trained under the Africa Adaptation Programme.
Palau	As part of the Education Master Plan 2017–2026, climate change and disaster risk management are integrated into science curriculum, and teachers have been trained. The National Environmental Protection Council, National Emergency Management Office and Red Cross run awareness-raising programmes.
Scotland (United Kingdom)	Efforts to improve education and awareness include the Royal Scottish Geographical Society's climate literacy qualification, public workshops to inform development of a public engagement strategy, the 2050 Climate Group's Young Leaders Development Programme, the Eco-Schools Scotland programme of Keep Scotland Beautiful, and Climate Ready Classrooms in secondary schools.

Source: Selected voluntary national review reports.

There is a lack of clear targeting of education in domestic and international investment to address and respond to climate change, which increased from US$342 billion in 2013 to US$579 billion in 2017–18 (Buchner et al., 2019). Disaggregated data from 2015–16 revealed that 90% of the total US$463 billion on mitigation and adaptation went to sustainable transport, renewable energy generation and energy efficiency. There is no evidence any of the US$10 billion for cross-sector programmes (2% of the total) was allocated, for instance, to scaling up education systems, girls' education, behavioural changes on food waste and diet, or indigenous approaches to land use and management (Oliver et al., 2018).

PROFESSIONAL CAPACITY NEEDS TO BE STRENGTHENED TO SUPPORT GENDER EQUALITY AND CLIMATE CHANGE EFFORTS

Empowering female decision making is critical and should extend to all levels of political, economic and social life. In Pakistan, building on a gender quota policy introduced in 2000 to improve female representation in local and national politics, a project in 2013–15 focused on developing female parliamentarians' capacity through training, coaching, media activities, and networking and leadership forums. An evaluation found that over half the participants valued the programme for improving their awareness and leadership skills (Surani, 2016). In Tunisia, prior to the 2018 local elections, UN Women and the women's rights organization Aswat Nissa (Women's Voices) organized a political academy to train female candidates on local governance, missions and roles of municipal councils, and media relations (UN Women, 2018).

The Rural Women's Leadership Programme, organized by the International Fund for Agricultural Development, focused on rural female leaders in community-based organizations, self-help groups and trade unions in Madagascar, Nepal, the Philippines and Senegal. In Nepal, training focused on negotiating skills, confidence building, self-development and technical knowledge about natural resource management (IFAD, 2014).

Gender-responsive training for law enforcement officials is needed to respond when victims of intimate partner violence and other abuse seek protection and support. In Liberia, efforts in 2003–13 to recruit female officers and train a special unit to address sexual and gender-based violence led to the percentage of female officers increasing from 2% to 17% (Bacon, 2015). The Rabta programme of community policing in Pakistan helped sensitize police and increased the sense of security, especially among women (Nair et al., 2017). In the US state of Illinois, 80% of sexual assault investigators received classroom training but needed further training after being appointed to positions and communicating with victims (Venema et al., 2019).

A wider range of capacity development initiatives is needed to address the causes and consequences of climate change, from research and development for scientific innovation to support for solutions based on indigenous knowledge and for local actors to engage with national processes.

Innovations for sustainability and green growth require investment in tertiary education institutions to build capacity in research and development. Low- and middle-income countries, those most vulnerable to climate change, are not active participants in or beneficiaries of such investment. There was substantial progress in research and development capacity in the past 20 years in some middle-income countries, such as China and Turkey, where capacity quadrupled, but wide disparity persists (**Figure 20.2**). Small-scale efforts include Climate Research for Development in Africa, an African-led initiative established in 2013, which received US$3.5 million in 2019 for demand-driven African climate research and aims to support 21 African climate scientists (UNECA, 2019). On a global scale, there is scope for enhancing existing mechanisms, such as the CGIAR (formerly the Consultative Group on International Agricultural Research) and the International Energy Agency's Technology Collaboration Programmes (UNFCCC, 2017).

With respect to indigenous knowledge-based approaches, a recent analysis of carbon storage in community lands finds that indigenous peoples and local communities manage at least 17% of total carbon stored in the forest lands of 52 tropical and subtropical countries (RRI, 2018). Indigenous knowledge experts in rural Zambia highlight agricultural practices proven to reduce deforestation, showing that better integrating indigenous knowledge into Western climate change adaptation knowledge can help the most vulnerable communities (Makondo and Thomas, 2018).

EDUCATION PARTNERSHIPS NEED TO BE INCLUSIVE AND MEANINGFUL

A hurdle in ensuring that international partnerships improve education is power dynamics that limit their effectiveness. An analysis of connections among transnational partnership-based organizations in the education sector shows that networks reproduce power hierarchies. Donors wield the greatest influence over resources and normative preferences, while recipient countries' participation has been primarily symbolic (Menashy, 2019). This is also a limiting factor in climate change partnerships, which are characterized by a focus on technical knowledge rather than transformative perspectives of how people are linked with each other and natural systems (Kwauk, 2020).

> " Innovations for sustainability and green growth require investment in tertiary education institutions to build capacity in research and development "

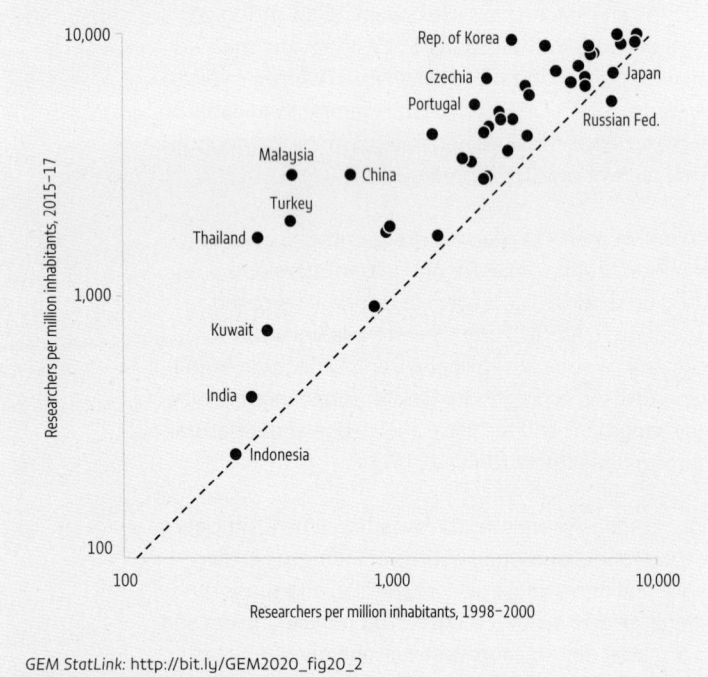

FIGURE 20.2:
Research and development increased in some middle-income countries, but disparity persists
Researchers and technicians (full-time equivalent) per 1 million inhabitants, 2000 and 2017

GEM StatLink: http://bit.ly/GEM2020_fig20_2
Note: Axes are on a logarithmic scale.
Source: UIS database.

> ## Business education does not emphasize inclusivity and sustainability

Examples of meaningful partnerships exist. The Canadian government partnered with provincial and territorial governments, municipalities, indigenous peoples, businesses, youth and civil society to be at the forefront of climate change action. The Pan-Canadian Framework on Clean Growth and Climate Change commits the federal government to strengthen collaboration with the indigenous community to ensure they are true partners in transitioning to a lower-carbon economy and building resilience (Canada Government, 2016). Canada's Arctic Policy Framework is grounded in both scientific and indigenous knowledge (Canada Government, 2016).

Building knowledge networks, capacity and technical skills is essential. The Partnering Initiative offers training courses on essential skills and tools for cross-sector partnerships for sustainable development (The Partnership Initiative, 2019). The Forest Carbon Partnership Facility, a global multi-stakeholder partnership for climate action, includes a US$10 million capacity-building programme for indigenous peoples and civil society to enhance their understanding of forest carbon stock efforts, commonly known as REDD+, and their engagement in REDD+ readiness and implementation (Forest Carbon Partnership, 2019).

It is important to build capacity to challenge the status quo and aspire to equitable, meaningful partnerships. This requires behavioural change at the top echelons of influence. The Association to Advance Collegiate Schools of Business, representing some 1,500 business schools in more than 100 countries and territories, advocates for a new vision for business education. It recommends that curricula pay closer attention to ethics, diversity and well-being and promote pursuing non-private-sector careers (AACSB International, 2016). The UN Principles for Responsible Management Education initiative, started in 2007, engages with higher education institutions to motivate business students to deliver change on global challenges. In 2017, 179 universities shared information on their engagement with the SDGs in teaching, research and campus activity (UN PRME, 2017).

Still, business education does not emphasize inclusivity and sustainability. An analysis of management education programmes found that most had a focus on narrow functional knowledge; curricula with a narrow, market-centric world view; limited real-world application; and an overtly American or European perspective. Critical thinking, soft skills, and values and ethics were less emphasized. Transforming education for sustainability and social responsibility requires major changes in business education, research and faculty incentives (Dyllick, 2015).

Bottom-up, disruptive participation should be nurtured. The Australian government developed Closing the Gap to improve indigenous peoples' outcomes. However, only after 10 years of failure to meet its goals and complaints that it ignored indigenous voices is there agreement on a partnership and joint leadership with Aboriginal and Torres Strait Islander representatives (Council of Australian Governments, 2018).

The Roma Early Childhood Development and Education Initiative in Serbia supports programmes, including the children's club pictured here, that focus on the development of primarily Roma children, through activities for children and their families.

CREDIT: Sanja Knezevic/Open Society Foundations

CHAPTER

21

Finance

KEY MESSAGES

Of the 141 countries with data for 2014–18, 47, or one-third, met neither of two public education expenditure benchmarks: spend at least 4% of GDP or at least 15% of total public expenditure. Many countries, including Cambodia and Uganda, have consistently missed both benchmarks.

Public education expenditure is 4.4% of GDP and 13.8% of total public expenditure, although data were missing for 54% of countries in 2017. The global trend since 2000 appears flat for both indicators, with important regional variations. In Latin America and the Caribbean, education increased from 3.9% to 5.6% of GDP, as both total public expenditure and the share of education grew.

Aid has stagnated at 0.3% of rich countries' income since 2005. As low-income countries' economies have grown faster than their donors', aid as a share of low-income countries' GDP fell from 13.6% in 2003 to 9.1% in 2018. Aid to education peaked at US$15.6 billion in 2018, but only 47% was directed to basic or secondary education in low- and lower-middle-income countries.

Household education spending accounted for 1.1% of GDP in 72 countries' data in 2013–18 or for 11% of total spending in high-income, 23% in middle-income and 43% in low-income countries; household spending tends to compensate for insufficient government spending.

The *Global Education Monitoring Report* has argued that it is necessary to examine the actions of the three main sources of education funding jointly to understand national investment in education. Such actions include prioritization of education in government budgets, degree of donor solidarity with poorer countries and household preparedness to pay out of pocket for education.

PUBLIC EXPENDITURE

The Education 2030 Framework for Action recognizes domestic resource mobilization as the key priority for achieving SDG 4. It sets two public education expenditure benchmarks: at least 4% of gross domestic product (GDP) and at least 15% of total public expenditure. Neither is binding, but failure to meet both indicates insufficient prioritization of education.

Of the 141 countries with data for 2014–18, 47, or one-third, met neither benchmark. The top 10 meeting the GDP benchmark were 4 Nordic countries, 3 in Latin America and the Caribbean, 2 in sub-Saharan Africa and 1 in Oceania. The top 10 for the public expenditure benchmark were low- and middle-income countries: Sierra Leone allocated the highest share (32.5%), followed by Ethiopia, Costa Rica, Eswatini, Guatemala, Uzbekistan, Honduras, Bhutan, Burkina Faso and Tunisia.

Many countries that missed one or both benchmarks struggled to prioritize education consistently. Cambodia, one of the lowest spenders globally at 2.2% of GDP and 8.8% of total public expenditure, has not changed its spending pattern in nearly 20 years, nor has Uganda in

nearly 10. In other countries, education expenditure has expanded and contracted to a lesser (Peru) or greater degree (Mauritania) (**Figure 21.1**).

The UNESCO Institute for Statistics (UIS) does not report regional and global averages for either indicator. *Global Education Monitoring Report* statistical tables have reported medians. Globally, median public education expenditure is 4.4% of GDP and 13.8% of total public expenditure.

The set of countries that report expenditure data changes yearly and the number of observations for each region is small. Hence it is necessary to impute data for countries with missing information to estimate consistent trends. Data were missing for 35% of countries in 2000–14, 39% in 2015–16, 54% in 2017 and over 66% in 2018. Data may be weighted by countries' GDP or total public expenditure (which indicates how much of the world's or region's GDP is spent on education, with the result driven by the countries with the largest economies), or unweighted (indicating general country-level tendencies).

The global trend in education expenditure in 2000–17 was strikingly flat for both indicators. Expenditure as a share of GDP fluctuated around 4.5% (or 4.7% when weighted

> "
> The Education 2030 Framework for Action recognizes domestic resource mobilization as the key priority for achieving SDG 4
> "

FIGURE 21.1:

Some countries are stuck in a low education spending cycle

Education expenditure as a share of GDP and of total public expenditure, selected countries, 2000–18

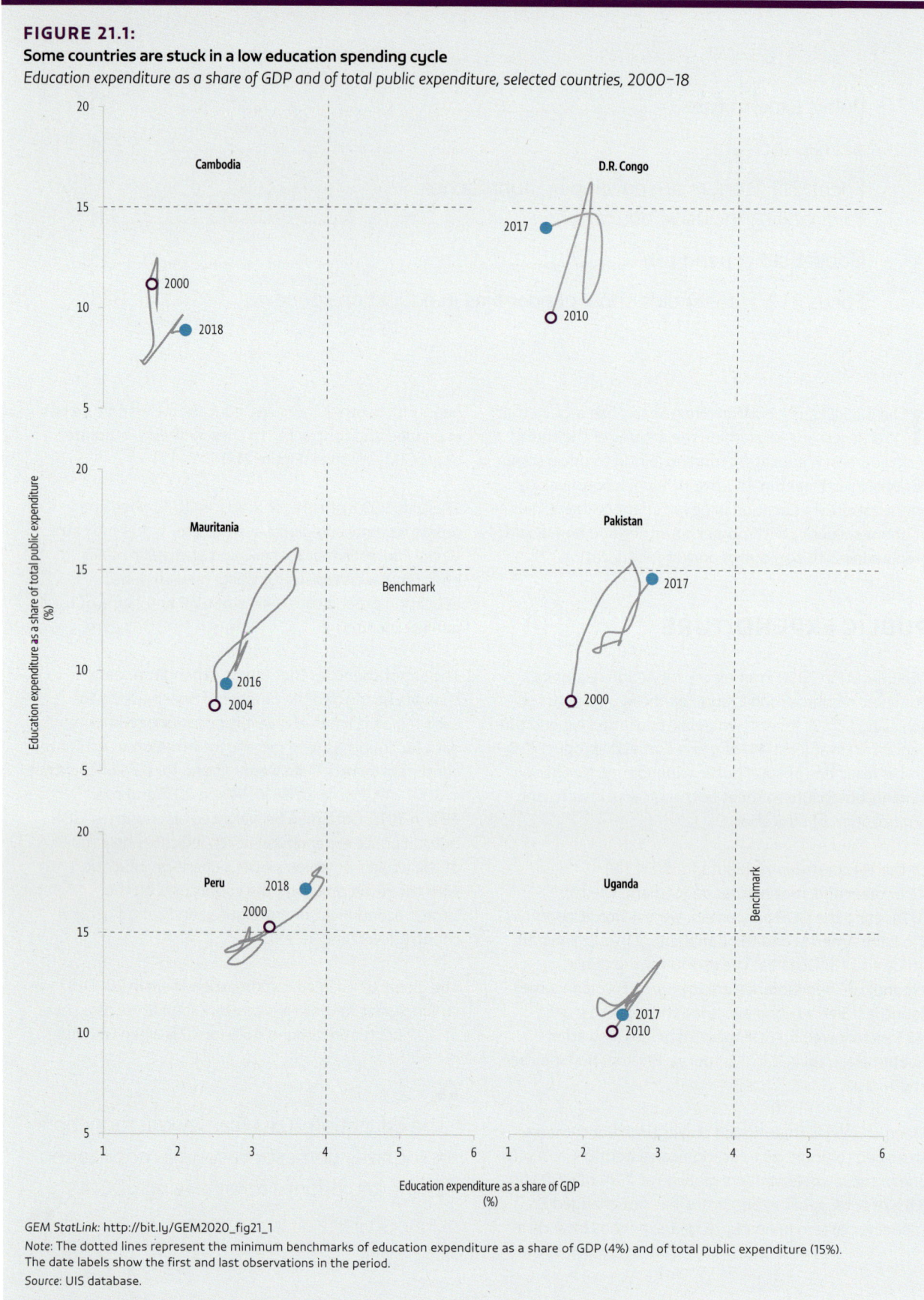

GEM StatLink: http://bit.ly/GEM2020_fig21_1

Note: The dotted lines represent the minimum benchmarks of education expenditure as a share of GDP (4%) and of total public expenditure (15%). The date labels show the first and last observations in the period.

Source: UIS database.

FIGURE 21.2:
Despite flat global public education expenditure, some regions had large changes in the past two decades
Education expenditure, global and regional averages, 2000–17

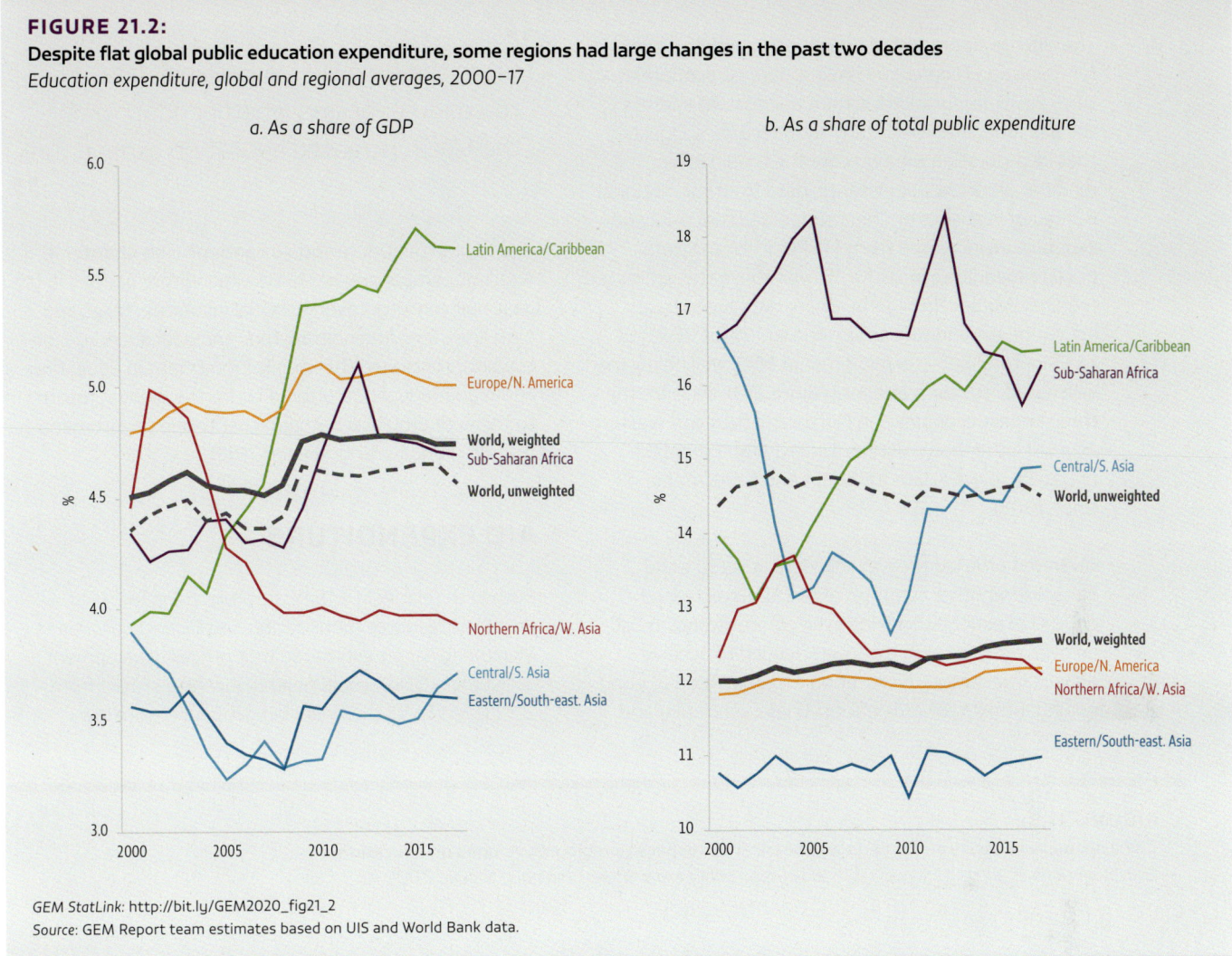

GEM StatLink: http://bit.ly/GEM2020_fig21_2
Source: GEM Report team estimates based on UIS and World Bank data.

by size of GDP). Expenditure as a share of total public expenditure fluctuated around 14.6% (or, when weighted by size of total public expenditure, rose from 12% in 2000 to 12.5% in 2017) (**Figure 21.2**).

Global stability masks regional movement. Latin America and the Caribbean had the largest increase in education expenditure as a share of GDP, from 3.9% in 2000 to 5.6% in 2017 (that level also being the highest among the regions). This resulted from rises in both public expenditure, from 22.6% of GDP in 2000 to 27.2% in 2015 (ECLAC, 2018), and priority on education in total public expenditure, from 13.1% in 2002 to 16.5% in 2017. Both indicators declined in Northern Africa and Western Asia: GDP dropped by more than one percentage point in 2001–08 and has since stagnated at 4% while total public expenditure fell by more than one percentage point in 2003–08 before stagnating at 12% in recent years.

> "
> **Latin America and the Caribbean had the largest increase in education expenditure as a share of GDP, from 3.9% in 2000 to 5.6% in 2017**
> "

Expenditure as a share of GDP grew rapidly in sub-Saharan Africa, from 4.3% in 2008 to 5.1% in 2012, a rise possibly associated with aid to education peaking during this period before declining to 4.5% since 2015. It is the only region to have allocated over 15% of total public expenditure to education every year since 2000. Eastern and South-eastern Asia had the lowest spending levels in terms of both GDP (around 3.5%) and total public expenditure (11%).

The UIS has not reported education expenditure data for China and Nigeria, the regions' largest economies, since 2000. Imputations cannot adequately address the gap, but complementary national data suggest that incorporating the two countries could affect regional averages. For instance, data from the National Bureau of Statistics of China suggested that education expenditure increased from 13.8% to 14.8% of total public expenditure in 2000–16, well above the estimated regional average. In Nigeria, where data are scarce, education expenditure amounted to 1.7% of GDP and 12.5% of total public expenditure in 2013, well below the estimated regional averages (**Figure 21.3**). Data for the three largest economies in Northern Africa and Western Asia are either non-existent (United Arab Emirates) or patchy (e.g. no data for Egypt and Saudi Arabia since 2008).

Given the time lag for available data, it is too early to assess whether adoption of the SDGs increased education expenditure. However, current trends must be overcome to reach the levels needed to achieve universal secondary completion and education of good quality. Efforts towards effectiveness, efficiency and

> *Given the time lag for available data, it is too early to assess whether adoption of the SDGs increased education expenditure*

equity in expenditure should continue (see **Chapter 4**). A recent comparison of 133 US expenditure policies in the past half century, covering social insurance, taxes and cash transfers, in-kind transfers, and education and job training, concluded that public investment in education and higher education offered by far the highest return to the economy at a net-zero cost to the government (Hendren and Sprung-Keyser, 2019).

AID EXPENDITURE

Even with relatively optimistic projections for domestic resource mobilization, the *Global Education Monitoring Report* estimated that official development assistance (ODA) would need to increase sixfold from 2012 levels to fill the financing gap and ensure low-

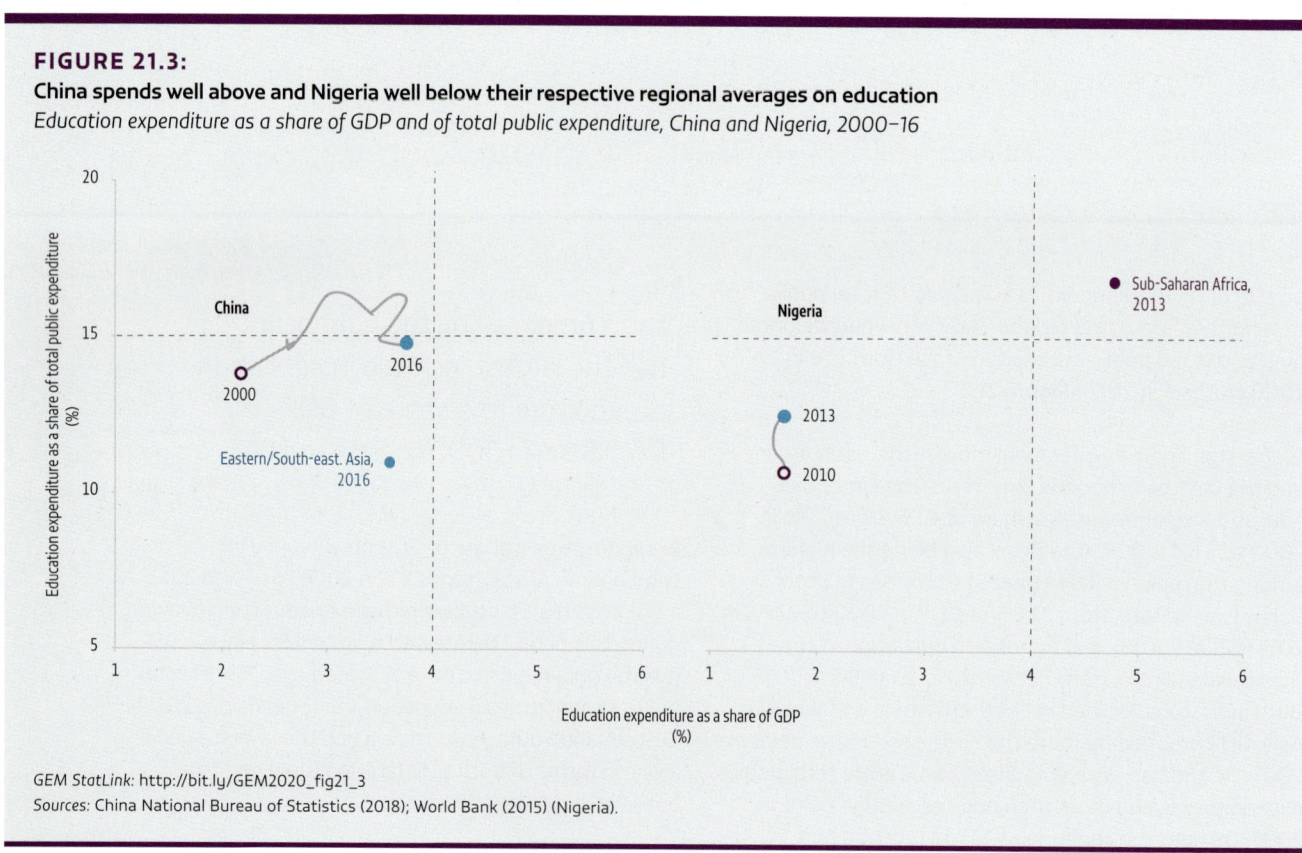

FIGURE 21.3:
China spends well above and Nigeria well below their respective regional averages on education
Education expenditure as a share of GDP and of total public expenditure, China and Nigeria, 2000–16

GEM StatLink: http://bit.ly/GEM2020_fig21_3
Sources: China National Bureau of Statistics (2018); World Bank (2015) (Nigeria).

and lower-middle-income countries achieve universal pre-primary, primary and secondary education completion by 2030 (UNESCO, 2015).

This is possible if all member countries of the Organisation for Economic Co-operation and Development (OECD) Development Assistance Committee (DAC), oil-rich Arab states, and Brazil, China, India, the Russian Federation and South Africa commit to two actions. The first is to allocate 0.7% of gross national income (GNI) to ODA. This target, formally adopted by the European Union and informally recognized by DAC countries, would require the latter to more than double their ODA from the current 0.3% of GNI. The second is to allocate 10% of ODA to primary and secondary education, up from 6% now (UNESCO, 2015).

DAC countries increased ODA from 0.21% to 0.30% of GNI between 2001 and 2019, but most of the increase

occurred in the early 2000s; levels have remained around 0.3% since 2005. Of the 30 DAC countries, only Denmark, Luxembourg, Norway, Sweden and the United Kingdom met the 0.7% target in 2017. Germany and the Netherlands spent over 0.6%. The United States is the largest donor in absolute terms (US$35 billion) but one of the smallest in relative terms (0.16%) (**Figure 21.4**).

While ODA levels in high-income countries remain constant in relative terms, ODA's relative significance as a source of financing is declining in low-income countries, which have had faster GDP growth rates since 2000 (albeit marginally faster in per capita terms). ODA as a share of GDP in low-income countries fell from 13.6% in 2003 to 7.9% in 2014, rebounding to 9.1% by 2018. In 2018, ODA amounted to 5% of GDP in least developed countries, 3% in sub-Saharan African countries and 0.6% in lower-middle-income countries (**Figure 21.5**). However, ODA remained high in some countries,

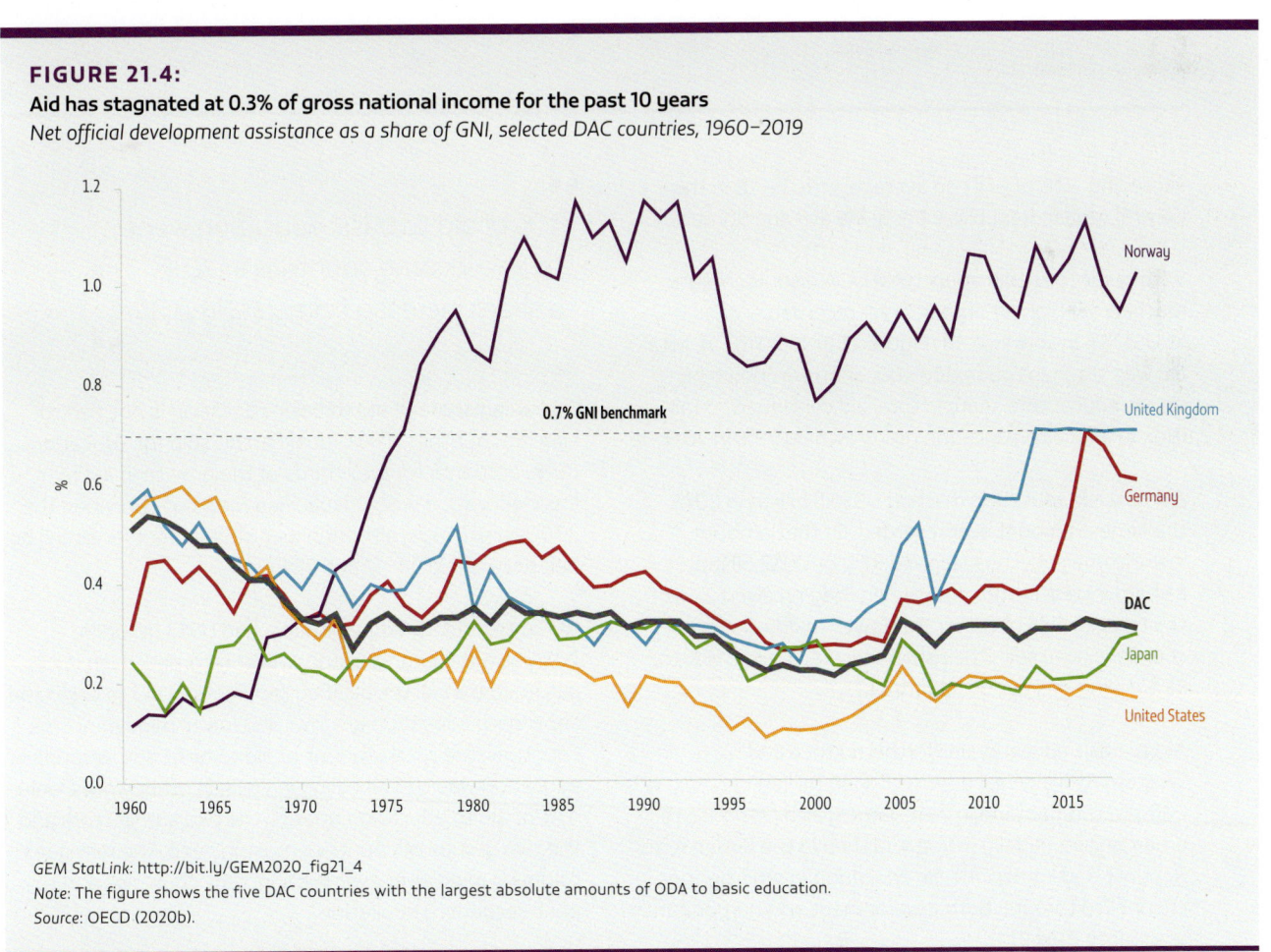

FIGURE 21.4:
Aid has stagnated at 0.3% of gross national income for the past 10 years
Net official development assistance as a share of GNI, selected DAC countries, 1960–2019

GEM StatLink: http://bit.ly/GEM2020_fig21_4
Note: The figure shows the five DAC countries with the largest absolute amounts of ODA to basic education.
Source: OECD (2020b).

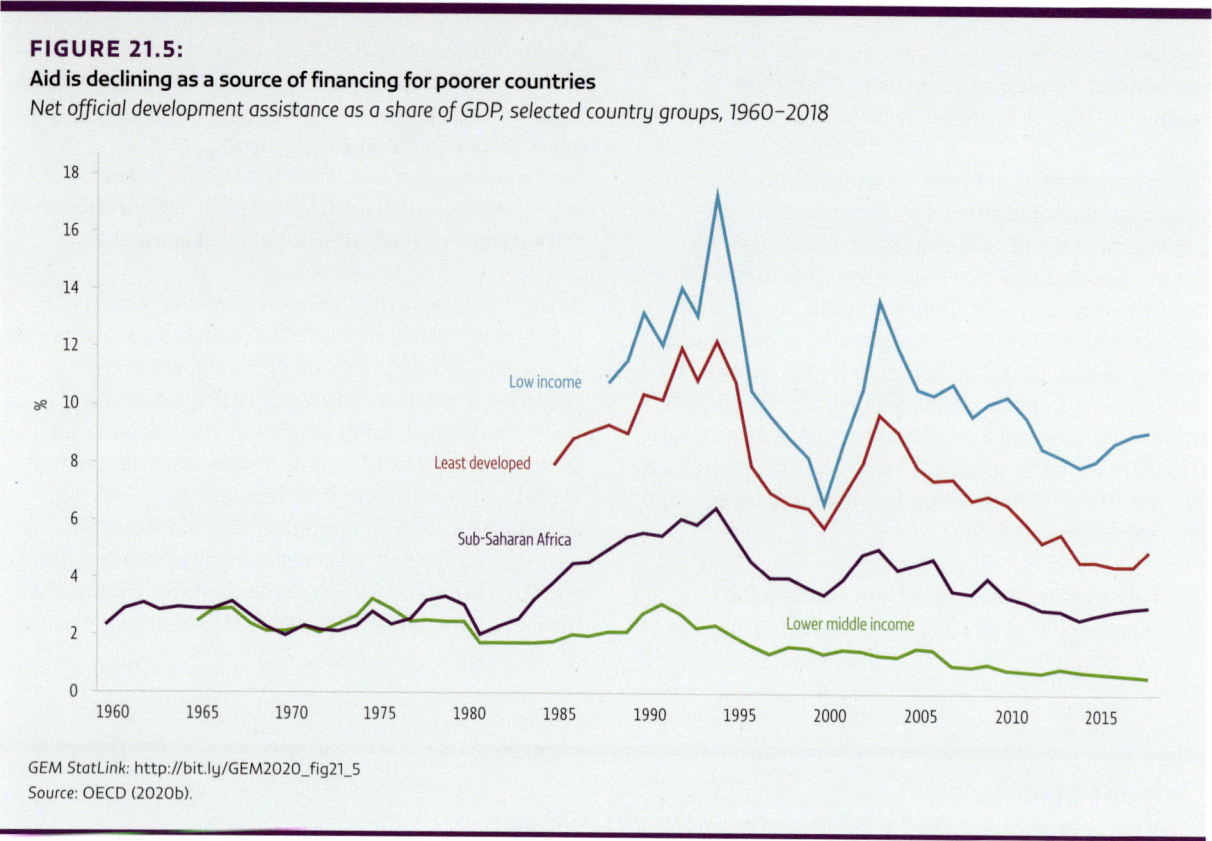

FIGURE 21.5:
Aid is declining as a source of financing for poorer countries
Net official development assistance as a share of GDP, selected country groups, 1960–2018

GEM StatLink: http://bit.ly/GEM2020_fig21_5
Source: OECD (2020b).

exceeding 20% of GDP, on average, in 2015–18 in the Central African Republic, Liberia, Malawi and Somalia.

With respect to education, total ODA disbursements reached the highest amount ever recorded, at US$15.6 billion, in 2018 (**Figure 21.6**). In 2010–14, total aid was stagnant but aid to education was down by 9%, as education's share in total aid continued to fall (**Box 21.3**). Aid to education has grown by 29% in 2012–18.

Aid to basic education reached US$6.5 billion in 2018, the largest amount ever recorded. Of that amount, low-income countries received 31%, or US$2 billion, a sharp increase from 2015, when they received 23% of the total, or US$1.3 billion. But lower-middle income countries have seen their share decrease from 46% to 33% during this period (**Figure 21.7**).

Aid to basic education in Northern Africa and Western Asia increased from US$148 million in 2002 to US$1.7 billion in 2018, largely as a response to emergencies, initially in Iraq and then in the Syrian Arab Republic and Yemen. Aid for education in emergencies is channelled through both development and humanitarian assistance (**Box 21.1**).

> **"**
> 31% of aid to basic education went to low-income countries in 2018, a sharp increase from 23% in 2015
> **"**

A growing share of aid to basic education is not tied to specific countries. The Global Partnership for Education (GPE) accounts for two-thirds of the growth in aid to basic education with unspecified recipients between the 2000s and 2010s, although its disbursement levels fell by half between 2014–17 and 2019.

Aid to secondary education reached US$3 billion in 2018, also the largest amount ever recorded. Even if it is assumed that all unspecified recipients of aid to basic and secondary education are low- and lower-middle-income countries, the total amount of aid to basic and secondary education was US$7.4 billion in 2018. In other words, only 47% of aid to education goes to the two sub-sectors and the two groups of countries most in need. The rest goes to upper-middle- or even high-income countries and to post-secondary education.

FIGURE 21.6:
Aid to basic education remains at 2010 levels
Total aid to education disbursements, by education level, 2002–18

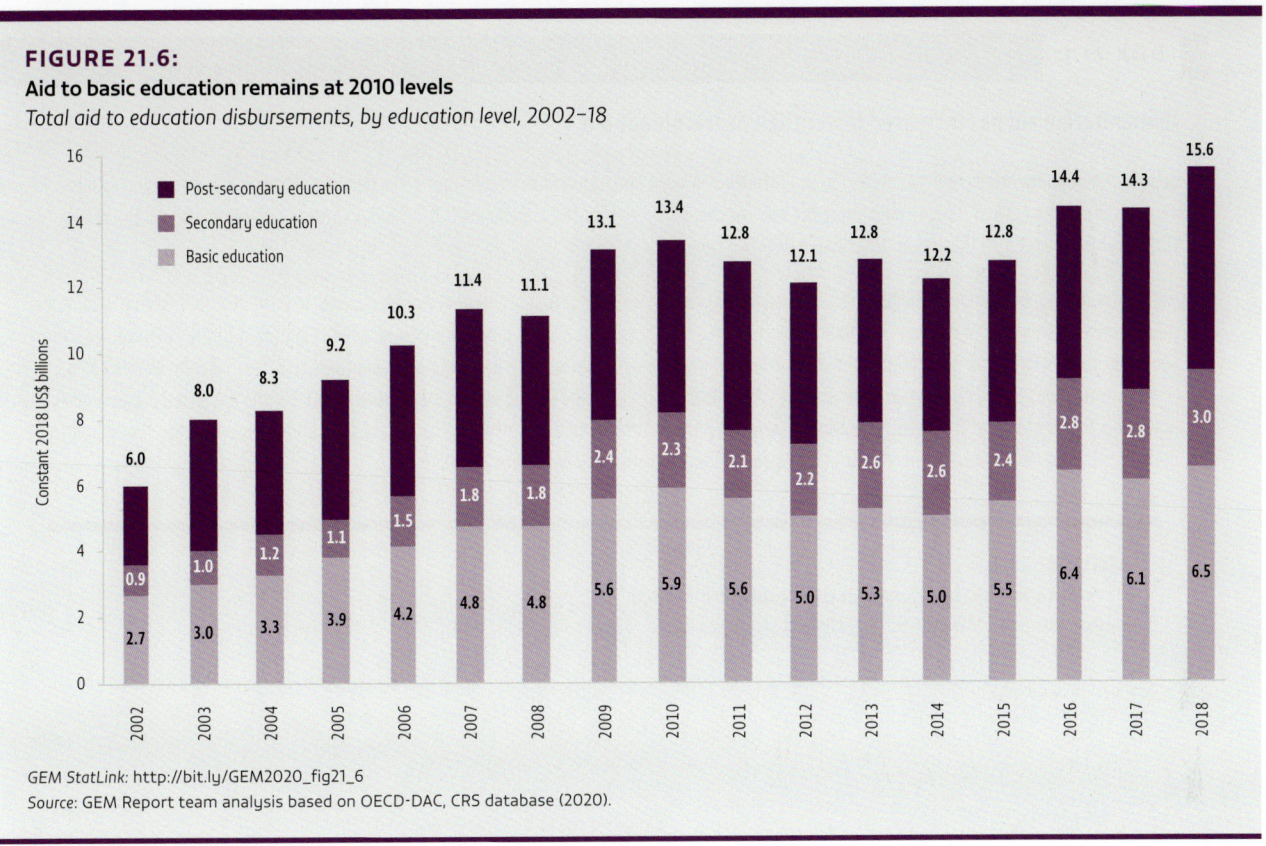

GEM StatLink: http://bit.ly/GEM2020_fig21_6
Source: GEM Report team analysis based on OECD-DAC, CRS database (2020).

FIGURE 21.7:
The share of low-income countries in aid to basic education has increased slightly since 2015
Share of total aid to basic education disbursements received, selected country groups, 2002–18

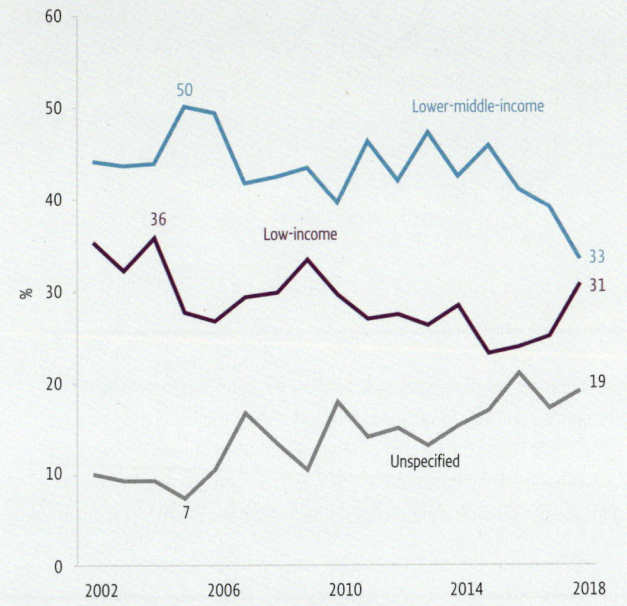

GEM StatLink: http://bit.ly/GEM2020_fig21_7
Source: GEM Report team analysis based on OECD-DAC, CRS database (2020).

The degree to which aid reaches those most in need also depends on what it is spent on. In recent years, for instance, donors have been increasing their emphasis on inclusion in education, with special reference to disability (**Focus 21.1**).

DEVELOPMENT FINANCE FLOWS EXTEND BEYOND ODA

Development finance comprises grants and loans with concessional or non-concessional terms. Whether countries receive concessional loans depends on their development level and the sector for which the loan is intended. Only low-income and selected lower-middle-income countries have access to concessional loans, and social sector loans are more likely to benefit from concessional terms.

" In recent years donors have been increasing their emphasis on inclusion in education, with special reference to disability "

BOX 21.1:

BOX 21.1:

Humanitarian aid has increased faster than development aid

Education in emergencies receives funding from both development and humanitarian assistance mechanisms. Although there are inconsistencies in reporting, in the case of refugee education, the two mechanisms contributed equally in 2016, excluding European Commission support to Turkey for Syrian refugee education (UNESCO, 2018).

Humanitarian support to education has increased in recent years due to the proliferation of protracted crises. In 2018, 16 countries had had more than 5 consecutive years of appeals coordinated by the United Nations (UN) (Development Initiatives, 2019). According to the Financial Tracking Service of the UN Office for the Coordination of Humanitarian Affairs, total humanitarian aid to education was US$705 million in 2019. Of this, US$457 million was based on appeals and response plans. Both have increased sixfold since 2012 (**Figure 21.8a**). Yet the increased support does not reflect increased prioritization of education in terms of proportion of education in humanitarian aid. Education amounted to 3% of global humanitarian aid and 2.6% of humanitarian appeals and response plans in 2019 (**Figure 21.8b**).

FIGURE 21.8:
Humanitarian aid to education continues to increase
Humanitarian aid to education, selected statistics, 2010–19

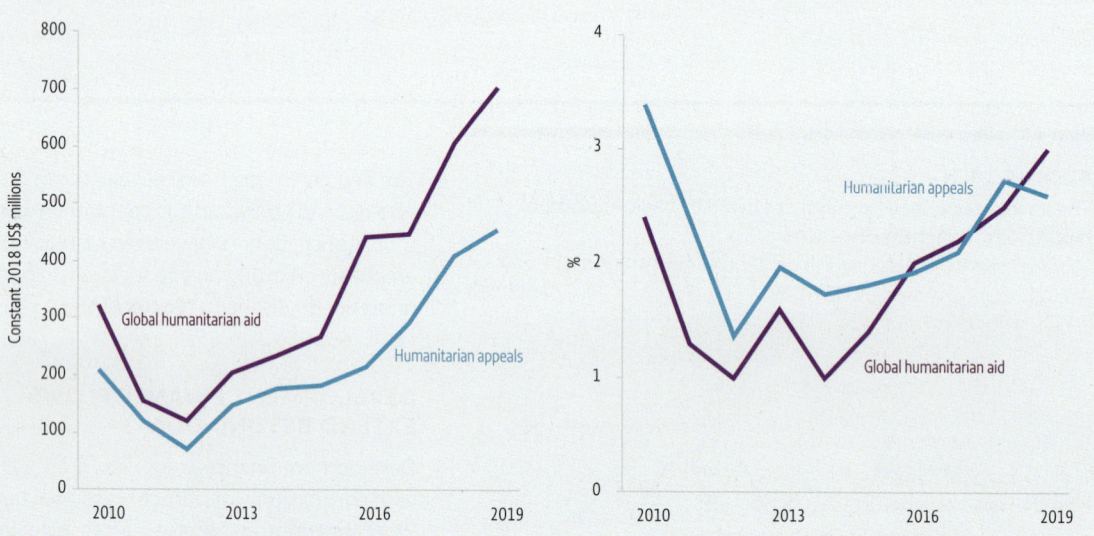

a. Volume of humanitarian aid to education

b. Share of education in humanitarian aid

GEM StatLink: http://bit.ly/GEM2020_fig21_8
Source: GEM Report team analysis based on OCHA FTS database (2020).

Education Cannot Wait, a multilateral body allowing donors to blend humanitarian and development funds for education in crises, disbursed US$255 million between its inception in 2016 and February 2020. Seven countries and two foundations pledged US$216 million in the replenishment announcement at the UN General Assembly in September 2019, bringing the total to US$614 million, which means the target of US$1.8 billion by 2021 remains ambitious (Education Cannot Wait, 2020b). In early 2020, Education Cannot Wait launched two new three-year programmes, in Chad for 230,000 children (US$21 million) and Ethiopia for almost 750,000 children (US$27 million), that will aim to catalyse additional support (Education Cannot Wait, 2020a).

A recent change in methodology means that, as of 2019, only the concessional grant-equivalent part of concessional loans will count as aid, alongside grants (**Box 21.2**).

As more countries graduate from eligibility for concessional terms, it will be important to monitor availability of non-concessional financing. The Addis Ababa Action Agenda stressed the need to tap into all funding sources as part of the 'billions to trillions' pledge to expand investment to levels needed to achieve the SDGs (International Monetary Fund, 2015).

According to the OECD-DAC Creditor Reporting System (CRS) database, the volume of non-concessional loans for education was US$1.5 billion in 2017, down from a peak of US$2.4 billion in 2010. The latter figure excludes the single largest project categorized as education: a US$667 million resettlement component of a World Bank project to support the Trans-Anatolian Natural Gas Pipeline in Azerbaijan and Turkey, for which no clear relationship with education could be identified. This example highlights the importance of how funds for multisector projects are allocated to sectors (**Box 21.3**). On average, more than 60% of these loans come from the International

BOX 21.2:

New development finance definitions will improve aid to education monitoring

Monitoring of development finance is undergoing significant change in response to the magnitude of the SDG challenge and changes in international financing. The main source of consolidated data on development finance, the OECD, is adopting a grant-equivalent methodology to calculate ODA, replacing the cash-flow basis. As grants are aid and market-rate non-concessional loans are not, the new definition will affect the treatment of concessional loans, which are a mixture of the two. Previously, loans by the official sector with a grant element of at least 25% were counted as ODA at their full face value, with repayments subtracted over time. Under the new methodology, only the grant portion of concessional loans will count as ODA (OECD, 2015).

This change is part of an initiative to improve monitoring of Total Official Support for Sustainable Development (TOSSD) and capture diverse development cooperation partners. TOSSD will cover ODA and two other flows in support of sustainable development (OECD, 2019c) (**Table 21.1**).

TOSSD will capture a greater variety of donors. In particular, donor codes for multilateral institutions, such as the GPE, will reduce the proportion of aid to education with a previously 'unspecified' country recipient. Sector-level information will be provided for the humanitarian sector, which will help identify humanitarian aid allocated to education. These changes will affect the database in mid-2020, but progress may vary depending on donor readiness. Education Cannot Wait will continue to be considered a recipient rather than a donor, but cases of 'unspecified amounts' of aid to education should be reduced if not eliminated.

TOSSD will also capture resources for regional and global activities and initiatives that indirectly support the SDGs, including promotion of global public goods, such as statistical databases and publications, and knowledge sharing across platforms aimed at enabling development and tackling global challenges, such as climate change and epidemics.

A task force of representatives from national statistics offices, DAC and other international organizations, non-DAC providers and other countries is developing statistical concepts, standards and methodologies for the TOSSD framework (OECD, 2019a, 2019b). It drafted reporting instructions for cross-border flows and global and regional expenditure, which have been piloted in countries including Burkina Faso, Costa Rica, Nigeria, the Philippines and Senegal. It aims to include South–South cooperation funders and multilateral institutions in the pilot projects (OECD, 2019d). It is also engaging with the Inter-agency and Expert Group on SDG Indicators to host the project at the United Nations and ensure that non-DAC countries can apply the TOSSD methodology. As an example of potential measurement challenges, the lines of credit that China and India, two non-DAC members, provide to partner countries are considered concessional under OECD but not World Bank criteria (Bhattacharya and Rashmin, 2019).

TABLE 21.1:
Total Official Support for Sustainable Development framework

Type of flow	Data implications
Official development assistance	Existing data
Other official flows	Additional data required
South–South cooperation	
Triangular cooperation	
Private finance mobilization	
International public goods for sustainable development, e.g. for research, peace and security	No data currently captured

Source: OECD (2019c).

> " According to the OECD-DAC CRS database, the volume of non-concessional loans for education was US$1.5 billion in 2017, down from a peak of US$2.4 billion in 2010 "

BOX 21.3:

Allocating aid to sectors is not always straightforward

Past editions of the *Global Education Monitoring Report* have shown education losing ground to other sectors. While the share of health, population and reproductive health was growing, the share of education in total aid fell from 14.8% in 2003 to 9.7% in 2013. It has increased slightly since, reaching 10.8% in 2018. The share of energy more than doubled from 3.6% in 2003 to 8.7% in 2018 (**Figure 21.10**). Recent research shows more nuances to the analysis, as classifying aid to sectors is complex.

AidData, an initiative based at William & Mary's Global Research Institute in the United States, developed methodology to analyse 1.25 million development project descriptions from the CRS database between 2000 and 2013 (except humanitarian and general budget support) to estimate the projects' contributions to SDG targets (DiLorenzo et al., 2017). Although descriptions included sector-specific purpose codes, reviewers exercised discretion as to whether descriptions fitted one or more sectors, splitting project budgets accordingly. Weights were applied to descriptions assigned to multiple SDG targets. Two review rounds ensured consistency.

Analysis for this report suggests that 82% of aid to education in the CRS was linked to SDG 4 and 18% to other goals, principally SDG 16 and SDG 9. As the leakage to other sectors was not fully offset by those sectors' contributions to education, the analysis concluded that aid concerning SDG 4 was overestimated by around 4% relative to CRS purpose codes, i.e. US$6 billion in aid to education was not spent on educational activities over the 13 years analysed.

AidData faced considerable methodological challenges. Donors are not obliged to provide detailed project descriptions when submitting data. CRS and AidData codes could be mapped on each other for 58% of cases. The interrelated nature of the SDGs further complicates assignment. CRS purpose codes, e.g. 'higher education' (11420) and 'advanced technical and managerial training' (11320), may not correspond to SDG 4 targets, yet many of these codes were assigned to targets 4.1 and 4.6 without sufficient explanation. Some projects in the CRS did not align with any SDG or SDG target.

AidData has updated coding guidelines to assist in assigning project records to SDGs (Turner and Burgess, 2019). Budget support and humanitarian aid, excluded in the first exercise, have been incorporated, which should be informative for donors that will report on how projects are linked to SDGs once TOSSD becomes operational.

FIGURE 21.10:
Education has lost ground to other donor priorities
Education, energy and health, population policies/programmes and reproductive health as a share of total sector allocable aid, 2003–2018

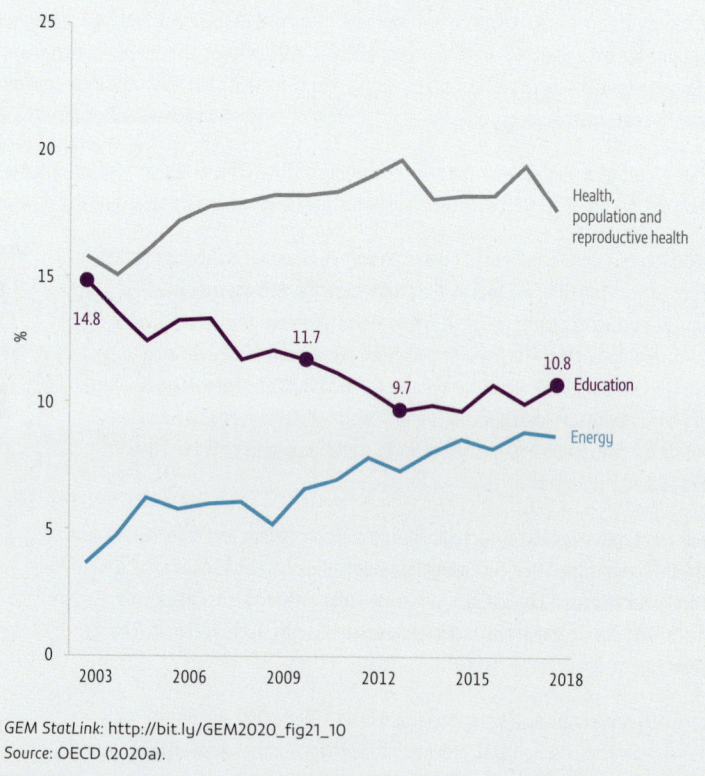

GEM StatLink: http://bit.ly/GEM2020_fig21_10
Source: OECD (2020a).

FIGURE 21.9:

The volume of loans to education has not changed in recent years

Non-concessional loans to education, 2002–17

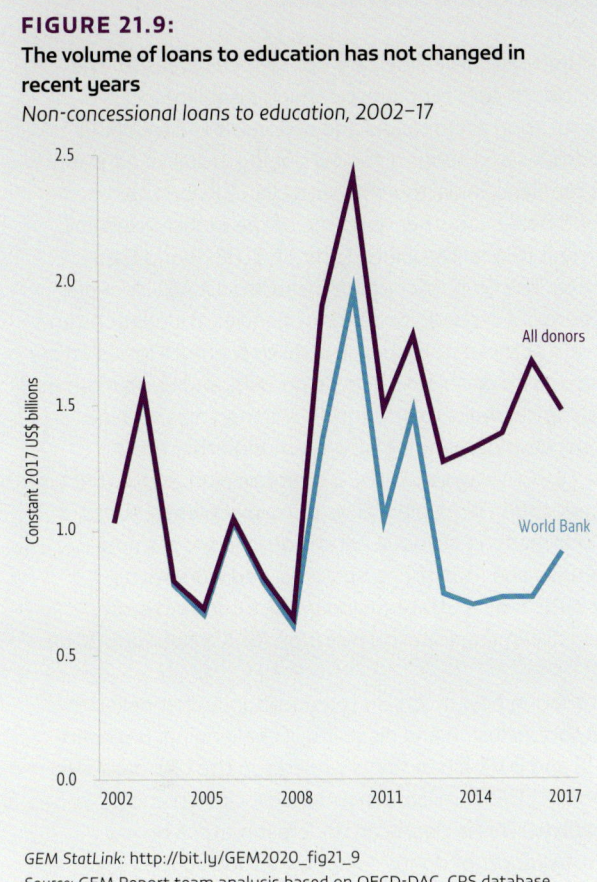

GEM StatLink: http://bit.ly/GEM2020_fig21_9
Source: GEM Report team analysis based on OECD-DAC, CRS database.

Bank for Reconstruction and Development, the World Bank branch serving middle-income countries, whose lending for this purpose is concentrated on Argentina, Brazil, Colombia, Mexico and the Philippines (**Figure 21.9**). The Inter-American Development Bank accounted for a further quarter and the Asian Development Bank (ADB) one-tenth of total non-concessional lending for education. However, such lending was a fraction of development banks' loan portfolios, e.g. 5.2% of ADB loans in 2018 (ADB, 2019).

The initiative to establish an International Finance Facility for Education, supported by the UN Special Envoy for Global Education, is meant to facilitate expansion of multilateral development banks' loans for education in middle-income countries. It aims to lower borrowing costs through grants and offer cash and written commitment guarantees to enable banks to raise more funds in capital markets (Education Commission, 2020). In September 2019, the Netherlands pledged

US$250 million in guarantees, and the United Kingdom pledged about US$125 million in grants and US$315 million in guarantees (Education Commission, 2019).

FOCUS 21.1: DONORS ARE DEVELOPING APPROACHES TO DISABILITY-INCLUSIVE EDUCATION

In recent years, inclusion, particularly with reference to disability, has gained prominence among global education and development priorities, aided by the UN Convention on the Rights of Persons with Disabilities and the 2030 Agenda for Sustainable Development. Donors can influence formal and informal governance processes, education plans and policy development. They can also routinely influence monitoring and reporting framework development and local engagement. The degree to which aid influences disability-inclusive education depends on the donor, provision channels and purpose.

Australia was among the first to formulate a disability-inclusive development assistance strategy: Development for All (Ausaid, 2008; Australia Department of Foreign Affairs and Trade, 2015). The Office of Development Effectiveness evaluated aid with respect to two disability-inclusiveness criteria. It found that, in 2017/8, 55% of aid to education actively involved people with disabilities and 73% identified and responded to barriers to participation. The levels were higher than those in any other sectors, including health and infrastructure (Australia Department of Foreign Affairs and Trade, 2018). Germany developed the 2013–15 Action Plan for the Inclusion of Persons with Disabilities (Germany Federal Ministry for Economic Cooperation and Development, 2013). However, an evaluation found that, despite education having been identified as a priority in the plan, only 2 of the 49 projects were actually linked to education (Schwedersky et al., 2017).

While most donors acknowledge the importance of targeting inclusion of people with disabilities, few set

> ❝ While most donors acknowledge the importance of targeting inclusion of people with disabilities, few set targets, especially in education ❞

targets, especially in education. Canada's Feminist International Assistance Policy prioritizes gender equality and women's and girls' empowerment, including through education, but has not prioritized disability inclusion (Global Affairs Canada, 2017a). The declaration on girls' education at the 2018 G7 summit in Charlevoix, Quebec, mentioned the need for attention to girls with disabilities (Canada Government, 2018). The 2017 European Consensus for Development calls on countries to 'take into account the specific needs of persons with disabilities in their development cooperation' but makes no commitments, including on education (European Council, 2017, p. 11). Organizations representing people with disabilities recently urged the European Commission's Directorate-General for International Cooperation and Development to improve disability inclusion in its policies and programmes (European Disability Forum, 2020).

The Global Disability Summit 2018 rallied development partners to commit to action. Norway had mentioned children with disabilities in its education and development agenda (Norway Government, 2014) but was criticized for inclusive education promises that were 'broad, vague, and non-binding' (Jennings, 2017, p. 4). At the summit, Norway joined the Inclusive Education Initiative with the United Kingdom and the World Bank and pledged to contribute NOK 50 million (US$5.3 million) over three years (Norway Ministry of Foreign Affairs, 2018). At the global level, the initiative aims to coordinate inclusive education planning and develop public goods for education of children with disabilities. At the country level, it aims to coordinate, financially and technically support and help implement disability-inclusive education programmes, and support disaggregated data collection (World Bank, 2019b).

Education is one of four pillars of the disability-inclusive development strategy of the United Kingdom's Department for International Development (DFID), which aims to double the proportion of disability-inclusive education programmes by 2023 (Department for International Development, 2018b). DFID's country and project targets include reaching up to 18,000 girls with disabilities through the Leave No Girl Behind programme by 2023, training 12,000 primary school teachers in Rwanda and establishing 687 inclusive education resource centres across Ethiopia by 2022 (Department for International Development, 2018a). As the first of 10 World Bank commitments to disability-inclusive development, all of its education

programmes will target people with disabilities by 2025 (World Bank, 2018b, 2018c).

Children with disabilities are 1 of 10 focus areas for the GPE, which calls for mainstreaming disability inclusion in education sector plans and policies. It is developing guidelines and support for developing inclusive education sector plans, in partnership with UNICEF and the World Bank – another outcome of the Global Disability Summit (Global Disability Summit, 2018; World Bank, 2019a). The Global Action on Disability (GLAD) Network, a coordination body of donors, agencies, foundations and private actors established in 2015 to promote inclusion of people with disabilities in development and humanitarian assistance, seeks to strengthen partnerships within global development initiatives, among other goals. The GLAD Network 2018–20 strategic plan, supported by an education work plan, aims to map activities, support mainstreaming inclusive education into programme agendas and monitoring systems, and work with the GPE and its Strategy and Impact Committee on mainstreaming disability inclusion (GLAD Network, 2018).

Estimating how much aid to education is channelled to support inclusion and disability is challenging. Between 2015 and 2017, a handful of projects in the CRS database (totalling US$17 million) mentioned inclusion and disability. This is clearly an underestimate: A review for this report of donor documents showed multiple programmes supporting education access for children with disabilities through safe and healthy learning environments and accessible buildings, disability-inclusive curricula, training of qualified teachers for children with disabilities and improving data availability.

The ADB is implementing a seven-year, US$240 million skills development project in India's Madhya Pradesh state. It includes a target of 6% enrolment and certification of people with disabilities in the technical and vocational education component. A five-year, US$27 million project on service delivery for people with disabilities in Mongolia includes a component

> " Children with disabilities are 1 of 10 focus areas for the GPE, which calls for mainstreaming disability inclusion in education sector plans and policies "

institutionalizing early identification to ensure access to education (ADB, 2017, 2018). A three-year, US$14 million Canadian project to improve access to education of good quality for more than 58,000 primary school children in Mali had three components, one of which focused on school construction and rehabilitation for children with disabilities (Global Affairs Canada, 2017b). The European Union is funding a five-year, US$40 million project in Egypt through UNICEF to expand access to education and protection, with a component upgrading 200 public primary schools to cater for 6,000 children with disabilities (European Union, 2016).

In 2017, the World Bank and US Agency for International Development established the Disability-Inclusive Education in Africa Program, a US$3 million trust fund to design and implement inclusive education programmes. It has funded analytical work on inclusion in mainstream and special schools in Ethiopia, the Gambia, Ghana, Lesotho, Liberia, Senegal and Zambia (World Bank, 2018a). The World Bank and GPE are co-financing a US$59.5 million project on early childhood education for 2019–24 in Uzbekistan. It will include provision of technical assistance to review or develop regulations promoting inclusive preschool education for children with disabilities or special education needs (World Bank, 2019c).

Tracking of the disability focus of donor-funded programmes will improve when the OECD introduces a disability inclusion and empowerment marker with the 2018 data, following the example of the gender equality marker (OECD, 2018a, 2018b).

HOUSEHOLD EXPENDITURE

Increasing data availability draws attention to the high levels of total education spending borne by households in poorer countries. Household education spending accounted for a median of 0.7% (from 0.5% in Europe and Northern America to 1.9% in sub-Saharan Africa) and a mean of 1.1% of GDP in 72 countries with data in 2013–18. Generally, the poorer the country, the larger the share of households in total education spending: Although the number of countries with data is insufficient to be representative for any income group except high-income countries, average values among those with data ranged from 11% in high-income to 23% in middle-income and 43% in low-income countries (**Figure 21.11**).

> " In six of nine countries where households spent at least 2.5% of GDP on education, governments spent less than 4% "

Household spending often makes up for insufficient government spending: In six of nine countries where households spent at least 2.5% of GDP on education, governments spent less than 4%. Lebanon is among the relatively richer countries where households spend a lot on education: Out-of-pocket expenditure was 2.7% of GDP, accounting for 52% of total education spending.

To reduce the burden on households, several governments have introduced programmes to abolish fees, but many struggle to implement them or to support schools and households through other means (see **Chapter 4**). Papua New Guinea, for instance, effectively eliminated tuition fees up to grade 10 in 2012 (Howes et al., 2014; UNICEF, 2017), but completion rates remain low (see **Chapter 9**). In Benin, while access to lower secondary education is nominally free, households pay out of pocket for other fees, books and school uniforms (Benin Ministry of Pre-Primary and Primary Education et al., 2013; Tiyab and Ndabananiye, 2013) and account for 55% of total national education spending. Globally, families facing high education costs make spending choices that sometimes reveal gender bias (**Focus 21.2**).

FOCUS 21.2: HOUSEHOLDS SHOW GENDER BIAS IN EDUCATION SPENDING

Household members do not share resources equally. Averages can therefore underestimate inequality, including in the distribution of resources for education. Studies have documented variation by birth order in education outcomes: Older sisters often have to look after younger siblings. There is ample evidence a child's gender informs education spending decisions. However, with education norms changing rapidly around the world, it is important to distinguish results by location, education level, and date of research.[1]

---

1   This Focus is based on Rodríguez Takeuchi (2020).

FIGURE 21.11:

The poorer the country, the higher the out-of-pocket share of national education spending

Distribution of total education expenditure, by source, 2013–18

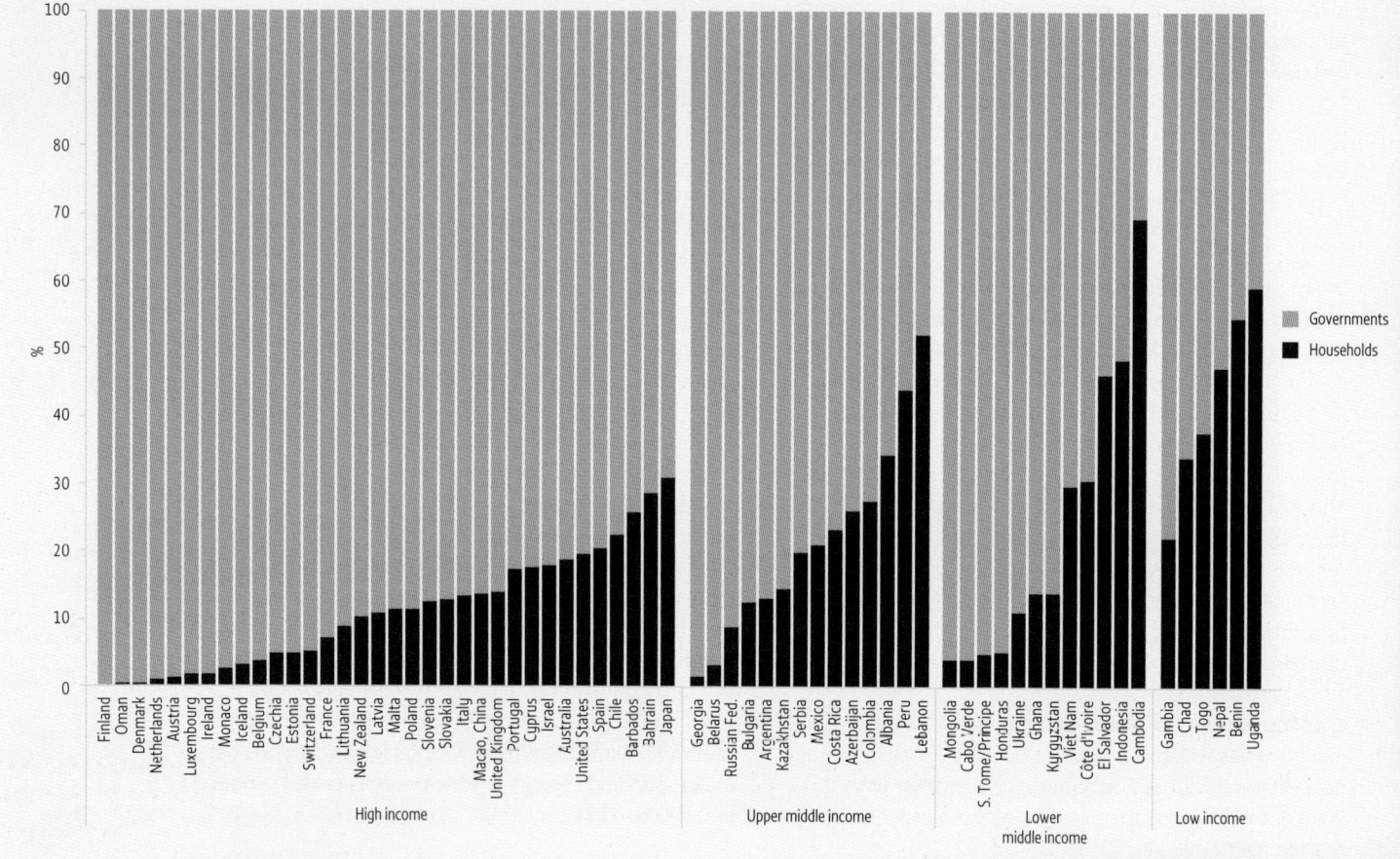

GEM StatLink: http://bit.ly/GEM2020_fig21_11
Source: UIS database.

> " In the 1990s, households in most Indian states spent more money on education for boys aged 5 to 14 than for girls, as more boys were enrolled "

Households decide (a) which children to send to school and (b) how much to spend on those enrolled. In the 1990s, households in most Indian states spent more money on education for boys aged 5 to 14 than for girls, as more boys were enrolled (Kingdon, 2005). Pakistan showed a similar bias concerning primary

school-aged children for the same reason, while in secondary education, the bias resulted from both higher enrolment rates for boys and higher spending on boys once in school (Aslam and Kingdon, 2008). By contrast, intra-household bias in Sri Lanka favoured girls across age groups, in line with higher national completion rates for girls (Himaz, 2010).

Bias often increases at higher education levels. In Ethiopia, household spending on the education of secondary school-aged children in 1994–2004 favoured boys (Delelegn, 2007). In Pakistan, the gap in the probability of boys receiving more household resources for education was 13 percentage

points for 5- to 9-year-olds and 24 points for
10- to 14-year-olds (Aslam and Kingdon, 2008).
In Paraguay, there was a bias towards boys for younger
children in rural areas and for children aged 15 to 19 in
all areas (Masterson, 2012).

However, more recent surveys show increasing
expenditure bias towards girls in some settings.
A comparison of surveys in 12 Latin American countries
found that households spent more on girls' secondary
and tertiary education than that of boys (Acerenza
and Gandelman, 2019). In Malaysia, while there was
no intra-household expenditure variation nationally,
it existed in some regions, favouring 5- to 14-year-old
girls, once children were enrolled (Kenayathulla, 2016).

Households in Ghana spent more on male children,
conditional on their enrolment at primary school
(Iddrisu et al., 2018). In India, while bias in enrolment fell
between 1995 and 2014, bias in conditional expenditure
rose significantly (Datta and Kingdon, 2019). This occurred
despite an economic liberalization drive around 2005 that
opened employment opportunities in the services
sector for women (Azam and Kingdon, 2013). In Thailand,
households were more likely to spend on girls' education,
especially at ages 12 to 19, an effect stronger in rural
areas. The bias towards girls was more apparent in the
amount spent on education than in the decision to enrol
children in school (Wongmonta and Glewwe, 2017).

Even when education is free and boys and girls enrol
in equal numbers, household spending on education

> " Even when education is free and boys and
> girls enrol in equal numbers, household
> spending on education that is perceived to
> be of better quality can be biased "

that is perceived to be of better quality can be biased.
In India, a bias towards boys means they are more likely
to be privately educated (Azam and Kingdon, 2013).
In the Republic of Korea, a study found that parents
spent US$23 more per month on private supplementary
education and tuition for academic subjects for first-born
boys than for first-born girls. These results were driven
by parental expectation that boys (especially the eldest)
would have higher education attainment and higher-wage
occupations (Choi and Hwang, 2015).

Such gendered labour market expectations interact
with cultural norms to shape parental attitudes and
household allocations. Households favour boys in
enrolment and education expenditure in every Indian
state except Meghalaya, the only one with a matrilineal
system in which women control household resources.
Matrilineal structures could also explain the absence
of bias towards boys in some of India's tribal regions
(Kaul, 2018; Saha, 2013). In Thailand, daughters are
favoured in education spending decisions because they
are expected to be primary caregivers to elderly parents
and more likely to send remittances (Wongmonta and
Glewwe, 2017).

A first grade girl copies homework from the blackboard in her classroom at the Héctor Abad Gómez Educational Institute in the Niquiato neighbourhood of Medellín, capital of the north-western department of Antioquia, Colombia.

CREDIT: UNICEF/Markisz

Statistical tables[1]

Table 1 presents basic information on demographic and education system characteristics as well as on domestic education finance. Tables 2–7 are organized by each of the seven SDG 4 targets (4.1–4.7) and three means of implementation (4.a–4.c). The tables mainly focus on the SDG 4 monitoring framework of 42 internationally comparable indicators: 12 global and 30 thematic indicators. The UNESCO Institute for Statistics (UIS) reported on 33 of the 42 indicators in 2019 (**Table I.1**).[2,3] The tables also include additional indicators, such as transition from primary to secondary education and student mobility, which are not formally part of the SDG 4 monitoring framework.

METHODOLOGICAL NOTES

Most data in the statistical tables come from the UIS. Where the statistical tables include data from other sources, these are mentioned in footnotes. The most recent UIS data on pupils, students, teachers and education expenditure presented in the tables are from the September 2019 release and refer to the school year or financial year ending in 2018.[4] They are based on results reported to and processed by the UIS before July 2019. For a limited number of indicators and countries, the UIS updated its database in February 2020 and these updates are also reflected. These statistics refer to formal education, both public and private, by level of education. The statistical tables list 209 countries and territories, all of which are UNESCO Member States or associate members. Most report their

data to the UIS using standard questionnaires issued by the UIS itself. For 46 countries, education data are collected by the UIS via the UIS/OECD/Eurostat (UOE) questionnaires.[5]

POPULATION DATA

The population-related indicators used in the statistical tables, including enrolment ratios, number of out-of-school children, adolescents and youth, and number of youth and adults, are based on the 2019 revision of population estimates produced by the UN Population Division (UNPD). Because of possible differences between national population estimates and those of the United Nations, these indicators may differ from those published by individual countries or by other organizations.[6] In the 2019 revision, the UNPD does not provide population data by single years of age for countries with total population of less than 90,000. For these countries, as well as some special cases, population estimates are derived from Eurostat (Demographic Statistics), the Secretariat of the Pacific Community (Statistics and Demography Programme) or national statistical offices.

ISCED CLASSIFICATION

Education data reported to the UIS are in conformity with the International Standard Classification of Education (ISCED), revised in 2011. Countries may have their own definitions of education levels that do not correspond to ISCED 2011. Differences between nationally

---

1   The statistical tables are accessible on the GEM Report website at http://en.unesco.org/gem-report/statistics.

2   The Inter-agency and Expert Group on SDG Indicators proposed the 11 SDG 4 global indicators. The UN Statistical Commission adopted them at its 48th session, in March 2017. The United Nations Economic and Social Council adopted them in June 2017.

3   The Technical Advisory Group on post-2015 education indicators originally proposed 43 indicators. The Technical Cooperation Group (TCG), whose secretariat is at the UIS, endorsed them, with some changes, to monitor progress towards the SDG 4 targets. At its meeting in Dubai in January 2018, the TCG agreed the UIS would report on 33 indicators in 2018. Several indicators, including some of those for which the UIS is currently reporting data, are at varying stages of methodological development.

4   This means 2017/18 for countries with a school year that overlaps two calendar years, and 2018 for those with a calendar school year. The most recent reference year for education finance for the UOE countries is the year ending in 2017.

5   The countries concerned are most European countries, non-European OECD countries, and a changing set of other countries.

6   Where obvious inconsistencies exist between enrolment reported by countries and the United Nations population data, the UIS may decide not to calculate or publish enrolment ratios for some or all levels of education.

and internationally reported education statistics may be due to the use of nationally defined education levels rather than the ISCED level, in addition to the population issue raised above.

ESTIMATES AND MISSING DATA

Regarding statistics produced by the UIS, both observed and estimated education data are presented throughout the statistical tables. The latter are marked with subscript (i). Wherever possible, the UIS encourages countries to make their own estimates. Where this does not happen, the UIS may make its own estimates if sufficient supplementary information is available. Gaps in the tables may arise where data submitted by a country are found to be inconsistent. The UIS makes every attempt to resolve such problems with the countries concerned, but reserves the final decision on omitting data it regards as problematic. If information for the year ending in 2018 is not available, data for earlier or later years are used. Such cases are indicated by footnotes.

AGGREGATES

Figures for regional and other aggregates represent either sums, the percentage of countries meeting some condition, medians or weighted averages, as indicated in the tables, depending on the indicator. Weighted averages take into account the relative size of the relevant population of each country, or more generally of the denominator in case of indicators that are ratios. The aggregates are derived from both published data and imputed values, for countries for which no recent data or reliable publishable data are available. Aggregates marked with (i) in the tables are based on incomplete country coverage of reliable data (between 33% and 60% of the population [or aggregate denominator value] of a given region or country grouping). GEM Report calculated sums are flagged for incomplete coverage if less than 95% of the population of a given region or country income group is represented among the countries for which data are available.

REGIONAL AND COUNTRY INCOME GROUPS

In terms of regional groups, the statistical tables use the SDG regional classification of the United Nations Statistical Division (UNSD), with some adjustments. The UNSD classification includes all territories, whether independent national entities or parts of bigger entities. However, the list of countries presented in the statistical tables includes only full UNESCO Member States and associate members, as well as Bermuda and Turks and Caicos Islands, non-member states that were included in the EFA statistical tables. The UIS does not collect data for the Faroe Islands, so this territory is not included in the GEM Report despite its status as a UNESCO associate member. In terms of country income groups, the statistical tables use the World Bank groups, which are updated each year on 1 July.

SYMBOLS USED IN THE STATISTICAL TABLES

± n   Reference year differs (e.g. -2: reference year 2015 instead of 2017).

i   Estimate and/or partial coverage

-       Magnitude nil or negligible

…   Data not available or category not applicable

Notes by indicator (**Table I.2**), footnotes to the tables and a glossary provide additional help to interpret the data.

TABLE I.1: SDG 4 monitoring framework indicators

Indicator		UIS reports in 2018
	Target 4.1	
4.1.1	Proportion of children and young people (a) in Grade 2 or 3; (b) at the end of primary education; and (c) at the end of lower secondary education achieving at least a minimum proficiency level in (i) reading and (ii) mathematics, by sex	Yes
4.1.2	Completion rate (primary education, lower secondary education, upper secondary education)	Yes
4.1.3	Gross intake ratio to the last grade (primary education, lower secondary education)	Yes
4.1.4	Out-of-school rate (primary education, lower secondary education, upper secondary education)	Yes
4.1.5	Percentage of children over-age for grade (primary education, lower secondary education)	Yes
4.1.6	Administration of a nationally-representative learning assessment (a) in Grade 2 or 3; (b) at the end of primary education; and (c) at the end of lower secondary education	Yes
4.1.7	Number of years of (a) free and (b) compulsory primary and secondary education guaranteed in legal frameworks	Yes
	Target 4.2	
4.2.1	Proportion of children under 5 years of age who are developmentally on track in health, learning and psychosocial well-being, by sex	Yes
4.2.2	Participation rate in organized learning (one year before the official primary entry age), by sex	Yes
4.2.3	Percentage of children under 5 years experiencing positive and stimulating home learning environments	Yes
4.2.4	Gross early childhood education enrolment ratio in (a) pre-primary education and (b) and early childhood educational development	Yes
4.2.5	Number of years of (a) free and (b) compulsory pre-primary education guaranteed in legal frameworks	Yes
	Target 4.3	
4.3.1	Participation rate of youth and adults in formal and non-formal education and training in the previous 12 months, by sex	Yes
4.3.2	Gross enrolment ratio for tertiary education by sex	Yes
4.3.3	Participation rate in technical-vocational programmes (15- to 24-year-olds) by sex	Yes
	Target 4.4	
4.4.1	Proportion of youth and adults with information and communications technology (ICT) skills, by type of skill	Yes
4.4.2	Percentage of youth/adults who have achieved at least a minimum level of proficiency in digital literacy skills	No
4.4.3	Youth/adult educational attainment rates by age group and level of education	Yes
	Target 4.5	
4.5.1	Parity indices (female/male, rural/urban, bottom/top wealth quintile and others such as disability status, indigenous peoples and conflict-affected, as data become available) for all education indicators on this list that can be disaggregated	Yes
4.5.2	Percentage of students in primary education whose first or home language is the language of instruction	No
4.5.3	Extent to which explicit formula-based policies reallocate education resources to disadvantaged populations	No
4.5.4	Education expenditure per student by level of education and source of funding	Yes
4.5.5	Percentage of total aid to education allocated to least developed countries	Yes
	Target 4.6	
4.6.1	Percentage of population in a given age group achieving at least a fixed level of proficiency in functional (a) literacy and (b) numeracy skills, by sex	Yes
4.6.2	Youth/adult literacy rate	Yes
4.6.3	Participation rate of illiterate youth/adults in literacy programmes	Yes
	Target 4.7	
4.7.1	Extent to which (i) global citizenship education and (ii) education for sustainable development are mainstreamed in: (a) national education policies, (b) curricula, (c) teacher education and (d) student assessment	No
4.7.2	Percentage of schools that provide life skills-based HIV and sexuality education	Yes
4.7.3	Extent to which the framework on the World Programme on Human Rights Education is implemented nationally (as per the UNGA Resolution 59/113)	No
4.7.4	Percentage of students by age group (or education level) showing adequate understanding of issues relating to global citizenship and sustainability	No
4.7.5	Percentage of students in the final grade of lower secondary education showing proficiency knowledge of environmental science and geoscience	No
	Target 4.a	
4.a.1	Proportion of schools offering basic services, by type of service	Yes
4.a.2	Percentage of students experiencing bullying in the last 12 months	Yes
4.a.3	Number of attacks on students, personnel and institutions	Yes
	Target 4.b	
4.b.1	Volume of official development assistance flows for scholarships by sector and type of study	Yes
	Target 4.c	
4.c.1	Proportion of teachers with the minimum required qualifications, by education level	Yes
4.c.2	Pupil-trained teacher ratio by education level	Yes
4.c.3	Proportion of teachers qualified according to national standards by education level and type of institution	Yes
4.c.4	Pupil-qualified teacher ratio by education level	Yes
4.c.5	Average teacher salary relative to other professions requiring a comparable level of qualification	No
4.c.6	Teacher attrition rate by education level	Yes
4.c.7	Percentage of teachers who received in-service training in the last 12 months by type of training	No

Notes: Global indicators are highlighted in grey shading.
Source: UIS.

TABLE I.2: Notes of indicators in the statistical tables

	Indicator Notes
	Table 1
A	**Compulsory education by level** Number of years during which children are legally obliged to attend school.
B	**Free years of education, by level** Number of years during which children are legally guaranteed to attend school free of charge.
C	**Official primary school starting age** The official age at which students are expected to enter primary school. This is expressed in whole years, not accounting for cut-off dates other than the beginning of the school year. The official entrance age to a given programme or level is typically, but not always, the most common entrance age.
D	**Duration of each education level** Number of grades or years in a given level of education.
E	**Official school-age population by level** Population of the age group officially corresponding to a given level of education, whether enrolled in school or not.
F	**Total absolute enrolment by level** Individuals officially registered in a given educational programme, or stage or module thereof, regardless of age.
G	**Initial government expenditure on education as percentage of GDP** Total general (local, regional and central, current and capital) initial government funding of education includes transfers paid (such as scholarships to students), but excludes transfers received, in this case international transfers to government for education (when foreign donors provide education sector budget support or other support integrated in the government budget).
H	**Expenditure on education as percentage of total government expenditure** Total general (local, regional and central) government expenditure on education (current, capital, and transfers), expressed as a percentage of total general government expenditure on all sectors (including health, education, social services, etc.). It includes expenditure funded by transfers from international sources to government.
I	**Initial government expenditure per pupil by level, in constant 2016 PPP US$ and as percentage of GDP per capita** Total general (local, regional and central, current and capital) initial government funding of education per student, which includes transfers paid (such as scholarships to students), but excludes transfers received, in this case international transfers to government for education (when foreign donors provide education sector budget support or other support integrated in the government budget).
J	**Initial household expenditure on education as percentage of GDP** Total payments of households (pupils, students and their families) for educational institutions (such as for tuition fees, exam and registration fees, contribution to parent-teacher associations or other school funds, and fees for canteen, boarding and transport) and purchases outside of educational institutions (such as for uniforms, textbooks, teaching materials, or private classes). 'Initial funding' means that government transfers to households, such as scholarships and other financial aid for education, are subtracted from what is spent by households.
	Table 2
A	**Out-of-school children, total number and as percentage of corresponding age group** Children in the official school age range who are not enrolled in either primary or secondary school.
B	**Education completion rate by level** Percentage of children aged 3–5 years older than the official age of entry into the last grade of an education level who have reached the last grade of that level. For example, the primary completion rate in a country with a 6-year cycle where the official age of entry into the last grade is 11 is the percentage of 14- to 16-year-olds who have reached grade 6.
C	**Percentage of pupils over-age for grade by level** The percentage of pupils in each level of education whose age is two years or more above the intended age for their grade.
D	**Gross enrolment ratio in primary education** Total enrolment in primary education, regardless of age, expressed as a percentage of the population in the official age group. It can exceed 100% because of early or late entry and/or grade repetition.
E	**Primary adjusted net enrolment rate** Enrolment of the official age group for primary education either at that level or the levels above, expressed as a percentage of the population in that age group.
F	**Gross intake ratio to last grade of primary education** Total number of new entrants to the last grade of primary education, regardless of age, expressed as a percentage of the population at the official school entrance age for that grade.
G	**Effective transition from primary to lower secondary general education** Number of new entrants to the first grade of lower secondary education in the following year expressed as a percentage of the students enrolled in the last grade of primary education in the given year who do not repeat that grade the following year.
H	**Lower secondary total net enrolment rate** Number of pupils of the official school age group for lower secondary education who are enrolled in any level of education, expressed as a percentage of the corresponding school age population.
I	**Gross intake ratio to last grade of lower secondary education** Total number of new entrants to the last grade of lower secondary education, regardless of age, expressed as a percentage of the population at the official school entrance age for that grade.
J	**Upper secondary total net enrolment rate** Number of pupils of the official school age group for upper secondary education who are enrolled in any level of education, expressed as a percentage of the corresponding school age population.
K	**Administration of nationally representative learning assessment in early grades (grade 2 or 3), or final grade of primary or lower secondary** The definition includes any nationally representative, national or cross-national formative low-stake learning assessment.
L	**Percentage of students achieving at least a minimum proficiency level in reading and mathematics** The minimum proficiency level in reading and mathematics is defined by each assessment. Data need to be interpreted with caution since the different assessments are not comparable. In the absence of assessments conducted in the proposed grade, surveys of student learning achievement in the grade below or above the proposed indicator grade are used as placeholders.

Table 3

A   **Percentage of children aged 36 to 59 months who are developmentally on track in health, learning and psychosocial well-being**
The UNICEF Early Childhood Development Index (ECDI) is collected through the UNICEF Multiple Indicator Cluster Surveys (MICS) and is a measure of fulfilment of developmental potential that assesses children aged 36 to 59 months in four domains: (a) literacy-numeracy, (b) physical development, (c) social-emotional development and (d) learning (ability to follow simple instructions, ability to occupy themselves independently). The percentage of children who are developmentally on track overall is the percentage of children on track in at least three of the four domains.

B   **Under-5 moderate or severe stunting rate**
Proportion of children in a given age group whose height for their age is below minus two standard deviations from median height for age established by the National Center for Health Statistics and the World Health Organization (WHO). (Source: March–August 2019 UNICEF, WHO and World Bank Joint Child Malnutrition Estimates [JME]. Regional aggregates are JME statistical estimates for the reference year, not weighted averages of the observed country values in the country table.)

C   **Percentage of children aged 36 to 59 months experiencing positive and stimulating home learning environments**
Percentage of children 36 to 59 months old with whom an adult has engaged in four or more of the following activities to promote learning and school readiness in the previous three days: (a) reading books to the child, (b) telling stories to the child, (c) singing songs to the child, (d) taking the child outside the home, (e) playing with the child and (f) spending time with the child naming, counting or drawing things. (Source: UNICEF database.)

D   **Percentage of children under 5 years living in households with three or more children's books**
Percentage of children aged 0 to 59 months who have three or more books or picture books. (Source: UNICEF database.)

E   **Gross early childhood education enrolment ratio in pre-primary education**
Total enrolment in pre-primary education, regardless of age, expressed as a percentage of the population in the official age group. It can exceed 100% because of early or late entry.

F   **Adjusted net enrolment rate one year before the official primary school entry age**
Enrolment of children one year before official primary school entry age in pre-primary or primary education, expressed as a percentage of the population in that age group.

Table 4

A   **Participation rate in adult education and training**
Participation rate of adults (aged 25 to 64) in formal or non-formal education and training in the last 12 months. Estimates based on other reference periods, in particular 4 weeks, are included when no data are available on the last 12 months.

B   **Percentage of youth enrolled in technical and vocational education**
Youth (aged 15 to 24) enrolled in technical and vocational education at ISCED levels 2–5, as a percentage of the total population of that age group.

C   **Share of technical and vocational education in total enrolment by level**
Total number of students enrolled in vocational programmes at a given level of education, expressed as a percentage of the total number of students enrolled in all programmes (vocational and general) at that level.

D   **Transition from upper secondary to tertiary education (ISCED levels 5, 6 and 7 combined)**
Gross transition ratio from secondary to tertiary education, based on students in all secondary programmes.

E   **Gross entry ratio to first tertiary programmes (ISCED levels 5 to 7)**
Students who, during the course of the reference school or academic year, enter a programme at a given level of education for the first time, irrespective of whether the students enter the programme at the beginning or at an advanced stage of the programme.

F   **Gross enrolment ratio in tertiary education**
Total enrolment in tertiary education, regardless of age, expressed as a percentage of the population in the five-year age group above the official graduation age from upper secondary. It can exceed 100% because of early or late entry and prolonged study.

G   **Percentage of adults (15 and over) with specific ICT skills**
Individuals are considered to have such skills if they have undertaken certain computer-related activities in the last three months: copying or moving a file or folder; using copy and paste tools to duplicate or move information within a document; using basic arithmetic formulas in a spreadsheet; writing a computer program using a specialized programming language.

H   **Percentage of adults (25 and over) who have attained at least a given level of education**
Number of persons aged 25 and above by the highest level of education attained, expressed as a percentage of the total population in that age group. Primary refers to ISCED 1 or higher, lower secondary to ISCED 2 or higher, upper secondary to ISCED 3 or higher, post-secondary to ISCED 4 or higher.

I   **Percentage of population of a given age group achieving at least a fixed level of proficiency in functional literacy / numeracy skills**
The threshold level corresponds to level 2 on the Programme for the International Assessment of Adult Competencies scale.

J   **Youth (15 to 24)/Adult (15 and above) literacy rate**
K   **Number of youth (aged 15 to 24)/adult (aged 15 and above) illiterates**
Number of literate youth (aged 15 to 24) and adults (aged 15 and above), expressed as a percentage of the total population in that age group. Literacy data are for 2010–16 and include both national observed data from censuses or household surveys and UIS estimates. The latter are based on the most recent national observed data and the Global Age-specific Literacy Projections (GALP) model. As definitions and methodologies used for data collection differ by country, data need to be used with caution.

Table 5

   Adjusted gender parity index, by indicator
The gender parity index (GPI) is the ratio of female to male values of a given indicator. If the female value is less than or equal to the male value, adjusted gender parity index (GPIA) = GPI. If the female value is greater than the male value, GPIA = 2 - 1/GPI. This ensures the GPIA is symmetrical around 1 and limited to a range between 0 and 2. A GPIA equal to 1 indicates parity between females and males. (Sources: UIS database; GEM Report team calculations based on national and international household surveys.)

A   **Completion rate, by level**

B   **Percentage of students with minimum level of proficiency at the end of given level**

C   **Youth and adult literacy rate**

D   **Percentage of adults (16 and over) achieving at least a fixed level of proficiency in functional literacy and numeracy skills**

	Indicator Notes
E	**Gross enrolment ratio, by level**
	Location and wealth disparity The location parity index is the ratio of rural to urban values of a given indicator. The wealth parity index is the ratio of the poorest 20% to the richest 20% of values of a given indicator.
F	**Completion rate, by level**
G	**Percentage of students with minimum level of proficiency at the end of given level**
	Table 6
A	**Extent to which (i) global citizenship education and (ii) education for sustainable development are mainstreamed at all levels in (a) national education policies; (b) curricula; (c) teacher education; and (d) student assessment** Three levels are distinguished: low (not reflected or little reflected), medium (somewhat reflected) and high (fully reflected). (Source: UNESCO, 2019.)
B	**Percentage of schools providing life skills-based HIV/AIDS education** Percentage of lower secondary schools providing life skills-based HIV/AIDS education (all institutions)
C	**Percentage of 15-year-old students performing at or above level 2 of proficiency in scientific literacy** Scientific literacy is defined as (a) scientific knowledge and its use to identify questions, acquire new knowledge, explain scientific phenomena and draw evidence-based conclusions about science-related issues; (b) understanding of the characteristic features of science as a form of human knowledge and enquiry; (c) awareness of how science and technology shape the material, intellectual and cultural environments; and (d) willingness to engage in science-related issues, and with the ideas of science, as a reflective citizen. (Source: OECD PISA 2018; TIMSS 2015.)
	Percentage of students and youth with adequate understanding of HIV/AIDS and sexuality Youth (aged 15 to 24) who know at least two ways to prevent infection and reject at least three misconceptions. (Source: UNAIDS, 2019.)
D	**Percentage of schools with basic drinking water, basic (single-sex) sanitation or toilets, and basic handwashing facilities** Basic drinking water means drinking water from an improved source, and water available at the school at the time of the survey. Basic sanitation or toilets means improved sanitation facilities at the school that are single-sex and usable (available, functional and private) at the time of the survey. Basic handwashing facilities means handwashing facilities with water and soap available at the school at the time of the survey.
E	**Percentage of public schools with:** • **Electricity** Regularly and readily available sources of power (e.g. grid/mains connection, wind, water, solar and fuel-powered generator) that enable the adequate and sustainable use of ICT infrastructure by pupils and teachers to support course delivery or independent teaching and learning needs. • **Internet used for pedagogical purposes** Internet that is available for enhancing teaching and learning and is accessible by pupils irrespective of the device used. Access can be via a fixed narrowband, fixed broadband or mobile network. • **Computers** Use of computers to support course delivery or independent teaching and learning needs, including to meet information needs for research purposes, develop presentations, perform hands-on exercises and experiments, share information and participate in online discussion forums for educational purposes. The definition includes desktops, laptops and tablets.
F	**Percentage of public primary schools with access to adapted infrastructure and materials for students with disabilities** Any built environments related to education facilities that are accessible to all users, including those with various types of disability, enabling them to gain access to use and exit from them. Accessibility includes ease of independent approach, entry, evacuation and/or use of a building and its services and facilities (such as water and sanitation) by all of the building's potential users with an assurance of individual health, safety and welfare during the course of those activities.
G	**Level of bullying** Harmonized classification of overall risk of bullying according to the UNICEF Innocenti Global Bullying Database combining data from six international surveys on bullying prevalence among 11- to 15-year-olds in 145 countries (Richardson and Hiu, 2018).
H	**Level of attacks on students, teachers, or institutions** Categorical ranking of the extent to which a country is affected by violent attacks, threats or deliberate use of force in a given period (e.g. the last 12 months, a school year or a calendar year) directed against students, teachers and other personnel or against education buildings, materials and facilities, including transport. The indicator focuses on attacks carried out for political, military, ideological, sectarian, ethnic or religious reasons by armed forces or non-state armed groups. Five levels are captured: No incidents reported: No reports of attacks on education were identified Sporadic: Fewer than 5 reported attacks or fewer than 5 students and education personnel harmed. Affected: 5–99 reported attacks on education or fewer than 5–99 students and education personnel harmed. Heavily affected: 100–199 reported attacks or 100–199 students and education personnel harmed. Very heavily affected: More than 200 reported attacks or more than 200 students and education personnel harmed.
I	**Internationally mobile students, inbound and outbound numbers enrolled and mobility rates** Number of students from abroad studying in a given country, expressed as a percentage of total tertiary enrolment in that country.
	Number of students from a given country studying abroad, expressed as a percentage of total tertiary enrolment in that country.
J	**Volume of official development assistance for scholarships** Total gross disbursement of official development assistance flows (all sectors) for scholarships (all levels). The sum of the values of regions and country income groups does not add up to the global total because some aid is not allocated by country. **Imputed student costs** Costs incurred by donor countries' higher education institutions when they receive students from developing countries.

| **Table 7** |

A **Number of classroom teachers**
Persons employed full-time or part-time in an official capacity to guide and direct the learning experience of pupils and students, irrespective of their qualifications or the delivery mechanism, i.e. face-to-face and/or at a distance. This definition excludes educational personnel who have no active teaching duties (e.g. headmasters, headmistresses or principals who do not teach) or who work occasionally or in a voluntary capacity in educational institutions.

B **Pupil/teacher ratio**
Average number of pupils per teacher at a given level of education, based on headcounts of pupils and teachers.

C **Percentage of trained classroom teachers**
Trained teachers are defined as those who have received at least the minimum organized and recognized pre-service and in-service pedagogical training required to teach at a given level of education. Data are not collected for UOE countries.

D **Percentage of qualified classroom teachers**
Qualified teachers are defined as those who have the minimum academic qualification necessary to teach at a specific level of education according to national standards.

E **Teacher attrition rate**
Number of teachers at a given level of education leaving the profession in a given school year, expressed as a percentage of teachers at that level and in that school year.

F **Relative teacher salary level**
Teacher salary relative to other professionals with equivalent academic qualification. Data refer to actual salaries of all teachers relative to earnings for full-time, full-year workers with tertiary education (ISCED 5 to 8). The indicator is defined as a ratio of salary, using annual average salaries (including bonuses and allowances) of teachers in public institutions relative to the wages of workers with similar educational attainment (weighted average) and to the wages of full-time, full-year workers aged 25 to 64 with tertiary education. Values for secondary education are GEM Report team calculations and represent weighted averages of lower and upper secondary values, weighted by the number of teachers at each level.

TABLE 1: Education system characteristics and education expenditure

	EDUCATION SYSTEMS																
	A Compulsory		B Free		C Official primary school starting age	D Duration (years)				E School-age population (000,000)				F Enrolment (000,000)			
	1 year of pre-primary	9 years of primary-secondary	1 year of pre-primary	12 years of primary-secondary		Pre-primary	Primary	Lower secondary	Upper secondary	Pre-primary	Primary	Secondary	Tertiary	Pre-primary	Primary	Secondary	Tertiary
SDG indicator	4.2.5	4.1.7	4.2.5	4.1.7													
Reference year								2018									
Region	% of countries				Median					Sum							
World	23	73	49	52	6	3	6	3	3	350	722	787	588i	169	726	569	219
Sub-Saharan Africa	2	44	18	22	6	3	6	3	3	76	171	141	90i	17	158	51	6
Northern Africa and Western Asia	12	88	46	67	6	3	6	3	3	25	55	56	42i	7	45	37	18
Northern Africa	-	83	17	33	6	2	6	3	3	10	28	25	20i	3	27	15	6
Western Asia	17	89	56	78	6	3	6	3	3	15	27	31	22i	3	18	22	12
Central and Southern Asia	14	64	57	46	6	3	5	4	3	101	189	258	179	27	210	185	46
Central Asia	20	100	100	40	7	4	4	5	2	6	5	8	6	2	6	7	2
Southern Asia	11	44	33	50	6	2	5	3	4	94	183	250	173	24	204	177	45
Eastern and South-eastern Asia	22	78	44	31	6	3	6	3	3	81	177	180	156	66	182	145	72
Eastern Asia	29	100	57	43	6	3	6	3	3	58	113	112	101	51	113	97	53
South-eastern Asia	18	64	33	22	6	3	6	3	3	23	64	68	55	16	68	48	19
Oceania	18	59	55i	64i	6	2	6	4	3	1	4	4	3i	1	4	4	...
Latin America and the Caribbean	54	83	68	61	6	2	6	3	2	28	59	66	54i	19	60	63	25i
Caribbean	27	82	47	58	5	2	6	3	2	2	4	4	3	1	2	2	1i
Central America	100	86	86	57	6	3	6	3	2	10	19	19	16	6	19	17	6
South America	75	83	92	67	6	3	6	3	3	16	35	43	35	12	38	43	18
Europe and Northern America	26	93	63	72	6	3	6	3	3	38	67	82	64i	33	67	85	50
Europe	28	93	60	70	6	3	5	4	3	26	40	54	40i	24	40	58	29
Northern America	-	100	100	100	6	1	6	3	3	12	28	28	24i	9	27	27	21
Low income	6	42	32	20	6	3	6	3	3	56	112	98	63i	10	107	35	5
Middle income	23	69	47	45	6	3	6	3	3	257	533	604	454	128	542	444	160
Lower middle	17	60	35	31	6	3	6	3	3	151	324	382	269	50	336	249	65
Upper middle	28	76	56	56	6	3	6	3	3	106	209	222	186i	79	206	195	95
High income	31	93	61	75	6	3	6	3	3	37	77	85	71i	31	77	90	54

A   Years of compulsory education, by level.
B   Years of free education, by level.
C   Official primary school starting age.
D   Official duration of education levels in years.
E   Official school-age population by level (for tertiary: the five years following upper secondary).
F   Total absolute enrolment by level.
G   Initial government expenditure on education as % of GDP.
H   Initial government expenditure on education as % of total government expenditure.
I   Initial government expenditure per pupil by level, in constant 2016 PPP US$ and as % of GDP per capita.
J   Initial household expenditure on education as % of GDP.

Note: PPP = purchasing power parity.
Source: UIS unless noted otherwise. Data refer to school year ending in 2018 unless noted otherwise.
Aggregates represent countries listed in the table with available data and may include estimates for countries with no recent data.
(-) Magnitude nil or negligible.
(…) Data not available or category not applicable.
(± n) Reference year differs (e.g. -2: reference year 2016 instead of 2018).
(i) Estimate and/or partial coverage.

		FINANCE								
G	**H**	**I**								**J**
		Government education expenditure per pupil								
		2016 PPP US$				% of GDP per capita				
Government education expenditure (% of GDP)	Education share of total government expenditure (%)	Pre-primary	Primary	Secondary	Tertiary	Pre-primary	Primary	Secondary	Tertiary	Household education expenditure (% of GDP)
	1.a.2	4.5.4								
		2018								
		Median								
4.4	**14.0**	**1,407i**	**2,313i**	**3,169i**	**4,895i**	**11i**	**15i**	**19i**	**27i**	**...**
4.4	16.8	80i	271i	408i	2,635i	2i	12i	17i	76i	...
3.7i	11.6i	...	6,822i	7,147i	4,970i	...	14i	18i	22i	...
...	...	...	...	3,910i	...	...	...	33i	...	...
3.6i	11.0i	3,346i	8,248i	8,461i	3,398i	14i	14i	18i	19i	0.9i
4.1	15.2	211i	638i	817i	2,031	2i	11i	14i	28	...
5.3	16.1	831i	...	...	575i	22i	...	...	7i	0.7i
4.0	14.6	27	895	752	3,523	1	11	11	31	...
3.6	12.2	1,124i	4,842i	9,818i	7,888i	7i	13i	22i	21i	...
3.3	13.1i	4,484i	8,935i	10,660i	8,413	11i	15i	...	17i	0.4i
3.9	11.6	404i	1,514i	4,135i	7,364i	3i	9	13i	22i	...
4.7i	12.7i	...	...	...	...	...	...	...	...	...
4.7	16.1	1,521i	2,033i	2,602i	3,146i	11i	15i	18i	26i	...
3.4i	14.2i	695i	1,959i	2,612i	...	6i	15i	19i	...	...
4.6	20.4	905i	1,949i	1,965i	1,913	11i	15i	14i	30	...
5.2	16.1	2,600i	2,492	2,589	4,219	15	16	17	24	1.3i
4.8	12.3	6,082	7,914	8,148	9,065	18	21	23	26	0.5i
4.8	12.3	6,032	7,856	8,031	8,315	18	22	23	26	0.4i
3.2	10.6	6,877i	9,659	12,711i	12,657	15	18	17	28	1.2i
3.9	16.5	48i	192i	251i	1,704i	2i	10i	16i	83i	...
4.1	14.9	790i	1,317i	1,714i	3,057i	9i	13i	16i	27i	...
4.3	15.8	309i	544i	804i	2,268i	6i	13i	15i	41i	...
3.8i	13.9i	1,369i	1,959i	2,595i	3,394i	9i	15i	18i	24i	...
4.7	12.9	5,766i	8,420	9,100i	11,352	17	19	22	26	0.6i

TABLE 1: Continued

Country or territory	EDUCATION SYSTEMS																
	A Compulsory		B Free		C	D Duration (years)				E School-age population (000)				F Enrolment (000)			
	1 year of pre-primary	9 years of primary-secondary	1 year of pre-primary	12 years of primary-secondary	Official primary school starting age	Pre-primary	Primary	Lower secondary	Upper secondary	Pre-primary	Primary	Secondary	Tertiary	Pre-primary	Primary	Secondary	Tertiary
SDG indicator	4.2.5	4.1.7	4.2.5	4.1.7													
Reference year	2018																
Sub-Saharan Africa																	
Angola	⁻⁺¹	6+1	⁻⁺¹	6+1	6	2	6	3	3	2,136	5,699	4,533	2,713	784	5,621	2,034	253
Benin	-	6	-	6	6	2	6	4	3	677	1,869	1,817	1,028	172	2,224	993	126
Botswana	-	-	...	...	6	3	7	3	2	163	357	230	199	33	345	...	49
Burkina Faso	-	11	-	10	6	3	6	4	3	1,877	3,421	3,249	1,811	82	3,206	1,281	118
Burundi	-	-	...	...	7	2	6	4	3	700	1,860	1,655	1,020	108	2,171	675	62
Cabo Verde	-	10	-	8	6	3	6	3	3	32	62	60	49	23	64	53	12
Cameroon	-	6	-	6	6	2	6	4	3	1,497	4,161	4,016	2,275	516	4,202	2,207	290
Central African Republic	-	10	-	13	6	3	6	4	3	427	818	840	416	12	814	138	...
Chad	-	10	-	10	6	3	6	4	3	1,551	2,768	2,614	1,286	14	2,213	535	42
Comoros	-	6	-	6	6	3	6	4	3	71	128	127	76	15	124	74	6
Congo	-	10	3	13	6	3	6	4	3	466	859	806	433				55
Côte d'Ivoire	-	10	-	10	6	3	6	4	3	2,196	3,991	4,078	2,333	180	3,900	2,041	218
D. R. Congo	-	6	-	6	6	3	6	2	4	8,347	14,684	11,647	7,037	339	13,763	4,619	465
Djibouti	⁻⁺¹	10+1	2+1	12+1	6	2	5	4	3	40	91	126	87	4	69	65	...
Equat. Guinea	-	6	-	6	7	3	6	4	2	101	177	144	101	40	93	...	...
Eritrea	-	8	-	8	6	2	5	3	4	193	506	572	304	47	350	260	10
Eswatini	-	7	-	7	6	3	7	3	2	85	206	134	121	...	237	108	...
Ethiopia	-	8	-	8	7	3	6	4	2	9,002	16,834	15,490	9,342	2,513	16,198	5,029	757
Gabon	-	10	-	10	6	3	5	4	3	169	250	281	179	...	...	...	...
Gambia	-	9	-	9	7	4	6	3	3	283	369	305	198	118	350	...	...
Ghana	2	9	2	9	6	2	6	3	4	1,552	4,340	4,415	2,828	1,852	4,550	2,851	444
Guinea	-	6	-	6	7	3	6	4	3	1,107	2,052	2,068	1,020	...	1,777	716	118
Guinea-Bissau	-	9	...	...	6	3	6	3	3	169	306	254	167	...	...	...	...
Kenya	-	12	-	12	6	3	6	2	4	4,203	8,295	7,507	4,907	3,200	8,290	...	563
Lesotho	-	7	-	7	6	3	7	3	2	143	304	218	212	54	368	136	22
Liberia	-	6	-	6	6	3	6	3	3	412	773	675	388	510	635	227	...
Madagascar	-	5	3	12	6	3	5	4	3	2,207	3,468	4,320	2,687	874	4,861	1,548	144
Malawi	-	8	-	8	6	3	6	4	2	1,662	3,210	2,760	1,594	1,361	4,442	1,041	...
Mali	-	9	4	12	7	3	6	3	3	1,884	3,380	2,658	1,607	131	2,477	1,046	73
Mauritania	-	9	3	13	6	3	6	3	3	374	675	659	387	36	655	237	19
Mauritius	-	11	-	13	5	2	6	3	4	27	86	126	96	26	90	122	39
Mozambique	-	-	...	...	6	3	7	3	2	2,820	5,964	3,657	2,926	...	6,563	1,216	214
Namibia	-	7	...	7	7	2	7	3	2	127	406	245	245	43	491	...	56
Niger	-	-	...	...	7	3	6	4	3	2,321	4,015	3,541	1,815	187	2,768	787	80
Nigeria	-	9	-	9	6	1	6	3	3	5,930	32,752	26,967	15,867	...	25,591	10,315	...
Rwanda	-	6	-	9	7	3	6	3	3	1,009	1,913	1,652	1,126	227	2,504	658	76
Sao Tome and Principe	-	6	-	6	6	3	6	3	3	19	36	31	18	9	37	26	2
Senegal	-	11	-	11	6	3	6	4	3	1,492	2,646	2,487	1,449	247	2,142	1,087	185
Seychelles	-	10	-	11	6	2	6	3	4	3	9	9	7	3	9	7	1
Sierra Leone	-	9	-	9	6	3	6	3	4	653	1,232	1,235	663	91	1,370	492	...
Somalia	-	-	...	...	6	3	6	2	4	1,467	2,663	2,235	1,247	...	...	...	...
South Africa	-	9	-	12	7	3	7	2	3	3,510	7,815	4,911	4,990	862	7,582	5,052	1,116
South Sudan	-	8	-	8	6	3	6	2	4	982	1,784	1,527	1,022	111	1,274	164	...
Togo	-	10	-	5	6	3	6	4	3	682	1,274	1,252	702	156	1,549	728	102
Uganda	-	7	...	...	6	3	7	4	2	4,336	9,163	6,418	3,420	609	8,841	...	165
United Republic of Tanzania	-	7	2	7	7	2	7	2	2	3,437	11,016	7,585	4,876	1,423	10,112	2,148	179
Zambia	-	7	-	7	7	4	7	2	3	2,208	3,487	2,125	1,468	160	3,285	...	...
Zimbabwe	-	7	...	...	6	2	7	2	4	902	2,872	2,006	1,355	...	...	...	136

		FINANCE									
G	**H**	**I** Government education expenditure per pupil								**J**	
		2016 PPP US$				% of GDP per capita					
Government education expenditure (% of GDP)	Education share of total government expenditure (%)	Pre-primary	Primary	Secondary	Tertiary	Pre-primary	Primary	Secondary	Tertiary	Household education expenditure (% of GDP)	Country code
	1.a.2	4.5.4									
		2018									
...	...	...	...	...	...	...	...	...	...	...	AGO
4.0i	17.7i	260-3	200-3	237-3	1,595-3	12-3	9-3	11-3	73-3	...	BEN
...	...	...	...	...	...	...	...	...	...	...	BWA
6.0i	22.7i	172-2	280-3	335-2	6,348-2	10-2	16-3	19-2	351-2	...	BFA
5.0	19.9	...	...	...	...	...	...	...	...	...	BDI
5.2-1	16.4-1	87-1	1,171-1	1,382-1	2,693-1	1-1	17-1	20-1	38-1	...	CPV
3.1i	16.9i	...	...	...	...	...	...	...	...	...	CMR
...	...	...	...	...	...	...	...	...	...	...	CAF
2.2i	17.2i	...	...	...	...	...	...	...	...	...	TCD
2.5-3	13.3-3	315-4	271-4	236-4	690-4	11-4	10-4	8-4	25-4	...	COM
3.6i	15.6i	...	...	...	...	...	...	...	...	...	COG
4.3	18.3	862	544	751	5,889-1	21	13	18	150-1	2.3-3i	CIV
1.5-1i	14.0-1i	- -3	...	...	...	- -3	...	...	...	...	COD
5.6i	14.0i	...	...	...	...	...	37-2	...	...	...	DJI
...	...	...	...	...	...	...	...	...	...	...	GNQ
...	...	...	...	...	...	...	...	...	...	...	ERI
7.1-4	24.8-4	...	1,635-4	2,804-4	12,735-4	...	16-4	28-4	128-4	...	SWZ
4.7-3	27.1-3	54-3	120-3	256-3	3,791-4	4-3	8-3	17-3	266-4	...	ETH
2.7-4	11.2-4	...	...	...	...	...	...	...	...	...	GAB
2.4i	11.2i	- -3	136-3	...	...	- -3	8-3	...	...	...	GMB
4.0i	18.6i	68-4	243-4	804-4	2,298-4	2-4	6-4	19-4	55-4	...	GHA
2.6	14.9	...	150-2	167-4	1,812-4	...	7-2	8-4	90-4	...	GIN
...	...	...	...	...	...	...	...	...	...	...	GNB
5.3i	19.1i	41-3	321-3	...	2,239-3	1-3	11-3	...	76-3	...	KEN
6.5	13.9	...	636	922	1,373	...	21	30	45	...	LSO
2.6i	8.1i	130-2	192-2	241-3	...	10-2	14-2	18-3	...	...	LBR
3.2i	19.8i	...	...	...	1-2	...	...	...	- -2	...	MDG
4.7i	15.8i	- -2	101-2	296-2	...	- -2	8-2	24-2	...	...	MWI
3.8-1	16.5-1	40-1	271-1	563-1	3,692-1	2-1	12-1	25-1	166-1	- -1	MLI
2.6-2i	9.3-2i	...	413-2	575-2	3,889-2	...	10-2	14-2	96-2	...	MRT
4.8	19.6	635	3,415	6,872	2,026-1	3	16	31	10-1	...	MUS
5.6i	17.9i	...	...	...	...	...	...	...	...	...	MOZ
3.1-4	7.6-4	...	...	...	8,388-4	...	...	...	76-4	...	NAM
4.9i	16.8i	471-1	133-1	163-1	2,635-1	46-1	13-1	16-1	260-1	...	NER
...	...	...	...	...	...	...	...	...	...	...	NGA
3.1	10.8	43	87	443	1,996	2	4	22	98	...	RWA
5.1-2i	16.0-2i	391-4	371-4	267-4	1,309-4	13-4	12-4	9-4	42-4	5.1-2i	STP
4.7	21.5	67	403	422	4,838	2	11	11	131	...	SEN
4.4-2	11.7-2	3,415-2	4,004-2	4,314-2	19,938-2	12-2	14-2	15-2	71-2	...	SYC
7.1	32.5	-	194	220-1	...	-	12	14-1	...	...	SLE
...	...	...	...	...	...	...	...	...	...	...	SOM
6.2	18.9	785	2,377	2,832	6,356	6	18	21	48	...	ZAF
1.0-1	0.9i	8-2	94-2	246-2	...	0.4-2	5-2	12-2	...	...	SSD
5.4i	21.8i	83-3	267-2	...	1,299-1	5-3	16-2	...	77-1	...	TGO
2.5i	10.9i	- -4	103-4	...	...	- -4	6-4	...	...	3.9-4	UGA
3.7i	20.6i	243-4	252-4	395-4	...	9-4	10-4	15-4	...	...	TZA
4.7i	17.0i	76-2	527-1	...	...	2-2	13-1	...	...	...	ZMB
4.6i	19.0i	...	...	...	...	...	...	...	...	...	ZWE

Country or territory	A Compulsory — 1 year of pre-primary	A — 9 years of primary-secondary	B Free — 1 year of pre-primary	B — 12 years of primary-secondary	C Official primary school starting age	D Duration (years) — Pre-primary	D — Primary	D — Lower secondary	D — Upper secondary	E School-age population (000) — Pre-primary	E — Primary	E — Secondary	E — Tertiary	F Enrolment (000) — Pre-primary	F — Primary	F — Secondary	F — Tertiary
SDG indicator	4.2.5	4.1.7	4.2.5	4.1.7													
Reference year										2018							
Northern Africa and Western Asia																	
Algeria	-	10	1	12	6	1	5	4	3	912	4,208	4,322	3,116	...	4,430	...	1,601
Armenia	-	12	3	12	6	3	4	5	3	129	168	288	189	49	153	235	103
Azerbaijan	1	9	5	11	6	3	4	5	2	511i	637i	1,000i	724i	203	635	945	201
Bahrain	-	9	-	12	6	3	6	3	3	64	118	105	89	35	114	99	45
Cyprus	1	9	1	12	6	3	6	3	3	29i	57i	55i	60i	24	56	55	45
Egypt	-	12	-	12	6	2	6	3	3	4,798	12,466	10,520	8,288	1,377	12,643	9,137	2,914
Georgia	-	9	-	12	6	3	6	3	3	172	319	266	237	...	305	280	151
Iraq	-	6	2	12	6	2	6	3	3	2,071	5,715	5,041	3,445	...	...	...	...
Israel	3	12+1	3+1	12+1	6	3	6	3	3	493	916	807	609	535	917	819	377
Jordan	-	10	1	12	6	2	6	4	2	472	1,402	1,277	932	128	1,134	790	321
Kuwait	-	9	-	12	6	2	5	4	3	126	314	343	214	79	280	302	116
Lebanon	-	10	3	9	6	3	6	3	3	...	...	...	...	220	509	403	231
Libya	-	9	-	9	6	2	6	3	3	265	766	681	573	...	...	...	...
Morocco	-	9	-	9	6	2	6	3	3	1,362	3,862	3,598	2,939	693	4,323	2,871	1,056
Oman	-	10	-	12	6	2	4	6	2	152	282	408	315	79	279	422	120
Palestine	-	10	1	12	6	2	4	5	3	267	495	855	502	151	488	765	222
Qatar	-	9	-	9	6	3	6	3	3	80	154	125	188	48	154	108	34
Saudi Arabia	-	9	-	12	6	3	6	3	3	1,802	3,367	2,826	2,382	383	3,299	3,108	1,620
Sudan	-	8	-4	11-3	6	2	6	2	3	2,320	6,584	4,933	3,860	1,066	4,900	2,205	653
Syrian Arab Republic	-	9	3	12	6	3	6	3	3	1,116	2,170	1,950	1,741	...	...	...	697
Tunisia	-	9	-	11	6	3	6	3	4	608	1,077	1,109	858	251	1,202	1,047	272
Turkey	-	12	3	12	6	3	4	4	4	4,093	5,427	10,831	6,571	1,326	4,972	11,404	7,199
United Arab Emirates	-	6	-	12	6	2	5	4	3	203	484	544	518	156	486	528	192
Yemen	-	9	-	9	6	3	6	3	3	2,368	4,409	3,902	2,878	36	3,900	1,916	...
Central and Southern Asia																	
Afghanistan	-+1	9+1	1+1	12+1	7	1	6	3	3	1,086	6,352	5,653	3,826	...	6,545	3,064	371
Bangladesh	-	5	1	...	6	3	5	3	4	8,767	14,800	21,653	15,320	3,578	17,338	15,870	3,151
Bhutan	-	-	-	11	6	2	7	4	2	24	90	83	77	8	92	76i	12
India	-	8	-	8	6	3	5	3	4	71,285	123,996	177,433	122,370	10,004	143,227	133,144	34,338
Iran, Islamic Republic of	-	9	-	9	6	1	6	3	3	1,365	7,738	6,725	5,981	706	8,172	5,684	4,074
Kazakhstan	-+1	9+1	4+1	11+1	7	4	4	5	2	1,578	1,400	1,703	1,109	986	1,461	1,928	685
Kyrgyzstan	1	9	4	11	7	4	4	5	2	603	520	724	528	240	529	675	218
Maldives	-	-	-	12	6	3	7	3	2	23	50	26	46	21	45	...	14
Nepal	1+1	8+1	1+1	10+1	5	2	5	3	4	1,096	2,793	4,320	3,261	958	3,970	3,464	405
Pakistan	-	12	-	12	5	2	5	3	4	10,387	24,704	31,625	20,965	8,636	22,931	13,358	1,878
Sri Lanka	-+1	11+1	-+1	13+1	5	1	5	4	4	335	1,707	2,731	1,532	464	1,725	2,728	301
Tajikistan	-	9	4	11	7	4	4	5	2	960	839	1,180	849	91	771	...	265
Turkmenistan	-	12	3	12	6	3	4	6	2	404	473	788	558	189	359	651	44
Uzbekistan	-	12	4	12	7	4	4	4	3	2,622	2,451	4,181	2,974	733	2,485	3,893	300
Eastern and South-eastern Asia																	
Brunei Darussalam	-	9	...	...	6	3	6	2	5	21	39	46	35	14	39	44	11
Cambodia	-	-	-	9	6	3	6	3	3	1,061	2,032	1,785	1,545	253	2,147	...	211
China	-	9	-	9	6	3	6	3	3	52,219	102,354	99,114	88,797	46,001	101,873	84,322	44,935
DPR Korea	1	10	1	10	7	2	4	3	3	660	1,337	2,232	1,948	...	1,508	2,148	526
Hong Kong, China	-	9	-	12	6	3	6	3	3	172	344	317	388	183	366	349	298
Indonesia	-	9	-	12	7	2	6	3	3	9,479	27,740	28,009	22,134	5,909i	29,426	24,894	8,037
Japan	-	9	-	9	6	3	6	3	3	...	...	...	...	2,872	6,532	7,093	3,853
Lao PDR	-	9	-	9	6	3	5	4	3	467	770	1,013	704	218	786	678i	105
Macao, China	1	9	3	12	6	3	6	3	3	20	32	26	37	19	30	27	33
Malaysia	-	6	-	11	6	2	6	3	3	1,007	2,924	3,162	2,847	1,000	3,085	2,593	1,285
Mongolia	-	12	4	12	6	4	5	4	3	296	316	322	237	257	311	...	155
Myanmar	-	5	-	5	5	2	5	4	2	1,806	4,642	6,037	4,954	154	5,300	4,187	932
Philippines	1	10	1	10	6	1	6	4	2	2,273	13,174	12,568	10,118	1,815	14,040	9,007	3,589
Republic of Korea	-	9	3	9	6	3	6	3	3	1,359	2,730	2,938	3,324	1,291	2,682	3,072	3,136
Singapore	-	6	...	...	6	3	6	2	-	111i	233i	159i	230i	...	235	171	195
Thailand	-	9	3	12	6	3	6	3	3	2,310	4,848	5,227	4,888	1,824	4,901	6,266	2,411
Timor-Leste	-	-	-	9	6	3	6	3	3	94	185	186	123	21	213	156	...
Viet Nam	1	9	1	5	6	3	5	4	3	4,589	7,369	9,289	7,195	4,600	8,042	...	2,307

	FINANCE										
G	**H**	**I** Government education expenditure per pupil								**J**	
		2016 PPP US$				% of GDP per capita					
Government education expenditure (% of GDP)	Education share of total government expenditure (%)	Pre-primary	Primary	Secondary	Tertiary	Pre-primary	Primary	Secondary	Tertiary	Household education expenditure (% of GDP)	Country code
	1.a.2				4.5.4						
					2018						
...	...	...	...	...	...	...	...	...	...	...	DZA
2.7₋₁	10.4₋₁	1,407₋₁	977₋₁	1,276₋₄	951₋₁	15₋₁	10₋₁	15₋₄	10₋₁	...	ARM
2.5₋₁	7.0₋₁	2,593₋₁	...	...	3,398₋₁	15₋₁	...	...	19₋₁	0.9₋₁	AZE
2.3₋₁	7.2₋₁	...	5,395₋₃	8,461₋₃	...	...	11₋₃	18₋₃	...	0.9₋₁	BHR
6.3₋₂	16.7₋₂	4,099₋₂	11,137₋₂	13,725₋₂	9,263₋₂	12₋₂	32₋₂	39₋₂	27₋₂	1.3₋₂	CYP
...	...	1,145₋₁	1,112₋₁	1,558₋₁	...	10₋₁	10₋₁	14₋₁	...	...	EGY
3.8₋₁	13.0₋₁	...	...	...	1,070₋₁	...	...	...	10₋₁	0.1₋₁	GEO
...	...	...	...	...	...	...	...	...	...	...	IRQ
5.8₋₂	15.5₋₂	5,110₋₂	8,248₋₂	7,147₋₂	6,965₋₂	13₋₂	22₋₂	19₋₂	18₋₂	1.3₋₂	ISR
3.6	11.6	142	1,217	1,425	2,315	2	13	16	25	...	JOR
...	...	13,696₋₄	11,735₋₄	14,116₋₄ᵢ	...	17₋₄	14₋₄	17₋₄ᵢ	...	...	KWT
...	...	...	...	...	...	...	...	...	...	...	LBN
...	...	...	...	...	...	...	...	...	...	...	LBY
...	...	...	...	...	...	...	...	...	...	...	MAR
...	...	...	13,721₋₂	14,795₋₁	18,809₋₂	...	32₋₂	36₋₁	44₋₂	-₋₁	OMN
4.9₋₁	...	...	...	...	...	...	...	...	...	...	PSE
2.9₋₁	8.6₋₁	...	...	...	...	...	...	...	...	...	QAT
...	...	...	...	...	...	...	...	...	...	...	SAU
...	...	...	...	...	...	...	...	...	...	...	SDN
...	...	...	...	...	...	...	...	...	...	...	SYR
6.6₋₃	22.6₋₃	...	...	6,261₋₃	6,541₋₃	...	...	52₋₃	55₋₃	...	TUN
...	...	...	...	...	...	...	...	...	...	...	TUR
...	...	...	...	...	...	...	...	...	...	...	ARE
...	...	...	...	...	...	...	...	...	...	...	YEM
4.1₋₁ᵢ	15.7₋₁ᵢ	-₋₁	198₋₁	219₋₁ᵢ	835₋₄	-₋₁	10₋₁	11₋₁ᵢ	42₋₄	...	AFG
2.0	14.6	...	...	372₋₂	1,126₋₂	...	...	10₋₂	30₋₂	...	BGD
6.6ᵢ	22.8ᵢ	-₋₃	1,056₋₄	2,527₋₃	4,168₋₄	-₋₃	13₋₄	29₋₃	51₋₄	...	BTN
...	...	...	...	...	...	...	...	...	...	...	IND
4.0	21.1	211₋₂	2,240₋₁	3,532₋₁	4,868₋₁	1₋₂	11₋₁	18₋₁	24₋₁	...	IRN
2.8	13.9	1,837₋₂	64	5,471₋₂	2,031	7₋₂	0.2	21₋₂	7	0.5	KAZ
6.0₋₁	15.7₋₁	831₋₁	...	...	183₋₁	22₋₁	...	...	5₋₁	1.0₋₁	KGZ
4.1₋₂	11.3₋₂	1,349₋₂	2,303₋₂	...	4,520₋₄	9₋₂	16₋₂	...	32₋₄	...	MDV
5.2	14.1	53₋₃	318₋₃	269₋₃ᵢ	622₋₃	2₋₃	12₋₃	10₋₃ᵢ	24₋₃	...	NPL
2.9₋₁	14.5₋₁	...	380₋₃	752₋₃	3,346₋₁	...	8₋₃	16₋₃	67₋₁	...	PAK
1.9	11.3	-	895	881	3,700	-	7	7	28	...	LKA
5.2₋₃	16.4₋₃	808₋₃	...	...	575₋₃	28₋₃	...	...	20₋₃	...	TJK
...	...	...	...	...	...	...	...	...	...	...	TKM
5.3₋₁ᵢ	23.0₋₁ᵢ	...	...	...	...	...	...	...	...	...	UZB
4.4₋₂	11.4₋₂	826₋₂	7,192₋₂	19,165₋₂	25,879₋₂	1₋₂	9₋₂	24₋₂	32₋₂	...	BRN
2.2	8.8	102₋₄	183₋₄	...	...	3₋₄	5₋₄	...	...	...	KHM
...	...	...	...	...	...	...	...	...	...	...	CHN
...	...	...	...	...	...	...	...	...	...	...	PRK
3.3	18.8	5,261	8,979	13,341	14,656	9	15	22	24	...	HKG
3.6₋₃	20.5₋₃	303₋₄	1,514₋₃	1,199₋₃	2,367₋₃	3₋₄	13₋₃	11₋₃	21₋₃	3.4₋₃	IDN
3.2₋₂	8.4₋₂	3,707₋₂	8,891₋₂	9,818₋₂	8,413₋₂	9₋₂	...	...	...	1.3₋₂	JPN
2.9₋₄	11.8₋₄	505₋₄	539₋₄	742₋₄	1,205₋₄	9₋₄	9₋₄	13₋₄	20₋₄	...	LAO
2.7₋₁	13.5₋₁	...	...	...	22,105₋₁	...	...	...	19₋₁	0.4₋₁	MAC
4.5	19.7	1,422	4,842₋₁	7,071	7,364	5	16₋₁	23	24	...	MYS
3.8₋₁	12.6₋₁	1,759₋₁	1,674₋₁	...	406₋₁	14₋₁	13₋₁	...	3₋₁	0.2₋₃	MNG
2.0	10.5₊₁	...	...	...	...	...	8	10	17	...	MMR
...	...	...	...	...	...	...	...	...	...	...	PHL
4.6₋₂	...	6,207₋₂	10,535₋₂	10,660₋₂	5,684₋₂	16₋₂	28₋₂	28₋₂	15₋₂	...	KOR
...	...	...	16,021₋₁	19,788₋₁	21,529₋₁	...	18₋₁	22₋₁	24₋₁	...	SGP
...	...	...	...	...	...	...	...	...	...	...	THA
4.1ᵢ	7.9ᵢ	164₋₄	594₋₄	564₋₄	...	2₋₄	8₋₄	8₋₄	...	...	TLS
4.2	14.5	...	...	...	...	...	...	...	...	...	VNM

TABLE 1: Continued

	EDUCATION SYSTEMS																	
	A		B		C	D				E				F			
	Compulsory		Free		Official primary school starting age	Duration (years)				School-age population (000)				Enrolment (000)			
Country or territory	1 year of pre-primary	9 years of primary-secondary	1 year of pre-primary	12 years of primary-secondary		Pre-primary	Primary	Lower secondary	Upper secondary	Pre-primary	Primary	Secondary	Tertiary	Pre-primary	Primary	Secondary	Tertiary
SDG indicator	4.2.5	4.1.7	4.2.5	4.1.7													
Reference year						2018											
Oceania																	
Australia	-	10	1	13	5	1	7	4	2	322	2,270	1,829	1,569	528	2,217	2,650	1,775
Cook Islands	-	12	2	13	5	2	6	4	3	1	2	2	1	1	2	2	...
Fiji	-	-	...	...	6	3	6	4	3	54	104	108	74	...	110	...	...
Kiribati	-	9	-	9	6	3	6	3	4	9	17	15	11	...	17	...	...
Marshall Islands	1	12	1	12	6	2	6	4	2	3	9	9	5	1	8	6	...
Micronesia, F. S.	-	-	-	8	6	3	6	2	4	7	14	14	12	2	14	...	...
Nauru	2	12	2	12	6	3	6	4	2	1	2	1	1	1	2	1	...
New Zealand	-	10	2	13	5	2	6	4	3	122	382	432	327	118	384	486	269
Niue	-	11	1	12	5	1	6	4	3	-	0.2	0.2	0.1	-	0.2	0.2	...
Palau	-	12	-	12	6	3	6	2	4	1	1	1	2	1	2	2	...
Papua New Guinea	-	-	...	...	6	4	7	2	4	842	1,422	1,119	729	358	1,275	507	...
Samoa	-	8	-	8	5	2	6	2	5	10	29	29	17	5	33	26	...
Solomon Is	-	-	...	...	6	3	6	3	4	58	103	100	53	49	105	...	...
Tokelau	-	11	...	...	5	2	6	4	3	-	0.1	0.2	0.1	0.1	0.2	0.1	...
Tonga	2	13	-	8	6	2	6	5	2	5	15	16	9	2	17	16	...
Tuvalu	-	8	...	...	6	3	6	4	3	1	2	2	1	1	1	1	...
Vanuatu	-	-	...	...	6	2	6	4	3	16	46	44	24	14	46	21	...
Latin America and the Caribbean																	
Anguilla	-	12	-	12	5	2	7	3	2	...	...	...	...	...	...	...	...
Antigua and Barbuda	-	11	-	11	5	2	7	3	2	3	10	7	8	2	10	8	...
Argentina	2	12	3	12	6	3	6	3	3	2,242	4,383	4,269	3,492	1,695	4,754	4,613	3,141
Aruba	2	11	2	11	6	2	6	2	3	2	8	7	8	3	10	...	1
Bahamas	-	12	2	12	5	2	6	3	3	10	35	39	33	4	30	27	...
Barbados	-	11	2	11	5	2	6	3	2	6	20	19	19	5	20	20	...
Belize	-	8	2	12	5	2	6	4	2	15	46	47	38	7	51	40	9
Bolivia, P. S.	2	12	2	12	6	2	6	2	4	475	1,407	1,380	1,037	354	1,379	1,234	...
Brazil	2	12	2	12	6	2	5	4	3	5,299i	13,952i	22,928i	16,694i	5,102	16,107	23,118	8,571
British Virgin Islands	-	12	-	12	5	2	7	3	2	1	2	2	2	1	3	2	0.3
Cayman Islands	1	11	2	12	5	2	6	3	3	...	...	...	...	1	4	3	...
Chile	-	12	2	12	6	3	6	2	4	754	1,517	1,483	1,401	617	1,515	1,521	1,239
Colombia	1	11	3	11	6	3	5	4	2	2,217	3,740	4,869	4,352	...	4,304	4,821	2,408
Costa Rica	2	11	2	11	6	2	6	3	2	143	428	357	393	140	484	477	217
Cuba	-	9	3	12	6	3	6	3	3	377	730	769	715	370	741	795	296
Curaçao	2	12	...	...	6	2	6	2	4	4	12	13	10	...	...	...	...
Dominica	-	12	-	12	5	2	7	3	2	2	6	5	7	2	7	6	...
Dominican Republic	3	12	3	12	6	3	6	2	4	582i	1,159i	1,153i	929i	299	1,226	925	557
Ecuador	3+1	12+1	3+1	12+1	6	3	6	3	3	976	1,882	1,867	1,516	639	1,932	1,892	669
El Salvador	3	9+1	3+1	12+1	7	3	6	3	3	345	693	711	649	230	663	522	191
Grenada	-	12	2	12	5	2	7	3	2	4	13	8	9	4	13	9	9
Guatemala	3	9	3	12	7	3	6	3	2	1,190	2,322	1,954	1,683	604	2,362	1,227	367
Guyana	-	6	-	6	6	3	6	3	2	44	85	75	82	...	...	...	...
Haiti	-	6	-	6	6	3	6	3	4	755	1,469	1,619	1,059	...	...	...	...
Honduras	1	11	3	11	6	3	6	3	2	592	1,207	1,039	1,020	245	1,124	655	267
Jamaica	-	6	-	6	6	3	6	3	2	141	274	238	268	103	249	201	75
Mexico	2	12	2	12	6	3	6	3	3	6,731	13,389	13,479	11,013	4,943	14,182	14,035	4,430
Montserrat	-	12	-	12	5	2	7	3	2	0.1	0.4	0.3	0.2	0.1	0.5	0.3	...
Nicaragua	1	6	-	9	6	3	6	3	2	399	784	619	607	...	...	...	...
Panama	2	9	2	12	6	2	6	3	3	155	453	431	337	95	419	323	161
Paraguay	1	12	3	12	6	3	6	3	3	411	819	796	676	181	727	611	...
Peru	3	11	3	11	6	3	6	3	2	1,587	3,274	2,596	2,630	1,643	3,593	2,780	1,896
Saint Kitts and Nevis	-	12	-	12	5	2	7	3	2	1	5	4	4	1	5	4	4
Saint Lucia	-	10	-	10	5	2	7	3	2	4	15	13	16	3	16	12	2
Saint Vincent/Grenadines	-	12	2	12	5	2	7	3	2	3	12	9	9	3	13	10	2
Sint Maarten	2	11	2	11	6	3	6	2	3	2	3	2	3	1	4	3	0.2
Suriname	-+1	6+1	--3	6-3	6	2	6	4	3	21	62	71	49	18	68	58	...
Trinidad and Tobago	-	6	-	...	5	2	7	3	2	39	136	91	93	...	...	...	...
Turks and Caicos Islands	2	11	...	...	6	2	6	3	2	...	...	...	...	1	4	2	0.3
Uruguay	2	12	2	12	6	3	6	3	3	143	280	290	257	133	304	357	162
Venezuela, B. R.	3	11	3	11	6	3	6	3	2	1,688	3,290	2,638	2,661	1,190	3,285	2,391	...

Government education expenditure (% of GDP)	Education share of total government expenditure (%)	Government education expenditure per pupil 2016 PPP US$				Government education expenditure per pupil % of GDP per capita				Household education expenditure (% of GDP)	Country code
G	**H**	Pre-primary	Primary	Secondary	Tertiary	Pre-primary	Primary	Secondary	Tertiary	**J**	
	1.a.2				4.5.4						
					2018						
5.3_{-2}	13.8_{-2}	$5{,}192_{-2}$	$9{,}524_{-2}$	$7{,}392_{-2}$	$8{,}797_{-2}$	11_{-2}	19_{-2}	15_{-2}	18_{-2}	1.2_{-3}	AUS
4.7_{-2}	11.6_{-4}	...	...	...	...	...	...	...	...	...	COK
...	...	...	...	...	...	...	...	...	...	...	FJI
...	...	...	...	...	...	...	...	...	...	...	KIR
...	...	...	...	...	...	...	...	...	...	...	MHL
12.5_{-3}	22.3_{-3}	...	...	...	...	...	...	...	...	...	FSM
...	...	...	...	...	...	...	...	...	...	...	NRU
6.4_{-2}	16.8_{-2}	$7{,}186_{-2}$	$7{,}833_{-2}$	$8{,}139_{-2}$	$9{,}735_{-2}$	19_{-2}	20_{-2}	21_{-2}	25_{-2}	0.7_{-2}	NZL
...	...	...	...	...	$-_{-1}$	...	...	...	$-_{-1}$	...	NIU
...	...	...	...	...	...	...	...	...	...	...	PLW
1.9_i	8.7_i	...	...	...	...	...	...	...	...	...	PNG
4.1_{-2}	10.5_{-2}	104_{-2}	538_{-2}	782_{-2}	...	2_{-2}	9_{-2}	13_{-2}	...	...	WSM
...	...	...	...	...	...	...	...	...	...	...	SLB
...	...	...	...	...	...	...	...	...	...	...	TKL
...	...	...	...	...	...	...	...	...	...	...	TON
...	...	...	...	...	...	...	...	...	...	...	TUV
4.0_{-1}	12.7_{-1}	3_{-3}	408_{-3}	633_{-3}	...	0.1_{-3}	14_{-3}	21_{-3}	...	...	VUT
...	...	...	...	...	...	...	...	...	...	...	AIA
...	...	...	...	...	...	...	...	...	...	...	ATG
5.5_{-1}	13.3_{-1}	$2{,}600_{-1}$	$3{,}122_{-1}$	$4{,}298_{-1}$	$3{,}525_{-1}$	12_{-1}	15_{-1}	21_{-1}	17_{-1}	0.8_{-1}	ARG
5.9_{-2}	21.4_{-2}	$5{,}269_{-4}$	$6{,}574_{-4}$	...	$38{,}364_{-2}$	13_{-4}	17_{-4}	...	98_{-2}	...	ABW
...	...	...	...	...	...	...	...	...	...	...	BHS
4.7_{-1}	12.9_{-1}	...	$3{,}674_{-2}$	$4{,}964_{-2}$	...	...	21_{-2}	28_{-2}	...	1.6_{-1}	BRB
7.4_{-1}	21.3_{-1}	$1{,}388_{-1}$	$1{,}389_{-1}$	$2{,}292_{-1}$	$2{,}291_{-1}$	17_{-1}	17_{-1}	27_{-1}	27_{-1}	...	BLZ
...	...	...	...	...	...	...	...	...	...	...	BOL
6.2_{-3}	16.2_{-3}	...	$3{,}267_{-3}$	$3{,}507_{-3}$	$5{,}383_{-3}$	...	20_{-3}	22_{-3}	33_{-3}	...	BRA
2.4_{-1}	...	...	...	...	...	0.1_{-3}	6_{-1}	11_{-1}	40_{-3}	...	VGB
...	...	...	...	...	...	...	...	...	...	...	CYM
5.4_{-1}	21.3_{-1}	$5{,}416_{-1}$	$4{,}458_{-1}$	$4{,}530_{-1}$	$4{,}913_{-1}$	22_{-1}	18_{-1}	19_{-1}	20_{-1}	1.6_{-1}	CHL
4.5	16.0	...	2,492	2,589	3,175	...	17	18	22	1.0	COL
7.0	26.1	1,933	3,594	3,648	6,474	11	21	21	38	...	CRI
...	...	...	...	...	...	...	...	...	...	...	CUB
...	...	...	...	...	...	...	...	...	...	...	CUW
3.4_{-3}	10.5_{-3}	311_{-3}	$1{,}660_{-3}$	$2{,}128_{-3}$	...	3_{-3}	15_{-3}	19_{-3}	...	...	DMA
...	...	1,791	2,816	2,622	...	10	16	15	...	...	DOM
5.0_{-3}	12.6_{-3}	$2{,}847_{-2}$	$1{,}088_{-2}$	604_{-2}	$6{,}203_{-3}$	25_{-2}	10_{-2}	5_{-2}	53_{-3}	...	ECU
3.4	14.9	794	1,246	1,159	904	10	15	14	11	3.2	SLV
3.2_{-1}	14.0_{-1}	865_{-1}	$1{,}205_{-1}$	$1{,}605_{-1}$	766_{-1}	6_{-1}	8_{-1}	11_{-1}	5_{-1}	...	GRD
2.9	23.7	905	982	448	$1{,}449_{-3}$	11	12	5	18_{-3}	...	GTM
5.9_i	16.0_i	...	...	...	...	...	...	...	...	...	GUY
2.8	14.4	...	...	...	...	...	...	...	...	...	HTI
6.1	23.0	...	...	...	$1{,}913_{-3}$	...	...	...	41_{-3}	...	HND
5.4	18.6	524	1,896	2,602	$3{,}117_{-3}$	6	22	30	36_{-3}	...	JAM
4.9_{-2}	17.9_{-2}	...	$2{,}653_{-2}$	$2{,}771_{-2}$	$5{,}708_{-2}$	...	14_{-2}	14_{-2}	30_{-2}	1.3_{-2}	MEX
8.3	...	...	...	...	...	...	12	29	...	...	MSR
4.3_{-1}	17.9_{-2}	...	...	...	...	...	...	...	...	...	NIC
...	...	...	...	...	...	...	...	...	...	...	PAN
3.4_{-2}	18.2_{-2}	$1{,}403_{-2}$	$1{,}449_{-2}$	$1{,}486_{-2}$	...	11_{-2}	12_{-2}	12_{-2}	...	...	PRY
3.7	17.1	1,638	1,580	2,062	$1{,}488_{-1}$	12	11	15	11_{-1}	2.9	PER
2.6_{-3}	8.6_{-3}	$3{,}762_{-3}$	$1{,}561_{-3}$	$5{,}326_{-3}$	$1{,}747_{-3}$	13_{-3}	5_{-3}	18_{-2}	6_{-3}	...	KNA
3.5	14.4	-	1,959	2,660	-	-	15	20	-	...	LCA
5.7	18.8	368_{-3}	2,107	2,424	...	3_{-3}	18	20	...	...	VCT
...	...	...	...	...	...	...	...	...	...	...	SXM
...	...	...	...	...	...	...	...	...	...	...	SUR
...	...	...	...	...	...	...	...	...	...	...	TTO
2.9	12.1	...	...	...	...	17	6	18	88_{-3}	...	TCA
4.8_{-1}	14.9_{-1}	$3{,}153_{-1}$	$2{,}873_{-1}$	$3{,}673_{-1}$	$5{,}770_{-1}$	14_{-1}	13_{-1}	16_{-1}	25_{-1}	...	URY
...	...	...	...	...	...	18_{-3}	18_{-3}	15_{-3}	...	...	VEN

	EDUCATION SYSTEMS																
	A Compulsory		B Free		C	D Duration (years)				E School-age population (000)				F Enrolment (000)			
Country or territory	1 year of pre-primary	9 years of primary-secondary	1 year of pre-primary	12 years of primary-secondary	Official primary school starting age	Pre-primary	Primary	Lower secondary	Upper secondary	Pre-primary	Primary	Secondary	Tertiary	Pre-primary	Primary	Secondary	Tertiary
SDG indicator	4.2.5	4.1.7	4.2.5	4.1.7													
Reference year									2018								
Europe and Northern America																	
Albania	-	11	3	12	6	3	5	4	3	101	159	269	240	81	171	269	132
Andorra	-	11	-	10	6	3	6	4	2	...	...	...	...	2	4	5	1
Austria	1	12	1	12	6	3	4	4	4	249	332	690	506	256	335	687	430
Belarus	-	9	-	11	6	3	4	5	2	353	440	646	445	349	428	649	389
Belgium	-	12	3	12	6	3	6	2	4	395	802	765	661	456	815	1,187	527
Bermuda	-	13	1	13	5	1	6	3	4	1	4	5	4	0.4	4	4	1
Bosnia and Herzegovina	-	9	-	9	6	3	5	4	4	93	...	...	...	21	159	248	95
Bulgaria	2	9	4	12	7	4	4	4	4	278	299	521	352	224	265	486	250
Canada	-	10	1	12	6	1	6	3	3	399	2,384	2,326	2,359	...	2,365	2,653	1,626i
Croatia	-	8	-	8	7	4	4	4	4	165	171	326	243	119	163	340	165
Czechia	-	9	-	13	6	3	5	4	4	334	580	797	551	367	576	772	353
Denmark	-	10	-	10	6	3	7	3	3	179	461	406	387	179	473	534	312
Estonia	-	9	4	12	7	4	6	3	3	60	92	74	69	57	86	83	48
Finland	1	9	1	12	7	4	6	3	3	244	371	354	335	206	364	543	296
France	-+1	10+1	3+1	12+1	6	3	5	4	3	2,389i	4,177i	5,862i	3,859i	2,561	4,310	6,058	2,533
Germany	-	13	-	13	6	3	4	6		2,173	2,923	7,098	4,401	2,308	2,955	7,029	3,092
Greece	1+1	9+1	2+1	12+1	6	2	6	3	3	186	636	638	538	152	649	668	735
Hungary	3	10	3	12	7	4	4	4	4	363	382	778	592	306	391	808	287
Iceland	-+1	10+1	...	...	6	3	7	3	4	13	32	30	25	13	32	35	18
Ireland	-	10	...	...	5	1	8	3	2	67i	559i	317i	289i	113	559	392	225
Italy	-	12	-	8	6	3	5	3	5	1,599	2,808	4,586	2,966	1,535	2,902	4,602	1,837
Latvia	2	9	6	12	7	4	6	3	3	81i	122i	107i	94i	75	122	117	83
Liechtenstein	1	8	...	...	7	2	5	4	3	1i	2	3	2i	1	2	3	1
Lithuania	-	10	-	12	7	4	4	6	2	117i	112i	215i	174i	104	114	243	126
Luxembourg	2	10	2	13	6	3	6	3	4	19	37	47	37	17	37	48	7
Malta	-	11	2	13	5	2	6	3	4	9	25	28	27	9	26	31	14
Monaco	-+1	11+1	3+1	12+1	6	3	5	4	3	...	...	...	...	1	2	3	1
Montenegro	-	9	-	9	6	3	5	4	4	22	39	63	42	15	39	57	24
Netherlands	1	12	2	12	6	3	6	3	3	534	1,103	1,208	1,030	504	1,182	1,650	875
North Macedonia	-	13	-	13	6	3	5	4	4	69	112	192	145	28	109	161	61
Norway	-	10	-	10	6	3	7	3	3	187	448	382	346	181	445	448	284
Poland	1	9	4	12	7	4	6	3	3	1,550	2,380	2,113	2,286	1,299	2,297	2,408	1,550
Portugal	-+1	12+1	2+1	12+1	6	3	6	3	3	258	571	628	543	254	630	770	347
Republic of Moldova	-	11	4	12	7	4	4	5	2	153i	155i	260i	219i	132	140	226	87
Romania	-	10	3	13	6	3	5	4	4	561	1,064	1,638	1,076	521	928	1,502	532
Russian Federation	-	11	4	11	7	4	4	5	2	7,397	6,838	10,176	7,187	6,253	6,574	9,905	5,887
San Marino	-	10	-	13	6	3	5	3	5	1	2	2	2	1	2	2	1
Serbia	-	8	-	12	7	4	4	4	4	263i	266i	562i	381i	164	267	534	256
Slovakia	-+1	10+1	1+1	13+1	6	3	4	5	4	168	230	485	335	165	225	442	156
Slovenia	-	9	-	13	6	3	6	3	4	66	129	130	101	61	124	148	80
Spain	-+1	10+1	3+1	10+1	6	3	6	3	3	1,356	2,967	2,717	2,262	1,321	3,042	3,333	2,010
Sweden	1+1	9+1	1+1	12+1	7	4	6	3	3	472	705	634	636	462	861	916	426
Switzerland	2	9	2	9	7	2	6	3	4	169	493	593	505	173	508	609	301
Ukraine	-	11	-	11	6	3	4	5	2	1,505	1,701	2,827	2,596	1,117	1,677	2,377	1,615
United Kingdom	-	11	2	13	5	2	6	3	4	1,647	4,895	5,170	4,053	1,763	4,820	6,386	2,432
United States	-	12	1	12	6	3	6	3	3	12,000i	24,674i	25,050i	21,566i	8,752	25,124	24,788	19,015

		FINANCE									
G	H	I								J	
		Government education expenditure per pupil									
		2016 PPP US$				% of GDP per capita					
Government education expenditure (% of GDP)	Education share of total government expenditure (%)	Pre-primary	Primary	Secondary	Tertiary	Pre-primary	Primary	Secondary	Tertiary	Household education expenditure (% of GDP)	Country code
1.a.2		4.5.4									
2018											
2.5$_i$	8.4$_i$	...	4,420$_{-1}$	1,032$_{-1}$	1,782$_{-1}$	...	34$_{-1}$	8$_{-1}$	14$_{-1}$	2.1$_{-2}$	ALB
3.2	19.3	...	...	...	...	13	12	14	22	...	AND
5.5$_{-2}$	11.0$_{-2}$	9,460$_{-2}$	12,422$_{-2}$	14,666$_{-2}$	19,171$_{-2}$	18$_{-2}$	23$_{-2}$	28$_{-2}$	36$_{-2}$	0.1$_{-2}$	AUT
4.8$_{-1}$	12.3$_{-1}$	6,082$_{-1}$	...	6,747$_{-1}$	3,390$_{-1}$	32$_{-1}$	...	36$_{-1}$	18$_{-1}$	0.2$_{-1}$	BLR
6.5$_{-2}$	12.3$_{-2}$	8,488$_{-2}$	10,663$_{-2}$	...	15,670$_{-2}$	17$_{-2}$	22$_{-2}$	...	32$_{-2}$	0.3$_{-2}$	BEL
1.5$_{-1}$	7.8$_{-1}$	...	...	...	...	17$_{-3}$	8$_{-3}$	12$_{-3}$	24$_{-1}$	...	BMU
...	...	3,199$_{-2}$	...	5,734$_{-2}$	3,127$_{-2}$	24$_{-2}$	...	44$_{-2}$	24$_{-2}$	...	BIH
...	...	...	...	...	...	...	...	...	...	...	BGR
...	...	...	7,914$_{-3}$	...	14,156$_{-2}$	...	18$_{-3}$	...	31$_{-2}$	...	CAN
...	...	...	...	...	...	...	...	...	...	...	HRV
5.6$_{-2}$	14.2$_{-2}$	5,117$_{-2}$	5,066$_{-2}$	8,148$_{-2}$	7,431$_{-2}$	14$_{-2}$	14$_{-2}$	22$_{-2}$	20$_{-2}$	0.3$_{-2}$	CZE
7.6$_{-4}$	13.8$_{-4}$	...	12,980$_{-4}$	16,132$_{-4}$	22,345$_{-4}$	...	25$_{-4}$	31$_{-4}$	43$_{-4}$	...	DNK
4.9$_{-2}$	13.1$_{-2}$	...	6,099$_{-2}$	6,112$_{-2}$	11,472$_{-2}$	...	19$_{-2}$	19$_{-2}$	36$_{-2}$	0.3$_{-3}$	EST
6.9$_{-2}$	12.3$_{-2}$	10,051$_{-2}$	9,697$_{-2}$	11,160$_{-2}$	15,299$_{-2}$	22$_{-2}$	22$_{-2}$	25$_{-2}$	34$_{-2}$	...	FIN
...	...	...	...	...	...	...	...	...	...	...	FRA
4.8$_{-2}$	10.9$_{-2}$	8,492$_{-2}$	9,010$_{-2}$	11,860$_{-2}$	17,347$_{-2}$	16$_{-2}$	17$_{-2}$	23$_{-2}$	34$_{-2}$	...	DEU
...	...	4,971$_{-2}$	5,577$_{-2}$	6,308$_{-2}$	2,566$_{-2}$	18$_{-2}$	20$_{-2}$	22$_{-2}$	9$_{-2}$	...	GRC
4.7$_{-2}$	10.1$_{-2}$	6,747$_{-2}$	5,258$_{-2}$	6,359$_{-2}$	7,008$_{-2}$	24$_{-2}$	19$_{-2}$	23$_{-2}$	25$_{-2}$	...	HUN
7.5$_{-2}$	16.8$_{-2}$	11,582$_{-2}$	11,967$_{-2}$	10,503$_{-2}$	14,789$_{-2}$	21$_{-2}$	22$_{-2}$	19$_{-2}$	27$_{-2}$	0.3$_{-3}$	ISL
3.7$_{-2}$	13.4$_{-2}$	3,137$_{-3}$	8,591$_{-2}$	11,483$_{-2}$	11,233$_{-2}$	4$_{-3}$	12$_{-2}$	16$_{-2}$	15$_{-2}$	...	IRL
3.8$_{-2}$	7.8$_{-2}$	6,894$_{-2}$	7,856$_{-2}$	9,100$_{-3}$	9,790$_{-2}$	17$_{-2}$	20$_{-2}$	23$_{-3}$	24$_{-2}$	0.5$_{-2}$	ITA
4.6$_{-2}$	12.9$_{-2}$	5,602$_{-2}$	6,538$_{-2}$	6,985$_{-2}$	4,421$_{-2}$	21$_{-2}$	24$_{-2}$	26$_{-2}$	16$_{-2}$	0.6$_{-2}$	LVA
...	...	...	...	...	...	...	...	...	...	...	LIE
3.9$_{-2}$	12.0$_{-2}$	5,400$_{-2}$	6,080$_{-2}$	5,569$_{-2}$	5,276$_{-2}$	17$_{-2}$	19$_{-2}$	18$_{-2}$	17$_{-2}$	0.4$_{-2}$	LTU
4.0$_{-3}$	9.4$_{-3}$	21,057$_{-3}$	21,336$_{-3}$	21,031$_{-3}$	46,331$_{-3}$	19$_{-3}$	20$_{-3}$	19$_{-3}$	43$_{-3}$	0.1$_{-3}$	LUX
5.2$_{-3}$	13.2$_{-3}$	9,431$_{-3}$	8,834$_{-3}$	11,437$_{-3}$	17,197$_{-3}$	24$_{-3}$	23$_{-3}$	30$_{-3}$	44$_{-3}$	0.7$_{-3}$	MLT
1.5$_{-1}$	7.0$_{-1}$	...	...	...	...	2$_{-2}$	3$_{-2}$	5$_{-2}$	...	...$_{-4}$	MCO
...	...	...	...	...	...	...	...	...	...	...	MNE
5.5$_{-2}$	12.8$_{-2}$	6,130$_{-2}$	8,873$_{-2}$	12,306$_{-2}$	19,061$_{-2}$	12$_{-2}$	17$_{-2}$	23$_{-2}$	36$_{-2}$	...$_{-3}$	NLD
...	...	...	...	...	...	...	...	...	...	...	MKD
8.0$_{-2}$	16.0$_{-2}$	13,077$_{-2}$	13,342$_{-2}$	16,465$_{-2}$	24,478$_{-2}$	21$_{-2}$	22$_{-2}$	27$_{-2}$	40$_{-2}$	...	NOR
4.6$_{-2}$	11.3$_{-2}$	5,766$_{-2}$	6,562$_{-2}$	6,395$_{-2}$	7,132$_{-2}$	20$_{-2}$	23$_{-2}$	22$_{-2}$	25$_{-2}$	0.6$_{-2}$	POL
4.9$_{-3}$	10.2$_{-3}$	4,786$_{-3}$	6,955$_{-3}$	8,557$_{-3}$	8,183$_{-3}$	15$_{-3}$	23$_{-3}$	28$_{-3}$	26$_{-3}$	1.0$_{-3}$	PRT
5.5	17.5	2,522	2,313	2,200	1,902	35	32	31	27	...	MDA
3.0$_{-2}$	9.5$_{-2}$	2,817$_{-2}$	1,934$_{-2}$	3,747$_{-2}$	6,449$_{-2}$	11$_{-2}$	8$_{-2}$	15$_{-2}$	26$_{-2}$	...	ROU
3.7$_{-2}$	11.0$_{-2}$	...	...	...	5,031$_{-2}$	...	...	...	20$_{-2}$	0.4$_{-2}$	RUS
3.1$_{-1}$	13.1$_{-1}$	...	...	...	...	...	...	...	...	...	SMR
3.7$_{-1}$	9.3$_{-1}$	195$_{-3}$	6,731$_{-3}$	1,714$_{-3}$	4,895$_{-1}$	1$_{-3}$	44$_{-3}$	11$_{-3}$	30$_{-1}$	0.9$_{-1}$	SRB
3.8$_{-2}$	9.4$_{-2}$	5,360$_{-2}$	6,503$_{-2}$	6,268$_{-2}$	8,131$_{-2}$	17$_{-2}$	21$_{-2}$	20$_{-2}$	26$_{-2}$	0.6$_{-2}$	SVK
4.8$_{-2}$	11.7$_{-2}$	6,102$_{-2}$	8,112$_{-2}$	7,915$_{-2}$	8,340$_{-2}$	18$_{-2}$	24$_{-2}$	23$_{-2}$	24$_{-2}$	0.7$_{-3}$	SVN
4.2$_{-2}$	10.0$_{-2}$	5,983$_{-2}$	6,505$_{-2}$	7,175$_{-2}$	8,290$_{-2}$	16$_{-2}$	17$_{-2}$	19$_{-2}$	22$_{-2}$	1.1$_{-2}$	ESP
7.7$_{-2}$	15.7$_{-2}$	14,293$_{-2}$	11,094$_{-2}$	12,123$_{-2}$	22,068$_{-2}$	28$_{-2}$	22$_{-2}$	24$_{-2}$	43$_{-2}$	...	SWE
5.1$_{-2}$	15.5$_{-2}$	13,014$_{-2}$	16,325$_{-2}$	16,026$_{-3}$	24,634$_{-2}$	20$_{-2}$	25$_{-2}$	24$_{-3}$	37$_{-2}$	0.3$_{-2}$	CHE
5.4$_{-1}$	13.1$_{-1}$	3,157$_{-1}$	2,636$_{-1}$	2,631$_{-1}$	2,996$_{-1}$	36$_{-1}$	30$_{-1}$	30$_{-1}$	34$_{-1}$	0.7$_{-1}$	UKR
5.5$_{-2}$	13.8$_{-2}$	3,059$_{-2}$	10,280$_{-2}$	9,010$_{-2}$	16,155$_{-2}$	7$_{-2}$	24$_{-2}$	21$_{-2}$	38$_{-2}$	0.9$_{-3}$	GBR
5.0$_{-4}$	13.4$_{-4}$	6,877$_{-2}$	11,404$_{-2}$	12,711$_{-2}$	11,157$_{-2}$	12$_{-2}$	20$_{-2}$	22$_{-2}$	...	1.2$_{-4}$	USA

TABLE 2: SDG 4, Target 4.1 – Primary and secondary education

By 2030, ensure that all girls and boys complete free, equitable and quality primary and secondary education leading to relevant and effective learning outcomes

	PARTICIPATION / COMPLETION																		
	A Out-of-school children (000,000)			Out-of-school rate (%)			B Completion rate (%)			C Over-age for grade (%)		D GER primary (%)	E NERA primary (%)	F GIR last primary (%)	G Transition from primary to lower secondary (%)	H NERT lower secondary (%)	I GIR last lower secondary grade (%)	J NERT upper secondary (%)
Region	Primary	Lower secondary	Upper secondary	Primary	Lower secondary	Upper secondary	Primary	Lower secondary	Upper secondary	Primary	Lower secondary							
SDG indicator				4.1.4			4.1.2			4.1.5					4.1.3		4.1.3	
Reference year	2018											2018						
	Sum			Weighted average								Weighted average						
World	59i	61i	138i	8i	16i	35i	85	73	49	8i	11	104i	90i	90i	91-1i	84i	76i	65i
Sub-Saharan Africa	32i	28i	37i	19i	37i	58i	65	40	28	19	26	99i	79i	69i	75-2i	63i	44i	42i
Northern Africa and Western Asia	5i	4i	8i	9i	14i	30i	85i	76i	53i	7	9	99i	90i	87i	92-1i	86i	74i	70i
Northern Africa	3	1i	4i	9	12i	30i	83i	73i	56i	9	15	101	90i	91	95-1	88i	75	70i
Western Asia	2i	3i	4i	9i	16i	30i	88i	79i	49i	4	4	97i	91i	83i	89-2i	84i	73i	70i
Central and Southern Asia	13i	17i	65i	7i	15i	45i	85	74	38	3	8	110i	92i	93i	92-1i	85i	81i	55i
Central Asia	0.1	0.3i	1i	2	5i	27i	99i	98i	88i	0.1	0.2	103	97	103	100-1	95i	100	73i
Southern Asia	12i	17i	64i	7i	15i	45i	85	73	38	4	9	111i	92i	92i	91-1i	85i	80i	55i
Eastern and South-eastern Asia	6i	9i	18i	3i	10i	21i	95	82	59	3i	10i	103	96i	98i	97-1i	90i	86i	79i
Eastern Asia	3i	4i	9i	3i	7i	16i	96	85	59	...	...	101	97i	95i	100-1i	93i	87i	84i
South-eastern Asia	3i	5i	9i	4i	13i	29i	94	78	60	3	11	107i	94i	103i	94-1i	87i	84i	71i
Oceania	0.2i	0.1i	0.4i	5i	5i	25i	...	74	61	16	9	103i	88i	93i	64-2i	95i	77i	75i
Latin America and the Caribbean	2i	3i	7i	4i	7i	23i	90	80	60	6	13	109i	95i	99i	95-1i	93i	81i	77i
Caribbean	0.1	0.1i	0.3	...	...	...	77	65	43	7	13	...	...	...	94i	...	...	...
Central America	1	1	3	4	12	33	92	78	49	5	7	104	96	98	94	88	87	67
South America	1	1	4	2i	5i	18i	90	82	68	7	16	110i	97i	99i	98i	95i	86i	82i
Europe and Northern America	1i	1i	3i	2i	2i	7i	99i	97	88	2i	3i	101i	96i	98i	99-1i	98i	95i	93i
Europe	1i	1i	2i	3i	2i	8i	99i	96	84	1i	2i	101i	96i	97i	98-1i	98i	94i	92i
Northern America	0.1i	0.1i	1i	0.4i	0.4i	5i	99	99	92	3	4	102i	96i	99i	99-1i	100i	96i	95i
Low income	21i	21i	26i	19i	39i	61i	56i	28i	15i	25	29	103i	80i	67i	76-1i	61i	40i	39i
Middle income	37i	39i	108i	7i	13i	35i	87	76	47	5i	10	104i	92i	92i	92-1i	87i	79i	65i
Lower middle	30i	31i	88i	9i	17i	44i	84	71	42	5	10	105i	89i	91i	89-1i	83i	76i	56i
Upper middle	7i	8i	21i	3i	7i	20i	94	84	59	5i	11i	103i	96i	95i	98-1i	93i	84i	80i
High income	1i	1i	3i	2i	3i	8i	99i	97	88	2	4	102i	96i	98i	97-1i	97i	94i	92i

A Out-of-school children, total number (million) and out-of-school rate as percentage of the corresponding age group.

B Education completion rate by level, most recent survey year between 2014 and 2018 [Source: UIS and GEM Report analysis of household surveys].

C Percentage of pupils who are at least two years over-age for their current grade, by level.

D Gross enrolment ratio (GER) in primary education.

E Primary adjusted net enrolment rate (NERA) (%).

F Gross intake ratio (GIR) to last grade of primary education (%).

G Effective transition rate from primary to lower secondary general education (%).

H Lower secondary total net enrolment rate (NERT) (%).

I GIR to last grade of lower secondary education (%).

J Upper secondary total NERT (%).

K Administration of nationally representative learning assesssment in early grades (grade 2 or 3), or final grade of primary or lower secondary.

L Percentage of students achieving at least a minimum proficiency level in reading and mathematics.

Source: UIS unless noted otherwise. Data refer to school year ending in 2018 unless noted otherwise.

Aggregates represent countries listed in the table with available data and may include estimates for countries with no recent data.

(-) Magnitude nil or negligible.

(...) Data not available or category not applicable.

(± n) Reference year differs (e.g. -2: reference year 2016 instead of 2018).

(i) Estimate and/or partial coverage.

LEARNING											
K						L					
Administration of nationally representative learning assessment						Achieving minimum proficiency (%)					
Early grades		End of primary		End of lower secondary		Early grades		End of primary		End of lower secondary	
Reading	Mathematics	Reading	Mathematics	Reading	Mathematics	Reading	Mathematics	Reading	Mathematics	Reading	Mathematics
4.1.6						4.1.1					
2018											
% of countries						Weighted average					
67	65	60	61	51	54	...	...	...	...	...	...
73	69	73	71	15	17	...	...	...	...	...	...
54	46	29	33	54	75	...	...	...	...	...	...
50	33	17	17	50	67	...	...	...	...	...	...
56	50	33	39	56	78	...	...	...	...	...	...
57	57	57	57	57	57	...	...	...	...	...	...
20	20	60	60	40	40	...	...	...	...	...	...
78	78	56	56	67	67	...	...	...	...	...	...
61	72	44	44	78	78	...	...	...	...	...	...
57	71	43	43	86	86	...	...	...	...	...	...
64	73	45	45	73	73	...	...	...	...	...	...
100	100	94	94	41	41	...	...	...	...	...	...
73	73	56	56	41	39	...	...	...	...	...	...
68	68	41	41	18	14	...	...	...	...	...	...
86	86	86	86	71	71	...	...	...	...	...	...
75	75	67	67	67	67	...	...	...	...	...	...
57	52	61	65	89	91	...	...	...	...	...	...
56	51	63	67	88	91	...	...	...	...	...	...
67	67	33	33	100	100	...	...	...	...	...	...
84	77	68	65	13	13	...	...	...	...	...	...
60	59	60	61	50	53	...	...	...	...	...	...
62	60	66	66	43	43	...	...	...	...	...	...
59	59	55	57	55	62	...	...	...	...	...	...
69	67	55	58	75	79	...	...	...	...	...	...

TABLE 2: Continued

	PARTICIPATION / COMPLETION											D	E	F	G	H	I	J
	A						B			C								
	Out-of-school (000)			Out-of-school rate (%)			Completion rate (%)			Over-age for grade (%)		GER primary (%)	NERA primary (%)	GIR last primary (%)	Transition from primary to lower secondary (%)	NERT lower secondary (%)	GIR last lower secondary grade (%)	NERT upper secondary (%)
Country or territory	Primary	Lower secondary	Upper secondary	Primary	Lower secondary	Upper secondary	Primary	Lower secondary	Upper secondary	Primary	Lower secondary							
SDG indicator				4.1.4			4.1.2			4.1.5				4.1.3			4.1.3	
Reference year	2018											2018						
Sub-Saharan Africa																		
Angola	...	...	...	...	...	...	60-3	36-3	19-3	...	...	113-3	...	...	...	...	...	...
Benin	51	...	369-3i	3	...	56-3i	48-1	19-1	8-1	12	30-3	122	97	81-2	84-3	...	46-2	44-3i
Botswana	36-4i	...	...	11-4i	...	...	...	...	...	...	33-4	103-3	...	...	...	...	98-4	...
Burkina Faso	689	829	833	21	44	66	...	...	...	25	59	96	79	65	80-1	56	43	34
Burundi	114	240	399	6	33	60	50-2	23-2	10-2	31	64	121	93	63	76-1	67	33	40
Cabo Verde	4	4	8	6	13	27	...	...	...	10	29	104	94	87	94-1	87	68	73
Cameroon	259-1	808-2	778-3	7-1	37-2	54-3	74-4	43-4	16-4	21-1	28-3	103	93-1	64	66-3	63-2	47-2	46-3
Central African Republic	...	...	...	...	...	...	...	...	...	...	...	102-2	...	41-2	...	...	10-2	...
Chad	675-2	869-2	748-2	26-2	61-2	80-2	27-3	14-3	10-3	29-2	46-2	87-2	73-2	41-2	74-3	39-2	15-2	20-2
Comoros	23	14	25	18	19	50	...	...	...	27-1	48-4	100	82	77-1	...	81	48-4	50
Congo	...	...	...	...	...	...	80-3	50-3	23-3	...	...	...	...	...	...	...	...	...
Côte d'Ivoire	242	1,088	992	6	46	61	56-2	28-2	16-2	13	32	100	94	72-1	92-1	54	49	39
D. R. Congo	...	...	...	...	...	...	...	...	...	...	...	108-3	...	70-3	...	...	50-4	...
Djibouti	30+1	35-3	36-3	33+1	48-3	66-3	...	...	...	7+1	19+1	75+1	67+1	66	86-1	52-3	50+1	34-3
Equat. Guinea	84-3	...	...	55-3	...	...	...	...	...	39-3	49-3	62-3	44-3	41-3	...	...	24-3	...
Eritrea	242	95	138	47	36	49	...	...	...	34	48	68	52	60	95-1	64	51	51
Eswatini	36-1	2-3i	8-3i	17-1	3-3i	16-3i	71-4	51-4	32-4	45-1	69-1	115-1	83-1	96-1	98-2	97-1	67-1	84-1
Ethiopia	2,307-3i	4,638-3i	3,356-3i	14-3i	47-3i	74-3i	52-2	21-2	13-2	22-3	26-3	101-3	85-3i	54-3	91-4	53-3i	29-3	26-3i
Gabon	...	...	...	...	...	...	...	...	...	...	...	...	...	...	...	...	...	...
Gambia	65	...	...	18	...	...	66	46	29	33	41	98	82	69-2	...	...	59-4	...
Ghana	35+1	208+1	889+1	1+1	11+1	36+1	66-4	52-4	20-4	31	41+1	105+1	87+1	94	94-1	89+1	78+1	64+1
Guinea	425-2	559-4	491-4	22-2	51-4	67-4	45	26	16	16-2	30-2	92-2	78-2	60-2	...	49-4	35-4	33-4
Guinea-Bissau	...	...	...	...	...	...	30-4	17-4	7-4	...	...	...	...	...	...	...	...	...
Kenya	...	...	...	...	...	...	84-4	71-4	42-4	...	...	103-2	...	100-2	99-1	...	79-2	...
Lesotho	7-1i	23-2	29-2	2-1i	17-2	34-2	80	44	31	30-1	50-1	121-1	91-1	86-2	88-3	83-2	47-1	66-2
Liberia	159-1	65-4	70-4	21-1	21-4	26-4	...	...	...	71-1	79-1	85-1	45-1	61-1	80-2	79-4	44-1	74-4
Madagascar	67	628	1,127	2	25	65	56	24	9	40	46	143	97	65	73-3	75	37	35
Malawi	...	308	534	...	17	66	47-3	22-3	14-3	36	...	142	...	80-4	...	83	...	34
Mali	1,343	719	893	41	53	75	47	20	5	11	17-1	76	59	50-1	78-2	47	30-1	25
Mauritania	129	143	167	20	38	64	58-3	47-3	25-3	42	55	100	80	76	66-1	62	42	36
Mauritius	1	2	15	1	5	20	...	...	...	1	6	101	95	101	99-1	95	87	80
Mozambique	354	860-3	827-3	6	43-3	69-3	...	...	...	39	46	113	94	52	74-3	57-3	23-1	31-1
Namibia	6i	...	...	2i	...	...	...	...	...	26	48-1	124	98i	94	...	...	77-1	...
Niger	1,241-1	1,287-1	1,087-1	34-1	65-1	86-1	...	...	...	6-1	25	75-1	66-1	72-2	58-3	35-1	19	14-1
Nigeria	...	...	...	...	...	...	71	62	49	–-4	–-4	85-2	...	...	...	...	...	...
Rwanda	81	74	336	4	9	44	54-3	28-3	18-3	35	44	133	95	87	73-1	91	37	56
Sao Tome and Principe	2-1	1-3	2-3i	6-1	10-3	17-3i	83-4	34-4	8-4	15-1	43-1	107-1	94-1	84-1	97-2	90-1	74-1	83-1
Senegal	586-1	667-1	598-1	24-1	48-1	63-1	50-1	27-1	12-1	7-1	10-1	81	76-1	57	73-2	52-1	37-1	37-1
Seychelles	0.3	...	1	3	...	14	...	...	...	0.3	0.5	100	93	102	97-1	...	108	86
Sierra Leone	6-2	268	432	1-2	49	65	64-1	44-1	22-1	1	18	113	99-2	82	90-1	51	51	35
Somalia	...	...	...	...	...	...	...	...	...	...	...	...	...	...	...	...	...	...
South Africa	568-1i	369-1	486-1	8-1i	19-1	17-1	97-2	89-2	49-2	6-1	30-1	101-1	92-1i	87-2i	96-3	81-1	81-2	83-1
South Sudan	1,088-3i	290-3i	625-3i	62-3i	56-3i	64-3i	...	...	...	77-3	91-3	73-3	35-3i	...	...	44-3i	...	36-3i
Togo	66	152-1	265-1	5	21-1	57-1	61-4	24-4	15-4	23-1	30	124	95	90	82-1	79-1	48	43-1
Uganda	...	...	...	...	...	...	44-2	26-2	18-2	34-1	48-1	103-1	...	53-1	59-2	...	26-1	...
United Republic of Tanzania	1,895	3,363-2i	1,783-2i	18	72-2i	86-2i	80-3	29-3	8-3	9-2	18-2	94	82	69	71-1	28-2i	30	14-2i
Zambia	496-1	...	...	15-1	...	...	72	52	30	27-1	...	99-1	85-1	...	...	...	...	...
Zimbabwe	...	...	...	...	...	...	89+1	72+1	8+1	...	...	...	...	...	...	...	...	...

Administration of nationally representative learning assessment (K)						Achieving minimum proficiency (%) (L)						
Early grades		End of primary		End of lower secondary		Early grades		End of primary		End of lower secondary		
Reading	Mathematics	Reading	Mathematics	Reading	Mathematics	Reading	Mathematics	Reading	Mathematics	Reading	Mathematics	Country code
4.1.6						4.1.1						
2018												
No	No	No	No	No	No	...	...	...	...	...	...	AGO
Yes	Yes	Yes	Yes	No	No	9-4	34-4	23-4	11-4	...	...	BEN
Yes	Yes	Yes	Yes	No	Yes	...	...	...	16-3	...	...	BWA
Yes	Yes	Yes	Yes	No	No	36-4	59-4	21-4	22-4	...	...	BFA
Yes	Yes	Yes	Yes	No	No	79-4	97-4	7-4	40-4	...	...	BDI
Yes	Yes	Yes	Yes	No	No	...	...	...	...	...	...	CPV
Yes	Yes	Yes	Yes	No	No	30-4	57-4	24-4	12-4	...	...	CMR
No	No	No	No	No	No	...	...	...	...	...	...	CAF
Yes	Yes	Yes	Yes	No	No	18-4	48-4	3-4	3-4	...	...	TCD
No	No	No	No	No	No	...	...	...	...	...	...	COM
Yes	Yes	Yes	Yes	No	No	38-4	72-4	17-4	6-4	...	...	COG
Yes	Yes	Yes	Yes	No	No	17-4	33-4	22-4	3-4	...	...	CIV
Yes	Yes	Yes	No	No	No	...	...	...	...	...	...	COD
No	No	Yes	Yes	No	No	...	...	...	...	...	...	DJI
No	No	No	No	No	No	...	...	...	...	...	...	GNQ
Yes	Yes	Yes	Yes	No	No	...	...	...	...	...	...	ERI
No	No	Yes	Yes	No	No	...	...	...	...	...	...	SWZ
Yes	Yes	Yes	Yes	Yes	Yes	...	...	...	...	...	...	ETH
No	No	No	No	No	No	...	...	...	...	...	...	GAB
Yes	Yes	Yes	Yes	Yes	Yes	...	...	...	...	...	...	GMB
Yes	Yes	Yes	Yes	No	No	...	...	...	...	...	...	GHA
Yes	Yes	No	No	No	No	...	...	...	...	...	...	GIN
Yes	Yes	Yes	Yes	No	No	...	...	...	...	...	...	GNB
Yes	Yes	Yes	Yes	No	No	53	42	...	...	...	...	KEN
Yes	Yes	Yes	Yes	No	No	...	...	...	...	...	...	LSO
Yes	Yes	No	No	No	No	...	...	...	...	...	...	LBR
Yes	No	Yes	Yes	No	No	...	...	4-4	5-4	...	...	MDG
No	No	Yes	Yes	No	No	...	...	...	...	...	...	MWI
Yes	Yes	Yes	Yes	No	No	...	...	...	...	...	...	MLI
No	No	No	No	No	No	...	...	...	...	...	...	MRT
No	No	Yes	Yes	Yes	Yes	...	...	...	...	...	...	MUS
Yes	Yes	Yes	Yes	No	No	...	...	...	...	...	...	MOZ
No	No	Yes	Yes	No	No	...	...	...	...	...	...	NAM
Yes	Yes	Yes	Yes	No	No	9-4	27-4	2-4	1-4	...	...	NER
Yes	Yes	No	No	No	No	...	...	...	...	...	...	NGA
Yes	Yes	Yes	Yes	No	No	...	...	...	...	...	...	RWA
No	No	No	No	No	No	...	...	...	...	...	...	STP
Yes	Yes	Yes	Yes	Yes	Yes	29-4	63-4	35-4	29-4	9-3	8-3	SEN
No	No	Yes	Yes	No	No	...	...	...	...	...	...	SYC
Yes	Yes	No	No	Yes	Yes	...	...	...	...	...	...	SLE
Yes	No	No	No	No	No	...	...	...	...	...	...	SOM
Yes	Yes	Yes	Yes	Yes	Yes	22-2	...	...	13-3	...	...	ZAF
Yes	Yes	No	No	No	No	...	...	...	...	...	...	SSD
Yes	Yes	Yes	Yes	No	No	19-4	40-4	16-4	20-4	...	...	TGO
Yes	Yes	Yes	Yes	No	No	33-3	21-3	...	...	...	...	UGA
Yes	Yes	Yes	Yes	No	No	...	...	...	...	...	...	TZA
Yes	Yes	Yes	Yes	Yes	Yes	...	...	...	...	5-3	2-3	ZMB
Yes	Yes	Yes	Yes	No	No	...	...	...	...	...	...	ZWE

TABLE 2: Continued

Country or territory	A Out-of-school (000) Primary	Lower secondary	Upper secondary	A Out-of-school rate (%) Primary	Lower secondary	Upper secondary	B Completion rate (%) Primary	Lower secondary	Upper secondary	C Over-age for grade (%) Primary	Lower secondary	D GER primary (%)	E NERA primary (%)	F GIR last primary (%)	G Transition from primary to lower secondary (%)	H NERT lower secondary (%)	I GIR last lower secondary grade (%)	J NERT upper secondary (%)
SDG indicator					4.1.4			4.1.2			4.1.5				4.1.3		4.1.3	
Reference year					2018											2018		
Northern Africa and Western Asia																		
Algeria	14	...	...	0.4	...	...	...	...	...	6	23	110	100	105	99-1	...	85	...
Armenia	11	15	...	7	8	...	99-2	99-2	94-2	0.3	1	93	91	90	98-1	92	93	...
Azerbaijan	25i	3i	5i	4i	1i	1i	...	...	...	2	3-1	100i	93i	100i	99-1	99i	85i	99i
Bahrain	1	3	4	1	5	9	...	...	...	1	3	99	98	98	99-1	95	94	91
Cyprus	1-1i	0.1-1i	2-1i	1-1i	0.4-1i	5-1i	100-1	99-1	90-1	0.3-1	2-1	99-1i	98-1i	101-1i	100-2	100-1i	99-1i	95-1i
Egypt	78	221	1,247	1	4	24	91-4	80-4	70-4	2	4	106	98	101	97-1	96	85	76
Georgia	2	0.2	9	1	0.2	7	100	98	82	1	1	99	99	96	100-1	100	102	93
Iraq	...	...	...	...	...	...	76	46	28	...	...	...	...	...	...	...	...	...
Israel	2-1	...	6-1	0.3-1	...	2-1	...	...	...	0.4-1	1-1	105-1	97-1	106-1	100-2	...	103-1	98-1
Jordan	265	262	197	19	31	49	...	...	...	1	2	81	81	73	98-1	69	59	51
Kuwait	7-2	11-3	24-3	3-2	6-3	18-3	...	...	...	2	4	92	88	92	98-1	94-3	94	82-3
Lebanon	...	...	...	...	...	...	...	...	...	9	12	...	...	...	96-1	...	...	...
Libya	...	...	...	...	...	...	...	...	...	...	...	...	...	...	...	...	...	...
Morocco	8	194	511	0.2	11	29	...	...	...	15	31	114	99	94	91-1	89	65	71
Oman	9	8	11	3	3	12	...	...	...	0.3	5	103	95	100	98-1	97	104	88
Palestine	13	14	87	3	3	28	99-4	86-4	62-4	0.3	1	99	97	97	97-1	97	90	72
Qatar	3	3	...	2	6	...	...	...	...	1	5	104	98	96-1	99-2	94	88	...
Saudi Arabia	134	21	50i	4	1	4i	...	...	...	5	9	100	95	97	98-1	99	105	96i
Sudan	2,443-1i	...	...	38-1i	...	...	67-4	53-4	32-4	28-1i	...	77-1	62-1i	62-1	92-2	...	58-1	...
Syrian Arab Republic	...	...	...	...	...	...	...	...	...	...	...	...	...	...	...	...	...	...
Tunisia	...	...	...	...	...	...	95	74	49	6	16	115	...	95-1	98-2	...	77	...
Turkey	273-1	478-1	787-1	5-1	9-1	15-1	98-4	92-4	56-4	2-1	2-1	93-1	95-1	90-1	100-1	91-1	88-1	85-1
United Arab Emirates	6-1	2-1	25-1	1-1	1-1	12-1	...	...	...	2-1	5-1	108-1	99-1	104-3	...	99-1	82-4	88-1
Yemen	650-2	543-2	1,019-2	16-2	28-2	56-2	...	...	...	9-2	11-2	94-2	84-2	72-2	...	72-2	53-2	44-2
Central and Southern Asia																		
Afghanistan	...	...	1,510i	...	...	57i	55-3	37-3	23-3	...	11	104	...	86	91-1	...	55	43i
Bangladesh	...	...	4,817i	...	...	38i	80-4	55-4	19-4	...	4-1	116	...	...	...	...	88	62i
Bhutan	7i	7i	8i	8i	12i	28i	...	...	...	14-1	32	100	90i	100-1	100-2	88i	82	72i
India	...	...	...	...	...	...	92-3	81-3	43-3	3	4	113-1	...	92	91-1	...	84	...
Iran, Islamic Republic of	17-1	157-1	854-1	0.2-1	5-1	26-1	...	...	...	3-1	3-1	111-1	100-1	99-1	96-2	95-1	90-1	74-1
Kazakhstan	13+1	...	5	1+1	...	1	100-3	100-3	94-3	0.3+1	0.3+1	104+1	99+1	106+1	100	...	118+1	99
Kyrgyzstan	1	15	56	0.3	3	28	99	99	87	0.4	1	108	99	105	100-1	97	95	72
Maldives	2-1	...	...	4-1	...	...	98-1	91-1	40-1	0.3-1	11-1	97-1	95-1	97-1	99-2	...	108-1	...
Nepal	103+1	47+1	490+1	4+1	3+1	19+1	73-2	63-2	...	36+1	43+1	142+1	96+1	120+1	82-2	97+1	99+1	81+1
Pakistan	6,006	4,426	9,133	25	32	52	60	50	23	...	48	94	68	71	88-1	68	48	48
Sri Lanka	9	2	211	1	0.1	16	...	...	...	1	1	100	99	103	99-1	100	96	84
Tajikistan	4-1	...	...	1-1	...	...	98-1	96-1	74-1	-1	-1	101-1	99-1	95-1	99-2	...	96-1	...
Turkmenistan	...	...	...	...	...	...	100-3	99-3	97-3	...	...	88-4	...	...	...	...	...	...
Uzbekistan	17i	95i	261-1	1i	4i	16-1	...	...	...	0.1	0.2	104	97i	103	100-1	96i	96	84-1
Eastern and South-eastern Asia																		
Brunei Darussalam	0.3	-	6	1	0.3	18	...	...	...	1	3	103	96	108	100-1	100	106	82
Cambodia	186	120-3i	...	9	13-3i	...	72-4	41-4	21-4	19	20	107	91	88	90-1	87-3i	58	...
China	...	...	...	...	...	...	96-4	85-4	59-4	...	...	100	...	...	...	...	...	...
DPR Korea	...	...	...	...	...	...	...	...	...	...	...	113	...	102	...	...	...	...
Hong Kong, China	8i	0.1i	3i	2i	0.1i	2i	...	...	...	2i	6i	109	96i	104	100-1	100i	107	98i
Indonesia	1,555	2,299	3,137	6	16	23	97-1	87-1	65-1	0.3	9	106	94	102	91-2	84	90-1	77
Japan	...	...	...	...	...	...	...	...	...	-3	...	...	...	...	100-2	...	...	...
Lao PDR	65	146i	170i	9	25i	40i	83-1	54-1	31-1	11	26	102	91	98	86-1	75i	67	60i
Macao, China	1	0.3	2	3	2	13	...	...	...	2	13	100	96	101	99-1	98	98	87
Malaysia	10-1i	206-1	605-1	0.4-1i	13-1	37-1	...	...	...	-1	-	105-1	100-3	99-1	91-2	87-1	82	63-1
Mongolia	2i	...	...	1i	...	...	99	83	69	1	2	104	99i	102	99-1	...	105	...
Myanmar	92	848	884	2	21	43	83-2	44-2	17-2	...	9	112	98	95	...	79	65	57
Philippines	424-1	894-1	424-3	3-1	11-1	21-3	92-1	81-1	78-1	9-1	17-1	108-1	95-1	109-1	97-2	89-1	78-1	79-3
Republic of Korea	66-1	80-1	5-1	2-1	...	...	...	...	...	...	0.4-1	98-1	98-1	91-1	100-2	94-1	96-1	100-1
Singapore	0.1-1i	-1i	0.1-1i	-1i	0.1-1i	0.1-1i	...	...	...	0.2-1i	3-1	101-1i	100-1i	99-1i	99-2	100-1i	105-1i	100-1i
Thailand	...	331-3i	603-3i	...	12-3i	21-3i	98-3	83-3	56-3	...	6	100	...	93	98-1	88-3i	81	79-3i
Timor-Leste	8	12	24	4	13	26	80-2	66-2	52-2	23	35	115	95	104	93-1	87	91	74
Viet Nam	...	...	...	...	...	...	97-4	84-4	56-4	1-2	...	111	...	110	100-3	...	98	...

| Administration of nationally representative learning assessment (4.1.6) | | | | | | Achieving minimum proficiency (%) (4.1.1) | | | | | | Country code |
| Early grades | | End of primary | | End of lower secondary | | Early grades | | End of primary | | End of lower secondary | | |
Reading	Mathematics	Reading	Mathematics	Reading	Mathematics	Reading	Mathematics	Reading	Mathematics	Reading	Mathematics	
No	No	No	No	Yes	Yes	...	...	...	...	21-3	19-3	DZA
No	No	No	Yes	No	Yes	...	...	...	55-3	...	50-3	ARM
No	No	Yes	No	No	No	...	...	81-2	...	...	...	AZE
Yes	Yes	No	No	No	Yes	69-2	40-3	...	...	...	39-3	BHR
No	Yes	No	No	Yes	Yes	...	74-3	...	...	56	63	CYP
Yes	No	No	No	No	Yes	...	...	...	...	...	21-3	EGY
Yes	Yes	No	No	Yes	Yes	86-2	47-3	...	...	36	39	GEO
No	No	No	No	No	No	...	...	...	...	...	...	IRQ
Yes	No	Yes	Yes	Yes	Yes	91-2	...	...	...	69	66	ISR
Yes	Yes	Yes	Yes	Yes	Yes	...	...	...	...	59	41	JOR
Yes	Yes	No	No	Yes	Yes	...	12-3	...	...	...	18-3	KWT
No	No	No	No	Yes	Yes	...	...	...	...	32	35-3	LBN
No	No	No	No	No	No	...	...	...	...	...	...	LBY
Yes	Yes	No	No	Yes	Yes	36-2	16-3	...	...	27	14-3	MAR
Yes	Yes	No	No	No	Yes	59-2	32-3	...	...	...	23-3	OMN
Yes	No	Yes	Yes	Yes	Yes	...	...	...	...	...	...	PSE
Yes	Yes	Yes	Yes	Yes	Yes	66-2	36-3	...	...	49	36-3	QAT
Yes	Yes	No	No	No	Yes	63-2	16-3	...	...	48	11-3	SAU
No	No	No	No	No	No	...	...	...	...	...	...	SDN
No	No	No	No	No	No	...	...	...	...	...	...	SYR
Yes	Yes	Yes	Yes	Yes	Yes	...	...	...	...	28-3	25-3	TUN
No	No	No	Yes	Yes	Yes	...	...	...	57-3	74	42-3	TUR
Yes	Yes	Yes	Yes	Yes	Yes	68-2	42-3	...	...	57	46-3	ARE
No	No	No	No	No	No	...	...	...	...	...	...	YEM
Yes	Yes	Yes	Yes	No	No	22-2	24-2	...	...	...	...	AFG
Yes	Yes	Yes	Yes	Yes	Yes	47-1	34-1	44-1	32-1	54-3	57-3	BGD
No	No	No	No	Yes	No	...	...	...	...	56-3	...	BTN
Yes	Yes	Yes	Yes	Yes	Yes	47-1	53-1	46-1	44-1	...	...	IND
Yes	Yes	No	No	No	Yes	66-2	33-3	...	...	...	34-3	IRN
No	No	Yes	Yes	Yes	Yes	...	...	98-2	80-3	36	51	KAZ
Yes	Yes	Yes	Yes	Yes	Yes	...	...	36-4	35-4	...	...	KGZ
No	No	No	No	No	No	...	...	...	...	...	...	MDV
Yes	Yes	Yes	Yes	Yes	Yes	...	...	...	...	...	...	NPL
Yes	Yes	Yes	Yes	Yes	Yes	35-4	...	...	...	...	...	PAK
Yes	Yes	No	No	Yes	Yes	...	...	...	...	...	...	LKA
No	No	No	No	No	No	...	...	...	...	...	...	TJK
No	No	No	No	No	No	...	...	...	...	...	...	TKM
No	No	Yes	Yes	No	No	...	...	...	...	...	...	UZB
Yes	Yes	No	No	Yes	Yes	...	...	...	...	48	52	BRN
No	Yes	Yes	Yes	Yes	Yes	...	...	...	...	8-3	10-3	KHM
Yes	Yes	No	No	Yes	Yes	82-2	85-3	...	...	80-2	79-3	CHN
Yes	Yes	No	No	No	No	...	...	...	...	...	...	PRK
Yes	Yes	Yes	Yes	Yes	Yes	99-2	98-3	...	...	87	91	HKG
Yes	Yes	No	No	Yes	Yes	...	18-3	...	...	30	28	IDN
No	Yes	Yes	Yes	Yes	Yes	...	95-3	...	...	83	89-3	JPN
No	Yes	No	No	No	No	...	...	...	...	...	...	LAO
Yes	No	No	No	Yes	Yes	98-2	...	...	...	89	95	MAC
Yes	Yes	Yes	Yes	Yes	Yes	...	...	...	...	54	59	MYS
No	No	Yes	Yes	Yes	Yes	...	...	...	...	...	...	MNG
No	No	No	No	No	No	...	...	...	...	...	...	MMR
Yes	Yes	Yes	Yes	Yes	Yes	...	...	...	...	19	19	PHL
No	Yes	No	No	Yes	Yes	...	97-3	...	...	85	85	KOR
Yes	Yes	No	No	Yes	Yes	97-2	93-3	...	...	89	94-3	SGP
Yes	Yes	Yes	Yes	Yes	Yes	...	...	...	...	40	47	THA
No	No	No	No	No	No	...	...	...	...	...	...	TLS
Yes	No	Yes	Yes	Yes	Yes	...	...	55-4	51-4	86-3	81-3	VNM

LEARNING — K / L — 2018

TABLE 2: Continued

Country or territory	Out-of-school (000) Primary	Out-of-school (000) Lower secondary	Out-of-school (000) Upper secondary	Out-of-school rate (%) Primary	Out-of-school rate (%) Lower secondary	Out-of-school rate (%) Upper secondary	Completion rate (%) Primary	Completion rate (%) Lower secondary	Completion rate (%) Upper secondary	Over-age for grade (%) Primary	Over-age for grade (%) Lower secondary	GER primary (%)	NERA primary (%)	GIR last primary (%)	Transition from primary to lower secondary (%)	NERT lower secondary (%)	GIR last lower secondary grade (%)	NERT upper secondary (%)
Oceania																		
Australia	7_{-1}	22_{-1}	10_{-1}	0.3_{-1}	2_{-1}	2_{-1}	...	98_{-4}	87_{-4}	0.2_{-1}	2_{-1}	100_{-1}	96_{-1}	...		98_{-1}	...	98_{-1}
Cook Islands	$-_{2}$	$-_{2}$	0.3_{-2}	1_{-2}	1_{-2}	33_{-2}	...	...	...	0.3_{-2}	0.2_{-2}	109_{-2}	99_{-2}	107_{-2}	100_{-3}	99_{-2}	93_{-2}	67_{-2}
Fiji	1_{-2}	...	...	1_{-2}	...	...	...	...	...	2_{-2}	4_{-2}	106_{-2}	99_{-2}	107_{-2}	98_{-3}	...	103_{-2}	...
Kiribati	1_{-1}	...	...	4_{-1}	...	...	...	...	...	2_{-1}	10_{-1}	101_{-1}	96_{-1}	101_{-1}	96_{-3}	...	95_{-2}	...
Marshall Islands	2_{-2}	2_{-2i}	1_{-2i}	24_{-2}	31_{-2i}	44_{-2i}	...	...	...	11_{-2}	23_{-2}	85_{-2}	75_{-2}	71_{-2}	...	69_{-2i}	...	56_{-2i}
Micronesia, F. S.	2_{-3}	1_{-4}	...	15_{-3}	13_{-4}	...	...	...	...	$-_{3}$	$-_{3}$	97_{-3}	85_{-3}	...	...	87_{-4}	...	...
Nauru	$-_{2}$	0.1_{-2}	0.2_{-2}	3_{-2}	11_{-2}	56_{-2}	...	...	...	0.3_{-2}	...	126_{-2}	94_{-2}	131_{-2}	...	89_{-2}	...	44_{-2}
New Zealand	1_{-1}	5_{-1}	4_{-1}	1_{-2}	2_{-1}	2_{-1}	...	...	...	0.1_{-1}	0.3_{-1}	100_{-1}	99_{-1}	...	...	98_{-1}	...	98_{-1}
Niue	...	...	$-_{4}$	...	...	9_{-4}	...	...	...	$-_{2}$	2_{-3}	127_{-2}	...	112_{-2}	77_{-4}	...	104_{-3}	91_{-4}
Palau	0.1_{-4}	...	...	5_{-4}	...	...	...	...	...	14_{-4}	15_{-4}	113_{-4}	95_{-4}	100_{-4}	...	...	109_{-4}	...
Papua New Guinea	86_{-2}	53_{-2}	320_{-2}	7_{-2}	14_{-2}	46_{-2}	62_{-1}	35_{-1}	17_{-1}	47_{-2}	50_{-2}	109_{-2}	76_{-2}	77_{-2}	...	86_{-2}	62_{-2}	54_{-2}
Samoa	0.4	$-_{4}$	2_{-2}	1	0.3_{-4}	10_{-2}	...	...	...	9	9	111	96	105	96_{-1}	100_{-4}	105	90_{-2}
Solomon Is	4	...	...	4	...	...	...	...	...	74	75	106	67	87	88_{-1}	...	71	...
Tokelau	...	...	$-_{2}$	...	...	62_{-2}	...	...	...	2_{-2}	12_{-2}	138_{-2}	...	...	...	...	...	38_{-2}
Tonga	0.2_{-3}	1_{-3}	2_{-3}	1_{-3}	5_{-3}	38_{-3}	...	...	...	0.2_{-3}	2_{-3}	116_{-3}	99_{-3}	...	...	95_{-3}	...	62_{-3}
Tuvalu	0.2_{-2}	$0.2i$	$0.3i$	12_{-2}	$23i$	$48i$	...	...	...	0.2_{-2}	1_{-2}	86	88_{-2}	79	94_{-3}	$77i$	61_{-2}	$52i$
Vanuatu	3_{-3}	1_{-3}	7_{-3}	8_{-3}	3_{-3}	44_{-3}	...	...	...	...	...	109_{-3}	92_{-3}	...	...	97_{-3}	...	56_{-3}
Latin America and the Caribbean																		
Anguilla	...	...	...	...	...	...	...	...	...	...	...	...	...	...	...	...	...	...
Antigua and Barbuda	0.1	0.1	0.4	1	1	13	...	...	...	2	13	105	99	96	99_{-1}	99	99	87
Argentina	19_{-1}	0.2_{-1}	219_{-1}	0.4_{-1}	$-_{1}$	10_{-1}	...	...	...	3_{-1}	14_{-1}	110_{-1}	99_{-1}	100_{-1}	100_{-2}	100_{-1}	90_{-1}	90_{-1}
Aruba	$-_{4i}$	...	...	0.1_{-4i}	...	...	...	...	...	9_{-4}	31_{-4}	117_{-4}	99_{-4i}	101_{-4}		...	99_{-4}	...
Bahamas	9	6	6	24	29	33	...	...	...	6	...	81	74	76		71	...	67
Barbados	0.3	0.4	0.4	2	4	6	...	...	...	0.1	3	99	98	89		96	...	94
Belize	0.3	3	6	1	10	38	74_{-3}	37_{-3}	14_{-3}	8	15	112	99	104	97_{-1}	90	67	62
Bolivia, P. S.	95	62	193	7	13	21	97	92	76	4	12	98	93	95	97_{-1}	87	83	79
Brazil	54_{-1i}	616_{-1i}	$1,943_{-1i}$	0.4_{-1i}	5_{-1i}	19_{-1i}	85_{-3}	82_{-3}	63_{-3}	8_{-1}	17_{-1}	115_{-1i}	98_{-1i}	...	...	95_{-1i}	...	81_{-1i}
British Virgin Islands	$-_{4}$	0.4_{-1}	0.2_{-1}	1_{-4}	29_{-1}	18_{-1}	...	...	...	4_{-1}	18_{-1}	129_{-1}	94_{-4}	95_{-1}	98_{-3}	71_{-1}	81_{-1}	82_{-1}
Cayman Islands	...	...	...	...	...	...	...	...	...	0.2	0.4	...	...	...	...	...	...	...
Chile	34_{-1}	25_{-1}	52_{-1}	2_{-1}	5_{-1}	5_{-1}	99_{-3}	98_{-3}	87_{-3}	5_{-1}	9_{-1}	101_{-1}	95_{-1}	95_{-1}	98_{-2}	95_{-1}	94_{-1}	95_{-1}
Colombia	$84i$	192	359	$2i$	6	21	92_{-3}	76_{-3}	73_{-3}	13	22	115	$98i$	106	98_{-4}	94	76	79
Costa Rica	1	8	14	0.1	4	10	96	73	58	6	31	113	97	99	92_{-1}	96	70	90
Cuba	16	21	85	2	5	21	99_{-4}	98_{-4}	87_{-4}	0.4	1	102	98	84	98_{-1}	95	93	79
Curaçao	...	...	...	...	...	...	...	...	...	...	...	...	...	...	...	...	...	...
Dominica	0.1_{-2}	0.1_{-3}	0.4_{-2}	1_{-2}	2_{-3}	16_{-2}	...	...	...	5_{-2}	14_{-2}	115_{-2}	98_{-2}	114_{-2}	96_{-4}	98_{-3}	91_{-3}	84_{-2}
Dominican Republic	$66i$	$62i$	$142i$	$6i$	$11i$	$25i$	91_{-4}	83_{-4}	57_{-4}	12	23	$106i$	$94i$	$93i$	93_{-1}	$89i$	$89i$	$75i$
Ecuador	25	45	184	1	5	20	99	91	72	3	7	103	98	104	100_{-1}	95	97	80
El Salvador	96	60	126	14	17	34	86_{-4}	73_{-4}	35_{-4}	13	20	95	82	87	95_{-1}	83	77	66
Grenada	0.1	0.2_{-4}	0.1_{-1}	1	3_{-4}	3_{-1}	...	...	...	2	9	107	99	123	98_{-1}	97_{-4}	107	97_{-1}
Guatemala	246	386	680	11	33	59	78_{-3}	48_{-3}	35_{-3}	16	27	102	89	80	90_{-1}	67	56	41
Guyana	...	...	...	...	...	...	98_{-4}	85_{-4}	57_{-4}	...	...	...	...	...	...	...	...	...
Haiti	...	...	...	...	...	...	53_{-1}	34_{-1}	14_{-1}	...	...	...	...	...	...	...	...	...
Honduras	214_{-1}	239_{-1}	331_{-1}	17_{-1}	38_{-1}	53_{-1}	87	53	38	12_{-1}	33_{-3}	92_{-1}	80_{-1}	82_{-1}	71_{-3i}	62_{-1}	46_{-2}	47_{-1}
Jamaica	43	26	25	16	18	25	...	...	...	1	3	91	81	86	97_{-1}	82	82	75
Mexico	98_{-1}	402_{-1}	$1,745_{-1}$	1_{-1}	6_{-1}	26_{-1}	96_{-3}	88_{-3}	52_{-3}	1_{-1}	3_{-1}	106_{-1}	99_{-1}	104_{-1}	97_{-2}	94_{-1}	97_{-1}	74_{-1}
Montserrat	$-_{2}$	-	0.1	3_{-2}	10	...	...	...	...	0.4	-	110	97_{-2}	95	...	90	74	47
Nicaragua	...	...	...	...	...	...	74_{-4}	50_{-4}	41_{-4}	...	...	...	...	...	...	...	...	...
Panama	59_{-1}	26_{-1}	92_{-1}	13_{-1}	12_{-1}	44_{-1}	96	85	67	8_{-1}	11_{-1}	94_{-1}	87_{-1}	90_{-1}	99_{-2}	88_{-1}	77_{-1}	56_{-1}
Paraguay	...	...	130_{-2}	...	...	32_{-2}	92_{-2}	78_{-2}	59_{-2}	14_{-2}	14_{-2}	...	...	...	...	...	...	68_{-2}
Peru	48	28	185	1	2	18	97	91	86	4	7	107	99	96	95_{-1}	98	98	82
Saint Kitts and Nevis	0.1_{-2}	...	0.1_{-2}	1_{-2}	...	4_{-2}	...	...	...	1_{-2}	2_{-2}	109_{-2}	96_{-2}	98_{-2}	99_{-3}	...	111_{-2}	96_{-2}
Saint Lucia	0.2	1	1	1	12	20	...	...	...	1	2	103	98	95	98_{-1}	88	86	80
Saint Vincent/Grenadines	0.1_{-1}	0.1	1	0.5_{-1}	2	15	...	...	...	1	14	113	98_{-1}	106	95_{-1}	98	92	85
Sint Maarten	...	...	0.4_{-4}	...	...	22_{-4}	...	...	...	15_{-4}	18_{-4}	128_{-4}	...	123_{-4}	...	...	42_{-4}	78_{-4}
Suriname	9	6_{-3}	11_{-3}	14	15_{-3}	38_{-3}	86	50	28	18	36	109	86	85	66_{-1}	85_{-3}	45	62_{-3}
Trinidad and Tobago	...	...	...	...	...	...	...	...	...	...	...	...	...	...	...	...	...	...
Turks and Caicos Islands	...	...	...	...	...	...	...	...	...	4	3	...	...	...	...	...	...	...
Uruguay	1_{-1}	0.4_{-1}	18_{-1}	0.3_{-1}	0.3_{-1}	12_{-1}	98	73	40	3_{-1}	14_{-1}	108_{-1}	100_{-1}	99_{-1}	...	100_{-1}	...	88_{-1}
Venezuela, B. R.	325_{-1}	232_{-1}	249_{-1}	10_{-1}	14_{-1}	23_{-1}	94_{-4}	80_{-4}	70_{-4}	8_{-1}	12_{-1}	97_{-1}	90_{-1}	93_{-1}	99_{-2}	86_{-1}	75_{-1}	77_{-1}

SDG indicator: 4.1.4 (columns A out-of-school rate); 4.1.2 (B completion rate); 4.1.5 (C over-age for grade); 4.1.3 (F, G); 4.1.3 (I)

Reference year: 2018

Early grades Reading	Early grades Mathematics	End of primary Reading	End of primary Mathematics	End of lower secondary Reading	End of lower secondary Mathematics	Early grades Reading	Early grades Mathematics	End of primary Reading	End of primary Mathematics	End of lower secondary Reading	End of lower secondary Mathematics	Country code
Yes	Yes	Yes	Yes	Yes	Yes	94$_{-2}$	70$_{-3}$	...	64$_{-3}$	80	78	AUS
Yes	Yes	Yes	Yes	No	No	...	...	...	...	...	...	COK
Yes	Yes	Yes	Yes	No	No	...	...	...	...	...	...	FJI
Yes	Yes	Yes	Yes	Yes	Yes	...	...	...	...	...	...	KIR
Yes	Yes	Yes	Yes	Yes	Yes	...	...	...	...	...	...	MHL
Yes	Yes	Yes	Yes	Yes	Yes	...	...	...	...	...	...	FSM
Yes	Yes	Yes	Yes	Yes	Yes	...	...	...	...	...	...	NRU
Yes	Yes	No	No	Yes	Yes	90$_{-2}$	59$_{-3}$	...	...	81	78	NZL
Yes	Yes	Yes	Yes	No	No	...	...	...	...	...	...	NIU
Yes	Yes	Yes	Yes	Yes	Yes	...	...	...	...	...	...	PLW
Yes	Yes	Yes	Yes	No	No	...	...	...	...	...	...	PNG
Yes	Yes	Yes	Yes	No	No	...	...	...	...	...	...	WSM
Yes	Yes	Yes	Yes	No	No	...	...	...	...	...	...	SLB
Yes	Yes	Yes	Yes	No	No	...	...	...	...	...	...	TKL
Yes	Yes	Yes	Yes	No	No	...	...	...	...	...	...	TON
Yes	Yes	Yes	Yes	No	No	...	...	...	...	...	...	TUV
Yes	Yes	Yes	Yes	No	No	...	...	...	...	...	...	VUT
Yes	Yes	Yes	Yes	Yes	No	...	...	...	...	...	...	AIA
Yes	Yes	Yes	Yes	No	No	...	...	...	...	...	...	ATG
Yes	Yes	Yes	Yes	Yes	Yes	...	...	...	...	48	31	ARG
No	No	No	No	No	No	...	...	...	...	...	...	ABW
Yes	Yes	Yes	Yes	No	No	...	...	...	...	...	...	BHS
No	No	No	No	No	No	...	...	...	...	...	...	BRB
No	No	No	No	No	No	...	...	...	...	...	...	BLZ
No	No	No	No	No	No	...	...	...	...	...	...	BOL
Yes	Yes	Yes	Yes	Yes	Yes	...	...	...	...	50	32	BRA
Yes	Yes	Yes	Yes	No	No	...	...	...	...	...	...	VGB
Yes	Yes	Yes	Yes	Yes	Yes	...	...	...	...	...	...	CYM
Yes	Yes	Yes	Yes	Yes	Yes	...	...	...	...	68	28$_{-3}$	CHL
Yes	Yes	Yes	Yes	Yes	Yes	...	...	...	...	50	35	COL
Yes	Yes	Yes	Yes	Yes	Yes	...	...	...	...	58	40	CRI
No	No	No	No	No	No	...	...	...	...	...	...	CUB
No	No	No	No	No	No	...	...	...	...	...	...	CUW
Yes	Yes	Yes	Yes	No	No	...	...	...	...	...	...	DMA
Yes	Yes	Yes	Yes	Yes	Yes	...	...	...	...	21	9	DOM
Yes	Yes	Yes	Yes	Yes	Yes	...	...	...	...	49$_{-3}$	29$_{-3}$	ECU
No	No	No	No	No	No	...	...	...	...	...	...	SLV
Yes	Yes	No	No	No	No	...	...	...	...	...	...	GRD
Yes	Yes	Yes	Yes	Yes	Yes	...	...	...	...	30$_{-3}$	11$_{-3}$	GTM
Yes	Yes	No	No	No	No	...	...	...	...	...	...	GUY
Yes	Yes	Yes	Yes	No	No	...	...	...	...	...	...	HTI
Yes	Yes	Yes	Yes	Yes	Yes	...	...	...	...	30$_{-3}$	15$_{-3}$	HND
Yes	Yes	No	No	No	No	...	...	...	...	...	...	JAM
Yes	Yes	Yes	Yes	Yes	Yes	...	...	...	...	55	44	MEX
Yes	Yes	No	No	No	No	...	...	...	...	...	...	MSR
Yes	Yes	Yes	Yes	No	No	...	...	...	...	...	...	NIC
Yes	Yes	Yes	Yes	Yes	Yes	...	...	...	...	36	19	PAN
Yes	Yes	Yes	Yes	Yes	Yes	...	...	...	...	32$_{-3}$	8$_{-3}$	PRY
Yes	Yes	Yes	Yes	Yes	Yes	...	...	...	...	46	40	PER
Yes	Yes	Yes	Yes	No	No	...	...	...	...	...	...	KNA
Yes	Yes	No	No	No	No	...	...	...	...	...	...	LCA
Yes	Yes	No	No	No	No	...	...	...	...	...	...	VCT
No	No	No	No	No	No	...	...	...	...	...	...	SXM
No	No	No	No	No	No	...	...	...	...	...	...	SUR
Yes	Yes	No	No	Yes	Yes	80$_{-2}$	...	...	...	58$_{-3}$	48$_{-3}$	TTO
No	No	No	No	No	No	...	...	...	...	...	...	TCA
Yes	Yes	Yes	Yes	Yes	Yes	...	...	...	...	58	49	URY
No	No	No	No	No	No	...	...	...	...	...	...	VEN

TABLE 2: Continued

Country or territory	Out-of-school (000) Primary	Out-of-school (000) Lower secondary	Out-of-school (000) Upper secondary	Out-of-school rate (%) Primary	Out-of-school rate (%) Lower secondary	Out-of-school rate (%) Upper secondary	Completion rate (%) Primary	Completion rate (%) Lower secondary	Completion rate (%) Upper secondary	Over-age for grade (%) Primary	Over-age for grade (%) Lower secondary	GER primary (%)	NERA primary (%)	GIR last primary (%)	Transition from primary to lower secondary (%)	NERT lower secondary (%)	GIR last lower secondary grade (%)	NERT upper secondary (%)
	A						B			C		D	E	F	G	H	I	J
SDG indicator				4.1.4			4.1.2			4.1.5					4.1.3		4.1.3	
Reference year	2018											2018						
Europe and Northern America																		
Albania	4	5	22	3	3	17	92-1	94-1	81-1	3	3	107	97	102	99-1	97	96	83
Andorra	...	...	...	...	...	...	...	...	...	2	7	...	...	...	...	...	...	...
Austria	0.1-1	1-1	31-1	--1	0.2-1	9-1	100-3	98-1	87-1	5-1	7-1	103-1	89-1	99-1	100-2	100-1	98-1	91-1
Belarus	6	5	2	1	1	1	...	...	...	1	1	101	95	105	98-1	99	98	99
Belgium	2-1	3-1	4-1	0.3-1	1-1	1-1	99-1	94-1	72-1	1-1	5-1	104-1	99-1	...	...	99-1	94-1	99-1
Bermuda	...	...	...	...	...	...	...	...	...	--3	--3	101-3	...	92-3	51-4	...	87-3	...
Bosnia and Herzegovina	...	...	...	...	...	...	...	...	...	1	1	...	...	...	98-1	...	...	...
Bulgaria	35-1	26-1	23-1	12-1	10-1	10-1	...	92-1	85-1	1-1	5-1	89-1	88-1	90-1	99-2	90-1	47-1	90-1
Canada	3-1i	1-3	88-1	0.1-1i	0.1-3	7-1	...	...	...	...	...	101-1	100-2i	...	...	100-3	...	93-1
Croatia	2-1	2-2	28-1	1-1	1-2	15-1	100-1	99-1	94-1	0.2-1	2-2	96-1	98-1	96-1	99-2	99-2	96-1	85-1
Czechia	2-1	3-1	6-1	0.3-1	1-1	2-1	100-1	99-1	90-1	3-1	5-1	101-1	89-1	98-1	100-2	99-1	96-1	98-1
Denmark	1-1	1-1	25-1	0.2-1	1-1	12-1	100-1	99-1	79-1	0.3-1	1-1	101-1	99-1	104-1	100-2	99-1	99-1	88-1
Estonia	2-1	0.5-1	0.4-1	2-1	1-1	1-1	100-1	98-1	88-1	1-1	4-1	97-1	94-1	97-1	100-1	99-1	105-1	99-1
Finland	4-1	1-1	8-1	1-1	0.5-1	4-1	100-1	100-1	91-1	...	...	100-1	99-1	101-1	100-2	100-1	99-1	96-1
France	3-1i	42-1i	127-1i	0.1-1i	1-1i	5-1i	...	97-1	88-1	...	1-1	103-1i	99-1i	...	...	99-1i	100-1i	95-1
Germany	15-1	217-1	291-1	1-1	5-1	11-1	...	92-1	88-1	...	...	104-1	90-1	99-1	100-2	95-1	...	89-1
Greece	8-1	12-1	21-1	1-1	4-1	7-1	100-1	98-1	93-1	1-1	5-1	100-1	98-1	97-1	99-2	96-1	95-1	93-1
Hungary	10-1	14-1	48-1	3-1	4-1	12-1	...	97-1	85-1	1-1	3-1	101-1	97-1	105-1	100-2	96-1	94-1	88-1
Iceland	--1	0.1-1	2-1	--1	0.5-1	14-1	100-1	100-3	67-3	--1	--1	100-1	100-1	...	100-1	...	...	86-1
Ireland	0.2-1i	1-1i	1-1i	--1i	0.5-1i	1-1	100-1	99-3	95-3	--1	0.2-1	101-1i	100-1i	...	...	100-1i	100-1i	99-1
Italy	72-1	28-1	149-1	3-1	2-1	5-1	100-1	100-1	86-1	0.4-1	2-1	102-1	97-1	99-1	100-2	98-1	99-1	95-1
Latvia	2-1i	1-1i	2-1i	2-1i	1-1i	4-1i	100-1	98-1	83-1	1-1	3-1	99-1i	97-1i	99-1i	99-2	99-1i	99-1i	96-1i
Liechtenstein	--2i	0.2-1i	0.2-1i	0.3-2i	13-1i	13-1i	...	...	...	0.1-1	1-1	105-1i	99-2i	90-1i	98-2	87-1i	98-1i	87-1i
Lithuania	0.2-1	--1	2-1	0.2-1	--1	3-1	...	98-1	87-1	0.3-1	1-1	104-1	100-1i	102-1i	99-2	100-1	98-1	97-1i
Luxembourg	0.2-1	1-1	5-1	1-1	6-1	19-1	...	87-1	79-1	2-1	8-1	102-1	98-1	80-1	...	94-1	95-1	81-1
Malta	0.1-1	0.1-1	2-1	0.2-1	1-1	13-1	...	99-4	75-4	0.2-1	1-1	105-1	100-1	102-1	99-2	99-1	107-1	87-1
Monaco	...	...	...	...	...	...	...	...	...	0.1+1	0.3+1	...	...	...	...	...	...	...
Montenegro	1	2	4	2	7	12	...	...	...	2	1-1	100	97	94	100-1	93	95	88
Netherlands	11-1	11-1	0.4-1	1-1	2-1	0.1-1	100-1	93-1	83-1	...	...	104-1	99-1	...	...	98-1	...	100-1
North Macedonia	1-1	...	...	1-1	...	...	...	...	...	1-1	1-1	97-1	96-1	91-1	100-4i	...	85-1	...
Norway	0.2-1	1-1	15-1	--1	1-1	8-1	99-3	99-3	72-3	--1	--1	100-1	100-1	101-1	100-2	99-1	98-1	92-1
Poland	60-1	34-1	59-1	3-1	3-1	5-1	100-1	98-1	92-1	...	...	100-1	97-1	106-1	100-2	97-1	98-1	95-1
Portugal	4-1	1-1	4-1	1-1	0.3-1	1-1	99-1	93-1	79-1	...	...	106-1	98-1	...	100-1	...	...	99-1
Republic of Moldova	14i	28i	27i	9i	15i	35i	...	...	...	0.3	1	91i	90i	89i	98-1	85i	85i	65i
Romania	126-1	60-1i	172-1	12-1	7-1i	21-1	...	98-1	74-1	2-2	4-1	85-1	86-1	92-2	100-2	93-1i	87-1	79-1
Russian Federation	9-1	11-1i	106-1i	0.1-1	0.2-1i	4-1i	...	...	...	...	...	103-1	98-1	96-2	100-3	100-1i	96-2	96-1i
San Marino	...	-i	1i	...	3i	55i	...	...	...	-	1	108	...	107	...	97i	103	45i
Serbia	4i	5i	33i	1i	2i	12i	99-4	99-3	92-3	1	1	100i	98i	99i	100-1	98i	98i	88i
Slovakia	13-1	12-1	23-1	5-1	5-1	10-1	100-1	99-1	95-1	...	...	99-1	83-1	92-1	99-2	95-1	87-3	90-1
Slovenia	0.2-1	0.4-1	3-1	0.2-1	1-1	4-1	100-1	100-1	92-1	1-1	1-1	100-1	98-1	96-1	100-2	99-1	98-1	96-1
Spain	75-1	2-1	51-1	3-1	0.2-1	4-1	97-1	94-1	70-1	0.2-1	8-1	103-1	97-1	101-1	100-2	100-1	95-1	96-1
Sweden	2-1	0.5-3	4-2	0.3-1	0.2-3	1-2	100-1	100-1	92-1	0.1-1	0.4-1	127-1	99-1	105-1	100-2	100-3	110-1	99-2
Switzerland	1-1	4-1	60-1	0.1-1	1-1	17-1	100-3	99-3	90-3	0.1-1	1-1	105-1	100-1	97-1	100-2	99-1	96-1	83-1
Ukraine	136-4	71-4i	51-4i	8-4	4-4i	6-4i	...	...	...	1	1	99-4	92-4	103-4	100-1	96-4i	94-4	94-4i
United Kingdom	21-1	3-1	108-1	0.4-1	0.1-1	4-1	100-3	100-3	82-3	--1	--1	101-1	100-1	100-1	100-2	100-1	101-1	96-1
United States	96-1i	28-1i	607-1i	0.4-1i	0.2-1i	5-1i	99-2	99-2	92-2	3-1	4-1	102-1i	96-1i	99-1i	99-2	100-1i	105-1i	95-1i

LEARNING												
K — Administration of nationally representative learning assessment						L — Achieving minimum proficiency (%)						
Early grades		End of primary		End of lower secondary		Early grades		End of primary		End of lower secondary		
Reading	Mathematics	Reading	Mathematics	Reading	Mathematics	Reading	Mathematics	Reading	Mathematics	Reading	Mathematics	Country code
4.1.6						4.1.1						
2018												
Yes	Yes	Yes	Yes	Yes	Yes	...	...	...	...	48	58	ALB
No	No	No	No	No	No	...	...	...	...	...	...	AND
No	No	Yes	Yes	Yes	Yes	...	...	98_{-2}	...	76	79	AUT
No	No	Yes	No	Yes	Yes	...	...	...	...	77	71	BLR
Yes	Yes	Yes	Yes	Yes	Yes	...	...	...	...	79	80	BEL
No	No	Yes	Yes	Yes	Yes	...	...	...	...	...	...	BMU
No	No	No	No	Yes	Yes	...	...	...	...	46	42	BIH
No	No	Yes	Yes	Yes	Yes	...	...	95_{-2}	75_{-3}	53	56	BGR
Yes	Yes	No	No	Yes	Yes	96_{-2}	69_{-3}	...	...	86	84	CAN
No	No	No	Yes	Yes	Yes	...	...	...	67_{-3}	78	69	HRV
Yes	Yes	Yes	Yes	Yes	Yes	97_{-2}	78_{-3}	...	...	79	80	CZE
Yes	Yes	Yes	Yes	Yes	Yes	97_{-2}	80_{-3}	...	...	84	85	DNK
Yes	Yes	Yes	Yes	Yes	Yes	...	...	...	...	89	90	EST
Yes	Yes	No	No	Yes	Yes	98_{-2}	82_{-3}	...	...	86	85	FIN
Yes	Yes	Yes	Yes	Yes	Yes	...	...	94_{-2}	58_{-3}	79	79	FRA
Yes	Yes	Yes	Yes	Yes	Yes	...	...	95_{-2}	77_{-3}	79	79	DEU
No	No	No	No	Yes	Yes	...	...	...	...	69	64	GRC
No	No	Yes	Yes	Yes	Yes	...	...	97_{-2}	75_{-3}	75	67_{-3}	HUN
No	No	No	No	Yes	Yes	...	...	...	...	74	79	ISL
Yes	Yes	Yes	Yes	Yes	Yes	98_{-2}	84_{-3}	...	...	88	84	IRL
Yes	Yes	Yes	Yes	Yes	Yes	98_{-2}	69_{-3}	...	...	77	62_{-3}	ITA
Yes	No	No	No	Yes	Yes	99_{-2}	...	...	...	78	83	LVA
No	No	No	No	No	No	...	...	...	...	...	...	LIE
Yes	Yes	Yes	Yes	Yes	Yes	...	...	97_{-2}	81_{-3}	76	74	LTU
Yes	Yes	Yes	Yes	Yes	Yes	...	...	...	...	71	73	LUX
Yes	No	No	Yes	Yes	Yes	73_{-2}	...	...	...	64	62_{-3}	MLT
No	No	No	No	No	No	...	...	...	...	...	...	MCO
No	No	No	No	Yes	Yes	...	...	...	...	56	54	MNE
Yes	Yes	Yes	Yes	Yes	Yes	99_{-2}	83_{-3}	...	...	76	84	NLD
Yes	Yes	Yes	Yes	Yes	Yes	...	...	...	...	45	39	MKD
Yes	Yes	Yes	Yes	Yes	Yes	99_{-2}	86_{-3}	...	70_{-3}	81	81	NOR
Yes	Yes	No	No	Yes	Yes	98_{-2}	80_{-3}	...	...	85	85	POL
Yes	Yes	Yes	Yes	Yes	Yes	97_{-2}	82_{-3}	...	...	80	77	PRT
No	No	No	No	Yes	Yes	...	...	...	...	57	50	MDA
Yes	Yes	Yes	Yes	Yes	Yes	...	...	...	...	59	53	ROU
No	No	Yes	Yes	Yes	Yes	...	...	99_{-2}	89_{-3}	78	78	RUS
No	No	No	No	No	No	...	...	...	...	...	...	SMR
No	No	No	Yes	No	Yes	...	...	...	72_{-3}	62	60	SRB
No	No	Yes	Yes	Yes	Yes	...	...	93_{-2}	65_{-3}	69	75	SVK
Yes	Yes	Yes	Yes	Yes	Yes	96_{-2}	75_{-3}	...	...	82	84	SVN
Yes	Yes	Yes	Yes	Yes	Yes	97_{-2}	67_{-3}	...	...	84_{-3}	75	ESP
Yes	Yes	Yes	Yes	Yes	Yes	98_{-2}	75_{-3}	...	...	82	81	SWE
No	No	No	No	Yes	Yes	...	...	...	...	76	83	CHE
No	No	Yes	Yes	Yes	Yes	...	...	...	...	74	64	UKR
Yes	Yes	Yes	Yes	Yes	Yes	...	...	...	...	83	81	GBR
Yes	Yes	No	No	Yes	Yes	96_{-2}	79_{-3}	...	...	81	73	USA

TABLE 3: SDG 4, Target 4.2 – Early childhood

By 2030, ensure that all girls and boys have access to quality early childhood development, care and pre-primary education so that they are ready for primary education

	A	B	C	D	E	F
	Children under 5 developmentally on track (%)	Under-5 stunting (%)	Stimulating home environment (%)	Children under 5 with 3+ children's books (%)	GER pre-primary (%)	NERA one year before primary entry (%)
SDG indicator	4.2.1		4.2.3		4.2.4	4.2.2
Reference year			2018			
Region			Weighted average			
World	...	22	...	...	52ᵢ	67ᵢ
Sub-Saharan Africa	60ᵢ	32	51ᵢ	3ᵢ	33ᵢ	42ᵢ
Northern Africa and Western Asia	...	16	...	...	32ᵢ	50ᵢ
Northern Africa	...	17	...	...	41	54ᵢ
Western Asia	...	15	...	...	26ᵢ	45ᵢ
Central and Southern Asia	...	32	...	...	26ᵢ	59ᵢ
Central Asia	85ᵢ	11	84ᵢ	45ᵢ	36	47
Southern Asia	...	33	...	...	26ᵢ	59ᵢ
Eastern and South-eastern Asia	...	13	...	...	82	87₋₂ᵢ
Eastern Asia	...	5	...	...	87	...
South-eastern Asia	88	25	65ᵢ	25ᵢ	68	91ᵢ
Oceania		38	...	...	76ᵢ	80ᵢ
Latin America and the Caribbean	...	9	...	...	78ᵢ	96ᵢ
Caribbean	72	8	63	17	...	...
Central America	82	13	75	34	69	95
South America	...	7	...	...	85ᵢ	96ᵢ
Europe and Northern America	...	4ᵢ	...	...	86ᵢ	94ᵢ
Europe	...	...	...	...	92ᵢ	95ᵢ
Northern America	...	3	...	...	73ᵢ	91
Low income	60ᵢ	34	50ᵢ	3ᵢ	24ᵢ	41ᵢ
Middle income	...	22	...	...	54ᵢ	69ᵢ
Lower middle	...	31	...	...	37ᵢ	61ᵢ
Upper middle	...	6	...	...	78ᵢ	83ᵢ
High income	...	3	...	...	83ᵢ	91ᵢ

A Percentage of children aged 36 to 59 months who are developmentally on track in health, learning and psychosocial well-being [UNICEF Early Childhood Development Index (ECDI)].

B Under-5 moderate or severe stunting rate (%) [Source: UNICEF, WHO, World Bank Joint Child Malnutrition Estimates (JME)].
    (Regional aggregates are weighted averages of statistical JME estimates for the reference year, not of the observed country values in the country table; Eastern Asia excludes Japan, Oceania excludes Australia and New Zealand, Northern America is based only on United States.)

C Percentage of children aged 36 to 59 months experiencing positive and stimulating home learning environments [Source: UNICEF database].

D Percentage of children under age 5 living in households with three or more children's books [Source: UNICEF database].

E Gross enrolment ratio (GER) in pre-primary education.

F Adjusted net enrolment rate (NERA) one year before the official primary school entry age.

Source: UIS unless noted otherwise. Data refer to school year ending in 2018 unless noted otherwise.

Aggregates represent countries listed in the table with available data and may include estimates for countries with no recent data.

(-) Magnitude nil or negligible.

(...) Data not available or category not applicable.

(± n) Reference year differs (e.g. -2: reference year 2016 instead of 2018).

(i) Estimate and/or partial coverage.

TABLE 3: Continued

	A	B	C	D	E	F	
	Children under 5 developmentally on track (%)	Under-5 stunting (%)	Stimulating home environment (%)	Children under 5 with 3+ children's books (%)	GER pre-primary (%)	NERA one year before primary entry (%)	Country code
SDG indicator	4.2.1		4.2.3		4.2.4	4.2.2	
Reference year				2018			
Sub-Saharan Africa							
Angola	...	38_{-2}	...	...	40_{-2}	65_{-2i}	AGO
Benin	61_{-4}	32	39	2	25	85	BEN
Botswana	...	...	...	...	21_{-3}	21_{-3i}	BWA
Burkina Faso	...	21_{-1}	...	...	4	16	BFA
Burundi	41_{-1}	56_{-2}	58_{-1}	0.1_{-1}	15	45	BDI
Cabo Verde	...	...	...	...	73	81	CPV
Cameroon	61_{-4}	32_{-4}	44_{-4}	4_{-4}	34	45_{-1}	CMR
Central African Republic	...	...	...	...	3_{-1}	...	CAF
Chad	33_{-3}	40_{-3}	46_{-3}	1_{-3}	1_{-2}	10_{-2}	TCD
Comoros	...	...	...	...	22	30	COM
Congo	61_{-3}	21_{-3}	59_{-3}	3_{-3}	...	...	COG
Côte d'Ivoire	63_{-2}	22_{-2}	29_{-2}	1_{-2}	8	22_{-1}	CIV
D. R. Congo	66_{-4}	...	52_{-4}	1_{-4}	4_{-3}	...	COD
Djibouti	...	...	...	...	9_{+1}	12_{+1}	DJI
Equat. Guinea	...	...	...	...	43_{-3}	44_{-3}	GNQ
Eritrea	...	...	...	...	23	27	ERI
Eswatini	65_{-4}	26_{-4}	...	...	...	...	SWZ
Ethiopia	...	38_{-2}	...	...	29_{-3}	37_{-3}	ETH
Gabon	...	...	...	...	...	...	GAB
Gambia	...	...	...	...	42	...	GMB
Ghana	...	19_{-4}	...	...	115	87_{+1}	GHA
Guinea	49_{-2}	32_{-2}	31_{-2}	0.4_{-2}	...	42_{-2}	GIN
Guinea-Bissau	61_{-4}	28_{-4}	34_{-4}	$-_{4}$	...	...	GNB
Kenya	...	26_{-4}	...	...	76_{-2}	...	KEN
Lesotho	...	33_{-4}	...	...	39_{-2}	42_{-2}	LSO
Liberia	...	...	...	...	125_{-1}	79_{-1}	LBR
Madagascar	...	...	...	...	40	61	MDG
Malawi	60_{-4}	37_{-3}	29_{-4}	1_{-4}	84_{-3}	...	MWI
Mali	62_{-3}	30_{-3}	55_{-3}	0.3_{-3}	7	45	MLI
Mauritania	60_{-3}	28_{-3}	44_{-3}	1_{-3}	10_{-3}	...	MRT
Mauritius	...	...	...	...	98	89	MUS
Mozambique	...	...	...	...	...	...	MOZ
Namibia	...	...	...	...	34	69	NAM
Niger	...	41_{-2}	...	...	8	22_{-1}	NER
Nigeria	61_{-1}	44_{-2}	63_{-2}	6_{-2}	...	...	NGA
Rwanda	63_{-3}	38_{-3}	44_{-3}	1_{-3}	22	48	RWA
Sao Tome and Principe	54_{-4}	17_{-4}	63_{-4}	6_{-4}	50_{-2}	52_{-3}	STP
Senegal	67_{-1}	16_{-1}	29_{-1}	1_{-1}	17	$16i$	SEN
Seychelles	...	...	...	...	95	95	SYC
Sierra Leone	51_{-1}	...	19_{-1}	2_{-1}	14	42	SLE
Somalia	...	...	...	...	...	...	SOM
South Africa	...	27_{-2}	...	...	25_{-1}	...	ZAF
South Sudan	...	...	...	...	11_{-3}	21_{-3i}	SSD
Togo	51_{-4}	28_{-4}	26_{-4}	1_{-4}	23	97	TGO
Uganda	63_{-2}	29_{-2}	53_{-2}	2_{-2}	14_{-1}	...	UGA
United Republic of Tanzania	...	34_{-3}	...	...	41	55	TZA
Zambia	...	...	...	...	8_{-2}	...	ZMB
Zimbabwe	62_{-4}	27_{-3}	43_{-4}	3_{-4}	...	...	ZWE

TABLE 3: Continued

	A Children under 5 developmentally on track (%)	B Under-5 stunting (%)	C Stimulating home environment (%)	D Children under 5 with 3+ children's books (%)	E GER pre-primary (%)	F NERA one year before primary entry (%)	Country code
SDG indicator	4.2.1		4.2.3		4.2.4	4.2.2	
Reference year				2018			
Northern Africa and Western Asia							
Algeria	...	...	...	...	...	...	DZA
Armenia	...	9_{-2}	...	...	38	48	ARM
Azerbaijan	...	...	...	...	40_i	69_i	AZE
Bahrain	...	...	...	...	54	71	BHR
Cyprus	...	...	...	...	84_{-1i}	96_{-1i}	CYP
Egypt	...	22_{-4}	...	...	29	37	EGY
Georgia	88_{-3}	...	83_{-3}	58_{-3}	...	...	GEO
Iraq	79	...	44	3	...	...	IRQ
Israel	...	...	...	...	111_{-1}	99_{-1}	ISR
Jordan	...	...	92	16	27	43	JOR
Kuwait	...	5_{-3}	...	...	62	81	KWT
Lebanon	...	...	...	...	...	...	LBN
Libya	...	...	...	...	...	...	LBY
Morocco	...	...	36	...	51	50	MAR
Oman	68_{-4}	14_{-4}	81_{-4}	25_{-4}	52	81	OMN
Palestine	72_{-4}	7_{-4}	78_{-4}	20_{-4}	56	68	PSE
Qatar	...	...	...	...	60	92	QAT
Saudi Arabia	...	...	...	...	21	46	SAU
Sudan	...	38_{-4}	...	2_{-4}	47_{-1}	...	SDN
Syrian Arab Republic	...	...	...	...	...	...	SYR
Tunisia	...	...	...	...	45_{-2}	...	TUN
Turkey	...	...	...	...	33_{-1}	68_{-1}	TUR
United Arab Emirates	...	...	...	...	78_{-1}	99_{-1}	ARE
Yemen	...	...	...	...	2_{-2}	...	YEM
Central and Southern Asia							
Afghanistan	...	...	...	...	...	...	AFG
Bangladesh	...	36_{-4}	...	...	41	...	BGD
Bhutan	...	...	...	...	34	35	BTN
India	...	38_{-3}	...	...	14_{-1}	...	IND
Iran, Islamic Republic of	...	...	...	...	54_{-2}	51_{-2}	IRN
Kazakhstan	86_{-3}	8_{-3}	86_{-3}	51_{-3}	62_{+1}	90_{+1}	KAZ
Kyrgyzstan	78_{-4}	13_{-4}	72_{-4}	27_{-4}	40	91	KGZ
Maldives	...	...	96_{-1}	59_{-1}	92_{-1}	96_{-1}	MDV
Nepal	64_{-4}	36_{-2}	67_{-4}	5_{-4}	87_{+1}	87_{+1}	NPL
Pakistan	...	38	...	...	83	94	PAK
Sri Lanka	...	17_{-2}	...	...	91_{-3}	...	LKA
Tajikistan	...	18_{-1}	...	...	10_{-1}	12_{-1}	TJK
Turkmenistan	91_{-2}	12_{-3}	94_{-2}	48_{-2}	58_{-4}	...	TKM
Uzbekistan	...	...	...	...	28	37	UZB
Eastern and South-eastern Asia							
Brunei Darussalam	...	...	...	...	...	...	BRN
Cambodia	...	36_{-4}	...	...	41	...	KHM
China	...	...	...	...	34	35	CHN
DPR Korea	...	38_{-3}	...	...	14_{-1}	...	PRK
Hong Kong, China	...	...	...	...	54_{-2}	51_{-2}	HKG
Indonesia	86_{-3}	8_{-3}	86_{-3}	51_{-3}	62_{+1}	90_{+1}	IDN
Japan	78_{-4}	13_{-4}	72_{-4}	27_{-4}	40	91	JPN
Lao PDR	...	...	96_{-1}	59_{-1}	92_{-1}	96_{-1}	LAO
Macao, China	64_{-4}	36_{-2}	67_{-4}	5_{-4}	87_{+1}	87_{+1}	MAC
Malaysia	...	38	...	...	83	94	MYS
Mongolia	...	17_{-2}	...	...	91_{-3}	...	MNG
Myanmar	...	18_{-1}	...	...	10_{-1}	12_{-1}	MMR
Philippines	91_{-2}	12_{-3}	94_{-2}	48_{-2}	58_{-4}	...	PHL
Republic of Korea	...	...	...	...	28	37	KOR
Singapore							SGP
Thailand							THA
Timor-Leste							TLS
Viet Nam							VNM

TABLE 3: Continued

	A	B	C	D	E	F	
	Children under 5 developmentally on track (%)	Under-5 stunting (%)	Stimulating home environment (%)	Children under 5 with 3+ children's books (%)	GER pre-primary (%)	NERA one year before primary entry (%)	Country code
SDG indicator	4.2.1		4.2.3		4.2.4	4.2.2	
Reference year				2018			
Oceania							
Australia	...	...	...	...	165[-1]	86[-1]	AUS
Cook Islands	...	...	...	...	94[-2]	98[-2]	COK
Fiji	...	...	...	...	...	...	FJI
Kiribati	...	...	...	...	...	...	KIR
Marshall Islands	79[-1]	35[-1]	72[-1]	18[-1]	38[-2]	63[-2]	MHL
Micronesia, F. S.	...	...	...	...	31[-3]	73[-3]	FSM
Nauru	...	...	...	...	82[-2]	98[-2]	NRU
New Zealand	...	...	...	...	91[-2]	92[-2]	NZL
Niue	...	...	...	...	115[-2]	63[-3]	NIU
Palau	...	...	...	...	72[-4]	91[-4]	PLW
Papua New Guinea	...	...	...	...	43[-2]	71[-2]	PNG
Samoa	...	5[-4]	...	...	49	38	WSM
Solomon Is	...	32[-3]	...	...	84	59	SLB
Tokelau	...	...	...	...	124[-2]	88[-2]	TKL
Tonga	...	...	...	...	46[-3]	...	TON
Tuvalu	...	...	...	...	83	88[i]	TUV
Vanuatu	...	...	...	...	90[-3]	...	VUT
Latin America and the Caribbean							
Anguilla	...	...	...	...	...	...	AIA
Antigua and Barbuda	...	...	...	...	70	91	ATG
Argentina	...	...	...	...	76[-1]	98[-1]	ARG
Aruba	...	...	...	...	106[-4]	100[-4]	ABW
Bahamas	...	...	...	...	35	38	BHS
Barbados	...	...	...	...	87	...	BRB
Belize	82[-3]	15[-3]	88[-3]	44[-3]	47	86	BLZ
Bolivia, P. S.	...	16[-2]	...	...	74	90	BOL
Brazil	...	...	...	...	96[-1i]	98[-1i]	BRA
British Virgin Islands	...	...	...	...	132[-1]	99[-1]	VGB
Cayman Islands	...	...	...	...	...	...	CYM
Chile	...	2[-4]	...	...	82[-1]	94[-1]	CHL
Colombia	...	...	...	...	...	99	COL
Costa Rica	...	...	...	...	98	97	CRI
Cuba	89[-4]	...	89[-4]	48[-4]	98	100	CUB
Curaçao	...	...	...	...	...	...	CUW
Dominica	...	...	...	...	96[-2]	77[-3]	DMA
Dominican Republic	84[-4]	...	58[-4]	10[-4]	51[i]	88[i]	DOM
Ecuador	...	24[-4]	...	...	66	95	ECU
El Salvador	81[-4]	14[-4]	59[-4]	18[-4]	67	82	SLV
Grenada	...	...	...	...	100	90[-1]	GRD
Guatemala	...	47[-3]	...	...	51	85	GTM
Guyana	86[-4]	11[-4]	87[-4]	47[-4]	...	...	GUY
Haiti	55[-1]	22[-1]	54[-1]	8[-1]	...	...	HTI
Honduras	...	...	...	...	41[-1]	78[-1]	HND
Jamaica	...	6[-4]	...	...	73	91	JAM
Mexico	82[-3]	10[-2]	76[-3]	35[-3]	74[-1]	99[-1]	MEX
Montserrat	...	...	...	...	73	93	MSR
Nicaragua	...	...	...	...	...	...	NIC
Panama	...	...	...	...	62[-1]	76[-1]	PAN
Paraguay	82[-2]	6[-2]	64[-2]	23[-2]	44[-2]	69[-2]	PRY
Peru	...	13[-1]	...	...	104	99	PER
Saint Kitts and Nevis	...	...	...	...	90[-2]	89[-2]	KNA
Saint Lucia	...	...	...	...	74	96	LCA
Saint Vincent/Grenadines	...	...	...	...	76	95[-1]	VCT
Sint Maarten	...	...	...	...	78[-4]	95[-4]	SXM
Suriname	...	...	...	...	86	90	SUR
Trinidad and Tobago	...	...	...	...	...	...	TTO
Turks and Caicos Islands	...	...	...	...	...	...	TCA
Uruguay	...	...	...	...	93[-1]	98[-1]	URY
Venezuela, B. R.	...	...	...	...	70[-1]	86[-1]	VEN

	A	B	C	D	E	F	
	Children under 5 developmentally on track (%)	Under-5 stunting (%)	Stimulating home environment (%)	Children under 5 with 3+ children's books (%)	GER pre-primary (%)	NERA one year before primary entry (%)	Country code
SDG indicator	4.2.1		4.2.3		4.2.4	4.2.2	
Reference year				2018			
Europe and Northern America							
Albania	...	11₋₁	78	...	80	88₋₃	ALB
Andorra	...	...	...	...	...	...	AND
Austria	...	...	...	...	104₋₁	100₋₁	AUT
Belarus	...	...	...	...	99	98	BLR
Belgium	...	...	...	...	115₋₁	98₋₁	BEL
Bermuda	...	...	...	...	69₋₃	...	BMU
Bosnia and Herzegovina	...	...	...	...	...	...	BIH
Bulgaria	...	...	...	...	77₋₁	84₋₁	BGR
Canada	...	...	...	...	...	...	CAN
Croatia	...	...	...	...	70₋₁	99₋₁	HRV
Czechia	...	...	...	...	106₋₁	89₋₁	CZE
Denmark	...	...	...	...	96₋₁	94₋₁	DNK
Estonia	...	...	...	...	92₋₁	93₋₁	EST
Finland	...	...	...	...	84₋₁	99₋₁	FIN
France	...	...	...	...	106₋₁ᵢ	100₋₁ᵢ	FRA
Germany	...	...	...	...	109₋₁	99₋₁	DEU
Greece	...	...	...	...	74₋₁	93₋₁	GRC
Hungary	...	...	...	...	82₋₁	87₋₁	HUN
Iceland	...	...	...	...	94₋₁	94₋₁	ISL
Ireland	...	...	...	...	163₋₁ᵢ	100₋₁ᵢ	IRL
Italy	...	...	...	...	94₋₁	94₋₁	ITA
Latvia	...	...	...	...	96₋₁ᵢ	98₋₁ᵢ	LVA
Liechtenstein	...	...	...	...	103₋₁ᵢ	100₋₂ᵢ	LIE
Lithuania	...	...	...	...	88₋₁ᵢ	100₋₁ᵢ	LTU
Luxembourg	...	...	...	...	92₋₁	98₋₁	LUX
Malta	...	...	...	...	108₋₁	100₋₁	MLT
Monaco	...	...	...	...	...	...	MCO
Montenegro	...	...	...	...	69	75	MNE
Netherlands	...	...	...	...	94₋₁	100₋₁	NLD
North Macedonia	...	...	...	...	41₋₁	46₋₁	MKD
Norway	...	...	...	...	95₋₁	96₋₁	NOR
Poland	...	3₋₄	...	...	81₋₁	99₋₁	POL
Portugal	...	...	...	...	94₋₁	99₋₁	PRT
Republic of Moldova	...	...	...	...	87ᵢ	93ᵢ	MDA
Romania	...	...	...	...	84₋₁	78₋₁	ROU
Russian Federation	...	...	...	...	87₋₁	93₋₁	RUS
San Marino	...	...	...	...	96	94ᵢ	SMR
Serbia	95₋₄	6₋₄	96₋₄	72₋₄	62ᵢ	94ᵢ	SRB
Slovakia	...	...	...	...	95₋₁	82₋₁	SVK
Slovenia	...	...	...	...	92₋₁	94₋₁	SVN
Spain	...	...	...	...	92₋₁	93₋₁	ESP
Sweden	...	...	...	...	96₋₁	100₋₁	SWE
Switzerland	...	...	...	...	104₋₁	99₋₁	CHE
Ukraine	...	...	...	...	...	...	UKR
United Kingdom	...	...	...	...	106₋₁	100₋₁	GBR
United States	...	4₋₂	...	...	73₋₁ᵢ	...	USA

TABLE 4: SDG 4, Target 4.3 – Technical, vocational, tertiary and adult education

By 2030, ensure equal access for all women and men to affordable and quality technical, vocational and tertiary education, including university

SDG 4, Target 4.4 – Skills for work

By 2030, substantially increase the number of youth and adults who have relevant skills, including technical and vocational skills, for employment, decent jobs and entrepreneurship

	A	B	C	D	E	F	G % of adults 15+ with ICT skills			H % of adults 25+ having attained at least			
	Participation in adult education & training (%)	% of youth enrolled in TVET	TVET share of secondary enrolment (%)	Transition from upper secondary to tertiary (%)	Gross entry ratio into tertiary (%)	GER tertiary (%)	Copy & paste within document	Use formula in spreadsheet	Write computer program	Primary	Lower secondary	Upper secondary	Post-secondary
SDG indicator:	4.3.1	4.3.3				4.3.2	4.4.1			4.4.3			
Reference year:	2018						2018						
Region	Weighted average						Weighted average						
World	...	5i	11i	97	49	38i	...	...	...	...	...	...	...
Sub-Saharan Africa	...	1i	6i	...	...	9i	...	...	...	...	...	25i	8i
Northern Africa and Western Asia	...	8i	14i	91	55	46i	40	21	7	87i	69i	57i	23i
Northern Africa	...	7i	14i	57	36	35i	33	11	4	...	70i	67i	13i
Western Asia	24i	9i	13i	115i	75i	56i	47	31	9	88i	69i	52i	28i
Central and Southern Asia	...	1i	3i	121	40	26	...	...	...	...	...	...	...
Central Asia	...	13i	18i	24	34	24	19	19	...	100	99	94	63
Southern Asia	...	1i	3i	124	41	26	...	...	...	...	...	...	...
Eastern and South-eastern Asia	...	6	16	83	57	45	...	...	...	...	...	...	...
Eastern Asia	...	6	18	85	63	51	...	...	...	...	...	...	...
South-eastern Asia	...	6i	12i	77i	43	34i	40i	10i	...	77	52	36i	14i
Oceania	...	12i	28i	...	...	73i	...	...	...	100i	94	76	48
Latin America and the Caribbean	...	7i	13i	90i	...	52i	...	...	...	81	60	45	18
Caribbean	...	7i	17i	94i	...	...	...	...	...	...	...	...	...
Central America	...	11	27	80	49	37	...	26	9	79	58	34	15
South America	...	5i	8	...	...	59i	25	17	4	83	61	50	19
Europe and Northern America	44i	11i	16i	78	67i	77i	52i	35i	...	...	...	...	...
Europe	44	18i	24i	86	76	72i	52	35	...	...	...	...	...
Northern America	...	-i	0.5i	64	...	86i	...	...	...	99	96	...	...
Low income	...	1i	5i	...	11i	9i	...	...	...	...	...	...	...
Middle income	...	4i	10i	103	50i	36	...	...	...	...	57i	...	...
Lower middle	...	3i	6i	111i	39	25	...	...	...	...	50i	...	14i
Upper middle	...	7i	15i	93	66	53i	...	...	...	...	64i	...	...
High income	48i	10i	15i	72	61i	75i	...	...	...	...	...	...	...

A Participation rate of adults (25 to 64) in formal or non-formal education and training in the last 12 months (%).

 Estimates based on other reference periods, in particular 4 weeks, are included in the country when no data are available on the last 12 months, but not in regional aggregates.

B Percentage of youth (15 to 24) enrolled in technical and vocational education and training (TVET) programmes (ISCED levels 2 to 5) (%).

C Share of technical and vocational education and training (TVET) in total secondary enrolment (%).

D Gross transition ratio from secondary (all programmes) to tertiary education (ISCED levels 5 to 7).

E Gross entry ratio to first tertiary programmes (ISCED levels 5 to 7).

F Gross enrolment ratio (GER) in tertiary education.

G Percentage of adults (15 and over) with specific information and communication technology (ICT) skills.

H Percentage of adults (25 and over) who have attained at least a given level of education.

I Percentage of population of a given age group achieving at least a fixed level of proficiency in functional literacy and numeracy skills.

J Literacy rate, among youth (15 to 24) and adults (15 and above).

K Number of youth and adult illiterates, and percentage female.

Source: UIS unless noted otherwise. Data refer to school year ending in 2018 unless noted otherwise.

Aggregates include countries listed in the table with available data and may include estimations for countries with no recent data.

(-) Magnitude nil or negligible.

(…) Data not available or category not applicable.

(± n) Reference year differs (e.g. -2: reference year 2016 instead of 2018).

(i) Estimate and/or partial coverage.

SDG 4, Target 4.6 – Literacy and numeracy

By 2030, ensure that all youth and a substantial proportion of adults, both men and women, achieve literacy and numeracy

	I				J		K			
	% achieving proficiency in				Literacy rate (%)		Illiterates			
	Literacy		Numeracy				% female		Number (000,000)	
	Youth	Adults	Youth	Adults	Youth	Adults	Youth	Adults	Youth	Adults
	4.6.1				4.6.2					
					2018					
	Weighted average								Sum	
	...	...	...	...	92	86	56	63	100	773
	...	...	...	...	77	66	56	61	48	204
	...	...	...	...	89	80	57	63	9	70
	...	...	...	...	89	73	51	62	4	44
	...	56ᵢ	...	51ᵢ	89	86	62	63	5	27
	...	...	...	...	90	74	57	64	36	368
	...	...	...	...	100	100	45	64	-	0.1
	...	...	...	...	90	73	57	64	36	368
	...	...	...	...	99	96	48	69	3	78
	...	...	...	...	100	97	47	73	1	47
	...	...	...	...	98	94	49	64	3	30
	...	...	...	...	...	...	...	...	...	...
	...	...	...	...	99	94	43	55	2	30
	...	...	...	...	...	...	...	...	...	3ᵢ
	...	...	...	...	98	93	46	60	1	8
	...	...	...	...	99	95	38	53	1	18
	...	...	...	...	...	...	...	...	0.1ᵢ	2ᵢ
	...	...	...	...	...	...	...	...	0.1ᵢ	2ᵢ
	...	...	...	...	...	...	...	...	...	...
	...	...	...	...	76	63	56	62	36	157
	...	...	...	...	93	86	56	63	62	581
	...	...	...	...	90	77	56	63	56	481
	...	...	...	...	98	95	49	65	6	100
	...	...	...	...	...	...	43ᵢ	55ᵢ	0.2ᵢ	5ᵢ

Country or territory	A Participation in adult education & training (%)	B % of youth enrolled in TVET	C TVET share of secondary enrolment (%)	D Transition from upper secondary to tertiary (%)	E Gross entry ratio into tertiary (%)	F GER tertiary (%)	G % of adults 15+ with ICT skills — Copy & paste within document	G — Use formula in spreadsheet	G — Write computer program	H % of adults 25+ having attained at least — Primary	H — Lower secondary	H — Upper secondary	H — Post-secondary
SDG indicator:	4.3.1	4.3.3				4.3.2	4.4.1			4.4.3			
Reference year:			2018					2018					
Sub-Saharan Africa													
Angola	...	...	14-2	...	10-3	9-2	...	...	...	44-4	29-4	16-4	3-4
Benin	...	1-2	3-2	...	17-1	12-1	...	...	...	...	...	...	...
Botswana	...	...	...	...	45-4	25-1	31-4	20-4	5-4	...	...	...	...
Burkina Faso	...	1-1	2	...	...	7	...	...	...	...	8-4	3-4	--4
Burundi	2-4	3	10	9-1	2-1	6-1	...	...	...	11-4	6-4	3-4	1-4
Cabo Verde	...	1	2	63	30	24	38-3	22-3	5-3	52-3	29-3	20-3	12-3
Cameroon	...	7-2	22-2	159-2i	19-1	13-1	...	...	...	...	...	...	...
Central African Republic	...	...	4-1	...	...	...	...	...	...	...	...	...	...
Chad	...	--2	1-2	...	...	3-3	...	...	...	...	...	...	...
Comoros	...	-	-	...	13-4	9-4	...	...	...	...	...	...	...
Congo	...	...	...	...	...	13-1	...	...	...	...	...	...	...
Côte d'Ivoire	...	2	6	...	...	9-1	11-1	3-1	1-1	35-4	21-4	11-4	5-4
D. R. Congo	...	...	19-3	...	10-2	7-2	...	...	...	64-2	51-2	27-2	9-2
Djibouti	...	...	7+1	...	...	...	16-1	12-1	4-1	...	...	...	...
Equat. Guinea	...	...	...	...	...	...	...	...	...	...	...	...	...
Eritrea	...	0.5	1	18-2	4-2	3-2	...	...	...	...	...	...	...
Eswatini	2-2	--3	4-2	...	...	...	...	...	...	...	...	...	...
Ethiopia	...	2-3i	7-3	...	...	8-4	...	...	...	...	...	...	...
Gabon	...	...	...	...	...	...	...	...	...	...	...	...	...
Gambia	...	...	...	...	...	...	...	...	...	39-3	31-3	23-3	8-3
Ghana	2-1	1+1	3+1	38	20	16	...	...	...	...	...	...	...
Guinea	...	1-4	4-4	...	18-4	12-4	...	...	...	16-4	11-4	7-4	5-4
Guinea-Bissau	...	...	...	...	...	...	...	...	...	...	...	...	...
Kenya	...	...	...	...	...	11-1	...	...	...	...	...	...	...
Lesotho	...	1-3i	2-1	...	14	10	...	...	...	...	...	...	...
Liberia	...	...	...	...	...	...	...	...	...	...	...	...	...
Madagascar	...	1	2	80	9	5	...	...	...	...	...	...	...
Malawi	1-1	-	...	...	...	...	...	...	...	...	...	...	...
Mali	1-2	4	12	...	...	5-1	...	...	...	16	10	7	6
Mauritania	...	0.1	0.5	...	6-1	5-1	...	...	...	...	...	...	...
Mauritius	2-1	2	10	...	...	41-1	...	...	...	...	...	43	14
Mozambique	...	1-3	9-1	45-2	8	7	...	...	...	46-1	15-1	9-1	2-1
Namibia	7	...	...	...	38-1	23-1	...	...	...	...	...	...	...
Niger	...	1-1	7-1	...	4	4	8-1	1-1	1-1	...	...	...	...
Nigeria	...	...	...	...	...	...	...	...	...	...	...	...	...
Rwanda	3-1	4	13	28-1	7-1	7	...	...	...	36	13	10	4
Sao Tome and Principe	...	5-3i	6-1	...	...	13-3	...	...	...	...	...	...	...
Senegal	6-3	--1	2	...	...	13	...	...	...	22-1	18-1	11-1	10-1
Seychelles	...	14	1	10	25	17	...	...	...	...	...	...	...
Sierra Leone	3-4	...	...	...	...	...	...	...	...	...	...	...	...
Somalia	...	...	...	...	...	...	...	...	...	...	...	...	...
South Africa	3	5-1	7-1	...	...	22-1	...	...	...	82-3	77-3	65-3	15-3
South Sudan	...	...	...	...	...	...	...	...	...	...	...	...	...
Togo	...	3-1	6-1	...	...	15	4-1	1-1	--1	...	...	...	...
Uganda	...	...	...	...	...	5-4	...	...	...	...	...	...	...
United Republic of Tanzania	...	0.1-1	0.4	...	...	4-3	...	...	...	...	...	...	...
Zambia	3-1	...	...	...	...	...	...	...	...	...	...	...	...
Zimbabwe	...	...	...	...	...	10-3	4-4	2-4	1-4	82-1	65-1	12-1	9-1

% achieving proficiency in				Literacy rate (%)		Illiterates				Country code
Literacy		Numeracy		Literacy rate (%)		% female		Number (000)		
Youth	Adults	Youth	Adults	Youth	Adults	Youth	Adults	Youth	Adults	
				2018						
...	...	...	...	77-4	66-4	66-4	71-4	1,165-4	4,778-4	AGO
...	...	...	...	61i	42i	61i	61i	890i	3,810i	BEN
...	...	...	...	...	...	...	...	...	...	BWA
...	...	...	...	58i	41i	53i	58i	1,652i	6,391i	BFA
...	...	...	...	88-1	68-1	62-1	63-1	248-1	1,851-1	BDI
...	...	...	...	98-3	87-3	34-3	68-3	2-3	48-3	CPV
...	...	...	...	85i	77i	59i	62i	745i	3,317i	CMR
...	...	...	...	38i	37i	58i	60i	623i	1,627i	CAF
...	...	...	...	31-2	22-2	57-2	56-2	2,021-2	5,903-2	TCD
...	...	...	...	78i	59i	49i	57i	35i	207i	COM
...	...	...	...	82i	80i	59i	65i	176i	602i	COG
...	...	...	...	58i	47i	57i	56i	2,154i	7,691i	CIV
...	...	...	...	85-2	77-2	69-2	75-2	2,181-2	9,561-2	COD
...	...	...	...	...	...	...	...	...	...	DJI
...	...	...	...	...	...	...	...	...	...	GNQ
...	...	...	...	93i	77i	54i	67i	42i	470i	ERI
...	...	...	...	95i	88i	36i	52i	11i	81i	SWZ
...	...	...	...	73-1i	52-1i	51-1i	58-1i	6,273-1i	30,147-1i	ETH
...	...	...	...	90i	85i	42i	53i	37i	205i	GAB
...	...	...	...	67-3	51-3	55-3	61-3	140-3	562-3	GMB
...	...	...	...	92i	79i	51i	60i	435i	3,894i	GHA
...	...	...	...	46-4	32-4	59-4	62-4	1,239-4	4,156-4	GIN
...	...	...	...	60-4i	46-4i	64-4i	67-4i	136-4i	526-4i	GNB
...	...	...	...	88i	82i	49i	60i	1,291i	5,714i	KEN
...	...	...	...	87-4i	77-4i	23-4i	33-4i	56-4i	317-4i	LSO
...	...	...	...	55-1i	48-1i	60-1i	64-1i	409-1i	1,423-1i	LBR
...	...	...	...	81i	75i	51i	55i	1,017i	3,926i	MDG
...	...	...	...	73-3i	62-3i	50-3i	61-3i	934-3i	3,471-3i	MWI
...	...	...	...	50	35	57	59	1,831	6,422	MLI
...	...	...	...	64-1i	53-1i	59-1i	61-1i	297-1i	1,190-1i	MRT
...	...	...	...	99i	91i	33i	62i	2i	90i	MUS
...	...	...	...	71-1	61-1	61-1	67-1	1,659-1	6,178-1	MOZ
...	...	...	...	95i	92i	40i	53i	24i	131i	NAM
...	...	...	...	...	...	...	...	...	...	NER
...	...	...	...	75i	62i	63i	62i	9,365i	41,764i	NGA
...	...	...	...	86	73	43	59	327	1,968	RWA
...	...	...	...	98i	93i	48i	73i	1i	9i	STP
...	...	...	...	69-1	52-1	60-1	66-1	923-1	4,236-1	SEN
...	...	...	...	99i	96i	21i	43i	0.1i	3i	SYC
...	...	...	...	67i	43i	56i	58i	518i	2,561i	SLE
...	...	...	...	...	...	...	...	...	...	SOM
...	...	...	...	95-1	87-1	33-1	54-1	464-1	5,229-1	ZAF
...	...	...	...	48i	35i	50i	55i	1,157i	4,181i	SSD
...	...	...	...	84-3	64-3	68-3	69-3	224-3	1,522-3	TGO
...	...	...	...	89i	77i	48i	64i	940i	5,323i	UGA
...	...	...	...	86-3	78-3	54-3	62-3	1,417-3	6,240-3	TZA
...	...	...	...	92i	87i	53i	65i	285i	1,266i	ZMB
...	...	...	...	90-4i	89-4i	37-4i	56-4i	267-4i	884-4i	ZWE

Country or territory	A Participation in adult education & training (%)	B % of youth enrolled in TVET	C TVET share of secondary enrolment (%)	D Transition from upper secondary to tertiary (%)	E Gross entry ratio into tertiary (%)	F GER tertiary (%)	G % of adults 15+ with ICT skills Copy & paste within document	G Use formula in spreadsheet	G Write computer program	H % of adults 25+ having attained at least Primary	H Lower secondary	H Upper secondary	H Post-secondary
SDG indicator:	4.3.1	4.3.3				4.3.2	4.4.1			4.4.3			
Reference year:	2018						2018						
Northern Africa and Western Asia													
Algeria	...	...	...	34-4	32-4	51	...	...	...	...	...	...	...
Armenia	...	...	8	129-1	91-1	55	...	...	...	99-1	97-1	90-1	47-1
Azerbaijan	...	15i	16	55-3	33-3i	28i	64-1	21-1	1-1	98-1	96-1	89-1	30-1
Bahrain	...	4	7	75	67	50	62-1	44-1	20-1	87	80	65	32
Cyprus	48-2	7-1i	9-1	...	...	76-1i	43-2	24-1	3-1	95-2	80-2	71-2	38-2
Egypt	1-1	11	22	49-4	32-4	35-1	41-1	11-2	4-2	...	73-1	67-1	13-1
Georgia	2-1	2	4	...	...	64+1	36-1	12-1	1-1	99-1	98-1	92-1	59-1
Iraq	...	...	...	...	...	...	25-4	7-4	5-4	...	...	...	...
Israel	53-3	17-1	20-1	70-3	...	63-1	...	...	...	96-3	89-3	81-3	47-3
Jordan	...	1	3	...	...	34	98-2	87-2	91-2	...	...	...	...
Kuwait	...	"-3	2-3	...	75	54	60-1	...	...	62	56	31	19
Lebanon	...	...	16	...	...	...	...	...	...	...	...	...	...
Libya	...	...	...	...	...	...	...	...	...	...	...	...	...
Morocco	...	6	9	113	55	36	46-1	20-1	7-1	...	...	...	...
Oman	...	0.4	0.4	72	57	38	...	...	...	84-3	66-3	50-3	21-3
Palestine	2	3	1	82	56	44	30-4	17-4	...	95	64	43	26
Qatar	...	1	1	65	33	18	42-1	27-1	5-1	88-1	68-1	41-1	24-1
Saudi Arabia	...	0.3-1	1	67-3	75-3	68	72-1	55-1	10-1	81-1	69-1	54-1	31-1
Sudan	...	...	1-1	...	...	17-1	4-2	2-2	2-2	...	...	...	...
Syrian Arab Republic	...	...	...	...	34-3	40-2	...	...	...	...	...	...	...
Tunisia	...	...	9-2	...	33	32	12-1	6-1	2-1	74-2	45-2	...	15-2
Turkey	21-2	26-1	24-1	138-4	97-1	...	36-4	26-2	3-1	90-1	61-1	39-1	19-1
United Arab Emirates	...	0.5-1	2-1	77-2	46-1	...	64-1	36-1	12-1	91	83	69	55
Yemen	1-4	"-2	0.3-2	...	...	...	...	...	...	...	...	...	...
Central and Southern Asia													
Afghanistan	...	0.2-1i	1	41-4	15-4	10	...	...	...	...	...	...	...
Bangladesh	...	2	5	...	37	21	...	...	...	58	44	31	16
Bhutan	...	"-i	2i	...	...	16	...	...	...	...	...	...	...
India	...	...	2-1	125-2	41	28	...	...	...	...	...	...	...
Iran, Islamic Republic of	...	6-1	13-1	134-1	61-1	68-1	21-1	7-1	1-1	...	70-2	48-2	23-2
Kazakhstan	17-1	19+1	11+1	73+1	117+1	62+1	14-1	34-1	5-1	100	99	97	79
Kyrgyzstan	...	6	8	...	...	41	...	...	...	...	...	...	...
Maldives	9-2	...	...	...	51-1	31-1	...	...	...	...	...	...	...
Nepal	...	"-1	1+1	...	...	12	...	...	...	...	...	...	...
Pakistan	...	1	3	...	...	9	4-2	2-2	2-2	49-1	36-1	27-1	9-1
Sri Lanka	1-2	4	4	...	28	20	...	...	...	...	83	63	...
Tajikistan	...	...	...	"-1	"-1	31-1	...	...	...	...	95-1	81-1	23-1
Turkmenistan	...	...	8-4	...	...	8-4	...	...	...	...	...	...	...
Uzbekistan	...	23-1	35-1	12-1	11-1	10	22	10	...	100	100	96	64
Eastern and South-eastern Asia													
Brunei Darussalam	2-4	7	12	...	...	31	68-2	25-2	17-2	...	...	...	...
Cambodia	...	...	...	...	...	14	27-1	9-1	0.1-1	23-3	12-3	9-3	6-3
China	...	6i	19	85	63	51	...	...	...	...	...	...	...
DPR Korea	...	"-3	...	...	...	27	...	...	...	...	...	...	...
Hong Kong, China	...	3i	2	...	...	77	...	...	...	96-1	79-1	63-1	29-1
Indonesia	1-4	13	20	53	36	36	50-2	8-2	...	78	51	35	10
Japan	...	...	11-1	83-1	...	...	...	...	...	...	...	...	...
Lao PDR	1-1	0.4i	1i	60-2	27	15	...	...	...	...	...	...	...
Macao, China	...	1	4	...	...	91	...	...	...	90-2	73-2	52-2	26-2
Malaysia	...	5	11	59-1	37	45	55-1	25-1	8-1	94-2	74-2	58-2	21-2
Mongolia	1-1	6	6	86	102	66	...	...	...	...	...	...	...
Myanmar	0.4-1	0.3	0.2	223	29	19	...	...	...	...	...	...	...
Philippines	...	"-3	6-1	...	...	35-1	...	...	...	84-1	59-1	...	20-1
Republic of Korea	...	15-1	10-1	...	...	94-1	62-1	44-1	5-1	96-3	86-3	76-3	40-3
Singapore	57-3	"-1i	...	...	...	85-1i	51-1	37-1	6-1	88	81	74	56
Thailand	0.5-2	6-3	10	117-3	76-3	49-2	5-4	...	...	66-2	45-2	33-2	...
Timor-Leste	...	5	9	...	...	...	...	...	...	...	...	...	...
Viet Nam	0.2-3	...	...	111-1	58-1	29-2	...	...	...	...	...	...	...

% achieving proficiency in				Literacy rate (%)		Illiterates				Country code
Literacy		Numeracy		Literacy rate (%)		% female		Number (000)		
Youth	Adults	Youth	Adults	Youth	Adults	Youth	Adults	Youth	Adults	
				2018						
...	...	...	...	97i	81i	52i	66i	156i	5,484i	DZA
...	...	...	...	100-1	100-1	40-1	67-1	1-1	6-1	ARM
...	...	...	...	100-1	100-1	67-1	68-1	1-1	16-1	AZE
...	...	...	...	100	97	96	67	1	32	BHR
...	...	...	...	...	...	...	...	...	...	CYP
...	...	...	...	88-1	71-1	54-1	59-1	1,976-1	18,519-1	EGY
...	...	...	...	100-1	99-1	67-1	59-1	2-1	21-1	GEO
...	...	...	...	94-1	86-1	60-1	69-1	487-1	3,321-1	IRQ
78-3	73-3	70-3	69-3	...	...	...	...	...	...	ISR
...	...	...	...	99i	98i	38i	61i	13i	116i	JOR
...	...	...	...	99	96	25	48	4	130	KWT
...	...	...	...	100i	95i	33i	68i	3i	250i	LBN
...	...	...	...	...	...	...	...	...	...	LBY
...	...	...	...	98i	74i	56i	69i	134i	6,885i	MAR
...	...	...	...	99	96	29	51	9	161	OMN
...	...	...	...	99	97	46	76	7	83	PSE
...	...	...	...	95-1i	93-1i	17-1i	17-1i	21-1i	154-1i	QAT
...	...	...	...	99-1	95-1	50-1	63-1	34-1	1,157-1	SAU
...	...	...	...	73i	61i	49i	57i	2,296i	9,774i	SDN
...	...	...	...	...	...	...	...	...	...	SYR
...	...	...	...	96-4	79-4	54-4	68-4	67-4	1,774-4	TUN
63-3	54-3	60-3	50-3	100-1	96-1	81-1	85-1	33-1	2,380-1	TUR
...	...	...	...	99-3i	93-3i	62-3i	19-3i	6-3i	539-3i	ARE
...	...	...	...	...	...	...	...	...	...	YEM
...	...	...	...	65i	43i	61i	60i	2,791i	12,054i	AFG
...	...	...	...	93	74	37	55	2,053	30,392	BGD
...	...	...	...	93-1	67-1	49-1	60-1	10-1	183-1	BTN
...	...	...	...	92i	74i	56i	64i	20,538i	252,864i	IND
...	...	...	...	98-2	86-2	54-2	66-2	229-2	8,700-2	IRN
...	...	...	...	100i	100i	70i	63i	2i	29i	KAZ
...	...	...	...	100i	100i	37i	62i	3i	18i	KGZ
...	...	...	...	99-2	98-2	24-2	29-2	1-2	9-2	MDV
...	...	...	...	92i	68i	62i	71i	481i	6,275i	NPL
...	...	...	...	75-1	59-1	62-1	64-1	10,534-1	54,876-1	PAK
...	...	...	...	99	92	39	59	38	1,331	LKA
...	...	...	...	100-4i	100-4i	41-4i	63-4i	2-4i	13-4i	TJK
...	...	...	...	100-4i	100-4i	30-4i	63-4i	2-4i	12-4i	TKM
...	...	...	...	100	100	50	100	-	2	UZB
...	...	...	...	100i	97i	35i	64i	0.2i	9i	BRN
...	...	...	...	92-3	81-3	47-3	67-3	249-3	2,067-3	KHM
...	...	...	...	100i	97i	47i	75i	375i	37,038i	CHN
...	...	...	...	...	...	...	...	...	...	PRK
...	...	...	...	...	...	...	...	...	...	HKG
...	...	...	...	100	96	50	69	133	8,527	IDN
...	...	...	...	...	...	...	...	...	...	JPN
...	...	...	...	92-3	85-3	63-3	67-3	106-3	687-3	LAO
...	...	...	...	100-2	97-2	32-2	75-2	0.2-2	19-2	MAC
...	...	...	...	97	95	46	61	177	1,234	MYS
...	...	...	...	99i	98i	33i	44i	6i	35i	MNG
...	...	...	...	85-2i	76-2i	51-2i	61-2i	1,468-2i	9,360-2i	MMR
...	...	...	...	99-3	98-3	39-3	49-3	182-3	1,257-3	PHL
...	...	...	...	...	...	...	...	...	...	KOR
92-3	74-3	90-3	72-3	100	97	37	76	1	128	SGP
...	...	...	...	98	94	37	63	176	3,589	THA
...	...	...	...	84i	68i	46i	56i	45i	252i	TLS
...	...	...	...	98i	95i	50i	65i	224i	3,670i	VNM

Country or territory	A Participation in adult education & training (%)	B % of youth enrolled in TVET	C TVET share of secondary enrolment (%)	D Transition from upper secondary to tertiary (%)	E Gross entry ratio into tertiary (%)	F GER tertiary (%)	G % of adults 15+ with ICT skills — Copy & paste within document	G — Use formula in spreadsheet	G — Write computer program	H % of adults 25+ having attained at least — Primary	H — Lower secondary	H — Upper secondary	H — Post-secondary
SDG indicator:	4.3.1	4.3.3				4.3.2	4.4.1			4.4.3			
Reference year:	2018						2018						
Oceania													
Australia	...	20[-1]	37[-1]	...	...	113[-1]	...	20[-1]	37[-1]	...	...	113[-1]	
Cook Islands	1[-2]	-[-2]	...	...	...	...	1[-2]	-[-2]	...	...	...	...	
Fiji	1[-2]	...	...	...	...	...	1[-2]	...	...	...	...	...	
Kiribati	...	...	...	...	...	...	...	...	...	...	...	...	
Marshall Islands	...	1[-2]	2[-2]	...	...	...	...	1[-2]	2[-2]	...	...	...	
Micronesia, F. S.	...	...	...	...	...	...	...	...	...	...	...	...	
Nauru	...	-[-2]	...	...	...	...	...	-[-2]	...	...	...	...	
New Zealand	67[-3]	5[-1]	14[-1]	70[-1]	93[-1]	82[-1]	67[-3]	5[-1]	14[-1]	70[-1]	93[-1]	82[-1]	
Niue	...	-[-3]	...	...	...	...	...	-[-3]	...	...	...	...	
Palau	...	-[-4]	...	...	...	...	...	-[-4]	...	...	...	...	
Papua New Guinea	...	2[-2]	9[-2]	...	...	...	...	2[-2]	9[-2]	...	...	...	
Samoa	...	-[-2]	...	...	...	...	...	-[-2]	...	...	...	...	
Solomon Is	...	...	...	...	...	...	...	...	...	...	...	...	
Tokelau	...	-[-2]	...	...	...	...	...	-[-2]	...	...	...	...	
Tonga	...	2[-3]	3[-3]	...	...	...	...	2[-3]	3[-3]	...	...	...	
Tuvalu	...	1	2	...	...	...	...	1	2	...	...	...	
Vanuatu	...	1[-3]	2[-3]	...	...	...	...	1[-3]	2[-3]	...	...	...	
Latin America and the Caribbean													
Anguilla	...	...	...	...	...	...	...	...	...	...	...	...	...
Antigua and Barbuda	...	2	4	...	...	...	...	...	...	...	...	...	...
Argentina	6[-1]	-[-1]	...	138[-2]	88[-2]	90[-1]	...	...	...	93	57	...	20
Aruba	...	...	...	25[-2]	16[-2]	...	54[-1]	45[-1]	5[-1]	...	...	...	...
Bahamas	...	-	...	...	...	...	...	...	...	...	...	...	...
Barbados	...	-	...	...	...	...	...	...	...	...	...	...	...
Belize	...	3	8	44[-1]	22[-1]	25[-1]	...	...	...	...	...	...	...
Bolivia, P. S.	5[-1]	29	64	...	...	...	...	...	...	72[-3]	59[-3]	43[-3]	24[-3]
Brazil	...	3[-1i]	4[-1]	...	...	51[-1i]	21[-1]	12[-1]	3[-1]	80	60	47	17
British Virgin Islands	...	2[-1]	4[-1]	...	...	16	...	...	...	...	...	...	...
Cayman Islands	...	...	...	...	...	...	...	...	...	99[-3]	95[-3]	90[-3]	55[-3]
Chile	47[-3]	17[-1]	19[-1]	96[-1]	87[-1]	88[-1]	...	43[-1]	12[-1]	88[-1]	80[-1]	59[-1]	22[-1]
Colombia	...	9	8	58	...	55	38[-1]	25[-1]	8[-1]	79	54	50	21
Costa Rica	...	8	23	...	...	55	...	...	...	81[-2]	53[-2]	38[-2]	21[-2]
Cuba	...	13	26	67	44	41	17[-1]	17[-1]	0.1[-1]	...	...	...	...
Curaçao	...	...	...	...	...	...	29[-1]	21[-1]	4[-1]	...	...	...	...
Dominica	...	-[-2]	-[-3]	...	...	...	...	...	...	...	...	...	...
Dominican Republic	6[-1]	4i	8	124[-1]	...	60[-1i]	22[-3]	11[-3]	7[-3]	67[-3]	57[-3]	35[-3]	12[-3]
Ecuador	3	8	14	...	...	45[-3]	...	...	...	83[-1]	53[-1]	44[-1]	14[-1]
El Salvador	2[-4]	7	18	37	23	29	...	...	...	59[-1]	43[-1]	30[-1]	8[-1]
Grenada	...	2	...	60[-2]	49[-2]	105	...	...	...	...	...	...	...
Guatemala	3[-1]	9	29	...	...	22[-3]	...	...	...	62[-4]	37[-4]	27[-4]	10[-4]
Guyana	2[-1]	...	...	...	...	...	...	...	...	...	...	...	...
Haiti	...	...	...	...	...	...	...	...	...	...	...	...	...
Honduras	3[-1]	10[-1]	39[-1]	...	...	26	...	...	...	60	31	23	10
Jamaica	...	-	...	...	...	27[-3]	14[-2]	5[-2]	1[-3]	...	...	...	...
Mexico	30[-1]	12[-1]	27[-1]	82[-1]	50[-1]	40[-1]	...	26[-1]	9[-1]	83	63	36	16
Montserrat	...	-	...	...	...	...	...	...	...	...	...	...	...
Nicaragua	4[-4]	...	...	...	...	...	...	...	...	...	...	...	...
Panama	4[-1]	7[-1]	17[-1]	...	...	48[-2]	...	...	...	...	...	...	...
Paraguay	...	5[-2]	16[-2]	...	...	...	...	...	...	76	50	39	15
Peru	34[-1]	1	2	...	...	71[-1]	26	16	3	82	64	58	22
Saint Kitts and Nevis	...	-[-2]	...	97[-3]	66[-3]	87[-3]	...	...	...	...	...	...	...
Saint Lucia	...	0.4	1	...	...	14	...	...	...	...	...	...	...
Saint Vincent/Grenadines	...	-[-1]	-[-1]	...	...	24[-3]	...	...	...	91[-1]	...	42[-1]	4[-1]
Sint Maarten	...	16[-4]	59[-4]	8[-4]	3[-3]	6[-3]	...	...	...	...	...	...	...
Suriname	...	18[-3]	44	...	...	...	...	...	...	...	...	...	...
Trinidad and Tobago	...	...	...	...	...	...	...	...	...	...	...	...	...
Turks and Caicos Islands	...	...	...	...	...	...	...	...	...	...	...	...	...
Uruguay	6	11[-1]	23[-1]	...	...	63[-1]	77[-2]	51[-2]	8[-2]	91	57	30	13
Venezuela, B. R.	...	2[-3]	5[-1]	...	...	...	...	...	...	93[-2]	74[-2]	62[-2]	35[-2]

Literacy Youth	Literacy Adults	Numeracy Youth	Numeracy Adults	Literacy rate (%) Youth	Literacy rate (%) Adults	% female Youth	% female Adults	Number (000) Youth	Number (000) Adults	Country code
										2018
...	20_{-1}	37_{-1}	...	...	113_{-1}					AUS
1_{-2}	$-_{-2}$	...	...	...	...					COK
1_{-2}	...	...	...	...	...					FJI
...	...	...	...	...	...					KIR
...	1_{-2}	2_{-2}	...	...	...					MHL
...	...	...	...	...	...					FSM
...	$-_{-2}$	...	...	...	...					NRU
67_{-3}	5_{-1}	14_{-1}	70_{-1}	93_{-1}	82_{-1}					NZL
...	$-_{-3}$	...	...	...	...					NIU
...	$-_{-4}$	...	...	...	...					PLW
...	2_{-2}	9_{-2}	...	...	...					PNG
...	$-_{-2}$	...	...	...	...					WSM
...	...	...	...	...	...					SLB
...	$-_{-2}$	...	...	...	...					TKL
...	2_{-3}	3_{-3}	...	...	...					TON
...	1	2	...	...	...					TUV
...	1_{-3}	2_{-3}	...	...	...					VUT
...	...	...	...	...	...	...	...	...	...	AIA
...	...	...	...	...	99_{-3}	...	29_{-3}	...	1_{-3}	ATG
...	...	...	...	100	99	24	49	35	333	ARG
...	...	...	...	100_i	98_i	60_i	53_i	0.1_i	2_i	ABW
...	...	...	...	...	...	...	...	...	...	BHS
...	...	...	...	100_{-4i}	100_{-4i}	55_{-4i}	53_{-4i}	$-_{-4i}$	1_{-4i}	BRB
...	...	...	...	...	...	...	...	...	...	BLZ
...	...	...	...	99_{-3}	92_{-3}	49_{-3}	77_{-3}	13_{-3}	548_{-3}	BOL
...	...	...	...	99	93	35	50	270	11,168	BRA
...	...	...	...	...	...	...	...	...	...	VGB
...	...	...	...	...	...	...	...	...	...	CYM
61_{-3}	47_{-3}	47_{-3}	38_{-3}	99_{-1}	96_{-1}	49_{-1}	52_{-1}	28_{-1}	531_{-1}	CHL
...	...	...	...	99	95	40	49	100	1,875	COL
...	...	...	...	99_i	98_i	41_i	49_i	4_i	84_i	CRI
...	...	...	...	...	...	...	...	...	...	CUB
...	...	...	...	...	...	...	...	...	...	CUW
...	...	...	...	...	...	...	...	...	...	DMA
...	...	...	...	99_{-2}	94_{-2}	48_{-2}	50_{-2}	22_{-2}	462_{-2}	DOM
...	...	...	...	99_{-1}	93_{-1}	39_{-1}	56_{-1}	23_{-1}	851_{-1}	ECU
...	...	...	...	98	89	44	63	26	515	SLV
...	...	...	...	99_{-4i}	99_{-4i}	32_{-4i}	49_{-4i}	0.1_{-4i}	1_{-4i}	GRD
...	...	...	...	94_{-4}	81_{-4}	59_{-4}	66_{-4}	190_{-4}	$1,873_{-4}$	GTM
...	...	...	...	97_{-4i}	86_{-4i}	44_{-4i}	53_{-4i}	5_{-4i}	77_{-4i}	GUY
...	...	...	...	83_{-2i}	62_{-2i}	51_{-2i}	56_{-2i}	366_{-2i}	$2,741_{-2i}$	HTI
...	...	...	...	97	87	26	50	71	838	HND
...	...	...	...	96_{-4i}	88_{-4i}	16_{-4i}	31_{-4i}	20_{-4i}	256_{-4i}	JAM
...	...	...	...	99	95	44	61	151	4,273	MEX
...	...	...	...	...	...	...	...	...	...	MSR
...	...	...	...	92_{-3i}	83_{-3i}	37_{-3i}	51_{-3i}	102_{-3i}	744_{-3i}	NIC
...	...	...	...	99	95	61	56	6	139	PAN
...	...	...	...	98	94	32	53	23	293	PRY
...	...	...	...	99	94	54	75	52	1,334	PER
...	...	...	...	...	...	...	...	...	...	KNA
...	...	...	...	...	...	...	...	...	...	LCA
...	...	...	...	...	...	...	...	...	...	VCT
...	...	...	...	...	...	...	...	...	...	SXM
...	...	...	...	99_i	94_i	57_i	65_i	1_i	24_i	SUR
...	...	...	...	...	...	...	...	...	...	TTO
...	...	...	...	...	...	...	...	...	...	TCA
...	...	...	...	99	99	37	40	6	35	URY
...	...	...	...	99_{-2}	97_{-2}	36_{-2}	49_{-2}	63_{-2}	615_{-2}	VEN

TABLE 4: Continued

Country or territory	A — Participation in adult education & training (%) [4.3.1]	B — % of youth enrolled in TVET [4.3.3]	C — TVET share of secondary enrolment (%)	D — Transition from upper secondary to tertiary (%)	E — Gross entry ratio into tertiary (%)	F — GER tertiary (%) [4.3.2]	G — Copy & paste within document [4.4.1]	G — Use formula in spreadsheet	G — Write computer program	H — Primary [4.4.3]	H — Lower secondary	H — Upper secondary	H — Post-secondary
Europe and Northern America													
Albania	9$_{-2}$	5	8	66	50	55	...	...	...	...	...	...	...
Andorra	...	...	11	28	...	...	...	...	6$_{-1}$	97$_{-2}$	72$_{-2}$	47$_{-2}$	32$_{-2}$
Austria	60$_{-2}$	28$_{-1}$	35$_{-1}$	77$_{-2}$	75$_{-1}$	85$_{-1}$	63$_{-2}$	45$_{-2}$	7$_{-1}$	...	99$_{-4}$	79$_{-2}$	29$_{-2}$
Belarus	...	10	13	...	...	87	...	...	...	...	...	...	...
Belgium	45$_{-2}$	25$_{-1}$	44$_{-1}$	83$_{-1}$	79$_{-1}$	80$_{-1}$	65$_{-1}$	44$_{-1}$	9$_{-1}$	96$_{-2}$	85$_{-2}$	67$_{-2}$	34$_{-2}$
Bermuda	...	-$_{-2}$	...	...	22	19	...	...	...	...	...	87$_{-2}$	55$_{-2}$
Bosnia and Herzegovina	9$_{-2}$	...	38	57	...	...	28$_{-1}$	9$_{-1}$	2$_{-1}$	84$_{-2}$	81$_{-2}$	62$_{-2}$	12$_{-2}$
Bulgaria	25$_{-2}$	16$_{-1}$	29$_{-1}$	98$_{-1}$	77$_{-1}$	71$_{-1}$	26$_{-2}$	14$_{-2}$	1$_{-1}$	...	95$_{-2}$	76$_{-2}$	...
Canada	...	...	5$_{-1}$	...	...	69$_{-1i}$	...	...	...	...	...	84$_{-2}$	60$_{-2}$
Croatia	32$_{-2}$	22$_{-1}$	39$_{-1}$	...	...	68$_{-1}$	42$_{-1}$	32$_{-1}$	5$_{-1}$	...	...	...	...
Czechia	46$_{-2}$	26$_{-1}$	37$_{-1}$	80$_{-1}$	70$_{-1}$	64$_{-1}$	56$_{-1}$	41$_{-1}$	4$_{-1}$	100$_{-2}$	100$_{-2}$	90$_{-2}$	20$_{-2}$
Denmark	50$_{-2}$	12$_{-1}$	22$_{-1}$	75$_{-1}$	81$_{-1}$	81$_{-1}$	68$_{-2}$	56$_{-1}$	14$_{-1}$	...	94	79	37
Estonia	44$_{-2}$	12$_{-1}$	23$_{-1}$	...	...	70$_{-1}$	56$_{-2}$	44$_{-2}$	7$_{-1}$	...	...	88	40
Finland	54$_{-2}$	21$_{-1}$	48$_{-1}$	39$_{-1}$	62$_{-1}$	88$_{-1}$	72$_{-4}$	47$_{-1}$	9$_{-1}$	...	...	76$_{-1}$	36$_{-1}$
France	51$_{-2}$	19$_{-1i}$	18$_{-1}$	...	...	66$_{-1i}$	53$_{-2}$	40$_{-2}$	6$_{-1}$	98$_{-1}$	84$_{-1}$	70$_{-1}$	30$_{-1}$
Germany	52$_{-2}$	21$_{-1}$	19$_{-1}$	76$_{-1}$	63$_{-1}$	70$_{-1}$	62$_{-2}$	38$_{-2}$	6$_{-1}$	100	96	83	36
Greece	17$_{-2}$	13$_{-1}$	16$_{-1}$	49$_{-1}$	48$_{-1}$	137$_{-1}$	52$_{-2}$	41$_{-2}$	9$_{-2}$	91$_{-2}$	65$_{-2}$	55$_{-2}$	27$_{-2}$
Hungary	56$_{-2}$	13$_{-1}$	12$_{-1}$	54$_{-1}$	45$_{-1}$	49$_{-1}$	53$_{-2}$	37$_{-2}$	4$_{-1}$	100$_{-2}$	97$_{-2}$	76$_{-2}$	29$_{-2}$
Iceland	...	9$_{-1}$	19$_{-1}$	...	73$_{-3}$	72$_{-1}$	80$_{-4}$	72$_{-1}$	13$_{-1}$	...	...	...	...
Ireland	54$_{-2}$	7$_{-1i}$	5$_{-1}$	...	...	78$_{-1i}$	47$_{-1}$	35$_{-1}$	5$_{-1}$	...	86$_{-1}$	71$_{-1}$	43$_{-1}$
Italy	42$_{-2}$	22$_{-1}$	34$_{-1}$	73$_{-3}$	52$_{-1}$	62$_{-1}$	42$_{-2}$	31$_{-2}$	4$_{-2}$	95$_{-3}$	78$_{-3}$	49$_{-3}$	15$_{-3}$
Latvia	48$_{-2}$	17$_{-1i}$	20$_{-1}$	...	...	88$_{-1i}$	46$_{-2}$	31$_{-1}$	2$_{-1}$	100$_{-3}$	100	90	44
Liechtenstein	...	25$_{-1i}$	35$_{-1}$	52$_{-3}$	25$_{-1i}$	36$_{-1i}$	...	...	...	...	...	...	...
Lithuania	28$_{-2}$	9$_{-1i}$	10$_{-1}$	91$_{-1}$	80$_{-1i}$	72$_{-1i}$	45$_{-1}$	41$_{-1}$	4$_{-1}$	99$_{-1}$	96$_{-1}$	87$_{-1}$	55$_{-1}$
Luxembourg	48$_{-2}$	22$_{-1}$	33$_{-1}$	42$_{-2}$	35$_{-1}$	19$_{-1}$	83$_{-2}$	68$_{-1}$	11$_{-1}$	...	100$_{-3}$	80$_{-4}$	69$_{-3}$
Malta	36$_{-2}$	10$_{-1}$	16$_{-1}$	54$_{-1}$	80$_{-1}$	54$_{-1}$	44$_{-1}$	39$_{-1}$	6$_{-1}$	99	82	45	30
Monaco	...	...	9$_{+1}$	46$_{+1}$	...	...	...	...	...	...	...	...	...
Montenegro	...	23	33	...	...	56	...	32$_{-1}$	3$_{-1}$	...	...	...	...
Netherlands	64$_{-2}$	23$_{-1}$	37$_{-1}$	56$_{-1}$	65$_{-1}$	85$_{-1}$	73$_{-1}$	52$_{-1}$	8$_{-1}$	99	90	71	33
North Macedonia	13$_{-2}$	...	28$_{-1}$	74$_{-1}$	60$_{-1}$	42$_{-1}$	32$_{-2}$	21$_{-2}$	3$_{-2}$	...	...	...	...
Norway	60$_{-2}$	18$_{-1}$	28$_{-1}$	67$_{-1}$	71$_{-1}$	82$_{-1}$	68$_{-2}$	55$_{-1}$	12$_{-1}$	100$_{-1}$	99$_{-1}$	78$_{-1}$	40$_{-1}$
Poland	26$_{-2}$	19$_{-1}$	28$_{-1}$	91$_{-1}$	81$_{-1}$	68$_{-1}$	41$_{-2}$	28$_{-1}$	3$_{-1}$	99$_{-2}$	85$_{-2}$	85$_{-2}$	28$_{-2}$
Portugal	46$_{-2}$	17$_{-1}$	25$_{-1}$	71$_{-1}$	62$_{-1}$	64$_{-1}$	58$_{-4}$	38$_{-1}$	8$_{-1}$	92	54	37	19
Republic of Moldova	...	10$_{i}$	14	...	...	40$_{i}$	...	...	...	99	97	75	...
Romania	7$_{-2}$	...	28$_{-1}$	114$_{-2}$	80$_{-1}$	49$_{-1}$	22$_{-1}$	14$_{-1}$	1$_{-1}$	99$_{-1}$	91$_{-1}$	67$_{-1}$	18$_{-1}$
Russian Federation	...	17$_{-1i}$	14$_{-1}$	114$_{-1}$	107$_{-1}$	82$_{-1}$	47$_{-1}$	24$_{-1}$	1$_{-1}$	...	...	...	...
San Marino	...	2	7	269	89	42	...	...	...	97	83	54	16
Serbia	20$_{-2}$	24$_{i}$	35	113$_{-2}$	97$_{-2i}$	67$_{i}$	34$_{-3}$	24$_{-1}$	4$_{-1}$	98$_{-1}$	90$_{-1}$	72$_{-1}$	23$_{-1}$
Slovakia	46$_{-2}$	23$_{-1}$	31$_{-1}$	79$_{-1}$	55$_{-1}$	47$_{-1}$	51$_{-1}$	42$_{-1}$	4$_{-1}$	100$_{-1}$	99$_{-1}$	87$_{-1}$	23$_{-1}$
Slovenia	46$_{-2}$	35$_{-1}$	45$_{-1}$	72$_{-1}$	75$_{-1}$	79$_{-1}$	54$_{-2}$	42$_{-2}$	4$_{-1}$	100$_{-1}$	98$_{-1}$	83$_{-1}$	28$_{-1}$
Spain	43$_{-2}$	15$_{-1}$	19$_{-1}$	87$_{-1}$	80$_{-1}$	89$_{-1}$	52$_{-2}$	37$_{-2}$	6$_{-2}$	92	78	50	31
Sweden	64$_{-2}$	12$_{-1}$	20$_{-1}$	105$_{-1}$	74$_{-1}$	67$_{-1}$	70$_{-1}$	51$_{-1}$	12$_{-1}$	100$_{-1}$	91$_{-1}$	76$_{-1}$	39$_{-1}$
Switzerland	69$_{-2}$	23$_{-1}$	37$_{-1}$	77$_{-1}$	89$_{-1}$	60$_{-1}$	...	57$_{-1}$	9$_{-1}$	...	97	86	...
Ukraine	...	4$_{-4}$	7	159	...	83$_{-4}$	...	...	...	...	...	...	...
United Kingdom	52$_{-2}$	19$_{-1}$	35$_{-1}$	...	62$_{-4}$	60$_{-1}$	62$_{-2}$	47$_{-2}$	8$_{-2}$	100$_{-1}$	100$_{-1}$	77$_{-1}$	44$_{-1}$
United States	59$_{-1}$	1$_{-1i}$	...	64$_{-3}$	53$_{-3i}$	88$_{-1i}$	...	...	...	99	96	90	45

% achieving proficiency in (I)				Literacy rate (%) (J)		Illiterates (K)				Country code
Literacy		Numeracy		Literacy rate (%)		% female		Number (000)		
Youth	Adults	Youth	Adults	Youth	Adults	Youth	Adults	Youth	Adults	
				2018						
										ALB
...	...	...	...	99i	98i	26i	60i	3i	44i	AND
										AUT
...	...	...	...	...	...	...	...	...	...	BLR
...	...	...	...	100i	100i	42i	61i	1i	19i	BEL
...	...	...	...	...	...	...	...	...	...	BMU
										BIH
...	...	...	...	...	...	...	...	...	...	BGR
...	...	...	...	...	...	...	...	...	...	CAN
...	...	...	...	...	...	...	...	...	...	HRV
...	...	...	...	...	...	...	...	...	...	CZE
...	...	...	...	...	...	...	...	...	...	DNK
...	...	...	...	...	...	...	...	...	...	EST
...	...	...	...	...	...	...	...	...	...	FIN
...	...	...	...	...	...	...	...	...	...	FRA
...	...	...	...	...	...	...	...	...	...	DEU
...	...	...	...	...	...	...	...	...	...	GRC
77-3	73-3	73-3	71-3	99i	98i	54i	65i	9i	187i	HUN
...	...	...	...	99-4i	99-4i	42-4i	55-4i	14-4i	73-4i	ISL
...	...	...	...	...	...	...	...	...	...	IRL
...	...	...	...	...	...	...	...	...	...	ITA
...	...	...	...	100i	99i	37i	63i	4i	444i	LVA
				100i	100i	37i	47i	0.3i	2i	LIE
...	...	...	...	...	...	...	...	...	...	LTU
92-3	85-3	90-3	83-3	...	...	...	...	...	...	LUX
...	...	...	...	...	...	...	...	...	...	MLT
				99i	95i	30i	37i	0.3i	21i	MCO
...	...	...	...	...	...	...	...	...	...	MNE
				99i	99i	55i	77i	1i	6i	NLD
				...	...	...	...	...	...	MKD
...	...	...	...	99-4i	98-4i	53-4i	74-4i	4-4i	39-4i	NOR
...	...	...	...	...	...	...	...	...	...	POL
...	...	...	...	...	...	...	...	...	...	PRT
				100i	96i	44i	68i	4i	343i	MDA
				100-4	99-4	48-4	71-4	1-4	22-4	ROU
				99i	99i	47i	63i	12i	190i	RUS
				100i	100i	41i	54i	42i	323i	SMR
				100	100	32	59	-	-	SRB
				100-2	99-2	48-2	79-2	3-2	86-2	SVK
...	...	...	...	...	...	...	...	...	...	SVN
88-3	75-3	86-3	74-3	100-4i	100-4i	31-4i	57-4i	0.3-4i	6-4i	ESP
				100	98	44	67	13	623	SWE
...	...	...	...	...	...	...	...	...	...	CHE
...	...	...	...	...	...	...	...	...	...	UKR
...	...	...	...	...	...	...	...	...	...	GBR
...	...	...	...	...	...	...	...	...	...	USA

TABLE 5: SDG 4, Target 4.5 – Equity

By 2030, eliminate gender disparities in education and ensure equal access at all levels of education and vocational training for the vulnerable, including persons with disabilities, indigenous peoples and children in vulnerable situations

	GENDER														
	A			B				C		D		E			
	GPIA in completion			GPIA in minimum proficiency				GPIA in literacy rate		GPIA in adult proficiency		GPIA in gross enrolment ratio			
				End of primary		End of lower secondary									
Region	Primary	Lower secondary	Upper secondary	Reading	Mathematics	Reading	Mathematics	Youth	Adults	Literacy	Numeracy	Pre-primary	Primary	Secondary	Tertiary
SDG indicator						4.5.1									
Reference year						2018									
						Median									
World	1.00i	1.00i	1.03i	...	...	1.15i	1.00i	1.00	0.97	...	...	1.01	0.99	1.01	1.17
Sub-Saharan Africa	1.04i	0.88i	0.79i	...	...	...	...	0.97	0.80	...	...	1.03	0.98	0.97	0.73
Northern Africa and Western Asia	1.00i	1.01i	1.08i	...	...	1.32i	1.07	1.00	0.96	...	...	1.00	1.00	1.01	1.20
Northern Africa	1.01i	1.02i	0.97i	...	...	1.31i	1.10	0.99	0.86	...	...	1.01	0.96	1.00	1.03
Western Asia	1.00i	1.01i	1.08i	...	...	1.33i	1.05	1.00	0.98	...	...	1.00	1.00	1.01	1.25
Central and Southern Asia	1.00	0.98	0.95i	...	...	...	...	1.00	0.95	...	...	0.99	1.00	1.00	0.93
Central Asia	1.00	1.00	0.99	...	...	...	...	1.00	1.00	...	...	0.97	0.99	0.99	0.76
Southern Asia	1.00	0.96	0.85i	...	...	...	...	1.00	0.80	...	...	1.00	1.02	1.04	0.99
Eastern and South-eastern Asia	1.02i	1.07i	1.12i	...	...	1.17	1.04	1.00	0.97	...	...	1.01	1.00	1.01	1.18
Eastern Asia	...	...	...	...	...	1.09i	1.01i	1.00i	0.97i	...	...	1.00	1.00	1.00i	1.14
South-eastern Asia	1.03	1.06	1.10	...	...	1.27	1.07	1.00	0.97	...	...	1.01	0.98	1.02	1.19
Oceania	...	...	...	...	...	...	...	...	...	...	...	0.99	0.98	1.04	...
Latin America and the Caribbean	1.03i	1.09i	1.12i	...	...	1.13i	0.82i	1.00i	1.00i	...	...	1.02	0.98	1.03	1.36i
Caribbean	...	...	...	...	...	...	...	...	1.00i	...	...	1.03	0.98	1.03	1.44i
Central America	1.02	1.05	1.11	...	...	1.11	0.82	1.00	0.99	...	...	1.02	0.99	1.06	1.16
South America	1.02	1.09	1.13	...	...	1.13	0.76	1.00	1.00	...	...	1.01	0.97	1.04	1.14i
Europe and Northern America	1.00i	1.00	1.04	...	...	1.13	1.00	1.00i	1.00i	...	...	0.99	1.00	1.00	1.25
Europe	1.00i	1.00	1.04	...	...	1.13	1.00	1.00i	1.00i	...	...	0.99	1.00	1.00	1.24
Northern America	1.00i	1.01i	1.03i	...	...	1.09	0.99	...	...	...	...	0.93	0.99	1.01	1.26
Low income	1.01i	0.87i	0.69i	...	...	...	...	0.90	0.70	...	...	1.03	0.98	0.86	0.54
Middle income	1.02i	1.02i	1.03i	...	...	1.22i	1.00i	1.00	0.98	...	...	1.01	0.99	1.02	1.18
Lower middle	1.03	1.02	0.97	...	...	...	...	1.00	0.90	...	...	1.01	0.98	1.02	1.03
Upper middle	1.01i	1.01i	1.10i	...	...	1.22i	1.00i	1.00	0.99	...	...	1.01	0.99	1.03	1.25
High income	1.00i	1.00i	1.05i	...	...	1.13	1.01	1.00i	1.00i	...	...	1.00	1.00	1.00	1.27

A   Adjusted gender parity index (GPIA) in school completion rate by level.
B   GPIA in percentage of students with minimum level of proficiency at the end of given level.
C   GPIA in youth and adult literacy rate.
D   GPIA in percentage of adults aged 16 and over achieving at least a fixed level of proficiency in functional literacy and numeracy skills.
E   GPIA in gross enrolment ratio by level.
F   Adjusted parity index for location (rural-urban) and wealth (poorest to richest quintile) in school completion by level.
G   Adjusted parity index for wealth (poorest to richest quintile) in achievement of minimum proficiency.

Source: UIS and GEM Report analysis of household surveys. Data refer to school year ending in 2018 unless noted otherwise.

Aggregates represent countries listed in the table with available data and may include estimates for countries with no recent data.

(-) Magnitude nil or negligible.

(...) Data not available or category not applicable.

(± n) Reference year differs (e.g. -2: reference year 2016 instead of 2018).

(i) Estimate and/or partial coverage.

	F											G			
Disparity in primary completion				Disparity in lower secondary completion				Disparity in upper secondary completion				Wealth disparity in minimum proficiency			
Adjusted parity index		% of poorest completing		Adjusted parity index		% of poorest completing		Adjusted parity index		% of poorest completing		End of primary		End of lower secondary	
Location	Wealth	M	F	Location	Wealth	M	F	Location	Wealth	M	F	Reading	Mathematics	Reading	Mathematics
4.5.1															
2018															
Median															
0.94i	0.72i	71i	79i	0.88i	0.70i	47i	55i	0.66i	0.36i	18i	21i	...	...	0.61i	0.58i
0.66i	0.38i	31i	30i	0.40i	0.15i	9i	5i	0.25i	0.05i	2i	1i	...	...	...	...
0.98i	0.93i	92i	93i	0.95i	0.81i	70i	73i	0.84i	0.63i	32i	42i	...	...	0.47i	0.52
0.93i	0.89i	85i	87i	0.72i	0.55i	49i	56i	0.52i	0.30i	17i	32i	...	...	0.34i	0.40
1.00i	...	...	...	0.98i	0.88i	...	...	0.87i	0.66i	...	...	...	...	0.48i	0.53
0.98	0.89	89	88	0.93	0.74	69	72	0.65i	0.34i	20i	22i	...	...	...	...
1.00	1.01	99	100	1.00	0.99	98	98	0.95	0.88	84	85	...	...	...	...
0.90	0.75	65	68	0.84	0.50	44	38	0.49i	0.18i	16i	4i	...	...	...	...
0.96i	0.86i	80i	90i	0.83i	0.58i	48i	66i	0.63i	0.28i	21i	28i	...	...	0.63	0.51
...	...	...	...	...	...	...	...	...	...	...	...	...	...	0.85i	0.90i
0.94	0.75	68	77	0.76	0.46	36	50	0.58	0.22	17	22	...	...	0.41	0.42
...	...	...	...	...	...	...	...	...	...	...	...	...	...	...	...
0.94i	0.84i	79i	90i	0.83i	0.60i	48i	58i	0.69i	0.36i	20i	31i	...	...	0.41i	0.26i
...	...	...	...	...	...	...	...	...	...	...	...	...	...	...	...
0.91	0.76	73	78	0.72	0.49	47	46	0.46	0.36	17	25	...	...	0.35	0.20
0.97	0.95	91	93	0.88	0.72	61	76	0.71	0.44	36	43	...	...	0.43	0.26
1.00i	...	...	...	1.00i	0.99	98i	97i	0.97i	0.83	79i	81i	...	...	0.70	0.67
1.00i	...	...	...	1.00	0.99	98i	97i	0.97	0.81	79i	81i	...	...	0.70	0.67
...	0.99i	99i	99i	...	0.99i	97i	99i	...	0.90i	87i	89i	...	...	0.81	0.71
0.63i	0.35i	26i	29i	0.38i	0.12i	8i	5i	0.24i	0.04i	2i	1i	...	...	...	...
0.93i	0.79i	72i	81i	0.81i	0.54i	47i	55i	0.61i	0.26i	18i	21i	...	...	0.44i	0.40i
0.83	0.65	57	65	0.62	0.32	28	26	0.46	0.13	10	6	...	...	...	...
0.98i	0.94i	91i	94i	0.92i	0.81i	74i	80i	0.77i	0.41i	36i	41i	...	...	0.45i	0.45i
1.00i	...	...	...	1.00i	0.99i	...	...	0.97i	0.83i	...	...	...	...	0.72	0.68

TABLE 5: Continued

Country or territory	GENDER														
	A GPIA in completion			B GPIA in minimum proficiency				C GPIA in literacy rate		D GPIA in adult proficiency		E GPIA in gross enrolment ratio			
				End of primary		End of lower secondary									
	Primary	Lower secondary	Upper secondary	Reading	Mathematics	Reading	Mathematics	Youth	Adults	Literacy	Numeracy	Pre-primary	Primary	Secondary	Tertiary
SDG indicator	4.5.1														
Reference year	2018														
Sub-Saharan Africa															
Angola	0.89_{-3}	0.76_{-3}	0.64_{-3}	...	...	...	...	0.83_{-4}	0.67_{-4}	...	...	0.89_{-2}	0.87_{-3}	0.64_{-2}	0.83_{-2}
Benin	0.87_{-1}	0.54_{-1}	0.45_{-1}	0.78_{-4}	1.10_{-4}	...	...	0.74i	0.58i	...	...	1.03	0.94	0.76_{-2}	0.44_{-1}
Botswana	...	...	...	...	1.15_{-3}	...	...	...	...	...	...	1.03_{-3}	0.98_{-3}	...	1.30_{-1}
Burkina Faso	...	...	...	0.88_{-4}	0.74_{-4}	...	...	0.88i	0.65i	...	...	0.99	0.98	1.00	0.58
Burundi	1.16_{-2}	0.75_{-2}	0.70_{-2}	1.30_{-4}	1.47_{-4}	...	...	0.94_{-1}	0.80_{-1}	...	...	1.04	1.01	1.10	0.45_{-1}
Cabo Verde	...	...	...	...	...	...	...	1.01_{-3}	0.89_{-3}	...	...	1.01	0.93	1.09	1.33
Cameroon	0.94_{-4}	0.88_{-4}	0.78_{-4}	1.17_{-4}	0.94_{-4}	...	...	0.94i	0.87i	...	...	1.02	0.90	0.86_{-2}	0.81_{-1}
Central African Republic	...	...	...	...	...	...	...	0.60i	0.52i	...	...	1.04_{-1}	0.78_{-2}	0.67_{-1}	...
Chad	0.78_{-3}	0.55_{-3}	0.37_{-3}	0.72_{-4}	0.32_{-4}	...	...	0.55_{-3}	0.45_{-2}	...	...	0.92_{-2}	0.77_{-2}	0.46_{-2}	0.29_{-3}
Comoros	...	...	...	...	...	...	...	1.00i	0.82i	...	...	1.03	1.00	1.06	0.81_{-1}
Congo	1.04_{-3}	0.79_{-3}	0.69_{-3}	1.11_{-4}	1.01_{-4}	...	...	0.92i	0.87i	...	...	...	...	...	0.67_{-1}
Côte d'Ivoire	0.89_{-2}	0.61_{-2}	0.85_{-2}	1.15_{-4}	0.71_{-4}	...	...	0.83i	0.75i	...	...	1.02	0.93	0.77	0.69_{-1}
D. R. Congo	...	...	...	...	...	...	...	0.88_{-2}	0.75_{-2}	...	...	1.07_{-3}	0.99_{-3}	0.64_{-3}	0.56_{-2}
Djibouti	...	...	...	...	...	...	...	...	...	...	...	0.95_{+1}	1.00_{+1}	1.03_{+1}	...
Equat. Guinea	...	...	...	...	...	...	...	...	...	...	...	1.02_{-3}	0.99_{-3}	...	...
Eritrea	...	...	...	...	...	...	...	0.99i	0.82i	...	...	0.99	0.86	0.91	0.71_{-2}
Eswatini	1.17_{-4}	1.13_{-4}	1.07_{-4}	...	...	...	...	1.02i	1.00i	...	...	...	0.92_{-1}	0.99_{-2}	...
Ethiopia	1.01_{-2}	0.96_{-2}	1.11_{-2}	...	...	...	...	0.98_{-1i}	0.75_{-1i}	...	...	0.95_{-3}	0.91_{-3}	0.96_{-3}	0.48_{-4}
Gabon	...	...	...	...	...	...	...	1.04i	0.97i	...	...	...	...	...	...
Gambia	1.12	1.09	0.90	...	...	...	...	0.91_{-3}	0.67_{-3}	...	...	1.06	1.09	...	...
Ghana	1.05_{-4}	1.00_{-4}	1.02_{-4}	...	...	...	...	0.99i	0.89i	...	...	1.02	1.01_{+1}	1.00_{+1}	0.77
Guinea	0.75	0.61	0.51	...	...	...	...	0.65_{-4}	0.50_{-4}	...	...	...	0.82_{-2}	0.65_{-4}	0.43_{-4}
Guinea-Bissau	0.78_{-4}	0.69_{-4}	0.49_{-4}	...	...	...	...	0.70_{-4i}	0.50_{-4i}	...	...	...	...	...	...
Kenya	1.06_{-4}	1.12_{-4}	0.85_{-4}	...	...	...	...	1.01i	0.92i	...	...	0.97_{-2}	1.00_{-2}	...	0.74_{-1}
Lesotho	1.25	1.40	1.29	...	...	...	...	1.15_{-4i}	1.20_{-4i}	...	...	1.04_{-2}	0.95_{-1}	1.26_{-1}	1.35
Liberia	...	...	...	...	...	...	...	0.70_{-1i}	0.54_{-1i}	...	...	1.01_{-1}	0.99_{-1}	0.77_{-3}	...
Madagascar	1.14	0.98	0.97	...	...	...	...	0.99i	0.94i	...	...	1.09	1.01	1.03	0.95
Malawi	1.18_{-3}	0.92_{-3}	0.84_{-3}	...	...	...	...	1.01_{-3i}	0.79_{-3i}	...	...	1.01_{-3}	1.01	0.98	...
Mali	0.81	0.84	0.43	...	...	...	...	0.75	0.56	...	...	1.03	0.90	0.82	0.42_{-1}
Mauritania	0.85_{-3}	0.85_{-3}	0.66_{-3}	...	...	...	...	0.80_{-1}	0.68_{-1}	...	...	1.21_{-3}	1.05	1.02	0.50_{-1}
Mauritius	...	...	...	...	...	...	...	1.01i	0.96i	...	...	1.01	1.03	1.05	1.29_{-1}
Mozambique	...	...	...	...	...	...	...	0.85_{-1}	0.69_{-1}	...	...	...	0.93	0.89_{-1}	0.81
Namibia	...	...	...	...	...	...	...	1.02i	1.00i	...	...	1.03	0.97	...	1.49_{-1}
Niger	...	...	...	1.16_{-4}	0.71_{-4}	...	...	...	...	...	...	1.07	0.86_{-1}	0.75_{-1}	0.41
Nigeria	1.00	0.90	0.76	...	...	...	...	0.84i	0.74i	...	...	...	0.94_{-2}	0.90_{-2}	...
Rwanda	1.22_{-3}	1.16_{-3}	0.84_{-3}	...	...	...	...	1.05	0.89	...	...	1.03	0.99	1.11	0.81
Sao Tome and Principe	1.08_{-4}	1.10_{-4}	1.46_{-4}	...	...	...	...	1.00i	0.93i	...	...	1.09_{-2}	0.97_{-1}	1.13_{-1}	1.04_{-3}
Senegal	1.06_{-1}	0.85_{-1}	0.69_{-1}	0.97_{-4}	0.75_{-4}	1.11_{-3}	0.86_{-3}	0.84_{-1}	0.61_{-1}	...	...	1.11	1.12	1.09	0.68
Seychelles	...	...	...	...	...	...	...	1.01i	1.01i	...	...	1.02	1.06	1.06	1.52
Sierra Leone	1.03_{-1}	0.89_{-1}	0.64_{-1}	...	...	...	...	0.89i	0.67i	...	...	1.10	1.03	0.97_{-1}	...
Somalia	...	...	...	...	...	...	...	...	...	...	...	...	...	...	...
South Africa	1.03_{-2}	1.06_{-2}	1.13_{-2}	...	1.14_{-3}	...	...	1.03_{-1}	0.99_{-1}	...	...	1.00_{-1}	0.97_{-1}	1.08_{-1}	1.30_{-1}
South Sudan	...	...	...	...	...	...	...	0.98i	0.72i	...	...	0.95_{-3}	0.71_{-3}	0.54_{-3}	...
Togo	0.89_{-4}	0.64_{-4}	0.49_{-4}	1.14_{-4}	0.87_{-4}	...	...	0.87_{-3}	0.66_{-3}	...	...	1.03	0.96	0.73_{-1}	0.51
Uganda	1.07_{-2}	0.87_{-2}	0.79_{-2}	...	...	...	...	1.01i	0.86i	...	...	1.04_{-1}	1.03_{-1}	...	0.73_{-4}
United Republic of Tanzania	1.10_{-3}	0.86_{-3}	0.69_{-3}	...	...	...	...	0.97_{-3}	0.88_{-3}	...	...	1.00	1.03	1.05	0.54_{-3}
Zambia	1.03	0.92	0.80	...	...	1.46_{-3}	1.26_{-3}	0.99i	0.92i	...	...	1.07_{-2}	1.02_{-1}	...	...
Zimbabwe	1.06_{+1}	1.08_{+1}	0.79_{+1}	..	...	...	...	1.06_{-4i}	0.99_{-4i}	...	...	...	...	...	0.84_{-3}

LOCATION/WEALTH																
F												G				
Disparity in primary completion				Disparity in lower secondary completion				Disparity in upper secondary completion				Wealth disparity in minimum proficiency				
Adjusted parity index		% of poorest completing		Adjusted parity index		% of poorest completing		Adjusted parity index		% of poorest completing		End of primary		End of lower secondary		
Location	Wealth	M	F	Location	Wealth	M	F	Location	Wealth	M	F	Reading	Mathematics	Reading	Mathematics	Country code
4.5.1																
2018																
0.37[-3]	0.21[-3]	21[-3]	16[-3]	0.20[-3]	0.06[-3]	5[-3]	3[-3]	0.15[-3]	0.03[-3]	2[-3]	1[-3]	...	...	...	...	AGO
0.70[-1]	0.28[-1]	24[-1]	18[-1]	0.43[-1]	0.08[-1]	5[-1]	3[-1]	0.25[-1]	0.02[-1]	1[-1]	0.2[-1]	0.15[-4]	0.20[-4]	...	...	BEN
...	...	...	...	...	...	...	...	...	...	...	...	...	...	0.35[-3]	...	BWA
												0.28[-4]	0.50[-4]	...	...	BFA
0.67[-2]	0.40[-2]	21[-2]	31[-2]	0.46[-2]	0.16[-2]	12[-2]	3[-2]	0.20[-2]	0.03[-2]	2[-2]	-[-2]	0.18[-4]	0.94[-4]	...	...	BDI
																CPV
0.69[-4]	0.37[-4]	46[-4]	26[-4]	0.37[-4]	0.16[-4]	20[-4]	4[-4]	0.12[-4]	0.01[-4]	1[-4]	-[-4]	0.03[-4]	0.05[-4]	...	...	CMR
																CAF
0.35[-3]	0.27[-3]	19[-3]	12[-3]	0.15[-3]	0.12[-3]	8[-3]	2[-3]	0.08[-3]	0.02[-3]	2[-3]	-[-3]	0.09[-4]	0.08[-4]	...	...	TCD
																COM
0.61[-3]	0.43[-3]	42[-3]	41[-3]	0.30[-3]	0.08[-3]	7[-3]	6[-3]	0.09[-3]	0.01[-3]	1[-3]	0.2[-3]	0.08[-4]	0.07[-4]	...	...	COG
0.56[-2]	0.32[-2]	30[-2]	15[-2]	0.26[-2]	0.08[-2]	8[-2]	2[-2]	0.13[-2]	0.04[-2]	4[-2]	-[-2]	0.20[-4]	0.40[-4]	...	...	CIV
																COD
...	...	...	...	...	...	...	...	...	...	...	...				...	DJI
...	...	...	...	...	...	...	...	...	...	...	...				...	GNQ
																ERI
0.77[-4]	0.60[-4]	50[-4]	57[-4]	0.67[-4]	0.32[-4]	26[-4]	25[-4]	0.64[-4]	0.22[-4]	12[-4]	13[-4]	...	...	...	...	SWZ
0.52[-2]	0.35[-2]	28[-2]	28[-2]	0.20[-2]	0.08[-2]	3[-2]	5[-2]	0.13[-2]	0.04[-2]	1[-2]	2[-2]	...	...	...	...	ETH
																GAB
0.63	0.55	42	50	0.40	0.29	18	22	0.24	0.16	10	7	...	...	...	...	GMB
0.75[-4]	0.51[-4]	42[-4]	43[-4]	0.61[-4]	0.36[-4]	28[-4]	26[-4]	0.42[-4]	0.10[-4]	7[-4]	2[-4]	...	...	...	...	GHA
0.40	0.20	23	7	0.17	0.06	8	0.3	0.06	0.01	1	-	...	...	...	...	GIN
0.23[-4]	0.13[-4]	8[-4]	7[-4]	0.22[-4]	0.09[-4]	6[-4]	1[-4]	0.14[-4]	0.12[-4]	4[-4]	-[-4]	...	...	...	...	GNB
0.88[-4]	0.65[-4]	61[-4]	65[-4]	0.78[-4]	0.45[-4]	41[-4]	43[-4]	0.52[-4]	0.16[-4]	17[-4]	7[-4]	...	...	...	...	KEN
0.80	0.60	40	79	0.45	0.17	6	19	0.42	0.06	1	6	...	...	...	...	LSO
																LBR
0.68	0.20	14	21	0.41	0.05	4	2	0.47	0.07	2	1	...	...	...	...	MDG
0.58[-3]	0.35[-3]	22[-3]	29[-3]	0.31[-3]	0.11[-3]	7[-3]	5[-3]	0.28[-3]	0.07[-3]	4[-3]	2[-3]	...	...	...	...	MWI
0.49	0.32	29	21	0.30	0.15	8	5	0.15	-	-	-	...	...	...	...	MLI
0.64[-3]	0.39[-3]	38[-3]	28[-3]	0.56[-3]	0.29[-3]	18[-3]	23[-3]	0.39[-3]	0.14[-3]	10[-3]	4[-3]	...	...	...	...	MRT
																MUS
...	...	...	...	...	...	...	...	...	...	...	...	...	...	...	...	MOZ
...	...	...	...	...	...	...	...	...	...	...	...				...	NAM
												0.02[-4]				NER
0.65	0.27	26	26	0.58	0.19	21	13	0.48	0.13	18	6	...	...	...	...	NGA
0.76[-3]	0.48[-3]	26[-3]	38[-3]	0.49[-3]	0.24[-3]	11[-3]	12[-3]	0.30[-3]	0.08[-3]	2[-3]	4[-3]	...	...	...	...	RWA
0.91[-4]	0.76[-4]	69[-4]	74[-4]	0.85[-4]	0.17[-4]	8[-4]	10[-4]	0.64[-4]	0.08[-4]	-[-4]	5[-4]	...	...	...	...	STP
0.58[-1]	0.37[-1]	30[-1]	26[-1]	0.41[-1]	0.14[-1]	9[-1]	5[-1]	0.26[-1]	0.06[-1]	4[-1]	-[-1]	0.17[-4]	0.23[-4]	0.28[-3]	0.36[-3]	SEN
																SYC
0.54[-1]	0.38[-1]	31[-1]	34[-1]	0.30[-1]	0.11[-1]	10[-1]	7[-1]	0.16[-1]	0.04[-1]	4[-1]	1[-1]	...	...	...	...	SLE
																SOM
0.97[-2]	0.92[-2]	87[-2]	95[-2]	0.93[-2]	0.76[-2]	73[-2]	76[-2]	0.61[-2]	0.29[-2]	19[-2]	27[-2]	...	0.10[-3]	...	...	ZAF
																SSD
0.67[-4]	0.48[-4]	46[-4]	34[-4]	0.29[-4]	0.11[-4]	7[-4]	2[-4]	0.14[-4]	0.03[-4]	2[-4]	-[-4]	0.06[-4]	0.11[-4]	...	...	TGO
0.59[-2]	0.26[-2]	20[-2]	17[-2]	0.38[-2]	0.12[-2]	10[-2]	4[-2]	0.34[-2]	0.07[-2]	3[-2]	3[-2]	...	...	...	...	UGA
0.83[-3]	0.64[-3]	54[-3]	67[-3]	0.35[-3]	0.12[-3]	9[-3]	5[-3]	0.26[-3]	0.01[-3]	0.4[-3]	-[-3]	...	...	...	...	TZA
0.69	0.42	37	40	0.47	0.17	20	12	0.27	0.05	5	1	...	...	0.04[-3]	0.04[-3]	ZMB
0.88[+1]	0.79[+1]	75[+1]	81[+1]	0.71[+1]	0.48[+1]	45[+1]	45[+1]	0.06[+1]	-[+1]	-[+1]	-[+1]	...	...	...	...	ZWE

TABLE 5: Continued

Country or territory	GENDER														
	A GPIA in completion			B GPIA in minimum proficiency				C GPIA in literacy rate		D GPIA in adult proficiency		E GPIA in gross enrolment ratio			
				End of primary		End of lower secondary									
	Primary	Lower secondary	Upper secondary	Reading	Mathematics	Reading	Mathematics	Youth	Adults	Literacy	Numeracy	Pre-primary	Primary	Secondary	Tertiary
SDG indicator	4.5.1														
Reference year	2018														
Northern Africa and Western Asia															
Algeria	...	...	...	...	...	1.46-3	1.16-3	1.00i	0.86i	...	...	...	0.95	...	1.40
Armenia	1.00-2	1.01-2	1.04-2	...	1.04-3	...	1.07-3	1.00-1	1.00-1	...	...	1.08	1.00	1.04	1.25
Azerbaijan	...	...	...	1.06-2	...	...	...	1.00-1	1.00-1	...	...	0.99i	1.01i	1.00i	1.13i
Bahrain	...	...	...	...	...	...	1.17-3	0.99	0.96	...	...	1.03	0.99	1.06	1.45
Cyprus	1.00-1	1.00-1	1.09-1	...	...	1.32	1.09	...	...	...	...	0.99-1i	1.00-1i	0.98-1i	1.16-1i
Egypt	1.01-4	1.02-4	0.97-4	...	...	...	1.13-3	0.97-1	0.86-1	...	...	1.00	1.00	0.99	1.03-1
Georgia	1.00	1.00	1.08	...	...	1.37	1.04	1.00-1	1.00-1	...	...	...	1.01	1.01	1.12+1
Iraq	0.94	1.01	1.19	...	...	...	...	0.97-1	0.88-1	...	...	...	...	...	...
Israel	...	...	...	...	...	1.22	1.09	...	...	1.01-3	0.92-3	1.00-1	1.01-1	1.02-1	1.29-1
Jordan	...	...	...	...	...	1.35	1.01	1.00i	0.99i	...	...	0.99	0.98	1.03	1.16
Kuwait	...	...	...	...	...	...	0.84-3	1.01	0.98	...	...	1.05	1.09	1.06-3	1.53
Lebanon	...	...	...	...	...	1.22	0.95-3	1.00i	0.96i	...	...	...	...	...	...
Libya	...	...	...	...	...	...	...	...	...	...	...	...	...	...	...
Morocco	...	...	...	...	...	1.31	1.07-3	0.99i	0.78i	...	...	0.86	0.96	0.91	0.99
Oman	...	...	...	...	...	...	1.27-3	1.01	0.96	...	...	1.05	1.09	0.92	1.53
Palestine	1.01-4	1.14-4	1.28-4	...	...	...	...	1.00	0.97	...	...	1.00	1.00	1.09	1.36
Qatar	...	...	...	...	...	1.41	1.03-3	1.02-1i	1.02-1i	...	...	1.01	1.01	...	1.87
Saudi Arabia	...	...	...	...	...	1.44	0.91-3	1.00-1	0.95-1	...	...	1.05	1.01	0.94	1.05
Sudan	0.96-4	1.02-4	0.85-4	...	...	...	...	1.01i	0.86i	...	...	1.02-1	0.94-1	1.01-1	1.02-3
Syrian Arab Republic	...	...	...	...	...	...	...	...	...	...	...	...	...	...	1.12-2
Tunisia	1.03	1.15	1.30	...	...	1.28-3	0.87-3	0.99-4	0.84-4	...	...	1.02-2	0.99	1.13-2	1.45
Turkey	...	...	...	...	0.98-3	1.14	1.05-3	1.00-1	0.95-1	0.87-3	0.71-3	0.96-1	0.99-1	0.95-1	...
United Arab Emirates	...	...	...	...	...	1.33	1.07-3	0.99-3i	1.03-3i	...	...	0.95-1	0.98-1	0.92-1	...
Yemen	...	...	...	...	...	...	...	...	...	...	...	0.90-2	0.87-2	0.73-2	...
Central and Southern Asia															
Afghanistan	0.56-3	0.49-3	0.46-3	...	...	...	...	0.76i	0.54i	...	...	...	0.67	0.57	0.35
Bangladesh	1.11-4	1.02-4	0.82-4	...	...	0.98-3	0.84-3	1.03	0.93	...	...	1.04	1.07	1.14	0.71
Bhutan	...	...	...	...	...	...	...	1.00-1	0.76-1	...	...	1.01	1.00	1.11i	0.99
India	1.00-3	0.96-3	0.85-3	1.04-1	1.00-1	...	...	0.97i	0.80i	...	...	0.92-1	1.13-1	1.04i	1.07
Iran, Islamic Republic of	...	...	...	...	...	...	1.01-3	1.00-2	0.89-2	...	...	1.03-2	1.05-1	0.96-1	0.86-1
Kazakhstan	1.00-3	1.00-3	1.02-3	1.01-2	1.02-3	1.31	1.00	1.00i	1.00i	...	...	1.02+1	1.02+1	1.01+1	1.19+1
Kyrgyzstan	1.00	1.00	0.95	...	...	...	...	1.00i	1.00i	...	...	1.00	0.99	1.00	1.23
Maldives	1.02-1	1.09-1	1.29-1	...	...	...	...	1.01-2	1.01-2	...	...	1.03-1	1.02-1	...	1.72-1
Nepal	0.99-2	0.97-2	...	...	...	...	...	0.97i	0.76i	...	...	0.91+1	1.02+1	1.07+1	1.07
Pakistan	0.87	0.82	0.97	...	...	...	...	0.83-1	0.65-1	...	...	0.87	0.84	0.85	0.87
Sri Lanka	...	...	...	...	...	...	...	1.01	0.98	...	...	0.99-3	0.99	1.04	1.33
Tajikistan	0.99-1	0.97-1	0.79-1	...	...	...	...	1.00-4i	1.00-4i	...	...	0.87-1	0.99-1	...	0.76-1
Turkmenistan	1.00-3	1.00-3	1.03-3	...	...	...	...	1.00-4i	1.00-4i	...	...	0.97-4	0.98-4	0.96-4	0.64-4
Uzbekistan	...	...	...	...	...	...	...	1.00	1.00	...	...	0.96	0.99	0.99-1	0.70
Eastern and South-eastern Asia															
Brunei Darussalam	...	...	...	...	...	1.23	1.07	1.00i	0.98i	...	...	1.01	1.01	1.02	1.36
Cambodia	1.12-4	0.96-4	0.97-4	...	...	1.31-3	0.83-3	1.01-3	0.87-3	...	...	1.04	0.98	...	0.90
China	1.02-4	1.08-4	1.15-4	...	...	...	...	1.00i	0.97i	...	...	1.01	1.01	...	1.18
DPR Korea	...	...	...	...	...	...	...	...	...	...	...	...	1.00	1.01-3	0.51
Hong Kong, China	...	...	...	...	...	1.10	1.03	...	...	...	...	1.05	1.04	0.97	1.10
Indonesia	1.02-1	1.05-1	1.03-1	...	...	1.31	1.13	1.00	0.97	...	...	0.90i	0.97	1.02	1.13
Japan	...	...	...	...	...	1.09	1.01-3	...	...	...	...	...	...	...	...
Lao PDR	1.00-1	0.98-1	0.97-1	...	...	...	...	0.96-3	0.88-3	...	...	1.03	0.96	0.93i	1.07
Macao, China	...	...	...	...	...	1.06	1.00	1.00-2	0.97-2	...	...	0.97	0.99	1.00	1.26
Malaysia	...	...	...	...	...	1.23	1.07	1.00	0.97	...	...	1.02	1.01-1	1.08	1.18
Mongolia	1.02	1.10	1.13	...	...	...	...	1.01i	1.00i	...	...	1.00	0.98	...	1.29
Myanmar	1.03-2	1.03-2	1.33-2	...	...	...	...	0.99-2i	0.90-2i	...	...	1.02	0.96	1.08	1.29
Philippines	1.06-1	1.15-1	1.11-1	...	...	1.34	1.11	1.00-3	1.00-3	...	...	0.96-1	0.96-1	1.10-1	1.24-1
Republic of Korea	...	...	...	...	...	1.08	1.01	...	...	...	...	1.00-1	1.00-1	0.99-1	0.79-1
Singapore	...	...	...	...	...	1.07	1.03-3	1.00	0.97	0.96-3	0.93-3	...	1.00-1i	0.99-1i	1.13-1i
Thailand	1.00-3	1.12-3	1.19-3	...	...	1.38	1.16	1.01	0.97	...	...	1.00	1.00	0.98	1.29-2
Timor-Leste	1.10-2	1.10-2	1.10-2	...	...	...	...	1.03i	0.89i	...	...	1.01	0.96	1.08	...
Viet Nam	1.01-4	1.07-4	1.18-4	...	...	1.11-3	1.04-3	1.00i	0.97i	...	...	0.99	1.02	...	1.20-2

LOCATION/WEALTH																
F												G				
Disparity in primary completion				Disparity in lower secondary completion				Disparity in upper secondary completion				Wealth disparity in minimum proficiency				
Adjusted parity index		% of poorest completing		Adjusted parity index		% of poorest completing		Adjusted parity index		% of poorest completing		End of primary		End of lower secondary		
Location	Wealth	M	F	Location	Wealth	M	F	Location	Wealth	M	F	Reading	Mathematics	Reading	Mathematics	Country code
4.5.1																
2018																
...	...	...	...	...	...	...	...	...	...	...	...	...	...	0.61_{-3}	0.49_{-3}	DZA
1.01_{-2}	0.99_{-2}	99_{-2}	100_{-2}	0.99_{-2}	0.99_{-2}	98_{-2}	100_{-2}	0.91_{-2}	0.87_{-2}	82_{-2}	87_{-2}	...	0.94_{-3}	...	0.99_{-3}	ARM
...	...	...	...	...	...	...	...	...	...	...	...	0.90_{-2}	...	...	...	AZE
...	...	...	...	...	...	...	...	...	...	...	...	...	...	...	0.69_{-3}	BHR
1.00_{-1}	...	...	...	1.01_{-1}	0.96_{-4}	...	...	0.92_{-1}	0.93_{-4}	...	...	...	...	0.58	0.62	CYP
0.97_{-4}	0.89_{-4}	87_{-4}	87_{-4}	0.89_{-4}	0.74_{-4}	70_{-4}	71_{-4}	0.84_{-4}	0.64_{-4}	61_{-4}	51_{-4}	...	...	...	0.66_{-3}	EGY
1.00	1.00	100	100	0.96	0.93	95	91	0.84	0.69	65	64	...	...	0.39	0.40	GEO
0.87	0.58	62	45	0.76	0.32	26	19	0.81	0.23	11	10	...	...	...	...	IRQ
...	...	...	...	...	...	...	...	...	...	...	...	...	...	0.57	0.53	ISR
...	...	...	...	...	...	...	...	...	...	...	...	...	...	0.60	0.52	JOR
...	...	...	...	...	...	...	...	...	...	...	...	...	...	...	0.44_{-3}	KWT
...	...	...	...	...	...	...	...	...	...	...	...	...	...	0.25	0.52_{-3}	LBN
...	...	...	...	...	...	...	...	...	...	...	...	...	...	...	...	LBY
...	...	...	...	...	...	...	...	...	...	...	...	...	...	0.33	0.27_{-3}	MAR
...	...	...	...	...	...	...	...	...	...	...	...	...	...	...	0.70_{-3}	OMN
1.00_{-4}	0.99_{-4}	98_{-4}	100_{-4}	1.03_{-4}	0.83_{-4}	69_{-4}	84_{-4}	1.03_{-4}	0.63_{-4}	37_{-4}	62_{-4}	...	...	...	...	PSE
...	...	...	...	...	...	...	...	...	...	...	...	...	...	0.46	0.76_{-3}	QAT
...	...	...	...	...	...	...	...	...	...	...	...	...	...	0.42	0.24_{-3}	SAU
0.73_{-4}	0.47_{-4}	47_{-4}	42_{-4}	0.62_{-4}	0.31_{-4}	31_{-4}	24_{-4}	0.47_{-4}	0.18_{-4}	16_{-4}	9_{-4}	...	...	...	...	SDN
...	...	...	...	...	...	...	...	...	...	...	...	...	...	...	...	SYR
0.93	0.89	85	92	0.72	0.55	49	56	0.52	0.30	17	32	...	...	0.34_{-3}	0.31_{-3}	TUN
0.98_{-1}	0.97_{-4}	...	...	...	...	...	...	...	...	...	...	...	...	0.71	0.52_{-3}	TUR
...	...	...	...	...	...	...	...	...	...	...	...	...	...	0.48	0.58_{-3}	ARE
...	...	...	...	...	...	...	...	...	...	...	...	...	...	...	...	YEM
0.67_{-3}	0.58_{-3}	57_{-3}	31_{-3}	0.54_{-3}	0.42_{-3}	38_{-3}	13_{-3}	0.42_{-3}	0.26_{-3}	20_{-3}	4_{-3}	...	...	...	...	AFG
0.99_{-4}	0.70_{-4}	57_{-4}	68_{-4}	0.94_{-4}	0.40_{-4}	30_{-4}	27_{-4}	0.61_{-4}	0.10_{-4}	4_{-4}	3_{-4}	...	...	...	...	BGD
...	...	...	...	...	...	...	...	...	...	...	...	...	...	...	...	BTN
0.97_{-3}	0.82_{-3}	81_{-3}	80_{-3}	0.92_{-3}	0.62_{-3}	62_{-3}	56_{-3}	0.65_{-3}	0.18_{-3}	18_{-3}	9_{-3}	...	...	...	...	IND
...	...	...	...	...	...	...	...	...	...	...	...	...	...	...	0.34_{-3}	IRN
1.00_{-3}	1.00_{-3}	100_{-3}	100_{-3}	1.00_{-3}	0.99_{-3}	100_{-3}	99_{-3}	0.96_{-3}	0.90_{-3}	88_{-3}	89_{-3}	1.00_{-2}	0.82_{-2}	0.56	0.75	KAZ
1.00	1.01	100	100	0.99	0.97	96	97	0.92	0.81	74	81	...	...	...	...	KGZ
0.98_{-1}	0.97_{-1}	96_{-1}	97_{-1}	0.93_{-1}	0.86_{-1}	75_{-1}	89_{-1}	0.49_{-1}	0.34_{-1}	16_{-1}	22_{-1}	...	...	...	...	MDV
0.83_{-2}	0.80_{-2}	73_{-2}	69_{-2}	0.77_{-2}	0.57_{-2}	50_{-2}	50_{-2}	...	...	...	...	...	...	...	...	NPL
0.68	0.31	39	19	0.59	0.15	22	4	0.44	0.03	3	1	...	...	...	...	PAK
...	...	...	...	...	...	...	...	...	...	...	...	...	...	...	...	LKA
1.02_{-1}	1.01_{-1}	98_{-1}	96_{-1}	1.01_{-1}	1.00_{-1}	98_{-1}	92_{-1}	0.94_{-1}	0.87_{-1}	81_{-1}	59_{-1}	...	...	...	...	TJK
1.00_{-3}	0.99_{-3}	99_{-3}	99_{-3}	1.00_{-3}	1.00_{-3}	98_{-3}	99_{-3}	1.01_{-3}	0.98_{-3}	91_{-3}	99_{-3}	...	...	...	...	TKM
...	...	...	...	...	...	...	...	...	...	...	...	...	...	...	...	UZB
...	...	...	...	...	...	...	...	...	...	...	...	...	...	0.40	0.47	BRN
0.83_{-4}	0.52_{-4}	42_{-4}	54_{-4}	0.53_{-4}	0.26_{-4}	15_{-4}	19_{-4}	0.31_{-4}	0.09_{-4}	5_{-4}	4_{-4}	...	...	0.22_{-3}	0.19_{-3}	KHM
0.95_{-4}	0.98_{-4}	97_{-4}	99_{-4}	0.85_{-4}	0.95_{-4}	79_{-4}	87_{-4}	0.70_{-4}	0.69_{-4}	43_{-4}	57_{-4}	...	...	...	...	CHN
...	...	...	...	...	...	...	...	...	...	...	...	...	...	...	...	PRK
...	...	...	...	...	...	...	...	...	...	...	...	...	...	0.89	0.89	HKG
0.97_{-1}	0.92_{-1}	89_{-1}	95_{-1}	0.89_{-1}	0.71_{-1}	65_{-1}	73_{-1}	0.69_{-1}	0.36_{-1}	31_{-1}	35_{-1}	...	...	0.39	0.37	IDN
...	...	...	...	...	...	...	...	...	...	...	...	...	...	0.80	0.91_{-1}	JPN
0.83_{-1}	0.59_{-1}	61_{-1}	55_{-1}	0.57_{-1}	0.18_{-1}	21_{-1}	12_{-1}	0.35_{-1}	0.06_{-1}	5_{-1}	4_{-1}	...	...	...	...	LAO
...	...	...	...	...	...	...	...	...	...	...	...	...	...	0.96	0.96	MAC
...	...	...	...	...	...	...	...	...	...	...	...	...	...	0.45	0.48	MYS
0.98	0.97	95	98	0.80	0.70	65	70	0.58	0.39	32	43	...	...	...	...	MNG
0.91_{-2}	0.70_{-2}	64_{-2}	65_{-2}	0.47_{-2}	0.18_{-2}	18_{-2}	9_{-2}	0.31_{-2}	0.04_{-2}	1_{-2}	2_{-2}	...	...	...	...	MMR
0.98_{-1}	0.80_{-1}	71_{-1}	89_{-1}	0.92_{-1}	0.54_{-1}	40_{-1}	68_{-1}	0.89_{-1}	0.51_{-1}	42_{-1}	56_{-1}	...	...	0.11	0.16	PHL
...	...	...	...	...	...	...	...	...	...	...	...	...	...	0.82	0.80	KOR
...	...	...	...	...	...	...	...	...	...	...	...	...	...	0.83	0.28_{-3}	SGP
1.01_{-3}	1.00_{-3}	99_{-3}	99_{-3}	0.96_{-3}	0.81_{-3}	70_{-3}	83_{-3}	0.77_{-3}	0.32_{-3}	24_{-3}	31_{-3}	...	...	0.41	0.54	THA
0.82_{-2}	0.62_{-2}	57_{-2}	63_{-2}	0.63_{-2}	0.37_{-2}	33_{-2}	35_{-2}	0.48_{-2}	0.23_{-2}	18_{-2}	20_{-2}	...	...	...	...	TLS
0.97_{-4}	0.91_{-4}	88_{-4}	92_{-4}	0.91_{-4}	0.61_{-4}	56_{-4}	64_{-4}	0.68_{-4}	0.21_{-4}	15_{-4}	24_{-4}	...	...	0.84_{-3}	0.78_{-3}	VNM

TABLE 5: Continued

Country or territory	A GPIA in completion			B GPIA in minimum proficiency				C GPIA in literacy rate		D GPIA in adult proficiency		E GPIA in gross enrolment ratio			
				End of primary		End of lower secondary									
	Primary	Lower secondary	Upper secondary	Reading	Mathematics	Reading	Mathematics	Youth	Adults	Literacy	Numeracy	Pre-primary	Primary	Secondary	Tertiary
SDG indicator				4.5.1											
Reference year				2018											
Oceania															
Australia	...	1.00-4	1.04-4	...	0.97-3	1.11	0.99	...	...	...	...	0.96-1	1.00-1	0.89-1	1.30-1
Cook Islands	...	...	...	...	...	...	...	...	...	...	...	1.06-2	0.98-2	1.04-2	...
Fiji	...	...	...	...	...	...	...	1.00-1	1.00-1	...	...	...	0.98-1	...	...
Kiribati	...	...	...	...	...	...	...	...	...	...	...	...	1.07-1	...	...
Marshall Islands	...	...	...	...	...	...	...	...	...	...	...	0.92-2	1.00-2	1.06-2	...
Micronesia, F. S.	...	...	...	...	...	...	...	...	...	...	...	0.89-3	0.98-3	...	...
Nauru	...	...	...	...	...	...	...	...	...	...	...	0.94-2	0.95-2	1.02-2	...
New Zealand	...	...	...	...	...	1.11	0.99	...	...	1.01-3	0.95-3	1.01-2	1.00-1	1.06-1	1.30-1
Niue	...	...	...	...	...	...	...	...	...	...	...	1.13-2	1.00-2	1.18-3	...
Palau	...	...	...	...	...	...	...	1.01-3	1.00-3	...	...	1.15-4	0.88-4	1.10-4	...
Papua New Guinea	1.02-1	1.00-1	0.88-1	...	...	...	...	...	...	...	...	0.99-2	0.91-2	0.73-2	...
Samoa	...	...	...	...	...	...	...	1.01i	1.00i	...	...	1.14	1.00	1.09-2	...
Solomon Is	...	...	...	...	...	...	...	...	...	...	...	1.02	1.00	...	...
Tokelau	...	...	...	...	...	...	...	...	...	...	...	0.94-2	0.83-2	0.91-2	...
Tonga	...	...	...	...	...	...	...	1.00i	1.00i	...	...	1.06-3	0.99-3	1.03-3	...
Tuvalu	...	...	...	...	...	...	...	...	...	...	...	0.94	0.92	1.12	...
Vanuatu	...	...	...	...	...	...	...	1.01i	0.98i	...	...	0.97-3	0.97-3	1.03-3	...
Latin America and the Caribbean															
Anguilla	...	...	...	...	...	...	...	...	...	...	...	...	...	...	...
Antigua and Barbuda	...	...	...	...	...	...	...	...	1.01-3	...	...	1.10	0.99	0.96	...
Argentina	...	...	...	...	...	1.11	0.78	1.01	1.00	...	...	1.01-1	1.00-1	1.04-1	1.40-1
Aruba	...	...	...	...	...	...	...	1.00i	1.00i	...	...	0.98-4	0.97-4	...	1.48-2
Bahamas	...	...	...	...	...	...	...	...	...	...	...	1.08	1.00	1.06	...
Barbados	...	...	...	...	...	...	...	1.00-4i	1.00-4i	...	...	1.02	0.96	1.04	...
Belize	1.13-3	1.27-3	1.23-3	...	...	...	...	...	...	...	...	1.05	0.95	1.04	1.38-1
Bolivia, P. S.	1.01	0.99	1.03	...	...	...	...	1.00-3	0.92-3	...	...	1.02	0.99	0.98	...
Brazil	1.09-3	1.10-3	1.19-3	...	...	1.20	0.88	1.00	1.00	...	...	1.01-1i	0.97-1i	1.03-1i	1.27-1i
British Virgin Islands	...	...	...	...	...	...	...	...	...	...	...	1.11-1	0.96-1	1.10-1	1.44
Cayman Islands	...	...	...	...	...	...	...	...	...	...	...	...	...	...	...
Chile	1.00-3	1.01-3	1.05-3	...	...	1.13	0.74-3	1.00-1	1.00-1	0.90-3	0.70-3	0.98-1	0.97-1	1.00-1	1.13-1
Colombia	1.04-3	1.10-3	1.12-3	...	...	1.07	0.75	1.00	1.00	...	...	...	0.97	1.05	1.14
Costa Rica	1.02	1.05	1.16	...	...	1.11	0.80	1.00i	1.00i	...	...	1.01	1.01	1.07	1.18
Cuba	1.00-4	1.01-4	1.03-4	...	...	...	...	...	...	...	...	1.00	0.96	1.02	1.37
Curaçao	...	...	...	...	...	...	...	...	...	...	...	...	...	...	...
Dominica	...	...	...	...	...	...	...	...	...	...	...	1.03-2	0.97-2	0.99-3	...
Dominican Republic	1.07-4	1.15-4	1.27-4	...	...	1.37	0.94	1.00-2	1.00-2	...	...	1.02i	0.94i	1.07i	1.44-1i
Ecuador	1.00	1.01	1.05	...	...	1.09-3	0.71-3	1.00-1	0.98-1	...	...	1.05	1.02	1.03	1.14-3
El Salvador	1.05-4	1.02-4	1.08-4	...	...	...	...	1.00	0.96	...	...	1.02	0.97	0.99	1.12
Grenada	...	...	...	...	...	...	...	1.01-4i	1.00-4i	...	...	1.03	0.98	1.03	1.20
Guatemala	0.95-3	0.87-3	0.91-3	...	...	1.15-3	0.84-3	0.98-4	0.88-4	...	...	1.01	0.97	0.95	1.15-3
Guyana	1.03-4	1.04-4	1.23-4	...	...	...	...	1.01-4i	0.99-4i	...	...	...	...	...	...
Haiti	1.16-1	1.17-1	0.97-1	...	...	...	...	0.99-2i	0.89-2i	...	...	...	...	...	...
Honduras	1.07	1.09	1.24	...	...	1.11-3	0.66-3	1.03	1.00	...	...	1.02-1	1.00-1	1.13-1	1.27
Jamaica	...	...	...	...	...	...	...	1.05-4i	1.10-4i	...	...	1.04	0.96	1.03	1.43-3
Mexico	0.99-3	0.99-3	0.97-3	...	...	1.11	0.88	1.00	0.98	...	...	1.03-1	1.00-1	1.07-1	1.02-1
Montserrat	...	...	...	...	...	...	...	...	...	...	...	1.22	1.09	1.11	...
Nicaragua	1.22-4	1.17-4	1.30-4	...	...	...	...	1.04-3i	1.00-3i	...	...	...	...	...	...
Panama	1.01	1.07	1.11	...	...	1.16	0.82	1.00	0.99	...	...	1.02-1	0.98-1	1.05-1	1.36-2
Paraguay	1.07-2	1.09-2	1.13-2	...	...	1.12-3	0.56-3	1.01	0.99	...	...	1.01-2	...	...	...
Peru	1.00	1.01	1.01	...	...	1.13	0.85	1.00	0.94	...	...	1.00	0.97	0.95	1.05-1
Saint Kitts and Nevis	...	...	...	...	...	...	...	...	...	...	...	0.80-2	0.97-2	1.03-2	1.50-3
Saint Lucia	...	...	...	...	...	...	...	...	...	...	...	1.09	1.01	1.00	1.49
Saint Vincent/Grenadines	...	...	...	...	...	...	...	...	...	...	...	1.02	0.99	1.03	1.40-3
Sint Maarten	...	...	...	...	...	...	...	...	...	...	...	0.95-4	1.01-4	0.95-4	1.70-3
Suriname	1.11	1.27	1.35	...	...	...	...	1.00i	0.97i	...	...	1.00	1.00	1.24-3	...
Trinidad and Tobago	...	...	...	...	...	1.28-3	1.16-3	...	...	...	...	...	...	...	...
Turks and Caicos Islands	...	...	...	...	...	...	...	...	...	...	...	...	...	...	...
Uruguay	1.02	1.13	1.27	...	...	1.17	0.93	1.01	1.01	...	...	1.00-1	0.98-1	1.10-1	...
Venezuela, B. R.	1.02-4	1.13-4	1.15-4	...	...	...	...	1.01-2	1.00-2	...	...	1.01-1	0.98-1	1.07-1	...

LOCATION/WEALTH												G				
F												Wealth disparity in minimum proficiency				
Disparity in primary completion				Disparity in lower secondary completion				Disparity in upper secondary completion				End of primary		End of lower secondary		
Adjusted parity index		% of poorest completing		Adjusted parity index		% of poorest completing		Adjusted parity index		% of poorest completing						
Location	Wealth	M	F	Location	Wealth	M	F	Location	Wealth	M	F	Reading	Mathematics	Reading	Mathematics	Country code
4.5.1 / 2018																
...	...	...	...	...	0.97-4	96-4	96-4	...	0.82-4	70-4	82-4	...	0.52-3	0.76	0.71	AUS
...	...	...	...	...	...	...	...	...	...	...	...	...	...	...	...	COK
...	...	...	...	...	...	...	...	...	...	...	...	...	...	...	...	FJI
...	...	...	...	...	...	...	...	...	...	...	...	...	...	...	...	KIR
...	...	...	...	...	...	...	...	...	...	...	...	...	...	...	...	MHL
...	...	...	...	...	...	...	...	...	...	...	...	...	...	...	...	FSM
...	...	...	...	...	...	...	...	...	...	...	...	...	...	...	...	NRU
...	...	...	...	...	...	...	...	...	...	...	...	...	...	0.75	0.70	NZL
...	...	...	...	...	...	...	...	...	...	...	...	...	...	...	...	NIU
...	...	...	...	...	...	...	...	...	...	...	...	...	...	...	...	PLW
0.74-1	0.47-1	42-1	38-1	0.60-1	0.14-1	11-1	6-1	0.41-1	0.04-1	3-1	0.2-1	...	...	...	...	PNG
...	...	...	...	...	...	...	...	...	...	...	...	...	...	...	...	WSM
...	...	...	...	...	...	...	...	...	...	...	...	...	...	...	...	SLB
...	...	...	...	...	...	...	...	...	...	...	...	...	...	...	...	TKL
...	...	...	...	...	...	...	...	...	...	...	...	...	...	...	...	TON
...	...	...	...	...	...	...	...	...	...	...	...	...	...	...	...	TUV
...	...	...	...	...	...	...	...	...	...	...	...	...	...	...	...	VUT
...	...	...	...	...	...	...	...	...	...	...	...	...	...	...	...	AIA
...	...	...	...	...	...	...	...	...	...	...	...	...	...	...	...	ATG
...	...	...	...	...	...	...	...	...	...	...	...	...	...	0.36	0.20	ARG
...	...	...	...	...	...	...	...	...	...	...	...	...	...	...	...	ABW
...	...	...	...	...	...	...	...	...	...	...	...	...	...	...	...	BHS
...	...	...	...	...	...	...	...	...	...	...	...	...	...	...	...	BRB
0.94-3	0.67-3	51-3	67-3	0.74-3	0.20-3	11-3	15-3	0.47-3	0.02-3	1-3	--3	...	...	...	...	BLZ
0.98	0.98	95	97	0.88	0.92	87	88	0.69	0.63	59	55	...	...	...	...	BOL
0.88-3	0.78-3	69-3	82-3	0.81-3	0.70-3	61-3	75-3	0.66-3	0.44-3	33-3	43-3	...	...	0.45	0.26	BRA
...	...	...	...	...	...	...	...	...	...	...	...	...	...	...	...	VGB
...	...	...	...	...	...	...	...	...	...	...	...	...	...	...	...	CYM
1.00-3	0.99-3	98-3	99-3	1.00-3	0.97-3	97-3	98-3	0.90-3	0.76-3	70-3	77-3	...	...	0.63	0.28-3	CHL
0.90-3	0.84-3	79-3	85-3	0.69-3	0.54-3	47-3	55-3	0.58-3	0.41-3	36-3	41-3	...	...	0.44	0.34	COL
1.00	0.93	91	94	0.91	0.60	57	57	0.89	0.38	34	33	...	...	0.50	0.37	CRI
1.01-4	...	...	...	0.99-4	...	...	...	0.94-4	...	...	...	...	...	...	...	CUB
...	...	...	...	...	...	...	...	...	...	...	...	...	...	...	...	CUW
...	...	...	...	...	...	...	...	...	...	...	...	...	...	...	...	DMA
0.93-4	0.77-4	71-4	83-4	0.88-4	0.60-4	48-4	71-4	0.71-4	0.28-4	20-4	30-4	...	...	0.22	0.12	DOM
0.99	1.00	98	98	0.92	0.86	83	85	0.72	0.62	55	57	...	...	0.41-3	0.27-3	ECU
0.89-4	0.73-4	67-4	75-4	0.72-4	0.49-4	47-4	46-4	0.44-4	0.12-4	8-4	9-4	...	...	...	...	SLV
...	...	...	...	...	...	...	...	...	...	...	...	...	...	...	...	GRD
0.83-3	0.58-3	58-3	54-3	0.55-3	0.17-3	21-3	10-3	0.43-3	0.06-3	7-3	3-3	...	...	0.25-3	0.10-3	GTM
1.01-4	0.95-4	91-4	97-4	0.90-4	0.72-4	58-4	76-4	0.79-4	0.33-4	20-4	31-4	...	...	...	...	GUY
0.61-1	0.26-1	17-1	24-1	0.46-1	0.12-1	7-1	9-1	0.28-1	0.02-1	0.5-1	1-1	...	...	...	...	HTI
0.91	0.76	73	76	0.45	0.32	25	29	0.39	0.20	10	16	...	...	0.35-3	0.20-3	HND
...	...	...	...	...	...	...	...	...	...	...	...	...	...	...	...	JAM
1.00-3	0.92-3	90-3	93-3	0.91-3	0.76-3	74-3	76-3	0.72-3	0.36-3	38-3	25-3	...	...	0.47	0.44	MEX
...	...	...	...	...	...	...	...	...	...	...	...	...	...	...	...	MSR
0.74-4	0.71-4	55-4	78-4	0.51-4	0.46-4	28-4	36-4	0.46-4	0.37-4	17-4	31-4	...	...	...	...	NIC
0.94	0.90	89	91	0.83	0.72	66	75	0.70	0.45	39	41	...	...	0.27	0.15	PAN
0.94-2	0.82-2	74-2	90-2	0.76-2	0.48-2	45-2	49-2	0.56-2	0.20-2	17-2	20-2	...	...	0.34-3	0.15-3	PRY
0.97	0.95	95	93	0.89	0.83	82	80	0.82	0.73	71	69	...	...	0.29	0.24	PER
...	...	...	...	...	...	...	...	...	...	...	...	...	...	...	...	KNA
...	...	...	...	...	...	...	...	...	...	...	...	...	...	...	...	LCA
...	...	...	...	...	...	...	...	...	...	...	...	...	...	...	...	VCT
...	...	...	...	...	...	...	...	...	...	...	...	...	...	...	...	SXM
0.88	0.69	60	77	0.68	0.30	16	32	0.44	0.18	11	10	...	...	0.60-3	0.51-3	SUR
...	...	...	...	...	...	...	...	...	...	...	...	...	...	...	...	TTO
...	...	...	...	...	...	...	...	...	...	...	...	...	...	...	...	TCA
1.01	0.97	96	97	0.95	0.53	46	58	0.75	0.18	10	17	...	...	0.46	0.39	URY
...	0.94-4	89-4	93-4	...	0.84-4	65-4	80-4	...	0.74-4	54-4	66-4	...	...	...	...	VEN

Country or territory	A — GPIA in completion			B — GPIA in minimum proficiency				C — GPIA in literacy rate		D — GPIA in adult proficiency		E — GPIA in gross enrolment ratio			
				End of primary		End of lower secondary									
	Primary	Lower secondary	Upper secondary	Reading	Mathematics	Reading	Mathematics	Youth	Adults	Literacy	Numeracy	Pre-primary	Primary	Secondary	Tertiary
SDG indicator	4.5.1														
Reference year	2018														
Europe and Northern America															
Albania	1.01-1	1.00-1	1.02-1	...	...	1.35	1.06	1.01i	0.99i	...	...	1.01	1.04	1.01	1.36
Andorra	...	...	...	...	...	...	...	...	...	...	...	...	...	...	...
Austria	1.00-3	1.02-1	0.98-1	1.01-2	...	1.13	0.99	...	...	...	...	0.99-1	1.00-1	0.96-1	1.16-1
Belarus	...	...	...	...	...	1.13	0.99	1.00i	1.00i	...	...	0.96	1.00	0.99	1.16
Belgium	1.02-1	1.02-1	1.04-1	...	...	1.08	0.97	...	...	...	...	1.00-1	1.00-1	1.11-1	1.23-1
Bermuda	...	...	...	...	...	...	...	...	...	...	...	0.85-3	0.98-3	1.11-3	1.33
Bosnia and Herzegovina	...	...	...	...	...	1.30	1.01					...	...	...	...
Bulgaria	...	0.99-1	1.01-1	1.02-2	1.03-3	1.27	1.03	...	...	...	...	0.98-1	0.99-1	0.97-1	1.19-1
Canada	...	...	...	...	...	1.09	1.00	...	...	...	...	...	1.00-1	1.01-1	1.26-1i
Croatia	1.00-1	0.99-1	1.00-1	...	0.92-1	1.16	0.98	...	...	...	...	0.98-1	1.00-1	1.05-1	1.27-1
Czechia	1.00-1	1.01-1	1.08-1	...	...	1.13	1.01	...	...	...	...	0.97-1	1.01-1	1.01-1	1.29-1
Denmark	1.00-1	1.00-1	1.19-1	...	...	1.11	1.01	...	...	...	...	0.99-1	0.99-1	1.01-1	1.27-1
Estonia	1.00-1	1.03-1	1.08-1	...	...	1.07	1.00	...	...	...	...	0.99-1	1.00-1	1.02-1	1.35-1
Finland	1.00-1	1.00-1	1.08-1	...	...	1.13	1.04	...	...	...	...	1.00-1	0.99-1	1.09-1	1.15-1
France	...	1.02-1	1.05-1	1.02-2	0.97-3	1.11	1.00	...	...	...	...	1.00-1i	0.99-1i	1.01-1i	1.19-1i
Germany	...	0.97-1	1.06-1	1.01-2	0.98-3	1.10	1.00	...	...	...	...	0.99-1	1.00-1	0.94-1	1.01-1
Greece	1.00-1	1.01-1	1.01-1	...	...	1.22	1.04	1.00i	0.99i	1.05-3	0.94-3	1.01-1	1.00-1	0.94-1	1.01-1
Hungary	...	0.98-1	1.04-1	1.01-2	0.99-3	1.12	0.95-3	1.00-4i	1.00-4i	...	...	0.96-1	0.99-1	1.00-1	1.20-1
Iceland	1.00-3	1.00-3	1.32-3	...	...	1.19	1.07	...	...	...	...	1.03-1	1.00-1	0.99-1	1.46-1
Ireland	1.00-3	1.01-3	1.04-3	...	...	1.07	1.00	...	...	...	...	0.99-1i	1.00-1	0.98-1	1.10-1i
Italy	1.00-1	1.00-1	1.02-1	...	...	1.11	0.96-3	1.00i	1.00i	...	...	0.98-1	0.97-1	0.99-1	1.26-1
Latvia	0.99-1	1.02-1	1.14-1	...	...	1.16	1.00	1.00i	1.00i	...	...	0.99-1i	1.00-1i	0.99-1i	1.31-1i
Liechtenstein	...	...	...	...	...	...	...	...	...	...	...	1.04-1i	0.97-1i	0.81-1i	0.63-1i
Lithuania	...	0.99-1	1.12-1	1.01-1	1.03-3	1.18	1.05	...	...	1.01-3	0.99-3	0.99-1i	1.00-1i	0.96-1i	1.27-1i
Luxembourg	...	0.97-1	1.00-1	...	...	1.13	0.97	...	...	...	...	0.98-1	0.99-1	1.02-1	1.10-1
Malta	...	1.02-4	1.05-4	...	...	1.26	1.03-3	1.01i	1.03i	...	...	0.99-1	1.00-1	1.00-1	1.27-1
Monaco	...	...	...	...	...	...	...	...	...	...	...	...	...	...	...
Montenegro	...	...	...	...	...	1.24	0.94	1.00i	0.99i	...	...	0.90	0.95	1.01	1.26
Netherlands	1.00-1	1.05-1	1.03-1	...	...	1.13	1.02	...	...	...	...	1.00-1	1.00-1	1.01-1	1.13-1
North Macedonia	...	...	...	...	...	1.41	1.09	1.00-4i	0.98-4i	...	...	1.03-1	1.00-1	0.97-1	1.24-1
Norway	1.00-3	0.99-3	1.05-3	...	0.99-3	1.16	1.05	...	...	...	...	1.00-1	1.00-1	0.96-1	1.33-1
Poland	1.00-1	1.00-1	1.02-1	...	...	1.11	1.02	...	...	...	...	0.99-1	1.00-1	0.97-1	1.34-1
Portugal	1.01-1	1.00-1	1.10-1	...	...	1.10	1.00	1.00i	0.98i	...	...	0.99-1	0.97-1	0.98-1	1.11-1
Republic of Moldova	...	...	...	...	...	1.26	1.02	1.00-4	1.00-4	...	...	1.00i	1.00i	0.99i	1.25i
Romania	...	1.00-1	0.98-1	...	...	1.22	0.98	1.00i	0.99i	...	...	1.00-1	0.99-1	1.00-1	1.21-1
Russian Federation	...	...	...	1.01-2	1.00-3	1.12	1.00	1.00i	1.00i	...	...	0.98-1	1.00-1	0.98-1	1.16-1
San Marino	...	...	...	...	...	...	...	1.00	1.00	...	...	1.04	1.14	0.89	0.74
Serbia	1.00-4	1.01-3	1.02-3	...	1.01-3	1.22	1.01	1.00-2	0.99-2	...	...	0.99i	1.00i	1.01i	1.28i
Slovakia	1.00-3	0.99-1	1.01-1	1.01-1	0.93-3	1.18	1.01	...	...	...	...	0.98-1	0.99-1	1.01-1	1.34-1
Slovenia	1.00-1	1.00-1	1.03-1	...	...	1.16	1.01	1.00-4i	1.00-4i	1.02-3	0.98-3	0.98-1	1.00-1	1.02-1	1.30-1
Spain	0.94-1	1.03-1	1.05-1	...	...	1.08-3	1.00	1.00	0.99	...	...	1.00-1	1.02-1	1.01-1	1.16-1
Sweden	1.00-1	1.00-1	1.06-1	...	...	1.11	1.02	...	...	...	...	0.99-1	1.01-1	1.06-1	1.36-1
Switzerland	1.00-3	1.00-3	0.96-3	...	...	1.12	0.99	...	...	...	...	0.99-1	0.99-1	0.96-1	1.02-1
Ukraine	...	...	...	...	...	1.16	0.97	...	...	...	...	...	1.02-4	0.98-4	1.13-4
United Kingdom	1.00-3	1.00-3	1.10-3	...	...	1.07	0.97	...	...	...	...	1.00-1	1.00-1	1.03-1	1.27-1
United States	1.00-2	1.01-2	1.03-2	...	...	1.09	0.98	...	...	...	...	1.01-1i	0.99-1i	0.99-1i	1.26-1i

LOCATION/WEALTH																
F												G				
Disparity in primary completion				Disparity in lower secondary completion				Disparity in upper secondary completion				Wealth disparity in minimum proficiency				
Adjusted parity index		% of poorest completing		Adjusted parity index		% of poorest completing		Adjusted parity index		% of poorest completing		End of primary		End of lower secondary		
Location	Wealth	M	F	Location	Wealth	M	F	Location	Wealth	M	F	Reading	Mathematics	Reading	Mathematics	Country code
								4.5.1								
								2018								
0.95[-1]	0.89[-1]	84[-1]	92[-1]	1.01[-1]	0.91[-1]	91[-1]	89[-1]	0.87[-1]	0.65[-1]	61[-1]	63[-1]	...	...	0.51	0.75	ALB
...	...	...	...	...	...	...	...	...	...	...	...	...	...	...	...	AND
1.00[-3]	...	...	...	0.99[-1]	0.94[-4]	...	...	1.11[-1]	0.79[-4]	...	...	0.92[-2]	...	0.70	0.70	AUT
...	...	...	...	...	...	...	...	...	...	...	...	...	...	0.61	0.54	BLR
...	...	...	...	0.98[-1]	0.84[-4]	...	...	1.04[-1]	0.78[-4]	...	...	...	...	0.68	0.67	BEL
...	...	...	...	...	...	...	...	...	...	...	...	...	...	...	...	BMU
...	...	...	...	...	...	...	...	...	...	...	...	...	...	0.50	0.45	BIH
...	...	...	...	1.00[-1]	0.79[-4]	91[-1]	90[-1]	0.86[-1]	0.41[-4]	79[-1]	80[-1]	0.91[-2]	0.70[-3]	0.40	0.45	BGR
...	...	...	...	...	...	...	...	...	...	...	...	...	...	0.85	0.81	CAN
...	...	100[-1]	100[-1]	1.01[-1]	0.99[-4]	100[-1]	100[-1]	0.98[-1]	0.94[-4]	91[-1]	91[-1]	...	0.83[-3]	0.80	0.68	HRV
1.00[-3]	...	100[-3]	...	1.01[-1]	1.00[-4]	100[-3]	98[-3]	1.00[-1]	0.90[-4]	...	79[-3]	...	...	0.68	0.66	CZE
1.00[-1]	...	...	...	1.01[-1]	1.00[-4]	...	...	0.86[-1]	0.94[-4]	...	...	...	...	0.78	0.80	DNK
1.00[-1]	...	100[-3]	100[-1]	0.98[-1]	1.00[-4]	99[-1]	99[-1]	0.97[-1]	0.76[-4]	79[-1]	89[-1]	...	...	0.90	0.88	EST
1.00[-1]	...	...	...	1.00[-1]	1.00[-4]	...	...	0.84[-1]	0.98[-4]	...	...	...	...	0.85	0.80	FIN
...	...	...	...	1.01[-1]	0.97[-4]	...	...	1.02[-1]	0.83[-4]	...	...	0.92[-2]	0.52[-3]	0.70	0.64	FRA
...	...	...	...	1.00[-4]	0.96[-4]	...	...	1.03[-4]	0.83[-4]	...	...	0.82[-2]	0.68[-3]	0.71	0.68	DEU
1.00[-1]	...	100[-1]	100[-1]	1.01[-1]	0.99[-4]	97[-1]	96[-1]	0.94[-1]	0.83[-4]	89[-1]	93[-1]	...	...	0.63	0.57	GRC
...	...	...	...	1.02[-1]	0.96[-4]	98[-1]	96[-1]	0.92[-1]	0.70[-4]	79[-1]	78[-1]	0.94[-2]	0.60[-3]	0.58	0.53[-3]	HUN
1.00[-3]	...	...	...	1.00[-3]	1.00[-4]	...	...	0.65[-3]	1.04[-4]	...	...	...	...	0.73	0.76	ISL
1.00[-3]	...	...	...	1.01[-3]	1.00[-4]	...	...	1.05[-3]	0.93[-4]	...	...	...	...	0.84	0.78	IRL
1.00[-1]	1.00[-1]	100[-1]	100[-1]	1.00[-1]	1.00[-1]	100[-1]	100[-1]	1.01[-1]	0.75[-1]	59[-1]	83[-1]	...	...	0.72	0.64[-3]	ITA
0.99[-1]	...	100[-1]	98[-1]	0.99[-1]	0.95[-4]	98[-1]	100[-1]	0.83[-1]	0.73[-4]	51[-1]	81[-1]	...	...	0.78	0.78	LVA
...	...	...	...	...	...	...	...	...	...	...	...	...	...	...	...	LIE
...	...	...	100[-3]	0.96[-1]	1.03[-4]	96[-1]	94[-1]	0.83[-1]	0.95[-4]	70[-1]	86[-1]	0.91[-2]	0.79[-3]	0.68	0.65	LTU
...	...	...	...	1.04[-1]	0.85[-4]	...	...	1.10[-1]	0.59[-4]	...	...	...	...	0.58	0.59	LUX
...	...	...	...	...	0.99[-4]	...	...	...	0.73[-4]	...	...	...	...	0.64	...	MLT
...	...	...	...	...	...	...	...	...	...	...	...	...	...	...	...	MCO
...	...	...	...	...	...	...	...	...	...	...	...	...	...	0.63	0.60	MNE
...	...	...	...	...	0.95[-4]	...	...	...	1.10[-1]	...	...	...	...	0.73	0.78	NLD
...	...	...	...	...	...	...	...	...	...	...	...	...	...	0.45	0.39	MKD
1.00[-3]	...	...	...	1.00[-3]	0.99[-4]	...	...	1.20[-3]	0.93[-4]	...	...	...	0.79[-3]	0.81	0.78	NOR
1.00[-1]	...	100[-1]	100[-1]	0.98[-1]	0.97[-4]	98[-1]	95[-1]	0.97[-1]	0.85[-4]	92[-1]	89[-1]	...	...	0.81	0.78	POL
1.01[-1]	...	100[-1]	100[-1]	1.00[-1]	0.88[-4]	87[-1]	85[-1]	0.93[-1]	0.49[-4]	68[-1]	74[-1]	...	...	0.71	0.65	PRT
...	...	...	...	...	...	...	...	...	...	...	...	...	...	0.44	0.38	MDA
...	...	...	...	0.98[-1]	0.91[-4]	98[-1]	98[-1]	0.83[-1]	0.62[-4]	73[-1]	72[-1]	...	...	0.47	0.40	ROU
...	...	...	...	...	...	...	...	...	...	...	...	0.99[-2]	0.96[-3]	0.79	0.76	RUS
...	...	...	...	...	...	...	...	...	...	...	...	...	...	...	...	SMR
0.99[-4]	0.96[-4]	95[-4]	100[-3]	0.98[-3]	0.91[-4]	98[-3]	99[-3]	0.97[-1]	0.49[-4]	91[-3]	92[-3]	...	0.89[-3]	0.62	0.60	SRB
1.00[-3]	...	100[-1]	100[-3]	0.99[-1]	1.00[-4]	100[-1]	97[-1]	1.01[-1]	0.80[-4]	86[-1]	79[-1]	0.59[-2]	0.46[-3]	0.56	0.57	SVK
...	...	...	...	...	1.00[-4]	...	...	...	0.90[-4]	...	...	...	...	0.79	0.77	SVN
1.01[-3]	...	...	...	0.97[-1]	0.84[-1]	77[-1]	91[-1]	0.83[-1]	0.41[-1]	40[-1]	40[-1]	...	...	0.77[-3]	0.68	ESP
1.00[-1]	...	...	...	1.00[-1]	1.02[-4]	...	...	1.04[-1]	0.93[-4]	...	...	...	...	0.77	0.73	SWE
1.00[-3]	...	...	...	1.01[-3]	1.00[-4]	...	...	1.11[-3]	0.64[-4]	...	...	...	...	0.68	0.76	CHE
...	...	...	...	...	...	...	...	...	...	...	...	...	...	0.63	0.54	UKR
1.00[-3]	...	...	...	1.00[-3]	1.00[-4]	...	...	1.02[-3]	0.95[-4]	...	...	...	...	0.81	0.76	GBR
...	0.99[-2]	99[-2]	99[-2]	...	0.99[-2]	97[-2]	99[-2]	...	0.90[-2]	87[-2]	89[-2]	...	...	0.76	0.62	USA

TABLE 6: SDG 4, Target 4.7 – Education for sustainable development and global citizenship

By 2030, ensure that all learners acquire the knowledge and skills needed to promote sustainable development, including, among others, through education for sustainable development and sustainable lifestyles, human rights, gender equality, promotion of a culture of peace and non-violence, global citizenship and appreciation of cultural diversity and of culture's contribution to sustainable development

	A Extent to which global citizenship education and education for sustainable development are mainstreamed				B % of schools providing life skills-based HIV/AIDS education	C % of students and youth with understanding of	
	Education policies/ frameworks	Curriculum	In-service teacher training	Student assessment		HIV/AIDS and sexuality	Scientific literacy
SDG indicator	4.7.1				4.7.2	4.7.4	4.7.5
Reference year	2017				2018		
Region	% of countries					Median	
World	...	...	...	...	...	...	...
Sub-Saharan Africa	...	...	...	...	...	32i	...
Northern Africa and Western Asia	...	...	...	...	99i	...	...
Northern Africa	-i	100i	-i	100i	-i	...	...
Western Asia	...	...	...	...	100i	...	...
Central and Southern Asia	50i	33i	17i	100i	...	...	...
Central Asia	100i	-i	-i	100i	...	...	...
Southern Asia	25i	50i	25i	100i	100i	23i	...
Eastern and South-eastern Asia	57i	57i	...	86i	...	31i	...
Eastern Asia	33i	67i	33i	67i	...	...	...
South-eastern Asia	75i	50i	...	100i	...	40i	...
Oceania	...	...	...	...	...	...	...
Latin America and the Caribbean	...	50i	...	...	...	...	...
Caribbean	...	...	...	...	...	...	...
Central America	50i	50i	25i	50i	...	...	...
South America	...	43i	...	71i	...	46i	...
Europe and Northern America	...	83i	...	...	...	...	...
Europe	69	83	...	...	...	...	...
Northern America	...	100i	-i	100i	100i	...	...
Low income	...	...	...	...	...	24i	...
Middle income	...	68i	...	...	...	33i	...
Lower middle	...	...	...	...	...	32i	...
Upper middle	...	65i	...	...	...	...	...
High income	...	77i	...	...	...	...	...

A   Extent to which (i) global citizenship education and (ii) education for sustainable development (including climate change education) are mainstreamed at all levels in (a) national education policies; (b) curricula; (c) teacher education; and (d) student assessment [*Source:* UNESCO, 2019]. (Low = reflected not at all or little/not included in student assessment. Medium = reflected somewhat. High = fully reflected/included in student assessment.)

B   Percentage of lower secondary schools providing life skills-based HIV/AIDS education.

C   Percentage of students and youth with adequate understanding of issues relating to global citizenship and sustainable development [*Sources:* OECD (PISA 2018 Annex B1); TIMSS 2015; UNAIDS].

D   Percentage of primary schools with water, sanitation and hygiene (WASH): basic drinking water, basic (single-sex) sanitation or toilets, and basic handwashing facilities.

E   Percentage of public schools with electricity, and computers or internet used for pedagogical purposes.

F   Percentage of public primary schools with access to adapted infrastructure and materials for students with disabilities.

G   Level of attacks on students, teachers or institutions [*Source:* Global Coalition to Protect Education from Attack].

H   Level of bullying [*Source:* UNICEF].

I   Internationally mobile students, inbound and outbound numbers enrolled (thousand) and inbound and outbound mobility rates (as a percentage of total tertiary enrolment in the country).

J   Volume of official development assistance flows (all sectors) for scholarships (all levels) and imputed student costs, total gross disbursements (million constant 2017 US$).
Region totals include flows unallocated to specific countries. World total includes flows unallocated to specific countries or regions.

Note: ICT = information and communication technology.

Source: UIS unless noted otherwise. Data refer to school year ending in 2018 unless noted otherwise.

Aggregates represent countries listed in the table with available data and may include estimates for countries with no recent data.

(-) Magnitude nil or negligible.

(…) Data not available or category not applicable.

(± n) Reference year differs (e.g. -2: reference year 2016 instead of 2018).

(i) Estimate and/or partial coverage.

SDG 4, Means of implementation 4.a – Education facilities and learning environments

By 2030, build and upgrade education facilities that are child, disability and gender sensitive and provide safe, non-violent, inclusive and effective learning environments

SDG 4, Means of implementation 4.b – Scholarships

By 2020, substantially expand globally the number of scholarships available to developing countries

D			E			F	G	H
% of schools with WASH facilities			% of schools with ICT for pedagogical purposes			% of schools with adapted infrastructure and materials for students with disabilities	Level of bullying	Level of attacks on education
Basic drinking water	Basic sanitation or toilets	Basic handwashing	Electricity	Internet	Computers			
4.a.1							4.a.2	4.a.3
2018							2017	2018
Median								—
100i	100i	100i	100i	85i	90i	...	...	...
54i	...	34i	29	6i	14i	...	...	...
100i	100i	100i	100	90i	95	...	...	...
93i	90i	100i	98	49i	78	...	...	...
100i	100i	100	100	100	100	...	...	...
79i	90i	90i	100i	46i	42i	...	...	...
...	...	95i	100i	65i	93i	10i	...	...
69	88i	53i	87i	32i	18i	...	...	...
96i	100i	95	99i	97i	99i	...	...	...
100i	100i	100i	100i	99	100i	...	...	...
71i	57i	65	93i	...	...	...	...	...
...	100i	...	100i	63i	33i	...	...	...
100i	100i	100i	100i	61i	83i	29i	...	...
100i	100i	100i	100i	97i	100i	23i	...	...
82i	75i	...	96i	23	38i	30i	...	...
67i	...	...	95	41i	75i	...	...	...
100i	100i	100i	100i	100i	100i	...	...	...
100i	100i	100i	100i	100i	100i	...	...	...
...	...	100i	100i	100i	100i	100i	...	...
48i	...	24i	16i	...	...	...	...	...
83i	92i	90i	96i	42i	65i	...	...	...
78i	82i	73i	81	20i	35i	...	...	...
100i	100i	100i	100i	50i	78i	...	...	...
100i	100i	100i	100i	100i	100i	...	...	...

I				J	
Internationally mobile tertiary students				Official development assistance, in US$ (000,000)	
Mobility rate (%)		Number (000)			
Inbound	Outbound	Inbound	Outbound	Scholarships	Imputed student costs
2018				4.b.1	
				2017	
Median		Sum			
4i	6	5,113i	5,309-1	1331	2224
2i	7	118i	390-1	192	304
4	8	336i	625-1	188	604
2	2	35i	159-1	92	350
6	8	301	466-1	96	255
0.4i	7	110i	814-1	88	302
1	12	42	197-1	16	25
0.3i	5	68i	617-1	72	277
1	3	638	1,422-1	131	453
3	3	468	1,117-1	26	337
0.5i	3	169i	305-1	105	116
...	...	...	31-1	55	1
2i	2i	...	341-1	72	174
...	20i	...	38	10	8
1i	2	29i	57	12	41
0.4i	2	124i	246	50	125
7	5	3,307	1,116-1	78	209
7	6	2,112	978-1	78	209
10	3	1,195	138-1		
1i	6	...	321-1	137	203
2i	6	1,331i	3,150-1	620	1831
1i	5	202i	1,208-1	377	861
4i	6	1,129i	1,942-1	243	970
9	5	3,754	1,268-1	..	..

	Extent to which global citizenship education and education for sustainable development are mainstreamed				% of schools providing life skills-based HIV/AIDS education	% of students and youth with understanding of	
	A				B	C	
	Education policies/ frameworks	Curriculum	In-service teacher training	Student assessment	% of schools providing life skills-based HIV/AIDS education	HIV/AIDS and sexuality	Scientific literacy
SDG indicator	4.7.1				4.7.2	4.7.4	4.7.5
Reference year	2017					2018	
Sub-Saharan Africa							
Angola	…	…	…	…	…	32[-3]	…
Benin	…	…	…	…	…	24[-4]	…
Botswana	…	…	…	…	…	47[-2]	…
Burkina Faso	…	…	…	…	21	…	…
Burundi	High	Low	Low	High	100[-1]	…	…
Cabo Verde	…	…	…	…	100[-1]	…	…
Cameroon	Medium	High	Medium	High	…	35[-4]	…
Central African Republic	High	Low	Medium	High	…	…	…
Chad	Medium	Medium	Medium	High	…	13[-4]	…
Comoros	…	…	…	…	…	…	…
Congo	…	…	…	…	…	33[-3]	…
Côte d'Ivoire	Medium	High	Medium	High	…	27[-3]	…
D. R. Congo	Medium	Medium	Low	High	–[-3]	20[-4]	…
Djibouti	…	…	…	…	…	…	…
Equat. Guinea	…	…	…	…	…	…	…
Eritrea	…	…	…	…	…	…	…
Eswatini	…	…	…	…	100[-1]	50[-4]	…
Ethiopia	Medium	High	Medium	High	…	31[-2]	…
Gabon	…	…	…	…	…	…	…
Gambia	…	…	…	…	…	…	…
Ghana	…	…	…	…	…	22[-4]	…
Guinea	…	…	…	…	…	20[-2]	…
Guinea-Bissau	…	…	…	…	…	22[-4]	…
Kenya	…	…	…	…	…	60[-4]	…
Lesotho	…	…	…	…	…	36[-4]	…
Liberia	…	…	…	…	…	…	…
Madagascar	…	…	…	…	…	24[-3]	…
Malawi	…	…	…	…	…	42[-2]	…
Mali	High	High	Medium	High	…	23[-3]	…
Mauritania	…	…	…	…	…	58[-2]	…
Mauritius	High	Low	Medium	Low	…	32[-4]	…
Mozambique	…	…	…	…	…	31[-3]	…
Namibia	Medium	High	Medium	Low	…	…	…
Niger	…	…	…	…	100[-2]	22[-2]	…
Nigeria	…	…	…	…	…	29[-1]	…
Rwanda	…	…	…	…	100	64[-3]	…
Sao Tome and Principe	…	…	…	…	100[-1]	43[-4]	…
Senegal	High	High	Medium	High	76	28[-3]	…
Seychelles	…	…	…	…	81	…	…
Sierra Leone	…	…	…	…	53	…	…
Somalia	…	…	…	…	…	…	…
South Africa	…	…	…	…	…	46[-2]	…
South Sudan	…	…	…	…	…	…	…
Togo	…	…	…	…	…	26[-4]	…
Uganda	…	…	…	…	…	46[-2]	…
United Republic of Tanzania	…	…	…	…	…	…	…
Zambia	High	High	High	High	…	44[-4]	…
Zimbabwe	…	…	…	…	…	46[-3]	…

% of schools with WASH facilities			% of schools with ICT for pedagogical purposes			% of schools with adapted infrastructure and materials for students with disabilities	Level of bullying	Level of attacks on education	Internationally mobile tertiary students — Mobility rate (%)		Internationally mobile tertiary students — Number (000)		Official development assistance, in US$ (000,000)		Country code
Basic drinking water	Basic sanitation or toilets	Basic handwashing	Electricity	Internet	Computers				Inbound	Outbound	Inbound	Outbound	Scholarships	Imputed student costs	
			4.a.1				4.a.2	4.a.3					4.b.1		
			2018				2017	2018	2018				2017		
20-2	...	...	22-2	3-2	7-2	...	...	Sporadic	...	6-2	...	14-1	3	3	AGO
45-2	...	...	26	...	...	...	...	Sporadic	7-1	6-1	9-1	7-1	2	12	BEN
...	...	...	...	...	...	...	...		2-1	5-1	1-1	3-1	1	0.1	BWA
58	...	30	19	0.1	0.3	2-1	...	Affected	3	6-1	3	6-1	3	7	BFA
39	35	21	8	-	-	-	...	Affected	3-1	5-1	2-1	3-1	2	2	BDI
99	92	78	79	16	42	...	...	...	1	28-1	0.2	3-1	2	6	CPV
34-1	39-1	...	28	...	...	...	...	Very heavy	1-1	9-1	4-1	26-1	9	64	CMR
14-2	...	...	4-2	...	...	...	...	...	...	...	...	2-1	2	2	CAF
...	17-3i	...	...	...	...	...	...	Sporadic	...	14-3	...	7-1	2	3	TCD
...	...	...	41-1	8-1	31-1	...	...	...	-4	79-4i	-4	6-1	6	6	COM
...	...	...	...	...	...	...	...	Sporadic	...	18-1	...	10-1	6	11	COG
43	...	31	38	...	...	...	...	Sporadic	2-1	6-1	5-1	14-1	6	23	CIV
-3	...	-3	9-3	-3	-3	-3	...	Very heavy	0.4-2	2-2	2-2	11-1	5	5	COD
88-1	98-1	...	95-1	...	...	...	...	...	...	...	...	2-1	1	4	DJI
...	...	...	...	...	...	...	...	...	...	...	...	1-1	0.3	0.2	GNQ
...	26	3	29	...	...	...	...	...	...	20-2	...	2-1	1	1	ERI
79-1	...	...	100-1	16-2	15-2	12-2	...	...	...	...	...	2-1	1	-	SWZ
...	...	...	...	...	...	...	Medium-4	Affected	...	1-4i	...	7-1	7	6	ETH
...	...	...	...	...	...	...	...	Sporadic	...	...	...	7-1	2	14	GAB
84	84	...	36-1	...	100-1	...	...	...	...	...	...	2-1	2	0.4	GMB
33	...	35	25	8	3	...	...	Sporadic	2	3-1	10	15-1	10	10	GHA
25-2	...	85-2	14-2	-2	-2	...	...	Affected	...	6-4i	...	9-1	4	16	GIN
...	...	...	...	...	...	...	...	...	...	...	...	3-1	1	5	GNB
...	...	...	83-2	...	...	...	...	Affected	1-1	3-1	5-1	15-1	8	7	KEN
...	...	...	...	...	...	...	...	...	0.4	13-1	0.1	3-1	0.4	0.1	LSO
59-1	...	62-1	10-1	...	...	...	...	...	...	...	...	1-1	1	0.2	LBR
...	...	...	8	0.4	2	...	...	Sporadic	1	3-1	2	5-1	4	9	MDG
87-1	...	28-1	25	...	...	...	...	Sporadic	...	...	...	3-1	2	0.2	MWI
...	17-2i	...	16-1	...	...	...	...	Affected	1-1	10-3	0.4-1	9-1	4	11	MLI
44	...	...	40	...	14-1	...	...	Sporadic	1-1	24-1	0.3-1	5-1	2	4	MRT
100	100	89	100	27	100	31	...	...	5-1	22-1	2-1	9-1	2	6	MUS
...	48-2i	15-2i	...	...	...	...	...	Sporadic	0.4	1-1	1	3-1	3	3	MOZ
...	...	...	73	...	...	...	High-4	...	6-1	9-1	3-1	5-1	1	1	NAM
16i	...	10	5	-	2	-2	...	Affected	5	7-1	4	5-1	1	4	NER
...	...	...	...	...	...	...	...	Heavy	...	...	...	85-1	10	17	NGA
54	...	66	74	30	75	24	...	...	4	6-1	3	5-1	4	3	RWA
88-1	72-1	88-1	87-1	...	59-1	...	...	...	...	28-3i	...	1-1	1	1	STP
78	...	34	50	13	28	...	...	Sporadic	8	8-1	14	13-1	7	39	SEN
100	100	100	100	100	100	7	...	...	-	37-1	-	0.5-1	2	0.2	SYC
52	47	66	6	1	3	5	...	...	...	...	...	1-1	1	0.3	SLE
...	...	...	...	...	...	...	...	Affected	...	...	...	6-1	2	1	SOM
...	...	...	...	...	...	...	High-4	Affected	4-1	1-1	45-1	8-1	7	3	ZAF
...	...	...	...	...	...	...	...	Affected	...	...	...	1-1	1	0.1	SSD
...	58	...	25	...	3	...	...	Sporadic	...	7-1	...	6-1	2	10	TGO
...	...	41-1	...	...	...	...	...	Affected	...	3-4i	...	6-1	4	2	UGA
...	...	20-2i	85-2	...	...	...	...	...	...	4-2	...	7-1	5	2	TZA
82-1	...	...	36-1	6-1	85-1	4-2	...	Sporadic	...	...	...	5-1	4	0.4	ZMB
...	...	...	...	...	...	...	...	Affected	0.5-3	13-3	1-3	19-1	3	2	ZWE

TABLE 6: Continued

	Extent to which global citizenship education and education for sustainable development are mainstreamed (A)				% of schools providing life skills-based HIV/AIDS education (B)	% of students and youth with understanding of (C)	
	Education policies/ frameworks	Curriculum	In-service teacher training	Student assessment		HIV/AIDS and sexuality	Scientific literacy
SDG indicator	4.7.1				4.7.2	4.7.4	4.7.5
Reference year	2017				2018		
Northern Africa and Western Asia							
Algeria	…	…	…	…	-	…	29-3
Armenia	Medium	High	Medium	High	100	18-2	…
Azerbaijan	…	…	…	…	…	…	…
Bahrain	…	…	…	…	100	…	73-3
Cyprus	…	…	…	…	…	…	61
Egypt	Medium	High	Medium	High	-‑2	5-3	42-3
Georgia	High	High	Medium	High	…	…	36
Iraq	Medium	Low	Medium	High	…	…	…
Israel	…	…	…	…	…	…	67
Jordan	…	…	…	…	…	…	60
Kuwait	High	High	High	High	…	…	49-3
Lebanon	…	…	…	…	…	…	38
Libya	…	…	…	…	…	…	…
Morocco	Medium	High	Medium	High	…	…	31
Oman	High	High	Medium	High	99	…	72-3
Palestine	…	…	…	…	3	…	…
Qatar	High	Medium	Medium	High	100	…	52
Saudi Arabia	…	…	…	…	100-1	…	38
Sudan	…	…	…	…	…	…	…
Syrian Arab Republic	…	…	…	…	…	…	…
Tunisia	…	…	…	…	…	…	34-3
Turkey	High	High	Medium	High	…	…	75
United Arab Emirates	…	…	…	…	…	…	57
Yemen	…	…	…	…	…	…	…
Central and Southern Asia							
Afghanistan	…	…	…	…	…	2-3	…
Bangladesh	Medium	Low	Low	High	100	…	…
Bhutan	…	…	…	…	…	23-2	…
India	…	…	…	…	…	26-2	…
Iran, Islamic Republic of	Medium	Medium	Medium	High	…	…	73-3
Kazakhstan	…	…	…	…	…	…	40
Kyrgyzstan	…	…	…	…	100-1	…	…
Maldives	High	High	Medium	High	100-1	…	…
Nepal	…	…	…	…	…	…	…
Pakistan	Medium	High	High	High	…	…	…
Sri Lanka	…	…	…	…	100	…	…
Tajikistan	High	Low	Medium	High	…	…	…
Turkmenistan	…	…	…	…	…	…	…
Uzbekistan	High	Low	Medium	High	…	…	…
Eastern and South-eastern Asia							
Brunei Darussalam	…	…	…	…	…	…	54
Cambodia	High	High	Medium	High	…	40-4	…
China	…	…	…	…	…	…	98
DPR Korea	…	…	…	…	…	…	…
Hong Kong, China	…	…	…	…	95[i]	…	88
Indonesia	…	…	…	…	…	…	40
Japan	High	High	High	High	…	…	89
Lao PDR	…	…	…	…	…	…	…
Macao, China	…	…	…	…	100	…	94
Malaysia	…	…	…	…	100	41-3	63
Mongolia	Medium	High	Medium	Low	…	22-4	…
Myanmar	High	Low	Low	High	85	17-2	…
Philippines	…	…	…	…	…	…	22
Republic of Korea	Medium	Medium	Medium	High	…	…	86
Singapore	Medium	High	Medium	High	…	…	91
Thailand	High	Low	…	High	…	46-2	56
Timor-Leste	…	…	…	…	…	11-2	…
Viet Nam	…	…	…	…	…	…	96

D % of schools with WASH facilities			E % of schools with ICT for pedagogical purposes			F % of schools with adapted infrastructure and materials for students with disabilities	G Level of bullying	H Level of attacks on education	I Internationally mobile tertiary students — Mobility rate (%)		Number (000)		J Official development assistance, in US$ (000,000)		Country code
Basic drinking water	Basic sanitation or toilets	Basic handwashing	Electricity	Internet	Computers				Inbound	Outbound	Inbound	Outbound	Scholarships	Imputed student costs	
4.a.1							4.a.2	4.a.3					4.b.1		
2018							2017	2018	2018				2017		
...	...	...	...	...	...	...	Low-4	Sporadic	1	2-1	9	26-1	20	107	DZA
...	...	...	100	100	100	...	...	...	4	6-1	5	6-1	5	11	ARM
100	100	100	100	54	94	...	...	...	2	21-1	5	43-1	5	11	AZE
100	100	100	100	100	100	100	...	...	13	14-1	6	6-1	...	...	BHR
...	...	...	...	...	...	...	...	...	23-1	69-3	10-1	24-1	...	...	CYP
...	100-2	100-2	100-2	48-2	78-1	...	...	Sporadic	2-2	1-1	...	35-1	15	43	EGY
100	100	100	100	100	100	...	...	...	8+1	8-1	12+1	11-1	5	17	GEO
...	...	...	...	...	...	...	...	Affected	...	...	...	30-1	6	8	IRQ
100-2	100-2	100-2	100-2	85-2i	85-2i	...	Medium-4	Affected	3-4	4-1	...	15-1	...	...	ISR
36	36	36	36	13	13	...	...	...	14	9-1	45	25-1	12	15	JOR
100i	100i	100i	100i	...	...	...	...	...	...	20-1	...	23-1	...	...	KWT
...	...	100	100	90	66	...	...	Sporadic	9	8-1	22	17-1	4	27	LBN
...	...	...	...	...	...	...	...	Affected	...	...	...	12-1	2	6	LBY
75	90	81	96	79	77	17	...	...	2	5-1	20	51-1	23	144	MAR
100	100	100	100	100	100	...	...	...	3	12-1	3	14-1	...	...	OMN
100	99	96	100	85	74	46	...	Very heavy	-	11-1	-	25-1	6	17	PSE
100	100	100	100	100	100	100	...	...	34	21-1	12	7-1	...	...	QAT
100-1	100-1	100-1	100-1	100-1	100-1	100-1	...	Sporadic	5	5-1	74	84-1	...	...	SAU
93-2	73-2	...	54-2	...	13-2	...	...	Very heavy	...	2-3	...	13-1	3	4	SDN
...	...	...	...	...	...	...	...	Heavy	...	7-2	...	54-1	15	96	SYR
98	...	100	100	49	96	...	...	Sporadic	2	8-1	6	22-1	17	82	TUN
...	...	...	...	...	...	...	High-4	Heavy	2-1	1-1	108-1	46-1	22	76	TUR
100-1	100-1	100-1	100-1	100-1	100-1	...	...	Sporadic	49-2	6-1	...	11-1	...	...	ARE
...	...	...	...	...	...	...	...	Very heavy	...	...	...	25-1	3	14	YEM
60	26	5	...	...	...	...	...	Very heavy	--4	7-4i	...	30-1	11	6	AFG
79-2	37-2	29-2	43-2	4-2	18-2	...	...	Affected	...	2-1	...	58-1	11	20	BGD
...	...	...	87-3	52	14-3	...	...	...	...	...	...	4-1	3	0.2	BTN
...	92	53	52	...	10-2	64	...	Very heavy	0.1	1-1	45	332-1	19	142	IND
...	...	...	...	...	...	...	...	Affected	1-1	1-2	21-1	53-1	7	79	IRN
...	...	...	100+1	...	...	7	...	...	3+1	14-1	23+1	85-1	4	12	KAZ
...	...	100-1	100-1	41-1	89-1	...	...	...	8	5-1	17	11-1	3	4	KGZ
100-1	100-1	100-1	100-1	100-1	100-1	100-1	...	...	...	20-1	...	3-1	2	0.1	MDV
39-2i	...	...	...	...	...	...	High-4	Sporadic	...	17-1	...	64-1	4	13	NPL
52-2i	...	...	...	...	...	...	...	Affected	...	3-1	...	53-1	15	41	PAK
90	88	90	100	12	42	...	...	Affected	0.4	7-1	1	21-1	7	3	LKA
...	...	...	...	...	...	...	...	...	1-1	7-1	2-1	20-1	2	2	TJK
...	...	...	...	...	...	...	...	Sporadic	0.2-4	107-4i	0.1-4	46-1	1	1	TKM
90	92	90	100	89	97	13-1	...	...	0.2	12-1	1	35-1	3	6	UZB
...	...	100	100	...	...	...	Medium-3	...	5	29-1	0.5	3-1	...	...	BRN
...	48-2i	49-2i	...	...	...	...	Medium-4	...	...	3-1	...	6-1	14	3	KHM
100	99i	97	99	96	97	...	...	Affected	0.4	2-1	178	928-1	22	349	CHN
...	...	...	...	...	...	...	...	...	...	0.3-3i	...	1-1i	0.1	1	PRK
100	100	100	100	99i	99i	95i	...	...	13	12-1i	37	36-1i	...	...	HKG
58	50	69	93	...	40	...	...	Affected	0.1	1-1	8	48-1	55	41	IDN
...	...	...	...	...	...	...	...	Sporadic	4-1	1-1	164-1	32-1	...	...	JPN
...	...	...	37-2	...	...	...	...	...	0.5	5-1	0.5	5-1	11	0.4	LAO
100	100	100	100	100	100	64	...	...	49	11-1i	16	4-1i	...	...	MAC
92	100	92	98	97	100-1	40	...	Sporadic	10	5-1	123	63-1	6	14	MYS
...	...	...	...	71-2	...	...	Medium-4	...	1	7-1	2	11-1	11	6	MNG
75	64	56	27-1	0.2	1	1	...	Heavy	-	1-1	0.5	9-1	14	1	MMR
49-2i	33-2i	49-2i	...	...	...	...	...	Affected	...	0.5-1	...	17-1	81	3	PHL
100-2	100-2	100-2	100-2	100-2	100-2	...	Low-4	...	2-1	3-1	71-1	105-1	...	...	KOR
100-1	100-1	100-1	100-1	...	...	...	...	...	...	...	...	24-1	...	...	SGP
...	...	...	...	...	...	...	...	Affected	1-2	1-2	32-2	32-1	6	9	THA
67	...	61	82	...	...	...	...	...	...	...	...	3-1	5	2	TLS
...	...	...	...	...	...	...	Medium-4	...	0.2-2	4-2	6-2	95-1	31	52	VNM

TABLE 6: Continued

	A				B	C	
	Extent to which global citizenship education and education for sustainable development are mainstreamed				% of schools providing life skills-based HIV/AIDS education	% of students and youth with understanding of	
	Education policies/ frameworks	Curriculum	In-service teacher training	Student assessment		HIV/AIDS and sexuality	Scientific literacy
SDG indicator	4.7.1				4.7.2	4.7.4	4.7.5
Reference year	2017					2018	
Oceania							
Australia	...	High	...	High	...	...	81
Cook Islands	High	Medium	...	High	32_{-2}	...	...
Fiji	...	...	...	...	...	...	...
Kiribati	...	...	...	...	...	...	...
Marshall Islands	...	...	...	...	...	...	...
Micronesia, F. S.	...	...	...	...	...	...	...
Nauru	...	...	...	...	50_{-2}	...	...
New Zealand	High	High	High	High	...	...	82
Niue	...	...	...	...	100_{-2}	...	...
Palau	...	...	...	...	...	...	...
Papua New Guinea	...	...	...	...	...	...	...
Samoa	...	...	...	...	...	...	...
Solomon Is	...	...	...	...	...	...	...
Tokelau	...	...	...	...	...	...	...
Tonga	...	...	...	...	...	...	...
Tuvalu	Medium	High	Medium	Low	...	...	...
Vanuatu	...	...	...	...	...	...	...
Latin America and the Caribbean							
Anguilla	...	...	...	...	...	...	...
Antigua and Barbuda	...	...	...	...	100	86_{-2}	...
Argentina	...	High	Medium	High	...	...	47
Aruba	...	...	...	...	...	...	...
Bahamas	...	...	...	...	...	4_{-4}	...
Barbados	...	...	...	...	...	46_{-4}	...
Belize	...	...	...	...	...	43_{-2}	...
Bolivia, P. S.	High	High	High	High	...	...	...
Brazil	...	...	...	...	...	...	45
British Virgin Islands	...	...	...	...	...	...	...
Cayman Islands	...	...	...	...	100	...	...
Chile	Medium	Medium	Low	Low	...	...	65
Colombia	High	Low	Low	High	...	30_{-3}	50
Costa Rica	...	...	...	...	73	...	52
Cuba	...	...	...	...	100	60_{-4}	...
Curaçao	...	...	...	...	...	...	...
Dominica	...	...	...	...	100_{-2}	...	...
Dominican Republic	...	...	...	...	...	0.4_{-4}	15
Ecuador	High	Low	...	High	...	...	...
El Salvador	Medium	Low	Medium	Low	...	36_{-4}	...
Grenada	...	...	...	...	92	...	...
Guatemala	High	Medium	High	Low	...	22_{-3}	...
Guyana	...	...	...	...	...	49_{-4}	...
Haiti	Medium	Medium	Medium	High	...	37_{-1}	...
Honduras	Medium	High	Medium	High	...	...	...
Jamaica	...	...	...	...	...	...	...
Mexico	High	High	Medium	High	...	...	53
Montserrat	...	...	...	...	-	...	...
Nicaragua	...	...	...	...	...	...	...
Panama	...	...	...	...	...	...	29
Paraguay	...	...	...	...	...	...	...
Peru	High	High	Medium	High	...	75_{-2}	46
Saint Kitts and Nevis	Medium	High	Medium	...	...	...	...
Saint Lucia	...	...	...	...	...	...	...
Saint Vincent/Grenadines	...	...	...	...	96	...	...
Sint Maarten	...	...	...	...	...	...	...
Suriname	...	...	...	...	...	...	...
Trinidad and Tobago	Medium	High	Low	Low	...	...	54_{-3}
Turks and Caicos Islands	...	...	...	...	...	...	...
Uruguay	Medium	Low	Medium	Low	100_{-1}	...	56
Venezuela, B. R.	...	...	...	...	...	...	...

% of schools with WASH facilities			% of schools with ICT for pedagogical purposes			% of schools with adapted infrastructure and materials for students with disabilities	Level of bullying	Level of attacks on education	Internationally mobile tertiary students				Official development assistance, in US$ (000,000)		Country code
Basic drinking water	Basic sanitation or toilets	Basic handwashing	Electricity	Internet	Computers				Mobility rate (%) Inbound	Mobility rate (%) Outbound	Number (000) Inbound	Number (000) Outbound	Scholarships	Imputed student costs	
4.a.1							4.a.2	4.a.3					4.b.1		
2018							2017	2018	2018				2017		
100-2	100-2	100-2	100-2	100-2	100-2	...	...	...	21-1	1-1	381-1	13-1	...	...	AUS
100-2	100-2	100-2	100-2	100-2	100-2	4-2	...	...	...	...	...	0.2-1i	0.3	-	COK
...	...	...	98-2	...	...	...	...	...	...	...	...	1-1	6	-	FJI
...	...	...	...	...	...	...	...	...	...	...	...	1-1	4	-	KIR
3-2	27-2	36-2	54-2	26-2	22-2	21-2	...	...	...	...	...	0.3-1	0.1	...	MHL
...	...	...	...	...	...	...	...	...	...	...	...	0.2-1	0.3	-	FSM
...	100-2	...	67-2	...	33-2	...	...	...	...	...	...	0.2-1i	1		NRU
...	...	...	...	...	...	...	...	...	20-1	2-1	53-1	5-1	...	...	NZL
100-2	100-2	100-2	100-2	100-2	100-2	100-2	...	...	...	...	...	--1	0.4		NIU
...	...	...	...	...	...	...	...	...	...	...	...	--1	0.1	-	PLW
...	...	...	...	...	...	...	...	...	...	...	...	1-1	15	-	PNG
100	100	100	100	14-1	14-1	...	...	...	...	...	...	1-1	8	-	WSM
...	...	...	50	-	-	...	...	...	...	...	...	3-1	5	-	SLB
...	...	...	...	...	...	...	...	...	...	...	...	0.1-1i	-		TKL
...	...	...	...	...	...	...	...	...	...	...	...	1-1	3		TON
...	...	...	100	...	...	...	Medium-4	...	...	...	...	0.5-1	1		TUV
...	...	...	...	...	...	...	...	...	...	...	...	2-1	3	2	VUT
...	...	...	...	...	...	...	...	...	...	...	...	0.2-1	...	...	AIA
100	100	100	100	90	90	5	...	...	...	...	...	1-1	0.1	-	ATG
...	...	...	97-1	40-1	65-1	...	High-4	...	3-1	0.3-1	89-1	9-1	4	7	ARG
...	...	...	...	...	...	...	...	...	28-2	20-2	0.3-2	0.2-1	...	...	ABW
...	...	...	...	...	...	...	Medium-4	...	...	...	...	4-1	...	...	BHS
100	100	100	100	...	...	...	...	...	...	...	...	1-1	...	...	BRB
...	...	...	...	...	...	...	...	...	...	9-1	...	1-1	0.4	0.1	BLZ
...	...	...	...	...	...	...	...	Sporadic	...	...	...	20-1	2	3	BOL
...	...	95-1	96-1	62-1	54-1	28-1	Medium-4	Sporadic	0.2-1	1-1	21-1	59-1	14	45	BRA
100-1	100-1	81-1	100-1	100-1	89-1	63-1	...	...	17-2	43-2	...	0.4-1	...	...	VGB
100	100	100	100	100	100	100	...	...	...	...	...	1-1	...	...	CYM
...	...	...	...	...	...	...	Low-4	Sporadic	0.4-1	1-1	5-1	16-1	3	11	CHL
...	...	...	88	43	81	...	High-4	Affected	0.2	2-1	5	44-1	8	36	COL
83	68	66	96	59	63	55	Low-4	...	...	1-1	...	3-1	1	3	CRI
100	100	100	100	13	100	...	...	...	...	1-1	...	2-1	1	2	CUB
...	...	...	...	...	...	...	...	...	...	...	...	0.2-1	...	...	CUW
100-2	100-2	100-2	100-2	100-2	100-2	2-2	...	...	...	...	...	1-1	0.3	0.2	DMA
...	90-2i	...	...	23-2	...	...	High-4	...	2-1	1-1	10-1	4-1	1	1	DOM
40	...	83	79	39	75	...	High-4	...	1-3	3-3	5-3	22-1	3	8	ECU
82-1	...	...	98	23	61	30	Medium-4	...	1	2-1	1	5-1	1	2	SLV
100	...	100	100	72	72	22	...	...	85	6-1	8	1-1	0.1	-	GRD
...	76-2i	...	...	9-2	12-2	...	Low-4	...	...	1-3	...	3-1	1	2	GTM
...	...	...	...	...	...	...	...	...	...	...	...	2-1	1	0.1	GUY
...	...	...	...	...	...	...	...	...	...	...	...	10-1	4	6	HTI
65-2i	...	...	48-2	16-2	16-2	5-2	Medium-4	...	1	2-3	3	5-1	1	1	HND
...	...	100	100	84-1	85	12-1	...	...	...	6-3	...	5-1	1	1	JAM
...	75-2i	...	...	39-2	...	...	Low-4	...	1-1	1-1	25-1	35-1	8	34	MEX
100	100	100	100	100	100	25	...	...	...	...	...	--1	0.1		MSR
...	...	...	...	...	...	...	Medium-4	Heavy	...	...	...	3-1	1	1	NIC
...	82-2i	...	...	...	...	...	Medium-4	...	...	2-2	...	4-1	1	1	PAN
67-2	...	62-2	94-2	5-2	5-2	...	Medium-4	...	...	...	...	14-1	1	1	PRY
55	...	...	80	41	78	30	High-4	...	...	2-1	...	33-1	3	12	PER
79-2	...	79-2	100-2	...	...	...	...	...	73-4	13-3i	...	1-1	...	...	KNA
100	100	100	100	100	100	...	...	...	13	31-1	0.3	1-1	1	0.1	LCA
100	100	100	100	100	100	100	...	...	...	33-3i	...	1-1	0.2	-	VCT
...	...	...	...	...	...	...	...	...	36-3	49-3i	0.1-3	0.1-1	...	...	SXM
...	...	...	...	...	...	...	...	...	...	...	...	1-1	1	0.1	SUR
...	...	...	...	...	...	...	...	...	...	...	...	3-1	...	...	TTO
100	100	100	100	93	97	...	...	...	...	54-3i	...	0.2-1	...	...	TCA
100-1	...	...	100-1	100-1	100-1	100-1	Low-4	...	...	3-1	...	5-1	1	1	URY
97-2	90-2	...	99-2	...	...	...	...	Affected	...	...	...	21-1	1	7	VEN

TABLE 6: Continued

	A Extent to which global citizenship education and education for sustainable development are mainstreamed				B	C % of students and youth with understanding of	
	Education policies/ frameworks	Curriculum	In-service teacher training	Student assessment	% of schools providing life skills-based HIV/AIDS education	HIV/AIDS and sexuality	Scientific literacy
SDG indicator	4.7.1				4.7.2	4.7.4	4.7.5
Reference year	2017					2018	
Europe and Northern America							
Albania	High	High	Low	High	95	...	53
Andorra	Medium	High	Medium	High	100	...	...
Austria	Medium	High	Medium	...	...	...	78
Belarus	...	...	...	...	...	...	76
Belgium	Medium	High	Low	High	...	...	80
Bermuda	...	...	...	...	100-2	...	...
Bosnia and Herzegovina	Medium	Medium	Medium	...	...	...	43
Bulgaria	High	High	High	High	...	19-2	53
Canada	...	High	Medium	High	...	...	87
Croatia	...	...	...	...	...	...	75
Czechia	High	High	Medium	Low	...	...	81
Denmark	Medium	High	Medium	High	...	...	81
Estonia	Medium	Medium	Medium	High	...	...	91
Finland	Medium	High	...	High	100+1i	...	87
France	High	Medium	High	High	...	...	80
Germany	High	High	High	High	...	...	80
Greece	Medium	High	Medium	High	...	...	68
Hungary	Medium	High	Medium	High	...	...	76
Iceland	...	...	...	...	...	...	75
Ireland	High	High	Medium	High	...	...	83
Italy	...	...	...	...	...	...	74
Latvia	High	High	High	High	...	...	82
Liechtenstein	...	...	...	...	...	...	...
Lithuania	High	High	Low	High	...	71-4	78
Luxembourg	...	...	...	...	...	...	73
Malta	High	High	Medium	High	...	...	66
Monaco	High	Medium	Medium	High	100+1	...	...
Montenegro	...	...	...	...	...	...	52
Netherlands	High	High	...	...	...	...	80
North Macedonia	High	High	...	High	...	...	51
Norway	...	...	...	...	...	...	79
Poland	High	High	High	High	...	...	86
Portugal	High	High	...	High	...	...	80
Republic of Moldova	...	...	...	...	100	...	57
Romania	High	High	Medium	High	...	...	56
Russian Federation	High	High	High	High	...	...	79
San Marino	...	...	...	...	...	...	...
Serbia	High	High	Medium	High	...	...	62
Slovakia	High	Medium	Medium	Low	...	...	71
Slovenia	...	...	...	...	...	...	85
Spain	High	High	Medium	High	...	...	79
Sweden	High	High	High	High	...	...	81
Switzerland	...	...	...	...	...	...	80
Ukraine	...	...	...	...	...	23-4	74
United Kingdom	...	...	...	...	...	...	83
United States	...	...	...	...	...	...	81

D			E			F	G	H	I				J		Country code
% of schools with WASH facilities			% of schools with ICT for pedagogical purposes			% of schools with adapted infrastructure and materials for students with disabilities	Level of bullying	Level of attacks on education	Internationally mobile tertiary students				Official development assistance, in US$ (000,000)		
Basic drinking water	Basic sanitation or toilets	Basic handwashing	Electricity	Internet	Computers				Mobility rate (%)		Number (000)				
									Inbound	Outbound	Inbound	Outbound	Scholarships	Imputed student costs	
4.a.1							4.a.2	4.a.3	4.b.1						
2018							2017	2018	2018				2017		
55	83	71	94	47	50	5	...	...	1	12-1	2	17-1	6	23	ALB
100	100	100	100	100	100	100	...	...	44	247-1	0.3	1-1	...	...	AND
...	...	...	...	...	...	...	...	...	17-1	4-1	74-1	19-1	...	...	AUT
100	100	100	100	87	100	...	...	...	4	5-1	17	22-1	3	28	BLR
100	...	100	100	100	100	...	...	...	9-1	3-1	45-1	15-1	...	...	BEL
...	...	100-2	100-2	100-2	100-2	100-2	...	...	10	243-1	0.1	2-1	...	...	BMU
...	...	...	...	...	...	...	...	...	7	13-1	7	13-1	4	29	BIH
...	...	...	...	...	...	...	...	...	5-1	9-2	14-1	25-1	...	...	BGR
...	...	...	...	...	...	...	...	...	13-1i	3-1i	210-1i	49-1	...	...	CAN
...	...	...	...	...	...	...	...	...	3-1	6-2	5-1	10-1	...	...	HRV
...	...	...	...	...	...	...	...	...	13-1	4-1	44-1	13-1	...	...	CZE
100-2	100-2	100-2	100-2	100-2	100-2	...	...	...	11-1	2-1	34-1	5-1	...	...	DNK
100-2	100-2	100-2	100-2	100-2	100-2	...	Medium-4	...	8-1	8-1	4-1	4-1	...	...	EST
100+1i	100+1i	100+1i	100+1i	100+1i	100+1i	100+1i	...	...	8-1	4-1	24-1	11-1	...	...	FIN
100	100	100	100	98-1i	99-1i	...	...	...	10-1	4-1	258-1	89-1	...	...	FRA
100	100	100	100		...	...	Low-4	...	8-1	4-1	259-1	122-1	...	...	DEU
...	...	...	...	...	...	...	...	Sporadic	3-1	5-1	25-1	37-1	...	...	GRC
100-2	100-2	100-2	100-2	100-2	100-2	...	...	...	10-1	4-1	29-1	12-1	...	...	HUN
...	...	...	...	...	...	...	...	...	7-1	15-1	1-1	3-1	...	...	ISL
...	...	...	...	...	...	...	...	...	9-1	7-1	20-1	15-1	...	...	IRL
100-2	100-2	100-2	100-2	70-2i	...	...	...	...	5-1	4-1	98-1	74-1	...	...	ITA
100-2	100-2	100-2	100-2	100-2	100-2	18-2	...	...	7-1	6-1	6-1	5-1	...	...	LVA
...	...	...	...	...	...	...	...	...	88-1	133-2	1-1	1-1	...	...	LIE
...	...	...	...	...	...	...	...	...	5-1	8-1	6-1	10-1	...	...	LTU
...	...	...	...	...	...	...	...	...	47-1	156-1	3-1	11-1	...	...	LUX
...	...	...	...	...	...	...	High-4	...	8-1	8-2	1-1	1-1	...	...	MLT
100+1	100+1	100+1	100+1	100+1	100+1	100+1	...	...	0.3-1	50-1	...	0.4-1	...	...	MCO
...	...	...	...	...	...	...	...	...	...	20-1	...	5-1	1	2	MNE
100+1	100+1	100+1	100+1	100+1	100+1	...	...	...	11-1	2-1	96-1	18-1	...	...	NLD
...	...	...	...	...	...	...	...	...	5-1	7-3	3-1	5-1	3	9	MKD
100+1	100+1	100+1	100+1	100+1	100+1	...	Medium-4	...	3-1	6-1	9-1	18-1	...	...	NOR
100-2	100-2	100-2	100-2	100-2	100-2	...	Medium-4	...	4-1i	2-1	64-1i	25-1	...	...	POL
100	100	100	100	100	100	...	...	...	6-1	4-1	22-1	14-1	...	...	PRT
100	100	100	100	91	100	...	...	...	5	19-1	4	18-1	34	6	MDA
...	...	...	...	...	...	...	High-4	...	5-1	6-2	28-1	36-1	...	...	ROU
...	...	...	...	...	...	...	...	Sporadic	4-1	1-1	251-1	57-1	...	...	RUS
100	100	100	100	100	100	100	...	...	91	...	1	1-1	...	...	SMR
...	...	...	...	...	...	...	...	...	4	6-1	11	15-1	8	23	SRB
100-2	100-2	100-2	100-2	100-2i	100-2i	14-2i	...	...	7-1	21-1	11-1	32-1	...	...	SVK
100-2	100-2	100-2	100-2	100-2	100-2	...	...	...	4-1	4-1	3-1	3-1	...	...	SVN
100	100	100	100	100	100	...	Medium-4	...	3-1	2-1	65-1	41-1	...	...	ESP
...	...	...	...	...	...	...	...	...	7-1	4-1	29-1	17-1	...	...	SWE
100-2	100-2	100-2	100-2	100-2	100-2	...	...	...	18-1	5-1	53-1	14-1	...	...	CHE
...	...	78	100	58	82	66	...	Affected	3	5-1	50	78-1	11	110	UKR
...	...	...	...	...	...	...	...	...	18-1	1-1	436-1	35-1	...	...	GBR
...	...	...	...	...	...	...	...	Sporadic	5-1	0.5-1	985-1	87-1	...	...	USA

TABLE 7: SDG 4, Means of implementation 4.c – Teachers

By 2030, substantially increase the supply of qualified teachers, including through international cooperation for teacher training in developing countries, especially least developed countries and small island developing States

	PRE-PRIMARY A Classroom teachers (000)	B Pupil/teacher ratio	C % of trained classroom teachers (4.c.1)	D % of qualified classroom teachers (4.c.3)	E Teacher attrition rate (%) (4.c.6)	F Relative teacher salary level (4.c.5)	PRIMARY A Classroom teachers (000)	B Pupil/teacher ratio	C % of trained classroom teachers (4.c.1)	D % of qualified classroom teachers (4.c.3)	E Teacher attrition rate (%) (4.c.6)	F Relative teacher salary level (4.c.5)	SECONDARY A Classroom teachers (000)	B Pupil/teacher ratio	C % of trained classroom teachers (4.c.1)	D % of qualified classroom teachers (4.c.3)	E Teacher attrition rate (%) (4.c.6)	F Relative teacher salary level (4.c.5)
Reference year	2018						2018						2018					
Region	Sum	Median					Sum	Median					Sum	Median				
World	7,659	16	85i	98i	...	...	28,541	18	95i	100i	...	...	30,135	13	91i	98i	...	...
Sub-Saharan Africa	454	24	55i	82	...	...	2,951	36	86i	95	8i	...	1,917	24	70i	84i	...	...
Northern Africa and Western Asia	290	17	100i	100i	...	...	2,012	15	100i	100i	...	...	2,273	10	100i	100i	...	...
Northern Africa	111i	26i	88i	100i	...	...	949	24	100	100	9i	...	838i	17i	100i	100i	...	...
Western Asia	180	16	100i	100i	...	...	1,064	13	100i	100i	...	...	1,435	10	100i	100i	...	...
Central and Southern Asia	621i	12i	99i	88i	...	...	6,435	25	96	97	2i	...	7,139	19	83i	100i	...	...
Central Asia	71i	11i	100i	100i	...	...	256	22	100	98	4i	...	688i	10i	97i	100i	...	...
Southern Asia	550i	16i	86i	88i	...	...	6,179	30	86	93	1	...	6,451	24	83	94	...	...
Eastern and South-eastern Asia	3,759	18	97i	99i	4i	...	10,371	17	98	100	2i	...	10,108	13	95i	97	4i	...
Eastern Asia	2,873	17	97i	99i	3i	...	6,898	16	97i	100	2i	...	7,408	12	91i	100	4i	...
South-eastern Asia	886	18	97i	99i	9i	...	3,473	20	99	99	4i	...	2,700	18	96i	97	...	...
Oceania	28	14	85i	100i	...	...	70	21	86i	100i	...	...	55i	15i	...	89i	...	...
Latin America and the Caribbean	776i	16i	73i	97i	...	...	2,407	18	90i	98i	...	...	3,235	13	89i	93i	...	...
Caribbean	28i	11i	70i	96i	...	...	169	15	85	100	...	...	158	11	74	93	...	...
Central America	235	19	93i	100i	...	...	778	24	96i	97i	...	...	1,070	15	94i	99i	...	...
South America	514i	19i	...	91i	...	...	1,460	19	95i	93i	...	...	2,008i	18i	90i	93i	...	...
Europe and Northern America	1,730	12	...	...	...	0.68i	4,296	12	...	...	...	0.78i	5,408	9	...	...	...	0.90i
Europe	1,117	12	...	...	...	0.68i	2,526	12	...	...	...	0.79i	3,712	9	...	...	...	0.91i
Northern America	613	11	100i	100i	...	0.62i	1,770	12	100i	100i	...	0.63i	1,696	10	100i	99i	...	0.67i
Low income	272	28	46i	81	...	...	2,341	40	86i	96	6i	...	1,302	27i	61i	85i	...	...
Middle income	5,467	17	90i	96i	...	...	21,269	22	95i	98i	5i	...	22,647	15	91i	96i	...	...
Lower middle	1,771	20	90i	98i	...	...	10,557	27	95	94i	5i	...	10,570	19	89i	94i	...	...
Upper middle	3,697i	16	90i	94i	...	...	10,713	17	97i	99i	...	...	12,077	12	92i	97i	...	...
High income	1,919	13	...	...	...	...	4,931	12	97i	100i	...	0.83i	6,186	10	...	100i	...	...

A   Number of classroom teachers.

B   Pupil/teacher ratio, headcount basis.

C   Percentage of teachers who have received at least the minimum organized and recognized pre-service and in-service pedagogical training required to teach at a given level of education.

D   Percentage of teachers qualified according to national standards.

E   Teacher attrition rate (%).

F   Ratio of actual teacher salaries to comparable workers [*Sources*: OECD; for secondary: GEM Report weighted average of OECD lower secondary and upper secondary data].

Source: UIS unless noted otherwise. Data refer to school year ending in 2018 unless noted otherwise.

Aggregates represent countries listed in the table with available data and may include estimates for countries with no recent data.

(-) Magnitude nil or negligible.

(…) Data not available or category not applicable.

(± n) Reference year differs (e.g. -2: reference year 2016 instead of 2018).

(i) Estimate and/or partial coverage.

TABLE 7: Continued

Country or territory	PRE-PRIMARY						PRIMARY						SECONDARY						Country code
	A	B	C	D	E	F	A	B	C	D	E	F	A	B	C	D	E	F	
	Classroom teachers (000)	Pupil/teacher ratio	% of trained classroom teachers	% of qualified classroom teachers	Teacher attrition rate (%)	Relative teacher salary level	Classroom teachers (000)	Pupil/teacher ratio	% of trained classroom teachers	% of qualified classroom teachers	Teacher attrition rate (%)	Relative teacher salary level	Classroom teachers (000)	Pupil/teacher ratio	% of trained classroom teachers	% of qualified classroom teachers	Teacher attrition rate (%)	Relative teacher salary level	
SDG indicator			4.c.1	4.c.3	4.c.6	4.c.5			4.c.1	4.c.3	4.c.6	4.c.5			4.c.1	4.c.3	4.c.6	4.c.5	
Reference year	2018						2018						2018						
Sub-Saharan Africa																			
Angola	12₋₂	63₋₂	...	72₋₂	...	...	96₋₂	50₋₃	...	63₋₂	15₋₂	...	76₋₂	27₋₂	51₋₃	52₋₂	...	...	AGO
Benin	7	24	25	100	...	...	57	39	70	100	13₋₁	...	90₋₂	11₋₂	18₋₂	69₋₂	...	...	BEN
Botswana	2₋₄	19₋₄	...	...	...	...	15₋₃	24₋₃	...	100₋₄	...	...	...	...	...	...	...	...	BWA
Burkina Faso	5	17	42	71₋₁	4₋₂	...	81	40	88	95	5	...	55	23	60	99	2	...	BFA
Burundi	3	38	100	69₋₄	5	...	51	43	100	100	11₋₂	...	25	27	100	96	-₂	...	BDI
Cabo Verde	1	16	30	30	...	...	3	21	99	94	4	...	3	15	96	93	13	...	CPV
Cameroon	25	20	67₋₁	61₋₁	...	...	94	45	81₋₁	73₋₁	9₋₁	...	115₋₂	19₋₂	53₋₃	54₋₂ᵢ	...	...	CMR
Central African Republic	0.3₋₂	...	...	100₋₂	...	...	10₋₂	83₋₂	...	100₋₂	...	...	4₋₁	32₋₁	45₋₂	...	...	...	CAF
Chad	0.4₋₂	32₋₂	24₋₂	76₋₂	...	...	39₋₂	57₋₂	...	55₋₂	...	...	20₋₂	27₋₂	44₋₂	51₋₂	...	...	TCD
Comoros	1	28	56₋₁	44₋₁	22	...	4	28	...	...	31	...	9	8	...	...	30	...	COM
Congo	...	...	...	...	...	...	...	...	...	...	...	...	...	...	...	...	...	...	COG
Côte d'Ivoire	9	21	100	100	...	...	93	42	100	100	6	...	75	27	100	100	...	...	CIV
D. R. Congo	15₋₃	23₋₃	21₋₃	100₋₄	...	...	415₋₃	33₋₃	95₋₄	95₋₃	...	...	324₋₃	14₋₃	24₋₄	100₋₄	...	...	COD
Djibouti	0.2	14	...	100	...	...	2	29	100	100	3₋₁	...	2₊₁	27₊₁	100₋₃	100₊₁	6	...	DJI
Equat. Guinea	2₋₃	17₋₃	89₋₃	8₋₃	...	...	4₋₃	23₋₃	37₋₃	61₋₃	...	...	...	...	...	...	...	...	GNQ
Eritrea	2	29	42	...	4₋₁	...	9	39	84	84	...	...	7	35	...	84₋₁	...	...	ERI
Eswatini	...	...	...	...	...	...	9₋₁	27₋₁	88₋₁	75₋₁	...	...	7₋₂	16₋₂	73₋₃	73₋₂	...	...	SWZ
Ethiopia	23₋₁	...	...	100₋₁	...	...	...	...	...	...	...	...	...	...	...	...	...	...	ETH
Gabon	...	...	...	...	...	...	...	...	...	...	...	...	...	...	...	...	...	...	GAB
Gambia	2	48	69₋₁	69₋₁	19	...	10	36	100	100	...	...	8	...	100	100	...	...	GMB
Ghana	62₊₁	30₊₁	59₊₁	55	...	...	169₊₁	27₊₁	62₊₁	60	...	...	188₊₁	15₊₁	77	77	...	...	GHA
Guinea	...	...	...	...	...	...	38₋₂	47₋₂	75₋₂	92₋₂	22₋₂	...	...	...	...	...	...	...	GIN
Guinea-Bissau	...	...	...	...	...	...	...	...	...	...	...	...	...	...	...	...	...	...	GNB
Kenya	111₋₂	29₋₂	82₋₄	82₋₄	...	...	267₋₃ᵢ	31₋₃ᵢ	...	...	...	...	199₋₃ᵢ	...	...	...	...	...	KEN
Lesotho	3₋₂	18₋₂	100₋₃	100₋₃	...	...	11₋₁	33₋₁	87₋₂	83₋₂	...	...	5₋₁	25₋₁	89₋₂	91₋₂	...	...	LSO
Liberia	14₋₁	37₋₁	55₋₁	55₋₁	5₋₁	...	28₋₁	22₋₁	70₋₁	70₋₁	6₋₁	...	18₋₁	18₋₃	62₋₃	64₋₃	...	...	LBR
Madagascar	40	22	10	100	...	...	122	40	15	100	...	...	80	19	20	85	...	...	MDG
Malawi	32₋₃	42₋₃	...	100₋₃	...	...	76	59	...	100	...	...	14	72	...	56	...	...	MWI
Mali	7	20	...	100	...	...	65	38	...	...	...	...	58₋₁	17₋₁	...	...	...	...	MLI
Mauritania	2₋₃	19₋₃	...	...	...	...	19	34	91	...	11₋₂	...	9	26	97₋₁	...	...	...	MRT
Mauritius	2	12	100	100	7	...	6	16	100	100	7	...	11	11	53	100	...	...	MUS
Mozambique	...	...	...	...	...	...	119	55	97	100	...	...	33₋₁	37₋₁	85₋₃ᵢ	100₋₂	...	...	MOZ
Namibia	2	23	...	76	...	...	20	25	...	90	...	...	11₋₁	...	...	...	...	...	NAM
Niger	6	33	36	94	8	...	69	36₋₁	62	95	9	...	29	30₋₁	11₋₁	100	12₋₁	...	NER
Nigeria	...	...	...	...	...	...	...	...	...	...	...	...	...	...	...	...	...	...	NGA
Rwanda	6	36	46	86	1₋₁	...	42	60	94	99	2₋₁	...	23	28	63	81	5₋₁	...	RWA
Sao Tome and Principe	...	13₋₃	28₋₃	...	...	...	1₋₁	31₋₁	27₋₁	...	...	...	1₋₂	25₋₂	36₋₃	26₋₃	...	...	STP
Senegal	8	30	44	100	...	...	59	36	79	100	-₃	...	57₋₁	19₋₁	77₋₂ᵢ	76₋₃	...	...	SEN
Seychelles	0.2	18	86	90	7₋₁	...	1	14	85	92	10₋₁	...	1	11	100	99	12₋₁	...	SYC
Sierra Leone	...	14₋₁	37₋₁	21₋₁	...	...	50	28	61	46	11₋₁	...	...	22₋₁	70₋₁	37₋₂	...	...	SLE
Somalia	...	...	...	...	...	...	...	...	...	...	...	...	...	...	...	...	...	...	SOM
South Africa	...	30₋₄ᵢ	...	...	...	...	249₋₃	30₋₃	...	...	...	...	183₋₁	28₋₁	100₋₂	80₋₃	...	...	ZAF
South Sudan	3₋₃	35₋₃	...	87₋₃	...	...	27₋₃ᵢ	47₋₃ᵢ	...	84₋₃ᵢ	...	...	6₋₃ᵢ	27₋₃ᵢ	...	64₋₃ᵢ	...	...	SSD
Togo	5	28	63	32	...	...	39	40	73₋₃	33₋₃	2	...	...	...	...	...	...	...	TGO
Uganda	28₋₁	22₋₁	60₋₁	40₋₁	...	...	207₋₁	43₋₁	80₋₁	...	...	...	64₋₄	...	...	85₋₄	...	...	UGA
United Republic of Tanzania	13₋₁	114₋₁	50₋₂	52₋₁	...	...	200	51	99₋₂	98	0.3ᵢ	...	103	21	...	99	...	...	TZA
Zambia	...	...	...	...	...	...	78₋₁	42₋₁	99₋₁	94₋₁	...	...	...	...	...	...	...	...	ZMB
Zimbabwe	...	...	...	...	...	...	...	...	...	...	...	...	...	...	...	...	...	...	ZWE

Country or territory	PRE-PRIMARY						PRIMARY						SECONDARY						Country code
	A	B	C	D	E	F	A	B	C	D	E	F	A	B	C	D	E	F	
	Classroom teachers (000)	Pupil/teacher ratio	% of trained classroom teachers	% of qualified classroom teachers	Teacher attrition rate (%)	Relative teacher salary level	Classroom teachers (000)	Pupil/teacher ratio	% of trained classroom teachers	% of qualified classroom teachers	Teacher attrition rate (%)	Relative teacher salary level	Classroom teachers (000)	Pupil/teacher ratio	% of trained classroom teachers	% of qualified classroom teachers	Teacher attrition rate (%)	Relative teacher salary level	
SDG indicator			4.c.1	4.c.3	4.c.6	4.c.5			4.c.1	4.c.3	4.c.6	4.c.5			4.c.1	4.c.3	4.c.6	4.c.5	
Reference year	2018						2018						2018						
Northern Africa and Western Asia																			
Algeria	…	…	…	…	…	…	182	24	100_{-3}	100	13	…	…	…	…	…	…	…	DZA
Armenia	8	6	82_{-1}	100	…	…	10	15	…	100	…	…	29	8	…	100	…	…	ARM
Azerbaijan	11	18	91	96	…	…	41	15	100	100	…	…	124	8	92	100	…	…	AZE
Bahrain	2	14	100	100	12	…	10	12	100	100	5	…	10	10	100	100	7	…	BHR
Cyprus	2_{-1}	14_{-1}	…	…	…	…	5_{-1}	12_{-1}	…	…	…	…	7_{-1}	8_{-1}	…	…	…	…	CYP
Egypt	53	26	77_{-2}	100_{-2}	…	…	534	24	83	100_{-2}	…	…	603	15	82	100_{-2}	…	…	EGY
Georgia	…	…	…	…	…	…	34	9	…	…	…	…	37	8	…	…	…	…	GEO
Iraq	…	…	…	…	…	…	…	…	…	…	…	…	…	…	…	…	…	…	IRQ
Israel	…	…	…	…	…	0.85_{-1}	74_{-2}	12_{-2}	…	…	…	0.88_{-1}	…	…	…	…	…	…	ISR
Jordan	7	18	100	100	3_{-1}	…	61	19	100	100	3	…	64	12	100	100	14	…	JOR
Kuwait	9	8	75_{-3}	74_{-3}	…	…	32	9	79_{-3}	77_{-3}	…	…	45	8_{-3}	…	…	…	…	KWT
Lebanon	15_{-1}	16_{-1}	…	…	…	…	40_{-1}	12_{-1}	…	…	…	…	50_{-2}	8_{-2}	…	…	…	…	LBN
Libya	…	…	…	…	…	…	…	…	…	…	…	…	…	…	…	…	…	…	LBY
Morocco	…	…	…	…	…	…	161	27	100	100	4_{-1}	…	148	19	100	100	…	…	MAR
Oman	4	21	100	100	…	…	29	10	100	100	…	…	41	10	100	100	…	…	OMN
Palestine	9	17	100	…	6	…	20	24	100	70	5	…	44	17	100	50	5_{-1}	…	PSE
Qatar	3	15	…	100	10_{-1}	…	13	12	…	100	7_{-1}	…	10	11	…	100	6_{-1}	…	QAT
Saudi Arabia	25	15	100	100	…	…	239	14	100	100	…	…	270	12	100	100	…	…	SAU
Sudan	41_{-1}	26_{-1}	…	96_{-4}	…	…	…	…	…	…	…	…	…	…	…	…	…	…	SDN
Syrian Arab Republic	…	…	…	…	…	…	…	…	…	…	…	…	…	…	…	…	…	…	SYR
Tunisia	16_{-2}	15_{-2}	100_{-2}	100_{-2}	…	…	71	17	100	100	…	…	87	…	…	100	…	…	TUN
Turkey	77_{-1}	17_{-1}	…	…	…	0.85_{-1}	293_{-1}	17_{-1}	…	…	…	0.85_{-1}	657_{-1}	17_{-1}	…	…	…	0.85_{-1i}	TUR
United Arab Emirates	5_{-2}	29_{-2}	100_{-2}	100_{-2}	…	…	19_{-2}	25_{-2}	100_{-2}	100_{-2}	…	…	46_{-2}	10_{-2}	100_{-2}	100_{-2}	…	…	ARE
Yemen	1_{-2}	26_{-2}	…	54_{-2}	…	…	145_{-2}	27_{-2}	…	59_{-2}	…	…	…	…	…	…	…	…	YEM
Central and Southern Asia																			
Afghanistan	…	…	…	…	…	…	134	49	…	79	…	…	91	34	…	79	…	…	AFG
Bangladesh	…	…	…	…	…	…	577_i	30_i	50_{-1i}	100_i	5_{-2}	…	452	35	66_{-1}	100	1_{-1}	…	BGD
Bhutan	1	11	100	100	…	…	3	35	100	100	2_{-1}	…	7_i	11_i	100_i	100_i	…	…	BTN
India	461_{-3}	20_{-3}	…	…	…	…	$4,373_{-1}$	33_{-1}	70_{-1}	89_{-1}	1_{-1}	…	4,668	29	76_{-1}	94_{-1}	3_{-1}	…	IND
Iran, Islamic Republic of	…	…	…	…	…	…	286_{-1}	29_{-1}	100_{-1}	100_{-1}	…	…	299_{-1}	19_{-1}	98_{-1}	100_{-1}	…	…	IRN
Kazakhstan	…	9_{-4}	100_{-4}	100_{-4}	…	…	85_{+1}	17_{+1}	100_{+1}	100_{+1}	7_{-1}	…	251_{+1}	8_{+1}	100_{+1}	100_{+1}	…	…	KAZ
Kyrgyzstan	…	…	…	…	…	…	21	25	95_{-1}	74_{-1}	…	…	63	11	75_{-1}	…	…	…	KGZ
Maldives	1_{-1}	16_{-1}	88_{-1}	81_{-3}	8_{-1}	…	4_{-1}	10_{-1}	90_{-1}	83_{-3}	0.4_{-1}	…	…	…	…	…	…	…	MDV
Nepal	51_{+1}	19_{+1}	83_{+1}	88_{+1}	$-_{-1}$	…	201_{+1}	20_{+1}	97_{+1}	97_{+1}	$-_{-1}$	…	123_{+1}	28_{+1}	83_{+1}	89_{+1}	…	…	NPL
Pakistan	…	…	…	…	…	…	520	44	78	…	…	…	655_i	20_i	…	…	…	…	PAK
Sri Lanka	35	13	51	87	…	…	79	22	83	83	1_{-1}	…	156	18	82	79	…	…	LKA
Tajikistan	8_{-1}	11_{-1}	100_{-2}	57_{-1}	…	…	35_{-1}	22_{-1}	100_{-1}	97_{-1}	…	…	…	…	…	…	…	…	TJK
Turkmenistan	…	…	…	…	…	…	…	…	…	…	…	…	…	…	…	…	…	…	TKM
Uzbekistan	63	12	99	100	1_{-2}	…	116	22	99	100	2_{-2}	…	374	10_{-1}	97	100	3_{-2}	…	UZB
Eastern and South-eastern Asia																			
Brunei Darussalam	1	15	62	100	4	…	4	10	86	100	3	…	5	8	89	92	7_{-1}	…	BRN
Cambodia	8	33	100	100	…	…	51	42	100	100	…	…	…	…	…	…	…	…	KHM
China	2,647	17	…	90	…	…	6,202	16	…	96	1	…	6,360	13	…	93	1	…	CHN
DPR Korea	…	…	…	…	…	…	74	20	…	100	…	…	124	17_{-3}	…	100	…	…	PRK
Hong Kong, China	14	…	96	100	7	…	27	13	97	100	2_{-1}	…	31	11	97	100	3_{-2i}	…	HKG
Indonesia	466_i	13_i	…	60_i	…	…	1,727	17	…	90	7_{-4}	…	1,637	15	…	96	…	…	IDN
Japan	104_{-1}	28_{-1}	…	…	…	…	417_{-1}	16_{-1}	…	…	…	…	638_{-1}	11_{-1}	…	…	…	…	JPN
Lao PDR	12_i	18_i	90_i	42_i	1_{-1}	…	35_i	22_i	97_i	90_i	2_{-1}	…	37_i	18_i	96_i	81_i	…	…	LAO
Macao, China	1	14	99	100	3	…	2	13	99	100	0.5	…	3	10	91	100	4	…	MAC
Malaysia	55	18	97	98	14_i	…	240	12_{-1}	97	98	2_{-1}	…	227	11	93	97	…	…	MYS
Mongolia	8	33	97	97	1	…	10	30	93	94	2_{-1}	…	21	…	89	95	5	…	MNG
Myanmar	10	15	81	100	…	…	218	24	95	91	12	…	154	27	89	97	…	…	MMR
Philippines	67_{-1}	27_{-1}	100_{-1}	99_{-1}	19_{-2}	…	483_{-1}	29_{-1}	100_{-1}	100_{-1}	5_{-1}	…	377_{-1}	24_{-1}	100_{-1}	100_{-1}	2_{-3}	…	PHL
Republic of Korea	99_{-1}	13_{-1}	…	…	…	…	165_{-1}	16_{-1}	…	…	…	…	232_{-1}	13_{-1}	…	…	…	…	KOR
Singapore	…	…	…	…	…	…	16_{-1}	15_{-1}	99_{-1i}	100_{-1}	…	…	15_{-1}	11_{-1}	99_{-1i}	100_{-1}	…	…	SGP
Thailand	…	…	…	…	…	…	295	17	100	100	…	…	241	26	100	100	…	…	THA
Timor-Leste	1	32	…	…	…	…	8	27	…	76	…	…	6	27	…	84	…	…	TLS
Viet Nam	266	17	99	…	…	…	397	20	100	…	…	…	…	…	…	…	…	…	VNM

TABLE 7: Continued

Country or territory	PRE-PRIMARY						PRIMARY						SECONDARY						Country code
	A	B	C	D	E	F	A	B	C	D	E	F	A	B	C	D	E	F	
	Classroom teachers (000)	Pupil/teacher ratio	% of trained classroom teachers	% of qualified classroom teachers	Teacher attrition rate (%)	Relative teacher salary level	Classroom teachers (000)	Pupil/teacher ratio	% of trained classroom teachers	% of qualified classroom teachers	Teacher attrition rate (%)	Relative teacher salary level	Classroom teachers (000)	Pupil/teacher ratio	% of trained classroom teachers	% of qualified classroom teachers	Teacher attrition rate (%)	Relative teacher salary level	
SDG indicator			4.c.1	4.c.3	4.c.6	4.c.5			4.c.1	4.c.3	4.c.6	4.c.5			4.c.1	4.c.3	4.c.6	4.c.5	
Reference year	2018						2018						2018						
Oceania																			
Australia	...	...	...	...	...	0.93-2	...	...	...	...	...	0.93-2	...	...	...	...	...	...	AUS
Cook Islands	--2	16-2	78-2	84-3	...	...	0.1-2	17-2	95-2	100-3	...	...	0.1-2	16-2	98-3	98-3	...	...	COK
Fiji	...	...	...	...	...	...	...	...	...	...	...	...	...	...	...	...	...	...	FJI
Kiribati	...	...	...	...	...	...	1-1	25-1	73-2	100-1	...	...	...	...	...	...	...	...	KIR
Marshall Islands	...	...	...	...	...	...	...	...	...	...	...	...	...	...	...	...	...	...	MHL
Micronesia, F. S.	...	...	...	...	...	...	1-3i	20-3i	...	...	...	...	...	...	...	...	...	...	FSM
Nauru	--2	22-2	100-2	100-2	...	...	--2	40-2	100-2	100-2	...	...	--2	25-2	...	89-4	...	...	NRU
New Zealand	15-1	8-1	...	...	...	...	26-1	15-1	...	...	...	0.86-1	36-1	14-1	...	...	...	0.92-1i	NZL
Niue	--2	6-2	100-2	100-2	...	...	--2	15-2	92-2	100-2	...	...	--3	8-3	100-3	100-3	...	...	NIU
Palau	--4	18-4	...	100-4	...	...	...	...	...	...	...	...	...	...	...	...	...	...	PLW
Papua New Guinea	9-2	42-2	...	...	...	...	36-2	36-2	...	...	...	...	15-2	34-2	...	...	...	...	PNG
Samoa	0.4	12	100	100-2	...	...	...	...	...	...	...	...	...	...	...	...	...	...	WSM
Solomon Is	2	23	25	26	5	...	4	25	76	80	4	...	2-3	...	76-3	84-3	...	...	SLB
Tokelau	--2	4-2	42-2	...	...	...	--2	12-2	67-2	...	...	...	...	...	...	...	...	...	TKL
Tonga	0.2-3	11-3	...	...	...	...	1-3	22-3	92-3	92-3	...	...	1-3	15-3	59-3	80-3	...	...	TON
Tuvalu	0.1	8	91	100	...	...	0.1	16	80	100	...	...	0.1	9	65	98	...	...	TUV
Vanuatu	1-3	16-3	46-3	52-3	...	...	2-3	27-3	...	72-3	...	...	1-3	21-3	...	79-3	...	...	VUT
Latin America and the Caribbean																			
Anguilla	...	...	...	...	...	...	...	...	...	...	...	...	...	...	...	...	...	...	AIA
Antigua and Barbuda	...	...	65-3	100-3	...	...	1	12	53	100	...	...	1	9	48	98	...	...	ATG
Argentina	...	...	...	...	...	...	...	...	...	...	...	...	...	...	...	...	...	...	ARG
Aruba	...	...	...	...	...	...	...	...	...	...	...	...	...	...	...	...	...	...	ABW
Bahamas	0.2	21	63	63	...	...	2	19	90	90	...	...	2	12	83	83	...	...	BHS
Barbados	0.3	16	72	100	...	...	1	14	76	100	...	...	1	18	49	100	...	...	BRB
Belize	0.4	16	47	53	...	...	3	20	79	21	...	...	2	17	61	39	...	...	BLZ
Bolivia, P. S.	11	31	83	...	5	...	77	18	90	...	5	...	67	18	89	...	3	...	BOL
Brazil	310-1	16-1	...	...	...	...	796-1	20-1	...	...	...	...	1,382-1	17-1	...	...	...	0.86-3i	BRA
British Virgin Islands	...	8-2	...	...	...	...	0.3-1	12-1	80-1	92-1	...	...	0.3-1	9-1	89-3	86-1	...	...	VGB
Cayman Islands	...	...	...	...	...	...	0.3	16	100	100	...	...	0.3	11	100	100	...	...	CYM
Chile	24-1	25-1	...	99-1	...	0.89-1	85-1	18-1	...	100-1	...	0.87-1	83-1	18-1	...	100-1	...	0.93-1i	CHL
Colombia	51-4	...	97-4	94-4	...	...	185	23	97	97	...	...	186	26	98	98	...	...	COL
Costa Rica	11	13	90	97	...	1.15-1	40	12	94	97	...	1.21-1	38	12	96	99	...	1.47-1i	CRI
Cuba	...	...	...	...	...	...	81	9	100	76	...	...	83	10	100	76	...	...	CUB
Curaçao	...	...	...	...	...	...	...	...	...	...	...	...	...	...	...	...	...	...	CUW
Dominica	0.1-2	11-2	19-2	39-2	...	...	1-2	13-2	66-2	100-2	...	...	1-2	11-3	49-2	52-2	...	...	DMA
Dominican Republic	16	19	90	90	...	...	65	19	95	95	14	...	50-1	19-1	83-3	83-3	...	...	DOM
Ecuador	33	19	...	89	9	...	80	24	...	89	7	...	92	21	...	93	7	...	ECU
El Salvador	8	28	95	100	4	...	25	27	95	100	9-1	...	19	28	92	100	4	...	SLV
Grenada	0.3	12	38	36-2	3	...	1	16	63	100	7	...	1	13	46	100	7	...	GRD
Guatemala	...	...	...	...	...	...	117	20	...	...	...	...	117	10	...	...	...	...	GTM
Guyana	...	...	...	...	...	...	...	...	...	...	...	...	...	...	...	...	...	...	GUY
Haiti	...	...	...	...	...	...	...	...	...	...	...	...	...	...	...	...	...	...	HTI
Honduras	12-2	19-2	...	...	...	...	44-1	26-1	...	...	4-2	...	39-1	17-1	...	...	...	...	HND
Jamaica	10	11	70	94-2	3	...	10	25	100	100	13	...	12	17	100	100	14	...	JAM
Mexico	198-1	25-1	85-2	...	...	...	534-1	27-1	97-2	...	...	...	833-1	17-1	92-2	...	...	...	MEX
Montserrat	-	8	73	100	-	...	-	17	67	100	10	...	-	9	...	100	-	...	MSR
Nicaragua	...	...	...	...	...	...	...	...	...	...	...	...	...	...	...	...	...	...	NIC
Panama	6-1	15-1	100-1	100-2	...	...	19-1	22-1	99-1	90-1	...	...	24-1	14-1	96-4	84-1	...	...	PAN
Paraguay	...	...	...	...	...	...	...	...	...	...	...	...	...	...	...	...	...	...	PRY
Peru	84	20	...	...	...	...	207	17	95i	87	...	...	196	14	91	82	...	...	PER
Saint Kitts and Nevis	...	11-3	...	100-3	...	...	0.4-2	14-2	72-2	99-2	14-3	...	1-2	8-2	62-2	100-2	5-3	...	KNA
Saint Lucia	...	6-2	70-4	...	...	...	1	15	89	100	...	...	1	11	74	100	...	...	LCA
Saint Vincent/Grenadines	0.4	6	...	...	...	...	1	14	61	27	...	...	1	14	58-3	54	...	...	VCT
Sint Maarten	...	...	...	...	...	...	...	...	...	...	...	...	0.4-4	8-4	...	93-4	...	...	SXM
Suriname	1	20	100	98	...	...	5	13	99	98	...	...	5-3	12-3	71-3	60-3	...	...	SUR
Trinidad and Tobago	...	...	...	...	...	...	...	...	...	...	...	...	...	...	...	...	...	...	TTO
Turks and Caicos Islands	-	43	...	...	...	...	0.2	18	89-4	55	...	...	0.2	10	98-3	90	...	...	TCA
Uruguay	...	...	...	...	...	...	28-1	11-1	100-1	100-1	...	...	...	...	...	...	...	...	URY
Venezuela, B. R.	...	...	...	...	...	...	...	...	...	...	...	...	...	...	...	...	...	...	VEN

TABLE 7: Continued

Country or territory	PRE-PRIMARY						PRIMARY						SECONDARY						Country code
	A	B	C	D	E	F	A	B	C	D	E	F	A	B	C	D	E	F	
	Classroom teachers (000)	Pupil/teacher ratio	% of trained classroom teachers	% of qualified classroom teachers	Teacher attrition rate (%)	Relative teacher salary level	Classroom teachers (000)	Pupil/teacher ratio	% of trained classroom teachers	% of qualified classroom teachers	Teacher attrition rate (%)	Relative teacher salary level	Classroom teachers (000)	Pupil/teacher ratio	% of trained classroom teachers	% of qualified classroom teachers	Teacher attrition rate (%)	Relative teacher salary level	
SDG indicator			4.c.1	4.c.3	4.c.6	4.c.5			4.c.1	4.c.3	4.c.6	4.c.5			4.c.1	4.c.3	4.c.6	4.c.5	
Reference year	2018						2018						2018						
Europe and Northern America																			
Albania	5	17	86	73	-	...	10	18	90	84	2	...	24	11	...	97-1	3	...	ALB
Andorra	0.2	13	100	100	1	...	0.4	10	100	100	2	...	1	8	100	100	0.2	...	AND
Austria	22-1	12-1	...	...	...	...	33-1	10-1	...	...	...	0.74-1	74-1	9-1	...	...	...	0.91-1i	AUT
Belarus	44	8	93	46	2	...	22	19	100	100	6	...	76	9	97	100	...	...	BLR
Belgium	36-1	13-1	...	...	...	...	72-1	11-1	...	...	...	...	132-1	9-1	...	...	...	...	BEL
Bermuda	0.1-2	9-4	100-2	100-2	...	...	0.4-2	10-3	100-2	100-2	...	...	1-2	6-3	100-2	99-2	...	...	BMU
Bosnia and Herzegovina	2	14	...	...	...	...	9	17	...	...	...	...	27	9	...	...	...	...	BIH
Bulgaria	18-1	12-1	...	...	...	...	17-1	15-1	...	...	...	...	39-2	13-2	...	...	...	...	BGR
Canada	...	...	...	...	...	...	...	...	...	...	...	...	...	...	...	...	...	...	CAN
Croatia	9-2	13-2	...	...	...	...	12-2	14-2	...	...	...	...	52-2	7-2	...	...	...	...	HRV
Czechia	...	...	...	...	...	0.54-3	...	...	...	...	...	0.64-3	...	...	...	...	...	...	CZE
Denmark	...	...	...	...	...	0.68-1	44-4	11-4	...	...	...	0.81-1	49-4	11-4	...	...	...	...	DNK
Estonia	...	...	...	...	...	0.63-1	8-1	11-1	...	...	...	0.91-1	9-1	9-1	...	...	...	0.91-1i	EST
Finland	19-1	11-1	...	...	...	0.66-2	27-1	14-1	...	...	...	0.89-2	40-1	14-1	...	...	...	1.05-2i	FIN
France	...	...	...	...	...	0.79-3	...	...	...	...	...	0.77-3	...	...	...	...	...	0.94-4i	FRA
Germany	300-1	8-1	...	...	...	...	240-1	12-1	...	...	...	0.91-1	587-1	12-1	...	...	...	1.02-1i	DEU
Greece	15-1	10-1	...	...	...	0.78-1	69-1	9-1	...	...	...	0.78-1	78-1	9-1	...	...	...	0.83-1i	GRC
Hungary	26-2	12-2	...	...	...	0.64-1	37-2	11-2	...	...	...	0.68-1	81-2	10-2	...	...	...	0.71-1i	HUN
Iceland	3-3	5-3	...	...	...	...	3-3	10-3	...	...	...	...	...	...	...	...	...	...	ISL
Ireland	...	...	...	...	...	...	...	...	...	...	...	...	...	...	...	...	...	...	IRL
Italy	132-1	12-1	...	...	...	0.65-3	253-1	11-1	...	...	...	0.65-3	461-1	10-1	...	...	...	0.69-3i	ITA
Latvia	8-1	10-1	...	...	...	1.05-1	11-1	12-1	...	...	...	1.35-1	14-1	8-1	...	...	...	1.44-1i	LVA
Liechtenstein	0.1-1	8-1	...	...	...	...	0.3-1	8-1	...	...	...	...	0.3-1	10-1	...	...	...	...	LIE
Lithuania	11-1	10-1	...	...	...	0.92-4	8-1	14-1	...	...	...	0.92-4	31-1	8-1	...	...	...	0.92-4i	LTU
Luxembourg	2-2	10-2	...	...	...	...	4-2	8-2	...	...	...	...	5-2	9-2	...	...	...	...	LUX
Malta	1-1	12-1	...	...	...	...	2-1	13-1	...	...	...	...	4-1	7-1	...	...	...	...	MLT
Monaco	-+1	20+1	78+1	...	35+1	...	0.2+1	12+1	64+1	...	11+1	...	0.4-1i	9-1i	...	...	...	...	MCO
Montenegro	...	...	...	...	...	...	...	...	...	...	...	...	...	...	...	...	...	...	MNE
Netherlands	32-1	16-1	...	...	...	0.71-1	100-1	12-1	...	...	...	0.71-1	114-1	15-1	...	...	...	0.89-1i	NLD
North Macedonia	...	...	...	...	...	...	7-1	15-1	...	...	...	...	18-1	9-1	...	...	...	...	MKD
Norway	14-1	13-1	...	...	...	0.68-1	52-1	9-1	...	...	...	0.76-1	52-1	9-1	...	...	...	0.79-1i	NOR
Poland	100-1	13-1	...	...	...	0.68-2	226-1	10-1	...	...	...	0.79-2	265-1	9-1	...	...	...	0.81-2i	POL
Portugal	15-1	17-1	...	...	...	1.53-1	51-1	12-1	...	...	...	1.40-1	81-1	10-1	...	...	...	1.44-1i	PRT
Republic of Moldova	11	12	91	...	...	...	8	18	99	...	...	...	23	10	98	...	...	...	MDA
Romania	34-1	15-1	...	...	...	...	48-1	19-1	...	...	...	...	124-1	12-1	...	...	...	...	ROU
Russian Federation	...	...	...	...	...	...	309-1	21-1	...	...	...	...	...	...	...	...	...	...	RUS
San Marino	0.1	7	95	...	...	...	0.2	7	90	...	...	...	0.3	6	...	100	...	...	SMR
Serbia	14	12	...	100	...	...	19	14	...	100	...	...	67	8	...	100	...	...	SRB
Slovakia	14-1	12-1	...	...	...	0.50-1	15-1	16-1	...	...	...	0.65-1	40-1	11-1	...	...	...	0.66-1i	SVK
Slovenia	7-2	9-2	...	...	...	0.74-1	9-2	14-2	...	...	...	0.87-1	15-2	10-2	...	...	...	0.91-1i	SVN
Spain	98-1	13-1	...	...	...	...	232-1	13-1	...	...	...	...	288-1	12-1	...	...	...	...	ESP
Sweden	84-1	6-1	...	...	...	0.74-1	70-1	12-1	...	...	...	0.84-1	70-1	13-1	...	...	...	0.88-1i	SWE
Switzerland	15-1	12-1	...	...	...	...	51-1	10-1	...	...	...	...	62-1	10-1	...	...	...	...	CHE
Ukraine	...	...	...	...	...	...	129	13	87	...	...	...	324	7	93	...	...	...	UKR
United Kingdom	29-1	62-1	...	...	...	...	319-1	15-1	...	...	...	...	384-1	17-1	...	...	...	...	GBR
United States	613-1	14-1	...	...	...	0.62-1	1,769-1	14-1	...	...	...	0.63-1	1,695-1	15-1	...	...	...	0.67-1i	USA

Sophea Meng, 10 years old, at school in Cambodia. Sophea is a beneficiary of the Humanity and Inclusion programme.

CREDIT: Veuve/Humanity and Inclusion

Aid tables

INTRODUCTION

Data in the following four tables on official development assistance (ODA) are derived from the International Development Statistics (IDS) database of the Organisation for Economic Co-operation and Development (OECD). The IDS database records information provided annually by all members of the OECD Development Assistance Committee (DAC), as well as a growing number of non-DAC donors. Figures for ODA come from the DAC database, while figures for aid to education from the Creditor Reporting System (CRS), a database of individual projects. Figures in the DAC and CRS databases are expressed in constant 2018 US dollars. The DAC and CRS databases are available at www.oecd.org/dac/stats/idsonline.htm.

In 2019, the methodology of defining ODA changed:

- The *cash-flow* approach, used for 2010–12 and 2017 data, includes both grants and loans that (a) are undertaken by the official sector, (b) have promotion of economic development and welfare as their main objective and, for loans, (c) are at concessional financial terms (having a grant element of at least 25%).

- The new *grant-equivalent* approach, which is used for 2018 and 2019 data, counts only grants and the grant element of concessional loans as ODA.

The DAC glossary of terms and concepts is available at www.oecd.org/dac/financing-sustainable-development/development-finance-data/dac-glossary.htm.

AID RECIPIENTS AND DONORS

The DAC list of ODA recipients consists of all low- and middle-income countries, based on the World Bank income classification. For further information, see www.oecd.org/development/financing-sustainable-development/development-finance-standards/historyofdaclistsofaidrecipientcountries.htm.

Bilateral donors are countries that provide development assistance directly to recipient countries. Most are DAC members. Bilateral donors also contribute substantially to the financing of multilateral donors through contributions recorded as multilateral ODA.

Multilateral donors are international institutions with government membership that conduct many or all of their activities supporting development and aid recipient countries. They include multilateral development banks (e.g. World Bank, regional development banks), UN agencies and regional agencies.

- 'Bilateral flows' refers to bilateral donors contracting with multilateral donors to deliver a programme.

- 'Multilateral flows' refers to bilateral donor contributions pooled with other contributions and disbursed at the discretion of the multilateral donor to fund its own programmes and running costs.

For a list of bilateral and multilateral donors, see the 'Donors' worksheet at www.oecd.org/dac/financing-sustainable-development/development-finance-standards/DAC-CRS-CODES.xls.

TABLE 1: DEVELOPMENT AND HUMANITARIAN ASSISTANCE

ODA comprises bilateral and multilateral *development assistance*, both sector allocable and non-allocable (e.g. general budget support, humanitarian aid, debt relief). ODA disbursements are reported as follows:

- Total ODA
  - As volume, in million US dollars
  - As share of gross national income (GNI)

- Contributions to multilateral donors (a subset of total ODA)
  - As volume, in million US dollars
  - As share of total ODA disbursements.

Reported *humanitarian assistance* is a subset of total ODA from the OECD CRS database. It has been estimated using the cash-flow approach.

TABLES 2 AND 3: DEVELOPMENT ASSISTANCE TO EDUCATION BY DONOR AND BY RECIPIENT

Direct aid to education is aid reported in the CRS database as direct allocations to the education sector. Four education levels are distinguished:

- *Basic* covers primary education, basic life skills for youth and adults, and early childhood education.

- *Secondary* covers general secondary education and vocational training.

- *Post-secondary* covers tertiary education as well as advanced technical and managerial training.

- *Level unspecified* refers to any activity that cannot be attributed solely to the development of a particular level of education, such as education research and teacher training. General education programme support is often reported in this subcategory.

Total aid to education adds to direct aid a component of general budget support (i.e. aid provided to governments without being earmarked for specific projects or sectors). It is reported as follows:

- *Total aid to education* is direct aid to education plus 20% of general budget support.

- *Total aid to basic education* is direct aid to basic education plus 50% of 'level unspecified' and 10% of general budget support.

- *Total aid to secondary education* is direct aid to secondary education plus 25% of 'level unspecified' and 5% of general budget support.

- *Total aid to post-secondary education* is direct aid to post-secondary education plus 25% of 'level unspecified' and 5% of general budget support.

The *share of education in total ODA* is calculated using total ODA as reported in Table 1.

TABLE 4: DEVELOPMENT ASSISTANCE TO EDUCATION BY DONOR – TOP 3 RECIPIENTS

This table reports the amount and share of bilateral and multilateral donor assistance to education and to basic education allocated to the top three recipients of assistance from each donor.

TABLE 1: Development and humanitarian assistance

[Handwritten annotation pointing to "Disbursements": The payment of money from a fund. Paying out money.]

Country	OFFICIAL DEVELOPMENT ASSISTANCE (ODA)****																TOTAL HUMANITARIAN ASSISTANCE****			
	Disbursements																			
	Total				As a share of gross national income (%)				Of which, contributions to multilaterals								Constant 2018 US$ millions			
	Constant 2018 US$ millions								Constant 2018 US$ millions				As a share of total net disbursements (%)							
	2010–2012	2017	2018	2019	2010–2012	2017	2018	2019	2010–2012	2017	2018	2019	2010–2012	2017	2018	2019	2010–2012	2017	2018	2019
Australia	3,857	3,025	3,149	3,070	0.34	0.23	0.23	0.22	599	621	599	693	16	21	19	23	302	206	183	91
Austria	1,147	1,332	1,170	1,256	0.29	0.30	0.26	0.27	598	693	684	803	52	52	58	64	19	62	27	42
Belgium	2,662	2,335	2,312	2,259	0.55	0.45	0.43	0.42	958	958	981	1,039	36	41	42	46	124	177	190	200
Canada	4,646	4,385	4,660	4,684	0.32	0.26	0.28	0.27	1,209	1,200	1,147	1,439	26	27	25	31	400	656	661	562
Czechia	224	336	305	313	0.12	0.15	0.13	0.13	152	247	205	214	68	74	67	68	5	8	17	23
Denmark	2,670	2,582	2,590	2,654	0.86	0.74	0.72	0.71	732	769	780	810	27	30	30	31	160	367	359	430
Estonia*	24	47	49	43	0.11	0.16	0.16	0.13	17	25	27	28	69	53	56	64	...	3	3	4
Finland	1,348	1,159	984	1,163	0.54	0.42	0.36	0.42	525	520	508	547	39	45	52	47	114	72	50	56
France**	11,810	11,957	12,136	12,651	0.47	0.43	0.43	0.44	4,192	4,940	5,457	4,958	35	41	45	39	73	85	109	83
Germany	13,121	26,576	24,977	24,627	0.38	0.67	0.61	0.60	4,803	5,513	6,212	5,852	37	21	25	24	374	2,798	2,646	2,538
Greece	357	330	290	322	0.15	0.16	0.13	0.14	223	241	252	245	62	73	87	76	2	13	7	5
Hungary*	119	158	285	326	0.10	0.11	0.21	0.22	92	116	156	177	78	74	55	54	...	0	7	13
Iceland	36	69	74	73	0.22	0.28	0.28	0.27	8	14	13	11	23	21	18	15	2	4	7	4
Ireland	872	884	934	976	0.50	0.32	0.31	0.31	297	364	404	420	34	41	43	43	91	122	125	119
Italy	3,174	6,187	5,190	5,136	0.16	0.30	0.25	0.24	2,208	3,043	2,958	3,052	70	49	57	59	65	281	234	0
Japan	8,344	11,634	14,164	15,224	0.18	0.23	0.28	0.29	3,005	3,433	3,407	3,655	36	30	24	24	559	764	589	487
Kazakhstan*	0	37	40	...	...	0.02	...	...	0	12	...	...		33	...	...	...	0	5	0
Kuwait*	189	593	838	...	...	0.41	...	...	27	39		...	14	7	...	...	...	10	0	0
Lithuania*	48	64	65	60	0.12	0.13	0.12	0.11	28	48	53	47	58	74	81	79	...	1	2	1
Luxembourg	406	455	473	486	1.01	1.00	0.98	1.05	133	129	130	130	33	28	27	27	45	58	61	54
Netherlands	5,779	5,306	5,659	5,429	0.76	0.60	0.62	0.59	1,643	1,525	1,871	1,850	28	29	33	34	171	307	289	212
New Zealand**	410	443	556	575	0.27	0.23	0.28	0.28	85	78	93	106	21	18	17	18	25	36	39	22
Norway	3,740	4,437	4,258	4,671	0.98	0.99	0.94	1.02	925	1,073	1,028	1,063	25	24	24	23	273	578	513	572
Poland	372	719	766	707	0.09	0.13	0.14	0.12	280	484	521	557	75	67	68	79	...	48	36	19
Portugal	627	405	411	389	0.29	0.18	0.18	0.16	216	283	256	268	34	70	62	69	0	13	7	9
Republic of Korea	1,560	2,273	2,358	2,686	0.12	0.14	0.14	0.15	389	605	624	658	25	27	26	24	22	101	131	90
Romania*	135	229	249	256	0.08	0.11	0.11	0.10	106	188	190	190	79	82	76	74	...	6	8	10
Slovakia	74	127	138	132	0.09	0.13	0.13	0.12	55	90	105	110	75	70	77	83	...	1	0	1
Slovenia	58	81	84	88	0.13	0.16	0.16	0.16	38	54	54	56	66	67	65	63	...	2	2	2
Spain	3,695	2,710	2,890	3,006	0.29	0.19	0.20	0.21	1,486	1,986	1,882	1,945	40	73	65	65	191	65	62	58
Sweden	4,503	5,592	6,001	5,711	0.99	1.02	1.07	0.99	1,512	1,745	2,163	2,022	34	31	36	35	381	476	494	504
Switzerland	2,657	3,177	3,101	3,121	0.44	0.47	0.44	0.44	600	816	766	720	23	26	25	23	248	340	325	345
United Arab Emirates*	604	4,123	3,863	2,279	0.19	1.03	0.93	0.55	48	127	75	84	8	3	2	4	88	401	1,199	564
United Kingdom**	12,945	19,109	19,410	19,829	0.57	0.70	0.70	0.70	4,978	7,145	7,055	6,614	38	37	36	33	616	1,914	1,739	1,969
United States	34,256	35,578	34,152	34,009	0.20	0.18	0.16	0.16	4,735	4,841	3,853	3,913	14	14	11	12	4,913	7,146	7,087	6,914
TOTAL*	**146,919**	**187,358**	**189,922**	**187,732**	**0.31**	**0.33**	**0.35**	**0.35**	**37,920**	**45,556**	**45,594**	**45,149**	**26**	**24**	**24**	**24**	**11,139**	**25,774**	**27,372**	**25,842**

[Handwritten notes in margins: Chile 2010, Israel, Korea, Latvia, Mexico, Turkey, Colombia, Costa rica.]

Source: OECD-DAC (2020).

   * Estonia, Hungary, Kazakhstan, Kuwait, Lithuania, Romania and the United Arab Emirates are not part of the Development Assistance Committee (DAC) but are included in its Creditor Reporting System (CRS) database.

  ** ODA from France, New Zealand and the United Kingdom includes funds disbursed to overseas territories.

 *** The total includes ODA from other bilaterals and multilaterals not listed above.

**** ODA disbursements in 2018 and 2019 are calculated using a new grant-equivalent methodology except for humanitarian assistance. ODA disbursements for 2010-2012 and 2017 are calculated using the previous cash-flow methodology.

 (...) indicates that data are not available.

TABLE 2 : Development assistance to education by donor

Region	TOTAL ODA Education		Basic education		Secondary education		Post-secondary education		DIRECT ODA Education		Basic education		Secondary education		Post-secondary education		SHARE Education in total ODA		Basic education in total ODA to education		Secondary education in total ODA to education	
	Constant 2018 US$ millions								Constant 2018 US$ millions								%					
	2017	2018	2017	2018	2017	2018	2017	2018	2017	2018	2017	2018	2017	2018	2017	2018	2017	2018	2017	2018	2017	2018
Australia	196	217	135	126	37	47	25	44	195	216	89	89	14	28	2	26	8	8	69	58	19	22
Austria	168	160	10	4	12	19	146	138	168	160	1	2	8	18	142	137	35	37	6	2	7	12
Belgium	113	113	26	21	38	37	48	55	113	113	17	16	34	35	44	52	10	10	23	19	34	33
Canada	211	231	110	110	52	70	49	51	210	229	65	58	29	44	26	24	8	8	52	48	25	30
Czechia	9	9	1	1	2	1	6	6	9	9	0	0	1	1	6	6	13	11	9	13	18	12
Denmark	88	129	59	80	11	21	18	28	85	127	36	40	0	1	7	8	5	7	67	62	13	17
Estonia*	2	3	0	0	0	0	1	2	2	3	0	0	0	0	1	2	9	17	13	15	8	10
Finland	46	46	28	29	5	7	13	10	46	46	22	20	2	3	10	6	8	11	60	62	11	16
France**	1,491	1,355	200	159	289	191	1,002	1,006	1,318	1,272	87	105	232	164	945	979	18	16	13	12	19	14
Germany	2,197	2,552	310	376	372	507	1,514	1,668	2,196	2,498	152	172	293	405	1,435	1,566	12	14	14	15	17	20
Greece	1	2	1	1	...	...	0	1	1	2	1	1	0	0	0	1	8	21	99	65	...	...
Hungary*	27	63	0	3	0	1	27	58	27	63	0	1	0	0	27	57	70	50	0	6	0	2
Iceland	1	0	1	0	0	0	0	0	1	0	1	0	0	0	0	0	3	1	92	60	4	20
Ireland	39	43	21	27	9	9	9	8	39	43	14	21	6	5	6	4	8	9	53	63	24	20
Italy	106	124	49	48	21	23	36	53	106	124	27	22	10	11	25	40	7	11	46	38	20	19
Japan	702	644	208	180	128	120	365	343	568	577	58	64	53	62	290	285	5	5	30	28	18	19
Kazakhstan*	0	1	0	...	0	...	0	1	0	1	0	0	0	0	0	1	0	3	16	...	8	...
Kuwait*	43	202	21	68	11	61	11	74	43	202	0	0	0	27	0	40	5	10	50	33	25	30
Lithuania*	2	3	1	1	0	0	2	2	2	3	0	0	0	0	1	2	16	28	25	23	13	15
Luxembourg	44	52	12	11	30	37	2	3	44	52	11	7	29	35	1	1	13	15	27	21	69	72
Netherlands	96	182	16	117	11	17	68	48	96	182	12	114	9	16	66	47	3	6	17	64	12	9
New Zealand**	75	76	14	16	9	4	53	56	72	70	10	12	7	2	51	54	21	17	19	22	11	5
Norway	417	377	311	287	44	40	63	50	411	374	260	252	19	22	38	32	13	12	74	76	11	11
Poland	88	93	3	2	1	1	84	90	88	93	2	2	0	0	84	89	34	36	3	3	1	1
Portugal	52	57	12	13	10	10	30	34	52	57	0	0	4	3	24	27	30	32	23	24	18	17
Republic of Korea	229	228	53	63	76	62	100	103	229	228	42	50	71	55	94	97	13	12	23	28	33	27
Romania*	33	47	0	2	3	4	30	41	33	47	0	0	2	3	30	40	81	79	1	4	8	9
Slovakia	4	4	1	1	1	1	2	2	4	4	1	1	0	1	2	2	12	13	28	24	16	20
Slovenia	11	12	0	0	0	0	10	11	11	12	0	0	0	0	10	11	42	43	0	0	2	3
Spain	53	61	20	23	15	17	18	20	53	61	8	10	9	11	12	13	6	7	38	38	28	28
Sweden	114	164	58	100	14	20	42	44	114	164	43	79	7	10	35	33	4	5	51	61	12	12
Switzerland	133	136	53	50	54	59	27	27	131	134	34	32	45	51	18	18	6	6	40	37	40	44
United Arab Emirates*	568	488	265	237	137	118	166	133	95	83	7	5	7	2	37	17	13	12	47	49	24	24
United Kingdom**	967	933	532	483	217	209	219	241	967	933	396	326	149	131	151	162	8	8	55	52	22	22
United States	1,614	1,636	1,319	1,368	46	56	248	211	1,594	1,609	1,270	1,321	22	33	224	188	5	6	82	84	3	3
TOTAL bilaterals*	**10,226**	**11,730**	**3,979**	**4,417**	**1,722**	**1,983**	**4,526**	**5,330**	**9,303**	**10,565**	**2,667**	**2,830**	**1,066**	**1,190**	**3,870**	**4,537**	**8**	**9**	**39**	**38**	**17**	**17**
African Development Fund	145	118	22	10	49	44	74	64	120	118	0	0	38	40	63	60	5	6	15	8	34	38
Asian Development Bank	288	281	69	119	180	142	40	21	288	281	14	85	153	125	12	4	11	12	24	42	63	50
EU Institutions	1,393	1,313	649	633	359	305	386	375	1,259	1,199	301	281	185	129	212	200	7	7	47	48	26	23
World Bank (International Development Association)	1,300	1,297	603	626	363	400	334	270	1,299	1,297	469	427	296	301	267	170	9	9	46	48	28	31
International Monetary Fund (Concessional Trust Funds)	252	243	126	121	63	61	63	61	0	0	0	0	0	0	0	0	20	20	50	50	25	25
UNICEF	92	87	62	54	18	17	12	16	92	87	38	23	6	1	0	0	6	6	67	62	20	20
UN Relief and Works Agency for Palestine Refugees	523	458	523	458	0	0	0	0	523	458	523	458	0	0	0	0	56	60	100	100	0	0
TOTAL multilaterals*	**4,107**	**3,855**	**2,121**	**2,062**	**1,045**	**974**	**942**	**819**	**3,692**	**3,496**	**1,396**	**1,311**	**683**	**599**	**579**	**444**	**7**	**7**	**52**	**53**	**25**	**25**
TOTAL	**14,334**	**15,585**	**6,100**	**6,478**	**2,766**	**2,958**	**5,467**	**6,149**	**12,995**	**14,061**	**4,063**	**4,140**	**1,748**	**1,789**	**4,449**	**4,980**	**8**	**8**	**43**	**42**	**19**	**19**

Source: OECD-DAC, CRS database (2020).

* Estonia, Hungary, Kazakhstan, Kuwait, Lithuania, Romania and the United Arab Emirates are not part of the Development Assistance Committee (DAC) but are included in its Creditor Reporting System (CRS) database.

** ODA from France, New Zealand and the United Kingdom includes funds disbursed to overseas territories.

*** The total includes ODA from other bilaterals and multilaterals not listed above.

(...) indicates that data are not available.

All data represent gross disbursements. ODA is net of refugee costs.

TABLE 3: Development assistance to education by recipient

Region	TOTAL ODA Education		Basic education		Secondary education		Post-secondary education		DIRECT ODA Education		Basic education		Secondary education		Post-secondary education		SHARE Education in sector allocable ODA		Basic education in total ODA to education		Secondary education in total ODA to education	
	Constant 2018 US$ millions								Constant 2018 US$ millions								%					
	2017	2018	2017	2018	2017	2018	2017	2018	2017	2018	2017	2018	2017	2018	2017	2018	2017	2018	2017	2018	2017	2018
Sub-Saharan Africa	3,547	3,678	1,655	1,741	868	888	1,024	1,049	3,115	3,288	1,119	1,219	600	627	756	788	9	9	47	47	24	24
Unallocated within the region	84	75	28	35	23	14	33	26	84	75	15	23	16	8	26	20	4	3	34	47	27	19
Angola	36	27	22	17	9	3	6	8	36	27	20	15	8	2	5	7	13	12	60	61	23	10
Benin	83	73	34	26	26	22	22	25	69	59	23	16	21	17	17	19	14	14	41	36	32	31
Botswana	20	4	10	2	5	1	6	1	20	4	1	1	0	0	1	1	18	4	49	46	23	19
Burkina Faso	88	107	40	47	25	33	22	27	72	88	27	30	19	24	15	19	10	12	46	44	29	31
Burundi	20	18	8	5	6	7	6	6	19	17	6	2	4	5	5	5	5	5	42	27	28	37
Cabo Verde	24	29	5	7	7	9	11	13	18	27	0	0	5	6	9	9	21	32	21	26	31	31
Cameroon	184	156	51	40	26	19	106	97	100	102	8	10	4	4	85	82	23	21	28	26	14	12
Central African Republic	30	26	14	11	6	6	11	9	8	6	1	1	0	1	4	4	16	8	45	42	20	22
Chad	52	78	25	38	13	20	13	21	23	27	7	8	4	5	4	6	14	23	49	48	26	25
Comoros	16	18	2	3	2	2	12	13	16	18	2	2	1	2	12	12	24	21	14	17	10	12
Congo	20	31	2	10	2	3	16	19	20	31	1	9	2	2	15	18	20	23	11	31	11	8
Côte d'Ivoire	153	109	77	41	33	26	44	42	119	86	57	24	23	17	34	34	20	13	50	37	21	24
D. R. Congo	127	154	61	72	42	54	24	28	127	154	47	54	35	45	17	19	7	8	48	47	33	35
Djibouti	22	23	9	10	5	4	8	9	16	16	5	6	3	2	6	7	18	15	41	45	23	17
Equatorial Guinea	1	2	0	1	0	0	1	1	1	2	0	1	0	0	1	1	13	21	32	52	10	8
Eritrea	9	5	0	0	2	2	7	2	9	5	0	0	2	2	6	2	13	6	4	11	26	38
Eswatini	6	8	5	4	1	2	1	2	6	8	5	2	1	1	1	1	4	6	74	57	12	22
Ethiopia	217	316	133	222	46	55	38	39	217	316	114	195	36	41	28	25	7	8	61	70	21	17
Gabon	40	40	10	10	10	7	21	22	22	22	1	1	5	2	16	17	69	76	24	26	24	18
Gambia	19	29	10	12	4	4	5	13	10	21	2	4	0	0	2	9	9	15	52	41	20	13
Ghana	166	131	47	53	85	41	34	37	145	93	29	28	75	28	24	25	13	13	29	41	51	31
Guinea	61	91	23	37	9	27	28	27	49	76	10	29	3	23	22	22	15	21	38	41	15	30
Guinea-Bissau	22	17	11	5	1	2	10	10	20	16	9	3	0	1	9	9	21	12	51	31	6	9
Kenya	112	142	56	62	17	40	39	40	112	142	50	47	14	33	36	33	4	5	50	43	16	28
Lesotho	11	7	6	4	3	2	2	1	11	7	4	3	2	1	0	0	7	4	57	61	27	22
Liberia	38	44	30	31	2	11	6	2	32	41	26	29	0	10	4	2	7	8	78	71	6	24
Madagascar	82	65	36	29	20	15	26	20	52	53	13	19	8	10	15	15	14	11	44	45	24	24
Malawi	162	134	95	75	37	33	30	26	155	127	81	63	30	26	23	20	11	11	59	56	23	24
Mali	134	161	79	96	27	31	29	34	104	125	57	69	16	18	17	21	12	14	59	60	20	19
Mauritania	27	49	8	7	9	9	10	33	20	40	2	1	7	5	7	30	8	12	28	15	36	17
Mauritius	12	11	1	1	3	2	8	8	12	11	1	1	3	2	8	8	21	9	12	9	22	18
Mozambique	206	202	131	123	41	50	33	28	206	202	97	94	24	36	16	14	11	11	64	61	20	25
Namibia	18	29	5	20	5	5	8	5	18	29	2	18	4	4	7	4	8	16	25	68	29	16
Niger	109	106	54	50	35	42	19	15	85	94	26	31	21	32	6	6	12	12	50	47	33	39
Nigeria	181	232	87	98	37	74	57	60	181	232	58	65	23	58	42	44	7	9	48	42	21	32
Rwanda	134	111	48	50	55	29	30	32	118	106	37	42	49	25	25	28	12	10	36	45	41	26
Sao Tome and Principe	5	6	2	2	1	1	3	3	5	6	0	1	0	0	2	2	14	14	34	39	19	19
Senegal	140	155	44	50	29	32	67	73	139	153	36	35	25	24	63	65	14	15	31	32	21	21
Seychelles	1	…	0	…	0	…	1	…	1	…	0	…	0	…	1	…	5	…	28	…	2	…
Sierra Leone	69	47	42	24	18	15	9	7	53	36	26	13	10	10	1	2	15	10	61	52	26	33
Somalia	41	46	24	23	8	12	9	10	39	40	11	13	2	7	3	5	6	6	58	51	19	26
South Africa	64	62	24	24	13	10	28	28	64	62	13	15	8	6	23	24	6	6	37	39	20	16
South Sudan	82	59	67	51	6	3	9	5	82	59	57	46	1	1	3	3	10	11	82	86	8	5
Togo	44	45	13	13	13	12	18	21	25	27	2	2	8	7	12	15	15	20	30	28	30	27
Uganda	113	128	40	47	27	31	46	50	113	128	32	41	24	28	42	47	7	7	35	37	24	24
United Republic of Tanzania	193	190	98	114	52	43	43	33	193	190	70	79	38	26	30	16	7	7	51	60	27	23
Zambia	37	39	21	14	10	15	7	10	37	39	14	7	6	12	4	6	3	4	56	35	25	39
Zimbabwe	33	42	16	24	10	11	6	7	32	42	13	21	9	10	5	5	5	6	49	57	31	27
Northern Africa and Western Asia	3,211	3,876	1,458	1,740	526	678	1,227	1,458	2,740	2,923	917	879	256	247	957	1,028	16	21	45	45	16	17
Unallocated within the region	22	43	9	34	1	4	12	5	22	43	9	33	1	3	12	5	3	5	41	79	5	9
Algeria	131	143	3	3	6	3	122	137	131	143	1	1	6	3	121	137	56	64	2	2	5	2
Armenia	40	25	13	4	4	1	23	19	39	25	5	4	1	0	19	18	11	10	32	20	11	4
Azerbaijan	25	35	1	4	9	10	14	21	25	35	0	2	9	10	13	20	10	16	6	10	37	30
Egypt	278	410	113	161	53	94	112	155	278	357	53	24	23	26	82	87	17	14	41	39	19	23
Georgia	69	78	16	20	15	17	37	41	69	78	5	4	10	9	32	33	13	11	23	25	22	22
Iraq	140	118	60	56	38	25	42	38	49	56	8	17	12	6	16	18	11	14	43	47	27	21
Jordan	489	385	332	291	54	26	103	69	397	375	241	259	8	10	57	53	21	18	68	75	11	7
Lebanon	279	280	161	171	57	43	61	66	279	280	148	134	51	25	54	48	33	31	58	61	21	15

TABLE 3: Continued

Region	TOTAL ODA Education		Basic education		Secondary education		Post-secondary education		DIRECT ODA Education		Basic education		Secondary education		Post-secondary education		Education in sector allocable ODA		Basic education in total ODA to education		Secondary education in total ODA to education	
	Constant 2018 US$ millions								Constant 2018 US$ millions								%					
	2017	2018	2017	2018	2017	2018	2017	2018	2017	2018	2017	2018	2017	2018	2017	2018	2017	2018	2017	2018	2017	2018
Libya	9	11	0	1	0	1	9	9	9	11	0	0	0	1	9	9	3	6	2	5	0	13
Morocco	439	326	111	46	103	71	225	209	328	314	18	18	56	57	178	194	15	22	25	14	23	22
Palestine	486	473	404	367	36	47	46	59	460	435	371	314	20	20	30	33	32	34	83	78	7	10
Sudan	48	45	19	18	12	10	16	18	21	37	2	9	4	6	8	13	11	13	40	39	26	22
Syrian Arab Republic	148	202	50	62	8	11	90	129	148	202	41	45	3	2	86	120	22	20	34	31	5	5
Tunisia	147	154	18	9	19	19	110	126	144	153	4	4	12	17	102	123	11	11	12	6	13	13
Turkey	253	339	63	99	68	93	123	147	253	339	2	4	37	45	92	99	6	13	25	29	27	27
Yemen	211	809	84	396	42	201	85	212	91	40	7	8	3	6	46	18	20	74	40	49	20	25
Central and Southern Asia	**2,303**	**2,417**	**1,029**	**989**	**474**	**478**	**801**	**950**	**2,240**	**2,377**	**783**	**723**	**351**	**345**	**678**	**817**	**11**	**12**	**45**	**41**	**21**	**20**
Unallocated within the region	13	27	1	1	5	4	8	22	13	27	0	0	5	4	8	22	4	8	4	3	38	16
Afghanistan	251	290	116	152	39	48	96	90	224	264	91	113	27	28	84	70	8	9	46	52	16	16
Bangladesh	617	625	311	357	195	181	111	87	617	625	230	276	155	141	70	46	15	14	50	57	32	29
Bhutan	2	7	1	3	0	2	1	2	2	7	1	1	0	1	1	1	2	6	44	38	13	27
India	507	418	233	104	29	53	244	261	487	406	209	60	17	31	232	238	8	8	46	25	6	13
Iran, Islamic Republic of	91	96	1	1	1	1	89	93	91	96	0	0	1	1	88	93	71	70	1	1	2	1
Kazakhstan*	25	75	2	3	1	2	22	70	25	75	0	0	0	1	21	69	31	64	8	4	4	3
Kyrgyzstan	66	156	26	27	25	20	15	109	61	156	13	14	19	13	9	103	19	37	39	17	38	13
Maldives	5	4	2	1	1	0	2	2	4	4	0	0	0	0	1	2	9	3	35	26	21	12
Nepal	165	205	80	119	47	47	39	39	156	205	61	94	38	34	30	27	13	15	48	58	28	23
Pakistan	422	380	217	186	77	76	127	118	421	379	153	141	45	54	95	96	13	17	52	49	18	20
Sri Lanka	83	78	25	23	39	25	20	30	83	78	18	18	35	23	16	27	11	11	30	29	46	32
Tajikistan	27	25	11	9	8	9	8	8	27	25	5	5	5	7	5	6	7	6	42	35	30	34
Turkmenistan	3	6	0	1	1	3	2	3	3	6	0	0	0	3	2	3	10	27	9	10	19	45
Uzbekistan	25	24	3	3	5	6	18	15	25	24	0	0	4	5	16	14	4	4	11	12	19	25
Eastern and South-eastern Asia	**1,558**	**1,658**	**372**	**348**	**355**	**386**	**831**	**924**	**1,480**	**1,658**	**188**	**165**	**263**	**295**	**738**	**832**	**13**	**13**	**24**	**21**	**23**	**23**
Unallocated within the region	11	6	2	3	1	2	7	2	11	6	2	2	1	2	7	2	5	3	19	42	11	30
Cambodia	122	132	41	66	52	32	28	35	122	132	21	33	42	15	18	18	13	16	34	50	43	24
China	514	674	34	53	92	189	388	432	514	674	5	4	78	165	373	408	38	45	7	8	18	28
DPR Korea	1	1	0	0	0	0	1	1	1	1	0	0	0	0	1	1	3	4	18	0	1	0
Indonesia	172	185	46	55	23	25	104	105	172	185	13	15	6	5	87	85	7	6	27	30	13	14
Lao PDR	89	103	55	58	20	31	13	14	89	103	51	49	18	26	11	9	16	17	62	57	23	30
Malaysia	37	35	2	3	1	1	34	31	37	35	0	1	0	0	33	30	45	48	6	8	3	3
Mongolia	113	51	46	12	27	11	41	29	55	51	13	8	10	9	24	27	20	13	40	23	24	21
Myanmar	106	72	48	26	27	23	31	23	106	72	26	14	16	18	19	17	8	5	45	36	26	33
Philippines	73	125	41	30	8	6	24	89	73	125	32	22	3	3	19	85	10	11	56	24	11	5
Thailand	35	36	9	8	3	3	23	25	35	36	5	4	2	2	21	23	7	9	25	23	9	10
Timor-Leste	30	35	11	17	8	7	11	11	30	35	4	6	4	1	8	6	13	18	37	49	26	19
Viet Nam	255	203	36	19	92	55	127	128	235	203	15	7	82	49	116	122	8	8	14	10	36	27
Oceania	**250**	**234**	**101**	**92**	**81**	**58**	**68**	**84**	**226**	**200**	**47**	**49**	**54**	**36**	**40**	**63**	**13**	**11**	**40**	**39**	**32**	**25**
Unallocated within the region	73	36	22	6	38	12	13	18	73	36	10	2	32	10	7	16	16	10	30	17	52	33
Cook Islands	6	1	0	0	5	0	0	1	6	1	0	0	5	0	0	0	24	3	6	34	88	18
Fiji	25	19	10	8	8	3	7	9	25	19	2	3	4	0	3	7	21	17	40	39	31	13
Kiribati	11	10	8	7	0	1	3	3	11	10	8	7	0	0	2	3	15	15	74	68	4	5
Marshall Islands	15	14	7	10	4	2	4	2	5	8	0	7	0	0	0	0	55	51	50	74	24	12
Micronesia, F. S.	12	11	7	6	3	2	3	3	3	3	2	1	0	0	0	0	39	25	56	55	21	21
Nauru	3	2	1	0	2	2	1	0	3	2	0	0	2	2	0	0	13	7	17	4	64	80
Niue	2	2	1	1	0	0	1	1	1	1	0	0	0	0	0	0	18	15	37	38	21	19
Palau	1	14	1	7	0	3	0	4	1	1	0	0	0	0	0	0	7	74	48	50	19	24
Papua New Guinea	38	48	20	16	7	17	10	15	37	48	9	8	2	14	5	11	7	6	52	33	20	36
Samoa	13	17	5	7	1	1	7	8	12	16	2	4	0	0	5	7	10	13	37	43	11	8
Solomon Islands	20	25	6	11	6	7	8	7	20	25	4	7	5	5	7	5	10	13	31	43	29	27
Tokelau	2	3	1	2	0	1	0	1	1	1	1	1	0	0	0	0	58	24	61	60	21	20
Tonga	7	8	2	2	2	2	3	4	7	8	1	2	1	2	3	3	9	11	32	29	22	26
Tuvalu	3	2	1	1	0	0	2	1	3	2	0	0	0	0	1	1	12	15	27	31	14	10
Vanuatu	18	20	9	8	4	5	6	8	18	20	8	6	3	4	5	7	15	19	50	38	20	22
Latin America and the Caribbean	**2327**	**2091**	**751**	**598**	**328**	**295**	**1235**	**1198**	**1815**	**1917**	**333**	**355**	**132**	**174**	**1026**	**1077**	**12**	**10**	**32**	**29**	**14**	**14**
Unallocated within the region	39	23	17	11	3	1	18	10	39	23	14	10	2	1	17	10	4	2	43	49	9	5
Antigua and Barbuda	0	0	...	0	0	0	0	0	0	0	0	0	0	0	0	0	7	5	...	1	83	63
Argentina	30	32	7	8	4	5	18	18	30	32	2	2	2	3	15	15	35	16	24	24	15	17

Region	TOTAL ODA Education (Constant 2018 US$ millions) 2017	2018	Basic education 2017	2018	Secondary education 2017	2018	Post-secondary education 2017	2018	DIRECT ODA Education (Constant 2018 US$ millions) 2017	2018	Basic education 2017	2018	Secondary education 2017	2018	Post-secondary education 2017	2018	SHARE Education in sector allocable ODA (%) 2017	2018	Basic education in total ODA to education 2017	2018	Secondary education in total ODA to education 2017	2018
Belize	3	2	1	1	0	0	1	1	3	2	1	0	0	0	0	0	7	6	53	43	14	17
Bolivia, P. S.	43	31	8	7	7	7	28	16	43	31	5	4	5	6	26	14	4	4	19	23	17	24
Brazil	98	103	18	18	10	10	71	75	98	103	3	4	2	2	64	68	11	15	18	18	10	9
Chile	30	...	7	...	4	...	19	...	30	...	3	...	2	...	16	...	29	...	24	...	14	...
Colombia	70	77	14	14	7	9	48	54	70	77	9	9	5	7	45	52	8	4	21	18	11	12
Costa Rica	13	14	4	5	3	3	6	6	13	14	3	4	2	2	5	5	10	12	33	40	22	19
Cuba	8	10	1	1	1	0	6	8	8	10	0	1	1	0	6	8	6	5	9	14	14	4
Dominica	2	4	0	2	0	1	1	1	1	3	0	0	0	0	1	0	10	34	28	44	14	22
Dominican Republic	20	21	10	12	6	5	3	4	20	21	10	11	6	5	3	3	12	16	53	56	31	25
Ecuador	28	34	9	14	4	4	14	16	28	34	6	11	3	3	13	15	14	8	33	40	16	13
El Salvador	32	49	17	18	6	21	9	9	32	49	15	16	5	21	8	9	18	19	53	37	17	44
Grenada	1	0	0	0	0	0	0	0	0	0	0	0	0	0	0	0	5	1	39	20	20	13
Guatemala	68	79	51	59	7	12	10	7	68	79	46	55	4	10	8	5	18	20	75	76	10	15
Guyana	7	7	2	2	1	4	4	1	7	7	2	1	0	4	3	1	10	6	34	26	9	54
Haiti	100	90	74	56	12	16	14	18	96	81	65	45	8	10	10	12	13	12	74	62	12	18
Honduras	42	43	35	34	4	5	3	4	42	43	33	32	3	4	2	3	8	6	84	79	9	12
Jamaica	8	9	5	6	2	1	2	2	8	9	4	5	1	1	2	2	10	8	54	60	19	16
Mexico	63	68	9	10	6	7	48	51	63	68	3	4	3	4	45	48	7	10	14	15	9	10
Montserrat	2	3	1	1	1	1	1	1	2	3	0	0	0	0	0	0	7	6	48	47	24	24
Nicaragua	51	48	25	25	21	17	5	6	51	48	21	20	20	14	3	3	9	13	49	53	42	35
Panama	4	4	2	2	0	0	2	2	4	4	0	0	0	0	2	2	8	8	48	50	7	5
Paraguay	27	27	12	13	7	6	7	8	27	27	2	3	2	1	2	3	13	13	47	49	25	23
Peru	44	45	15	13	8	8	21	23	44	45	9	7	5	5	19	20	8	8	34	30	18	18
Saint Lucia	2	1	0	0	0	0	1	1	2	1	0	0	0	0	1	1	9	11	29	29	14	12
Saint Vincent/Grenadines	0	1	0	1	0	0	0	0	0	1	0	1	0	0	0	0	4	7	19	62	11	11
Suriname	3	2	0	0	1	1	2	1	3	2	0	0	1	1	2	1	11	13	3	2	38	44
Uruguay	7	...	3	...	1	...	3	...	7	...	1	...	1	...	2	...	15	...	39	...	19	...
Venezuela, B. R.	15	17	3	4	1	2	10	10	15	17	1	3	1	1	9	9	44	42	22	26	10	12
Europe and Northern America	**735**	**624**	**199**	**129**	**100**	**74**	**429**	**421**	**481**	**542**	**37**	**53**	**25**	**36**	**348**	**383**	**15**	**12**	**27**	**21**	**14**	**12**
Unallocated within the region	93	100	37	37	3	7	46	56	93	100	21	30	2	4	38	52	7	7	40	37	4	7
Albania	40	46	5	4	8	10	27	32	40	46	2	4	6	9	26	31	15	10	13	9	19	21
Belarus	46	42	2	2	4	4	40	36	46	42	1	0	3	3	39	35	36	37	5	4	8	10
Bosnia and Herzegovina	46	51	5	6	3	5	38	40	46	51	2	2	1	3	36	37	9	11	12	12	6	10
Montenegro	5	5	0	0	0	1	4	4	5	5	0	0	0	0	4	4	3	3	7	8	8	9
North Macedonia	17	22	3	6	1	3	13	13	17	22	2	4	0	2	12	12	8	9	19	26	4	15
Republic of Moldova	49	58	5	8	9	8	35	43	46	56	2	3	7	6	34	41	17	20	10	13	18	13
Serbia	299	144	131	51	70	32	98	60	49	64	1	1	4	7	33	35	34	14	44	36	23	22
Ukraine	141	156	10	15	3	4	128	137	141	156	6	10	1	2	126	134	14	15	7	10	2	3
Unallocated by region or country	1,872	2,256	934	1,100	227	249	711	908	1,860	2,240	714	803	118	101	602	759	8	9	50	49	12	11
Low income	3,037	3,873	1,532	1,996	680	888	825	989	2,621	2,833	1,054	1,192	441	486	586	587	10	13	50	52	22	23
Lower middle income	5,628	5,627	2,392	2,163	1,168	1,157	2,068	2,308	5,184	5,354	1,645	1,405	795	778	1,695	1,929	11	12	43	38	21	21
Upper middle income	3,406	3,492	1,111	1,080	597	615	1,699	1,797	2,942	3,313	574	636	328	393	1,431	1,575	15	16	33	31	18	18
High income	44	18	13	9	6	4	25	6	44	5	6	2	3	0	21	2	18	24	30	49	14	20
Unallocated by income	2,218	2,575	1,052	1,230	315	295	851	1,049	2,204	2,555	785	905	181	132	717	887	8	8	47	48	14	11
Least developed countries	4,223	5,046	2,097	2,603	1,057	1,233	1,069	1,210	3,764	3,978	1,445	1,620	731	742	743	718	11	12	50	52	25	24
Sub-Saharan Africa	3,547	3,678	1,655	1,741	868	888	1,024	1,049	3,115	3,288	1,119	1,219	600	627	756	788	9	9	47	47	24	24
Northern Africa and Western Asia	3,211	3,876	1,458	1,740	526	678	1,227	1,458	2,740	2,923	917	879	256	247	957	1,028	16	21	45	45	16	17
Central and Southern Asia	2,303	2,417	1,029	989	474	478	801	950	2,240	2,377	783	723	351	345	678	817	11	12	45	41	21	20
Eastern and South-eastern Asia	1,558	1,658	372	348	355	386	831	924	1,480	1,658	188	165	263	295	738	832	13	13	24	21	23	23
Oceania	250	234	101	92	81	58	68	84	226	200	47	49	54	36	40	63	13	11	40	39	32	25
Latin America and the Caribbean	858	843	353	340	129	148	376	356	852	833	260	249	82	102	329	310	9	9	41	40	15	18
Europe and Northern America	735	624	199	129	106	74	429	421	481	542	37	53	25	36	348	383	15	12	27	21	14	12
Unspecified by region	1,872	2,256	934	1,100	227	249	711	908	1,860	2,240	714	803	118	101	602	759	8	9	50	49	12	11
TOTAL	**14,334**	**15,585**	**6,100**	**6,478**	**2,766**	**2,958**	**5,467**	**6,149**	**12,995**	**14,061**	**4,063**	**4,140**	**1,748**	**1,789**	**4,449**	**4,980**	**11**	**12**	**43**	**42**	**19**	**19**

Source: OECD-DAC, CRS database (2020).

(…) indicates that data are not available. (-) represents a nil value.

The country groupings by level of income are as defined by the World Bank but include only countries shown in the table. They are based on the list of countries by income group as revised in July 2019.

All data represent gross disbursements.

TABLE 4 : Development assistance to education by donor – top 3 recipients

Donor		Recipient	TOTAL Constant 2018 US$ millions	Recipient %	Recipient	BASIC EDUCATION Constant 2018 US$ millions	Recipient %
Bilateral	Australia	Papua New Guinea	29.7	14	Bilateral, unspecified	12.0	13
		Oceania, regional	22.6	10	Lebanon	11.4	13
		Bilateral, unspecified	20.0	9	Bangladesh	9.8	11
	Austria	Turkey	21.0	13	Mexico	1.6	69
		Bosnia/Herzeg.	20.8	13	Albania	0.2	8
		Serbia	12.7	8	Bilateral, unspecified	0.2	8
	Belgium	Bilateral, unspecified	24.4	22	Bilateral, unspecified	7.7	48
		D. R. Congo	15.9	14	Viet Nam	1.4	9
		Uganda	8.9	8	South Africa	1.3	8
	Canada	Senegal	42.0	18	Senegal	10.6	19
		Jordan	22.8	10	Afghanistan	9.4	16
		Afghanistan	20.3	8	Bangladesh	7.5	13
	Czechia	Ukraine	0.9	11	Ukraine	0.2	53
		Ethiopia	0.9	10	Syrian Arab Republic	0.2	47
		Bosnia/Herzeg.	0.5	6			
	Denmark	Bilateral, unspecified	93.2	66	Afghanistan	25.2	63
		Afghanistan	25.3	18	Bilateral, unspecified	7.9	20
		Burkina Faso	13.5	10	Myanmar	4.4	11
	Estonia	Europe, regional	1.1	33	Myanmar	0.0	87
		Bilateral, unspecified	0.7	20	Bilateral, unspecified	0.0	13
		Georgia	0.5	15			
	Finland	Mozambique	9.4	20	Mozambique	7.2	36
		Nepal	5.8	13	Turkey	2.4	12
		Bilateral, unspecified	5.0	11	Palestine	2.0	10
	France	Morocco	184.1	11	Bilateral, unspecified	22.9	22
		Cameroon	141.8	8	Niger	8.2	8
		Algeria	133.1	8	Mali	6.3	6
	Germany	China	464.9	17	Jordan	36.0	21
		Egypt	342.6	12	Northern Africa, regional	29.5	17
		India	164.7	6	Mozambique	17.4	10
	Greece	Ukraine	0.4	16	Ukraine	0.3	24
		Albania	0.3	14	Albania	0.3	21
		Egypt	0.3	13	Egypt	0.2	16
	Hungary	Jordan	7.0	11	Iraq	1.0	90
		Iraq	5.6	9	Montenegro	0.1	5
		Syrian Arab Republic	4.0	6	Armenia	0.0	2
	Iceland	Kenya	0.2	59	South Africa	0.1	100
		South Africa	0.1	19			
		Bilateral, unspecified	0.0	13			
	Ireland	Bilateral, unspecified	14.1	33	Bilateral, unspecified	12.6	61
		Mozambique	7.5	17	Uganda	1.9	9
		Uganda	4.7	11	India	0.6	3
	Italy	Bilateral, unspecified	26.0	21	Jordan	3.9	18
		Senegal	6.7	5	Lebanon	3.4	15
		India	6.5	5	Bilateral, unspecified	2.0	9
	Japan	Iraq	273.0	30	Guinea	6.5	10
		Bilateral, unspecified	144.7	16	Myanmar	4.9	8
		India	71.8	8	Nepal	3.8	6
	Kazakhstan	Afghanistan	0.7	85			
		Kyrgyzstan	0.1	9			
		Mongolia	0.0	5			
	Kuwait	China	73.0	36			
		Lebanon	52.4	26			
		Mauritania	24.5	12			
	Lithuania	Ukraine	1.2	41	Ukraine	0.1	79
		Belarus	1.2	38	Argentina	0.0	10
		Georgia	0.2	7	Belarus	0.0	6
	Luxembourg	Niger	8.9	17	Niger	3.3	45
		Senegal	7.2	14	Bangladesh	0.5	7
		Cabo Verde	5.8	11			
	Netherlands	Bilateral, unspecified	102.7	56	Bilateral, unspecified	59.0	52
		Lebanon	25.1	14	Lebanon	19.3	17
		Ethiopia	10.9	6	Syrian Arab Republic	8.3	7

TABLE 4: Continued

Donor	Recipient	TOTAL		BASIC EDUCATION		
		Constant 2018 US$ millions	Recipient %	Recipient	Constant 2018 US$ millions	Recipient %
New Zealand	Tokelau	13.8	14	Solomon Islands	4.5	37
	Samoa	10.2	10	Timor-Leste	3.7	30
	Solomon Islands	7.7	8	Oceania, regional	1.8	15
Norway	Bilateral, unspecified	184.1	47	Bilateral, unspecified	158.7	63
	Palestine	30.3	8	Malawi	13.8	5
	Malawi	19.4	5	South Sudan	13.7	5
Poland	Ukraine	57.6	62	Ukraine	1.1	61
	Belarus	20.0	22	U. R. Tanzania	0.3	16
	India	1.3	1	Europe, regional	0.1	7
Portugal	Timor-Leste	13.2	23	Guinea-Bissau	0.0	94
	Mozambique	11.4	20	Cabo Verde	0.0	6
	Cabo Verde	10.3	18			
Republic of Korea	Bilateral, unspecified	50.0	22	Mali	4.2	8
	Rwanda	14.3	6	Iraq	4.0	8
	Viet Nam	12.7	6	Mozambique	3.7	7
Romania	Republic of Moldova	37.5	80	Bilateral, unspecified	0.0	100
	Serbia	2.2	5			
	Ukraine	1.3	3			
Slovakia	Kenya	1.3	32	Lebanon	0.4	64
	Serbia	0.9	23	Kenya	0.1	9
	Lebanon	0.4	10	Iraq	0.0	7
Slovenia	North Macedonia	3.8	33	Gambia	0.0	100
	Bosnia/Herzeg.	3.8	33			
	Serbia	2.8	24			
Spain	Morocco	6.6	12	Haiti	2.4	25
	America, regional	4.7	8	Guatemala	0.9	9
	Bilateral, unspecified	3.6	6	Senegal	0.7	7
Sweden	Bilateral, unspecified	54.5	33	Bilateral, unspecified	49.8	63
	Afghanistan	31.6	19	Afghanistan	22.7	29
	UR. R. Tanzania	28.6	17	U. R. Tanzania	2.5	3
Switzerland	Bilateral, unspecified	22.7	16	Niger	4.2	13
	Burkina Faso	14.4	10	Burkina Faso	3.8	12
	Sub-Saharan Africa, regional	8.0	6	Mali	3.4	11
United Arab Emirates	Yemen	1311.8	62			
	Serbia	398.0	19			
	Palestine	177.4	8			
United Kingdom	Bilateral, unspecified	328.9	19	Bilateral, unspecified	102.9	32
	Pakistan	153.7	9	Pakistan	81.4	25
	Bangladesh	40.0	2	Rwanda	17.8	5
United States	Bilateral, unspecified	224.7	13	Bilateral, unspecified	211.9	16
	Jordan	109.5	6	Jordan	99.4	8
	Afghanistan	83.7	5	Pakistan	53.1	4
Multilateral African Development Fund	Uganda	29.2	25			
	Kenya	16.4	14			
	Africa, regional	14.8	13			
Asian Development Bank	Bangladesh	129.1	46	Bangladesh	67.8	80
	Nepal	46.5	17	Nepal	16.5	19
	Viet Nam	26.7	9	Marshall Islands	0.5	1
EU Institutions	Bilateral, unspecified	383.1	22	Bilateral, unspecified	131.1	47
	Turkey	153.9	9	Bangladesh	31.4	11
	Afghanistan	117.1	7	Nepal	24.0	9
World Bank (International Development Association)	Bangladesh	332.7	26	Ethiopia	133.6	31
	India	169.9	13	Bangladesh	123.8	29
	Ethiopia	166.0	13	India	47.1	11
IMF (Concessional Trust Funds)	Ghana	188.1	15			
	Cameroon	156.3	13			
	Chad	148.9	12			
UNICEF	D .R. Congo	8.1	9	India	2.2	9
	Afghanistan	6.6	8	Somalia	0.9	4
	India	5.4	6	Nigeria	0.9	4

Source: OECD CRS database (2019).

Glossary

Attainment rate. Number of persons in a particular age group by the highest level of education attained, expressed as a percentage of the total population in that age group (see **Completion rate**).

Age-specific enrolment ratio. Enrolment of a given age or age group, regardless of the level of education in which pupils or students are enrolled, expressed as a percentage of the population of the same age or age group. An example is global indicator 4.2.2, the participation rate in organized learning (one year before the official primary entry age).

Completion rate. Percentage of children aged three to five years older than the official age of entry into the last grade of an education level who have reached the last grade of that level. For example, the primary completion rate in a country with a 6-year cycle where the official age of entry into the last grade is 11 years is the percentage of 14- to 16-year-olds who have reached grade 6.

Conflict-affected country. For a given year, any country with 1,000 or more battle-related deaths (including fatalities among civilians and military actors) over the preceding 10-year period and/or more than 200 battle-related deaths in any 1 year over the preceding 3-year period, according to the Uppsala Conflict Data Program Battle-Related Deaths Dataset.

Constant price. Price of a particular item adjusted to remove the overall effect of general price changes (inflation) since a given baseline year.

Early childhood care and education. Services and programmes that support children's survival, growth, development and learning – including health, nutrition and hygiene, and cognitive, social, emotional and physical development – from birth to entry into primary school.

Early Childhood Development Index. Index of fulfilment of developmental potential that assesses children aged 36 to 59 months in four domains: literacy/numeracy, and physical, social-emotional, and cognitive development. The information is collected through the UNICEF Multiple Indicator Cluster Surveys. A child is 'on track' overall if it is 'on track' in at least three of the four domains. The index is currently being revised.

Education levels according to the International Standard Classification of Education (ISCED), which is the classification system designed to serve as an instrument for assembling, compiling and presenting comparable indicators and statistics of education both within countries and internationally. The system, introduced in 1976, was revised in 1997 and 2011.

- *Pre-primary education (ISCED level 0).* Programmes at the initial stage of organized instruction, primarily designed to introduce very young children, aged at least 3 years, to a school-type environment and provide a bridge between home and school. Upon completion of these programmes, children continue their education at ISCED 1 (primary education).

- *Primary education (ISCED level 1).* Programmes generally designed to give pupils a sound basic education in reading, writing and mathematics, and an elementary understanding of subjects such as history, geography, sciences, art and music.

- *Secondary education (ISCED levels 2 and 3).* Lower secondary education (ISCED 2) is generally designed to continue the basic programmes of the primary level but the teaching is typically more subject-focused, requiring more specialized teachers for each subject area. The end of this level often coincides with the end of compulsory education. Teaching in upper secondary education (ISCED 3) is often organized even more along subject lines and teachers typically need a higher or more subject-specific qualification.

- *Post-secondary non-tertiary education (ISCED level 4).* It provides learning experiences building on secondary education, preparing for labour market entry as well as tertiary education.

- *Tertiary education (ISCED levels 5–8).* It builds on secondary education, providing learning activities in specialized fields of education. It aims at learning at a high level of complexity and specialization. It comprises:

  □ Level 5: Short-cycle tertiary education, often designed to provide participants with professional knowledge, skills and competences. It is practically based and occupationally specific, and prepares students to enter the labour market.

- Level 6: Bachelor's, often designed to provide participants with intermediate academic and/or professional knowledge, skills and competences, leading to a first degree or equivalent qualification.

- Level 7: Master's or equivalent level, often designed to provide participants with advanced academic and/or professional knowledge, skills and competences, leading to a second degree or equivalent qualification.

- Level 8: Doctoral or equivalent level, designed primarily to lead to an advanced research qualification.

Education for Sustainable Development. A type of education that aims to enable learners to constructively and creatively address present and future global challenges and create more sustainable and resilient societies.

Global Citizenship Education. A type of education that aims to empower learners to assume active roles to face and resolve global challenges and to become proactive contributors to a more peaceful, tolerant, inclusive and secure world.

Gross domestic product (GDP). The value of all final goods and services produced in a country in one year.

Gross enrolment ratio. Enrolment in a specific level of education, regardless of age, expressed as a percentage of the population in the official age group corresponding to this level of education. It can exceed 100% because of early or late entry and/or grade repetition.

Gross intake rate. Total number of new entrants to a given grade of primary education, regardless of age, expressed as a percentage of the population at the official school entrance age for that grade.

Gross national income. The value of all final goods and services produced in a country in one year (GDP) plus income that residents have received from abroad, minus income claimed by non- residents.

Information and communication technology skills. Individuals are considered to have such skills if they have undertaken certain computer-related activities in the last three months: copying or moving a file or folder; using copy and paste tools to duplicate or move information within a document; sending emails with attached files; using basic arithmetic formulas in a spreadsheet; connecting and installing new devices; finding, downloading, installing and configuring software; creating electronic presentations with presentation software; transferring files between a computer and other devices; and writing a computer program using a specialized programming language.

Literacy. According to UNESCO's 1958 definition, the term refers to the ability of an individual to read and write with understanding a simple short statement related to his/her everyday life. The concept of literacy has since evolved to embrace several skill domains, each conceived on a scale of different mastery levels and serving different purposes.

Literacy rate. Number of literate people in a particular age group, expressed as a percentage of the total population in that age group.

- Adult. Aged 15 and above.

- Youth. Aged 15 to 24.

Minimum proficiency level. Benchmark of basic knowledge in mathematics and reading, measured through learning assessments. Until such time as common standards are validated by the international community or countries, the definitions of minimum proficiency published by agencies specialized in cross-national learning assessments are being used.

Net attendance rate. Number of students in the official age group for a given level of education who attend school at that level, expressed as a percentage of the population in that age group.

Net enrolment rate. Enrolment of the official age group for a given level of education, expressed as a percentage of the population in that age group. There are two additional variations of this indicator:

- Adjusted net enrolment rate. Enrolment of the official age group for a given level of education *either at that level or the levels above*, expressed as a percentage of the population in that age group.

- Total net enrolment rate. Enrolment of the official age group *in any level of education*, expressed as a percentage of the population in that age group.

New entrants. Students entering a given level of education for the first time; the difference between enrolment and repeaters in the first grade of the level.

Never been to school rate. Percentage of children aged three to five years older than the official entrance age into primary education who have never been to school. For example, in a country where the official entrance age is 6 years, the indicator is calculated over the age group 9 to 11 years.

Out-of-school number. Those not enrolled, defined over the following populations:

- Children of official primary school age.
- Adolescents of official lower secondary school age.
- Youth of official upper secondary school age.

Out-of-school rate. Those of the official age group for a given level of education not enrolled, expressed as a percentage of the population in that age group.

Over-age for grade rate. The percentage of students in each level of education (primary, lower secondary and upper secondary) who are two years or more above the intended age for their grade.

Parity index. A measure of inequality defined as the ratio of the values of an education indicator of two population groups. Typically, the numerator is the value of the disadvantaged group and the denominator is the value of the advantaged group. An index value between 0.97 and 1.03 indicates parity. A value below 0.97 indicates disparity in favour of the advantaged group. A value above 1.03 indicates disparity in favour of the disadvantaged group. An adjusted parity index is symmetrical around 1 and limited to a range between 0 and 2. Groups can be defined by:

- Gender. Ratio of female to male values of a given indicator.
- Location. Ratio of rural to urban values of a given indicator.
- Wealth/income. Ratio of the poorest 20% to the richest 20% of a given indicator.

Private institutions. Institutions that are not operated by public authorities but are controlled and managed, whether for profit or not, by private bodies such as non-government organizations, religious bodies, special interest groups, foundations or business enterprises.

Public expenditure on education. Total current and capital expenditure on education by local, regional and national governments for public and private institutions.

Pupil/teacher ratio. Average number of pupils per teacher at a specific level of education.

Purchasing power parity. An exchange rate adjustment that accounts for price differences between countries, allowing international comparisons of real output and income.

Qualified teacher. Teacher who has the minimum academic qualification necessary to teach at a specific level of education in a given country.

Teacher attrition rate. Number of teachers at a given level of education leaving the profession in a given school year, expressed as a percentage of teachers at that level and in that school year.

Technical and vocational education and training. Programmes designed mainly to prepare students for direct entry into a particular occupation or trade (or class of occupations or trades).

Trained teacher. Teacher who has fulfilled at least the minimum organized teacher-training requirements (preservice or in-service) to teach a specific level of education according to national policy or law.

Transition rate. Number of new entrants to the first grade of an education level in a given year, expressed as a percentage of the number of students who were enrolled in the final grade of the previous education level in the previous year and who do not repeat that grade the following year.

INCLUSION TERMS

Ability. Individual talent, skill or proficiency in a particular area.

Accessibility. Of facilities and services: the quality of being easily reached, entered or used by people with disabilities on an equal basis with others.

Accommodation. Alteration of curriculum, teaching, assessment, environment or equipment that, without altering what is being taught, allows an individual with a disability to gain access to content and/or complete assigned tasks. It allows students with disabilities to pursue a regular course of study.

Affirmative action. Measures aimed at promoting access by members of certain groups to services to the same extent as members of other groups.

Assessment. Process of defining, selecting, designing, collecting, analysing, interpreting and using information about a student's achievement and development level in academic, behavioural or social areas.

Assistive technology. Equipment, devices, apparatuses, services, systems, processes and environmental modifications used by people with disabilities to overcome social, infrastructural and other barriers to learning independence, safe and easy participation in learning activities, and full participation in society.

Background. Individual education, experience and social circumstances.

Curriculum. Description of what, why, how and how well students should learn in a systematic and intentional way. This definition refers to what is written during curriculum design and development, but through misunderstanding, disagreement or lack of resources, school-level implementation and enactment may diverge from original intentions. For instance:

- *Experienced curriculum* refers to learning as students experience it, including the knowledge and perspectives learners bring, their ability to learn and their interaction with the curriculum.

- *Hidden curriculum* refers to student experiences of school beyond the formal curriculum structure, such as messages communicated by the school or education system concerning values, beliefs,

behaviours and attitudes, which may complement or undermine the curriculum as intended and implemented.

Developmental delay. Delay in reaching a normal stage of development, such as sitting or talking.

Disability. A limitation in one or multiple functional domains (e.g. walking, seeing), on a spectrum from minimal to severe, arising from the interaction between a person's intrinsic capacity and environmental and personal factors that hinder their full, effective participation in society on an equal basis with others.

Discrimination. Failure to treat people equally.

Diversity. Presence of people of different backgrounds, abilities and identities in a group.

Equality. A state of affairs or result whereby all members of a group enjoy the same inputs, outputs or outcomes in terms of status, rights and responsibilities.

Equity. A process or actions aimed at ensuring equality.

Exclusion. Any form of direct or indirect prevention of access.

Gender expression. Individual expression of gender through names, clothes, walking style, speaking, communication, societal roles and general behaviour.

Gender identity. Deeply felt internal and individual experience of gender, which may or may not correspond with the sex assigned at birth.

Identification. Recognition or detection of special education needs in a child or student.

Identity. Qualities of a person or group that make them different from others.

Impairment. Problem in body function or structure.

Inclusion. A process consisting of actions and practices that embrace diversity and build a sense of belonging, rooted in the belief that every person has value and potential and should be respected.

Inclusive education. An education that promotes mutual respect and value for all persons and builds educational environments in which the approach to learning, the institutional culture and the curriculum reflect the value of diversity.

Individualized education plan. Written plan setting out a student's present performance level along with goals and objectives, as well as services and timelines to meet those goals and objectives.

Integration. Process of placing people with disabilities in mainstream educational institutions to whose standardized requirements the individuals can adjust.

Mainstream. Regular education settings where students of different backgrounds, identities and abilities learn together.

Marginalized. Of a group within a given culture, context or history: at risk of being excluded and discriminated against because of the interplay of differing personal characteristics or grounds. In this report it is used interchangeably with **disadvantaged**.

Modification. Alteration of curriculum, teaching or assessment in which content and learning expectations are changed for students with intellectual disabilities.

Segregation. For students with a particular characteristic in terms of background, identity or ability, provision of education in separate classes or schools isolated from students without this characteristic.

Sexual orientation. Capacity for profound emotional and sexual attraction to, and intimate and sexual relations with, individuals of a different gender, the same gender or more than one gender.

Special. Of education settings: where students with disabilities and/or special needs learn separately from those without special needs or disabilities.

Special education need. Learning difficulty and/or disability that may require special education support. Countries define these needs differently.

Universal design. Design of products, environments, programmes and services to be usable by all to the greatest extent possible, with no need for adaptation or specialised design.

Universal design for learning. Design of curriculum that gives all individuals equal opportunities to learn.

Zero reject. Principle that everyone, regardless of circumstance, has a right to education.

Abbreviations

ADB	Asian Development Bank
AECD	Australia Early Childhood Development Census
AES	Adult Education Survey (EU)
AIDS	Acquired immunodeficiency syndrome
ASER	Annual Status of Education Report (India)
CBE	Community-based education
CCTV	Closed-circuit television
Covid-19	COrona VIrus Disease of 2019
CRPD	Convention on the Rights of Persons with Disabilities (UN)
CRS	Creditor Reporting System (OECD)
CSO	Civil society organization
DAAD	Deutscher Akademischer Austauschdienst (German Academic Exchange Service)
DAC	Development Assistance Committee (OECD)
DFID	Department for International Development (UK)
DHS	Demographic and Health Survey
DPO	Disabled people's organization
ECCE	Early childhood care and education
ECDI	Early Childhood Development Index
EFA	Education for All
EMIS	Education management information system
EU	European Union
Eurostat	Statistical office of the European Union
FAO	Food and Agriculture Organization of the United Nations
FTS	Financial Tracking Service (OCHA)
GDP	Gross domestic product
GEM Report	*Global Education Monitoring Report*
GER	Gross enrolment ratio
GLAD Network	Global Action on Disability Network
GNI	Gross national income
GPE	Global Partnership for Education
GPI	Gender parity index
GRALE	Global Report on Adult Learning and Education
HIV	Human immunodeficiency virus
IAEG	Inter-agency and Expert Group (on SDG Indicators)
IBE	International Bureau of Education (UNESCO)
ICETEX	Instituto Colombiano de Crédito Educativo y Estudios Técnicos en el Exterior
ICF	International Classification of Functioning, Disability and Health (WHO)

ICT	Information and communication technology
IDA	International Development Association (World Bank)
IEA	International Association for the Evaluation of Educational Achievement
IFAD	International Fund for Agricultural Development
IIEP	International Institute for Educational Planning (UNESCO)
ILO	International Labour Office/Organization
IMF	International Monetary Fund
IRT	Item response theory
ISCED	International Standard Classification of Education
ITU	International Telecommunication Union
JMP	Joint Monitoring Programme (WHO/UNICEF)
LAMP	Literacy Assessment and Monitoring Programme (UIS)
LGBTI	Lesbian, gay, bisexual, transgender and intersex
LLECE	Laboratorio Latinoamericano de Evaluación de la Calidad de la Educación
LWC	Living Water Community (Venezuela)
MDG	Millennium Development Goal
MICS	Multiple Indicator Cluster Survey
NADA	National Data Archive
NER	Net enrolment rate
NGO	Non-government organization
OCHA	Office for the Coordination of Humanitarian Affairs (UN)
ODA	Official development assistance
OECD	Organisation for Economic Co-operation and Development
OHCHR	Office of the United Nations High Commissioner for Human Rights
PASEC	Programme d'analyse des systèmes éducatifs de la CONFEMEN
PEER	Profiles Enhancing Reviews in Education
PIAAC	Programme for the International Assessment of Adult Competencies (OECD)
PILNA	Pacific Islands Literacy and Numeracy Assessment
PIRLS	Progress in International Reading Literacy Study
PISA	Programme for International Student Assessment (OECD)
PISA-D	PISA for Development (OECD)
PPP	Purchasing power parity
RTE Act	Right of Children to Free and Compulsory Education Act (India)
SCOPE	Scoping Progress in Education
SDG	Sustainable Development Goal
SIAS	Screening, Identification, Assessment and Support (South Africa)
STEP	Skills Toward Employment and Productivity (World Bank)
TALIS	Teaching and Learning International Survey (OECD)
TaRL	Teaching at the Right Level
TCG	Technical Cooperation Group
TIMSS	Trends in International Mathematics and Science Study

TOSSD	Total Official Support for Sustainable Development (OECD)
TVET	Technical and vocational education and training
UIL	UNESCO Institute for Lifelong Learning
UIS	UNESCO Institute for Statistics
UK	United Kingdom
UN	United Nations
UNAIDS	Joint United Nations Programme on HIV/AIDS
UNDP	United Nations Development Programme
UNESCO	United Nations Educational, Scientific and Cultural Organization
UNFCCC	United Nations Framework Convention on Climate Change
UNFPA	United Nations Population Fund
UNHCR	United Nations High Commissioner for Refugees
UNICEF	United Nations Children's Fund
UNODC	United Nations Office on Drugs and Crime
UNPD	United Nations Population Division
UNSD	United Nations Statistical Division
UOE	UIS/OECD/Eurostat
US	United States
WASH	Water, sanitation and hygiene
WFP	World Food Programme (United Nations)
WHO	World Health Organization (United Nations)

References

THEMATIC SECTION

CHAPTER 1

Action on Albinism. 2019. *About the Regional Action Plan (RAP) on Albinism in Africa.* Action on Albinism. https://actiononalbinism.org/uploaded_documents/15326742809925p85jaqb1dobp0kn49u5o2yb9.pdf.

Ahmed, K. 2020. Bangladesh grants Rohingya refugee children access to education. *The Guardian,* 29 January.

Al Ju'beh, K. 2015. *Disability Inclusive Development Toolkit.* Bensheim, Germany, CBM International.

Albert, G., Matache, M., Taba, M. and Zimová, A. 2015. *Segregation of Roma Children in Education: Successes and Challenges.* Budapest, Roma Education Fund.

Amnesty International. 2019. *Kuwait 2018.* www.amnesty.org/en/countries/middle-east-and-north-africa/kuwait/report-kuwait. (Accessed 24 July 2019.)

Amnesty International and European Roma Rights Centre. 2017. *A Lesson in Discrimination: Segregation of Romani Children in Primary Education in Slovakia.* www.errc.org/uploads/upload_en/file/report-lesson-in-discrimination-english.pdf.

Anastasiou, D., Gregory, M. and Kauffman, J. M. 2018. Article 24: Education. Bantekas, I., Stein, M. A. and Anastasiou, D. (eds), *The UN Convention on the Rights of Persons with Disabilities: A Commentary.* Oxford, UK, Oxford University Press.

Antón, J. 2020. *La Población Afrodescendiente e Inclusión Escolar en Ecuador [Afro-descendant Populations and School Inclusion in Ecuador].* Paris, UNESCO. (Background paper for *Global Education Monitoring Report on Inclusion and Education in Latin America and the Caribbean 2020.*)

Baker, C. 2018. Children with albinism find it hard to navigate school. Teachers can help. *The Conversation,* 21 November.

Baker, C., Lund, P., Nyathi, R. and Taylor, J. 2010. The myths surrounding people with albinism in South Africa and Zimbabwe. *Journal of African Cultural Studies,* Vol. 22, No. 2, pp. 169–81.

Beaugrand, C. B. M. 2010. Statelessness and transnationalism in northern Arabia: Biduns and state building in Kuwait, 1959–2009. Ph.D. thesis, London School of Economics and Political Science, London.

___. 2017. *Stateless in the Gulf: Migration, Nationality, and Society in Kuwait.* London/New York, I. B. Tauris.

Bilken, G. 1985. *Achieving the Complete School: Strategies for Effective Mainstreaming.* New York, Teachers College Press.

Burke, J., Kaijage, T. J. and John-Langba, J. 2014. Media analysis of albino killings in Tanzania: a social work and human rights perspective. *Ethics and Social Welfare,* Vol. 8, No. 2, pp. 117–34.

Chagas, W. F. 2017. Afro-Brazilian and African history and culture in K–12 education in Paraíba state, Brazil. *Educação e Realidade,* Vol. 42, No. 1, pp. 79–98.

Cisternas Reyes, M. S. 2019. Inclusive education: perspectives from the UN Committee on the Rights of Persons with Disabilities. de Beco, G., Quinlivan, S. and Lord, J. E. (eds), *The Right to Inclusive Education in International Human Rights Law.* Cambridge, UK, Cambridge University Press, pp. 403–23.

Committee on the Rights of Persons with Disabilities. 2016. *General Comment No. 4: Article 24 – Right to Inclusive Education.* New York, United Nations Committee on the Rights of Persons with Disabilities.

Council of Europe. 2017. *Fighting School Segregation in Europe through Inclusive Education: A Position Paper.* Strasbourg, France, Commissioner for Human Rights, Council of Europe.

___. 2019. *Inclusive Schools: Making a Difference for Roma children – About the Project.* Strasbourg, France, Council of Europe. https://pjp-eu.coe.int/en/web/inclusive-education-for-roma-children/about-the-project.

De Beco, G. 2018. The right to inclusive education: why is there so much opposition to its implementation? *International Journal of Law in Context,* Vol. 14, No. 3, pp. 396–415.

Dupuy, K., Gjerløw, H., Ashraful Haque, M., Mahmud, S., Nilsen, M. and Østby, G. 2019. *Mapping Education Programmes for Rohingya Refugees in Bangladesh.* Oslo, Peace Research Institute Oslo. (PRIO Policy Brief 11/2019.)

ECLAC. 2017. *Situación de las Personas Afrodescendientes en América Latina y Desafíos de Políticas para la Garantía de sus Derechos [Situation of Afro-descendants in Latin America and Policy Challenges to Guaranteeing their Rights]*. Santiago, Economic Commission for Latin America and the Caribbean.

___. 2018. *Afrodescendent Women in Latin America and the Caribbean: Debts of Equality*. Santiago, Economic Commission for Latin America and the Caribbean.

Ecuador Ministry of Heritage Coordination. 2009. *Plan Plurinacional para Eliminar la Discriminación Racial y la Exclusión Étnica y Cultural [Plurinational Plan for the Elimination of Racial Discrimination and Ethnic and Cultural Exclusion]*. Quito, Ministry of Heritage Coordination.

Elgayar, A. 2014. Kuwait's stateless residents struggle for education. *Al-Fanar Media*, 24 November.

European Commission. 2016. *Commission requests Hungary to put an end to the discrimination of Roma children in education*. Brussels, European Commission.

___. 2019a. *Education and Training Monitor: Hungary*. Brussels, European Commission.

___. 2019b. *Anti-discrimination: Commission sends reasoned opinion to Slovakia urging the country to comply with EU rules on equal treatment of Roma schoolchildren*. Brussels, European Commission.

European Council. 2013. *Council Recommendation of 9 December 2013 on Effective Roma Integration Measures in the Member States*. Brussels, Council of the European Union. (2013/C 378/01.)

European Court of Human Rights. 2013. *Case of Horváth and Kiss v. Hungary (Application no. 11146/11): Judgement*. Strasbourg, France, European Court of Human Rights.

Forlin, C. I., Chambers, D. J., Loreman, T., Deppler, J. and Sharma, U. 2013. *Inclusive Education for Students with Disability: A Review of the Best Evidence in Relation to Theory and Practice*. Canberra, Australian Research Alliance for Children and Youth.

FRA. 2014. *Roma Survey – Data in Focus. Poverty and Employment: The Situation of Roma in 11 EU Member States*. Vienna, European Union Agency for Fundamental Rights.

___. 2016. *EU MIDIS II: Second European Union Minorities and Discrimination Survey: Roma – Selected Findings*. Vienna, European Union Agency for Fundamental Rights.

Haug, P. 2017. Understanding inclusive education: ideals and reality. *Scandinavian Journal of Disability Research*, Vol. 19, No. 3, pp. 206–17.

Human Rights Council. 2013. *Persons with Albinism: Report of the Office of the United Nations High Commissioner for Human Rights*. New York, United Nations, Human Rights Council.

___. 2018. *Report of the Detailed Findings of the Independent International Fact-Finding Mission on Myanmar*. New York, United Nations, Human Rights Council. (Thirty-ninth session, 10–28 September.)

Human Rights Watch. 2009. *Perilous Plight: Burma's Rohingya Take to the Seas*. New York, Human Rights Watch.

___. 2011. *Prisoners of the Past: Kuwaiti Bidun and the Burden of Statelessness*. New York, Human Rights Watch.

___. 2019a. *'Are We Not Human?' Denial of Education for Rohingya Refugee Children in Bangladesh*. New York, Human Rights Watch.

___. 2019b. *Bangladesh: Rohingya refugee students expelled – ensure formal education is available to all children*. New York, Human Rights Watch. www.hrw.org/news/2019/04/01/bangladesh-rohingya-refugee-students-expelled. (Accessed 11 December 2019.)

___. 2019c. *World Report 2019: Events of 2018*. New York, Human Rights Watch.

IBGE. 2017. *Pesquisa Nacional por Amostra de Domicílios Contínua: Características Gerais dos Moradores 2012–2016 [Continuous National Household Sample Survey: General Characteristics of Residents 2012–2016]*. Rio de Janeiro, Brazilian Institute of Geography and Statistics.

Institute on Statelessness and Inclusion. 2017. *The World's Stateless Children*. Oisterwijk, Netherlands, Institute on Statelessness and Inclusion.

Lipsky, D. K. and Gartner, A. 1997. *Inclusion and School Reform: Transforming America's Classrooms*. Baltimore, Md., Paul H. Brookes.

Lynch, P. and Lund, P. 2011. *Education of Children and Young People with Albinism in Malawi*. London/Lilongwe, Commonwealth Secretariat/Malawi Ministry of Education, Science and Technology/Sightsavers.

Lynch, P., Lund, P. and Massah, B. 2014. Identifying strategies to enhance the educational inclusion of visually impaired children with albinism in Malawi. *International Journal of Educational Development*, Vol. 39, pp. 216–24.

Mena García, M. I. 2009. La ilustración de las personas Afrocolombianas en los textos escolares para enseñar historia [Presentation of Afrocolombians in history textbooks]. *Historia Caribe*, Vol. 15, No. 5, pp. 105–22.

MENA Rights Group. 2018. *Inconsistencies in Qatar's approach to civil and political rights in era of Gulf crisis.* https://menarights.org/en/documents/qatar-upr. (Accessed 24 July 2019.)

Middle East Eye. 2016. Comoros ready to take Kuwait's stateless. 16 May.

Miles, S. 2011. Exploring understandings of inclusion in schools in Zambia and Tanzania using reflective writing and photography. *International Journal of Inclusive Education*, Vol. 15, No. 10, pp. 1087–102.

Mulat, M., Lehtomäki, E. and Savolainen, H. 2018. Academic achievement and self-concept of deaf and hard-of-hearing and hearing students transitioning from the first to second cycle of primary school in Ethiopia. *International Journal of Inclusive Education*, Vol. 23, No. 6, pp. 609–23.

Muñoz, N. 2003. *Guatemala: New law recognises indigenous languages.* Rome, Inter Press Service News Agency. www.ipsnews.net/2003/05/guatemala-new-law-recognises-indigenous-languages. (Accessed 11 December 2019.)

Myanmar Ministry of Health and Sports and ICF. 2017. *Myanmar Demographic and Health Survey 2015–16.* Nay Pyi Taw, Myanmar/Rockville, Md., Ministry of Health and Sports/ICF.

Norwich, B. 2014. Recognising value tensions that underlie problems in inclusive education. *Cambridge Journal of Education*, Vol. 44, No. 4, pp. 495–510.

OECD. 2019. *PISA 2018 Results: What Students Know and Can Do – Volume I.* Paris, Organisation for Economic Co-operation and Development.

OEI. 2010. *2021 Metas Educativas: La Educación que Queremos para la Generación de los Bicentenarios – Documento Final [2021 Education Goals: The Education We Want for the Bicentenary Generation – Final Document].* Madrid, Organization of Ibero-American States.

OHCHR. 2019. *Statement to the Media by the United Nations' Working Group of Experts on People of African Descent, on the Conclusion of Its Official Visit to Ecuador, 16–20 December 2019.* Geneva, Switzerland, Office of the High Commissioner for Human Rights. www.ohchr.org/EN/NewsEvents/Pages/DisplayNews.aspx?NewsID=25451&LangID=E. (Accessed 11 February 2020.)

Parashar, A. and Alam, J. 2019. The national laws of Myanmar: making of statelessness for the Rohingya. *International Migration*, Vol. 57, No. 1, pp. 94–108.

Paschel, T. S. 2016. *Becoming Black Political Subjects: Movements and Ethno-Racial Rights in Colombia and Brazil.* Princeton, NJ, Princeton University Press.

Pedneault, J. and Labaki, L. 2019. *'It Felt Like A Punishment': Growing Up with Albinism in Tanzania.* New York, Human Rights Watch.

Plan International and REACH. 2015. *Joint Education Sector Needs Assessment, North Rakhine State, Myanmar: Assessment Report.* Woking, UK/Geneva, Switzerland, Plan International/REACH.

Rimmerman, A. 2013. *Social Inclusion of People with Disabilities: National and International Perspectives.* Cambridge, UK, Cambridge University Press.

Rodríguez, M. and Mallo, T. 2014. *Los Afrodescendientes Frente a la Educación: Panorama Regional de América Latina [Afro-descendants Facing Education: Latin America Regional Panorama].* Madrid, CeALCI Fundación Carolina. (Avances de Investigación 75.)

Save the Children. 2017. *Stolen Childhoods: End of Childhood Report 2017.* London, Save the Children International.

Silver, H. 2015. *The Contexts of Social Inclusion.* New York, United Nations Department of Economic and Social Affairs. (DESA Working Paper 144.)

Slee, R. 2020. *Defining the Scope of Inclusive Education.* Paris, UNESCO. (Background paper for *Global Education Monitoring Report 2020*.)

Standing Voice. 2017. *Opening Doors, Unlocking Potential: Bure's Story.* https://medium.com/@StandingVoice/opening-doors-unlocking-potential-bures-story-727705696664.

Stubbs, S. 2008. *Inclusive Education Where There Are Few Resources.* Oslo, The Atlas Alliance.

Tomaševski, K. 2001. *Human Rights Obligations: Making Education Available, Accessible, Acceptable and Adaptable.* Lund, Sweden/Stockholm, Raoul Wallenberg Institute/Swedish International Development Cooperation Agency. (Right to Education Primer 3.)

Tones, M., Pillay, H., Carrington, S., Chandra, S., Duke, J. and Joseph, R. M. 2017. Supporting disability education through a combination of special schools and disability-inclusive schools in the Pacific Islands. *International Journal of Disability, Development and Education*, Vol. 64, No. 5, pp. 497–513.

Torres Fuentes, D. M. 2014. La primera infancia en los pueblos afrodescendientes de Colombia: una mirada pedagógica y cultural [Early childhood in Afro-descendant populations in Colombia: a pedagogical and cultural perspective]. Marchesi, Á., Blanco, R. and Hernández, L. (eds), *Avances y Desafíos de la Educación Inclusiva en Iberoamérica* [Progress and Challenges of Inclusive Education in Ibero-America]. Madrid, Organization of Ibero-American States.

UNDP. 2019. *Human Development Report 2019: Beyond Income, Beyond Averages, Beyond Today – Inequalities in Human Development in the 21st Century*. New York, United Nations Development Programme.

UNESCO. 2009. *Policy Guidelines on Inclusion in Education*. Paris, UNESCO.

___. 2017. *A Guide for Ensuring Inclusion and Equity in Education*. Paris, UNESCO.

UNESCO and Spain Ministry of Education and Science. 1994. *The Salamanca Statement and Framework for Action on Special Needs Education*. Paris, UNESCO.

UNHCR. 2020. *Rohingya Emergency*. Geneva, Switzerland, United Nations High Commissioner for Refugees. www.unhcr.org/rohingya-emergency.html. (Accessed 11 February 2020.)

United Nations. 2006. *Convention on the Rights of Persons with Disabilities and Optional Protocol*. New York, United Nations.

___. 2015. *Transforming Our World: The 2030 Agenda for Sustainable Development*. New York, United Nations. https://sustainabledevelopment.un.org/post2015/transformingourworld.

___. 2019. *Disability Statistics*. New York, United Nations Statistics Division. https://unstats.un.org/unsd/demographic-social/sconcerns/disability/statistics/#/home.

United Nations General Assembly. 2017a. *Report of the Independent Expert on the Enjoyment of Human Rights by Persons with Albinism on the Regional Action Plan on Albinism in Africa (2017–2021)*. New York, United Nations. (Human Rights Council, 37th Session, 26 February–23 March.)

___. 2017b. *Report of the Independent Expert on the Enjoyment of Human Rights by Persons with Albinism on Her Mission to the United Republic of Tanzania*. New York, United Nations. (Human Rights Council, 37th Session, 26 February–23 March.)

Van den Bogaert, S. 2018. *Segregation of Roma Children in Education: Addressing Structural Discrimination through the Framework Convention for the Protection of National Minorities and the Racial Equality Directive 2000/43/EC*. Leiden, Netherlands, Brill | Nijhoff.

WHO. 2001. *International Classification of Functioning, Disability and Health*. Geneva, Switzerland, World Health Organization. http://apps.who.int/classifications/icfbrowser.

World Bank. 2018. *Afro-descendants in Latin America: Toward a Framework of Inclusion*. Washington, DC, World Bank.

World Bank and UNICEF. 2016. *Ending Extreme Poverty: A Focus on Children*. Washington, DC/New York, World Bank/UNICEF.

Zacharias, A. 2018. Explained: Who are the bidoon? A look at the history of the stateless in the Gulf. *The National*, 5 September.

Zemandl, E. J. 2018. *The Roma Experience of Political (In)justice: The Case of School (De)segregation in Hungary*. Utrecht, Netherlands, ETHOS Towards a European Theory of Justice and Fairness.

CHAPTER 2

Abdou, E. 2020. *Arab States: Solid Steps on a Long Path Towards Inclusive Education*. Paris, UNESCO. (Background paper for Global Education Monitoring Report 2020.)

Abramo, L., Cecchini, S. and Morales, B. 2019. *Social Programmes, Poverty Eradication and Labour Inclusion: Lessons from Latin America and the Caribbean*. Santiago, United Nations Economic Commission for Latin America and the Caribbean.

Adair, J. K. 2015. *The Impact of Discrimination on the Early Schooling Experiences of Children from Immigrant Families*. Washington, DC, Migration Policy Institute.

African Commission on Human and Peoples' Rights. 2019. *Statement of the Working Group on the Rights of Older Persons and People with Disabilities in Africa of the African Commission on Human and Peoples' Rights, on the Occasion of the World Braille Day – 4th January 2019*. Banjul, African Commission on Human and Peoples' Rights.

African Union. 2018. *Protocol to the African Charter on Human and Peoples' Rights on the Rights of Persons with Disabilities in Africa*. Addis Ababa, African Union.

Agarwal, M. 2020. *Retain, Promote or Support: How to Reduce Inequality in Elementary Education*. Paris, UNESCO. (Global Education Monitoring Report Fellowship Paper.)

AgCom. 2020. *Broadband Map*. Naples, Italy, Authority for Communications Guarantees. https://maps.agcom.it. (Accessed 6 May 2020.)

AHEAD. 2019. *The Global University Disability and Inclusion Network (GUDIN)*. Huntersville, NC, Association on Higher Education and Disability. www.ahead.org/about-ahead/gudin. (Accessed 11 December 2019.)

Ahmed, A. Y. and Mihiretie, D. M. 2015. Primary school teachers and parents' views on automatic promotion practices and its implications for education quality. *International Journal of Educational Development*, Vol. 43, pp. 90–99.

Ainscow, M. 1991. *Effective Schools for All*. London, David Fulton.

Algraigray, H. and Boyle, C. 2017. The SEN label and its effect on special education. *Educational and Child Psychology*, Vol. 34, No. 4, pp. 70–79.

Alla-Mensah, J. 2020. *Virtual Conference on Inclusive TVET: Virtual Conference Report*. Paris, UNESCO. (Background paper for *Global Education Monitoring Report 2020*.)

Allen, C. S., Chen, Q., Willson, V. L. and Hughes, J. N. 2009. Quality of research design moderates effects of grade retention on achievement: a meta-analytic, multilevel analysis. *Educational Evaluation and Policy Analysis*, Vol. 31, No. 4, pp. 480–99.

Alper Dinçer, M. and Erten, B. 2015. Does compulsory schooling reduce child labor? Evidence from Turkey. Istanbul/Boston, Sabancı University/Northeastern University. (Unpublished.)

Amin, S., Saha, J. S. and Ahmed, J. A. 2018. Skills-building programs to reduce child marriage in Bangladesh: a randomized controlled trial. *Journal of Adolescent Health*, Vol. 63, No. 3, pp. P293–300.

Anastasiou, D. and Keller, C. E. 2014. Cross-national differences in special education coverage. *Exceptional Children*, Vol. 80, No. 3, pp. 353–67.

___. 2017. Cross-national differences in special education: a typological approach. Kauffman, J. M., Hallahan, D. P. and Pullen, C. P. (eds), *Handbook of Special Education*, 2nd edition. Routledge.

Argentina Ministry of Education. 2019. *Terminar la primaria o la secundaria con el Plan FinEs [Completing Primary or Secondary Education with Plan FinEs]*. Buenos Aires, Ministry of Education. www.argentina.gob.ar/terminar-la-primaria-o-la-secundaria-con-el-plan-fines. (Accessed 11 December 2019.)

Armenia Government. 2016. *The 2012–2015 National Report of the Republic of Armenia on the Implementation of the Provisions of the UNESCO Convention against Discrimination in Education of 14 December 1960*. Yerevan, Government of Armenia.

Asanov, I., Flores, F., McKenzie, D., Mensmann, M. and Schulte, M. 2020. *Remote-learning, Time-use, and Mental Health of Ecuadorian High-School Students during the COVID-19 Quarantine*. Washington, DC, World Bank. (Policy Research Working Paper 9252.)

Australia Department of Education, Skills and Employment. 2020. *Higher Education Disability Support Program: Changes to the Higher Education Disability Support Program from 1 January 2020*. Canberra, Department of Education, Skills and Employment.

Austria Ministry of Science Research and Economy. 2017. *National Strategy on the Social Dimension of Higher Education: Towards More Inclusive Access and Wider Participation*. Vienna, Federal Ministry of Science, Research and Economy.

Autin, C. 2020. *Coronavirus : le CNED lance «Ma classe à la maison» pour suivre des cours à distance [Coronavirus: the CNED launches 'My class at home' to follow distance courses]*. Paris, France Bleu. www.francebleu.fr/infos/education/coronavirus-le-cned-lance-ma-classe-a-la-maison-pour-suivre-des-cours-a-distance-1583244985. (Accessed 6 May 2020.)

Ball, J. and Smith, M. 2019. *Independent Evaluation of the Multilingual Education National Action Plan in Cambodia*, Vol. I. Phnom Penh, UNICEF.

Basque Country Department of Education. 2019. *Plan Marco para el Desarrollo de una Escuela Inclusiva 2019–2022 [Framework for the Development of an Inclusive School 2019–2022]*. Vitoria-Gasteiz, Spain, Department of Education.

Battaglia, M. and Lebedinski, L. 2015. Equal access to education: an evaluation of the Roma Teaching Assistant Program in Serbia. *World Development*, Vol. 76, pp. 62–81.

___. 2017. The curse of low expectations. *Economics of Transition*, Vol. 25, No. 4, pp. 681–721.

BBC News. 2019. *The Cape Town schools learning from transgender students*. London, BBC. www.bbc.com/news/world-africa-46213884. (Accessed 11 December 2019.)

Beech, J. 2019. The long and winding road to inclusion. Ornelas, C. (ed.), *Politics of Education in Latin America: Reforms, Resistance and Persistence*, pp. 17–42. Leiden, Netherlands, Brill | Sense. (Comparative and International Education: Diversity of Voices, Vol. 49.)

Belize National Resource Center for Inclusive Education. 2019. *Referral Process*. Belmopan, Education Support Services, Ministry of Education.

Bertrand, M., Hanna, R. and Mullainathan, S. 2010. Affirmative action in education: evidence from engineering college admissions in India. *Journal of Public Economics*, Vol. 94, No. 1–2, pp. 16–29.

Bessho, S., Noguchi, H., Kawamura, A., Tanaka, R. and Ushijima, K. 2019. Evaluating remedial education in elementary schools: administrative data from a municipality in Japan. *Japan and the World Economy*, Vol. 50, pp. 36–46.

Bhattacharjea, S. and Ramanujan, P. 2019. *What Do Children in Rural India Do in their Early Years?* New Delhi, Ideas for India. www.ideasforindia.in/topics/macroeconomics/what-do-children-in-rural-india-do-in-their-early-years.html. (Accessed 11 December 2019.)

Bhattacharya, S., Woods, M. and Lykes, M. B. 2017. Can educational policy redress historical discrimination? Exploring a university community's experiences with India's caste-based affirmative action policy. *Community Psychology in Global Perspective*, Vol. 3, No. 2, pp. 38–59.

Biegon, J. 2019. The scope of recognition and protection of the right to inclusive education in the African human rights system. de Beco, G., Quinlivan, S. and Lord, J. E. (eds), *The Right to Inclusive Education in International Human Rights Law*. Cambridge, UK, Cambridge University Press, pp. 473–94.

Blomgren, L. 2013. *Child Marriage in Bangladesh: Impact of Discriminatory Personal Laws*. Ithaca, NY, Avon Global Center for Women and Justice at Cornell Law School.

Blume, H. and Kohli, S. 2020. 15,000 L.A. high school students are AWOL online, 40,000 fail to check in daily amid coronavirus closures. *Los Angeles Times*, 30 March.

Braun, A. 2020. *Referral and Identification of Special Educational Needs*. Paris, UNESCO. (Background paper for *Global Education Monitoring Report 2020*.)

Brauner, J. M., Sharma, M., Mindermann, S., Stephenson, A. B., Gavenčiak, T., Johnston, D., Salvatier, J., Leech, G., Besiroglu, T. and Altman, G. 2020. The effectiveness and perceived burden of nonpharmaceutical interventions against COVID-19 transmission: a modelling study with 41 countries. *medRxiv*.

Broderick, A. 2019. Emerging trends in the jurisprudence of the European Court of Human Rights. de Beco, G., Quinlivan, S. and Lord, J. E. (eds), *The Right to Inclusive Education in International Human Rights Law*. Cambridge, UK, Cambridge University Press, pp. 424–46.

Cambodia Ministry of Education, Youth and Sport. 2019. *Education Strategic Plan 2019–2023*. Phnom Penh, Ministry of Education, Youth and Sport.

CAMFED. 2020. *Leading Community Action for Vulnerable Girls: Young African Women at the Forefront of COVID-19*. Cambridge, UK, CAMFED. https://camfed.org/latest-news/african-women-leading-community-action-vulnerable. (Accessed 16 May 2020.)

Canada Supreme Court. 2002. *Chamberlain v. Surrey School District No. 36*. Ottawa, Supreme Court of Canada.

Center for Education Innovations. 2018a. *Empowering Marginalized Girls*. Washington, DC, Center for Education Innovations. www.educationinnovations.org/page/empowering-marginalized-girls. (Accessed 11 December 2019.)

___. 2018b. *Fabretto Children's Foundation's Early Education Program*. Washington, DC, Center for Education Innovations. www.earlylearningtoolkit.org/program/fabretto-childrens-foundations-early-education-program. (Accessed 11 December 2019.)

Chang, G.-C. and Yano, S. 2020. *How Are Countries Addressing the Covid-19 Challenges in Education? A Snapshot of Policy Measures*. Paris, UNESCO. https://gemreportunesco.wordpress.com/2020/03/24/how-are-countries-addressing-the-covid-19-challenges-in-education-a-snapshot-of-policy-measures. (Accessed 6 May 2020.)

Chapman, B., Higgins, T. and Stiglitz, J. E. 2014. Introduction and summary. Chapman, B. and Stiglitz, J. E. (eds), *Income Contingent Loans: Theory, Practice and Prospects*. London, Palgrave Macmillan UK.

China Ministry of Education. 2015. 散发材料三 《国家中长期教育改革和发展规划纲要》中期评估特殊教育专题评估报告 [*Distributing Materials 3: The National Mid- and Long-term Education Reform and Development Plan Outline – Mid-term Assessment, Special Education Special Evaluation Report*]. Beijing, Ministry of Education. (Accessed 11 December 2019.)

Chiwandire, D. and Vincent, L. 2019. Funding and inclusion in higher education institutions for students with disabilities. *African Journal of Disability*, Vol. 8, p. 336.

ClassTag. 2020. *Special Report: How Teachers Are Turning to Technology amid COVID-19 School Closings*. New York, ClassTag.

Colombia Constitutional Court. 2016. *Sentencia T-281A/16: Johana Andrea Céspedes Hernández, en representación de Juan Esteban Parra Céspedes contra el Colegio Tolimense [Decision T-281A/16: Johana Andrea Céspedes Hernández, on behalf of Juan Esteban Parra Céspedes against Colegio Tolimense]*. Bogotá, Constitutional Court.

Colombia Ministry of National Education. 2017. *Decreto 1421 de 2017 por el cual se Reglamenta en el Marco de la Educación Inclusiva la Atención Educativa a la Población con Discapacidad [Decree 1421 of 2017 Regulating Education Care for People with Disabilities in the Framework of Inclusive Education]*. Bogotá, Ministry of National Education.

Committee on the Rights of Persons with Disabilities. 2011. *Concluding observations of the Committee on the Rights of Persons with Disabilities: Spain*. New York, Committee on the Rights of Persons with Disabilities. (Consideration of Reports Submitted by States Parties Under Article 35 of the Convention.)

___. 2016. *General Comment No. 4: Article 24 – Right to Inclusive Education*. New York, Committee on the Rights of Persons with Disabilities.

___. 2019. *Concluding Observations of the Committee on the Combined Second and Third Periodic Reports of Spain*. New York, Committee on the Rights of Persons with Disabilities.

Cooper, H., Nye, B., Charlton, K., Lindsay, J. and Greathouse, S. 1996. The effects of summer vacation on achievement test scores: a narrative and meta-analytic review. *Review of Educational Research*, Vol. 66, No. 3, pp. 227–68.

Cortes, K. E., Goodman, J. S. and Nomi, T. 2015. Intensive math instruction and educational attainment: long-run impacts of double-dose algebra. *Journal of Human Resources*, Vol. 50, No. 1, pp. 108–58.

Council of Europe. 2016. *Resolution 2097 (2016): Access to School and Education for All Children*. Strasbourg, France, Parliamentary Assembly, Council of Europe.

___. 2018a. *Digest of the Case Law of the European Committee of Social Rights: Appendix – Relevant Abstracts, Decisions and Conclusions of the European Committee of Social Rights*. Strasbourg, France, Council of Europe.

___. 2018b. *Report by Dunja Mijatović Commissioner for Human Rights of the Council of Europe Following Her Visit to Albania from 21 to 25 May 2018*. Strasbourg, France, Commissioner for Human Rights, Council of Europe.

Cruz, R. A. and Rodl, J. E. 2018. An integrative synthesis of literature on disproportionality in special education. *Journal of Special Education*, Vol. 52, No. 1, pp. 50–63.

Cuba Government. 2019. *List of Issues in Relation to the Initial Report of Cuba: Addendum – Replies of Cuba to the List of Issues*. New York, Committee on the Rights of Persons with Disabilities.

Daflon, V. T., Feres Júnior, J. and Campos, L. A. 2013. Ações afirmativas raciais no ensino superior público brasileiro: um panorama analítico [Racial affirmative action in Brazilian public higher education: an analytical panorama]. *Cadernos de Pesquisa*, Vol. 43, No. 148, pp. 302–27.

de Hoop, T., Ring, H., Coombes, A., Rothbard, V., Holla, C., Hunt, K., Seidenfeld, D. and Connolly, H. 2019. *Scaling Education Innovations in Complex Emergencies: Evidence from the Humanitarian Education Accelerator*. Washington, DC, American Institutes for Research with UNICEF, UNHCR and DFID.

Degener, T. and Uldry, M. 2018. *Towards Inclusive Equality: 10 Years Committee on the Rights of Persons with Disabilities*. Bochum, Germany, Protestant University of Applied Sciences Rhineland-Westphalia-Lippe.

Delavarian, M., Afrooz, A., Towhidkhah, F. and Rasoolzadeh Tabatabaei, K. 2017. Designing a computerized neuro-cognitive program for early diagnosing children at risk for dyslexia. *Iranian Rehabilitation Journal*, Vol. 15, No. 2, pp. 103–10.

Dewi, K., Irmanda, H. N. and Solek, P. 2017. *Indonesian Dyslexia Early Identification System*. Paper for UnITE SpLD 2017, Singapore, 19–21 June.

DHS Program. 2020. *StatCompiler*. Rockville, Md., DHS Program. www.statcompiler.com/en. (Accessed 6 May 2020.)

Djibouti Government. 2000. *Loi n°96/AN/00/4ème L portant Orientation du Système Educatif Djiboutien [Law n°96/AN/00/4ème L on Orientation of the Djiboutian Education System]*. Djibouti, Ministry of National Education and Higher Education.

Dufranc, M. 2017. Reintegrating children in street situations into schools in Haiti. *Enabling Education Review* No. 6, pp. 40–41.

Dyslexia International. 2014. *Better Training, Better Teaching*. Brussels, Dyslexia International with the Center for Child and Family Policy at Duke University.

Economic Times. 2015. Universities asked to include column for transgenders in forms. 7 May.

Education Development Trust and UNICEF. 2016. *Eastern and Southern Africa Regional Study on the Fulfilment of the Right to Education of Children with Disabilities*. Reading, UK, Education Development Trust.

El Nagar, S., Mahjoub, M., Idris, A. and Tønnessen, L. 2018. *Community Views on Child Marriage in Kassala: Prospects for Change*. Bergen, Norway, Chr. Michelsen Institute. (CMI Sudan Report 1.)

Elango, S., García, J. L., Heckman, J. and Hojman, A. 2015. *Early Childhood Education*. Cambridge, Mass., National Bureau of Economic Research. (Working Paper 21766.)

Elder, T. E., Figlio, D. N., Imberman, S. A. and Persico, C. I. 2019. *School Segregation and Racial Gaps in Special Education Identification*. Cambridge, Mass., National Bureau of Economic Research. (Working Paper 25829.)

Elston, J., Moosa, A., Moses, F., Walker, G., Dotta, N., Waldman, R. J. and Wright, J. 2016. Impact of the Ebola outbreak on health systems and population health in Sierra Leone. *Journal of Public Health*, Vol. 38, No. 4, pp. 673–78.

Endeley, M. N. 2016. School characteristics and the implementation of automatic promotion: implications for literacy in English-speaking primary schools in Cameroon. *Journal of Education and Social Policy* Vol. 3, No. 6, pp. 54–61.

E-Nenasala. 2019. *E-Nenasala, Gampaha: About Us*, E-Nenasala. www.enenasala.com. (Accessed 11 December 2019.)

Esposito, S. and Principi, N. 2020. School closure during the coronavirus disease 2019 (COVID-19) pandemic: an effective intervention at the global level? *JAMA Pediatrics*.

European Agency for Special Needs and Inclusive Education. 2016. *Inclusive Early Childhood Education: An Analysis of 32 European Examples*. Odense, Denmark, European Agency for Special Needs and Inclusive Education.

European Agency for Special Needs and Inclusive Education and UNESCO. 2019. *1+5+N: Using a Three-level Resource Room System to Promote Inclusive Education (Learning in Mainstream Classrooms) in China*. Paris, UNESCO. www.inclusive-education-in-action.org/case-study/15n-using-three-level-resource-room-system-promote-inclusive-education-learning.

European Commission/EACEA/Eurydice. 2019. *Key Data on Early Childhood Education and Care in Europe: 2019 Edition*. Eurydice Report. Luxembourg, Publications Office of the European Union.

European Committee of Social Rights. 2017. *Decision on Admissibility and the Merits: Mental Disability Advocacy Center (MDAC) v. Belgium: Complaint No. 109/2014*. Strasbourg, France, Council of Europe, European Committee of Social Rights.

European Court of Human Rights. 2007. *Case of D.H. and Others v. The Czech Republic (Application no. 57325/00): Judgement*. Strasbourg, France, European Court of Human Rights.

Faramarzi, S., Abedi, A. and Ghamarani, A. 2019. Designing the Comprehensive Diagnostic Test of Dyslexia (CDTD) and investigating its validity and reliability for primary school students of Isfahan in 2015–2016. *Journal of Paramedical Sciences and Rehabilitation*, Vol. 8, No. 2, pp. 17–28.

Fenwick, T. B. 2017. From CCTs to a social investment welfare state? Brazil's 'new' pro-poor strategy. *Development Policy Review*, Vol. 35, No. 5, pp. 659–74.

Ferguson, V. 2017. Enabling education for long-term street connected young people in Kenya. *Enabling Education Review*, No. 6, pp. 45–47.

Fiala-Butora, J. 2019. Financing inclusive education. de Beco, G., Quinlivan, S. and Lord, J. E. (eds), *The Right to Inclusive Education in International Human Rights Law*. Cambridge, UK, Cambridge University Press, pp. 213–36.

Fiji Ministry of Education, Heritage and Arts. 2016. *Policy on Special and Inclusive Education*. Suva, Ministry of Education, Heritage and Arts.

Firstpost. 2020. *CBSE Class 10 and 12 Exams, JEE Main 2020 Cancelled: List of Universities, Recruitment Tests Impacted by Coronavirus Outbreak*. www.firstpost.com/india/cbse-class-10-and-12-exams-jee-main-2020-cancelled-list-of-universities-recruitment-tests-impacted-by-coronavirus-outbreak-8166961.html. (Accessed 6 May 2020.)

Fletcher, J. M., Lyon, G. R., Fuchs, L. S. and Barnes, M. A. 2018. *Learning Disabilities: From Identification to Intervention*. New York, Guilford.

Fraillon, J., Ainley, J., Schulz, W., Friedman, T. and Duckworth, D. 2020. *Preparing for Life in a Digital World: IEA International Computer and Information Literacy Study 2018 International Report*. Amsterdam, International Association for the Evaluation of Educational Achievement.

France Education International. 2019. *Second-chance School: Overcoming School Dropout in Tunisia*. Sevres, France, France Education International. (www.ciep.fr/en/actualites/2019/03/28/second-chance-school-overcoming-school-dropout-in-tunisia. (Accessed 11 December 2019.)

France Inter. 2020. *Quelles plateformes, quels formats, quelle durée : les cours à distance, comment ça marche? [What platforms, what formats, what duration: how does distance education work?]*. Paris, France Inter. www.franceinter.fr/education/quelles-plateformes-quels-formats-quelle-duree-les-cours-a-distance-comment-ca-marche. (Accessed 6 May 2020.)

Frisancho Robles, V. and Krishna, K. 2016. Affirmative action in higher education in India: targeting, catch up, and mismatch. *Higher Education*, Vol. 71, No. 5, pp. 611–49.

Fundación Corona, Fundación ANDI and USAID ACDI/VOCA. 2020. *Informe Nacional de Empleo Inclusivo 2018–2019 [National Inclusive Employment Report 2018–2019]*. Bogotá, Fundación Corona/Fundación ANDI/ USAID ACDI/VOCA.

Gambia Ministries of Basic and Secondary Education and Higher Education, Research, Science and Technology. 2016. *Education Sector Policy 2016 – 2030: Accessible, Equitable and Inclusive Quality Education for sustainable Development*. Banjul, Ministries of Basic and Secondary Education and Higher Education, Research, Science and Technology.

Ghana Ministry of Education. 2015. *Inclusive Education Policy*. Accra, Ministry of Education.

Girade, H. A. 2018. 'Criança Feliz': A programme to break the cycle of poverty and reduce the inequality in Brazil. *Early Childhood Matters: Advances in Early Childhood Development*, Vol. 127, pp. 34–38.

Girls' Education Challenge. 2018. *Project: Marginalised no More (MnM)*. London, Department for International Development. https://girlseducationchallenge.org/#/article/marginalised-no-more-mnm.

Goos, M., Schreier, B. M., Knipprath, H. M. E., de Fraine, B., van Damme, J. and Trautwein, U. 2013. How can cross-country differences in the practice of grade retention be explained? A closer look at national educational policy factors. *Comparative Education Review*, Vol. 57, No. 1, pp. 54–84.

Gordon, N. 2017. *Race, Poverty, and Interpreting Overrepresentation in Special Education*. Washington, DC, Brookings Institution.

Guerra Botello, R., Mohamedbhai, G., Pijano, C. and Salmi, J. 2019. *Is Free Tuition the Panacea to Improve Equity in Higher Education?* Washington, DC, Council for Higher Education Accreditation. (Policy Brief 13.)

Hai, N. X., Villa, R. A., Thousand, J. S. and Muc, P. M. 2020. Inclusion in Vietnam: more than a quarter century of implementation. *International Electronic Journal of Elementary Education*, Vol. 12, No. 3, pp. 257–64.

Hande Sart, Z., Barış, S., Düşkün, Y. and Sarıışık, Y. 2016. *The Right of Children with Disabilities to Education: Situation Analysis and Recommendations for Turkey*. Istanbul, Education Reform Initiative.

Heath, J. 2019. *TEVET Codes of Conduct and Trainee Orientation Programme Impact Report*. Lilongwe, Skills and Technical Education Programme (STEP TEVET Orientation Impact Report.)

Herbaut, E. and Geven, K. 2019. *What Works to Reduce Inequalities in Higher Education? A Systematic Review of (Quasi-) Experimental Literature on Outreach and Financial Aid*. Washington, DC, World Bank. (Policy Research Working Paper 8802.)

Hodge, H., Carson, D., Carson, D., Newman, L. and Garrett, J. 2017. Using Internet technologies in rural communities to access services: the views of older people and service providers. *Journal of Rural Studies*, Vol. 54, pp. 469–78.

Human Rights Watch. 2018a. *"I Would Like to Go to School": Barriers to Education for Children with Disabilities in Lebanon*. New York, Human Rights Watch. www.hrw.org/report/2018/03/22/i-would-go-school/barriers-education-children-disabilities-lebanon. (Accessed 11 December 2019.)

___. 2018b. *Leave No Girl Behind in Africa: Discrimination in Education against Pregnant Girls and Adolescent Mothers*. New York, Human Rights Watch. www.hrw.org/report/2018/06/14/leave-no-girl-behind-africa/discrimination-education-against-pregnant-girls-and. (Accessed 11 December 2019.)

___. 2018c. *Nepal: Barriers to Inclusive Education Segregation – Lack of Accessibility for Children with Disabilities*. New York, Human Rights Watch. www.hrw.org/news/2018/09/13/nepal-barriers-inclusive-education. (Accessed 11 December 2019.)

___. 2019a. *Africa: Pregnant Girls, Young Mothers Denied School*. New York, Human Rights Watch. www.hrw.org/news/2019/06/16/africa-pregnant-girls-young-mothers-denied-school. (Accessed 11 December 2019.)

___. 2019b. *"Just Like Other Kids": Lack of Access to Inclusive Quality Education for Children with Disabilities in Iran*. New York, Human Rights Watch.

Hunt, P. F. 2020. *Including Children with Disabilities in Education*. Paris, UNESCO. (Background paper for *Global Education Monitoring Report 2020*.)

ICAI. *Accessing, Staying and Succeeding in Basic Education: UK Aid's Support to Marginalised Girls – A Performance Review*. London, Independent Commission for Aid Impact.

IITE. 2020. *Inclusive Education Policy in the Russian Federation*. Paris, UNESCO. (Background paper for *Global Education Monitoring Report 2020*.)

ILO. 2017a. *Disability Inclusion in the Bangladesh Skills System*. Geneva, Switzerland, International Labour Office.

___. 2017b. *Global Estimates of Child Labour: Results and Trends, 2012–2016*. Geneva, Switzerland, International Labour Office.

___. 2017c. *Making TVET and Skills Systems Inclusive of Persons with Disabilities*. Geneva, Switzerland, International Labour Office. (Policy Brief.)

India Ministry of Health and Family Welfare. 2016. *Menstrual Hygiene Scheme*. New Delhi, , Ministry of Health and Family Welfare. https://nhm.gov.in/index1.php?lang=1&level=3&sublinkid=1021&lid=391. (Accessed 6 May 2020.)

India Ministry of Women and Child Development. 2018. *State/UT-wise Number of Anganwadi Centres, Anganwadi Workers and Helpers under Anganwadi Services*. New Delhi, Ministry of Women and Child Development.

India Parliament. 2016. *The Rights of Persons with Disabilities Act*. New Delhi, Ministry of Law and Justice.

India Supreme Court. 2014. *National Legal Services Authority v. Union of India Judgement*. New Delhi, Supreme Court of India.

India University Grants Commission. 2012. *Guidelines for Persons with Disabilities Scheme in Universities XII Plan (2012–2017)*. New Delhi, University Grants Commission.

Indonesia Ministry of Education and Culture. 2020. *Pelaksanaan Kebijakan Pendidikan dalam Masa Darurat Penyebaran Covid-19 [Implementation of Education Policies in an Emergency for the Spread of Covid-19]*. Jakarta, Ministry of Education and Culture.

Ireland Government. 2019. *Early Childhood Care and Education (ECCE) or Free Preschool*. Dublin, Government of Ireland. www.gov.ie/en/publication/d7a5e6-early-childhood-care-and-education-ecce-or-free-preschool. (Accessed 11 December 2019.)

Italy Ministry of Education, Universities and Research. 2012. *Strumenti d'Intervento per Alunni con Bisogni Educativi Speciali e Organizzazione Territoriale per l'Inclusione Scolastica [Intervention Tools for Pupils with Special Education Needs and Territorial Organization for School Inclusion]*. Rome, Ministry of Education, Universities and Research.

ITU. 2018a. *Argentinian seniors learn about digital literacy to access financial services*. Geneva, Switzerland, International Telecommunication Union. http://digitalinclusionnewslog.itu.int/2018/11/19/argentinian-seniors-learn-about-digital-literacy-to-access-financial-services. (Accessed 11 December 2019.)

___. 2018b. *Digital Skills Toolkit*. Geneva, Switzerland, International Telecommunication Union.

___. 2018c. *Government of La Plata, Argentina Launched a Programe to Increase ICT Skills and Awareness among Seniors*. Geneva, Switzerland, International Telecommunication Union. http://digitalinclusionnewslog.itu.int/2018/08/27/government-of-la-plata-argentina-launched-a-program-to-increase-ict-skills-and-awareness-among-seniors. (Accessed 11 December 2019.)

___. 2018d. *New ITU Statistics Show More than Half the World Is Now Using the Internet*. Geneva, Switzerland, International Telecommunication Union. https://news.itu.int/itu-statistics-leaving-no-one-offline. (Accessed 11 December 2019.)

___. 2019. *Key ICT Indicators for Developed and Developing Countries and the World (Totals and Penetration Rates)*. Geneva, Switzerland, International Telecommunication Union. https://www.itu.int/en/ITU-D/Statistics/Documents/statistics/2019/ITU_Key_2005-2019_ICT_data_with%20LDCs_28Oct2019_Final.xls. (Accessed 6 May 2020.)

ITU and UNESCO. 2019. *The State of Broadband 2019: Broadband as a Foundation for Sustainable Development*. Geneva, Switzerland, Broadband Commission for Sustainable Development.

Jap, B. A. J., Borleffs, E. and Maassen, B. A. M. 2017. Towards identifying dyslexia in Standard Indonesian: the development of a reading assessment battery. *Reading and Writing*, Vol. 30, No. 8, pp. 1729–51.

Jenkins, L. D. and Moses, M. S. 2014. Affirmative action initiatives around the world. *International Higher Education*, No. 77, pp. 5–6.

Jimerson, S. R. and Ferguson, P. 2007. A longitudinal study of grade retention: academic and behavioral outcomes of retained students through adolescence. *School Psychology Quarterly*, Vol. 22, No. 3, pp. 314–39.

Jolley, E., Lynch, P., Virendrakumar, B., Rowe, S. and Schmidt, E. 2018. Education and social inclusion of people with disabilities in five countries in West Africa: a literature review. *Disability and Rehabilitation*, Vol. 40, No. 22.

Jordan, C., Sifuma, E. and Kombo, N. 2015. *What Works in ECD? A CEI Case Study of Five Innovative Programs in Kenya*. Washington, DC, Center for Education Innovations.

Jyoti, D. 2019. SC/ST activists oppose reservation for economically weaker sections. *The Hindustan Times*, 8 January.

Kadiri, G. 2020. Au Maroc, le coronavirus fait exploser la facture de l'école à distance [In Morocco, the coronavirus makes the cost of distance schooling skyrocket]. *Le Monde*, 20 April.

Kanter, A. 2019. The right to inclusive education for students with disabilities under international human rights law. de Beco, G., Quinlivan, S. and Lord, J. E. (eds), *The Right to Inclusive Education in International Human Rights Law*. Cambridge, UK, Cambridge University Press, pp. 15–57.

Kaul, V., Bhattacharjea, S., Chaudhary, A. B., Ramanujan, P., Banerji, M. and Nanda, M. 2017. *The India Early Childhood Education Impact Study*. New Delhi, UNICEF.

Kenya Institute of Curriculum Development. 2020. *Media and Extension Services Broadcast to School Timetable 2020*. Nairobi, Kenya Institute of Curriculum Development.

Keogh, B. K. and MacMillan, D. L. 1996. Exceptionality. Berliner, D. C. and Calfee, R. C. (eds), *Handbook of Educational Psychology*. New York, Routledge, pp. 311–30.

KPMG. 2015. *Department of Education and Training: Evaluation of the Disability Support Programme – Final Report*. Sydney, Australia, KPMG.

Kuhfeld, M. 2018. *Summer Learning Loss: What We Know and What We're Learning*. Portland, Ore., Northwest Evaluation Association. www.nwea.org/blog/2018/summer-learning-loss-what-we-know-what-were-learning. (Accessed 6 May 2020.)

Kuhfeld, M. and Tarasawa, B. 2020. *The COVID-19 Slide: What Summer Learning Loss Can Tell Us about the Potential Impact of School Closures on Student Academic Achievement*. Portland, Ore., Northwest Evaluation Association. (Collaborative for Student Growth Brief.)

Kyama, R. and Pérez-Peña, R. 2019. Kenya's High Court Upholds a Ban on Gay Sex. *The New York Times*, 24 May.

Lao PDR Government. 2016. *Initial Report of the Lao PDR on the Implementation of the Convention on the Rights of Persons with Disabilities*. Geneva, Switzerland, United Nations.

Lao PDR Ministry of Education. 2007. *Strategic Plan for the Development of Technical and Vocational Education and Training from 2006 to 2020*. Vientiane, Ministry of Education.

Lao PDR Ministry of Education and Sports. 2015. *Education and Sports Sector Development Plan (2016–2020)*. Vientiane, Ministry of Education and Sports.

Leighton, M., Souza, P. and Straub, S. 2019. Social promotion in primary school: effects on grade progression. *Brazilian Review of Econometrics*, Vol. 39, No. 1, pp. 1–33.

Leonard Cheshire Disability. 2017. *Inclusive Education and Accountability Mechanisms*. Paris, UNESCO. (Background paper for *Global Education Monitoring Report 2017/8*.)

LGL. 2018. *IGLYO Inclusive Education Report 2018: Lithuania*. Vilnius, Lithuanian Gay League. www.lgl.lt/en/?p=21003. (Accessed 11 December 2019.)

Light for the World and Imprint Consultants. 2016. *Project Evaluation: Beyond the Darkness – Tanzania 2015–2016*. Brussels/The Hague, Light for the World Belgum/Imprint Consultants.

Lobo d'Avila, D. A., Alves Pantoja, S. and de Carvalho, P. 2019. Em tempos de guerra e de paz: a educação especial em Angola [In times of war and peace: special education in Angola]. *Revista Educação Especial*, Vol. 32.

Lyytinen, H., Erskine, J., Hamalainen, J., Torppa, M. and Ronimus, M. 2015. Dyslexia: Early identification and prevention – highlights from the Jyväskylä Longitudinal Study of Dyslexia. *Current Developmental Disorders Reports*, Vol. 2, No. 4, pp. 330–38.

Maadhyam. 2017. *No Detention Policy for Schools: Is the No Fail System Hurting Our Students?* thebetterindia. www.thebetterindia.com/117644/no-detention-policy-right-education-failing-school. (Accessed 11 December 2019.)

Madhav, N., Oppenheim, B., Gallivan, M., Mulembakani, P., Rubin, E. and Wolfe, N. 2017. Pandemics: risks, impacts, and mitigation. Jamison, D. T., Gelband , H. and Horton, S. (eds), *Disease Control Priorities: Improving Health and Reducing Poverty*. Washington, DC, World Bank.

Malawi Ministry of Labour, Youth, Sports and Manpower Development. 2018a. *Gender Equality and Inclusion Analysis of the Technical, Entrepreneurial, Vocational Education and Training System*. Lilongwe, Skills and Technical Education Programme, Ministry of Labour, Youth, Sports and Manpower Development. (STEP Research Series 3.)

___. 2018b. *Situational Analysis on the Status of Sexual and Reproductive Health of Students and Gender-Based Violence in Technical and Vocational Colleges in Malawi*. Lilongwe, Skills and Technical Education Programme, Ministry of Labour, Youth, Sports and Manpower Development. (STEP Research Series 2.)

Mamedova, S. and Pawlowski, E. 2018. *A Description of U.S. Adults Who Are not Digitally Literate*. Washington, DC, National Center for Education Statistics. (Stats in Brief.)

Martin, A. J. 2011. Holding back and holding behind: grade retention and students' non-academic and academic outcomes. *British Educational Research Journal,* Vol. 37, No. 5, pp. 739–63.

Martin, J. P. 2018. *Skills for the 21st Century: Findings and Policy Lessons from the OECD Survey of Adult Skills.* Bonn, IZA Institute of Labor Economics. (IZA Policy Paper 138.)

Martin, S. 2015. *'n Plek van liefde waar dié Kinders tuis voel [A place of love where children feel at home].* Cape Town, Netwerk 24. www.netwerk24.com/Nuus/n-Plek-van-liefde-waar-die-kinders-tuis-voel-20150501. (Accessed 11 December 2019.)

Martínez-Alcalá, C. I., Rosales-Lagarde, A., Alonso-Lavernia, M. Á., Ramírez-Salvador, J. Á., Jiménez-Rodríguez, B., Cepeda-Rebollar, R. M., López-Noguerola, J. S., Bautista-Díaz, M. L. and Agis-Juárez, R. A. 2018. Digital inclusion in older adults: a comparison between face-to-face and blended digital literacy workshops. *Frontiers in ICT,* Vol. 5.

Mauritania Government. 1975. *Loi No 75-023 du 20 Janvier 1975 Portant Réorganisation de l'Enseignement Fondamental Public [Law N 75-023 of 20 January 1975 Reorganizing Public Basic Education]* Nouakchott, Ministry of National Education.

McCombs, J. S., Whitaker, A. A. and Yoo, P. Y. 2017. *The Value of Out-of-School Time Programs.* Santa Monica, Calif., RAND Corporation.

Melhuish, E., Ereky-Stevens, K., Petrogiannis, K., Ariescu, A., Penderi, E., Rentzou, K., Tawell, A., Slot, P., Broekhuizen, M. and Leseman, P. 2015. *A Review of Research on the Effects of Early Childhood Education and Care (ECEC) upon Child Development.* CARE Project. (Curriculum Quality Analysis and Impact Review of European Early Childhood Education and Care.)

Mendos, L. R. 2019. *State-Sponsored Homophobia 2019.* Geneva, Switzerland, International Lesbian, Gay, Bisexual, Trans and Intersex Association.

Mexico Supreme Court. 2015. *Resuelve Corte Primer Caso de Bullying: Ordena a Escuela Indemnizar a Niño de 7 Años [Court Decides First Case of Bullying: Orders School to Compensate 7-Year-Old Child].* Mexico City, Supreme Court of Justice of the Nation. www.internet2.scjn.gob.mx/red2/comunicados/noticia.asp?id=3088. (Accessed 11 December 2019.)

Mnyanyi, C. B. F. 2014. *Changing Teachers' Practices in Regular Schools Enrolling Children with Visual Impairment: An Action Research Project in Tanzania.* Åbo, Finland, Åbo Akademi University Press.

Modan, N. 2019. *50 States of Ed Policy: Do 3rd-grade Retention Policies Work?*, EducationDive, 30 July. www.educationdive.com/news/the-50-states-of-education-policy-do-3rd-grade-retention-policies-work/559741.

Mojib, I. 2020. MoE trains 42,000 teachers in distance learning. *Gulf Today,* 15 March.

Munir, M. A., Sarfaraz, H., Raza Jamil, B. and Aslam, M. 2020. *Reviewing the Status of Inclusive Education in Pakistan: Where Do We Stand?* Paris, UNESCO. (Background paper for *Global Education Monitoring Report 2020.*)

Myanmar Ministry of Education. 2016. *National Education Strategic Plan 2016–21.* Naypyitaw, Ministry of Education.

Namibia Ministry of Education, Arts and Culture. 2018a. *Assessing Inclusive Education in Practice in Namibia: Challenges and Opportunities in Leaving No Child Behind.* Windhoek, Ministry of Education, Arts and Culture.

___. 2018b. *National Promotion Policy Guide for Junior and Senior Secondary School Phases.* Okahandja, Namibia, National Institute for Educational Development.

Nepal Law Commission. 2017. *Act Relating to Rights of Persons with Disabilities, 2074.* Kathmandu, Nepal Law Commission.

New Brunswick Government. 2013. *Policy 322: Inclusive Education.* Frederickton, Canada, Department of Education and Early Childhood Development.

New Delhi Times. 2019. 27 Delhi schools get 'trans-friendly' certification. 12 July.

Ngololo Kamara, E., Kasanda, C. and Van Rooy, G. 2018. Provision of integrated early childhood development in Namibia: Are we on the right track? *Education Sciences,* Vol. 8, No. 3, p. 117.

Niazi, S. 2019. *Extension of Caste Quotas to Shake Up Higher Education.* New Delhi, University World News. www.universityworldnews.com/post.php?story=20190117124356721. (Accessed 11 December 2019.)

NITI Aayog and UNDP. 2015. 2.33 Samarpan: Early identification and intervention to check disability in Madhya Pradesh. *Social Sector Service Delivery: Good Practices Resource Book 2015.* New Delhi, NITI Aayog/United Nations Development Programme, pp. 237–43.

Norões, K. and McCowan, T. 2016. The challenge of widening participation to higher education in Brazil: injustices, innovations, and outcomes. Shah, M., Bennett, A. and Southgate, E. (eds), *Widening Higher Education Participation: A Global Perspective.* Kidlington, UK, Elsevier, pp. 63–80.

OECD. 2008. *Tertiary Education for the Knowledge Society: OECD Thematic Review of Tertiary Education – Synthesis Report.* Paris, Organisation for Economic Co-operation and Development.

___. 2016. *Society at a Glance.* Paris, Organisation for Economic Co-operation and Development.

___. 2020. *A Framework to Guide an Education Response to the COVID-19 Pandemic of 2020*. Paris, Organisation for Economic Co-operation and Development.

OHCHR. 2016. *General Comment on the Right to Inclusive Education*. Geneva, Switzerland, Office of the High Comissioner of Human Rights. www.ohchr.org/EN/HRBodies/CRPD/Pages/GCRightEducation.aspx. (Accessed 11 December 2019.)

___. 2019. *Committee on the Rights of Persons with Disabilities*. Geneva, Switzerland, Office of the High Comissioner of Human Rights. www.ohchr.org/EN/HRBodies/CRPD/Pages/CRPDIndex.aspx. (Accessed 11 December 2019.)

___. 2020. *Status of Ratification Interactive Dashboard*. Geneva, Switzerland, Office of the High Comissioner of Human Rights. https://indicators.ohchr.org. (Accessed 10 January 2020.)

Okyere, C., Aldersey, H. M., Lysaght, R. and Sulaiman, S. K. 2019a. Implementation of inclusive education for children with intellectual and developmental disabilities in African countries: a scoping review. *Disability and Rehabilitation*, Vol. 41, No. 21, pp. 2578–95.

Okyere, C., Aldersey, H. M. and Lysaght, R. 2019b. The experiences of children with intellectual and developmental disabilities in inclusive schools in Accra, Ghana. *African Journal of Disability*, Vol. 8, p. 542.

Oxfam India. 2020. *Inclusive Education in India*. Paris, UNESCO. (Background paper for *Global Education Monitoring Report 2020*.)

Pakistan Higher Education Commission. 2019. *Policy for Students with Disabilities at Higher Education Institutions in Pakistan*. Islamabad, Higher Education Commission.

Pantea, M.-C. 2014. Affirmative action in Romania's higher education: Roma students' perceived meanings and dilemmas. *British Journal of Sociology of Education*, Vol. 36, No. 6, pp. 896–914.

Peru Ministry of Education. 2020. *Resolución Ministerial N° 176-2020-MINEDU [Ministerial Resolution N° 176-2020-MINEDU]*. Lima, Ministry of Education.

Peyton, N. 2020. *Sierra Leone lifts ban on pregnant girls attending school*. Reuters, 30 March. www.reuters.com/article/leone-education-women/sierra-leone-lifts-ban-on-pregnant-girls-attending-school-idUSL8N2BN4R4. (Accessed 31 March 2020.)

Pinnock, H. 2020. *Inclusive Education in Nigeria: Policy Progress Weakened by Financing*. Paris, UNESCO. (Background paper for *Global Education Monitoring Report 2020*.)

Portugal Presidency of the Council of Ministers. 2008. *Decreto-Lei n.º 3/2008 [Decree Law No. 3/2008]*. Lisbon, Council of Ministers. (Diário da República, Series 1, No.4.)

___. 2018. *Decreto-Lei n.º 54/2018 [Decree Law No. 54/2018]*. Lisbon, Council of Ministers. (Diário da República, Series 1, No. 129.)

Pouretemad, H. R., Khatibi, A., Zarei, M. and Stein, J. 2011. Manifestations of developmental dyslexia in monolingual Persian speaking students. *Archives of Iranian Medicine*, Vol. 14, No. 4.

Powers, S. and Azzi-Huck, K. 2016. *The Impact of Ebola on Education in Sierra Leone*. Washington, DC, World Bank. https://blogs.worldbank.org/education/impact-ebola-education-sierra-leone. (Accessed 9 January 2020.)

Quinlivan, S. 2019. Emerging jurisprudence on inclusive education under the European Social Charter (Revised). de Beco, G., Quinlivan, S. and Lord, J. E. (eds), *The Right to Inclusive Education in International Human Rights Law*. Cambridge, UK, Cambridge University Press, pp. 447–72.

R4V. 2020. *RMRP 2020 for Refugees and Migrants from Venezuela: Refugee and Migrant Response Plan 2020*. Response for Venezuelans (R4V).

RDC Nepal. 2019. *Sang Sangai: The Learning Together*. Rautahat, Nepal, Rural Development Centre Nepal.

Richard, G. and MAG Jeunes LGBT. 2018. *Summary Report of the Global Consultation on Inclusive Education and Access to Health of LGBTI+ Youth Around the World*. Paris, MAG Jeunes LGBT with the support of UNESCO.

Rieser, R. 2013. *Teacher Education for Children with Disabilities: Literature Review*. Hyde, UK, Enabling Education Network.

Right to Education Initiative. 2017. *The Right to Education of Transgender People*. London, ActionAid International. www.right-to-education.org/news/right-education-transgender-people. (Accessed 11 December 2019.)

Rofiah, N. H. 2015. Proses identifikasi: mengenal anak kesulitan belajar tipe disleksia bagi guru sekolah dasar inklusi [Identification process: getting to know children with learning difficulties by dyslexia type for inclusive elementary school teachers]. *Inklusi*, Vol. 2, No. 1, pp. 109–24.

Rwanda Ministry of Education and UNICEF. 2017. *Understanding Dropout and Repetition in Rwanda: Full Report*. Kigali, Ministry of Education/UNICEF.

Saavedra, J. E., Näslund-Hadley, E. and Alfonso, M. 2019. Remedial inquiry-based science education: experimental evidence from Peru. *Educational Evaluation and Policy Analysis*, Vol. 41, No. 4, pp. 483–509.

Salmi, J. 2017. *The Tertiary Education Imperative: Knowledge, Skills and Values for Development*. Rotterdam, Sense Publishers/Center for International Higher Education, Boston College.

___. 2018. *All Around the World: Higher Education Equity Policies Across the Globe*. Indianapolis, Ind., Lumina Foundation.

___. 2020. *Higher Education and Inclusion*. Paris, UNESCO. (Background paper for *Global Education Monitoring Report 2020*.)

Salmi, J. and Bassett, R. M. 2014. The equity imperative in tertiary education: promoting fairness and efficiency. *International Review of Education*, Vol. 60, No. 3, pp. 361–77.

Salmi, J. and Sursock, A. 2018. Access and completion for underserved students: international perspectives. de Wit, H., Rumbley, L. E. and Melnyk, D. (eds), *The Boston College Center for International Higher Education: Year in Review 2017–2018*. Boston, Center for International Higher Education. (CIHE Perspectives 9.)

Samadi, S. A. and McConkey, R. 2018. Perspectives on inclusive education of preschool children with autism spectrum disorders and other developmental disabilities in Iran. *International Journal of Environmental Research and Public Health*, Vol. 15, No. 10.

Sanatullova-Allison, E. and Robison-Young, V. A. 2016. Overrepresentation: an overview of the issues surrounding the identification of English language learners with learning disabilities. *International Journal of Special Education*, Vol. 31, No. 2.

Santiago, P., Fiszbein, A., García Jaramillo, S. and Radinger, T. 2017. *Chile*. Paris, Organisation for Economic Co-operation and Development. (OECD Reviews of School Resources.)

Santos Calderón, J. M. 2018. 'De Cero a Siempre', a commitment to our children's early years. *Early Childhood Matters: Advances in Early Childhood Development*, No. 127.

Schwartz, A. C. 2012. *Remedial Education Programs to Accelerate Learning for All*. Washington, DC, Global Partnership for Education. (GPE Working Paper Series on Learning, No. 11.)

Shaywitz, S. E., Morris, R. and Shaywitz, B. A. 2008. The education of dyslexic children from childhood to young adulthood. *Annual Review of Psychology*, Vol. 59, pp. 451–75.

Sichombe, B., Nambira, G., Tjipueja, G. and Kapenda, L. 2011. *No 4: Evaluation of Promotion Policy Requirements in Namibian Schools*. Okahandja, Namibia, National Institute for Educational Development.

South Africa Department of Basic Education. 2010. *Guidelines for Full-service/Inclusive Schools*. Pretoria, Department of Basic Education. (Education White Paper 6: Special Needs Education – Building an Inclusive Education and Training System.)

___. 2014. *Policy on Screening, Identification, Assessment and Support*. Pretoria, Department of Basic Education.

___. 2016a. *Minister Motshekga hosts National Education Excellence Awards*. Pretoria, Department of Basic Education. www.education.gov.za/DBEandtheMotsepeFoundationlaunch/tabid/990/Default.aspx. (Accessed 11 December 2019.)

___. 2016b. *Revised Five-Year Strategic Plan 2015/16–2019/20*. Pretoria, Department of Basic Education.

___. 2019. *Annual Report 2018/2019*. Pretoria, Department of Basic Education.

Special Olympics. 2019. *Play Unified. Learn Unified: Annual Report 2019*. Washington, DC, Special Olympics/Stavros Niarchos Foundation.

Special Olympics Kenya. 2018. *Progress Review*. Nairobi, Special Olympics Kenya.

Sri Lanka University Grants Commission. 2018. *University Admission Handbook 2018–2019*. Colombo, University Grants Commission.

St Vincent and the Grenadines Government. 2005. *Education Bill 2005*. Kingstown, Ministry of Education, National Reconciliation, Ecclesiastical Affairs and Information.

Statistics Sierra Leone. 2018. *Sierra Leone Multiple Indicator Cluster Survey 2017: Survey Findings Report*. Freetown, Statistics Sierra Leone.

Statistics Sierra Leone and UNICEF-Sierra Leone. 2011. *Sierra Leone Multiple Indicator Cluster Survey 2010: Final Report*. Freetown, Statistics Sierra Leone/UNICEF-Sierra Leone.

Street Child. 2020. *Annual Report for the Year Ended 31st March 2019*. London, Street Child.

Tadesse Mergia, A. 2020. *The Practice of Inclusive Education in Ethiopia*. Paris, UNESCO. (Background paper for *Global Education Monitoring Report 2020*.)

Tang, C., Zhao, L. and Zhao, Z. 2020. Does free education help combat child labor? The effect of a free compulsory education reform in rural China. *Journal of Population Economics*, Vol. 33, No. 2, pp. 601–31.

Taylor, E. 2014. Spending more of the school day in math class: Evidence from a regression discontinuity in middle school. *Journal of Public Economics*, Vol. 117, pp. 162–81.

Teff, M. 2019. *Forced into Illegality: Venezuelan Refugees and Migrants in Trinidad and Tobago*. Washington, DC, Refugees International.

Thomson, D. 2020. *Moderating Teacher Judgments in 2020*. London, fft Education Data Lab. https://ffteducationdatalab. org.uk/2020/03/moderating-teacher-judgments-in-2020. (Accessed 6 May 2020.)

Thorat, S., Shyamprasad, K. M. and Srivastava, R. K. 2007. *Report of the Committee to Enquire into the Allegation of Differential Treatment of SC/ST Students in All India*. New Delhi, Institute of Medical Science.

Thoreson, R. 2017. *The Philippines Affirmed Equal Rights in Schools – Now It Should Protect Them*. New York, Human Rights Watch. www.hrw.org/news/2017/07/19/philippines-affirmed-equal-rights-schools-now-it-should-protect-them. (Accessed 11 December 2019.)

Tomlinson, S. 1982. *A Sociology of Special Education*. London, Routledge.

Trinidad and Tobago Office of the Prime Minister. 2019. *T&T Responds to Humanitarian Needs: Venezuelan Registration Policy*. Port of Spain, Office of the Prime Minister.

Tugend, A. 2020. Teachers of special-needs students struggle with feelings of helplessness. *The New York Times*, 23 April.

UCAS. 2016. *Through the Lens of Students: How Perceptions of Higher Education Influence Applicants' Choices*. London, Universities and Colleges Admissions Service.

Uganda Ministry of Education and Sports. 2018. *Education Response Plan for Refugees and Host Communities in Uganda: May 2018*. Kampala, Ministry of Education and Sports.

UNDESA. 2004a. *Comments on the draft text: Draft Article 17 – Education*. New York, United Nations Department of Economic and Social Affairs. www.un.org/esa/socdev/enable/rights/wgdca17.htm.

___. 2004b. *Daily Summary of Discussions Related to Article 17: Education*. New York, United Nations Department of Economic and Social Affairs. www.un.org/esa/socdev/enable/rights/ahc3sum17.htm.

___. 2004c. *Draft Article 17: Education*. New York, United Nations Department of Economic and Social Affairs. www.un.org/ esa/socdev/enable/rights/ahcwgreporta17.htm.

___. 2019. *Monitoring of the Implementation of the Convention*. New York, United Nations Department of Economic and Social Affairs. www.un.org/development/desa/disabilities/convention-on-the-rights-of-persons-with-disabilities/ monitoring-of-the-implementation-of-the-convention.html. (Accessed 11 December 2019.)

UNESCO. 1960. *Convention Against Discrimination in Education*. Paris, UNESCO.

___. 1990. *World Declaration on Education for All and Framework for Action to Meet Basic Learning Needs*. Paris, UNESCO.

___. 2000. *World Education Forum, Dakar, Senegal, 26–28 April 2000: Final Report*. Paris, UNESCO.

___. 2015a. *Education 2030 Incheon Declaration and Framework for Action for the Implementation of Sustainable Development Goal 4*. Paris, UNESCO.

___. 2015b. *Leveraging ICT for Achieving Education 2030: Qingdao Declaration (2015) – Seize Digital Opportunities, Lead Education Transformation*. Paris, UNESCO.

___. 2018a. *Gender Review 2018: Meeting Our Commitments to Gender Equality in Education*. Paris, Global Education Monitoring Report.

___. 2018b. *Progress towards LGBTI Inclusion in Education in Europe*. Paris, UNESCO. https://en.unesco.org/news/progress-towards-lgbti-inclusion-education-europe. (Accessed 11 December 2019.)

___. 2019a. *Beyond Commitments: How Countries Implement SDG 4*. Paris, UNESCO.

___. 2019b. *N for Nose: State of the Education Report for India 2019 – Children with Disabilities*. New Delhi, UNESCO.

UNESCO and Spain Ministry of Education and Science. 1994. *The Salamanca Statement and Framework For Action of Special Needs Education*. Paris, UNESCO.

UNHCR. 2018a. *Uganda: July 2018*. Geneva, Switzerland, United Nations High Commissioner for Refugees.

___. 2018b. *Uganda Country Refugee Response Plan: The Integrated Response Plan for Refugees from South Sudan, Burundi and the Democratic Republic of the Congo – January–December 2018*. Nairobi, United Nations High Commissioner for Refugees.

___. 2019. *Equal Place: Education Programme*. Port of Spain, United Nations High Commissioner for Refugees.

UNICEF. 2013. *The Situation Analysis of Children with Disabilities*. Belmopan, UNICEF.

___. 2015. *School Drop-Out and Out-of-School Children in Namibia: A National Review* Windhoek, Namibia Ministry of Education Arts and Culture/UNESCO Institute for Statistics/UNICEF. (Global Initiative on Out-of-School Children.)

___. 2018. *Child Marriage: Latest Trends and Future Prospects*. New York, UNICEF.

___. 2019. *A World Ready to Learn: Prioritizing Quality Early Childhood Education.* New York, UNICEF.

___. 2020. *Child Marriage Database.* New York, UNICEF.

United Nations. 1989. *Convention on the Rights of the Child: Adopted and Opened for Signature, Ratification and Accession by General Assembly Resolution 44/25 of 20 November 1989.* New York, United Nations.

___. 2006. *Convention on the Rights of Persons with Disabilities and Optional Protocol.* New York, United Nations.

US Department of Education. 2019. *Individuals with Disabilities Education Act: Statute and Regulations.* Washington, DC, Office of Special Education Programs, Department of Education. https://sites.ed.gov/idea/statuteregulations. (Accessed 11 December 2019.)

___. 2020. *Secretary DeVos Makes Available Over $13 Billion in Emergency Coronavirus Relief to support Continued Education for K-12 Students.* Washington, DC, Department of Education. www.ed.gov/news/press-releases/secretary-devos-makes-available-over-13-billion-emergency-coronavirus-relief-support-continued-education-k-12-students. (Accessed 6 May 2020.)

University of Auckland. 2019. *MAPTES Admissions.* Auckland, New Zealand, University of Auckland. www.auckland.ac.nz/en/engineering/study-with-us/maori-and-pacific-at-the-faculty/maptes-admissions.html. (Accessed 11 December 2019.)

Ünver, O., Burcan, T. and Nicaise, I. 2016. *D 5.2.2: Accessibility and Use of Early Childhood Education and Care – A Comparative Analysis of 34 European Countries.* Leuven, Belgium, HIVA, Catholic University of Leuven. (Curriculum Quality Analysis and Impact Review of European Countries: Early Childhood Education and Care: Promoting Quality for Individual, Social and Economic Benefits.)

Usher, A. and Burroughs, R. 2018. *Targeted Free Tuition: A Global Analysis.* Toronto, Canada, Higher Education Strategy Associates.

Vargas-Barón, E., Small, J., Wertlieb, D., Hix-Small, H., Botero, R. G., Diehl, K., Vergara, P. and Lynch, P. 2019. *Global Survey of Inclusive Early Childhood Development and Early Childhood Intervention Programs.* Washington, DC, The RISE Institute/UNICEF/Early Childhood Development Taskforce.

Verneau, L. 2020. A Madagascar, les radios au service des enfants [In Madagascar, radios in the service of children]. *Le Monde*, 23 April.

Victoria University of Wellington. 2019. *New Zealand University Entrance.* Wellington, Victoria University of Wellington. www.wgtn.ac.nz/study/apply-enrol/admissions/nz-university-entrance.

Vieira, R. S. and Arends-Kuenning, M. 2019. *Affirmative Action in Brazilian Universities: Effects on the Enrollment of Targeted Groups.* Urbana, Ill., University of Illinois at Urbana-Champaign.

Viet Nam General Statistics Office. 2018. *Viet Nam National Survey on People with Disabilities 2016.* Hanoi, General Statistics Office.

Viet Nam Government and World Bank. 2019. *Digital Government and Open Data Readiness Assessment.* Hanoi, Office of the Government/World Bank.

VVOB. 2018. *Learning through Play.* Brussels, VVOB. (Putting SDG 4 into Practice 3.)

Wadhwa, W., Bhattacharjea, S. and Banerji, M. 2019. Does Participation in Preschool Help Children's Early Grade Learning? Kaul, V. and Bhattacharjea, S. (eds), *Early Childhood Education and School Readiness in India.* Singapore, Springer.

Wainer, J. and Melguizo, T. 2017. Políticas de inclusão no ensino superior: avaliação do desempenho dos alunos baseado no Enade de 2012 a 2014 [Inclusion policies in higher education: assessing student performance based on Enade from 2012 to 2014]. *Educação e Pesquisa*, Vol. 44.

Whyte, G. 2019. Litigating the right to inclusive education under Irish Law. de Beco, G., Quinlivan, S. and Lord, J. E. (eds), *The Right to Inclusive Education in International Human Rights Law.* Cambridge, UK, Cambridge University Press, pp. 497–513.

World Bank. 2019a. *Bangladesh: Reaching Out of School Children II (P131394) – Implementation Status and Results Report.* Washington, DC, World Bank.

___. 2019b. *A Second Chance to Education.* Dhaka, World Bank. (Reaching Out-Of-School Children II Project.)

___. 2020. *Access to Electricity.* Washington, DC, World Bank. https://data.worldbank.org/indicator/eg.elc.accs.zs. (Accessed 6 May 2020.)

World Federation of the Deaf, European Union of the Deaf, World Federation of the Deaf Youth Section and European Union of the Deaf Youth. 2015. *Submission on the Draft General Comment No. 4 on Article 24.* Geneva, Switzerland, Committee on the Rights of Persons with Disabilities.

Yi, T. X. 2019. Outcry over retaining ethnic quota for pre-university admission in Malaysia. *Channel News Asia*, 8 May.

Yohannes, B., Sintayehu, B., Alebachew, Y. and Kay, L. 2017. Catch-up education: the door to future possibilities in Ethiopia. *Enabling Education Review*, No. 6, pp. 20–21.

Ziegler, J. C. and Goswami, U. 2005. Reading acquisition, developmental dyslexia, and skilled reading across languages: a psycholinguistic grain size theory. *Psychological Bulletin*, Vol. 131, No. 1, pp. 3–29.

CHAPTER 3

Abubakar, A., Ssewanyana, D. and Newton, C. R. 2016. A systematic review of research on autism spectrum disorders in sub-Saharan Africa. *Behavioural Neurology*.

Ainscow, M. 2005. Developing inclusive education systems: What are the levers for change? *Journal of Educational Change*, Vol. 6, No. 2, pp. 109–24.

Aksoy, C. G. and Poutvaara, P. 2019. *Refugees' and Irregular Migrants' Self-Selection into Europe: Who Migrates Where?* Munich, Germany, ifo Institute. (Working Paper 289.)

Al-Hroub, A. 2010. Perceptual skills and Arabic literacy patterns for mathematically gifted children with specific learning difficulties. *British Journal of Special Education*, Vol. 37, No. 1, pp. 25–38.

Altman, B. M. (ed.). 2016. *International Measurement of Disability: Purpose, Method and Application*. Cham, Switzerland, Springer.

Alton-Lee, A. 2003. *Quality Teaching for Diverse Students in Schooling: Best Evidence Synthesis*. Wellington, New Zealand, Medium Term Strategy Policy Division, Ministry of Education.

Ametepee, L. K. and Chitiyo, M. 2009. What we know about autism in Africa: a brief research synthesis. *Journal of the International Association of Special Education*, Vol. 10, No. 1.

Armstrong, A. C., Armstrong, D. and Spandagou, I. 2010. *Inclusive Education: International Policy and Practice*. Los Angeles, Calif., Sage.

Asadullah, M. N. and Chaudhury, N. 2016. To madrasahs or not to madrasahs: the question and correlates of enrolment in Islamic schools in Bangladesh. *International Journal of Educational Development*, Vol. 49, pp. 55–69.

Asadullah, M. N. and Maliki. 2018. Madrasah for girls and private school for boys? The determinants of school type choice in rural and urban Indonesia. *International Journal of Educational Development*, Vol. 62, pp. 96–111.

Aşlamacı, İ. and Kaymakcan, R. 2017. A model for Islamic education from Turkey: the Imam-Hatip schools. *British Journal of Religious Education*, Vol. 39, No. 3, pp. 279–92.

Bangladesh Bureau of Education Information and Statistics. 2018. *Bangladesh Education Statistics 2018*. Dhaka, Bangladesh Bureau of Education Information and Statistics. https://data.banbeis.gov.bd/index.php.

Bangladesh Directorate of Primary Education. 2017. *Bangladesh Primary Education Annual Sector Performance Report 2017*. Dhaka, Directorate of Primary Education.

Barshay, J. 2018. Is Providence the poster child for the worst increase in school segregation? Depends on how you measure it. *Hechinger Report*, 25 June.

Bassok, D., Latham, S. and Rorem, A. 2016. Is kindergarten the new first grade? *AERA Open*, Vol. 2, No. 1.

Bearak, M. and Ombour, R. 2019. A new census in Kenya is counting people never counted before. *Washington Post*, 12 September.

Begum, H. A., Perveen, R., Chakma, E., Dewan, L., Afroze, R. S. and Tangen, D. 2019. The challenges of geographical inclusive education in rural Bangladesh. *International Journal of Inclusive Education*, Vol. 23, No. 1, pp. 7–22.

Booth, T. and Ainscow, M. 2002. *Index for Inclusion: Developing Learnng and Participation in Schools*. London, Centre for Studies on Inclusive Education.

Braddick, F. and Jané-Llopis, E. 2008. *Mental Health in Youth and Education*. Brussels, Directorate-General for Health and Consumers, European Commission.

Brüggemann, C. 2012. *Roma Education in Comparative Perspective: Analysis of the UNDP/World Bank/EC Regional Roma Survey 2011*. Bratislava, United Nations Development Programme. (Roma Inclusion Working Papers.)

Buckley, S. J. 2000. *Living with Down Syndrome*. Portsmouth, UK, The Down Syndrome Educational Trust.

Burden, R. and Burdett, J. 2005. Factors associated with successful learning in pupils with dyslexia: a motivational analysis. *British Journal of Special Education*, Vol. 32, No. 2, pp. 100–04.

Butler, D. 2018. *With more Islamic schooling, Erdogan aims to reshape Turkey*. London, Reuters, 25 January. www.reuters. com/investigates/special-report/turkey-erdogan-education. (Accessed 11 December 2019.)

Çakmaklı, A. D., Boone, C. and van Witteloostuijn, A. 2017. When does globalization lead to local adaptation? The emergence of hybrid Islamic schools in Turkey, 1985–2007. *American Journal of Sociology*, Vol. 122, No. 6, pp. 1822–68.

Cappa, C. 2014. *Collecting Data on Child Disability*. New York, UNICEF. (Webinar 4: Companion Technical Booklet.)

Carr-Hill, R. 2013. Missing millions and measuring development progress. *World Development*, Vol. 46, pp. 30–44.

Carrington, S. and Duke, J. 2014. Learning about inclusion from developing countries: using the Index for Inclusion. Forlin, C. and Loreman, T. (eds), *Measuring Inclusive Education*. Bingley, UK, Emerald, pp. 189–203. (International Perspectives on Inclusive Education, Vol. 3.)

Chang, A. 2018. The data proves that school segregation is getting worse. *Vox*, 5 March.

Chile Ministry of Social Development. 2016. *Estudio Nacional de la Discapacidad: Informe Metodológico – Marco de Referencia Conceptual, Diseño del Instrumento y Medición de la Discapacidad [National Disability Study: Methodological Report – Conceptual Reference Framework, Instrument Design and Disability Measurement]*. Santiago, National Disability Service, Ministry of Social Development.

Cioè-Peña, M. 2017. The intersectional gap: How bilingual students in the United States are excluded from inclusion. *International Journal of Inclusive Education*, Vol. 21, No. 9, pp. 906–19.

Connor, D. J. 2014. Social justice in education for students with disabilities. Florian, L. (ed.), *SAGE Handbook of Special Education*. London, Sage, pp. 111–28.

Costa Rica National Institute of Statistics and Census. 2019. *Encuesta Nacional sobre Discapacidad 2018: Resultados Generales [National Disability Survey 2018: General Results]*. San José, National Institute of Statistics and Census/National Council of People with Disabilities.

d'Aiglepierre, R. and Bauer, A. 2018. The choice of Arab-Islamic education in sub-Saharan Africa: findings from a comparative study. *International Journal of Educational Development*, Vol. 62, pp. 47–61.

Dare, L., Nowicki, E. and Felimban, H. 2017. Saudi children's thoughts on inclusive education. *International Journal of Inclusive Education*, Vol. 21, No. 5, pp. 532–43.

Davis, P., Florian, L., Ainscow, M., Dyson, A., Farrell, P., Hick, P., Humphrey, N., Jenkins, P., Kaplan, I., Palmer, S., Parkinson, G., Polat, F., Reason, R., Byers, R., Dee, L., Kershner, R. and Rouse, M. 2004. *Teaching Strategies and Approaches for Pupils with Special Educational Needs: A Scoping Study*. Nottingham, UK, Department for Education and Skills Publications. (Research Report 516.)

De Vroey, A., Struyf, E. and Petry, K. 2016. Secondary schools included: a literature review. *International Journal of Inclusive Education*, Vol. 20, No. 2, pp. 109–35.

Delobel-Ayoub, M., Ehlinger, V., Klapouszczak, D., Maffre, T., Raynaud, J.-P., Delpierre, C. and Arnaud, C. 2015. Socioeconomic disparities and prevalence of autism spectrum disorders and intellectual disability. *PloS one*, Vol. 10, No. 11.

Dia, H., Hugon, C. and d'Aiglepierre, R. 2016. Le monde des écoles coraniques: essai de typologie pour le Sénégal [The world of Koranic schools: an attempted typology for Senegal]. *Afrique contemporaine*, Vol. 257, pp. 106–10.

Durkin, M. S., Maenner, M. J., Meaney, F. J., Levy, S. E., DiGuiseppi, C., Nicholas, J. S., Kirby, R. S., Pinto-Martin, J. A. and Schieve, L. A. 2010. Socioeconomic inequality in the prevalence of autism spectrum disorder: evidence from a U.S. cross-sectional study. *PloS one*, Vol. 5, No. 7.

Elsabbagh, M., Divan, G., Koh, Y.-J., Kim, Y. S., Kauchali, S., Marcín, C., Montiel-Nava, C., Patel, V., Paula, C. S., Wang, C., Yasamy, M. T. and Fombonne, E. 2012. Global prevalence of autism and other pervasive developmental disorders. *Autism Research*, Vol. 5, No. 3, pp. 160–79.

Ettinger, A. B., Weisbrot, D. M., Nolan, E. E., Gadow, K. D., Vitale, S. A., Andriola, M. R., Lenn, N. J., Novak, G. P. and Hermann, B. P. 1998. Symptoms of depression and anxiety in pediatric epilepsy patients. *Epilepsia*, Vol. 39, No. 6, pp. 595–99.

European Agency for Special Needs and Inclusive Education. 2018. *European Agency Statistics on Inclusive Education: 2016 Dataset Cross-Country Report*. Odense, Denmark, European Agency for Special Needs and Inclusive Education.

Fall, A. S. and Cisse, R. 2017. *Jàngandoo: Barometre de la Qualité des Apprentisages au Sénégal [Jàngandoo: Barometer of Learning Quality in Senegal]*. Dakar, Laboratoire de Recherche sur les Transformations Économiques et Sociales, Institut Fondamental d'Afrique Noire Cheick Anta Diop.

Fastenau, P. S., Shen, J., Dunn, D. W. and Austin, J. K. 2008. Academic underachievement among children with epilepsy: proportion exceeding psychometric criteria for learning disability and associated risk factors. *Journal of Learning Disabilities*, Vol. 41, No. 3, pp. 195–207.

Fayette, R. and Bond, C. 2017. A systematic literature review of qualitative research methods for eliciting the views of young people with ASD about their educational experiences. *European Journal of Special Needs Education*, Vol. 33, No. 3, pp. 349–65.

Ferguson, D. L. 2008. International trends in inclusive education: the continuing challenge to teach each one and everyone. *European Journal of Special Needs Education*, Vol. 23, No. 2, pp. 109–20.

Fiji Ministry of Education, Heritage and Arts. 2016. *Policy on Special and Inclusive Education*. Suva, Ministry of Education, Heritage and Arts.

___. 2017. *Fiji Education Management Information System (FEMIS): Disability Disaggregation Package – Guidelines and Forms*. Suva, Access to Quality Education Program, Ministry of Education, Heritage and Arts.

Florian, L. 2014. Reimagining special education: Why new approaches are needed. Florian, L. (ed.), *SAGE Handbook of Special Education*. London, Sage, pp. 9–22.

Florian, L., Hollenweger, J., Simeonsson, R. J., Wedell, K., Riddell, S., Terzi, L. and Holland, A. 2006. Cross-cultural perspectives on the classification of children with disabilities: Part I – Issues in the classification of children with disabilities. *Journal of Special Education*, Vol. 40, No. 1, pp. 36–45.

Fotso, A. S., Duthé, G. and Odimegwu, C. 2019. *A Comparative Analysis of Disability Measures in Cameroonian Surveys*. Paris, Institut National d'Études Démographiques. (Document de travail 249.)

Fotso, A. S., Solaz, A., Diene, M. and Nanfosso, R. T. 2018. Human capital accumulation of children in Cameroon: Does disability really matter? *Education Economics*, Vol. 26, No. 3, pp. 305–20.

Frederickson, N. 2010. Bullying or befriending? Children's responses to classmates with special needs. *British Journal of Special Education*, Vol. 37, No. 1, pp. 4–12.

Global Partnership for Education. 2018. *Disability and Inclusive Education: A Stocktake of Education Sector Plans and GPE-Funded Grants*. Washington, DC, Global Partnership for Education. (Working Paper.)

Goldstein, D. 2019. San Francisco had an ambitious plan to tackle school segregation. It made it worse. *The New York Times*, 25 April.

Goswami, U. 2004. Neuroscience, education and special education. *British Journal of Special Education*, Vol. 31, No. 4, pp. 175–83.

Grant, T. 2018. Statistics Canada begins testing non-binary gender options in surveys. *Globe and Mail*, 13 May.

Groce, N. and Mont, D. 2017. Counting disability: emerging consensus on the Washington Group questionnaire. *The Lancet Global Health*, Vol. 5, No. 7, pp. 649–50.

Gustafsson, M. 2019. An analysis of school segregation in South Africa grade 12 examination data. Stellenbosch, South Africa, University of Stellenbosch. (Unpublished.)

Gutiérrez, G., Jerrim, J. and Torres, R. 2020. School segregation across the world: Has any progress been made in reducing the separation of the rich from the poor? *Journal of Economic Inequality*. Vol. 18, pp. 157–79.

Hanford, E. 2017. Hard to read: How American schools fail kids with dyslexia. *APM Reports*, 11 September.

Harry, B. 2014. The disproportionate placement of ethnic minorities in special education. Florian, L. (ed.), *SAGE Handbook of Special Education*. London, Sage, pp. 73–95.

Hart, S. and Drummond, M. J. 2014. Learning without limits: constructing a pedagogy free from determinist beliefs about ability. Florian, L. (ed.), *SAGE Handbook of Special Education*. London, SAGE, pp. 439–58.

Hartas, D. 2011. Children's language and behavioural, social and emotional difficulties and prosocial behaviour during the toddler years and at school entry. *British Journal of Special Education*, Vol. 38, No. 2, pp. 83–91.

Hedegaard-Soerensen, L., Jensen, C. R. and Tofteng, D. M. B. 2018. Interdisciplinary collaboration as a prerequisite for inclusive education. *European Journal of Special Needs Education*, Vol. 33, No. 3.

Hehir, T., Grindal, T., Freeman, B., Lamoreau, R., Borquaye, Y. and Burke, S. 2016. *A Summary of the Evidence on Inclusive Education*. São Paulo, Brazil, Instituto Alana.

Hollenweger, J. 2014. *Definition and Classification of Disability*. New York, UNICEF. (Webinar 2: Companion Technical Booklet.)

Hornby, G. 2015. Inclusive special education: development of a new theory for the education of children with special educational needs and disabilities. *British Journal of Special Education*, Vol. 42, No. 3, pp. 234–56.

Index for Inclusion Network. 2019. *Brazil*. Cambridge, UK, Index for Inclusion Network. www.indexforinclusion.org/brazil.php. (Accessed 11 December 2019.)

Jordan, A. and McGhie-Richmond, D. 2014. Identifying effective teaching practices in inclusive classrooms. Forlin, C. and Loreman, T. (eds), *Measuring Inclusive Education*. Bingley, UK, Emerald, pp. 133–64. (International Perspectives on Inclusive Education, Vol. 3.)

Kamenov, K., Cabello, M., Ballert, C. S., Cieza, A., Chatterji, S., Rojas, D., Cerón, G., Bickenbach, J., Ayuso-Mateos, J. L. and Sabariego, C. 2018. What makes the difference in people's lives when they have a mental disorder? *International Journal of Public Health*, Vol. 63, No. 1, pp. 57–67.

Kaphle, D., Marasini, S., Kalua, K., Reading, A. and Naidoo, K. S. 2015. Visual profile of students in integrated schools in Malawi. *Clinical and Experimental Optometry*, Vol. 98, No. 4, pp. 370–74.

Kauffman, J. M. and Badar, J. 2014. Better thinking and clearer communication will help special education. *Exceptionality*, Vol. 22, No. 1, pp. 17–32.

Keddie, A. 2014. Indigenous representation and alternative schooling: prioritising an epistemology of relationality. *International Journal of Inclusive Education*, Vol. 18, No. 1, pp. 55–71.

Keil, S., Miller, O. and Cobb, R. 2006. Special educational needs and disability. *British Journal of Special Education*, Vol. 33, No. 4, pp. 168–72.

Kuper, H., Saran, A. and White, H. 2018. *Rapid Evidence Assessment (REA) of What Works to Improve Educational Outcomes for People with Disabilities in Low- and Middle-Income Countries*. London, International Centre for Evidence in Disability, London School of Hygiene and Tropical Medicine/Campbell Collaboration.

Leonard Cheshire and Department for International Development. 2018. *Disability Data Review: A Collation and Analysis of Disability Data from 40 Countries*. London, Leonard Cheshire/Department for International Development.

Loeb, M., Mont, D., Cappa, C., De Palma, E., Madans, J. and Crialesi, R. 2018. The development and testing of a module on child functioning for identifying children with disabilities on surveys: I – Background. *Disability and Health Journal*, Vol. 11, No. 4, pp. 495–501.

Loreman, T., Forlin, C., Chambers, D., Sharma, U. and Deppeler, J. 2014. Conceptualising and measuring inclusive education. Forlin, C. and Loreman, T. (eds), *Measuring Inclusive Education*. Bingley, UK, Emerald, pp. 3–17. (International Perspectives on Inclusive Education, Vol. 3.)

Lund, I. 2014. Dropping out of school as a meaningful action for adolescents with social, emotional and behavioural difficulties. *Journal of Research in Special Educational Needs*, Vol. 14, No. 2, pp. 96–104.

MacTaggart, I., Polack, S., Kuper, S., Murthy, G. V. S., Oye, J., Sagar, J. and Tamo, V. 2014. *Measuring Disability in Surveys and Programs: A Summary*. London, International Centre for Evidence in Disability, London School of Hygiene and Tropical Medicine.

Male, C. and Wodon, Q. 2017. *The Price of Exclusion: Disability and Education – Disability Gaps in Educational Attainment and Literacy*. Washington, DC, World Bank.

Marks, S. U. and Kurth, J. A. 2013. Examination of disproportionality of autism in school-aged populations. *Journal of the International Association of Special Education*, Vol. 14, pp. 9–21.

Massey, M. 2018. The development and testing of a module on child functioning for identifying children with disabilities on surveys: II – Question development and pretesting. *Disability and Health Journal*, Vol. 11, No. 4, pp. 502–09.

Messiou, K. 2008. Understanding children's constructions of meanings about other children: implications for inclusive education. *Journal of Research in Special Educational Needs*, Vol. 8, No. 1, pp. 27–36.

Mont, D. 2007. Measuring health and disability. *The Lancet*, Vol. 369, No. 9573, pp. 1658–63.

Morning, A. 2008. Ethnic classification in global perspective: a cross-national survey of the 2000 census round. *Population Research and Policy Review*, Vol. 27, No. 2, pp. 239–72.

Moyse, R. and Porter, J. 2015. The experience of the hidden curriculum for autistic girls at mainstream primary schools. *European Journal of Special Needs Education*, Vol. 30, No. 2, pp. 1–15.

Munro, J. 2002. The reading characteristics of gifted literacy disabled students. *Australian Journal of Learning Difficulties*, Vol. 7, No. 2, pp. 4–12.

Murenzi, V. and McGeown, J. 2015. Developing inclusive education standards and norms in Rwanda. *Enabling Education Review*, No. 4, pp. 12–13.

Murillo, J. F. and Martínez-Garrido, C. 2017. Estimación de la magnitud de la segregación escolar en América Latina [Estimating the magnitude of school segregation in Latin America]. *magis: Revista Internacional de Investigación en Educación*, Vol. 9, No. 19, pp. 11–30.

Naidoo, K. 2007. Poverty and blindness in Africa. *Clinical and Experimental Optometry*, Vol. 90, No. 6, pp. 415–21.

National Center for Education Statistics. 2016. *Private School Enrolment*. Washington, DC, US Department of Education, National Center for Education Statistics, Private School Universe Survey. https://nces.ed.gov/programs/coe/indicator_cgc.asp. (Accessed 11 December 2019.)

Nedeljkovic, V. 2019. *SDG 4: Quality Inclusive Education in Serbia*. Paper for Regional Forum on Sustainable Development for the UNECE Region, 19 March, Geneva, Switzerland, United Nations Economic Commission for Europe.

New Zealand Education Review Office. 2016. *School Evaluation Indicators: Effective Practice for Improvement and Learner Success*. Wellington, Education Review Office.

Nie, J., Pang, X., Wang, L., Rozelle, S. and Sylvia, S. 2020. Seeing is believing: experimental evidence on the impact of eyeglasses on academic performance, aspirations, and dropout among junior high school students in rural China. *Economic Development and Cultural Change*, Vol. 68, No. 2, pp. 335–55.

Nieuwenhuis, J. and Hooimeijer, P. 2016. The association between neighbourhoods and educational achievement, a systematic review and meta-analysis. *Journal of Housing and the Built Environment*, Vol. 31, No. 2, pp. 321–47.

Nind, M. and Wearmouth, J. 2004. *Pedagogical Approaches that Effectively Include Children with Special Educational Needs in Mainstream Classrooms: A Systematic Literature Review*. London, EPPI-Centre, Social Science Research Unit, Institute of Education. (Research Evidence in Education Library.)

Norwich, B. 2014. Categories of special educational needs. Florian, L. (ed.), *SAGE Handbook of Special Education*. London, Sage, pp. 55–72.

O'Hare, W. P. 2018. *Citizenship Question Nonresponse: A Demographic Profile of People Who Do Not Answer the American Community Survey Citizenship Question*. Washington, DC, Georgetown Law, Center on Poverty and Inequality, Economic Security and Opportunity Initiative.

OECD. 2015. *Helping Immigrant Students to Succeed at School – and Beyond*. Paris, Organisation for Economic Co-operation and Development.

___. 2019. *PISA 2018 Results: What School Life Means for Students' Lives*. Vol. III. Paris, Organisation for Economic Co-operation and Development.

Oravec, J. A. 2012. Digital image manipulation and avatar configuration: implications for inclusive classrooms. *Journal of Research in Special Educational Needs*, Vol. 12, No. 4, pp. 245–51.

Orfield, G. and Frankenberg, E. 2014. *Brown at 60: Great Progress, a Long Retreat and an Uncertain Future*. Los Angeles, Calif., Civil Rights Project/Proyecto Derechos Civiles.

Park, A. 2016. *Reachable: Data Collection Methods for Sexual Orientation and Gender Identity*. Los Angeles, Calif., Williams Institute, UCLA School of Law.

Park, J. and Niyozov, S. 2008. Madrasa education in South Asia and Southeast Asia: current issues and debates. *Asia Pacific Journal of Education*, Vol. 28, No. 4, pp. 323–51.

Porter, J. 2014. Research and pupil voice. Florian, L. (ed.), *SAGE Handbook of Special Education*. London, Sage, pp. 405–19.

Porter, J., Daniels, H., Feiler, A. and Georgeson, J. 2011. Recognising the needs of every disabled child: the development of tools for a disability census. *British Journal of Special Education*, Vol. 38, No. 3, pp. 120–25.

Porter, J., Daniels, H., Georgeson, J., Feiler, A., Hacker, J., Tarleton, B., Gallop, V. and Watson, D. 2008. *Disability Data Collection for Children's Services*. Nottingham, UK, Department of Children, Schools and Families. (Research Report 62.)

Porter, J., Georgeson, J., Daniels, H., Martin, S. and Feiler, A. 2013. Reasonable adjustments for disabled pupils: What support do parents want for their child? *European Journal of Special Needs Education*, Vol. 28, No. 1, pp. 1–18.

Powell, J. J. W. 2014. Comparative and international perspectives on special education. Florian, L. (ed.), *SAGE Handbook of Special Education*. London, Sage, pp. 335–49.

Price, R. 2018. *Inclusive and Special Education Approaches in Developing Countries*. Brighton, UK, Institute of Development Studies. (K4D Helpdesk Report.)

Reardon, S. and Owen, A. 2014. 60 years after Brown: trends and consequences of school segregation. *Annual Review of Sociology*, Vol. 40, pp. 199–218.

Riddick, B. 2000. An examination of the relationship between labelling and stigmatisation with special reference to dyslexia. *Disability and Society*, Vol. 15, No. 4, pp. 653–67.

Rix, J. and Sheehy, K. 2014. Nothing special: the everyday pedagogy of teaching. Florian, L. (ed.), *SAGE Handbook of Special Education*. London, Sage, pp. 459–74.

Rose, P. and Sabates, R. 2017. *Mobilizing the Power of Volunteers through Citizen Led Assessments.* Nairobi, People's Action for Learning Network. https://palnetwork.org/mobilizing-the-power-of-volunteers-through-citizen-led-assessments. (Accessed 11 December 2019.)

Rwanda Education Board. 2016. *Guide to Inclusive Education in Pre-primary, Primary, and Secondary Education.* Kigali, Rwanda Education Board.

Sarton, E. and Smith, M. 2018. The challenge of inclusion for children with disabilities. Chakera, S. and Tao, S. (eds), *The UNICEF Education Think Piece Series: Innovative Thinking for Complex Educational Challenges in the SDG 4 Era.* Nairobi, UNICEF Eastern and Southern Africa Regional Office.

Save the Children. 2016. *Inclusive Education: What, Why, And How – A Handbook for Program Implementers.* London, Save the Children.

Serbia Social Inclusion and Poverty Reduction Unit and UNICEF. 2014. *Monitoring Framework for Inclusive Education in Serbia.* Belgrade, Social Inclusion and Poverty Reduction Unit.

Shakespeare, T. 2006. *Disability Rights and Wrongs.* London, Routledge.

Sharma, U. 2016. *Pacific Indicators for Disability-Inclusive Education: The Guidelines Manual 2016.* Clayton, Australia, Nossal Institute for Global Health/CBM/Pacific Disability Forum/Pacific Islands Forum Secretariat/Monash University.

Shaw, A. 2017. Inclusion: the role of special and mainstream schools. *British Journal of Special Education,* Vol. 44, No. 3, pp. 292–312.

Sightsavers. 2020. *Education of Children with Visual Impairments in sub-Saharan Africa: Challenges and Opportunities.* Paris, UNESCO. (Background paper for *Global Education Monitoring Report 2020.*)

Simon, P. and Piché, V. 2012. Accounting for ethnic and racial diversity: the challenge of enumeration. *Ethnic and Racial Studies,* Vol. 35, No. 8, pp. 1357–65.

Singal, N. 2014. Entry, engagement and empowerment: dilemmas for inclusive education in an Indian context. Florian, L. (ed.), *SAGE Handbook of Special Education.* London, Sage, pp. 203–16.

Singal, N., Salifu, E. M., Iddrisu, K., Casely-Hayford, L. and Lundebye, H. 2015. The impact of education in shaping lives: reflections of young people with disabilities in Ghana. *International Journal of Inclusive Education,* Vol. 19, No. 9, pp. 908–25.

Southwell, N. 2006. Truants on truancy: a badness or a valuable indicator of unmet special educational needs? *British Journal of Special Education,* Vol. 33, No. 2, pp. 91–97.

Sprunt, B. 2014. *Efforts to Improve Disability Disaggregation of the Fiji Education Management Information System.* Paper for expert group meeting on Disability Data and Statistics, Monitoring and Evaluation: The Way Forward – A Disability Inclusive Development Agenda towards 2015 and Beyond, Paris, UNDESA and UNESCO, 8-10 July.

Swift, A. 2003. *How Not to be a Hypocrite: School Choice for the Morally Perplexed Parent.* London, Routledge.

The Leadership Conference Education Fund. 2018. *Will You Count? Latinos in the 2020 Census.* Washington, DC, Georgetown Law, Center on Poverty and Inequality, Economic Security and Opportunity Initiative.

Tymms, P. and Merrell, C. 2006. The impact of screening and advice on inattentive, hyperactive and impulsive children. *European Journal of Special Needs Education,* Vol. 21, No. 3, pp. 321–37.

UIS. 2018. *Education and Disability: Analysis of Data from 49 Countries.* Montreal, Canada, UNESCO Institute for Statistics. (Information Paper 49.)

___. 2019. *The Use of UIS Data and Education Management Information Systems to Monitor Inclusive Education.* Montreal, Canada, UNESCO Institute for Statistics. (Information Paper 60.)

UNESCO. 2011. *Regional Education System on Students with Disabilities (SIRIED): Methodological Proposal.* Santiago, UNESCO Regional Bureau of Education for Latin America and the Caribbean.

___. 2013. *Sistema Regional de Información Educativa de los Estudiantes con Discapacidad: SIRIED – Resultados de la Primera Fase de Aplicación [Regional Education Information System on Students with Disablity: SIRIED – Results of the First Phase of Implementation].* Santiago, UNESCO Regional Bureau for Education in Latin America and the Caribbean.

___. 2014. *EFA Global Monitoring Report 2013/4: Teaching and Learning – Achieving Quality for All.* Paris, UNESCO.

___. 2018. *Global Education Monitoring Report 2019: Migration, Displacement and Education – Building Bridges, not Walls.* Paris, UNESCO.

UNICEF. 2016. *Guide for Including Disability in Education Management Information Systems.* New York, UNICEF.

___. 2017. *Orphans.* New York, UNICEF. www.unicef.org/media/media_45279.html. (Accessed 11 December 2019.)

___. 2018. *Equity Index Outline Paper.* Kathmandu, UNICEF.

___. 2019. *The State of the World's Children*. New York, UNICEF.

UNICEF and World Bank. 2016. *Ending Extreme Poverty: A Focus on Children*. New York, UNICEF. (Briefing Note.)

UK House of Commons. 2010. *London's Population and the 2011 Census: First Report of Session 2009–10*. London, The Stationery Office.

UK Office of National Statistics. 2015. *Census Coverage Survey: 2011 Census General Report for England and Wales*. London, Office of National Statistics.

United Nations. 2005. *Household Sample Surveys in Developing and Transition Countries*. New York, Statistics Division, United Nations Department of Economic and Social Affairs.

___. 2018. *Disability and Development Report: Realizing the Sustainable Development Goals by, for and with Persons with Disabilities*. New York, United Nations Department of Economic and Social Affairs.

Valencia Lopez, E. 2020. *Improving and Aligning Measurement of Ethnicity in Latin America*. Paris, UNESCO. (Global Education Monitoring Report Fellowship Paper.)

Virkkunen, J., Newnham, D. S., Nleya, P. and Engestroöm, R. 2012. Breaking the vicious circle of categorizing students in school. *Learning, Culture and Social Interaction*, Vol. 1, No. 3–4, pp. 183–92.

Watkins, A., Ebersold, S. and Lénárt, A. 2014. Data collection to inform international policy issues on inclusive education. Forlin, C. and Loreman, T. (eds), *Measuring Inclusive Education*. Bingley, UK, Emerald, pp. 53–74. (International Perspectives on Inclusive Education, Vol. 3.)

WHO. 2019. *Disability: Data*. Geneva, Switzerland, World Health Organization. www.who.int/disabilities/data/en.

WHO and World Bank. 2011. *World Report on Disability*. Geneva, Switzerland, World Health Organization.

Wines, M. 2019. A census whodunit: why was the citizenship question added? *The New York Times*, 30 November.

Wodon, Q. 2014. *Education in Sub-Saharan Africa: Comparing Faith-Inspired, Private Secular, and Public Schools*. Washington, DC, World Bank.

Wodon, Q., Male, C., Montenegro, C. and Nayihouba, A. 2018. *The Price of Exclusion: Disability and Education – The Challenge of Inclusive Education in Sub-Saharan Africa*. Washington, DC, World Bank.

Yuxiao, W. and Chao, H. 2017. School socioeconomic segregation and educational expectations of students in China's junior high schools. *Social Sciences in China*, Vol. 38, No. 3, pp. 112–26.

CHAPTER 4

Abu-Hamour, B. and Al-Hmouz, H. 2014. Special education in Jordan. *European Journal of Special Needs Education*, Vol. 29, No. 1, pp. 105–15.

Accountability Initiative. 2013. *Paisa District Surveys: Mid Day Meals (2012)*. New Delhi, Centre for Policy Research.

ActionAid, Education International and Light for the World. 2020. *Collaborative, Multi-Country Research: Investment in Inclusive Education*. London/Brussels/Vienna, ActionAid/Education International/Light for the World. (Policy Brief.)

Ahimbisibwe, P. 2018. Govt to stop funding to 800 private USE schools. *Daily Monitor*.

Ahmed, A., Adato, M., Kudat, A., Gilligan, D. and Colasan, R. 2007. *Impact Evaluation of the Conditional Cash Transfer Program in Turkey: Final Report*. Washington, DC, International Food Policy Research Institute.

Aïdara, C. 2019. Éducation Primaire en Mauritanie : Quel Rôle pour les Associations des Parents d'Élèves (APE)? [Primary Education in Mauritania: What Role for Parent Associations?]. Nouakchott, Thaqafa. https://aidara.mondoblog. org/2019/04/12/education-primaire-mauritanie-role-associations-parents-deleves-ape. (Accessed 11 December 2019.)

Akita, T., Riadi, A. A. and Rizal, A. 2019. *Fiscal Disparities in Indonesia under Decentralization: To What Extent Has General Allocation Grant (DAU) Equalized Fiscal Revenues?* Minamiuonuma, International University of Japan. (Economics and Management Series 2019-05.)

Anindita, A. and Sahadewo, G. A. 2020. Lighten the burden: assessing the impact of a for-poor-students cash transfer program on spending behaviour. *Journal of Development Studies*, Vol. 56, No. 7, pp. 1367–83.

Araujo, M. C., Bosch, M. and Schady, N. 2017. *Can Cash Transfers Help Households Escape an Inter-Generational Poverty Trap?* Washington, DC, Inter-American Development Bank. (Working Paper 767.)

Arenson, M., Hudson, P. J., Lee, N. and Lai, B. 2019. The evidence on school-based health centers: a review. *Global Pediatric Health*, Vol. 6.

Argentina Government. 2006. *Ley de Financiamiento Educativo [Education Financing Law]*. Buenos Aires, Ministry of Justice and Human Rights.

Asian Development Bank. 2019. *Performance Evaluation Report: Nepal – School Sector Program*. Kathmandu, Asian Development Bank.

Asim, S., Chugunov, D. and Gera, R. M. C. 2019. *Fiscal Implications of Free Education: The Case of Tanzania*. Washington, DC, World Bank.

Aurino, E., Gelli, A., Adamba, C., Osei-Akoto, I. and Alderman, H. 2018. *Food for Thought? Experimental Evidence on the Learning Impacts of a Large-Scale School Feeding Program in Ghana*. Washington, DC, International Food Policy Research Institute. (Discussion Paper 1782.)

Baird, S., Ferreira, F. H., Özler, B. and Woolcock, M. 2014. Conditional, unconditional and everything in between: a systematic review of the effects of cash transfer programmes on schooling outcomes. *Journal of Development Effectiveness*, Vol. 6, No. 1, pp. 1–43.

Barrera-Osorio, F., De Barros, A. and Filmer, D. 2018. *Long-term Impacts of Alternative Approaches to Increase Schooling: Evidence from a Scholarship Program in Cambodia*. Washington, DC, World Bank. (Policy Research Working Paper 8566.)

Bate, A. and Foster, D. 2017. *Sure Start (England)*. London, House of Commons. (Briefing Paper 7257.)

Benin Ministry of Pre-Primary and Primary Education. 2018. *Plan Sectoriel de l'Éducation Post 2015 (2018–2030) [Post-2015 Education Sector Plan (2018–2030)]*. Cotonou, Ministry of Pre-Primary and Primary Education.

Bertoni, E., Elacqua, G., Marotta, L., Martinez, M., Soares, S., Santos, H. and Vegas, E. 2018. *School Finance in Latin America: A Conceptual Framework and a Review of Policies*. Washington, DC, Inter-American Development Bank. (Education Division Social Sector Technical Note 1503.)

Bezzina, L. 2018. *Malta: Fact Sheet on Social Care and Support Services Sector for Persons with Disabilities*. Brussels, European Associaton of Service Providers for Persons with Disabilities.

Biewer, G., Buchner, T., Shevlin, M., Smyth, F., Šiška, J., Káňová, Š., Ferreira, M., Toboso-Martin, M. and Díaz, S. R. 2015. Pathways to inclusion in European higher education systems. *ALTER: European Journal of Disability Research/Revue Européenne de Recherche sur le Handicap*, Vol. 9, No. 4, pp. 278–89.

Bolivia Ministry of Education. 2018. *Informe de Gestión 2017 [Management Report 2017]*. La Paz, Ministry of Education.

Brazil National Secretariat of Youth. 2017. *Guia operacional do Programa Estação Juventude 2.0 [Operational Guide of the Youth Station 2.0 Programme]*. Brasilia, National Secretariat of Youth, Government Secretariat of the Presidency of the Republic.

Brudevold-Newman, A. 2017. The impacts of lowering the costs of secondary education: evidence from a fee reduction in Kenya. College Park, Md., University of Maryland. (Unpublished.)

Bundy, D., Silva, N. d., Horton, S., Jamison, D. T., Patton, G. C., Schultz, L., Galloway, R., Bing Wu, K., Azzopardi, P. and Kennedy, E. 2018. *Child and Adolescent Health Development: Re-Imagining School Feeding – A High-Return Investment in Human Capital and Local Economies*. Washington, DC, World Bank. (Disease Control Priorities Volume 8.)

Cahyadi, N., Hanna, R., Olken, B. A., Prima, R. A., Satriawan, E. and Syamsulhakim, E. 2018. *Cumulative Impacts of Conditional Cash Transfer Programs: Experimental Evidence from Indonesia*. Cambridge, Mass., National Bureau of Economic Research. (Working Paper 24670.)

CDC. 2019. *Autism Data Vizualization Tool*. Atlanta, Ga., Centers for Disease Control and Prevention. www.cdc.gov/ncbddd/autism/data/index.html.

Center for Educational Research and Consulting. 2013. *Assessment of Implementation of Inclusive Education in the Republic of Armenia*. Yerevan, Open Society Foundations-Armenia/Center for Educational Research and Consulting.

Center for Inclusive Policy. 2019. *Clarification Needed: Inclusive, Disability Responsive or CRPD Compliant Budgeting?* Washington, DC, Center for Inclusive Policy.

CfBT Education Trust. 2010. *An International Perspective on Integrated Children's Services*. Reading, UK, CfBT Education Trust.

Chambers, J. G., Parrish, T. B. and Harr, J. J. 2004. *What Are We Spending on Special Education Services in the United States, 1999-2000? Report: Special Education Expenditure Project (SEEP)*. Washington, DC, Department of Education/American Institutes for Research.

Claus, A. and Sanchez, B. 2019. *El Financiamiento Educativo en la Argentina: Balance y Desafíos de Cara al Cambio de Década [Educational Financing in Argentina: Record and Challenges as the Decade Changes]*. Buenos Aires, CIPPEC. (Documento de Travajo 178.)

Colombia Ministry of National Education. 2017. *Decreto 1421 de 2017 por el cual se Reglamenta en el Marco de la Educación Inclusiva la Atención Educativa a la Población con Discapacidad [Decree 1421 of 2017 Regulating Education Care for People with Disabilities in the Framework of Inclusive Education]*. Bogotá, Ministry of National Education.

Cornman, S. Q., Ampadu, O., Wheeler, S., Hanak, K. and Zhou, L. 2019. *Revenues and Expenditures for Public Elementary and Secondary School Districts: School Year 2015–16 (Fiscal Year 2016)*. Washington, DC, National Center for Education Statistics, Department of Education. (NCES 2019-303.)

Corter, C. 2019. Integrated early childhood development services. Tremblay, R. E., Boivin, M. and Peters, R. D. (eds.), *Encyclopedia on Early Childhood Development*. Montreal, Canada, Centre of Excellence for Early Childhood Development.

Cullen, J. B. 2003. The impact of fiscal incentives on student disability rates. *Journal of Public Economics*, Vol. 87, No. 7–8, pp. 1557–89.

Dachelet, K. 2019. *50-State Comparison: K-12 Funding*. Denver, Colo., Education Commission of the States. www.ecs.org/50-state-comparison-k-12-funding. (Accessed 23 August 2019.)

Davis, B. 2013. *Financial Sustainability and Funding Diversification: The Challenge for Indonesian NGOs*. Canberra, Cardno for the Australia Department of Foreign Affairs and Trade.

Department for International Development. 2016. *Business Case: Rwanda Learning for All Education Programme*. London, Department for International Development.

Dominican Republic Ministry of Education. 2008. *Manual Funcionamiento: Centro de Recursos para la Atención a la Diversidad [Operational Manual: Resource Center for Attention to Diversity]*. Santo Domingo, Ministry of Education.

Donohue, D. and Bornman, J. 2014. The challenges of realising inclusive education in South Africa. *South African Journal of Education*, Vol. 34, No. 2.

Drèze, J. and Khera, R. 2017. Recent social security initiatives in India. *World Development*, Vol. 98, pp. 555–72.

Duflo, E., Dupas, P. and Kremer, M. 2017. *The Impact of Free Secondary Education: Experimental Evidence from Ghana*. Boston, Mass., Massachusetts Institute of Technology. (Working Paper.)

Ebersold, S., Watkins, A., Óskarsdóttir, E. and Meijer, C. 2019. Financing inclusive education to reduce disparity in education: trends, issues and drivers. Schuelka, M. J., Johnstone, C. J., Thomas, G. and Artiles, A. J. (eds), *The SAGE Handbook of Inclusion and Diversity in Education*. London, Sage, pp. 232–48.

European Agency for Special Needs and Inclusive Education. 2015. *Education for All: Special Needs and Inclusive Education in Malta – External Audit Report*. Odense, Denmark, European Agency for Special Needs and Inclusive Education.

___. 2016. *Financing of Inclusive Education: Mapping Country Systems for Inclusive Education*. Odense, Denmark, European Agency for Special Needs and Inclusive Education.

___. 2017a. *Decentralisation in Education Systems: Seminar Report*. Odense, Denmark, European Agency for Special Needs and Inclusive Education.

___. 2017b. *Education for All in Iceland: External Audit of the Icelandic System for Inclusive Education*. Odense, Denmark, European Agency for Special Needs and Inclusive Education.

European Commission. 2016. *Prevention and Early Intervention Services to Address Children at Risk of Poverty: Peer Review in Social Protection and Social Inclusion 2015–2016 – Short Report*. Brussels, European Commission.

Eurydice. 2018. *Finland: National Reforms in Early Childhood Education and Care*. Brussels, European Commission. https://eacea.ec.europa.eu/national-policies/eurydice/content/national-reforms-early-childhood-education-and-care-21_en. (Accessed 11 December 2019.)

Evans, P. 2013. *Evaluation of Implementation of the National Strategy & Action Plan for the Reform of the Residential Childcare System in Moldova 2007–2012*. New York, UNICEF.

Figueiredo Walter, T. 2018. *The Allocation of Teachers across Public Primary Schools in Zambia*. London, International Growth Centre.

Finland National Institute for Health and Welfare. 2019. *Lastenneuvola [Child Health Clinics]*. Helsinki, National Institute for Health and Welfare. https://thl.fi/fi/web/lapset-nuoret-ja-perheet/peruspalvelut/aitiys_ja_lastenneuvola/lastenneuvola. (Accessed 11 December 2019.)

Finnish Education Evaluation Centre. 2019. *Ongoing National Evaluation: Evaluation of the Experiment for Free of Charge Early Childhood Education and Care for Five-year-olds*. Helsinki, Finnish Education Evaluation Centre. https://karvi.fi/en/early-childhood-education/evaluation-of-the-experiment-for-free-early-childhood-education-and-care-for-five-year-olds. (Accessed 10 December 2019.)

Florida Department of Education. 2019. *Funding for Florida School Districts*. Tallahassee, Fla., Department of Education.

Ghana Ministry of Education. 2013. *Ghana Inclusive Education Policy: Implementation Plan 2015–2019*. Accra, Ghana Ministry of Education.

Glewwe, P., Kremer, M. and Moulin, S. 2009. Many children left behind? Textbooks and test scores in Kenya. *American Economic Journal: Applied Economics*, Vol. 1, No. 1, pp. 112–35.

Global Partnership for Education. 2018a. *Disability and Inclusive Education: A Stocktake of Education Sector Plans and GPE-Funded Grants*. Washington, DC, Global Partnership for Education. (Working Paper 3.)

___. 2018b. *GPE Replenishment Pledge for Ghana for 2017–2020*. Washington, DC, Global Partnership for Education. www.globalpartnership.org/sites/default/files/2018-gpe-third-replenishment-ghana-pledge.pdf. (Accessed 18 December 2019.)

González, L. I. 2019. Federal transfers, inequality, and redistribution: contrasting theories and empirical evidence for five Latin American cases. *Regional and Federal Studies*, Vol. 29, No. 2, pp. 165–85.

Griffith, M. 2015. *A Look at Funding for Students with Disabilities*. Denver, Colo., Education Commission of the States. (The Progress of Education Reform, Vol. 16, No. 1.)

Gubbels, J., Coppens, K. M. and de Wolf, I. 2018. Inclusive education in the Netherlands: How funding arrangements and demographic trends relate to dropout and participation rates. *International Journal of Inclusive Education*, Vol. 22, No. 11, pp. 1137–53.

Hahn, Y., Islam, A., Nuzhat, K., Smyth, R. and Yang, H.-S. 2018. Education, marriage, and fertility: long-term evidence from a female stipend program in Bangladesh. *Economic Development and Cultural Change*, Vol. 66, No. 2, pp. 383–415.

Hill, L., Warren, P., Murphy, P., Ugo, I. and Pathak, A. 2016. *Special Education Finance in California*. San Francisco, Calif., Public Policy Institute of California.

Holmes, L., McDermid, S., Padley, M. and Soper, J. 2012. *Exploration of the Costs and Impact of the Common Assessment Framework*. Loughborough, UK, Centre for Child and Family Research, Loughborough University, for the Department for Education.

Humanitarian Information Unit. 2018. *Yemen: A Severe Food Security Crisis*. Washington, DC, Humanitarian Information Unit, State Department. https://reliefweb.int/sites/reliefweb.int/files/resources/Yemen_FoodSecurityCrisis_2018Dec17_HIU_U1957.pdf. (Accessed 11 December 2019.)

Hunt, P. and Poudyal, N. 2019. *Education for Children with Disabilities in Nepal: Baseline Data – 2019*. New York, International Disability Alliance.

IDDC and Light for the World. 2016. *#Costing Equity: The Case for Disability-Responsive Education Financing*. Brussels/Vienna, International Disability and Development Consortium/Light for the World.

IIEP. 2018. *Ghana: Making Inclusive Education a Reality*. Paris, UNESCO International Institute for Educational Planning. www.iiep.unesco.org/en/ghana-making-inclusive-education-reality-4564. (Accessed 9 July 2019.)

India Committee on the Welfare of Scheduled Castes and Scheduled Tribes. 2013. *Thirtieth Report on Ministry of Human Resource Development: Prevention of Untouchability in Mid Day Meal Scheme in Government Run Schools*. New Delhi, Ministry of Human Resource Development.

India Ministry of Social Justice and Empowerment. 2017. *Scheme of Assistance to Disabled Persons for Purchase/Fitting of Aids/Appliances (ADIP Scheme)*. New Delhi, Ministry of Social Justice and Empowerment.

___. 2019. *Assistance to Disabled Persons for Purchase/Fitting of Aids and Appliances (ADIP)*. New Delhi, Department of Empowerment of Persons with Disabilities, Ministry of Social Justice and Empowerment. http://disabilityaffairs.gov.in/content/page/adip.php. (Accessed 4 November 2019.)

Ireland Department of Public Expenditure and Reform. 2017. *Spending Review 2017: Disability and Special Education Related Expenditure*. Economic and Evaluation Service, Department of Public Expenditure and Reform.

Jackson, E. 2018. *Indonesian NGOs Can Now Access Government Funds to Provide Services to Communities*. The Conversation, 24 August. https://theconversation.com/indonesian-ngos-can-now-access-government-funds-to-provide-services-to-communities-101451. (Accessed 1 November 2019.)

Jenkins, L. D. and Moses, M. S. 2014. *Affirmative Action Matters: Creating Opportunities for Students Around the World*. London, Routledge.

John, E., Thomas, G. and Touchet, A. 2019. *The Disability Price Tag 2019: Policy Report*. London, Scope.

Jordan Government. 2016. *Education for Prosperity: Delivering Results – A National Strategy for Human Resources Development 2016–2025*. Amman, Government of Jordan.

Jordan Ministry of Education. 2020. *The 10-Year Strategy for Inclusive Education Based on the Text of Article (18/h) of the Law on the Rights of Persons with Disabilities (20) of the Year 2017*. Amman, Ministry of Education/Higher Council for the Rights of Persons with Disabilities. (Unpublished.)

Kaga, Y., Bennett, J. and Moss, P. 2010. *Caring and Learning Together: A Cross-National Study on the Integration of Early Childhood Care and Education Within Education.* Paris, UNESCO.

Kekkonen, M., Montonen, M. and Viitala, R. 2012. *Family Centre in the Nordic Countries: A Meeting Point for Children and Families.* Copenhagen, Nordic Council of Ministers.

Kenya Ministry of Education. 2018. *Sector Policy for Learners and Trainees with Disabilities.* Nairobi, Ministry of Education.

Kiru, E. W. 2019. Special education in Kenya. *Intervention in School and Clinic,* Vol. 54, No. 3, pp. 181–88.

Kristjansson, E., Gelli, A., Welch, V., Greenhalgh, T., Liberato, S., Francis, D. and Espejo, F. 2016. Costs, and cost-outcome of school feeding programmes and feeding programmes for young children: evidence and recommendations. *International Journal of Educational Development,* Vol. 48, pp. 79–83.

Kwan Chan, C. and Lei, J. 2017. Contracting social services in China: the case of the integrated family services centres in Guangzhou. *International Social Work,* Vol. 60, No. 6, pp. 1343–57.

Lamichhane, K. 2015. *Disability, Education and Employment in Developing Countries: From Charity to Investment.* New Delhi, Cambridge University Press.

Lawrence, J. and Thorne, E. 2016. *A Systems Approach to Integrating Health in Education.* Louisville, Ky., Cairn Guidance for the Robert Wood Johnson Foundation.

Leer, J. 2016. After the Big Bang: estimating the effects of decentralization on educational outcomes in Indonesia through a difference-in-differences analysis. *International Journal of Educational Development,* Vol. 49, pp. 80–90.

Léveillé, S. and Chamberland, C. 2010. Toward a general model for child welfare and protection services: a meta-evaluation of international experiences regarding the adoption of the Framework for the Assessment of Children in Need and their Families (FACNF). *Children and Youth Services Review,* Vol. 32, No. 7, pp. 929–44.

Lord, P., Kinder, K., Wilkin, A., Atkinson, M. and Harland, J. 2008. *Evaluating the Early Impact of Integrated Children's Services: Round 1 – Final Report.* Slough, UK, National Foundation for Educational Research.

Luschei, T. F. and Chudgar, A. 2016. *Teacher Distribution In Developing Countries: Teachers of Marginalized Students in India, Mexico, and Tanzania.* Cham, Switzerland, Springer.

Malouf Bous, K. and Farr, J. 2019. *False Promises: How Delivering Education through Public-Private Partnerships Risks Fueling Inequality Instead of Achieving Quality Education for All.* Oxford, UK, Oxfam.

Mauritania Government. 2015. *Plan d'Action Triennal du secteur de l'éducation 2016–2018 [Three-year Education Sector Action Plan 2016–2018].* Nouakchott, Government of Mauritania.

Mauritius Government Information Service. 2019. *Budget 2018–2019: Advancing a More Inclusive and Equitable Quality Education.* Port Louis, Government Information Service, Prime Minister's Office. www.govmu.org/English/News/Pages/Budget-2018-2019-Advancing-a-more-inclusive-and-equitable-quality-education-.aspx. (Accessed 19 October 2019.)

Medellín, N. and Sánchez Prada, F. 2015. *How Does Más Familias en Acción Work? Best Practices in the Implementation of Conditional Cash Transfer Programs in Latin America and the Caribbean.* Washington, DC, Inter-American Development Bank. (Social Protection and Health Division Technical Note 884.)

Milligan, L. O., Tikly, L., Williams, T., Vianney, J.-M. and Uworwabayeho, A. 2017. Textbook availability and use in Rwandan basic education: a mixed-methods study. *International Journal of Educational Development,* Vol. 54, pp. 1–7.

Milman, H. M., Castillo, C. A., Sansotta, A. T., Delpiano, P. V. and Murray, J. 2018. Scaling up an early childhood development programme through a national multisectoral approach to social protection: lessons from Chile Crece Contigo. *The BMJ,* Vol. 363.

Mitra, S., Palmer, M., Kim, H., Mont, D. and Groce, N. 2017. Extra costs of living with a disability: a review and agenda for research. *Disability and Health Journal,* Vol. 10, No. 4, pp. 475–84.

Molina Millán, T., Barham, T., Macours, K., Maluccio, J. A. and Stampini, M. 2019. Long-term impacts of conditional cash transfers: review of the evidence. *The World Bank Research Observer,* Vol. 34, No. 1, pp. 119–59.

Morando Rhim, L. 2018. Quality must remain the focus as Vermont and other states overhaul special education. *Washington Post,* 9 October. www.washingtonpost.com/education/2018/10/09/quality-must-remain-focus-vermont-other-states-overhaul-special-education. (Accessed 11 December 2019.)

Moriña, A. 2017. Inclusive education in higher education: challenges and opportunities. *European Journal of Special Needs Education,* Vol. 32, No. 1, pp. 3–17.

Munday, B. 2007. *Integrated Social Services in Europe.* Strasbourg, France, Council of Europe.

Murenzi, V. and McGeown, J. 2015. Developing inclusive education standards and norms in Rwanda. *Enabling Education Review*, No. 4, pp. 12–13.

Mutegeki, G. 2019. Understanding Sh3.28 Trillion Education Ministry Budget. *New Vision*, 29 April.

Muttaqin, T., van Duijn, M., Heyse, L. and Wittek, R. 2016. The impact of decentralization on educational attainment in Indonesia. Holzhacker, R. L., Wittek, R. and Woltjer, J. (eds), *Decentralization and Governance in Indonesia*. Cham, Switzerland, Springer, pp. 79–103.

Namibia Ministry of Education. 2013. *Ministry of Education Sector Policy on Inclusive Education*. Windhoek, Ministry of Education.

National Campaign on Dalit Human Rights. 2017. *Exclusion in Schools: A Study on Practice of Discrimination and Violence*. New Delhi, National Campaign on Dalit Human Rights.

National Council on Disability. 2018. *Broken Promises: The Underfunding of IDEA*. Washington, DC, National Council on Disability. (IDEA Series.)

Nepal Ministry of Education. 2016. *School Sector Development Plan 2016–2023*. Kathmandu, Ministry of Education.

New York City Department of Education. 2018. *NYC Department of Education: FY 2017 System Wide Report*. New York, Department of Education.

New Zealand Office for Disability Issues. 2015. *Disability Action Plan 2014–2018: Update 2015 – Cross-government Priorities to Improve Disabled People's Ability to Participate and Contribute to New Zealand*. Wellington, Office for Disability Issues, Ministry for Social Development.

___. 2018. *Disability Action Plan 2014–2018 Progress Report: September 2018*. Wellington, Office for Disability Issues, Ministry for Social Development.

NOOIS. 2018. *Situation Analysis: Position of Children with Disabilities in the Republic of Serbia*. Belgrade, National Organization of Persons with Disabilities of Serbia.

Nordic Welfare Centre. 2019. *Adolescent Health in the Nordic Region: Health Promotion in School Settings*. Stockholm, Nordic Welfare Centre.

Norway Government. 2019. *Meld. St. 6 (2019–2020) Tett På – Tidlig Innsats og Inkluderende Fellesskap i Barnehage, Skole og SFO [White Paper 6 (2019–2020] Close-up: Early Interventions and Inclusive Community in Kindergartens, Schools and After-school Care]*. Oslo, Ministry of Education.

O'Donoghue, J., Crawfurd, L., Makaaru, J., Otieno, P. and Perakis, R. 2018. *A Review of Uganda's Universal Secondary Education Public Private Partnership Programme*. London, Education Partnerships Group.

OECD. 2000. *Inclusive Education at Work: Students with Disabilities in Mainstream Schools*. Paris, Centre for Educational Research and Innovation, Organisation for Economic Co-operation and Development.

___. 2014. *Investing in Youth: Brazil*. Paris, Organisation for Economic Co-operation and Development. (OECD Youth Action Plan.)

___. 2015. *Integrating Social Services for Vulnerable Groups: Bridging Sectors for Better Service Delivery*. Paris, Organisation for Economic Co-operation and Development.

___. 2017a. *Education in Chile*. Paris, Organisation for Economic Co-operation and Development. (Reviews of National Policies for Education.)

___. 2017b. *Starting Strong V: Transitions from Early Childhood Education and Care to Primary Education*. Paris, Organisation for Economic Co-operation and Development.

OECD and ADB. 2015. *Education in Indonesia: Rising to the Challenge*. Paris/Manila, Organisation for Economic Co-operation and Development/Asian Development Bank.

Palmer, M., Williams, J. and McPake, B. 2016. The cost of disability in a low income country. Melbourne, Australia, University of Melbourne. (Unpublished.)

Patana, P. 2020. *Inclusive Education and Cross-Sectoral Collaboration between Education and Other Sectors*. Paris, UNESCO. (Background paper for *Global Education Monitoring Report 2020*.)

Paxton, W. and Mutesi, L. 2012. *School Funding and Equity in Rwanda: Final Report*. Kigali, Institute of Policy Analysis and Research – Rwanda.

Prakash, R. 2017. *Why Aren't Students of Delhi's Government Schools Getting Their Textbooks on Time?* New Delhi, Scroll.in. https://scroll.in/article/833900/why-arent-students-of-delhis-government-schools-getting-their-textbooks-on-time. (Accessed 1 December 2019.)

Pulkkinen, J. 2019. *Reforming Policy, Changing Practices? Special Education in Finland after Educational Reforms.* Jyväskylä, Finland, Finnish Institute for Educational Research, University of Jyväskylä. (Studies 34.)

Qin, L. and Bowen, D. H. 2019. The distributions of teacher qualification: a cross-national study. *International Journal of Educational Development,* Vol. 70.

Ranasinghe, A., Arunathilake, N. and Dunusinghe, D. D. P. M. 2016. *Study on Investment in General Education in Sri Lanka.* Colombo, National Education Commission. (Research Series [2014] No. 7.)

Reddy, A. 2018. *How Caste is Marring Mid-Day Meals.* New Delhi, DownToEarth.

Republic of Korea Ministry of Health and Welfare. 2019. *DreamStart.* Seoul, Ministry of Health and Welfare. www.dreamstart.go.kr/eng/index.asp. (Accessed 11 December 2019.)

Republic of Moldova Ministry of Education, Culture and Research. 2017. *Educație Incluzivă: Unitate de Curs − Ediție Revăzută și Completată [Inclusive Education: Course Unit − Revised and Completed Edition].* Chișinău, Ministry of Education, Culture and Research.

Rivas, A. and Dborkin, D. 2018. ¿Qué Cambió en el Financiamiento Educativo en Argentina? [*What Changed in Education Financing in Argentina?*]. Buenos Aires, CIPPEC. (Documento de Trabajo 162.)

Rose, P. 2011. Strategies for engagement: government and national non-government education providers in South Asia. *Public Administration and Development,* Vol. 31, No. 4, pp. 294–305.

Rwanda Ministry of Finance and Economic Planning. 2017. *2017–2018 Earmarked Transfers Guidelines to Decentralized Entities.* Kigali, Ministry of Finance and Economic Planning.

Sabarwal, S., Evans, D. K. and Marshak, A. 2014. *The Permanent Input Hypothesis: The Case of Textbooks and (No) Student Learning in Sierra Leone.* Washington, DC, World Bank. (Policy Research Working Paper 7021.)

Sabharwal, N. S., Naik, A. K., Diwakar G, D. and Sharma, S. 2014. Swallowing the humiliation: the mid-day meal and excluded groups. *Journal of Social Inclusion Studies,* Vol. 1, No. 1, pp. 169–82.

Salmi, J. 2018. *All Around the World: Higher Education Equity Policies Across the Globe.* Indianapolis, Ind./London, Lumina Foundation/World Access to Higher Education Day.

Samal, J. and Dehury, R. K. 2017. Family impact analysis of mid-day meal (MDM) scheme in India with special focus on child education and nutrition. *Journal of Development Policy and Practice,* Vol. 2, No. 2, pp. 151–62.

Sarker, S. 2019. Distribution of Braille textbooks needs to be more 'even'. *Dhaka Tribune,* 5 January. www.dhakatribune.com/uncategorized/2019/01/05/distribution-of-braille-textbooks-needs-to-be-more-even. (Accessed 10 November 2019.)

Serbia Prime Minister's Office. 2019. *Voluntary National Review of the Republic of Serbia on the Implementation of the 2030 Agenda for Sustainable Development.* Belgrade, Prime Minister's Office.

Sharma, U., Forlin, C. and Furlonger, B. 2015. *Contemporary Models of Funding Inclusive Education for Students with Autism Spectrum Disorder.* Clayton, Australia, Monash University.

Sierra Leone Government. 2011. *Persons with Disability Act.* Freetown, *Sierra Leone Gazette,* 5 May.

Sloper, P. 2004. Facilitators and barriers for co-ordinated multi-agency services. *Child: Care, Health and Development,* Vol. 30, No. 6, pp. 571–80.

Smart, A. and Jagannathan, S. 2018. *Textbook Policies in Asia: Development, Publishing, Printing, Distribution, and Future Implications.* Manila, Asian Development Bank.

Snilstveit, B., Stevenson, J., Phillips, D., Vojtkova, M., Gallagher, E., Schmidt, T., Jobse, H., Geelen, M., Pastorello, M. G. and Eyers, J. 2015. *Interventions for Improving Learning Outcomes and Access to Education in Low- and Middle-Income Countries: A Systematic Review.* London, International Initiative for Impact Evaluation (3ie). (Systematic Review 24.)

South Africa Department of Basic Education. 2014. *Policy on Screening, Identification, Assessment and Support.* Pretoria, Department of Basic Education.

___. 2015. *Action Plan to 2019 towards the Realisation of Schooling 2030: Taking Forward South Africa's National Development Plan 2030.* Pretoria, Department of Basic Education.

Sri Lanka Finance Commission. 2014. *Recommendation 2014 to H.E. the President in Terms of the Article 154R (4) of the Constitution of Sri Lanka.* Colombo, Finance Commission.

Statham, J. 2011. *A Review of International Evidence on Interagency Working, to Inform the Development of Children's Services Committees in Ireland.* Dublin, Department of Children and Youth Affairs.

Tabazah, S. 2017. *New Anti-Discriminatory Law Seeks to Improve Lives of People with Disabilities. Jordan Times,* 20 September. www.jordantimes.com/news/local/new-anti-discriminatory-law-seeks-improve-lives-people-disabilities.

Tigere, B. and Moyo, T. 2019. *Actualizing the Rights of People Living with Disabilities (PWDS) in Development Policies, Planning and Programming in Africa: A Review of Selected Country Experiences.* Paper for International Conference on Public Administration and Development Alternatives, Johannesburg, South Africa, 3–5 July.

Turkey Government and European Commission. 2019. *Conditional Cash Transfer for Education (CCTE) Programme for Syrian and Other Refugee Children.* https://www.unicef.org/turkey/en/media/8001/file. (Accessed 11 December 2019.)

UNDP. 2019. *Fiscal Transfers in Asia: Challenges and Opportunities for Financing Sustainable Development at the Local Level.* Bangkok, United Nations Development Programme.

UNESCO. 2006. *EFA Global Monitoring Report 2007: Strong Foundations: – Early Childhood Care and Education.* Paris, UNESCO.

___. 2018. *Estado del Arte de los Servicios de Apoyo para Estudiantes en Situación de Discapacidad Residentes en Países Miembros de la RIINEE [State of the Art of Support Services for Students with Disabilities Resident in Member States of the Iberoamerican Network of Special Education Needs].* Santiago, UNESCO.

___. 2019a. *Beyond Commitments: How Countries Implement SDG 4.* Paris, Global Education Monitoring Report under the auspices of the SDG – Education 2030 Steering Committee.

___. 2019b. *Global Monitoring Report 2019: Migration, Displacement and Education – Building Bridges, not Walls.* Paris, UNESCO.

UNICEF. 2017. *Education Budget Brief: FY 2011/12 – FY 2015/16.* New York, UNICEF.

Vieira, R. S. and Arends-Kuenning, M. 2018. *Affirmative Action in Brazilian Universities: Effects on the Enrollment of Targeted Groups.* Urbana, Ill., University of Illinois at Urbana-Champaign.

Viet Nam Ministry of Planning and Investment 2018. *Viet Nam's Voluntary National Review on the Implementation of the Sustainable Development Goals.* Hanoi, Department for Science, Education, Natural Resoruces and Environment, Ministry of Planning and Investment.

Vogel, C. A. and Xue, Y. 2018. *Lessons Learned from the Early Head Start Program.* Tremblay, R. E., Boivin, M. and Peters, R. D. (eds.), *Encyclopedia on Early Childhood Development.* Montreal, Canada, Centre of Excellence for Early Childhood Development.

Weale, S. 2019. Special-needs children lose out on £1.2bn of support, says union. *The Guardian,* 14 April.

WFP. 2019a. *The Impact of School Feeding Programmes.* Rome, World Food Programme.

___. 2019b. *Yemen: Systems Approach to Better Education Results (SABER) – Investing in Capacities in Conflict to Implement Inclusive and Better-Quality School Feeding Programs.* Rome, World Food Programme. (Unpublished.)

WHO. 2018. *Global Nutrition: Policy Review 2016–2017.* Geneva, Switzerland, World Health Organization.

Williams, T. P. 2017. The political economy of primary education: Lessons from Rwanda. *World Development,* Vol. 96, pp. 550–61.

Wingender, P. 2018. *Intergovernmental Fiscal Reform in China.* Washington, DC, International Monetary Fund. (Working Paper 18/88.)

Wisconsin Taxpayer. 2019. *Special Education Funding in Wisconsin: Why it Works and Why it Matters.* Madison, Wis., Wisconsin Policy Forum.

World Bank. 2014. *Georgia: Technical Assistance to Support Preparation of Education Sector Strategy – Education Sector Policy Review: Strategic Issues and Reform Agenda.* Washington, DC, World Bank.

___. 2017a. *Indonesia Social Assistance Public Expenditure Review Update: Towards a Comprehensive, Integrated, and Effective Social Assistance System in Indonesia.* Jakarta, World Bank.

___. 2017b. *Pakistan Tertiary Education: SABER Country Report.* Washington, DC, World Bank.

___. 2017c. *World Bank Approves Financing to Expand Indonesia's Social Assistance Program.* Washington, DC, World Bank. www.worldbank.org/en/news/press-release/2017/05/09/world-bank-approves-financing-to-expand-indonesias-social-assistance-program. (Accessed 11 December 2019.)

___. 2018. *Implementation Completion and Results Report for the Cambodia Global Partnership for Education Second Education Support Project (P144715).* Washington, DC, World Bank.

World Blind Union. 2016. *Millions of People Are Denied Access to Books and Printed Materials: WBU Press Release for World Book and Copyright Day.* Toronto, Canada, World Blind Union. www.worldblindunion.org/English/news/Pages/Millions-of-People-are-Denied-Access-to-.aspx. (Accessed 9 December 2019.)

CHAPTER 5

Abdou, E. D. 2016. 'Confused by multiple deities, ancient Egyptians embraced monotheism': analysing historical thinking and inclusion in Egyptian history textbooks. *Journal of Curriculum Studies*, Vol. 48, No. 2, pp. 226–51.

___. 2017. Copts in Egyptian history textbooks: towards an integrated framework for analyzing minority representations. *Journal of Curriculum Studies*, Vol. 50, No. 4, pp. 476–507.

Abudu, A. M. and Mensah, M. A. 2016. Basic school teachers' perceptions about curriculum design in Ghana. *Journal of Education and Practice*, Vol. 7, No. 19.

Adewumi, T. M., Rembe, S., Shumba, J. and Akinyemi, A. 2017. Adaptation of the curriculum for the inclusion of learners with special education needs in selected primary schools in the Fort Beaufort District. *African Journal of Disability*, Vol. 6, p. 377.

African Union. 2016. *Continental Education Strategy for Africa 2016–2025*. Addis Ababa, African Union.

___. 2018. *Workshop on the Launch of CESA Curriculum Cluster*. Addis Ababa, African Union. https://au.int/fr/node/35594. (Accessed 11 December 2019.)

AHEAD. 2017. *Universal Design for Learning*. Dublin, Association for Higher Education Access and Disability. www.ahead.ie/udl. (Accessed 11 December 2019.)

Ali, M. I. 2016. BRAC roles in non-formal education: a study on BRAC education for ethnic children program in Bangladesh. MA dissertation, Institute of Governance and Development, BRAC University, Dhaka.

Alkahtani, M. A. and Kheirallah, S. A. 2016. Background of individual education plans (IEPs) policy in some countries: a review. *Journal of Education and Practice* Vol. 7, No. 24.

All Children Reading. 2018. *eKitabu*. Washington, DC, US Agency for International Development/World Vision/Australian Government. https://allchildrenreading.org/innovator/ekitabu-2. (Accessed 11 December 2019.)

Altinyelken, H. K. 2015. *Evolution of Curriculum Systems to Improve Learning Outcomes and Reduce Disparities in School Achievement*. Paris, UNESCO. (Background paper for *EFA Global Monitoring Report 2015*.)

Altrichter, H. 2019. School autonomy policies and the changing governance of schooling. Jahnke, H., Kramer, C. and Meusburger, P. (eds), *Geographies of Schooling, Knowledge and Space 14*, pp. 55–73.

Anderson, G. D. S. 2015. *The Munda Languages*. New York, Routledge.

Apple, M. and Christian-Smith, L. 1991. *The Politics of the Textbook*. New York, Routledge.

Arphattananon, T. 2011. The shift of policy on language of instruction in schools in three southernmost provinces of Thailand. *Pertanika Journal of Social Sciences and Humanities*, Vol. 19, No. 1, pp. 113–22.

Atuhurra, J. and Alinda, V. 2018. *Basic Education Curriculum Effectiveness in East Africa: A Descriptive Analysis of Primary Mathematics in Uganda Using the 'Surveys of Enacted Curriculum'*. Paper for RISE annual conference, Oxford, UK, 21–22 June.

Australia Education Council. 2017. *2017 Data on Students in Australian Schools Receiving Adjustments for Disability*. Canberra, Education Council.

Ávila, R. 2018. *LGBTQI Inclusive Education Report*. Brussels, International Lesbian, Gay, Bisexual, Transgender, Queer and Intersex Youth and Student Organisation.

Ball, J. and Smith, M. 2019. *Independent Evaluation of the Multilingual Education National Action Plan in Cambodia: July 2018– February 2019 – Cambodia*. Phnom Penh, UNICEF.

Banerjee, S. 2018. Quebec spends $1.6M to replace word 'Amerindian' from history textbooks with proper Indigenous terms. *National Post*, 27 September.

Baranovitch, N. 2010. Others no more: the changing representation of non-Han peoples in Chinese history textbooks, 1951–2003. *The Journal of Asian Studies*, Vol. 69, No. 1, pp. 85–122.

Beckett, A., Ellison, N., Barrett, S. and Shah, S. 2010. 'Away with the fairies?' Disability within primary-age children's literature. *Disability and Society*, Vol. 25, No. 3, pp. 373–86.

BEQUAL. 2018. *Basic Education Quality and Access in Lao PDR Implementation Plan Phase 1 (October 2018–August 2020)*. Vientiane, Ministry of Education and Sport/Australian Aid/European Union. www.bequal-laos.org/wp-content/uploads/2019/03/BEQUAL-Implementation-plan-2018-2020_March-2019.pdf. (Accessed 11 December 2019.)

___. 2019. *Provinces and Teacher Training Colleges (TTC) Getting Ready for the Implementation of the New Primary Curriculum*. Vientiane, Ministry of Education and Sport/Australian Aid/European Union. www.bequal-laos.org/provinces-and-teacher-training-colleges-ttc-getting-ready-for-the-implementation-of-the-new-primary-curriculum. (Accessed 11 December 2019.)

Berkvens, J. 2020. *An Inclusive Education Curriculum: A Utopian Dream, or Is It Really Possible? What We Can Learn from Countries Developing Inclusive Education Curricula.* Paris, UNESCO. (Background paper for *Global Education Monitoring Report 2020.*)

Blackwell, W. H. and Rossetti, Z. S. 2014. The development of individualized education programs. *SAGE Open,* Vol. 4, No. 2.

Blatchford, P., Bassett, P., Brown, P., Koutsoubou, M., Martin, C., Russell, A., Webster, R. and Rubie-Davies, C. 2009. *Deployment and Impact of Support Staff in Schools: The Impact of Support Staff in Schools (Results from Strand 2, Wave 2).* London, Institute of Education, University of London. (Research Report DCSF-RR148.)

Bold, T., Filmer, D., Martin, G., Molina, E., Stacy, B., Rockmore, C., Svensson, J. and Wane, W. 2017. Enrollment without learning: teacher effort, knowledge, and skill in primary schools in Africa. *Journal of Economic Perspectives,* Vol. 31, No. 4, pp. 185–204.

Bourke, R. and Mentis, M. 2010. *Research and Evaluation of Narrative Assessment and Curriculum Exemplars for Students with Special Education Needs: Final Report.* Palmerston, New Zealand, Centre for Educational Development, Massey University College of Education.

Bradley, D. 2019. Language policy and language planning in mainland Southeast Asia: Myanmar and Lisu. *Linguistics Vanguard,* Vol. 5, No. 1.

Carrington, S. and MacArthur, J. 2012. *Teaching in Inclusive School Communities.* Milton, Australia, Wiley.

Çayır, K. 2014. *Who are We? Identity, Citizenship and Rights in Turkey's Textbooks.* Istanbul, Turkey, Tarih Vakfı, History Foundation Publications. (Human Rights in Textbooks.)

Centre for Budget and Policy Studies. 2017. *Reviewing the Status of Education in Tribal Areas in Maharashtra: A Comprehensive Report.* Bangalore, India, Centre for Budget and Policy Studies.

Chen, S., Lawrence, J. F., Zhou, J., Min, L. and Snow, C. E. 2018. The efficacy of a school-based book-reading intervention on vocabulary development of young Uyghur children: a randomized controlled trial. *Early Childhood Research Quarterly,* Vol. 44, pp. 206–19.

Chile Ministry of Education. 2019. *Currículum Nacional: Lengua Indígena 1° Básico [National Curriculum: Indigenous Language Grade 1].* Santiago, Curriculum and Evaluation Unit, Ministry of Education.

China Government. 2001. 1984年5月31日第六届全国人民代表大会第二次会议通过　根据2001年2月28日第九届全国人民代表大会常务委员会第二十次会议《关于修改〈中华人民共和国民族区域自治法〉的决定》修正 [*'People's Republic of China Regional Ethnic Autonomy Law' issued by the Second Session of the Sixth National People's Congress on 31 May 1984 and amended in accordance with the 'Decision on Revising the People's Republic of China Regional Ethnic Autonomy Law' made at the 12th Meeting of the Standing Committee of the Ninth National People's Congress on 28 February 2001*]. Beijing, Central People's Government of the People's Republic of China. http://www.gov.cn/ziliao/flfg/2005-09/12/content_31168.htm. (Accessed 19 November 2019.)

Choksi, N. 2017. From language to script: graphic practice and the politics of authority in Santali-language print media, eastern India. *Modern Asian Studies,* Vol. 51, No. 5, pp. 1519–60.

Chu, Y. 2018. Visualizing minority: images of ethnic minority groups in Chinese elementary social studies textbooks. *The Journal of Social Studies Research,* Vol. 42, No. 2, pp. 135–47.

Cobano-Delgado, V. C. and Llorent-Bedmar, V. 2019. Identity and gender in childhood: representation of Moroccan women in textbooks. *Women's Studies International Forum,* Vol. 74, pp. 137–42.

Committee on the Rights of Persons with Disabilities. 2016. *General Comment No. 4: Article 24 – Right to Inclusive Education.* New York, United Nations Committee on the Rights of Persons with Disabilities.

Cortina, R. 2014. *The Education of Indigenous Citizens in Latin America.* Bristol, UK, Multilingual Matters. (Bilingual Education and Bilingualism.)

Council of Europe. 2017. *Fighting School Segregation in Europe through Inclusive Education.* Strasbourg, Commissioner for Human Rights, Council of Europe.

___. 2019. *Working towards a Recommendation on Including Roma and Travellers' History in School Curricula: Meeting in Toulouse.* Strasbourg, France, Council of Europe.

Covacevich, C. and Quintela-Dávila, G. 2014. *Desigualdad de Género, el Currículo Oculto en Textos Escolares Chilenos [Gender Inequality, the Hidden Curriculum in Chilean Textbooks].* Washington, DC, Education Division, Inter-American Development Bank. (Technical Note 694.)

Cumming, J. J. and Maxwell, G. S. 2013. Expanding approaches to summative assessment for students with impairment. Florian, L. (ed.), *The SAGE Handbook of Special Education.* London, Sage, pp. 573–96.

Curwood, J. S. 2013. Redefining normal: a critical analysis of (dis)ability in young adult literature. *Children's Literature in Education,* Vol. 44, No. 1, pp. 15–28.

Darak, K. 2018. Language textbooks and politically active citizenship: assisting or hindering the national project? *Studies in Indian Politics,* Vol. 6, No. 1, pp. 132–39.

Deaf Child Worldwide. 2018. *Language and Communication.* London, Deaf Child Worldwide.

Doi, K. 2016. *Japan's Chance at an LGBT-Inclusive Curriculum: School Guidelines Should Address Sexual Orientation, Gender Identity.* New York, Human Rights Watch. www.hrw.org/news/2016/10/12/japans-chance-lgbt-inclusive-curriculum. (Accessed 11 December 2019.)

Doi, K. and Knight, K. 2017. *Japan's Missed Opportunity to Support LGBT Children: At Least 10 More Years of Official Silence on LGBT Lives in Schools.* New York, Human Rights Watch.

Dubai KHDA. 2017. *Dubai Inclusive Education Policy Framework.* Dubai Knowledge and Human Development Authority.

ECLAC. 2014. *Guaranteeing Indigenous People's Rights in Latin America: Progress in the Past Decade and Remaining Challenges.* Santiago, Economic Commission for Latin America and the Caribean.

Education International. 2019. *Resolution on Education for Democracy.* Bangkok, Education International. https://ei-ie.org/en/detail/16429/resolution-on-education-for-democracy.

Enable-Ed and Uganda Society for Disabled Children. 2017. *Inclusive Education in Uganda: Examples of Best Practice.* Kampala, Enable-Ed/Uganda Society for Disabled Children.

Ethiopia Ministry of Education. 2012. *Guideline for Curriculum Differentiation and Individual Education Programme 2012.* Addis Ababa, Ministry of Education.

___. 2016. *A Master Plan for Special Needs Education/Inclusive Education in Ethiopia 2016–2025.* Addis Ababa, Ministry of Education.

ETS. 2013. *The Gordon Commission on the Future of Assessment in Education.* Princeton, NJ, Educational Testing Service. www.ets.org/research/policy_research_reports/gordon_commission.

European Agency for Development in Special Needs Education. 2007. *Assessment in Inclusive Settings: Key Issues for Policy and Practice.* Odense, Denmark, European Agency for Development in Special Needs Education.

___. 2008. *Cyprus Recommendations on Inclusive Assessment.* Odense, Denmark, European Agency for Development in Special Needs Education.

European Commission. 2019. *Portugal: National Reforms in School Education – Curricular Flexibility and Autonomy (Update).* Brussels, Education, Audiovisual and Culture Executive Agency. https://eacea.ec.europa.eu/national-policies/eurydice/content/national-reforms-school-education-53_en. (Accessed 11 December 2019.)

European External Action Service. 2018. *Eswatini Launches New Schools Curriculum Framework, Thanks to EU Support.* Brussels, European External Action Service. https://eeas.europa.eu/delegations/african-union-au/48118/eswatini-launches-new-schools-curriculum-framework-thanks-eu-support_en. (Accessed 11 December 2019.)

Expert Mechanism on the Rights of Indigenous Peoples. 2010. *Trabajo Infantil y Niñez Indígena en América Latina: Encuentro Latinoamericano de Trabajo Infantil, Pueblos Indígenas y Gobiernos – De la Declaración a la Acción [Child Labour and Indigenous Children in Latin America: Latin American Meeting on Child Labour, Indigenous Peoples and Governments – From Declaration to Action].* Geneva, Switzerland, UN Human Rights Council, Expert Mechanism on the Rights of Indigenous Peoples.

Finnish National Board of Education. 2014. *Perusopetuksen Opetussuunnitelman Perusteet 2014 [National Core Curriculum for Basic Education 2014].* Helsinki, National Board of Education.

First Nations Development Institute. 2018. *Research Findings: Compilation of All Research.* Longmont, Colo., First Nations Development Institute/Echo Hawk Consulting. (Reclaiming Native Truth.)

Flecha, R. 2015. *Successful Educational Actions for Inclusion and Social Cohesion in Europe.* Cham, Switzerland, Springer.

Fleisch, B. 2018. *The Education Triple Cocktail: System-Wide Instructional Reform in South Africa.* Cape Town, South Africa, University of Cape Town Press.

Fleisch, B., Gultig, J., Allais, S. and Maringe, F. 2019. *Curriculum Reform, Assessment and National Qualifications Frameworks.* Johannesburg, South Africa, University of the Witwatersrand. (Background paper for *Secondary Education in Africa: Preparing Youth for the Future of Work,* Toronto, Canada, Mastercard Foundation.)

Fuchs, E. and Bock, A. 2018. Introduction. Fuchs, E. and Bock, A. (eds), *The Palgrave Handbook of Textbook Studies.* New York, Palgrave Macmillan US, pp. 1–9.

Fuchs, E., Otto, M. and Yu, S. 2020. *Textbooks and Inclusive Education*. Paris, UNESCO. (Background paper for *Global Education Monitoring Report 2020*.)

Garner, P., Forbes, F., Fergusson, A., Aspland, T. and Datta, P. 2012. *Curriculum, Assessment and Reporting in Special Educational Needs and Disability: A Thematic Overview of Recent Literature*. Sydney, Australia, Australian Curriculum, Assessment and Reporting Authority.

Geldenhuys, J. L. and Wevers, N. E. J. 2013. Ecological aspects influencing the implementation of inclusive education in mainstream primary schools in the Eastern Cape, South Africa. *South African Journal of Education*, Vol. 33, No. 3.

Glatthorn, A. A., Boschee, F., Whitehead, B. M. and Boschee, B. F. 2018. *Curriculum Leadership: Strategies for Development and Implementation*. London, Sage.

Global Partnership for Education. 2018. *Disability and Inclusive Education: A Stocktake of Education Sector Plans and GPE-Funded Grants*. Washington, DC, Global Partnership for Education. (Working Paper.)

Global Voices. 2019. *The Indian State of Odisha Publishes Online Dictionaries in 21 Indigenous Languages*. Global Voices. https://globalvoices.org/2019/10/19/the-indian-state-of-odisha-publishes-online-dictionaries-in-21-indigenous-languages. (Accessed 18 November 2019.)

Hailombe, O. 2011. Education equity and quality in Namibia: a case study of mobile schools in the Kunene region. Ph.D. thesis, Department of Education Management and Policy Studies, University of Pretoria.

Halinen, I. 2018. The new educational curriculum in Finland. Matthes, M., Pulkkinen, L., Clouder, C. and Heys, B. (eds), *Improving the Quality of Childhood in Europe*, Vol. 7. Brussels, Alliance for Childhood European Network Foundation, pp. 75–89.

Hegarty, S. 2020. *Inclusion and Learning Assessment: Policy and practice*. Paris, UNESCO. (Background paper for *Global Education Monitoring Report 2020*.)

Hodkinson, A., Ghajarieh, A. and Salami, A. 2016. An analysis of the cultural representation of disability in school textbooks in Iran and England. *Education 3–13*, Vol. 46, No. 1, pp. 27–36.

Hohenberger, A. 2007. The possible range of variation between sign languages: Universal Grammar, modality, and typological aspects. Perniss, P. M., Pfau, R. and Steinbach, M. (eds), *Visible Variation: Comparative Studies on Sign Language Structure*. Berlin and New York, Mouton de Gruyter. (Trends in Linguistic Studies.)

Hunt, P. F. 2020. *Inclusive Education: Children with Disabilities*. Paris, UNESCO. (Background paper for *Global Education Monitoring Report 2020*.)

IBE. 2008. *Inclusive Education: The Way of the Future*. Paper for International Conference on Education, Geneva, Switzerland, 25–28 November.

___. 2019. *Inclusive Curriculum*. Geneva, Switzerland, UNESCO International Bureau of Education. www.ibe.unesco.org/en/glossary-curriculum-terminology/i/inclusive-curriculum. (Accessed 11 December 2019.)

Illinois Safe Schools Alliance. 2019. *LGBTQ Inclusive Curriculum Bill Approved by Illinois Gov. JB Pritzker*. Chicago, Ill., Illinois Safe Schools Alliance, Public Health Institute of Metropolitan Chicago. www.ilsafeschools.org/latest-news/lgbtq-inclusive-curriculum-bill-approved. (Accessed 11 December 2019.)

Islam, K. M. M. and Asadullah, M. N. 2018. Gender stereotypes and education: a comparative content analysis of Malaysian, Indonesian, Pakistani and Bangladeshi school textbooks. *PLoS ONE*, Vol. 13, No. 1.

Kadenge, M. and Muzengi, M. 2018. Zimbabwean sign language. Kamusella, T. and Ndhlovu, F. (eds), *The Social and Political History of Southern Africa's Languages*. Cham, Switzerland, Springer, pp. 339–46.

Kelly, J. and McKenzie, J. 2018. *Teacher Education: An Analysis of the Availability of Teacher Education Addressing the Educational Needs of Learners with Severe to Profound Sensory or Intellectual Impairments*. Cape Town, University of Cape Town/Christoffel-Blindenmission Deutschland e.V. (Teacher Empowerment for Disability Inclusion.).

Kenya Institute of Curriculum Development. 2017. *Basic Education Curriculum Framework*. Nairobi, Kenya Institute of Curriculum Development.

Kosciw, J. G., Greytak, E. A., Zongrone, A. D., Clark, C. M. and Truong, N. L. 2018. *The 2017 National School Climate Survey: The Experiences of Lesbian, Gay, Bisexual, Transgender, and Queer Youth in Our Nation's Schools*. New York, GLSEN.

Kosonen, K. 2017. *Language of Instruction in Southeast Asia*. Paris, UNESCO. (Background paper for *Global Education Monitoring Report 2017/8*.)

Kwon, K.-A., Elicker, J. and Kontos, S. 2011. Social IEP objectives, teacher talk, and peer interaction in inclusive and segregated preschool settings. *Early Childhood Education Journal*, Vol. 39, No. 4, pp. 267–77.

Laitusis, C., Buzick, H., Stone, E., Hansen, E. and Hakkinen, M. 2012. *Literature Review of Testing Accommodations and Accessibility Tools for Students with Disabilities.* Princeton, NJ, Educational Testing Service.

Laveault, D. and Allal, L. 2016. Implementing assessment for learning: theoretical and practical issues. Laveault, D., Allal, L. (eds), *Assessment for Learning: Meeting the Challenge of Implementation.* Cham, Switzerland, Springer.

Lebeer, J., Birta-Székely, N., Demeter, K., Bohács, K., Candeias, A. A., Sønnesyn, G., Partanen, P. and Dawson, L. 2011. Re-assessing the current assessment practice of children with special education needs in Europe. *School Psychology International,* Vol. 33, No. 1, pp. 69–92.

Leininger, M., Dyches, T. T., Prater, M. A. and Heath, M. A. 2010. Newbery award winning books 1975–2009: How do they portray disabilities? *Education and Training in Autism and Developmental Disabilities,* Vol. 45, No. 4, pp. 583–96.

Lin, M. M. 2019. Malaysia revises 'victim-shaming' school text book. *BBC News,* 16 January.

Little, A. W. (ed.). 2006. *Education for All and Multigrade Teaching: Challenges and Opportunities.* Cham, Switzerland, Springer.

Lo Bianco, J. 2019. Uncompromising talk, linguistic grievance, and language policy: Thailand's Deep South conflict zone. Kelly, M., Footit, H. and Salama-Carr, M. (eds), *The Palgrave Handbook of Languages and Conflict.* London/New York, Palgrave MacMillan, pp. 295–330.

López Navajas, A. and López García-Molins, Á. 2009. *La Presencia de las Mujeres en la E.S.O [The Presence of Women in Compulsory Secondary Education].* Valencia, Spain, University of Valencia. http://meso.uv.es/informe/index.php.

Mahidol University and UNICEF. 2018. *Bridge to a Brighter Tomorrow: The Patani Malay-Thai Multilingual Education Programme.* Bangkok, Research Institute for Languages and Cultures of Asia, Mahidol University/UNICEF.

Malawi Government. 2016. *Convention on the Rights of Persons with Disabilities: Initial and Second State Party Reports.* Lilongwe, Ministry of Justice.

Maurer, E. L., Patrick, J., Britto, L. M. and Millar, H. 2018. *Where Are the Women? A Report on the Status of Women in the United States Social Studies Standards.* Alexandria, Va., National Women's History Museum.

McCausland, D. 2005. *International Experience in the Provision of Individual Education Plans for Children with Disabilities.* Dublin, National Disability Authority.

McEwan, P. J. 2008. Evaluating multigrade school reform in Latin America. *Comparative Education,* Vol. 44, No. 4, pp. 465–83.

McKenzie, J., Kelly, J. and Shanda, N. 2018. *Starting Where We Are: Situational Analysis of the Educational Needs of Learners with Severe to Profound Sensory or Intellectual Impairments in South Africa.* Cape Town, University of Cape Town/Christoffel-Blindenmission Deutschland e.V. (Teacher Empowerment for Disability Inclusion.).

Mercator. 2017. *Dutch Sign Language in the Netherlands.* Leeuwarden, Netherlands, Mercator European Research Centre on Multilingualism and Language Learning. www.mercator-research.eu/wiki/languages:dutch_sign_language_in_nl. (Accessed 11 December 2019.)

Mergia, A. T. 2020. *Inclusive Education Country Profile: Ethiopia.* Paris, UNESCO. (Background paper for *Global Education Monitoring Report 2020.*)

Meyer, A., Rose, D. H. and Gordon, D. 2016. *Universal Design for Learning: Theory and Practice.* Wakefield, Mass., Center for Applied Special Technology.

Mitchell, D. 2014. *What Really Works in Special and Inclusive Education: Using Evidence-Based Teaching Strategies.* Abingdon, UK, Routledge.

Mohanty, A. K. 2019. Language policy in education in India. Kirkpatrick, A. and Liddicoat, A. J. (eds), *Routledge International Handbook of Language Education Policy in Asia.* New York, Routledge.

Mohanty, S. 2017. Education in mother tongue: impact of multilingual education in Odisha. *Economic and Political Weekly,* Vol. 52, No. 7, p. 31.

Moya-Mata, I., Ruiz Sanchis, L., Ruiz, J. M., Pérez Alonso-Geta, P. M. and Ros Ros, C. 2017. La representación de la discapacidad en las imágenes de los libros de texto de Educación Física: ¿inclusión o exclusión? [Representation of disability in physical education textbook images: inclusion or exclusion?]. *Retos. Nuevas Tendencias en Educación Física, Deporte y Recreación,* Vol. 32, No. July–December, pp. 88–95.

Mullaney, T. 2010. *Coming to Terms with the Nation Ethnic Classification in Modern China.* Berkeley, Calif., University of California Press.

Munde-Mana, A. 2019. Malawi: inclusive education that excludes others. *Nyasa Times,* 26 May.

Musengi, M. 2019. *The Right to Sign Language in Inclusive Education Curricula for Deaf Learners: Illustrations from Zimbabwe.* Paper for Inclusion, Mobility and Multilingual Education Conference, Bangkok, 24–26 September.

Musengi, M. and Chireshe, R. 2012. Inclusion of deaf students in mainstream rural primary schools in Zimbabwe: challenges and opportunities. *Studies of Tribes and Tribals*, Vol. 10, No. 2, pp. 107–16.

Musengi, M., Ndofirepi, A. and Shumba, A. 2012. Rethinking education of deaf children in Zimbabwe: challenges and opportunities for teacher education. *Journal of Deaf Studies and Deaf Education*, Vol. 18, No. 1, pp. 62–74.

Namatende-Sakwa, L. 2018. Networked texts: discourse, power and gender neutrality in Ugandan physics textbooks. *Gender and Education*, Vol. 31, No. 3, pp. 362–76.

National Association of the Deaf. 2018. *States that Recognize American Sign Language: List Current as of 2/15/2016*. Silver Spring, Md., National Association of the Deaf.

National Confederation of Disabled People. 2019. *Human Rights and Persons with Disabilities: Alternative Report Greece 2019*. Ilioupoli, Greece, National Confederation of Disabled People.

National Congress of American Indians. 2019. *Becoming Visible: A Landscape Analysis of State Efforts to Provide Native American Education for All*. Washington, DC, National Congress of American Indians.

New Zealand Ministry of Education. 2015. *Effective Pedagogy for All Students*. Wellington, Ministry of Education.

___. 2017. *Implementing an Inclusive Curriculum*. Wellington, Ministry of Education.

New Age. 2017. Santali writing system debate must be ended. 20 April. www.newagebd.net/article/13834/santali-writing-system-debate-must-be-ended (Accessed 15 November 2019.)

News18. 2019. Goodbye, gender stereotypes: Maharashtra school textbooks do away with 'traditional' roles. 21 June.

Ng'asike, J. T. 2019. Indigenous knowledge practices for sustainable lifelong education in pastoralist communities of Kenya. *International Review of Education*, Vol. 65, No. 1, pp. 19–46.

Niehaus, I. 2018. How diverse are our textbooks? Research findings in international perspective. Fuchs, E. and Bock, A. (eds), *The Palgrave Handbook of Textbook Studies*. New York, Palgrave Macmillan, pp. 329–43.

Njeng'ere Kabita, D. and Ji, L. 2017. *The Why, What and How of Competency-Based Curriculum Reforms: The Kenyan Experience*. Geneva, Switzerland, UNESCO International Bureau of Education.

Norway Ministry of Education and Research. 2015. *Curriculum for Physical Education*. Oslo, Ministry of Education and Research.

Nyamnjoh, F. B. 2012. 'Potted plants in greenhouses': a critical reflection on the resilience of colonial education in Africa. *Journal of Asian and African Studies*, Vol. 47, No. 2, pp. 129–54.

O'Mara, A., Akre, B., Munton, T., Marrero-Guillamon, I., Martin, A., Gibson, K., Llewellyn, A., Clift-Matthews, V., Conway, P. and Cooper, C. 2012. *Curriculum and Curriculum Access Issues for Students with Special Educational Needs in Post-Primary Settings: An International Review*. Trim, Ireland, National Council for Special Education (Research Report 10.)

Odisha Government. 2014. *No. XII-SME-SSA 64/2013-14118*. Bhubaneswar, India, Government of Odisha.

OECD. 2016. *PISA 2015 Results: Policies and Practices for Successful Schools – Volume II*. Paris, Organisation for Economic Co-operation and Development.

OHCHR. 2019a. *Civil Society's Suggestions to the UN Committee on the Rights of Persons with Disabilities Regarding the 'List of Issues Prior to Reporting' on the Kingdom of Denmark*. Copenhagen, Disabled People's Organisations Denmark.

___. 2019b. *Concluding Observations on the Initial Report of Turkey*. Geneva, Switzerland, Committee on the Rights of Persons with Disabilities.

Opertti, R. and Ji, L. 2017. *Training Tools for Curriculum Development: Inclusive Student Assessment*. Geneva, Switzerland, UNESCO International Bureau of Education.

Opertti, R., Kang, H. and Magni, G. 2018. *Comparative Analysis of the National Curriculum Frameworks of Five Countries: Brazil, Cambodia, Finland, Kenya and Peru*. Geneva, Switzerland, UNESCO International Bureau of Education. (Current and Critical Issues in Curriculum, Learning and Assessment.)

OSCE. 2018. *'Two Schools Under One Roof': The Most Visible Example of Discrimination in Education in Bosnia and Herzegovina*. Sarajevo, Mission to Bosnia and Herzegovina, Organization for Security and Co-operation in Europe.

Paivandi, S. 2008. *Discrimination and Intolerance in Iran's Textbooks*. Washington, DC, Freedom House.

Peru Ministry of Education. 2016. *Currículo Nacional de la Educación Básica [National Basic Education Curriculum]*. Lima, Ministry of Education.

___. 2017. *Los 6 Mitos del Currículo Nacional [The Six Myths of the National Curriculum]*. Lima, Ministry of Education.

Pietarinen, J., Pyhältö, K. and Soini, T. 2016. Large-scale curriculum reform in Finland: exploring the interrelation between implementation strategy, the function of the reform, and curriculum coherence. *The Curriculum Journal*, Vol. 28, No. 1, pp. 22–40.

Portugal Presidency of the Council of Ministers. 2018. Decreto-Lei n.º 55/2018 [Decree-Law No. 55/2018]. *Diário da República Series 1*, No. 129, pp. 2928–43.

Premsrirat, S. 2019. *Patani Malay: Thai Mother Tongue Based Bi/Multilingual Education in Thailand's 4 Southern Border Provinces*. Salaya, Research Institute for Languages and Cultures of Asia, Mahidol University.

Prengel, A. 2016. Didaktische Diagnostik als Element alltäglicher Lehrerarbeit: 'Formative Assessment' im inklusiven Unterricht [Didactic diagnostics as an element of everyday teacher work: 'formative assessment' in inclusive lessons]. Amrhein, B. and Ziemen, K. (eds), *Diagnostik im Kontext inklusiver Bildung: Theorien, Ambivalenzen, Akteure, Konzepte [Diagnostics in the Context of Inclusive Education: Theories, Ambivalences, Actors, Concepts]*. Bad Heilbrunn, Germany, Klinkhardt.

Pritchard, A. E., Koriakin, T., Carey, L., Bellows, A., Jacobson, L. and Mahone, E. M. 2016. Academic testing accommodations for ADHD: Do they help? *Learning Disabilities: A Multidisciplinary Journal*, Vol. 21, No. 2, pp. 67–78.

Pritchett, L. and Beatty, A. 2012. *The Negative Consequences of Overambitious Curricula in Developing Countries*. Cambridge, Mass., John F. Kennedy School of Government, Harvard University. (Research Working Paper 12–035.)

Queensland Government. 2017. *2016 State Review Panel Report: Moderation of Authority Subjects Offered in 2016*. South Brisbane, Australia, Queensland Curriculum and Assessment Authority. (State Reviews Panel Reports.)

Reid, G. 2016. *Dyslexia: A Practitioner's Handbook*. Hoboken, NJ, Wiley-Blackwell.

Republic of Korea Ministry of Gender Equality and Family. 2018. 교과서 속의 성차별, 이렇게 바꿔주세요! [Gender discrimination in textbooks, change it like this!]. Seoul, Ministry of Gender Equality and Family. www.mogef.go.kr/nw/enw/nw_enw_s001d.do;jsessionid=RAKBAWd9vB1YlyW8VGCwsAkL.mogef21?mid=mda700&bbtSn=706569. (Accessed 11 December 2019.)

Rogers, C. M., Lazarus, S. S. and Thurlow, M. L. 2016. *A Summary of the Research on the Effects of Test Accommodations: 2013–2014*. Minneapolis, Minn., National Center on Educational Outcomes, University of Minnesota. (NCEO Report 402.)

Rosky, C. 2017. Anti-Gay Curriculum Laws. *Columbia Law Review*, Vol. 117, pp. 1461–541.

Royal Dutch Kentalis. 2019. *The Reading Project, a Method to Develop the Literacy Skills of Young Deaf Children in Africa*. Sint-Michielsgestel, Netherlands, Kentalis International. https://www.kentalis.com/reading-project-method-develop-literacy-skills-young-deaf-children-africa. (Accessed 11 December 2019.)

Sarker, P. and Davey, G. 2009. Exclusion of indigenous children from primary education in the Rajshahi Division of northwestern Bangladesh. *International Journal of Inclusive Education*, Vol. 13, No. 1, pp. 1–11.

Sarvarzade, S. and Wotipka, C. M. 2017. The rise, removal, and return of women: gender representations in primary-level textbooks in Afghanistan, 1980–2010. *Comparative Education*, Vol. 53, No. 4, pp. 578–99.

Schaefli, L., Godlewska, A. and Lamb, C. 2019. Securing indigenous dispossession through education: an analysis of Canadian curricula and textbooks. Jahnke, H., Kramer, C. and Meusburger, P. (eds), *Geographies of Schooling, Knowledge and Space 14*. Cham, Switzerland, Springer, pp. 145–61.

Schmelkes, S. 2018. What is 'learning' in the case of marginalized populations in low-income countries? Wagner, D. A., Wolf, S. and Boruch, R. F. (eds), *Learning at the Bottom of the Pyramid: Science, Measurement, and Policy in Low-Income Countries*. Paris, UNESCO International Institute of Educational Planning.

Scierri, I. D. M. 2017. Stereotipi di genere nei sussidiari di lettura per la scuola primaria [Gender stereotypes in supplementary reading in primary schools]. *Gender Rivista Internationale di Studi di Genere*, Vol. 6, No. 12.

Scotland Government. 2018. *LGBTI Education: Scotland Will Lead the Way in Inclusive Education*. Edinburgh, UK, Scottish Government. www.gov.scot/news/lgbti-education. (Accessed 11 December 2019.)

Selaibeekh, L. 2017. Citizenship Education in Bahrain: An Investigation of the Perceptions and Understandings of Policymakers, Teachers and Pupils. Ph.D. thesis, School of Politics, Faculty of Arts and Human Sciences, University of Surrey, Guildford, UK.

Sharif, S. 2014. Education and skill development of Santal children and youth in Bangladesh. *Bangladesh Education Journal*, Vol. 13, No. 1, pp. 7–26.

Shear, S. B., Knowles, R. T., Soden, G. J. and Castro, A. J. 2015. Manifesting destiny: re/presentations of Indigenous peoples in K–12 U.S. history standards. *Theory and Research in Social Education*, Vol. 43, No. 1, pp. 68–101.

Siddique, A. and Vlassopoulos, M. 2020. Competitive preferences and ethnicity: experimental evidence from Bangladesh. *Economic Journal*, Vol. 130, No. 627, pp. 793–821.

Smit, R. and Humpert, W. 2012. Differentiated instruction in small schools. *Teaching and Teacher Education*, Vol. 28, No. 8, pp. 1152–62.

South Africa Department of Basic Education. 2019. *Textbook Evaluation Report of the Ministerial Task Team: Evaluation of a Broad Sample of Existing Textbooks and Learning Materials Towards Developing a Textbook Policy that Promotes Diversity.* Pretoria, Department of Basic Education.

South Carolina Code of Laws. 2013. *Title 59 – Education; Chapter 32 – Comprehensive Health Education Program; Section 59-32-30. Local School Boards to Implement Comprehensive Health Education Program; Guidelines and Restrictions.* Columbia, S.C., South Carolina Legislature.

Spielman, A. 2017. *HMCI's Commentary: Recent Primary and Secondary Curriculum Research.* London, Ofsted. www.gov.uk/government/speeches/hmcis-commentary-october-2017. (Accessed 11 December 2019.)

Ssentanda, M. 2014. The challenges of teaching reading in Uganda: curriculum guidelines and language policy viewed from the classroom. *Apples – Journal of Applied Language Studies*, Vol. 8, No. 2, pp. 1–22.

Ssentanda, M., Southwood, F. and Huddlestone, K. 2019. Curriculum expectations versus teachers' opinions and practices in teaching English in rural primary schools in Uganda. *Language Matters*, Vol. 50, No. 2, pp. 141–63.

Stevenson, B. and Zlotnick, H. 2018. Representations of men and women in introductory economics textbooks. *AEA Papers and Proceedings*, Vol. 108, pp. 180–85.

Stoianova, A. and Angermann, M. 2018. The HCNM impact on minority and state language promotion and on the social integration of diverse societies through education: the cases of Kazakhstan and Kyrgyzstan. Ulasiuk, I., Hadîrcă, L. and Romans, W. (eds), *Language Policy and Conflict Prevention.* Leiden, Netherlands, Brill | Nijhoff, pp. 93-120.

Stone-Macdonald, A. and Fettig, A. 2019. Culturally relevant assessment and support of grade 1 students with mild disabilities in Tanzania: an exploratory study. *International Journal of Disability, Development and Education*, Vol. 66, No. 4, pp. 374–88.

Surk, B. 2018. In a divided Bosnia, segregated schools persist. *The New York Times,* 1 December.

Tedesco, J. C., Opertti, R. and Ginebra, M. A. 2013. *Porqué importa Hoy el Debate Curricular [Why the Curriculum Debate Matters Today].* Geneva, Switzerland, UNESCO International Bureau of Education. (IBE Working Papers on Curriculum Issues.)

Texas Health and Safety Code. 2018. *Chapter 163: Education Program about Sexual Conduct and Substance Abuse – Sec. 163.002, Instructional Elements.* Austin, Tex., Texas Legislature Online.

Thai PBS News. 2019. *สำเร็จ! บรรจุหลักสูตร "ความหลากหลายทางเพศ" ตั้งแต่ ป.1 [Success! Packing course 'Sexual Diversity' from Primary 1].* Bangkok, Thai PBS News. https://news.thaipbs.or.th/content/280153.

Thurlow, M. L. 2013. Instructional and assessment accommodations in the 21st century. Florian, L. (ed.), *The SAGE Handbook of Special Education.* London, Sage, pp. 597–612.

Tremblay, P. 2013. Comparative outcomes of two instructional models for students with learning disabilities: inclusion with co-teaching and solo-taught special education. *Journal of Research in Special Educational Needs*, Vol. 13, No. 4, pp. 251–58.

U. R. Tanzania Ministry of Education, Science and Technology. 2018. *Education Sector Development Plan (2016/17–2020/21) Tanzania Mainland.* Dar es Salaam, Ministry of Education, Science and Technology.

UNECE. 2014. *National Review of the Republic of Armenia on Implementation of the Beijing Declaration and Platform for Action (1995) and the Outcomes of the Twenty-Third Special Session of the General Assembly (2000) in the Context of the Twentieth Anniversary of the Fourth World Conference on Women and the Adoption of the Beijing Declaration and Platform for Action 2015.* Geneva, Switzerland, United Nations Economic Commission for Europe.

UNESCO. 2015. *From Insult to Inclusion: Asia-Pacific Report on School Bullying, Violence and Discrimination on the basis of Sexual Orientation and Gender Identity.* Paris/Bangkok, UNESCO.

___. 2016a. *If You Don't Understand, How Can You Learn?* Paris, UNESCO. (Global Education Monitoring Report Policy Paper 24.)

___. 2016b. *Out in the Open.* Paris, UNESCO.

___. 2016c. *Textbooks Pave the Way to Sustainable Development.* Paris, UNESCO. (Global Education Monitoring Report Policy Paper 28.)

___. 2017. *Making Textbook Content Inclusive: A Focus on Religion, Gender, and Culture.* Paris, UNESCO.

___. 2018. *Ensuring the Right to Equitable and Inclusive Quality Education: Results of the Ninth Consultation of Member States on the Implementation of the UNESCO Convention and Recommendation against Discrimination in Education.* Paris, UNESCO.

___. 2019. *Beyond Commitments: How Countries Implement SDG 4.* Paris, Global Education Monitoring Report.

UNESCO and UNFPA. 2012. *Sexuality Education: A Ten-Country Review of School Curricula in East and Southern Africa.* Paris/New York, UNESCO/UNFPA.

UNICEF. 2014. *Thailand Case Study in Education, Conflict and Social Cohesion.* Bangkok, UNICEF East Asia and Pacific Regional Office.

___. 2016. *The Impact of Language Policy and Practice on Children's Learning: Evidence from Eastern and Southern Africa.* Nairobi, UNICEF.

___. 2019. *Early Literacy and Multilingual Education in South Asia.* Kathmandu, UNICEF.

United Nations. 2001. *Annex IX General Comment No. 1 (2001): Article 29 (1) – The Aims of Education,* United Nations.

United Nations General Assembly. 1994. *Standard Rules on the Equalization of Opportunities for Persons with Disabilities: Adopted by General Assembly resolution 48/96 of 20 December 1993.* New York, United Nations General Assembly.

US Code. 2011. *Title 20 Education. Chapter 33: –Education of Individuals with Disabilities. Subchapter I – General Provisions. §1400. Short Title; Findings; Purposes.* Washington, DC, U.S. Government Publishing Office.

US Department of Education. 2010. *National Education Technology Plan 2010: Transforming American Education Learning Powered by Technology.* Washington, DC, Office of Educational Technology, Department of Education.

US Office of the Federal Registers. 2019. *Title 34 - Education. Subtitle B - Regulations of the Offices of the Department of Education. Chapter III. Part 300. Assistance to States for the Education of Children with Disabilities.* Washington, DC, Office of the Federal Registers.

Uzbekistan Ministry of Education. 2019. *Education Sector Plan (ESP) of Uzbekistan 2019–2023.* Tashkent, Ministry of Education.

Victoria State Government. 2016. *The Education State: Review of the Program for Students with Disabilities.* Melbourne, Australia, Department of Education and Training Victoria.

VSO and Deaf Child WorldWide. 2018. *Achieving Academic Excellence for Deaf Learners: The Influence of Early Exposure to Rich Language.* London, VSO/Deaf Child Worldwide.

Ware, J., Butler, C., Robertson, C., O'Donnell, M. and Gould, M. 2011. *Access to the Curriculum for Pupils with a Variety of Special Educational Needs in Mainstream Classes: An Exploration of the Experiences of Young Pupils in Primary School.* Trim, Ireland, National Council for Special Education. (Research Report 8.)

Warotamasikkhadit, U. and Person, K. 2011. Development of the National Language Policy (2006–2010): Committee to Draft the National Language Policy. *The Journal of the Royal Institute of Thailand,* Vol. III.

Wauters, L., Knoors, H., Aarnoutse, C. and Vervloed, M. 2001. Dove kinderen leren lezen: perspectieven van woordherkenningstraining [Deaf children learn to read: perspectives of word recognition training]. *Pedagogische Studiën,* Vol. 78, pp. 256–70.

Webb, A. and Radcliffe, S. 2013. Mapuche demands during educational reform, the Penguin Revolution and the Chilean Winter of Discontent. *Studies in Ethnicity and Nationalism,* Vol. 13, No. 3, pp. 319–41.

WHO. 2018. *Deafness.* Geneva, Switzerland, World Health Organization. www.who.int/news-room/facts-in-pictures/detail/deafness.

WIPO. 2016. *Main Provisions and Benefits of the Marrakesh Treaty (2013).* Geneva, Switzerland, World Intellectual Property Organization.

Wood, B. 2017. Senate approves lifting ban on 'advocacy of homosexuality' in Utah schools. *The Salt Lake Tribune,* 1 March.

Wopperer, E. 2011. Inclusive literature in the library and the classroom: the importance of young adult and children's books that portray characters with disabilities. *Journal of the American Association of School Librarians* Vol. 39, No. 3.

World Bank. 2015. *Indigenous Latin America in the Twenty-First Century: The First Decade.* Washington, DC, World Bank.

World Bank, Inclusion International and Leonard Cheshire. 2019. *Every Learner Matters: Unpacking the Learning Crisis for Children with Disabilities.* Washington, DC, World Bank.

World Federation of the Deaf. 2017. *The Legal Recognition of Sign Languages by Country.* Helsinki, World Federation of the Deaf. https://wfdeaf.org/news/resources/legal-recognition-sign-languages-country. (Accessed 11 December 2019.)

Yan, F. and Vickers, E. 2019. Portraying 'minorities' in Chinese history textbooks of the 1990s and 2000s: the advance and retreat of ethnocultural inclusivity. *Asia Pacific Journal of Education,* Vol. 39, No. 2, pp. 190–208.

CHAPTER 6

Ahmmed, M., Sharma, U. and Deppeler, J. 2012. Variables affecting teachers' attitudes towards inclusive education in Bangladesh. *Journal of Research in Special Educational Needs,* Vol. 12, No. 3, pp. 132–40.

Albert, G., Matache, M., Taba, M. and Zimová, A. 2015. *Segregation of Roma Children in Education: Successes and Challenges.* Budapest, Roma Education Fund.

Alisic, E., Bus, M., Dulack, W., Pennings, L. and Splinter, J. 2012. Teachers' experiences supporting children after traumatic exposure. *Journal of Traumatic Stress,* Vol. 25, No. 1, pp. 98–101.

Bakhshi, P. 2020. *Unpacking Inclusion in Education: Lessons from Afghanistan for Achieving SDG 4.* Paris, UNESCO. (Background paper for *Global Education Monitoring Report 2020.*)

Ball, J. and Smith, M. 2019. *Independent Evaluation of the Multilingual Education National Action Plan in Cambodia: Final Report – Volume I.* Phnom Penh, UNICEF.

Banerjee, A., Banerji, R., Berry, J., Duflo, E., Kannan, H., Mukerji, S., Shotland, M. and Walton, M. 2017. *Using Learning Camps to Improve Basic Learning Outcomes of Primary School Children in India.* Cambridge, Mass., J-PAL, Abdul Latif Jameel Poverty Action Lab.

Ben-Peretz, M. and Flores, M. A. 2018. Tensions and paradoxes in teaching: implications for teacher education. *European Journal of Teacher Education,* Vol. 41, No. 2, pp. 202–13.

BEQUAL. 2018. *Gender and Inclusive Education Strategy.* Vientiane, BEQUAL Consortium.

Bett, H. K. 2016. The cascade model of teachers' continuing professional development in Kenya: a time for change? *Cogent Education,* Vol. 3, No. 1.

Blatchford, P., Bassett, P., Brown, P. and Webster, R. 2009. The effect of support staff on pupil engagement and individual attention. *British Educational Research Journal,* Vol. 35, No. 5, pp. 661–86.

Borker, G. 2017. Tribal identity in education: Does teacher ethnicity affect student performance? Providence, RI, Brown University. (Unpublished.)

Burns, E. and Bell, S. 2010. Voices of teachers with dyslexia in Finnish and English further and higher educational settings. *Teachers and Teaching,* Vol. 16, No. 5, pp. 529–43.

Butt, R. 2018. 'Pulled in off the street' and available: What qualifications and training do teacher assistants really need? *International Journal of Inclusive Education,* Vol. 22, No. 3, pp. 217–34.

Cambodia Ministry of Education, Youth and Sport. 2015. *Teacher Policy Action Plan.* Phnom Penh, Ministry of Education, Youth and Sport.

Canada Public Health Agency. 2018. *Autism Spectrum Disorder among Children and Youth in Canada 2018: Report of the National Autism Spectrum Disorder Surveillance System.* Ottawa, Public Health Agency of Canada.

Carew, M. T., Deluca, M., Groce, N. and Kett, M. 2019. The impact of an inclusive education intervention on teacher preparedness to educate children with disabilities within the Lakes Region of Kenya. *International Journal of Inclusive Education,* Vol. 23, No. 3, pp. 229–44.

Carlana, M. 2019. Implicit stereotypes: evidence from teachers' gender bias. *Quarterly Journal of Economics,* Vol. 134, No. 3, pp. 1163–1224.

Catholic Relief Services. 2016. *Right to Learn: An Inclusive Approach to Education.* Baltimore, Md., Catholic Relief Services.

CBM. 2018a. *Case Study on Callan Network.* Bensheim, Germany, Christoffel-Blindenmission.

___. 2018b. *My Right Is Our Future: The Transformative Power of Disability-Inclusive Education.* Bensheim, Germany, Christoffel-Blindenmission.

Census India. 2011. *Scheduled Castes and Scheduled Tribes Population.* New Delhi, India Office of the Registrar General and Census Commissioner. http://censusindia.gov.in/Census_Data_2001/India_at_glance/scst.aspx. (Accessed 24 September 2019.)

Cherng, H.-Y. S. and Halpin, P. F. 2016. The importance of minority teachers: student perceptions of minority versus white teachers. *Educational Researcher,* Vol. 45, No. 7, pp. 407–20.

Chile Ministry of Education. 2017. *Educación para la Igualdad de Género Plan 2015–2018 [Education for Gender Equality Plan 2015–2018].* Santiago, Ministry of Education.

Chopra, R. V. and Giangreco, M. F. 2019. Effective use of teacher assistants in inclusive classrooms. Schuelka, M. J., Johnstone, C. J., Thomas, G. and Artiles, A. J. (eds), *The SAGE Handbook of Inclusion and Diversity in Education.* London, Sage, pp. 193–207.

Chounlamany, K. 2014. School education reform in Lao PDR: good intentions and tensions? *Revue Internationale d'éducation de Sèvres. Colloque: L'Éducation en Asie en 2014: Quels Enjeux Mondiaux? [Colloquium on Education in Asia in 2014: What Global Issues?]*.

Cochran-Smith, M. and Dudley-Marling, C. 2012. Diversity in teacher education and special education: the issues that divide. *Journal of Teacher Education*, Vol. 63, No. 4, pp. 237–44.

Colbert, V. and Arboleda, J. 2016. Bringing a student-centered participatory pedagogy to scale in Colombia. *Journal of Educational Change*, Vol. 17, No. 4, pp. 385–410.

Colombia Ministry of National Education. 2013. *Lineamientos: Política de Educación Superior Inclusiva [Guidelines: Inclusive Higher Education Policy]*. Bogotá, Ministry of National Education.

Cook Islands Ministry of Education. 2010. *Towards an Inclusive Society: The Cook Islands Inclusive Education Policy*. Avarua, Ministry of Education.

___. 2014. *Education for All 2015 National Review Report: Cook Islands*. Paris, UNESCO.

___. 2017a. *2017 Education Statistics Report*. Avarua, Ministry of Education.

___. 2017b. *Inclusive Education*. Avarua, Ministry of Education. (Draft.)

Coyle, D., Hood, P. and Marsh, D. 2010. *CLIL: Content and Language Integrated Learning*. Cambridge, UK, Cambridge University Press.

CREW. 2017. *46 Secondary School Teachers Trained on Gender Based Violence Prevention and Response*. Juba, Crown the Woman. https://crownthewoman.org/46-secondary-school-teachers-trained-on-gender-based-violence-prevention-and-response. (Accessed 12 June 2019.)

Cuba Ministry of Education. 2011. *Resolucion Ministerial n. 134/2011 [Ministerial Resolution 134/2011]*. Havana, Ministry of Education.

Deluca, M., Pinilla-Roncancio, M. and Kett, M. 2017. *Promoting the Provision of Inclusive Primary Education for Children with Disabilities in Mashonaland, West Province, Zimbabwe*. London, University College London.

Donlevy, V., Meierkord, A. and Rajania, A. 2017. *Study on the Diversity within the Teaching Profession with Particular Focus on Migrant and/or Minority Background*. Brussels, Directorate-General for Education, Youth, Sport and Culture, European Commission.

Dowd, A. J., Friedlander, E., Guajardo, J., Mann, N. and Pisani, L. 2013. *Literacy Boost: Cross Country Analysis Results*. Fairfield, Conn., Save the Children.

Education International. 2017. *Education Support Personnel*. Brussels, Education International. https://ei-ie.org/en/detail_page/4646/education-support-personnel. (Accessed 26 March 2019.)

___. 2018. *Are We There Yet? Education Unions Assess the Bumpy Road to Inclusive Education*. Brussels, Education International.

Egalite, A. J., Kisida, B. and Winters, M. A. 2015. Representation in the classroom: the effect of own-race teachers on student achievement. *Economics of Education Review*, Vol. 45, pp. 44–52.

Elder, B. C. and Kuja, B. 2019. Going to school for the first time: inclusion committee members increasing the number of students with disabilities in primary schools in Kenya. *International Journal of Inclusive Education*, Vol. 23, No. 3, pp. 261–79.

Engelbrecht, P., Nel, M., Smit, S. and van Deventer, M. 2016. The idealism of education policies and the realities in schools: the implementation of inclusive education in South Africa. *International Journal of Inclusive Education*, Vol. 20, No. 5, pp. 520–35.

Espinosa, O. 2017. Educación superior para indígenas de la Amazonía peruana: balance y desafíos [Higher education for Indigenous peoples of the Peruvian Amazon region: record and challenges]. *Anthropologica*, Vol. 35, pp. 99–122.

European Agency for Special Needs and Inclusive Education. 2010. *Policy Review on Teacher Education for Inclusion*. Odense, Denmark, European Agency for Special Needs and Inclusive Education.

___. 2012. *Teacher Education for Inclusion: Profile of Inclusive Teachers*. Odense, Denmark, European Agency for Special Needs and Inclusive Education.

___. 2015. *Empowering Teachers to Promote Inclusive Education: A Case Study of Approaches to Trainiing and Support for Inclusive Teacher Practice*. Odense, Denmark, European Agency for Special Needs and Inclusive Education.

Ewing, D., Monsen, J. and Kielblock, S. 2017. Teachers' attitudes towards inclusive education: a critical review of published questionnaires. *Educational Psychology in Practice*, Vol. 34, pp. 1–16.

Fiji Ministry of Education, Heritage and Arts. 2016. *Policy on Special and Inclusive Education.* Suva, Ministry of Education, Heritage and Arts.

Florian, L. 2019. Preparing teachers for inclusive education. Peters, M. (ed.), *Encyclopedia of Teacher Education.* Singapore, Springer.

Florian, L. and Pantić, N. 2017. Teacher education for the changing demographics of schooling: pathways for future research. Florian, L. and Pantić, N. (eds), *Teacher Education for the Changing Demographics of Schooling: Issues for Research and Practice.* Cham, Switzerland, Springer, pp. 229–36.

Florian, L. and Spratt, J. 2013. Enacting inclusion: a framework for interrogating inclusive practice. *European Journal of Special Needs Education,* Vol. 28, No. 2, pp. 119–35.

FNPH. 2018. *Rapport Alternatif sur la Mise en Œuvre de l'Agenda 2030 au Niger [Altervative Report on Implementation of the 2030 Agenda in Niger].* Niamey, Fédération Nigérienne des Personnes Handicapées.

Furuta, H. and Alwis, K. A. C. 2017. Teaching students with special educational needs in an inclusive educational setting in Sri Lanka: regular class teacher's view. *Journal of International Cooperation in Education,* Vol. 19, No. 2, pp. 1–18.

Gazeley, L. 2012. The impact of social class on parent–professional interaction in school exclusion processes: deficit or disadvantage? *International Journal of Inclusive Education,* Vol. 16, No. 3, pp. 297–311.

Ghana Ministry of Education. 2015. *Inclusive Education Policy.* Accra, Ministry of Education.

Global Partnership for Education. 2018. *Summative Evaluation of GPE's Country-level Support to Education.* Washington, DC, Global Partnership for Education.

Griffiths, S. 2012. 'Being dyslexic doesn't make me less of a teacher'. School placement experiences of student teachers with dyslexia: strengths, challenges and a model for support. *Journal of Research in Special Educational Needs,* Vol. 12, No. 2, pp. 54–65.

Hannås, B. M. and Bahdanovich Hanssen, N. 2016. Special needs education in light of the inclusion principle: an exploratory study of special needs education practice in Belarusian and Norwegian preschools. *European Journal of Special Needs Education,* Vol. 31, No. 4, pp. 520–34.

Hayes, A., Turnbull, A. and Moran, N. 2018. *Universal Design for Learning to Help All Children Read: Promoting Literacy for Learners with Disabilities.* Washington, DC, US Agency for International Development.

Hehir, T., Grindal, T., Freeman, B., Lamoreau, R., Borquaye, Y. and Burke, S. 2016. *A Summary of the Research Evidence on Inclusive Education.* São Paulo, Brazil, Instituto Alana.

Honkasilta, J., Ahtiainen, R., Hienonen, N. and Jahnukainen, M. 2019. Inclusive and special education and the question of equity in education: the case of Finland. Schuelka, M. J., Johnstone, C. J., Thomas, G. and Artiles, A. J. (eds), *The SAGE Handbook of Inclusion and Diversity in Education.* London, Sage, pp. 481–95.

Humanity and Inclusion. 2017. *West Africa: Breaking Down Barriers So Kids Can Attend School* London, Humanity and Inclusion. www.hi-us.org/west_africa_breaking_down_barriers_so_kid_s_can_attend_school. (Accessed 15 May 2019.)

___. 2018. *Tchad [Chad].* Lyon, Handicap International. https://handicap-international.fr/fr/pays/tchad. (Accessed 11 December 2019.)

IBE. 2017. *A Resource Pack for Gender-responsive STEM Education.* Geneva, Switzerland, UNESCO International Bureau of Education

ILGA Europe. 2019. *Annual Review of the Human Rights Situation of Lesbian, Gay, Bisexual, Trans and Intersex People.* Brussels, International Lesbian, Gay, Bisexual, Trans and Intersex Association Europe.

Ireland Department of Education and Skills. 2017. *Guidelinesfor Primary Schools Supporting Pupils with Special Educational Needs in Mainstream Schools.* Dublin, Department of Education and Skills.

Kartika, D. and Kuroda, K. 2019. Implications for teacher training and support for inclusive education: empirical evidence from Cambodia. Schuelka, M. J., Johnstone, C. J., Thomas, G. and Artiles, A. J. (eds), *The SAGE Handbook of Inclusion and Diversity in Education.* London, Sage, pp. 446–67.

Khochen, M. and Radford, J. 2012. Attitudes of teachers and headteachers towards inclusion in Lebanon. *International Journal of Inclusive Education,* Vol. 16, No. 2, pp. 139–53.

Lamichhane, K. 2016. Individuals with visual impairments teaching in Nepal's mainstream schools: a model for inclusion. *International Journal of Inclusive Education,* Vol. 20, No. 1, pp. 16–31.

Lao PDR Ministry of Education. 2005. *Education for All: National Plan of Action, 2003–15.* Bangkok, UNESCO.

Lao PDR Ministry of Education and Sports. 2015. *Education and Sports Sector Development Plan (2016–2020).* Vientiane, Ministry of Education and Sports.

Le, H. M. 2018. The reproduction of 'best practice': following Escuela Nueva to the Philippines and Vietnam. *International Journal of Educational Development,* Vol. 62, pp. 9–16.

Lehtomäki, E., Posti-Ahokas, H., Beltrán, A., Edjah, H., Hirvonen, M., Juma, S., Mulat, M. and Shaw, C. 2020. *Teacher Education for Inclusion.* Paris, UNESCO. (Background paper for *Global Education Monitoring Report 2020.*)

Lindsay, S., Cagliostro, E., Albarico, M., Mortaji, N. and Karon, L. 2018. A systematic review of the benefits of hiring people with disabilities. *Journal of Occupational Rehabilitation,* Vol. 28, No. 4, pp. 634–55.

Main, S., Chambers, D. J. and Sarah, P. 2016. Supporting the transition to inclusive education: teachers' attitudes to inclusion in the Seychelles. *International Journal of Inclusive Education,* Vol. 20, No. 12, pp. 1270–85.

Makhalemele, T. and Payne-van Staden, I. 2018. Enhancing teachers' self-efficacy within full-service schools: a disregarded aspect by the District-Based Support Team. *International Journal of Inclusive Education,* Vol. 22, No. 9, pp. 983–96.

Masdeu Navarro, F. 2015. *Learning Support Staff: A Literature Review.* Paris, Organisation for Economic Co-operation and Development. (Education Working Paper 125.)

Miesera, S. and Gebhardt, M. 2018. Inclusive vocational schools in Canada and Germany: a comparison of vocational pre-service teachers attitudes, self-efficacy and experiences towards inclusive education. *European Journal of Special Needs Education,* Vol. 33, No. 5, pp. 707–22.

Mora, R. A., Chiquito, T. and Zapata, J. D. 2019. Bilingual education policies in Colombia: seeking relevant and sustainable frameworks for meaningful minority inclusion. Johannessen, B. G. G., (ed.), *Bilingualism and Bilingual Education: Politics, Policies and Practices in a Globalized Society.* Cham, Switzerland, Springer, pp. 55–77.

Namibia Ministry of Education. 2013. *Sector Policy on Inclusive Education.* Windhoek, Ministry of Education.

NASUWT. 2015. *Disabled Teachers' Consultation Conference.* London, NASUWT: The Teachers' Union.

New Brunswick Government. 2019. *Autism Learning Partnership: Building Collective Capacity for Supporting Learners with Autism.* Fredericton, Canada, Department of Education and Early Childhood Development.

NUEPA. 2016. *Teachers in the Indian Education System.* New Delhi, National University of Educational Planning and Administration.

O'Nions, H. 2010. Divide and teach: educational inequality and the Roma. *International Journal of Human Rights,* Vol. 14, No. 3, pp. 464–89.

OECD. 2009. *Reviews of National Policies for Education: Kazakhstan, Kyrgyz Republic and Tajikistan 2009 – Students with Special Needs and Those with Disabilities.* Paris, Organsation for Economic Co-operation and Development.

___. 2019. *TALIS 2018 Results (Volume I): Teachers and School Leaders as Lifelong Learners.* Paris, Organisation for Economic Co-operation and Development.

OECD and World Bank. 2015. *OECD Reviews of School Resources: Kazakhstan.* Paris, Organisation for Economic Co-operation and Development.

OHCHR. 2016. *Initial Report Submitted by Singapore under Article 35 of the Convention.* New York, United Nations Committee for the Rights of Persons with Disabilities.

___. 2017. *Consideration of Reports Submitted by States Parties under Article 18 of the Convention: Sixth Periodic Report of States Parties Due in 2015: Nepal.* New York, United Nations Committee on the Elimination of Discrimination Against Women.

___. 2018. *Initial Report Submitted by Bangladesh under Article 35 of the Convention.* New York, United Nations Committee on the Rights of Persons with Disabilities.

___. 2019. *Initial Report Submitted by Viet Nam under Article 35 of the Convention.* New York, United Nations Committee on the Rights of Persons with Disabilities.

Osorio Vázquez, M. C. 2017. *Understanding Girls' Education in Indigenous Maya Communities in the Yucatán Peninsula: Implications for Policy and Practice.* Washington, DC, Brookings Institution.

Peru Ministy of Education. 2016. *Plan Nacional de Educación Intercultural Bilingüeal 2021 [National Plan for Bilingual Intercultural Education 2021].* Lima, Ministry of Education.

Pink Ambasada. 2018. 66% of Albanian teachers stay silent when pupils are bullied because of homophobia and transphobia. Tirana, Pink Ambasada. www.pinkembassy.al/en/66-albanian-teachers-stay-silent-when-pupils-are-bullied-because-homophobia-and-transphobia. (Accessed 23 June 2019.)

Porter, G. L. and AuCoin, A. 2012. *Strengthening Inclusion, Strengthening Schools: Report of the Review of Inclusive Education Programs and Practices in New Brunswick Schools – An Action Plan for Growth.* Fredericton, Canada, Government of New Brunswick.

Porter, G. L. and Towell, D. 2017. *Advancing Inclusive Education: Keys to Transformational Change in Public Education Systems*. Toronto, Canada, Inclusive Education Canada/Centre for Inclusive Futures.

Pratham. 2020. *Teaching at the Right Level: From Concern with Exclusion to Challenges of Implementation*. Paris, UNESCO. (Background paper for *Global Education Monitoring Report 2020*.)

Queensland Department of Education. 2019. *Rural and Remote Incentives*. Brisbane, Australia, Queensland Government. https://teach.qld.gov.au/teaching-with-us/pay-and-benefits/rural-remote-incentives. (Accessed 14 May 2019.)

Quinn, D. M. 2017. Racial attitudes of preK–12 and postsecondary educators: descriptive evidence from nationally representative data. *Educational Researcher,* Vol. 46, No. 7, pp. 397–411.

Radford, J., Bosanquet, P., Webster, R. and Blatchford, P. 2015. Scaffolding learning for independence: clarifying teacher and teaching assistant roles for children with special educational needs. *Learning and Instruction,* Vol. 36, pp. 1–10.

Rahaman, M. M. 2017. Inclusive education aspirations: exploration of policy and practice in Bangladesh secondary schools. Ph.D. thesis, University of Canterbury, New Zealand.

Rose, R. 2020. *The Use of Teacher Assistants and Education Support Personnel in Inclusive Education*. Paris, UNESCO. (Background paper for *Global Education Monitoring Report 2020*.)

Rouse, M. and Florian, L. 2012. *The Inclusive Practice Project: Final Report*. Aberdeen, UK, University of Aberdeen.

Save the Children. 2019. *Children's Literacy Programs: Literacy Boost*. Fairfield, Conn., Save the Children. www.savethechildren.org/us/what-we-do/global-programs/education/literacy-boost. (Accessed 9 December 2019.)

Scottish Government. 2018. *LGBTI Inclusive Education Working Group: Report to the Scottish Ministers*. Edinburgh, UK, Scottish Government.

Sharma, U. and Salend, S. 2016. Teaching assistants in inclusive classrooms: a systematic analysis of the international research. *Australian Journal of Teacher Education,* Vol. 36, No. 3, pp. 118–34.

Shastri, P. 2019. Gujarat government to identify dyslexia, learning disabilities early. *Times of India,* 31 January.

Singal, N., Pedder, D., Malathy, D., Shanmugam, M., Manickavasagam, S. and Govindarasan, M. 2018. Insights from within activity based learning (ABL) classrooms in Tamil Nadu, India: teachers perspectives and practices. *International Journal of Educational Development,* Vol. 60, pp. 165–71.

Song, S. 2015. Cambodian teachers' responses to child-centered instructional policies: a mismatch between beliefs and practices. *Teaching and Teacher Education,* Vol. 50, pp. 36–45.

South Africa Department of Basic Education. 2010. *Guidelines for Inclusive Teaching and Learning*. Pretoria, Department of Basic Education.

___. 2011. *Guidelines for Responding to Learner Diversity in the Classroom*. Pretoria, Department of Basic Education.

Swinburne University. 2018. *Young Mums Programme*. Melbourne, Australia, Swinburne University. www.swinburne.edu.au/giving/why-giving-matters/young-mums-program. (Accessed 25 March 2019.)

Symeonidou, S. 2017. Initial teacher education for inclusion: a review of the literature. *Disability and Society,* Vol. 32, No. 3, pp. 401–22.

Teaching at the Right Level. 2019a. *Ghana*. Teaching at the Right Level. www.teachingattherightlevel.org/tarl-in-action/ghana. (Accessed 2 December 2019.)

___. 2019b. *Zambia*. Teaching at the Right Level. www.teachingattherightlevel.org/tarl-in-action/zambia-case-study. (Accessed 2 December 2019.)

The Right to Education for Children with Disabilities Alliance. 2016. *Alternative Report to the UN Committee on the Rights of Persons with Disabilities in Response to South Africa's Baseline Country Report of March 2013 on the UN Convention on the Rights of Persons with Disabilities, with Particular Reference to the Provisions of Article 24*. Geneva, Switzerland, United Nations Committee on the Rights of Persons with Disabilities.

Thompson, O. 2019. *School Desegregation and Black Teacher Employment*. Cambridge, Mass., National Bureau of Economic Research. (Working Paper 25990.)

Uganda Ministry of Education and Sports. 2015. *National Strategy for Girls' Education (NSGE) in Uganda (2015–2019)*. Kampala, Ministry of Education and Sports.

Uganda Ministry of Finance, Planning and Economic Development. 2018. *Provision of Inclusive Education in Uganda: What Are the Challenges?* Kampala, Ministry of Finance, Planning and Economic Development. (BMAU Briefing Paper 13/18.)

Ukrainian Step by Step Foundation. 2015. *Submission to the Committee for the UN Convention on the Rights of Persons with Disabilities Day of General Discussion on Article 24: Education*. Kyiv, Ukrainian Step by Step Foundation.

UNESCO. 2016. *Closing the Gender Gap in STEM: Drawing More Girls and Women into Science, Technology, Engineering and Mathematics*. Bangkok, UNESCO. (Education Thematic Brief.)

___. 2019. *Strengthening Gender Responsive Pedagogy for STEM in Uganda*. Paris, UNESCO. https://en.unesco.org/news/strengthening-gender-responsive-pedagogy-stem-uganda. (Accessed 23 September 2019.)

UNICEF. 2015a. *Case Study on Inclusive Education Development*. Rabat, UNICEF.

___. 2015b. *Readiness for Education of Children with Disabilities in Eight Provinces of Viet Nam*. Hanoi, UNICEF.

US National Center for Education Statistics. 2016. *Digest of Education Statistics*. Washington, DC, Institute of Education Sciences. https://nces.ed.gov/programs/digest/2016menu_tables.asp. (Accessed 11 December 2019.)

Villegas, A. M. and Lucas, T. 2007. The culturally responsive teacher. *Educational Leadership*, Vol. 64, No. 6, pp. 28–33.

Wodon, Q. T., Male, C., Montenegro, C. E. and Nayihouba, K. A. 2018. *The Challenge of Inclusive Education in Sub-Saharan Africa*. Washington, DC, World Bank. (The Price of Exclusion: Disability and Education.)

Woodcock, S. and Hardy, I. 2017. Probing and problematizing teacher professional development for inclusion. *International Journal of Educational Research*, Vol. 83, pp. 43–54.

Yada, A. and Savolainen, H. 2017. Japanese in-service teachers' attitudes toward inclusive education and self-efficacy for inclusive practices. *Teaching and Teacher Education*, Vol. 64, pp. 222–29.

Zero Project. 2016. *Innovative Policy 2016 on Inclusive education and ICT: Canada´s New Brunswick Forbids Segregated Education*. Vienna, Zero Project.

CHAPTER 7

Access Exchange International. 2017. *Bridging the Gap*. San Francisco, Calif., Access Exchange International.

Ace Centre. 2019. *Case Studies*. Oldham, UK, Ace Centre. http://acecentre.org.uk/people-we-support. (Accessed 19 December 2019.)

Agarwal, A. 2019. *School Accessibility and Universal Design in School Infrastructure*. (Background paper for *Global Education Monitoring Report 2020*.)

Ahmad, F. K. 2015. Use of assistive technology in inclusive education: making room for diverse learning needs. *Transcience*, Vol. 6, No. 2, pp. 62–77.

Ainscow, M. 2011. Some lessons from international efforts to foster inclusive education. *Innovación Educativa*, Vol. 2, No. 21.

Ainscow, M., Dyson, A., Goldrick, S. and West, M. 2016. Using collaborative inquiry to foster equity within school systems: opportunities and barriers. *School Effectiveness and School Improvement*, Vol. 27, No. 1, pp. 7–23.

Ainscow, M., Fox, S. and O'Kane, J. C. 2003. *Leadership and Management in Special Schools*. London, National College for School Leadership.

Ajuwon, P. M. and Chitiyo, G. 2015. Survey of the use of assistive technology in schools in Nigeria. *Journal of the International Association of Special Education*, Vol. 16, pp. 4–13.

Allen, K., Kern, M. L., Vella-Brodrick, D., Hattie, J. and Waters, L. 2018. What schools need to know about fostering school belonging: a meta-analysis. *Educational Psychology Review*, Vol. 30, No. 1, pp. 1–34.

Armstrong, P. W. and Ainscow, M. 2018. School-to-school support within a competitive education system: views from the inside. *School Effectiveness and School Improvement*, Vol. 29, No. 4, pp. 614–33.

Ashraf, M. M., Hasan, N., Lewis, L., Hasan, M. R. and Ray, P. 2017. A systematic literature review of the application of information communication technology for visually impaired people. *International Journal of Disability Management*, Vol. 11.

Ault, M. J., Bausch, M. E. and Mclaren, E. M. 2013. Assistive technology service delivery in rural school districts. *Rural Special Education Quarterly*, Vol. 32, No. 2, pp. 15–22.

AusAID. 2013. *Accessibility Design Guide: Universal Design Principles for Australia's Aid Program*. Canberra, AusAID.

Baars, S., Shaw, B., Mulcahy, E. and Menzies, L. 2018. *School Cultures and Practices: Supporting the Attainment of Disadvantaged Pupils*. London, Department for Education.

Bădescu, G. 2020. *Fostering Inclusive Education by Enhancing Cooperative Skills*. Paris, UNESCO. (Global Education Monitoring Report Fellowship Paper.)

Barrett, P., Treves, A., Shmis, T., Ambasz, D. and Ustinova, M. 2019. *The Impact of School Infrastructure on Learning: A Synthesis of the Evidence*. Washington, DC, World Bank.

Batorowicz, B., Missiuna, C. A. and Pollock, N. A. 2012. Technology supporting written productivity in children with learning disabilities: a critical review. *Canadian Journal of Occupational Therapy*, Vol. 79, No. 4, pp. 211–24.

Bauman University. 2019. *History of the Center*. Moscow, Center for Complex Rehabilitation of the Deaf and Hard-of-Hearing. https://guimc.bmstu.ru/en/history-of-the-center. (Accessed 19 December 2019.)

Baxter, S., Enderby, P., Evans, P. and Judge, S. 2012. Barriers and facilitators to the use of high-technology augmentative and alternative communication devices: a systematic review and qualitative synthesis. *International Journal of Language and Communication Disorders*, Vol. 47, No. 2, pp. 115–29.

Bell, J. and McKay, T. M. 2011. The rise of 'class apartheid' in accessing secondary schools in Sandton, Gauteng. *Southern African Review of Education*, Vol. 17.

Bennett, T. 2017. *Creating a Culture: How School Leaders Can Optimise Behaviour*. London, Department for Education.

Bernardo, F. B. and Rust, N. M. 2018. A utilização de materiais grafo-táteis para o ensino de ciências e matemática para alunos com deficiência visual [The use of graphical-tactile materials for teaching science and mathematics to visually impaired students]. *Annals of the 2018 Brazilian Congress of Special Education*, Vol. 3.

Bichard, J.-A., Coleman, R. and Langdon, P. 2007. Does my stigma look big in this? Considering acceptability and desirability in the inclusive design of technology products. Stephanidis, C. (ed.), *International Conference on Universal Access in Human-Computer Interaction*. Berlin/Heidelberg, Springer, pp. 622–31.

Blake, J. J., Lund, E. M., Zhou, Q., Kwok, O.-m. and Benz, M. R. 2012. National prevalence rates of bully victimization among students with disabilities in the United States. *School Psychology Quarterly*, Vol. 27, No. 4, pp. 210–22.

Blitz, L. V., Yull, D. and Clauhs, M. 2016. Bringing sanctuary to school: assessing school climate as a foundation for culturally responsive trauma-informed approaches for urban schools. *Urban Education*, Vol. 55, No. 1, pp. 95–124.

Bond, L., Patton, G., Glover, S., Carlin, J. B., Butler, H., Thomas, L. and Bowes, G. 2004. The Gatehouse Project: Can a multilevel school intervention affect emotional wellbeing and health risk behaviours? *Journal of Epidemiology and Community Health*, Vol. 58, No. 12, pp. 997–1003.

Borgwald, K. and Theixos, H. 2012. Bullying the bully: Why zero-tolerance policies get a failing grade. *Social Influence*, Vol. 8, No. 2–3.

Bouck, E. C., Maeda, Y. and Flanagan, S. M. 2011. Assistive technology and students with high-incidence disabilities. *Remedial and Special Education*, Vol. 33, No. 5, pp. 298–308.

Bradshaw, C. P., Waasdorp, T. E., Debnam, K. J. and Johnson, S. L. 2014. Measuring school climate in high schools: a focus on safety, engagement, and the environment. *Journal of School Health*, Vol. 84, No. 9, pp. 593–604.

Brazil Government. 2014. *Education for All 2015 National Review*. Brasilia, Ministry of Education.

Brown, V., Kelly, M. and Mabugu, T. 2017. *The Education System in Karamoja*. Oxford, UK, High-Quality Technical Assistance for Results.

Bubb, S. 2009. Coaching in a special school: making teachers and support staff feel more valued. Porritt, V. and Earley, P. (eds), *Effective Practices in Continuing Professional Development: Lessons from Schools*. London, Institute of Education, University of London.

Burdette, P. 2010. *Principal Preparedness to Support Students with Disabilities and Other Diverse Learners: A Policy Forum Proceedings Document*. Alexandria, Va., Project Forum.

Campbell, C. 2011. *How to Involve Hard-to-Reach Parents: Encouraging Meaningful Parental Involvement with Schools*. Nottingham, UK, National College for School Leadership.

Campigotto, R., McEwen, R. and Demmans Epp, C. 2013. Especially social: exploring the use of an iOS application in special needs classrooms. *Computers and Education*, Vol. 60, pp. 74–86.

Centers for Disease Control and Prevention. 2009. *School Connectedness: Strategies for Increasing Protective Factors among Youth*. Atlanta, Ga., Department of Health and Human Service.

Centre for Education Statistics and Evaluation. 2016. *Does Changing School Matter?* Sydney, Centre for Education Statistics and Evaluation, New South Wales Government. (Learning Curve 13.)

Centre for Excellence in Universal Design. 2019. *The 7 Principles*. Dublin, Centre for Excellence in Universal Design. http://universaldesign.ie/What-is-Universal-Design/The-7-Principles. (Accessed July 2019.)

Cobb, C. 2014. Principals play many parts: a review of the research on school principals as special education leaders 2001–2011. *International Journal of Inclusive Education*, Vol. 19, No. 3, pp. 213–34.

Coffey. 2016. *Kiribati Education Improvement Program Phase II: Completion Report*. Canberra, Coffey/Australian Aid.

Cooc, N. 2018. *Who Needs Special Education Professional Development? International Trends from TALIS 2013.* Paris, Organisation for Economic Co-operation and Development. (Education Working Paper 181.)

Danso, A. K., Owusu-Ansah, F. E. and Alorwu, D. 2012. Designed to deter: barriers to facilities at secondary schools in Ghana. *African Journal of Disability,* Vol. 1, No. 1, p. 2.

Department for Education. 2015. *Special Educational Needs and Disability Code of Practice: 0 to 25 years – Statutory Guidance for Organisations which Work with and Support Children and Young People Who Have Special Educational Needs or Disabilities.* London, Department for Education/Department of Health.

Devries, K., Kuper, H., Knight, L., Allen, E., Kyegombe, N., Banks, L. M., Kelly, S. and Naker, D. 2018. Reducing physical violence toward primary school students with disabilities. *Journal of Adolescent Health,* Vol. 62, No. 3, pp. 303–10.

Donnelly, C. 2000. In pursuit of school ethos. *British Journal of Educational Studies,* Vol. 48, No. 2.

European Agency for Development in Special Needs Education. 2013. *Organisation of Provision to Support Inclusive Education: Developing a Support Service for Learners with Visual Impairment – Ljubljana, Slovenia.* Odense, Denmark, European Agency for Development in Special Needs Education.

European Agency for Special Needs and Inclusive Education. 2017a. *Financing Policies for Inclusive Education Systems: Country Report – Lithuania.* Odense, Denmark, European Agency for Special Needs and Inclusive Education.

___. 2017b. *Financing Policies for Inclusive Education Systems: Country Study Visit Report – Slovenia.* Odense, Denmark, European Agency for Special Needs and Inclusive Education.

___. 2017c. *Raising the Achievement of All Learners in Inclusive Education: Lessons from European Policy and Practice.* Odense, Denmark, European Agency for Special Needs and Inclusive Education.

___. 2018a. *Key Actions for Raising Achievement: Guidance for Teachers and Leaders.* Odense, Denmark, European Agency for Special Needs and Inclusive Education.

___. 2018b. *Supporting Inclusive School Leadership: Policy Review.* Odense, Denmark, European Agency for Special Needs and Inclusive Education.

___. 2019. *Innovative New Inclusive Education Law for Portugal's Schools.* Odense, Denmark, Eurpean Agency for Special Needs and Inclusive Education. https://www.european-agency.org/news/innovative-new-inclusive-education-law-portugals-schools. (Accessed 21 May 2019.)

Faas, D., Smith, A. and Darmody, M. 2018. Between ethos and practice: Are Ireland's new multi-denominational primary schools equal and inclusive? *Compare,* Vol. 49, No. 6, pp. 602–18.

Falvey, M. A. and Givner, C. C. 2005. What is an inclusive school? Villa, R. A. and Thousand, J. S. (eds), *Creating an Inclusive School.* Alexandria, Va., Association for Supervision and Curriculum Development.

Fitzpatrick Associates. 2018. *School Leadership in Ireland and the Centre for School Leadership: Research and Evaluation – Final Report.* Dublin, Fitzpatrick Associates.

Fleming, M., Fitton, C. A., Steiner, M. F. C., McLay, J. S., Clark, D., King, A., Mackay, D. F. and Pell, J. P. 2019. Educational and health outcomes of children treated for asthma: Scotland-wide record linkage study of 683716 children. *European Respiratory Journal,* Vol. 54, No. 3.

Foley, A. and Ferri, B. A. 2012. Technology for people, not disabilities: ensuring access and inclusion. *Journal of Research in Special Educational Needs,* Vol. 12, No. 4, pp. 192–200.

Foundation House. 2016. *School's In for Refugees: A Whole-School Approach to Supporting Students and Families of Refugee Background.* Brunswick, Australia, Foundation House.

Garner, P. and Forbes, F. 2013. School leadership and special education: challenges, dilemmas and opportunities from an Australian context. *Support for Learning,* Vol. 28, No. 4, pp. 154–61.

Gleason, M., Cicutto, L., Haas-Howard, C., Raleigh, B. M. and Szefler, S. J. 2016. Leveraging partnerships: families, schools, and providers working together to improve asthma management. *Current Allergy and Asthma Reports,* Vol. 16, No. 10.

Glover, D. and Coleman, M. 2005. School culture, climate and ethos: interchangeable or distinctive concepts? *Journal of In-service Education,* Vol. 31, No. 2.

Goldberg, J. M., Sklad, M., Elfrink, T. R., Schreurs, K. M. G., Bohlmeijer, E. T. and Clarke, A. M. 2019. Effectiveness of interventions adopting a whole school approach to enhancing social and emotional development: a meta-analysis. *European Journal of Psychology of Education,* Vol. 34, No. 4, pp. 755–82.

Gotlib, S. 2018. *Action Must Be Taken to Stop Bullying of Students with Disability.* Melbourne, Australia, Probono Australia. https://probonoaustralia.com.au/news/2018/05/action-must-taken-stop-bullying-students-disability. (Accessed 19 December 2019.)

Granvik Saminathen, M., Brolin Låftman, S., Almquist, Y. B. and Modin, B. 2018. Effective schools, school segregation, and the link with school achievement. *School Effectiveness and School Improvement*, Vol. 29, No. 3, pp. 464–84.

Hawe, P., Bond, L., Ghali, L. M., Perry, R., Davison, C. M., Casey, D. M., Butler, H., Webster, C. M. and Scholz, B. 2015. Replication of a whole school ethos-changing intervention: different context, similar effects, additional insights. *BMC Public Health*, Vol. 15.

Hehir, T., Grindal, T., Freeman, B., Lamoreau, R., Borquaye, Y. and Burke, S. 2017. *A Summary of the Evidence on Inclusive Education*. São Paulo, Instituto Alana.

Hersh, M. 2013. Deaf people's experiences, attitudes and requirements of contextual subtitles: a two-country survey. *Telecommunications Journal of Australia*, Vol. 63, No. 2.

___. 2014. Evaluation framework for ICT-based learning technologies for disabled people. *Computers & Education*, Vol. 78, pp. 30–47.

___. 2019. *Technology for Inclusion*. Paris, UNESCO. (Background paper for *Global Education Monitoring Report 2020*.)

Hersh, M. and Johnson, M. 2008. On modelling assistive technology systems: Part I – Modelling framework. *Technology and Disability*, Vol. 20.

Hersh, M. and Mouroutsou, S. 2015. *A Comparative Evaluation of ICT to Support Lifelong Learning by Disabled People in 15 Different Countries*. Glasgow, UK, University of Glasgow. (Enable Network of ICT Supported Learning for Disabled People.)

Hersh, M. and Mouroutsou, S. 2019. Learning technology and disability: overcoming barriers to inclusion – evidence from a multicountry study. *British Journal of Educational Technology*, Vol. 50, pp. 3329–44.

Hoodline. 2018. *Tenderloin's Safe Passage program celebrates 10 years of helping kids, seniors walk safely*. San Francisco, Calif., Hoodline. https://hoodline.com/2018/11/tenderloin-s-safe-passage-program-celebrates-10-years-of-helping-kids-seniors-walk-safely. (Accessed 19 December 2019.)

Humphrey, N. and Symes, W. 2010. Perceptions of social support and experience of bullying among pupils with autistic spectrum disorders in mainstream secondary schools. *European Journal of Special Needs Education*, Vol. 25, No. 1, pp. 77–91.

Ipingbemi, O. and Aiworo, A. B. 2013. Journey to school, safety and security of school children in Benin City, Nigeria. *Transportation Research Part F: Traffic Psychology and Behaviour*, Vol. 19, pp. 77–84.

Jahnukainen, M. 2014. Inclusion, integration, or what? a comparative study of the school principals' perceptions of inclusive and special education in Finland and in Alberta, Canada. *Disability and Society*, Vol. 30, No. 1, pp. 59–72.

Johnson, G. 2013. Using tablet computers with elementary school students with special needs: the practices and perceptions of special education teachers and teacher assistants/Utilisation des tablettes électroniques avec des enfants d'école primaire à besoins spéciaux. *Canadian Journal of Learning and Technology/La revue canadienne de l'apprentissage et de la technologie*, Vol. 39, No. 4.

Johnson, L. S. 2003. The diversity imperative: building a culturally responsive school ethos. *Intercultural Education*, Vol. 14, No. 1.

Jones, F. W., Long, K. and Finlay, W. M. L. 2007. Symbols can improve the reading comprehension of adults with learning disabilities. *Journal of Intellectual Disability Research*, Vol. 51, No. 7, pp. 545–50.

Jones, H. 2011. *Inclusive Design of School Latrines: How Much Does It Cost and Who Benefits?* Loughborough, UK, Water, Engineering and Development Centre, Loughborough University. (Briefing Note 1.)

Kamarudin, H., Hashim, A. E., Mahmood, M., Ariff, N. R. M. and Ismail, W. Z. W. 2012. The implementation of the Malaysian Standard Code of Practice on access for disabled persons by local authority. *Procedia: Social and Behavioral Sciences*, Vol. 50, pp. 442–51.

Kamenetz, A. 2018. *Century-old decisions that impact children every day*. Washington, DC, National Public Radio. www.npr.org/sections/ed/2018/06/09/611079188/century-old-decisions-that-impact-children-every-day. (Accessed 11 December 2019.)

Khan, M. S. H., Hasan, M. and Clement, C. K. 2012. Barriers to the introduction of ICT into education in developing countries: the example of Bangladesh. *International Journal of Instruction*, Vol. 5, No. 2.

Knight, L., Allen, E., Mirembe, A., Nakuti, J., Namy, S., Child, J. C., Sturgess, J., Kyegombe, N., Walakira, E. J., Elbourne, D., Naker, D. and Devries, K. M. 2018. Implementation of the Good School Toolkit in Uganda: a quantitative process evaluation of a successful violence prevention program. *BMC Public Health*, Vol. 18.

Kugelmass, J. W. 2006. Sustaining cultures of inclusion: the value and limitation of cultural analyses. *European Journal of Psychology of Education*, Vol. 21, No. 3.

Leithwood, K., Harris, A. and Hopkins, D. 2008. Seven strong claims about successful school leadership. *School Leadership and Management*, Vol. 28, No. 1.

Lynch, J. M. 2012. Responsibilities of today's principal: implications for principal preparation programs and principal certification policies. *Rural Special Education Quarterly*, Vol. 31, No. 2, pp. 40–47.

Manrique, A. L., Kozma, E. V. B., Dirani, E. A. T., da Silva, M. L. and Frere, A. F. 2016. ICTs in the classroom, multiliteracy and special education: a required interface. *Creative Education*, Vol. 7, No. 7, pp. 963–70.

McMaster, C. 2013. Building inclusion from the ground up: a review of whole school re-culturing programmes for sustaining inclusive change. *International Journal of Whole Schooling*, Vol. 9, No. 2, pp. 1–24.

McNaughton, D. and Light, J. 2013. The iPad and mobile technology revolution: benefits and challenges for individuals who require augmentative and alternative communication. *Augmentative and Alternative Communication*, Vol. 29, No. 2, pp. 107–16.

Meng, L.-f. 2007. The rate of handedness conversion and related factors in left-handed children. *Laterality*, Vol. 12, No. 2, pp. 131–38.

Messinger-Willman, J. and Marino, M. T. 2010. Universal design for learning and assistive technology: leadership considerations for promoting inclusive education in today's secondary schools. *NASSP Bulletin*, Vol. 94, No. 1, pp. 5–16.

Modin, B., Laftman, S. B. and Ostberg, V. 2017. Teacher rated school ethos and student reported bullying: a multilevel study of upper secondary schools in Stockholm, Sweden. *International Journal of Environmental Research and Public Health*, Vol. 14, No. 12.

Muijs, D. 2017. Can schools reduce bullying? The relationship between school characteristics and the prevalence of bullying behaviours. *British Journal of Educational Psychology*, Vol. 87, No. 2, pp. 255–72.

Muijs, D., Ainscow, M., Dyson, A., Raffo, C., Goldrick, S., Kerr, K., Lennie, C. and Miles, S. 2010. Leading under pressure: leadership for social inclusion. *School Leadership and Management*, Vol. 30, No. 2, pp. 143–57.

Mullis, I. V. S., Martin, M. O., Foy, P. and Hooper, M. 2016. *TIMSS 2015 International Results in Mathematics*. Boston, Mass., TIMSS & PIRLS International Study Center.

NBACL. 2011. *Creating an Inclusive School: Indicators of Success*. Fredericton, Canada, New Brunswick Association for Community Living.

New Zealand Government. 2014. *What an Inclusive School Looks Like*. Wellington, Ministry of Education.

OECD. 2017. *PISA 2015 Results: Students' Well-Being – Volume III*. Paris, Organisation for Economic Co-operation and Development.

___. 2019a. *Have Students' Feelings of Belonging at School Waned Over Time?* Paris, Organisation for Economic Co-operation and Development. (PISA in Focus 100.)

___. 2019b. *PISA 2018 Results: What School Life Means for Students' Lives – Volume III*. Paris, Organisation for Economic Co-operation and Development.

___. 2019c. *TALIS 2018 Results: Teachers and School Leaders as Lifelong Learners – Volume I*. Paris, Organisation for Economic Co-operation and Development.

Oralbekova, A. K., Arzymbetova, S. Z., Begalieva, S. B., Ospanbekova, M. N., Mussabekova, G. A. and Dauletova, A. S. 2016. Application of information and communication technologies by the future primary school teachers in the context of inclusive education in the Republic of Kazakhstan. *International Journal of Environmental and Science Education*, Vol. 11, No. 9, pp. 2813–27.

Osterman, K. F. and Hafner, M. M. 2009. Curriculum in leadership preparation: understanding where we have been in order to know where we might go. Young, M. D., Crow, G. M., Murphy, J. and Ogawa, R. T. (eds), *Handbook of Research on the Education of School Leaders*. New York, Routledge, pp. 269–318.

Park, A. 2014. Switching schools may give your kids psychotic symptoms. *Time*, 20 February.

Phifer, L. W. and Hull, R. 2016. Helping students heal: observations of trauma-informed practices in the schools. *School Mental Health*, Vol. 8, No. 1, pp. 201–05.

Philippines Senate. 2019. *Angara to schools: provide neutral desks for students*. Manila, Senate of the Philippines.

Plan International. 2014. *Hear Our Voices*. Woking, UK, Plan International.

Poon-McBrayer, K. F. and Wong, P.-m. 2013. Inclusive education services for children and youth with disabilities: values, roles and challenges of school leaders. *Children and Youth Services Review*, Vol. 35, No. 9, pp. 1520–25.

Ramos, S. I. M. and de Andrade, A. M. V. 2016. ICT in Portuguese reference schools for the education of blind and partially sighted students. *Education and Information Technologies*, Vol. 21, No. 3, pp. 625–41.

Rix, J. and Sheehy, K. 2014. Nothing special: the everyday pedagogy of teaching. Florian, L. (ed.), *The SAGE Handbook of Special Education*. London, Sage, pp. 459–74.

Robyler, M. D. and Doering, A. H. 2013. *Integrating Educational Technology into Teaching*. Boston, Mass., Pearson.

Roffey, S. 2013. Inclusive and exclusive belonging: the impact on individual and community well-being. *Educational and Child Psychology*, Vol. 30, No. 1.

Roland, E., Bru, E., Midthassel, U. V. and Vaaland, G. S. 2010. The Zero programme against bullying: effects of the programme in the context of the Norwegian manifesto against bullying. *Social Psychology of Education*, Vol. 13, No. 1, pp. 41–55.

Rose, D. H., Meyer, A., Strangman, N. and Rappolt, G. 2002. *Teaching Every Student in the Digital Age: Universal Design for Learning*. Alexandria, Va., ASCD.

Rumberger, R. W. 2015. *Student Mobility: Causes, Consequences and Solutions*. Boulder, Colo., National Education Policy Center.

Rutter, M., Maughan, B., Mortimore, P., Ouston, J. and Smith, A. 1979. *Fifteen Thousand Hours: Secondary Schools and their Effects on Children*. Cambridge, Mass., Harvard University Press.

Salmivalli, C., Kärnä, A. and Poskiparta, E. 2011. Counteracting bullying in Finland: the KiVa program and its effects on different forms of being bullied. *International Journal of Behavioral Development*, Vol. 35, No. 5, pp. 405–11.

Schuelka, M. J. 2018. *Implementing Inclusive Education*. London. (K4D Helpdesk Report.)

Schuster, M. A., Bogart, L. M., Klein, D. J., Feng, J. Y., Tortolero, S. R., Mrug, S., Lewis, T. H. and Elliott, M. N. 2015. A longitudinal study of bullying of sexual-minority youth. *New England Journal of Medicine*, Vol. 372, No. 19, pp. 1872–74.

Schwartz, A. E., Stiefel, L. and Cordes, S. A. 2017. Moving matters: the causal effect of moving schools on student performance. *Education Finance and Policy*, Vol. 12, No. 4, pp. 419–46.

Scott, S. and McNeish, D. 2013. *Leadership of Special Schools: Issues and Challenges*. London, National Centre for Social Research.

Scottish Government. 2008. *Curriculum for Excellence: Building the Curriculum 3 – A Framework for Learning and Teaching*. Edinburgh, UK, Scottish Government.

Seale, J., Draffan, E. A. and Wald, M. 2010. Digital agility and digital decision making: conceptualising digital inclusion in the context of disabled learners in higher education. *Studies in Higher Education*, Vol. 35, No. 4, pp. 445–61.

Shane, H. C., Laubscher, E. H., Schlosser, R. W., Flynn, S., Sorce, J. F. and Abramson, J. 2012. Applying technology to visually support language and communication in individuals with autism spectrum disorders. *Journal of Autism and Developmental Disorders*, Vol. 42, No. 6, pp. 1228–35.

Southall, C. 2013. Use of technology to accommodate differences associated with autism spectrum disorder in the general curriculum and environment. *Journal of Special Education Technology*, Vol. 28, No. 1, pp. 23–34.

Stephenson, J. and Limbrick, L. 2015. A review of the use of touch-screen mobile devices by people with developmental disabilities. *Journal of Autism and Developmental Disorders*, Vol. 45, No. 12, pp. 3777–91.

Topping, B. 2014. *Access to School and the Learning Environment I: Physical, Information and Communication*. New York, UNICEF. (Webinar 10: Companion Technical Booklet.)

Ttofi, M. M. and Farrington, D. P. 2011. Effectiveness of school-based programs to reduce bullying: a systematic and meta-analytic review. *Journal of Experimental Criminology*, Vol. 7, No. 1, pp. 27–56.

UIS. 2018. *SDG Indicator 4.a.1(d): Review of Definitions and Data Collection Approaches – TCG Fifth Meeting, 15–16 November 2018, Mexico City, Mexico*. Montreal, Canada, UNESCO Institute for Statistics.

UNDESA. 2019a. *Disability and Development Report*. New York, United Nations Department of Economic and Social Affairs.

___. 2019b. Review of national reports under Article 35 of the Convention on the Rights of Persons with Disabilities. New York, United Nations Department of Economic and Social Affairs. (Unpublished.)

UNESCO. 1994. *The Salamanca Statement and Framework for Action on Special Needs Education*. Paris, UNESCO.

___. 2011. *ICTs in education for people with disabilities*. Moscow, UNESCO Institute for Information Technologies in Education.

___. 2016. *Out in the Open: Education Sector Responses to Violence based on Sexual Orientation and Gender Identity/Expression*. Paris, UNESCO.

___. 2017. *School Violence and Bullying: Global Status Report*. Paris, UNESCO.

___. 2018. *PIRLS 2016: Correlations between the Incidence of Bullying, Students' Sense of Belonging and Learning Outcomes.* Paris, UNESCO. https://en.unesco.org/news/pirls-2016-correlations-between-incidence-bullying-students-sense-belonging-and-learning. (Accessed May 20 2019.)

___. 2019. *Behind the Numbers: Ending School Violence and Bullying.* Paris, UNESCO.

United Arab Emirates Ministry of Education. 2009. *General Rules for the Provision of Special Education Programs and Services (Public and Private Schools).* Abu Dhabi, Special Education Department, Ministry of Education.

United Nations. 2006. *Convention on the Rights of Persons with Disabilities and Optional Protocol.* New York, United Nations.

___. 2019. *Report of the Secretary-General A/74/146: Accessibility and the Status of the Convention on the Rights of Persons with Disabilities and the Optional Protocol Thereto.* New York, United Nations.

U. R. Tanzania Ministry of Education, Science and Technology. 2016. *Basic Education Statistics in Tanzania (BEST) 2012–2016: National Data.* Dar es Salaam, Ministry of Education, Science and Technology.

Van Cleave, J., Gortmaker, S. L. and Perrin, J. M. 2010. Dynamics of obesity and chronic health conditions among children and youth. *JAMA Network,* Vol. 303, No. 7, pp. 623–30.

Victoria Department of Education and Training. 2019. *Building Quality Standards Handbook.* East Melbourne, Australia, Victorian School Building Authority, Department of Education and Training.

WAO. 2011. *WAO White Book on Allergy.* Milwaukee, Wis., World Allergy Organization.

Wheeler, L. S., Merkle, S. L., Gerald, L. B. and Taggart, V. S. 2006. Managing asthma in schools: lessons learned and recommendations. *Journal of School Health,* Vol. 76, No. 6, pp. 340–44.

WHO. 2011. *World Report on Disability.* Geneva, Switzerland, World Health Organization/World Bank.

Wilichowski, T. and Molina, E. 2018. *The School Leadership Crisis Part 2: From Administrators to Instructional Leaders.* Washington, DC, World Bank. http://blogs.worldbank.org/education/school-leadership-crisis-part-2-administrators-instructional-leaders. (Accessed 20 May 2019.)

Winsper, C., Wolke, D., Bryson, A., Thompson, A. and Singh, S. P. 2016. School mobility during childhood predicts psychotic symptoms in late adolescence. *Journal of Child Psychology and Psychiatry,* Vol. 57, No. 8, pp. 957–66.

Wynne, R., McAnaney, D., MacKeogh, T., Stapleton, P., Delaney, S., Dowling, N. and Jeffares, I. 2017. *Assistive Technology/Equipment in Supporting the Education of Children with Special Educational Needs: What Works Best?* Trim, Ireland, National Council for Special Education. (Research Report 22.)

CHAPTER 8

Adams-Byers, J., Whitsell, S. S. and Moon, S. M. 2004. Gifted students' perceptions of the academic and social/emotional effects of homogeneous and heterogeneous grouping. *Gifted Child Quarterly,* Vol. 48, No. 1, pp. 7–20.

Afghanistan Ministry of Education. 2016. *National Education Strategic Plan (2017–2021).* Kabul, Ministry of Education.

___. 2018. *Community Based Education Policy and Guidelines.* Kabul, Ministry of Education.

Alberta Teachers' Association. 2019. *Indigenous Education and Walking Together.* Edmonton, Canada, Alberta Teachers' Association. www.teachers.ab.ca/For%20Members/Professional%20Development/IndigenousEducationandWalkingTogether/Pages/WalkingTogether.aspx. (Accessed 11 December 2019.)

Alnahdi, G. H. 2019. The positive impact of including students with intellectual disabilities in schools: children's attitudes towards peers with disabilities in Saudi Arabia. *Research in Developmental Disabilities,* Vol. 85, pp. 1–7.

Alur, M. 2010. Family perspectives: parents in partnership. Rose, R. (ed.), *Confronting Obstacles to Inclusion: International Responses to Developing Inclusive Education.* Abingdon, UK, Routledge, pp. 61–74.

Antoninis, M. 2010. *Education Sector Support Programme in Nigeria (ESSPIN): Community Survey Report.* Abuja, Education Sector Support Programme in Nigeria.

Asendorpf, J. and Motti, F. 2017. A longitudinal study of immigrants' peer acceptance and rejection: immigrant status, immigrant composition of the classroom, and acculturation. *Cultural Diversity and Ethnic Minority Psychology,* Vol. 23.

Australia Government. 2008. *Apology to Australia's Indigenous Peoples.* Canberra, Australian Government.

Australian National University. 2019. *Students face "confronting" levels of racism.* Canberra, Australian National University. www.anu.edu.au/news/all-news/students-face-confronting-levels-of-racism. (Accessed 12 November 2019.)

Avramidis, E., Avgeri, G. and Strogilos, V. 2018. Social participation and friendship quality of students with special educational needs in regular Greek primary schools. *European Journal of Special Needs Education,* Vol. 33, No. 2, pp. 221–34.

Bae, H.-o., Choo, H. and Lim, C. 2019. Bullying experience of racial and ethnic minority youth in South Korea. *Journal of Early Adolescence,* Vol. 39, No. 4, pp. 561–75.

Bakhshi, P. 2019. *Unpacking Inclusion in Education: Lessons from Afghanistan for Achieving SDG 4.* Paris, UNESCO. (Background paper for *Global Education Monitoring Report 2020.*)

Baytiyeh, H. 2017. Has the educational system in Lebanon contributed to the growing sectarian divisions? *Education and Urban Society,* Vol. 49, No. 5, pp. 546–59.

Beauregard, F., Petrakos, H. and Dupont, A. 2014. Family-school partnership: practices of immigrant parents in Quebec, Canada. *The School Community Journal,* Vol. 24, No. 1, pp. 177–210.

Bernewasser, J. 2018. Wie geht weltbeste Bildung? [How is the world's best education doing?]. *Die Zeit,* 3 January.

Billingham, C. M. and Hunt, M. O. 2016. School racial composition and parental choice: new evidence on the preferences of white parents in the United States. *Sociology of Education,* Vol. 89, No. 2, pp. 99–117.

Blackman, S. 2016. Barbadian students' attitudes towards including peers with disabilities in regular education. *International Journal of Special Education,* Vol. 31, pp. 135–43.

Bodkin-Andrews, G. and Carlson, B. 2016. The legacy of racism and Indigenous Australian identity within education. *Race, Ethnicity and Education,* Vol. 19, No. 4, pp. 784–807.

Bollmer, J. M., Milich, R., Harris, M. J. and Maras, M. A. 2005. A friend in need: the role of friendship quality as a protective factor in peer victimization and bullying. *Journal of Interpersonal Violence,* Vol. 20, No. 6, pp. 701–12.

Booth, T., Booth, W. and McConnell, D. 2005. Care proceedings and parents with learning difficulties: comparative prevalence and outcomes in an English and Australian court sample. *Child and Family Social Work,* Vol. 10, No. 4, pp. 353–60.

Botelho, F., Madeira, R. A. and Rangel, M. A. 2015. Racial discrimination in grading: evidence from Brazil. *American Economic Journal: Applied Economics,* Vol. 7, No. 4, pp. 37–52.

Brede, J., Remington, A., Kenny, L., Warren, K. and Pellicano, E. 2017. Excluded from school: autistic students' experiences of school exclusion and subsequent re-integration into school. *Autism and Developmental Language Impairments,* Vol. 2, pp. 1–20.

Brunello, G. and De Paola, M. 2017. *School Segregation of Immigrants and Its Effects on Educational Outcomes in Europe: EENEE Analytical Report No. 30,* European Expert Network on Economics of Education.

Brydges, C. and Mkandawire, P. 2020. Perceptions and experiences of inclusive education among parents of children with disabilities in Lagos, Nigeria. *International Journal of Inclusive Education,* Vol. 24, No. 6, pp. 645–59.

Burde, D., Kapit, A., Lisiecki, M., Middleton, J., Misic, V., Sadiqi, M. A. and Samii, C. 2017. *The Assessment of Learning Outcomes and Social Effects on Community-Based Education: A Randomized Field Experiment in Afghanistan – Phase One Outcomes Report.* New York, New York University Steinhardt School of Culture, Education, and Human Development.

Burde, D., Middleton, J. and Samii, C. 2015. *The Assessment of Learning Outcomes and Social Effects of Community-Based Education: A Randomized Field Experiment in Afghanistan – Baseline Report.* New York, New York University Steinhardt School of Culture, Education, and Human Development

Byrne, A. 2013. What factors influence the decisions of parents of children with special educational needs when choosing a secondary educational provision for their child at change of phase from primary to secondary education? A review of the literature. *Journal of Research in Special Educational Needs,* Vol. 13, No. 2, pp. 129–41.

CAIR. 2017. *Unshakable: The Bullying of Muslim Students and the Unwavering Movement to Eradicate It.* Santa Clara, Calif., California Chapter, Council on American-Islamic Relations.

Campbell, J. M. and Barger, B. D. 2014. Peers' knowledge about and attitudes towards students with autism spectrum disorders. Patel, V. B., Preedy, V. R. and Martin, C. R. (eds), *Comprehensive Guide to Autism.* New York, Springer, pp. 247–61.

Canada Government. 2008. *Statement of Apology to Former Students of Indian Residential Schools.* Ottawa, Indigenous and Northern Affairs Canada.

Candlelight. 2015. *Basic Education for Pastoralist Children.* Hargeisa, Candlelight for Environment, Education and Health. www.candlelightsomal.org/?p=2070. (Accessed 19 November 2019.)

Carter, E. W., Asmus, J., Moss, C. K., Biggs, E. E., Bolt, D. M., Born, T. L., Brock, M. E., Cattey, G. N., Chen, R., Cooney, M., Fesperman, E., Hochman, J. M., Huber, H. B., Lequia, J. L., Lyons, G., Moyseenko, K. A., Riesch, L. M., Shalev, R. A., Vincent, L. B. and Weir, K. 2016. Randomized evaluation of peer support arrangements to support the inclusion of high school students with severe disabilities. *Exceptional Children,* Vol. 82, No. 2, pp. 209–33.

Çelik, Ç. and İçduygu, A. 2018. Schools and refugee children: the case of Syrians in Turkey. *International Migration*, Vol. 57, No. 2, pp. 253–67.

Chae, S., Park, E.-Y. and Shin, M. 2019. School-based interventions for improving disability awareness and attitudes towards disability of students without disabilities: a meta-analysis. *International Journal of Disability, Development and Education*, Vol. 66, No. 4, pp. 343–61.

Chamberlain, N. 2019. *Principal's Welcome*. Leederville, Australia, School of Isolated and Distance Education. www.side.wa.edu.au/about/welcome/principals-welcome.html. (Accessed 21 November 2019.)

Charema, J. 2007. From special schools to inclusive education: the way forward for developing countries south of the Sahara. *Journal of the International Association of Special Education*, Vol. 8, pp. 88–97.

Cherng, H.-Y. S. and Han, W.-J. 2018. *Who Teaches and How Do They View Different Groups of Students and Parents? The Case of China*. Paris, UNESCO. (Background paper for *Global Education Monitoring Report 2019*.)

Chia, J. 2017. *China's New Regulations for Persons with Disabilities Are a Good Step – But Not Enough*. New York, Open Society Foundations. (Accessed 11 December 2019.)

Children and Young People with Disability Australia. 2017. *CYDA Education Survey 2017: Summary*. Collingwood, Australia, Children and Young People with Disability Australia.

Chu, S.-Y. and Lo, Y.-L. S. 2016. Taiwanese families' perspectives on learning disabilities: an exploratory study in three middle schools. *Journal of Research in Special Educational Needs*, Vol. 16, No. 2, pp. 77–88.

Cimpian, J. P., Lubienski, S. T., Ganley, C. M. and Copur-Gencturk, Y. 2014. Teachers' perceptions of students' mathematics proficiency may exacerbate early gender gaps in achievement. *Developmental Psychology*, Vol. 50, No. 4, pp. 1262–81.

Cimpian, J. R., Lubienski, S. T., Timmer, J. D., Makowski, M. B. and Miller, E. K. 2016. Have gender gaps in math closed? Achievement, teacher perceptions, and learning behaviors across two ECLS-K cohorts. *AERA Open*, Vol. 2, No. 4.

Cortina, R. 2014a. Introduction. Cortina, R. (ed.), *The Education of Indigenous Citizens in Latin America*. Bristol, UK, Multilingual Matters, pp. 1–18.

___. 2014b. Partnerships to promote the education of indigenous citizens. Cortina, R. (ed.), *The Education of Indigenous Citizens in Latin America*. Bristol, UK, Multilingual Matters, pp. 50–73.

Council of Europe. 2006. *Information Note No. 89 on the Case-law of the Court: September 2006*. Strasbourg, France, European Court of Human Rights, Council of Europe.

Crooks, C. V., Burleigh, D., Snowshoe, A., Lapp, A., Hughes, R. and Sisco, A. 2015. A case study of culturally relevant school-based programming for First Nations youth: improved relationships, confidence and leadership, and school success. *Advances in School Mental Health Promotion*, Vol. 8, No. 4, pp. 216–30.

Dastambuev, N. 2015. Speeding up progress towards inclusive education in Tajikistan. *Enabling Education Review*, Special Issue, pp. 9–11.

Dave, H. 2017. "Safe schools": keeping vulnerable and working children in education in Peru. *Enabling Education Review*, No. 6, pp. 36–37.

de Beco, G. 2014. *Study on the Implementation of Article 33 of the UN Convention on the Rights of Persons with Disabilities in Europe*. Geneva, Switzerland, Regional Office for Europe of the UN High Commissioner for Human Rights.

de Boer, A., Pijl, S. J. and Minnaert, A. 2010. Attitudes of parents towards inclusive education: a review of the literature. *European Journal of Special Needs Education*, Vol. 25, No. 2, pp. 165–81.

___. 2012. Students' attitudes towards peers with disabilities: a review of the literature. *International Journal of Disability, Development and Education*, Vol. 59, No. 4, pp. 379–92.

de Boer, A. A. and Munde, V. S. 2015. Parental attitudes toward the inclusion of children with profound intellectual and multiple disabilities in general primary education in the Netherlands. *Journal of Special Education*, Vol. 49, No. 3, pp. 179–87.

Donnelly, M. 2019. *Homeschool Freedom Advances in Ukraine, Philippines, Mexico, and Taiwan*. Purcellville, Va., Home School Legal Defense Association. https://hslda.org/post/homeschool-freedom-advances-in-ukraine-philippines-mexico-and-taiwan. (Accessed 11 December 2019.)

Edmonton Public Schools. 2018. *Strategic Plan Update Report: First Nations, Métis, and Inuit Students*. Edmonton, Canada, Edmonton Public Schools.

Elbeheri, G., Reid, G. and Everatt, J. 2017. *Motivating Children with Specific Learning Difficulties: A Teacher's Practical Guide*. London, Routledge.

Elkins, J., Van Kraayenoord, C. E. and Jobling, A. 2003. Parents' attitudes to inclusion of their children with special needs. *Journal of Research in Special Educational Needs*, Vol. 3, No. 2, pp. 122–29.

Equal Rights Trust. 2017. *Learning InEquality: Using Equality Law to Tackle Barriers to Primary Education for Out-of-school Children*. London, Open Society Foundations.

Ethiopia Ministry of Education. 2016. *A Master Plan for Special Needs Education/Inclusive Education in Ethiopia 2016–2025*. Addis Ababa, Ministry of Education.

Finnvold, J. E. 2018. School segregation and social participation: the case of Norwegian children with physical disabilities. *European Journal of Special Needs Education*, Vol. 33, No. 2, pp. 187–204.

Frankenberg, E., Hawley, G. S., Ee, J. and Orfield, G. 2017. *Southern Schools: More than a Half-Century after the Civil Rights Revolution*. Los Angeles, Calif., Civic Rights Project.

Furuta, H. and Thamburaj, R. 2014. Promoting inclusive education in India: roles played by NGOs under the Sarva Shiksha Abhiyan scheme in the state of Tamil Nadu. *Journal of Special Education Research*, Vol. 3, No. 1, pp. 15–22.

Gerdes, C. 2013. Does immigration induce 'native flight' from public schools? *The Annals of Regional Science*, Vol. 50, No. 2, pp. 645–66.

Gershoff, E. T. 2017. School corporal punishment in global perspective: prevalence, outcomes, and efforts at intervention. *Psychology, Health and Medicine*, Vol. 22, No. sup1, pp. 224–39.

Ghana Ministry of Education. 2015. *Inclusive Education Policy*. Accra, Ministry of Education.

Glazzard, J. 2010. The impact of dyslexia on pupils' self-esteem. *Support for Learning*, Vol. 25, No. 2, pp. 63–69.

Graham, S. 2018. Race/ethnicity and social adjustment of adolescents: how (not if) school diversity matters. *Educational Psychologist*, Vol. 53, No. 2, pp. 64–77.

Gur, A. and Stein, M. A. 2020. Social worker attitudes toward parents with intellectual disabilities in Israel. *Disability and Rehabilitation*, Vol. 42, No. 13, pp. 1803–13.

Hanford, E. 2018. *Rethinking How Students with Dyslexia Are Taught to Read*. Washington, DC, National Public Radio. www.npr.org/sections/ed/2018/03/11/591504959/rethinking-how-students-with-dyslexia-are-taught-to-read. (Accessed 11 December 2019.)

Hong, S.-Y., Kwon, K.-A. and Jeon, H.-J. 2014. Children's attitudes towards peers with disabilities: associations with personal and parental factors. *Infant and Child Development*, Vol. 23, No. 2, pp. 170–93.

Hooja, V. 2009. Parents of students included in mainstream schools: a narrative exploration. Alur, M. and Timmons, V. (eds), *Inclusive Education across Cultures: Crossing Boundaries, Sharing Ideas*. New Delhi, Sage, pp. 352–64.

Hornby, G. 2010. Supporting parents and families in the development of inclusive practice. Rose, R. (ed.), *Confronting Obstacles to Inclusion: International Responses to Developing Inclusive Education*. Abingdon, UK, Routledge.

Huang, S. 2019. Ten years of the CRPD's adoption in China: challenges and opportunities. *Disability and Society*, Vol. 34, No. 6, pp. 1004–09.

Human Rights Watch. 2019. *South Africa: Children with Disabilities Shortchanged – Adopt Free, Inclusive Education for All*. New York, Human Rights Watch. www.hrw.org/news/2019/05/24/south-africa-children-disabilities-shortchanged. (Accessed 11 December 2019.)

Humphrey, N. and Lewis, S. 2008. `Make me normal': the views and experiences of pupils on the autistic spectrum in mainstream secondary schools. *Autism*, Vol. 12, No. 1, pp. 23–46.

Humphries, T., Kushalnagar, P., Mathur, G., Napoli, D. J., Padden, C., Rathmann, C. and Smith, S. R. 2012. Language acquisition for deaf children: reducing the harms of zero tolerance to the use of alternative approaches. *Harm Reduction Journal*, Vol. 9, No. 1, p. 16.

IDDC. 2018. *IE Call to Action Endorsement by Global Partnership for Education*. Brussels, International Disability and Development Consortium. https://www.iddcconsortium.net/news/CTA-endorsement-by-GPE. (Accessed 20 June 2019.)

IDDC and Light for the World. 2016. *#Costing Equity: The Case for Disability-Responsive Education Financing*. Brussels/Vienna, International Disability and Development Consortium/Light for the World.

Inclusion International. 2006. *Hear Our Voices: A Global Report – People with an Intellectual Disability and their Families Speak Out on Poverty and Exclusion*. London, Inclusion International.

Jigyel, K., Miller, J. A., Mavropoulou, S. and Berman, J. 2018. Parental communication and collaboration in schools with special educational needs (SEN) programmes in Bhutan. *International Journal of Inclusive Education*, Vol. 22, No. 12, pp. 1288–305.

Johnson, D. M. 2013. Confrontation and cooperation: the complicated relationship between homeschoolers and public schools. *Peabody Journal of Education*, Vol. 88, No. 3, pp. 298–308.

Keith, J. M., Bennetto, L. and Rogge, R. D. 2015. The relationship between contact and attitudes: reducing prejudice toward individuals with intellectual and developmental disabilities. *Research in Developmental Disabilities*, Vol. 47, pp. 14–26.

Khan, M. A., Kanwal, N. and Wang, L. 2018. Violent attacks on education in the tribal areas of Pakistan and the role of NGOs in providing educational services. *Conflict, Security and Development*, Vol. 18, No. 2, pp. 113–36.

Kippels, S. and Ridge, N. 2019. *International and Other Migrant Schools in Gulf Cooperation Council Countries*. Paris, UNESCO. (Background paper for *Global Education Monotoring Report Arab States 2019*.)

Kosciw, J. G., Greytak, E. A., Zongrone, A. D., Clark, C. M. and Truong, N. L. 2018. *The 2017 National School Climate Survey: The Experiences of Lesbian, Gay, Bisexual, Transgender, and Queer Youth in Our Nation's Schools*. New York, GLSEN.

Lall, A. 2016. *'Don't Tell Them Where We Live': Caste and Access to Education in Northern Sri Lanka*. London, Centre for Poverty Analysis, Overseas Development Institute. (Secure Livelihoods Research Consortium Working Paper 49.)

Lang, R. and Officer, A. 2009. Behind the scenes disability advocacy. Alur, M. and Timmons, V. (eds), *Inclusive Education across Cultures: Crossing Boundaries, Sharing Ideas*. New Delhi, Sage, pp. 380–94.

Le Fanu, G. 2013. The inclusion of inclusive education in international development: lessons from Papua New Guinea. *International Journal of Educational Development*, Vol. 33, pp. 139–48.

Lee, Y., Lee, M. and Park, S. 2019. The mental health of ethnic minority youths in South Korea and its related environmental factors: a literature review. *Journal of the Korean Academy of Child and Adolescent Psychiatry*, Vol. 30, No. 3, pp. 88-99.

Leseyane, M., Mandende, P., Makgato, M. and Cekiso, M. 2018. Dyslexic learners' experiences with their peers and teachers in special and mainstream primary schools in North-West Province. *African Journal of Disability*, Vol. 7.

Leyser, Y. and Kirk, R. 2004. Evaluating inclusion: an examination of parent views and factors influencing their perspectives. *International Journal of Disability, Development and Education*, Vol. 51, No. 3, pp. 271–85.

Lohmann, A., Wulfekühler, H., Wiedebusch, S. and Hensen, G. 2019. Parents' attitudes towards inclusive education in day care facilities. *International Journal of Inclusive Education*, Vol. 23, No. 12, pp. 1232–47.

Lüke, T. and Grosche, M. 2018. What do I think about inclusive education? It depends on who is asking: Experimental evidence for a social desirability bias in attitudes towards inclusion. *International Journal of Inclusive Education*, Vol. 22, No. 1, pp. 38–53.

Lyons, E. M., Simms, N., Begolli, K. N. and Richland, L. E. 2018. Stereotype threat effects on learning from a cognitively demanding mathematics lesson. *Cognitive Science*, Vol. 42, No. 2, pp. 678–90.

Macedo, D. M., Smithers, L. G., Roberts, R. M., Paradies, Y. and Jamieson, L. M. 2019. Effects of racism on the socio-emotional wellbeing of Aboriginal Australian children. *International Journal for Equity in Health*, Vol. 18, No. 1.

MacMillan, M., Tarrant, M., Abraham, C. and Morris, C. 2014. The association between children's contact with people with disabilities and their attitudes towards disability: a systematic review. *Developmental Medicine and Child Neurology*, Vol. 56, No. 6, pp. 529–46.

Macura-Milovanović, S., Munda, M. and Peček, M. 2013. Roma pupils' identification with school in Slovenia and Serbia: case studies. *Educational Studies*, Vol. 39, No. 5, pp. 483–502.

Makarova, E., Aeschlimann, B. and Herzog, W. 2019. The gender gap in STEM fields: the impact of the gender stereotype of math and science on secondary students' career aspirations. *Frontiers in Education*, Vol. 4, No. 60.

Makin, C., Hill, V. and Pellicano, E. 2017. The primary-to-secondary school transition for children on the autism spectrum: a multi-informant mixed-methods study. *Autism and Developmental Language Impairments*, Vol. 2.

Mann, G., Cuskelly, M. and Moni, K. 2018. An investigation of parents' decisions to transfer children from regular to special schools. *Journal of Policy and Practice in Intellectual Disabilities*, Vol. 15, No. 3, pp. 183–92.

Mariga, L., McConkey, R. and Myezwa, H. 2014. *Inclusive Education in Low-Income Countries: A Resource Book for Teacher Educators, Parent Trainers and Community Development Workers*. Cape Town, Atlas Alliance and Disability Innovations Africa.

Martinez Novo, C. and de la Torre, C. 2010. Racial discrimination and citizenship in Ecuador's educational system. *Latin American and Caribbean Ethnic Studies*, Vol. 5, No. 1, pp. 1–26.

Mawene, D. and Bal, A. 2018. Factors influencing parents' selection of schools for children with disabilities: a systematic review of the literature. *International Journal of Special Education*, Vol. 33, pp. 313–29.

McDonald, J. and Lopes, E. 2014. How parents home educate their children with an autism spectrum disorder with the support of the Schools of Isolated and Distance Education. *International Journal of Inclusive Education*, Vol. 18, No. 1, pp. 1–17.

McGeown, J. 2019. HI case study for *Global Education Monitoring Report 2020*. London, Humanity and Inclusion. (Unpublished.)

McQuiggan, M., Megra, M. and Grady, S. 2017. *Parent and Family Involvement in Education: Results from the National Household Education Surveys Program of 2016*. Washington, DC, National Center for Education Statistics.

Meresman, S. 2014. *Parents, Family and Community Participation in Inclusive Education*. New York, UNICEF. (Webinar 13: Companion Technical Booklet.)

Merry, M. S. and Driessen, G. 2012. Equality on different terms: the case of Dutch Hindu schools. *Education and Urban Society*, Vol. 44, No. 5, pp. 632–48.

Mont, D. and Nguyen, C. 2013. Does parental disability matter to child education? Evidence from Vietnam. *World Development*, Vol. 48, pp. 88–107.

Moodie, N., Maxwell, J. and Rudolph, S. 2019. The impact of racism on the schooling experiences of Aboriginal and Torres Strait Islander students: a systematic review. *The Australian Educational Researcher*, Vol. 46, No. 2, pp. 273–95.

Mukhopadhyay, S., Mangope, B. and Moorad, F. 2019. Voices of the voiceless: inclusion of learners with special education needs in Botswana primary schools. *Exceptionality*, Vol. 27, No. 3, pp. 232–46.

Ngalomba, S. 2016. *Taunts and Bullying Drive Children with Albinism from Tanzanian Schools*. https://theconversation.com/taunts-and-bullying-drive-children-with-albinism-from-tanzanian-schools-63559. (Accessed 11 December 2019.)

Nicoletti, I. and Kunz, A. 2018. *The Impact of School De-segregation for Children in Stolipinovo on their Right to Education*. Graz, Austria, European Training and Research Centre for Human Rights and Democracy.

North-Rhine Westphalia Ministry of Schools and Education. 2018. *Neuausrichtung der Inklusion in den öffentlichen allgemeinbildenden weiterführenden Schulen [Realignment of inclusion in public general secondary schools]*. Düsseldorf, Germany, North-Rhine Westphalia Ministry of Schools and Education.

Norwich, B. and Kelly, N. 2004. Pupils' views on inclusion: moderate learning difficulties and bullying in mainstream and special schools. *British Educational Research Journal*, Vol. 30, No. 1, pp. 43–65.

Nowicki, E. A. 2006. A cross-sectional multivariate analysis of children's attitudes towards disabilities. *Journal of Intellectual Disability Research*, Vol. 50, No. 5, pp. 335–48.

Nuth, M. 2018. How context influences the ideologies and strategies of disabled people's organisations: a case study from Cambodia. *Disability and Society*, Vol. 33, No. 7, pp. 1046–60.

Obeid, R., Daou, N., DeNigris, D., Shane-Simpson, C., Brooks, P. J. and Gillespie-Lynch, K. 2015. A cross-cultural comparison of knowledge and stigma associated with autism spectrum disorder among college students in Lebanon and the United States. *Journal of Autism and Developmental Disorders*, Vol. 45, No. 11, pp. 3520–36.

Odom, S. L., Buysse, V. and Soukakou, E. 2011. Inclusion for young children with disabilities: a quarter century of research perspectives. *Journal of Early Intervention*, Vol. 33, No. 4, pp. 344–56.

OECD. 2017. *Promising Practices in Supporting Success for Indigenous Students*. Paris, Organisation for Economic Co-operation and Development.

Ogando Portela, M. J. and Pells, K. 2015. *Corporal Punishment in Schools: Longitudinal Evidence from Ethiopia, India, Peru and Viet Nam*. Florence, UNICEF. (Office of Research – Innocenti Discussion Paper 2015-02.)

Opoku, M. 2020. *Parental Attitude towards Inclusive Education*. Paris, UNESCO. (Background paper for *Global Education Monitoring Report 2020*.)

OSCE/ODIHR. 2015. *Activism, Participation and Security among Roma and Sinti Youth*. Warsaw, Office for Democratic Institutions and Human Rights, Organization for Security and Co-operation in Europe.

Page, J., Whitting, G. and Mclean, C. 2007. *Engaging Effectively with Black and Minority Ethnic Parents in Children's and Parental Services*. London, GHK Consulting Ltd.

Paraguay Ministry of Education and Sciences, USAID and Fundación Saraki. 2018. *Lineamientos para un Sistema Educativo Inclusivo en el Paraguay [Guidelines for an Inclusive Education System in Paraguay]*. Asunción, Ministry of Education and Sciences.

Parveen, N. 2019. Birmingham school stops LBGT lessons after parents protest. *The Guardian*, 4 March.

Pedneault, J. and Labaki, L. 2019. *'It Felt Like a Punishment': Growing Up with Albinism in Tanzania*. New York, Human Rights Watch.

Pells, K., Ogando Portela, M. J. and Espinoza, P. 2016. Poverty and inequity: multi-country evidence on the structural drivers of bullying. United Nations (ed.), *Ending the Torment: Tackling Bullying from the Schoolyard to Cyberspace.* New York, Office of the Special Representative of the Secretary-General on Violence against Children, United Nations, pp. 41–48.

Pierpoint, G. 2019. College admissions scandal: the extreme lengths parents go to. *BBC News,* 12 March.

Prats, J., Deusdad, B. and Cabre, J. 2017. School xenophobia and interethnic relationships among secondary level pupils in Spain. *Education as Change,* Vol. 21, No. 1.

Priest, N., Mackean, T., Davis, E., Waters, E. and Briggs, L. 2012. Strengths and challenges for Koori kids: harder for Koori kids, Koori kids doing well – Exploring Aboriginal perspectives on social determinants of Aboriginal child health and wellbeing. *Health Sociology Review,* Vol. 21, No. 2, pp. 165–79.

Purdie, N., Reid, K., Frigo, T., Stone, A. and Kleinhenz, E. 2011. *Literacy and Numeracy Learning: Lessons from the Longitudinal Literacy and Numeracy Study for Indigenous Students.* Camberwell, Australia, Australian Council for Educational Research.

Raman, S. R. and Sua, T. Y. 2010. Ethnic segregation in Malaysia's education system: enrolment choices, preferential policies and desegregation. *Paedagogica Historica,* Vol. 46, No. 1–2, pp. 117–31.

Rich, P. M. and Jennings, J. L. 2015. Choice, information, and constrained options: school transfers in a stratified educational system. *American Sociological Review,* Vol. 80, No. 5, pp. 1069–98.

Rieser, R. 2009. Inclusion, empowerment and the vital role of disabled people and their thinking. Alur, M. and Timmons, V. (eds), *Inclusive Education across Cultures: Crossing Boundaries, Sharing Ideas.* New Delhi, Sage, pp. 365–79.

Roda, A. and Wells, A. S. 2013. School choice policies and racial segregation: where white parents' good intentions, anxiety, and privilege collide. *Faculty Works: Education,* Vol. 46.

Rollan, K. and Somerton, M. 2019. Inclusive education reform in Kazakhstan: civil society activism from the bottom-up. *International Journal of Inclusive Education.*

Runswick-Cole, K. 2008. Between a rock and a hard place: parents' attitudes to the inclusion of children with special educational needs in mainstream and special schools. *British Journal of Special Education,* Vol. 35, No. 3, pp. 173–80.

Rwanda Ministry of Education. 2018. *Special Needs and Inclusive Education Policy.* Kigali, Ministry of Education.

Ryder, A. 2015. Raising Roma educational participation and achievement: collaborative relationships, transformative change, and a social Europe. *Alberta Journal of Educational Research,* Vol. 61, pp. 417–31.

Sahni, U. 2019. *Prerna Girls School: About.* Lucknow, Study Hall Educational Foundation www.studyhallfoundation.org/ prerna-girls/index.php. (Accessed 19 November 2019.)

Sayeed, Z. 2009. Families: the cornerstone of society – building a global family movement. Alur, M. and Timmons, V. (eds), *Inclusive Education across Cultures: Crossing Boundaries, Sharing Ideas.* New Delhi, Sage, pp. 342–51.

Schwab, S. 2017. The impact of contact on students' attitudes towards peers with disabilities. *Research in Developmental Disabilities,* Vol. 62, pp. 160–65.

___. 2018. *Attitudes towards Inclusive Schooling: A Study on Students', Teachers' and Parents' Attitudes.* Münster, Germany, Waxmann Verlag.

Scior, K. 2011. Public awareness, attitudes and beliefs regarding intellectual disability: a systematic review. *Research in Developmental Disabilities,* Vol. 32, No. 6, pp. 2164–82.

Shuayb, M. 2016. Education for social cohesion attempts in Lebanon: reflections on the 1994 and 2010 education reforms. *Education as Change,* Vol. 20, pp. 225–42.

Simopoulos, G. and Alexandridis, A. 2019. Refugee education in Greece: integration or segregation? *Forced Migration Review,* Vol. 60, pp. 27–29.

Sin, K. F., Forlin, C., Au, M. L., Ho, F. C., Lui, M. and Yan, Z. 2012. *Study on Equal Learning Opportunities for Students with Disabilities under the Integrated Education System.* Hong Kong, China, Equal Opportunities Commission/Centre for Special Educational Needs and Inclusive Education.

Singal, N. 2020. *Role of Non-Government Organisations as Providers of and Advocates for Inclusive Education.* Paris, UNESCO. (Background paper for *Global Education Monitoring Report 2020.*)

Srivastava, M., de Boer, A. and Pijl, S. J. 2015. Inclusive education in developing countries: a closer look at its implementation in the last 10 years. *Educational Review,* Vol. 67, No. 2, pp. 179–95.

Stein, T. 2019. *Immer mehr Gymnasien in NRW steigen aus der Inklusion aus: und das ist politisch gewollt [More and more secondary schools in North-Rhine Westphalia are getting out of inclusion: and that is politically desirable].* Cologne, Germany,

Watson. www.watson.de/deutschland/politik/560297467-immer-mehr-gymnasien-in-nrw-steigen-aus-der-inklusion-aus. (Accessed 11 December 2019.)

Stevens, L. and Wurf, G. 2020. Perceptions of inclusive education: A mixed methods investigation of parental attitudes in three Australian primary schools. *International Journal of Inclusive Education*, Vol. 20, No. 4, pp. 351-65.

Stewart, H. 2019. LGBT education in the UK must not stop with children when adults are part of the problem. Euronews, 10 April. www.euronews.com/2019/04/10/lgbt-education-in-the-uk-must-not-stop-with-children-when-adults-are-part-of-the-problem-v. (Accessed 11 December 2019.)

Strnadová, I., Hájková, V. and Květoňová, L. 2015. Voices of university students with disabilities: inclusive education on the tertiary level – a reality or a distant dream? *International Journal of Inclusive Education*, Vol. 19, No. 10, pp. 1080–95.

Stubbs, S. 2008. *Inclusive Education: Where There Are Few Resources*. Oslo, The Atlas Alliance.

Symeou, L., Karagiorgi, Y., Roussounidou, E. and Kaloyirou, C. 2009. Roma and their education in Cyprus: reflections on INSETRom teacher training for Roma inclusion. *Intercultural Education*, Vol. 20, No. 6, pp. 511–21.

Tadevosyan, S. and Ghukasyan, H. 2015. Moving from special schools to inclusive schooling: Bridge of Hope's advocacy in Armenia. *Enabling Education Review*, Special Issue, pp. 5–8.

Tamil Nadu School Education Department. 2019. *Policy Note 2019–20*. Chennai, Tamil Nadu School Education Department.

Tchintcharauli, T. and Javakhishvili, N. 2017. Inclusive education in Georgia: current trends and challenges. *British Journal of Special Education*, Vol. 44, No. 4, pp. 465–83.

Tesemma, S. T. 2011. *Educating Children with Disabilities in Africa: Towards a Policy of Inclusion*. Addis Ababa, The African Child Policy Forum.

The Economist. 2019. British Muslim parents propose LGBT lessons in primary school. 7 March.

Theirworld. 2018. *Charity Helps Latin American Street Children Find an Identity and an Education*. London, Theirworld. https://theirworld.org/news/street-children-el-salvador-guatemala-helped-into-school. (Accessed 18 November 2019.)

Thoms, E.-M. 2017. *NRW nach der Wahl: und Inklusion? [North-Rhine Westphalia after the election: and incluson?]*. Cologne, Germany, mittendrin e.V. – Beratungsstelle für Inklusion www.mittendrin-koeln.de/blog/artikel/nrw-nach-der-wahl-und-inklusion. (Accessed 11 December 2019.)

Through the Looking Glass. 2013. *Parents with Disabilities and their Children: Promoting Inclusion and Awareness in the Classroom*. Berkeley, Calif., Through the Looking Glass.

Timmer, A. D. 2010. Constructing the "needy subject": NGO discourses of Roma need. *PoLAR: Political and Legal Anthropology Review*, Vol. 33, No. 2, pp. 264–81.

___. 2017. *Educating the Hungarian Roma: Nongovernmental Organizations and Minority Rights*. Lanham, Md., Lexington Books.

Torgbenu, E. L., Oginni, O. S., Opoku, M. P., Nketsia, W. and Agyei-Okyere, E. 2018. Inclusive education in Nigeria: exploring parental attitude, knowledge and perceived social norms influencing implementation. *International Journal of Inclusive Education*.

Truth and Reconciliation Commission of Canada. 2015a. *Honouring the Truth, Reconciling for the Future: Summary of the Final Report of the Truth and Reconciliation Commission of Canada*. Winnipeg, Canada, Truth and Reconciliation Commission of Canada.

___. 2015b. *Truth and Reconciliation Commission of Canada: Calls to Action*. Winnipeg, Canada, Truth and Reconciliation Commission of Canada.

Ullman, J. and Ferfolja, T. 2016. The elephant in the (class)room: parental perceptions of LGBTQ-inclusivity in K–12 educational contexts. *Australian Journal of Teacher Education*, Vol. 41, No. 10, pp. 15–29.

UNESCO. 2019. *Beyond Commitments: How Countries Implement SDG 4*. Paris, Global Education Monitoring Report.

United Nations. 2019. *Disability and the Media*. New York, United Nations. www.un.org/development/desa/disabilities/resources/disability-and-the-media.html. (Accessed 28 February 2019.)

US Department of Education 2012. *Statistics about Nonpublic Education in the United States*. Washington, DC, Department of Education. www2.ed.gov/about/offices/list/oii/nonpublic/statistics.html. (Accessed 17 May 2019.)

Valenzuela, J. P., Bellei, C. and Ríos, D. d. l. 2014. Socioeconomic school segregation in a market-oriented educational system: the case of Chile. *Journal of Education Policy*, Vol. 29, No. 2, pp. 217–41.

van Baar, H. 2013. Travelling activism and knowledge formation in the Romani social and civil movement. Miskovic, M. (ed.), *Roma Education in Europe: Practices, Policies and Politics*. Abingdon, UK, Routledge.

Wasserberg, M. J. 2014. Stereotype threat effects on African American children in an urban elementary school. *Journal of Experimental Education*, Vol. 82, No. 4, pp. 502–17.

World Vision. 2007. *Including the Excluded: Integrating Disability into the EFA Fast Track Initiative Processes and National Education Plans in Cambodia.* Phnom Penh, World Vision.

Xiong, Y. and Li, M. 2017. Citizenship education as NGO intervention: turning migrant children in Shanghai into 'new citizens'. *Citizenship Studies*, Vol. 21, No. 7, pp. 792–808.

Yohannes, B., Sintayehu, B., Alebachew, Y. and Kay, L. 2017. Catch-up education: the door to future possibilities in Ethiopia. *Enabling Education Review*, No. 6, pp. 20–21.

Yukon Government. 2019. *How First Nations perspectives are incorporated into schools.* Whitehorse, Canada. https://yukon.ca/en/first-nations-perspectives. (Accessed 13 November 2019.)

Zine, J. 2007. Safe havens or religious 'ghettos'? Narratives of Islamic schooling in Canada. *Race, Ethnicity and Education*, Vol. 10, No. 1, pp. 71–92.

MONITORING SECTION

CHAPTER 9

Barakat, B., Alkema, L. and Antoninis, M. 2019. Adjusted Bayesian completion rates (ABC) estimation: technical report. Paris, Global Education Monitoring Report. (Unpublished.)

Bexell, M. and Jönsson, K. 2018. Country reporting on the Sustainable Development Goals: the politics of performance review at the global-national nexus. *Journal of Human Development and Capabilities*, Vol. 20, No. 4, pp. 403–17.

Burke, S. and Rürup, B. L. 2019. Political thriller exposes the underbelly of global goals. *Global Policy*, Vol. 10, No. S1, p. 137.

European Commission. 2019. *European policy cooperation (ET 2020 framework).* Brussels, European Commission. https://ec.europa.eu/education/policies/european-policy-cooperation/et2020-framework_en. (Accessed 11 December 2019.)

European Council. 2020. *Draft Council Resolution on Education and Training in the European Semester: Ensuring Informed Debates on Reforms and Investment.* Brussels, European Council.

Fritz, S., See, L., Carlson, T., Haklay, M. M., Oliver, J. L., Fraisl, D., Mondardini, R., Brocklehurst, M., Shanley, L. A., Schade, S., Wehn, U., Abrate, T., Anstee, J., Arnold, S., Billot, M., Campbell, J., Espey, J., Gold, M., Hager, G., He, S., Hepburn, L., Hsu, A., Long, D., Masamp, J., McCallum, I., Muniafu, M., Moorthy, I., Obersteiner, M., Parker, A. J., Weisspflug, M. and West, S. 2019. Citizen science and the United Nations Sustainable Development Goals. *Nature Sustainability*, Vol. 2, No. 10, pp. 922–30.

Fukuda Parr, S. and McNeill, D. 2019. Knowledge and politics in setting and measuring the SDGs: introduction to special issue. *Global Policy*, Vol. 10, No. S1, pp. 5–15.

Fukuda Parr, S. and Muchhala, B. 2020. The Southern origins of sustainable development goals: ideas, actors, aspirations. *World Development*, Vol. 126.

GPSDD. 2019a. *About the Global Partnership for Sustainable Development Data*, Global Partnership for Sustainable Development Data. www.data4sdgs.org/about-gpsdd. (Accessed 11 December 2019.)

___. 2019b. *Inclusive Data Charter*, Global Partnership for Sustainable Development Data. www.data4sdgs.org/inclusivedatacharter. (Accessed 11 December 2019.)

IHSN. 2013. *Activities.* Paris/Washington, DC, International Household Survey Network. https://ihsn.org/content/about/activities. (Accessed 11 December 2019.)

IPUMS. 2019. *IPUMS International.* University of Minnesota, Minneapolis, Minn. https://ipums.org/projects/ipums-international. (Accessed 11 December 2019.)

LIS. 2019. *About LIS.* Luxembourg, Luxembourg Income Study. www.lisdatacenter.org/about-lis. (Accessed 11 December 2019.)

Mahajan, M. 2019. The IHME in the shifting landscape of global health metrics. *Global Policy*, Vol. 10, No. S1, pp. 110–20.

Merry, S. E. 2019. The Sustainable Development Goals confront the infrastructure of measurement. *Global Policy*, Vol. 10, No. S1, pp. 146–48.

Pacific Community. 2013. *Demographic and Health Survey: Papua New Guinea, 2006-2007.* Noumea, Pacific Community. https://microdata.pacificdata.org/index.php/catalog/30/study-description. (Accessed 11 December 2019.)

Papua New Guinea National Statistical Office and ICF. 2019. *Papua New Guinea Demographic and Health Survey 2016-18.* Port Moresby/Rockville, Md., National Statistical Office/ICF.

PARIS21. 2019. *Statistical Capacity Monitor.* Paris, Partnership in Statistics for Development in the 21st Century. https://statisticalcapacitymonitor.org. (Accessed 11 December 2019.)

Pérez Piñán, A. and Vibert, E. 2019. The view from the farm: gendered contradictions of the measurement imperative in global goals. *Journal of Human Development and Capabilities,* Vol. 20, No. 4, pp. 436–50.

Sánchez-Páramo, C. and Fu, H. 2019. *From Data Day to a Data Decade.* Washington, DC, World Bank. https://blogs.worldbank.org/opendata/data-day-data-decade. (Accessed 11 December 2019.)

Serajuddin, U., Yoshida, N. and Uematsu, H. 2015. *Much of the World Is Deprived of Poverty Data: Let's Fix This.* Washington, DC, World Bank. https://blogs.worldbank.org/developmenttalk/much-world-deprived-poverty-data-let-s-fix. (Accessed 11 December 2019.)

Spaull, N. 2016. *Serious Technical Concerns about SACMEQ IV Results Presented to Parliament.* https://nicspaull.com/2016/09/14/serious-technical-concerns-about-sacmeq-iv-results-presented-to-parliament. (Accessed 11 December 2019.)

UIS. 2018. *Instruction Manual: Survey of Formal Education.* Montreal, Canada, UNESCO Institute for Statistics.

___. 2019a. *Monitoring Progress: Benchmarking – Group Discussion.* Montreal, Canada, UNESCO Institute for Statistics. (TCG6/REF/12.)

___. 2019b. *The Quality of International Data on Teachers to Report on SDG Target 4.c.* Montreal, Canada, UNESCO Institute for Statistics. (TCG6/REF/5.)

UNESCO. 2016. *Incheon Declaration and Framework for Action for the Implementation of Sustainable Development Goal 4.* Paris, UNESCO.

___. 2019a. *Global Education Monitoring Report 2019: Gender Report – Building Bridges for Gender Equality.* Paris, UNESCO.

___. 2019b. *Meeting Commitments: Are Countries on Track to Achieve SDG 4?* Montreal, Canada/Paris, UNESCO Institute for Statistics/Global Education Monitoring Report.

UNSC. 2019. *Achieving the Full Potential of Household Surveys in the SDG Era.* New York, Inter-Secretariat Working Group on Household Surveys, United Nations Statistical Commission.

UNSD. 2020. *Global Indicator Framework for the Sustainable Development Goals and Targets of the 2030 Agenda for Sustainable Development.* New York, Inter-agency and Expert Group on SDG Indicators, United Nations Statistical Division.

World Bank. 2019. *About the Microdata Library.* Washington, DC, World Bank. https://microdata.worldbank.org/index.php/about. (Accessed 11 December 2019.)

Yap, M. L.-M. and Watene, K. 2019. The Sustainable Development Goals (SDGs) and indigenous peoples: another missed ppportunity? *Journal of Human Development and Capabilities,* Vol. 20, No. 4, pp. 451–67.

CHAPTER 10

Bacher-Hicks, A., Billings, S. B. and Deming, D. J. 2019. *The School to Prison Pipeline: Long-Run Impacts of School Suspensions on Adult Crime.* Cambridge, Mass., National Bureau of Economic Research. (Working Paper 26257.)

Burton, R. F. 2001. Quantifying the effects of chance in multiple choice and true/false tests: question selection and guessing of answers. *Assessment and Evaluation in Higher Education,* Vol. 26, No. 1, pp. 41–50.

Chmielewski, A. K. 2019. The global increase in the socioeconomic achievement gap, 1964 to 2015. *American Sociological Review,* Vol. 84, No. 3, pp. 517–44.

Christle, C. A., Jolivette, K. and Nelson, C. M. 2007. School characteristics related to high school dropout rates. *Remedial and Special Education,* Vol. 28, No. 6, pp. 325–39.

Cuellar, A. E. and Markowitz, S. 2015. School suspension and the school-to-prison pipeline. *International Review of Law and Economics,* Vol. 43, pp. 98–106.

Daniels, H. and Cole, T. 2010. Exclusion from school: short-term setback or a long term of difficulties? *European Journal of Special Needs Education,* Vol. 25, No. 2, pp. 115–30.

Department for Education. 2019. *Permanent and Fixed Period Exclusions in England: 2017 to 2018.* Darlington, UK, Department for Education.

Gustafsson, M. 2020. *Floor Effects and the Comparability of Developing Country Student Test Scores.* Paris, UNESCO. (Background paper for *Global Education Monitoring Report 2020.*)

Hutchinson, J. and Crenna-Jennings, W. 2019. *Unexplained Pupil Exits from Schools*. London, Education Policy Institute and National Education Union. (Social Mobility and Vulnerable Learners.)

Kauffman, E. 2012. The worst "school-to-prison" pipeline: was it in Mississippi? *Time*, 11 December.

Kebede, T. A. 2018. *Strømme Foundation's Speed School Program in Burkina Faso, Mali and Niger*. Oslo, Fafo. (Fafo-report 2018:27.)

Kim, S., Richardson, D. and Mizunoya, S. 2020. *Out of Sight, Out of Mind: Inclusion in Learning Assessments and Measurement Challenges*. Paris, UNESCO. (Background paper for *Global Education Monitoring Report 2020*.)

Kipruto, I. 2019. *PAL Network Embarks on a Multi-country Study in Early Grade Numeracy*. Nairobi, People's Action for Learning Network. https://palnetwork.org/pal-network-embarks-on-a-multi-country-study-on-early-grade-numeracy. (Accessed 11 December 2019.)

Lewis, T. and Vásquez Solótzano, E. 2006. Unraveling the heart of the school-to-prison pipeline. Rosatto, C. A., Allen, R. L. and Pruyn, M. (eds), *Reinventing Critical Pedagogy*. Lanham, Md., Rowman & Littlefield, pp. 63–78.

Lowden, J. 2018. *Speed School as a Model for Accelerated Education: Emerging Evidence*. Paper for Comparative and International Education Society, Mexico City, 25–29 March.

Martin, M. O., Mullis, I. and Hooper, M. (eds). 2016. *Methods and Procedures in TIMSS 2015*. Chestnut Hill, Pa., International Association for the Evaluation of Educational Achievement.

Miller, J. 2019. A sea change in New York City public schools that prioritizes student well-being? As students head back to class, arrests for minor misbehavior are set to end. *The Hechinger Report*, 5 September.

Montoya, S. and Senapaty, H. 2019. *Linking Data to Get Results: India Shows How Countries Can Use Their National Assessments for Global Reporting*. Paris, Global Education Monitoring Report. https://gemreportunesco.wordpress.com/2019/11/18/linking-data-to-get-results-india-shows-how-countries-can-use-their-national-assessments-for-global-reporting. (Accessed 11 December 2019.)

Morris, M. 2016. *Pushout: The Criminalization of Black Girls in Schools*. New York, The New Press.

Mullis, I., Martin, M. O., Foy, P. and Hooper, M. 2016. *TIMSS 2015 International Results in Mathematics*. Chestnut Hill, Pa., International Association for the Evaluation of Educational Achievement.

Myers, J., Pinnock, H. and Lewis, I. 2016. *Accelerated Education Programmes: A Toolkit for Donors, Practitioners and Evaluators*. Geneva, Switzerland, United Nations High Commissioner for Refugees.

National Women's Law Center. 2015. *School Reform and Dropout Prevention: Addressing Disparities in Discipline for African American Girls*. Washington, DC, National Women's Law Center and NAACP Legal Defense and Educational Fund.

Oddy, J. 2019. *Accelerated Education Programming (AEP): Children, Families, Teachers and Educational Stakeholders Experiences of AEP in Uganda*. London, Save the Children.

OECD. 2018. *PISA for Development*, Paris, Organisation for Economic Co-operation and Development.

___. 2019. *PISA 2018 Results: Volume I, What Students Know and Can Do*. Paris, Organisation for Economic Co-operation and Development.

Pacific Community. 2019. *Pacific Islands Literacy and Numeracy Assessment 2018 Regional Report*. Suva, Fiji, Educational Quality and Assessment Division, Pacific Community.

Pritchett, L. and Beatty, A. 2012. *The Negative Consequences of Overambitious Curricula in Developing Countries*. Cambridge, Mass., Harvard Kennedy School.

Razer, M., Friedman, V. J. and Warshofsky, B. 2013. Schools as agents of social exclusion and inclusion. *International Journal of Inclusive Education*, Vol. 17, No. 11, pp. 1152–70.

Rutkowski, L., Rutkowski, D. and Liaw, Y.-L. 2019. The existence and impact of floor effects for low-performing PISA participants. *Assessment in Education: Principles, Policy & Practice*, Vol. 26, No. 6, pp. 1–22.

Sullivan, A. L., Van Norman, E. R. and Klingbeil, D. A. 2014. Exclusionary discipline of students with disabilities. *Remedial and Special Education*, Vol. 35, No. 4, pp. 199–210.

Thomson, P. and Russell, L. 2009. Data, data everywhere – but not all the numbers that count? Mapping alternative provisions for students excluded from school. *International Journal of Inclusive Education*, Vol. 13, No. 4, pp. 423–38.

UIS. 2019. *UIS-IEA Rosetta Stone Meeting*. Montreal, Canada, UNESCO Institute for Statistics. http://gaml.uis.unesco.org/uis-iea-rosetta-stone-meeting. (Accessed 11 December 2019.)

UNESCO. 2019a. *Beyond Commitments: How Countries Implement SDG 4*. Paris, UNESCO.

___. 2019b. *Meeting Commitments: Are Countries on Track to Achieve SDG 4?* Montreal, Canada/Paris, UNESCO Institute for Statistics/Global Education Monitoring Report.

United Nations. 2019. *World Population Prospects 2019*. New York, Department of Economic and Social Affairs, Population Division. https://population.un.org/wpp/DataQuery. (Accessed 11 December 2019.)

US Department of Education. 2019. *Indicator 15: Retention, Suspension, and Expulsion*. Washington, DC, National Center for Education Statistics. https://nces.ed.gov/programs/digest/d17/tables/dt17_233.28.asp. (Accessed 11 December 2019.)

US Department of Education Office for Civil Rights. 2014. *Data Snapshot: School Discipline*. Washington, DC, Department of Education. (Civil Rights Data Collection, Issue Brief.)

World Bank. 2019. *Learning poverty*. Washington, DC, World Bank. www.worldbank.org/en/topic/education/brief/learning-poverty. (Accessed 11 December 2019.)

CHAPTER 11

Barakat, B. F. and Bengtsson, S. 2017. What do we mean by school entry age? Conceptual ambiguity and its implications: the example of Indonesia. *Comparative Education*, Vol. 54, No. 2, pp. 203–24.

Boller, K. and Harman-Smith, Y. 2019. *Measuring Up: Learning About Improving Equity from Australia's Early Childhood Development Census*. Princeton, NJ, Mathematica Policy Research. (InFOCUS.)

Cappa, C., Petrowski, N. and Britto, P. 2019. *Measuring Milestones: Developing a Tool to Assess Early Childhood Development Outcomes*. New York, UNICEF.

Djibouti Ministry of National Education and Professional Training. 2017. *Plan d'Action de l'Éducation 2017–2019 [Education Action Plan 2017–2019]*. Djibouti, Ministry of National Education and Professional Training.

Djibouti Ministry of National Education and Professional Training and UNICEF. 2019. *Document de la Stratégie Nationale du Préscolaire à Djibouti [Djibouti National Pre-primary Education Strategy Document]*. Djibouti, Ministry of National Education and Professional Training.

Dyer, C., Bhattacharjea, S., Alcott, B., Thomas, S. E., Imran, W. and Loyo, D. 2019. *Left Behind in School*. Nairobi/Leeds, PAL Network/University of Leeds. (Leave No One Behind Evidence Brief 1.)

Inui, M. 2020. Impact of the 'Grade Zero'system on minority children in Lao PDR: a qualitative study of pre-primary schools in a rural province. *Education 3-13*, Vol. 48, No. 1, pp. 118–30.

Kuger, S., Marcus, J. and Spiess, C. K. 2019. Day care quality and changes in the home learning environment of children. *Education Economics*, Vol. 27, No. 3, pp. 1–22.

Morocco Higher Council of Education, Training and Scientific Research. 2017. *Un préscolaire équitable et de qualité [Equitable and Quality Pre-primary Education]*. Rabat, Higher Council of Education, Training and Scientific Research. (Rapport préparatoire à l'avis n° 3/2017.)

Nguyen, H. T. M. and Lewis, B. D. 2019. Teenage marriage and motherhood in Vietnam: the negative effects of starting school early. *Population Research and Policy Review*, Vol. 54, No. 3, pp. 1–24.

OECD. 2019. *Education at a Glance 2019*. Paris, Organisation for Economic Co-operation and Development.

Sweet, J. 2019. New Brunswick: Education minister says age-based grade levels to be phased out, CBC News, 3 October. www.cbc.ca/news/canada/new-brunswick/grade-level-phase-out-1.5307605. (Accessed 11 December 2019.)

UNICEF. 2019. *A World Ready to Learn: Prioritizing Quality Early Childhood Education*. New York, UNICEF.

World Bank. 2019. *Lao PDR: Early Childhood Education Project (P145544) IDA Credit Number 5370-LA and IDA Grant Number H910-LA Implementation Support Review, November 12–15, 2019 – Aide-Memoire*. Washington, DC, World Bank.

Zerrour, L. 2018. Préscolaire : Près de 800.000 enfants bénéficiaires en 2018-2019 [Pre-primary education: nearly 800,000 beneficiary children in 2018-2019]. *Aujourd'hui le Maroc*, 22 July. http://aujourdhui.ma/societe/prescolaire-pres-de-800-000-enfants-beneficiaires-en-2018-2019. (Accessed 11 December 2019.)

CHAPTER 12

American School Counselor Association. 2019. *Student-to-School-Counselor Ratio 2016-2017*. Alexandria, Va., American School Counselor Association.

Broton, K. M. and Goldrick-Rab, S. 2017. Going without: an exploration of food and housing insecurity among undergraduates. *Educational Researcher*, Vol. 47, No. 2, pp. 121–33.

Burchell, B., Hardy, V., Rubery, J. and Smith, M. 2014. *A New Method to Understand Occupational Gender Segregation in European Labour Markets*. Brussels, European Commission, Directorate-General for Justice.

Chrisco Brennan, L. 2019. When it comes to college and career support, the counselor shortage is only part of the problem. *The Hechinger Report*, 23 July.

Coates, S. 2016. *Unlocking Potential: A Review of Education in Prison*. London, Ministry of Justice.

Costelloe, A., Langelid, T. and Wilson, A. 2012. *Survey on Prison Education and Training in Europe: Final Report*. Birmingham, GHK.

Council of Europe. 2006. *Recommendation Rec (2006) 2 of the Committee of Ministers to Member States on the European Prison Rules*. Strasbourg, France, Council of Europe.

___. 2018. *Detainees with Disabilities in Europe*. Strasbourg, France, Council of Europe.

Cross, K. P. 1981. *Adults as Learners. Increasing Participation and Facilitating Learning*. San Francisco, Calif., Jossey-Bass.

D'Orio, W. 2019. Propelling prisoners to bachelor's degrees in California. *The Hechinger Report*, 12 July.

Davis, L. M., Bozick, R., Steele, J. L., Saunders, J. and Miles, J. N. V. 2013. *Evaluating the Effectiveness of Correctional Education: A Meta-Analysis of Programs that Provide Education to Incarcerated Adults*. Santa Monica, Calif., RAND Corporation.

Durkin, E. 2019. US college admissions scandal: how did the scheme work and who was charged? *The Guardian*, 13 March.

Escobar, N. 2019. The Reasoning Behind the SAT's New 'Disadvantage' Score. *The Atlantic*, 17 May.

European Commission. 2018. *Guidance to Facilitate the Implementation of Targets to Promote Gender Equality in Research and Innovation*. Brussels, European Commission, Directorate-General for Research and Innovation.

European Institute for Gender Equality. 2019. Proportion of men graduates in tertiary (ISCED levels 5-8) and vocational (ISCED levels 3-4) education and training in the field of education, health and welfare (EHW) – of all graduates in the study field. *Gender Statistics Database*. Vilnius, European Institute for Gender Equality. https://eige.europa.eu/gender-statistics/dgs/indicator/bpfa_b_offic_b1__uoe_share_stem_ehw2. (Accessed 11 December 2019.)

Eurostat. 2019. *Participation Rate in Education and Training by Sex*. Luxembourg, Eurostat. https://appsso.eurostat.ec.europa.eu/nui/show.do?dataset=trng_aes_100&lang=en. (Accessed 11 December 2019.)

Farley, H. and Pike, A. 2018. Research on the inside: overcoming obstacles to completing a postgraduate degree in prison. Padró, F., Erwee, R., Harmes, M., Harmes, M. and Danaher, P. (eds), *Postgraduate Education in Higher Education*. Singapore, Springer, pp. 211–34.

Farley, H., Pike, A., Demiray, U. and Tanglang, N. 2016. Delivering digital higher education into prisons: the cases of four universities in Australia, UK, Turkey and Nigeria. *GLOKALde*, Vol. 2, No. 2, pp. 147–66.

Friess, S. 2019. Rural students often go unnoticed by colleges. Can virtual counseling put them on the map? *The Hechinger Report*, 11 June.

Gertz, E. 2017. *Why These Prisoners Are Getting Law Degrees behind Bars*, TED. https://ideas.ted.com/why-these-prisoners-are-getting-law-degrees-behind-bars. (Accessed 11 December 2019.)

Golden, D. and Burke, D. 2019. The unseen student victims of the 'Varsity Blues' college-admissions scandal. *The New Yorker*, 8 October.

Gonser, S. 2019. College dreams often melt away in summer months. 'Near-peer' counseling is helping keep them alive. *The Hechinger Report*, 30 August.

Hartocollis, A. 2019. SAT 'Adversity Score' is abandoned in wake of criticism. *The New York Times*, 27 August.

Hoibian, S. and Millot, C. 2018. *Aider les Jeunes à Mieux Identifier leurs Goûts et Motivations Personnelles : Un Levier pour Améliorer l'Orientation – Enquête sur l'Orientation des 18-25 Ans [Helping Young People to Better Identify their Personal Tastes and Motivations: A Lever to Improve Orientation – Survey on the Orientation of 18-25 Year Olds]*. Paris, Conseil National d'Évaluation du Système Scolaire.

India Ministry of Home Affairs. 2003. *Model Prison Manual for the Superintendence and Management of Prisons in India*. New Delhi, Bureau of Police Research and Development, Ministry of Home Affairs.

India Ministry of Women and Child Development. 2018. *Women in Prisons: India*. New Delhi, Ministry of Women and Child Development.

Institute for Women's Policy Research. 2014. *4.8 Million College Students Are Raising Children*. Washington, DC, Institute for Women's Policy Research. (Fact Sheet.)

___. 2018. *Time Demands of Single Mother College Students and the Role of Child Care in their Postsecondary Success*. Washington, DC, Institute for Women's Policy Research. (Briefing Paper.)

Juneja, A. 2019. The most reprehensible part of the admissions scandal: faking disability accommodations. *Vox*, 14 March.

Justice Trends. 2019. Singapore Prison Service towards total digitisation. Covilhã, Portugal, IPS_ Innovative Prison Systems. https://justice-trends.press/singapore-prison-service-towards-total-digitisation. (Accessed 11 December 2019.)

Klocker, N. and Drozdzewski, D. 2012. Career progress relative to opportunity: how many papers is a baby 'worth'? *Environment and Planning A: Economy and Space*, Vol. 44, No. 6, pp. 1271–77.

Krolak, L. 2019. *Books Beyond Bars: The Transformative Potential of Prison Libraries*. Hamburg, UNESCO Institute for Lifelong Learning.

Lindeque, B. 2018. Ground breaking prison education programme launched in South Africa. *GoodThingsGuy*. www. goodthingsguy.com/business/ground-breaking-prison-education-programme. (Accessed 11 December 2019.)

Mayer, A. K., Kalamkarian, H. S., Cohen, B., Pellegrino, L., Boynton, M. and Yang, E. 2019. *Integrating Technology and Advising: Studying Enhancements to Colleges' iPASS Practices*. New York: MDRC and Community College Research Center, Teachers College, Columbia University.

Miller, R. 2020. The need for more black school counselors, and four ways to get better information about HBCUs. *The Hechinger Report*, 9 January.

Miller, S. 2016. The banning of books in prisons: 'It's like living in the dark ages'. *The Guardian*, 25 September.

Moss, S. 2017. Half of Britain's prisoners are functionally illiterate. Can fellow inmates change that? *The Guardian*, 15 June.

Nadworny, E. 2019. Congress considers making college more accessible to people in prison. *NPR*, 20 April.

Oakford, P., Brumfield, C., Goldvale, C., Tatum, L., diZerega, M. and Patrick, F. 2019. *Investing in Futures: Economic and Fiscal Benefits of Postsecondary Education in Prison*. New York, Vera Institute of Justice.

OECD. 2019a. *Future-Ready Adult Learning Systems*. Paris, Organisation for Economic Co-operation and Development. (Getting Skills Right.)

___. 2019b. *OECD Skills Strategy 2019*. Paris, Organisation for Economic Co-operation and Development.

Perry, A. M. 2019. *In Higher Education, the Wand Chooses the Wizard*, Brookings Institution. www.brookings.edu/blog/the-avenue/2019/05/23/in-higher-education-the-wand-chooses-the-wizard. (Accessed 11 December 2019.)

Prison Insider. 2019. *Guinea*. Lyon, France, Prison Insider. www.prisoninsider.com/en/countryprofile/guinee-2015. (Accessed 11 December 2019.)

Rafferty, L., Dalton, B., Hill, B., Saris, I., Atkinson-Barrett, L. and Maynard, L. 2010. *Consideration of Merit Relative to Opportunity in Employment-Related Decisions*. Canberra, Group of Eight HR Directors Staff Equity Subcommittee Project.

RFI. 2019. Students demand anti-poverty measures ahead of national strike. *Radio France International*, 26 November. www.rfi.fr/en/france/20191126-french-students-demand-anti-poverty-measures-ahead-general-strike. (Accessed 11 December 2019.)

Robbins, A. 2019. Kids are the victims of the elite-college obsession. *The Atlantic*, 12 March.

Rubenson, K. 2011. Barriers to participation in adult education. Rubenson, K. (ed.), *Adult Learning and Education*. Saint Louis, Mo., Academic Press, pp. 216–21.

___. 2018. Conceptualizing participation in adult learning and education: equity issues. Milana, M., Webb, S., Holford, J., Waller, R. and Jarvis, P. (eds), *The Palgrave International Handbook on Adult and Lifelong Education and Learning*. London, Palgrave Macmillan, pp. 337–57.

Rubiano-Matulevich, E. and Viollaz, M. 2019. *Gender Differences in Time Use: Allocating Time between the Market and the Household*. Washington, DC, World Bank. (Policy Research Working Paper 8981.)

Sawahel, W. 2017. University in prisons: the 'best rehabilitation tool'. *University World News*, 27 September. www. universityworldnews.com/post.php?story=20170927104116664. (Accessed 11 December 2019.)

Schaub, M. 2016. Texas prisons ban books by Langston Hughes and Bob Dole but 'Mein Kampf' is OK. *Los Angeles Times*, 27 September.

Torlone, F. and Vryonides, M. (eds). 2016. *Innovative Learning Models for Prisoners*. Florence, Firenze University Press. (Studies on Adult Learning and Education 4.)

Tough, P. 2019. What college admissions offices really want. *The New York Times*, 10 September.

UIL. 2019. *4th Global Report on Adult Learning and Education*. Hamburg, UNESCO Institute for Lifelong Learning.

UNICEF and Universidad Diego Portales. 2017. *Situación Educativa de las y los Adolescentes Privados de Libertad por Causas Penales en América Latina y el Caribe [Education Situation of Adolescents Deprived of Liberty for Penal Reasons in Latin America and the Caribbean]*. Panama City, UNICEF Latin America and the Caribbean Regional Office.

US Department of Education. 2018. *The Guidance Counselor's Role in Ensuring Equal Educational Opportunity*. Washington, DC, Department of Education, Office of Civil Rights. www2.ed.gov/about/offices/list/ocr/docs/hq43ef.html. (Accessed 11 December 2019.)

UNODC. 2015. *The United Nations Standard Minimum Rules for the Treatment of Prisoners (the Nelson Mandela Rules)*. Vienna, United Nations Office on Drugs and Crime.

___. 2017. *Roadmap for the Development of Prison-based Rehabilitation Programmes*. Vienna, United Nations Office on Drugs and Crime. (Criminal Justice Handbook Series.)

Vorhaus, J. 2014. Prisoners' right to education: a philosophical survey. *London Review of Education*, Vol. 12, No. 2, pp. 162–74.

Walmsley, R. 2018. *World Prison Population List*. London, Institute for Criminal Policy Research.

Welsch, D. M. and Windeln, M. 2019. Student gender, counselor gender, and college advice. *Education Economics*, Vol. 27, No. 2, pp. 112–31.

Wikeley, F., Bullock, K., Muschamp, Y. and Ridge, T. 2009. Educational relationships and their impact on poverty. *International Journal of Inclusive Education*, Vol. 13, No. 4, pp. 377–93.

CHAPTER 13

Brewer, J. and Gibson, S. W. 2016. The Academy for Creating Enterprise. Brewer, J. and Gibson, S. W. (eds.), *Institutional Case Studies on Necessity Entrepreneurship*. Cheltenham, UK, Edward Elgar.

Cummings, S., Seferiadis, A. A., Maas, J., Bunders, J. F. and Zweekhorst, M. B. 2019. Knowledge, social capital, and grassroots development: insights from rural Bangladesh. *Journal of Development Studies*, Vol. 55, No. 2, pp. 161–76.

Friedson-Ridenour, S. and Pierotti, R. S. 2018. *Competing Priorities: Women's Microenterprises and Household Relationships*. Washington, DC, World Bank. (Policy Research Working Paper 8550.)

ILO. 2015. *International Labour Conference Recommendation 204 Concerning the Transition from the Informal to the Formal Economy, Adopted by the Conference at its One Hundred and Fourth Session*. Geneva, Switzerland, International Labour Organization.

___. 2017. *ILO Business Management Training Programme Has Led to the Creation of 9 Million Jobs Globally*. Geneva, Switzerland, International Labour Organization. www.ilo.org/global/about-the-ilo/newsroom/news/WCMS_560493/lang--en/index.htm. (Accessed 11 December 2019.)

___. 2018. *Women and Men in the Informal Economy: A Statistical Picture*. Geneva, Switzerland, International Labour Organization.

Jayachandran, S. 2020. Microentrepreneurship in Developing Countries. Evanston, Ill., Northwestern University. (Unpublished.)

Leifels, A. and Metzger, G. 2019. *Migrant Start-ups: A Stronger Desire for Self-employment*. Frankfurt, Germany, KfW. (Research Focus on Economics 240.)

Lingelbach, D. C., De La Vina, L. and Asel, P. 2005. *What's Distinctive about Growth-oriented Entrepreneurship in Developing Countries?* San Antonio, Tex., College of Business Center for Global Entrepreneurship, University of Texas. (Working Paper 1.)

McCallum, E., Weicht, R., McMullan, L. and Price, A. 2018. *EntreComp into Action: Get Inspired, Make it Happen – A User Guide to the European Entrepreneurship Competence Framework*. Seville, Spain, Joint Research Centre.

Mersha, T., Sriram, V. and Hailu, M. 2010. Nurturing opportunity entrepreneurs in Africa: some lessons from Ethiopia. *Journal for Global Business Advancement*, Vol. 3, No. 2, pp. 155–75.

Roberts, J. and Myrrha, N. 2016. SEBRAE: Serviço Brasileiro de Apoio às Micro e Pequenas Empresas. Brewer, J. and Gibson, S. W. (eds), *Institutional Case Studies on Necessity Entrepreneurship*. Cheltenham, UK, Edward Elgar.

Singer, S., Amorós, J. E. and Moska Arreola, D. 2015. *Global Entrepreneurship Monitor: 2014 Global Report*. London, Global Entrepreneurship Research Association.

Valerio, A., Parton, B. and Robb, A. 2014. *Entrepreneurship Education and Training Programs Around the World: Dimensions for Success*. Washington, DC, World Bank.

Webb, P. and Fairbourne, J. 2016. Microfranchising: a solution to necessity entrepreneurship. Brewer, J. and Gibson, S. W. (eds), *Institutional Case Studies on Necessity Entrepreneurship*. Cheltenham, UK, Edward Elgar.

World Bank. 2018. *Nearly Half the World Lives on Less than $5.50 a Day*. Washington, DC, World Bank.

Xie, J., Basham, J. D., Marino, M. T. and Rice, M. F. 2017. Reviewing research on mobile learning in K–12 educational settings. *Journal of Special Education Technology*, Vol. 33, No. 1, pp. 27–39.

CHAPTER 14

Arms, E. 2007. Gender equity in coeducational and single-sex environments. Klein, S. S., Richardson, B., Grayson, D. A., Fox, L. H., Kramarae, C., Pollard, D. S. and Dwyer, C. A. (eds), *Handbook for Achieving Gender Equity through Education*, Vol. 2. London, Routledge, pp. 171–90.

Aslam, M. and Kingdon, G. G. 2008. Gender and household education expenditure in Pakistan. *Applied Economics*, Vol. 40, No. 20, pp. 2573–91.

Ávila, R. 2018. *LGBTQI Inclusive Education Report*. Brussels, International Lesbian, Gay, Bisexual, Transgender, Queer and Intersex Youth and Student Organisation.

Bigler, R. S., Roberson Hayes, A. and Liben, L. S. 2014. Analysis and evaluation of the rationales for single-sex schooling. *Advances in Child Development and Behavior*, Vol. 47, pp. 225–60.

Bustillo, I., Artecona, R. and Perrotti, D. 2018. *Inequality and Growth in Latin America: Achievements and Challenges*. New York, Group of 24 and Friedrich-Ebert-Stiftung.

CDI. 2017. *Indicadores Socioeconómicos de los Pueblos Indígenas de México, 2015 [Socioeconomic Indicators of Indigenous Peoples of Mexico, 2015]*. Mexico City, National Commission for the Development of Indigenous Peoples.

Dajani, H. and Rizvi, A. 2018. Boys and girls to be educated together in major shift for UAE's public schools. *The National*, 1 July. www.thenational.ae/uae/boys-and-girls-to-be-educated-together-in-major-shift-for-uae-s-public-schools-1.745934. (Accessed 11 December 2019.)

Del Popolo, F. 2008. *Los Pueblos Indígenas y Afrodescendientes en las Fuentes de Datos: Experiencias en América Latina [Indigenous Peoples and Afro-descendants in Data Sources: Experiences in Latin America]*. Santiago, United Nations Economic Commission for Latin America and the Caribbean.

Dustmann, C., Ku, H. and Kwak, D. W. 2018. Why are single-sex schools successful? *Labour Economics*, Vol. 54, pp. 79–99.

ECLAC. 2016. *Los Censos de la Ronda 2020: Desafíos ante la Agenda 2030 para el Desarrollo Sostenible, los Objetivos de Desarrollo Sostenible y el Consenso de Montevideo sobre Población y Desarrollo [The 2020 Round Censuses: Challenges for Agenda 2030 for Sustainable Development, the Sustainable Development Goals and the Montevideo Consensus on Population and Development]*. Santiago, United Nations Economic Commission for Latin America and the Caribbean.

Fabes, R. A., Pahlke, E., Martin, C. L. and Hanish, L. D. 2013. Gender-segregated schooling and gender stereotyping. *Educational Studies*, Vol. 39, No. 3, pp. 315–19.

Flores, R. and Telles, E. 2012. Social stratification in Mexico: disentangling color, ethnicity, and class. *American Sociological Review*, Vol. 77, No. 3, pp. 486–94.

Giardili, S. 2019. *Single-Sex Primary Schools and Student Achievement: Evidence from Admission Lotteries*. London, School of Economics and Finance, Queen Mary University of London.

Gomez Murillo, A. R. 2008. *Indígena Urbano en América Latina: Etnogénesis en el Distrito Metropolitano de Quito [Urban Indigenous Populations in Latin America: Ethnogenesis in the Quito Metropolitan District]*. Editorial Académica Española.

Hall, G. and Patrinos, H. 2012. *Indigenous Peoples, Poverty, and Development*. Cambridge, UK, Cambridge University Press.

INEE. 2017. *Breve Panorama Educativo de la Poblacion Indigena [Brief Education Panorama of Indigenous Peoples]*. Mexico City, National Institute of Education Evaluation.

Jackson, K. 2012. Single-sex schools, student achievement, and course selection: evidence from rule-based student assignments in Trinidad and Tobago. *Journal of Public Economics*, Vol. 96, No. 1–2, pp. 173–87.

Link, S. 2012. *Single-Sex Schooling and Student Performance: Quasi-Experimental Evidence from South Korea*. Munich, Ifo Institute, Leibniz Institute for Economic Research at the University of Munich (Working Paper 146.)

Marcus, R. and Page, E. 2016. *Evidence Review: Girls' Learning and Empowerment – the Role of School Environments*. New York/London, United Nations Girls' Education Initiative/Overseas Development Institute.

Pahlke, E., Hyde, J. S. and Allison, C. M. 2014. The effects of single-sex compared with coeducational schooling on students' performance and attitudes: a meta-analysis. *Psychological Bulletin*, Vol. 140, No. 4, p. 1042–72.

Park, H., Behrman, J. R. and Choi, J. 2013. Causal effects of single-sex schools on college entrance exams and college attendance: random assignment in Seoul high schools. *Demography*, Vol. 50, No. 2, pp. 447–69.

Planas, M.-E., Middelkoop, B., Cruzado, V. and Richters, A. 2016. Navigating ethnicity in Peru: a framework for measuring multiple self-identification among indigenous Quechua women. *Latin American and Caribbean Ethnic Studies*, Vol. 11, No. 1, pp. 70–92.

Riordan, C. 2015. *Single-Sex Schools: A Place to Learn*. London, Rowman & Littlefield.

Sax, L. J., Arms, E., Woodruff, M., Riggers, T. and Eagan, K. 2009. *Women Graduates of Single-Sex and Coeducational High Schools: Differences in their Characteristics and the Transition to College.* Los Angeles, Calif., Sudikoff Family Institute for Education and New Media, UCLA Graduate School of Education and Information Studies.

Smyth, E. 2010. Single-sex education: what does research tell us? *Revue française de pédagogie: Recherches en éducation,* No. 171, pp. 47–58.

Sperling, G. and Winthrop, R. 2015. *What Works in Girls' Education: Evidence for the World's Best Investment.* Washington, DC, Brookings Institution.

Telles, E., Flores, R. D. and Urrea-Giraldo, F. 2015. Pigmentocracies: educational inequality, skin color and census ethnoracial identification in eight Latin American countries. *Research in Social Stratification and Mobility,* Vol. 40, pp. 39–58.

Telles, E. and Torche, F. 2019. Varieties of indigeneity in the Americas. *Social Forces,* Vol. 97, No. 4, pp. 1543–70.

Telles, E. E. 2007. Race and ethnicity and Latin America's United Nations Millennium Development Goals. *Latin American and Caribbean Ethnic Studies,* Vol. 2, No. 2, pp. 185–200.

TWB. 2019. *The Words Between Us: How Well Do Enumerators Understand The Terminology Used in Humanitarian Surveys? A Study from Northeast Nigeria.* Danbury, Conn., Translators Without Borders.

___. 2020. *Language data fills a critical gap for humanitarians.* Danbury, Conn., Translators Without Borders. www.translatorswithoutborders.org/blog/language-data-gap. (Accessed 20 February 2020.)

Unterhalter, E., North, A., Arnot, M., Lloyd, C., Moletsane, L., Murphy-Graham, E., Parkes, J. and Saito, M. 2014. *Interventions to Enhance Girls' Education and Gender Equality.* London, Department for International Development. (Education Rigorous Literature Review.)

Valencia Lopez, E. 2020. *Improving and Aligning Measurement of Ethnicity in Latin America.* Paris, UNESCO. (*Global Education Monitoring Report Fellowhip Paper.*)

Villarreal, A. 2014. Ethnic identification and its consequences for measuring inequality in Mexico. *American Sociological Review,* Vol. 79, No. 4, pp. 775–806.

Wong, W. I., Shi, S. Y. and Chen, Z. 2018. Students from single-sex schools are more gender-salient and more anxious in mixed-gender situations: results from high school and college samples. *PLOS ONE,* Vol. 13, No. 12.

Yoshioka, H. 2010. Indigenous language use and maintenance patterns among indigenous people in the era of neoliberal multiculturalism in Mexico and Guatemala. *Latin American Research Review,* Vol. 45, No. 3, pp. 5–34.

CHAPTER 15

Alidou, H. 2006. *Use of African Languages and Literacy: Conditions, Factors and Processes (Benin, Burkina Faso, Cameroon, Tanzania and Zambia).* Paper for Association for the Development of Education in Africa Biennale on Education in Africa, Libreville, 27–31 March.

Copeland, S. R., McCord, J. A. and Kruger, A. 2016. A review of literacy interventions for adults with extensive needs for supports. *Journal of Adolescent and Adult Literacy,* Vol. 60, No. 2, pp. 173–84.

Dyslexia Association of Ireland. 2016. *Adult Dyslexia.* Dublin, Dyslexia Association of Ireland.

Dyslexia International. 2014. *Better Training, Better Teaching.* Brussels, Dyslexia International.

Eberhard, D. M., Simons, G. F. and Fennig, C. D. 2020. *Ethnologue: Languages of the World.* Dallas, Tex., SIL International. www.ethnologue.com. (Accessed 7 February 2020.)

European Commission. 2012. *EU High-level Group of Experts on Literacy: Final Report.* Brussels, European Commission.

Groce, N. E. and Bakhshi, P. 2011. Illiteracy among adults with disabilities in the developing world: a review of the literature and a call for action. *International Journal of Inclusive Education,* Vol. 15, No. 10, pp. 1153–68.

Hanemann, U. and McKay, V. 2019. Learning in the mother tongue: examining the learning outcomes of the South African Kha Ri Gude literacy campaign. *International Review of Education,* Vol. 65, No. 3, pp. 351–87.

International Dyslexia Association. 2019. *Resources to Support Implementation.* Baltimore, Md. https://dyslexiaida.org/resources-to-support-implementation. (Accessed 11 December 2019.)

Kutner, M., Greenberg, E., Jin, Y., Boyle, B., Hsu, Y.-c. and Dunleavy, E. 2007. *Literacy in Everyday Life: Results From the 2003 National Assessment of Adult Literacy.* Washington, DC, National Center for Education Statistics.

Latch-On. 2020. *Welcome to Latch-On: literacy, confidence and independence for young people with intellectual disabilities.* Brisbane, Australia, University of Queensland. www.latch-on.net. (Accessed 4 February 2020.)

LDA. 2015. *Adult Literacy Reading Programs.* Pittsburgh, Pa., Learning Disabilities Association of America.

Limerick, N. 2017. Kichwa or Quichua? Competing alphabets, political histories, and complicated reading in indigenous languages. *Comparative Education Review*, Vol. 62, No. 1, pp. 103–24.

National Research Council. 2012. *Improving Adult Literacy: Instruction Options for Practice and Research*. Washington, DC, National Academies Press.

Ng'asike, J. T. 2019. Indigenous knowledge practices for sustainable lifelong education in pastoralist communities of Kenya. *International Review of Education*, Vol. 65, No. 1, pp. 19–46.

OECD. 2019. *Skills Matter: Additional Results from the Survey of Adult Skills*. Paris, Organisation for Economic Co-operation and Development.

Patterson, M. B. 2008. Learning disability prevalence and adult education program characteristics. *Learning Disabilities Research and Practice*, Vol. 23, No. 1, pp. 50–59.

Patterson, M. B. and Mellard, D. 2008. Contrasting adult literacy learners with and without specific learning disabilities. *Learning Disabilities Research and Practice*, Vol. 29, No. 3, pp. 133–44.

Rabkin, G., Geffers, S., Hanemann, U., Heckt, M. and Pietsch, M. 2018. Hamburg's Family Literacy project (FLY) in the context of international trends and recent evaluation findings. *International Review of Education*, Vol. 64, No. 5, pp. 651–77.

Robinson, C. 2016. Languages in adult literacy: policies and practices in Education for All and beyond. *Prospects*, Vol. 46, No. 1, pp. 73–91.

South Africa Department of Basic Education. 2019. *Kha Ri Gude Mass Literacy Programme*. Pretoria, Department of Basic Education. www.education.gov.za/Programmes/KhaRiGude.aspx.

Tamassia, C., Lennon, M., Yamamoto, K. and Kirsch, I. 2007. *Adult Education in America: A First Look at Results from the Adult Education Program and Learner Surveys*. Princeton, NJ, Educational Testing Service, Center for Global Assessment.

UIS. 2017. *Implementation in Diverse Settings of the Literacy Assessment and Monitoring Programme (LAMP): Lessons for Sustainable Development Goal 4 (SDG 4)*. Montreal, Canada, UNESCO Institute for Statistics.

___. 2018. *Mini-LAMP for Monitoring Progress towards SDG 4.6.1*. Montreal, Canada, UNESCO Institute for Statistics.

UNDP. 2004. *Human Development Report 2004: Cultural Liberty in Today's Diverse World*. New York, United Nations Development Programme.

UNESCO. 2003. The mother-tongue dilemma. *Education Today: The Newsletter of UNESCO's Education Sector*, No. 6, pp. 4–7.

___. 2019a. *Algeria's Multilingual National Literacy Strategy Wins UNESCO Prize*. Paris, UNESCO. https://en.unesco.org/news/algerias-multilingual-national-literacy-strategy-wins-unesco-prize. (Accessed 11 December 2019.)

___. 2019b. *Learning literacy as a family in Mozambique*. Paris, UNESCO. https://en.unesco.org/news/learning-literacy-family-mozambique%20. (Accessed 11 December 2019.)

Wittgenstein Centre. 2019. *Human Capital Data Explorer*. Vienna, Wittgenstein Centre for Demography and Global Human Capital. http://dataexplorer.wittgensteincentre.org/wcde-v2. (Accessed 11 December 2019.)

World Bank. 2015. *Skills Toward Employment and Productivity: Global Initiative to Generate Internationally Comparable Data on Skills of Adult Population*. Washington, DC, World Bank.

CHAPTER 16

African Youth Initiative on Climate Change. 2020. *About AYICC*. Nairobi, African Youth Initiative on Climate Change. http://ayicckenya.blogspot.com/p/about-ayicc.html. (Accessed 4 February 2020.)

Buckler, C. and Creech, H. 2014. *Shaping the Future we Want: UN Decade of Education for Sustainable Development (2005–2014): Final Report*. Paris, UNESCO.

Cunningham, W. and Villasenor, P. 2016. *Employer Voices, Employer Demands, and Implications for Public Skills Development Policy Connecting the Labor and Education Sectors*. Washington, DC, World Bank. (Policy Research Working Paper 7582.)

Durlak, J. A., Weissberg, R. P., Dymnicki, A. B., Taylor, R. D. and Schellinger, K. B. 2011. The impact of enhancing students' social and emotional learning: a meta-analysis of school-based universal interventions. *Child Development*, Vol. 82, No. 1, pp. 405–32.

Education International. 2019. *Defending education, sustaining the world*. Bangkok, Education International. www.ei-ie.org/en/detail/16421/resolution-on. (Accessed 11 December 2019.)

Engelbrecht, A. 2006. Textbooks in South Africa from apartheid to post-apartheid: ideological change revealed by racial stereotyping. Roberts-Schweitzer, E. (ed.), *Promoting Social Cohesion through Education: Case Studies and Tools for Using Textbooks and Curricula*. Washinton, DC, World Bank, pp. 71–80.

Fredriksen, B. and Brar, S. 2015. *Getting Textbooks to Every Child in Sub-Saharan Africa: Strategies for Addressing the High Cost and Low Availability Problem*. Washington, DC, World Bank.

Global Climate Strike. 2019. *7.6 million people demand action after week of climate strikes*. New York, Global Climate Strike. https://globalclimatestrike.net/7-million-people-demand-action-after-week-of-climate-strikes. (Accessed 11 December 2019.)

Greaney, V. 2006. Textbooks, respect for diversity, and social cohesion. Roberts-Schweitzer, E. (ed.), *Promoting Social Cohesion through Education: Case Studies and Tools for Using Textbooks and Curricula*. Washinton, DC, World Bank, pp. 47–69.

Hanemann, U. 2019. How are target 4.7 themes and related issues addressed in non-formal and youth and adult education from a lifelong learning perspective? Smart, A., Sinclair, M., Benavot, A., Bernard, J., Chabbott, C., Russell, S. G. and Williams, J. (eds), *NISSEM Global Briefs: Educating for the Social, the Emotional and the Sustainable – Diverse Perspectives from over 60 Contributors Addressing Global and National Challenges*, Networking to Integrate SDG Target 4.7 and Social and Emotional Learning Skills into Educational Materials.

Jiménez, J. D. and Lerch, J. C. 2019. Waves of diversity: depictions of marginalized groups and their rights in social science textbooks, 1900–2013. *Comparative Education Review*, Vol. 63, No. 2, pp. 166–88.

Kennedy, B. and Hefferon, M. 2019. *What Americans Know About Science*. Washington, DC, Pew Research Center.

OECD. 2001. *Thematic Review of National Policies for Education: Romania – Stability Pact for South Eastern Europe*. Paris, Organisation for Economic Co-operation and Development.

___. 2017. *Preparing our Youth for an Inclusive and Sustainable World: The OECD PISA Global Competence Framework*. Paris, Organisation for Economic Co-operation and Development.

___. 2019. *TALIS 2018 Results: Teachers and School Leaders as Lifelong Learners – Volume I*. Paris, Organisation for Economic Co-operation and Development.

Our Children's Trust. 2019. *Global legal actions*. Eugene, Ore., Our Children's Trust. www.ourchildrenstrust.org/global-legal-actions. (Accessed 11 December 2019.)

Pingel, F. 2010. *UNESCO Guidebook Textbook Research and Textbook Revision*, Paris/Braunschweig, Germany, UNESCO/ Georg Eckert Institute for International Textbook Research.

Preston, C. 2019. The silence of school leaders on climate change. *The Hechinger Report*, 12 June.

Smart, A., Sinclair, M., Benavot, A., Bernard, J., Chabbott, C., Russell, S. G. and Williams, J. 2019. *NISSEM Global Briefs: Educating for the Social, the Emotional and the Sustainable – Diverse Perspectives from over 60 Contributors Addressing Global and National Challenges*. Networking to Integrate SDG Target 4.7 and Social and Emotional Learning Skills into Educational Materials.

The Aspen Institute. 2019. *From a Nation at Risk to a Nation at Hope: Recommendations from the National Commission on Social, Emotional, and Academic Development*. Washington, DC, The Aspen Institute.

UIS. 2019a. *Report on Indicator 4.7.1*. Montreal, Canada, Technical Cooperation Group, UNESCO Institute for Statistics. (TCG6/REF/2.)

___. 2019b. *SDG Indicator 4.7.1: Proposal for a Measurement Strategy*. Monteal, Canada, Technical Cooperation Group, UNESCO Institute for Statistics. (TCG6/REF/4.)

___. 2019c. *SDG Indicator 4.7.1: Proposal for Monitoring*. Montreal, Canada, Technical Cooperation Group, UNESCO Institute for Statistics. (TCG6/REF/3.)

UNESCO. 2018. *Progress on Education for Sustainable Development and Global Citizenship Education: Findings of the 6th Consultation on the Implementation of the 1974 Recommendation Concerning Education for International Understanding, Co-operation and Peace and Education Relating to Human Rights and Fundamental Freedoms (2012-2016)*. Paris, UNESCO.

Unigwe, C. 2019. It's not just Greta Thunberg: why are we ignoring the developing world's inspiring activists? *The Guardian*, 5 October.

Vista, A., Kim, H. and Care, E. 2018. *Use of Data from 21st Century Skills Assessments: Issues and Key Principles*. Washington, DC, Brookings Institution.

World Bank. 2008. *Textbooks and School Library Provision in Secondary Education in Sub-Saharan Africa*. Washington, DC, World Bank. (African Human Development Series Working Paper 126.)

WWF. 2018. *Environmental and indigenous rights activist to receive WWF's top youth conservation award*. Gland, Switzerland, WWF International. wwf.panda.org/?327434. (Accessed 11 December 2019.)

CHAPTER 17

Agrasar. 2018. *Choking Childhood: School Corporal Punishment – Everyday Violence Faced by Disadvantaged Children in India.* Gurugram, India, Agrasar.

Alevriadou, A. 2010. Promoting road safety for preadolescent boys with mild intellectual disabilities: the effect of cognitive style and the role of attention in the identification of safe and dangerous road-crossing sites. *International Journal of Special Education,* Vol. 25, No. 2, pp. 127–35.

Bader, L. 2019. *'They Are Making Us into Slaves, Not Educating Us': How Indefinite Conscription Restricts Young People's Rights, Access to Education in Eritrea.* New York, Human Rights Watch.

Bakó-Biró, Z., Clements-Croome, D. J., Kochhar, N., Awbi, H. B. and Williams, M. J. 2012. Ventilation rates in schools and pupils' performance. *Building and Environment,* Vol. 48, pp. 215–23.

Baron, J. 2019. Bringing attention to indoor air pollution. *Forbes,* 19 February.

Barrett, P., Treves, A., Shmis, T., Ambasz, D. and Ustinova, M. 2019. *The Impact of School Infrastructure on Learning: A Synthesis of the Evidence.* Washington, DC, World Bank.

Barshay, J. 2020. The learning effect of air quality in classrooms. *The Hechinger Report,* 20 January.

Bastin, J.-F., Clark, E., Elliott, T., Hart, S., van den Hoogen, J., Hordijk, I., Ma, H., Majumder, S., Manoli, G., Maschler, J., Mo, L., Routh, D., Yu, K., Zohner, C. M. and Crowther, T. W. 2019. Understanding climate change from a global analysis of city analogues. *PLOS ONE,* Vol. 14, No. 7.

Borker, G. 2018. Safety first: perceived risk of street harassment and educational choices of women. Providence, RI, Department of Economics, Brown University. (Unpublished.)

Burdick-Will, J., Stein, M. L. and Grigg, J. 2019. Danger on the way to school: exposure to violent crime, public transportation, and absenteeism. *Sociological Science,* Vol. 6, pp. 118–42.

Costa, L. G., Cole, T. B., Coburn, J., Chang, Y.-C., Dao, K. and Roqué, P. J. 2017. Neurotoxicity of traffic-related air pollution. *Neurotoxicology,* Vol. 59, pp. 133–39.

EASO. 2016. *Eritrea: National Service and Illegal Exit.* Valletta, European Asylum Support Office. (Country of Origin Information Report.)

Ebenstein, A., Lavy, V. and Roth, S. 2016. The long-run economic consequences of high-stakes examinations: evidence from transitory variation in pollution. *American Economic Journal: Applied Economics,* Vol. 8, No. 4, pp. 36–65.

FIA Foundation. 2016. *Child Health Initiative launched to support 'safe journey for every child'.* London, FIA Foundation. www.fiafoundation.org/blog/2016/june/child-health-initiative-launched-to-support-safe-journey-for-every-child. (Accessed 11 December 2019.)

___. 2020. *These Are Our Streets: Manifesto 2030 – Safe and Healthy Streets for Children, Youth and Climate.* London, Child Health Initiative, FIA Foundation.

Gershoff, E. T. 2017. School corporal punishment in global perspective: prevalence, outcomes, and efforts at intervention. *Psychology, Health and Medicine,* Vol. 22, Supplement 1, pp. 224–39.

Global Coalition to Protect Education from Attack. 2020. *Safe Schools Declaration Endorsements.* New York, Global Coalition to Protect Education from Attack. https://ssd.protectingeducation.org/endorsement. (Accessed 11 February 2020.)

Global Initiative to End All Corporal Punishment of Children. 2019. *Teaching Without Violence: Prohibiting Corporal Punishment.* London, Global Initiative to End All Corporal Punishment of Children. (Briefing Paper.)

Goodman, J., Hurwitz, M., Park, J. and Smith, J. 2018. *Heat and Learning.* Cambridge, Mass., National Bureau of Economic Research. (Working Paper 24639.)

Greene, M., Robles, O., Stout, K. and Suvilaakso, T. 2011. *A Girl's Right to Learn Without Fear: Working to End Gender-based Violence at School.* Woking, UK, Plan International.

Heissel, J., Persico, C. and Simon, D. 2019. *Does Pollution Drive Achievement? The Effect of Traffic Pollution on Academic Performance,* Cambridge, Mass., National Bureau of Economic Research. (Working Paper 25489.)

Heywood, J. S. and Weber, B. 2019. University-provided transit and crime in an urban neighborhood. *The Annals of Regional Science,* Vol. 62, pp. 467–95.

IFRTD. 2010. *A Moving Issue: Children and Young People's Transport and Mobility Constraints in Africa.* London, International Forum for Rural Transport and Development. (Forum News 15 (1).)

Kann, L., Olsen, E. O. M., McManus, T., Harris, W. A., Shanklin, S. L., Flint, K. H., Queen, B., Lowry, R., Chyen, D., Whittle, L., Thornton, J., Lim, C., Yamakawa, Y., Brener, N. and Zaza, S. 2016. Sexual identity, sex of sexual contacts, and health-related behaviors among students in grades 9–12: United States and selected sites, 2015. *Surveillance Summaries,* Vol. 65, No. 9, pp. 1–202.

Koppensteiner, M. F. and Menezes, L. 2017. *Afraid to Go to School? Estimating the Effect of Community Violence on Schooling Outcomes*. Paper for second IZA Workshop: The Economics of Education, Bonn, Germany, 25–27 September.

Kunn, S., Palacios, J. and Pestel, N. 2019. *The Impact of Indoor Climate on Human Cognition: Evidence from Chess Tournaments*. Paper for seventh IZA Workshop on Environment and Labor Markets, Bonn, Germany, 8–9 May.

Le, K. and Nguyen, M. 2019. 'Bad apple' peer effects in elementary classrooms: the case of corporal punishment in the home. *Education Economics*, Vol. 27, No. 6, pp. 557–72.

Lin, P.-S., Guo, R., Bialkowska-Jelinska, E., Kourtellis, A. and Zhang, Y. 2019. Development of countermeasures to effectively improve pedestrian safety in low-income areas. *Journal of Traffic and Transportation Engineering*, Vol. 6, No. 2, pp. 162–74.

Matthews, T. 2019. Heatwave: think it's hot in Europe? The human body is already close to thermal limits elsewhere. *The Conversation*, 25 July. http://theconversation.com/heatwave-think-its-hot-in-europe-the-human-body-is-already-close-to-thermal-limits-elsewhere-121003. (Accessed 11 December 2019.)

Moser-Mercer, B. 2018. *Local Knowledge Production: Kakuma Refugee Camp (Kenya)*. Geneva, Switzerland, Connected Learning in Crisis Consortium. https://connectedlearning4refugees.org/case-studies/local-knowledge-production. (Accessed 11 December 2019.)

Mumovic, D., Chatzidiakou, L., Williams, J. J. and Burman, E. 2018. *Indoor Air Quality in London's Schools*. London, Greater London Authority.

Munns, C. 2019. *Afghan Schools Left Unprotected by Government and International Community*. Inter Press Service News Agency, 6 June. www.ipsnews.net/2019/06/afghan-schools-left-unprotected-government-international-community. (Accessed 11 December 2019.)

Naylor, R. 2019. *Not Just Ramps and Girls' Toilets: Seeing beyond the 'Inclusionwash' of Inclusive Education*. www.ukfiet.org/2019/not-just-ramps-and-girls-toilets-seeing-beyond-the-inclusionwash-of-inclusive-education. (Accessed 11 December 2019.)

Porras-Salazar, J. A., Wyon, D. P., Piderit-Moreno, B., Contreras-Espinoza, S. and Wargocki, P. 2018. Reducing classroom temperature in a tropical climate improved the thermal comfort and the performance of elementary school pupils. *Indoor Air*, Vol. 28, No. 6, pp. 892–904.

Power of Zero. 2018. *Early Learning for a Connected World: Life Skills for Young Children*. San Francisco, Calif., No Bully.

Rames, V., Jean-Gilles, S. and Seisun, C. 2016. *USAID/Haiti Gender Assessment Report*. Washington, DC, Banyan Global.

Randell, H. and Gray, C. 2019. Climate change and educational attainment in the global tropics. *Proceedings of the National Academy of Sciences*, Vol. 116, No. 18, pp. 8840–45.

Rees, D. I., Sabia, J. J. and Kumpas, G. 2020. *Anti-Bullying Laws and Suicidal Behaviors among Teenagers*. Cambridge, Mass., National Bureau of Economic Research. (Working Paper 26777.)

Republic of Korea National Human Rights Commission. 2017. *Independent Report of National Human Rights Commission of Korea for Consideration of Third to Fifth Periodic Reports submitted by Republic of Korea under Convention against Torture and Other Cruel, Inhuman or Degrading Treatment or punishment*. Seoul, National Human Rights Commission of Korea.

Silverman, A. 2016. *Rights of Way: Child Poverty and Road Traffic Injury in the SDGs*. New York/London, UNICEF/FIA Foundation.

Silverman, A. and Billingsley, S. 2015. *Safe to Learn: Safe Journeys to School Are a Child's Right*. New York/London, UNICEF/FIA Foundation.

Sunyer, J., Esnaola, M., Alvarez-Pedrerol, M., Forns, J., Rivas, I., López-Vicente, M., Suades-González, E., Foraster, M., Garcia-Esteban, R., Basagaña, X., Viana, M., Cirach, M., Moreno, T., Alastuey, A., Sebastian-Galles, N., Nieuwenhuijsen, M. and Querol, X. 2015. Association between traffic-related air pollution in schools and cognitive development in primary school children: a prospective cohort study. *PLOS Medicine*, Vol. 12, No. 3.

The Economist. 2019. How air pollution can ruin schoolchildren's lives. 2 November.

Theirworld. 2019. *Safe Schools: The Hidden Crisis – A Framework for Action to Deliver Safe, Non-Violent, Inclusive and Effective Learning Environments*. New York, Theirworld.

Tigre, R., Sampaio, B. and Menezes, T. 2017. The impact of commuting time on youth's school performance. *Journal of Regional Science*, Vol. 57, No. 1, pp. 28–47.

UNESCO. 2017. *Global Education Monitoring Report 2017/8: Accountability in Education – Meeting Our Commitments*. Paris, UNESCO.

___. 2018. *School Violence and Bullying: Global Status and Trends, Drivers and Consequences*. Paris, UNESCO.

___. 2019a. *Behind the Numbers: Ending School Violence and Bullying*. Paris, UNESCO.

___. 2019b. *Bringing It out in the Open: Monitoring School Violence Based on Sexual Orientation, Gender Identity or Gender Expression in National and International Surveys.* Paris, UNESCO. (Technical Brief.)

UNICEF. 2019a. *Guidance on Menstrual Health and Hygiene.* New York, UNICEF.

___. 2019b. *School Closures in the Sahel Double in the Last Two Years due to Growing Insecurity.* New York, UNICEF. www.unicef.org/press-releases/school-closures-sahel-double-last-two-years-due-growing-insecurity-unicef. (Accessed 11 December 2019.)

Wang, D., Xu, Y., Liu, Y., Wang, Y., Jiang, J., Wang, X. and Liu, J. 2018. Experimental investigation of the effect of indoor air temperature on students' learning performance under the summer conditions in China. *Building and Environment,* Vol. 140, pp. 140–52.

Wargocki, P., Porras-Salazar, J. A. and Contreras-Espinoza, S. 2019. The relationship between classroom temperature and children's performance in school. *Building and Environment,* Vol. 157, pp. 197–204.

Welle, B., Bray Sharpin, A., Adriazola-Steil, C., Job, S., Shotten, M., Bose, D., Bhatt, A., Alveano, S., Obelheiro, M. and Imamoglu, T. 2016. *Sustainable and Safe: A Vision and Guidance for Zero Road Deaths.* Washington, DC, World Resources Institute/Global Road Safety Facility.

CHAPTER 18

European Commission. 2019. *Intra-Africa Academic Mobility Scheme.* Brussels, Education, Audiovisual and Culture Executive Agency, European Commission. https://eacea.ec.europa.eu/intra-africa/actions/intra-africa-academic-mobility-scheme_en. (Accessed 11 December 2019.)

Gardner, M. 2016. *Tuition fees to be reintroduced for non-EU students.* University World News, 11 November. www.universityworldnews.com/post.php?story=20161111124506846. (Accessed 11 December 2019.)

Hansrod, Z. 2019. France will increase university fees for for non-EU students. Radio France International, 22 April. www.rfi.fr/en/france/20190422-france-will-increase-university-fees-non-eu-students. (Accessed 11 December 2019.)

UNESCO. 2018. *Global Education Monitoring Report 2019: Migration, Displacement and Education – Building bridges, Not Walls.* Paris, UNESCO.

CHAPTER 19

Cambodia Ministry of Education Youth and Sport. (2017). *Public Education Statistics and Indicators 2016-2017.* Phnom Penh, Ministry of Education Youth and Sport.

Dolton, P., Marcenaro, O., De Vries, R., & She, P.-W. (2018). *Global Teacher Status Index.* London, Varkey Foundation.

Education Commission. (2019). *Transforming the Education Workforce: Learning Teams for a Learning Generation.* New York, Education Commission.

Edwards, D. (2019). Is the World Bank taking the right approach to ensure #successfulteachers? *World of Education,* 25 February. https://worldsofeducation.org/en/woe_homepage/woe_detail/16134/%E2%80%9Cis-the-world-bank-taking-the-right-approach-to-ensure-successfulteachers%E2%80%9D-by-david-edwards. (Accessed 11 December 2019.)

Ginsburg, M., Ansari, N., Goyee, O. N., Hatch, R., Morris, E., and Tuowal, D. (2018). Where have all the (qualified) teachers gone? Implications for measuring sustainable development goal target 4.c from a study of teacher supply, demand and deployment in Liberia. *African Educational Research Journal,* Vol. 6, No. 2, pp.30–47.

Henshaw, C. (2019). Teachers work more unpaid overtime than anyone else. *Tes,* 1 March. www.tes.com/news/teachers-work-more-unpaid-overtime-anyone-else. (Accessed 11 December 2019.)

India Ministry of Human Resource Development. (2018). *Educational Statistics at a Glance.* New Delhi, Ministry of Human Resource Development.

Kim, H. (2019). *To Teach or Not to Teach? It's a Little More Complicated Than That.* Washington, Brookings Institution. www.brookings.edu/blog/education-plus-development/2019/02/11/to-teach-or-not-to-teach-its-a-little-more-complicated-than-that. (Accessed 11 December 2019.)

Kim, H., Cameron, C. E., Kelly, C. A., West, H., Mashburn, A. J., and Grissmer, D. W. (2018). Using an individualized observational measure to understand children's interactions in underserved kindergarten classrooms. *Journal of Psychoeducational Assessment,* Vol. 37, No. 8, pp. 935–56.

Masdeu Navarro, F. (2015). *Learning Support Staff: A Literature Review.* Paris, Organisation for Economic Co-operation and Development. (Education Working Paper 125.)

OECD. (2018). *OECD Handbook for Internationally Comparative Education Statistics 2018: Concepts, Standards, Definitions and Classifications*. Paris, Organisation for Economic Co-operation and Development.

OECD. (2019a). *PISA 2018 Results: What Students Know and Can Do – Volume I*. Paris, Organisation for Economic Co-operation and Development.

OECD. (2019b). *Providing Quality Early Childhood Education and Care: Results from the Starting Strong Survey 2018*. Paris, Organisation for Economic Co-operation and Development.

OECD. (2019c). *TALIS 2018 Results (Volume I): Teachers and School Leaders as Lifelong Learners*. Paris, Organisation for Economic Co-operation and Development.

Rose, R. (2020). *The Use of Teacher Assistants and Education Support Personnel in Inclusive Education*. Paris, UNESCO. (Background paper for *Global Education Monitoring Report 2020*.)

Schuhmacher, K., and Burkert, M. (2013). Time is relative: how framing of time estimation affects measurement error in cost systems. Atlanta, Ga./Fribourg, Switzerland, Emory University/University of Fribourg. (Unpublished.)

South Africa Department of Basic Education. (2018). *Education Statistics in South Africa 2016*. Pretoria, Department of Basic Education.

UNESCO. (2016). *Incheon Declaration and Framework for Action for the Implementation of Sustainable Development Goal 4*. Paris, UNESCO.

UNICEF. (2016). *Guide for Including Disability in Education Management Information Systems*. New York, UNICEF.

UOE. (2019). *UOE Data Collection on Formal Education. Manual on Concepts, Definitions and Classifications*. Montreal, Canada/Paris/Luxembourg, UNESCO Institute for Statistics/Organisation for Economic Co-operation and Development/Eurostat.

Uwezo. (2018). *Are Our Children Learning Beyond the Basic Skills? Findings from the 2016 Uwezo Beyond Basics Assessment in Uganda*. Kampala, Twaweza East Africa.

World Bank. (2019). *Teach: Observer Manual*. Washington, DC, World Bank.

CHAPTER 20

AACSB International. 2016. *A Collective Vision for Business Education*. Tampa, Fla., The Association to Advance Collegiate Schools of Business.

Adukia, A. 2017. Sanitation and education. *American Economic Journal: Applied Economics*, Vol. 9, No. 2, pp. 23–59.

Bacon, L. 2017. Liberia's Gender-Sensitive Police Reform: Improving Representation and Responsiveness in a Post-Conflict Setting. *International Peacekeeping*, Vol. 22, No. 4, pp. 1–26.

Birchall, J. 2018. *Early Marriage, Pregnancy and Girl Child School Dropout*. Brighton, UK, Institute of Development Studies. (K4D Helpdesk Report.)

Buchner, B., Clark, A., Falconer, A., Macquarie, R., Meattle, C., Tolentino, R. and Wetherbee, C. 2019. *Global Landscape of Climate Finance 2019*. London, Climate Policy Initiative.

Canada Government. 2016. *Pan-Canadian Framework on Clean Growth and Climate Change*. Ottawa, Government of Canada.

Chakravarty, S., Haddock, S. and Botea, I. 2016. *Providing Out-of-School Adolescent Girls with Skills: A Review of the Global Evidence*. Washington, DC, World Bank.

Council of Australian Governments. 2018. *COAG Meeting Communique, 12 December 2018*. Canberra, Council of Australian Governments.

Drummond, C. and Fischhoff, B. 2017. Individuals with greater science literacy and education have more polarized beliefs on controversial science topics. *Proceedings of the National Academy of Sciences*, Vol. 114, No. 36, pp. 9587–92.

Dyllick, T. 2015. Responsible management education for a sustainable world: the challenges for business schools. *Journal of Management Development*, Vol. 34, No. 1, pp. 16–33.

Erten, B. and Keskin, P. 2018. For better or for worse? Education and the prevalence of domestic violence in Turkey. *American Economic Journal: Applied Economics*, Vol. 10, No. 1, pp. 64–105.

Evans, D. and Yuan, F. 2019. *What We Learn about Girls' Education from Interventions that Do Not Focus on Girls*. Washington, DC, Center For Global Development. (Working Paper 513.)

Forest Carbon Partnership Facility. 2019. *Capacity Building Program for Indigenous Peoples and Civil Society*. www.forestcarbonpartnership.org/capacity-building-program. (Accessed 11 December 2019.)

Grépin, K. A. and Bharadwaj, P. 2015. Maternal education and child mortality in Zimbabwe. *Journal of Health Economics*, Vol. 44, pp. 97–117.

Hawken, P. (ed.) 2017. *Drawdown: The Most Comprehensive Plan Ever Proposed to Reverse Global Warming.* New York, Penguin Books.

Heath, R. and Jayachandran, S. 2016. *The Causes and Consequences of Increased Female Education and Labor Force Participation in Developing Countries.* Cambridge, Mass., National Bureau of Economic Research. (Working Paper 22766.)

IBE. 2016. *Global Monitoring of GCED and ESD: Themes in School Curricula.* Paris, UNESCO (Background paper for *Global Education Monitoring Report 2016.*)

IFAD. 2014. *Rural Women's Leadership Programme: Madagascar, Nepal, the Philippines and Senegal – Good Practices and Lessons Learned, 2010-2013.* Rome, International Fund for Agricultural Development.

IPCC. 2018. *Special Report: Global Warming of 1.5° C.* Geneva, Switzerland, Intergovernmental Panel on Climate Change.

Jewkes, R., Flood, M. and Lang, J. 2015. From work with men and boys to changes of social norms and reduction of inequities in gender relations: a conceptual shift in prevention of violence against women and girls. *The Lancet,* Vol. 385, No. 9977, pp. 1580–89.

Khanna, M. 2019. The precocious period: the impact of early menarche on schooling in India. Washington, DC, Georgetown University. (Unpublished.)

Kwauk, C. 2020. *Roadblocks to Quality Education in a Time of Climate Change.* Washington, DC, Brookings Institution.

Lewandowsky, S., Ecker, U. K. and Cook, J. 2017. Beyond misinformation: understanding and coping with the 'post-truth' era. *Journal of Applied Research in Memory and Cognition,* Vol. 6, No. 4, pp. 353–69.

Makondo, C. C. and Thomas, D. S. G. 2018. Climate change adaptation: linking indigenous knowledge with western science for effective adaptation. *Environmental Science and Policy,* Vol. 88, pp. 83–91.

Male, C. and Wodon, Q. 2018. Girls' education and child marriage in West and Central Africa: trends, impacts, costs, and solutions. *Forum for Social Economics,* Vol. 47, No. 2, pp. 262–74.

Menashy, F. 2019. *International Aid to Education: Power Dynamics in an Era of Partnership.* New York, Teachers College Press.

Mensch, B. S., Chuang, E. K., Melnikas, A. J. and Psaki, S. R. 2019. Evidence for causal links between education and maternal and child health: systematic review. *Tropical Medicine and International Health,* Vol. 24, No. 5, pp. 504–22.

Muralidharan, K. and Prakash, N. 2017. Cycling to school: increasing secondary school enrollment for girls in India. *American Economic Journal: Applied Economics,* Vol. 9, No. 3, pp. 321–50.

Nair, N. S., Darak, S., Bhumika, T.V. Darak, T., Mathews, M., Devi, L. D., Ratheebhai, V. and Dave, A. 2017. *'Gender-Responsive Policing' Initiatives Designed to Enhance Confidence, Satisfaction in Policing Services and Reduce Risk of Violence Against Women in Low and Middle Income Countries: A Systematic Review.* London, EPPI-Centre, Social Science Research Unit, UCL Institute of Education, University College London.

OECD. 2019. Labour force participation rate, by sex and age group. *OECD Statistics: Employment.* Paris, Organisation for Economic Co-operation and Development. https://stats.oecd.org/index.aspx?queryid=54741. (Accessed 11 December 2019.)

Oliver, P., Clark, A. and Meattle, C. 2018. *Global Climate Finance: An Updated View 2018.* London, Climate Policy Initiative.

RRI. 2018. *A Global Baseline of Carbon Storage in Collective Lands.* Washington, DC, Rights and Resources Initiative.

Surani, M. N. 2016. *Strengthening Women's Political Participation and Leadership for Effective Democratic Governance in Pakistan.* Washington, DC, Search for Common Ground.

The Partnership Initiative. 2019. *Research and Learning.* Oxford, UK, The Partnership Initiative. https://thepartneringinitiative.org/research-and-learning. (Accessed 11 December 2019.)

Tonga Government. 2019. *Kingdom of Tonga Voluntary National Review.* Nuku'alofa, National Planning Division, Prime Minister's Office.

UN PRME. 2017. *2017 Annual Report and 2018 Outlook.* New York, United Nations Principles for Responsible Management.

UN Women. 2018. *Historic Leap in Tunisia: Women Make Up 47 per cent of Local Government.* New York, UN Women. https://www.unwomen.org/en/news/stories/2018/8/feature-tunisian-women-in-local-elections. (Accessed 11 December 2019.)

UNECA. 2019. *Climate Research for Development in Africa.* www.uneca.org/cr4d. (Accessed 11 December 2019.)

UNESCO. 2019. *Global Education Monitoring Report: Gender Report – Building Bridges for Gender Equality.* Paris, UNESCO.

UNFCCC. 2017. *Enhancing Financing for the Research, Develpment and Demonstration of Climate Technologies.* New York, United Nations Framework Convention on Climate Change.

Venema, R. M., Lorenz, K. and Sweda, N. 2019. A descriptive study of training and its perceived helpfulness among Illinois sexual assault investigators. *Journal of Crime and Justice,* Vol. 43, No. 1, pp. 1–15.

Wodon, Q., Nguyen, M. C. and Tsimpo, C. 2016. Child marriage, education, and agency in Uganda. *Feminist Economics*. Vol. 22, No. 1, pp. 54–79.

World Economic Forum. 2018. *Global Gender Gap Report 2018*. Geneva, Switzerland, World Economic Forum. (Insight Report.)

CHAPTER 21

Acerenza, S. and Gandelman, N. 2019. Household education spending in Latin America and the Caribbean: evidence from income and expenditure surveys. *Education Finance and Policy*, Vol. 14, No. 1, pp. 61–87.

ADB. 2017. *Mongolia: Ensuring Inclusiveness and Service Delivery for Persons with Disabilities Project – Project Administration Manual*. Manila, Asian Development Bank.

___. 2018. *Madhya Pradesh Skills Development Project: Gender Equality and Social Inclusion Plan*. Manila, Asian Development Bank.

___. 2019. *2018 Financial Report*. Manila, Asian Development Bank.

Aslam, M. and Kingdon, G. G. 2008. Gender and household education expenditure in Pakistan. *Applied Economics*, Vol. 40, No. 20, pp. 2573–91.

Ausaid. 2008. *Development for All: Towards a Disability-inclusive Australian Aid Program 2009-2014*. Canberra, Australian Agency for International Development.

Australia Department of Foreign Affairs and Trade. 2015. *Development for All 2015-2020 Strategy for Strengthening Disability-inclusive Development in Australia's Aid Program*. Canberra, Department of Foreign Affairs and Trade.

___. 2018. *Development for All: Evaluation of Progress Made in Strengthening Disability Inclusion in Australian Aid*. Canberra, Office of Development Effectiveness, Department of Foreign Affairs and Trade.

Azam, M. and Kingdon, G. G. 2013. Are girls the fairer sex in India? Revisiting intra-household allocation of education expenditure. *World Development*, Vol. 42, pp. 143–64.

Benin Ministries of Pre-Primary and Primary Education; Secondary Education, Technical and Professional Education and Youth Training and Integration; Higher Education and Scientific Research; and Culture, Literacy, Crafts and Tourism. 2013. *Plan Decennal de Developpement du Secteur de l'Education Actualisé [Updated 10-Year Education Sector Development Plan]*. Cotonou, Ministries of Pre-Primary and Primary Education; Secondary Education, Technical and Professional Education and Youth Training and Integration; Higher Education and Scientific Research; and Culture, Literacy, Crafts and Tourism.

Bhattacharya, D. and Rashmin, R. 2019. Financial flows from China and India: how concessional are they? *Forum for Development Studies*, Vol. 47, No. 1, pp. 181–99.

Canada Government. 2018. *G7 2018 Charlevoix Declaration on Quality Education for Girls, Adolescent Girls and Women in Developing Countries*. La Malbaie, PQ, Government of Canada.

China National Bureau of Statistics. 2018. *China Statistical Yearbook 2018*. Beijing, National Bureau of Statistics. www.stats.gov.cn/tjsj/ndsj/2018/indexeh.htm. (Accessed 11 December 2019.)

Choi, E. J. and Hwang, J. 2015. Child gender and parental inputs: no more son preference in Korea? *American Economic Review*, Vol. 105, No. 5, pp. 638–43.

Datta, S. and Kingdon, G. G. 2019. *Gender Bias in Intra-Household Allocation of Education in India: Has It Fallen over Time?* Bonn, Germany, Institute of Labor Economics. (IZA Discussion Paper 12671.)

Delelegn, A. 2007. Intra-household gender bias in child educational spending in rural Ethiopia: panel evidence. *Ethiopian Journal of Economics*, Vol. XVI, No. 2, pp. 1–38.

Department for International Development. 2018a. *DFID Disability Inclusion Strategy Delivery Plan*. London, Department for International Development.

___. 2018b. *DFID's Strategy for Disability Inclusive Development 2018-23* London, Department for International Development.

Development Initiatives. 2019. *Global Humanitarian Assistance Report 2019*. Bristol, UK, Development Initiatives.

DiLorenzo, M., Ghose, S. and Turner, J. 2017. *Estimating Baseline Aid to the Sustainable Development Goals*. Williamsburg, Va., AidData, College of William and Mary.

ECLAC. 2018. *Fiscal Panorama of Latin America and the Caribbean: Public Policy Challenges in the Framework of the 2030 Agenda*. Santiago, United Nations Economic Commission for Latin America and the Caribbean.

Education Cannot Wait. 2020a. *Education Cannot Wait Invests $48 Million in Chad and Ethiopia*. New York, Education Cannot Wait. www.educationcannotwait.org/chad-ethiopia-myrp-launches. (Accessed 20 February 2020.)

___. 2020b. *Results Dashboard*. New York, Education Cannot Wait.

Education Commission. 2019. *Breakthrough in Global Campaign to Double Education Funding for Countries Most in Need*. Washington, DC, International Commission on Financing Global Education Opportunity. http://educationcommission. org/press-releases/september-30-2019-breakthrough-in-global-campaign-to-double-education-funding-for-countries-most-in-need. (Accessed 11 February 2020.)

___. 2020. *2020 Update: the International Finance Facility for Education (IFFEd)*. Washington, DC, International Commission on Financing Global Education Opportunity. http://educationcommission.org/updates/2020-update-the-international-finance-facility-for-education-iffed. (Accessed 11 February 2020.)

European Council. 2017. *The New European Consensus on Development 'Our World, Our Dignity, Our Future'*. Brussels, European Council.

European Disability Forum. 2020. *Successful meeting with the European Commission to advance disability inclusion in international development*. Brussels, European Disability Forum and International Disability Alliance. www.edf-feph.org/ newsroom/news/successful-meeting-european-commission-advance-disability-inclusion-international. (Accessed 2 March 2020.)

European Union. 2016. *European Union supports Egypt in collaboration with UNICEF to expand educational opportunities and enforce child protection systems*. Cairo, European Union External Action.

Germany Ministry for Economic Cooperation and Development. 2013. *Action Plan for the Inclusion of Persons with Disabilities (2013-2015)*. Bonn/Berlin, Ministry for Economic Cooperation and Development. (BMZ Strategy Paper 1.)

GLAD Network. 2018. *Strategic Plan 2018-2020*. Geneva, Switzerland, Global Action on Disability Network.

Global Affairs Canada. 2017a. *Canada's Feminist International Assistance Policy*. Ottawa, Global Affairs Canada.

___. 2017b. *Project Profile: Improving Access to Healthy and Safe Primary Schools and Preschools*. Ottawa, Global Affairs Canada. https://w05.international.gc.ca/projectbrowser-banqueprojets/project-projet/details/a035565001?Lang=eng. (Accessed 11 December 2019.)

Global Disability Summit. 2018. *Global Disability Summit 2018: Summary of Commitments*. London, UK Government with the International Disability Alliance and the Government of Kenya.

Hendren, N. and Sprung-Keyser, B. 2019. *A Unified Welfare Analysis of Government Policies*. Cambridge, Mass., National Bureau of Economic Research. (Working Paper 26144.)

Himaz, R. 2010. Intrahousehold allocation of education expenditure: the case of Sri Lanka. *Economic Development and Cultural Change*, Vol. 58, No. 2, pp. 231–58.

Howes, S., Mako, A. A., Swan, A., Walton, G., Webster, T. and Wiltshire, C. 2014. *Service Delivery and Reforms in Papua New Guinea 2002-2012*. Canberra, Papua New Guinea Promoting Effective Public Expenditure Project, National Research Institute and Development Policy Centre, Australian National University.

Iddrisu, A. M., Danquah, M., Quartey, P. and Ohemeng, W. 2018. Gender bias in households' educational expenditures: does the stage of schooling matter? *World Development Perspectives*, Vol. 10-12, pp. 15–23.

International Monetary Fund. 2015. *From Billions to Trillions: Transforming Development Finance – Post-2015 Financing for Development, Multilateral Development Finance*. Washington, DC, International Monetary Fund.

Jennings, K. 2017. *Tracking Inclusion in Norwegian Development Support to Global Education*. Oslo, Fafo Research Foundation for the Atlas Alliance.

Kaul, T. 2018. Intra-household allocation of educational expenses: gender discrimination and investing in the future. *World Development*, Vol. 104, pp. 336–43.

Kenayathulla, H. B. 2016. Gender differences in intra-household educational expenditures in Malaysia. *International Journal of Educational Development*, Vol. 46, pp. 59–73.

Kingdon, G. G. 2005. Where has all the bias gone? Detecting gender bias in the intrahousehold allocation of educational expenditure. *Economic Development and Cultural Change*, Vol. 53, No. 2, pp. 409–51.

Masterson, T. 2012. An empirical analysis of gender bias in education spending in Paraguay. *World Development*, Vol. 40, No. 3, pp. 583–93.

Norway Government. 2014. *White Paper 25: Education for Development (2013-2014)*. Oslo, Government of Norway.

Norway Ministry of Foreign Affairs. 2018. *Norway supports new initiative to strengthen education for children with disabilities.* Oslo, Ministry of Foreign Affairs. www.regjeringen.no/en/aktuelt/new-initiative-to-strengthen-education-for-children-with-disabilities/id2607536. (Accessed 11 December 2019.)

OECD. 2015. *Why Modernise Official Development Assistance?* Paris, Organisation for Economic Co-operation and Development.

___. 2018a. *Handbook for the Marker for the Inclusion and Empowerment of Persons with Disabilities.* Paris, Development Assistance Committee Working Party on Development Finance Statistics, Organisation for Economic Co-operation and Development.

___. 2018b. *Proposal to Introduce a Policy Marker in the CRS to Track Development Finance that Promotes the Inclusion and Empowerment of Persons with Disabilities.* Paris, Development Assistance Committee Working Party on Development Finance Statistics, Organisation for Economic Co-operation and Development.

___. 2019a. *TOSSD International Task Force Members/Alternates and Observers as of 1 October 2019.* Paris, Organisation for Economic Co-operation and Development.

___. 2019b. *TOSSD Task Force: Updated Terms of Reference.* Paris, Organisation for Economic Co-operation and Development.

___. 2019c. *Total Official Support for Sustainable Development (TOSSD): A New Statistical Measure for the SDG Era.* Paris, Organisation for Economic Co-operation and Development.

___. 2019d. *Total Official Support for Sustainable Development: Country Pilot Studies.* Paris, Organisation for Economic Co-operation and Development. www.oecd.org/dac/financing-sustainable-development/development-finance-standards/tossd-country-pilot-studies.htm. (Accessed 11 February 2020.)

___. 2020a. Aid (ODA) by sector and donor [DAC5]. *OECD Statistics: Development – Flows by Provider.* Paris, Organisation for Economic Co-operation and Development. https://stats.oecd.org/Index.aspx?DataSetCode=TABLE5#. (Accessed 11 February 2020.)

___. 2020b. Net ODA. *OECD Data.* Paris, Organisation for Economic Co-operation and Development. https://data.oecd.org/oda/net-oda.htm. (Accessed 11 February 2020.)

Rodríguez Takeuchi, L. 2020. *Intrahousehold Inequalities in Education Spending.* Paris, UNESCO. (Background paper for *Global Education Monitoring Report 2020.*)

Saha, A. 2013. An assessment of gender discrimination in household expenditure on education in India. *Oxford Development Studies*, Vol. 41, No. 2, pp. 220–38.

Schwedersky, T., Ahrens L. and Steckhan, H. 2017. *Evaluation of the BMZ Action Plan for the Inclusion of Persons with Disabilities.* Bonn, German Institute for Development Evaluation.

Tiyab, B. K. and Ndabananiye, J.-C. 2013. *Household Education Spending: Approach and Estimation Techniques Using Household Surveys – Methodological Guidelines.* Dakar, Pôle de Dakar, International Institute for Educational Planning.

Turner, J. and Burgess, B. 2019. *Estimating Financing to the Sustainable Development Goals: Methodology Note for V2.0.* Williamsburg, Va., AidData, College of William and Mary.

UNESCO. 2015. *Pricing the Right to Education: The Cost of Reaching New Targets by 2030.* Paris, UNESCO. (Education For All Global Monitoring Report Policy Paper 18.)

___. 2018. *Global Education Monitoring Report 2019: Migration, Displacement and Education – Building Bridges, Not Walls.* Paris, UNESCO.

UNICEF. 2017. *PNG 2018-2022 Programme Strategy Note: Education.* New York, UNICEF.

Wongmonta, S. and Glewwe, P. 2017. An analysis of gender differences in household education expenditure: the case of Thailand. *Education Economics*, Vol. 25, No. 2, pp. 183–204.

World Bank. 2015. *Governance and Finance Analysis of the Basic Education Sector in Nigeria* Washington, DC, World Bank.

___. 2018a. *Disability-Inclusive Education in Africa Program.* Washington, DC, World Bank.

___. 2018b. *Inclusive education.* www.worldbank.org/en/topic/education/brief/inclusive-education. (Accessed 11 December 2019.)

___. 2018c. *World Bank Group Announces New Commitments on Disability Inclusion.* Washington, DC, World Bank. www.worldbank.org/en/news/press-release/2018/07/24/world-bank-group-announces-new-commitments-on-disability-inclusion. Institute for Development Evaluation (Accessed 11 December 2019.)

___. 2019a. *Disability and Inclusion.* Washington, DC, World Bank. www.worldbank.org/en/topic/disability#2. (Accessed 11 December 2019.)

___. 2019b. *Inclusive Education Initiative: Transforming Education for Children with Disabilities*. Washington, DC, World Bank.

___. 2019c. *International Development Association Project Appraisal Document on a Proposed Credit in the Amount of US$59.5 Million Equivalent and Proposed Grants from the Global Partnership for Education (US$9.5 million) and Global Partnership for Results-Based Approaches (US$4.85 million) for a Total of US$73.85 Million Equivalent to the Republic of Uzbekistan for Promoting Early Childhood Development Project*. Washington, DC, World Bank.